05/07

UNIVERSITY OF
WOLVERHAMPTON

Harrison Learning Centre
Wolverhampton Campus
University of Wolverhampton
St Peter's Square
Wolverhampton WV1 1RH
Telephone: 0845 408 1631

Telephone Renewals: 01902 321333 or 0845 408 1631
Please RETURN this item on or before the last date shown above.
Fines will be charged if items are returned late.
See tariff of fines displayed at the Counter.   (L2)

The Grub-street Journal, 1730–33

THE
GRUB-STREET JOURNAL,
1730–33

Edited by
Bertrand A. Goldgar

Volume 3
1732

MUNDUS
INTELLECTUALIS

LONDON
PICKERING & CHATTO
2002

Published by Pickering & Chatto (Publishers) Limited
21 Bloomsbury Way, London WC1A 2TH

2252 Ridge Road, Brookfield, Vermont 05036, USA

www.pickeringchatto.com

BRITISH LIBRARY CATALOGUING IN PUBLICATION DATA
A catalogue record for this title is available from the British Library.

LIBRARY OF CONGRESS CATALOGING-IN-PUBLICATION DATA
A catalogue record for this title is available from the Library of Congress

Set ISBN 1 85196 744 3

New material typeset by
P&C

Printed and bound by
Antony Rowe Ltd.,
Chippenham

CONTENTS

The Grub-ſtreet Journal.

NUMB. 105

Thurſday, JANUARY 6, 1731

Still dancing in an airy round,
Still pleas'd with their own verſes ſound,
Brought back, how faſt ſo e'er they go,
Always aſpiring, always low Prior.

An ODE to His Majeſty, on New-year's day, 1732. By Mr. CIBBER, ſervant to His Majeſty

Recit

AWAKE with joyous ſongs the day
That leads the op'ning year,
The year advancing to prolong,
Auguſtus' ſway demands our ſong,
And calls for univerſal cheer

Air

Your antient Annals, *Britain*, read,
And mark the Reign you moſt admire:
The preſent ſhall the paſt exceed,
And yield enjoyment to deſire
Or if you find the coming year
In bleſſings ſhould tranſcend the laſt,
The diff'rence only will declare
The preſent ſweeter than the paſt

Recit

But, ah! the ſweets his ſway beſtows,
Are greater far than Greatneſs knows.
With various penſive cares oppreſs'd,
Unſeen, alas, the Royal Breaſt
Endures his many a weight,
Unfelt by ſwains of humble ſtate

Air

Thus brooding on her lonely neſt,
Aloft the Eagle wakes,
Her due delights forſakes,
Tho' Monarch of the air confeſs'd,
Her drooping eyes refuſe to cloſe;
While fearleſs of annoy,
Her young belov'd enjoy
Protection, food, and ſweet repoſe.

Recit

What thanks, ye *Britons*, can repay
So mild, ſo juſt, ſo tender ſway?

Air

Your annual aid when he deſires,
Leſs the King than land requires,
All the dues to him that flow
Are ſtill but Royal wants to you
So the ſeaſons lend the earth
Their kindly rains to raiſe her birth;
And well the mutual labours ſuit,
His the glory, yours the fruit

Recit

Aſſiſt, aſſiſt, ye ſplendid throng,
Who now the Royal circle form,
With duteous wiſhes blend the ſong,
And every grateful wiſh be warm

CHORUS

May *Cæſar's* health his reign ſupply,
'Till faction ſhall be pleas'd, or die,
'Till loyal hearts deſire his fate
'Till happier ſubjects know,
Or foreign realms can ſhow
A land ſo bleſs'd, a King ſo great!

It is no uncommon thing for the Publiſhers of Weekly Memoirs, either through inadvertency, or too great a deference to their Correſpondents, to print ſuch things as ought intirely to be ſuppreſſed, or at leaſt to be altered before they appear in publick In this reſpect, I think, my Brother Fog has been a little blameable, in his laſt *Journal*, where, in the Introduction to the *Epilogue*, we find the following words 'It was always thought eſſential to verſe, to have either ſome wit or ſome rhime in it, 'till the preſent excellent LAUREAT thought fit to change that cuſtom, and to publiſh nothing but nonſenſe, and in ſuch curſed numbers, as would almoſt choak the Devil, if he was obliged to read them over' Which words, I fear, were they to come under the cognizance of a learned Jury, would probably be interpreted to be ſeditious, as they are certainly falſe and ſcandalous For tho' our learned LAUREAT no doubt, has frequently *publiſhed nonſenſe*, (a privilege, from which to debar him, would be extremely hard, ſince it is claimed by the generality of Poets, who are all inferior to him) yet to ſay, that he has *publiſhed nothing but nonſenſe*, is as far from truth, as it is from that decent reſpect, which is due to a Poet of ſo ſuperior a rank —Since it is as morally impoſſible, that all learned or witty men ſhould be of one opinion, as that the illiterate or ſtupid ſhould be ſo; the former ought to manifeſt the effects of a liberal education, by their decent treatment of one another in all differences that may ariſe And this decorum ought to be obſerved ſtill more exactly by thoſe, who either are, or have been Members of the ſame Society, for the honour of that in general, as well as of each other in particular Which obligation ſtill riſes higher, in regard to any one Member, who for his extraordinary merit has been dignified with an advantageous place, and diſtinguiſhed by an illuſtrious title This ſhould be ſo far from raiſing the envy of the leſs fortunate, and provoking them to ſhew their reſentment in ill language, that it ought to excite in them a noble emulation, upon the proſpect of the like ſucceſs, in an age when ingenuity and learning are ſo much incouraged

But there are two obſervations which ought to make Writers a little more cautious in their attaques upon perſons ſo eminent as Mr CIBBER, the truth of both which is exemplified in the Caſe before us One is, that they are apt, in the heat of the onſet, to run into ſome abſurdity; as this Critic has certainly done, in repreſenting the LAUREAT as writing without either *wit* or *rhime*, becauſe he *publiſhes nothing but nonſenſe, and in curſed numbers*, neither of which is inconſiſtent with *rhime*, tho' one of them is with *wit* —— The other obſervation is, that the abſurdity proves very often a real Encomium upon the perſon, againſt whom it was intended as a ſatire Thus the LAUREAT's *numbers* are here branded with the epithet of *curſed*, for a reaſon, which if true, would juſtly intitle them to an epithet directly contrary, they being aſſerted to be *ſuch as would almoſt choak the Devil* This is to make a poor weak *Devil* of him indeed, *weaker* even than many ingenious perſons, weaker even than myſelf, who in admiration of theſe *numbers* have *read them over* ſeveral times.

There are ſome *numbers*, I own, not altogether unlike theſe, which tend to the *choaking* of the perſons who are obliged to repeat them but this happens, becauſe they are accompanied with the odd ceremony of putting on an *anodyne necklace* However, even thoſe do not deſerve to be called *curſed*, having frequently, I believe, at laſt a very *bleſſed* conſequence And could we ingage a Popiſh Prieſt in his Exorciſms, to uſe this Hymn of the LAUREAT in the *vulgar* tongue, inſtead of one in a more *learned* language, I do not doubt that it would have as powerful an effect And if the experiment ſhould ſucceed according to this Gentleman's aſſurance, and my hope, it would juſtly intitle the Poet, and even the Popiſh Prieſt to the character of *Bleſſed*

Another Gentleman has thought fit to abuſe the LAUREAT in an *Ode* publiſhed in the *Whitehall Evening Poſt* of *Jan* 3 This *Ode* is pretended to be written *in his ſtile and manner*; the Author ſhould rather have ſaid, in his very words, ſome of which he has altered, in order to make him abuſe himſelf, which is certainly the eaſieſt way of ſatiric writing Againſt the ſevere cenſures of both theſe Gentlemen, I hope the following illuſtrations of this Ode, will be looked upon as a ſufficient defence

1 *Awake with joyous ſongs the day*] The laſt ſtanza of the LAUREAT's *Ode* on his Majeſty's Birth Day, begins thus *With ſong, ye Britons, lead the day*. Which bold expreſſion, tho' juſtifiable in Lyric Poetry; he has thought it better to ſoften, to reconcile it to the ears of *True Britons*, who will more readily endeavour to *awake the day*, than to *lead* it *with ſongs*, and will rather leave one *day* to *lead* another As he has preſerved both theſe words in the beginning of this *Ode*, it certainly exceeds the ending of the laſt; and conſequently he has *outdone his own outdoings*

2 *The op'ning year*], Both the firſt day of the new year, and the new year itſelf, being here very poetically repreſented as perſons, we are bid to *awake* the former, that it may *lead* the latter It has been objected, that tho' the epithet *opening*, which frequently ſignifies *beginning*, may be properly applied to the *year*, conſidered as a term of time, yet it cannot be applied to it, when introduced as a perſon But that this is a great miſtake, and that the word *opening* is to be underſtood in a literal ſenſe of the *year's opening* its mouth, is evident from the three verſes which immediately follow For in them the year is repreſented as *advancing* forward, *demanding* a ſong, and *calling* for univerſal cheer, which it cannot be ſuppoſed to do without *opening* its mouth

6 *Your antient Annals, &c*] I muſt own, I think the Poet has here conſidered the muſic, more than the matter of his verſe, which I could wiſh had run thus, *Antient and modern Annals read* For by thus confining us within ſo narrow a compaſs as *our antient Annals*, he has rendered his advice in the next line abſolutely impracticable. How can we, in *reading only* our *antient Annals*, poſſibly *mark the Reign we moſt admire*, when That is to be found only in our modern and lateſt Annals?

10 *Or if you find, &c*] Some envious Criticks have paſſed a general cenſure upon our Authors *Odes*, as written in the Unintelligible Sublime But I defie them to produce four *plainer* lines than theſe before us; which contain this ſelf-evident propoſition, That if the coming year have more bleſſings than the laſt, it will be ſweeter.

14 *But, ah! What ſweets, &c*] Theſe two lines are capable of two different ſenſes, and both extremely good. One is, That the *Sweets* his Majeſty's Reign *beſtows* upon his ſubjects are *far greater*, than He himſelf, in his extenſive thought, can comprehend The other, That they *are far greater* than He himſelf injoys; which is confirmed by the following lines But take them which way you will, they are a fine complement; and the *ſweets* and the *ſway* in one verſe, and the *greater* and the *Greatneſs* in the other, make them both very harmonious.

16 *With various penſive, &c*] Obſerve the *various* expreſſions in this, and in the 18th verſe Here theſe *cares* are ſaid to be not only *penſive*, but *various*, which they might be, though they were but very few There the Climax is carried much higher, and we are informed, that they are likewiſe *many* But we are not directly informed of this, but left to infer it from a lamentation moſt ſurprizingly poetical, *Alas! the Royal Breaſt endures his many a weight* His *many a weight*! Admirable!

20 *Thus brooding on her lonely neſt, &c*] Some Copies have *lovely* but the ſenſe of either reading is equally good

22 *Her due delights forſakes*] There was ſome diſpute in the Society, about the meaning of this expreſſion; which was ended by Mr DACTYL, who obſerved, that this *Eagle* had had her *due delights*, otherwiſe ſhe would not have ſate *brooding* there

23 *Tho' Monarch of the air confeſt*] All the Poets make the Male *Eagle* the *Monarch* of the birds; and therefore it has been thought ſomewhat odd, that the Female ſhould be here called the *Monarch of the air*, and be introduced by way of compariſon, to illuſtrate the greatneſs of his Majeſty's Royal *cares* Tho' I ſhall not pretend to make any conjectures in a matter, as to which I am intirely in the dark yet I do not in the leaſt queſtion, but the Poet himſelf can aſſign a ſufficient reaſon for this extraordinary compariſon.

24. *Her drooping eyes*] It has been diſputed, whether this ſhould not be *dropping*, which is more applicable to the eyes, as *drooping* is to the head

32. *All the dues, &c*] This and the following line were above the comprehenſion of the whole Society; nor did any one pretend to put any conſtruction upon them.

37 *His the Glory, yours the Fruit*] This is a plain proof, *how well the mutual labours of the Seaſons and the Earth ſuit*

41 *And every grateful wiſh be warm*] There is a great propriety in this verſe for to make a *wiſh* the more *grateful* at this ſeaſon, one muſt make it *warm*

Mr BAVIUS,

YOU having made my Brother NOKES famous in your laſt Paper, I hope you will not refuſe me the ſame honour in your next, by diſplaying the following lines, otherwiſe I ſhall highly reſent it, and you may expect a Satyr from me upon your Society, written in *Keybertian* verſe, ſuch as the following, which will make you all as ridiculous as

I am, Sir, your humble ſervant,
THOMAS STINAS.

If when at all, ſuppoſe it ſhould be ſo,
Without regarding either to or lo,
Some, not in vain, together, blindly go,
Then only them, however, I abhor,

Not that becauſe, which ſome I know will ſay,
Indubitable reaſons may be giv'n;
Yet, if bright Phœbus gilds the golden day,
Our thoughts aſcend inſenſibly to heav'n!

If ought there be, who own, that is, if there
Be any, who will not this truth deny,
None for *Parnaſſus'* hill e'er bid ſo fair,
Or eaſier climb'd the ſteep aſcent than I.

Our Correſpondents are deſired to ſend no more of this nonſenſical kind of wit. BAVIUS.

DOMESTIC NEWS.

C. *Courant.*	E P. *Evening Poſt.*
P. *Poſt-Boy.*	S J. *S. James's Evening Poſt.*
D P. *Daily Poſt.*	WE. *Whitehall Evening P.*
D J. *Daily Journal.*	LE. *London Evening Poſt.*

THURSDAY, *Dec.* 30.

The Hon. —— Boſcawen, youngeſt ſon to the L. Viſc. Falmouth, being appointed an Enſign in the 1ſt Regiment of Foot-guards, yeſterday mounted the King's guard as ſuch, with Col. Pierſon. —— The Serjeant that threw down his halbert and ſaſh, and refuſed his orders laſt ſaturday on the Parade in S. James's Park, was laſt tueſday try'd by a Court Martial at Whitehall, and by them ordered to private Centinel's pay and duty. *D J.* —— *Thoſe are fitteſt to command, who know how to obey.*

They write from Oxford, that with great ſurprize they obſerved a paragraph in ſome of the Daily Papers, relating to a deſign of applying to Parliament for redreſs againſt deciſions made by their Viſitors; whereas the preſent Set of Heads, Fellows, and Scholars, are ſo ſtrictly bound down by their ſeveral oaths to obſerve their reſpective ſtatutes, (of which that againſt the final determination of Viſitors is a very material one) that they can never admit of ſuch an indulgence, without incurring the guilt of perjury: tho' they admit, that a law may, for the future, remove that part of their oath, and to poſterity give ſome relief: a repeal of certain ſtatutes was formerly attempted, but to no purpoſe. *D P.*

There is an account from France, that the L. Viſc. Dunkeron, Mr. Kinnerſly, and Mr. Stuart, had made their eſcapes, as they were bringing from Tours to Paris; and that two of their Keepers were gone along with them. *D P.*

Yeſterday Geo. Bramſton of the Middle Temple, Eſq; ſon of Tho. Bramſton of the Waterhouſe in Eſſex, Eſq; [illegible] between 4 and 5 the Glouceſter ſtage coach was robb'd near Tyburn, by 2 Highwaymen, well mounted, who took from the paſſengers to the value of near 300 l. and detain'd the coach near half an hour. *D P.*

They write from Baſingſtoke, that an unfortunate accident happened at Wincheſter Church, in that neighbourhood, on ſunday ſe'nnight laſt, when a mad dog ran in in the time of Divine Service, and bit ſeveral of the congregation, who were carried to Southampton to be dipt in the ſea. *S J.*

Yeſterday morning about 6 died at his houſe in James's-ſtreet, Weſtm. after a long illneſs with the ſtone and gravel, the Hon. Tho. Cornwallis, Eſq; Brother to the R. Hon. the L. Cornwallis: he was the firſt Projector of the State-Lotteries, and was always choſe by the Lords of the Treaſury to be the firſt Manager of the State-Lotteries; in which ſtation he was when he died. He was an ingenuous man, and a ſincere friend, which makes his death lamented by all that had the happineſs of his acquaintance. *W E.* —— He was Member of Parliament for Eye in Suffolk. *P.*

Laſt tueſday morning died of the palſy, in the 58th year of his age, at Malden in Eſſex, Sir Tho. Seatoun, a Scots Baronet. *D J.*

FRIDAY, *Dec.* 31.

Laſt tueſday the R. Hon. the L. Tilney gave a grand entertainment at his fine ſeat at Wanſtead, to his Tenants and all the Pariſh of Wanſtead, of both ſexes, which were about 100 in number; and in the evening was a Ball, which continued 'till 2 the next morning. *D P.*

On tueſday in the evening the corpſe of John Olmius, Eſq; Dep. Governor of the Bank, was interred with great funeral ſolemnity, from his houſe in the Old Jewry, at the Church of the ſaid Pariſh; and purſuant to his laſt will and teſtament, it was performed by day-light, and the funeral proceſſion on foot, &c. *C.*

On wedneſday morning died the Lady Katharine Edwin, who was ſiſter to the late Duke of Mancheſter, at her houſe in Groſvenor-ſtreet, near Groſvenor-ſquare. *P.*

SATURDAY, *Jan.* 1.

Yeſterday the R. Hon. the E. of Effingham received his gold ſtaff out of the Jewel Office, which is of curious workmanſhip, and weighs 16 ounces; and this day he will enter on his office. *C.*

Yeſterday was held a Board of Admiralty at the Admiralty Office, when their Lordſhips admitted ſeveral ſuperannuated ſeamen into the penſion of Greenwich Hoſpital; and alſo minuted a great number more, who are to be provided for as ſoon as the new additional building adjoining to the ſaid Hoſpital is finiſh'd. *D J.* —— They ordered upwards of 100 to be minuted. *D P.* —— To the number of 300. *P.*

Our letters from Oxford whiſper, that a Juvenile Piece, in defence of the oaths of Allegiance, wrote by that excellent Antiquary, Mr. Hearne, has been, contrary to his conſent, printed, and privately handed about there; which work was much encouraged by two able perſonages, who have clubb'd their heads to throw together a Preface, which, like the French, they call Memoirs, tho' deſtitute of the advantages of amuſement theirs are ſtuff'd with. *D P.*

Col. La Fountaine, commonly called the Daniſh Colonel, is imbark'd, with his rich chariot, in the river, for Holland. *D P.*

We hear the ſo much talk'd of equeſtrian ſtatue of King William is propoſed to be erected in Lincolns-Inn-fields; and that the promoters of that deſign intend to wait on his Grace the D. of Newcaſtle for his leave and encouragement. *D P.* —— *This is a much more convenient place than* Cheapſide.

We hear that a contribution is ſetting on foot by a great number of Printers of this city, and other parts of the Kingdom, for erecting of *Lyon*'s mouths, *All Uzanza Veneziana*, as receivers of intelligence, for the benefit and diverſion of the Publick; and that others have agreed to leave open their windows, like the *Old Oxford terræ filius*, or erect wheels like thoſe for foundlings in foreign parts, all to ſerve to the ſame moſt glorious uſe, and to baffle the curious philoſophical enquiries of the *ſapientum Octurus* *D P.* —— *This is an odd mixture of Engliſh, Italian, and Latin, and is ſcarce any of the three.*

On thurſday died, at Kingſton, Edw. Whitaker, Eſq; Barriſter at Law, Steward to his Royal Highneſs the Prince, in his manor at Kennington, and Steward to the Borough Court in Southwark. *D J.* Judge of the Borough Court. *P.* —— Yeſterday, about 11, died at Chelſea, the Lady Gough, late wife of Sir Ric. Gough. *D P.* —— And about 4 in the afternoon died of the ſtone, the Lord Derwentwater. *D P.*

This day being the firſt of the new year, their Majeſties, &c. received the compliments from the Nobility and Gentry on that occaſion. The Ode for the day, compoſed by Colley Cibber, Eſq; Poet Laureat, was performed in the Council Chamber, before their Majeſties, &c. *S J.* — [illegible] Rowe, accompanied [illegible] his Majeſty's Chapel. *S J. L E.* —— This day the 40 boys, educated in Chriſt's Hoſpital, in the Mathematical School founded by King Charles II. were preſented to his Majeſty, according to annual cuſtom. *S J.*

Yeſterday, about 4 in the afternoon, the E. of Derwentwater died of the ſtone, at Sir John Webb's in great Marlborough-ſtreet. *L E. E P. S J.* He was the only ſurviving ſon of the late E. of Derwentwater, who was beheaded in the year 1716, by Anna-Maria, eldeſt Daughter of Sir John Webb, Bar. We hear the reverſion of this Lord's eſtate, of near 7000 l. per ann. was ſold ſome few years ſince, for about 2000 l. The title on the death of this young Lord would have gone to his Uncle, the Hon. Charles Ratcliffe, Eſq; but he breaking out of Newgate, with others, in the year 1716, having been taken in rebellion at Preſton, was attainted of high treaſon. *L E.*

Chriſtened: Males 158, Females 134. In all 292.
Buried: Males 123, Females 229. In all 452.
Increaſed in the burials this week 4. *E P.*

MONDAY, *Jan.* 3.

Yeſterday being the laſt ſunday within the 12 days, it was obſerved at S. James's as a feſtival, the Knights of the Garter, Thiſtle, and Bath, wearing the collars of their reſpective orders. Their Majeſties, the Prince, and the 3 eldeſt Princeſſes, went to the Royal Chapel, preceded by the King's Heralds, &c. The Rev. Dr. John Lynch preached. *D J. C. P.* —— The Rev. Dr. Clarke preached before his Royal Highneſs the Duke, &c. *C.*

Yeſterday morning, about 1, a fire happened in a chimney in his Highneſs the D. of Cumberland's apartment at S. James's, which was diſcovered by the Patrole in the Park, who immediately fired a piſtol, which alarmed the Centinel, who diſcharged his piece; whereupon the whole guard went immediately under arms; but proper means being uſed, the fire was extinguiſhed without doing any damage. *D P.* — As the Patrole was riding by S. James's houſe. It was occaſioned by leaving a ſtove ſhut to draw up the fire. *P.*

A few days ſince a man was committed to New priſon, being charged with the murder of his own wife, by confining her up in a cloſe room upwards of one year and a half, and in a moſt cruel and barbarous manner ſtarved her to death: ſhe having found means to break looſe from her confinement, died on wedneſday laſt, and on friday the Coroner's inqueſt ſat on her body, and brought in their verdict *Wilful murder.* *C.*

Laſt night about 6, a Gentleman and his wife going over Fleet-bridge, were ſet upon by 5 or 6 foot-pads, who beat and bruiſed the Gentleman in a cruel manner, and afterwards took his hat, wig, and cane, and made off. *P.*

The Rev. Dr. Middleton is choſen Dr. Woodward's Philoſophical Profeſſor in Cambridge, with a ſalary of 150 l. per ann. *P.*

On ſaturday a man went into the Tower, and at the Governor's door uttered ſeveral treaſonable and ſeditious words againſt his Majeſty, and proclaimed the Pretender, by the name of James III. of England; on which he was ſecured, and committed to Newgate by the Governor, under a file of Muſqueteers. *C.* —— A man, ſuppoſed to be diſorder'd in his ſenſes, rode on horſeback into the Tower, &c. *P.* —— We hear that orders have lately been ſent to the Tower, to repair the ſeveral apartments where State-priſoners were uſual confined. *P.* — *This Mad*man *ought to have been* confined *in one the firſt.*

TUESDAY, *Jan* 4.

On ſunday night an expreſs arrived at the R. Hon. Sir Rob. Walpole's from Paris, with the melancholy news of the death of the Lady of the R. Hon. the L. Malpas, who died in Provence, in France, in her way to the Spaw, for the recovery of her health, &c. *P.* —— Yeſterday an expreſs arrived at the R. Hon. the E. of Cholmondley's, with an account of the death of the Lady Malpas, who died at the Spaw in Germany, &c. *D J.* —— She was the only ſurviving daughter of Sir Robert: ſhe has left 3 ſons, the eldeſt of whom is about 8 years old. *D P.*

The ſame night the body of the late E. of Derwentwater was opened by Mr. Cheſelden, and ſeveral other eminent Surgeons, when it was found that his Lordſhip had died of an ulcer in his kidney. The family have ordered his corpſe to be carried over to Bruſſels, to be interr'd with that of his mother. *D P.* —— The corpſe [illegible]y to be carried to Northumberland, to be interr'd in a [v]ault with his father. *P.*

The people of Trinity College ſay, that the motion intended againſt the power of Viſitors was not deſigned by any of Oxford; (as ſeveral of the News Papers had got it) however, it may alarm them; but will, if offer'd to the Parliament, come from another place, and 'tis believed the Lords, the Viſitors, will move for a Clauſe for excepting all caſes now under proſecution, as is uſual in general pardons. *D J. C.*

The R. Rev. Dr. Tanner, L. Biſhop of S. Aſaph, has had a box of curious books and manuſcripts ſunk in the Thames, by th[illegible] of the Watermen. *C. D J.*

His Majeſty has been pleaſed to appoint Rob. Dickſon, Eſq; to be one of the Puiſney Judges of the Court of Common-Pleas in Ireland, in the room of Mr. Juſtice Barnard; and an order is ſent over for his Patent to paſs the ſeals for that purpoſe. *D J.*

Yeſterday began the Gen. Quarter Seſſions for the Royalty of the Tower, at the new Court-houſe on Great Tower-hill, where Sir John Gonſon opened the Seſſions with a *learned and excellent* ſpeech, or charge, of about half an hour. *D P*

On ſaturday laſt died Mr. Griffith Williams, one of the Grooms belonging to his Majeſty's kitchen. *P.* — Yeſterday morning died of a dropſey, at his houſe in Lincoln's-Inn fields, Counſellor Jones. *D P.* —— On friday died at Wigmore, near Bromley in Kent, Tho. Weſt, Eſq; one of the Juſtices for that County. *P.* On ſaturday at his houſe at Wapping, Tho. Weſt, Eſq; one of the Juſtices for the County of Middleſex. *C.*

WEDNESDAY, *Jan.* 5.

Whitehall, Jan. 1. Mr. Money, one of his Majeſty's Meſſengers, arrived here this evening, with letters from Mr. Colman, his Majeſty's Miniſter at Florence, of the 28th of laſt month, N. S. giving an account, that the Infante Don Carlos, Duke of Parma, &c. arrived the day before at Leghorn, about 4 in the afternoon, in good health. They had met with a ſtorm in their paſſage, which had diſperſed ſome of the Gallies; however, two of thoſe of Spain, and the Grand Dukes three Gallies, were got ſafe into Leghorn, and the reſt were hourly expected. *C. &c.*

His Majeſty has been pleaſed to confer the dignity of a Baronet of Great Britain upon Will. Clayton, of Marden, in Surrey, Eſq; *C. P. D P.* —— Who poſſeſſes the great eſtate of the late Sir Rob. Clayton. *D J.*

The Earl of Leiceſter, as Conſtable of the Tower, has been pleaſed to beſtow the place of Wharfinger at the Tower, worth about 200 l. per annum, upon Mr. Joſeph Williams, his Lordſhip's Steward. *D P.*

On the 4th of February will be held a Seſſion of Admiralty at Juſtice-Hall in the Old Baily, for trying crimes committed on the high ſeas. *Ibid.*

We hear, that notwithſtanding the artifices uſed to prevent it, the Proprietors of the Charitable Corporation are determined to ſeek redreſs in Parliament, as appears by the following reſolution propoſed by Mr. Clarke in a late General Court: —— Reſolved, That a General Court of

this Corporation be held on wednesday the 12th of January next, to receive a Report from the Gentlemen appointed to inspect the affairs of this Corporation; and to appoint a Committee to draw up a Petition to the Hon. House of Commons, humbly imploring their assistance in detecting the frauds by which this Corporation is reduced to so deplorable a state, and for giving them such relief as in their wisdom they shall think meet. —— And as the said resolution was passed almost unanimously, it is hoped the Proprietors will give their attendance on the above-mentioned day. *Ibid.*

Yesterday at a board of Admiralty, the Lords Commissioners put the 3 following ships in commission, viz. the Kingston, Capt. Lestock, of 60 guns, and 365 men; the Dolphin, Capt. Vincent, and the Sheerness, Capt. Fitch, each of 20 guns and 130 men. Capt. Lestock is to go Commodore with the Squadron to the West Indies, to relieve Admiral Stewart; and we hear the other two are to be stationed, one on the Coast of Ireland, and the other at New York. The Dolphin and the Sheerness were launched yesterday at Deptford. *D J.*

On sunday last died at her house in Basing-hall-street, the Dowager Lady Colerain, of the kingdom of Ireland. *D J.* On monday, aged upwards of 90 years. *C.* —— A few days ago died at Bednal-green, Nath. Hubbard, Esq; one of the oldest Captains belonging to his Majesty's navy. *D J.*

From the PEGASUS *in Grub-street.*

Mr. Bavius,

I Have constantly observed in one of the Daily Papers mention made of the *King of France's Children having cut their teeth all safely, and thrived extremely with* Dr. Chamberlen's *famous Anodyne Necklace*; which advertisements I always looked on, and, I believe, the generality of people did so too, to be only profitable inventions: but the contrary I am now convinced of, from what has happened at Belfast in Ireland, to one Jane Hooks, a woman of 112 years old, whom you took notice of in your *Journal* of thursday last. But the Gentleman who gave that account has been short in his information of that surprising Phænomenon: and therefore I think myself obliged to tell you the whole fact, which happened during my residence at Belfast. And I doubt not, but for the publick good, and in justice to that most excellent *Necklace*, your Paper will generously make it universally *known, even without* being paid for so doing. —— Jane Hooks, that good old woman, is certainly near 112, and this account I had from herself. Her teeth were all decay'd and worn out; so that for some years past she has lived upon spoon meat and puddings; but having fortunately heard of that inestimable *Necklace*, in less than 3 months time after she put it on, she cast her old stumps, and has now got a new set of teeth, as good as ever she had in her life: so that she can now eat a beef stake as easily as she before could swallow spoon-meat and pudding. —— The truth of this account, Mr. Bavius, you may as much depend on, tho' it come from Ireland, as upon those which are said to have come from France. And whoever doubts in the least of it, may receive full satisfaction from

Dublin, 27, *Dec.* 1731. Your constant Reader, and humble Servant,
TEAGUE.

ADVERTISEMENTS.

This day is published, A Book proper for New-year's Gifts, viz. A Conference between the Soul and the Body, &c. By Dr. Nicholson. Containing 1. 2. 3. 4. 5. 6. 7. 8. 9. 10. 11. 12. Printed for, and only to be had of E. Curle. *D J. Jan.* 3.

This Book design'd for the Direction of the Soul. — Of the same Author may be had for the Diversion of the Body. 1. Fornication spiritualiz'd. 2. The Nun in her smock. 3. Cases of impotency and divorce. 4. Rochester's Poems. 5. The Altar of love, or the Art of kissing in all its varieties. 6. The school of Venus: with the Art of Flogging, &c.

Long [1] look'd for is come at last, for lo!
This day are published,

(Very proper to be given by Bishops and Deans for New-year's gifts, &c.) ---- An Assertion of the late Rev. Dr. Clarke's principles, under these heads. 1. His manner of subscribing to the Church. 2. His study of Divinity, &c. 3. Opinion of the irony in writing, &c. 4. Opinion of the use of pictures, &c. 5. An Allegorical lecture on Butchers in white frocks, &c. 6. An opening discourse for a grand Cathartic, with a few other Miscellanies. —— Sold only by Mr. Roberts, at the corner of Lincoln's-Inn fields, near Clare-market. Pr. 4s. 6d. with allowance to such as buy a quantity. —— N. B. The place is situated between dust and ashes, that is to say, between a Snuff-shop and a Coffee-house. *D J. Jan.* 1. — We hear that the Subscribers to the Oratory [2] increasing, have [3] engaged a Sermon, &c. *D J. Dec.* 31. —— N B. [4] A new impression is to be had at the Oratory of the first numbers of the Oratory Transactions, &c. *D J. Dec.* 31. —

1. *Rather never* look'd for, *nor* upon, *tho' it has* come *over and over again.* 2. *If they* increased *they would publish it sufficiently themselves.* 3. Oratory English. 4. *If it be* a new impression, *why are the* Titles *and the* Publisher's *name altered?*

N. B. The *Original* Art of Advertising *was stolen from* Mr. Curle's Literatory, *by Grub* Orators, and Hyp-Doctors, *by Paper-mongers, by Pamphleteers, by Titles of books, &c.* and Mr. Curle's *Native Right to that* ingenious and profitable Art is indisputable, *which is mimick'd by those Jackanapes.* See D J. Jan. 4.

Dublin, Dec. 18. The Hon. Hiacenthius Ric. Nugent, commonly called Lord Riverston, of the Kingdom of Ireland, who was outlaw'd (at 7 years old) in the year 94; but by the clemency of his present Majesty, obtained an Act of Parliament in the first year of his Majesty's reign, to sue for his estate, and has now obtained a decree, to put him in possession of a very considerable estate in the Counties of Westmeath and Galway, which has been possessed by his younger brother for 17 years past. *C. Dec.* 30. Hiacinthus. *D P.* Hyacinthus. *P.* ------ The same day Joan Allen, near 50 years old, who delivered herself, and buried her child naked and alive, which about an hour after it was found and christened, died of the cold it got, was likewise convicted of the said murder, but she pleaded pregnancy. *P. D J.* --- *Dec.* 21. Last saturday his Grace the Duke of Dorset went to the Parliament house, and gave the royal assent to the Bills which were transmitted from England. *C. &c.* ——A Society consisting of a great number of Gentlemen, being form'd in this city, for improving the husbandry arts and manufactures of this Kingdom, the Lord Lieutenant has done them the honour to be President, and the Lord Primate Vice-President. *C. D P. D J.*

Edinburgh, Dec. 23. Last monday a servant drawing water out of a well on the back of the Cannongate, observed a bundle floating in it, and going thither again yesterday, observed it to be still there, and after some pains brought it up in the bucket, and opening it, found therein a new born male child, with his throat cut from ear to ear. Presently after, enquiry was made for women newly delivered, and a woman was taken up on suspicion. *D P. D J. Dec.* 30.

Leith, Dec. 27. On saturday last a west country Gentleman taking the air in his coach on the sands near this place, made a stop at the sea side, and ordered his coachman hither to buy some speldings; the 'Squire in the mean while, it seems, was so busied in his lucubrations, that he never once thought of the tide, 'till it so effectually surrounded him, that he stood but a very poor chance for his life: when he look'd on the shore, he saw numbers of people willing, but incapable to help him; on the other hand, nothing but the croaking of the sea fowls, and Neptune threatning to swallow him up: by this time you'd believe he would willingly give 100l. for a boat. The only shift now left him was to cut the harness, and get out on horseback; whereby with great difficulty, he got to dry land, where he sat down, and while he eat his speldings, had the mortification to see his coach carried off, which yesterday drove ashore all in pieces, near the Saw-mills. *C. P. Jan.* 4.

'Tis written from *Jamaica*, Sept. 27. that his Majesty's sloop the Sharke had taken at sea, and brought in there, 2 Spanish sloops, on suspicion of their being Guarde Costa's, and as such having committed pyratical acts on the subjects of Great Britain; but on examination, nothing criminal appearing against them, Rear Adm. Stewart ordered them to be released. — From *Porto Bello*, Sept. 25. N. S. They write, that they had there and at Carthagena a sad mortality, and that great number of considerable people were dead. 'Tis added, that the Spaniards had made full satisfaction to the South-Sea Company's Factors, for what they had seized of the Company's during the late rupture. *D J.*

FOREIGN NEWS.

THURSDAY, *Dec.* 30.

Extract of a letter from Lisbon, *Dec.* 11. —— We now have the agreeable news of our fleet from Rio in Brazil being safe arrived here, in all, 2 men of war and 14 merchant ships, after a passage of 99 days. They are immensely rich, having in diamonds register'd about 5,000,000, and an exceeding great sum in gold, besides other merchandize. Guards are posted all along the coast, to prevent any diamonds, &c. being run, and they search all as they come ashore. *D J.*

This day arrived the Mails from France.

Paris, Jan. 2. Letters from Seville of the 14th past advise, that the King of Spain has been ill of a swelling in his legs, but at the departure of the Courier was grown better. *L E. E P. W E.*

Paris, Jan. 5 The Grand Prior of France arrived at Cannes on the 17th past, just as the serene Infante Duke was on his departure, where, having paid the King's compliment, he attended his Highness to Antibes, and there presented him with the sword set with diamonds, from his most Christian Majesty. *L E. E P.*

FRIDAY, *Dec.* 31.

Paris, Jan. 2. The King's library at Versailles is going to be enlarged one half; so that it will inclose the 4 sides of Diana's Court, the expence whereof is reckon'd at about 200,000 livres. —— The Italian Comedians have a new Comedy in rehearsal, of 5 acts, call'd *L'Amante difficile*, done by the late M. de la Motte, which has the character of the finest piece lately written of that kind. *D P.*

'Tis written from Cadiz the 18th, N. S. that the order was come there for delivering the treasure by the Almirante, and the Galleons merchandize, on the same terms as the last Flota's, altho' there was not the least pretence for its exceeding the antient Indulto, and that an additional charge of 2 per cent. was laid, to defray the expence of sending 2 men of war with mails, &c. to bring home the Capitana from Puerto Rico, which brings out the account to about 18 per cent. in specie. *D J.*

From *Dunkirk, Jan.* 6. They write, that 7 fine large Dutch ships had a few days before been driven on shore between that place and Calais; and that four were almost in pieces, and could not be got off. *L E. S J.*

MONDAY, *Jan.* 3.

Paris, Dec. 19 N. S. Yesterday the famous Poet *Fuselier* was committed to the *Chatelet*, a Commissary having first sealed up his Papers. He is charged with being the Author of a satyrical Epigram upon a certain Abbot, and some other persons, who are blamed for supporting Father Girard in his scandalous process against Mademoiselle Cadiere. He was the Author of *Momus turned Fabulist*, a Comedy that has met with very good success, and of some other theatrical pieces. *C.*

Paris, Dec. 26. The famous Father Girard is now in the Jesuites Cloister at Lyons; and as he is a man of admirable parts, and is reckoned one of the best preachers of the age, great interest is making, that he may have the liberty of preaching again. *C.*

Yesterday arrived a Mail from France *and 2 from* Holland.

Paris, Jan. 9. Letters from Antibes say, that upon Christmas-Eve about 10 in the forenoon, the Galleys of Spain, and those of the Great Duke of Tuscany, having on board the Infante Don Carlos, and all his retinue, sailed from thence with a fair wind. *C. D J.* —— There is to be seen at M. de Rivry's *Rue Quinquenpoix*, a curious piece of Mechanicks, being a Wind-mill a foot and half diameter, which is to be sold. There you see the sails of the mill turn round, and hear the corn grind: the Miller opens his door, walks, and takes his hat off: above is a cat running away with a rat in her mouth; and below in the meadow is a little flock of sheep, which pass along, and part as they go, followed by a Shepherd, who strikes them with his crook. His dog makes them turn about, and keep all together. *C.*

Vienna, Dec. 29. 'Tis said that his Polish Majesty, as well as the Courts of Bavaria and Palatine, has declared that for divers important reasons, he cannot yet resolve to give his consent to the Guaranty of the *Pragmatick Sanction. C. D P. D J.*

TUESDAY, *Jan.* 4.

Smyrna, Nov. 3. N. S. Our Letters from Constantinople advise, that the Persians having made several mines under ground about Tauris, they broke up, and marched to meet the Turks, who were coming to relieve the place; that they were repulsed with loss, and being pursued by our troops as far as their concealed mines, the Persians set fire to them, and blew up a great number of our men, and among them the five following Bashaws, who were found among the slain, namely, the Bashaw of Acre or Acon, Bashaw Ali, Bashaw Damur, Bashaw Rustan, and Bashaw Mustapha; and that the Persians having thus gained their point, they pursued the gross of our army towards Erivan. *P.*

This day arrived a Mail from Holland.

Amsterdam, Jan. 11. We learn from Warsaw, that the King of Poland set out from thence the 26th past, accompanied by Messieurs de Bruhl, Thioli and Pauli; and that his Majesty expected to be at Dresden, by the 2d or 3d instant. *E P.*

Turin, Dec. 24. The Marq. de Vaugrenan, French Embassador, has had an Audience of the King, and delivered a letter from the King his Master, in behalf of the late King Victor, which his Excellency, back'd with a very moving speech: his Majesty's answer is variously represented. *L E.*

Moscow, Dec. 14. By our last letters from Persia, the peace appears to be a suspension of arms agreed on between the Sultan and Prince Thamas, in order for a peace, in case the first will comply with the demands of the latter, which are said to be very exorbitant. *L E.*

WEDNESDAY, *Jan.* 5.

Berlin, Jan. 1. The King set out this day for Potsdam, to receive the Duke of Lorrain there. His Majesty is so nearly touch'd with the miseries which the poor Saltzburg-

ers suffer for the sake of religion, and with what conftancy they endure them, that he has refolved to grant lands, and other great advantages to fuch as fhall come and fettle in his dominions. *D J. C. DP.—*

Jan. 4. Married laft year in this city and fuburbs 481 couple: born 3064 children of both fexes, befides 336 baftards: and died, men, women and children, 3153. *C.*

Hamburgh, Jan. 4. On March the 10th, the entire cargo of the fhip Apollo will be expofed to fale; and here they give her the title of the royal fhip of Pruffia. *C. DP*

Books and Pamphlets publifhed fince our laft.

31. Modern Hiftory, &c. by Mr. Salmon, No. 89. Vol. XV. P. 4.

Hiftoria Literaria, No. 14. Vol. III. P. 2.

Confiderations upon the South-Sea trade. &c.

Jan. 1. Philofophical Tranfactions, No. 419. for June and July.

Love and Ambition, a Tragedy : by James Darcey, Efq; An Ode to his Majefty on New-year's-day, by Mr. Cibber. Pr. 6 d.

3. The unhappy Lovers : or the Hiftory of James Welton, Gent. &c. Pr. 1 s.

The Cafe of the oppofition ftated between the Craftfman and the People. Pr. 1 s.

Memoirs of Maritime Affairs of G. Britain, &c. By John Pullen, Efq; Pr. 1 s. 6 d.

Of Dullnefs and Scandal, &c. By Mr. Welfted. Pr. 6 d.

4. A Cloud of Witneffes, proving that the Bifhop of Litchfield has mifreprefented the Quakers. Pr. 4 d.

4. The 4th volume of the Annals of the Church of England, &c. by John Strype, M. A.

5. A Propofal for the better regulation of the Stage, &c. Pr. 1 s.

On Tuefday Stocks were

South Sea Stock 102 3 8ths, 102 1 qr. 102 1 half, 102 3 8ths to 1 half, for the Opening. South Sea Annuity 109 7 8ths, to 110. Bank 149. New Bank Circulation 6 l. 2 s. 6 d. Premium. India 182, 181 3 qrs. 182 1 qr. for the Opening. Three per Cent Annuity 97 1 half, for the Opening. Royal Exchange Affurance 100, for ditto. London Affurance 13 1 8th. York Buildings 14 1 qr. to 1 half, for the Opening. African 46, for ditto. Englifh Copper 2 l. 16 s. Welch ditto 2 l. 1 s. South Sea Bonds 6 l. 17 s. Premium. India ditto 6 l. 19 s. ditto. Blanks 7 l. 4 s. 6 d. 20 l. Prizes 19 l. 5 s.

❋❋❋❋❋❋❋❋❋❋❋❋❋❋❋❋❋❋❋❋❋❋❋❋❋❋❋

LONDON: Printed by S. PALMER and J. HUGGONSON, in *Bartholomew-Clofe,* for Captain GULLIVER, near the *Temple,* where Letters and Advertifements are taken in : As alfo at the *Rainbow Coffee-Houfe* in *Cornhill,* and *John's Coffee-Houfe* in *Sheer-Lane,* near *Temple-Bar.* [Price Two Pence.]

The Grub-ſtreet Journal.

NUMB. 106

Thurſday, JANUARY 13, 1731.

A general murmur ran quite through the Hall,
To think that the Bays to an Actor ſhould fall.
Seſſions of the Poets in Dryden's Miſcellanies, Vol. II.

ALTHO' the following Letter, ſent at a time when it could not conveniently be inſerted in our *Journal*, was written above a year ago: yet, it is not doubted, but the fame of the LAUREAT, which conſtantly receives an annual augmentation at this ſeaſon, will render this Piece acceptable now to the Public.

To Mr. BAVIUS, Secretary to the Grubean Society.

SIR,

THE entertaining account you gave us, in * one of your *Journals*, of the rites and ceremonies practiſed at the inauguration of a Poet-Laureat, under the Pontificate of LEO X, occaſioned my falling into ſeveral reflections upon the preſent ſtate of Engliſh Poetry, the injudiciouſneſs of Patrons, and the proper methods of retrieving the honour of the Muſes, and reſtoring the moſt elegant of all the ſciences to its ancient luſtre and reputation; which diſpoſed me for the following dream or viſion, when I went to bed.

I fancied myſelf walking up and down in the ſhady groves of Parnaſſus, amidſt a very large company of Poets of all nations and languages; of whom few made a better figure than thoſe of the Engliſh. I had not long wandered in this agreeable ſcene, before ſome of theſe welcomed my arrival in the moſt obliging manner, and with the moſt ſenſible demonſtrations of joy for the acceſſion of a new brother and aſſociate to thoſe delightful regions of ſerenity and repoſe. For they made me to underſtand, that the little grudges and heart-burnings of jealouſy, and that narrowneſs of ſoul with which paltry mortals are ſo much upon the fret at the thoughts of a rival, are unknown to the more candid and exalted ſpirits of Parnaſſus, who think a partnerſhip of fame, and the immortality it gives, an accumulation of their happineſs. I never was ſo much mortified with not being in reality what I was taken for, as now; nor ſo heartily regretted any thing, as that I had not purſued ſuch elevated and refined ſtudies, as might have entitled me to a place in ſo much good company.—— However, before I undeceived them as to their favourable conceptions of me, I preſumed to enquire, whether any of our nation had of late been thought worthy to be admitted among them, becauſe they ſeemed to entertain with ſo much pleaſure the acceſſion of a youth, who had a juſter opinion of himſelf, than to think he had a title to the great honour they were pleaſed to do him. To which it was anſwered, that, on what account they knew not, but the Engliſh genius, they apprehended, had very much declined. For a great number of our Countrymen had made pretenſions to their Society of late; but for want of good credentials, they were ſtill rejected. Why, alas! then, Gentlemen, I replied, it is no ſmall affliction to me to be obliged to declare to you, that I am not the happy perſon you miſtake me for. This is but an excurſion into theſe flowery regions, like the accidental adventures of my Muſe; I am not ſo fortunate as to be free of your company, and enrolled a Parnaſſian; for, being no profeſſed Poet, how ſhould I obtain the privileges of your community under the hand of APOLLO?

Upon this, a venerable Bard, whom I now apprehended to be the great DRYDEN, whoſe aſpect carried ſomething more auguſt, ſince his Apotheoſis, as I may call it, than the pictures he has left us of himſelf, during his mortality: Why, Brother, for I will call you ſo, it is a greater indication of merit, as well as more truly honourable, to decline honours than to court them with never ſo much ſucceſs; nor is he leſs to be eſteemed a Poet who can write, and does not, or who conceals what he has written, either out of modeſty, or want of ambition. What farther paſſed betwixt us, I ſhall not preſume to mention: but our conference was ſoon interrupted by a ſurprizing clamour, which aſcended the mountain; when approaching nearer, we heard, Make way there for the noble LAUREAT of Great Britain! This drew our curioſity to know who this illuſtrious perſonage ſhould be, and the reception APOLLO would give him. Big with this expectation, we were carried to the preſence-room, where his Parnaſſian Majeſty gives audience, and determines the pretenſions of the candidates for the laurel.

We were no ſooner arrived, than the undaunted Britiſh Bard was introduced to his Majeſty, and, with an air of confidence, challenged the laurel, as inconteſtably his own: which was attended with a general acclamation of all the ſcouts and ſcavengers of Parnaſſus, and did not contribute a little to the elevation of his creſt. To be ſhort, APOLLO was pleaſed to demand his credentials, telling him he had never yet heard of his name. May it pleaſe your Majeſty, replies his Laureatſhip, not at all abaſhed with the ſeverity of the rebuke, here are my Works, which will ſpeak for me. With that he preſented APOLLO with two large volumes in Quarto, finely bound and gilt; and, added he, Who has yet trod the Engliſh ſtage with better grace, or ever acted a character, or written one, better than your Majeſty's moſt obedient ſervant? APOLLO opening the Books, found they were Plays; whereupon knitting his brows, I tell thee, Bard, ſays he, I am ſo ſurfeited with the productions of you modern Play-wrights, that I have ordered moſt of the Plays that have been written in this laſt age, to be diſpoſed of in a library adjoining to the Temple of CLOACINA, at the foot of Parnaſſus, where alone they can be of uſe to mankind. Beſides, for me to beſtow the never-fading crown of Poets, which Princes and Conquerors have been ambitious of wearing, upon a Player, without ſome extraordinary merit, will be degrading the dignity of the laurel.

Here the Bard interrupted: But, Sir, with reverence, LAUREAT I am, and LAUREAT I muſt be; for the greateſt Prince of the preſent age, has commanded it to be ſo; and therefore I am, with authority, chief Poet in his dominions. This really, rejoined APOLLO, is like NERO's taking the laurel by ſtrength of his legions, and crowning himſelf with it; at the ſame time cauſing himſelf to be proclaimed, with ſound of trumpet, the beſt Poet in his dominions, let any man ſay the contrary at his peril. Well, Mr. LAUREAT, proceeds he, as great a veneration as I have for every thing that comes ſigned by the authority of the Prince, whoſe ſervant you now write your ſelf, and whoſe ſanction and recommendation generally have the place of law with me, as being the true teſtimonial of merit; I cannot yet admit your claim to the laurel in my Parnaſſian territories, without ſome formal proofs of your abilities, according to the ſtatutes of theſe our poetical dominions; and 'till I ſee your compliments to your Sovereign, in return for the honour he has done you. You have likewiſe to paſs your examination, and the rites of inauguration, before you can be endenizoned in the Heliconian climes.

And now I perceived an indignation to ſpread and redden the faces of ſome venerable Bards, who, one and all, requeſted that the Candidate might be examined in the antient Writers of the Drama; and that he might be required to tranſlate ſome paſſages of the antient Poets; which, as a right line diſcovers its contrary, would try the truth of his genius, and how far his manner of compoſing would bear the touch-ſtone of nature and good ſence. But this examination he had the modeſty to decline.—Upon which a draught of the water of *Hippocrene*, was ordered to be given him, which having a ſudorific quality, if the Candidate had juſt pretenſions to the poetical ſpirit, would refine and defecate his upper parts, by an inſenſible perſpiration, and prepare him for breathing the purer air of the Parnaſſian climate; if the contrary, like the water of jealouſy, it would work violently downward, and ſhew its effects in the nether regions. And this laſt happened to be the caſe, to the very great offence of our noſes; which threw the aſſembly into ſo loud a fit of laughter, that it awaked

Your moſt humble ſervant, A. B.

* *Journal the 46th.*

SIR,

SOon after I ſent you that Letter upon *eaſy writing*, &c. I was obliged to go into the country; from whence I returned not 'till yeſterday. The firſt thing I did was to read your three Journals that have been publiſhed in my abſence; and I read them indeed with a great deal of pleaſure. You ſeem to hate heartily, and to be reſolved to encounter ſtoutly all nonſence and abſurdity, all villainy and impoſition upon the Public, in whatſoever ſubject you ſhall find them. A moſt audacious and truly *Herculean* undertaking. Pray never flinch from that deſign, which is ſo very laudable; and you'll certainly have ſucceſs, and do good. It was particularly a lucky thought of yours, to give us the news of the paſt week, with remarks. I look upon your Paper as a ſort of *Expurgatory Index*, to purge away, and clear us of all the traſh and filth that we have been gorged and ſurfeited with, for a whole week together.

I fancy, Mr. BAVIUS, you would not like a Letter with nothing in it but your own praiſes; therefore I'll write down a few verſes of HORACE, Epiſt. L. I. Ep. XVI. ver. 25, &c.

Si quis bella tibi terra pugnata marique
Dicat, & his verbis vacuas permulceat aures;
*'*TENE *magis ſalvum populus velit, an populum tu,*
'Servet in ambiguo, qui conſulit & tibi & urbi,
'Jupiter; Auguſti laudes agnoſcere poſſis.

Whilſt I was reading this moſt beautiful Epiſtle at my friend's houſe in the country, I happened to look into the old Scholiaſt upon HORACE, and there I found that this compliment to AUGUSTUS is quoted by HORACE out of a panegyrical Poem of VARIUS upon AUGUSTUS, *Hæc enim*, ſays the Scholiaſt, *Varius de Auguſto ſcripſerat; ſunt autem ex notiſſimo Panegyrico Auguſti.* HORACE makes a great compliment both to AUGUSTUS and VARIUS, by producing theſe verſes, and 'tis pity we have not more remains of that excellent Poet. For, in my opinion, theſe are the fineſt lines, and contain the fineſt compliment that ever was made by any mortal. The more you conſider, the more you admire. There's the judgment and ſolidity of VIRGIL, the eaſe and unaffectedneſs of OVID. 'Tis as lofty and ſtrong as HOMER; and, as to expreſſion, ſhort and natural as HORACE himſelf. I wiſh I could tranſlate them into † two Engliſh ones as good; I would give 50 pounds. Let POPE himſelf do it, if he can, and apply them to our AUGUSTUS.

I can't forbear tranſcribing out of the ſame Epiſtle, four or five moſt admirable lines, both becauſe they contain a very good moral, and becauſe there's a reading intolerably falſe and nonſenſical. Ver. 39, 40.

Falſus honor juvat, & mendax infamia terret,
Quem niſi mendoſum & mendacem?

Dr. BENTLEY's edition has *mendoſum & medicandum?* and *medicandum* is undoubtedly the true reading for *egentem Helleboro, non ſanum.* Indeed *mendacem* makes downright nonſenſe, as the Critic has fully demonſtrated; beſides, *medicandum* is in the beſt MSS. yet *mendacem* ſticks in our vulgate Editions, and there ſtick it will, perhaps, in ſpite of BENTLEY and common ſenſe. To ſpeak truth, the whole paſſage was very obſcure and ill underſtood before he took it in hand.

'Tis bold, perhaps, to meddle with HORACE after BENTLEY, and yet I'll mention to you ‡ a conjecture of mine, upon a paſſage that he has not touched *Carm. Lib* I. Ode XV. v. 13. NEREUS, foretelling the deſtruction of Troy, ſays to PARIS,

Nequicquam Veneris præſidio ferox
Pectes cæſariem, grataque fœminis
Imbelli cithara carmina divides:
Nequicquam thalamo graves
Haſtas & calami ſpicula Cnoſſii
Vitabis, ſtrepitumque, & celerem ſequi
Ajacem: tamen, heu ſerus, adulteros
Crines *pulvere collines.*

I was thinking the Poet would not uſe *crines* ſo ſoon after *cæſariem*, and I believe he wrote *adulteros cultus.* It came into my mind, upon reading theſe verſes, *Carm. Lib.* IV. Ode IX. v. 13.

† It is, no doubt, impoſſible to do this, the Latin containing thirty ſix ſyllables; and two Engliſh verſes, but twenty. However, the very thought of applying them to our AUGUSTUS, incited Mr. MÆVIUS to attempt them in four lines, in which there are but four ſyllables more than in the Latin. The Society highly approved them, and ordered that they ſhould be ſubjoined to this Letter, as a ſhort ſpecimen of unpenſioned Panegyric; intirely different from ſome *New-years Odes*, which, if the Author was not well known, might juſtly be looked upon as grave burleſques upon the Court.

‡ I wiſh this Gentleman would ſend us for the future only his own conjectures, or at the moſt ſuch criticiſms of other learned men as are not commonly known; the two preceding being in ſeveral editions of *Horace*, particularly in that by Mr. BAXTER.

Non sola comptos arsit adulteri
Crines & aurum vestibus illitum,
Mirata regalesque cultus
Et comites, Helene Lacæna.

Cultus in both places means the whole dress and exterior garb, with all its attractions and allurements of gold, silver, gems, &c. which are very properly called *adulteros; aurum vestibus illitum, regalesque* cultus. SUETONIUS, in his life of NERO, has, *insignes pinguissima* coma *& excellentissimo* cultu *pueri*; and FLORUS says of CLEOPATRA, that she was *induta maximos cultus*. Besides, *cultus* has been found in some MSS.

Pour la bonne bouche, I'll give you a very honest verse of PLAUTUS,

Pulchrum ornatum *pejus cœno turpes mores collinunt.*

where you'll observe, *ornatum collinunt*, as in HORACE, *cultus collines*.

Jan. 1. 1731. I am yours, PHILARCHÆUS.

P. S. I must go into the country again before I can send you any more upon MILTON: when I come back I will, *omnes nervos intendere*; in the mean time you may, if you please, print what you have already.

To the KING.

Whether for your, or for your People's weal,
Or They, or You are fir'd with warmer zeal;
May JOVE, to whom You Both your safety owe,
Still keep a secret from the world below.

BAVIUS.

DOMESTIC NEWS.

C. *Courant.*	E P. *Evening Post.*
P. *Post-Boy.*	S J. *S. James's Evening Post.*
D P. *Daily Post.*	WE. *Whitehall Evening P.*
D J. *Daily Journal.*	LE. *London Evening Post.*

THURSDAY, *Jan.* 6.

We hear that his Majesty will send a solemn Embassy to compliment Don Carlos on his peaceable and happy entry into the dominions of Tuscany and Parma. *D P.*

On tuesday last his Excellency Gov. Phillips, upon his return from his Government went to Court, had the honour to kiss their Majesties hands, and was graciously received. *D P.*

On friday last Mr. Anderson and Mr. Milborn, 2 of his Majesty's Grooms, landed in Holland with the set of fine horses that his Majesty presented to his most serene Highness the Duke of Lorain. *C.* And his Highness's Master of the horse was there ready to receive them, and proceeded directly to Lorrain with the said horses. *P.*

A few days ago the R. Hon. the E. of Rockingham set out on his travels for France, Spain, &c. for about 3 years. *P.*

Yesterday the Court of Directors of the East India Company appointed John Brown, Esq; one of the Representatives in Parliament for Dorchester, to be their standing Council, in the room of Dr. Exton Sayer, deceased. *D J.*

We hear the books and manuscripts of the R. Rev. the L. Bishop of S. Asaph, which we mentioned in our Paper of the 4th instant, lay 20 hours below water; and there were as many of them, when opened, as loaded 7 waggons; among which were between 2 and 300 volumes of manuscripts, which his Lordship has been collecting near these 40 years: they are so much damaged, that they are obliged to take them in pieces, and dry them on lines; several of them are lost, and many so much damaged as to be useless. So *fatal* has the last year been to the *History and Antiquities* of our nation. *D J.*

Yesterday John Yorke, Esq; Member of Parliament for the Borough of Richmond, in the County of York, was married to the Hon. Miss Ann D'Arcy, Daughter to the late R. Hon. James L. D'Arcy, of Sedbury in the same County; an agreeable young Lady of great merit and fortune; and they are gone to reside at their house in Queen's-square, near Ormond-street. *D P.*

On tuesday last died, at his father's in Golden-square, Mr. Burroughs, a young Gentleman of a pretty good fortune: it is said the loss he sustained in the Charitable Corporation broke his heart. *D P.*

Cambridge, Jan. 3. Dr. Needham left his estate, which is very considerable, to his relations; but in case they die without issue, it comes to the *Corporation of the Sons of the Clergy*. *D J.*

We are informed that the Rev. Mr. Doiley, Minister of Ingarston in Essex, has lately given to the Corporation for support of poor widows and children of Clergymen, the sum of 3000 l. in consideration of which, they settle 000 l. [100 l. *D P. Jan.* 7.] to be paid yearly for ever; 70 l. to 7 such widows with families of small children as they shall find to be most in want, at 10 l. a year each, and 30 l. to such Clergymens children as shall be named from time to time by Trustees, to be appointed by his will. *L E.*

The Christmas Jury have collected, for discharging poor Debtors out of the Gatehouse prison in Westminster, and for other charitable purposes, in the said City and Liberty, upwards of 250 l. *LE.*

This day began the Gen. Quarter Sessions for Westminster, when Sir John Gonson gave a very useful charge on that occasion. *WE.* A learned charge. *D J. Jan.* 7.

Gloucester, Jan. 1. About the middle of this week a young woman going to push off her father's barge, a little above the key, accidentally slipt into the river, and was drowned; the news whereof so surprized her mother, that she died soon after; and both were interred together this evening. —— We have received advice, that on Nov. 27. was paid into the hands of the R. Hon. the L. Mayor of London, the sum of 55 l. 6 s. 9 d. collected in the parishes of S. Nicholas, S. Michael, S. Mary de Grace, and S. Mary de Load; which money is apply'd as follows, viz. to Blandford 36 l. 15 s. 9 d. and to Tiverton 18 l. 11 s. *S J. WE.*

There is lately erected a Society who call themselves FREE SAWYERS, who claim a priority to the Free Masons, the order of Gormogon, and Antient Hums; for as the Free Masons pretend to date their standing from the building of Babel, so these FREE SAWYERS say, they cut the stones for those mad builders; and what is very remarkable among them, they have a fine silver Saw laid on their table at their meetings, with this Motto, LET IT WORK. *LE.*

FRIDAY, *Jan.* 7.

Yesterday being Twelfth-day, the Knights Companions of the most noble orders appeared at Court in their Collars, where their Majesties, &c. heard divine service, and made the usual offerings of purses of gold, myrrhe, and frankincense. The same evening there was a great Drawing-room, when the King play'd at cards for the benefit of the Groom-Porter; and according to annual custom, he received his usual present of a handful of gold from a bowl at the King's table, besides other presents from the several Nobility and Quality. *C. D J.*

We hear that the persons who bought the reversion of the late E. of Derwentwater's estate, are Mr. Smith of Aldgate, Sir Jos. Eyles, Mr. Bond, and Mr. White. *D P.*

We hear that the E. of Crawford has resign'd his Troop in the Scotch grey regiment of Dragoons. *D P.*

On wednesday night, about 11 o'clock, Mr. John Yerbury was knock'd down by 2 street-robbers, near Child's Coffee-house in S. Paul's Church yard, who robbed him of 5 s. and abused him in a very severe manner. *D J.*

Last wednesday died at Weybridge in Surrey, Jonathan Beesaiz, Esq; and has left 5000 l. by his will to a private Centinel of the foot guards. *D J.* —— Last friday died George Heneage, Esq; at his seat in Lincolnshire, a Gentleman possessed of about 8000 l. per ann. *P.* —— On saturday last died at Islington, Mr. Emlyn, an eminent dissenting Minister *D. D P But the same day was seen well on horseback in Aldersgate-street.* —— On wednesday last died Sir John Blount, Bar. who in the year 1720 was a Director of the South Sea Company. *P. D P.* —— The report of the death of Sir John Blount is without foundation. *C. Jan.* 8.

We hear that the increasing Subscribers of the Oratory having desired the sundays lectures to be for some time on particular chosen subjects, the burlesque Orations of the week days will be for the present discontinued, &c. *D J.* —— *He should have said* the decreasing wednesday Auditors *occasioned this. As these* orations will be discontinued for the present, *they will perhaps be revived* for the time past.

SATURDAY, *Jan.* 8.

Last thursday night at S. James's her Royal Highness the Princess Amelia, his Grace the D of Grafton, and the Lady Betty Germaine lost very considerably; and the R. Hon. the E. of Portmore won several thousand pounds. *D J.*

On wednesday last a dealer in hogs went down to Rumford market, and received 21 l. which he put in a bag into his pocket; on his return home a poor man (seemingly) on the road desired him to give him a lift to London; accordingly he took him up behind him, and carried him to White-Chappel; in which time he found means to pick the Hog merchant's pocket of all his money; and, after he had returned him thanks for his civility, walked off. *C.* —— *This person was not only* seemingly, *but* really a poor man, *when* the Hog-merchant took him up.

Two more Footmen are appointed his Royal Highness the Prince, which will make the number eight. *WE.*

This week the Earl of Yarmouth arrived in town from his seat in Norfolk, in a very advanced age, to be present at the meeting of the Parliament on thursday next. *L E.*

Last thursday evening a Gentleman was robbed on Finchley Common, by a man and woman on horseback; as were the night before a Gentleman and his Wife, by an old man and a boy on horseback. *W E.* —— *This is a very heroic age, when* old men, women, and boys, *dare undertake such hazardous enterprizes.*

On thursday last died in Norfolk-street in the Strand, Trafford Smith, Esq; Barrister at Law, eldest son of Sir Robert Smyth, of Hampshire, Bart. *L E. WE*

A few days since died in the 84th year of his age, the Rev. Mr. Harman, Vicar of Market end near Chelmsford in Essex, which living, tho' but small, he enjoy'd near 60 years: he was a man of excellent principles, and of so exemplary a life, that he may be said to be an honour to the religion he professed: Bishop Compton would several times have preferr'd him; but he chose a quiet and retired life, and would not undertake the charge of a large parish, where he could not himself discharge the duty required of him; thinking he should not discharge his duty to God with serving it by a Curate; a rare example! and if our dignified Clergy would but seriously consider this, it is to be hoped their parishes would be better supplied than at present. *L E.*

Yesterday a melancholy accident happened at Mr. Bentley's, the King's Arms tavern, near Hungerford-market in the Strand, the particulars of which are as follow: about nine in the morning, a young Gentleman and a Lady came in a Hackney coach, and some time after sent for Mr. Turnor, a Clerk in the East India house, who came to them, and then having drank some time, Turnor sent the Porter of the tavern to Mr. Freeman's in S. Martin's lane, to hire a pistol, on pretence of going to Windsor, leaving half a guinea for the use of it, and gave Mr. Freeman's son particular Directions about the charging of it, which was done before them both, and then the Gunsmith withdrew: Mr. Bentley and one of the Drawers, about one of the clock, hearing a pistol go off, run into the fore-room next the street, and found Mr. Turnor shot thro' the head, in at the right ear, and the person who was with him, gone, (the woman being gone about an hour before.) the surprize and confusion was so great, that the other, being so near the door, escaped, and run up Hewit's court, and so thro' Round court. There was a letter found in the deceased's pocket, directed to a *Clerk in the India House*, the person supposed to be fled, from the Lady who was with them, appointing him to meet her at a certain place in Holbourn, but not to bring that *Villain Turnor* with him. It is supposed this letter being shewn to Turnor by the person that fled, was the occasion either of Turner's killing himself, or the other person's doing it; tho' its something strange, that a letter directed to another person, with such words in it, should be found in Turnor's pocket, unless he snatched it from the other. *L E.*

There is advice by a private letter from Ireland, that 2 women were poison'd *there*, by taking some of the juice of laurel leaves, which it seems is an agreeable *bitter*, and hath by nurses frequently been mixed with childrens spoon meat, being reckoned good for the wind; whereupon a very eminent Chymist of this town try'd it upon 2 or 3 *several* dogs this week, and they immediately fell into convulsions *upon taking it*, and dy'd on the spot; so that it appears to be rank poison. *D P.* —— *This* bitter it seems *is* agreeable *to* children, *but not to* dogs *and* women.

We hear that the Rev. Mr. Billingsby, an eminent dissenting Minister at Dover, has lately conformed to the Church; he formerly married a sister of Sir Phil. Yorke, Knt. his Majesty's Attorney General. *C.* —— *If this Gentleman* had *only pretended to* conform, *he would have been, according to* Cathelicus's *letter in one of our late Journals, a person of much greater* merit.

Oratory advertisement. N. B At the instance of several Friends and Subscribers, mov'd with pity at the enemies crying *Quarter*, the Burlesque week day Lectures of the Oratory shall, for some time be discontinued, to prepare for Lectures, &c. *Fog's Journal* —— Mr. Orator's *quondam* Auditors, *whom he now calls his* enemies, *but indeed* cryed quarter; *insomuch, that* (to *imitate his* burlesque *manner*) not a quarter *of a* quarter *of a hundred will come once* a quarter, *to see and hear learning hang'd, drawn, and* quartered.

MONDAY, *Jan.* 10.

Yesterday the Rev. Dr. Clarke preached before their Majesties, his Royal Highness the Prince, &c. And the Rev. Dr. Gilbert preached before his Royal Highness the Duke. *C.* The Rev. Dr. Lynch preached before his Highness the Duke. *P. D P.* —— Last saturday his Majesty was pleased to sign a Commission to Sir Charles Hotham, one of his Grooms of the Bedchamber, appointing him Lieut. Col. of the regiment of foot on the Irish establishment, commanded by Col. Legonier. *D J.* Late Col. Cosby's, who is made Governor of New York. *DP.* —— And appointed the Hon. Col Step. Cornwallis, Esq; to be Col. of a regiment of foot, now at Jamaica, in the room of the Hon. —— Hays, deceased. *P.* —— Mr. Tho. Turner and Mr. Hen. Clarke, are appointed Pages to the Princess Mary, with a salary of 80 l. per ann. each. *P.*

The corpse of the late E. of Derwentwater is to be put on board a ship for Flanders, in order to be interred at Louvain, where the Lady his Mother was buried. *D P.*

On saturday morning the D. of Lorrain, Capt. Wilson, the Bedford, Capt. Wells, and the Prince of Orange, Capt. Hudson, in the service of the East India Company, sailed from Blackwall for Graveend, in order to proceed on their respective voyages. *C.*

We hear that Will. Collins has purchased the place of Serjeant at Mace, at the Poultry Counter, formerly Mr. Beer's, for 300 guineas, of Sam. Russel, Esq; one of the Sheriffs. *C.*

We hear from the East India Coffee-house in Cornhill, that Sir Isaac will, in his to morrow's Paper, answer the late Craftsman's objections, &c. which no Writer has yet undertaken. Courage! *D J.* —— Sir Isaac's *will always be a* To morrow's Paper.

Yesterday died Jeremy Gough, Esq; at his Chambers in the Temple, and has left a large estate to his Sister, a widow Lady in Gloucestershire. *D P.* About 1500 l. per ann. *P.* ——— On friday night one Capt. John Weeden, Commander of the Hanover Grenadiers, &c. went to bed seemingly in perfect health, having supt cheerfully with some friends, and was found dead in his bed on saturday morning. *C.*

Last saturday the Coroner's inquest sat on the body of Mr. Turner, and it appeared to the Jury, by the deposition of the Father of the Gentleman who was in the room when the misfortune happened, and has since absconded, that Mr. Turner was to have fought a duel that afternoon, for which purpose he had sent for his sword into Johnson's Court the same morning by a porter. *D J.*

TUESDAY, *Jan.* 11.

It is now certain that his Majesty will visit his German dominions the ensuing summer. ——— Sunday last his Excellency Col. Cosby kissed his Majesty's hand, upon being appointed Capt. General and Governor, and Chief in and over New York and New Jersey, &c. *D J.*

We hear that Mr. Davis has purchased the place of one of the Ushers of the Court of Exchequer, in the room of Mr. Monk, deceased. *P.*

Last week the Lord Mayor received 20 guineas from the Society of Clifford's-Inn, to be distributed, 14 l. to the sufferers of Blandford, and 7 l. to Tiverton. *D P.*

From Leghorn it is written, that it has been observed, that from the time of the British Admiral making a signal for weighing, to the time of the fleet being all under sail, was but an hour and a quarter; but that the Spanish squadron was 30 hours doing the same. *D J.* ——— *And yet the* Spaniards outsail'd *us in the* West Indies.

Yesterday morning, about 7, a poor woman about 25 years of age, having drank too plentifully of gin, sat herself down by a Geneva shop, the corner of Buckingham-court, at Charing-cross, and expired in a short time. She was immediately carried to S. Martin's Bone-house, but no body *knew her*; and this day the Coroner's Jury is to sit on her body. Just before she died, she was raving mad. *P.* —— *Death equals all. My Brother justly pays the same respect to this* poor woman, *which he wou'd do to one of much greater fortune: he gives us her age, the place, and manner of her death, and the removal of her body to a* Bone-house, *instead of an* Upholders, *in order to her interment. in his next we may expect an account of her funeral solemnity.*

A few days since, —— Davenport, of Shropshire, Esq; a Gentleman of about 3000 l. per annum, was married to the celebrated Miss Rodd, of Lincoln's-Inn fields, niece to Mr. Justice Price. *L E.*

We hear from Preston in Lancashire, that Mr. Molineux having declined standing as a candidate for Member of Parliament for that place, in the room of Daniel Pulteney, Esq; deceased, Counsellor Fazakerley will be elected without opposition. *Ibid.*

Her Grace the Dutchess of Buckinghamshire gave an elegant entertainment this day to several persons of distinction, upon its being the birth-day of her son the Duke of Buckinghamshire, who enter'd into the 18th year of his age. *S J.*

WEDNESDAY, *Jan.* 12.

Whitehall, Jan. 11. Yesterday M. Como, Agent from the Court of Parma, deliver'd to his Grace the Duke of Newcastle, one of his Majesty's principal Secretaries of State, a letter from the Dutchess dowager Dorothea of Parma, wherein she acquaints his Majesty with the due and happy accomplishments of the succession to the dominions of Parma and Placentia, formerly allotted to the most serene royal Infante Duke Don Carlos, the possession and Government thereof having been delivered up to her as his Guardian; and desires his Majesty's acceptance of a medal struck upon this occasion; and her Highness expresses her sense of his Majesty's friendship to the Royal Infante Duke, and to herself, and of the great share his Majesty has had in this important event. *C.* &c.

The Burlesque wednesdays discourses of the Oratory are discontinued for some time, on an obligation which the Rev. Mr. Henley has entered into, &c. *D J.* —— *This* obligation *was rather* layed upon *him, than voluntarily* entered into; *which occasioned these* quotidian Puffs.

From the PEGASUS *in Grub-street.*

ODE for the new year; faithfully translated into English, for the use of Readers unskilled in the *Cibberine* style; and, consequently, not able to interpret the figurative *sublime of the* original.

N. B. Our courteous Readers are desired, for our honour, and their own emolument, to compare the exalted original, stanza by stanza, with this our elaborate, and almost literal translation.

Recitativo.

AWake, with Songs, the opening day,
That calls for general *cheer:*
Since nothing *good* can live too *long,*
Let AUGUSTUS have a *song;*
And, *hey,* for gambols, and strong beer

Air.

Britons, your Chronicles go read;
See what King's reign you most admire:
The present shall the past exceed,
And *be* whate'er your hearts *desire.*
For if, by chance, the *next* new year
But proves as lucky as the *last,*
Why, *then* —— the *present,* 'tis most *clear,*
Is far more happy than the *past.*

Recitativo.

But, ah! —— so sweet a Prince as he,
Is greater far than *great can be!*
With cares, which none can *see,* oppress'd,
And *thoughtful too,* the Royal breast
Endures full many a weight,
Unfelt by *Cottagers of state.*

Air.

Thus *brooding, single,* in her nest,
The *she* King Eagle wakes;
Nor half her due of pleasure takes,
Tho' Monarch of the air confess'd:
Nay, tho' she *wakes,* her eyes don't *close;* ——
She keeps strict watch and ward,
Her young ones, *yet unhatch'd,* to guard;
That they may *eat, unborn,* in sweet repose.

Recitative.

What thanks, ye *Britons!* can repay
So mild, so just, so soft, a sway?

Air.

When once a year he asks your aid,
The *Land,* and not the *King,* is paid.
Nay, and what's *more,* his *Royal due*
Is but a *Royal want* in *you.*
Air, *moist* or *dry,* alike sends rain,
To raise up earth, that's *born again:*
Blessings more grateful, uninvok'd:
His fame well *spred,* your land well *soak'd.*

Recitativo.

Help me, O help me, shining *crown,*
Who now stand round in *Royal form:*
Sing, sing your wishes, clear and loud;
And, *ah!* be grateful, and be *warm.*

Chorus.

The reign of CÆSAR let his health *supply*
'Till faction shall be *pleas'd to die;*
Or they who *love* him, wish him *down:*
'Till happier tolls than *we,*
In some far country, *see*
A King, *so prais'd,* in so *be mus'd* a Town.

N. B. To the last line, I shall presume, beyond the sphere of a *Translator,* to add an *humble praise;* in reverence of an excellence, which my great Author is well known to be *too modest* to assert his claim to.

With such a LAUREAT to insure renown.

Whereas in Mr. WELSTED's *Dullness and Scandal,* occasioned by the character of *Timon,* there was *false Latin* in the Motto, viz. *Turnus te hoc vulnere* DONIT, instead of DONAT; which false Latin is repeated in what is said to be the *second* and *third* edition: two Gentlemen have laid a considerable wager, the one, that Mr. WELSTED *understood not Latin,* as not having corrected the same in three Editions; the other, that the title of *second* and *third* Edition was only an imposition on the publick, so that Mr. WELSTED could not correct it, as having never been re printed: it is humbly desired of Mr. WELSTED, that he will please to decide this wager, by declaring in this Paper, *which of these is the truth?*

Edinburgh, Dec. 30. On tuesday one Mrs. Eliz. Hogg' of North Berwick, gained the highest prize of 7 l. sterling, for yarn of her own spinning of 7 spindles in the pound. One Margaret Tenier, near Glasgow, gained the next prize of 6 l. for yarn of her own spinning, of 6 spindles in the pound. One Mrs. Bruce, in Edinburgh, gained the lowest prize of 3 l. for yarn of her own spinning, of 3 spindles, And the Trustees for the manufactures were so well satisfied with some yarn shewn to them by a girl of the Merchants Hospital, that they ordered her a compliment of 2 guineas. *C. P.*

FOREIGN NEWS.

THURSDAY, *Jan.* 6.

Naples, Dec. 11. N. S. On saturday arrived here a Courier from Vienna, with the Emperor's commission, constituting the Count de Harrach Viceroy of this kingdom for 3 years longer. *C.*

Copenhagen, Jan. 1. Letters from Stockholm take notice, that altho' the accession to the Vienna Treaty has been twice proposed to the Senate since the King's return, they have come to no resolution, on pretence they wait to see what measures will be taken by other Powers. *D P.*

This day arrived a Mail from France.

Paris, Jan. 12. They have newly printed at the Royal Printing house, the third volume of the ordinances of the Kings of France, from the time of Hugo Capet, collected by Mr. Seconsse, Advocate of the Parliament in place of the late Mr. Lauriere, who had begun that work, and an impression of the 4th volume will be forwarded suddenly. *E P.* M. Secourse. *D P.* Secousse. *P.* Secousses. *C.*

FRIDAY, *Jan.* 7.

Paris, Jan. 12. They write from Grenoble, that M. Raymont, husband to the 2d Madam de France's Nurse, has revived at S. Gervaix, the Royal foundery of iron cannon, which had been laid aside there for 10 or 12 years; and that he is actually casting guns of all sorts and sizes *C.* &c. —— They write from Genoa, that the Duke de S. Aignan arrived there the 29th past. —— We have received advice, that the Princess of Monaco died there of the Small-pox, in the 35th year of her age. *C. P. D P.* —— Some days ago, 3 Attorneys of Pontoise murdered M. Le Fevre, another Attorney of the same place, who had some time before won of them about 60 livres at bowls. They met him in the country, and demanded the 60 livres, which he refusing to pay, they beat out his brains with their sticks, and afterwards threw him into the river, and made their escape. *C.* &c.

Hague, Dec. 18. N. S. Mynheer Hochaver, formerly Secretary to the Imperial Chancery, 'till he was charged with communicating to the French Ministers copies of the Treaty of Vienna of March last, and also of the Count Von Kofstein's instructions, has been tried for that fact, and condemned to work in the mines at Raab in Hungary for 6 years, and then to be banished the Emperor's dominions. ——— The English Merchants settled in the Monarchy of Spain, still complain in their letters, that they do not feel the benefit of the alliance between their Britannick and Catholick Majesties. The Spanish Privateers still take their ships under the *Guarda Costa's,* who at least search their vessels, and make them pay exorbitant duties: which if continued must in time end in repelling force by force; the Court of Spain, which has been informed of all these hardships seeming to turn a deaf ear to the frequent representations that have been made to them upon this subject. *P.*

Extract of a private letter from Liege. —— The Pamphlet by some attributed to Monsieur de Chavigny, entitled *Reflexions of an impartial German Patriot, upon the Emperor's demand of the Guarantee of the Pragmatick Sanction,* makes a great noise. *P.*

SATURDAY, *Jan.* 8.

Hague, Dec. 18. N. S. Our last letters from Brussels advise, that the 2 ships equipping at Ostend by the Directors of the Company of the Austrian Netherlands will speedily sail, notwithstanding the opposition made by certain Powers. —— Private letters from Vienna inform us, that the Electors of Cologn and Bavaria have lately had an interview at Rothenberg, and resolved to rebuild that fortress, demolished many years since: and confirm, that the Electors of Bavaria, Saxony, and Palatine, have no inclination to come into the *Pragmatick Sanction.* —— *Dec.* 21. The Duke de Ripperda is arrived at Tangier; and the next news we hear of him, he will be at Miquenez. We are assured, that he is gone to bring some fatal catastrophe upon the monarchy of Spain: others say his design is against England; but all that we know for certain is, that he is gone away full fraught with some grand enterprise. *P.*

MONDAY, *Jan.* 10.

Extract of a private letter from Hamburgh. —— Upon their High Mightinesses insisting, that the Ostend Company having sent the ship Apollo to India, since the Preliminaries, they could now send but one more by virtue of the Treaty of Vienna, the Emperor has declared, that he had nothing to do with that ship, neither did it belong to any of his subjects. The pasport of the Court of Prussia was given with blanks, for the names of the ship, the Owner, and Captain; and therefore it is plain she belongs to *Nobody*; Signor Rezzmi sells the merchandizes, for *Nobody*: *Nobody* is paid for them; and 2 smacks of this town, loaden with tea from on board her, having been

sken upon the coast of Holland, and confiscated, *Nobody* burns them and therefore *Nobody* defires all the News Papers to insert the following advertisement — A Ship Found, There is arrived in the Elbe, a ship freighted by *Nobody*, commanded by *Nobody*, loaded with tea, china ware, India silks, muslins, and other commodities, which *Nobody* in England or Holland can buy; her passport was too *Nobody*. If any person has lost such a ship, let him apply to Signer Rezani at Hamburgh, who sells the cargo, and will sell the ship for *Nobody*, if *Nobody* reclaims her *P*

Yesterday arrived the Mail from France

Paris, Jan 16 On the 10th, the Deputies of the Parliament went to Verfailles, in obedience to the order they had received from the King, when his Majesty told them, he was very much diffatisfied with his Parliament, and commanded them to erase out of their Registers all that has been done since September in relation to the affairs of the times. *C*

WEDNESDAY, *Jan* 11

Paris, Dec. 31 N S They write from Cahors, that 4 Vicars in that Diocese being interdicted upon account of the Constitution *Unigenitus*, the Recollects perform'd the service in their room. These Gentlemen make no scruple to forbid the reading of the Gospel, upon pain of excommunication for laymen; alledging, among other things, that it is better not to read at all, than to concern themselves with reading the Gospel —— There has been a new fashion started here within these few weeks, occasioned by the famous process between Father Girard and Mademoiselle Cadiere It consists in a sort of ribbons, upon which those two celebrated persons are painted in miniature, much like the figures upon fans; and to these they give the name of *Girards* and *Cadieres* The eagerness of the *Coquets* and *Beaux* at the first appearance of these ribbons, was such, that the price of them rose to a crown a yard the former wore them upon their heads, and the latter upon their fwords. but this mode was soon put down as scandalous, all the ribbon shops in this City having received warning from the Lieutenant General *de Police*, not to sell any more of those ribbons, upon pain of fine and imprisonment, and accordingly several that were exposed to sale in the *Palais*, were seized, together with those that uttered them *C*

Extract of a private Letter from Paris Councils of war are continually holding at Court, and in all appearance, our forces, instead of suffering a diminution either by sea or land, will be augmented —— Our last letters from Tours advise, that an English Gentleman named Hamilton, who had resided there for some time, having invited several friends to his house, he went out, during the repast, to look for a friend that was not yet come, and by accident met in the street one Brochine, a common gamester and bully, who insulted him they drew and the other English gentlemen coming to Mr Hamilton's assistance, Brochine was killed upon the spot Mr Hamilton made his escape; but one of the English gentlemen was taken It is said, there are several witnesses, that will prove Brochine to be the aggressor *P*

Books and Pamphlets published since our last.

5 The Gentleman's Magazine, Numb XII. Pr 6 d
The Englishman's Right, &c By Sir John Hawles Pr 1s.
Alkibla. Part II on worshipping towards the East, &c.
10 Numb I of Elements of Chemistry. Pr 1s 6 d
11 The Peace of Europe a Poem, by Mr. Seagrave Pr 6 d.
A Scheme demonstrating how several hundred thousand pounds may be raised yearly without Officers, &c by Tho Downes Pr 4 d.
A Sermon preached at Christ-Church, Dublin, Oct 23. by Edw Lord Bishop of Clonfert Pr 6 d.
The Political State of Great Britain, for December
Remarks on a Letter to Dr Waterland, &c Pr 6 d.
A character of Ansfelmus, or a view of Parnassus a Poem Pr 1s
12 A Soldier and a Scholar Pr 6 d

On Tuesday Stocks were

South Sea Stock 102 1 half, 102 1 qr for the Opening South Sea Annuity 110 1 half to 5 8ths Bank 149 3 8ths. New Bank Circulation 6 l 2 s 6 d. Premium. India 182 3 qis. 182 1 8th, for the Opening Three per Cent Annuity 97 1 half, for ditto Royal Exchange Assurance 100, for ditto London Assurance 13 1 8th. York Buildings 14, Books open. African 46, for the Opening English Copper 2 l. 16 s. Welch ditto 11 16s South Sea Bonds 6 l. 18 s Premium India ditto 7 l. 2 s. ditto. Blanks 7 l 4 s 6 d. to 5 s 20 l. Prizes 19 l. 6 s

---

LONDON. Printed by S. PALMER and J HUGGONSON, in *Bartholomew-Close*, for Captain GULLIVER, near the *Temple*, where Letters and Advertisements are taken in : As also at the *Rainbow Coffee-House* in *Cornhill*, and *John's Coffee-House in Sheer-Lane*, near *Temple-Bar*. [Price Two Pence.]

The Grub-ſtreet Journal.

NUMB. 107

Thurſday, JANUARY 20, 1731.

OUR kind Correſpondents have frequently expreſſed ſome uneaſineſs, that we neither print their Papers, nor acknowledge the receipt of them; which has occaſioned ſome of them to ſend two copies, on ſuppoſition that the firſt has miſcarried. As in doing this, they have hitherto given themſelves an unneceſſary trouble: ſo they may juſtly believe it will be ſuch for the future; eſpecially, if their Letters are directed to be left at Captain Gullivers near the Temple. It would be very inconvenient to acknowledge the receipt of every Paper; which, if done to one, every Correſpondent would have an equal right to expect. In compliance however with their importunity, we ſhall here publiſh ſeveral which have no relation to one another: the firſt of the three following regarding Arithmetic; the ſecond, Metaphyſics; and the third, Phyſics.

NOtwithſtanding the great perfection to which Arithmetic is now brought, for ought I can find, in multitudes of writers, from Bp. TONSTAL down to Col. AYRES; the grand rule of that excellent Science (deſervedly called the *golden rule*) remains yet unfiniſh'd. As it now ſtands, in the books I have peruſ'd, it is ſo perplex'd and defective, that there are few learners but are ſtrangely at a loſs in ſtating of moſt queſtions; and, for the ſolving of many, they have no directions at all.

On account of theſe inconveniencies, I ſet myſelf to diſembroil this doctrine, and hope I have hit upon a method which will render the practice of the rule of Three, in its utmoſt extent, abundantly *more eaſy, certain, and uſeful.*

The *only difficulty* is to diſtinguiſh, in the terms of a queſtion, the producing from the produced. —— *Producing* terms are ſuch as jointly produce any effect, e. g. whatever is conſidered as a Cauſe, with the adjuncts of Time, Diſtance, Length, Breadth, Depth, &c. —— *Produced* terms are ſuch as are connected with the others, under the character of Price, Produce, Proviſion, Gain, Loſs, Intereſt, Advantage, value or quantity of Work, &c.

Theſe things being premiſed, there will be no difficulty in the following account of

A NEW METHOD

Of anſwering one way, and at one ſtating, all manner of queſtions in the rule of three.

'*Firſt*, Place the conditional terms in one line, in any 'order, and their correſponding terms under each re'ſpectively. —— *Then* having, if neceſſary, prepar'd the 'terms (by bringing the heterogeneous to one deno'mination, and the correſponding to the ſame,) mul'tiply the producing terms of one line by the produced of 'the other, for a dividend; and the reſt of the terms 'together for a diviſor: the quotient will be the term 'required of the ſame denomination with the term over 'the blank.

For inſtance, (I) in the Single rule (1) Direct: *What is the price of* 6 *yards, at the rate of* 5 *s. for* 3 *yards?* (2) Inverſe: *How much ſtuff, yard-broad, will line* 10 *yards of cloth, yard-and quarter-broad?* (II) in the Double rule (i) of five terms (3) Direct: *What is the intereſt of* 200 *l. for* 18 *months, at the rate of* 6 *per cent. per annum?* (4) Inverſe: *At the rate of* 50 *s. for* 50 *l. in* 10 *months, what is the principal of* 6 *l. for* 12 *months?* (ii) of more terms (5) *There is* 48,000 *pounds worth of proviſions to be diſtributed among* 1600 *men for* 40 *days, at ten pennyworth a man a day: I demand, if the ſame was to be diſtributed among* 800 *men, how much would come to each man a day, for* 20 *days?*

The ſtating of theſe queſtions, according to this method, is ſo eaſy and obvious; that even learners will be fore-hand with me in obſerving, that the produced term (1) in the 1ſt queſtion, is 5 s (2) in the 2d, none at all; as generally happens in the ſingle rule inverſe: in which caſe, in each line, inſtead thereof, ſubſtitute an unit; or, which will amount to the ſame, only multiply the terms of the former line for a dividend; and the term of the other, or the product of its terms will be the diviſor; (3) in the 3d, 6 l. intereſt; (4) in the 4th, 50 s. and 6 l. intereſt; (5) in the 5th, 48,000 l. —— So the placing will conſequently be in the

(1) { 5 s. —— 3 y. / 6 } or { 3 y. —— 5 s. / 6 } 5 × 6 = 30 - - - - Dividend
3 - - - - Diviſor.

(2) { 1 —— 5 q. br. —— 10 y lo. / 1 4 } or { 10 y lo. —— 5 q. br. —— 1 / 4 1 } or, &c.

Now, Mr. BAVIUS, if *this method* be new, as I apprehend it is, you will be glad to oblige the Public with it; and if it ſhould prove as *uſeful*, as I conceive it may, all the returns I crave are, that thoſe Gentlemen who are ſkillful and curious in this way, would publiſh their emendations and improvements of this firſt ſketch, in your Paper; where I ſhall be ſure to meet with it: for, to be plain with you, there are ſuch ſwarms of your renegado Members, almoſt in every ſhop, that I dare hardly venture upon any thing, and ſo read but very little of our modern productions. I am, your humble ſervant,

The SEEKER.

Mr. BAVIUS,

SOME years ago, Mr. BERKELEY of Trinity College, Dublin, and Mr. COLLIER of Langford-Magna, near Sarum; without having communicated their thoughts to each other, hit upon *a new ſcheme of the principles of philoſophy:* which, notwithſtanding the character of the authors, and the importance of the thing, has not yet been publickly canvaſs'd.

The titles of their eſſays are, *The principles of human knowledge*, and *The impoſſibility of an external world.* To engage the attention of the curious, pray juſt inform the Public, that the great point they advance, is, that IN NATURE THERE IS, THERE CAN BE, NOTHING BUT SPIRIT AND IDEAS.

This principle, they argue, will not only cut off innumerable ſuperfluities in Philoſophy, but alſo derive a great light on all the parts of human knowledge. Appris'd hereof, and pleas'd with a diſcovery of ſo great compaſs and conſequence, a very young Gentleman of my acquaintance ſtruck out at a heat the following Panegyric: which, unleſs you think it unſeaſonable, or unworthy, you will enter in the Journals of your Society.

On the Reverend Mr. ARTHUR COLLIER'S CLAVIS UNIVERSALIS.

Long have I rang'd through ev'ry ſchool, with pain,
Try'd various ſchemes, yet found the projects vain:
Like NOAH's dove, ſtill anxious was my mind,
And could no reſt to ſatiſy her find:
'Till, by ſome gentle Spirit adviſ'd, ſhe flew;
And, joyful, a ſure footing found in you.
LUCRETIUS, tho' from Heav'n he ſtole his fire,
To dreſs his thoughts in fancy's gay attire;
I ſcorn his doctrine, but his Muſe admire.
In *Academus'* ſhady groves I've walk'd,
And with the ancient Sages hourly talk'd:
Nor they, nor yet CARTESIUS could reſolve
The doubts that did my' unſettled ſoul involve.
But now inform'd, ſhe views each object right;
Free from th' impediments of vulgar light:
By your new ſcheme, corrects her erring ſence,
And gives her reaſon up to evidence.
The Sages' doctrine, which for ages ſtood,
By powerful wit and reaſon unſubdu'd;
By you attack'd can no reſiſtance make:
Your arguments its very baſis ſhake.
For whilſt their occult qualities you diſown,
With eaſe you pull the tottering fabrick down.
The unſeen atoms too, the Modern's boaſt,
By you rejected, are entirely loſt;
Who make all things exiſting in his mind,
Who firſt the beings of each ſeed aſſign'd:
So that, in ſolid body, nothing lies
Too nice to be perceiv'd by human eyes;
Which may uphold its ſeveral properties:
But he that made the world, ſupports the whole;
And next to him, each vaſt inferior ſoul.
For all that's ſeen depends upon ſome eye,
Which what it liſts, can inſtantly deſtroy;
As well as the ideas that we feign,
Chimeras only of a ſickly brain.
In this each man his Maker's image wears,
And, great in power, a Demi-god appears;
That when he will, he's able to create,
What the next hour he can annihilate.
For if around the objects that we ſee,
Trees, purling ſtreams, and fields, ideas be;
The mind, being free, may its ideas chuſe,
Inform new objects, and the old refuſe.
Thus, e'er he fell, once happy ADAM thought,
By holy converſe with the Angels taught:
And thus, by you inſtructed, once again
Our ſouls their ancient privilege attain.
Oh, that the Muſes would ſome bard inſpire,
To ſing your ſyſtem with the Roman's fire!
For, if his verſe preſerves ſo weak a ſcheme,
And gains its Author ſuch a laſting fame:
Yours, ably ſung, would hardly ever die,
'Till age, compar'd to his, a vaſt eternity.
But tho' in proſe, leſs gay is its attire;
Yet evidence gives proſe poetic fire:
Which from groſs ignorance our ſoul refines,
And like the pearl, a gem, tho' not ſo gaudy ſhines.
Needs muſt we all your wond'rous ſcheme approve,
That does Philoſophy's dark miſt remove,
And with new ſenſe of things our brighten'd minds improve.
So when the ſky night's darkſome face o'erhales,
And from our eyes each beauteous object vails;
The day's great ruler with thrice welcome light,
Shows, as a-new, the world, and baniſhes the night.

H. P——R.

SIR,

HAving lately ſeen ſome very mean Pieces popt into publick Papers, I thought it a proper time to get my poor performance publiſhed. You will eaſily diſcern the lowneſs of my accompiſhments, but perhaps not the loftineſs of my expectations, without my unboſoming a little to you. And to tell you the truth, tho' I have had but ill ſucceſs in the former part of my life, yet I expect to live to be a great man; that is, Sir, I am in hopes you will admit me into your Society: and then, as what I here ſend you tends greatly to the improving of natural knowledge, I don't doubt but I ſhall be admitted Fellow of the R——l Society. Now with theſe honours, without doubt, I ſhall paſs for *un bel Eſprit:* and who knows what I may come to be? For, tho' I was brought up behind the counter, and have kept a ſhop in the country, 'till the Hawkers and Pedlars came in ſuch ſwarms amongſt us, that I had nothing left to do, but to trot up to Town and try for a place; and tho' I have, as yet, got nothing but promiſes; yet I am reſolved not to deſpair. Who can tell, but after all, I may come to be LAUREAT; to qualify me for which honourable Poſt, I am glad to find it is not neceſſary to be a Poet. —— But, dear Sir, if you ſhould undervalue this my firſt performance, and not afford it a place in your Paper, all my tow'ring hopes will vaniſh. 'Tis neceſſary that I inform you, that a neighbour of mine, who has ſtretch'd his abdomen by much toping to a remarkable ſize, has obtain'd the appellation of BACCHUS: and he, being one night very flatuous, went into the ſtreet and made a very loud diſcharge, which occaſion'd the following lines, by,

Sir, your moſt obedient, humble ſervant, *W. H.*

Ye Sages, who the cauſes know
Of things above, and things below;
Your mighty wiſdoms ſometimes blunder,
As I ſhall prove, in caſe of thunder.
Your vapours, and your exhalations,
Your flames produc'd by agitations,
Your heat and cold, your wet and dry,
And min'ral juices in the ſky,
Are all a philoſophic lie.
Think not, by ſubtil diſputation,
To overthrow a true relation.
Know then, that BACCHUS late one night,
When all, he thought, were out of ſight,
Replete with wine, and ſwoln with wind,
Retir'd to vent it from behind:
Th' exploſions were like claps of thunder;
You'd ſworn his b——ch was burſt aſunder.
From which this inference does ariſe,
Atteſted by my ears and eyes;
From fact moſt plain: there's no more art in
Making of thunder, than in f——ting.
Mighty diſcov'ry, mighty fame,
On this account I ſure may claim;
Since I, the firſt of all mankind,
Did this important ſecret find.
'Tis true, that ancient Poets ſing,
That JOVE alone his bolts did fling;
That he diſcharg'd his 'vengeful ire
In flaſhing, loud, ſulphureous fire.
But that's all fable, all miſtake:
For all the Gods can thunder make,
Whene'er their bellies chance to ake.
This Tale, when once I was a drinking
With ſparks that boaſted of Free-thinking,

told, —— They swore 'twas wond'rous pretty,
Extremely arch, severely witty:
That well it ridicul'd the noise,
Which frighted women, girls, and boys.
At this was heard a sudden rumbling,
As if the house at once, was tumbling:
The cause unknown, the more they wonder'd;
And all concluded that it thunder'd.
At which our Sparks, of late so pert,
So loud, profane, and so alert,
Dumb-founder'd now, look'd plaguy silly;
And seem'd for once, to *think* not *freely*.
Their thoughts, which, with their visage alter'd,
With trembling lips, and tongue that faulter'd,
In words they plainly could not tell,
They more than told, by looks, and smell.

BAVIUS.

DOMESTIC NEWS.

C. *Courant.*	E P. *Evening Post.*
P. *Post-Boy.*	S J. *S. James's Evening Post.*
D P. *Daily Post.*	WE. *Whitehall Evening P.*
D J. *Daily Journal.*	L E. *London Evening Post.*

THURSDAY, *Jan.* 13.

We are assured, that the report of his Majesty's intention of visiting his German dominions this summer, is without foundation. —— Yesterday his Majesty held a Chapter of the most Hon. order of the Bath, in the Council room at S. James's, his Grace the D. of Mountague, Grand Master, with the Right Rev. Father in God, the L. Bishop of Rochester, Dean of that order; the Hon. Grey Longueville, Esq; King at Arms, being present, with Edm. Sawyer, Esq; Gent. Usher of the order. His Majesty was pleased to create 4, viz. the R. Hon. the Marq. of Carnarvon, the R. Hon. the L. Bateman, Sir Geo. Downing, and Gunter Nichols, Esq; Member of Parliament for Peterborough, to be Knights Companions; and his Majesty put the red ribbons about their necks with the usual ceremony. —— There were 5 red ribbons vacant, viz. his Grace the D. of Richmond's, and Sir Rob. Walpole's, who resigned them for the blue; the L. Deloraine's, L. Sussex's, and Sir Will. Morgan's, deceased. —— We hear that the above 4 new Knights of the Bath will be enstalled in King Henry VIIth's Chappel in Westminster-Abbey, the beginning of March next. *P.*

Yesterday Mr. Crawford, one of his Majesty's Messengers, was sworn into the place of Messenger to the R. Hon. the L. Chancellor, in the room of —— Briscoe, Esq; which place is worth upwards of 200 l. per ann. *P.* —— Mr. Ric. Higgerson is appointed to succeed Mr. Griffith Williams, as one of the Grooms of his Majesty's privy kitchen: and Mr. John Gordon, one of the Children of the privy kitchen, in the room of Mr. Higgerson. *S J. L E.*

On tuesday last, in the afternoon, a person properly called a PUFF, went to several Proprietors in the Charitable Corporation, to desire they would be at the Gen. Court held yesterday, and hoped they would be against petitioning the Parliament for relief, alledging it would be of great detriment to the Company, and that several of the Proprietors were against it, &c. So its very plain, that these Charitable Gentlemen, are afraid of a Parliamentary enquiry. *D P.*—Yesterday was held in Spring-Gardens, a Gen. Court of the Charitable Corporation, when a Petition (drawn up pursuant to an order made at their last meeting) to lay before the Parliament, setting forth the great sufferings of the unhappy Proprietors, and praying such relief as to them shall seem meet, was read and agreed to, with some amendments, and ordered to be printed, and 16 of their Members were nominated to lay the same before the House, of whom five or more are to be present at the delivering the said Petition. *D J.*

Gloucester, Jan. 8. We hear from Trowbridge in Wilts, that on the top of West Ashton-hill, within 2 miles of that place, a mineral spring was discovered of the nature of the Holt Wells, and strongly impregnated with salts, sulphur, steel, allom, and oaker; as appears by the tryals made by Mr. Godfrey, Chymist, in London, and by the strata of earth, stone, &c. dug from the well, viz. oaker very full of small pieces of tulk, veins of living sulphur, stones which produce much steel, the selenites or moon stars, the Ammon's horn in various shapes; cockle, muscle, and oister shells; the lynk-stone, and divers other fossils, &c. 'Tis added, that more than 30 persons, by drinking and washing with those waters, have been already cured of old running wounds and sores, of eruptions, breakings out in the body, arms, and legs; of sore breasts, sore eyes, scurvy in the gums, and some in the King's Evil have received great relief. *S J.* —— *This seems to be a* Puff *against the* Holt Water man.

We are credibly informed, that Mr. Knoaks intends to surrender himself at the Sessions at the Old Bailey, to take his trial. *W E.*

This day the price of South Sea Bonds fell above 20 shillings. *W E.*

This day his Majesty went to the House of Peers, and opened the Session with a most gracious speech to both Houses. 4 *Ev.*

On sunday last died at his seat at Aldenham, near Bridgenorth, in the County of Salop, Sir Whitmore Acton, Bar. He is succeeded in his honour and estate by his only son Sir Ric. Acton, Bar. a young Gentleman of about 20 years of age. *P.* —— Lineally descended from John de Acton, High Sheriff for the County of Salop, 33 Edw. I. *L E.* —— Yesterday died, at Hampstead, Will Ashurst, Esq; Comptroller of the Stamp-Office. *S J. W E.*

FRIDAY, *Jan.* 14.

On tuesday last Mr. Bentley, the son of Dr. Bentley, presented to their Majesties, and their Royal Highnesses, the new edition of Milton. *C.* —— We hear the fees for creating the Knights of the Hon. order of the Bath, are for each near 600 l. besides the charge of a dinner at their installment. *P.*

Yesterday his Grace the D. of Ancaster, Lord Chamberlain of England, went to the House of Lords, and with lighted flamboys searched the vaults under the said house, which has been a custom every time the King comes to the house, since the Gunpowder treason. *P.*

Yesterday there was a Board of Admiralty, when their Lordships put the Kingston man of war, a 4th rate, into commission, and appointed Lieut. John Ogilvy, to be Captain of her. *DP. P.*

We hear from the Theatre in Drury-lane, that the new Comedy, called, *The Modish Couple*, which met with great opposition the 2 first nights, but was acted the third with success, before one of the finest assemblies of persons of Quality that has been seen, was last night again so interrupted, that the Players could not perform, but were forc'd to dismiss the audience, &c. —— Success *before* one of the finest assemblies of Quality, the third night, *whose Taste is the true standard of* Wit, *as well as* Fashions, *is a strong consolation under* Damnation *from the* Vulgar, *and turns it into* Purgatory.

On tuesday last died Will. Davis, Esq; a Gentleman of a very plentiful estate. *P.* —— And yesterday Will. Steele, the Tobacconist, in Newgate: confined there for giving a false information relating to a barrel of gunpowder, &c. *C.*

We hear the Rev. Mr. Henley is required by some of his Subscribers, to propose to the Publick, that his next Sunday Evening's Lecture, engaged by them, to be fully advertised in Fog To-morrow, on God's voice to the Parliament; or, the Practice of Policy, be compared with *that* which is to be preached by a Dignified Divine on monday next. —— The Rev. Dr. Herring, Dean of Rochester is to preach, &c. on monday morning next, &c. *D J.* —— *If the* Oratory Lecture *be but as* intelligible *as this* Puff, *it must needs be more* admired than Dr. Herring's: *who is certainly here level'd at by the* Orator, *on account of his name; it having been usual in* Lincoln's Inn Fields, *as well as* Smithfield, *for a* Merry Andrew *to attaque a* Pickle Herring.

SATURDAY, *Jan.* 15.

His Majesty has been pleased to grant the Archdeaconry of S. David's to the Rev. Mr. Walter Morgan, A. M. *P.* —— Yesterday the Lords spiritual and temporal waited on his Majesty in a body at S. James's, with their address of thanks for his most gracious speech to both Houses of Parliament. *P. DP. DJ.* —— To which his Majesty was pleased to make the following most gracious answer: My Lords, I thank you for this affectionate and loyal address. As the interests of my people, and the securing the peace and balance of power in Europe, has been my chief care and concern; the satisfaction you shew in the success of my endeavours, cannot but be extreamly acceptable to me. You may depend upon my favour and protection; and I am persuaded I may always rely upon your duty and support. *D P.*

Yesterday was held a General Court of the South Sea Company, when a dividend of 2 *per cent.* was agreed on. A General state of the Company's affairs was communicated to the Court; it appear'd, that in the year 1720, the Company owed on bonds above 4,400,000, and that they do not owe now 2,000,000 l. that since Mar. 25, 1721, to Christmas last, they had received by the Assiento trade 250,000 l. more than sent out, and very considerable demands they still have: that by the Greenland trade they had lost about 50,000 l. and the Court of Directors were of opinion it would not be adviseable to pursue that trade after the present year, without the Parliament should give them some further encouragement. The General Court seemed well pleased with the management of their affairs, and returned thanks to the Directors. *C.* —— In the year 1721, 640,000 had been lost or sunk in the Assiento trade; but since that time 250,000 had been received more than sent out. *D J.*

His Majesty has been pleased to grant unto Tho. Liveings, of Woodburn in Bucks, &c. the sole use and benefit of making and vending a compound manure, for mending and improving land for 14 years. *P.* —— *Puff.*

Christened: Males 198, Females 198. In all 396.
Buried: Males 248, Females 248. In all 496.
Decreased in the burials this week 70. *E P.*

N. B. The Oratory-Transactions, lately republished to be had there, are, &c. *Fog's Journal.* —— *This seems to be an honest retraction of a Puff in the* D J. *of Dec.* 31. N. B. A new impression is to be had at the Oratory of the first numbers of the Oratory-Transactions, &c. —— *These* Transactions *are it seems only* republished; *a word of great propriety, invented by* Mr. CURLE, *who scorns to put off an* old *Edition, by* putting on *persons* a New Imposition, *under the title of a* New Impression.

MONDAY, *Jan.* 17.

On saturday in the afternoon the Hon. the House of Commons waited on his Majesty at S. James's, with a very dutiful and loyal address, and was most graciously received. —— Yesterday the Rev. Dr. Lynch preached before their Majesties, his Royal Highness the Prince, &c. And the Rev. Dr. Clarke before his Royal Highness the Duke, &c. *C.*

On saturday Sir John Tash, Alderman of Walbrook Ward, declared Mr. Hezekiah Walker to be duly elected Common-Council-man upon the scrutiny, in the room of Mr. Rob. Henshaw. *D P. D J.*

Wednesday last Will. Folkes, of the Inner-Temple, Esq; was married to Miss Ursula Taylor, a young Lady of great merit and considerable fortune. —— Yesterday the wife of an eminent Attorney in Smith-street, Westm. was brought to bed of 3 children, viz. 2 girls and 1 boy: she was delivered of two children the last time she was brought to bed. *D P.*

On saturday Corbet Vesey was try'd on an indictment for starving his wife to death, and, after a long tryal, was acquitted. *D J.* It lasted 5 hours. *C.* About 6 hours. *D P.* 8 hours, *P.* —— We hear the relations of Mrs. Vesey intend to bring an appeal; Lewis Hussar, a French Barber, who was executed some years ago for the murder of his wife, being acquitted by the Jury on the indictment, but found guilty on the appeal. *D P.* —— Ric. Pool (lately committed to Newgate, being charged with perjury, &c.) was on friday try'd at Hicks's Hall, for assaulting Justice Lawton in the execution of his office, and found guilty, and received judgment to be 3 month's confined in Bridewell, to hard labour, and to receive the correction of the house, when the time is expired. The assault was committed upon his examination concerning the said perjury. *D J.*

On saturday notice was given, that Mr. Noakes will surrender himself this day at the Old Baily, &c. *D J.*

Yesterday morning died the R. Hon. the Lady Diana Feilding. She was youngest Daughter of Francis, Earl of Bradford. Her first Husband was Tho. Howard, Esq; one of the Tellers of the Exchequer, (Son of the Hon. Sir Rob. Howard, Brother of the Earl of Berkshire) who left issue one Son, who died at Westminster school, and one Daughter, married to the R. Hon. Lord Dudley and Ward. She married afterwards the Hon. Will. Fielding, Esq; Brother to the E. of Denbigh. This Lady's Grandson, the L. Dudley and Ward, dying last summer unmarried; the estates, both in Norfolk and Surrey, descend to the present E. of Berkshire. *C.* &c.

TUESDAY, *Jan.* 18.

The installation of the 4 new Knights of the Bath, is to be on Mar. 1. at Westminster-hall. *D J.* —— Some time since Mr. Hurst was appointed one of the Yeomen of the Guard, which place he purchased for 350 l. *P.*

Yesterday was preached at Bow Church, by the Rev. Dr. Herring, Dean of Rochester, an excellent Sermon before the Societies for the reformation of manners; at which were present the R. Rev. the Lords Bishops of London, Durham, Rochester, Ely, Carlisle, Litchfield and Coventry, Chichester, Landaff, and S. David's. Several Aldermen, and a great number of Justices of peace, and of the Rev. the Clergy, and a very numerous auditory. *C.*

On saturday the L. James Cavendish, with M. Gurley and Mr. Ewer, arrived here from their travels. *P.* —— Yesterday Mr. Noke surrendered himself at the Old Bailey, &c. *C. P.* Mr. Nokes. *D J.* Mr. Noakes. *D P.*

Yesterday morning the South Sea Company received the agreeable news of the safe arrival of their ship the Eaton, Capt. Kettle, in the Downs, from Buenos Ayres and Guiney, richly loden. *P.* —— Received letters of Oct. 8, from Buenos Ayres, by the ship City of London, Capt. Kettle, who delivered there near 390 negroes. She had a long passage, and the negroes were reduced to a very low estate. —— The Eaton Galley Capt. Upton, arrived there July 20, and delivered upwards of 230 slaves. *D J.*

On saturday night died Mr. Tomlinson, Professor of Geometry, at Gresham College. *P.* —— On sunday: to which place is annexed a salary of 50 l. per ann. and a house, with other conveniences. *D P.*

On friday morning dy'd suddenly at his seat at Mannington in Norfolk, Sir Cha. Potts, Bar. who was a Woollen Draper at the Naked Boy in Fleet-street about 1718, who having no issue, the title is extinct. *L E.*

WEDNESDAY, *Jan.* 18.

We hear from Bear-Key, that there is a very small

dispute between the Distillers and the Maltsters on the one hand, and the Farmers and Kentish-hoymen on the other; the cause whereof is —— The Distillers and Maltsters have lately combined to pay no longer certain charges on such corn as they shall buy, tho' these charges have been paid by them, and all other buyers, time out of mind, and were at first wisely settled by an act of Common Council: now these Gentlemen are endeavouring not only to overcome this act, but also to throw these charges on the poor Farmers. — The Factors and Kentish-Hoymen, who act for the Farmers, and who ought to use all their endeavours for their interest, have agreed not to sell any corn to the Distillers and Malsters, or any other buyer, unless they will pay such charges as formerly they have done; so that hereby there is almost a stagnation of business at Bear-Key. — But how little regard soever the Distillers have for the Farmers interests, yet it is still remembered, that when the Gin act was a-foot, these very Gentlemen made all the interest they could with the landed men and Farmers, to speak to their representatives in their favour; and perhaps a like occasion may offer again. *C.*

Yesterday Mr. Nokes was try'd at the Old Baily, for the murder of Mr. Turnor, &c. and acquitted. It held 7 hours. *D P.* 8 hours. *C.* 9 hours. *D J.* — Mrs. Faulkner, the woman that was in company, proved that the deceased offered to kill himself with a red hot poker, and afterwards with his sword, which Mr. Nokes desired her to take with her. Several persons gave the prisoner a good character, as not given to quarrelling. *P.* —— He is not discharged out of Newgate, by reason the deceased's Brother intends this day, as we hear, to lodge an appeal against him. *P. D J.*

Ric. Pool, committed to Newgate, on oath of Col. Wingfield and *his wife* for perjury, was brought before the bench of Justices at Hicks's-Hall to be try'd, but not caring to be try'd before *their Worships*, travers'd the indictment 'till next Sessions: however, we hear the same will be mov'd by Certiorari into the Court of King's Bench, to be try'd before the L. C. Justice Raymond. *D P.*

Tho. Moreton, Esq; Senior City Counsel, is sworn in Steward of the Borough of Southwark. *P.*

Yesterday, about 12, died Mr. Jones, at the Fleece tavern in Cornhill, a very eminent Merchant of this City. *P.*

From the PEGASUS *in Grub-street.*

We hear the following short Letter was sent yesterday to every Member of the Honourable House of Commons.

SIR, *Jan.* 13, 1731.

YOUR *commiseration* is most humbly *craved*, in behalf of all *aggrieved Suitors* at *Law*, that the GRAND COMMITTEE for *Courts* of *Justice* may sit to chuse a CHAIRMAN to do *business*; then will the *oppression* of the *Law* appear, and the *numerous, burthensome*, and *useless offices* thereof, with the *exorbitancy* of their *fees*, be *exposed*.

BRITANNIA.

Whereas it was said in the P. and *D P.* of Jan. 7. that 'On sunday last died at Islington, Mr. Emlyn, an eminent Dissenting Minister;' this is to assure the world, that he is at this very time as much alive, as he has been for many years past.

To Mr. CONUNDRUM, at the Pegasus in Grub-street.

Dear Cousin,

YOU know I am a Gentleman of very good parts, and excellent application; and that I have, with very great applause, done all the exercices which our *Alma Mater* requires, in order to commence *Batchelor*. I have had the honour of wearing this gown some time, and hope soon to exchange it for a *Master's*. During my residence at College, I have made it my chief business to qualify my self for the conversation of the polite part of the world; and, at length, have obtained a very happy talent in *Punning*. But, Cousin, there are now in our University a great number of plodding, old, testy Fellows, who are ready to sound at a *Pun*; nay, a great many of our young whipsters begin to affirm, that *Punning* is false wit: I beg you would be so good as to reason them into another opinion, which I cannot do, on account of an old grudge they owe me. This unreasonable ill-will I have gained, it seems, by telling a young Gentleman, who said, my wig was not *upright*, that it was an emblem of a P——r; and yet this is two or three years ago. The D—— rs were affronted soon after, because as one of them passed by in his robes, and a country acquaintance, who never saw the University before, asking me, if all the D——rs wore such gowns? I answered, yes, They are *all as bis*; for which (an ill-natur'd Fellow over-hearing) I was accused of calling the D——rs *all asses*. In short, some way or other, I have affronted all Orders in the University, tho' it is very unreasonable they should be angry at a joke from, dear Cousin, your most affectionate Kinsman,

HENRY CONUNDRUM.

P. S. *I forgot to tell you, that our young men have got a very unmannerly phrase amongst them, whenever a man begins to be witty, they insolently cry out, Cork him: pray persuade them to be more mannerly.*

An EPITAPH on THEOPHILUS CAVE, Esq; in the Chancel at Barrow upon Stowre.

HERE in this grave
There lies a *Cave*.
We call a Cave a Grave:
If Cave be Grave, and Grave be Cave,
Then Reader judge, I crave,
Whether does Cave here lye in Grave,
Or Grave here lye in Cave?
If Grave and Cave here buried lye,
Then, Grave, where is thy victory!
Go, Reader, and report here lyes a Cave,
Who conquers Death, and buries his own Grave.
Cave, Ave in æternitatem.

Dublin, Jan. 1. At Mr. Mac Donald's, Merchant, at Castlebar, one of his Apprentices went with a shoemaker into a room next to the shop, to take out some goods, where lay a barrel of gun-powder: and as they were clandestinely taking some of it, the snuff of a candle fell in, and [the powder] taking fire, forced the Apprentice through the loft and roof, and blew him 100 yards from the house: the shoemaker being on one side of the barrel, was only lifted up to the reeves of the house, where he was kept fast by the roof, which came plump down the minute the powder was fired: the shoemaker was found almost dead: 2 other Apprentices were in the shop, where they had like to have been smother'd, the roof and loft coming down on them. There was not 20 s. worth of damage done to all Mr. Mac Donald's goods. *P. Jan.* 15.

Dublin, Dec. 28. On friday last our Parliament adjourned to thursday, Feb. 3. —— *Jan* 4. His Grace the L. Lieutenant has been pleased to grant Letters Patent unto James Wall, Esq; and Charles his son, and the survivor of them, of the office of second Chamberlain of the Court of Exchequer. —— Letters Patent are passing, containing a grant unto Edw. Digby, Esq; of the office of Gentleman Porter of his Majesty's Castle of Dublin. — *Jan.* 8. We hear that Alderman Sam. Burton was lately knighted by his Grace the D. of Dorset. *C. P. Jan.* 15. —— On thursday died the Rev. Dr. Will. Gore, Dean of Down. *P. D P.*

Edinburgh, Jan. 10. On friday died of a consumption the Hon. Geo. Ogilvie, Advocate, Son to the late E. of Finlater and Seafield, much regretted for his parts and learning. *C. D P.*

FOREIGN NEWS.

THURSDAY, *Jan.* 13.

Yesterday arrived a Mail from France, *and one from* Holland.

Paris, Jan. 19. We find that the Lead-mine lately discovered in Brittany, promises beyond expectation, so that 'tis reckoned lead enough will be extracted thence in time to supply the whole Kingdom, and save the expence of importing it from abroad. *D P.*

Vienna, Jan. 5. An express arrived from Constantinople brings advice, that the Turks are resolved on a war with the Republick of Venice; that the Grand-Seignior is actually equipping 18 men of war, with a great number of other vessels, to go and attack the Isles of Zante and Corfou; and that the famous Gianon Coggia, late Admiral, who fell under disgrace last year, and was banished to Retimo, will be deputed to command in this expedition. *D P.* — They have actually set up the Horse-tail against the Christians. *D J.*

Seville, Dec. 28. Orders are sent to the Sea-ports for building several new men of war, the Court being resolved to put the navy in a flourishing condition. Mean while the works of Gibraltar are suspended, those already done being sufficient to hinder the running of contraband goods. *D P.*

FRIDAY, *Jan.* 14.

Venice, Jan. 5. Gianun Coggia, who had been the most instrumental in establishing the new Sultan upon the throne, &c. was seized May 17, and carried to the point of the Arsenal, to be strangled within sight of the Sultan, who went for that purpose, with the *Sultana Valide*, or Queen Mother, into a Kioske situate upon the sea-side. Gianun Coggia was no sooner arrived here, but the *Bostangi* Bashaw, who was charged with the execution, took off his furred robe, bidding him not to make any motion, because the Grand Seignior observed his actions. But he cried out as loud as he could to his Master, beseeching him not to put him to death, at least without a hearing; adding, that 50 years service done the Empire, and what he had lately done in person, and his great age, might plead in his favour. But if not, he ought to reflect, that he was going to embrue his hands in the blood of an innocent man, for which he must give an account to God. Upon this the Grand Seignior opened one of the windows of the *Kioske*, and made signs with his hand that they should not put him to death, but that he should be carried to the Point of Chalcedonia, where they should wait his farther orders. *P.*

SATURDAY, *Jan.* 15.

Rome, Dec. 29. N. S. We have a confirmation that the old King of Sardinia has obtained the favour of having his wife with him again. It is reported here, that the titular Lord Hay and his Lady are turn'd Roman Catholicks in the County of Avignon. *P.*

MONDAY, *Jan.* 17.

Hague, Jan. 8. Our letters from Vienna say, that the Spanish troops lately landed at Leghorn, were [perpetually quarrelling with those of the Great Duke; who begins to be tired already] with the complaints continually made to him. —— Our letters from Warsaw are full of the factions and divisions of that unhappy kingdom. King Stanislaus's party is now grown strong enough to appear almost barefaced; and this is in a great measure attributed to the intrigues of the Marq. de Monti, Ambassador of France, who is justly esteemed one of the ablest Ministers in the service of that Crown. *P.*

On saturday arrived the Mail from Holland, *and yesterday that from* Flanders.

Hague, Jan. 20. They write from Osnabrug, that the Duke of Lorrain arrived the 15th; and the next day set out for Berlin. *C.*

Berlin, Jan. 12. Two days ago, the Hereditary Prince of Bareith set out, with the Princess his Consort, on his return to Bareith. *C.*

Leghorn, Dec. 31. The Infante Don Carlos arrived here the 27th, landed in the evening, and made his public entry into this city, where he was received as Great Prince of Tuscany, with all the grandeur and magnificence possible. *C.*

Ratisbon, Jan. 14. In the assembly of the Dyet on friday last, the affair of the *Pragmatick Sanction* was concluded, by a majority of voices, according to the Emperor's intention. *P.*

Copenhagen, Jan. 12. They write from Norway, that the foreign East India ship which arrived in a harbour of that Kingdom some time ago, staid there 'till 2 other vessels had loaded themselves with her cargo, and sailed no body knows whither. —— We hear from Stockholm, that the affair of that Crown's accession to the Treaty of Vienna is protracted, somewhat like that of the States General. *P.*

Vienna, Jan. 9. 'Tis advised from the Frontiers, that the French are fortifying several posts in the neighbourhood of Landau. *D P.* —— And that the Court of France has given orders for buying up several thousand horses, to remount their Cavalry. *D P. P.*

TUESDAY, *Jan.* 18.

Yesterday arrived the Mail from France.

Paris, Jan. 22. Letters of Dispensation being arrived from Rome, for the marriage of Mademoiselle de Chartres, on the 21st she was betrothed, and married on the 22d. *D P.* —— The Court has given orders for the immediate equipping of several men of war, and some bomb vessels. 'Tis assured this Armament is made purely on account of the Algerines, who have, on several occasions, infring'd on former Treaties. *D P. P. D J.*

WEDNESDAY, *Jan.* 19.

Extract of a private letter from Vienna.

We are told, that the King of Sweden has consented to his imperial Majesty's request, to send two ships every year to the East-Indies under Swedish colours; which permission his imperial Majesty can transfer to such of his subjects, as he thinks fit. *P.*

Extract of a private letter from Paris.

We hear it has been represented to this Court, on the part of a neighbouring Crown, that it was not easy to comprehend with what view his most Christian Majesty was so augmenting his forces both by sea and land, at a time when the general tranquillity of Europe seemed to be settled upon the most solid and unalterable foundation: that this conduct of the Court of France justly alarmed their neighbours, who found themselves under the hard necessity of keeping up their armaments, though they had resolved to ease their people of the great burden of maintaining an extraordinary force both by sea and land. Wherefore they think it reasonable to demand a positive answer in relation thereto; which has occasioned several conferences at our Court, to consider of means of satisfying our neighbours, as we are informed. *P.*

Books and Pamphlets published since our laſt.

13. Liberty: or the meeting of the Parliament. A Poem.
The Aſſembled Patriots: or the meeting of the Parliament. A Poem. Pr. 6 d.
The ſeaſonable Enquiry, &c. Pr. 2 d.
Free Parliaments: or an Argument on their Conſtitution, &c.
A Treatiſe of Feme Coverts: or the Ladies Law, &c.
14. A Letter to the Author of Chriſtianity as old as, &c. by Anthony Holbrook. Pr. 6 d.
Milton's Paradiſe Loſt. By Ric. Bentley, D. D.
The Modiſh Couple: a Comedy: by Cha. Bodens, Eſq;
The monthly Chronicle, for December.
Malpaſia: a Poem: by Mr. Humphreys. Pr. 6 d.
15. Faithful Memoirs of the Life and Actions of James Butler, late Duke of Ormonde, &c. Pr. 1 s. Grub.
Mr. Pope's Poem on Taſte: with a compleat key, and nótis variorum, &c. Pr. 1 s. Grub.
Original Poems, &c. by Will. Bowman, M. A. Pr. 1 s. Grub.
The Report of the Gentlemen appointed by the Charitable Corporation, &c. Pr. 1 s.
17. Don Carlos de Lara: or the Spaniſh Bean. Pr. 1 s.
An Enquiry into the Origin of Honour, &c.
The Ambitious Father: or, the Politician's Advice to his Son: a Poem in 5 Cantoes: by Edw. Ward. Pr. 1 s.
Verres and his Scribblers: a Satire in 3 Cantoes. Pr. 1s.
A Deſcription of Devils, &c. Pr. 6 d.
19. The Third Part of the Merry Thought, &c. Pr. 6 d.
The Court Biſhop no Apoſtolical Biſhop, &c. Pr. 1 s.

On Tueſday Stocks were
South Sea Stock 103 7 8ths, 103 3 qrs. for the Opening.
South Sea Annuity 110 1 8th, to 1 qr. Bank 149 1 qr.
New Bank Circulation 6 l. 10 s. Premium. India 182 3 qrs. Books open. Three per Cent Annuity 97 3 qrs.
Books open. Royal Exchange Aſſurance 100, Books open. London Aſſurance 13 1 qr. to 3 8ths. York Buildings 13 1 qr. to 1 half. African 46, for the Opening. Engliſh Copper 2 l. 15 s. Welch ditto 1 l. 16 s. South Sea Bond. 8 l. 13 s. Premium. India ditto 6 l. 19 s. ditto. Blanks 7 l. 4 s. 6 d. to 5 s. 20 l. Prizes 19 l. 6 s.

ADVERTISEMENTS.

Lately Publiſhed the two following Books.

I. Practical Diſcourſes on the ſeveral Parts and Offices of the Liturgy of the Church of England: Wherein are laid open the Harmony, Excellency, and Uſefulneſs of its Compoſure. In four Volumes. By Matthew Hole, D. D. late Rector of Exeter College in Oxford. Vol. I. Containing 58 Diſcourſes on all the Parts of Morning and Evening Prayer, including the Creed of St. Athanaſius. Vol. II. and III. Containing 55 Diſcourſes on the Litany, and the Prayers and Thankſgiving that follow it. Vol. IV. Containing 174 Diſcourſes (in 3 large Parts) on all the Collects, Epiſtles and Goſpels, to be us'd throughout the Year. The Second Edition.
II. A practical Expoſition of the Church Catechiſm. In two Volumes. By the ſame Author. The Third Edition, with the Addition of two Diſcourſes; one on the Duty of confeſſing Chriſt, the other on the Danger of denying him; both preach'd at St Mary's in Oxford.

Sold by J. and J. Knapton, and C. Rivington in St. Paul's Church-Yard; A. Bettesworth and C. Hitch in Paternoſter Row; and S. Birt in Avemary-Lane.

This Day is publiſhed,

Dedicated to the Gentlemen of the Navy of England,

THE MEMOIRS of Monſieur du Gué Trouin, Chief of a Squadron of the Royal Navy of France, and Great Croſs of the Military Order of S. Lewis; containing all his Sea-Actions with the Engliſh, Dutch, and Portugueſe, in the late Wars of King William and Queen Ann.

Tranſlated from the French by a Sea-Officer.

Printed for J. Batley, at the Dove, in Pater-noſter Row
Where may be had,
The TRADITIONS of the CLERGY no way Deſtructive of Religion: A Sermon preach'd at Bingle Church, on Sunday September 12th, 1731.

By IS. SMITH.

Miniſter of Haworth, near Kighley, Yorkſhire.
ALSO.

I. The Religion of Nature conſidered. To which is added a Poſtſcript, containing Reflections on Mr. Chubs's Diſcourſe concerning Reaſon, &c. ſo far as it reſpects this Subject.
II. Some Thoughts concerning Virtue and Happineſs. In a Letter to a Clergyman.

Juſt publiſhed,

The Second and Laſt Volume of

THE SACRED CLASSICS defended and illuſtrated. In Three Parts. Containing,
I. A further Demonſtration of the Purity, Purity, and formal Eloquence of the Language of the NEW TESTAMENT WRITERS.
II. An Account of the wrong Diviſion of Chapters and Verſes, and faulty Tranſlations of the DIVINE BOOK, which weaken its Reaſonings, and ſpoil its Eloquence and native Beauties.
III. A DISCOURSE on the various Readings of the New Teſtament.
With a PREFACE, wherein is ſhewn the Neceſſity and Uſefulneſs of a new Verſion of the Sacred Books. By the late Reverend and Learned A. BLACKWALL, A. M. Author of the Firſt Volume.
To which is added, A Copious INDEX.
Printed for C. RIVINGTON, at the Bible and Crown in S. Paul's Church-Yard.
Where may be had,
I. Mr. BLACKWALL'S SACRED CLASSICS, Firſt Vol. Second Edition.
II. —— New Latin Grammar, for the Uſe of Schools.
III. —— Introduction to the Claſſics: Containing a ſhort Diſcourſe on their Excellencies, and Directions how to ſtudy them to Advantage, &c. for the Uſe of Schools.

This Day is publiſhed,

In Two Vol. Twelves,

And ſold by C. Davis in Pater-Noſter-Row, and A. Lyon in Ruſſel-Street, Covent-Garden,

HISTOIRE de Charles XII. Roi de Suede, par M. de Voltaire.
N. B. The Tranſlation of the above Book is near finiſhed, and will be publiſhed in a few Days.
Where may be had, lately printed,
1. Les Voyages de Cyrus, avec un Diſcours ſur la Mythologie, par M. Ramſay.
2. Dr. Lobb's Treatiſe of the Small-Pox. In 2 Parts.

This Day is publiſhed,

LOVE and AMBITION. A Tragedy. As it is Acted at the Theatre-Royal in Dublin by his Majeſty's Servants.
Abeat Fortuna Superbis. Hor.

By JAMES DARCY, Eſq;

Dublin, Printed: London, Re-printed for J Roberts in Warwick-lane. Price 1 s. 6 d.
Where may be had, juſt publiſh'd,
I. SCHEMES from Ireland for the Benefit of the Body Natural, Eccleſiaſtical and Politick. The firſt humbly offer'd for making Religion and the Clergy uſeful. With the Author's Obſervations on the Cauſe and Cure of the Piles: And ſome uſeful Directions about wiping the Poſteriors. The ſecond, an infallible Scheme to pay the publick Debt of this Nation in ſix Months. Humbly offer'd to the Conſideration of the P—— t. Pr. 6d.
II. POEMS on ſeveral Occaſions; containing the Progreſs of Wit in Ireland. The Poet's Well; an Eſſay towards a Tranſlation of Anacreon. An Ode on his Majeſty's Birth-Day: To which is added, the Plague of Wealth, occaſion'd by the Author's receiving Fifty Pounds from his Excellency the Lord Carteret for the aforemention'd Ode. With ſeveral Poems not in the Dublin Edition, and a curious Frontiſpiece engrav'd by Mr. Vertue. By Matthew Pilkington, M. A. Price 3 s. 6 d.
III. The DRAPIER's Letters to the People of Ireland, concerning Mr. Wood's Braſs Half-pence, with Conſiderations on the Attempts made to paſs that Coin, and Reaſons for the People of Ireland's refuſing it.
O thou whatever Title pleaſe thine Ear,
Dean, Drapier, Bickerſtaff, or Gulliver, &c.
IV. The TRIBUNES. Part I. and II. being a Collection of entertaining Papers on various Subjects. Price 2 s.
V. The PARISH-PRIEST: a Poem of much Piety, and not a little Satire. Price 6 d.

This Day is publiſhed,

And Sold by J. Brotherton at the Bible over-against the Royal-Exchange in Cornhill,

A NEW EDITION of

LES Aventures de Telemaque, Fils d'Ulyſſe. Par feu Meſſire François de Salignac de la Motte Fenelon, Precepteur de Meſſeigneurs les Enfans de France, & depuis Archevêque-Duc de Cambrai, Prince due Saint-Empire, &c. Nouvelle Edition, conforme au Manuſcript Original. Enrichie d'un grand Nombre de Figures en Taille Douce. Avec des Remarques pour l'intelligence de ce Ouvrage.
This new Edition is correctly printed, with a good Letter, upon a fine Paper, with 25 Cuts and a Map, all engrav'd by the beſt Hands, and is no way inferior to the Hamburgh edition, and is ſold 30 per Cent. cheaper than that Edition; and beſides, farther Allowance will be made to all Gentlemen who take Numbers to uſe in Schools.
N. B. This Edition has 12 Cuts more than that of Hamburgh.

LONDON: Printed by S. PALMER and J. HUGGONSON, in Bartholomew-Cloſe, for Captain GULLIVER, near the Temple, where Letters and Advertiſements are taken in: As alſo at the Rainbow Coffee-Houſe in the North, and John's Coffee-Houſe in Shoar-Lane, near Temple-Bar. [Price Two Pence.]

The Grub-street Journal.

NUMB. 108

Thursday, JANUARY 27, 1731.

Here studious I unlucky Moderns save;
Nor sleeps one error in its father's grave.
Dunciad, B. I.

To Mr. BAVIUS, Secretary to the Grubean Society.

SIR,

I Always imagined, that MILTON made use of an Amanuensis, for no other reason but because he was blind himself. But his late learned Editor has assigned three other substantial reasons for this; namely, because he was *obnoxious to the Government, poor, and friendless*, Pref. pag. 1. These circumstances, at first sight, seem to be such as would rather oblige a man to write his own copy himself; and none, but a person of an uncommon way of thinking, could have alleged them in proof, that a Poet *dictated his verses to be writ by another.*

However, from this manner of writing them from his mouth, it is certain, that many *errors in spelling*, and *pointing*, must needs have creeped into the first copy; and highly probable, that *even in whole words of a like or near sound*, one word was sometimes written down for another. These errors, being followed and augmented by those of the Printer in the first impression, received still an additional increase in the succeeding editions. The like has happened to many other English books, in prose, as well as in verse, which have borne several editions, the last of which are generally the most incorrect; insomuch that in some of them it is necessary to have recourse to the first, as to a manuscript, to discover the true original meaning of the Author. This observation was made to the Public, not long ago, in relation to Mr. CHILLINGSWORTH's *Safe guide*, &c. and I fear it may be justly applied to many other pieces. Which incorrectness is, I believe, chiefly owing to the inadvertency, and sometimes ignorance of Printers, who frequently undertake the correction of English books themselves.

And if this be the case of the prosaical pieces, that of the poetical must necessarily be much worse; which even a learned person is not capable of correcting, unless he have likewise a taste for Poetry, and somewhat of a poetical Genius himself. —— Of this our learned Editor being throughly sensible, to prepare his readers for a more candid reception of his Emendations of *Paradise Lost*, assures them, in VIRGIL's words, 'That he has verses by him of 'his own composing, that some Pastors call him a Poet; 'but that he does not believe them.

Sunt & mihi carmina; me quoque dicunt
Vatem pastores: sed non ego credulus illis.

Now altho' this has been hitherto so great a secret to the world, that they never entertained the least suspicion of any such thing: yet I doubt not, but they will not only believe the two former parts of the Doctor's affirmation, but will likewise readily join with him in the last part, and not presume to differ in this point from the faith of so great a Divine.

Many of these *typographical errors* are obvious to a diligent Reader; who will not be surprized at them, if he consider the two sources above-mentioned, from which they must necessarily flow. But there are besides many other *blemishes* in this Poem, which no man ever discovered, or even suspected, till our Learned Editor took it in hand. MILTON himself was guilty of many *slips and inadvertencies*, which *cannot be redressed without a change both of the words and sense. There are* likewise *some inconsistencies in the very system and plan of his Poem.* Pag. 4. To these, he declares, the *Author may fairly plead Not guilty*, because he had lost his *eye sight*; which it seems is as necessary to draw *the plan* of an Epic Poem, as of a magnificent Palace. For these *inconsistencies in the plan* are declared to have happened *for want of his revisal of the whole before its publication.* Where by the word *revisal*, is meant, not a *mental revisal*, (which the Author must necessarily have often made) but an *ocular*; it being said immediately before, that *had he had his eye-sight, he would have prevented all complaints.*

But what is worst of all, the Author's *suppos'd friend*, the last *Editor* of this Poem, *knowing* MILTON's *bad circumstances, thought he had a fit opportunity to foist into the book several of his own verses, without the blind Poet's discovery*; which the learned Doctor has now first *detected by their silliness and unfitness.* Pag 3, 4. — To this perhaps it may be objected, that the Editor had little temptation to this piece of infidelity; and that the danger was very great of a discovery, unless the Poet had been *as deaf as blind*. But this is fully answered by the learned Doctor in the next page, where he tells us, *That the proof-sheets of the first Edition were never read to* MILTON: *nay the Edition, when published, was never read to him in seven years time.* —— And this rascally Editor, being thus incouraged by the success, had the impudence to *insert* more of *his forgeries, even in the second Edition, when the Poem and its Author had slowly grown to a vast reputation.* Pag. 5. So that he, not only in the Poets *bad circumstances*, but even in his good, *thought he had a fit opportunity to foist into his book several of his own verses*; and consequently there was no security against such a villain.

If it be asked, What proof the Doctor has brought of the truth of these two pieces of Secret History, 'That 'this Poem was thus interpolated, and 'That the Author 'never heard it read in seven years? As to the first, he says, *the Editor's interpolations are detected by their own silliness and unfitness*: and as to the second, *an attentive Reader will be throughly convinc'd of it.* The latter of which he corroborates by *a farther confirmation; That when* MILTON *afterwards publish'd his* Paradise Regain'd, *and* Samson Agonistes; *that edition is without faults; because he was then in high credit, and had chang'd his old Printer and Supervisor.* Thus this blind Author, who, when the first edition of his *Paradise Lost* was printed, having *threescore years weight upon his shoulders, might be reckoned more than half dead*, could not prevent the errors of that edition; nor being *grown to vast reputation seven years* afterwards, could not prevent the propagation of those errors in the second; being at last got in to *high credit*, and grown older, revived on a sudden, *chang'd his old Printer and Supervisor*, and *published* his Paradise Regain'd *in an edition without faults.* This account may seem strange to vulgar apprehensions: but every thing is wonderful, which relates to this wonderful man.—Thus much for this learned *Preface*, the foundation of all the succeeding criticisms: and if I see this letter in your next Journal, it is probable I may send you some instances of the *sagacity and happy conjecture* of this Great Critic, in his alterations of the first Book.

I am, Sir, your most humble servant,

Jan. 21, 1731. J. T.

A List of the Commissioners of the High Court of Justice, who sate in judgment upon King CHARLES I. and condemned him to be beheaded on Jan. 30, 1648.

THE decollation of King CHARLES I. was an action, which, at the distance of above fourscore years, is now variously represented; being approved, as well as condemned by many. The posterity of the greatest number of those who had the boldness to sit in judgment upon their Sovereign, and condemn him to lose his head, has been long extinct; so that very few of the Off-spring of any of them remain alive, to be either applauded or reproached for the actions of their Fore-fathers. There is therefore the greater occasion to preserve the memory of the JUDGES, who signalized themselves in so unparallelled a manner; and to spread their names as much as possible, to be an object either of admiration, or abhorrence to the present age.

John Bradshaw, President
* John Lisle
William Say
Oliver Cromwell
Henry Ireton 5
Sir Hardress Waller, Knt
Sir John Bourcher, Knt
* William Hevenningham
* Isaac Penington, Alderman of London
Henry Marten 10
William Purefoy
John Barkstead
* Matthew Thomlinson
John Blackistone
Gilbert Millington 15
Sir William Constable, Bar
Edmund Ludlow
John Hutchinson
Sir Michael Livesey, Bar
Robert Tichburne 20
Owen Roe
Robert Lilburn
Adrian Scroope
Richard Deane
John Okey 25
John Huson
William Goffe
* Cornelius Holland
John Carew
John Jones 30
Miles Corbet
* Francis Allen
Peregrine Pelham
Daniel Blagrave
Valentine Walton 35
Thomas Harrison
Edward Whaley
Thomas Pride
Isaac Ewer
Thomas Lord Grey of Groby 40
Sir John Danvers
Sir Thomas Maleverer, Bar
John Moore
John Alured
Henry Smith 45
Humphry Edwards
Gregory Clement
Thomas Wogan
Sir Gregory Norton, Bar.
* Edmund Harvey 50
John Ven
Thomas Scot
Thomas Andrews, Alderman of London
William Cawley
Anthony Stapley 55
John Downs
Thomas Horton
* Thomas Hammond
* Nicholas Love
Vincent Potter 60
Augustine Garland
John Dixwell
George Fleetwood
Simon Meyne
James Temple 65
Peter Temple
Thomas Wayte

Those marked with an * did not sign the Warrant for his execution; which was signed by all the rest, and likewise by Richard Ingoldsby, and Thomas Chaloner, who were not present at the Tryal.

SIR,

IT is rare to meet with a Preface or Dedication to any new Book, without an invective against mankind, for not giving a more publick encouragement to learning, and men of wit. The general run of Authors take all opportunities of calumniating the present age, beyond any that has preceded. In this, in short, consists the whole mystery of writing; for tho' in reality genius and learning are, in a modern Author's Arithmetick, but of small value or consideration; yet if he cries out in an angry tone, that men of parts are neglected, there are thousands of charitable Readers, who are immediately for ranking him in that class. I may take upon me to affirm, that learning is, in this age, so far from being discouraged, that even the meanest pretenders to it meet with constant protection and assistance.

The Authors of this Town, by a moderate reckoning, may be computed at six thousand; four thousand that are concerned in political discourses, one in dramatick performances, and the other odd thousand in petit pieces. A formidable army to be maintained by the pure benevolence of the publick. Disband half our Writers, and the Hessians may be maintained another year, without any great burthen. In the forementioned six thousand 'tis probable there may be ten men that have a tolerable share of learning; the remaining 5990 consist either of such as have taken up the trade of writing from an observation, that as it is at present managed, fewer abilities and less genius are required in it, than in any other profession; or else of men of fortune and quality, who write for fame, and often to gain the reputation of Wits, lose that of having common-sense; or else of Beaux and Lovers, who, to soften their obdurate Mistresses, think it necessary to attack them in the harmonious strains of Poetry.

Some, 'tis true, have made Poetry the daughter of love: but if this was to be admitted as a truth, then every man that was fool enough to be in love, must be at the same time wise enough to be a Poet. Rhime, it must be confessed, has often been produced by love: but rhime and poetry, are far from being synonymous. If indeed the spirit of rhiming always ended with the passion that created it, the Criticks would have no great cause of complaint. But the misfortune of it is, that, like thieving, when once a person is initiated, he can't leave off 'till he has committed some crime too enormous to be passed over. From a love song to CAELIA, many a man has been led to the writing of a very bad Play; or what is high treason in Poetry, the attempting at even an heroick Poem itself without a genius.

There is scarce a day passes that does not afford us some instance of that whereof I am now speaking. The last new performance at Drury-lane is an irrefragable argument to prove the truth of this assertion. A Play, which is one of the most arduous tasks of which human wisdom is capable, requires not only the strongest judgment and observation, but the utmost delicacy in the working up. Every person ought therefore to ponder well his own abilities, before he ventures on so bold an undertaking.

I would ask the Author of *The Modish Couple*, upon a supposition that he was at the head only of fifty men, whether he would venture to give battle to an army of 50,000? and if he did, whether all mankind would not justly condemn him for a temerarious, precipitate Hero. For my own part, I see but little difference between this

caſe, and that of a Writer, who audaciouſly attempts the moſt difficult performance, without either wit or humour, without genius or capacity; and, in ſhort, without being poſſeſſed of even one qualification neceſſary to the accompliſhment of ſo great a work. What can we then think of an Audience, that with noiſe and violence are reſolutely bent to ſupport a wretched Rhapſody of the loweſt chit-chat? A thing, call'd a *Comedy*, without plot, language, or ſentiments. The moſt charitable thoughts that can ſurely be entertained, are either to pity their folly and ignorance; or elſe to conclude, that there muſt be ſomething worſe in their endeavours to impoſe upon mankind, by applauding what indiſputably ought to have been condemned to the Flames. A man that claps out of time is making the moſt poignant Satire againſt himſelf: 'tis like laughing in company at no Jeſt. How far beneath his quality does a Nobleman appear, when at the head of a formidable party to countenance ſuch a piece! The reproach does not lye in being a friend to a bad Poet, but in patronizing his Works.

Among the Greeks and Romans, their Captains and Generals were freqnently men of the fineſt parts, improved by the moſt liberal education. They were ſcholars, as well as Soldiers, and could command the pen, as readily as the ſword. But the education of moſt of our military Gentlemen is very different from theirs. And tho' many of them are ingenious, and ſome of them learned Perſons: yet they act out of their ſphere; if they endeavour to ſecure the ſucceſs even of a good Play, by bringing a large party into the houſe, liſted under them on purpoſe to make a noiſe in its behalf. This conduct will naturally provoke a contrary party to hiſs it off the ſtage undeſervedly. But if the Play be really bad, nothing can effectually protect it from the contempt of the Audience, but a detachment of the Foot-Guards, ready to fire upon any perſon who ſhall preſume to ſhew the leaſt token of diſlike.

I am, Sir,

Your humble ſervant, E. P.

The Society expect, that this Gentleman ſhould ſend ſome criticiſms upon this Play, to make good in particular inſtances, what he has here only alledged againſt it in general.

A Recipe to make a Modern Dramatick Poet. To C—— B——, Eſq;

Since a Bard to commence, you are fir'd with a paſſion,
And write in Dramaticks — becauſe 'tis the faſhion;
Since dire Heathen Greek ne'er puzzled your noddle,
Nor Precepts antique from old ARISTOTLE;
A few modern ones take, which will teach you much better,
To dictate a Play, tho' you can't write a letter.
Take of learning a grain for the Critics in Pit;
Of good Humour a ſcruple, and a dram of good Wit;
An ounce of good ſenſe far too much will be found;
Half will do: but of Laureate-Aſſurance a pound.
Five *Double Entendres* in your Epilogue put,
To leave in the Ladies an impreſſion of Smut.
Theſe precepts can't fail a gay Modern to raiſe,
As fam'd for Dramatick as T——d or BAYS.

DOMESTIC NEWS.

C. *Courant.*	EP. *Evening Poſt.*
P. *Poſt-Boy.*	SJ. *S. James's Evening Poſt.*
DP. *Daily Poſt.*	WE. *Whitehall Evening P.*
DJ. *Daily Journal.*	LE. *London Evening Poſt.*

Omitted in our laſt.

Mr. *D'Anvers*, in his Journal of the 8th, ſays in his note at the bottom of the page, that 'the *higheſt* calculation of the Army Debentures was at firſt 400,000 l.' ——In the laſt year of Q. *Anne*, the houſe of Commons, appointed a ſelect Committee, who drew up a ſtate of that Debt to Chriſtmas, 1713, which amounted to 1,854,859 l. 3 s. 9 d. ½, beſides which, there were 2 Papers annex'd, containing farther demands of 733,334 l. 9 s. 6 d. ½ on which no judgment was given by the Committee; but they were mark'd with theſe words *Paſs'd over*. This was the *firſt calculation* of that Debt; *this* was enter'd into the Journals of the Houſe of Commons; *this* lay before them the next year; *this* was freſh in the memory of all who had been Members of the former Parliament, and was ſo commonly known without doors, that it is hardly to be conceived it ſhould have eſcaped Mr. *D'Anvers* reſearches. If he did *not* know of it, I hope that, upon this information, he will abate of his anger towards thoſe who have ſometimes blamed him for raſhneſs in his aſſertions. If he *did* know of it, I would beg of him to try, by his own rules, Whether a wilful miſrepreſentation to the People, may proceed from a *Spirit of Liberty*. *C. Jan.* 15.

THURSDAY, *Jan.* 20.

Yeſterday came on the election of Governors of the Royal African Company for the year enſuing, when the King's moſt excellent Majeſty was rechoſen Governor; Sir Bibye Lake, Bar. Sub-Governor, in the room of Rob. Sutton, Knight of the Bath; and James Oglethorpe, Eſq; Dep. Governor, in his room. *DJ.*

The ſame day Mr. Ald. Barber declared on the ſcrutiny for Common-Council men for the Ward of Caſtle Baynard, that the following Gentlemen were duly elected, viz. Mr. Valentine Grimſtead, Mr. Trubey, Mr. Belchier, Mr. Innys, and Mr. Williams. *C.* —— The Alderman, who could not be there, deputed a Common-Council man to declare for the old Common-Council. *DP.* —— Mr. John Cordwell was appointed, who declared the numbers of good Pollers to ſtand as follows.

Mr. Grimſtead ——	140	Mr. Peachey ——	105
Mr. Trubey —	133	Mr. Perkins —	110
Mr. Belchier —	139	Mr. Clear ——	95
Mr. Innys ——	129	Mr. Williamſon ——	107
Mr. Williams —	133	Mr. Atkinſon —	94 *P.*

Dr. Hare, Biſhop of Chicheſter, is appointed to preach before the Houſe of Lords on the 31ſt inſt. *DP. P.* —— Dr. Alured Clarke, one of the Prebendaries of Wincheſter, is appointed to preach before the Houſe of Commons. 4 *Even.*

Laſt night the Seſſions ended at the Old-Bailey, when Rob. Hallam, for murdering his wife, and Geo. Scrogs, for robbing a Clergyman, received ſentence of death. *DJ.* Of 13 s. 6 d. *P.* On a ſunday morning. *C.* —— Hallam deſired to relate the Caſe as it really was, or he ſhould not be eaſy, which the Court granted, and was in ſubſtance, 'That he came home one night about 12, and knocking at the door longer than uſual, when let in, he ſcolded at his wife for making him ſtay; that they both went up ſtairs, in order to go to bed, he went into bed, but ſhe did not, ſo he aſked her the reaſon; upon which ſhe ran down ſtairs; he followed her, and ſtruck her with his fiſt; that then ſhe ran up, and locked herſelf into the chamber, and he ſtood in his ſhirt without, threatning to break the door open, and ſaid he would fetch his cane. After ſeveral words paſſing between them, ſhe flung herſelf out of the window, for when he broke the door open, he heard a cry in the ſtreet of murder, not knowing, 'till he had enter'd the room, that ſhe was gone: that he ran down into the ſtreet, and took her up in his arms, and carried her up to bed: that he frequently aſked her if ſhe was hurt, or any limb broke, but ſhe did not then complain, or accuſe him; tho' afterwards ſhe complained of a pain in her belly, &c. and died. He pretended that he was proſecuted out of malice, &c. and ſaid, he could not fling her out of the window, it being but 16 inches and a half wide.' He proteſted his innocency, as did the other priſoner, and begged for tranſportation. —— No appeal being brought againſt Mr. Nokes before the Court roſe, he was diſcharged. —— The perſon who proclaimed the Pretender in the Tower, appearing to be a Lunatick, was not tried, but ordered for Bethlehem. *DP.*

Yeſterday morning died Tho. Mauley, Eſq; a Gentleman of a very great Eſtate in Cornwall. *DJ.*

Laſt monday a melancholy accident happened at Canterbury: as Mr. Lade, the Leatherſellller, was writing in his room, a man brought home his fowling-piece, and ſet it down a little diſtance from him: Mr. Lade's Son, about 7 or 8 years of age, playing with the trigger, the gun went off, and ſhot the Apprentice in the back and out at the breaſt, as he overlooked his maſter, and the unfortunate youth died within a few hours after. *LE.*

FRIDAY, *Jan.* 21.

His Majeſty was pleaſed to return the following moſt gracious anſwer to the addreſs of the Hon. Houſe of Commons.

'Gentlemen, I return you my thanks for this dutiful and loyal addreſs: I make no doubt of the continuance of your duty, affection, and confidence in me: and you will always find, that all my views tend to the honour, intereſt, and ſecurity of my Crown and People.' *C.* —— Yeſterday being the Birth-day of his Royal Highneſs the Prince of Wales, when he entered into the 25th year of his age, there was a great appearance at Court. *C. DJ.* —— *The* SJ. *of yeſterday has* the 26th year.

Morgan Vane, Eſq; is appointed Comptroller of the Stamp Duties. *C.* —— We hear he will be made, &c. a place of 400 l. per ann. *DP.* —— Cha. Bodens, Eſq; is made Secretary to the Commiſſioners of Hackney-Coaches. *C.* —— Regiſter to the Commiſſioners for regulating and licenſing Hackney coaches and chairs. *DP. Jan.* 24. —— *It is pity there are not* Commiſſioners for regulating Hackney Writers, *as well as* coaches.

Yeſterday Lieut. Col. Sam. Weſtal was elected Muſter-Maſter for this City. *DP.* &c. —— The ſame day a Gen. Court was held at the Bank, when they came to a final reſolution for building a new houſe in Threadneedle-ſtreet, according to a plan laid down by Mr. Sampſon; and likewiſe reſolved, that an handſome Equeſtrian ſtatue be erected to the memory of our great and glorious Deliverer King WILLIAM the 3d, in the Court-yard leading to the houſe. C. &c.

Yeſterday came on the election of 24 Aſſiſtants of the Royal African Company, when the following Gentlemen were choſen, viz. Col. Aſhby, John Baker, Tho. Bodicoate, John Bodicoate, * Fran. Boteler, Tho. Bradſhaw, * Joſ. Bradſhaw, Chriſtian Cole, Rob. Cruikſhank, Joſ. Danvers, Dan. Finch, * John Gaſcoyne, Cha. Hayes, * John Laroche, Cha. Lloyd, Hen. Parſons, Ben. Periam, Tho. Revell, Eſq; the Hon. Sir Tho. Saunderſon, * the R. Hon. Sir Rob. Sutton, Knights of the Bath, John Thompſon, Fran. Townley, Tho. Watts, and Phi. Wilkinſon, Eſqs; Thoſe marked with * were not Aſſiſtants the preceding year. *DJ. DP.*

Yeſterday morning, between 12 and 1, died the Rev. Mr. And. Tooke, F. R. S. 2d Maſter of the Charter-houſe ſchool near 30 years, and choſen head Maſter upon the demiſe of Dr. Walker. He had his education in that ſchool; ſo that his excellent natural parts wanted no ſort of culture, and being endowed with an admirable facetiouſneſs in converſation, his company was coveted and admired by perſons of all ranks. *P.* —— Laſt tueſday died at Watford in Hertfordſhire, Mr. Iſaac Finch, aged 104 years. He followed the trade of a Leather-dreſſer 80 years, and died worth near 15,000 l. He was a great benefactor to the poor. *P.*

SATURDAY, *Jan.* 22.

Laſt night, about 7, a Meſſenger arrived at Whitehall, from the R. Hon. E. of Waldegrave at the Court of France, on ſome extraordinary affairs. *P.*

Tho. Lloyd, Gent. Surveyor General of the duty on houſes, lately diſcharged from being Clerk of the peace for Cardiganſhire, is reſtored into that office by the Lieutenancy and Juſtices of the peace. —— Capt Rob. Trevor is made Commander of the Exeter, a Guardſhip at Plymouth. *DR.*

We hear that the moſt valuable collection of manuſcripts belonging to Dr. Tanner, Biſhop of S. Aſaph, were on their removal from Norwich to Chriſt-Church in Orford, (of which he is alſo Canon) and that they formely belong'd to that great and truly primitive Prelate, Archbiſhop Sancroft, by whoſe Nephew they were ſold, to the late Mr. Bateman, a Bookſeller, from whom they were purchaſed by the preſent owner; and that they were very great curioſities which have ſuffer'd ſo much. *DP.*

Yeſterday at a Gen. Court of the worſhipful Company of Mercers, came on the choice of a Lecturer for Wakefield in Yorkſhire. The Candidates were the Rev. Mr. Diſney, Mr. Fenton, and Mr. Lamplugh; *but being* reduced to the 2 former, upon a diviſion the numbers ſtood, viz. for Mr. Diſney, 120; Mr. Fenton, 82. *C.* Mr. Diſney had a majority of 36. *P.*

A few days ſince the R. Hon. the L. Viſc. Bulkeley, Member of Parliament for Beaumaris in Angleſea, was married to Miſs Owen, daughter and heir of the late Lewis Owen, of Peniarth in Merionethſhire, Eſq; a fortune of 60,000 l. *DP.*

Yeſterday morning died Tho. Bonds, Eſq; a Gentleman of a great eſtate in Warwickſhire. *DJ.*

MONDAY, *Jan.* 24.

Yeſterday morning the Rev. Dr. Greenwood preached before the King and Queen, &c. and the Rev. Dr. Birch before his Royal Highneſs the Duke, &c. *C.*

On ſaturday night laſt his Grace the D. of Cleaveland and Southampton was married to the Lady Harriet Finch, one of the daughters of the late E. of Nottingham, and ſiſter to the preſent E. of Winchelſea. *DP.*

George Heathcoate, Eſq; one of the Directors of the South Sea Company, has diſqualified himſelf by ſelling his ſtock. *DJ.*

On ſaturday morning laſt, Sir John Williams, Knt. Alderman of Cripplegate Ward, declared the 4 old Common Council-men for the Ward of Cripplegate without, duly elected on the ſcrutiny; when the poll ſtood as follows, viz. for Mr. Dep. Farrington 187, Mr. Will. Meredith 175, Mr. Will. Cooper 181, Mr. John Deeton 177, Mr. Tho. Tew 160. *P.* —— *The* C. *and* DJ. *leave out the word* four.

Laſt ſummer at Paris, the L. Derwentwater having ſymptoms like thoſe of the ſtone, was ſearched by 3 eminent Surgeons, 2 of which declared they could not diſcover any; but the 3d declaring, that he diſcovered one, my Lord was immediately brought to London to be cut; where Mr. Cheſelden ſearching him, declared he could not find any; and Mr. Ferne declared the ſame alſo. About a month after, Mr. Cheſelden ſearched again carefully, and gave as full aſſurance as ſuch a caſe admits of, that there was none; and therefore would not cut him. When my Lord was opened, there was neither ſtone, gravel, nor ſand, found in his bladder; but his right kidney was very large, ulcerated, and full of matter, and the ureter (or the paſſage from the kidney into the bladder) was alſo diſeaſed; the matter from the kidney continually flowing with the urine into the bladder, cauſed the ſymptoms uſually found in ſtone-caſes, and this diſeaſed kidney was the ſole cauſe of his death. *P.*

Laſt night died at his houſe at Tottenham High-Croſs, Mr. Abrah. Craieſteyn, an eminent Dutch Merchant.— On friday died Mr. Turner an eminent Brewer in Bar

naby-ſtreet, Southwark, as is thought, of exceſſive grief for the loſs of his only ſon, who died about 3 months ago, being on the point of marriage to a young Gentlewoman of conſiderable fortune, who is given over by her Phyſicians. *C.*

Lent Preachers appointed to preach before his Majeſty, for the year 1731-32.

Feb.
23 *Aſhwedn.* Dean of the Chappel, L. Bp, of London
25 *Frid.* Dean of York, Dr. Oſbaldeſton
27 *Sund.* L. Bp. of Durham
March
1 *Wedn.* Mr. Chamberlain
3 *Frid.* Dean of Durham, Dr. Bland
5 *Sund.* L. Bp. of Sarum
8 *Wedn.* Dr. Waterland
10 *Frid.* Dean of Exeter, Dr. Gilbert
12 *Sund.* L. Bp. of Chicheſter
15 *Wedn.* Dr. Benſon
17 *Frid.* Dean of Litchfield, Dr. Penny
19 *Sund.* L. Bp. of Bangor
22 *Wedn.* Mr. Bundy
24 *Frid.* Dean of Peterborough, Dr. Lockyer
26 *Sund.* L. B. of Glouceſter
29 *Wedn.* Dr. Foulkes
31 *Frid.* Dean of Sarum, Dr. Clarke
April
2 *Palm Sund.* L. Bp. of Wincheſter
5 *Wedn.* Dr. Terry
7 *Good Frid.* Dean of Weſtminſter, L. Bp. of Rocheſter
9 *Eaſter day*, L. Almoner, L. Archbiſhop of York

Appointed to preach at his Majeſty's Chappel at Whitehall.

Feb.
23 *Aſh-Wedn.* Dean of Glouceſter, Dr. Newcome
25 *Frid.* Dr. Pearce
Mar.
1 *Wedn.* Dr. Lovell
3 *Frid.* Dr Hutton
8 *Wedn.* Dr. Day
10 *Frid.* Dr. Thiſtlethwate
15 *Wedn.* Dr. Crow
17 *Frid.* Dr. Hargraves
22 *Wedn.* Mr. Bernard
24 *Frid.* Dr. Lewis
29 *Wedn.* Dr. Cobden
31 *Frid.* Dr. Littleton
Apr.
5 *Wedn.* Mr. Lavington
7 *Good Frid.* Dean of Rocheſter, Dr. Herring.

C. D P.

TUESDAY, *Jan.* 25.

Mrs. Allworthy, a maiden Lady, who died lately vaſtly rich, has left her eſtate to be laid out in a purchaſe, and intailed ſuch eſtate ſo purchaſed on Mr. Allworthy, a Corn-Chandler at New Brentford, and his heirs (which are pretty numerous) and for want of heirs, to Chriſt's Hoſpital, &c. *L E.* 50,000l. *S J.* ——— *I hear ſhe was not at all related to him.*

The R. Hon. the E. of Portmore is appointed his Majeſty's *Ambaſſador* extraordinary to Italy, to compliment Don *Carlos* in his Majeſty's name, on his happy arrival in the Dominions of Parma and Placentia. ——— Yeſterday Dr. Anderſon was introduced by the R. Hon. the L. Baltimore, to his Royal Highneſs the Prince of Wales, to whom he preſented in form, his book of Royal Genealogies, dedicated to his Royal Highneſs, which was graciouſly received. *P.*

The Rev. Mr. Geo. Stephens, Rector of Weſt-Clandon in Surry, and Chaplain to the R. Hon. the L. Onſlow, is appointed by the R. Hon. the Speaker of the Houſe of Commons, to be his 2d Chaplain, and accordingly officiated yeſterday in that Hon. Houſe. *D P.*

Laſt ſunday ——— Vane, Eſq; Comptroller of the Stamp-Office, was married to Miſs Knight, a Lady of 8000 l. fortune, at S. James's Chappel. *P.*

We hear from Oxford, that ſome Gentlemen, who promoted the placing of a MS. in the Bodleian Library, and the publiſhing it from thence lately, contrary to the intention of the Author, begin to diſcover their error by the reception the world gives it, and the ſlowneſs of its ſale. *D P.*

We hear that the Gentlemen who purchaſed the reverſion of the eſtate of the late L. Derwentwater, are obliged to pay that Family about 30,000 l. before they can be let into the benefit of that purchaſe. *D P.*

On new-year's day, a private Gentlewoman, living near S. James's, received a letter from an unknown hand, with a Bank bill incloſed. This account is publiſhed in hopes it may help the perſon aſſiſted to a knowledge of her benefactor, that ſhe may have it in her power to repay the charity with a virtue full as rare, viz. gratitude. *P.*

A few days ſince died Mr. Pet. Whitton, an eminent wholeſale Grocer of the City of York, Receiver General of the Eaſt and Weſt riding of the ſaid Country. *C.—viz. the* City of York.

Yeſterday being the firſt day of the term, &c. Mr. Francklin appeared at the King's Bench, Bar, but the judgment awarded againſt him was deferred for ſome days. *C.* — He has 'till 4 days within the term to move in arreſt of judgment. *D P.* — He will receive ſentence the laſt day of this term. *P. D J.*

On friday laſt the Hon. Rob. Byng, Eſq; was unanimouſly re-elected to ſerve in Parliament for the Borough of Plymonth. *D P. D J.* — And on ſaturday the Hon. John Spencer, Brother to the R. Hon. the E. of Sunderland, was unanimouſly elected for Woodſtock. *P. D J.* — And was yeſterday introduced into the Houſe of Commons by Will. Pultney, Eſq; *D J.*

Canterbury, Jan. 22. His Grace the Archbiſhop hath granted a Patent to John Shelden and Will. Churchill, Eſqs; for the Officers for the Conſiſtory Court of the Dioceſe of Canterbury. *W E.*

WEDNESDAY, *Jan.* 26.

An order has paſs'd his Majeſty's Board of works, for the neceſſary repairs and beautifying the Royal Palace at Kenſington, for the reception of the Royal Family, their Majeſties deſigning to reſide there early in the ſpring. *C.*— His Majeſty has been pleaſed to appoint Enſign Scot to ſucceed Capt. Fog. deceaſed, in the command of a company in the firſt Regiment of Foot Guards. *C.*

Geo. Purvis, Eſq; a Captain belonging to his Majeſty's Navy, is choſe a Member of Parliament for Alborough in Suffolk. *P. D. P.*

Yeſterday Mr. Francklin's Council moved in relation to his conviction; but the Poſtea of that conviction not being brought into Court, they were directed to move again. *D P.*

On monday Mr. Wright, a wholeſale Druggiſt in Lawrence-lane, was married to Miſs Hammond, an agreeable young Gentlewoman, with a fortune of 6000 l. —— And yeſterday Mr. Naſh, an eminent Woollen Draper in S. Paul's Church-yard, to the only daughter of Mr. Bateman, in partnerſhip with him; a young Gentlewoman of fine accompliſhments, with a fortune of 5000 l. *C.*

From the PEGASUS *in Grub-ſtreet.*

The Art of turning a thought round and round, in imitation of a Squirrel turning a cage with bells, or of a Dog turning a ſpit, exemplified in a *Penitential Letter from the Craftsman*, &c, publiſhed in the *C.* of *Jan.* 13.

Dear BAVY,

BEing at the tavern with ſome friends to'ther night, as his Majeſty's ſpeech lay before us, one of the Company, preſuming on the good conſequences of a peace ſo eſtabliſhed, ſcribbled over this ſong, which you may inſert in your next Grub, or not, just as you think fit. Yours,

Jan. 18th, 1731-2. BRITANNICUS.

Peace, return'd on downy wings,
Fame and Triumph with her brings:
Happy Britain! bleſs the day
When the jarring powers agreed:
Such is Mighty GEORGE's ſway,
Who has Europes's fate decreed.
To Great GEORGE and CAROLINE
Let our hearts and glaſſes join.

War no more, deſtructive war,
Shall alarm us from afar.
Now ye Hinds ſecurely plow;
Reap the fruitful years increaſe:
Baniſh Sorrow every Brow;
Wealth and Honor flow from Peace.
To Great GEORGE, &c.

Lo! the Merchant truſts the Main:
His the hazard, his the gain.
Traffic free, and Taxes waining,
Sep'rate Int'reſts now no more;
Freedom too her Rights maintaining
Shall the Golden Age reſtore.
To Great GEORGE, &c.

Each ſcene I view'd did but my woes proclaim,
At home an Exile, — baniſh'd from my fame!
Life without glory, what a worthleſs prize?
Recall'd to ſink beneath a weight of ſhame,
And bear the load of life without its fame.

Curſe on that pity then, which meanly gave
My body freedom —— kept my mind a ſlave.
'Twas cruelty, not love, an art could find
To ſave the man —— yet captivate the mind.
Scorning that mercy, which my ſoul detains
In ſlavery ſtill — with freedom held in chains.

Treaſon, if once reſolv'd to ſtrike, whene'er
She draws the ſword ——— muſt bleed, or perſevere.
Who injure States, muſt either die or kill;
Firſt draw the ſteel, then caſt the ſheath away.
In all, thro' guilt, to greatneſs who aſpire,
Safe to purſue —— but fatal to retire.
From treaſon once begun, whoever fly
Sharpen that ſword by which themſelves ſhall die.
In ſhallow plots their danger when they ſee,
A deeper plunge alone can ſet them free.

FOREIGN NEWS.

THURSDAY, *Jan.* 20.

Yeſterday arrived the Mail due from Holland.

Rome, Jan. 5. On monday was celebrated, with a great deal of magnificence, in the Palace of the Chevalier de S. George, the birth-day of his eldeſt ſon, who then entered into the 12th year of his age. *P.*

Genoa, Jan. 5. On ſunday we received advice, by a veſſel from Corſica, that the 2000 men, under the command of the Commiſſary Gen. Doria and Col. Wachtendonk, were returned to Baſtia with a booty of 3000 head of cattle; having burnt the Towns of Luciana, Borgo, and Venceláſco, with ſeveral magazines of corn, cheſnuts, and ſalt, and killed above 500 Rebels, with the loſs only of 8 or 10 men. *P. DP.*

Ratisbon, Jan. 17. The Miniſters of Bavaria, Saxony, and Palatine, have delivered to the Protocol in the Electoral College, and that of the Princes, a proteſtation, couched in very ſtrong terms, againſt all that had been done in their preſence, relating to the affair of the Guarantee of the Pragmatick Sanction, and againſt all that ſhall be done on that ſubject during their abſence, theſe Miniſters being returned home. *D J.*

Madrid, Jan 1. They write from Liſbon, that in the town of Barreiro, Juan Roderigo, aged 125 years, and his wife, aged 105 years, died Octob. 17. They had been married 87 years. *P.*

Moſcow, Jan. 11. The Czarina having ordered Gen. Soltikoff to draw up the 3 Regiments of Guards in the Cremelin, ſummoned an Aſſembly yeſterday in the evening, of all the Generals, Miniſters and Synod; and having made a ſpeech to them, which laſted near a quarter of an hour, ſhe ordered the Archbiſhop to read the form of an oath, whereby the ſaid Generals, &c. promiſed and engaged to acknowledge thoſe for their Sovereigns, whom her Czarian Majeſty ſhould nominate to be her ſucceſſors in the Empire; which was accepted and executed by all the Aſſembly *nemine contradicente*; and the Dutcheſs of Mecklemburg, the Princeſs her daughter, and the Princeſs Elizabeth were the firſt who ſubſcribed that oath. *P. DP. D J.*

FRIDAY, *Jan.* 21.

Yeſterday arrived the Mail due from France.

Paris, Jan. 26. N. S. On monday laſt we had here ſuch a thick fog, that the like was never known in the memory of man; and we have heard of ſeveral ſad accidents occaſioned by it. *C. P. D P.*

Rome, Jan. 5. Card. Coſcia has ſent a very ſubmiſſive letter to Card. Albani, to intreat his protection, acquainting him that he is ready to obey the Pope's orders, and return to Rome to proſtrate himſelf at his feet. *D P.*

Extract of a letter from Cadiz, *Jan.* 8. —— We learn by way of Nantes, that 2 of the Galleons, which ſuffer'd in the ſtorm, are put into Guarica in the iſle of Santo Domingo. *P.* ——— *Cadiz, Jan.* 8. In the year 1731, have arrived in this bay 301 Britiſh ſhips, 130 French, 7 Dutch men of war, and 53 Merchant ſhips, 9 Swedes, 3 Hamburghers, 1 Imperial, 1 Daniſh, and 1 Genoeſe; ſo that the Britiſh ſhips amount to 96 more than thoſe of all other nations added together. *D J.*

SATURDAY, *Jan.* 22.

Yeſterday arrived the Mail due from Holland.

Hanover, Jan. 22. The Duke of Lorrain arrived at Herenhauſen on the 19th, about 3 in the afternoon, with a retinue of 40 perſons. And yeſterday about 9 he ſet out for Pein in the Dioceſe of Hildeſheim. *D P. D J.*

Vienna, Jan. 16. Born here laſt year 6006: died 6710 *D J.*

Moſcow, Jan. 3. The Veldt-Marſhal Dolhorucki, has been condemned to loſe his head: but her Imperial Majeſty has been graciouſly pleaſed to commute his puniſhment for perpetual impriſonment at Schluſſemberg. *D P.* Schuſſelburg. *D J.*

MONDAY, *Jan.* 24.

Hague, Jan. 29. On friday laſt the States of the Province of Holland came to a reſolution to accede to the Treaty of Vienna; which reſolution was the next day reported to the States General, when the Deputies of Utrecht, Overyſſel, Frieſland and Gelderland, declared themſelves ready to concur in it. Thoſe of Zealand and Groningen deſired time to conſult their reſpective Provinces, who are to aſſemble on monday next. *P. DP. D J.*

Paris, Jan. 30. The King has bought of M. de Seignelay, all the manuſcripts collected by the late M. Colbert, for which he is to give him 300,000 livres; and they were carried to his Majeſty's library ſome days ago. —— Before the Imperial Troops evacuated the Dutchies of Parma and Placentia, General Stampa, who commanded them, made the Marq. de Monteleone, the King of Spain's Miniſter, ſign an inſtrument, wherein he promiſes, in the name of his Catholick Majeſty, to leave but 3000 of the Spaniſh Troops in the Dutchy of Tuſcany, inſtead of the 6000 ſtipulated by the laſt Treaty of Vienna. *C. D P.*

TUESDAY, *Jan.* 25.

Copenhagen, Jan. 15. The Gov. of Tranquebar having written to Court, that the number of the inhabitants there, who are converted to Chriſtianity, increaſe ſo conſiderably, that Eccleſiaſticks are wanting for their inſtruction, his Majeſty has given orders to the Biſhop of this City to chuſe ſome perſons duly qualify'd, who are willing under a convenient ſalary, to go and ſettle there, in order to ſend them by the next veſſel which ſails to thoſe parts. *D P.*

Moſcow, Dec. 31. The Princeſs Elizabeth-Petrowna, Daughter of Peter the Great, having, on the 29th, enter'd into the 23d year of her age, received thereon the compliments of all the Nobility and perſons of diſtinction. *D P.*

WEDNESDAY, *Jan.* 26.

Extract of a private letter from Paris. The King has ſent Orders to the proper officers in all the Sea-Ports of France, to take exact liſts of all the men of war that

are fit for service in cafe of need, and to tranfmit the fame immediately to the Minifters of war; which makes *certain people* jealous, that they have formed fome fecret and finifter defign, grounded perhaps upon the ill-will they have conceived againft *certain people*: but France will hardly be able to deceive *any people* with her outward grimaces, if the defigns war while fhe feems to breathe nothing but peace and tranquility. —— Abbot Paris's Grave has lately wrought a prodigious miracle indeed! The Chevalier Folart, known for his learned commentary upon Polybius, had pafs'd for a man of excellent judgment to this day, had he not taken a great deal of pains to undeceive the world. That Janfenifical Saint's grave occafioned our learned officer to fay fomething in relation to miracles; and thus he declared, that he believed it was God, that (at the requeft of that Saint) wrought the miracles whereof all Paris rings. This fentiment of the Minifter of war; and as people are not permitted in this country to think as they really think, but muft think as the King or his Minifters think, Monfieur Dangervilliers gave the Chevalier Folart to underftand, that he would have caufe to repent, if he continued to believe what he could not help believing of the miracles of Abbot Paris. The Chevalier anfwer'd with an Englifh freedom, that they fhould not make him refufe his belief to a thing of which he was convinced, were he even to lofe his penfion and his place by it. And thus he is like to be a Martyr to miracles, as his Thaumaturgus was a Martyr to the fect of the Janfenifts. *P.*

Books and Pamphlets publifhed fince our laft.
20. War with Prieftcraft; or the Free-thinker's Iliad: A Burlefque Poem. Pr. 1 s.
The Craftfman's Doctrine and Practice of the Liberty of the Prefs, explained to the meaneft capacity. Pr. 1 s.
The London Medley. Pr. 6d.
A Mifcellany of Tafte: by Mr. Pope, &c. *Curleax Grubbifm.*
A Vindication of thofe who take the Oath of Allegiance to his prefent Majefty, &c. By Mr. Hearne, Pr. 2 s. 6 d.
22. Of Good Nature. An Epiftle to his Grace the D—ke of C—s. Pr. 6d.
Luke-warmnefs in Religion reprefented and reproved: in two Sermons, by William Harris, D. D.
24. The Beauties of the Univerfe: A Poem. Pr. 1 s.
The Britifh Spy's Tour through London and Weftminfter, &c. Pr. 1 s.
25. A Propofal fully to prevent the fmugling of Wool, &c. Pr. 1 s.
The Traditions of the Jews, &c. No. II. Pr. 1 t.
Mifcellaneous Obfervations on Authors, &c. No. XIII. Pr. 6d.
The Nature and Neceffity of preaching the Gofpel: a vifitation Sermon, June 9, 1731, at Wye in Kent: By Francis Cull, Rect. of Snave.
Love-a-la-mode: or the Amours of Florelia and Phillis, &c. Pr. 1 s.
26. The Proceedings at the Seffions at the Old Baily, &c. Pr. 6 d.

On Tuefday Stocks were
South Sea Stock 104 1 8th, 104, for the Opening.
South Sea Annuity 110 1 8th, to 1 qr. Bank 149 to 1 qr.
New Bank Circulation 6 l. 10 s. Premium. India 180,
179 3 qrs. Three per Cent Annuity 96 5 8ths. Royal
Exchange Affurance 97 3 qts. London Affurance 13
1 half. York Buildings 13. African 46. Englifh Copper 2 l. 10 s. Welch ditto 1 l. 15 s. South Sea Bonds
6 l. 10s. Premium. India ditto 6 l. 19 s. ditto. Blanks
7 l. 5 s. 20 l. Prizes 19 l. 6 s. 4 d.

ADVERTISEMENTS.

At the Boarding School lately fet up at *Highgate*,

YOUNG Ladies are taught READING, WRITING and ACCOMPTS; DANCING, FRENCH, and all forts of Work.
PHILIPPA JEYNSON.

This Day is publifhed.

MILTON's Paradife Loft, by *Richard Bentley*, D.D. Printed for Jacob Tonfon; and for John Poulfon; and for J. Darby, A. Bettefworth, and F. Clay, in Truft for Richard, James and Bethel Wellington.

Juft publifhed,

The Second and Laft VOLUME of

THE SACRED CLASSICS defended and illuftrated. In Three Parts. Containing,
I. A further Demonftration of the Propriety, Purity, and found Eloquence of the Language of the NEW TESTAMENT WRITERS.
II. An Account of the wrong Divifion of Chapters and Verfes, and faulty Tranflations of the DIVINE BOOK, which weaken its Reafonings, and fpoil its Eloquence and native Beauties.
III. A DISCOURSE on the various Readings of the New Teftament.
With a PREFACE, wherein is fhewn the Neceffity and Ufefulnefs of a new Verfion of the Sacred Books.
By the late Reverend and Learned A. BLACKWALL, A.M
Author of the Firft Volume.
To which is added, A Copious INDEX.
Printed for C. RIVINGTON, at the Bible and Crown in S. Paul's Church-Yard.
Where may be had,
I. Mr. BLACKWALL's SACRED CLASSICS, Firft Vol. Second Edition.
II. —— New Latin Grammar, for the Ufe of Schools.
III. —— Introduction to the Claffics: Containing a fhort Difcourfe on their Excellencies, and Directions how to ftudy them to Advantage, &c. for the Ufe of Schools.

To be Lett,

At *Stamford Hill, Middlefex*, near the *Turn-Pike*,

SEveral Houfes, four or five Rooms on a Floor, with five or fix Acres of Orchard or Garden Ground; great Plenty of Spring Water running through the fame, and Fifh Ponds there; with Coach-Houfes and Stables, and other good Conveniences.
Inquire of Mr. Halfted there, and know further.

This Day is publifhed,

A Collection of PIECES in VERSE and PROSE, which have been publifhed on occafion of the Dunciad. Dedicated to the Right Honourable the Earl of Middlefex. By Mr. Savage;
Likewife
ATHELWOLD: A Tragedy. By A. Hill, Efq; as it is acted at the Theatre Royal in Drury-Lane.
2. OF FALSE TASTE; an Epiftle to the Right Honourable Richard, Earl of Burlington. By Mr. POPE. The 3d Edition, with an additional Letter.
Printed for Lawton Gilliver, at Homer's Head, againft St. Dunftan's-Church, Fleet-ftreet.

This Day is publifhed,

Price Six Pence.
The Third Edition of,

A SOLDIER and a SCHOLAR; or the Lady's Judgment upon thofe two Characters, in the Perfons of Captain — and D—n S—t.
Printed for J Roberts in Warwick-lane.
Where may be had, juft publifh'd,
I. LOVE and AMBITION. A Tragedy. As it is Acted at the Theatre-Royal in Dublin by his Majefty's Servants.
About Fortuna Superbis. Hor.
By JAMES DARCY, Efq; Price 1 s. 6 d.
II. The Second Edition of SCHEMES from Ireland for the Benefit of the Body Natural, Ecclefiaftical and Politick. The firft humbly offer'd for making Religion and the Clergy ufeful. With the Author's Obfervations on the Caufe and Cure of the Plies: And fome ufeful Directions about wpng the Pofteriors. The fecond, an infallible Scheme to pay the publick Debt of this Nation in fix Months. Humbly offer'd to the Confideration of the P—— t P . 6 d.
III. POEMS on feveral Occafions, containing the Progrefs of Wit in Ireland. The Poet's Well; an Effay towards a Tranflation of Anacreon. An Ode on his Majefty's Birth-Day: To which is added, the Plague of Wealth, occafion'd by the Author's receiving Fifty Pounds from his Excellency the Lord Carteret for the aforemention'd Ode. With feveral Poems not in the Dublin Edition, and a curious Frontifpiece engrav'd by Mr. Vertue. By *Matthew Pilkington*, M. A. Price 3 s. 6 d.
IV. The DRAPIER's Letters to the People of Ireland, concerning Mr. Wood's Brafs Half-pence, with Confiderations on the Attempts made to pafs that Coin, and Reafons for the People of Ireland's refufing it.
O thou whatever Title pleafe thine Ear,
Dean, Drapier, Bickerftaff, or Gulliver, &c. Price 1 d.
V. The TRIBUNES. Part I. and II. being a Collection of entertaining Papers on various Subjects. Price 2 s.
VI. The PARISH-PRIEST; a Poem of much Pity, and not a little Satire. Price 6 d.

To be LETT in *James-Street, Weftminfter,*

A Strong, well-built Brick Houfe, handfomely fitted up, with Marble Chimney-Pieces, and proper Wainfcotting: It has convenient Clofets, and a Room ufeful for a Library: Alfo, for the better Security againft Fire, it has a Stone-Stair from the Cellar to the Attick Floor, befides the great Stair, and ftands clear from other Houfes.
It has a Profpect into St. James's Park, and into Garden-Grounds and open Fields, backward. The late Bifhop of Peterborough lived in it feveral Years The is by it.
Door into St. James's Park.
If any Perfons can find a Pleafure in living in a Houfe not likely to fall on their Heads, or that (in all human Probability) is free from burning, this Houfe may fuit them.
Enquire of Mr. Doyly, at the Black Peruwig in Pany, France, Weftminfter.

This Day is publifhed,

AN Enquiry into the Origin of HONOUR, and the Ufefulnefs of Chriftianity in WAR.
By the Author of the *Fable of the Bees.*
Price bound 3 s. 6 d.
Printed for J. Brotherton at the Bible, next the Royal Exchange Tavern in Cornhill.

This Day is publifhed,

Dedicated to the Gentlemen of the Navy of England,

THE MEMOIRS of Monfieur *du Gai Troin*, Chief of a Squadron of the Royal Navy of France, and Great Crofs of the Military Order of S. Lewis: containing all his Sea-Actions with the Englifh, Dutch, and Portuguefe, in the late Wars of King William and Queen Anne.
Tranflated from the French by a *Sea-Officer.*
Printed for J. Batley, at the Dove, in Pater-nofter-Row,
Where may be had,
The TRADITIONS of the CLERGY the way Deftructive of Religion: A Sermon preach'd at Bingley-Church, on Sunday September 12th, 1731.
By IS. SMITH.
Minifter of Haworth, near Kighley, Yorkfhire.
ALSO,
I. The Religion of Nature confidered. To which is added a Poftfcript, containing Reflections on Mr. Clarke's Difcourfe concerning Reafon, &c. fo far as it refpects this Subject.
II. Some Thoughts concerning Virtue and Happinefs in a Letter to a Clergyman.

Jan. 4. was publifhed, Price 6d.

No. XII. for December, 1731.

THE Gentleman's Magazine: Or, *Monthly Intelligencer.*
Very proper for private Families, or to fend into the Country, and Places abroad, where the Englifh refide, being a compendious View of all our publick Papers and Tranf-actions.

NO. XIII. for JANUARY, will be publifhed Feb. 4, and with it the latter Part of the Index to VOL. I. which with the former Part given in No. XII containing, in alphabetical Order, all the Names mention'd throughout the whole, will be extremely convenient for thofe who may have occafion to look for any Occurence, Birth, Marriage, Preferment, Death, Accident, Adventure, Date, or other Circumftance relating to them. And befides a particular Table of Contents to each Month, a general one of the Subjects is added, referring to the Pages when they are treated of, in order to render this Defign as ufeful as poffible, and fo far to anfwer the Character given it in the following Lines:

Never more Authors! ne'er fo bufy known!
Preffes unlicenc'd, as unlicens'd, grown;
Projects, like Maggots, in their Brains abound,
News, Effays, Contefts, an eternal Round!
And crabbed Politicks the World confound.
Midft Love, Intrigues, and Wit's unbounded Themes
We lofe, unfeen, juft half their fruitful Schemes.
But where's a Remedy? Can none reduce
Their various Merits into Form and Ufe?
Tis done———
From a wild CHAOS fpringing forth is feen
A beauteous World, —— The Monthly Magazine.
Printed and fold by A. Dod, near Temple-Bar, E. Jeffries, in Ludgate-ftreet.
Where may be had,
An exact LIST of the prefent Parliament.

LONDON: Printed by S. PALMER and J. HUGGONSON, in *Bartholomew-Clofe*, for Captain GULLIVER, near the *Temple*, where Letters and Advertifements are taken in: As alfo at the *Rainbow Coffee-Houfe* in *Cornhill*, and *John's Coffee-Houfe* in *Sheer-Lane*, near *Temple-Bar*. [Price Two Pence.]

The Grub-ſtreet Journal.

NUMB. 109

Thursday, *FEBRUARY* 3, 1731.

OUR laſt Journal exhibited a Catalogue of the Judges who condemned K. CHARLES I. and it was intended, that in this a Liſt of the Witneſſes againſt him ſhould have appeared. But theſe Gentlemen, (like their Brother the Executioner in a maſk) were too averſe to vain-glory to permit their names to be tranſmitted to poſterity at full length. And therefore nothing but the initial letters, with their places of abode, and their profeſſions, could be recovered, as they are preſerved in *Ruſhworth's Hiſtorical Collections*; where they ſtand in the ſame manner, as the initial and final letters of the names of ſome modeſt Convicts at the Old Bailey appear in our modern Seſſions Papers.

W. C. of *Patrington* in *Holderneſs*, Gent.
J. B. of *Harwood* in the County of *York*, Gent.
W. T. of *Wixhall* in the County of *Salop*, Gent.
H. H. of *Stratford* upon *Avon* in *Warwickſhire*
[illegible] L. of *Nottingham*, Painter
E. R. of *Biſhops-Caſtle* in the County of *Salop*, Ironmonger.
R. A. of *Cottam* in *Northamptonſhire*, Tyler
G. P. of *Wellington* in the County of *Salop*, Feltmaker
J. W of *Roſſe* in *Herefordſhire*, Shoe-maker
J. P. of *Hayner* in the County of *Derby*, Yeoman
G. [illegible] of *Nottingham*, Maltſter
[illegible] J. of *London*, Citizen and Barber-Surgeon
T. W. of *Nottingham*, Shoe-maker
J. C. of *Llangellen* in the County of *Denbigh*, Husbandman.
R. T. of *London*, Citizen and Weaver
W. J. of *Uskk* in the County of *Monmouth*, Husbandman
H. B. of *Witſondine* in the County of *Rutland*, Husbandman
D. E. of *Abergenny* in the County of *Monmouth*, Smith
D. C. of *Carſton* in the County of *Salop*, Butcher
G. G. of *Wellington* in *Shropſhire*, Gent.
J. [illegible] of *Damorham* in the County of *Wilts*, Gent.
S. G. of *London*, Cordwainer
J. P. of the City of *Cork* in *Ireland*, Gent.
T. J. of *Boyſet* in the County of *Northampton*, Husbandman
T. R. of *Hanſlop* in the County of *Bucks*
T. R. of *Maidſtone* in the County of *Kent*, Gent.
J. C. of *Dublin* in *Ireland*, Barber
G. T. of *Lyneham* in the County of *Wilts*, Gent.
M. B. of *Sharpereton*, in the County of *Northumberland*, Vintner
G. C. of *Aſton* in the County of *Hereford*, Ferryman
H. S. of *Grays-Inn* in the County of *Middleſex*, Gent.
B. W. of S. *Martin*'s in the County of *Cornwall*, Husbandman
R. P. of *London*, Scrivener
J. C. a Member of the Houſe of Commons

'When through the anger of Providence, a thriving 'army of Rebels had worſted Juſtice, cleared the field, 'ſubdued all oppoſition and riſings, even to the very *inſurrections* of *Conſcience* itſelf; ſo that impunity grew at 'length into the reputation of piety, and ſucceſs gave Re'bellion the varniſh of Religion; that they might con'ſummate their villany, the Gown was called in to com'plete the execution of the Sword; and to make *Weſt'minſter-Hall*, a place for taking *away lives*, as well as '*eſtates*, a new Court was ſet up, and Judges pack'd, 'who had nothing to do with *Juſtice*, but ſo far as they 'were fit to be the *objects* of it. ——— Such an infe'rior crew, ſuch a mechanick rabble were they, having 'not ſo much as *any arms* to ſhew the world, but what 'they wore and *uſed in the Rebellion*; that when I ſur'vey the Liſt of the King's Judges, and the Witneſſes 'againſt him, I ſeem to have before me a Catalogue of '*all trades*, and ſuch as might better have filled the *ſhops* 'in *Weſtminſter-Hall*, than ſat upon the *benches*. Some 'of which came to be poſſeſſors of the *King's houſes*, 'who before had no certain dwelling but the *King's high'way*. And ſome might have continued tradeſmen ſtill, 'had not want, and inability to trade, ſent them to a 'quicker and ſurer way of traffick, the wars.

'Now, that a King, that ſuch a King, ſhould be mur'dered by ſuch, the baſeſt of his ſubjects; and not like a '*Nimrod*, (as ſome ſanctified railing Preachers have called 'him) but like an *Actæon*, be torne by a pack of blood'hounds; that the ſteam of a dunghill ſhould thus ob'ſcure the ſun; this ſo much enhaunces the calamity of 'this Royal Perſon, and makes his death as different from 'his, who is conquer'd and ſlain by another King, as it 'is between being torne by a *Lion*, and being eaten up 'with *vermin*. An expreſſion too proper, (I am ſure) 'as coarſe as it is: for where we are ſpeaking of *beg'gars*, nothing can be more natural than to think of '*vermin* too.

'For, that the feet ſhould *trample upon*, nay kick off 'the Head, who would not look upon it as a monſter? But 'indeed of all others, theſe were the fitteſt inſtruments for 'ſuch a work: for baſe deſcent, and poor education, diſ'poſe the mind to imperiouſneſs and cruelty, as the moſt 'ſavage beaſts are bred in dens, and have their extraction 'from *under ground*. Theſe therefore were the worthy 'Judges and condemners of a great King, even the re'fuſe of the people, and the very ſcum of the nation; 'that is, at that time both the *uppermoſt*, and the *baſeſt* 'part of it.' Dr. SOUTH's *Sermon at Whitehall, before King* CHARLES II. *Jan.* 30, 166$\frac{2}{3}$, Vol. V. Pag. 71, 72, 73.

One Yeoman, five Huſband-men, ſeven Engliſh, one Iriſh
Gent.
One Honourable Member of the Rump of Parliament,
One Scrivener, Iron-monger, Glover, and Felt-maker,
An Independent Vintner, who for rhime I wiſh had been
a Quaker,
A Maltſter, Ferry-man, Barber Surgeon, and a Painter,
A Tyler, a Butcher, an Iriſh Barber turn'd Saint here,
A Weaver, Smith, two Shoe-makers, and a Cordwainer:
Every one of whom ought to have been a Cord-ſtrainer.

Mr. BAVIUS, *Hereford, Jan.* 15, 1731.

I Doubt not but you have long ſince read the *Spectator's* parallel between the two celebrated Comedians, Mr. BULLOCK and Mr. PENKETHMAN. I have here attempted one between two more conſiderable perſons, viz. Mr. CARPENTER, Poet Laureat of this City, and the renowned Laureat in London.

Mr. CARPENTER and Mr. CIBBER are perſons of the ſame ſex, education, profeſſion, occupation and complexion; and 'tis obſervable, that the initial and final letters are the ſame in both their names. Mr. CARPENTER is Deputy Bellman of the City of Hereford. As for Mr. CIBBER, in your City, *vicem gerit ille tonantis*, which is as much as to ſay, he is Director of the Play-houſe thunder, as Deputy to the ingenious Mr. DENNIS, inventor thereof. [See *the Dunciad*.]

If you inquire into their education, 'tis well known the learned Mr. CARPENTER has read *Cato, Corderius*, and *Æſop's Fables*; in which he has ſome advantage over Mr. CIBBER, whoſe ſtudies, 'tis evident, were never extended beyond *Sententiæ Pueriles*. It has, indeed, been pretended, that he was no ſtranger to *Lucan*; but it muſt be acknowledged, that acquaintance was contracted by the mediation of Mr. ROWE; by whoſe aſſiſtance and recommendation JULIUS CÆSAR ſo far honoured him as to be his gueſt *in Egypt*, where he gave that Hero but a ſcurvy entertainment, almoſt as bad as that wherewith he has ſince regaled AUGUSTUS.

Mr. CIBBER is a profeſſed Poet, ſo is Mr. CARPENTER: and, with due ſubmiſſion I ſpeak it, in my opinion, the better of the two; as will appear from an impartial view of their reſpective performances on new year's day. I have herewith ſent you that of Mr. CARPENTER in print.

The year its ſteady courſe doth conſtant run,
No ſooner ends but 'tis again begun;
One is no ſooner paſt but ſtill appears
An other new; thus years are chain'd to years,
Whoſe fruitful ſeaſons does for man provide,
And all the creatures on the earth beſide:
Thus doth the year its active courſe maintain,
It comes to go, and goes to come again.

From theſe verſes you may perhaps obſerve, that the one Laureat has ſtolen ſome thoughts from the other. But 'tis apparent, that our Countryman was not the Plagiary; for honeſt STEPHEN BRYAN, the Worceſter Printer, can teſtify, that Mr. CARPENTER's verſes were publiſhed, among other of his miſcellaneous works, for the entertainment of his good friends againſt Chriſtmas; whereas Mr. CIBBER's did not make their appearance 'till new year's day.

Mr. CIBBER is an Actor; and, I can aſſure you, Mr. CARPENTER has formerly made no inconſiderable figure among a ſet of Strollers. It has been obſerv'd, that Players act thoſe parts beſt, to which they are moſt naturally inclined; but to this obſervation the action of either of theſe Gentlemen is a direct contradiction: for Mr. CIBBER is ſaid to perform the parts of a Coxcomb and a Villain to the greateſt perfection. And tho' it muſt be confeſſed, that Mr. CARPENTER is no Tragedian, yet he has acted the part of *Scrub*, in the *Beaux Stratagem*, and that of SHAKESPEAR's drunken *Tinker*, in the *Taming of the Shrew*, with general applauſe.

Mr. CARPENTER's occupation is that of a Shoemaker; and he does not cut out his work amiſs, always obſerving the old rule of *Ne ſutor ultra crepidam*. Happy were it for others, if they could take the ſame *meaſures!* but, he has ever been allowed to be an excellent *Tranſlator* or Cobler; and will piece on a ſole with that exactneſs, that the moſt curious eye can ſcarce obſerve the ſtitches. Mr. CIBBER is alſo a *Tranſlator* and Cobler, but in no degree equal to his rival. He has *tranſlated*, as I am told, two pair of CORNEILLE's and MOLIERE's old ſhoes, in ſuch a manner as to fit no mortal. The *Pompey*, the *Cid*, &c. were deſpiſed by many of our Society, who wear none but ſecond-hand ſhoes: and even the *Nonjurors* themſelves have choſen to go almoſt barefoot, rather than to appear in a pair of patch'd ſhoes of *Tartuffe*, or to tread one *ſtep* like him. As a Cobler, in his Comedy called the *Fop's Fortune*, he has ingrafted the former part of FLETCHER's *Elder Brother* upon an old Play, called the *Loyal Lovers*, in ſo bungling a manner, that the chaſms are to be diſcerned even with half an eye.

As to the complexion of theſe two great men, 'tis in both tending toward the ſubfusk; only Mr. CIBBER's is the deeper copper of the two. Mr. CIBBER has the more years, but then Mr. CARPENTER has the more wit: and yet, wonderful to relate! Mr. CIBBER drinks ſack, while Mr. CARPENTER, alas! is doom'd to cyder. To conclude, in the words of the *Spectator*, Mr. CIBBER *has the more money*, but Mr. CARPENTER *is the taller man*.

I am your humble ſervant,
PHILO VERMI-GENERIS.

Mr. MÆVIUS looking upon the Banquetting-houſe at White-hall, Jan. 30, 1731.

1.

When this fine Palace ſunk in riſing flame,
What providence preſerv'd this nobleſt part?
A laſting Monument conſign'd to fame,
Of STUARTS grandeur, and of JONES's art?

2.

No doubt, for wiſeſt purpoſe Heav'n decreed,
This pompous Dome, ſecure to lateſt time,
Should mark the ſcene of one unrivall'd Deed,
A glorious virtue, or a heinous crime.

3.

If that, a bleſſing; but if this, a curſe
Has ever ſince purſu'd Britannia's land:
When the third Age has run its dubious courſe,
The fourth may plainly ſee Heav'ns vengeful hand.

4.

'Till then this Dome here opportunely ſhines,
For deprecation, and thanks-giving too:
Which may retard, or haſten Heav'ns deſigns,
In ſcenes of laſting happineſs, or woe.

5.

Whilſt ſome, deteſting that vile barbarous Age,
What Fiend poſſeſs'd thoſe godly Villains, aſk:
Others declare, had they then trod the Stage,
They'd ſtruck the glorious ſtroke without a maſk.

6.

From thoughts directly oppoſite as theſe,
Paſſions as oppoſite inceſſant flow:
Exhilarating hopes of laſting peace;
Dejecting fears of ſome dire ſudden blow.

7.

Th' Egyptians thus, as Nile's vaſt floods retreat,
See Monſters creeping from their oozy bed;
And while the Sun darts down prolific heat,
Both plenty hope, and ſwift deſtruction dread.

DOMESTIC NEWS.

C. *Courant*.	EP. *Evening Poſt*.
P. *Poſt-Boy*.	SJ. *S. James's Evening Poſt*.
DP. *Daily Poſt*.	WE. *Whitehall Evening P.*
DJ. *Daily Journal*.	LE. *London Evening Poſt*.

THURSDAY, *Jan.* 27.

We hear that his Majeſty has given orders that the O[illegible]

ficers u on half-pay shall be provided for as vacancies shall happen from time to time in the Army, in order to reduce the establishment of half-pay. *P.*

The annual Feast of the sons of the Clergy will be held at Merchant Taylor's-Hall on Feb. 17. *P. D P.* —— Yesterday there was an elegant entertainment at the Archbishop of Canterbury's Palace at Lambeth, on account of its being his Grace's Birth-day, who then entered into the 75th year of his age. *D J.*

A few days since Sir John Glynne of Hawarden in Flintshire, Bar. was married to Miss Conway, a very rich Heiress, Daughter and Heir of the late Sir John Conway, Bar. a fortune of 50,000 l. *D P.* —— This day —— Anderson, Esq; eldest son to Sir Steph. Anderson of Queen-square, Ormond-street, is to be married to Miss Barns of Leaden-hall-street, a beautiful young Lady, of 20,000 l. fortune. *P.* This day was married, &c. *E P. L E.*

This day Dr. Newland was elected Geometry Professor at Gresham College, without opposition. *L E. W E.*

We hear the tryal of Corbet Vesey, for locking up his wife in a garret upwards of a twelve month, whereby she was starved to death, is laid before an eminent Counsel, for his opinion, in order to bring an appeal against him. —— We hear great intercession is making to his Majesty for Hallam the Waterman (condemned for the murder of his wife, by flinging her out of a window when big with child) that he may be transported. *D P.*

Last night the Dutchess of Ancaster was brought to bed of a son, to the great joy of that noble Family. *L E.* Of a Daughter. *C. Jan.* 29.

Last week Letters patent, under the Great Seal, were granted to the Rev. Mr. Rowning, Fellow of Magdalen College in Cambridge, for the sole privilege of making and vending his new invented clock, which (we hear) is contrived in a much shorter way, and will be afforded at a much lower price than common clocks the multiplicity of wheels and steel-work being much lessen'd by this new invention. *L E.*

Yesterday Mr. Serjeant Raby was seized suddenly with an apoplectick fit, in the Court of Common-Pleas at Westminster, and dropt down dead: he was carried into Oliver's Coffee-house, and all means were used to restore him, but to no purpose; he having had 2 fits before of the like nature. He was Recorder of Huntington, and Judge of the Isle of Ely. *C. E P.* He was obliged to be carried home directly in a coach. *D P.* Being carried to his lodgings in Southampton-Buildings, he died last night about 7. *S J.* About 11. *W E.* He died in the coach before he got there. *L E.*

Last monday died at Kensington, —— Gordon, Esq; a Gentleman of great estate. *D J.* —— The same day died the Lady Meux, at her house in Dartmouth-street, in an advanc'd age. —— The Lady Fielding, who died lately, left a considerable sum of money to Mrs. Fanshaw, who has been her companion for upwards of 20 years; but she grieving so much at her death, died last monday. *S J.* —— *This was a very extraordinary case: considerable legacies generally occasioning so much* consideration, *as to prevent these fatal excesses of* grief.

Last night, between 9 and 10, died, in the 75th year of his age, at his house on the Parade in S. James's Park, Count Bothmar, Prime Minister at this Court for the affairs of Hanover, and one of the Regency for the management of his Majesty's German Dominions. *S J.* He had lived in England above 20 years. *L E.* —— Aged 84. *D P. Jan.* 28. —— The latter end of last week died at his lodgings near Lancaster-Court in the Strand, Capt. Stephens. He has left, by his will, 1000 l. to a poor Cobler in Southwark. *D J.* —— *If this* Cobler *buy a Place, civil or military, it will make him a* Gentleman.

This day Sir Will. Thompson made his report to his Majesty of the 2 condemned Malefactors. *W E.* —— The report is put off 'till next week. *C. Jan.* 28.—Yesterday Mr. Baron Thomson made the report, &c. *D P.* Mr. Serjeant Urling Deputy Recorder made his report, &c. *P.* —— And they are ordered for execution on monday next. *S J.* — *No report has been made, but this false one.*

FRIDAY, *Jan.* 28.

On monday last the R. Hon. L. Visc. Tyrconnel, was married at his seat at Belton-Hall near Grantham, to Miss Carteret, of the County of Southampton. *D P.*

Yesterday Sir Phil. York, his Majesty's Attorney-Gen. and Mr. Reeves, the King's Counsel, moved the Court of King's Bench, that a day might be fixed for giving Judgment against Mr. Ric. Francklin, they have given notice of this motion to the Defendant. Mr. Bootle, sen. and Mr. Fazakerley replied, that the *Postea* was not entered in the Crown Office regularly; but after a long argument on both sides, the Court was of opinion, that the *Postea* was regularly entered, and ordered that Judgment be given in 4 days, and that the Defendant be at liberty, if he thinks proper, then to move in arrest of Judgment. *P.*

In 1731, 6990 barrels of Herrings were imported at Koningsburgh, which, with 5162 tons and a half imported at Riga, were all white, and (a very few from Scotland excepted) all from Holland, and as the greatest part, if not all, were caught on the coast of Scotland, it is not doubted, but if proper encouragement be given, that beneficial branch of trade may be carried on, so as not only to rival, but exclude, all Foreigners. *D J.*

On wednesday morning last died Mrs. Bolton of Enfield, a widow Gentlewoman: she was sister to the Hon. Sir Cha. Wager, was a good Christian, and a person of so agreeable conversation, that her death is very much regretted by all who knew her. *D P.* An exceeding good Christian. *D J.*

SATURDAY, *Jan.* 29.

Baron Bothmar, Nephew of the late Count Bothmar, will be appointed Prime Minister for the affairs of the electorate of Hanover, in the room of his Uncle, with a salary of 50 l. per week. *D J.* —— My Brother *speaks as positively, as if he had 'this from the* Prime Minister of Great Britain.

On saturday Phil. Lloyd of Greenwich, Esq; one of his Majesty's Equerries, and Captain of a Troop, &c. was unanimously elected a Representative in Parliament for Christ-Church. —— On monday came on the election for Preston: the numbers on the Poll were as follow; Nich. Fazakerley, Esq; 378, Major Haldane 132, which latter made no interest 'till the day of election. The former was returned. —— On tuesday, at the election for Totness, Sir Hen. Gough, Bar. was chosen, having 61 votes, and Arthur Champernoune, Esq; but 6. *D J.*

Rodolphe White, Esq; succeeds Cha. Bolton, Esq; deceased, as Register and Clerk to the Commissioners for licensing Hackney coaches. *C.* —— *The* D P. *of* Jan. 24. *conferred this place upon* Cha. Bodens, Esq; *whom the* C. *of* Jan. 21. *had dignified with the Title of* Secretary to the Commissioners of Hackney Coaches.

The following Gentlemen are to read the Lectures at Gresham College every morning during the term, at 9 o' clock in Latin, and at 3 in the afternoon in English, viz. *Monday*, John Bridgen, M. A. in Divinity; *tuesday*, John Cuming, of the Middle Temple, Esq; Civil Law; *wednesday*, Dr. Geo. Newland, in Geometry; *friday*, John Ward, F. R. S. Rhetorick; *saturday*, Hen. Pemberton, M.D. Physick; *ditto*, John Gordon in musick, at 4. *P.*

Yesterday in the Court of Common Pleas in Westminster-hall, a Cause was tried before the L. C. Just. Eyre, between Mr. Gouldney, Plaintiff. and Mr. Harvey, Defendant, both of the County of Wilts, upon an action brought against the Defendant, for criminal conversation with the Plaintiff's wife, which being fully proved, the Jury brought in a verdict for the Plaintiff, and allowed him 1000 l. damage. *D J.*

This morning the twelve Judges met at the Exchequer Chamber at Westminster, and chose their Circuits for the Lent Assizes, as follows, viz.

Norfolk Circuit.	*Midland Circuit.*
L. Raymond	Mr. Just. Page
Mr. Baron Comyns.	Mr. Just. Price
Home Circuit.	*Western Circuit.*
L. C. Justice Eyre	Mr. Just. Probyn
Mr. Baron Thomson	Mr. Just. Lee
Oxford Circuit.	*Northern Circuit.*
L. C. Baron Reynolds	Mr. Just. Denton
Mr. Just. Fortescue Aland	Mr. Baron Carter.

S J. W E. L E.

Sittings in the Court of King's Bench and Common Pleas, in and after Hillary term, 1732.

In the King's Bench.	In the Common Pleas.
Middlesex, Feb. 1, 7, 10. After term, 14	*Middlesex*, Jan. 28. Feb. 1, 5. After term, 14
London, Jan. 27. Feb. 3, 11. After term, 15	*London*, Jan. 29. Feb. 3, 8. After term 15

E P. W E. L E.

Last week christen'd Males 167, Females 175: in all 342. Buried Males 278, Females 293: in all 571. Increased in the burials this week 15. *E P.*

Cambridge, Jan. 27. On tuesday last a Citation was sent from the L. Bishop of Ely, summoning the Rev. Dr. Bentley, Master, and Dr. Craister, Sen. Dean of Trinity College, to appear before him on Feb. 1. to answer upon an appeal made by Porter Thompson, of Trumpington, Esq; a Gentleman of a large fortune, and unexceptionable character, whom the said Master and Dean lately expelled the College. —— N.B. This is the Gentleman that threaten'd to make the very Rev. and pious Dr. Hacket, late Vicar of Trumpington, reside there; according to the terms of the will of Dr. Thorndike, a great Benefactor to that Vicarage. *W E.*

This morning Geo. Hill of Hertfordshire, Esq; was married to Miss Eliz. Backwell, eldest Daughter of Tyringham Backwell, of Tyringham in Buckinghamshire, Esq; *L E.*

On thursday morning died, at Stamford in Lincolnshire, William Langhorne Games, Esq; Lord of the Manor of Hampstead in Middlesex. *L E.*

Last night one John Tapper was committed to Newgate, being charged with the murder of Joseph Cannon, by stabbing him with a penknife. *C.*

A widow woman, one Haggard, at Shrivenham in the County of Berks, has been tapp'd for the dropsy 20 times, since Ap. 1, 1730, being about once a-month; and at every time about 6 gallons of water were drawn from her. *L E.*

MONDAY, *Jan.* 31.

Yesterday the Rev. Dr. Byrch preached before the King and Queen, his Royal Highness the Prince, &c. And the Rev. Dr. Greenwood preached before his Royal Highness the Duke, &c. —— We hear that Baron Hattorf is appointed to have the care of the affairs of Hanover, in the room of the late Count Baron de Bothmar, 'till a Minister is appointed for that purpose. *C.* —— We hear that Baron Bothmar has, by his will, left all his personal estate to his daughter, which is valued at 50 000 l. *D J.*

On saturday last, at the King's Bench, Westm. Mr. Francklin, by his Counsel, mov'd to have the verdict given against him set aside: the chief argument for this was, that the Rule given by the Court for the trial by a *Special Jury*, was taken for the sittings after Trinity term, and the trial came on after Michaelmas term; Mr. Francklin's Counsel pleaded very learnedly on this affair, and the Counsel for the King have taken 'till to-morrow to give their answer. *D P.*

The Writ of error hath been returned by the proper Officers into the House of Lords, for carrying the Appeal of the R. Rev. the L. Bishop of Ely thither, from a sentence of the Court of King's Bench, in the case between his Lordship and Dr. Bentley. *D J.*

Last week died at her seat in Cheshire, the Hon. Mrs. Cholmondley, sister to the present Earl of Ashburnham; her first husband was Rob. Cholmondley, of Holford in Cheshire, Esq; by her death a stop is, for the present, put to a great Law-suit, which was to have been heard next thursday, between her husband and her, Plaintiffs, and Mr. Asheton, a Cheshire Gentleman, (an intimate acquaintance of her first husband) Defendant; Mrs. Cholmondley having (during her widowhood) by deed, given to Mr. Asheton 1000 l. per ann. after her decease, the validity of which deed of gift was then to be try'd; but her death will occasion great alterations in the proceedings. *D P.*

Yesterday morning the head of the late Col. Oxburgh, who was executed for being in the Preston rebellion, and had his head stuck on a pole, fell off from the top of Temple-Bar. *D P.*

This day the corpse of Mrs. Mary Badam is to be carried to Chippenham in Wiltshire, to be interr'd in great funeral solemnity. She was a Maiden Gentlewoman, in the 48th year of her age, and has left by her will, to 12 of her poor relations, 1000 l. each. *D J.*

We hear that the new edition of Milton has been sent as a present to divers persons of Quality; but we can't learn, whether a CASE went with it, or is to follow it. *D J.*

TUESDAY, *Feb.* 1.

Yesterday being kept for the Anniversary of the 30th of January. *C.* The Anniversary of the Martyrdom of K. Charles I. *P. D J.* The R. Rev. Dr. Hare, L. Bishop of Chester. *C.* Of Chichester. *P. D P. D J.* Preached before the House of Lords, on Prov. xxiv. 21. *My son, fear thou the Lord, and the King, and meddle not with them that are given to change. P. D P.* An excellent sermon. *P. D J.* A most extraordinary sermon, in which he vindicated the King's honour and sincerity in his concessions to the Parliament, and made several very just remarks; also pleaded strongly for the keeping up the day. That before the Commons by Dr. Clark, was somewhat different. *D P.* —— The Rev. Dr. Clarke preached on Ps. lxxviii. vers. 8. latter part; *A Generation that set not their hearts aright, and whose spirits were not stedfast with God.* P. —— The same day also, the Rev. Dr. Warren preached an excellent sermon before the R. Hon. the L. Mayor, *&c. P.*

On Saturday the R. Hon. the Lords of the Admiralty were pleased to put the Scarborough, a 6th rate of 20 guns and 120 men, into commission, and appointed Capt. Robert Commander. *P.*

Last sunday died suddenly, James Reynardson, Esq; one of the Band of Gentlemen Pensioners. *D J.* —— None of that name belongs to the Band. *C. Feb.* 2.

This day the Attorney General, Solicitor Gen. &c. answer'd the objections made by Mr. Franklin's council on saturday last; and after arguing the same near 3 hours, Mr. Francklin's Counsel desired till thursday next to make a reply; which was granted by the Court. *L E.*

WEDNESDAY, *Feb* 2.

Last friday Sir Phil York, his Majesty's Attorney General, received a letter by the Penny Post, dated two days before, and signed A B C. demanding 300 guineas to be put at a place therein specified, and threatening in case of failure, his house should be set on fire in less than 24 hours, and that he himself should not long survive it. — His Majesty has since promised his most gracious pardon, and a reward of 500 l. to any one concerned, who shall discover his accomplices, or to any one who shall apprehend any person concerned; to be paid immediately after conviction, out of his Majesty's Exchequer. *D J.*

His Honour the Master of the Rolls continues ...

much indiſpoſed. *C.* —— The Hon. Sir Joſ. Jeckyll, Maſter of the Rolls, is now very well recovered, and laſt night ſat upon cauſes at his houſe in Chancery-Lane. *P.*

Laſt friday the Rev. Mr. Jeale was choſen Head-maſter of the Free ſchool at Guildford in Surrey, by the Corporation there without oppoſition. *D P.*

Laſt week died at Kingſtown Wick, Mr. Iſ. Jackſon, an eminent Malſter and Cornfactor, reputed to be worth 30000 l. *P.* — Laſt ſunday died at New-Windſor, Mrs. Abigail Bendon, an heireſs of 12000 l. fortune. *D J.*

From the PEGASUS *in Grub-ſtreet.*

In our laſt, pag. 1. col. 2. l. 31. *Read* and being grown. Pag. 3. In the article from the Pegaſus, the four firſt lines ought to have been placed immediately after the Song on the Peace.

To the honourable Society of Grub-ſtreet.

Gentlemen,

HAveing procured ſeveral original manuſcripts In defence of the laſt new Comedy, written by the very honourable patrons of that performance, I beg your aſſiſtance in the publication of them. As they are the works of perſons of diſtinction, you cannot doubt the intreſt your Society has in them: tho' I muſt confeſs I cannot yet ſay any thing with entire certainty in relation to them; by reaſon of ſome obſcuritys in carracter and arthography, which you very well know manuſcripts, eſpecially of this ſort, are very liable too.

I have indeed done all in my powr to obviate this misfortune, by a dilligent camparion of the papers now in my hands, with that valuable edition of the former works of the ſame authors, publiſh'd in three Tomes by Mr. JOHN ROBERTS, under the title of the *Boghouſe Miſcellany.* I have alſo had recourſe to the originals of that work upon moſt of the Tavern windows in Pell-mell and St. Jameſe'ſtreet; and I take this oppertunity of acknowledging the great humanity of Mother WILLIAMS, who very freely exhibitted to my peruſall all the valuable remains of this kind in her houſe that had eſcaped the Gothick fury of her cuſtomers. For you muſt know, Gentlemen, that where ſcrauling a glaſs is reckon'd wit, the criticiſm conſiſts only in breaking the pane —— but to return

By the dilligence of my ſearch I have arrived at a pretty good gueſs as to the letter and ſpelling; and for the language I have vſed no other help, than a carefull peruſall of the Comedy itſelf to which theſe Manuſcripts relate, and which doubleſs is the ſtandard to which theſe Gentlemen write.

But all this notwithſtanding, I cannot but own myſelf much at a loſs with relation to the ſenſe of theſe valuable pieces; and therefore humbly hope you will appoint the learned Doctor ZOILUS of your Society, to aſſiſt me in tranſmitting to poſterity theſe laſting monuments of the preſent Taſte.

I deſire leave to inform the publick, that I intend ſoon to publiſh ſome curious obſervations on the Roman Drama, in which many errors of the Learned are refuted, particularly that with relation to the *Tibiæ:* it being plainly proved, that the *dextræ* could be nothing elſe but certain loud vociferations uſed by the friends of the Author, to terrifie the audience into an approbation; as by the *ſiniſtræ* could only be meant the Catcalls. A due mixture of both theſe gave riſe to a third diſtinction; as a very great prevalence of either did to the *impares:* tho' a certain learned Modern is rather inclined to think this latter might allude to the different quality of the audience, being very well aſſured that SCIPIO and LÆLIUS did in perſon aſſiſt at the head of a very conſiderable body of theſe performers, from which ſome vain *litterati* would ignorantly fix the carracter of authors, upon theſe two great men.

N. B. as a work of this kind cannot but require many references to the learned languages, the Author will anex a verſion of the latin ſentences, together with a Gloſſary of hard words to a few Copys, which ſhall be printed on a royal paper and neatly bound and gilt for perſons of diſtinction. I am, Gentlemen, your moſt humble ſervant,

W. F.

P. S. I am afraid, Sirs, you will conclude my Emanuenſis a perſon of quality: I cannot mortifie him better, than by makeing him write my appology for the many errors he has committed, and which I fear will render this as illegible as my manuſcripts.

Whereas ſome perſons in Grub ſtreet pretend to ſell *Strops for razors*; this is to inform the Publick, that *The true original Strops for razors* are ſold only by the firſt Inventor, Mr. Roberts at the Corner of Lincoln's-Inn fields near Clare-market, with allowance to ſuch as buy a quantity. —— N B. The ſhop is ſituated between duſt and aſhes, that is to ſay, between a Snuff-ſhop and a Coffee-houſe: [*See* D J. *Jan.* 1.] and is not open now on Wedneſdays, as formerly; but only on Sundays, for the convenience of Journeymen, Apprentices, &c.

Fungor vice cotis, acutum
Reddere quæ ferrum valet, exors ipſe ſecandi.

FOREIGN NEWS.

THURSDAY, *Jan.* 27.

Yeſterday arrived the Mails due from France *and* Holland.

Paris, Feb. 2. The 30th of laſt month, Father de la Sante, the Jeſuite, one of the Profeſſors of Rhetorick in the Coll. of *Lewis the Great,* made a very eloquent latin ſpeech. The ſubject was, *That of all Hiſtories, that of France is one of the moſt difficult to write, and one of the moſt agreeable to read.* The French Academy will, on Aug. 25. S. Lewis's day, give the prize of Eloquence, founded by the late Monſ. de Balzac: the theme whereof will be, *The Miſchiefs and Inconveniencies of double dealing;* according to thoſe words, *Ecclus.* ii. 14. *Væ duplici corde, & labiis ſceleſtis, & peccatori terram ingredienti duabus viis.* —— The ſame day, the Academy will give the prize of Poetry; the theme to be, *The progreſs of Tragedy, in the reign of* Lewis the Great. *P.* —— The new Academy of Surgery propoſes for the ſubject of their prize, *Why ought certain tumours to be extirpated, and others only opened? in what caſes, in both thoſe operations, is the Cautery to be preferred to the inciſion knife? and the reaſons for ſuch preference.* The prize is a gold medal, valued at 200 livres, and will be given to him, native or Foreigner, that ſhall give the beſt ſolution, &c. The Papers in anſwer to it will not be received 'till the 30th of September next. *P.* Will be received only 'till the 30th of September next. *D P.* ——

Ratiſbon, Jan. 24. Upon the Miniſters of Bavaria, Saxony and Palatine, preſenting to the electoral College, their Proteſts againſt the affair of the Pragmatick Sanction, all the other Miniſters immediately withdrew, nor would receive the ſaid Proteſts, much leſs ſuffer them to be recorded among the acts of the Empire. *D P.*

FRIDAY, *Jan.* 28.

Hambourg, Jan. 25. 'Tis not yet aſcertain'd whom her Imperial Majeſty will name her ſucceſſor; but 'tis ſtrongly ſurmiſed the young Princeſs of Mecklembourg is fixed upon, the Czarina having, on her ſerene Highneſs's Name-day, added the name of Anne, to that of Elizabeth-Chriſtina. *D P.*

SATURDAY, *Jan.* 29.

Yeſterday arrived the Mail from Holland.

Seville, Jan. 13. N.S. On the 10th, between 8 and 9 o'clock in the morning, we felt here a ſlight ſhock of an earthquake, which laſted near a minute: half an hour after, we felt another, which was more violent: it did very little damage, however; there being but 2 houſes and ſome old walls ſhook down, and a woman buried under the ruins. *P. D J.* An old woman. *D P.*

Hambourg, Feb. 1. Letters from Stockholm mention a ſtrange accident which happen'd at Torna, to a boy that was born blind, and at 11 years of age got his ſight by having the Small-pox. *DP.* —*It is plain, he was not* inoculated.

MONDAY, *Jan.* 31.

Extract of a private letter from Italy. —— The Spaniſh Troops lately landed in the Dutchy of Tuſcany, continue to teaſe and harraſs the Officers and Soldiers belonging to the great Duke, and pretend even to turn them out of their old poſts. Upon the whole matter, it is certain, that the Spaniards are ſo far from having hitherto agreed with the Italians ſo well as the Germans, that there has been more wrangling in the little time that the Spaniards have been landed in Italy, than there was with the Germans for ſeveral years before. *P.*

Extract of a private letter from Paris. —— There is much talk here, of a ſpeedy promotion of Marſhals of France, and of the nomination of Generals; which, joined with ſome other indications, makes us terribly apprehenſive, that this Court meditates a war early in the ſpring. —Abbot Paris's grave ſeems to have brought convulſions into faſhion throughout this capital City. The Chevalier de Folard, ſo well known in the world for his learned Commentary upon Polybius, is viſited by an innumerable multitude of people, to ſee the extraordinary agitations with which he is ſeized every evening regularly at 5. M. Dangervilliers, Secretary at war, ſent him a letter *de Cachet* the other day, forbidding him to make himſelf a publick ſpectacle any more: but the Chevalier de Folard is too fond of his new Saint: he declared, he could not conceal the gifts that God ſhower'd down upon him in abundance; and that he would ſooner loſe all he had in the world *P.*

Vienna, Jan. 23. The Elector of Bavaria is actually raiſing 18000 men, which his Highneſs propoſes to have in readineſs againſt the ſummer, and has further ordered an account to be taken of all the horſes fit for ſervice in his Electorate; all the diſbanded Heſſians have reſolved to enter into his ſervice. *D P.*

TUESDAY, *Feb.* 1.

This day arrived the Mail from Holland.

Amſterdam, Feb. 8. We have an account from Liſbon of the ſeizure of 700 reals in the houſe of a Britiſh Merchant, and 1,400,000 in another's of the ſame nation, by the King's order: the reaſon of this ſeizure is not mention'd, but ſuppos'd to be upon ſuſpicion of that money belonging to the Jews.— Letters from Leghorn of the 21ſt ſay, the ſerene Infante Duke appeared on that day out of danger, being the criſis day of his diſtemper. —— They write from Peterſbourg, that the Czarina is arrived there. *D P.* With a retinue of about 600 perſons. *D J.*

Berlin, Feb. 2. Upon advice from Kuſtrin, that the Prince Royal is relaps'd, and dangerouſly ill, his Majeſty immediately diſpatched M. Stahl, an eminent Phyſician, to attend his Royal Highneſs. We have juſt received an account that the Prince is ſomewhat better. *D P. C.*

Vienna, Jan. 26. We have received advice from Conſtantinople, that Mehemet Effendi, lately Ambaſſador at this Court, was ſtrangled immediately after his return. *C. D P. D J.* —— Some will have it, that the Crown of France has made a new Treaty with the Elector of Bavaria. *D J*

WEDNESDAY, *Feb.* 2.

Hague, Feb. 8. N. S. Yeſterday in the evening arrived from Zealand, the reſolution of the States of that Province to agree to the acceſſion of this Republick, to the Treaty of Vienna. *C. D P. D J.*

Extract of a private from Vienna. —— Certain Foreign Miniſters at this Court ſeem very much confounded upon the information they have received, that there is a ſecret negotiation carrying on between the Imperial Miniſters and thoſe of Spain, tending to obtain of his Catholick Majeſty a general permiſſion for all the ſubjects of his Imperial Majeſty to trade to all the parts of the Spaniſh Monarchy, and even to the Indies depending upon that Crown. *P.*

ADVERTISEMENTS.

Speedily will be publiſhed,

The Third Volume of

A General Collection of Treaties, Manifeſtoes, Declarations of War, and other publick Papers, from the Year 1640, to the preſent Time. In which will be inſerted ſeveral remarkable Treaties made after the Death of King CHARLES I. and during the Protectorſhip of Oliver Cromwell. In Octavo. Printed by J. Darby and T. Browne in Bartholomew-Cloſe

The Firſt Volume of this Work, which has been ſome Years out of Print, will, at the ſame Time, be re-publiſhed. Printed for J. and J. Knapton; J. Darby; D. Midwinter and A. Ward; A. Bettesworth and C. Hitch; F. Fayram and T. Hatchett; J. Pemberton; J. Osborn and T. Longman; C. Rivington; F. Clay; J. Batley; and R. Hett.

Lately Publiſhed the two following Books.

I. Practical Diſcourſes on the ſeveral Parts and Offices of the Liturgy of the Church of England: Wherein are laid open the Harmony, Excellency, and Uſefulneſs of its Compoſure. In four Volumes. By Matthew Hole, D. D. late Rector of Exeter College in Oxford. Vol. I Containing 58 Diſcourſes on all the Parts of Morning and Evening Prayer, including the Creed of St. Athanaſius Vol. II. and III. Containing 55 Diſcourſes on the Litany, and the Prayers and Thankſgiving that follow it. Vol. IV. Containing 174 Diſcourſes (in 3 large Parts) on all the Collects, Epiſtles and Goſpels, to be us'd throughout the Year. The Second Edition.

II. A practical Expoſition of the CHURCH-CATECHISM. In two Volumes By the ſame Author. The Third Edition, with the Addition of two Diſcourſes; one on the Duty of confeſſing Chriſt, the other on the Danger of denying him; both preach'd at St Mary's in Oxford

Sold by J and J. Knapton, and C. Rivington in St. Paul's Church-Yard; A. Bettesworth and C. Hitch in Pater-noſter-Row; and S. Birt in Avemary-Lane.

The *Cœleſtial Anodyne Tincture:* Or, The *Great Pain-Eaſing Medicine.*

FOund and approv'd of for its wonderful and never-failing Succeſs, in giving immediate Eaſe and Relief in all manner of pains, either inward or outward, and is the moſt certain Remedy in the World for a ſure and ſpeedy Cure of the Cholick, and expelling Wind, Gripes and pains in the ſtomach, the Pleuriſy, ſtitches or pains in the ſide, back, loins, or any other part; Rheumatick Ailments, which cauſe pain and dolor. It has given eaſe to a Miracle, when all other Remedies have fail'd. In the Gravel and Stone in the Kidneys, it gives eaſe forthwith, and brings them away to Admiration. It alſo facilitates and cauſes a ſpeedy Delivery in Child-birth. 'Tis no Quack trifling thing to allure the World with, but a real and well-experienced Medicine, not acting by Stupefaction (as Opiates) but by a friendly, balſamick, and ſubtile Nature, pacifying the moſt ſevere and terrible racking pains, and carries off the Cauſe, not by purging, but by [illegible], by Urine, or breaking Wind. No Family ought to be without it. And uſed outwardly, it cures Swellings, Aches, pains, Numbneſs, or Weakneſs of the Joints; 'tis excellent for Cramps, and [illegible] Infirmities, [illegible] Wonders in Agues, Fevers, Small-pox, &c. No Family ought to be without it.

It is ſold only by Mr. PARKER, Printer, at his Houſe in Saliſbury-Court, or by ſuch perſons as he ſhall depute, viz. at Mr. Parker's, a Printer, in Bull-Head Court, Jewin-ſtreet; at the White Gallon Pot, a Chandler's Shop in Bandy-leg-Walk, Southwark, and at Mr. Neal's, a Toy-ſhop over againſt the White Hart Inn in the Borough, at Eighteen pence a bottle, with printed Directions; and, if requeſted, will be brought to any Perſon, by the Hawker who ſells his Penny-poſt. [illegible]

This Day, being February *the* 3*d, and all this Week; the Libraries of the Reverend* LEWIS ATTERBURY, LL. D. *and* PETER WENTWORTH, *Eſq; both lately deceaſed, will continue to be ſold very Cheap (the Price fix'd in eachBook) at* THO. OSBORNE's *Shop in* Gray's-Inn. *Among ſeveral Thouſand Volumes are the following Books,* Viz.

FOLIO, Gr. & Lat. &c.

RYMER's Fœdera, 17 vols. curiouſly bound in Ruſſia Leather, paned with Gold, beſt Edit.
Montfaucon's Antiq. 15. vol. large P.
Sir William Dugdale's Works
Stephens's Gr. & Lat. Theſaurus
Mezeray's Hiſt. 3 vol. beſt Edit.
Selden's Works, large and ſmall paper
Bacon's Works, large and ſmall paper
Hiſt. Anglicanæ Scriptores X
Rerum Anglicar. Script. per Gale, 3 v
Matth. Weſtmonaſterienſium
Camdeni Anglicana-Normannica
Mat. Paris Hiſtoriæ
Uptoni de Studio Militari
Wood Hiſt. & Antiq. Oxonienſes
Rerum Angl. Script. poſt Bedam
Beda Hiſt. Eccleſiæ
Chroniques de Menſtrelet
Lindenbrogii Codex Legum Antiq
Etat de la France, 3 vol.
Skenæ Regiam Majeſtatem Scotia.
Uſſerii Britan. Eccleſ. Antiq.
Dion. Caſſii Hiſt. Romana
Camdeni Britannia
Cavei Hiſtoria Litteraria, 2 vol.
Prideaux Marmora Oxonienſes
Thuani Hiſtoria, 3 vol beſt Edit.
Wilkins Leges Ang. Sax. l. pap. & ſm.
Flamſtedi Hiſt. Cœleſtis
Vaillant Numiſmata, 2 vol.
Regiſtrum Honoris de Richmond
Joſephi Opera, per Hudſon, 2 vol.
Bocharti Opera, 3 vol.
Architecture, par Blondel, 2 vol.
Parellele de Architecture
Willoughby de Piſcibus
Willis Opera Mathematica, 3 vol.
Ciceronis Opera, a Lambini, 2 vol.
Ariſtotelis Opera, 2 vol.
Ciceronis Opera, 2 vol. Car. Steph.
——— 2 vol. Rob. Steph.
——— Verburgius, 2 vol.
C. Plinii Hiſt. Notis Aarduini, 3 vol.
Ariſtophanes, per Kuſteri
Dion. Halicarnaſſenſis, per Hud. 2 vol.
Euripidis, Gr. & Lat. per Barnes
Scapulæ Lexicon. apud Elzev.
Spelmanni Gloſſarium
Cooperi Theſaurus
Vocabulario della Cruſca, 3 vol.
Torranio's Italian Dictionary
Conſtantini Lexicon, 2 vol.
Harris's Lexicon, 2 vol. l. p. & ſm.
Suidæ Lexicon, 3 vol.
Skinneri Etymologicon, l. p. & ſm.
Bayles Dictionary, Fr. & Eng.
Somners Saxon Dictionary
Fabri Theſaurus
Furetieres Dictionary, 4 vol.
Colliers Dictionary, 4 vol.
Hickeſii Theſaurus, 3 vol. large paper
Biblia Polyglotta, 8 vol. ruled
Poli Synopſis, 5 vol.
Critica Sacra, 9 vol
Grotii Opera, 4 vol.
S. Cypriani Opera, 2 vol.
Mills's Gr. Teſtament
Clerici Comment. Philologici, 4 vol.
Collectio Fratrum Polonorum, 8 vol.
Coteleri Patrum Apoſtolicis, 2 vol.
Euſebii R. Steph.
Uſſerii Annales, 2 vol.
Forbeſii Opera, 2 vol.
Bidloo's Anatomy
Whartoni Anglia Sacra, 2 vol. l. p.
Buchanani Opera, 2 vol.
Oeuvres de Bayle, 4 vol.
Grabei Septuaginta, 4 vol.
Suiceri Theſaurus. 2 vol.
Strabonis Geographia, 2 vol.
Julii Pollucis, 2 vol.
Coll. Nummaria Siſtertii Theſaurus
Caſauboni Epiſtolæ
Du Freſne Gloſſarium, 2d & 3d vol. Græcum, 2 vol.
Caviſii Theſau. Monumentorum, 6 vol.
Molinæi Opera, 3 vol.

English Folio.

Gibſon's Codex
Bundy's Roman Hiſtory, 4 vols.
Kennet's Hiſtory of England, 3 vol.
Montfaucon's Antiquities, 7 vol.
Dews Journal of the Parliament
Lewis's Hiſtory of Great Britain
Stevens's Hiſtory of Spain
Baker's Chronicle
Ruſhworth's Collections, l. p. and ſ.
Brandts Hiſt. of the Reformation, 4 vol. large paper
Gordon's Journey through Scotland
Puffendorff's Law of Nature
Sir Will. Temples Works, 2 vol.
Locke's Works, 3 vols
Scheuchzers Hiſt. of Japan, 2 vol.
Clarend. Hiſt. of the Rebellion, 6 vol.
State Trials, 6 vol. l. p. and ſmall
Hiſtory of Naples, 2 vol.
Madox's Firmaburgi
Collier's Eccleſiaſtical Hiſtory, 2 vol.
Wood's Athenæ Oxonienſes
Burnet's Hiſt. of the Reformat. 3 vol.
——— Hiſtory of his own Time
Cambden's Britannia, by Gibſon, 2 vol. large paper and ſmall
Melvil's Memoirs
Winwood's State-papers, 3 vol. large paper and ſmall
Vertot's hiſt. of the Knights of Malta, with 60 heads, 2 vol. large paper and ſmall
Spelman's Engliſh Works, l. p. and ſ.
Sandford's Hiſtory of the Coronation of K. James II. with finecuts.
Loggan's Cuts of all the Colleges in Oxford and Cambridge, 2 vol.
Aſhmole's Order of the Garter, fine Cuts, large paper and ſmall
Cabala, or Myſteries of State, beſt Edit.
Sandford's Genealogical Hiſtory of the Kings of England, fine cuts
Jones's Antiq. of Stone Henge, fine cuts
Howel's Hiſtory of the World, 3 vol.
Hobbes's Leviathan
Biondi's Civil Wars of Eng. compl.
Brady's Hiſtory of England, 3 vol.
Newcourts Hiſtory of the Dioceſe of London, with cuts
Davila's Civil Wars of France
Weever's Funeral Monuments
Sydney on Government
Hume on the Houſe of Douglas
Sir John Pettus on Metals
State Tracts, 3 vol.
Fabian's Chronicle
Polycronicon, very fair
Froiſſart's Chronicle
Stow's Chronicle
Hollingſhead's Chronicle, with Caſtrations, 2 vol. very fair
The Caſtrations alone
Kennet's Chronicle
Hall's Chronicle
Grafton's Chronicle
Fuller's Worthies
Plott's Nat. Hiſt. of Oxfordſhire
King's Deſcription of Cheſter
Burton's Deſcription of Leiceſterſhire
Leiceſter's Antiquities of Cheſter
Wright's Antiquities of Rutlandſhire
Thoroton's Antiq. of Nottinghamſhire
Dart's Antiq. of Canterbury
Prince's Worthies of Devon
Peck's Antiq. of Stamford
Philpot's Survey of Kent
Chauncey's Antiq. of Hertfordſhire
Purchas's Pilgrims, 5 vol.
Hickluyt's Voyages, 3 vol. with the Voyage to Cadiz
Langley's Pomona; or, the Fruit Garden illuſtrated, l. p. and ſmall
Willoughby on Birds
Burton's Commentary on Antoninus's Itinerary
Conqueſt of Mexico
Hope's compleat Horſeman
Gordon's Tacitus, 2 vol.
——— Life of Cæſar Borgia
Moll's Geographer
L'Eſtrange's Joſephus
Pope's Homers Iliads and Odyſſes, 11 vol. large paper and ſmall
Blome's Gentleman's Rec. with cuts
Chaucer's Works, beſt Edition
Domat's Civil Law, large paper
Harris's Voyages, 2 vol.
Tavernier's Voyages
Hook's Micographia
Cuſtoms of London (very rare)
Spencer's Works
Machiavel's Works
Parkinſon's Herbal
Salmon's Herbal
L'Eſtrange's Obſervators, 2 vol.
Sir Thomas Brown's Works
Milton's Paradiſe Loſt, l. p. fine cuts
Ben Johnſon's Works
Knox's Relat. of the Iſland of Ceylon
Clelia, a Romance
Hammond's Works, 4 vol.
——— On the New Teſtament
Cambridge Concordance
Hooker's Eccleſiaſtical Polity
Poole's Annotations, 2 vol.
Kidder on the Meſſiah
Newman's Concordance
Book of Martyrs, 3 vol. l. p. and ſ.
Barrow's Works, 4 vol.
Prideaux's Connection of the Old and New Teſtament, 2 vol.
Pearſon on the Creed
Cudworth's Intellectual Syſtem, with the Sacrament
Du Pin's Eccleſ. Hiſt. 8 vol. compleat
Scott's Chriſtian Life
Fidde's Body of Divinity 2 vol.
Stackhouſe's Body of Divinity
Tillotſon's Works, 3 vol.
Kettlewell's Works, 2 vol.
Cauſſin's Holy Court
Whitby on the New Teſtament
Patrick, Whitby, and Lowth's Commentaries on the Old and New Teſtament, 6 vol. compleat
Pocock on Hoſea, Joel, Micah, and Malachi, 2 vol.
Bedford's Scripture Chronology, large paper and ſmall
Blome's Hiſt. of the Bible
Leſlie's Works, 2 vol.
Religious Ceremonies, 3 vol. fine cuts
Mede's Works, beſt Edition
Gentlemens Seats, 4 vol. fine cuts
New General Atlas, with Maps
A general View of the World, relating to Trade and Navigation
Campbels Vitruvius, 3 vol. large paper and ſmall 3d vol. alone
Raleigh's Hiſt. of the World
Moreton's Hiſt. of Northamptonſhire
Harris's Hiſt. of Kent, l. p. and ſ.
Burchet's Naval Hiſt.
Paul's Hiſt. of the Council of Trent
Sam. Johnſon's Works
Fifth and 6th vol. of State-Trials
Seventh and 8th vol. Ruſhworth's Col.
Lawrence on Gardening
Guillims Heraldry, beſt Edition
Blackhall's Works, 2 vol.
Fidde's Life of Cardinal Woolſey
Brevall's Travels
Chambers's Dictionary, 2 vol.
Byngham's Works, 2 vol.
Shakeſpear's Plays, beſt Edition.

LAW Folio

Rolles's }
Nelſon's } Abridgment
Danvers's }
Bracton de Legibus
Cotton's Records in the Tower
Caſes in Parliament
Swinburne on Wills
Watſon's Clergyman's Law
Wood's Inſtitutes of the Common-Law
——— Civil Law
Cowel's Law Dictionary
Bird's Practiſing Scrivener
Dalton's Juſtice, beſt
Bridgman's Conveyances
Prynne on the 4th Inſtitute
Coke on Littleton, beſt
——— 2d, 3d, and 4th Inſtit. beſt
Jacob's Law Dictionary
Maxims of Equity
Tremaine's Pleas of the Crown
Regiſtrum Brevium
Vidian }
Coke }
Handſard } Entries
Raſtal }
Clift's }
Townſend's Tables, 2 vol.
Raſtal's Statutes
Corpus Juris-Civilis, 2 vol. Elz.
Lyndewoodi Provincialia
Modern Caſes in Law and Equity
Caſes in Chancery
Jenkins's Century.]

Reports.

Coke's	Comberbatch
Hardreſs	Dyers
Jones (Sir Will.)	Vernon
Jones (Sir Tho.)	Keble's, 3 vol.
Styles, l. p. and ſ.	Plowden
Rolles, 2 vol.	Maynards (Ed.) 2d
Levinz, both Fr. and Eng.	Lutwyche, 2 vol.
	Yelvertons
Vaughan	Huttons
Sanderſon	Davis
Bulſtrode	Owens
Moore	Allens
Palmer	Popham
Finche	Keyling
Pollexfen	Noye's
Croke, 3 vol.	Hetlys
Carter	Latche's
Leonard	Leys
Benloe	Winches
Saunders, both Fr. and Eng.	Saviles
	Bridgmans
Syderfin	Modern, 5 vol.
Ventris	Lane's
Keilway	Lee's
Hobart	Owens
Carters	Godbolts
Showers, 2 vol.	Lilly's

QUARTO.

Acta Eruditorum, 65 vol. in 35
Rapin's Hiſtory, 10 vol.
Hiſtoire de l'Academie Royale de Sciences, 29 vol.
Philoſophical Tranſactions, compleat in 16 vol.
Hooke's Lectures and Philoſoph. Col.
Lowthorp's and Jones's Abr. 5 vol.
Kennet's Parochial Antiquities
Willis's Survey of the Cathedrals, l. p.
Somner on Gavel kind
L'Efant's Hiſtory of the Council of Conſtance, 2 vol.
Pope's Homers Iliads, 6 vol. l. p.
——— Odyſſes, 5 vol.
Gay's Poems
Thompſon's Seaſons, large paper
Waller's Works by Fenton.
Bradley on Gardening
Pembert. View of Sir Iſaac Newton
Switzer's Syſtem of Hydroſtaticks, 2 v.
Anderſon's Collections, 4 vol.
Religion of Nature
Tournefort's Voyages
Addiſon's Works, 4 vol.
A curious Collection of all the Sermons that ever were preached before the Sons of the Clergy, bound in red Turky Leather, in 2 vol.

In uſum Delphini.

Ovidij Opera	Cæſaris Comment.
Corn. Nepos	Suetonius
Q. Curtij	Pompei Feſti
Juvenalis & Perſius	Plinij Hiſt. 5 vol.
Juſtini	Livij Hiſt. 6 vol.

Daniel's Hiſt. of France, 10 vol. l. p.
Pearſe's Longinus
Grotius, 2 vol.
James on Gardening
Cibber's Plays
Bentley's Horace
——— Terence
Wright's Travels, 2 vol.
Pomet on Drugs.
Hiſt. of Harwich
Parſons's Anſwer to Coke's Repor.

OCTAVO.

A curious Collect. of Hearne's Pieces in 40 vol. curiouſly bd. and g. l. p.
Grævius's Tully, 4 vol.
Davie's Continuation of Tully

Notis Variorum.

L. Florus	Macrobij Opera
Livij, 3 vol.	Auſonij Opera
Plinij, 3 vol.	Eraſmus
Virgilij, 3 vol.	Plauti Comedia
Corn. Tacitus, 2 v.	Minut. Fœlix
Quintilian, 2 vol.	Val. Maximus
Æliani variaH. 2 v.	Cæſaris Comment.
Suetonius, 2 vol.	Vell. Paterculus
Q. Curtis,	Seneca
Juven. & Perſius	Martialis
C. Nepos	Lactantij
Juſtini Hiſtoria	Boethij

Rapin's Hiſt. 15 vol.
Echard's Roman Hiſt. 5 vol.
Daniel's Hiſt. of France, 5 vol.
Vertot's Works
Doleman on Succeſſion
Ecton's Liber Valorum.
Acta Reg. 4 vol.
Buckingham's Works
Hiſtorical Regiſter, 14 vol.
Shaftsbury's Characteriſticks.

With ſeveral Thouſands of other Volumes, in Folio, Quarto, and Octavo, in *Greek*, *Latin*, *Engliſh*, *French*, *Italian*, and *Spaniſh*; containing a Curious Collection relating to the Hiſtory, Antiquities, Laws, and Parliamentary Affairs of *Great Britain* and *Ireland*, as alſo of divers other Nations; alſo a great many of the Claſſics *in Uſum Delphini*, and ſeveral *Cum Notis Variorum*; likewiſe many printed by *Colinæus*, *Giolito*, *Aldus*, *Juntæ*, *Rob. Char. & Hen. Stephens*, *Elzevir*, and others the moſt Celebrated Printers. Together with a curious Collection of Hiſtorians, Books of Architecture, Coins, Medals, Husbandry, Trade, Voyages, Travels, Mathematicks; Civil, Canon, and Common Law; Lexicography, Natural Hiſtory, Phyſick and Surgery, moſtly gilt Backs, Letter'd, and many Large Paper.

CATALOGUES to be had at the Place of Sale, and Money for any Library of Book.

Lately publiſhed, Modern Caſes in Law and Equity, in two Parts: containing, 1ſt, Reports of Special Caſes argued and adjudged in the Court of *King's-Bench*, in the 7th, 8th, 9th, 10th, 11th and 12th Years of King *George* I. 2dly, Caſes argued and decreed in the High Court of *Chancery*, in the 8th, 9th, 10th and 11th Years of King *George* I. To which are added ſome Special Caſes on Appeals.

LONDON: Printed by S. PALMER and J. HUGGONSON, in *Bartholomew-Cloſe*, for Captain GULLIVER, near the *Temple*, where Letters and Advertiſements are taken in: As alſo at the *Rainbow Coffee-Houſe* in *Cornhill*, and *John's Coffee-Houſe* in *Sheer-Lane*, near *Temple-Bar*. [Price Two Pence.]

The Grub-street Journal.

NUMB. 110

Thursday, *FEBRUARY* 10, 1731.

For Mr. BAVIUS, Secretary to the Grub-street Society.

Mr. BAVIUS,

THE Gentleman who wrote the letter signed PHILARCHÆUS, printed in your Journal, No. 106, mistook his genius, and deserved a severer remark than you made upon him. Either he had no friend, on whose judgment he might rely, or else he was *not so wise as to consult his friend*, before he committed his thoughts to writing. Which ever [1] is the case, he might have continued happy in his own opinion of his parts and learning, if he had not exposed himself to censure and ridicule, through too strong an inclination to appear in print. But however, he should not have pretended to criticism, before he knew how to express his own thoughts naturally: and he should have remembered what he was doing when he talked of *imposition upon the public*. To give another man's criticism for his own, to use his own words, is *villainy and imposition*. Indeed I don't wonder at his expressing himself after so odd a *manner*; *for he seems to be but little* acquainted with the force and meaning of *words*. For if he had had a true knowledge of his subject, or even any tolerable notion of language, or of accuracy of stile, he would have been more careful in the choice of his epithets. Your Society's undertaking ought to be encouraged, because it is really just and good; and as the Gentlemen concerned execute their design with so much prudence and temper, it will certainly be of great service to the Public. To attempt the reformation of our taste is truly laudable and any one speaking of *that* attempt, is justifiable, if he calls it a bold or daring undertaking; for so it is, considering the difficulty that must necessarily attend the execution of it: but if he calls it a *most audacious* one, what he meant a praise, proves a severe reflection. For if words have any meaning, *audacious* conveys a very bad idea: I am so positive of it, that I challenge PHILARCHÆUS to produce so much as one good authority where the word *audacious* is used in a good sense.

[2] VIRGIL, OVID, HOMER, HORACE, were great men: PHILARCHÆUS should read their works a little more, before he presumes to give his opinion of them. What he says in this letter is perfect common-place; but his censures and his praises are equally proper, neither of them ought to be regarded.

I am not at all surprized at the great character which he gives to BENTLEY. A good index, well read over, makes both of them critics and authors; but neither of them understands HORACE, however it came into their heads to think they did. PHILARCHÆUS is as yet but a young man, and so may possibly be reclaimed; but as for the *Great* BENTLEY, it is in vain to endeavour to work any good upon him. He is *backney'd in the ways of criticism*. The attempt must be unsuccessful, as unsuccessful

——— ut si quis asellum
In campo doceat parentem currere frænis.

Nothing can make him ashamed, who has murdered HORACE, and laid violent hands on MILTON.

I have no old scholiast upon HORACE before me; and I believe, honest Mr. BAXTER, or some other modern Commentator was the only *scholiast* which PHILARCHÆUS *happened to look into*, notwithstanding what he says of his *reading this most beautiful Epistle at his friend's house in the country*. The laying a formal scene of action is only the solemn affectation of a [3] vain methodical Coxcomb. But he is a young man; when he comes to have more judgment, he will laugh at these silly airs. Tho' he is perfectly in raptures *with the finest lines, the finest complement that ever was made by any mortal*; yet I believe, he must look again into his *old scholiast* for the meaning of the whole passage.

I own, Mr. BAVIUS, I can see no obscurity in these verses,

Falsus honor juvat & mendax infamia terret
Quem? nisi mendosum & mendacem. ——

The thought is just, and very properly exprest. If PHILARCHÆUS knew the meaning of *mendacem*, he would not say it *makes downright nonsense*; he would have spared his furious criticism on the common reading, and his great encomium upon BENTLEY. *Mendacem* is *non bonum*, and what HORACE afterwards calls

Introrsum turpem, speciosum pelle decorâ.

Medicandum would be rightly interpreted *non sanum, egentem medicamine* or *belleboro*, if you please; but that very interpretation is a demonstration, that *medicandum* is improper in the place before us. If it is to be allowed, which I think it is not, yet the common reading is much better.

There is then no reason for discarding *mendacem*; and there is no more for the alteration of *crines* into *cultus*. There is, indeed, an advantage in the original, which must be wanting in a translation into English, because we have but one word to express *cæsariem* and *crines*. But if you put *cultus* instead of *crines*, the ideas are changed, and the change is for the worse. *Why do you value yourself upon having so fine an head of hair? that fine head of hair will be laid in the dust.* That is the sense of the passage: I am sensible, that this translation is not a literal one, and I know very well that *collines* signifies anointed, or daubed. Put *cultus* instead of *crines*, and what a pretty figure it makes then! *Why do you value yourself upon having so fine an head of hair? your fine clothes will be* [4] *daubed in the dust*. HORACE could never use *cultus* in Lib. I. Od. xv. 20. and his subject obliged him to use *cultus*, or some word implying the same sense in Lib. IV. Od. xv. 13. The verse in PLAUTUS is nothing to the purpose; but I commend PHILARCHÆUS for introducing it with [5] a vile scrap of French. I believe he would be puzzled to give a reason for his *Pour la bonne bouche*; but I fancy I can give one, for it is pity a letter which bears the least relation to criticism, should go without a conjecture. It was for the same reason, that the Duke of BUCKINGHAM made his two Kings of Brentford talk French, *to shew their breeding*.

I have done with PHILARCHÆUS: but I must beg of you, Mr. BAVIUS, to tell him, and all other second-hand critics and judges, [6] that there is no reason to alter any passage in an Author, because an expression of a like nature occurs in another part of his works; and that there is less reason to make an alteration, because an expression nearly the same occurs in another Author. For supposing PLAUTUS had said, *cultum collinunt*, is that any reason why HORACE should say so too?

The citing a great many passages in *Virgil, Lucan, Statius, Silius Italicus, Ovid, Propertius* —— to prove the propriety of a passage in *Horace* shews much reading; and fools, who are delighted with appearances, will call it learning: but in reality it signifies just nothing. [7] Indeed when a sentence is obscure, and no good sense can be drawn from the words as they stand, then recourse must be had to an expression of the same nature in another part of the work, or even to another author, in order to bring in a word which may throw a proper light upon the place. But how seldom is that the case! Bentleian Editors take up their murderous pens, and set to work with a full purpose and resolution of making alterations; and every Author is sure to suffer from them. What has poor HORACE suffer'd! [8] How has he been dismembered, mangled, cut, castrated! And what will become of him, now he is fallen under the hands of the Doctor of Gainsborough! I am, dear Mr. BAVIUS,

Your most humble servant,

31 *January* 1731 HORATIANUS.

The desire of the Gentleman who wrote this Letter, That *no alterations should be made, except in the spelling*, has been exactly complied with: however, it may not be amiss to subjoin a few short notes.

1. It is supposed, that *is* was by a mistake put here instead of *was*.

2. If these Authors, and those mentioned below, had been placed according to their seniority, they would not have made a worse appearance.

3. This appellation seems too severe.

4. *Daubed with dirt* seems to be more proper, than *daubed in the dust*.

5. This is unjustly called *a vile scrap of French*, because it is really very expressive, and no expression in English answers it exactly. To keep a thing *pour la bonne bouche*, is to keep the best for the last; as is done in entertainments, where the *Dessert* consists of the most exquisite fruits, &c. to leave an agreeable relish in the mouths of the Guests. And for this *reason*, PHILARCHÆUS concludes with *a very honest verse of* PLAUTUS.

6. These are both excellent negative Rules in Criticism.

7. This is an excellent positive Rule.

8. This Gentleman had said above, that BENTLEY had *murdered* HORACE: and therefore it is thought, that this passage would run better thus, *How has he been cut, castrated, dismembered, mangled, murdered!* – Whether he has been used in this barbarous manner, or not, let HORATIANUS and PHILARCHÆUS dispute: whose arguments shall be presented to the Public in this Paper with the greatest impartiality.

Some account of the state of Prisons since the late Act, entituled, *An Act for the relief of Debtors, with respect to the imprisonment of their persons*; humbly offered to the consideration of the Legislature.

THE late Act for the *relief of Debtors*, &c. was doubtless intended, by the wisdom and goodness of Parliament, to answer its *title*; but such have been the abuses thereof, by the toils of law, and sinister practices of artful and designing men, that few have been relieved thereby; for they who are entituled thereto, may receive no benefit from it 'till two or three Terms after they are charged in *execution*, which is often the case, by their extreme poverty and incapacity to compel their Creditors to comply therewith, who, tho' they have no mind to release their Debtors, drill on the time, under pretence of not being satisfied with the Schedule; by the dilatoriness of their own Attornies, few being ready to assist an helpless man, when his misfortunes have banished his friends; and by the odious proceedings of the Law in our Courts of Justice: so that the unhappy relinquished prisoner may perish with want, or drag on a miserable life above twelve months before his Creditor is obliged, by law, to allow him any support: and even then, if the Creditor neglects to pay him his weekly allowance, tho' several weeks together, and the prisoner thereby, according to the express tenour of the Act, be intituled to a discharge, yet fruitless are all his applications, many times, to justice; the only relief he finds, is an order for his Creditor to pay him his due from the first time of omission; but, alas! how seldom is it in the power of the miserable, destitute of friends, to obtain this small satisfaction, when perhaps he is not even able to get subsistance to rescue him from the most cruel death!

Besides, if after all, the first persecuting Creditor does release him upon the receipt of his *all*, yet is he still liable to be charged in execution by others, who may severally defer the allowance two or three Terms afterwards, and alternately lengthen the duration of his trouble, which too many, alas! are maliciously prone to do, when being already stripped by the first, he has nothing left to mitigate their fury, none of them all the while allowing him any manner of support; so that the unhappy Debtor, if he has but five Creditors, be each debt ever so small, may serve an apprenticeship of seven years to a miserable confinement, before he can possibly be discharged, and in such a deplorable a condition as is only to be *felt*; but if he has many more Creditors, he must inevitably linger out his days, without any relief from them, in prison. And further, if his debt to one be ever so little above the limitation of the Act, that person only shall hold him in execution; by which means he is entirely deprived of all manner of relief, and hopes of releasement. How many also are there, who, tho' their Creditors, to save paying the allowance, decline suing them to execution, yet breathe out their last in confinement, for want of so small a matter as might supersede their respective actions? This is a punishment more severe than is inflicted by our laws on thieves and murtherers: for death to the poor confined debtor, is not less certain than to the felon, but more dreadful, as he perishes by the lingering and tormenting rack of hunger. Thus is the honest trader, and unfortunate Gentleman, only for being liable to the vicissitudes of human affairs, from which no man living is exempt, condemned to be entombed alive, cut off from the common Society, and given up to want, and complicated misery, if he escapes with life. Thus also are the charitable views of the Representatives of the *British* nation, to all intents and purposes, evaded, who, it cannot be imagined, ever meant that *Christian* Act should be made in vain.

Moreover, as the sum is limited to 100 l. many exclusive of the Act, who have lived, perhaps, in a higher

are, and are in a capacity of being more ſerviceable to their Country, are hereby rendered uſeleſs Members of the Commonwealth: nor is any manner of proviſion made for them. If ſuch a perſon be a reduced Gentleman, his condition is infinitely worſe than that of the meaneſt Mechanic, provided he be moneyleſs, and without friends; who ſoon grow cold, when long confinement, and all hopes of releaſement baniſhed, render the priſoner burthenſome. How many ſuch there are, whoſe wives and numerous pledges of their loves, daily cry to their *more diſtreſſed* parents for bread, there needs a viſit only to theſe ſad abodes for evident demonſtration. Such deplorable ſpectacles of human woe, one would think, muſt ſurely move a heart of ſtone. No tongue can tell the miſeries they bear, which would ſhrink the ſoul of a Chriſtian to ſee, and of which the *Great* cannot frame the leaſt idea: yet notwithſtanding their importunate prayers to their Creditors for liberty, upon the delivery of all their poſſeſſions, no regard or pity hath been had thereto.

But how unreaſonable a revenge is this, (however imprudent the Debtor may have been) how contrary to *Chriſtianity*, and the practice of all other nations; eſpecially if the Debtor be ready and willing to ſurrender up his *all*, under ſuch penalties as the wiſdom of Parliament ſhall think fit, is needleſs to repreſent to that *wiſe, honourable Aſſembly*, to whom this true ſtate of the affair is moſt humbly offered, in hopes of recommending them as real objects of parliamentary compaſſion.

The following Prologue and Epilogue were ſpoken at the acting of the *Orphan*, by ſome Scholars at a private School, about three years ago; and a few copies of them printed upon a ſheet by themſelves. We think them ſo good, that they ought to be made more public, and preſerved to poſterity in the *Memoirs* of our Society.

PROLOGUE *ſpoken by a young Nobleman, who acted* Polydor.

Wond'rous the Bard, whoſe happy tragic vein
Draws *joy* from *tears*, and *pleaſes* us with *pain!*
In this the tender OTWAY's Muſe was chief:
He *grieves* us, yet we *thank* him for our grief.
But never does the triumph of his art
So touch the paſſions, and command the heart;
As when we here ſee the ſoft, gentle *Fair*,
Young, innocent, deluded, in deſpair;
See with ſuch rage the *Rival Brothers* burn,
And with ſo ſweet a grace the lovely ORPHAN mourn.

Thus OTWAY wrote: but how ſhall *our* green age,
Ill ſuited to the labours of the Stage,
To ſuch a celebrated Piece be true,
And give the *elegant diſtreſs* it's due?
The raſh CHAMONT, we fear, you'll ſee ſcarce brave;
And mad CASTALIO *impotently* rave;
Fierce POLYDOR too *feebly* dare his foe;
And poor MONIMIA *robb'd* of half her *woe*.
If then you view this Action with neglect,
And with dry eyes; ours is the ſole defect:
Could *we* be juſt, *you'd* be ſo to this Scene;
And *weep* like *children*, could we *act* like *men*.

EPILOGUE *ſpoken by a young Gentleman, who acted* Caſtalio.

My *birthright*'s privilege is ſure but ſmall;
This *younger Brother*'s part is all in all.
He *trick'd* me in the Play: and now that's over,
In which I was a *Lord*, as well as *Lover*;
I *un-Caſtalio'd*, he *un-Polydor'd*,
I'm but plain *Joe*; he ſtill, forſooth, *My Lord*.
There's ſomething too, as we theſe matters rate,
In a third *circumſtance*; and that's —— *eſtate*.
For *his*; 'tis viſible, and well inroll'd:
But where *mine* lies — I never yet was told.
Well; be it — What is it that I would ſay?
Something to *cheer* you, after this *ſad* Play.
Fain would I make you merry —— but I can't:
For WIT runs low — what then? no WIT we want,
To raiſe a *laugh* —— where's *Harlequin, Scaramouch*,
Jonathan Wild, Jack Shepherd, and *Cartouch*?
What? *Farce* with *Tragedy*? —Yes; 'tis the faſhion —
No *Stage-Coach*? *Windmill-Dance*? — nor *Coronation*?
Where's Doctor *Fauſtus*, and the *flying letters*?
Alas! theſe *nobler ſports* are for our BETTERS:
For MEN, not CHILDREN —— We make no pretence
To ſuch *politeneſs*, and ſo great *expence*;
Forc'd to *take up* with POETRY —— and SENSE.

BAVIUS.

DOMESTIC NEWS.

C. *Courant*.	E P. *Evening Poſt*.
P. *Poſt-Boy*.	S J. *S. James's Evening Poſt*.
D P. *Daily Poſt*.	WE. *Whitehall Evening P.*
D J. *Daily Journal*.	LE. *London Evening Poſt*.

THURSDAY, *Feb.* 3.

His Majeſty has made a preſent to the R. Hon. Sir Rob. Walpole of the houſe lately inhabited by Count Bothmar, near the Treaſury Office, Whitehall. *P.* —— He has been pleaſed to appoint James Proſſer, Gent. to be one of the Surveyors of the Office of Ordnance at Woolwich, in the room of Wm. Sumpter, Gent. promoted to a Lieutenancy in the Royal Regiment of Artillery. *C.* —— James Herring is made an Enſign in the Foot-Guards. *D J.*

Yeſterday at a general Court of the South Sea Company, Sir John Eyles, the Sub-Governor acquainted them, that their Directors had examined the Accounts, and found they were exactly right, and directed him to declare they were unanimous. *C. P.* Their payments ſince 1721, to Dec. 1731, amounted to 2,088,000 l. and their receipts to 2,198,751 l. value of their ſhips and ſloops at home 11,900 l. Their profit in trade, about 110,000 l. and the debts due to the Company more than in 1721. —— Mr. Heathcote ſaid, that he would have had the Court of Directors examined into their advices from abroad, to ſee the entries in their books were right; but they declining that method, he proteſted againſt their proceedings, and acquainted them, that he would diſqualify himſelf; moving that a Committee might be appointed to examine the Accounts. *D J.* —— Mr. Heathcote declared, he had deſired to ſee the ſtate of the Accounts, and was refuſed. Mr. Stroud, in anſwer, denied that he was refuſed, and inſiſted, that Mr. Heathcote requiring vouchers for every particular, was anſwered, That they being foreign correſpondences, if at all poſſible, would take up ſeveral months to examine into, and that he was at liberty to make thoſe examinations. *D P.* —— Sir John Lade took notice, that tho' theſe accounts were ſaid to be very exact, yet there muſt be ſome doubt concerning them, by the difference between the price of the Stock and the Annuities; and was of opinion there ſhould be a Committee of Inquiry. —— An Account of the extraordinary receipts and payments was read: the former amounted to 7,381,848 l. 6 s. 1 d. and above 1,300,000 l. thereof had been made uſe of to pay the Dividends, over and above what they received from the Government. *D J.* — Sir John Eyles acquainted them, that the Bonds were under two millions; and that they had Bonds to the amount of 600,000 l. in their cheſt ever ſince 1721. — It was deſired for the ſatisfaction of the Proprietors, that the ſtate of their affairs might be more frequently laid before the General Courts, and then agreed to adjourn to ſome time in March, in order to have the ſtate of the Bonds, &c. laid before them. *D P.* —— Sir John Eyles was for putting off the Queſtion for a particular adjournment, becauſe by their Charter, an half-yearly Court was to be held in March. *D J.*

Yeſterday at a meeting of the R. Hon. the Governors of the Charter-houſe, the Rev. Mr. Hotchkis, the Uſher, was unanimouſly choſen School-maſter, and the Rev. Mr. Preſcot, Fellow of Catharine-Hall in Cambridge, was appointed Uſher. *D P. E P. S J. W E.* The Rev. Mr. Hotchkis, ſecond Maſter, was choſen to be Head Maſter, and the Rev. Mr. Smythies of Colcheſter, to be ſecond Maſter. *P.* — The Rev. Mr. Preſcot was appointed ſecond Maſter. *W E.*

Mr. Darby, Keeper of the Marſhalſea priſon, has lett the ſaid Gaol to Mr. Taylor, an Undertaker in the Borough. *D J.* —— An Undertaker *is a very proper perſon for a* Goaler *in a* Chriſtian Country, *where the conſequence of being* dead in Law, *is to be* buried alive.

On tueſday the Rev. Dr. Bentley and Dr. Craiſter appeared at Ely-Houſe before the Viſitor, the Bp. of Ely (his Lordſhip not allowing them to appear by proxy) &c. *D P.* —— We are well aſſured the ſame is entirely falſe, he having liberty granted to appear by proxy. *W E.*

Edw. Popham, Eſq; only ſon and heir to Francis Popham of the County of Wilts, Eſq; was married ſome time ſince to Mrs. Huddon, a young Lady of great beauty, merit, and fortune. *D P.*

FRIDAY, *Feb.* 4.

On tueſday laſt his Majeſty was pleaſed to appoint John Lumley, Eſq; Brother to the R. Hon. the E. of Scarborough, to be Colonel of a Company of Grenadiers in his Majeſty's Coldſtream regiment of Foot-guards in the room of the E. of Albemarle. *P.* — Laſt week was held a General Council, in which his Majeſty was graciouſly pleaſed to give his royal ſanction to a Charter for incorporating Truſtees for the relief of the poor, by ſettling a new Colony in the uncultivated parts of Carolina, which is to be called *Georgia*. *D P.*

Yeſterday there was a Board of Treaſury, when their Lordſhips were pleaſed to appoint Mr. Wright, a Domeſtick of the R. Hon. Sir Rob. Walpole, to be one of the Meſſengers of the Treaſury, in the room of Mr. Joſ. Richardſon, deceaſed. *P.* Footman to Sir Rob. Walpole. *D J.* — *A* Footman *is well qualified to be a* Meſſenger.

Cha. Clarke, Eſq; is choſen Recorder of Huntingdon, and likewiſe of Godmancheſter. *D P.* He is appointed Chief Juſtice of the Iſle of Ely, in the room of Mr. Serjeant Raby, deceaſed. *D J.*

By letters from Cambridge we learn, that the Univerſity intend to deprive of his preferments there (which are very conſiderable) an eminent Doctor of Divinity of that Univerſity (well known to the learned world) for being the Author of 2 Pamphlets againſt Dr. Waterland, and denying the authority of Moſes and the Prophets: unleſs he will make an affidavit of his not writing the ſame, his late advertiſements of recantation not ſatisfying that learned and orthodox body. *D P.*

Yeſterday the Petition againſt the *Charitable Corporation* (a deſign calculated for the rich to prey on the neceſſitous) was brought into the Houſe of Commons, when ſeveral excellent ſpeeches were made againſt that *Charitable undertaking*, which was very juſtly expoſed; and it was ordered to be referred to a Committee of 21, and to be ballotted for on tueſday next, which has put the Directors and Aſſiſtants into a terrible fright, ſince their Actions will now be expoſed to the Publick, and not huſhed up. *D P.*

SATURDAY, *Feb.* 5.

On monday Iſaac Leheup, Eſq; was choſen Member of Parliament for Grampound in Cornwall. —— By private letters from Edinburgh we hear, that the E. of Crawford was choſen by a great majority, to ſit in the Parliament of Great Britain. *C.*

Yeſterday the Proprietors of the Charitable Corporation delivered their Caſe to the Members of the Houſe of Commons, whereby they lay the entire blame on the Gentlemen in the direction, viz. 7 Committee Men and 11 Aſſiſtants; and that the Proprietors were wholly kept in ignorance; and in October laſt were made to believe, that their Capital was 518,370 l. 14 s. 6 d. upon which it was declared, that they were able to divide 10,614 l. 10 s. 6 d. being but part of their profits, and that this was only calculated to keep up the ſpirit of the Proprietors; for upon the ſtricteſt enquiry there has not been found in pledges or effects, in both houſes and out-warehouſes, above the ſum of 50,000 l. ſo that conſidering the various advanced prices paid by the Proprietors, together with the loſs that will ariſe to thoſe poſſeſſed of notes and bonds, the whole loſs will amount to much more than half a million of money. —— So theſe unhappy Proprietors are deſtitute of all manner of relief, but from the juſtice and compaſſion of Parliament, who, it is not doubted, will call the offenders to juſtice. —— The puniſhments inflicted upon the famous South Sea Directors in the ever memorable year 1720, is freſh in every one's memory; but their crimes are but ſmall, when compared with theſe *charitable Gentlemen*, who ſtripped the poor quite naked. — 'Tis ſaid, that four of the principal Managers *have gone out of Town for the recovery of their healths*, within a week paſt. *D P.*

We hear that Miſs Edwards of Kenſington, the rich heireſs, is coming out with one of the fineſt equipages that has been ſeen. *D P.* —— *Moſt of my Brethren were concerned in marrying this* Lady *to a* Lord, *three months ago*.

Yeſterday great quantities of ſilver were carried from the Eaſt-India Houſe in Leadenhall-ſtreet, in carts, and put on board lighters, in order to be convey'd to their ſhips now lying in the river, and which are ſhortly to proceed on their reſpective voyages to the Eaſt-Indies. *S J.*

This morning died at his houſe near Cavendiſh-ſquare, his Excellency Walter Chetwynd, Eſq; Governor of Barbadoes, and Member in ſeveral Parliaments for the City of Litchfield. *L E.*

Laſt week *chriſtned*, Males 201; Females 206. In all 407. *Buried*, Males 225; Females 262. In all 487. Decreaſed in the burials this week 87. *P.*

MONDAY, *Feb.* 7.

Yeſterday the Rev. Dr. Croxall preached before their Majeſties, his Royal Highneſs the Prince of Wales, &c. and the Rev. Dr. Hargrove before his Royal Highneſs the Duke, &c. *C.* —— We hear that —— Killigrew, Eſq; is appointed one of the Pages of Honour to her Majeſty. *P.*

On ſaturday it was argued in the Court of King's Bench, whether Dr. Bentley ſhould have a Prohibition granted him againſt the Biſhop of Ely, as Viſitor in the affair of Porter Thompſon of Trumpington, Eſq; and after a long debate, the Court agreed to enlarge the Rule of Court. *C.*

Yeſterday at noon died, at her houſe in Pall-Mall, in the 85th year of her age, her Grace the Dutcheſs of Buccleugh, commonly called Dutcheſs of Monmouth: ſhe was Conſort to the late Duke of Monmouth, who was beheaded in the reign of K. James II. By her death an eſtate of 15,000 l. per ann. and the title of Duke of Buccleugh, deſcend to the E. of Dalkeith, her Grandſon. *D J.* About 90. *D P.* Her Grace married in 1688, to her ſecond huſband, Charles Lord Cornwallis, and had iſſue a ſon and two daughters. *D P.* Her loſs will be almoſt inſupportable. *C.* —— *A great many ſuch* almoſt inſupportable loſſes *have been borne with Chriſtian patience*.

TUESDAY, *Feb.* 8.

On ſunday the Lady of the R. Hon. the Lord Baltimore was brought to bed of a ſon. *C.*

The Rev. Dr. Le Mothe, Chaplain to his Grace the Duke of Montagu, and to the firſt Troop of Horſe-guards, and Author of the late celebrated Treatiſe concerning Poetry and Painting, is appointed Suffragan Biſhop of Soder and Man, &c. *D J.*

Cambridge, Feb. 5. This day was delivered to the Vice-Chancellor a *Grace* to deprive Dr. Middleton of the Head Librarian's place, which the Vice-Chancellor proposed in Congregation to the CAPUT, in which it was stopt by Dr. *Adams*, Master of Sidney College, and Dr. Smith, Professor of Astronomy; by this means the *Grace* did not descend to the Body, where there was a good disposition to support it. The CAPUT consists of SIX, *whose concurrence is necessary to every Grace, before it can be read to the House, each having a negative vote.* ——— On the monday preceding, the said Dr. Middleton was admitted Lecturer for Dr. Woodward, upon the nomination of his Trustees, which the University is *obliged* to accept. *D P.* —— Mr. Conundrum *thinks this* Depriving Grace *ought rather to be called a* Dis-Grace; *and that the* admission *of the* Dr. *as* Lecturer *was no* act of Grace.

Yesterday came on a Tryal at Bar in the Court of Common-Pleas at Westminster, between the E. of Warwick, and Edward-Henry Edwards, Esq; in relation to the estate at Holland-House in Middlesex, and Chosely-Farm in Berks, &c. The chief point was, the validity of the marriage of the said Mr. Edwards's Father, with the Lady Betty Rich, sister to the late E. of Warwick: the Tryal lasted some hours, when the Jury gave a verdict for Mr. Edwards, confirming his Father's marriage with the said Lady. *D P.* John Edwards, Esq; Defendant: an estate of 4000 l. per ann. After a trial of 5 hours, the Earl of Warwick gave it up. *P.*

The same day the Court of King's Bench over-rul'd the motion made by Mr. Francklin's Council, to set aside his Tryal, because the Rule was not, as they suggested, regularly issued; and Mr. Francklin was committed to the King's Bench prison. *D P.* The Judges cited several Precedents, that the proceedings were legal. *P.* The Court declared the proceedings were regular, and the verdict good. *D J.*

The same morning died, the R. Hon. the Lord Carpenter, an old and experienced Field-Officer, &c. *C. E P. L E.*—Last night he lay at the point of death. *P.*

We hear that Col. Paget will be made Governor of Barbadoes in the room of Walter Chetwynd, Esq; *S J.* —— The Hon. Col. Paget, &c. *D J. Feb.* 9. The Hon. Charles Cathcart, Esq; *D P. Feb.* 9.

Last thursday Col. Reynolds of the 3d Regiment of Foot-Guards was married to Miss Duncombe, only Daughter of Col. Duncombe, of the 1st Regiment. *S J.*

WEDNESDAY, *Feb.* 9.

Yesternay Mr. Richard Francklin was brought up to the King's Bench Bar at Westminster; when his Council moved in Arrest of Judgment, 1st, That the return of the Jury from the Sheriff was not regular, by reason he returned but 24; when by Act of Parliament he should have returned 48, to be ballotted for. 2dly, That on this account the *Postea* was not regularly entered; and that the Defendant should have another Tryal. But the King's Counsel made answer, that those objections were of no weight; for that the Act of Parliament for regulating of Juries left that open, and as it was the practice in common Law to return 24 Jurors only, the return was regular from the Sheriff, and the *Postea* enter'd regularly. After many learned arguments on both sides, the Court was of the same opinion with the King's Counsel; so Mr. Francklin's Motion was over-ruled. *P.* —— The chief point insisted on was, That by the late Act, all Juries were to be chosen by ballotting, except on a motion a Special Jury was granted; and that as he was try'd by a Special Jury, it ought so to have been specify'd on the back of the Record, and that it was according to the form of the Statute. *D P.*—After this, Mr. Attorney General moved the Court, that a day might be appointed to give judgment against the said Mr. Francklin; and the Court was pleas'd to appoint Saturday next for the same, it being the last day of Term. *P.*

On Monday died the R. Hon. George Carpenter, Baron Carpenter &c. *D P.* —— His Lordship is in a better state of health than he has been for some time past. *D J.* In a fair way of recovery, and takes the air every day. *C. P.*

Last week died John Reynolds, Esq; a Gentleman of a very plentiful estate in the Bishoprick of Durham. *P.*

From the PEGASUS *in Grub-street.*

Dear BAVY,

A military Author of a late damn'd Dramatick performance, is continually complaining of the injustice of the Town; but what more particularly affects him is, the hard usage he has met from your illustrious Society. Even you, who ought to have espous'd the Cause of an oppress'd Brother, have, like a profess'd enemy, publish'd some things to his disadvantage. If you go on thus, you have not the good of your Community at heart; for you'll hinder several military Heroes from inlisting themselves into your Society, who might defend the Members of it against all opposition, by force of arms; which is a stronger, and therefore a better argument, than can be produced in your *Journal*. If upon mature deliberation you shall think fit to consult the interest of your Society, and to alter your conduct; I myself will write a Play against the latter end of this month; and contemn all Critics, aided by your *Journal*, and a file of Grenadiers.

S. James's Coffee-House, Feb. 2*d.*

I am yours eternally,
TIM. COCKADE.

At the late Trial of Mr. PETER NOAKES for the murder of Mr. WILLIAM TURNER; that celebrated Actor Mr. WILLIAM PENKETHMAN was produced as a witness in favour of the Prisoner. On which tragical occasion, he delivered his testimony in a most surprizingly proper manner; performing at once the parts of a good Witness, a good Actor, and a good Poet, —— To relate the common occurrences of life in the lofty strains of Poetry, is extremely difficult; but to do this extempore, is really wonderful. *To act a part* well at the *Theatre* in the Old Baily; before such severe *Judges*, and so numerous and polite an *Audience*, and to *come off* with applause, is a very great thing: but it is still greater, to bring off a Friend. —As all these circumstances concur to raise Mr. PENKETHMAN's reputation; the Society is sorry to observe, that our learned Brother the Historiographer of the Old Baily has not done him justice; having printed that fine speech of his in a prosaic manner, which is most sublime blank verse. As such it is therefore here republished, in a poetical manner, but without the change of one word; in order to transmit to posterity an illustrious *evidence* of a great genius for Poetry, and of a great act of Friendship.

On thursday night, or rather friday morning,
'Twixt two and three, the Prisoner and Deceased,
Rack punch were drinking at the Rummer Tavern
In Drury-Lane ——— for then I found 'em there,
And sociable they seem'd, and drank, and talk'd
Like friends, 'till watchmen cry'd, *Past four a clock.*
The reckoning was a crown, NOAKES paid it all.
From thence we rambled to King's Coffee-house,
In Covent-Garden. Ale and orange there
We drank: and still they cordial friends appear'd. ——
They told me, that they had been serenading
Some Ladies, but they did not tell me who.
And what (said they) is your opinion, Sir,
Of such Diversion? I assur'd 'em that
I was not fond of catterwauling frolicks.
At five I left 'em, and return'd at six,
And found 'em still together very friendly.
'Twas after seven when the Deceas'd arose,
And ask'd the Prisoner if he would go with him.
But he refus'd to go: then the Deceased
Bade him Good morrow, and went out alone.
No, Sir, I did not take him to be mad,
But rather thought he was a little silly.
For he would laugh at every thing that pass'd,
At every word was spoke, tho' nothing merry,
Not fit to raise a smile; the meerest trifle
Imaginable wou'd set him on the twitter. ———
When he was gone, I importun'd the Prisoner
To cross the water, with me, and two more,
Who were in company, to spend the day
In merriment, (for I had then no knowledge,
That I should at the Theatre be wanted)
The Prisoner gave consent, we all agreed,
And down Southampton-street we took our way:
A servant to the Theatre by chance
We met; his business was at Tavern doors,
And City gates the Play-house Bills to fix.
I view'd his Bills, and found, that very night
A Part appointed was for me to act,
In *Th' Amorous Widow, or the Wanton Wife*;
And by His Royal Highnesses command.
Our journey then was stopp'd; and to the Rummer
In Drury-Lane we all return'd at nine;
But did not tarry, for they had no fire.
We to the Play-house went, and breakfasted,
And after ten we parted.

FOREIGN NEWS.

THURSDAY, *Feb.* 3.

This day arrived the Mails from France and Flanders.

Hambourgh, Feb. 1. 'Tis generally reported, that the D. of Mecklembourg has resolved to embrace the Roman Catholick religion. Private letters assure us, that the Prince Royal of Prussia has, at length, consented to marry the Princess of Mecklenbourg, and will thereupon have the succession of the Russian Empire settled on him. *L E.* — *It is strange, his* Royal Highness *should be* long *in consenting to accept of a* beautiful Princess, *and an* Imperial Crown.

FRIDAY, *Feb.* 4.

Vienna, Jan. 26. On the 22d an express arrived from M. Tahlman, Imperial Resident at Constantinople, with advice that the Ottoman Porte shews no manner of inclination to a rupture with his Imperial Majesty, nor can his Excellency find the least room to suspect their designs. *D P.*

SATURDAY, *Feb.* 5.

Constantinople, Dec. 12. Gianum Coggia, who was sent for home to resume the office of Capt. Bashaw, or High Admiral, declined to return; making it his request, that he might be permitted to end his days in retirement, for that he was incapacitated by his great age to discharge that trust as he ought. *P.* —— Coggia *declined this preferment, not because he thought* his age *too* great, *but that it might be* greater.

Frankfort, Feb. 3. We see here the following distich,

Ripperda & Bonneval, numquid par nobile fratrum?
Unus enim Turca est, Barbarus alter erit.

Milan, Jan. 19. Notwithstanding the departure of several Regiments of Horse for Transylvania, 'tis computed no less than 20,000 men still remain in this State and the Dutchy of Mantua. *D P.*

Last night arrived the Mail from Holland.

Amsterdam, Feb. 12. Letters from Constantinople, dated Nov. 1. bring certain advice, that the Persian army, commanded by Prince Thamas, and the Ottoman army, commanded by Achmet Pascha, Governor of Babylon, had come to a general engagement, which lasted 7 hours, 2 hours in firing, and the other 5 sword in hand; in the issue whereof the Turks gained a complete victory, took most of their baggage, and among other things, the Royal ornaments of the young Sophy, and 30 pieces of heavy brass cannon: a great part of the Persian Infantry were killed on the spot, and the young Monarch narrowly escaped. This important action was succeeded by the taking of Hamadan, and 100 pieces of cannon therein, 70 whereof were left there when taken by the Persians, and 30 added by them. *D J.*

MONDAY, *Feb.* 7.

Hague, Feb. 1. N. S. At last the States of Holland acceded to the Treaty of Vienna on friday last, and the next day their resolution was communicated to the assembly of the States General. *P.*

Extract of our private advices from Vienna. ——— It is generally believed here, that France is preparing in good earnest for a war; and that in order to embarrass the Emperor as much as possible, she has engaged the Porte to declare against some Christian Princes. —— The Imperial forces both by sea and land are going to be put upon the foot of the augmentation projected some time ago: nay, some say, there will be 4 or 5 men added to every Troop of Horse, and every Company of Foot. All these preparations, and the keeping up of armies here, in France, in Spain, in England, and in short, in almost all parts of Christendom, do they certainly portend Peace? *P.*

Parma, Jan. 19. M. Oddi, as Apostolick Commissary, has protested against the taking possession of the Dutchies of Parma and Placentia, by Don Carlos's Guardians. *C.*

Books and Pamphlets published since Jan. 26.

Jan. 27. Fabulæ Æsopi selectæ, with an English Translation. By H. Clarke.

Royal Genealogies, &c. By James Anderson, D. D.

An Epistle to Mr. Pope. Pr. 6d.

The Honourable Lovers: or 2d Volume of Pylades and Corinna, &c. Pr. 5 s.

A Treatise of the suffocation of the matrix, &c. Pr. 6d.

28. Milton restored, and Bentley deposed, &c. *Grub.*

29. A Collection of Pieces in verse and prose, published on occasion of the Dunciad. By Mr. Savage.

The Proceedings at the Sessions at the Old Baily: 2d Part. Pr. 6 d.

A Letter to a Member of Parliament, concerning the reduction of interest. Pr. 4d.

The Craftsman's Apology: being a vindication of his conduct and writings. In several Letters to the King. Pr. 6 d. *Printed in 5 Courants.*

31. The present State of Europe, &c. for December.

A Description of the Peritonæum, &c. by James Douglass, Physician in extraordinary to Her Majesty, &c.

A Vindication of Mr. Nation's Sermon &c. Pr. 6 d.

Feb. 1. Malice Detected: a Pastoral Essay. Pr. 2 d.

Free-thinking proved Atheism, &c. Pr. 1 s. 6d.

A Review of the Text of Milton's Paradise Lost. Part I. Pr. 2 s.

Philosophical Transactions No. 420, for August and September.

The Occasional Monitor. Part II.

The way to be wise and wealthy, &c.

2. A true state of the South-Sea scheme, &c.

3. An Address to the Proprietors of the South Sea Capital, &c. Pr. 1 s.

A true state of the South Sea scheme, as first form'd, &c.

The Pall-Mall Miscellany, &c. Pr. 1 s.

4. The Quack's Miscellany, &c. Pr. 1 s.

5. Sermon before the Hon. House of Commons, Jan. 31. By Alured Clarke, D. D.

The English Lawyer, &c. By Will Bohun, Esq;

A Reply to the Defence of the Letter to Dr. Waterland.

Ecclesiastical Memoirs of the first 6 Centuries, &c. By M. de Tillemont, No. II. Pr. 2 s. 6 d.

7. An Ode occasioned by rejecting the Proposal for erecting a statue of K. Will. III. &c. Pr. 1 s.

The 4th Part of an Essay towards a natural History of Florida, &c. By M. Catesby.

8. A friendly Letter to Dr. Bentley, &c. Pr. 1 s.

The History of the Modern Patriots. Pr. 6 d.

A Sermon before the House of Lords Jan. 31, By Francis Lord Bishop of Chichester. Pr. 6 d.

Modern History by Mr. Salmon. N. 90, 91. Vol. xv. P. 5, 6.

On P——e and W——d; occasioned by their late Writings. Pr. 6 d.

Uprightness and Integrity requisite to attain and preserve a good conscience: A Sermon at Beverley Oct. 10. by Christopher Hildyard.

A Sermon, occasioned by the death of Mr. John Hurrion. By Thomas Ridgley. Pr. 6 d.

9. Readiness to good works, &c. recommended in a Sermon, Jan. 1. By James Wood, Pr. 4 d.

Whitlock's Memorials of English Affairs, with many additions never before printed.

A necessary Caution to the Sufferers by the Charitable Corporation. Pr. 2 d.

A Proposal for rendring Bankruptcies less frequent. Pr. 6 d.

South Sea Stock 99 3 qrs. 100, 99 3 qrs. to 7 8ths. South Sea Annuity 110 3 8ths. Bank 149 1 half. New Bank Circulation 6 l. 12 s. 6 d. Premium. India 177, 178 1 qr. 17 3 qrs. Three per Cent Annuity 98. Royal Exchange Assurance 98 1 half. London Assurance 13 3 8ths. York Buildings 12. African 46. English Copper 2 l. 10 s. Welch ditto 1 l. 15 s. South Sea Bonds 3 l. 3 s. Premium. India ditto 5 l. 2 s. ditto. Blanks 7 l. 7 s. 6 d. to 8 s. 20 l. Prizes 19 l. 13 s. 6 d.

ADVERTISEMENTS.

For the BENEFIT of
Mr. JOHN HEBDEN,
At Stationers Hall on Friday the 3d Day of March, 1732.

WILL be a Grand Concert of MUSICK by the best Masters. To begin exactly at Seven o' Clock. N.B. Tickets to be had at Will's Coffee-House, near the Royal Exchange; the George and Vulture Tavern in Cornhill; the Rummer Tavern in S. Mary's Church-yard, Southwark: and the Castle Tavern in Pater-Noster-Row, at Five Shillings each.

Just published,

M. J. JUSTINI ex Trogi Pompeii Historiis Extenuis Libri XLIV. quam diligentissime ex variorum exemplorum collatione recensiti & castigati.

To which is added,

The WORKS of JUSTIN, disposed in a Grammatical or Natural Order, in one Collumn, so as to answer, as near as can be, Word for Word, to an English Version, as literal as possible in the other. Design'd for the easy and expeditious Learning of JUSTIN, by those of the meanest Capacity, with Pleasure to the Learner, and without Fatigue to the Teacher. With Chronological Tables accommodated to JUSTIN's History; and also an Index of Words, Phrases, and most remarkable Things. For the Use of Schools. By N. Bailey.

Printed for J. Bickerton; J. Hazard; W. Meadows; T. Cox; W. Hinchcliffe; W. Bickerton; T. Astley; S. Austen; L. Gilliver, and R. Willock.

This day is published,

A TREATISE of Feme Coverts, or the Lady's Law. Containing all the Laws and Statutes relating to Women, under several Heads, (viz.) 1. Of Descents of Lands to Females Copartners, &c. 2. Of Consummation of Marriage, stealing of Women, Rapes, Polygamy. 3. Of the Laws of Procreation of Children, and therein of Bastards, or spurious Issue. 4. Of the Privileges of Feme Coverts, and their Power, with respect to their Husbands, and all others. 5. Of Husband and Wife, and in what Actions they are to join. 6. Of Estates Tail, Jointures; and Settlements real and personal on Women. 7. Of what the Wife is entitled to of the Husbands, and Things belonging to the Wife, the Husband gains Possession of the Marriage. 8. Of what Contracts by the Wife, Alimony, Separate Maintenance, Divorces, Elopements, &c.

To which are added, Judge Hide's very remarkable Argument in the Exchequer-Chamber, in the Case of Manby and Scot. Whether, and in what Cases, the Husband is bound by the Contract of his Wife. And select Presidents of Conveyances in all Cases concerning Feme Coverts Printed for B. Lintot, and sold by Henry Lintot, at the Cross-Keys against St. Dunstan's Church in Fleet-street.

This Day is published,

And sold by N. Prevost, over-against South-ampton-Street in the Strand,

THE Life of Mr. Cleveland, natural Son of Oliver Cromwell. Written by himself. Giving a particular Account of his Happiness in Love, Marriage, Friendship, &c. and his great Sufferings in Europe and America intermix'd with Reflexions, describing the Heart of Man, in all its variety of Passions and Languors. In four Volumes, 12mo.

N.B. The 3d and 4th Vol. may be had separate.

This Day is published,

A new Edition, with many Additions, never before printed, of

WHITELOCK's Memorials of the English Affairs: Or, An Historical Account of what passed from the Beginning of the Reign of King Charles the First, to King Charles the Second his happy Restoration. Containing the publick Transactions, Civil and Military: Together with the private Consultations and Secrets of the Cabinet. With a compleat Index.

——Quæque ipse miserrima vidi
Et quorum pars magna fui.   Virg.

Printed for J. Tonson: And sold by J. and J. Knapton; R. Knaplock; D. Midwinter and A. Ward; A. Bettesworth and C. Hitch; G. Strahan; J. Pemberton; F. Fayram and J. Hatchett; C. Rivington; J. Batley; J. Brotherton; F. Gyles; R. Will arnton; J. Stagg; T. Osborne; L. Gilliver and F. Cogan.

This Day is published, [Price 2 s. 6 d.]
[To be continued,]
NUMBER II. of

ECCLESIASTICAL MEMOIRS of the First Six Centuries, made good by Citations from Original Authors: With a Chronological Table, containing an Abridgment of the principal Things, placed according to the Order of Time; and with Notes, clearing the Difficulties of Facts and Chronology. Translated from the French of Lewis Sebastian Le Nain De Tillemont.

Nothing escapes her. Tillemont's Exactness; and there is no Fact so obscure and perplexed, but his Criticism dispels the Mists, and disentangles the Difficulties. These Works of Mr. Tillemont are the Product of a prodigious Labour, and almost infinite Industry, and are compos'd with all possible Exactness. He is most exact in his Expressions, just in his Citation, cautious in his Decisions, pious and judicious in his Observations. The World may gain a great deal of Improvement from this Work, which is calculated both for the Instruction and the Edification of Mankind.
Du Pin's Bibliotheque, Tom. 18.

Printed for the Author; and sold by Charles Rivington at the Bible and Crown in St. Paul's Church-yard; and William Clayton Bookseller in Manchester.

This Day is published,

AN Enquiry into the Origin of HONOUR, and the Usefulness of Christianity in WAR.

By the Author of the Fable of the Bees.

Price bound 3 s. 6 d.

Printed for J. Brotherton at the Bible, next the Fleece Tavern in Cornhill.

This Day is published,

Dedicated to the Gentlemen of the Navy of England.

THE MEMOIRS of Monsieur du Guè Trouin, Chief of a Squadron of the Royal Navy of France, and Great Cross of the Military Order of S. Lewis; containing all his Sea-Actions with the English, Dutch, and Portuguese, in the late Wars of King William and Queen Anne.

Translated from the French by a Sea-Officer.

Printed for J. Batley, at the Dove, in Pater-noster Row, Where may be had,

The TRADITIONS of the CLERGY no way Destructive of Religion: A Sermon preach'd at Bingley-Church, on Sunday September 12th, 1731.

By IS. SMITH.

Minister of Haworth, near Kighley, Yorkshire.

ALSO,

I. The Religion of Nature considered. To which is added a Postscript, containing Reflections on Mr. Chubs's Discourse concerning Reason, &c. so far as it respects this Subject.

II. Some Thoughts concerning Virtue and Happiness, in a Letter to a Clergyman.

This Day is published,

THE Compleat Store of the Overture, Songs and Chorus in the new Opera call'd Æthius, Compos'd by Mr. Handel. To which are added, the whole Transposed for the Flute. Engrav'd, Printed and Sold at the Printing-Office in Bow Church-yard, price 2 s 6 d.

Where may be had,

The Favourite Songs in the Opera of PORUS. Price 2 s. 6 d. As also the following Opera's in Score, by the same Author, viz. Julius Cæsar, Tamerlane, Rodelinda, Scipio, Alexander, Admetus, King Richard the First, and Lotharius.

Likewise, at the above Printing-Office is just publish'd, Mirth and Harmony, consisting of a Cantata, and other new Musick, with a Thorough-Bass, figur'd for the Harpsichord. Compos'd by Mr. George Vanbrught, and the whole transpos'd for the Flute; price 5 s. —Note, The Tunes may be had alone; price 1 s.

Also just published, at the same place,

Sententiæ Selectæ: Or, A Collection of Miscellaneous Sentences, Divine, Moral and Historical. In Prose and Verse. English and Latin. Excerpted from the Works of many learned and judicious Authors, and digested into Alphabetical Order. By Edward Curtey. To which are added, various Forms for indicting Letters. The Characters, Places and Significations of all Sorts of Stops, Points, Pauses and Marks used both in Writing and Printing, with their Explanations. A Table of the most common Abbreviations, or Contractions of Words. Pertinent Directions for fair and exact Writing, with Rules for making and managing the Pen, &c. The best approv'd Receipts for making Ink of many Colours. An ingenious Discourse and Poem on the unspeakable Advantages of Reading and Writing; also several Instructions and Rules to Behaviour; with many other useful and profitable Particulars.

As also

A curious Book of Select Fables, and other short Poems &c. finely engraved on 32 Copper Plates, for the Amusement of young Gentlemen and Ladies. To which are added, The most useful and ornamental Hands for their Improvement in the Art of Writing; price 1 s. 6 d. Also, a new Cyphering Book for the Use of Schools, being the best of the Kind ever yet extant. Engrav'd by George Bickham, Senr. price 1 s. 6 d.

This Day is published,

A Collection of PIECES in VERSE and PROSE, which have been published on occasion of the Dunciad. Dedicated to the Right Honourable the Earl of Middlesex. By Mr. Savage;

Likewise

ATHELWOLD: A Tragedy. By A. Hill, Esq; as it is acted at the Theatre Royal in Drury-Lane. 2. OF FALSE TASTE; an Epistle to the Right Honourable Richard, Earl of Burlington. By Mr. POPE. The 3d Edition, with an additional Letter.

Printed for Lawton Gilliver, at Homer's Head, against St. Dunstan's-Church, Fleet-street.

Feb. 4. was published, Price 6 d. small Paper; the fine Royal Paper, Margin open'd, 1 s.

THE GENTLEMAN'S MAGAZINE: Or, Monthly Intelligencer.

No. XIII. for January 1731.

Containing more in Quantity, and greater Variety, than any Book of the Kind and Price.

I. A View of the Weekly Essays, viz. 1. Vindication of Mankind; the Religion of Philosophers; Duell's Creed. Coffee-house Savages; Sir Wm. Page's New-year's Gift; Conjugal Love; Mr. Pope's Epistle on Taste censur'd and defended; Foolish Fondness; Love and Grandeur; the Lau eat's pretentions canvas'd; Female Heroism; Lessons of Morality; of the Stage; Love of Fame; Remarks on Dr. Bentley's Edition of Milton; on Authors; Rules in Courtship; of Immortality.

II. Political Points, viz. On the Jury Act; Severities in B——ke's Administration; the Craftsman's Huge Letter with Remarks; the King's Speech; of publick Credit. Monopolies, &c. Affidavits about S. Sea private Transactions; Charitable Corporation Accounts; on the Pragmatick Sanction; Sheriff's Act eluded; a Scheme to pay the publick Debts; political Charity; K. Charles II. vindicated; the Form of an Oath proposed to be taken by Popish Priests to his Majesty.

III. Poetry, viz. Ode for New-year's Day, burlesqued, translated into English; the Laureat's Answer; Keys to the manner 1 C—— prefer'd to P——pe.

IV. Domestic Occurrences, &c.
V. Prices of Goods, Grain, Stocks.
VI. Foreign Affairs.
VII. Books and Pamphlets.
VIII. A Table of Contents.

Printed and sold at St. John's Gate; and by E. Jeffries in Ludgate-street. Where may be had, the former Numbers. Also An exact LIST of the present Parliament, with the Places of their Abode in Town, &c.

LONDON: Printed by S. PALMER and J. HUGGONSON, in Bartholomew-Close, for Captain GULLIVER, near the Temple, where Letters and Advertisements are taken in: As also at the Rainbow Coffee House in Cornhill, and John's Coffee-House in Sheer-Lane, near Temple-Bar. [Price Two Pence.]

The Grub-ſtreet Journal.

NUMB. 111

Thurſday, *FEBRUARY* 17, 1731.

A Sermon before the Houſe of Lords, on Jan. 31, 1731. the day appointed to be kept as the day of the Martyrdom of K. Charles I. By FRANCIS Lord Biſhop of Chicheſter. ——— Prov. xxiv. 21. *My ſon, fear thou the Lord and the King, and meddle not with them that are given to change.*

THE Church was always true to the King, and they had little hopes of ſucceeding in their deſigns againſt him, as long as that ſtood; and therefore their main ſtrength was in the firſt place levell'd againſt that part of the Conſtitution. —— The great fault of the King was, that he loved the Church; and the Church muſt be ruined becauſe it will not deſert the King. The pretence, indeed, was pure religion, and a farther reformation; Prelacy and Popery were rung in the ears of the people, without ceaſing, 'till they were worked up to an incredible degree of infatuation and enthuſiaſm. The indiſcreet zeal of the friends of the Church, and the ſeverity with which they preſs'd a compliance in things indifferent, or of ſmall conſequence, upon perſons of different perſuaſions, whoſe averſion to compliance increaſed in proportion to the zeal with which it was preſs'd, prepared the fuel for that unhappy fire, which then broke out with ſo much fury. The warm heads of the lower people were full of reformation; they thought every injunction in Church matters an infringement of Chriſtian liberty; they could bear nothing that had any reſemblance to what was practiſed in the Church of *Rome*; every thing they did not like, was *Popery*, and *Popery* was *Antichriſt*, and that ſanctified all the vows that could be made for its deſtruction; it was the cauſe of God. P. 15, 16.

A Sermon before the Hon. Houſe of Commons, on Jan. 31, 1731. By ALURED CLARKE, D. D. Prebendary of S. Peter's Weſtminſter, and Chaplain in ordinary to his Majeſty. —— Pſal. lxxviii. 8. *And might not be as their Fathers, a ſtubborn and rebellious generation.*

Nor was the *corrupt* part of the Clergy wanting to prepare the way for ſuch proceedings, by raiſing the Prerogative to a greater heighth than ever was known. P. 3.

But the Church was not leſs afflicted than the State; for another great occaſion of thoſe diſturbances was the erecting an Eccleſiaſtical Tribunal over the conſciences of men, and the introducing a diſcipline into the Church, not at all ſuited to thoſe, if to *any* times. Ceremonies, confeſſedly indifferent, were forc'd upon the people, and the neglect of them puniſhed with exorbitant ſeverity. ——The jealouſy of Popery had ſpread ſo wide, that the whole nation became in a manner poſſeſs'd with it, on which it is ſeverely remark'd, that the fire was kindled from the altar; and the heavy judgments, which followed began at the houſe of God. P. 4. After this it can be no wonder that the Nonconformiſts having been provok'd, with ſo much ill uſage from the heads of a Proteſtant Communion, ſhould take the advantage of theſe unwarrantable meaſures; and draw from our own Body, numbers of thoſe who had long contended (tho' in vain) againſt the many dangerous innovations and fanciful trappings of Public Worſhip, wherein the men of zeal and power did fondly imagine *the beauty of holineſs* to conſiſt. P. 5.

And here the example of a Prince (whoſe diſtreſſes were chiefly owing to the blind zeal of thoſe about him) ought to have its proper weight with us: for he ſoon found the ill conſequences of religious violence; and as he knew by ſad experience, that the paſſions of men were ſooner inflam'd by hardſhips of that kind than any other, &c. P. 17.

A Sermon before the R. Hon. the Lord Mayor, &c. being the Anniverſary Faſt for the Martyrdom, &c. By ROB. WARREN, D. D. Rect. of S. Mary of Stratford-Bow. —— Rev. iii. 21. *To him that overcometh will I grant to ſit with me in my throne, &c.*

The jealouſies and animoſities which were conceiv'd againſt him, as they were almoſt without number, ſo were they without reaſon. The charge of Popery has been always a piece of cunning in men of no religion at all, to blacken the Church of England: for, ſure I am, that this Church always has been, and I heartily pray God it always may be, the ſtrongeſt bulwark againſt the Romiſh religion. P. 17.

I will not ſay there had been no occaſions given on the part of the Court for jealouſies and fears, or that there was not ſufficient reaſon for oppoſition in a Parliamentary way to the then meaſures; but I think, in juſtice to the King, it may be truly ſaid, there was no neceſſity for fomenting thoſe popular tumults the troubles began with, much leſs for having recourſe to arms, and involving the nation in all the calamities of a civil war, and leaſt of all for carrying things to ſuch an extremity, as to take away the King's life, which muſt always, and always will be looked on by all indifferent perſons, by all nations round about us, as a moſt infamous and execrable action. —— Whatever wrong meaſures had been taken, which might endanger the liberties of the ſubject (tho' what was moſt offenſive of this kind was done by the advice of his Council, with the concurrence of all his Judges, Judges in general of good character, and well-eſteemed in their Profeſſion) the King not only ſhewed the greateſt diſpoſition to give his People all poſſible ſatisfaction by the moſt ſolemn Declarations, ... but gave the greateſt proof of his being ſo diſpoſed, by giving the Royal aſſent to Bills of the greateſt importance to the Crown. He gave up entirely thoſe branches of the Prerogative, which were moſt liable to be made an arbitrary uſe of; and denied nothing that could be aſked; . . . . Nothing would ſatisfy but an Act empowering the Parliament to ſit as long as they ſhould judge it neceſſary: and even this for peace ſake, ... the good King conſented to; by which, in effect, he unkinged himſelf; . . . . . As it was in itſelf the greateſt proof he could give, ſo it was done at the beginning of the Troubles, and before his affairs can be ſaid to have put him under a neceſſity of doing it. . . . . The King, in the times of his greateſt ſucceſs, was always willing to put an end to the effuſion of blood by a Treaty, and to make ſuch conceſſions as were below the Majeſty of a King, and which nothing could juſtify but the concern he had for the publick peace and welfare, to which he was always ready to ſacrifice his own moſt valuable rights. P. 11, 12.

It will be neceſſary to look into the beginning of his reign, when we ſhall find him ſurrounded with Miniſters, who, being averſe to our Conſtitution, as well as ignorant of it, were too ſtudious to eſtabliſh the authority of the Prince on the ruin of the liberties of the People. P. 3.

Though theſe and all former grievances were offered to be redreſs'd; and the royal conceſſions were ſo many, that more could not with ſecurity be made by the King, or even received by the Subject, they all came TOO LATE; for by this time the winds that mov'd theſe waters were too ſtrong to be laid; ——— The remembrance of paſt times, which ſet before men the many unwarrantable acts of power; the oppreſſions of ſome great Church-men; and the influence of a Popiſh Queen and her Attendants; together with a prevailing opinion, that the King diſguis'd his real intentions, or that his condeſcenſion proceeded from want of power, and not an inclination to promote the happineſs of his people; ——— Theſe, and other circumſtances of this kind, ſerv'd to create unconquerable fears in Many, and to give life to the wicked and ambitious hopes of a Few, whereby the public ruin was at length too effectually compaſſed. P. 5, 6.

There was another charge againſt the Royal Martyr, and that too of ſuch a malignant nature, as his righteous ſoul abhorred, and that was that he endeavoured to ſubvert the Laws and the Conſtitution: but as this objection was made againſt him by Thoſe that really did it, I cannot but conclude, that he endeavoured, to the utmoſt of his power, to maintain and preſerve them. For ſure I am, that the King, and thoſe unhappy men, his undutiful ſubjects, had never the ſame deſign. P. 18.

This makes it highly reaſonable we ſhould, in the moſt ſolemn manner, expreſs our deteſtation and abhorrence of ſo execrable an action, and deprecate the Divine vengeance, that God would not viſit upon us this great iniquity of our Fore-fathers, and thoſe other national ſins, which provoked God to give them up to ſuch ſtrong deluſions. —— But it will be ſaid, What is this to us? Why ſhould we obſerve a Day of faſting and humiliation for a Fact committed above fourſcore years ago, and which no body now alive could poſſibly be any way *concerned* in? I anſwer, That the judgments of God for great ſins may hang over a nation for many generations; and therefore it may ſtill be our concern to deprecate the wrath of God for ſo heinous a pollution of the Land. But there are other reaſons for ſuch commemorations; Men may be guilty now as truly as their Forefathers were then; they may conſent *ex poſt facto*, and approve a crime when it is done, and by that means make themſelves as guilty in the ſight of God, as if themſelves had had a hand in it, or had actually been conſenting to it. But further, ſuch Solemnities are of great uſe to keep up by this means a ſenſe of duty to God and the King, and to excite in the people a juſt abhorrence of ſuch great and flagrant ſins. And I wiſh I could not ſay, there is in the preſent age but too much cauſe to think this neceſſary; for tho' the men are gone who perpetrated this horrid Fact, the ſpirit ſtill remains. . . . . Republican principles are as induſtriouſly propagated now as they were then, tho' perhaps more covertly, and to the ſame ends: 'tis to introduce a change of Government, and in order to that to weaken it, by weakning firſt the influence of Religion, and introducing Infidelity, which attempts come chiefly from the Republican quarter now, as they did then. P. 16.

The deſign of all that has been ſaid, is to ſhew, that the *whole* of our duty *on this occaſion*, is to beg of God to keep away from us the evil of the days that are paſt; to pray for the continuance and improvement of the good ones we enjoy; and to arm ourſelves with a reſolute endeavour, at all worldly hazards, to continue down our civil and religious rights, at leaſt as pure as we receiv'd 'em, to the generations that are to come. P. 20.

But I hope it cannot be expected, that the weight of the guilt of thoſe times (on *either* hand) ſhould be laid upon any of the preſent generation of men; for it can hardly be with modeſty affirmed, that we are more particularly *concerned* in the confuſions of the late civil wars, than in the other general calamities which were ſo frequently felt in the ages that went before. As to public Bleſſings, —ſuch as the foundations of States and Kingdoms; or the preſervation of thoſe States from ruin and devaſtation; or ſuch a change in a Kingdom as promotes the only end of all Government, the good and happineſs of the people. —— Theſe ſhould be had in everlaſting remembrance, by men who continue to enjoy the effects of them. But a national humiliation for ſins which were committed in an age that is paſt and gone, cannot be a duty of like obligation to any people, and much leſs to a people in actual poſſeſſion of all thoſe bleſſings of heaven, which are the ordinary marks of the Divine favour and reconciliation. But however this be ——— ſo long as the wiſdom of our Governors ſhall think it proper to continue ſuch a Memorial of the paſt times, it becomes us to ſubmit to their direction, and to conſider that *All theſe things happ'ed to our Forefathers for euſamples*, &c. P. 10.

To mention no other proofs of his ſincerity and good intentions to his people, his Trial and death were undergone with that Chriſtian meekneſs, patience, reſignation and fortitude, as are inimitable by any one who is not thoroughly convinced of the righteouſneſs of his cauſe, and the uprightneſs of his heart; who takes not God for his help, and puts his confidence in him. Such was his behaviour and conſtancy in his laſt black ſcene, that he did nothing unbecoming a good King, nothing below a great one. P. 13.

As to his character, however it may be diſguis'd by panegyric on one hand, or ſatire on the other, yet may we certainly pronounce it of him, that tho' many Princes have equall'd him in his miſtakes, and the abuſe of his power, few have done it in his ſufferings, or in his behaviour under them, from the beginning of his impriſonment, to the laſt moments of his life. P. 7.

O! how ſteady! How manly was his whole behaviour! O! how calm and compoſed was his whole ſoul! There was nothing to be diſcovered in him, but what was Royal and majeſtic. No unmanly fears of dying diſturbed the ſerenity of his mind; no peeviſh reſentment againſt his murderers, but a ſpirit of reſignation to the whole will of God, and a ſurprizing appearance of inward peace and comfort, and joy in the Holy Ghoſt manifeſted it ſelf in all he ſaid or did. P. 18. He could never have arrived at ſuch an eminency of virtue, had he not been ſupported by a well grounded conſcience, an active and vigorous faith, the fulneſs of Divine grace, and the proſpect of eternal glory, which is the ſure reward of all thoſe who ſuffer for righteouſneſs ſake, and thereby *overcome* themſelves and the world. P. 20.

The Bishop's *Sermon.*

When ſuch men can't ruin the eſtabliſhed Religion this way, then they ſet up for zealous aſſerters of the rights of ſubjects in religious matters, and declare loudly for an abſolute exemption from all authority whatever, as an invaſion of their liberty; fault is found firſt with the Teachers of Religion, then with what is taught; the Law of Nature is cry'd up in oppoſition to the Chriſtian Revelation, and all reſtraint upon licentiouſneſs is Prieſtcraft. P. 8.

The nation never was ſo peſter'd with Libels againſt both the eſtabliſhed Religion and eſtabliſhed Government, as it is at preſent; which, where it will end, I dread to think. Whatever good ſome men may think there is in this licentiouſneſs, ſure I am there is great evil in it; and ſo have all Governments, and the freeſt States, ever thought in all times. 'Tis what, in my apprehenſion, no Government, be it ever ſo wiſely conſtituted, or ever ſo well adminiſtred, can long ſubſiſt under. Every Government, in a certain number of years, is by one incident or other diſtreſſed in its affairs: when ſuch a juncture finds a people greatly divided among themſelves, and alienated in their affections, by perpetual Libels from one another, and from their Governors; what can that Government do in its own defence, or the defence of the nation, againſt a foreign enemy, much more againſt a Pretender to the Crown, when its trueſt ſtrength is gone, the affections of the people, and a hearty union among themſelves? For we can't but obſerve, that under a Republican ſpirit there lurks one very different. The men who are ſo loud for liberty upon the Republican ſcheme are joined by a Party of men who mean nothing leſs than what in appearance they are ſo zealous for. They act by direction from another quarter, and to ſerve another Cauſe: 'tis for that they endeavour to weaken the King at home, and to expoſe him abroad; 'tis to bring in a Power deſtructive of the religion and liberty of their Country, that they eſpouſe ſo warmly the Cauſe of liberty, and join with men of quite different principles. P. 17, 18.

And after his Parliament had made ſo ill an uſe of this great power, [to ſit as long as they ſhould judge neceſſary] as to involve the nation in a war, they might at any time have put an end to it upon the moſt advantageous terms. P. 12.

Nor were his Adherents unworthy the greateſt Prince or the beſt Cauſe. They were not only the attendants of his Court, or ſuch as had a dependance on him; who either had received, or expected favours from him; they were not mercenary creatures, who could eaſily be bribed to betray their Country, or could hope to raiſe themſelves upon the ruins of it, or would give up the Conſtitution and the Laws to the will and pleaſure of an abſolute Prince; they were no friends to Popery, or arbitrary Power; they were the Nobility and chief Gentry of the nation: Theſe were the King's friends, who adhered to him in all his diſtreſſes; theſe commanded his armies, or rather compoſed them, and ſerved as private men in their perſons, while they ſupported him with their fortune. And many of them ſealed with their blood the juſtice of his Cauſe, not only in the field, but by ſuffering ſhameful and ignominious deaths. P. 13. Theſe were ſuch Adherents, as carry with them the greateſt weight in proof of the goodneſs of the cauſe they eſpouſed. They could have no intereſt ſeparate from that of their Country; they had themſelves the greateſt ſhare of property, and conſequently the ſtrongeſt inducement to keep from their necks the heavy yoke of arbitrary power, to which in every Country the Nobility are the firſt ſacrifice. As they had the greateſt eſtates to preſerve to themſelves and their poſterity, ſo it may be preſumed they had the beſt education, and underſtood the Conſtitution, the Laws of their Country, and the rights both of Prince and people, better than the lower part of the nation, much better than the populace can be ſuppoſed to do, or the factious Leaders at the head of them. . . . . . This was the King's caſe, ... from whence we may certainly conclude, he was far from deſerving thoſe black and odious characters with which his enemies have loaded him. P. 14.

Dr. Clark's *Sermon*

The many looſe and profane writings that are ſcattered amongſt us, have ſpread ſuch a coldneſs and indifference over the hearts of the people to every thing that regards the intereſts of Religion, as has almoſt extinguiſhed that antient laudable zeal, which one may affirm to be neceſſary to the very *being* of a Proteſtant Kingdom. And as this lethargic diſpoſition, into which we are fallen, moſt effectually favours the views of Popery, its Emiſſaries have accordingly increaſed their diligence in gaining Proſelytes, and are *now* more induſtriouſly imploy'd in every corner of our Metropolis than has been any time known in the preſent age. P. 18. And from hence we may conclude, that when the principles of Religion have no proper influence on the minds of men, and the moſt ſacred tyes have loſt their force, a Free Government muſt be haſting apace to its diſſolution. And 'tis as certain, that when a general ſpirit of luxury and expence has made it neceſſary for men to have recourſe to extraordinary methods for their ſupport, we can then be no longer in our own power: for the door being open to every ſort of corruption, public virtue muſt gradually die away, and we be left deſtitute of all the means of oppoſing any future attempt that might be made to bereave us of our liberties. And *ſuch* indeed ſeems to be our *preſent* caſe, that only an happy accident, or the immediate care of Providence will continue us in the enjoyment of our Rights; which can never be ordinarily ſecur'd, but by the virtues of induſtry, frugality and oeconomy. P. 22.

The miſchiefs that befell the Kingdom have been falſly imputed to this part of our Conſtitution; which is abundantly confuted by the King's own Declaration, preſently after the firſt battle, that there was *not above one part in ſix left in either Houſe.* P. 16.

The Parliament, which ſate for ſome time in the higheſt and moſt deſerved honour and credit, found themſelves enſlav'd, ſoon after the war broke out, by a deſpicable few of their own Body. P. 11.

And yet one would think *another* People was now appearing, and not They who are in the quiet, undoubted poſſeſſion of thoſe bleſſings, which our Forefathers had in view in *all* their ſtruggles from one generation to another. P. 21, 22.

This great iniquity. P. 16. The horrid fact. P. 5, 16. The impious murder. P. 18. A moſt infamous and execrable action. P. 11. | The murder of our unhappy King. P. 2.
No one in the Engliſh Hiſtory more execrable and impious. P. 5. The moſt flagrant crime a nation could be guilty of. P. 11.

Bp. Hare.	Dr. Clarke.	Dr. Warren.
The good King. P. 12.	The unhappy King. P. 3, 15.	The Royal Martyr. P. 14, 16, 17, 18. The Bleſſed Martyr. P. 4.

DOMESTIC NEWS.

C. *Courant.*	E P. *Evening Poſt.*
P. *Poſt-Boy.*	S J. *S. James's Evening Poſt.*
D P. *Daily Poſt.*	WE. *Whitehall Evening P.*
D J. *Daily Journal.*	LE. *London Evening Poſt.*

THURSDAY, *Feb.* 10.

It is ſaid, that Miſs Moſtyn, Daughter of Sir Rob. Moſtyn, Bar. is made one of the Maids of honour to her Majeſty, in the room of Miſs Vane. *D P.*

Yeſterday the Barons of the Exchequer gave their opinion concerning the ſpecial Verdict between the King, Plaintiff, and Mr. Huggins, late Warden of the Fleet, Defendant, relating to the eſcape of ſeveral priſoners (who were charged on the King's ſuit for large ſums of money) during his Wardenſhip; and the Court was of opinion, that it was no wilful eſcape as to the knowledge of the Defendant, and ſo gave it in favour of Mr. Huggins. *P.*

Yeſterday at Ipſwich in Suffolk, Sir Rob. Kemp of Ubbeſton in Suffolk, Bar. was elected Knight of the Shire without oppoſition. *D P.*

We hear that the names of Alderman Barnard and Alder. Perry were in both liſts, for two of the Committee for enquiring into the Charitable Corporation. *D P.*

The Truſtees of the Turnpike leading to Kenſington, Chelſea and Fulham, were reſolved to petition the Parliament, for leave to bring in a bill, to explain and amend the Act, in regard to the conduct of their Collectors, and toll having been reduced from upward of 2000 l. a year, to 1600 l. a year, and ſince they were turned out, the toll has produced 2200 l per ann. for which the Collectors were committed to Newgate by 5 Gentlemen in the Commiſſion of the Peace, of unblemiſhed character, againſt whom actions have been brought by the Collectors. *D J.*

On tueſday night laſt 3 perſons, who were committed to the New Goal in Southwark, for entering the houſe of Mr. Moor of Lambeth, mask'd and diſguis'd, made their eſcape. *D P.* ——— They went to a Smith in the Mint, threatning immediate death, if he would not knock off their fetters; but he aſſuring them he had no tools, they went away: the next morning their irons were found on the ſhore near Freſh Wharf. *C. Feb.* 12.

Chriſtened laſt week, Males 167: Females 175. In all 342. Buried, Males 278: Females 293. In all 571. Increaſed in the Burials laſt week 15. *E P.*

It having been inſerted in *The Daily Courant* of tueſday, That *on monday died the R. the Hon. the Lord Carpenter,* &c. the Evening Papers copy'd it, as alſo the Daily Papers of yeſterday: but the ſame is intirely falſe, his Lordſhip having been ſlightly indiſpoſed with a cold. *D P.* His Lordſhip being at preſent in a better ſtate of health than he has been for ſome time paſt. *E P.* ——— At 6 this morning died the R. Hon. George L. Carpenter, the eldeſt Lieutenant General, in the 74th year of his age: he had been 59 years in the army. He married Alice, Daughter to William L. Viſc. Charlemont, by whom he has left iſſue only one Son, who ſucceeds him in his honour, and is now Lieut. Col. of his Majeſty's Horſe Guards. *S J. L E.* ——— A few days ſince dy'd at Buſhy Park, the Wife of Mr. Simpſon, one of the Keepers; ſhe was aged 106 years, 4 months, and 8 days: ſhe enjoy'd all her ſenſes to the laſt. *L E.*

FRIDAY, *Feb.* 11.

A few days ſince James Calthrope, Eſq; was ſworn in one of the Gentlemen Uſhers, Quarterly Waiter to his Majeſty, in the room of Leonard Finkney, Eſq; deceaſed. *P.* —— On wedneſday the R. Hon. John Earl of Crawford, kiſs'd the King's hand for the command of a Troop of Dragoons in Brigadier Ker's Regiment. *D P.*

We hear that a noble Peer has paid 5000 l. to Beau Naſh, and agreed to allow him 400 l. per ann. during life, in lieu of 10,000 l. he was to pay him, in caſe he, the ſaid Nobleman, ſhould loſe at hazard above 2000 l. at one ſitting, which he did in the laſt October meeting at Newmarket. *D P.*

Tho. Pelham, Eſq; is newly arrived from Tours in France, where the Lord Dunkeron, Mr. Kinnerſley, and Mr. Stewart, remain confin'd on account of Mr. Hamilton's killing a Gameſter in that City. *D P.* —— *Theſe Gentlemen, according to the accounts of* ſome of my Brethren, *made their eſcapes; and according to thoſe of others, were ſet at liberty, two months ago.*

Yeſterday the Court of King's Bench granted a Rule to ſhew cauſe why an information ſhould not go againſt the Publiſher of the Daily Poſt, for ſome Paragraphs in that Paper of tueſday laſt, highly reflecting upon the York Buildings Company. *C.*

On ſunday dy'd of the gout, Tho. Byde, Eſq; at his fine ſeat at Ware Park in Hertfordſhire: by his death an eſtate of above 2000 l. per ann. falls to his eldeſt Son, a Minor. *D P.* ——— Yeſterday morning died Will. Jones, Eſq; a Proctor of Doctors Commons, and one of the Coalmeters of this City. *P.* ——— *I wonder whether his* Proctorſhip, *or his* Coalmeterſhip, *intitled him an* Eſquire.

Yeſterday morning died Tho. Howard, Eſq; a Gentleman of a plentiful fortune, and has left 2000 l. to one Stephens, a Journeyman Shoe-maker. *D J.* —— *Will not this legacy make* Criſpin *an* Eſquire?

SATURDAY, *Feb.* 12.

The R. Hon. the Earl of Shaftſbury being come to age on tueſday laſt, his Lordſhip took the oaths and his ſeat in the Houſe of Peers. *P.* He took the oaths, &c. on wedneſday. *C.*

A few days ſince, Benj. Pollen, Eſq; of Lincoln's-Inn, was married at Southampton to Mrs. Markland, Daughter of the late Rev. Dr. Markland, Maſter of S. Croſs, a Lady of a conſiderable fortune. *D P.*

At a meeting of the Royal Society laſt thurſday evening, Dr. John Martyn preſented his Tranſlation of *Tournefort's Hiſtory of Plants,* &c. in two volumes, 8vo. and Mr. Phil. Millar, Author of the Gardeners Dictionary, lately publiſhed, was ordered by the Society to peruſe the ſame, and give an account of it. *D J.* —— Mr. Orator-Wi-Hear, *has obſerv'd, That the* Dr. *having lately* given an account of Mr. Millar's Dictionary, *the* Gardener *now takes his* Tourn-for-*to tell* His-ſtory of Plants.

Yeſterday the Houſe of Commons appointed a Committee of 21 of their Members to inſpect the affairs of the Charitable Corporation. *D J.*

Yeſterday morning came on at the Arches Court at Doctors Commons, before Dr. Richard Chichley, the Hearing of the Cauſe relating to the Libel filed by a Lady againſt her Huſband, for inſufficiency, as formerly mention'd. The Affidavits, Interrogatories, and Certificates relating to the ſaid Cauſe were ſeverally read, as were alſo 19 letters that had paſſed between the Gentleman and his Lady. They have been married about 4 years; and a certificate of 3 Midwives was particularly read aſſerting the Lady to be *virgo intacta* at the time ſhe parted from her Huſband, and commenced this ſuit; and likewiſe his anſwer to his Wife's interrogatory of his not having had carnal knowledge of her for 3 years after their marriage, in which he aſſerted, that he *believed* he had ſuch knowledge of her twice within the firſt year. This point was learnedly argued by his Council, who aſſerted that to be ſufficient to prevent the marriage being ſet aſide; but this was anſwered by the oppoſite Council, that if the Gentleman could not ſwear *poſitively,* it look'd as if he was not a competent judge of what was meant by the words. The whole was merrily harangued on by both parties, and ſeveral ſmart repartees, as may be ſuppoſed from the nature of the ſubject, paſſed between the Council; but the Court took time to conſider of the judgment. The Lady's fortune was ſaid to be 30,000 l. *D J.*

This morning, at the Court of King's Bench Mr. Juft. Page gave judgment againſt Mr. Franklin, for printing and publishing the Craftſman of Jan. 2, 1731, viz. that he ſhould pay 100 l. fine, be imprisoned for 12 months, and give security for his good behaviour for 7 years; himself to be bound in 1000 l. and his two ſecurities in 500 l. each. *L.E. E.P. W.E.*

On ſunday laſt dy'd at his Seat at Rodborne Cheney in the County of Wilts, Tho. Webb, Esq; Serjeant at Law, by whoſe death an eſtate of 1000 l. per ann. deſcends to Borlace-Richmond Webb, Eſq; Member of Parliament for Ludgarſhall in the ſaid County, ſon to the late Gen. Webb. *L.E. W.E.* — Mr. Serj. Webb, Brother to the immortal Lieut Gen. Webb, who has been reported dead and buried in ſeveral Papers, is perfectly recovered, and deſigns to be in Town next Eaſter Term. *S.J.*

MONDAY, Feb. 14.

Yeſterday the Rev. Dr. Hargrave preached before their Majeſties, his Royal Highneſs the Prince, &c. and the Rev. Dr. Crozal before his Royal Highneſs the Duke, &c. *G.* — We hear that Mr. Geo. Foxgrave, one of the Under-Keepers of Buſhy Park, is made Keeper of Hampton-Court Houſe Park, in the room of Mr. Howard. *D.P.*

On thurſday was try'd at Guildhall an Action for treſpaſs, brought by Edw. Chapman, Esq; Plaintiff, againſt James Lamb and Hen. Jelly, Cuſtom-houſe Officers at Dover, Defendants, for taking from him (then come over from Calais) 1 ſilk night gown, 14 ſhirts, 1 black velvet cap, and 1 black ſilk cap. The Defendants gave evidence, that the clothes were new, and that they had often ſeiz'd wearing apparel for the Duty, and kept it; but not being able to ſhew any Law that lays any Duty on wearing apparel, unleſs brought in as merchandize, the Plaintiff recovered a verdict, with 20 l. damage; which plainly ſhews, that Travellers may paſs with their clothes. *D P.*

On ſaturday died, in a very advanced age, at his apartment in Somerſet-houſe, the Marquis of Marimont. *C.* He came here in the beginning of K. James II's reign, was made a Colonel of a Troop of Horſe in K. William's, and hath ſince been on half pay. *P.*

Yeſterday dy'd the R. Hon. Will. Bromley of Baginton in the County of Warwick, Eſq; Member of Parl. for the Univerſity of Oxford, in the preſent and 4 laſt Parliaments; He was Privy Counſellor to Q. Anne, Secretary of State, and Speaker of the Houſe of Commons in 1710. *D P.* Repreſentative in Parliament for Warwick. *D J.* At 6 o'clock. *C.* About 7. He was a Gentleman univerſally eſteemed by all who had the happineſs of his acquaintance. *P.*

By ſome private letters from the North, we hear, that about the beginning of the laſt week Col. Chartres died at his ſeat at Hornby Caſtle in Lancaſhire; and, 'tis ſaid, has left 80,000 l. to the 2d Son of the R. Hon. the E. of Wemes, his Grandſon, to whom he was Godfather. *C.* — Who railed a vaſt fortune by his induſtry. *D P. Feb. 15.*

TUESDAY, Feb. 15.

On ſunday in the evening a Cabinet Council was held at S. James's; at the breaking up of which, one of his Majeſty's Meſſengers was diſpatched to his Excellency Mr. Keene, his Majeſty's Miniſter at the Court of his Catholick Majeſty. *C.*

Samuel Sandys, Member of Parliament for Worceſter, is choſen Chairman to the Committee appointed to inſpect into the affairs of the Charitable Corporation. *P.*

On thurſday laſt a Member of the Royal Society preſented them a method to prevent children being over-laid by nurſes, &c. which is practiſed with great ſucceſs in Germany, and was tranſmitted to him by a friend who before theſe. *P.* Mr. Graham. *D P.*

We hear Sir Tho. Dyke, Bar. Maſter of Arts, of Chriſt-Church College, Oxford, is propoſed by ſeveral Members of that Univerſity to repreſent that learned body in Parliament, in the room of their late Member, William Bromley, Eſq; deceaſed. *D P.*

Yeſterday were rehearſed at S. Paul's for the Feſtival of the Sons of the Clergy, which is to be celebrated on thurſday next, the great Te Deum and Jubilate compoſed by Mr. Hardel, for the publick thankſgiving upon the peace of Utrecht; together with two Anthems made by him; one for his late Majeſty, and the other for the Coronation of his preſent Majeſty. As they are eſteemed by all good judges, ſome of the grandeſt compoſitions in Church-muſick, and were performed by a much greater number of voices and inſtruments than has ever yet been on the like occaſion; ſo there was a nobler audience, and a more generous contribution to the charity than has been known; the collection amounting to 250 l. 5 s. which is above 47 l. more than was given laſt year, altho' that was more double that had been collected in any former year. *P.* Upwards of 260 l. *C.*

Yeſterday morning died Tho. Weldon, Eſq; by whoſe death a very conſiderable eſtate falls to a Gardener at Ealing. He was a Gentleman of Iriſh extraction, and had an eſtate of about 1000 l. per ann. in King's County Ireland. *D J.*

The ſame day two Malefactors condemned the laſt Seſſions at the Old Bailey, were executed at Tyburn. Hallam denied the flinging his wife out of the window to which. *C.* Hallam and Scroggs. *P.* They both denied the facts for which they ſuffered, and Hallam received the ſacrament under Tyburn, of his innocence of throwing, *D J.* — This ſacrament of his innocence was new, as is the place of adminiſtring it.

WEDNESDAY, Feb. 16.

Dr. Iſham, Brother to Sir Juſtinian, is talked of for a candidate to repreſent the Univerſity of Oxford. *D P.* Yeſterday Dr. Betteſworth, Dean of the Arches at

Doctors Commons, gave Judgment in the affair in which a certain young Lady had libell'd her husband for inſufficiency. He gave his opinion in a learned ſpeech, ſetting forth, that though there were ſix midwives who ſwore the Lady was a pure Virgin, yet there were ſeveral eminent Surgeons who certified, that he was a man ſufficient to propagate his ſpecies; and that if he ſhould ſet aſide the Marriage, the caſe would be, that if the parties ſhould each marry again, and the man have children by his wife, and the woman by her husband, then the ſecond marriage on each ſide would be void, and the firſt marriage good, and the children on each ſide got in the ſecond Marriage would be baſtards; ſo that he confirmed the Marriage, and ordered the Lady to go home to her husband. *P.* —— We hear the ſaid Lady has lodged an appeal in the Court of Delegates againſt her ſaid husband *P.*

From the PEGASUS in Grub-ſtreet.

An Epilogue to the Comedy of *Ignoramus* lately acted by ſome young Gentlemen at Bury ſchool. Spoken by IGNORAMUS.

I, who ſo long have lorded at the Bar,
Still the great Champion of the gooſe-quill war;
Who, when a learned quotation would come pat in,
Could fill the Jury's gaping mouths with Latin;
To all my jargon now muſt quit pretence,　5
Nor ſpeak one word, forſooth, but ſimple ſenſe.
In ann. quart. Georg. ſecund. 'tis here decreed,
That Lawyers each Indenture, Bond, and Deed,
In plain pure Engliſh only write or read.
In plain pure Engliſh all; — oh, conſcience! conſcience!
Why downright ſenſe in Law is downright nonſenſe.
Dame Juſtice ſure no longer will be blind,
If Jury-men pretend their eyes to find.
Shall too each *Quorum*-Squire, juſt taught to ſee,
In wit and learning think to rival me?　15
Have I, for this, ſuch Folio's read, and wrote:
Made this poor head, with weighty volumes fraught,
Plunge 'through the vaſt profundity of thought?
Labour'd in terms abſtruſe t' amaſe the Nation;
Sought for learn'd nonſenſe thro' each rank and ſtation;　20
And after all — that ſenſe ſhould come in faſhion?
But ah! What makes yon Pulpit Heroes ſneer?
They think 'tis now their turn to domineer.
What! Then this Anti-Lawyer combination,
Was brought about by Clergy inſtigation.　25
And here ſome wiſeacres among 'em ſay,
Lawyers ſhould plead as cheap —— as Parſons pray;
Becauſe by your new-fangled reformation
The Pope's old Mumpſimus has loſt his ſtation,
And Prieſts no more have power to gull the nation.　30
Pray, Sirs, what's that to us? Who ever ſaw
Religion made a precedent in Law?
Muſt pulpit maxims then keep Barriſters in awe?
But, hold, don't think your victory compleat;
The Act, you know, is not in force as yet.　35
If any therefore cloath your brows in terrors,
I'll plague 'em with *Appeals* and *Writs of Errors*.
Dare not to frown then (if you do) th' event is,
I'll prove each mother's ſon *non compos mentis.*

FOREIGN NEWS.

THURSDAY, Feb. 10.

Paris, Feb. 8. The Archbishop of Paris has taken off the Prohibition laid on Foreign Curates, officiating in the Church of S. Medarde, on a plain diſcovery, that the perſons committed to the Baſtile, for pretending to be under convulſions from viſiting the tomb of L'Abbé Paris, are rank impoſtors; and a reaſonable ſuppoſition, that the people will be no longer ſeduced thereby. *D P.*

Vienna, Feb. 2. The Conſul Turk has had a ſpecial audience of Prince Eugene, to re-aſſure his Highneſs, that the report of the Grand Signor's deſigning a war with the Emperor or his Allies, was entirely groundleſs. *D P.* The Turkiſh Conful. *D J. Feb. 9.*

Amſterdam, Feb. 15. From Frankfort it is adviſed, that the French Troops on the frontiers keep quiet, but that orders were lately come to fill the magazines of all the frontier places with artillery, ammunition, and proviſions. *D P.*

Vienna, Feb. 2. 'Tis generally believed the Czar's choice of her Succeſſor will fall upon the Princeſs of Mecklemburg, who was born Dec. 18, 1718, and is going to be married. *C.*

Conſtantinople, Nov. 1. Some few weeks ago Michawoda, Hoſpodar (Prince) of Walachia, was ... a ſon of the late Prince Mauro Cordato, who ... plague in 1730, is made Hoſpodar in his room. *C.*

SATURDAY, Feb. 12.

This day arrived the Mail from France.

Paris, Feb. 16. Our laſt letters from Italy confirm the entire recovery of Don Carlos, and attribute the goodneſs thereof to his bleeding plentifully at the noſe, on the 3d and 4th days of his illneſs. *L.E. B.P.*

MONDAY, Feb. 14.

Extract of a letter from Barcelona, Feb. 3. N.S. —— There are orders come to the Intendant of this place to make preparations for embarking 30,000 troops, which are to be in readineſs to embark and take the field by Mar. 15. with artillery and every thing neceſſary to attend ſuch an army. *D P.*

TUESDAY, Feb. 15.

This day arrived the Mails from France and Holland.

Berlin, Feb. 16. The King has received advice, that the Duke of Lorrain having overheated himſelf in hunting, was taken ill of a fever and ſore throat. *W.E. L.E.*

Seville, Jan. 28. Men talk of forming a Camp in March next upon the frontiers of Catalonia, to conſiſt of 8 Regiments of Horſe, and 25 Battalions of Foot. *W E.*

WEDNESDAY, Feb. 16.

Hague, Feb. 20. The Earl of Cheſterfield, and Count Sinzendorf, went this day to the Aſſembly of the States General, and ſign'd jointly with them the Acceſſion of this Republick to the Treaty of Vienna. *C. P.D P.*

Petersburg, Jan. 28. On the 26th the Czarina arrived in one of our Suburbs, and yeſterday made her entrance into this City. *C.*

Books and Pamphlets published ſince our laſt.

10. Charity in all its branches, &c. Pr. 2 s.
Of falſe Fame. An Epiſtle to the Earl of Pembroke. By Mr. Welſted. Pr. 6 d.
The Political State of Great Britain: for January.
The Monthly Chronicle: for January.
11. Inſtitutiones Chirurgicæ: or Principles of Surgery, &c. By G. Smith.
Roma Antiqua & Recens; or the Conformity of ancient and modern Ceremonies, &c. Tranſlated from the French. Pr. 2 s.
Walteri Hemingford. Hiſtoria de rebus geſtis Edvar. di I, II, III, &c. in two Volumes, publicavit Tho. Hearne, A.M.

1731-32.	Norfolk.	Home.	Oxford.	Midland.	Northern.	Weſtern.
Lent Circuit.	Lt. Raymond Ch.Juſ. Bar. Comyns	Eyre Chief Baron Ju. Price	Chief Baron Bar. Thomp-ſon	Ju. Price	Ju Denton	Ju. Probyn Bar. Carter Ju Lee
			Reynolds Ju. Page	Reading	Northampt.	
M. Feb. 28:			iJ. Forteſcue			
T. 29.						Wilton
W. Mar. 1.			Oxford			N. Sarum
Fr. 3.				Oakham		
Sa. 4.	Aileſbury	Hertford	Gloucester	Lincoln		Dorcheſter
M. 6.		Chelmsford				
W. 8.						
T. 9.	Bedford		Monmouth			
Fr. 10.				Nottingham		
Sa. 11.	Huntington		Hereford	d. Town	York	
M. 13.	Cambridge			Derby		Launceſton
T. 14.		Rocheſter				
W. 15.				Shrop.		
Th. 16.	Thetford			Leiceſter		
Fr. 17.				d. Borough		
S. 18.						
M. 20.	Bury S. Ed.	E. Grimſtead		Stafford	Coven. & Warwick	Exeter
T. 21.		Guildford				
Th. 23.				Worceſter	Lancaſter	
M. 27.						Taunton

A Letter to a Member of Parliament in the North, concerning scandal and defamation, &c.

An Abstract of Sir Isaac Newton's Chronology: by Mr. Reid.

Speculum Crape-Gownorum, &c. Pr. 1 s.

A Dissertation on the Pox, &c. By Joseph Cam, M.D. Pr. 1 s. 6d.

12. The glorious reward of Christian fortitude: a Sermon before the Lord Mayor, &c. Jan. 31. By Rob. Warren, D.D. Pr. 6d.

Peace and unity recommended in a Sermon at S. Margaret's Lothbury, Jan. 30. By James How, A. M.

The History of Charles XII. King of Sweden, by M. de Voltaire: translated from the French.

A Scheme for a new Lottery: or a Husband, &c. for 40 s. Female Inconstancy display'd, &c. Pr. 1 s.

15. The faithful Pastor's duty and reward: a Sermon. A Consecration Sermon, at Lambeth, Jan. 23. By Sam. Knight, D.D.

The publick virtue of former times, and the present age compared. Pr. 6d.

On Tuesday Stocks were

South Sea Stock 100-1 8th, 100 3 8ths. South Sea Annuity 116 1 8th, a 1 4th. Bank 149 7 8ths. India 178 1 half. Three per Cent Annuity 97 3 4ths. Million Bank 111. African 46. York Buildings 11: Royal Exchange Assurance (100 l. paid in) 98 3 4ths. London ditto (13 l. paid in) 13 3 8ths. Bank Circulation 6 l. 17s. 6d. South Sea Bonds 3 l. 14s. India ditto 6 l. 1 s. ditto. English Copper 2 l. 12 s. Welch ditto 1 l. 16s. Blanks 7 l. 7 s. 6d. New Three per Cent. 97 1 4th, a 3 8ths.

ADVERTISEMENTS.

For the BENEFIT of
Mr. JOHN HEBDEN,
At Stationers Hall on Friday the 3d Day of March, 1732.

WILL be a Grand Concert of MUSICK by the best Masters. To begin exactly at Seven o' Clock. N. B. Tickets to be had at Will's Coffee-House, near the Royal Exchange; the George and Vultur Tavern in Cornhill; the Rummer Tavern in S. Mary's Church-yard, Southwark; and the Castle Tavern in Pater-Noster-Row, at Five Shillings each.

To be Lett,

At Stamford-Hill, Middlesex, near the Turn-Pike,

SEveral Houses, four or five Rooms on a Floor, with five or six Acres of Orchard or Garden Ground; great Plenty of Spring Water running through the same, and Fish Ponds there; with Coach-Houses and Stables, and other good Conveniences.
Inquire of Mr. Halsted there, and know further.

In a short Time will be published,

And delivered to the Subscribers, upon their sending in their Receipts and last Payment, to Mr. RICHARDSON at the Theatre in Oxford,

DR. FELTON's Sermons at the Lady MOYER's Lecture. After the Books are delivered to the Subscribers, the Remainder will be sold by Mr. Richardson; and any Booksellers, or others, may be furnished upon their sending to him.

This Day is published,

M. J. JUSTINI ex Trogi Pompeii Historiis Extenuis Libri XLIV. quam diligentissime ex variorum exemplorum collatione recensiti & castigati.
To which is added,
The WORKS of JUSTIN, disposed in a Grammatical or Natural Order, in one Column, so as to answer, as near as can be, Word for Word, to an English Version, as literal as possible in the other. Design'd for the easy and expeditious learning of JUSTIN, by those of the meanest Capacity, with Pleasure to the Learner, and without Fatigue to the Teacher. With Chronological Tables accommodated to JUSTIN's History; and also an Index of Words, Phrases, and most remarkable Things: For the Use of Schools. By N. Bailey.
Printed for J. Bickerton; J. Hazard; W. Meadows; T. Cox; W. Hinchcliffe; W. Bickerton; T. Astley; S. Austen; L. Gilliver; and R. Willock.

This Day is published,

AN Enquiry into the Origin of HONOUR, and the Usefulness of Christianity in WAR.
By the Author of the Fable of the Bees.
Price bound 3 s. 6d.
Printed for J. Brotherton at the Bible, next the Fleece Tavern in Cornhill.

This Day is published, [Price 2 s. 6d.] [To be continued,] NUMBER II. of

ECCLESIASTICAL MEMOIRS of the First Six Centuries, made good by Creations from Original Authors: With a Chronological Table, containing an Abridgment of the principal Things, placed according to the Order of Time; and with Notes, clearing the Difficulties of Facts and Chronology. Translated from the French of Lewis Sebastian Le Nain de Tillemont.

Nothing escapes Mr. Tillemont's Exactness; and there is no Fact so obscure and perplexed, but his Criticism dispels the Mists, and disentangles the Difficulties. These Works of Mr. Tillemont are the Product of a prodigious Labour, and almost infinite Industry, and are composed with all possible Exactness. He is most just in his Expressions, just in his Citations, cautious in his Decisions, pious and judicious in his Observations. The World may gain a great deal of Improvement from this Work, which is calculated both for the Instruction and the Edification of Mankind.
Du Pin's Bibliotheque, Tom. 18.
Printed for the Author; and sold by Charles Rivington at the Bible and Crown in St. Paul's Church-yard, and William Clayton Bookseller in Manchester.

This Day is published,

Dedicated to the Gentlemen of the Navy of England,

THE MEMOIRS of Monsieur du Guè Trouin, Chief of a Squadron of the Royal Navy of France, and Great Cross of the Military Order of S. Lewis, containing all his Sea-Actions with the English, Dutch, and Portuguese, in the late Wars of King William and Queen Anne.
Translated from the French by a Sea-Officer.
Printed for J. Batley, at the Dove, in Pater-noster Row, Where may be had,
The TRADITIONS of the CLERGY no way Destructive of Religion: A Sermon preach'd at Bingly-Church, on Sunday September 12th,
By I. S. SMITH,
Minister of Haworth, near Kighley, Yorkshire.
ALSO
I. The Religion of Nature considered. To which is add'd a Postscript, containing Reflections on Mr. Chubs's Discourse concerning Reason, &c. so far as it respects this Subject.
II. Some Thoughts concerning Virtue and Happiness, in a Letter to a Clergyman.

Feb. 4. was published, Price 6d. small Paper; the fine Royal Paper, Margin open'd, 1 s.

THE GENTLEMAN's MAGAZINE: Or, Monthly Intelligencer.
No. XIII. for January 1731.
Containing more in Quantity, and greater Variety, than any Book of the Kind and Price.
I. A View of the Weekly Essays, viz. a Vindication of Mankind; the Religion of Philosophers; Deist's Creed; Coffee-house Savages; Sir Wm. Paget's New-year's Gift; Conjugal Love; Mr. Pope's Epistle on Taste censur'd and defended; Foolish Fondness; Love and Grandeur; the Laureat's pretensions canvass'd; Female Heroism; Lessons of Morality of the Stage; Love of Fame; Remarks on Dr. Bentley's Edition of Milton; on Authors; Rules for Courtship; of Immortality.
II. Political Points, viz. On the Jury Act; Severities in B——ke's Administration; the Craftsman's Hague Letter with Remarks; the King's Speech; of publick Credit, Monopolies, &c. Affidavits about S. Sea private Trade; Charitable Corporation Accounts; on the Pragmatick Sanction; Sheriff's Act eluded; a Scheme to pay the publick Debts; political Charity; K. Charles II. vindicated; the Form of an Oath proposed to be taken by Popish Priests to his Majesty.
III. Poetry, viz. Ode for New-year's Day, burlesqued; translated into English; the Laureat's Answer; Keyberian manner; C—— preferr'd to P——pe.
IV. Domestic Occurrences, &c.
V. Prices of Goods, Grain, Stocks.
VI. Foreign Affairs.
VII. Books and Pamphlets.
VIII. A Table of Contents
Printed and sold at St. John's Gate; and by E. Jeffries in Ludgate-street. Where may be had, the former Numbers. Also An exact LIST of the present Parliament, with the Places of their Abode in Town, &c.

This Day is published,

THE Complete Score of the Overture, Favourite Songs and Chorus in the new Opera call'd Ætius. Compos'd by Mr. Handel. To which is added, the whole Transpos'd for the Flute. Engrav'd, Price 2 s. 6d.

Where may be had, The Favourite Songs in the Opera of PORUS. Price 2 s. 6d. As also the following Opera's in Score, by the same Author, viz. Julius Cæsar, Tamerlane, Rodelinda, Scipio, Alexander, Admetus, King Richard the First, Sosso, and Lotharius.

Likewise, at the above Printing-Office is just publish'd, Mirth and Harmony, consisting of a Cantata, and other new Musick, with a Thorough-Bass, figur'd, for the Harpsichord. Compos'd by Mr. George Vanbrughe, and the whole transpos'd for the Flute; price 5 s. Note, The Flute may be had alone; price 1 s.

Also just publish'd, at the same Place, Sententie Selecte: Or, A Collection of Miscellaneous Sentences, Divine, Moral and Historical. In Prose and Verse, English and Latin. Excerpted from the Works of many learned and judicious Authors, and digested into Alphabetical Order. By Edward Garray. To which are added, Various Forms for indicting Letters. The Characters, Places and Significations of all Sorts of Stops, Points, Pauses and Mirks used both in Writing and Printing, with their Explanations. A Table of the most common Abbreviations or Contractions of Words. Pertinent Directions for fair and exact Writing, with Rules for making and managing the Pen, &c. The best approv'd Precepts for making Ink of many Colours. An ingenious Discourse and Poem on the unspeakable Advantages of Reading and Writing; also several Instructions and Rules to Behaviour; with many other useful and profitable Particulars.

As also A curious Book of Select Fables, and other short Poems, &c. finely engraved on 32 Copper Plates, for the Amusement of young Gentlemen and Ladies. To which are added, The most useful and ornamental Hands for their Improvement in the Art of Writing; price 2 s. 6d. Also a new Cyphering Book for the Use of Schools, being the best of the Kind ever yet extant. Engrav'd by George Bickham, Sen. price 1 s. 6d.

To be LETT in James-Street, Westminster,

A Strong, well-built Brick House, handsomely fitted up, with Marble Chimney-Pieces, and proper Wainscotting: It has convenient Closets, and a Room useful for a Library: Also for the better Security against Fire, it has a Stone-Stair from the Cellar to the Attick Floor, besides the great Stairs, and stands clear from other Houses.
It has a prospect into St. James Park, and into Garden Grounds and open Fields backward. The late Bishop of Peterborough lived in it several Years. There is by it a Door into St. James's Park.
If any Persons can find a Pleasure in living in a House not likely to fall on their Heads, or that (in all human Probability) is free from burning, this House may suit them.
Enquire of Mr. Doyly, at the Black Perriwig in Petty-France, Westminster.

The Cælestial Anodyne Tincture: Or, The Great Pleasing Medicine,

FRam'd and approv'd of for its wonderful and never-failing Success in giving immediate Ease and Relief in all manner of pains, either inward or outward, and is the most certain Remedy in the World for a sure and speedy Cure of the Cholick, and expelling Wind, Gripes and pains in the Stomach, the Pleurisy, stitches or pains in the side, back, loins, or any other part; Rheumatick Ailments, which cause pain and dolor. It hath given ease to a Miracle, when all other remedies have fail'd. In the Gravel and Stone in the Kidneys, it gives ease forthwith, and brings them away to admiration. It also facilitates and causes a speedy Delivery in Child-birth. 'Tis no Quack trifling thing to allure the World with, but a real and well-experienced Medicine, and acting by Stupefaction (as Opiates) but by a friendly, benign and subtile Nature, pacifying the most fierce and terrible racking pains, and carries off the Cause, not by purging, but by Transpiration, by Urine, or breaking Wind. No Family ought to be without it. And used outwardly it cures Swellings, Aches, pains, Numbness, or Weakness of the Joints, 'tis excellent for Cramps, and all other such Infirmities, effecting Wonders in Agues, Fevers, Small pox, &c. No Family ought to be without it.
It is sold only by Mr. PARKER, Printer, at his House in Salisbury-Court, or by such persons as he shall depute, viz. at Mr. Parker's, a Printer, in Bell-Head Court, Jewin-street, at the White Gallon Pot, a Chandler's Shop in Bandy-Leg-Walk, Southwark, and at Mr. Neal's, a Toy-shop over against the White Hart Inn in the Borough. Eighteen pence a bottle, with printed Directions; and, requested, will be brought to any Person, by the Hands who sells his Penny-post. Sealed as above.

LONDON: Printed by S. PALMER and J. HUGGONSON, in Bartholomew-Close, for Captain GULLIVER, near the Temple, where Letters and Advertisements are taken in: As also at the Rainbow Coffee-House in Cornhill, and John's Coffee-House in Sheer-Lane, near Temple-Bar. [Price Two Pence.]

The Grub-street Journal.

NUMB. 112

Thursday, FEBRUARY 24, 1731.

Bombast and Farce, the Sock and Buskin blend;
Begin with bluster, and with bawdry end.
Harlequin Horace, pag. 8.

For Mr. BAVIUS, Secretary to the Grub-street Society.

SIR,

PLAYERS are a sort of an inferior order of *Grubeans*; or rather (to speak more properly) as they live by the labours of several of your Society, and may therefore be said to eat their bread, ought to be look'd upon as their servants. It is for this reason, that I think every thing that relates to them ought to be exhibited at your tribunal, and sentence past on them as the Society shall judge meet.

This premised, I beg leave, by you, to acquaint the illustrious Community, that I am an Author both in prose and verse; and think I have as good pretensions as any Writer whatsoever, to be elected a Member of the Society: as I shall shew, if ever I judge proper to stand Candidate for that honour. But this is only by the by: my present business, Mr. BAVIUS, is this. ——— Having written a Play lately, I was very desirous of bringing it upon the Stage; but as I had no personal acquaintance with any of the Managers, I apply'd to a friend, who spoke to one of his, that had. The Play was accordingly put into the hands of Mr. W. and it was expresly desired of him to give his impartial opinion of it; for which reason the Author was to remain unknown to him 'till then. In about a fortnight's time it was returned; but great difficulty made as to his giving this impartial opinion. Upon which I imagined of course, that my Play was look'd upon as a very bad, or silly piece. But, it seems, I was very much mistaken: for the sum total of this impartial opinion amounted to this, That *the Play was a very sensible performance, was really pretty, but not theatrical; so that he could not undertake to act it, on any account.*

Before I go any farther, I must acquaint you, that I have no pique at all against the Manager that deliver'd this opinion of my Play: for his behaviour, from first to last, had so much of the Gentleman, that I can say of him, as was said of a Great Man (whom I don't recollect at present) That his refusal had the air of a favour.

I was very much surprised at such a reason for rejecting it, having, as I thought, observed all the rules essential to the Drama that I had ever read. ——— My fable was natural; and the subject of it, I dare say, seen every day in common life. My characters, as well the principal as the under ones, properly distinguished, and kept up from the beginning to the end. The language, such as would be used by the polite world, that should find themselves in the circumstances of my Drama. There is not indeed any affectation of extraordinary wit, or introduction of unaccountable characters, such as the *Modish Couple* has furnish'd us with, in the persons of Sir *Lubberly Block*, his son *Chip*, and the lively Mr. *Grinly*. And really, to tell you a plain truth, I hugged myself, that I had naturally, and without foreseeing it, avoided the rock on which that ingenious Author split: for it has since appeared, that the Town was not greatly taken with those new out-of-the-way characters. As to the Plot of my Play, it was regularly carried on from Act to Act; and the *Denouement* in the fifth was neither too crouded, nor precipitated, as often happens, nor yet imperfect, or obscure. The time was only from morning to evening.

As to the meaning of the word *Theatrical*, tho' I have puzzled my brain ever since to find it out, I am as far off as ever, and despair now of coming at any tolerable idea of it, unless, Mr. BAVIUS, you will be so good as to help me in the search. ——— That the want of this quality should be assigned as a reason for rejecting a Play, that is allowed to be a *sensible performance*, and *really pretty*, is yet more surprising. Hitherto I have been used to think (and I believe I am not singular) that if a Play was *sensible* and *pretty*, it was a very proper entertainment for the Town. But, it seems, now Plays must be *theatrical*; and natural sense and wit, that arise (not from odd gestures in the Actor, or strain'd expressions in the Poet, but) from the situation in which the persons of the Drama find themselves, and the circumstances that occasion their shewing themselves, as they naturally would be off the stage, are no longer necessary in a Play, nor capable of pleasing the Town. 'Tis a melancholy reflection this, Mr. BAVIUS; but when things are at the worst, they must mend.

I shall beg leave now to lay before you, my conjectures about the meaning of the word *Theatrical*; and examine, if the Plays we have had this winter (which I presume were so) were one whit the better in themselves, or thought so by the Town, for wanting wit and sense, and being *theatrical*. ——— A Play may be call'd *theatrical*, that is, written by any person belonging to the Theatre, or that is given to the Theatre: in which case it becomes its property: such Plays are, strictly speaking, *theatrical*. Of this sort was *Athelwold*; which, as I am inform'd, was given to the House; but I don't find that its being *theatrical* could prevent it's dying a natural death soon after its birth. ——— A Play may likewise be call'd *theatrical*, that is revised and corrected by any person belonging to the Theatre. Of this kind was *The Modish Couple*, which, I am told, was lick'd into the form it now bears, and had the last touches given it by a person in the management of the House: famous lately for several Odes, in which he has shewn as much poetry, as judgment. The violent death this Play died of, after having been kept alive by as violent remedies, does not speak much in favour of this new quality so essential in dramatick performances. - - A Play that is forced upon the House by superior authority, may, I think, likewise be call'd *theatrical*, as the Actors are obliged to adopt it, and receive it as their own. *The Modish Couple* had this additional degree of *theatricality*. But alas! all this would not do, neither double Grenadiers, double Constables, nor double *theatricality* could save its tender life. It fell, hard fate! because the Town would not be imposed upon; nor could see with patience the stage reduced to a lower ebb, than at Bartholomew or Southwark Fair. ——— As to the last new piece, call'd *Injur'd Innocence*, it run indeed six nights; but, as I have been informed, the Author was obliged to make up the deficiency of some of them, the company that was there not paying the expence of the house: so that, however *theatrical* this Play may have been, in any other sense of the word, which I may be ignorant of, I don't find that the Town was over much edify'd by it. ——— All this, then, Mr. BAVIUS, seems to conclude, that wit and sense (I mean unforc'd wit and sense) are no legal cause to reject a Play, altho' it should want *theatricality*; and that the Town would receive much better a Play, that had wit and sense, even tho' it were destitute of the other, than they have done Plays, that have wanted both these, and yet been very *theatrical*.

I now, Mr. BAVIUS, am drawing to a conclusion; and shall only beg you would lay this before the Society at your first meeting. The request that I have to make of them is only, that they would favour me with their sentiment upon *theatricality*; how far they think it essential to a good Play, and whether it be a plausible reason for rejecting one that is allowed to be both a *sensible* and *pretty performance*. My reason for asking this favour of you, Mr. BAVIUS, is this; I have some thoughts of getting it in next winter at the New House. It is possible they may think *wit* and *sense* more essential than *theatricality*, and consequently will not reject it for that reason. But I should be sorry, Mr. BAVIUS, to undertake any thing of this kind, without the privity and approbation of your Body, for which reason I recommend myself to you, hoping, by your favour, to merit their consideration and regard. I am, Mr. BAVIUS, your unknown friend and admirer,

Feb. 14, 173$\frac{1}{2}$. DRAMATICUS.

Reverend SIR,

UPON reading the last *Grub-street Journal*, in which several paragraphs of the Bishop of Chichester's *Sermon* and your's are set opposite to each other, I observed, that tho' Both of you are for still observing the 30th of January, yet you differ very much in your sentiments, both as to the reasons why, and the manner in which it is to be observed. He tells us, that *the judgments of God for great sins may hang over a nation for many generations*; and that, by *approving a crime when done, men may make themselves as guilty in the sight of God, as if they had had a hand in it.* P. 16. - - You assure us, that *it cannot be expected, that the weight of the guilt of those times, on* either *hand* (which seems to intimate, that either hand was equally guilty) *should be laid upon any of the present generation of men*, who were no *more particularly concerned in the confusions of the late civil wars, than in the other general calamities so frequently felt in the ages that went before: but however, so long as the wisdom of our Governors shall think it proper to continue such a Memorial of the past times, it becomes us to submit to their direction.* P. 10.

In consequence of his doctrine, he teaches us, that *it is highly reasonable, that we should in the most solemn manner express our detestation and abhorrence of so execrable an action; and deprecate the divine vengeance, that God would not visit upon us this great iniquity of our Forefathers, &c.* P. 16. ——— You, in consequence of your doctrine, assure us, that *a national humiliation* for sins *which were committed in an age that is past and gone, cannot be a duty of like obligation* [as a commemoration of public blessings] *to any people, and much less to a people in actual possession of all those blessings of heaven, which are the ordinary marks of the Divine favour and reconciliation.* P. 10. ——— And declare, *that the* Whole *of our duty on this occasion, is to beg of God to keep far away from us the evil of those days that are past; to pray for the continuance and improvement of the good ones we enjoy; and to arm ourselves with a resolute endeavour, at all wordly hazards, to continue down our civil and religious Rights, at least as pure as we received 'em.* P. 20.

Now, Sir, tho' I like your doctrine, and your manner of keeping the day, much the best: yet I must own, I think his most agreeable to the public Office injoined to be used; which is intitled, *A Form of Prayer with Fasting . . . . . to implore the mercy of God, that neither the guilt of that sacred and innocent blood, nor those other sins . . . . may any time hereafter be visited upon us, or our posterity.* And accordingly, we are injoined to declare in the words of one of the Collects, that *we cannot reflect on so foul an act, but with horror and astonishment:* and in three others to use the following expressions, *Grant, that this our land may be freed from the vengeance of his righteous blood; Deliver this Nation from blood-guiltiness, that of this day especially; Lay not the guilt of this innocent blood (the shedding whereof nothing but the blood of thy son can expiate) lay it not to the charge of the people of this land, nor let it ever be required of us, or our posterity.*

This is to act exactly according to that which the Bishop declares to be our duty on this occasion, *In the most solemn manner to express our detestation and abhorrence of so execrable an action; and to deprecate the Divine vengeance:* and whoever is persuaded of the heinousness of the guilt, and of the likelihood of the Divine visitation even at this time, acts a very consistent and religious part in joining in a national humiliation. But for me, who entertain no such Tory notions, nor can ever think there is *any such obligation on a people in actual possession of all those blessings, which are the ordinary marks of the Divine favour*, I never go to Church on that day, till after the Prayers are over. And am glad to find my practice seemingly justified by your opinion; according to which, tho' I appear at Church only just as the Preacher mounts the pulpit, I have time sufficient to perform *the Whole of my duty on this occasion, in begging God to keep far away the evil of past days, in praying for the continuance and improvement of the present good ones, and in arming myself with a resolute endeavour, &c.*

But the satisfaction I received from this comfortable doctrine was a little interrupted by the sole reason you assign for the observation of this day, in the following words, *So long as the wisdom of our Governors shall think it proper to continue* SUCH *a Memorial of the past times, it becomes us to submit to their Direction*, p. 10. Where to *submit to their direction*, seems plainly to mean, to go fasting to the place of public worship, on that day, and to join in the Service appointed to be used for a *memorial of the past times.* Now if I do not *submit* in this manner, I refuse to obey my Governors, and to do that which it *becomes* me to do. And if I do thus *submit*, I fear I am guilty of hypocrisy, being fully persuaded, that, whatever crime there might be in shedding the King's blood, the *present generation* was not *concerned in* it; and that we are *in actual* possession of *all the blessings of heaven, which are the ordinary marks of the Divine favour, and reconciliation.* —I therefore beg your clear opinion in this complicated Case of Conscience, Whether I can [illegible]

in declining the public Office for the day: and if not, How I can ſafely join in it, and declare that I *turn to God in weeping, faſting, and praying*; when I neither *pray* from, nor are *grieved* at the heart, and have probably eaten a good Breakfaſt, and intend to eat a good dinner.

I am, Reverend Sir,
Your moſt humble ſervant,
Feb. 21. 1731. CONSCIENCIOUS DOUBTFUL.

Epitaph for the Tomb of a Gentleman, who, from a ſmall beginning, improv'd his fortune very conſiderably, and was very charitable to people in diſtreſs.

Ye ſons of Induſtry! learn, hence, to know,
How far in fortune patient hope will go.
By ſafe degrees, on honour's firm aſcent,
Slow-climbing care, at laſt, will reach Content.
Yet, ah! when up, forget not Want below,
But ſtretch your helping hand to diſtant Woe.
So roſe the man, whoſe duſt inſhrines this place;
So, gain'd with honour; and ſo gave, with Grace.
Alive, unenvied; dead, unloſt, he lies:
For, know, a good man's influence never dies.

DOMESTIC NEWS.

C. *Courant.*	E P. *Evening Poſt.*
P. *Poſt-Boy.*	S J. *S. James's Evening Poſt.*
D P. *Daily Poſt.*	WE. *Whitehall Evening P.*
D J. *Daily Journal.*	LE. *London Evening Poſt.*

THURSDAY, *Feb.* 17.

On monday the Rev. Dr. Hen. Stebbing was ſworn in Chaplain in ordinary to his Majeſty, in the room of the Rev. Dr. Herring, lately promoted to the Deanery of Rocheſter. —— Mr. Simonety Vincent was ſworn in Sewer of the Great Chamber in ordinary to his Majeſty. *P.*

Yeſterday came on a Cauſe in the Court of King's Bench, wherein Hugh Gatterell, one of the Collectors of the Toll of the Turnpikes by Hide-Park, was Plaintiff, and ſeveral Juſtices of the peace, Defendants, on an action brought for committing him to priſon for defrauding the Commiſſioners of the Toll; and after a Trial that laſted 6 hours, a verdict was given for the Defendants. *P. SJ. WE. LE.* For the Plaintiff, and 120 l. damages. *P. Feb.* 18.

Some of the Agents and Clerks of the Charitable Corporation are already order'd into cuſtody; and it is hoped in a few days ſome more of *thoſe charitable Gentlemen* will have the ſame fate, unleſs by an ample diſcovery they merit favour from the Honourable Committee. *D P.* —— *This is a very* charitable *wiſh, ſuch a* fate *being not very dreadful.*

About a week ſince was given to the Treaſurer of Bethlehem Hoſpital, by a perſon unknown, 100 l. for the uſe of incurables therein. *D P.*

Yeſterday the Coroner's Inqueſt ſat on the body of Mrs. Atkinſon, the Mother of Mr. Atkinſon, a Sadler at Charing Croſs, and brought in their verdict *Wilful Murder. C.* It was not brought in at 12 o' clock laſt night. *P. DJ.*

At the Lodge near Tower Hill, a muſical Inſtrument-maker was lately made a Free Maſon in the following manner; firſt, the Door-keeper pull'd off his wig, and held a drawn ſword over his head, while the 2 Wardens led him from one end of the Lodge-room to the other; then they put him on *Hiram's Mask*, which is painted half black and half white, with 3 noſes, the inſide was very *redolent*, with an ointment of *fæcal matter* of a *citron hue*; and at the ſame time the Maſter pinn'd a Fox's tail to his coat; when the maſk was taken off, the poor man began to complain of his *filthy uſage*; but to quiet him, they tied him in his chair, and the Maſter held a pair of red hot tongs ſo near his cheek, as to be ready to burn him, which put him into a terrible fright: the Wardens immediately roar'd in his ears *Swanko* 3 times; then they aſperſed his face with a *ſaline* liquor of a *diaphanous nature*, ſaying, *Now, Brother, you are in urine.* The wife hearing of this diſaſter, was afraid they had made him only fit for the Opera, but all was reconciled by uſing ſome means not proper to mention here. *D P.* —— *Theſe Ceremonies are, I believe, as ſignificant as thoſe of the* Original Free Maſons, *and much more diverting.*

Glouceſter, Feb. 12. They write from Tewkſbury, that a Collection of 55 l. 5 s. 6 d. was made there for the poor ſufferers at Blandford and Tiverton; 40 l. to be ſent to Blandford, and 15 l. 5 s. 6 d. to Tiverton: with this reſtriction, that no part is to be diſtributed to any perſon left worth above 500 l. *SJ.* —— On tueſday was interred an old maiden Gentlewoman, the pall being ſupported by 6 others, whoſe ages, with that the deceaſed, amount to 500 years. *WE.*

FRIDAY, *Feb.* 18.

Yeſterday was held the annual Feaſt of the Sons of the Clergy, when Mr. Handell's *Te Deum* and *Jubilate*, &c. were performed before a numerous and ſplendid audience at S. Paul's Cathedral; and the Rev. Dr. Warren preach'd an excellent Sermon, &c. *C.* The feaſt was held at Merchant-Taylors Hall, where was a great appearance, and a very handſome collection, which, with thoſe made at the rehearſal, and at the Church doors yeſterday, amounted to the ſum of 830 l. *P.*

We hear that Miſs Paget, daughter of Col. Paget, is appointed one of the Maids of Honour to the Queen. *D J.* —— Mr. Vane, one of the L. Barnard's ſons, and Page of Honour to his Majeſty, is made an Enſign in the firſt regiment of Foot-guards. *D P.* —— His Majeſty has been pleaſed to appoint the Hon. John Fane, Eſq; Col. of the firſt troop of Horſe-Grenadier Guards, to be Colonel of the regiment of Dragoons commanded by the late L. Carpenter. *D J. Feb.* 21.

Early yeſterday morning the Coroner's Jury broke up, without giving their verdict in relation to the death of Mrs. Atkinſon, who was murdered at Charing-Croſs; and yeſterday they met again, when 16 agreed for Wilful Murder, and 8 for Manſlaughter; but at laſt agreed to a verdict of Wilful Murder. —— The Surgeons, upon opening her head, found her ſcull broke in ſeveral places. *DJ.*

On tueſday night Rich. Chandler, Eſq; Sollicitor to the Exciſe, Son of the R. Rev. Biſhop of Durham, was marry'd to Mrs. Cavendiſh, daughter of the L. James Cavendiſh, at his Lordſhip's houſe in York Buildings. *D P.*

Yeſterday a Cauſe came on in the Court of King's Bench, on an Information againſt a perſon for dubliſhing a Libel againſt ſeveral eminent Cabinet-makers. The Libel certified, that any perſon might have ſuch work done better than ſuch matters, for that their beſt workmen had left them. They brought the perſon in guilty of publiſhing the Libel. *P.*

SATURDAY, *Feb.* 19.

On wedneſday a Tryal came on before the L. C. Juſtice Raymond, at Weſtminſter, upon an action brought by one Catheral, late a Collector of the Kenſington Turnpike, againſt Will. Cowper, Eſq; Sir Tho. Croſs, John Croſs, Chriſtian Cole, and Rich. Farwell, Eſqrs; 5 of his Majeſty's Juſtices of the peace, for committing him to Newgate for defrauding the Truſtees of very conſiderable ſums of money: and it being inſiſted upon by the Counſel for the Juſtices, that they had a juriſdiction given them by the Act of Parliament, and that therefore an action would not lie againſt them, his Lordſhip directed a caſe to be ſtated thereupon, for the opinion of the Court of King's Bench next term; and if the Court ſhall be of opinion, that the Juſtices had no authority for the Commitment, in that caſe the Plaintiff is to have 120 l. damages; but if the Court ſhall be of the contrary opinion, the verdict is to be for the Defendants, and the Plaintiff is to pay treble coſts. *C. WE.* —— *Notwithſtanding this particular account, the* SJ. *and* LE. *repeat the paragraph in the* P. *of Feb.* 18.

We hear that a Gent. has left by his will 200 l. towards erecting a ſtatue to the memory of our great and glorious Deliverer King William the 3d, in the middle of the Baſon of S. James's Square, which will be forwarded with expedition; and the reſt of the expence will be defray'd by the Veſtry of S. James's pariſh. *C.* —— *This is a proper way of* erecting a ſtatue to *his own* memory *at the ſame time.*

Mr. Venables, Accomptant to the Charitable Corporation, who was one of thoſe ordered into cuſtody, is diſcharged with honour from the cuſtody of the Serjeant at Arms, having made a fair and candid diſcovery of the proceedings of thoſe charitable Gentlemen; and 'tis hop'd the reſt, for their own ſakes, will do the like. *D P.*

The Town of Mancheſter has collected 500 l. to be divided, 300 l. to the poor ſufferers at Blandford, 150 l. for Tiverton, and 50 l. for Ramſay. —— And the pariſh of Biſhop's Waltham in Hants has collected 35 l. for Blandford. *D J.*

Fran. Hucheſon, Eſq; Nephew to the R. Hon. the E. of Effingham, is appointed Secretary to his Lordſhip, as Dep. Earl Marſhal of England. *P.*

A few days ſince Geo. Spike, Eſq; Repreſentative in Parliament for Taunton Dean, in the County of Somerſet, was married to Mrs. Pitt, a Gentlewoman of that County of a great eſtate. *D P.*

On thurſday laſt a Court of Common Council was held at Guildhall, at which the ſeveral Committees for managing the revenues of this City for the year enſuing were elected; when it was obſerved, that the oppoſition which had been given to ſome *preſuming Patriots* (who for many years paſt have, in a private cabal at the Half-moon in Cheapſide, ſettled liſts of Committees, conſiſting always of one Set of perſons of *their own Club*) had this good effect; that thoſe perſons this year thought proper to drop that *inſolent method* of impoſing liſts upon their Brethren of the Common Council; and therefore they ſummoned a general meeting of the Common Council at the Half-moon, to ſettle proper liſts of the ſeveral Committees, when their *uſual aſſurance* failed them to that degree that they durſt not inſiſt on their old Committee-men, but agreed to a liſt of worthy Gentlemen, moſt of whom were had, and probably, without this oppoſition, had not been choſen on any Committee: as to the diviſion ſo much boaſted of by the *Juncto*, it was not for the whole liſt, but only, whether Mr. Maſters, or Mr. Hamers ſhould be of the Iriſh Society; when the former divided againſt himſelf. —— Note, Thoſe with * are new Members.

For the IRISH SOCIETY.

Mr. Ald. Alſop, Haberdaſher, Governor	Mr. Tho. Sandford } Haberdaſhers
Mr. Edward Chowne, Goldſmith, Deputy-Governor	Mr. Thompſon Heyne } Haberdaſhers
Sir Will. Humphreys, Bar. and Ald. Ironmonger	Mr. Giles Vincent, Clothworker
Sir Charles Peers, Knt. and Ald. Salter	* Mr. Rich. Chauncey, ſen. } Mercers
Sir Richard Brocas, Knt. and Ald. Grocer	* Mr. John Spillet } Mercers
Sir John Taſh, Knt. and Ald. Vintner	* Mr. Sam. Smith, Grocer
Mr. Ald. Salter, Merchant-Taylor	* Mr John Hamers, Draper
Mr. Ja. Heywood, Draper	* Mr. John Cooper, Fiſhmon.
Mr. Hugh Bonfoy, Fiſhmonger	* Mr. Ric. Baily, Goldſmith
Mr. Henry King, Skinner	* Mr. Nat. Arnold, Skinner
	* Mr. R. Long, Merchant-T.
	* Mr. Robert Cary, Salter
	* Mr. Dep. Child, Ironmon.
	* Mr. Ja. Bedingfield, Vintn.
	* Mr. Ro. Burchal Cloth-w.

CITY LANDS.

The Right Hon. the Lord Mayor	Mr. Deputy J. Snart
Sir Richard Brocas, Knt. and Ald.	* Mr. Deputy Bateman
Humphrey Parſons, Eſq; Ald.	* Mr. John Wheeler
* Sir John Williams, Knt. and Ald.	* Joſeph Taylor, Eſq;
Robert Alſop, Eſq; Ald.	* Mr. James Danſie
John Salter, Eſq; Ald.	* Mr. Thomas Ridge
Mr. Henry Siſſon	* Mr. William Byrch
	* Mr. Thomas Naſh
	* Mr. Deputy Davis
	* Mr. Peter Roberts
	* Mr. William Lord

GRESHAM COMMITTEE.

The Right Hon. the Lord Mayor	Mr. Deputy Davis
Mr. Ald. Parſons	* Mr. Deputy Ayliffe
Mr. Ald. Barber	* Mr. Samuel Naſh
* Mr. Ald. Barnard	* Mr. William Poole
Mr. Deputy Child	* Mr. John Maſon
Mr. James Danſie	* Mr. Robert Mael

N. B. The Aldermen of each Ward are in courſe of the Committee of Sewers. *LE.*

MONDAY, *Feb.* 21.

Yeſterday the Rev. Dr. Jones preached before their Majeſties, his Royal Highneſs the Prince, &c. *C.* —— We are informed that his Majeſty will viſit his German dominions ſoon after the riſing of the Parliament. *D P.* —— His Royal Highneſs the Duke has raiſed a Company of young perſons of quality of the firſt rank; the Hon. Col. Catkart's ſon having the honour to command the ſame; his Royal Highneſs chooſing to act as Corporal: and yeſterday they were preſented to their Majeſties, being all clothed in the ſame manner as his Majeſty's Coldſtream Regiment of Foot-guards. *C* A new Company of Grenadiers, clothed as the ſecond Regiment, and conſiſts of a Captain, a Serjeant, a Corporal, and 12 private men; but it is to be augmented to a greater number. *P.*

On ſaturday the R. Hon. Sir Rob. Walpole gave an elegant entertainment to ſeveral Gentlemen of the Hon. Houſe of Commons, &c. at his houſe in Arlington-ſtreet. *C.*

Laſt thurſday Sir James Edwards, Bar. of Surrey, and the Rev. Mr. Jacob Serenius were elected Members of the Royal Society. *P.*

TUESDAY, *Feb.* 22.

On ſunday the R. Hon. the Earl of Cheſterfield, his Majeſty's Ambaſſador Extraordinary to the States General, landed from Holland. *C.*

Gilbert Vane, Eſq; is ſucceeded as Page of Honour to her Majeſty, by Mr. Killigrew, Page to the Princeſs Royal. *DP.*

On ſunday laſt Mr. Joſhua Vanneck, an eminent Dutch Merchant, Brother to Mr. Gerard Vanneck, one of the Directors of the Eaſt India Company, was married to Miſs Mary Anne Daubuz, youngeſt Daughter of Mr. Stephen Daubuz, an agreeable young Lady, of great merit, and 10,000 l. fortune. *D J.* —— *The* C. *of Feb.* 21. *married him on* ſaturday, *and made him* one of the Directors of the Eaſt India Company.

Briſtol, Feb. 19. Our Merchants have received advice, that the Alice and Elizabeth, Payne, was arrived at Jamaica; but that in her paſſage ſhe was taken by a pretended Spaniſh Privateer, who robbed her of the value of 3 or 400 l. *D J.*

The Rev. Dr. Henry Briggs, Rector of Holt in Norfolk, is made Chaplain in ordinary to his Majeſty. *SJ.*

We hear, that when the ſalt duty is reviv'd, it will be

put under the management of the Commissioners of the Excise. *S J. WE. LE.*

The Earl of Portmore has made a present of one of his fine running horses, valued at 400 l. to Count Kinski, the Imperial Envoy at this Court. *S J. LE.*

WEDNESDAY, *Feb.* 23.

His Majesty has been pleased to issue his Letters under his Royal Sign Manual, to his Grace the Lord Lieutenant of Ireland, to cause Letters patent to be passed under the great Seal of that Kingdom, for translating the Right Rev. Father in God Welbore, Lord Bishop of Kildare, to the Bishoprick of Meath, void by the death of Ralph, late Lord Bishop thereof; for translating the Right Rev. Father in God, Dr. Charles Cobb, Lord Bishop of Dromore, to the Bishoprick of Kildare; for translating the Right Rev. Father in God. Dr. Henry Maule, Lord Bishop of Cloyne, to the Bishoprick of Dromore; for translating the Right Rev. Father in God, Dr. Edward Synge Lord Bishop of Clonfert and Kilmacduagh, to the Bishoprick of Cloyne; and for promoting Dr. Mordecai Cary to the united Bishopricks of Clonfert and Kilmacdagh. —— His Majesty has been likewise pleased to issue his Letters under his Royal Sign Manual, to his Grace the Lord Lieutenant of Ireland, to cause Letters patent to be passed under the Great Seal of the said Kingdom, for granting to Richard Daniel the Deanry of Down, void by the death of William Gore, late Dean thereof; and for granting unto John Brandreth the Deanry of the Metropolitan Church of Ardmagh, void by the resignation of Richard Daniel, late Dean thereof. —— His Majesty has been pleased to appoint George Woodward, Esq; to be his Envoy extraordinary to the King of Poland. *C. P. D P.* —— Yesterday being the birth-day of her Royal Highness the Princess Mary, their Majesties received the Compliments from the several Nobility and Quality on that occasion, her Royal Highness being entered into the tenth Year of her Age. —— The same day came on a Tryal at Guild-hall, before the Lord Chief Justice Raymond, between a young Gentlewoman and Mr. Wilkinson, a Clergyman, on a Promise of Marriage: Several Evidences were examined, and many Letters produced, to prove the engagements he had been under to the Plaintiff, the jury found for the Plaintiff, and gave her 300 l. damage. *C. D P.*

They write from Lansworney in Glamorganshire, that a poor fellow of that place hang'd himself there a few days ago, the cause of which was very whimsical; it seems he had for some years past set up for a Fortune-teller among the vulgar, and to gain himself the greater repute in the knowledge of Astrology, pretended to foretell the year, month, day, and hour of his death, but happening to continue in perfect health to the time, and fearing he should be banter'd if he outliv'd it, he chose to dispatch himself as aforementioned, in order to verify the prediction. *D P.* —— *This* Welch Fortune-teller *might be a* Gentleman, *but he was certainly no* Conjurer.

From the PEGASUS *in Grub-street.*

Dear BAVY,

SOME few days ago, in the afternoon, as I was talking with my Sword Cutler at his shop door, near the end of Chancery-lane, I was surprised at an extraordinary and uncommon sight; which was a girl with an orange barrow, and a very little Gentleman about 4 foot ½ high, a fair man with large features, in a light tie wig, a band and bar gown on, throwing with dice in her barrow for oranges. He was pretty successful, and carried off his gains in triumph up Chancery-lane, in his way (as I suppose) to the Rolls; seeming highly pleased with carrying his Cause at the orange Bar, and looking on it, perhaps, as a good omen of success at the Chancery Bar before his Honour. Seeing this fortunate Counsellor t'other day in Westminster-Hall, I related the story to one of the Robe, who told me the Gentleman's name, and where he lives; and said he had been a considerable time at the Bar, and acquir'd great knowledge and skill, but takes a great deal of pleasure in such recreations and amusements.

I am yours,

Feb. 19, 1731. R. D.

SIR,

HAving read the following advertisement in several News Papers, [*This day is published, price* 1 *s.* A LECTURE ON HIGH FITS OF ZEAL, *or Miss* CADIERE'S RAPTURES. *In which, &c.* II. *The Third Edition of Miscellaneous Tracts. on various subjects of History, Polemical Divinity, Education, and Rhetorick. By J. Henley, M. A. Institutor of the Oratory.*] I bought the Pamphlet; the Title Page of which, as to the first part, runs as above; but the second part was altered thus, II. *Tracts on other subjects, in Humane and Divine Learning.* Then followed THE THIRD EDITION placed between two Rules, or Black lines; which in the plainest and most obvious construction, seemed to relate to the whole Pamphlet: but according to the Advertisement above, relates only to the *Miscellaneous Tracts.*

When I came to examine my purchase, I found I had been bit: for this THIRD EDITION is not more applicable to any part, than to the whole. For after the *Lecture on high fits,* &c. containing only 11 pages, follows on a spuare leaf, *Miscellaneous Tracts on several subjects: the third Edition.* Which *Miscellaneous Tracts* were printed in 1728, under the Title of *Oratory Transactions,* No. I. with which edition, this pretended *Third Edition* appears evidently to be the same, retaining the same typographical errors, the very same distances between the words, &c. so that unless there has been so great a demand for these *Miscellaneous Tracts,* as to keep the Letter standing above these 4 years, this *edition* is neither a *third,* nor even a *second.*

I shall now shew how these old Pieces answer the new Title, given then in the Advertisements, *Miscellaneous Tracts on various subjects of History, Polemical Divinity, Education,* and *Rhetorick.* The first *Tract* contains a very considerable piece of *History,* being *a Narrative of the Life of the* Reverend Mr. John Henley, *by* Mr. Welstede; and is followed by a *Defence, Idea, Plan,* and *Explanation of the Design of the Oratory;* which are all as *Polemico-theological,* as *Rhetorical,* and tend much to the improvement of the *Education* of young Butchers. —— Having bought these Pieces before under a different Title, I hope *The Institutor of the Oratory* will make me some amends, by presenting me with *The Sermon which it was expected Dr. Herring should have preached.* And since he has frequently inveigh'd against the impositions of Booksellers, it is expected, that he will not suffer this to pass without a severe animadversion; and that he will effectually prevent one *Roberts* in particular, with whom he is well acquainted, who keeps a shop *near Lincolns-Inn-Fields, between dust and ashes,* from imposing upon the Publick in the like manner.

I hope, Mr. BAVIUS, to see this published in your next, it being a matter of consequence, which concerns many other persons, as well as

Your most humble servant,

Feb. 21, 1731. T. D.

An EPIGRAM.

When you preach on the thirtieth day of January,
With your station and audience let your doctrine still vary:
If with Mitre you're grac'd, before the noble Peers,
You may Parliament blame, praise King and Cavaliers:
But if not — mind your hits — take a different tone;
Lay the blame on both sides alike, or on none:
Would you shine as a Dean, above Clerical Proctor,
Tho' you think like a BISHOP, still preach like a DOCTOR.

Dublin, Feb. 12. On wednesday morning died the Hon. Rob. Dixon, Esq; one of the Judges of his Majesty's Court of Common Pleas. *C.*

FOREIGN NEWS.

THURSDAY, *Feb.* 17.

Seville, Jan. 28. They write from Cadiz, that they had received advice, that the Capitana, and the other Galleons which were dispersed in a storm, were arrived in the Port of Guarico in the island of S. Domingo. *C.*

Extract of a letter from Cadiz, Feb. 5. —— We are assured, that there has been a proposal made to the Minister here, in relation to the privilege the South-Sea Company have of sending annual ships to America, which is, (as the said trade has been found destructive to the Merchants, and as the Court is willing to favour the English nation preferable to any other) that if the Company resign their right of sending a ship with the Flota and Galleons, the Court agrees to diminish the duty on the importation of English manufactures 2 or 3 per cent. less than usually paid: therefore 'tis be hoped, for the general good of us all, that this proposal may take, as it will be an infinite benefit to the nation, and revive our languishing trade in this country. *D J.*

Petersburg, Jan. 28. Although the Czarina has already named her successor, orders are issued for none to mention it in publick, under pain of death. *D P.*

FRIDAY, *Feb.* 18.

Paris, Feb. 20. The 15th being the anniversary of the King's birth-day, when he enter'd into the 23d year of his age, his Majesty received the compliments of the Princes and Princesses of the blood, &c. *C. P.*

Milan, Feb. 2. To reconcile different pretensions to the Farnese States, the following distinction is here made, into the Domain, the Possession and Jurisdiction; whereby the first as a Fief of the Empire rests in his Imperial Majesty; the second in the Holy See, to which will be continued the usual tribute of 12,000 ducatoons per ann. the third is vested in the Serene Infante Duke of Parma, together with the revenues thereto belonging, who goes first to Florence, and from thence to Parma. *D P.*

SATURDAY, *Feb.* 19.

Paris, Feb. 15. The Chevalier Folard, famous for his accurate Commentary on Polybius, persists in his sentiments of devotion, and has received orders to retire to Avignon, but reserves his Pension from the Crown of 6000 livres per ann. *D P.*

MONDAY, *Feb.* 21.

On saturday arrived the Mail from Holland, *and yesterday one from* France.

Paris, Feb. 27. Letters from Madrid of the 12th assure us, that they work incessantly in all the Spanish Ports of the Mediterranean, in order to equip a considerable armament; that 24,000 men are design'd for the expedition, which are actually on their march for Catalonia, where the embarkation is to be made; but to what intent is unknown, tho' some affirm 'tis to recover the City of Oran on the coast of Barbary. *D P. C. D J.*

TUESDAY, *Feb.* 22.

Yesterday arrived the Mail from Holland.

Brussels, Feb. 25. Some days ago the Directors of the Ostend Company received a Decree from the Emperor, whereby all his subjects in the Countries formerly possessed by Charles II. King of Spain, are forbid all commerce to the East Indies. The Actions are since fallen 4 per cent. *P. D J.*

WEDNESDAY, *Feb.* 23.

Hague, Feb. 15. *Extract of a private Letter from* Paris.—The general Farmers have made an advance of four millions to the King, and the general Receivers one of six millions; which looks as if this Court had some secret design, and that all our Speculations and Negotiations would end in a war. But upon the whole, unless the Cardinal de Fleury should happen to die, he is too old and too pacifick to advance the shield. *P.* — If he happens to die, *he will be somewhat* older, *and more* pacifick.

Extract of a private Letter from Vienna. —— Notwithstanding all that has been said in relation to the pacifick designs of the Ottoman Porte, it is plain that the Emperor does not lay any great stress upon it: the rather, because the present Grand Vizir is known to be a bold, enterprizing man, of affected subtlety and reserve, and withall, a friend to France; a Merchant of that nation having redeemed him from slavery among the Malteze when young, and after a series of kind usage, sent him home without a ransom: which is the reason that Minister has been so kind to the Count de Bonneval, with whom he keeps a strict correspondence, and gets as many of his projects approved as he can. *P.*

Milan, Feb. 9. Fresh advices from Corsica speak of a new action between the Genoese Troops and the malecontents, wherein the former lost four officers of distinction, with a great number of soldiers. Orders are come from Vienna for eight battalions to march thither, in case the Colonel Colmonero fails of success in his negotiations at Genoa, who waits there the last resolution of the Republick, touching an accommodation with the said Rebels. *D P.*

Books and Pamphlets published since Feb. 14.

15. The Theory and practice of Gardening, &c. by John James.

The History of the Puritans, &c. by Dan. Neal, M. A.

19. A serious Proposal for the entire destruction of Popery in Ireland. Pr. 6 d.

Miscellaneous Observations on Authors ancient and modern, No. 14. Vol. II. P. 2.

17. A Sermon occasion'd by the death of Mr. Mat. Madden: preached Jan. 16. By Sayer Rudd. Pr. 6 d.

Tournefort's History of Plants growing about Paris, &c. Translated into English by John Martyn, F. R. S. in 2 Vol. Pr. 10 s.

18. Britannia Major: the new scheme for discharging the debts, &c. Pr. 1 s.

21. The Modern Husband, a Comedy: by Hen. Fielding, Esq;

22. The present state of the Republick of Letters: for January.

The B——p and the D——r reconcil'd, &c. Pr. 6 d.

A T—d is as good for a sow as a Par[illegible], &c. Pr. 6 d.

Injur'd Innocence: a Tragedy.

A Sermon preached in the Chapel of Newgate, Feb. 6. at the desire of Rob. Hallam, &c. by James Guthrie, M. A. Pr. 4 d.

A Poem in praise of the Horn-Book. Pr. 6d.

23. The Gentleman's Pocket Companion; or Horseman's Tutor, &c. Pr. 6 d.

On Tueſday Stocks were

South Sea Stock 100 1 8th, 100 1 qr. 100. South Sea Annuity 110 3 8ths. Bank 149 7 8ths. New Bank Circulation 6 l. 15 s. Premium. India 178 1 8th. Three per Cent. Annuity 97 3 qrs. New 3 per Cent. Annuity 97 1 8th, to 1 qr. Royal Exchange Aſſurance 99. London Aſſurance 13 1 qr. to 3 8ths. York Buildings 10. African 46. Engliſh Copper 2 l. 10 s. Welch ditto 1 l. 15 s. South Sea Bonds 2 l. 12 s. Premium. India ditto 5 l. 13 s. ditto. Blanks 7 l. 7 s. 6 d. 20 l. Prizes 19 l. 13 s. 6 d.

ADVERTISEMENTS.

For the BENEFIT of
Mr. *JOHN HEBDEN*,
At Stationers Hall on Friday the 3d Day of March, 1732.

WILL be a Grand CONCERT of Vocal and Inſtrumental MUSICK by the beſt Maſters. To begin exactly at Seven o' Clock.

N. B. TICKETS to be had at Will's Coffee-Houſe, near the Royal Exchange; the George and Vulture Tavern in Cornhill; the Rummer Tavern in S. Mary's Church-yard, Southwark; the Caſtle Tavern and Gregg's Coffee-Houſe, both in Pater-Noſter-Row, at Five Shillings each.

Publick Notice is hereby given,

[*For the Information of all* GENTLEMEN *and* LADIES]

THAT *Charles Lyon, Grecian*, Maker of the JERUSALEM WASHBALLS, otherwiſe called GRECIAN WASHBALLS, ſo univerſally eſteem'd by all the Quality, who, for many Years, have made uſe of no other, being removed from Ironmonger-Lane, where he had carried on his Buſineſs about 40 years, to the Houſe of *Edward Hubbard*, over againſt Serjeant's-Inn, Chancery-Lane, where they may at any Time be furniſhed therewith, by ſending a Letter to the ſaid *Edward Hubbard*, who has, for ten Years paſt, aſſiſted Mr. *Lyon* in making them, being the only Perſon intruſted with the true Method of preparing them, and to whom alone the Receipt will be communicated upon the Deceaſe of the ſaid Mr. *Lyon*.

N. B. At the following Places is ſold an incomparable Tooth-Powder, which makes the Teeth as white as Ivory, and preſerves them from Rotting or Decaying. It effectually cures the Scurvy in the Gums Price one Shilling each Box.

Alſo a delicate Lip-Salve, that cures any rough and chopp'd Lips, and makes them of a fine lively red. Price one Shilling each Pot, viz. Cocoa-Tree Chocolate-Houſe, Pall-Mall; Will's Coffee-Houſe, Scotland-Yard, Charing-Croſs; Guildhall Coffee-Houſe, by Guildhall; Sword-Blade Coffee-Houſe, Birchin-Lane; and the East-India Coffee-Houſe, Leadenhall-Street.'

Feb. 4. **was publiſhed**, Price 6 d. ſmall Paper; the fine Royal Paper, Margin open'd, 1 s.

THE GENTLEMAN'S MAGAZINE: Or, *Monthly Intelligencer.*

No. XIII. for January 1731.

Containing more in Quantity, and greater Variety, than any Book of the Kind and Price.

I. A View of the Weekly Eſſays, viz. a Vindication of Mankind; the Religion of Philoſophers; Deiſt's Creed; Coffee-houſe Savages; Sir Wm. Paget's New-year's Gift; Conjugal Love; Mr. Pope's Epiſtle on Taſte cenſur'd and defended; Fooliſh Fondneſs; Love and Grandeur; the Laureat's pretenſions canvaſs'd; Female Heroiſm; Leſſons of Morality; of the Stage; Love of Fame; Remarks on Dr. Bentley's Edition of Milton; on Authors; Rules for Courtſhip; of Immortality.

II. Political Points, viz. On the Jury-Act; Severities in B——ke's Adminiſtration; the Craftſman's Hague Letter with Remarks; the King's Speech; of publick Credit, Monopolies, &c. Affidavits about S. Sea private Trade; Charitable Corporation Accounts; on the Pragmatick Sanction; Sheriff's Act eluded; a Scheme to pay the publick Debts; political Charity; K. Charles II. vindicated; the Form of an Oath propoſed to be taken by Popiſh Prieſts to his Majeſty.

III. Poetry, viz. Ode for New-year's Day burleſqued; tranſlated into Engliſh; the Laureat's Anſwer; Keyberian manner; C——r preferr'd to P——pe.

IV. Domeſtic Occurrences, &c.

V. Prices of Goods, Grain, Stocks.

VI. Foreign Affairs.

VII. Books and Pamphlets.

VIII. A Table of Contents

Printed and ſold at St. John's Gate; and by E. Jeffries in Ludgate-ſtreet. *Where may be had, the former Numbers.* Alſo

An exact LIST of the preſent Parliament, with the Places of their Abode in Town, &c.

This Day is publiſhed,

Beautifully Printed in Octavo.

PHILOSOPHICAL CONVERSATIONS: Or, a new Syſtem of Phyſics, by way of Dialogue, with 89 Copper Plates. Written in French by Father *Reginault*, of the Society of Jeſus. Tranſlated into Engliſh, and Illuſtrated with Notes by *Tho. Dale*, M. D. in 3 Vols. — N. B. The Deſign of this Author is like that of Monſ. *Fontenelle*, in his Plurality of Worlds, to render Natural Philoſophy no leſs plain to the meaneſt Readers, than entertaining to the brighteſt: At the ſame time his Reaſoning is founded upon ſuch Experiments as have imploy'd the Speculation of the greateſt Philoſophers in different Countries, that this laſt age has produced; particularly upon thoſe in the German Ephemerides, the French Journals, and the Royal Academy of Sciences. Printed for W. Innys, in St. Paul's Church-Yard; C. Davis, at the Corner of Pater-Noſter-Row; and N. Prevoſt, againſt Southampton-Street in the Strand.

To be Sold,

At Egham, near Stanes, in Surry (upon the Middle of the Hill leading to Inglesfield-Green, and thro' the Park to Windſor)

A Handſome Brick Houſe, moſt delightfully ſituated, and compleatly fitted up, conſiſting of four Rooms on a Floor, with large Cloſets, and Lodging Rooms for Servants, and other convenient Offices for a Family. The Houſe is all new ſaſh'd, floor'd, and leaded on the Roof; Marble Chimney-pieces and Slabs; a large Brew-houſe, with all Conveniencies for Brewing, and Vaults underneath it; a Coach-houſe, Barn, Dove-houſe, and Stables, wainſcotted, and paved with Dutch Clinkarts, and new built; a Kitchen-Garden paled in, and another Garden walled in, and well planted with the beſt ſort of Wall-fruit; together with a Fiſh-pond well ſtored.

N. B. There are very large Orchards, and ſeveral Parcels of Paſture Grounds adjoining to the Houſe, to be Let with it, if required.

Enquire of the Reverend M. Pagett in Egham, or of Mr. York, Goldſmith, in King-ſtreet, Weſtminſter.

This Day is publiſhed,

A Collection of PIECES in VERSE and PROSE, which have been publiſhed on occaſion of the Dunciad. Dedicated to the Right Honourable the Earl of Middleſex. By Mr. Savage.

Likewiſe,

ATHELWOLD: A Tragedy. By A. Hill, Eſq; as it is acted at the Theatre Royal in Drury-Lane.

2. Of FALSE TASTE: an Epiſtle to the Right Honourable Richard Earl of Burlington. By Mr. POPE. The 3d Edition, with an additional Letter.

Printed for Lawton Gilliver, at Homer's Head, againſt St. Dunſtan's Church, Fleet-ſtreet.

This Day is publiſhed,

AN Enquiry into the Origin of HONOUR, and the Uſefulneſs of Chriſtianity in WAR.

By the Author of the *Fable of the Bees.*

Price bound 3 s. 6 d.

Printed for J. Brotherton at the Bible, next the Fleece Tavern in Cornhill.

This Day is publiſhed,

Dedicated to the Gentlemen of the Navy of England.

THE MEMOIRS of Monſieur *du Gué Trouin*, Chief of a Squadron of the Royal Navy of France, and Great Croſs of the Military Order of S. Lewis; containing all his Sea-Actions with the Engliſh, Dutch, and Portugueſe, in the late *Wars* of *King William* and *Queen Anne.*

Tranſlated from the French by a *Sea-Officer.*

Printed for J. Batley, at the Dove, in Pater-noſter Row, Where may be had,

The TRADITIONS of the CLERGY no way Deſtructive of Religion: A Sermon preach'd at Bingley-Church, on Sunday September 12th, 1731.

By IS. SMITH,

Miniſter of Haworth, near Kighley, Yorkſhire.

ALSO,

I. The Religion of Nature conſidered. To which is added a Poſtſcript, containing Reflections on Mr. Chubb's Diſcourſe concerning Reaſon, &c. ſo far as it reſpects this Subject.

II. Some Thoughts concerning Virtue and Happineſs, in a Letter to a Clergyman.

This day is publiſhed,

With a curious Frontiſpiece by Mr. BICKHAM, *And at the End of the Book is prefixed, a fine ſatyrical Picture, which needs no Key to explain it.*

A SCHEME for a NEW LOTTERY: Or, A HUSBAND and COACH and SIX for Forty Shillings. Being very advantageous to both Sexes; where a Man may have a Coach and Six, and a Wife for nothing.

Here's a Whim-Wham newly come over,
And who will prick at my Lottery Book?

With a SCHEME to prevent the Downfal of the Charitable Corporation. By an old Sportſman.

In Female Service worn to Skin and Bone,
Fulfils the Proverb, to the World well known,
And yet to ſhew them I ne'er ſpare my Pains,
But freely do bequeath my future Gains,
Among the wanton Part o'th' Female Sex,
Take this laſt Legacy, and others vex.

To which is prefixed,

The Author's Picture, drawn to the Life; being fit to be hung in the Lodgings of all Ladies of Pleaſure, as a *Memento Mori*, with the following Lines under it:

Like an old Soldier, worn out in Campaigns,
Who's ſerv'd his Country many diff'rent Reigns,
When Wars are ended, homewards he returns,
And ſheaths his Sword, tho' with Ambition burns
For freſh Alarms; but when the Trumpet calls,
Finds his Decay, and on his Back he falls.

With a Recommendatory Poem, in Favour of the ſaid Lottery, to encourage Maids, Widows, ſingle Women, Batchelors and Widowers to put in. Alſo a Scheme where Ladies may divert themſelves before the Time of Drawing. And likewiſe a View of the Town, by the HIGHGATE SPY, taken thro' a Glaſs of the Projector's own making, and hopes it will be approv'd by the R---l S----, in which you may ſee thoſe who can't ſee themſelves: With an Account of what Perſons of both Sexes are excluded the Advantage of putting into the ſaid Lottery. And alſo the Author's Concluſion on Pawnbrokers, and the Difference between them and the Charitable Corporation.

Printed for T. DORMER at the Star and Garter, over againſt the Caſtle Tavern in Fleet-ſtreet, and ſold at the Pamphlet-ſhops; price 1 s. 6 d.

Where may be had, The Second Edition, of The UNHAPPY LOVERS: Or, The Tragical Hiſtory of *James Welſted*, Gent. price 1 s.

This Day is publiſhed,

In Four Volumes, Twelves,

And ſold by N. PREVOST, oppoſite to Southampton-Street in the Strand,

THE Life of Mr. CLEVELAND, natural Son of OLIVER CROMWELL. Written by himſelf. Giving a particular Account of his Unhappineſs in Love, Marriage, Friendſhip, &c. and his great Sufferings in *Europe* and *America*. Together with the ſecret AMOURS of the PROTECTOR, and his unnatural Uſage to his illegitimate Children. The whole intermix'd with Reflexions, deſcribing the Heart of Man, in all its Variety of Paſſions and Diſguiſes.

N.B. The 3d and 4th Vol. may be had ſeparate.

This day is publiſhed,

THE Benefit of FARTING explain'd: Or, the Fundamental Cauſe of the Diſtempers incident to the Fair Sex, inquir'd into; proving *a Poſteriori* moſt of the Diſ-ordures in-*tail'd* on them, are owing to *Flatulencies* not ſeaſonably vented. Wrote in Spaniſh, by Don *Fartinhando Puff-in-dorſt*, Profeſſor of *Bumbaſt* in the Univerſity of *Craccow*; and tranſlated into Engliſh at the Requeſt, and for the Uſe of the Lady *Damp-fart*, of *Her-fart-ſhire.*

A FART, tho' wholeſome, does not fail,
If barr'd of Paſſage by the Tail,
To fly back to the Head again,
And by its Fumes diſturb the Brain;
Thus Gun-powder confin'd, you know, Sir,
Grows ſtronger, as 'tis ramm'd the cloſer;
But, if in open air it fires,
In harmleſs Smoke its Force expires.

The Fourteenth Edition, reviſ'd by a College of Phyſicians. To which is added,

A Certificate of its Virtues, from the Court of the Princeſs *Arſemini*. Together with ſome

Verſes on a Lady's FART, in the Philippic ſtrain,
And on Squire NUMP'S FART in the *Brewers* ſtrain.

Alſo a Meditation on T——d, wrote in a Place of Eaſe. Price 6 d. Printed for A. MOORE, near St. Paul's, and ſold by the Bookſellers.

Where may be had,

1. TEA, a Poem, or Ladies into China Cups; price 6 d.
2. The Batchelor's Recantation, &c.

LONDON: Printed by S. PALMER and J. HUGGONSON, in *Bartholomew-Cloſe*, for Captain GULLIVER, near the *Temple*, where Letters and Advertiſements are taken in; As alſo at the *Rainbow Coffee-Houſe* in *Cornhill*, and *John's Coffee-Houſe* in *Sheer-Lane*, near *Temple-Bar*. [Price Two Pence.]

The Grub-ſtreet Journal.

NUMB. 113.

Thursday, *MARCH* 2, 1731.

—— Many monstrous Forms in sleep we see ;
That never were, nor are, nor e'er can be.
DRYDEN's Cock and Fox.

SIR,

SINCE I wrote the Letter concerning Dr. B.'s *Preface* to his *Paradise Lost*, published in your 108th *Journal*, I have met with several observations of others, and made some more myself upon that *Preface*. — At the beginning of my letter I took notice, that besides MILTON's *blindness*, the Doctor had assigned three other reasons why he made use of an Amanuensis, which could proceed only from an uncommon way of thinking, viz. because he was *obnoxious to the Government, poor*, and *friendless*: all which circumstances I find since directly contradicted. * To the first it has been answered, That after the Act of oblivion, having obtained a full protection from the Government, he appeared as much in Public, as formerly. To the second, That, tho' whilst he was Latin Secretary to the Parliament, and the two Protectors successively, he did not amass a very large fortune, which he had so good opportunities of doing ; yet no one, who pretends to give any account of his life, says, that he was poor or indigent. To the third, That his friends procured him a pardon, and a full protection from the Government, and a License for the printing of the first edition of his *Paradise Lost*. All which seems to amount to a full disproof of his *bad circumstances* ; and to shew, that he was neither *obnoxious to the Government, nor poor*, nor *friendless*.

As a confirmation, I suppose, of the badness of MILTON's circumstances, the Dr. tells us, p. 5. That *a poor Bookseller, living near Aldersgate, purchas'd the Copy for ten pounds, and (if a second edition follow'd) for five pounds more.* ——† In answer to this, it has been affirmed, that this *poor Bookseller* was Mr. SIMMONS, a Citizen of London, and Common Council-man, who died worth some thousands.

From the many supposed errors in the first edition of this Poem, the Doctor assures us, p. 5. that *an attentive Reader will be thoroughly convinc'd, That the proof-sheets were never read to* MILTON. Which, tho' a thing very strange and improbable, is immediately followed by a positive assertion, which is much stranger, and even incredible: *Nay, the edition, when publish'd, was never read to him in seven years time.* In proof of which he adds, *The first came out in* 1667, *and a second in* 1674; *in which all the faults of the former are continued, with the addition of some new ones.* —— But this I find contradicted by a person of as great authority, the Doctor himself; who in his note upon B. xi. 485, has these words, MILTON *made but two additions*, [in the second edition] *both proper and genuine* ; [certainly *genuine* if made by him] *three verses in the beginning of the* viii *Book, when he divided one Book into two ; and five in the beginning of the* xii, *when he divided another Book into two. The first edition comprised all in ten Books.* Let any one judge, whether MILTON could make these alterations and additions, without hearing the Poem *read to him* ; and whether is more probable, that it was *read* in the manuscript copy, or in the printed edition.

To prove that this Poem was corrupted and interpolated by the Editor, the Doctor in the same page of his *Preface* brings an argument, by way of *confirmation*, which very much invalidates both this, and the preceding assertions. For, having asked, *If the Editor durst insert his forgeries even in the second edition, when the Poem and its Author had slowly grown to a vast reputation ; what durst he not do in the first, under the Poets poverty, infamy, &c.* He subjoins, *Add to this a farther confirmation ; That when* MILTON *afterwards publish'd his* Paradise Regain'd *and* Samson Agonistes, *that edition is without faults ; because he was then in high credit, and had changed his old Printer and Supervisor.* —— In which sentence, the word *afterwards* plainly referring to the *second edition* of *Paradise Lost*, mentioned in the sentence foregoing, we are informed, that the first *edition* of *Paradise Regained*, &c. *is without faults*, because MILTON *was then in high credit, and had changed his old Printer and Supervisor*, who printed and *supervised* both the first and second edition of his *Paradise lost*. According to this account, the first edition of *Paradise Regain'd* must come out some time in 1674, the year in which, as the Doctor tells us above, the second edition of *Paradise Lost* was published: for the Author died in that very year. Now, supposing this account to be true (which it is not) the distance of time between the publications of the second edition of one, and the first of the other Poem, a distance perhaps of a few months, is too inconsiderable, for any great advancement of the Author's *credit* and reputation, and the change, supposed consequent thereupon, of his *old Printer and Supervisor*. —— Nor will it be of any advantage to the Doctor's argument, to give this sentence a forced construction, by supposing he knew that the first edition of *Paradise Regain'd* was published in 1671, and consequently that he designed the word *afterwards* should referr to the first edition of *Paradise Lost*, which appeared, according to his account, four years before, in 1667. For if MILTON *was in high credit, and had changed his old Printer and Supervisor* in 1671 ; would he not three years afterwards, in 1674, when his *credit* must needs have risen still *higher*, have employed his new *Printer*, or at least his new *Supervisor*, in publishing the second edition of *Paradise Lost*? Is it at all probable, that he should take so much care of his *Paradise Regain'd* and *Samson Agonistes*, (two Poems inconsiderable in comparison of the other) as to send those abroad into the world, the very first time, *without faults* ; and should so entirely neglect this grand Work, which had gotten him such *a vast reputation*, as to send it forth a second time, *polluted with* more than all the *monstrous faults* of the first impression? So that let us take this which way we will, and suppose that the first edition of *Paradise Regain'd* came out either in 1671, or in 1674 ; either before, or after the second edition of *Paradise Lost* ; this is so far from proving the *insertion of forgeries* by the *Editor* in this second edition, that it makes such an *insertion* still much more improbable, and almost impossible.

The real truth of the matter is this: The first edition of *Paradise Lost* was published, not in 1667, as the Doctor affirms, but in 1669 ; the first of *Paradise Regain'd* in 1671 ; and the second of *Paradise Lost* in 1674. Which makes it very surprising, and even astonishing, that the Doctor should pretend to draw arguments from the different times of the publication of these editions, and yet not know when two of them were published.

I am, Sir, your most humble servant,

Feb. 26, 1731. J. T.

* Milton Restor'd. Pref. † Ibid.

SIR,

I Have not as yet read any *Remarks on Dr.* BENTLEY's *Milton*, except the few that have been published in your Journal. I indeed am engaged in making some myself, and therefore avoid being led into ‡ other mens notions. If I find any willingness in you to receive my Letters, I may, perhaps, at my leisure, send you my thoughts concerning that extraordinary performance. As I perceive a great part of it to be founded on the supposal of an Editor, who altered, added to, and corrupted MILTON's text, I shall at present set myself to overturn that main pillar of the Doctor's structure.

This Critic, to prove the reality of his imagination, relies chiefly on the following argument, thus expressed in his *Preface*. P. 5. *If any one fancy this persona of an Editor to be a meer fantom, a fiction, an artifice to skreen* MILTON *himself ; let him consider these four and sole changes made in the second Edition.* I. 505. V. 638. XI. 485, 551. *These are proved here in the Notes, every one of them to be manifestly for the worse. And whoever allows them to be worse, and yet will contend, they are the Poet's own, betrays his ill judgment, as well as ill nature.*

I own myself one of them that take this Editor to be *a fantom, a fiction, an artifice* ; and am willing to be determin'd by these passages, which the Doctor appeals to. But why are these called the *sole changes made in the second Edition*, when the Doctor confesses in his notes, P. 364. that MILTON made two additions, three verses in 'the beginning of B. VIII. and five in the beginning of B. XII?' He cannot distinguish between *additions* and *changes* : for most of these *changes* imputed to the Editor, are only *additions*. But let us turn to them in order.

B. I. 504. MILTON, speaking of the nightly insolence of the *sons of Belial*, says,

Witness the streets of Sodom ; and that night
In Gibeah, when hospitable doors
Yielded their Matrons to avoid worse rape.

This was afterwards alter'd (either by MILTON or his Editor) to

—— *when* the *hospitable* door
Expos'd a Matron, *to avoid worse rape*.‖

Dr. B. affirms *the first Edition* to be most *agreeable to the Scriptures* : let us then decide this doubt by *the Scriptures. Gen.* xix. LOT, to save the two Angels from the outrage of the men of Sodom, *offers* them his two daughters, but did not *yield* them ; for they were not accepted. Neither were they *Matrons*, but *Virgins* (which this Editor opposes to each other in his note on B. IV. 501.) *Judges* xix. An *Ephraimite* sojourning in *Gibeah*, entertain'd in his house a Levite, with his Concubine or Wife (for the text calls him her *Husband*) who were distress'd for lodging ; but at night certain sons of Belial beset the house, and demanded the man, with the same vile intent, as the men of Sodom before-mention'd. To save him, the master of the house *offers* them his own daughter (not a *Matron*, but a *Virgin*) and the stranger's *Wife* or *Concubine*. It is not mentioned, that the Maiden was *given up* to them, tho' *offered* ; but only the *Concubine*, whom they barbarously abused. So that in Sodom two *Virgins* (no *Matron*) were *offered* only, not *yielded* : in Gibeah two were *offered*, a *Virgin* and a *Matron*, but only the *Matron* said to be ‖ *yielded*. I think no one can doubt, which of the editions is most agreeable to *Scripture* ; neither can it be doubted but that MILTON alter'd the passage, to make it more *agreeable to Scripture*. Besides, the *doors yielding* THEIR *Matrons*, implies, that the *Matrons* belonged to the house ; whereas the *Matron* exposed in *Gibeah* was the stranger's wife ; therefore MILTON, in his second edition, corrected this oversight also. Yet Dr. *B.* wonderfully asserts, that *two Matrons were yielded and offer'd in each place.* —— He adds another feeble objection to the reading in the second edition, that *the streets of Sodom are called on to witness nothing at all.* Yes, they are called on to *witness* to the *insolence* and drunkenness of *the sons of Belial*, mentioned but just before : but there is no necessity for the Poet to specify their particular actions in *Sodom*, tho' he might the more remarkable one in *Gibeah*.

Next let us consider, B V. 637. where, describing the repast of the Angels, MILTON (or rather RAPHAEL) said in the first edition ;

They eat, they drink, and with refection sweet
Are fill'd, before th' all-bounteous King. ——

It is probable the Author, upon farther consideration, might judge this to be a more proper description of an human feast, than of an angelic banquet in the presence of God, and for this reason might afterwards change it thus ;

On flours repos'd, and with fresh flourets crown'd,
They eat, they drink, and in communion *sweet*
Quaff Immortality and Joy, secure
Of surfeit, where full measure only bounds
Excess, *before th' all bounteous King.* ——

It would be no wonder if the description of an angelic repast could not stand the test of a cool philosophical examination : but let us hear this Editor's objections. He has nothing to say against the first of these verses, and therefore may fancy himself very cunning in giving it us, as tho' it were in the first edition. Nor does *communion* instead of *refection* offend him. : but concerning *Quaff Immortality and Joy*, he asks, *Whether the liquors here, that the Angels quaff, produced their Immortality?* and whether *they were not possessed of it before?* To these idle questions I answer, that (tho' according to MILTON, Angels require food) the word *Quaff* is here used in a metaphorical sense,

‡ Tho' this ingenious Gentleman is unwilling to be *led into other men's notions*, yet, after he has written his own, I wish he would compare them with those of others. By this means, if he have insisted upon the same things too largely, he may contract his Reflections ; if too briefly and obscurely, he may inlarge and illuminate them.

‖ The Author of the *Review of the Text of Milton's*, &c. p. 35. justly observes, that '*Yielded* was here changed, 'by M. into *Expos'd* ; because the Levite's wife was not 'only *yielded*, but put out of doors, and *expos'd* to the 'men's lewdness.

which is eaſier to be comprehended, than expreſſed. In *communion ſweet* they are tranſported with the poſſeſſion of *immortality and joy:* which may ſignify immortal joys, according to the Scripture idiom, which MILTON lov'd to imitate. —— But *ſecure of ſurfeit* puzzles him again, *for the conſtruction requires that it be a ſurfeit of immortality.* And what if it does *require* this, where is the fault? Is it not an high praiſe of immortality and heavenly joy, that they never ſatiate? But *ſecure of ſurfeit* may, without any violence or contrariety to MILTON's manner, be referr'd to *they eat, they drink:* tho' they have *piles of food* (ſays *Raphael*) *flowing nectar, fruit of delicious vines,* they are *ſecure of ſurfeit, where* plenty and *full meaſure* do not lead to, (as with mankind) but *only bound Exceſs*; prevent it, ſtop its approach. This is intelligible enough: and as to the queſtions concerning MILTON's *theory of Angels,* they are already anſwer'd by MILTON in this Book; That Angels have the lower faculties of man, and require food, v. 407, &c. that they eat heartily, v. 436; and that they *ſuffice nature with meats, and drinks, but do not burden it,* v. 451. As for the propriety of his theory, let MILTON himſelf be anſwerable for it; and let the Doctor raiſe a cloud of duſt about it: I am contented to have proved this paſſage in diſpute to be agreeable to it, and not unworthy of MILTON.

The next paſſage to be conſidered is, B. XI. 485. MICHAEL tells ADAM, a little before, that he will ſhew him *a monſtrous crew of dire diſeaſes,* v. 474. and the Author ſays *immediately a lazar houſe appear'd* to him, *wherein were laid numbers of all diſeas'd;* which he then proceeds to reckon up, and names *eleven ſorts,* ſays this Editor: perhaps there are more. However, MILTON forgot among theſe to reckon up any of the kinds of *madneſs, conſumption,* or *plague,* and therefore in his ſecond edition beſtows theſe three verſes on them:

Dæmoniac phrenſy, moping melancholy,
And moon ſtruck madneſs, pining atrophy,
Maraſmus, and wide-waſting peſtilence.

Good lines, which even this Critic can find no fault with, but only with the place of them: MILTON, ſays he, *had named eleven ſorts; enow for a Poem, if not too many.* I anſwer, that *ſeventeen* ſorts, if well expreſs'd, are not at all too many, when we are prepar'd to expect a *monſtrous crew, and numbers of all diſeas'd:* and theſe laſt inſerted are of as great conſequence as any. Indeed, conſidering the year when this Poem came out, 1669, it ſeems ſtrange that the Author ſhould on this occaſion omit to mention the plague, the terrible effects of which he muſt have been a witneſs of. But it is not unlikely, that this work might be finiſhed before the plague, and its publication prevented by the confuſion in the following years. If this was the caſe, 'tis no wonder this omiſſion was ſupplied in the ſecond edition. But ſtill the Dr. ſays, he ſhould not have brought in *phrenſy, and melancholy, and lunatic madneſs, for ſhapes of death;* becauſe they *are exempt from pain and ſickneſs, and often attended with long life.* This Gentleman, 'tis to be hoped, is free from *madneſs* himſelf; elſe he would have known it to be attended with ſevere *pain,* either in the fits or intervals, as *melancholy,* I believe always is with *ſickneſs.* But there is no need, that theſe ſhould be brought in for *ſhapes of death,* but for *diſeaſes* produced *by intemperance,* as this Editor muſt have ſeen at v. 472. But what he ſaid was thought more to his purpoſe; tho' even in that he was miſtaken: for tho' they are often attended with *long life,* do they not *kill* at laſt? and are not *heart-ſick qualms, ſtone, aſthmas,* and other diſeaſes here mention'd, often attended with *long life?* nay, does not MILTON himſelf, to aggravate thoſe evils, ſay the ſame, v. 491?

—— Over them triumphant death his dart
Shook; but delay'd to ſtrike, tho' oft invok'd
With vows, as their chief good, and final hope.

We have now but one paſſage to examine, and that will not create us much trouble. ADAM, ſpeaking of the *combrous charge* of life, ſays, B. XI. 550.

Which I muſt keep 'till my appointed day
Of rendring up.

To which, in the ſecond edition, is added,

—— and patiently attend
My diſſolution.

This Critic is forc'd to confeſs, that it is *a very good ſentence,* and he finds no fault with the expreſſion; but condemns it, as not *ſuiting the context,* and *contradicting* what ADAM ſaid before. I allow, that what ADAM ſaid before *ſhews rather ſome impatience to be rid of the combrous charge of life:* and this latter part of his ſpeech ſhews the ſame thing, not contradicting his former *impatience,* but declaring, with ſome regret, what is his duty; not ſaying what he deſires to do, but what he *muſt.* Tho' I am tir'd of life, and would chuſe to reſign it, yet, ſays he, *I muſt keep it 'till my appointed day:* to which he now adds another part of his duty; I muſt not only barely abſtain from ſelf-murder, but muſt, moreover, *patiently attend my diſſolution.* Very good ſenſe, beautiful expreſſion, ſound divinity, and properly inſerted. ADAM gives much the ſame inſtructions to EVE, upon her propoſal of killing themſelves, B. X. 1016. and the following verſes *.

But the *Dr's* main objection againſt this addition is, that it *gives* MICHAEL *three ſyllables,* which *the Author had here and elſewhere pronounc'd with two only.* It may be worth while to give a full anſwer to this, not to juſtify this paſſage (which does not now require it,) but to expoſe the trifling cavils of this Critic in ſeveral other places. The truth of the matter is this: MILTON (whether out of negligence, or deſign to vary his numbers, I will not determine) makes URIEL, GABRIEL, MICHAEL, RAPHAEL, and ſuch words, ſometimes two ſyllables, and ſometimes three. The learned *Dr.* poſſeſſed with the ſpirit of alteration, when he meets theſe words with three ſyllables, by ſome change or other contracts them into two, for this wiſe reaſon, becauſe MILTON *always gives them in two.* See note on B. XI. 466. A mighty ingenious proof this: I find theſe words in a dozen places to conſiſt of three ſyllables, and reduce them to two, becauſe MILTON *always* does! At B. II. 294. the Editor was not grown to ſo much boldneſs: MICHAEL is there firſt mentioned, and is given with three ſyllables: he alters it, but ſays only *our Author generally pronounces* MICHAEL, RAPHAEL, &c. *with two ſyllables;* tho' afterwards he takes courage, and ſays *always* inſtead of *generally.* In B. XI. 235. RAPHAEL has three ſyllables in all former editions: but the *Doctor,* to make it two, inſerts *as,* which makes † nonſenſe; and that the nonſenſe may not be imputed to him, very honeſtly ſays nothing of the change he has made, nor does he print it in a different character from the text. Yet ſtill, with all his *ſagacity,* he has overlook'd ſome of theſe ſad faults. B. III. 648. URIEL is left untouch'd with three ſyllables, tho' it has but two ſix lines afterwards. ITHURIEL is (I think) mention'd but thrice in the whole Poem. B. IV. 788, and 868, it has four ſyllables; and 810, but three. I have, upon this occaſion, taken the trouble to look over the whole Poem; and tho' it is but a dull concluſion of a letter, will preſent you with an index of the places, where theſe words are uſed with a different number of ſyllables, from what this Editor affirms them to be always uſed with.

MICHAEL, 3 ſyllables. B. II. 294. VI. 202, 411. XI. 466, 552. XII. 466.
GABRIEL, 3 ſyll. IV. 865.
URIEL, 3 ſyll. III. 648. VI. 363.
RAPHAEL, 3 ſyll. V. 561. VI. 363. VII. 40. XI. 235.
ITHURIEL, 4 ſyll. IV. 788, 868.

I hope, Sir, you will publiſh this, that it may be ſeen on what foundation Dr. BENTLEY's grand ſcheme of an *ignorant, pragmatical, corrupting Editor,* is raiſed. I am your humble ſervant. A. Z.

* A Gentleman at Oxford, who ſent us a letter dated Feb. 13. and ſubſcribed R. S. defends this paſſage, by giving the ſame explication of it, more at large, and ſubjoins the ſame obſervation about MICHAEL, RAPHAEL, &c. The Author of the *Review of the Text of Milton's,* &c. p. 56. obſerves, that FAIRFAX, in the Argument of B. IX. of his *Taſſo,* and elſewhere, makes MICHAEL three ſyllables. I find it likewiſe of two in Stanz. 58 of that Book.

† Mr. R. S. gives a like inſtance in B. IV. 865.

To whom their Chief
Gabriel from the front thus call'd aloud.

On which the Doctor makes this note: *A word is dropp'd here out of the verſe: for* GABRIEL *is but of two ſyllables. I believe he gave it,*

Gabriel from th' other *Front thus call'd aloud.*

He ſpeaks to UZZIEL *and his Party, that had wheel'd ſouthward.* v. 782.

But GABRIEL and UZZIEL were now met, and had now joined their two parties, in the *weſtern Point,* as appears from the verſes immediately preceding, which ſpeak of ITHURIEL and ZEPHON leading Satan whom they had ſeized.

Now drew they nigh
The weſtern Point, where thoſe half rounding guards
Juſt met, and cloſing *ſtood in* ſquadron join'd
Awaiting next command.

So that, as the Author of the *Review,* &c. ſays p. 145. '*The Front* was the Front of the whole Band of Angels.'

DOMESTIC NEWS.

C. *Courant.*	EP. *Evening Poſt.*
P. *Poſt-Boy.*	SJ. *S. James's Evening Poſt.*
DP. *Daily Poſt.*	WE. *Whitehall Evening P.*
DJ. *Daily Journal.*	LE. *London Evening Poſt.*

THURSDAY, *Feb.* 24.

Yeſterday being Aſh-wedneſday, the R. Rev. the Biſhop of Litchfield and Coventry preached before her Majeſty, his Royal Highneſs the Duke, and the Princeſſes, &c. *P.* Their Majeſties, and the 3 Princeſſes, &c. *C.* —— The Company of young ſoldiers which has been raiſed for the diverſion of his Royal Highneſs the Duke, conſiſting at preſent of only 15 young Gentlemen of diſtinction, the ſame will be augmented to about 3 times that number, and all completely clothed and armed at his Majeſty's coſt; and are to be trained up to the exerciſe of arms by an experienced Officer. *C.*

The ſame day a perſon was committed to Newgate by the Hon. Houſe of Commons, on his examination on ſome affairs relating to the Charitable Corporation, and ordered that no perſon ſhould viſit him, nor to have the uſe of pen, ink, or paper. *C.* A Gentleman. *DJ.* —— Mr. Leaſe, for groſly prevaricating in his examination: he is very ſullen, and don't reliſh his confinement in his new apartment. *DP. Feb.* 25.

The Directors of the Bank have agreed to build their new houſe behind the Royal Exchange, from the plan of Mr. Sampſon; and the Undertakers are 4 perſons, two Maſons and two Carpenters, viz. Mr. Townſend and Mr. Dunn, Maſons; and Mr. Edmonds and another Carpenter. *LE.*

Late laſt night the E. of Cheſterfield arrived at his houſe in S. James's-ſquare, from Holland; and this morning his Lordſhip waited on his Majeſty in his cloſet at S. James's. —— The Hon. Will. Finch, Eſq; will, in a few days, ſet out for the Hague, in the quality of his Majeſty's Envoy Extraord. to the States General. *LE.*

Dover, Feb. 22. We hear from Deal, that the Rev. Mr. Bullings, who lately embraced the Church of England, and had been Miniſter of a Preſbyterian Congregation in Dover many years, preached laſt ſunday morning at Weſtcliff, and in the afternoon at Ringſwould near this town, and made two excellent Sermons, greatly to the ſatiſfaction of his hearers. He has an extraordinary good character of a ſober, learned and pious man, and is well reſpected by all who know him. *P.* — *It was inſinuated not long ſince, by one of that perſuaſion, that no ſuch came over to the* Church of England.

Glouceſter, Feb. 22. From Crockerton, near Warminſter, Wilts, we have an account that a male child was lately born there with 24 fingers and toes, 6 fingers on each hand, and 6 toes on each foot, all ſtreight and proper. *SJ. WE.*

By letters from Bruſſels, dated Feb. 27. there is advice, that Mrs. Anne Plowden, an agreeable young Lady, and a great heireſs in England, the only child of Mr. Plowden, was profeſs'd a Nun at the Engliſh Benedictine Nunnery there, notwithſtanding all the endeavours of her Father to obſtruct the ſame, &c. *LE.* —— The endeavours of *a younger perſon than* her Father *might have probably been more ſucceſsful.*

FRIDAY, *Feb.* 25.

The King of Pruſſia, who for ſome years has, by contract, wholly ſupplied the Ruſſes with woollen cloth for cloathing their Troops in that Empire, has, in order to encourage that manufacture in his dominions, laid a new duty of 20 per cent. on all foreign cloth imported at Koningſburgh, as appears by letters from Dantzick, dated the 20th, N. S. ſo that our exports of woollen goods to that place, which formerly was very conſiderable, is now entirely at an end. *DJ.* —— Mr. Conundrum *obſerv'd, that the Wits of the Engliſh, inſtead of* wool-ſelling, *had been for a long time a* wool-gathering.

On tueſday night laſt a Sharper came to a houſe in Henrietta-ſtreet, Covent-garden, under pretence of taking lodgings for his Maſter, which he agreed for, and ſaid he was expected that night out of the country; but before his pretended Maſter came, he found means to carry off moſt of the valuable furniture. *P.* —— *If the man was ſuch a rogue, what was his* Maſter?

Monday laſt Mr. Abel Fonnereau, an eminent Hamburgh Merchant, was married to Miſs Heywood, Daughter of —— Heywood, Eſq; of Oxford, a very agreeable Lady, and 6000 l. fortune. *DP.*

Chriſtened: Males, 170. Females, 190. In all 360. Buried: Males, 190. Females, 185. In all 375. Decreaſed in the burials this week 75. *P.*

SATURDAY, *Feb.* 26.

Yeſterday his Majeſty went to the Houſe of Peers, with the uſual ſtate, and gave the Royal Aſſent to the Bill for continuing the Duty on malt, mum, mead, cyder, and perry, &c. and to 3 other private Bills. *C.* Three naturalization Bills. *DP.* Several. *DJ.* To ſeveral publick and private Bills. *P.*

The ſame day the Rev. Dr. Pearce preach'd before her Majeſty, his Royal Highneſs the Duke, and the three eldeſt Princeſſes. *C.*

On wedneſday the Lord Weymouth arrived at Dover, from France. *DJ. P.* —— The R. Hon. the Lord Noell, Knight of the ſhire for the County of Monmouth, only Brother to the D. of Beaufort, lies ill of the ſmall-pox, at his Grace's houſe in S. James's-ſquare. *DP.* —— He is thought by his Phyſicians to be in a fair way of recovery. *P. Feb.* 28.

Edw. Barker, Eſq; was on thurſday choſen Chairman to

the Middlesex Justices, in the Room of Tho. Abney, Esq; who resigns. *D J. W E.*

Yesterday at the Sessions at the Old Baily. Rob. Atkinson was try'd for the murder of his Mother, by flinging her down stairs. After a trial, which lasted 5 hours, the Jury brought in their verdict *Accidental death. P.* A trial of near 4 hours: gave in a verdict Not guilty; and to the indictment on the Coroner's inquest, Accidental death. *D P.*

Last night the Sessions ended, when 8 persons receiv'd sentence of death, viz. Tho. Smith and Tho. Faxton, for robbing Mr. Davis on the highway; and Tho. Edwards and Tho. Past, for robbing the Rev. Mr. Prior; Jane French, for robbing her Master of 15 l. and 2 gold rings; T. Andrews and Edw. Dell, for burglary; and John Brown, for returning from transportation. *C.* Katharine French. *P.* George Brown. *D P.* Tho. Brown, *D J.* Sam. Burroughs, alias Johnson, for returning from transportation. 30 were cast for transportation. *P.* —— Mr. Baron Thompson committed to Newgate one of the Sheriffs Officers, for refusing to admit witnesses, and others, without money. *D P.*

We hear that the installation of the 4 new Knights of the Bath will not be performed 'till the beginning of June. *L E.* —— We hear orders are given for all Officers to repair, with all convenient speed to their respective regiments at Gibraltar and Port Mahon. *P.*

Yesterday in the evening Mr. David Avery, a Merchant of this City, who had been several times examined before the Committee for enquiring into the affairs of the Charitable Corporation, was bail'd out of the custody of the Serjeant at Arms attending the House of Commons. *L E.*

On thursday morning died Mr. John Bellamy, in the 85th year of his age, &c. he was formerly an eminent money Scrivener, and was principally concerned in erecting the Bank of England. *C.*

MONDAY, *Feb.* 28.

Yesterday the R. Rev. the L. Bishop of Durham preached before their Majesties, his Royal Highness the Prince, &c. And the Rev. Mr. Lavington before his Royal Highness the Duke, &c. *C.* ——— The R. Hon. the L. Weymouth waited on their Majesties at S. James's, and was most graciously received. *C. D P. P.*

The Lords of the Admiralty having been pleased to appoint Capt. Ric. Lestock, Commadore of the squadron going *to the* West-Indies, have been pleased to appoint Capt. *Tho. Trevor* to be Commander of the Kingston under the said Commadore. *P.*

On saturday last, at Hicks's-Hall, the tryal of one Poole came on for perjury in the Court of King's Bench, for swearing that Col. Wingfield should say, He would hang 20 such men as Franklin was, on which the said Colonel was not admitted on the Jury that tried Mr. Franklin. After a trial, which lasted some time, he was convicted of the perjury, and sentenced to stand in the pillory, facing Westminster Hall gate, and to suffer 2 years imprisonment in Bridewell. *P.* Committed to the House of Correction to be kept to hard labour for 2 years. *C.*

The same day in the Court of King's-Bench at Guildhall, an issue directed out of Chancery was try'd, in which a Minor, and supposed son of one Mr. Pendreuell, deceased, was Plaintiff. The cause of action was, that Mr. Pendreuell being married to a woman in London, about 7 years ago, in a few days after marriage went into Staffordshire, and there lived upwards of two years, and then died: in the mean time his wife was delivered of a child in London. On the decease of Mr. Pendreuell, an estate of 100 l. a year devolved on the next heir of the family, given to the great grandfather of the deceased, by K. Charles II. for preserving him in the oak, which would have come to this child, had it been lawfully begotten: but it being sworn, that he had no conversation with his wife during that time, a verdict was given for the Defendant. *C.* —— *I imagined, that if the* Husband *was between the* 4 *seas, the* Wife *could have no* bastard.

Yesterday morning died, at his lodgings in Fleet-street, the Rev. Mr. Morgan, Minister of Hadly in Middlesex, who was lately appointed Archdeacon of S. Davids, &c. *P. D P.* — Mr. Hitchcock, a Tallow-chandler in White-cross street, was found dead in his bed; he had been used to take Laudanum for some time; and 'tis thought, took too large a dose. *C.* ——— On saturday morning, about 11, Mr. Skinner, an Attorney, shot himself into the head, at his house in Blewit's-buildings in Fetter-lane. He brought the pistols home but friday night. He had buckled one shoe, and laid his other buckle on the chair by him: there was a hole behind his ear big enough to thrust a man's fist in, and his brains were shot up against the cieling: he was a man of tolerable good business, but thought to be under some difficulties as to his fortune. *D P.* At his lodgings in Blewit's-buildings. *P.* —— He was lunatick some days before; the occasion of which was owing to his being beat and bruised in a barbarous manner by a Hackney Coach-man, who robb'd him of 70 guineas, his gold watch and rings, &c. *C. Feb.* 29.

TUESDAY, *Feb.* 29.

Yesterday his Majesty, with the rest of the Royal Family, viewed 12 fine horses lately imported from Hanover, and seemed very much pleased with them. *D J. C.*

Yesterday being the Birth-day of Peter Delme, Esq; eldest son of the late Sir Pet. Delme, who then became of age, whereby the executorship and trust devolves upon him of a very great estate, he gave a handsome entertainment to the Gentlemen concern'd for the management of his affairs at Pontack's. *D P.*

Yesterday a Sessions of Admiralty was held at the Old Bailey, when John Ellis was capitally convicted; and Lawrence Brown, Patrick Scott, and Rob. Halsey were acquitted. *D P. D J.* Ellis and Brown were try'd for running away with the Mahon Galley. It appeared, that the prisoners, with two others not yet taken, Dec. 20. about 20 leagues from Alicant, confined the Captain, and used him in a barbarous manner. *P.*

Last night the Hon. Morgan Vane, Esq; was married to Miss Knight, daughter of Rob. Knight, Esq; formerly Cashier to the South Sea Company, at her house in Grosvenor-street. *P.*

On sunday last died, in an advanced age, Andrew Card of Grey's-Inn, Esq; senior Bencher of that Hon. Society. *P.* ——— Yesterday in the 29th year of his age, of a convulsion in his nerves, at his house in Russel-street, Covent-garden, Francis Leigh, Esq; son of Sir John Leigh of Addington in the County of Surrey, Bar. *D J.* Sir John has upwards of 3000 l. per ann. part of which is a fine house and gardens at Addington, which he holds as a grant from the Crown, as being Grand Master of Serjeantry, whose place is to carry the first dish to the table at a Coronation feast. *C.*

On tuesday last died, at Paris, the R. Rev. Dr. Francis Atterbury, late Lord Bishop of Rochester, aged near 70 years; a man universally esteemed for his great parts, learning, judgment, and eloquence, and for his easy, polite, entertaining, and instructive conversation. He has left his son-in-law, Will. Morrice, Esq; Executor, who sets out for France this morning, to take care of his enterment; which (we hear) will be in Westminster Abbey. *P.*

WEDNESDAY, *March* 1.

Whitehall, Feb. 29. His Majesty has been pleased to grant unto John Baron, M. A. the Archdeaconry of Norfolk, void by the promotion of the R. Rev. Father in God, Dr. Tho. Tanner to the Bishoprick of S. Asaph. — And to confer the dignity of a Baronet of Great Britain upon Rob. Brown, of the City and Liberty of Westminster, Esq; *D P. P.*

This being her Majesty's Birth-day, when she enters into her 50th year, &c. *D P.* Into the 51st year. *D J.* — The Hon. Mrs. Vane is continued in her station of Maid of honour to her Majesty. *D P.*

On Saturday last, — Frederick of Gray's-Inn, Esq; was married to Miss Somerset, a young Lady of 10,000 l. fortune. *P.*

From the PEGASUS *in Grub-street.*

We have received several letters relating to Dr. BENTLEY's *Milton*, particularly two from A. Z. and two from R. S. one of the two former of which we have now published, and thereby compleated what we thought sufficient to overturn the greatest part of the Doctor's *Preface*; the foundation, upon which all his conjectural emendations are built. As we design to go through the whole Poem, in a methodical manner, we desire our ingenious and learned Correspondents, to make their observations upon the twelve Books in their proper order; and not to proceed in a desultory manner, forward and backward, from one to another. Which will be acknowledged as a very great addition to the favour of their correspondence, on this subject.

Mr. BAVIUS presented to the Society a Book intituled *Grubiana, or a compleat Collection of all the Poems and material Letters from the Grub-street Journals,* &c. Pr. 2 s. Which, after it had pass'd a while from hand to hand, was voted, *nemine contradicente,* to be a scandalous, impudent, and abominable imposition upon the Public; not containing half pretended to in the Title page; most injudiciously collected; and so incorrectly printed, as frequently to have several faults in a page, and sometimes two in a line. From whence it was concluded to be the Work of some hungry, stupid Renegado Member of our Society, printed and published by some mercenary Wretches, who are continually pestering the Town, either with pyrated good copies wretchedly printed, or with their own vile Copies, containing nothing but Nonsense, Bawdry, or Blasphemy. And a Committee was appointed to examine and draw up a particular account of this Book, against this day se'nnight; and in the mean time to take such methods, as to them should seem most proper to obstruct the running of this pick-pocket impression.

Edinburgh, Feb. 17. Yesterday the Lord Provost, &c. made choice of the Rev. Mr. Will. Hamilton, Professor of Divinity in this University, to be Principal thereof in the room of the Rev. Mr. Will. Wisheart, deceased; and of the Rev. Mr. James Smith, to be Professor of Divinity in the room of Mr. Hamilton. *P. D P. D J. Feb.* 24. — The same day Col. Francis Chartris arrived at his fine Country seat of Stonniehill. We hear he is much indisposed. *P.* Chartres: Stonichil, *D J.*

FOREIGN NEWS.

THURSDAY, *Feb.* 24.

Santa Cruz in Barbary, Jan. 25. N. S. King Muley Abdallah's army, which was advanced within 2 days journey of Morocco, was always victorious over the rebellious Arabs; but in the last battle they made such a slaughter of them, that it is generally believed they will never be able to appear in the field again. Thereupon the people in those parts have since made their submission, and the Blacks are marched within Cannon-shot of Morocco. *P, D J.*

FRIDAY, *Feb.* 25.

Hague, Feb. 25. *Extract of a private Letter from* Paris. ——— The Armaments that are making in this Kingdom and Spain, have quite a different view from what is given out. Our Ministers say, they will be revenged of the Algerines, whom they suggest to have insulted the French flag, but those who pretend to penetrate farther into the secrets of the Cabinet tells us, the 2 crowns begin to think in good earnest of re-uniting, now that Don Carlos is settled in Italy; and that possibly the House of Bourbon may have their eye upon all the ports of the Mediterranean: that in consequence they may grasp at the power of granting or refusing the liberty of trading to Africa or the Levant, to what nation they please. *P.*

SATURDAY, *Feb.* 26.

Hague, Feb. 19. N. S. According to our last advices from Germany, the Great Master of Malta had sent circular letters to Italy, France and Spain, &c. to warn the Knights to repair immediately to the Ports of Italy, where they are to wait 'till they hear farther from him. —— Tho' the publick Papers have lately mention'd the marriage of the Prince Royal of Prussia with the Princess of Mecklemburg, as a thing certain; we have it from good hands, that there is nothing in it; Count Goloffkin, the Muscovite Ambassador here, having declared so. *P.*

Extract of a private letter from Paris. —— The Power which has hitherto supported the Malecontents of Corsica, has at last taken off the mask. France has, in some measure, declared herself their Protector, by answering the Minister of Genoa, when he complain'd of it, that his most Christian Majesty expected they should respect his Flag wherever, or upon what occasion soever, they met it. *P.*

Yesterday arrived the Mails from France *and* Holland.

Barcelona, Feb. 3. 'Tis assured that the Troops, for whose embarkation preparations are making with all diligence, have orders to be ready to embark on the 15th of next month: that their number is to consist of 30,000 men, and that the tents, artillery, and all other necessaries for forming a camp, are to be embarked along with them. *D P.*

MONDAY, *Feb.* 28.

Hague, Feb. 22. We are still assured, that among the Malecontents [of Corsica] there are a great number of French Officers and Soldiers. This Island, which is separated from the Kingdom of Sardinia, only by a sea of about 2 leagues over, may be of use in case of an enterprize of France upon that Island, or upon Naples and Sicily. *P.*

TUESDAY, *Feb.* 29.

Yesterday arrived the Mail from France.

Paris, March 5. N. S. ——— M. Chirac, first Physician to the King, died the 1st instant, in the 74th year of his age. *C.* ——— Letters from Madrid advise the continuation of the armament lately mentioned, with the utmost diligence; adding, that 2 bomb-vessels are likewise equipping, and 14,000 bombs, with 50,000 bullets will be embark'd. *D P.* &c.

WEDNESDAY, *March.* 1.

Yesterday arrived the Mail from Holland.

Seville, Feb. 8. All the Officers of the Spanish forces are order'd to be at their respective posts by the 10th of March, upon pain of being cashier'd. *P.*

Bayonne, Feb. 20. We have advice, that over and above the 30,000 Spaniards formerly mentioned (part of whom are already march'd out of the Garrisons) 6000 Marines are likewise to be employed in that expedition, whatever it is. *P.*

Books and Pamphlets published since our last.

24. The Oxford Marbles: by Michael Mattaire.
25. Grubiana, &c. Pr. 2 s.
26 The Mountebank, &c No. I. for January. Pr. 6 d.
The Fall. In 4 Books By Mr. Thurston.
The nature and consequences of the sacramental Test, &c. Pr. 1 s.

Bes ... relies's Descent to the infernal Regions. Pr. 6 d.
28. The whole of the Proceedings in a Cause between
the Hon. Mrs Kath. Weld and Edw. Weld, Esq; &c. Pr. 1s.
29. The present state of Europe : for January.
Mar. 1. The Volunter Laureat : A Poem, by Ric. Savage, Esq;
A Letter to the R. Hon. Sir Ralph Gore, Bar, &c. Pr 6 d.

On Tuesday Stocks were
South Sea Stock 98 3 8ths, 98; 98 1 8th, to 1 qr.
South Sea Annuity 110 1 half. Bank 149 1 qr. to 1 half.
New Bank Circulation 6 l. 17 s. 6 d. Premium. India 178,
177. Three per Cent. Annuity 97 1 qr. to 1 half. New
3 per Cent. Annuity 96 3 qrs. Royal Exchange Assurance
99 1 qr. London Assurance 13 3 8ths, to 1 half. York
Buildings 8. African 44. English Copper 2 l. 10 s.
Welch ditto 1 l. 17 s. South Sea Bonds 1 l. 10 s. Pre-
mium. India ditto 5 l. 10 s. ditto. Blanks 7 l. 7 s. 20 l.
Prizes 19 l. 12 s.

ADVERTISEMENTS.
For the BENEFIT of
Mr. *JOHN HEBDEN*,
*At Stationers-Hall To morrow, being Friday
the 3d Day of March,* 1732,

WILL be a Grand CONCERT of Vocal and Instru-
mental MUSICK by the best Masters.
Act I. Overture of Richard III. with Trumpets, French
Horn, Kettle Drums, &c. First Concerto of Corelli. Two
Songs. A Concerto, the Solo Part to be performed upon
the Harpsicord ; and a Trumpet Piece.
Act II. Overture of Sofarmes. Solo for the German
Flute. Two Songs. Concerto for the Bassoon. Solo for
the Violin. A Grand Concerto for Trumpets, French
Horns, Kettle Drums, &c. With other Select Pieces.
To begin exactly at Seven o' Clock.
N. B. Tickets to be had at Will's Coffee-House, near
the Royal Exchange ; the George and Vulture Tavern in
Cornhill ; the Rummer Tavern in S. Mary Over's Church-
yard, Southwark ; the Castle Tavern and Gregg's Coffee-
House, both in Pater-Noster-Row, at Five Shillings each.

Just published,

A Full Answer to what the Authors of *Christianity*
as old as the Creation, and of the *Letter to Dr. Wat-*
land have advanced concerning the Confusion of Languages
at Babel ; proving it to have been miraculous, from the essential Difference between them. With an Enquiry into the
primitive Language, before that wonderful Event. By the
late learned WILLIAM WOTTON, D. D. Publish'd from
his original Manuscript.
Printed for J. Roberts, at the Oxford Arms in War-wick-
Lane ; price 1 s Where may be had,
I. The Publick Plea, a Poem. The second Edition ; price
4 d.
II. A Soldier and a Scholar ; or the Lady's Judgment upon
those two Characters in the Persons of Capt. —— and Dr.
S——t.
III. Love and Ambition, a Tragedy. By Mr. Darcy.

This Day is published,

AN Enquiry into the Origin of HONOUR,
and the Usefulness of Christianity in WAR.
By the Author of the *Fable of the Bees*.
Price bound 3 s. 6 d.
Printed for J. Brotherton at the Bible, next the Fleece
Tavern in Cornhill.

Books printed for J. BATLEY, at the Dove in *Pater-Noster-Row*.

1. MIscellaneous Essays, viz. 1. Of Company and
Conversation. 2. Of Solitariness and Retirement.
3. Of Nobility. 4. Of Contentment. 5. Of Woman.
6. Of the Knowledge of God, and against Atheism. 7. Of
Religion. 8. Of Kings, Princes, and the Education of
a Prince. 9. Of Greatness of Mind. 10 Of the Education
of Children. 11. Of Law. 12. Of Man. 13. Of old
Age ; with the Life and Conversion of St. Mary Magdalen,
and some Reflections upon the Conversion of the good Thief.
Also the Life and Conversion of St. Paul, by Sir Richard
Bulstrode, Kt. Envoy at the Court of Brussels from King
Charles II. and King James II. Published with a Preface
by his Son Whitlock Bulstrode, Esq; The second Edition.
Price 4s 6 d.
2. The memorable Things of Socrates. Written by Xenophon, in five Books Translated into English. The second
Edition. To which are prefixed, the Life of Socrates from
the French of Monsieur Charpentier, a Member of the
French Academy And the Life of Xenophon, collected
from several Authors; with some Account of his Writings.
Also complete Tables are added by Edward Bysse, Gent.
price 5 s

This Day is published,

A Collection of PIECES in VERSE and PROSE,
which have been published on occasion of the Dunciad.
Dedicated to the Right Honourable the Earl of Middlesex.
By Mr. Savage.
Likewise,
ATHELWOLD : A Tragedy. By A. Hill, Esq; as it
is acted at the Theatre Royal in Drury-Lane.
2. OF FALSE TASTE ; an Epistle to the Right
Honourable Richard Earl of Burlington. By Mr. POPE.
The 3d Edition, with an additional Letter.
Printed for Lawton Gilliver, at Homer's Head, against
St. Dunstan's Church, Fleet-street.

This Day is published,
Beautifully Printed in Octavo,

PHILOSOPHICAL CONVERSATIONS: Or, a new System of Physics, by way of Dialogue, with 89 Copper
Plates. Written in French by Father *Regnault*, of the Society of Jesus. Translated into English, and illustrated with
Notes by *The. Dale*, M. D. in 3 Vols. —— N. B. The Design
of this Author is like that of Mons. Fontenelle, in his Plurality
of Worlds, to render Natural Philosophy no less plain to
the meanest Readers, than entertaining to the brightest: At
the same time his Reasoning is founded upon such Experiments as have imploy'd the Speculation of the greatest Philosophers in different Countries, that this last age has produced ; particularly upon those in the German Ephemerides, the French Journals, and the Royal Academy of Sciences. Printed for W. Innys, at St. Paul's Church-Yard ;
C. Davis, at the Corner of Pater-Noster-Row ; and N. Prevost, against Southampton-Street in the Strand.

This Day is published,
[Price Six-Pence,]

THE GENTLEMAN's *Pocket Companion* ; Or,
Horseman's Tutor ; shewing how any Person may know
the Age of a Horse from one to eight Years old, and not be
imposed on. As also how a Road or Sporting Horse ought
to be framed or made ; the external Perfections and Imper-
fections ; Marks, good and bad ; a Collection of several
Receipts for Accidents which may happen to a Horse on the
Road or Sporting ; with several curious and necessary Ob-
servations, carefully collected from the best and approv'd
Writers on that Subject.
By W. L. Gent.
Printed for T. Payne, at the Crown in Pater-Noster-Row.

This Day is published,
In Four Volumes, Twelves,
And sold by N. PREVOST, opposite to South-
ampton-Street in the Strand,

THE Life of Mr. CLEVELAND, natural Son of
OLIVER CROMWELL. Written by himself. Giving a
particular Account of his Unhappiness in Love, Marriage,
Friendship, &c. and his great Sufferings in *Europe* and
America. Together with the secret AMOURS of the
PROTECTOR, and his unnatural Usage to his Il-
legitimate Children. The whole intermix'd with Reflexions,
describing the Heart of Man, in all its Variety of Passions
and Disguises.
N. B. The 3d and 4th Vol. may be had separate.

Just published,

MIscellaneous LETTERS on se-
veral Subjects in Philosophy and Astronomy, with
Cuts. Wrote to the learned Dr. Nicholson, late Archbishop
of Cashell, viz.
I. An Account of the great Variety of Plants, Shell-Stones,
and many other Curiosities, in the Parish of Magilligan,
in the County of Londonderry in Ireland ; together with a
curious Account of the forming the Land, being formerly
under Sea.
II. On the Declension of the Level of the Sea.
III. On the Aurora Borealis, or Northern Light.
IV. On the Bith Bogs, Timber found under these Bogs,
and several curious Remarks on the first planting the
World and Ireland, drawn from the Natural History of
such Bogs and Timber.
V. On the General Tides in the Atlantic Ocean, by a new
Hypothesis, and that the Moon hath no Influence on the
Tides.
VI. On the Cause of Gravity, and the Continuation of
Motion, by a new and curious Hypothesis.
VII. On the Load-stone, that the old Hypotheses were in-
sufficient, and a new one drawn from the Northern Light.
VIII An Endeavour to clear Astronomy of the Incredible,
by a new System of the World, wherein the projectile Power
and gravitating Principles of Sir Isaac Newton are proved
to be not according to Nature, and impossible ; and that the
Theory of the Moon is particularly very ill accounted for by Sir
Isaac's Principles ; and new Principles drawn from the Nature of Fluids, and a repelling Power in the Sun, and that the
long Telescopes help to deceive us. By Robert Innes, A. M.
Printed for S. Birt, at the Bible and Ball in Ave-Mary-
Lane; price 1 s 6 d.

On Saturday next will be publish'd,
Price 6 d.

THE GENTLEMAN's MAGAZINE : Or, Monthly
Intelligencer.
No. XIV. for February, being the 2d of Vol. II.
Containing, among other Heads, Arguments for and
against a Standing Army ; the Tax on Salt, Soap and
Candles ; Leather, Land and Windows ; Proposals for a
great many of the present burthensome Duties. On the
Pension Bill, Corruption and Indecency of Parliament ; of
Distillers and Farmers ; Parties changing Principles ; 30th
of January Sermons, &c. with Domestick Occurrences.
And next Week will be published the Second Edition of
No. X. for October,
The fifth Impression being near sold off, on Account of
several agreeable Pieces both in Prose and Verse, sent by
unknown Correspondents, particularly a Copy of the Will
of Samuel Travers, Esq; which was inserted entire with the
Letter prefixed. Another Correspondent was pleased to give
the Author a seasonable Hint (which was observed) in the
following exceeding Complaisant Epistle,
To Mr. Sylvanus Urban.

SIR,
THE Gentleman's Magazine is, perhaps, one of the most
useful Things of the Kind that has been at any time
set on Foot ; but this Usefulness must in Justice and Gratitude be attributed to your unbiass'd Impartiality and Industry ; It serves me, and to my Knowledge several others,
for what your Title truly expresses it, that is, a Magazine
or Repository of every Thing worthy remarking, and for
this Reason be many Years hence, an Authentick Collection for Historians to refer to, when Disputes shall arise
on the Manner and Spirit with which the present Controversies are carried on, the Force of their Arguments on both
Sides being fully retain'd ; besides many Historical Occurrences may be here found, which, tho' they escape the Notice of great and voluminous Historians, will serve to explain
and clear up the Truth of several Facts which in Time
may appear doubtful ; and the Reasons and Origin of some
Transactions will be here found, which might otherwise
be sought after in vain.
When I have promised this, I can't help thinking but
that you will excuse me for taking Notice of a Slip which you
made in July last, in Respect to Gibraltar ; and I am sure
it was no other than Inadvertency and Slip, for your whole
Design shows you mean no Wrong to any Party. The
Piece I mean was published in one of the Daily Papers,
and the Reason why, as I take it, you did not recite it was,
that by Eleven a-Clock the Morning of Publication it was
all sold off, and I gave myself a Shilling for one on Tuesday Morning following, however you may easily see it in
some Coffee-houses, and when you have to do, I am very
sure you will have the Materials of it up in your Magazine ;
for it is not a Temporary Thing, and therefore not worn
out by the Date, but will be as satisfactory now as on the Day
of Publication. I conclude, Sir, with my hearty Thanks to
you for the Benefit and Pleasure I receive from your Studies,
and am your Friend and Servant, tho' unknown,
Octob. 14, 1731. L. J.
Printed at St. John's Gate, and sold by P. Jefferies in
Ludgate-street ; A. Dodd, near Temple-bar ; E. Nutt, & at
the Royal-Exchange ; where may be had compleat Setts, and
an exact LIST of Parliament.

LONDON: Printed by S. PALMER and J. HUGGONSON, in *Bartholomew-Close*, for Captain GULLIVER, near the *Temple*, where Letters and Advertisements are taken in : As also at the *Rainbow Coffee-House* in *Cornhill*, and *John's Coffee-House* in *Shear-Lane*, near *Temple-Bar*. [Price Two Pence.]

The Grub-ſtreet Journal.

NUMB. 114.

Thurſday, *MARCH* 9, 1731.

Jura neget ſibi nata, nihil non arroget armis.
Hor.

A DESIRE to be happy is an inherent principle in all mankind. The whole world is equally addicted to pleaſure; tho' there are ſcarce any two perſons, who ſeek it by the ſame methods. Some take delight in Plays; ſome in Prayers: a pious Chriſtian is as great an Epicure, as the man that eats of ten diſhes at a meal. Our vanity, 'tis true, generally makes us think, that none really take pleaſure but thoſe who are in the ſame purſuits with ourſelves. The Beau wonders how any man can follow a fox for forty miles together: and the country Squire deſpiſes the Beau for an inſipid, puny wretch, who ſhrinks with horror at the approach of the ſmalleſt blaſt of wind.

Where ſociety is not affected by a man's taſte, or favourite pleaſure, I can ſee no ſufficient foundation for cenſuring him for it. Indeed, where private gratifications are detrimental to the Public, there we may juſtly find fault. As the Miſer's chief delight being in hoarding up, and ſpending nothing, he ought not to be free from reproof; becauſe the Public is in ſuch caſe injur'd for want of the circulation of his money.

PLUTARCH, in his life of CICERO, tells us, that when that great Orator conſulted at Delphi, how he ſhould arrive at the top of glory, the Pythia anſwered, by making his own genius, and not the opinion of the people, the guide of his life. Every one, ſays TULLY himſelf, in his *Offices*, ſhould follow his own genius, as far as it is agreeable to virtue and innocence: for while we purſue what other men fancy for us, and neglect our own inclinations, it is impoſſible we ſhould ever ſupport that neceſſary decorum in our lives which we ought to do.

But as no perſon therefore is intitled to lay down any particular plan of life for another; ſo none have a right of indulging themſelves in any appetites, that are not truly compatible with the rules of virtue, and the laws of a ſocial and orderly ſtate.

Ambition and avarice, upon examination, will appear, I believe, to be the moſt predominant paſſions in the mind of man. Ambition leads us on in our younger days; avarice governs our decline and ſilver hairs. Ambition, as it implies an unbounded deſire of conqueſt, is a barbarous, ſavage principle, inconſiſtent with humanity, and deſtructive of all order. True ambition is no other than a rational love of our fellow creatures; a tenderneſs and pity for virtue in diſtreſs; and an inclination and propenſity to promote the happineſs of all the world, as far as it lies in our power.

Narrow ſouls, and ſuch as are incapable of extending their reflections to the conſequences of things, are highly pleaſed, charmed, and even aſtoniſhed, at the falſe greatneſs of ALEXANDER, for weeping when he read the mighty actions of ACHILLES; and at that of CÆSAR, when, out of the ſame envy he wept at the victories of ALEXANDER. Theſe were all Heroes without juſtice; and conſequently, in the language of truth, no better than powerful robbers, and baſe invaders of the common rights and liberties of mankind.

In a Country of liberty (ſuch as ours is) I have been often amazed, that the names of men, thus barbarouſly romantic, ſhould ever have gained ſo general a veneration. —— A BRUTUS ſhall be condemned as guilty of a breach of friendſhip to a Tyrant; a PELOPIDAS forgotten, who reſtored the liberties of his country, and expelled the ſubverters of them; when a LEWIS ſhall be called Great, for a magnanimous conſpiracy againſt the freedom and independency of the largeſt part of the Chriſtian world.

The Mahometans have an eſtabliſhed maxim, that good ſucceſs is a ſure indication of the approbation of Heaven. In this reſpect, one would imagine, that all the world were Mahometans.

Proſperum ſcelus virtus vocatur.

Succeſs never fails to give a ſanction to the baſeſt actions. —The ſame ſpecies of villainy has often rendered one man's perſon ſacred, by gaining him a crown, for which another moſt deſervedly received a halter.

——————— *Multi*
Committunt eadem diverſo crimina fato:
Ille crucem ſceleris pretium tulit, hic diadema.
Juv. Sat. XIII. 103, &c.

Oft the ſame crimes unlike rewards have found:
That Rogue was crucify'd; but this was crown'd.

CHARLES XII. of Sweden, whoſe life the ingenious VOLTAIRE has lately preſented to the Public, ſhewed in all his actions the moſt remarkable inſtances of a brutal courage, conſtancy, and reſolution. His whole life is a ſeries of imprudence and temerity, revenge and folly. He had read of ALEXANDER's exploits; and he was reſolved to make mankind as unhappy, and to diſturb the world as much as that Grecian madman ever did. Whoever conſiders his behaviour at Bender, will without any difficulty pronounce him, I believe, fitter for Bedlam, than qualified to make a nation happy by a wiſe adminiſtration over it. He ſeems not to have had the leaſt ſenſe of gratitude for the generous hoſpitality he had met with. — Nothing was too difficult for him. — With 300 Swedes he thought to bully the whole Ottoman Empire.

The ſpeech which the Grand Seignior made upon this occaſion, will give us a true picture, as well of the Turkiſh generouſly as of CHARLES's ungovernable diſpoſition. I ſhall tranſcribe it out of the Engliſh Tranſlation of VOLTAIRE's *Hiſtory*, B. VI. The Sultan, having called an extraordinary Divan, ſpoke as follows:

'I ſcarce ever knew the King of Sweden, but by his defeat 'at Pultowa, and the requeſt he made to me to grant him 'a ſanctuary in my Empire. I have not, I believe, any 'need of him; nor any reaſon to love, or fear him: yet 'without conſulting any other motives than the hoſpitality of a Muſſulman, and my own generoſity, which 'ſheds the dew of its favours upon the great, as well as 'the little; upon ſtrangers, as well as my own ſubjects; 'I have received and aſſiſted him, his Miniſters, Officers, 'and Soldiers, in every reſpect, and for three years and 'a half have never held my hand from loading him with 'preſents.

'I have granted him a very conſiderable guard to con'duct him into his own Country. He has aſk'd for 1000 'purſes to defray ſome expences, tho' I pay them all: 'inſtead of 1000, I have granted him 1200. After get'ting theſe out of the hands of the Seraſquier of Bender, 'he deſires 1000 more, and refuſes to go, under a pretence 'that the guard is too little; whereas it is but too large to 'paſs through the Country of a friend and ally.

'I aſk you then, whether it is a breach of hoſpitality 'to ſend this Prince away; and whether foreign Princes 'ought to accuſe me of cruelty or injuſtice, in caſe I 'ſhould be obliged to make him go by force?'

The conſequence of this conſultation is but too well known. —— The Grand Seignior was reſolved, that he ſhould go, and CHARLES was determined not to ſtir: — upon which enſued that ſurpriſing affair at Bender; where the King of Sweden, with about 40 Domeſticks, defended himſelf againſt an army of near 30,000 Turks and Tartars.

VOLTAIRE makes the following general remark on this Prince's character, viz. That he was a man rather to be admired, than imitated. For my own part, I think he was neither to be admired, nor imitated. What we admire, we are, for the moſt part, but too apt to imitate: —and therefore in a country of freedom, (as 'tis to be preſumed ours is) ſuch true notions of virtue ſhould be eſtabliſhed, as that no man ſhould have the leaſt ſhare in our eſteem, who is not actuated by a ſpirit of humanity, and a love for his country.

A Dialogue between FIDLERO and NEWSCOUTERO, on thurſday March 2, 1731.

F. Hey! What makes you look ſo pale? You ſeem frighted.

N. Well I may. Here's a break-faſt for you. The Grub ſtreet Journal.

F. O! I have had that break faſt this morning already.

N. And, pray, how does it ſit upon your ſtomach?

F. Plaguy hard. You have drawn me into a fine ſcrape. I wiſh I had ne'er been concern'd in it.

N. Nor I ——. Theſe Grub Dogs are a parcel of Scrub Raſcals. But how the D——l they came by their information, I can't imagine. Why, they have plainly pointed us all out. But we'll be even with 'em.

F. Ay, and ſo we will. I have conſulted my Lawyer already; and he aſſures me, we have five good Actions againſt 'em.

N. I live amongſt the Lawyers; I can have law enough for nothing.

F. But, I believe, ſuch law will be good *for nothing*. If we ſue in *forma pauperis*, I fear we ſhall come *poorly* off. —— But I have money enough. I've 100 l. a year; and I'll ſpend it all, but I'll be reveng'd.

N. A 100 l. a year? Pray, where does it lye?

F. Why, in the Old Baily.

N. O! you mean the three old houſes there. —— One of them proved very fatal, both to our *Morning Poſt*, and to *Oedipus*. I fear there is ſomewhat ominous in them; and we ſhall bring an *old houſe* over our heads.

F. No, no, never fear. ———

N. But they charge us with incorrectneſs.

F. Ay, ſo they do, — and, between you and I, juſtly enough. I'll not pay *Hughes* a farthing more. 'Tis moſt abominably printed.

N. But why didn't you correct it better?

F. I correct it! I had nothing to do in it.

N. But, you lie: you had.

F. —— What ſignified correcting, if the Compoſitors would not alter it?

N. That will appear by the proofs. —— But what ſhall we do? If ſome ſtop be not put to theſe Grubs, there will be no living.

F. No more there won't. Our friends can never go on with their deſign of reprinting *Joſephus* and *Rapin*.

N. I hear Mr. CONUNDRUM declares 'tis down-right *Rapine*.

F. Don't the Bookſellers commit this *Rapine* upon one another? And why ſhould not we Printers and Pamphlet-ſellers do it upon them all?

N. This ſhews our impartiality. And as long as there is no Law againſt this way of Trade, it is certainly lawful; and what is lawful is rightful. —— But what ſhall be done with theſe GRUBS, who endeavour to ſpoil our trade.

F. I'll write againſt 'em myſelf. I can write as well as their BAVIUS or MÆVIUS either.

N. Why? Did you write the *Scheme for a new Lottery*, *The Quæriſt*, and *Love after Enjoyment*? You'll be in time as famous as Mr. CURLE.

F. 'Tis no matter. If I can't write myſelf, I can pay Thoſe that can, as well as he.

N. Ay and better too, if you've half an 100 l. a year.

F. But, ſuppoſe we try to make up the matter with theſe Scrubs? What think ye on't?

N. I think it certainly the beſt way; if we knew how to do it.

F. I'll go, and offer 'em Advertiſements.

N. 'Twill ſignify nothing. The Printers will inſert your Advertiſements; and the Authors will ridicule your Books.

F. They don't dare. The Bookſellers concerned in the Paper will turn 'em off, if they do.

N. Their Authors have done ſo, I am ſure, ſeveral times: and yet I don't find but the ſame perſons write in it now, who did at firſt.

F. 'Tis very ſtrange. The Writers I'm ſure in moſt other Papers are under a better regulation.

N. You ſeem to wonder at the boldneſs of the GRUBEANS. Why, they have banter'd the Books printed even for the Partners in that Paper; and in the very ſame Journal in which they have been advertiſed.

F. I wonder then, that any Bookſeller will advertiſe in the Paper.

N. You need not wonder at that. There are more printed of it than of any Daily Paper whatever; the number has riſen gradually from the very time of its firſt publication, whilſt that of ſome other Papers has ſunk; and it always goes into the hands of Theſe who are the beſt Cuſtomers for Books.

F. I'm ſure then we ought to advertiſe in it; let their Authors banter us as they will.

N. I think ſo too. — But then to be before-hand with 'em, I'll go to my Maſter HENLY. He'll maul 'em in the *Hyp-Doctor*.

F. The *Hyp-Doctor*! What will that ſignify? Hardly any body reads it; and thoſe few that do, don't underſtand it. Why 'tis nothing but mere Jargon. I can write better Engliſh myſelf.

N. No! ſure you can't. — He'll put 'em in his weekly Advertiſement in the *Daily Journal*; and then every body will ſee it.

F. Ay, That may do ſome good. For my Authors tell me, that he ſpends ſo much wit in the Advertiſements, that he has none left for the Paper itſelf. And I believe 'tis true.

B. I'll go to him then immediately.
F. And I to the Grub-street Printers.

DOMESTIC NEWS.

C. *Courant.*	EP. *Evening Post.*
P. *Post-Boy.*	SJ. *S. James's Evening Post.*
DP. *Daily Post.*	WE. *Whitehall Evening P.*
DJ. *Daily Journal.*	LE. *London Evening Post.*

THURSDAY, *March* 2.

On monday at Rotherhith a Sailor hang'd himself, *not born to be drown'd.*
Yesterday a man for stealing two cows was *put* into Newgate *pound.*
On Saffron Hill a Glazier, with liquor *brim full,*
Fell down one pair of stairs, and fractured his skull. *C.*

Yesterday being the anniversary of her Majesty's birthday, there was a more numerous and splendid appearance than has been known heretofore on that occasion, where upon her Majesty received the compliments from the several Nobility and Quality, who endeavoured to excel each other in richness of dress; and the evening was closed with a magnificent ball: and likewise, in honour of the day (being S. David's day, the titular Saint of Wales,) their Majesties, and all the Royal Family, wore the Leek. *C.* —— The suits made for this purpose were mostly of French silks. *LE.* ——— The Society of ancient Britons met at Christ-Church in Newgate street, and heard divine service, and a sermon preached by the Rev. Mr. Parry; after which they proceeded to Leathersellers-Hall, to dinner. *P.*

John Pollixfen, Esq; is made Surveyor General of all the roads on this side Tweed; a place worth 400 l. per ann. with the perquisites. *C. DJ.* — Last week Hutchinson Turck, Esq; was sworn into the office of Exiginter of the Common-Pleas, before the R Hon. the L. C. Justice Eyre, in the room of Francis Keyte Deighton, Esq; *DP.* —— *Mr* Brother N. Bailey *says it is* Exigenter; *which he explains.* One who makes out Exigents and Proclamations in Actions, in which process of outlawry lies.

On monday last, at the Sessions at Hick's-Hall, a French man was try'd for attempting to commit the detestable sin of Sodomy, on a young Gentleman, who by accident came into his company; the Jury brought him in guilty, and he was ordered to be sent to Bridewell to hard labour for a month. *DJ.* —— *This* Frenchman *pretended to teach* Italian.

Several Justices of the peace are under a terrible apprehension, fearing the qualification of Justices will be so high, as to strike all *Traders* out of the Commission. *SJ. WE. LE.* ——— *It can never exclude* all Traders *in* Justice.

Yesterday morning at 6, Will. Morice, Esq; &c. set out for Paris, to bring over the corpse of the R. Rev. Dr. Fran. Atterbury, &c. The said unfortunate Gentleman was taken with a fit of an Apoplexy, after he had eaten a hearty dinner, and died in a few hours. *DP.*

Saturday last, the R. Hon. the L. Visc. Cornbury, son and heir apparent to the R. Hon. the E. of Clarendon and Rochester, was unaminously elected by the University of Oxford, one of their Representatives in Parliament, in the place of the Hon. Will. Bromley, Esq; deceas'd. *LE.*

On tuesday died Miss South, the daughter of Mr. Humphrey South, an eminent West-India Merchant, &c. *DP.* —— On tuesday about 3 in the afternoon, died Mr. South, a very eminent Merchant in Billiter-lane, Leadenhall-street. *WE.*

We hear a young woman, about 30 years of age, very neat and clean dress'd, makes it her business, in company with a man, as a confederate, to go about the several parishes in the City and suburbs to hang herself, under pretence of great hardships she suffers by her husband's wasting her substance, in order to extort money from people who take pity on her; and on monday evening she was found hanging near Gravel-lane, in S. Saviour's, Southwark, another time at Hoxton, and another time at Westminster. *LE.* ——— *Many persons get a good livelihood by* hanging *others: but this is the first, who has done it by* hanging *herself.*

From Stamford *we hear,* that Mr. Anthony Drought,
Returning home from thence, his way *not finding out,*
Was unfortunately drown'd. From Lincoln they tell,
That a man drawing water fell into a **well.**
From James-Deeping in Lincolnshire, that *in tossing of a pot*
Two persons *try'd their strength,* 'till one died on the spot. *SJ.*

FRIDAY, *March* 3.

We hear that the duty on salt will commence from the 25th of March, 1732, and under the same Commissioners as before; and yesterday they met at their Office in York-Buildings, and took into their service several Clerks. *DP.*

Yesterday the R. Hon. the L. Visc. Weymouth was introduced into the House of Peers, and took the oaths and his seat accordingly. *DJ.*

The same day, by order of Council, part of 3 bars of iron, produced from Trissenden oar, at Mr. Wood's works near Chelsea road, in the presence of the Clerks of the Council, was manufactured into harrow tines, ship bolts, long nails, staples, and a hinge, and answered in the workmanship beyond expectation, especially as this iron was made out of oar, from which no iron could be produced in the ordinary way of making it, and was objected to by the opposers of Mr. Wood's project as an impossibility. *C.* —— *By this account,* Mr. Wood's posthumous iron *is like to succeed better in* England, *than his* living Copper *did in* Ireland.

On saturday last Will. Harris, servant to Mr. Tho. Plumsted, an eminent Ironmonger in Gracechurch-street, who went away last saturday se'nnight, with about 600 l of his Master's money, was taken at Ostend by a sailor, and secured there. *DJ.*

Mr. Palmer the Printer, who has been long ill of an Asthma, is not dead; and it's hoped will recover, and finish his History of Printing. *DP.*

Christned Males 190: Females 195: in all 385. Buried Males 196: Females 214: in all 410. Increased in the Burials this week 35. *P.*

SATURDAY, *March* 4.

Yesterday morning the Rev. Dr. Bland, Dean of Durham, preach'd before their Majesties, and the Royal Family, in the Chappel Royal at S. James's. *C.*

About 2 yesterday morning a fire broke out in Old-Bond street, S James's, in a large house belonging to the Lady Frederick, which in a short time burnt down the same to the ground; the wind being very high, the fire burnt with such excessive violence, that it was apprehended the most part of the street would have been consumed; but the wind happily changing from the north westward, the flames were suppressed. The fire was occasioned by an old Irish woman that was intrusted with the care of the house and furniture, the Family being out of Town. *DJ.*

We have received several letters from persons, desiring us to let the world know, that they are informed the Charity they sent to the poor sufferers at Blandford is not rightly apply'd; for their intention was to give it among the poorest sufferers, and not equally among the rich; and that no man (tho' with a large family) being now worth 2000 l. (or with a small family 1000 l.) should have one farthing, tho' his loss was ever so great; and if no family, (if now worth 500 l.) should not partake of the said Charity: for at the rate they are inform'd it is distributed, the rich are to be made richer, and the poor still poorer: therefore it is hoped all the sufferers will be examined upon oath, and if a Batchelor appears to have lost 200 l. and has 300 l. remaining, he should not have above 2 s. in the pound at most; and that man that had but 50 l. in the world, should have 40 l. if not the whole 50 l. and so in proportion. For if this excellent Charity, which has been so vigorously collected and contributed to, *even by the Clergy* as well as Laity, should not be rightly dispos'd of, it will be of very ill consequence, and prevent any attempts of the like nature for the future. *DP.* —— *I believe there was no occasion for the malicious* Italic *in this paragraph.*

Yesterday a Court of Honour, or High Court of Chivalry, was open'd in the Painted-Chamber, Westminster, in the following manner: About 12 o'clock, the Rt. Hon. the Earl of Effingham came into Court, preceded by the Proctors, Doctors of the Civil Law, and Officers of the Court, in their gowns; the Pursuivants and Heralds of Arms in their Tabaets and Collars, and Garter and Norroy Kings of Arms, and follow'd by the Lords hereafter mention'd, who assisted him upon this occasion, viz. the Dukes of Ancaster and Manchester; the Earls of Strafford, Warwick and Pomfret; the Lords Herbert, Haversham, Foley, Onslow, Howard and others. The Court being set, and proclamation made, the Duke of Norfolk's patent, constituting him Hereditary Earl Marshal of England, his Grace's nomination of the Earl of Effingham, his Deputy, and his Majesty's approbation of him, were severally read by the Register, and then the oaths of allegiance, abjuration, and oath of Office were administer'd to his Lordship: the patents of the several Officers of the Court were then read, and petitions of persons to be admitted Proctors, who were sworn accordingly, viz. Dr. Henchman, the King's Advocate; Mr. Mark Holman, Register; Mr. Sandford Nevill, the Earl Marshal's Proctor; and Mr. Greenley, Mr. Rawson, Mr. Smith, Mr. Farrant; Mr. Cook, Mr. Shelton, Proctors of the Court of Arches, to be Proctors of the said Court. The King's Advocate then exhibited a complaint against one Mrs. Radburne, Relict of one Mr. Radburne, Merchant, for using divers Ensigns of Honour not belonging to his condition, at the funeral of her said Husband; and likewise certain Arms both at the said funeral, and likewise since upon her Coach, not being intitled thereto in her own or Husband's right, and contrary to the law of Arms; whereupon his Lordship was pleased to grant a process, and to adjourn the Court to the Hall in the College of Arms on thursday the 30th instant. *DP.*

Last night her Grace the Dutchess of Bridgewater was safely deliver'd of a Daughter. *WE. LE.*

Marksbury in Somersetshire. A very melancholy accident has lately happened to this neighbourhood, viz. an hearse was hir'd to bring a corpse to be buried in our parish, and a great number of people (almost all our inhabitants, and many others) attended the funeral. But this very hearse (as it now appears) having just before carry'd a corpse that dy'd of the Small-pox, and burst in it, brought such an infection with it, as very few of the company escap'd. This distemper (so terrible to country people) broke out in above 40 families at once. *SJ.*

MONDAY, *March* 6.

Yesterday the R. Rev. the L. Bishop of Salisbury preach'd before their Majesties, his Royal Highness the Prince of Wales, &c. *C. P. DP.* — On friday Sir Hen. Penrice, Judge of the High Court of Admiralty, made his report to his Majesty in Council of John Ellis, who was convicted of Pyracy on the high seas at the Admiralty Sessions on monday last, and he was order'd for execution. *P.*

We hear that Mr. Thompson has intimated to the Committee of the Charitable Corporation, by letter, that he is willing to return home, and discover whatever he knows relating to the Company's affairs, protesting his own innocence, and declaring he is rather worse in his circumstances than better, by the said Company: and 'tis reported that his letter is the subject which Mr. Avery is gone over to treat with him upon. *C.*

On saturday night the wife of Mr. Salter, an eminent Surgeon in Bury-street, S. James's, being disorder'd in her senses, hang'd herself in a bed line, upon the bed-post. *DJ.*

TUESDAY, *March* 7.

We hear that the Banqueting-house at Whitehall will be fitted up for the safe keeping of the Cotton Library; and that a Royal Chappel will be built in the Privy Gardens, in lieu of that in the said building. *DP.*

On saturday last the R. Hon. the L. Hope arrived here from his travels beyond the seas. *P.*

Yesterday the 6 Malefactors were executed at Tyburn. *C.* &c. viz. Tho. Edwards and Tho. Past, for street-robberies; Tho. Smith and Tho. Faxton, for the highway; Geo. Brown, for returning from transportation; and Tho. Andrews for felony and burglary. *C. DP. Mar.* 6.

Bishop Atterbury died of the gout in his stomach. *P.*

On saturday died Miss Howard, Daughter of Sir Francis Howard, Bar. at her Brother-in-law's seat at Oxford. *P.*

On thursday the R. Hon. Ant. Visc. Montagu, was elected Grand Master of the ancient Society of Free and Accepted Masons, for the year ensuing, at the Devil Tavern in Fleet-street. *LE.* Viscount Montacute, a Roman Catholic Peer. *SJ.*

WEDNESDAY, *March* 8.

Yesterday a Board was held at the Admiralty-office, when the Dead Warrant was signed for executing this day John Ellis the Pirate, &c. *DP.* On monday next at Execution Dock. *P.*

On thursday next Richard Poole is to be put in the Pillory before Westminster-hall gate, pursuant to his sentence the last Sessions at Hicks's-Hall, in relation to the affair of summoning Col. Wingfield, to be upon the Jury for the tryal of Mr. Richard Francklin. *DP.*

From the PEGASUS *in Grub-street.*

The Representation of the Committee appointed to draw up an account of *Grubiana, or a Compleat Collection,* &c.

Tho' we have gone through no more than thirty pages of this Book; yet in obedience to your orders, we shall lay the result of our inquiries before you. In which we persuade ourselves, we have produced undeniable evidence of the truth of every particular of the unanimous Resolution, passed this day se'nnight; and have from that small part already examined, proved to a demonstration, that this Book is 'a scandalous, impudent, and abominable 'imposition upon the Public: 1. not containing half pretended to in the Title page: 2. most injudiciously collected; and 3. so incorrectly printed, as frequently to 'have several faults in a page, and sometimes two in 'a line.

I. Proofs of the first article.

It is declared in the Title page, to be a *Compleat Collection of all the Poems, and material Letters,* &c. but there is not in it even one of the First *Letters*; and only three of any length, which are taken from the first pages of our Journals. And it is so far from containing *all the Poems,* that in the compass of only the 30 pages now examined, which pretend to comprehend *all the Poems* in 37 Journals, the following are omitted.

1. A Latin Epigram of 6 verses, spoken to his Royal Highness the Duke, in Westminster-school: and a Translation of it in English, No. 20.

2. A Copy of 18 verses, in answer to an Epigram in No. 21. The former is in No. 27.

3. An Epitaph upon J. M. S. of 6 verses, N. 29.

4. An Epigram of 6 verses, in imitation of the six under Milton's picture, No. 33.

5. A Latin Epigram of 6 verses on his Royal Highness the Duke being present at the Hunting of the ram at Eaton school; and a Translation of it in English, No. 33.

If there are so many omissions in the first 30 pages; it is highly probable there are many more in the following.

II. Proofs of the second article.

The Collector has inserted 48 lines which are the beginning of Satire, called Blasphemy as old, &c. from Journal, No. 22. and 124 lines the beginning of another Satire, called an Essay on the Dunciad, from No. 24. both which were designed only to give a specimen of those two Pieces, and are of no use since they have been published. These are instances within the 30 first pages.

II. Proofs of the third article.

Page	
1. l. 7. for duller read dull.	20. l. 36. f. verdent r. verdant.
f. dull r. duller.	21. l. 12. f. passions r. passion.
uh. f. sawce r. source.	l. 20. f. Calebs r. Cælebs.
2. l. 12. f. fought r. sought.	22. l. 4. f. fulfil r. fulfill.
l. 27. Dele the.	l. 22. f. herolds r. Heralds.
4. l. 4. f. waggish r. Whiggish.	23. l. 4. f. mean r. means.
l. 12. f. laugh r. laugh'd.	l. 11. f. worth r. worth the.
l. 16. f. to r. too.	l. 20. f. Sherbone r. Sherborne.
l. 18. f. primers r. Primiers.	24. l. 10. your left out.
5. l. 2. f. lay r. lain.	25. l. 10. f. the dross. r. they dress.
l. 10. f. divorce thee r. me.	l. 11. f. recks r. rocks
l. 14. f. when by r. when thus by.	f. godesses r. Goddesses.
7. l. 3. Abbey left out.	26. l. 3. f. shoes string'd, who r. shoe-string'd SHORT, who.
l. 8. f. too r. two.	l. 7. f. liv'd and r. liv'd too short, and.
8. l. 12. f. Whoser. Whole.	l. 8. f. go far r. go so far.
l. 19. f. betray r. betray'd.	l. 9. f. rightly r. nightly.
9. l. 14. f. the r. thee.	l. 16. f. JOHN r. JOHN.
l. 17. f. on me r. on them.	l. 22. f. CHARTERS r. CHARTRES.
l. 23 f. Dawe r. Daw.	l. 30. f. author ask r. Author asks.
14. l. 8. f. so domy r. sodomy.	
15. l. 9. f. probaty r. probity.	27. l. 7. f. A r. As.
l. 31. f. roles r. rolls.	l. 16. f. princa'entry r. Prince's entry.
17. l. 15. f. the r. her.	
l. 32. f. the r. thee.	28 l. 13. f. delagate r. Delegate.
18. l. 3. f. peculary r. peculiar.	l. 22. f. deciples r. Disciples.
l. 25. f. repetia r. repetita.	
l. 28. f. pyritic r. pyratic.	29. l. 19. f. Dide ver r Did ever.
l. 32. f. streck'dr. stretch'd.	
l. 33. f. abhor'dr. abhorr'd.	
l. 37. f. those r. these.	
19. l. 12. f. Recal r. Recall.	
l. 26. f. veiw r. view.	

Instances of two faults in one line.

P. 1. l. 7. duller for dull, and dull for duller.

25. l. 10. the dross for they dress.

l. 11. recks for rocks, godesses for Goddesses

26. l. 3. shoes string'd, who for shoe-string'd SHORT, who.

l. 30. authors ask for Author asks.

This list of Errata consists of 60 in only 30 pages, without taking notice of false stops; small letters instead of Capitals in Proper names, want of Offices; and omissions of Italic, or some distinguishing character where proper; which we believe will amount to at least 60 more: of each of which we give only an instance. In p. 21 l. 8. gold; instead of gold, the last word in the Poem. P. 25. l. 23. room instead of Room an Undertaker. P. 29. l. 38. vice can instead of Vice Can. for Vice Chancellor.

But the most monitorous blunders are yet unmentioned. In p. 9. after An Epitaph, the next Copy has the title of Another; yet it is not an Epitaph, but an Epigram. In p. 2. after l. 6. a whole verse is left out. And in p. 25. after l. 19. four verses, which should conclude the next Poem on JOHN SHORT, ending p. 26. are added to conclude the Epigram on the Print in p 25. and so both Copies are made nonsense.

If the Erratas rise in the same proportion in the remaining part of the Book, the number instead of 400, as advertised by Mr. BAVIUS, will be increased to above 700. And yet these Proprietors of GRUBIANA, as they call themselves, have had the modesty to advertise it again in the Daily Journal yesterday, and in the Post-Boy to day, as beautifully and correctly printed; as complete, exact, and neat y printed; and to desire Gentlemen to all at Mr. Dormer's, to compare it with the Original Grub's. We have here performed this troublesome task them; and we hope they will excuse us for being so in exposing this outrageous imposture.——These Proprietors, who, we will not say have stolen, but borrowed our goods, tell the world in their Advertisements, that they defer answering the scandalous paragraphs in our last Journal, and our Advertisement, 'till they have an opportunity of reading our THREATENING Paper of thursday next. They do well to defer it 'till an oppor-

tunity which can never come. But their Advertisement-Cobler, did not express himself thus designedly: and therefore in his next let him avoid nonsense, if he can; and distinguish between a Paper threatening, and a Paper threatened: our threatening Paper was that of last thursday; and this, which may appear thursday next, being to morrow, is the Paper threatened in our last.

As a Warner look on me, my honest friend Dormer,
More just and sincere than Tim Birch the Reformer:
Still beware of nine Things: You'll remember the better;
They begin with the same, and yet with no letter:
Hemp, Halter, Hyp Doctor, and Henly haranging,
Hubbard, Hintone, and Hughes, High Holborn, and Hanging.

MÆVIUS.

Dublin, Feb. 26. On tuesday Sam. Cool, Esq; one of our late Sheriffs, was elected an Alderman, in the room of Alderman Berkey, deceased. C. P. Mar. 4.

Carlow, Feb. 26. On tuesday last, one Tho. Oliver, servant to Esq; Hamilton at this place, was coming from Dublin with a car laden with wine, sugar, &c. when he was overtaken by a man near Timolin, with whom he lay that night. The next morning about 10, he knocked Oliver down with a lathing hammer, and broke his scull, cut off his nose, and pulled out his eyes, stript off his breeches, and took from the car 2 bottles of wine, and a sugar loaf. Strict search is making after the inhuman murderer. P. Mar 6.

Edinburgh, Feb. 29. On the 24th died Col. Francis Chartres of Amsfield, Esq; in his 57th year; descended from an ancient and honourable family in this County. He married Mrs. Helen Swinton, Daughter of Sir Alexander Swinton, by whom he had one Daughter, married to the R. Hon. E. of Weems, to whose 2d Son he has left the bulk of his plentiful estate, and great portions to all the other children, with several legacies to friends and relations. C. P. D P.

FOREIGN NEWS.
THURSDAY, March 2.

Paris, Feb. 15. The King has granted M. Denis a patent for curing the Epilepsy, or Falling sickness, by a new method of his own invention, &c. C.

Vienna, Feb. 23. On wednesday arrived an express with advice, that Count Palfi, Palatine of Hungary, died some days ago. C.—— They write from Belgrade, that they have lately taken up several dead bodies at Rampieres, in the neighbourhood of that City; which, tho' buried a considerable while since, are found as fresh and full of blood, as if they were alive. D P.

This day arrived the Mails from France and Flanders.

Madrid, Feb. 19. The Duke de Ripperda not go to Tangier, as was reported, but is thought to be now at Smyrna or Constantinople. W E.

Versailles, Mar. 6. The 4th, Count Kinski, Ambassador extraordinary of the Emperor, had a private audience of the King, wherein he took leave of his Majesty. W E.

FRIDAY, March 3.

Paris, March 8. The 6th, Monsieur de Buffi Rabutin, Bishop of Luçon, was received into the French Academy, in the place vacant by the death of Monsieur de la Motte. ——They write from Madrid, that all the Troops that are to embarque, to the number of 21 battalions and and 21 squadrons, were already arrived in Catulonia. C. P.

Extract of a letter from Barcelona, Feb. 24. N. S.— The preparations for the army forming in this neighbourhood are carried on with the utmost diligence: the horse are to march to Carthagena; but the foot are to encamp near this city. D 7.

SATURDAY, March 4.

Paris, Feb. 25. N. S. M. Chinconneau, Physician of the Faculty of Montpelier, has the reversion of the Office of the first Physician to the King, with a Brevet de Retenue of 60,000 livres for his son.—— The library of the late M. Bouthlier de Chavigny, antient Bishop of Troyes, consisting of almost 18,000 volumes, is to be sold by auction. C.

MONDAY, March 6.

Gibraltar, Jan. 3. The Spanish line or wall before this place, from sea to sea, has been long finished; it is strongly glased, and covered to the top with earth and clay, so well secured, that all our shot could do them little or no harm: there are 2 large square fortifications at

each end, (and other works are designed for the center) that to the Bay will command the chief anchoring ground; the Old Mole will lie all open and exposed, even so far as the Water-gate. They have advanced their Centinels as far as the second tower; and will not suffer any from the Town to go near them by land or water: at present their number of workmen seem not lessened. We flattered ourselves the late services done to Spain, would have gained us some advantage.——Jan. 29. The Duke of Ripperda is at that Court [of Bubary] and was received by the Emperor, who offered him all he desire. D J.

TUESDAY, March 7.

Yesterday arrived one Mail from Holland.

Extract of a private letter from Russia. ... make it no longer a mystery here, ... of Prussia is to marry the Princess of ... sumptive Heir to the throne of Russia upon this expected condition, ... Elector of Brandenburg ... Prince William August ... will digest this article P

Books and Pamphlets published since our ...

Mar. 2. The Quack: or Merry Critic, &c. N. 1.

A Discourse of the nature of sudden deaths, &c. By Nic. Robinson, M D. Pr. 1 s. 6 d.

The Monthly Catalogue for January and February.

Morgan's Phoenix Britannicus, Numb. VI Pr. 2s. 6d.

The Clarendon Family vindicated, &c. Pr. 6 d.

Man and Woman: A Dissertation, &c. Pr. 6 d.

Literæ de re nummaria, &c. By Will. Smith, M. A.

A second plain and humble Address to the Clergy: A Sermon on 2 Cor. iii. 5. By Philanthropos.

The advantages proposed by repeating the sacramental Test, impartially considered. By Dr. Swift. Pr. 6 d

3. Liberty the support of Truth, and the natural property of Mankind. Pr. 1 s.

Interest at one view calculated to a farthing, &c. By Ric. Hayes.

4. The Proceedings at the Sessions at the Old Bailey, &c. Pr. 6 d.

On Tuesday Stocks were

South Sea Stock 97 7 8ths, to 98. South Sea Annuity 109 3 qrs. to 7 8ths. Bank 149 3 qrs. Books shut. New Bank Circulation 6 l. 17 s. 6 d. Premium. India 177, 176. Three per Cent. Annuity 96 1 half, to 3 qrs. New 3 per Cent. Annuity 96. Royal Exchange Assurance 99. London Assurance 13 3 8ths, to 1 half. York Buildings 7 1 qr. African 44. English Copper 2 l. 10 s. Welch ditto 1 l. 18 s. South Sea Bonds 2 l. 2 s. Prem. India ditto 5 l. 8 s. ditto. Blanks 7 l. 5 s. 6 d. 20 l. Prizes 19 l. 8 s. 6 d.

Next Week will be published,

In One Volume in Quarto,

THE Genuine Works in VERSE and PROSE, of the Right Hon GEORGE GRANVILLE, Lord LANSDOWNE. Printed for J. Tonson and L. Gilliver.

Just published,

Dedicated to the Gentlemen of the Navy of England.

THE MEMOIRS of Monsieur *du Gué Trouin*, Chief of a Squadron of the Royal Navy of France, and Great Cross of the Military Order of S. Lewis; containing all his Sea-Actions with the English, Dutch, and Portuguese, in the late Wars of King William and Queen Anne.

Translated from the French by a *Sea-Officer*.

Printed for J. Batley, at the Dove, in Pater-noster Row, Where may be had,

The TRADITIONS of the CLERGY no way Destructive of Religion: A Sermon preach'd at Bingley-Church, on Sunday September 12th, 1731.

By IS. SMITH,

Minister of Haworth, near Kighley, Yorkshire.

ALSO,

I. The Religion of Nature considered. To which is added a Postscript, containing Reflections on Mr. Chubb's Discourse concerning Reason, &c. so far as it respects this Subject.

II. Some Thoughts concerning Virtue and Happiness, in a Letter to a Clergyman.

On Saturday last was publish'd,

Price 6 d.

THE GENTLEMAN's MAGAZINE: Or, *Monthly Intelligencer*.

No. XIV. for February, being the 2d of Vol. II.

Containing, among other Heads, Arguments for and against a Standing Army; the Tax on Salt, Soap and Candles; Leather, Land and Windows; Proposals for a more equal and easier Tax to all People, and for abolishing a great many of the present burthensome Duties. Of the Pension Bill, Corruption and Independency of Parliament; of Distillers and Farmers; Parties changing Principles; 30th of January Sermons, &c. with Domestick Occurrences.

And next Week will be publish'd the Second Edition of No. X. for October,

The first Impression being near sold off, on Account of several agreeable Pieces both in Prose and Verse, sent by unknown Correspondents, particularly a Copy of the Will of *Samuel Travers*, Esq; which was inserted entire with the Letter prefixed. Another Correspondent was pleased to give the Author a seasonable Hint (which was observed) in the following exceeding Complaisant Epistle,

To Mr. *Sylvanus Urban*.

SIR,

THE *Gentleman's Magazine* is, perhaps, one of the most useful Things of the Kind that has been at any Time set on Foot; but this Usefulness must in Justice and Gratitude be attributed to your unbyass'd Impartiality and Industry: It serves me, and to my Knowledge several others, for what your Title truly expresses it, that is, a *Magazine* or Repository of every Thing worthy remarking, and for this Reason will be many Years hence, an Authentick Collection for Historians to refer to, when Disputes shall arise on the Manner and Spirit with which the present Controversies are carried on, the Force of their Arguments on both Sides being fully retain'd; besides many Historical Occurrences may be here found, which, tho' they escape the Notice of great and voluminous Historians, will serve to explain and clear up the Truth of several Facts which in Time may appear doubtful; and the Reasons and Origin of some Transactions will be here found, which might otherwise be sought after in vain.

When I have promised this, I can't help thinking but that you will excuse me for taking Notice of a Slip which you made in July last, in Respect to Gibraltar; and I am sure it was no other than Inadvertency and Slip, for your whole Design shows you mean no Wrong to any Party. The Piece I mean was published in one of the Daily Papers, and the Reason why, as I take it, you did not recite it was, that by Eleven a-Clock the Morning of Publication it was all sold off, and I gave myself a Shilling for one on Tuesday Morning following, however you may easily see it in some Coffee-houses, and when you have so done, I am very sure you will lay the Materials of it up in your Magazine; for it is not a Temporary Thing, and therefore not worn out by the Date, but will be as satisfactory now as on the Day of Publication. I conclude, Sir, with my harty Thanks to you for the Benefit and Pleasure I receive from your Studies, and am your Friend and Servant, tho' unknown,

Octob. 14, 1731. L. J.

Printed at St. John's Gate, and sold by F. Jeffries in Ludgate-street; A. Dodd, near Temple-bar; E. Nutt, &c. at the Royal-Exchange; where may be had compleat Setts; also an exact LIST of Parliament.

This Day is published,

With a curious Frontispiece by Mr. BICKHAM,

And at the End of the Book is prefixed, a fine Satyrical Picture, which needs no Key to explain it.

A SCHEME for a NEW LOTTERY: Or, A HUSBAND and COACH and SIX for Forty Shillings. Being very advantageous to both Sexes; where a Man may have a Coach and Six, and a Wife for nothing.

Here's a Whim-Wham newly come over,
And who will prick at my Lottery Book?

With a SCHEME to prevent the Downfal of the Charitable Corporation. By an old Sportsman.

In Female Service worn to Skin and Bone,
Fulfils the Proverb, to the World well known,
And yet to shew them I ne'er spare my Pains,
But freely do bequeath my future Gains,
Among the wanton Part o'th' Female Sex,
Take this last Legacy, and others vex.

To which is prefixed,

The Author's Picture, drawn to the Life; being fit to be hung in the Lodgings of all Ladies of Pleasure, as a *Memento Mori*, with the following Lines under it:

Like an old Soldier, worn out in Campaigns,
Who's serv'd his Country many diff'rent Reigns,
When Wars are ended, homewards he returns,
And sheaths his Sword, tho' with Ambition burns
For fresh Alarms; but when the Trumpet calls,
Finds his Decay, and on his Back he falls.

With a Recommendatory Poem, in Favour of the said Lottery, to encourage Maids, Widows, single Women, Batchelors and Widowers to put in. Also a Scheme where Ladies may divert themselves before the Time of Drawing. And likewise a View of the Town, by the HIGHGATE SPY, taken thro' a Glass of the Projector's own making, and hopes it will be approv'd by the R---l S----y, in which you may see those who can't see themselves: With an Account of what Persons of both Sexes are excluded the Advantage of putting into the said Lottery. And also the Author's Conclusion on Pawnbrokers, and the Difference between them and the Charitable Corporation.

Printed for T. DORMER at the Star and Garter, over against the Castle Tavern in Fleet-street, and sold at the Pamphlet-shops; price 1 s. 6 d.

Where may be had, The Second Edition, of

The UNHAPPY LOVERS: Or, The Tragical History of *James Welsted*, Gent. price 1 s.

This Day is published,

AN Enquiry into the Origin of HONOUR, and the Usefulness of Christianity in WAR.

By the Author of the *Fable of the Bees*.

Price bound 3 s. 6 d.

Printed for J. Brotherton at the Bible, next the Fleece Tavern in Cornhill.

WHEREAS other *Coffee-Houses*, and other *Publick Houses*, take of their Customers 8 s. for a Quart of Arrack, and 6 s. for a Quart of Rum or Brandy made into *Punch*, so that it is now become the settled Price thoughout the Town, and seldom less than a Bowl of 1 s. 6 d. is to be had: Therefore, for the better accommodating all Gentlemen, that are Lovers of *Punch*,

This is to give Notice,

That I have opened on Ludgate-hill, the *London-Coffee-House* and *Punch House*, (Two *Punch-Bowls* on Iron Pedestals before my Door,)

Where the finest and best old Batavia Arrack, Jamaica Rum, and French Brandy, are made into *Punch*, with the finest Ingredients, viz.

A Quart of Arrack made into *Punch* for 6 s. and so in Proportion to the smallest quantity, which is half a Quartern for four Pence Half-penny.

A Quart of Rum or Brandy made into *Punch* for 4 s. and so in Proportion to the smallest Quantity, which is half a Quartern for 3 d. And Gentlemen may have it as soon made, as a Gill of Wine can be drawn; with the best of Eating, Attendance, and Accommodation.

This Undertaking has occasion'd many, whose *Interest* it is to possess Gentlemen with such an Opinion, that the Liquors by me used are not good: The Publick is hereby assured, that I buy my Goods on the Keys, and at the best Hand, with Ready Money, and am at this Time provided with as well-chosen Brandies, Rum and Arrack, as any in Town, and will at all times procure the best that is imported: But what may convince Gentlemen of the Truth hereof, is, (not only by the Encouragement I meet with) that the Sherbet is always brought by itself, and the Brandy, Rum, or Arrack in the Measure, so there can be no Imposition, either in Quantity or Quality; for the Proof whereof I appeal to all Gentlemen who have done me the Honour to call at my House.

James Ashley.

Publick Notice is hereby given,

[*For the Information of all* GENTLEMEN *and* LADIES]

THAT *Charles Lyon, Grecian*, Maker of the JERUSALEM WASHBALLS, otherwise called GRECIAN WASHBALLS, so universally esteem'd by all the Quality, who, for many Years, have made use of no other, being removed from Ironmonger-Lane, where he had carried on his Business about 40 years, *to the House of Edward Hubbard*, over against Serjeant's-Inn, Chancery-Lane, where they may at any Time be furnished therewith, by sending a Letter to the said *Edward Hubbard*, who has, for ten Years past, assisted Mr. *Lyon* in making them, being the only Person intrusted with the true Method of preparing them, and to whom alone the Receipt will be communicated upon the Decease of the said Mr. *Lyon*.

N. B. At the following Places is sold an incomparable Tooth-Powder, which makes the Teeth as white as Ivory, and preserves them from Rotting or Decaying. It effectually cures the Scurvy in the Gums. Price one Shilling each Box.

Also a delicate Lip-Salve, that cures any rough and chopp'd Lips, and makes them of a fine lively red. Price one Shilling each Pot, viz. Cocoa-Tree Chocolate-House, Pall-Mall; Will's Coffee-House, Scotland-Yard, Charing-Cross; Guildhall Coffee-House, by Guildhall; Sword-Blade Coffee-House, Birchin-Lane; and the East-India Coffee-House, Leadenhall-Street.

This Day is published,

In Four Volumes, Twelves,

And sold by N. PREVOST, opposite to Southampton-Street in the Strand,

THE Life of Mr. CLEVELAND, natural Son of OLIVER CROMWELL. Written by himself. Giving a particular Account of his Unhappiness in Love, Marriage, Friendship, &c. and his great Sufferings in *Europe* and *America*. Together with the secret AMOURS of the PROTECTOR, and his unnatural Usage to his illegitimate Children. The whole intermix'd with Reflexions, describing the Heart of Man, in all its Variety of Passions and Disguises.

N. B. The 3d and 4th Vol. may be had separate.

This Day is published,

A Collection of PIECES in VERSE and PROSE, which have been published on occasion of the *Dunciad*. Dedicated to the Right Honourable the Earl of Middlesex. By Mr. Savage.

Likewise,

ATHELWOLD: A Tragedy. By A. Hill, Esq; as it is acted at the Theatre Royal in Drury-Lane.

2. OF FALSE TASTE; an Epistle to the Right Honourable Richard Earl of Burlington. By Mr. POPE. The 3d Edition, with an additional Letter.

Printed for Lawton Gilliver, at Homer's Head, against St. Dunstan's Church, Fleet-street.

This is to give Notice

To all Shopkeepers and Others,

THAT at the Printing-House in Bow Church Yard, Cheapside, London, all manner of Business in Printing, either at the Letter-Press or Rolling-press, continues to be carried on by THOMAS COBB, who married the Widow of the late Mr. JOHN CLUER, who kept the said Printing-House

Where Shopkeepers Bills, and Bills of Parcels are curiously engraved on Copper: Also Marks for Tobacconists, Haberdashers of Hats, &c. are engraved on Wood or Copper.

Labels for Surgeons Chests, Apothecaries, Grocers, &c. may be had there, painted or plain.

Also Blank Receipts for Taxes, &c. Titles for Hungary-Water, Directions for Daffey's Elixir, and Spirits of Scurvey-Grass.

Likewise Club-Orders and Funeral Tickets.

All Sorts of Pictures painted or plain, Lottery Pictures for Children, Copy-Book Covers, and a new Round-Hand Copy-Book with the Copies set on the Top of every Leaf for Learners to write underneath.

*** At the abovesaid Printing-Office may be had all Sorts of Paper for Writing Musick, sold cheaper than at any other Place.

Likewise Mr. Handel's Opera's, and many other Books of Musick, are there Engraved, Printed and Sold.

N. B. The Wholesale and Retale Warehouse for Dispensing Dr. Bateman's Pectoral Drops, by Letters Patent under the Great Seal of Great Britain, is still continued to be kept there.

Note also, That for those Persons who employ the said THOMAS COBB's Rolling-Press, he repairs their Copper-Plates, when necessary, gratis.

LONDON: Printed by S. PALMER and J. HUGGONSON, in *Bartholomew-Close*, for Captain GULLIVER, near the *Temple*, where Letters and Advertisements are taken in; As also at the *Rainbow Coffee-House* in *Cornhill*, and *John's Coffee-House* in *Sheer-Lane*, near *Temple-Bar*. [Price Two Pence.]

The Grub-ſtreet Journal.

NUMB. 115

Thurſday, *MARCH* 16, 1731.

Long labour'd RICH, *by Tragic verſe to gain*
The Town's applauſe---but labour'd long in vain.

Harlequin Horace, p. 30.

Feb. 26.

For Mr. BAVIUS, Secretary of the Grub-ſtreet Society.

SIR,

THE cacoethes of ſcribbling (if I may ſo call it) is ſo epidemical, that every one almoſt that can write his name, will turn Author. Hence ariſe the WALSINGHAM's and HYP-DOCTOR's in Politicks, the B——NS's and K—B--R's in Dramaticks, and the innumerable fry of ſmart Writers in the daily and weekly Papers. —— I can't but own I've found this malady growing on me ſometimes; but as I neither think myſelf dull enough for a Politician, nor pert enough for a Dramatick; the only way I can imagine to give me eaſe, is to endeavour, whenever the fit grows ſtrong, to carry it off by a letter to Mr. BAVIUS: nor can I doubt his admitting me a Correſpondent, which may put a ſtop to a diſeaſe that in time might prove incurable.

What at preſent has cauſed this itch of ſcribbling, is the obſervation I've made on a letter in your laſt *Journal*, Numb. 112, ſigned DRAMATICUS, and one in laſt ſaturday's *Daily Courant*, under the name of TAG-RHIME, that variouſly cenſure the Managers of either Theatre. DRAMATICUS, without any aſperſions on perſons, complains of the hardſhips an Author lies under, who even attempts to bring a Play on one ſtage: while Mr. TAG-RHIME very politely attacks the Manager of the other with all the rhetoric of Billingſgate. I have had an occaſion to obſerve what ſort of reception they both gave an Author; but beſides that, what I can infer from both letters is, that the Maſter of the New Houſe is moſt abuſed, but that the Managers of the Old deſerve it moſt. I have laid it down to myſelf for a general truth, That where there is moſt ſcurrility, there is the leaſt reaſon for it: this I take to be Mr. TAG-RHIME's caſe; who not knowing of what to accuſe the Maſter of the New Houſe in particular, retorts on him the accuſation of the Managers of the Old. But how ill it's ſuited to the Man, I ſhall make ſome obſervations from his own polite letter.

'About ſeven or eight years ago, he ſays, moſt 'of the dramatick Writers took it into their heads to 'be very angry with the Managers of the old Play-'houſe, whether with reaſons, or not, he can't ſay; but 'they accuſed them of avarice inſolence, and ſtupidity.' Tho' this Gentleman *can't ſay*, the dramatick Writers were uſed ill; yet he would inſinuate, they were not. If they were not, it is ſtrange Authors ſhould leave a ſett of Players, to whom themſelves and the Town had been ſo long bigotted, for a Company which then lay under not a little diſcouragement; nothing I think could induce them to this, but the ill treatment they met with from the Managers. But why ſhould I dwell on that of which every one knows the truth? Have not Plays, refuſed at the Old Houſe with contempt, and, I may venture to ſay, ill manners, been received at the New with that good nature, which gained the approbation of every one that made application to the Maſter? Should it be ſaid, that the Plays ſo rejected, were deſervedly rejected; I appeal only to the favourable reception they met with from the Town; which (with great deference to the judgment of the ingenious Mr. A—B—R, and the ceremonious Mr. W—KS) I think ought to be the beſt, and indeed the only judge, in all dramatick performances.

But he goes on, "When the Maſter of the New Houſe 'by theſe arts [ſome of which, he ſays, were to ſooth 'and flatter dramatic Writers] and the concurrence of 'ſome accidents, thought he had fully gained his point, 'and eſtabliſhed himſelf upon the Town; (where by the way he owns, that affability to the Poets was not a 'little recommendation) how did he behave? he put on 'the pride of a Grand Viſier, with the breeding of a 'Bum Baily'. Falſe reflection! no one would have imagined the accuſation of pride ſhould ever have been charged on Mr. R——, which has been ſo juſtly attributed by all to C—B—R; and if he is leſs ceremonious than the well-bred Mr. W—KS, it is becauſe he has more good nature.

'Did the Poets reſent the alterations made in their 'works by one who had good pretenſions to wit and 'taſte? they muſt now ſubmit to ſee 'em mangled by a 'Tumbler that can't ſpell.' This Gentleman of *wit and taſte* is that judicious and harmonious ſing-ſong writer Mr. C--LL--Y C--B--R, whoſe *Odes* are a demonſtrative proof of his wit, as his reception and eſpouſing *the Modiſh Couple* will be of his taſte. And I can think it not the leaſt reflection on any man, that he has not ſuch *wit*, and ſuch a *taſte*. As to the *mangling* of dramatick pieces charged on Mr. R——, I believe it's the firſt time the world ever heard of this accuſation, tho' they have long ſince been made ſenſible that every dramatick piece that appears at the Old Houſe, muſt have firſt paſſed the ordeal trial of the Managers; and ſuch often bear ſo little reſemblance of the original off-ſpring of the Poet, that he miſtakes it for ſome baſtard foiſted on him by the Managers.

But Mr. TAG-RHIME ſums up all Mr. R——'s male qualifications. 'In ſhort, the vanity complained of in 'W--KS, the pertneſs charged upon C——R, &c. are 'united in one ſingle little fellow, without the leaſt mix-'ture of the good qualities which the others had to atone '*for them.*' I own with Mr. TAG-RHIME, the Maſter of the New Houſe wants the good qualities, i. e. the *ceremony*, the *wit* and *taſte* of the Managers of the Old; but I affirm at the ſame time, he wants alſo the *vanity* of W——, and the *pertneſs* of a C--B--R.

This accuſation of the Maſter of the New Theatre, it ſeems, is ſo far from being ſecret hiſtory, 'that it is 'ſcarcely news; all the world knows it, the Poets have 'found their error, and repent it.' But if I'm not very much miſtaken, all Mr. TAG-RHIME's *world* is confin'd to Dr—y L—e Theatre, whoſe Managers would fain perſwade themſelves into the truth of every particular of Mr. R——: they are like a ſett of men, who tell things, not as the fact is, but as they would have it be.

That the Poets 'have met with ill uſage of various kinds 'at the New Houſe,' Mr. TAG RHIME has not made appear; tho' he ſays he could mention ſeveral inſtances. In his own caſe he does not ſay he was uſed ill; and if he was not uſed well, yet by his own confeſſion, he was not uſed better at the Old. I'm ſorry Mr. TAG-RHIME is ſo inconſiderate to mention again in this paragraph the *altering* and *amending* Plays, 'till they are *completely ſpoiled* at the New Houſe, when it has been ſo notoriouſly practiſed by that profound judge of *wit* and *taſte*, the refined Mr. Co--L--Y C--BB--R.

Was it not improper in this place, and would take up too much of your Paper, I believe I could let the Town into the knowledge, who Mr. TAG RHIME is: and notwithſtanding his letter proceeds neither from ſpleen, nor friendſhip, I could ſhew he has too great an *Intereſt* at Drury-lane for the Town to believe him.

I have took no notice of a third Manager at the Old Houſe, as I thought it would be ungenerous to attack a Gentleman under his misfortune; and who for a long time has been excluded from the management, and been even uſed ill both by his well-bred, and his ingenious brother-partners.

If I've aſſerted any falſity, I don't doubt, Sir, but you'll give Mr. TAG-RHIME an opportunity of juſtifying his letter, and be equally impartial to him, and

Mar. 1, 1731. Your humble ſervant,

PROSAICUS.

We are deſired to publiſh the following Epiſtle to DRAMATICUS, in order to clear up his Doubts about the true meaning of the word *Theatrical*, &c. and put him out of his pain.

To DRAMATICUS.

SIR,

I Conceive that the Epithet *Theatrical* apply'd to Plays, *in itſelf*, means *nothing*. But Mr. *W*. applies that word to the Pieces of theſe Authors, who have the knack of wriggling themſelves into his good graces; by what means I will readily communicate to you, or any other Brother of the Bathos in private, provided he will let me go ſnacks with him in the profits of his third night. Having written at leaſt twenty *theatrical* Pieces (tho' neither *ſenſible* nor *pretty*) which have ſucceeded by this very rule, and no other, I think, without the imputation of arrogance or vanity, I may ſafely pronounce it infallible.

C—-J——n.

Mr. DACTYL upon the reading of this letter obſerved, that tho' this might be the real meaning of the word *Theatrical* at the bottom, yet there was another, which to him ſeemed probable at leaſt. He imagined, that a Play might be ſaid to be *Theatrical*, when the characters in it were adapted to thoſe Parts in which the Actors might ſhine moſt. For inſtance, thoſe of a Beau, a Coxcomb, a Cuckold, or a Villain; of a Coquet, a Jilt, a Whore, or an Adultereſs. Beſides, as Actors are ſometimes Dramatic Authors themſelves, a Writer ſhould obſerve in what manner they deliver their own Comic jokes, or Tragic fuſtian; and endeavour to ſute the different ſneers, grimaces, rants, and poſtures, which he has obſerved to be moſt ſucceſsful. This, with the two former, he thought, took in *Theatricality* in its utmoſt extent.

Having given in our 109th Journal only the initial letters of the names of the Witneſſes againſt King CHARLES I, as they are modeſtly recorded in *Ruſhworth*, we ſhall now give them at full length, from the additional 7th Vol. to LORD CLARENDON's *Hiſtory*; that theſe worthy perſons, as good Gentlemen as many of the King's Judges, may not loſe any part of the glory due to them, for having joined with thoſe noble Patriots in the accompliſhment of ſo unparallelled an Action.

William Cuthbert.		David Evans.	
John Bennet.		Diogenes Edwards.	
William Brayne.		Giles Gryce.	20
Henry Hartford.		John Vinſon.	
Robert Lacy.	5	George Seely.	
Edward Roberts.		John More.	
Robert Loads.		Thomas Ives.	
Samuel Morgan.		Thomas Rawlins.	25
James Williams.		Thomas Read.	
John Pyneger.	10	James Croſby.	
Samuel Lawſon.		Samuel Burden.	
Arthur Young.		Michael Potts.	
Thomas Whittington		George Cornwal.	30
John Thomas.		Henry Gooche.	
Richard Blomfield.	15	Robert Williams.	
William Jones.		Richard Price.	
Humphry Browne.		Thomas Challoner.	

Mr. BAVIUS,

AS I was going up Chancery-lane t'other day, I ſaw at a diſtance before me, a coal cart unloading at one of the new houſes. The Carman had ſo placed his cart againſt the poſts, and ſome of his ſacks upon the pavement, that there was no paſſing without going beyond the middle of the ſtreet, and over the channel. Juſt as I came up, a very little Gentleman (who, I am ſure, is the ſame you mention in your Journal of the 24th of Feb. Numb. 112. on occaſion of his throwing for Oranges at a wheelbarrow, in his band and bar Gown) had finiſh'd his diſpute with the obſtinate Carman, who refuſed to make him way: whereby he was forc'd to go croſs the channel, and back through the dirt to come again upon the pavement. The little Gentleman's anger encreaſed, and ſeeing me juſt by him, deſired to borrow my cane; which I innocently, and little dreaming of the ill conſequence, immediately lent him. He received it very graciouſly, acknowledging my extreme kindneſs as a ſtranger; and, to my very great ſurprize, inſtantly ſet about belabouring the poor Carman, and gave him ſeveral ſmart blows. The Carman, tho' a very ſtout, ſturdy fellow, received the blows mildly, calmly, and gravely; and without any emotion of paſſion at all, not giving ſo much as an angry word or look, ſeized the little Gentleman by the collar with one hand, and held him ſo faſt againſt the rails, that he could not ſtir one jot; and having him fixed there with one hand, he with the other unbuttoned his breeches, pulled out his urine pipe, and piſſed in the little Gentleman's face, and all over his cloaths, turning the ſtream of his water as it paſt through his hand engine, firſt to one part, then to another, and ſo on, 'till he had thrown it all over the little Gentleman's face, hat, wig, collar, boſom, cloaths and ſtockings, and into his ſhoes: in ſhort, the Carman happened to be ſo very piſs-proud, that he made the poor little Gentleman in as bad a condition, as if he had drawn him through a pond; and when he had quite done piſſing on him, very quietly buttoned up his breeches, and diſmiſſed him with a contemptuous ſmile.

The little Gentleman went away ſeemingly ſorrowful, and whether the tears or urine were trickling down his face, I could not dinſtinguiſh; but he angrily threw

down my cane in the dirt, which the honeſt Carman ſnatched up and wiped, and returned me with a great deal of civility.

The little Gentleman went into a Coffee houſe, I did not care then to follow him in; but the next day I went in there to enquire the news of the houſe, and was told, that he there met one or two of his moſt intimate acquaintance, who enquiring of him the occaſion of his being in that ſad condition, he very pleaſantly told 'em, he had been held under an attachment of contempt, from which he was juſt then diſcharged. I am yours, &c.

Mar. 11, 1731. PHILOLUDICRI.

DOMESTIC NEWS.

C. *Courant.*	E P. *Evening Poſt.*
P. *Poſt-Boy.*	S J. *S. James's Evening Poſt.*
D P. *Daily Poſt.*	WE. *Whitehall Evening P.*
D J. *Daily Journal.*	L E. *London Evening Poſt.*

Hypochondriacal Puffs in January.

We have credible accounts from the Lord D — 's, that the Hyp-Doctor, &c. *D J. Jan.* 3. —— We hear from the Eaſt India Coffee-houſe in Cornhill, that Sir Iſaac the Hyp-Doctor, &c. *D J. Jan* 10. —— We hear from Capt. Ratcliff, that he has on board Sir Iſaac the Great Hyp Doctor, &c. *D J. Jan.* 17. —— We hear, that the Rev. Mr. Henley, &c. *D J. Jan.* 21. —— We hear, that at the Oratory next ſunday, &c. *D J. Jan.* 28. — We hear from Geo. Bickham, &c. that the Hyp-Doctor, &c. *D J. Jan.* 31. —— *Upon reading this, Mr.* Conundrum *declared, that for the future, inſtead of* Mr. Orator Henley, *he ſhould always ſay* Mr. Auditor Henley.

THURSDAY, *March* 9.

Yeſterday the Rev. Dr. Waterland preached before her Majeſty, his Royal Highneſs the Duke, and the 5 Princeſſes. *C.* —— We hear the Princeſs Royal is to accompany his Majeſty to Hanover. *D P.*

The latter end of laſt week died Walter Williams, Eſq; of the County of Caermarthen, a Gent. of a ſingular good character, and 600 l. per ann. *C.* —— A few days ſince died at his ſeat in North-Wales, Morgan Griffith, Eſq; a Gent. of a plentiful eſtate. *S J. WE.* —— On tueſday died of the Small-pox, at his lodgings in King-ſtreet, by Covent-garden, John Powel, Eſq; of Pennybank in Carmarthenſhire. *P.* —— The laſt week *was particularly fatal to the* Gentlemen of Wales.

On monday died Mrs. Herriman in S. Martin's Le Grand, about 115 years old. *P.*

They write from Biſceter in Oxfordſhire, that one Aldworth, who held 30 l. a year during the life of one Carpenter, which was his only ſupport, happening to quarrel with Carpenter, and called him Cuckold, which ſo enraged him, that he ſolemnly vow'd revenge; and laſt friday evening he drowned himſelf, to deprive the other of his annuity. *D P.* —— *And at the ſame time, I ſuppoſe, to get rid of his Wife.*

On ſunday night the corpſe of the late Dutcheſs of Monmouth and Buccleugh was interred with great funeral pomp at Dalkeith, &c. *L E.* —— *Edinburgh, Mar.* 3. Was privately interred laſt wedneſday night. *C.* &c. *Mar.* 11. —— With ſeveral hundreds of flambeaux, and the funeral ſervice was according to the rites of the Church of England. *C. P.*

This day the Dead Warrant came to Newgate for the execution of John Ellis, the Pyrate, at Execution Dock to morrow. *S J.* He will be carried from Newgate about 11. *WE.* On monday next. *L E.* —— This day John Ellis is appointed to be hanged at Execution Dock. *C. Mar.* 10. We hear that yeſterday a Reprieve was ſent to the Admiralty Office. *P. Mar.* 10. Thurſday night, about 10, a Reprieve came down to Newgate. *C. Mar.* 11. —Yeſterday a pardon was ſigned. *P. Mar.* 11. —— He was on ſaturday diſcharged out of Newgate. *P. Mar.* 13. *S J. WE. Mar.* 14. —— He is cloſely confined in one of the cells; and reprieved during his Majeſty's pleaſure. *C. Mar.* 15.

Miſs Cotton, and Miſs Hare, indiſpos'd, can't go out.
At Kenſington a Biſhop lies ill of the gout. *P.*

FRIDAY, *March* 10.

On wedneſday the R. Hon. the L. Hope, ſon to the E. of Hoptoun, lately arrived from his travels, was introduced to their Majeſties, and was moſt graciouſly received. *C.*

We hear that Mr. Robinſon and Mr. Thompſon are required to ſurrender themſelves in Great Britain in a month's time. *D P.*

This week the ſale of Teas in private trade belonging to the India Company began at their houſe in Leadenhall-ſtreet, and were ſold, their Congo from 12 s. to 16 s. per pound; and the Hyſſon from 22 s. to 28 s. per pound; beſides the inland duty of 4 s. per pound. *C. D P.*

On Wedneſday Mr. Stagg, an eminent Attorney at law, was elected Veſtry Clerk for S. Giles's Cripplegate. *C.*

Letters from Cambridge ſay, that the Rev. Dr. Davies, Maſter of Queen's College, Rector of Fen Ditton, and one of the Prebendaries of Ely, died there on monday laſt. *D P.*

Chriſtned, Males 199: Females 178: in all 377. *Buried*, Males 226: Females 220: in all 446. Increaſed in the burials this week, 36. *P.*

To Newgate yeſterday a fair Drury-lane Maid,
For picking a pocket, was decently convey'd. *D J.*

SATURDAY, *March* 11.

Yeſterday the Rev. Dr. Gilbert, Dean of Exeter, preached before her Majeſty and the 5 Princeſſes. *C.*

The ſame day one Jam. Thompſon having in his examination before the Committee of the Hon. Houſe of Commons for enquiring into the affairs of the Charitable Corporation, prevaricated in a groſs manner, was committed cloſe priſoner to Newgate. *D P.* — — *My Brother* S J. *archly obſerves, that* by the means and aſſiſtance of Dr. Mowbray, the famous Man-Midwife, he was *ſafely delivered* in Newgate.

The Rev. Mr. Williams of Trentham, who had been for many years Curate of Sandbatch, in the County of Cheſter, is preſented to the Rectory of Aſhbury in that neighbourhood, worth upwards of 600 l. per ann. *D P.*

We hear from Birmingham, that one Tho. Orton had a large leg cut off there lately of the moſt monſtrous ſize and form that ever was ſeen or heard of; it weighed 26 lb. and a half, and meaſured round the ſmall of the leg 3 quarters of a yard; there was only one large toe, which was ten inches and a half round: he never had any uſe of the leg, but always dragged it after him. The man, we hear, is perfectly well. *D P.*

Yeſterday was heard, at the bar of the Houſe of Lords, the Cauſe between John Wynne, Gent. Appellant, and Sir Geo. Wynne, Bar. Reſpondent, relating to an eſtate and mine in Flintſhire; and it being a family cauſe between Father and Son, their Lordſhips referred them to agree, which they did; Sir Geo. agreeing to allow his Son 1200 l. in money, and 400 l. per ann. during his life. *P.*

On thurſday died Counſellor Bugehill, in Norfolk-ſtreet in the Strand. *P. S J. WE.* Budgen. *L E.*

Tho' my Adverſaries ſay, I am but a Farce-Actor,
With my front I do engage to confront any detractor,
With Diſcourſe or Diputation, *in Divinity, or Hiſtory,*
Or any ſubject within the plan of the Oratory.
On a proper warning, and a reciprocal forfeit,
By a ſelf-evident teſt of the compariſon, *or feat.*
Of ad ertiſing THIRD-FIRST EDITION, which *clean-ly,*
And publick-ly I am ready to propoſe. J. HENLY.
Fog's Journal. S J.

N. B. The words in *Italic* are added, to make this advertiſement ſenſe, as well as rhime.

MONDAY, *March* 13.

Yeſterday the Right Honourable the L. Biſhop of Chicheſter preached before their Majeſties, his Royal Highneſs the Prince, &c. *C.* Right Reverend. *D P.* —— Yeſterday the R. Hon Sir Rob. Walpole gave a fine entertainment at his houſe at Chelſea to ſeveral of the Nobility and Foreign Miniſters. *P.*

On friday laſt a Gen. Court was held of the York Buildings Company, when it appeared that their affairs were in a very good way; and that upon a valuation of their eſtates only at 20 years purchaſe, there would remain clear, over and above all debts and incumbrances, upwards of 120,000 l. *D P.*

Laſt week began the uſual exerciſes of the determining Batchelors of Arts at Oxford, who were above 120 in number. *D P.*

Laſt week 400 l. was paid out of the Treaſury to the perſons concerned in apprehending Tho. Paſte, Tho. Faxton, Tho Smith and Will. Edwards, lately executed at Tyburn. *D J.*

On tueſday ſe'nnight John Owen, Eſq; of Angleſea in North Wales, was married at Pembroke to Miſs Owen, youngeſt daughter to Sir Arthur Owen of Rialton in Pembrokeſhire, an agreeable young Gentlewoman of 8000 l. fortune. *P.*

On ſaturday night died at her houſe in New Bond-ſtreet, the Lady Chetwynd, Relict of the Hon. Walter Chetwynd, Eſq; late Governor of Barbadoes. *P.* —— Mrs. Chetwynd. *D P. Mar.* 14. —— *The* S J. *of Mar.* 14. *reſolving to be right, puts this article in both ways.*

On ſaturday, a priſoner in the Compter, one Pick,
Threw himſelf into a bog-houſe, in mind being ſick:
He was almoſt ſuffocated before he was got out;
And ſtunk like to kill all that ſtood about. *C.*

TUESDAY, *March* 14.

The Writ of Error relating to the affair between the Biſhop of Ely and Dr. Bentley, is brought to the Houſe of Lords. *D P.*

Yeſterday James Thompſon was carried from Newgate, and examined before the Committee, &c. and remanded back to the ſaid priſon. *P.*

Joſ. Taylor, committed to Tothill-fields Bridewell, as an idle vagrant, and for hawking ſcandalous, lewd, and obſcene Pamphlets, was yeſterday brought before the R. Hon. the L. Raymond, at his chambers in Serjeants Inn; who, upon hearing the matter, remanded him again to Bridewell, to be kept to hard labour. *C.* —— *My Brother* D J. *mentions* the Pamphlet called the Fair Concubine, or, The ſecret Hiſtory of Vanella, *which he had puff'd in his Paper of Mar.* 9. *and* 11. *and very tenderly here ſays*, his Lordſhip ordered the priſoner to be continued in cuſtody 'till next Term.

Laſt week the Aſſizes ended at Saliſbury, when 4 perſons received ſentence of death; 2 were ordered to be tranſported; 1 was burnt in the hand for ſheep ſtealing; and Rob. Bullock and Daniel Croker (the latter a Hackney Writer from Chancery-lane, who in this dearth of buſineſs had ſtrolled down to Bath, and ſtole a Barber's waiſtcoat) were convicted of petty larcenies, and order'd to be whipt. *D P.* —— This Hackney Writer from Chancery-lane *had better have ſtayed here, and turned* Political Writer.

Two young children of —— Haſſel, of Lincoln's-Inn' Eſq; who were lately inoculated for the Small-pox, at his houſe in Bedford-Row, are ſince both dead. *D P.* —— *They are now ſecure from the* Small-pox *in the common way.*

In the News Papers of the 2d inſt. it was invidiouſly inſinuated, that moſt of the cloaths worn at Court on his Majeſty's birth-day, were French ſilks; which is ſo far from truth, that by her Majeſty's Royal encouragement to the manufacturers to invent new patterns, the making of gold and ſilver ſtuffs, and the richeſt ſilks, is brought to ſuch perfection in England as has never been excelled by the French; and all the Royal Family, and moſt of the Nobility and Gentry, did do honour to the Manufactories of their own country, by appearing in them on that joyful occaſion. *D P.* — *I did not ſee this circumſtance about* the French ſilks *mentioned in any other* News Paper of Mar. 2. *but the* L E.

Yeſterday a poor woman, who I ſuppoſe got up to ride,
Fell out of a duſt-cart, and immediately died.

WEDNESDAY, *March* 15.

The Hon. Mrs. Mary Vane having laſt week reſigned her place of Maid of Honour to her Majeſty, the Hon. Mrs. Martha Lovelace, only Siſter to the Right Hon. the Lord Lovelace, we hear is appointed to ſucceed her in that ſtation. *D P.*

We hear that the books and papers belonging to the Charitable Corporation have been diſcovered, and found concealed under a floor in a houſe in Broad-ſtreet. *D J.* —— *It is ſtrange, they ſhould be* be found concealed, *after they had* been diſcovered: *but this happens ſometimes.*

On ſunday laſt the Envoys from Algier went to Windſor, where they dined, ſaw the Caſtle, and return'd in the Evening to their Lodgings in Suffolk-ſtreet. *D P.*

Yeſterday, on a man, and boy, by coaches put out of breath,
The Coroner's Jury ſate: their verdict, *Accidental death*. P.

From the PEGASUS *in Grub-ſtreet.*

It has been related to the Society as a certain truth, that Mr. SAMUEL SHARP, late Apprentice to the famous Mr. CHESELDEN, and now a Surgeon in Fenchurch-ſtreet, was choſen one day laſt week Lecturer of Anatomy to S. Thomas's Hoſpital; where he read a very learned Lecture to a numerous Audience, which was much admired and applauded by all, particularly by thoſe Surgeons of our Society who were preſent.

It has always been an allowed privilege belonging to the Weekly Writers of our Society, to inſert in their Papers commendations of them dated from what places they pleaſe, even the remoteſt in the Kingdom. Our Brother HENRY STONECASTLE, Eſq; therefore acts very prudently in inſerting every now and then a panegyric of this kind, and particularly one from Wales in Numb. 177. written by TAFFIT MUARGAN AP SHENKIN, who by the elegancy of his verſes evidently ſhews how good a judge he is of theſe weekly performances. The two following lines contain a fine complement.

In you another ADDISON *we ſee,*
Whoſe loſs ca: only be ſupply'd by THEE.

And the two laſt give extraordinary good advice:

Go on and proſper in thy juſt deſign,
And foremoſt of the WEEKLY WRITERS *ſhine.*

In order to which, it is the opinion of our Society, that the next time he inſerts any verſes from his Correſpondent at Briſtol, he ſhould get them new-tagg'd: for thoſe in the laſt *Univerſal Spectator*, Numb. 179, are neither rhime, nor blank verſe; *Sir* and *far*, *ſcarce* and *commerce*, *abroad* and *Lord*, being no better rhimes, than *ſuppreſs* and *breaſt*, *taſte* and *as*, in another Weekly Paper of the ſame day.

The admirable defence of Punning in Numb. 178, received the approbation of the whole Society; and our Brother Fog is adviſed not to ſpeak ſo diſreſpectfully for

the future of that ingenious art, as he did in his Journal of laſt ſaturday.

The Letter in anſwer to the notes upon the letter of HORATIANUS, printed in our 110th Journal was received: but it was not thought that the Publick was intereſted enough in the diſpute to be entertained with it. Mr. BAVIUS intending to be a Moderator between PHILARCHÆUS and HORATIANUS, and not to ingage as an Antagoniſt againſt either of them; will leave his notes to the judgment of the Reader.

We informed the Public by three advertiſements in the Daily Papers laſt week, that there was actually in the preſs a beautiful and correct edition of *Select Memoirs of the Society of* GRUB-SRTEET, containing all the moſt curious Letters, Eſſays, Poems, and Remarks, printed in our Journals, with many alterations, additions, and explanatory notes upon the whole; adorned with Hogarthian Frontiſpieces, repreſenting to the life the Authors, Printers, Publiſhers, and Bookſellers of Grub-ſtreet. To make this edition as perfect and compleat as poſſible, all Gentlemen, who have favoured us with their correſpondence, are deſired to ſend us ſuch emendations of their particular Pieces, as they ſhall think proper; and directions by what capital letters they would have them diſtinguiſhed. -- — The Pyratical Publiſhers of *Grubiana* have again advertiſed it, as *beautifully and correctly printed*, tho' they have not been able to contradict one ſyllable advanced in our laſt concerning the multitude of blunders in it. In this advertiſement, they call the *Contents, A compleat Index to the whole*, which is only an *Index*, tho' not a *compleat* one, of their ignorance and impudence.

An Epigram occaſioned by a profane, lewd, and ſtupid Copy of verſes about a *Horſe* and an *Aſs*, printed laſt week in an obſcure Weekly Journal, and beginning,

See how unlimited is Beauty's ſway!
An *Aſs once ſpoke* (as *antient Records* ſay)
Charm'd with an *Angel* offer'd to his view;
The ſtory's ſtrange, but we muſt ſwear 'tis true.

Epigram.

Why ſhould we wonder, that in *old Records*,
An *Aſs* is ſaid to've ſpoke in human words?
Since, in theſe modern, learn'd, inlighten'd times,
Brutes ſpeak not only proſe, but oft in rhimes.
Such verſe ſome neighing Brute muſt ſure indite,
Or elſe ſome braying, duller Beaſt muſt write.
—— But hold, perhaps I'm wrong: this will not paſs:
'A heavy Mule is neither *Horſe*, nor *Aſs*.'

This day was held a general Court at the South-ſea houſe, where nothing material was done: only a great many Speeches were made on both ſides; and among the reſt, the famous Mr. C—y C—r, whoſe ſtock is large, delivered one with his uſual eloquence: and the Court adjourned till friday ſe'nnight.

SIR,

Since my retirement from publick affairs, your weekly performances have been my conſtant entertainment. I read them with pleaſure, and knowing you to be a lover of truth and liberty, recommend the following letter to a place in your next Paper, which will very much oblige,

Sir, your moſt humble ſervant and well-wiſher, &c.

BROTHER WOOLSTON,

Thou wilt, perhaps, think me a very buſy fellow to inſcribe this Letter to thee: but when thou art informed that I am one who delights much in ſpeculations on the conduct of extraordinary men, who daily furniſh the world with new and uncommon opinions, thou wilt undoubtedly receive my candid admoniſhments with calmneſs and good nature. In the firſt place I ſhall aſk thee, if thou haſt peruſed a certain Pamphlet juſt publiſhed, intitled a parallel between MUHAMED and SOSEM, by ZELIM, &c. and what is thy opinion of it? if not, I adviſe thee to read it over with deliberation; thou wilt find by the ſtrength of our Muſulman's arguments, that thou haſt been guilty of a * hugeous error, in thy late converſion from the Chriſtian belief to that of the Jews; for hadſt thou lately made choice of the Mahometan religion, thou mighſt have eſtabliſhed thy opinion upon a more rational foundation, as thou wilt acknowledge, when thou haſt made an impartial enquiry into the different grounds of the one and the other. However, do not imagine that I have any farther intereſt in recommending that work to thee, than the pure love I bear unto one who has made ſo conſiderable a figure in the world by his writings, and whoſe merit has in ſome manner been depreciated by thy late miſtaken rabbinical notions. Take this my friendly advice in good part, and if thou doſt * rape any benefit by it, my ambition will be gratified thereby, and I ſhall hereafter hold thee in greater eſteem, as I profeſs myſelf thy Brother and Servant, ALY. *Since the preceding two letters were compoſed, we have been informed, that the* Pamphlet *mentioned in the latter, is the work of one who ſeems to be neither* Jew, Chriſtian, *nor* Turk: *and therefore, we apprehend, the* Author *may deſign, (according to his own words)* a * hugeous rape *upon the pockets of the Public.*

Dublin, Mar. 4. We hear, that the perſon, who murdered the ſervant of Jam. Hamilton, Eſq; of Carlow, is taken and committed to the goal of Maryborough. *C. P. Mar.* 11. —— This night died Sir Chamberlen Walker, Knt. chief practiſer of Midwifery in this kingdom. *D P. Mar.* 11. — *The Villain here ſaid to be taken*, cut off the ſervant's noſe, and pull'd out his eyes.

Dublin, Mar. 7. We hear from Kilkenny, that a cruel robbery was lately committed within 2 or 3 miles of that place, by a gang of Villains, who broke into a houſe, and ſtript his family of all they had; they broke Mr. Smith's arm, cut his noſe off, ſtabbed him in ſeveral parts of his body, and almoſt broke his back. They almoſt hanged his mother, by tying her over the baniſter of the ſtairs: there is little hopes that either of them will recover. *P. Mar.* 14. —— *I expect a remark from ſome* Iriſh Gentleman *upon theſe ſtrange* robberies *and* murders *committed by his* Countrymen.

FOREIGN NEWS.

THURSDAY, *March* 9.

Yeſterday arrived the Mails from France *and* Holland.

Rome, Feb. 23. N. S. On the 15th the Chevalier de S. George's eldeſt ſon had a private audience of the Pope, who preſented him with a bill of 3000 crowns, and told him it was a prize he had drawn in the lottery called the Play of Genoa. *C.* —— *D P. Mar.* 10.

Venice, Feb. 23. It is written from Corſu, that they had had ſuch heavy rains for 3 days, that ſeveral villages were laid under water; that the rains were preceded by a violent ſhock of an earthquake; that a man of war in the harbour was 5 times thunder-ſtruck in one day; and that during the ſtorm, the air was filled with owls, bats, and other birds of the night, which perched upon the maſts and yards of the ſhip. *P.*

FRIDAY, *March* 10.

Medreyga in *Hungary, Jan.* 7, 1732. Upon a current report, that in the village of Medreyga certain dead bodies (called here *Vampyres*) had killed ſeveral perſons by ſucking out all their blood, the preſent enquiry was made by the Honourable Commander in Chief; and Capt. Gorſchutz of the Company of Stallater, the *Hadnagi* Bariacrar, and the Senior Heyduke of the village, were ſeverally examined: who unanimouſly declared, that about 5 years ago a certain Heyduke, named Arnold Paul, was killed by the overturning of a cart load of hay, who in his lifetime was often heard to ſay, that he had been tormented near Caſchaw, and upon the borders of Turkiſh Servia, by a *Vampyre*; and that to extricate himſelf, he had eaten ſome of the earth of the *Vampyres* graves, and rubbed himſelf with their blood. That 20 or 30 days after the deceaſe of the ſaid Arnold Paul, ſeveral perſons complained that they were tormented; and that, in ſhort, he had taken away the lives of four perſons. In order therefore to put a ſtop to ſuch a calamity, the inhabitants of the place, after having conſulted their *Hadnagi*, cauſed the body of the ſaid Arnold Paul to be taken up, 40 days after he had been dead, and found the ſame to be freſh, and free from all manner of corruption; that he bled at the noſe, mouth, and ears, as pure and florid blood as ever was ſeen; and that his ſhroud and winding ſheet were all over bloody; and laſtly, his finger and toe nails were fallen off, and new ones grown in their room —— As they obſerved from all theſe circumſtances, that he was a *Vampyre*, they, according to cuſtom, drove a ſtake through his heart; at which he gave a horrid groan, and loſt a great deal of blood. Afterwards they burnt his body to aſhes the ſame day, and threw them into his grave. —— Theſe good men ſay farther, that all ſuch as have been tormented or killed by the *Vampyres*, become *Vampyres* when they are dead; and therefore they ſerved ſeveral other dead bodies as they had done Arnold Paul's, for tormenting the living. Signed, *Bartuer*, firſt Lieutenant of the Regiment of *Alexander*. *Fickberger*, Surgeon Major to the Regiment of *Furſtemburch*. — Three other Surgeons. *Gurſchitz, Captain* a Stallath.

SATURDAY, *March* 11.

Camentz in *Upper Lauſnitz, Feb* 22. On tueſday laſt died here one John Hof, aged near 105 years, being born in 1628. He ſerved 82 years in the wars, and had made 36 campaigns: he had married 3 wives, the laſt of them when he was 100 years old. His conſtitution was ſo ſtrong and healthy, that 'till a few days before his death he was employed as a foot meſſenger, to carry letters ſeveral miles every day, and was ſick but 2 days. *P.*

Petersburgh, Feb. 19. The Princeſs of Mecklenbourgh's marriage with the Prince Royal of Pruſſia, is publickly talked of; the Czarina has augmented her Court, and given her the title of Imperial Highneſs. *D P.*

MONDAY, *March* 13.

Late laſt night arrived the Mail from Holland.

Amſterdam, March 18. Letters from Berlin of the 11th adviſe, that on the 10th the Prince Royal of Pruſſia was contracted to the Princeſs of Beveren, in the preſence of their Majeſties, the Royal Family, the Duke and Dutcheſs of Beveren, the Duke of Lorrain, and other perſons of diſtinction, with great ſplendor and ceremony; upon which occaſion, his Royal Highneſs preſented the Princeſs with a ring valued at 24,000 crowns, who gave another in exchange valued at 10,000. *D P. &c.*

TUESDAY, *March* 14.

Yeſterday arrived the Mail from Holland.

Hague, Mar. 16. The States of Holland have publiſhed a Placaert, to ſuppreſs an impious and profane Book, entituled, *The overthrow of the Worlds Idol, or the Faith of the Elect manifeſted in the Writings of* Pontian de Hattem, &c. His impious and prophane ſentiments are of a piece with thoſe of Spinoſa: for example, *That the tranſgreſſion of the commandments and law of God, or of the ſovereign, is no ſin at all*; no cauſe of repentance or remorſe for a Chriſtian. *C.*

This Mail brings a vacancy in the ſacred College by the death of Cardinal Mareſoſchi; and adviſes the arrival of the King of Poland at Warſaw. The Marquis de Caſtellar, Ambaſſador of Spain at Paris, is going to Italy in all haſte, which ſurprizes many Politicians. The French are fitting out 12 men of war at Breſt and Toulon. *P.*

Books and Pamphlets publiſhed ſince *Mar.* 4.

Alciphron: or, The minute Philoſopher. In 2 Vol.

The Chriſtian Faith aſſerted againſt Deiſts, Arians, and Socinians, in 8 Sermons at the Lady Moyer's Lecture, &c. By Hen. Felton, D. D.

The Compleat City and Country Cook, &c. By Charles Carter. Pr. 4 s. 6 d. A Work deſign'd for the good, and abſolutely neceſſary for all families. *Eſpecially thoſe of the Author and Bookſeller.*

Love after enjoyment in two Epiſtles, &c. Pr. 1 s.

The Ordinary of Newgate's Account of the behaviour and dying words of the 6 Malefactors executed Mar. 6.

~~Miſcellaneous Obſervations~~ on Authors, &c. No. 13.

A Parallel between Muhamed and Soſem, &c. Pr. 1 s.

Propoſals for a regulation or ſuppreſſion of Pawnbrokers, &c. Pr. 6 d.

7. Modern Hiſtory, &c. By Mr. Salmon. No. 92.

A ſermon on ſubmiſſion to Divine Chaſtiſements. By Sam. Savage.

Vanella; or the Amours of the Great. An Opera.

8. Symeonis Monachi Dunhelmenſis libellus de exordio & procurſu Dunhelmenſis Eccleſiæ, &c. Edidit. Tho. Bedford.

9 Of Modern Wit: an Epiſtle to the R. Hon. Sir Will. Yonge.

The danger of Faction to a free people. Pr. 6 d.

The whole ſequel of the Proceedings of Miſs Cadiere, &c. Pr. 2 s.

The Occaſional Hiſtorian, No. IV. By Mr. Earbery.

A letter to the R. Rev. the L. Biſhop of Chicheſter, occaſioned by his Lordſhip's Sermon before the Houſe of Lords.

An Hiſtorical and Law-Treatiſe againſt Jews and Judaiſm, &c. Pr. 1 s.

An Eſſay againſt incloſing common field land, &c.

The laborious works of the Craftſman impartially conſidered. Pr. 1 s.

11. The life and death of Sir Tho. Moore: by Will. Roper, Eſq; Pr. 3 s.

The Political State of Great Britain: for February.

The monthly Chronicle: for February.

City Cries, inſtrumental and vocal. Pr. 6 d.

Univerſal Hiſtory: Numb. V.

The Practical Farmer, &c. Pr. 2 s.

13. Hiſtoria Litteraria, Numb. XV.

14. The Caſes of Impotency and Virginity fully diſcuſs'd. By John Crawfurd, L. L. D. Printed for Thomas Gammon. *It was in relation to this Book, that Mr. Curl adviſed the Public to beware of Counterfeits.*

Two Sermons on charity of Temper and Affiance, &c. by Tho. Macro, D. D.

On Tueſday Stocks were

South Sea Stock 97 7 8ths. South Sea Annuity 109 7 8ths. Bank 149 1 half for the Opening. New Bank Circulation 7 l. Premium. India 176 3 qrs. Three per Cent. Annuity 97 1 8th. New 3 per Cent. Annuity 96 3 qrs. Royal Exchange Aſſurance 99 1 qr. London Aſſurance 13 3 8ths. York Buildings 8 1 qr. African 42. Engliſh Copper 2 l. 8 s. Welch ditto 1 l. 16 s. South Sea Bonds 1 l. 14 s. Prem. India ditto 5 l. 11 s. ditto. Blanks 7 l. 7 s. 20 l. Prizes 19 l. 12 s.

ADVERTISEMENTS.

This Day is published,

Number V. of

An UNIVERSAL HISTORY *from the earliest Account of Time to the present*;

WHICH comprizes not only the General History of the World, but also that of every particular Empire, Kingdom and State, from its first Foundation to its Dissolution, or to the present Time; with an exact Account of the Migrations and Conquests of every People, the Successions and Reigns of their respective Princes, their Religion and Government, Customs, Learning, &c.

The whole immediately extracted from the Original Authors, and illustrated with necessary Maps, Cuts, Chronological and other Tables. To be continu'd.

Printed for J. Batley, in Pater-Noster-Row; E. Symon, over-against the Royal-Exchange in Cornhill; N. Prevost, against Southampton-Street in the Strand; T. Osborne, in Gray's-Inn; J. Crokatt, at the Golden Key, over-against St. Dunstan's Church in Fleet-Street; and sold by Tho. Payne, at the Crown in Pater-Noster-Row. Where any of the former Numbers may be had.

This day is published,

STOWE, the *Gardens* of the Right Honourable *Richard* Lord Viscount *Cobham*. Address'd to Mr. *Pope*.

Devenere locos lætos, & amœna Vireta,
Fortunatorum nemorum, sedesque beatas. Virg.

Printed for Lawton Gilliver, at Homer's-Head, in Fleet-street.

And next Week will be Published, The *Progress of Love* In four ECLOGUES: *Uncertainty*, the First *Eclogue*, dedicated to Mr. *Pope*. *Hope* is the Second *Eclogue*, to the Right Honourable *George Dodington*, Esq; *Jealousy* the Third *Eclogue* to *Edward Walpole*, Esq; *Possession* the Fourth *Eclogue*, to the Right Honourable the Lord Viscount *Cobham*.

This Day is published,

AN Enquiry into the Origin of HONOUR, and the Usefulness of Christianity in WAR.

By the Author of the *Fable of the Bees.*

Price bound 3 s. 6 d.

Printed for J. Brotherton at the Bible, next the Fleece Tavern in Cornhill.

This day is published,

HISTORIA LITTERARIA: Or, An Exact and Early Account of the most valuable Books published in Europe. In this Number are contained the following Extracts, viz. The Life and Actoins of the famous Saladine. Part 3. Boerhaave's Chymistry. Part 1. Life of the Emperor Justinian, of the Empress Theodora, and of Trebonianus. History of the Island of Hispaniola, or San Domingo. Part 2. With the present State of Learning; or, the Books now printing or published in the Places following, viz.

Messina, Rome, Milan, Florence, Padua, Venice, Lucca, Leipsick, Nuremberg, Gena, Hamburg, Bourdeaux, Paris, Montpelier, Dijon, Rohan, Amsterdam, Francker, Hague, and London. Printed for N. Prevost, against Southampton-Street in the Strand; E. Symon in Cornhill; and sold by T. Payne in Pater-Noster-Row. Price 1 s.

Where also may be had,

The Two First Volumes of Historia Litteraria, containing 12 Numbers, with complete Indexes, or any single Number.

This Day is published,

A Collection of PIECES in VERSE and PROSE, on which have been published occasion of the Dunciad. Dedicated to the Right Honourable the Earl of Middlesex. By Mr. Savage.

Likewise,

ATHELWOLD: A Tragedy. By A. Hill, Esq; as it is acted at the Theatre Royal in Drury-Lane.

2. Of FALSE TASTE; an Epistle to the Right Honourable Richard Earl of Burlington. By Mr. POPE. The 3d Edition, with an additional Letter.

Printed for Lawton Gilliver, at Homer's Head, against St. Dunstan's Church, Fleet-street.

S. PALMER, Printer, near the Church in Bartholomew-Close, being oblig'd, thro' an ill State of Health, to remove his Business a little way out of Town (and his Partner, J. Huggonson, intending to remove elsewhere) his Apartment and his Printing Room, which is 65 Foot long and 27 Foot wide, with glaz'd Lights all round, and very strong and airy, is to be Lett, being very fit for any Tradesman that requires a great deal of Light and Room.

N. B. If the Apartment is not big enough, there is more Room to be had on reasonable Terms.

This Day is published,

In Four Volumes, Twelves,

And sold by N. PREVOST, opposite to Southampton-Street in the Strand,

THE Life of Mr. CLEVELAND, natural Son of OLIVER CROMWELL. Written by himself. Giving a particular Account of his Unhappiness in Love, Marriage, Friendship, &c. and his great Sufferings in *Europe* and *America*. Together with the secret AMOURS of the PROTECTOR, and his unnatural Usage to his illegitimate Children. The whole intermix'd with Reflexions, describing the Heart of Man, in all its Variety of Passions and Disguises.

N. B. The 3d and 4th Vol. may be had separate.

WHereas there is advertised in the *Universal Spectator*, and other Papers, that a new Edition of the most curious and uncommon Flowers of the twelve Months in the Year; Notice is hereby given to all Noblemen, Ladies, and Gentlemen, that those Prints are only Copies, and that we are not any ways concerned in 'em but the Original, which are only sold by us Robert Furbur, Gardener, at Kensington; Peter Casteels, Painter, in Long-Acre; Henry Fletcher, Engraver, in Nottingham-Street, the upper End of Plumbtree-Street, Bloomsbury; and at Mr. Tho. Bowle's in St. Paul's Church-Yard, Printseller, at Two Pounds Twelve Shillings and Six Pence coloured, and plain One Pound Five Shillings each Sett.

N. B. There's a thirteenth Plate, in which a List of the Subscribers Names, with a Border of Flowers about it, and our Names engrav'd at the Bottom of each Plate, and those are the Originals, and all without our Names are Copies; theirs are not above half the Bigness.

On Saturday, March 4, was publish'd, Price 6 d.

THE GENTLEMAN'S MAGAZINE: Or, *Monthly Intelligencer.*

No. XIV. for February, being the 2d of Vol. II.

Containing, among other Heads, Arguments for and against a Standing Army; the Tax on Salt, Soap and Candles; Leather, Land and Windows; Proposals for a more equal and easier Tax to all People, and for abolishing a great many of the present burthensome Duties. Of the Pension Bill, Corruption and Indepency of Parliament; of Distillers and Farmers; Parties changing Principles; 30th of January Sermons, &c. with Domestick Occurrences.

And this Day is published the Second Edition of

No. X. for October,

The first Impression being near sold off, on Account of several agreeable Pieces, both in Prose and Verse, sent by unknown Correspondents, particularly a Copy of the Will of *Samuel Travers*, Esq; which was inserted entire with the Letter prefixed. Another Correspondent was pleased to give the Author a seasonable Hint (which was observed) in the following exceeding Complaisant Epistle,

To Mr. *Sylvanus Urban.*

SIR,

THE *Gentleman's Magazine* is, perhaps, one of the most useful Things of the Kind that has been at any Time set on Foot; but this Usefulness must in Justice and Gratitude be attributed to your unbyass'd Impartiality and Industry: It serves me, and to my Knowledge several others, for what your Title truly expresses it, that is, a *Magazine* or Repository of every Thing worthy remarking, and for this Reason will be many Years hence, an Authentick Collection for Historians to refer to, when Disputes shall arise on the Manner and Spirit with which the present Controversies are carried on, the Force of their Arguments on both Sides being fully retain'd; besides many Historical Occurrences may be here found, which, tho' they escape the Notice of great and voluminous Historians, will serve to explain and clear up the Truth of several Facts which in Time may appear doubtful; and the Reasons and Origin of some Transactions will be here found, which might otherwise be sought after in vain.

When I have premised this, I can't help thinking but that you will excuse me for taking Notice of a Slip which you made in July last, in Respect to Gibraltar; and I am sure it was no other than Inadvertency and Slip, for your whole Design shows you mean no Wrong to any Party. The Piece I mean was published in one of the Daily Papers, and the Reason why, as I take it, you did not recite it was, that by Eleven a-Clock the Morning of Publication it was all sold off, and I gave myself a Shilling for one on Tuesday Morning following, however you may easily see it in some Coffee-houses, and when you have so done, I am very sure you will lay the Materials of it up in your Magazine; for it is not a Temporary Thing, and therefore not worn out by the Date, but will be as satisfactory now as on the Day of Publication. I conclude, Sir, with my harty Thanks to you for the Benefit and Pleasure I receive from your Studies, and am your Friend and Servant, tho' unknown,

Octob. 14, 1731. L. J.

Printed at St. John's Gate, and sold by F. Jeffries in Ludgate-street; A. Dodd, near Temple-bar; E. Nutt, &c. at the Royal-Exchange; where may be had compleat Setts; also an exact LIST of Parliament.

WHEREAS other *Coffee-Houses*, and other *Publick Houses*, take of their Customers 8 s. for a Quart of Arrack, and 6 s. for a Quart of Rum or Brandy made into *Punch*, so that it is now become the settled Price thoughout the Town, and seldom less than a Bowl of 1 s. 6 d. is to be had: Therefore, for the better accommodating all Gentlemen, that are Lovers of *Punch*,

This is to give Notice,

That I have opened on Ludgate-hill, the *London-Coffee-House* and *Punch-House*, (Two *Punch-Bowls* on Iron Pedestals before my Door,)

Where the finest and best old Batavia Arrack, Jamaica Rum, and French Brandy, are made into *Punch*, with the finest Ingredients, viz.

A Quart of Arrack made into Punch for 6 s. and so in Proportion to the smallest quantity, which is half a Quartern for four Pence Half-penny.

A Quart of Rum or Brandy made into *Punch* for 4 s and so in Proportion to the smallest Quantity, which is half a Quartern for 3 d. And Gentlemen may have it as soon made, as a Gill of Wine can be drawn; with the best of Eating, Attendance, and Accommodation.

This Undertaking has occasion'd many, whose *Interest* it is to possess Gentlemen with such an Opinion, that the Liquors by me used are not good; The Publick is hereby assured, that I buy my Goods on the Keys, and at the best Hand, with Ready Money, and am at this Time provided with as well-chosen Brandies, Rum and Arrack, as any in Town, and will at all times procure the best that is imported: But what may convince Gentlemen of the Truth hereof, is, (not only by the Encouragement I meet with) that the Sherbet is always brought by itself, and the Brandy, Rum, or Arrack in the Measure, so there can be no Imposition, either in Quantity or Quality; for the Proof whereof I appeal to all Gentlemen who have done me the Honour to call at my House.

James Ashley.

BOOKS printed for J. BATLEY, at the *Dove* in *Pater-Noster-Row.*

1. MIscellaneous Essays, viz. 1. Of Company and Conversation. 2. Of Solitariness and Retirement. 3. Of Nobility. 4. Of Contentment. 5. Of Women. 6. Of the Knowledge of God, and against Atheism. 7. Of Religion. 8. Of Kings, Princes, and the Education of a Prince. 9. Of Greatness of Mind. 10. Of the Education of Children. 11. Of Law. 12. Of Man. 13. Of old Age; with the Life and Conversion of St. Mary Magdalen, and some Reflections upon the Conversion of the good Thief. Also the Life and Conversion of St. Paul, by *Sir Richard* Bulstrode, Kt. Envoy at the Court of Brussels from King Charles II. and King James II. Published with a Preface, by his Son Whitlock Bulstrode, Esq; The second Edition. Price 4 s 6 d.

2. The memorable Things of Socrates. Written by *Xenophon*, in five Books. Translated into English. The second Edition. To which are prefixed, the Life of Socrates from the French of Monsieur Charpentier, a Member of the French Academy. And the Life of Xenophon, collected from several Authors; with some Account of his Writings. Also compleat Tables are added by *Edward Bysshe*, Gent. price 5 s.

The *Cælestial Anodyne Tincture*: Or, The *Great Pain-Easing Medicine*,

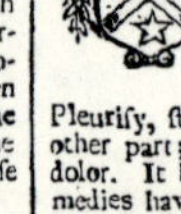

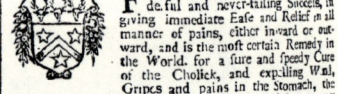

FAm'd and approv'd of for its wonderful and never-failing Success, in giving immediate Ease and Relief in all manner of pains, either inward or outward, and is the most certain Remedy in the World, for a sure and speedy Cure of the Cholick, and expelling Wind, Gripes and pains in the Stomach, the Pleurisy, stitches or pains in the side, back, loins, or any other part; Rheumatick Ailments, which cause pain and dolor. It hath given ease to a Miracle, when all other Remedies have fail'd. In the Gravel and Stone in the Kidneys, it gives ease forthwith, and brings them away to Admiration. It also facilitates and causes a speedy Delivery in Child-birth. 'Tis no Quack trifling thing to allure the World with, but a real and well-experienced Medicine, not acting by Stupefaction (as Opiates) but by a friendly, balsamick, and subtile Nature, pacifying the most severe and terrible racking pains, and carries off the Cause, not by purging, but by Transpiration, by Urine, or breaking Wind. No Family ought to be without it. And used outwardly, it cures Swellings, Aches, pains, Numbness, or Weakness of the Joints; 'tis excellent for Cramps, and all other aged Infirmities, effecting Wonders in Agues, Fevers, Small-pox, &c. No Family ought to be without it.

It is sold only by Mr. PARKER, Printer, at his House in Salisbury-Court, or by such persons as he shall depute, viz. at Mr. *Parker's*, a Printer, in Bull-Head Court, Jewin-street; at the White Gallon Pot, a Chandler's Shop in Bandy-Leg-Walk, Southwark, and at Mr. Neal's, a Toy-shop over against the White Hart Inn in the Borough, at Eighteen pence a bottle, with printed Directions; and, if requested, will be brought to any Person, by the Hawker who sells his Penny-post. Sealed as above.

LONDON: Printed by S. PALMER and J. HUGGONSON, in *Bartholomew-Close*, for Captain GULLIVER, near the *Temple*, where Letters and Advertisements are taken in: As also at the *Rainbow Coffee-House* in *Cornhill*, and *John's Coffee-House* in *Sheer-Lane*, near *Temple-Bar*. [Price Two Pence]

The Grub-ſtreet Journal.

NUMB. 116

Thurſday, *MARCH* 23, 1731.

To Mr. BAVIUS, Secretary to the Society of Grub-ſtreet.

SIR,

THO' I have not, as yet, complied with your advice in comparing my own obſervations with thoſe of others, I hope you will excuſe me; ſince you are at liberty, either to ſuppreſs my Letters, or to cut off their ſuperfluities. If therefore you will give me leave to go on in my own way, and to employ this Letter in ſome preliminary obſervations, I promiſe in my next to begin my Remarks on the ſeveral Books of Doctor B.'s *Milton* in order.

Firſt then, I muſt take notice of a paſſage in his *Preface*, p. 6. where he affirms, that 'this Poem has, for 'above 60 years time, paſſed upon the whole nation 'for a perfect, abſolute, faultleſs compoſition.' But what ſays Mr. ADDISON (to omit DRYDEN and others)? 'I have '(ſays that good-natur'd Critic, in *Spectator*, Vol. V. No. '369.) ſpoken of the cenſures which our Author may 'incur under each of theſe heads [the fable, the cha'racters, the ſentiments, and the language] which I have 'confined to two Papers, tho' I might have enlarged the 'number, if I had been diſpoſed to dwell on ſo ungrate'ful a ſubject. I believe, however, that the ſevereſt 'Reader will not find any little fault in Heroick Poetry, 'which this Author has fallen into, that does not come 'under one of thoſe heads, among which I have diſtributed 'his ſeveral blemiſhes.' And in another place, Vol. IV. No. 291, he declares, that 'he enters upon it as a very 'ungrateful work, and that he ſhall juſt point at the im'perfections, without endeavouring to enflame them with 'ridicule.' Tho' the Doctor did not think himſelf obliged to follow this Gentleman's example, yet it is certain that he has read his criticiſms: for he frequently quotes them. How then can he repreſent this Poem as being thought *faultleſs* by every one? So far from it, that I may venture to affirm, that no perſon, who had any juſt pretence to learning, *ever looked* on it as a *faultleſs compoſition*.

Indeed this Editor tells us, p. 149, 150. that 'thoſe 'verſes on which he has no note, he would be under'ſtood to approve, as wrought up to the higheſt per'fection.' And I doubt not but he would be *underſtood* to mean the ſame concerning the other verſes, as he has corrected them. If therefore in thoſe *approved verſes* we can find the ſame, or parallel ſuppoſed faults with thoſe which he finds in other places, which will be eaſily done, he muſt retract, either his cenſures, or his approbation. Or if we can find any real faults in theſe *approved verſes*, it is incumbent on the Doctor to defend them; which, I believe, will be an hard taſk.

Next, I cannot but obſerve the contradictory rules, by which the Doctor works. P. 32. he ſays, 'our Author 'generally rather aims at ſtrong expreſſion, than ſmooth 'and flowing numbers.' Whereas, p. 123. he ſays, 'our 'Author, well ſkilled in Muſic, could not be guilty of ſo 'abſonous an accent.' How ſhall we attack a man, who has ſuch different places of refuge? But it happens unfortunately for him, that neither of theſe rules is right, tho' oppoſite to each other: for MILTON is ſometimes guilty of low thoughts; and ſometimes of harſh numbers. Again, the Doctor ſometimes tells us, that what is beſt was dictated by MILTON; and that the faults are owing to the Printer, or Editor: at other times, he confeſſes, that MILTON was guilty of ſome ſlips and inadvertencies, by reaſon of his blindneſs. And thus, upon the ſtrength of theſe rules, he ſometimes lays the fault on MILTON; but oftener on the Editor, according to the humour he is in.

Laſtly, I muſt beſtow a word or two on the Doctor's very particular ſcheme of meliorating MILTON's Poem, ſo that no one fault ſhall remain in it, but all be *wrought up to the higheſt perfection*. How unneceſſary, and bold an attempt is this? Is it a national concern, that there ſhould be a perfect Poem amongſt us? No acceſſion of fame will accrue to MILTON by it; neither indeed does he want any: his own work, with all its defects, is a ſufficient ſubject of praiſe for one man. But if the Doctor would paſs upon us for a Poet himſelf (as his Preface informs us ſome people call him) let him produce ſomething of his own; and not perch upon MILTON's ſhoulders to make himſelf ſeem conſiderable. SCALIGER, whoſe courage and abilities were very great, in his *Hypercritic* has done ſomething like this to a few paſſages in ſome of the ancient Poets. But to pretend to correct and improve a whole Poem, and ſet it up for the ſtandard of perfection, was reſerved to one that exceeded SCALIGER in boldneſs: I wiſh he was equal to him in ability. If therefore the Doctor at any time ſucceeds in his attempt to improve MILTON, his labour is needleſs and impertinent; but if he fails, and, inſtead of mending, depraves the ſenſe, he then lays himſelf open to the utmoſt degree of ridicule, for voluntarily undertaking an unneceſſary taſk, which he is not capable of performing.

I have made theſe few reflections, becauſe they will furniſh me with ſome rules, by which to proceed in my remarks on the Doctor's alterations. I am, Sir,

March 9, 1731/2. Your moſt humble ſervant, A. Z.

P. S. In my laſt, I had mentioned MILTON's Poem to be firſt publiſhed in the year 1667, which you have changed to 1669, upon the authority (as I ſuppoſe) of your Correſpondent, J. T. Indeed I thought Doctor B. might be depended upon in a matter of ſo little conſequence: and I cannot but ſtill believe him to be in the right, as to this particular, tho' I am cautious of being guided ſolely by his authority. I have therefore looked over ſeveral old Catalogues of Books for auctions and ſale, between the years 1678, and 1684. In theſe I find MILTON's *Paradiſe Loſt, in ten Books*, mentioned eleven times. Four of which are dated in the year 1667; five in 1668; and two in 1669. I have now one of the date 1669 before me, which begins with this Advertiſement.

'The Printer to the Reader.

'Courteous Reader, there was no Argument at firſt in'tended to the Book; but for the ſatisfaction of *many that 'have deſired* it, I have procured it, and withall a reaſon 'of that which ſtumbled *many others*, why the Poem 'rhimes not. 'S SIMONS.

This ſeems to imply, that an impreſſion, or at leaſt part of an impreſſion, had been ſold off without the *Argument*, or the *Defence* of the blank verſe; unleſs by the *many* are meant thoſe who read it in manuſcript, or at the preſs. However, it muſt be confeſſed, there is ſomething ſtrange in this matter, which requires to be cleared up by thoſe who are able.

Paradiſe Regain'd was firſt publiſhed in Michaelmas term 1670, which I think Printers call 1671. Several of the old Catalogues before-mentioned, have *Paradiſe Loſt in 12 Books, Third Edition*, 1678, but none of them have it in the Second.

SIR,

THE account contained in the following extract of an old Letter, is undoubtedly true; and perhaps you may think it remarkable enough to be publiſhed in your Paper, when you ſhall have ſpare room. I believe you will think the ſufferer's honeſt way of telling it to be the beſt. I am, your humble ſervant, A. Z.

To Mr. A. H.

Metchelapatam, the 24th of *Septemb*. 1656.

I know not how far I may depend upon favour, altho' in conſcience we do deſerve ſome incouragement, in reſpect of our many hazards and hardſhips: one particular whereof I ſhall tell you; and 'tis the ſtrangeſt that ever you heard out of a Romance; which I ſhall tell, that you may join with me in praiſing the Lord for prolonging my days in the land of the living.

On thurſday the 24th of July (a day henceforth to be kept holy) Capt. WHITE, of the *Mayflower*, Capt. LUCAS, of the *Society*, and Capt. LOE, of the *Virgin*, had taken their leave of the ſhoar, and were going aboard their ſhips with all their retinue; and not without the company of near all the Engliſh Merchants on this place; intending to ſolemnize that day in valedictory ceremonies, and then to ſet ſail; and to this purpoſe, we had provided a common country boat, of about 30 tons, to go off in. So about 9 a clock, in a fair morning, we were all imbarked, being in number about 30 Engliſhmen, with 20 Blacks; the Engliſhmen lay moſt aloft upon the poop, only Capt. BROWNE, Capt. LUCAS, and myſelf, and ED. KING lay juſt under them in the hold. And while we were there ſerious, and the reſt aloft very merry in diſcourſe, going over the Bar, the boat ſtruck ground; and by means of her over-great main-ſail, ſuddenly over-ſet, and turned her keel upwards. Herewith, as many as were aloft, fell overboard: we that were in the hold, endeavoured to get out, and commit ourſelves to the mercy of the ſea, but could not, ſo ſuddenly the boat overturned, as a man can reckon to the number of 15. Suddenly we found ourſelves tumbled together in the water, among cheſts, caſes of liquor, and other ſuch lumber, with a ſcore of ſheep that were carrying aboard; and as within a diſh ſwimming with the bottom upwards, ſo were we all within the boat, and had the boat's keel in the zenith. It was there as dark as in the earth's center; but that air which was ſurprized within the concavous inſide of the boat's hold, wherein we were at her ſudden overturning, proved ſufficient for us (cloſe priſoners) to breathe in. And ſo we 4 Chriſtians, and ſome 20 Gentiles, ſat on *the thoughts*, with our heads above water, within ſide the boat, altho' without ſide the boat the water ran over her; and in this condition we lived 2 hours; in the mean time praying heartily, that mine and friend's eſtate might fall into merciful mens hands, and recommending my ſoul unto my Saviour's mercy for ſalvation; as for my body's, I had ſmall hopes; Capt. LUCAS often telling me, it was impoſſible to be preſerved, and a folly to think it. I anſwered him, that beſides the remembrance of miraculous JONAH in the whale's belly, in human reaſon, it was poſſible for us to continue alive a long time; and if any of thoſe men that were toſt overboard were ſaved, they would uſe ſome means for us alſo; unleſs they might give us over for dead (as indeed they did) the boat being a top of us, and water, for the moſt part, a top of the boat, ſo that but little of her appeared; and yet we that were within, had air, breath, and ſtood on *the thoughts*, with our heads above water. So I adviſed Capt. LUCAS to throw off all his cloaths, that we might be ready to ſwim, if any opportunity ſhould preſent, which he did, and I alſo, tho' I had 30 lb. in gold, beſides a little manuſcript book of 7 years Collections in my pocket; therefore I went wading through the water, groping about the inſide of the boat in that moſt perfect of darkneſs, until I found an hollow beam, and thereto I tied my breeching with a ſtrong tape, ſaying to my fellows, this ſhall be found whatever becomes of me. All this while, moſt hideous were the outcries of the diſtracted Gentiles, calling upon their Pagods, &c. In fine, the boat running aſhoar upon the ſands, and while the water was as high as our necks, with our feet we digged a pit in the ſand, near the boat's ſide, in doing whereof the current helped us; and then ſinking down into the water, and diving, crept out under the ſide of the boat, one by one. Then, after we were got out from under the boat, we found we had a water of ſome 180 paces over, and middle deep to wade through, the current whereof ran ſo ſtiff, that in attempting to ford it, 6 of our company had there periſhed before us: yet the major part eſcaping, Captain LUCAS and I held each other by the arms, and naked, waded through the current, ſuccouring each other in perilous ſteps; for if either had but loſt his footing, and fallen down, the violent torrent was ſo great, we ſhould never have riſen more in this world. At laſt, being got out of the water, as naked as ADAM, we had a mile and a half to run to the town, with the hot ſand ſcalding under our feet, and the ſun ſcorching over our heads, which cauſed all the ſkin of our bodies to peel off, altho' we ran apace; and the firſt Chriſtian we met, was a good Dutchman, who lent me his hat and ſlippers. The time we continued under the boat was about 2 hours; the perſons loſt were Mr. LEIGH, a tall, ancient Gentleman of 62 years, and an old ſervant to the Eaſt India Company; beſides Mr. MARTIN BRADGATE, the 2d Man, in the Company's ſervice at Metchel; alſo Mr. WATKINS, who went Merchant of the *Mayflower*, and three others.

That the Lord will teach us to walk worthy of his mercies, and vouchſafe me to ſee you, and friends, with comfort, is my daily prayer, and greateſt of temporal deſires: and ſo, committing you all to God's protection, I remain your moſt faithful friend and ſervant,

HUGH SQUIER.

An EPIGRAM, occaſioned by reading Doctor B's *Preface* to MILTON's *Paradiſe loſt*, in which he applies to himſelf theſe two lines of VIRGIL, Ec. IX. 33, 34.

—— *Sunt & mihi carmina; me quoque dicunt*
Vatem paſtores: ſed non ego credulus illis.

How could vile Sycophants contrive
A lie ſo groſs to raiſe;
Which even B———y can't believe,
Tho' ſpoke in his own praiſe!

DOMESTIC NEWS.

C. *Courant.*	E P. *Evening Post.*
P. *Post-Boy.*	S J. *S. James's Evening Post.*
D P. *Daily Post.*	WE. *Whitehall Evening P.*
D J. *Daily Journal.*	LE. *London Evening Post.*

Puffs of Hyp-oratorical wind in February.

The sunday evening Lectures of the Oratory are, and have been for these 3 or 4 months, as much encourag'd as when they were first begun at Newport Market. *D J. Feb.* 3.—*Shops, where trade is* much encouraged, *are seldom advertised, unless in order to be lett.* —— We hear that To-morrow's Hyp-Doctor will answer, &c. *D J.* 7. — *The* Doctor *to'd this, I suppose, to the Printers.* —— The Rev. Mr. Henley is desired to suit his next sunday's morning sermon, &c. *D J.* 11. —— *He, no doubt, complied with his own* desire. —— Sir Isaac Ratcliffe will publish to morrow, &c. *D J.* 14. —— This day is published in the Hyp Doctor, &c. Where may be had, there being a demand for it, the fourth edition of No. 39. *D J.* 15. —Where may be had, having been much demanded, &c. *D J.* 22. —— *This* fourth edition *came out the same day with the* third edition of the Lecture about Miss Cadiere. —— The Gentlemen concerned in the private subscription, have engaged two new Discourses at the Oratory, &c. *D J.* 18. —— *This* engagement *was as* private *as the* subscription. —— We hear from George's Coffee-house, that the Hyp-Doctor will, in his To-morrow's Paper, &c. *D J.* 21. —— Mr. Auditor's *Office being very considerable, he speaks in the Royal style,* We. — The morning subject of the Oratory, next sunday, is given out to be, &c. *D J.* 25. —— *Let it be* given out *as it will,* the morning, *as well as* evening subject of the Oratory, *is nothing but a* Coffee-house. —— The Craftsman having confess'd last saturday, that the Hyp-Doctor, &c. *D J.* 28. —— *It is to be wish'd, the* Hyp-Doctor *would come likewise to* confession.

THURSDAY, *March* 16.

Yesterday morning the Rev. Dr. Benson preached before her Majesty, his Royal Highness the Duke, and the Princesses. *C.* —— His Majesty has been pleased to appoint Col. Tho. Paget, Groom of his Bedchamber, to be Lieut. Col. to the Regiment of Horse in Ireland, commanded by Col. Legoniere. — Major Sowle to be Lieut. Col. to Col. Montague's Regiment of Foot in North-Britain; and Capt. Pool to be Major in his room. —— Major Patterson to be Lieut. Col. to Col. Cornwallis's Regiment of Foot at Jamaica; Capt. Tho. White to be Major in his room; Capt. Lieut. Robertson to be Capt. in his; and Ensign John Cole to be Lieut. in the room of Capt. Lieut. Seaman. *DP.*

Yesterday the claim to the Barony of Powis, between John Kynaston, Esq; and Sir Nath. Curzon, Bar. was further argued before the House of Lords. The further proceedings in this affair are adjourned to tuesday se'nnight. *D P. P.*

Yesterday there was a General Court of the South-Sea Company, when each Proprietor was examined, whether he had a 1000 l. stock, before he was suffered to go in: Sir John Eyles opened the Court, by offering a method to discharge part of their bond debts, which was, to annihilate 6 ¼ per cent. of the principal; but after several debates it was put to the vote and rejected. —— A Gentleman made a proposal, that a Committee of the Proprietors might be chosen to inspect the accounts; and the previous Question, whether this proposal should be put to the vote, was carry'd in the negative. —— Another proposal was made to discharge the bond debts, by reducing an half per cent. of the interest; which was also rejected. —— There were likewise many disputes relating to their trade; some were for carrying it on, others for dropping it, and others for farming both the Assiento and annual Trade, but they could not come to any resolution; so they agreed to leave it to the Directors, to consider of some method to put their affairs under a better regulation; and adjourned the Court till to-morrow se'nnight. *DP.*

This morning the Countess of Exeter, and her son the L. Burleigh, set out together for Winchester, his Lordship being to be entered of the College there. *LE.*

We hear that orders have been sent from the Admiralty-office, for all the Guardships to be cleaned and dock'd forthwith. *D P.*

On tuesday died at his seat at Berkhamstead in Hertfordshire, Sir Jos. Edmunds Moor, Bar. *P.* More, descended from Sir Will. la More, who was made Knight Banneret by Edward the Black Prince at the battle of Poictiers. He is succeeded in dignity and estate by his eldest son, who is in his minority. *D P.* 17. — Yesterday morning died the Hon. Mrs. Bellasys, sister to the R. Hon. the L. Visc. Falconbridge, at his Lordship's house in Poland-street. *C. P. DP.* — In the afternoon, the Hon. Brigadier Crofts, Brother to the late Dutchess of Bolton. *S J.* — Yesterday morning, Major General Crofts. *S J.* 17. — He was natural son of the late Duke of Monmouth. *LE.* 18.

A woman yesterday was committed to jail,
For hawking scandalous Libels, by Justice de Veil. *C.*

FRIDAY, *March* 17.

Hen. Davenant, Esq; formerly employ'd in several foreign Negotiations from this Court, set out some days since for Brussels, in order to reside there. *P.*

We hear Dr. Jurin has resign'd his place of Physician to Guy's Hospital, for which there are several Candidates, and 'tis thought will be succeeded by Dr. Clarke. *D J.* — My Brother, *I hear, sold his vote and interest in this election for* half a crown.

Yesterday Mary Price, commonly called the Witch of Westminster, and several other Hawkers and Venders of Pamphlets, were taken up in Westminster-hall, and the Court of Requests, and committed to hard labour in Tothill-fields Bridewell, for uttering a scandalous Pamphlet. *D P.*

We hear that the qualifications for Justices of the peace will be, being charged at 100 l. per ann. to the Land Tax. *D P.*

On the 3d died Margaret, Wife of Walt. Newberry, of Gracechurch-street, in the 33d year of her age, of the dropsy, with which she had been afflicted near 8 years. She was tapped 10 times, in the year 1728: in 1729, 15: in 1730, 18: and in 10 months of the year 1731, 14: in all 57 times: and had taken from her in the whole above 240 gallons of water. *D J.*

Yesterday the Reverend Mr. John Gwynn
Was presented to the Living of Llanvihangel-gonelglyn. *P.*

SATURDAY, *March* 18.

Yesterday the Rev. Dr. Penny, Dean of Litchfield, preached before their Majesties, and the Royal Family. *C.* — It being the anniversary of S. Patrick, the Tutelar Saint of Ireland, their Majesties, &c. appear'd in crosses. *P. D P.* A high Festival at Court. *C.*

The same day Mr. Leafe, some time since committed to Newgate by the Committee relating to the affair of the Charitable Corporation, was honourably discharged from his imprisonment. *P.*

On wednesday a general Court of the Bank agreed to a dividend of 3 *per cent.* for the half year ending at Lady Day 1732, which will begin to be paid Ap. 23. *P.*

The Cargo of the Heathcote from Mocha, on account of the united Company of Merchants of England trading to the East-Indies, viz. 979,000 lb. Coffee, besides several parcels of goods. *C. P. D J.* — By a private letter from Surat in the East Indies comes advice, that from May to September is the usual time of rain; but that they had not had one drop to Aug. 10. *C.*

Cambridge, Mar. 15. This day the Rev. Mr. Sedgwick, Fellow of Queen's Coll. was unanimously elected Master, in the room of the Rev. Dr. Davis. He had a Batchelor of Divinity's Degree given him by a Royal mandate, in order to qualify him for the Mastership. *C.*

The dispute about the Lectureship of S. Mary Whitechappel is decided between Dr. Simpson, Rect. of S. George in the East, and Mr. Smith, Lecturer of S. Giles's in the fields, who are to officiate alternately. *D J.*

A few days ago died at his seat at Monckton Farley, in the County of Wilts, Daniel Webb, Esq; &c. *D P.* — Last thursday morning died, at his apartment at the Cockpit, Whitehall, of the gout in his stomach, Mr. Edw. Dickinson, Chamber-keeper to his Majesty's Council office. *D J.* Chamber-keeper of the Hon. Committee of Council. *C.* Deputy-keeper of the Council Chamber at the Cockpit. *P.*

Cambridge, Mar. 16. This morning died of a sore throat the Rev. Dr. Myddleton, the supposed Author of a Letter to Dr. Waterland. *P.* Letters yesterday mention it, &c. *L E.* Some mention it, but others don't; it's hoped it is not true. *D P.*

Christned, Males, 178. Females, 174. In all, 352. *Buried,* Males, 236. Females, 236. In all, 472. Increased in the Burials this week, 25. *P.*

This day Ric. Poole stood in the pillory before Westminster-hall gate, for wilful and corrupt perjury, in relation to summoning Col. Wingfield on a Jury for the trial of Mr. Francklin. *LE. S J.*

On thursday died at his house in Salop, Sir Littleton Powis, Knt. many years one of the Justices of the Court of King's Bench, 'till he received his *Quietus est,* and had a pension allowed him. *LE.* In his 85th year. *P. Mar.* 20. — On thursday night last died —— Douglas, Esq; nephew to his Grace the Duke of Queensborough, at his lodgings at Charing-cross. *P.* —— On saturday died at New Woodstock, in Oxfordshire, Sir Will. Gordon, a Scotch Baronet. *S J.* —— This day died Mr. Lucas, an eminent Glazier in Warwick-lane, reckon'd worth 30,000 l. *L E.*

The Reverend Mr. Jenkins *has a place to be employ'd in,*
Being presented to the Living of Llanvihangel y Croyddin. *S J. WE. LE.*

MONDAY, *March* 20.

Yesterday the R. Rev. the L. Bishop of Bangor preached before their Majesties, &c. *C.* —— His Majesty was graciously pleased to issue out his Royal Proclamation on saturday last for apprehending Will. Burroughs, Esq; one of the Committee of the Charitable Corporation, and Will. Squire, one of the Assistants to the said Committee, offering a reward of 500 l. for discovering and apprehending each of them, &c. While the Proclamation was in the press, Will Burroughs, Esq; surrender'd himself. *D P.* and was order'd into the custody of the Serjeant at Arms. *C.*

The youngest son of Sir Tho. Lyttelton, Bart. and the youngest son of Sir Rog. Bradshaigh, Bart. are appointed Pages of Honour to her Majesty. *D P.*

We hear from Edinburgh, that the Magistrates of that City have clear'd the streets of Beggars, by putting them into a work-house, and placing boxes to receive charity for their support in the Kirks and Episcopal Meetings, which has had already a very good effect. *D P.*

The Rev. Mr. Alex. Chalmers was lately presented by the R. Hon. the L. High Chancellor to the Rectory of S. Stephen Coleman-street, void by the promotion of the R. Rev. Dr. Mordecai Cary to the See of Clonfert. *P.*

A woman was condemned last summer Assize at Rochester, for the murder of her bastard child, and now pleaded his Majesty's most gracious pardon; and was married immediately to the Gentleman by whom she was supposed to have had the said child. *D J.* — A Farmer.

Will. Ragley [late an eminent Smith at Gravesend. *D J.*] was found guilty, at the Assizes at Rochester, of the murder of his wife. It appear'd, that in December last he came home, and bid her make his bed; upon which she made answer, that she would not make it for him, nor his dog of a boy, and call'd him sodomitical dog: on which he took a gun loaded with shot, [with hob nails and bits of iron. *D J.*] and shot her in the breast, of which wound she languished for a week, and died. *P.* He was ordered for execution. *D J.* — *This and the foregoing instance shew,* that marriage *and* hanging *go by destiny.*

A few days since died at his seat at Leatherhead in Surrey, Hen. Lydcott, Esq; *P.* At his seat at Ashstead, near Banstead. *C. DP.* —— On the 5th died at East-Balsham in Norfolk, the Rev. Mr. Wright, formerly Rector of Wimfotsham in that County, deprived for non-compliance at the Revolution, but lived near that place, very much esteemed for his great modesty, learning, candour, and other valuable qualities, and his loss equally lamented. *D P.*

On saturday, a stain'd window of curious device,
In S. Andrew's Church Holborn was put up in a trice. *P.*
The Artist'*s name I'll tell, tho' I took nothing of* Price.

TUESDAY, *March* 21.

Yesterday his Majesty went to the House of Peers with the usual state, and gave the Royal assent to the Bill for punishing mutiny and desertion; the Bill relating to Messieurs Robinson and Thompson; and the Woolwich Church Bill. *C. P. D P.*

Yesterday came on the election of a Common-Council Man for Aldgate Ward, in the room of Mr. Dep. Atwood, deceased; the Candidates were Mr. Smith and Mr. Fludyer, and the numbers stood thus; for Mr. Fludyer 118, and Mr. Smith 121; whereupon Mr. Smith was declared duly elected; but a scrutiny being demanded, it was granted, and will begin on thursday next. *C. D P.* —— N. B. This is not Lutestring Smith, who was concerned in purchasing L. Derwentwater's estate. *L E.*

Yesterday morning died of a fever, Mrs. Sarah Abney, &c. *D P.* eldest daughter of the late Sir Tho. Abney, Knt. formerly L. Mayor of this City. *C.* —— In the afternoon died the Rev. Mr. Edgley, Vicar of Wandsworth. *D P.*

Cambridge, Mar. 20. Last week Mr. Hadderton of Trinity College, Under-Librarian to the University, departed this life: the place is worth 50 l. per ann. There were 5 Candidates to succeed him, out of whom, the Heads prick'd 2, viz. Mr. Taylor of S. John's, and Mr. Rookes of Christ's; the former carried it by 15. *D J.* His death occasion'd the report of the death of Dr. Middleton, Chief Librarian, who is in very good health. *D P.*

This morning the Countess of Portland, and her daughter the Lady Barbara, set out from her house, Whitehall, for Holland. *W E.*

March the 9th, at Leith died, as we are told,
Anne Ross, one hundred and eighteen years old.
C. P. D P.

WEDNESDAY, *March* 22.

On monday his Grace the Duke of Buccleugh was introduced to their Majesties and the Royal Family, and had the honour to kiss their several hands. *P.*

Extract of a Letter from a Merchant at Bristol *to his friend in London.* —— The Biddy Snow, of and from Bristol, John Roberts, Commander, in her way from Guiney, with upwards of 120 negroes, some Guiney wood, and Elephant's teeth on board, call'd at St. Christopher's to sell her cargo of negroes; but finding no market for them there, she sail'd for Jamaica; two days after the de-

parted from St. Christopher's, she was taken 30 leagues southward of the Island of Porto-Rico, by one Raphael Arman, Commander of the sloop St. Joseph Nostra Seignora delle Villa, belonging to the Margaritta's, and carried to Crab Island, where they took out 32 negroes, the best anchor and cable, all their spare sails and rigging, and sent away the snow to the Margarittas, with only two of Robert's men on board her, besides Spaniards: the Captain and all the rest were put on shore naked, at a place called Punk, 110 miles from the City of Porto-Rico, with a guard, to travel them through the woods, and over the mountains, with ill treatment and hungry bellies. *C. DP.*

Yesterday morn two men, a couple of sad dogs,
Were committed to the Gatehouse, for stealing two hogs. *C.*

From the PEGASUS *in Grub-street.*

The following paragraph begun our 107th Journal. 'Our kind Correspondents have frequently expressed some 'uneasiness, that we neither print their Papers, nor ac'knowledge the receipt of them; which has occasioned 'some of them to send two copies, on supposition that the 'first had miscarried. As in doing this, they have hither'to given themselves an unnecessary trouble: so they may 'justly believe it will be such for the future; especially, if 'their Letters are directed to be left at Captain GULLI'VER's, near the Temple.'

This paragraph has been taken by some Gentlemen in a sense directly contrary to that which was intended, as if we designed thereby to let them know, that they would give themselves *an unnecessary trouble for the future*, if they *directed their Letters to be left at the Captain's*, because if they were, we should take little notice of them. Whereas we intended to inform them, and we thought we had done it in plain words, That as in sending a second copy of some of their Letters, they had hitherto given themselves an unnecessary trouble, because the first copy had been received: so, they might justly believe their trouble in sending a second copy would be unnecessary for the future, especially if their first had been *directed to be left at Capt.* GULLIVER's, because then, in all probability it had come to our hands. —— This is particularly mentioned at this time, that those Gentlemen, who have favoured us with their correspondence, may send their alterations and emendations of their Pieces, so directed, in order to be inserted in the Volume of our *Memoirs*, which is now in the press.

Verses occasioned by reading the *London Journal of* February the 26th.

A Prelate, says OSBORNE, preach'd this doctrine o' late,
That the *Church* is the greatest support of the *State*;
A *traiterous* doctrine, for it is the same thing
With that *treacherous Maxim*, NO BISHOP, NO KING.
To *Protestant Dissenters*, this doctrine so spurious,
The King's faithful subjects, is highly injurious;
To the King and Government the highest insolence;
An arrogant imposition upon common sense;
The liberties of England it tends to subdue;
And is absolutely false; as now I shall shew.
When King CHARLES gave the Parliament leave by a Bill,
To sit, or to prorogue, or dissolve, at their will,
He himself then *unking'd*: this was in Forty one;
But 'twas in Forty four, that the BISHOPS went down.
The *Scots* march'd into England, soon finish'd the work;
And the Church was a Sacrifice made to the Kirk.
Brother OSBORNE, your Syllogism is out of joint,
Cries SPONDEE; and you quite have mistaken the Point.
You're to disprove, No BISHOP, no KING; and you dish up
An argument disproving NO KING, NO BISHOP.
But, as you are my Friend, and I like well your drift,
In your own way of arguing, I'll give you a lift.
In the year Forty-four, the Common Pray'r was outed;
Popish Priests, Chapters, Deans, and BISHOPS were routed;
The Great Little Arch-bishop, whom Saints all abhorr'd,
Felt a *laudable* stroak to the *laud* of the Lord.
But the KING, who was bigger, and younger, and stronger,
Kept his head on his shoulders full four years longer.
To them, MAVIUS replies, You have prov'd, to my wonder,
That BISHOP and KING have subsisted asunder:
But from both of your proofs this Conclusion I find,
That when One's gone, the Other ne'er stays long behind.

Edinburg, Mar. 13. Yesterday before noon (the Dyet appointed by the venerable Commissioners of the General Assembly of the edictal service of Mr Patrick Wotherspoon, his Majesty's Presentee, as one of the Ministers of the West Kirk) the Rev. Mr. Dawson preached a most excellent Sermon there, very suitable to the occasion, tending to promote love, peace, and other Christian virtues: but it was preaching to a rock to address the giddy rabble, who, it seems, were determined to play the Devil for God's sake; they had previously filled the locks of the Church door with rubbish, nail'd up the pulpit, and barricaded the avenues leading thereto; so that 'twas with much difficulty Mr. Dawson got access. After Sermon was over, while the Psalm was singing, a numerous mob of men and women, shaking off all regard to authority, or respect to the day, or place, got out of their seats, and in a most tumultuous manner attacked the Gentleman in the pulpit with sticks and stones, whom they had unquestionably tore to pieces, notwithstanding several Gentlemen, and others, opposed the fury, had not the Magistrates called in the City guard, which was posted hard by; so that at last the edict was got read. Seeing themselves disappointed here, and that the Magistrates had ordered the Proclamation for dispelling of mobs to be read, they got out of the Church, pulled down the copy of the edict, which was affix'd to the Kirk door, and seemed disposed to pull down the Church itself, had they not been beat off by the Guard: they afterwards renewed their attack at the West Port upon the City Guard, as they were carrying five of the rioters to goal; but after exchanging some blows, they thought proper to retire. —— This last detachment was led on by the fighing fisters. At night, when the Magistrates were returning to town, they repeated their attack on the City Guard with such fury, that the soldiers were obliged to fire on them, whereby a poor woman, standing at a distance, was wounded, as were also several of the guard. *C.*

Mount Jeuers, *in the County of* Clare, *March* 9. —— Last sunday night was seven weeks, Eliz. Hogan and Mary her daughter, were murdered near the six-mile Bridge, tho' not discovered till last night was se'nnight, when the two corpse were found in the house of the deceased, upon the breaking open the door by some of their friends, who had missed them for six weeks; the child of about seven years of age was strangled, and her neck twisted upon the bed where they lay; the mother had her neck broke and her throat cut, and one of the child's stockings thrust into the wound, and was dragg'd on the floor, without even a shift on her. The bodies were all mouldy; all the goods and money belonging to the deceased were carried off; and one Catherine Wing, now in Limerick goal, up on whom some of the cloaths were found, is all that can as yet be detected. *Ibid.*

FOREIGN NEWS.

THURSDAY, *March* 16.

Yesterday arrived the Mails from France.

Paris, Mar. 19. On the 15th, the French Academy chose the Abbot Terrasson of the Royal Academy of Sciences, to fill up the place vacant by the death of the Count de Morville. *C. P. DP.*

Extract of a private letter from Leyden, *dated Mar.* 14. —— This brings you an account of the severe usage the English receive here: 2 students going home the other night to their chambers, were attack'd, cut, beat, and taken into custody by the Town-guards, who carried them away to the Stadt-house, where they remain'd for 2 days and 3 nights, without being examin'd. The Grand Schout obliged them to pay 14 l. before he would release them. These fellows have 6 guilders a man for bringing them into the Stadt-house, and 6 guilders a man for swearing against each person: the fellow who imposes the fine is the aforesaid Grand Schout, and he himself receives the whole benefit thereof. In short, they are used so inhumanly on all occasions, that unless they are redress'd by the States, they must retire in their own defence from Leyden: they can neither go to College, or any where else on their lawful occasions, without being insulted by the Grand Schout's Myrmidons. One of the Gentlemen who was taken, was cut quite to the pericranium, and not one could lay any thing to his charge. *S J.*

FRIDAY, *March* 17.

Paris, Mar. 14. A deputation of 7 French Comedians, having at their head the two Sieurs Quinault, being introduced into the Hall of the French Academy, M. Quinault, the elder, made a polite compliment in the Academic stile, and declared the resolution they had taken to give all the Gentlemen of the Academy free entrance into their house, when, and as often as they please. *C.* —— *Our Academy justly expects the like* compliment *from* a deputation of English Comedians, *with* the two Sieurs CIBBER at their head.

Paris, Mar. 22. The Opera of *Jephthah* coming more and more in vogue, new Decorations are making for it. It is the first Dramatic Piece taken from the sacred Scriptures, that has been acted upon the French stage. *C.*

Hambourg, Mar. 14. On the 10th began the sale of the ship Apollo's cargo: the concourse of buyers was extraordinary. The Proprietors will make at least 100,000 crowns more of Tea than was expected. *D P.*

SATURDAY, *March* 18.

Hanover, Mar. 15. Recruits are raising to compleat the Companies against the arrival of his Britannic Majesty: who has been graciously pleas'd to lessen again the Tax upon Beer. *DP.*

MONDAY, *March* 20.

On saturday arrived the Mail from Holland.

Seville, Mar. 1. N. S. The King has nominated the Count de Mortemar to command the army that is assembling in Catalonia. *C. P.*

Yesterday arrived the Mail from France.

Paris, Mar. 26. About 6 in the evening a courier brought the news, that her Majesty was safely delivered of a Princess that afternoon, at 3 quarters after 4. *C. P. D P.* At Versailles. *D J.* —— The Actions are at above 1700. *C.* —— The French King was 22 years old Feb. 4. O. S. and has now 2 sons, and 4 daughters. *P.*

TUESDAY, *March* 21.

Late last night arrived the Mail from Holland.

Vienna, Mar. 5. An express from Milan, from the Governor General of that Dutchy brings advice, that the Malecontents of Corsica having implored the protection of the serene Infante Don Carlos, and a strong report being spread there, that the Spaniards intend a descent on that Island, he thought it very advisable to suspend the march of the Imperial Troops 'till new orders, and has further made such dispositions as to be able to call the Troops of that Dutchy together, and form an army on the first occasion. Upon the receipt of this express, the Emperor held a conference with Prince Eugene for 2 hours, at the issue whereof expresses were dispatch'd to Great Britain and Holland. Some advices from Italy say, that 12,000 Spaniards are actually lodg'd in the Isle of Elbe, on the coast of Tuscany. *D P. D J.*

WEDNESDAY, *March* 22.

Paris, Mar. 24. 'An embargo having been laid upon 'all ships in the Ports of Spain, from Cadiz to Barcelona, 'we expect to hear every day of an embarkation of the 'forces. *P.*

Pisa, Mar. 8. The Infante Duke set out hence the 3d, and lay at Ambrogiana, where he staid 'till the 6th, when he designed to set out for Florence. *C.*

Petersburg, Feb. 26. Admiral Severs, a Dane by birth, who was at the head of the Admiralty, is now in disgrace; so that Admiral Gordon is at the head of the Russian Admiralty. *C.*

Constantinople, Feb. 5. The famous General Count de Bonneval is at length arrived in this Capital, where he has been received with distinction by the Ottoman Ministers. He is now called *Achmet Bey*; and has a grand Palace assigned him, with a grand pension of 2000 crowns: and as an earnest of his being raised to the greatest dignities of the Empire, the Grand Seignior has nominated him Sangiac in the Archipelago, which will bring him in 2000 Ducats a year more. *P.*

Books and Pamphlets published since *Mar.* 14.

15. Of Spiritual Declensions, and the danger of being insensible under them: a Sermon by Abraham Taylor.

An Essay on the merchandize of slaves, and souls of men.

A vindication of the L. Bishop of Ely's visitatorial jurisdiction, &c.

16. Taste and Beauty; an Epistle to the E. of Chesterfield. Pr. 6 d.

An Hue and Cry after innocent blood, &c. Pr. 1 s.

Amelia: A new English Opera.

17. The Mountebank: for February, No. II. Pr. 6 d.

Sermons by the Rev. Dr. Nic. Brady, in 3 Vol.

A Voyage to Arabia the Happy, performed by the French, &c.

Stowe: the Gardens of Richard L. Visc. Cobham.

A compleat History of the intrigues of Priests and Nuns, &c.

A Tithing Table: by Will. Bohun, Esq; Pr. 1 s.

18. The Luscious Poet, &c. Pr. 1 s.

The Law of Pledges, or Pawns, &c. By John Ayliffe, L. L. D. Pr. 1 s.

20. A Letter to Sir John Eyles, Bar. &c. Pr. 3 d.

A Defence of the B. of Chichester's Sermon. Pr. 6 d.

The Footman: an opera.

A Treatise of Power, essential and mechanical, &c. By J. H.

The Happy Unfortunate: A Novel.

The Humours of the Court: a new Ballad Opera. Pr. 1 s. 6d.

The Wanton Jesuit: a new Ballad Opera. Pr. 1 s.

21. The Life of Will. Cecil, Lord Burleigh, &c. published by Arthur Collins, Esq;

Remarks on the 4 volumes of the lives of the Saints, published in 1729

A General History of the World, from the Creation to the Destruction of Jerusalem by Nebuchadnezzar, &c. By Tho. Brett, L. L. D.

A Sermon before the Sons of the Clergy, Feb. 17. By Rob. Warren, D. D.

On Tuesday Stocks were

South Sea Stock 98 to 98 1 8th. South Sea Annuity 110 3 8ths. Bank 150, for the Opening. New Bank Circulation 7 l. Premium. India 177 1 8th Three per. Cent. Annuity 97 1 half. Royal Exchange Assurance 99. London Assurance 13 3 8ths. York Buildings 8 3 qrs. African 42. English Copper 2 l. 8 s. Welch ditto 1 l. 16 s. South Sea Bonds 1 l. 18 s. Premium. India ditto 5 l. 17 s. ditto. Blanks 7 l. 7 s. 9 d. to 8 s. 20 l Prizes 19 l. 14 s to 6 d.

ADVERTISEMENTS.

This day is publiſhed,

INTEREST at one View calculated to a Farthing, at 3, 4, 5, 6, 7 and 8 per Cent. from 1000 l. to 1 l. for one Day to 96 Days; and for 1, 2, 3, 4, 5, 6, 7, 8, 9, 10, 11, and 12 Months: With Rules and Examples to caſt up Intereſt at any other Rates by the ſaid Tables. To which is added, A Table for the more ſpeedy caſting up of Salaries and Wages, from one Million to one Pound per Year. Beſides many other Tables of great Uſe in receiving and paying of Monies. The Whole being calculated, examined and corrected, and afterwards re-examined from the Preſs.

By RICHARD HAYES

Printed for W. MEADOWS, at the Angel in Cornhill.

Where may be had, by the ſame Author,

1. The Purchaſer's Pocket Companion; ſhewing at Sight what Intereſt is made by Money laid out in the Companies Stocks, or other publick Funds.

2. The Negotiator's Magazine of Monies and Exchanges, with a compleat Treatiſe of Arbitrations of Exchanges.

3. The Ship and Supercargo Book-Keeper, ſhewing the Manner of the Maſters ſettling Accounts with their Owners, the Privilege of Merchants, and Duty of Officers; with Supercargo's Accompts after the Italian Method of Double Entry.

4. An Eſtimate of Places for Life, calculated on the Chances of Lives in general, with an Account of Places in the Diſpoſal of the City of London, and their Value.

This Day is publiſhed,

The Seventh Edition, of

OGILBY and MORGAN's Pocket-Book of ROADS, with their Computed and Meaſured Diſtances, and the Diſtinction of Market and Poſt Towns. To which are added ſeveral ROADS, and above five hundred Market Towns; a TABLE for the ready finding any Road, City, or Market Town, and their Diſtance from London; A SHEET MAP of England, fitted to bind up with the Book, and an exact Account of all the FAIRS, both fixed and moveable, in Alphabetical Order, ſhewing the Days on which they are held. By W. MORGAN, Coſmographer to his Majeſty.

Printed for J. Brotherton, W. Meadows, T. Cox, W. Hinchliffe, R. Willock, in Cornhill; J. Hazard, over-againſt Stationers-Hall; W. Bickerton, without Temple-Bar; T. Aſtley, and S. Auſten in St. Paul's Church-Yard; and L. Gilliver in Fleet-ſtreet; price 1 s. 6 d.

This Day is Publiſhed.

M. J. JUSTINI ex Trogi Pompeii Hiſtoriis Externis Libri XLIV. quam diligentiſſime ex variorum exemplorum collatione recenſiti & caſtigati.

To which is added,

The WORKS of JUSTIN, diſpoſed in a Grammatical or Natural Order, in one Column, ſo as to anſwer, as near as can be, Word for Word, to an Engliſh Verſion, as literal as poſſible in the other. Deſign'd for the eaſy and expeditious learning of JUSTIN, by thoſe of the meaneſt Capacity, with Pleaſure to the Learner, and without Fatigue to the Teacher. With Chronological Tables accommodated to JUSTIN's Hiſtory; and alſo an Index of Words, Phraſes, and moſt remarkable Things. For the Uſe of Schools. By N. Bailey.

Printed for J. Brotherton; J. Hazard; W. Meadows; T. Cox; W. Hinchcliffe; W. Bickerton; T. Aſtley; S. Auſten; L. Gilliver, and R. Willock.

Of whom may be had,

I. Fundamenta Grammatices: Or, a Foundation of the Latin Tongue. By N. Farmborough, School-maſter of Watford. The Seventh Edition, reviſed by Mr N. Bailey, price 2 s.

II. The Rational Grammar; with eaſy Rules in Engliſh to learn Latin. Compared with the beſt Authors in moſt Languages, on this Subject. Written for the Uſe of his Royal Highneſs Prince William. By J. T. Philips, Preceptor to his Royal Highneſs. The Second Edition, in 12mo Price 2 s.

This day is publiſhed,

A TITHING TABLE. Shewing (by Way of Analyſis) of what Things TITHES are or are not due, either by Common Law, Cuſtom, or Preſcription. By W. BOHUN, of the Middle Temple, Eſq;

Printed for J. Brotherton, J. Hazard, W. Meadows, T. Cox, W. Hinchcliffe, W. Bickerton, T. Aſtley, S. Auſten, L. Gilliver, and R. Willock; price 1 s.

Of whom may be had, The Second Edition, of

The LAW of TITHES. Shewing their Nature, Kinds, Properties, and Incidents by whom, to whom, when, and in what Manner payable; how, and in what Courts to be ſued for and recovered; what Things, Land or Perſons are charged with or exempted therefrom. With the Nature, Incidents and Effects of Cuſtoms, Preſcriptions, real Compoſitions, Modus decimandi, Libels, Suggeſtions, Prohibitions, Conſultations, Cuſtoms of London, &c. wherein all the Statutes and adjudged Caſes, relative to the Subject, are introduced and conſidered. By W. BOHUN, Eſq; pr. 5 s. 6 d.

This Day is publiſhed,

(Price One Shilling)

Numb. I. *To be occaſionally continued*, of

THE QUÆRIST: Or, The Merry Critick. Containing Remarks ſerious and comical, on modern Plays, Pamphlets, Authors, &c. Together with an Examin of GEORGE BARNWELL, the Lover, and others. Interſpers'd with curious Poems on ſeveral Occaſions, never before made publick.

Scribimus Indocti; Doctique poëmata paſſim. Hor.

If Wits they have, 'tis of an evil Kind,
An impious Good, and a Debauch of Mind;
* * * * * *

Printed for, and ſold by T. Dormer, at the Star and Garter, over-againſt the Caſtle Tavern, in Fleet-Street; T. Warner, in Pater-Noſter-Row; E. Nutt, at the Royal-Exchange; A. Dodd, without Temple-Bar; and J. Crichley, at Charing-Croſs.

Where may be had,

A Scheme for a New Lottery: Or, a Huſband and Coach and Six for Forty Shillings, &c.

This Day is publiſhed,

The Second Edition corrected, of

A LETTER to Sir JOHN EYLES, Bar. Sub-Governor of the South-Sea Company, occaſioned by the Debates at the laſt General Court.

Printed for J. Brotherton at the Bible, next the Fleece Tavern in Cornhill; and ſold by A. Dodd, without Temple-Bar. Price Three Pence.

WHereas there is advertiſed in the *Univerſal Spectator*, and other Papers, that a new Edition of the moſt curious and uncommon Flowers of the twelve Months in the Year; Notice is hereby given to all Noblemen, Ladies, and Gentlemen, that thoſe Prints are only Copies, and that we are not any ways concerned in 'em but the Original, which are only ſold by us Robert Furbur, Gardener, at Kenſington; Peter Caſteels, Painter, in Long-Acre; Henry Fletcher, Engraver, in Nottingham-Street, the upper End of Plumbtree-Street, Bloomſbury; and at Mr. Tho. Bowle's in St. Paul's Church-Yard, Printſeller, at Two Pounds Twelve Shillings and Six Pence coloured, and plain One Pound Five Shillings each Sett.

N. B. There's a thirteenth Plate, in which a Liſt of the Subſcribers Names, with a Border of Flowers about it, and our Names engrav'd at the Bottom of each Plate, and thoſe are the Originals, and all without our Names are Copies; theirs are not above half the Bigneſs.

Juſt publiſhed,

Dedicated to the Gentlemen of the Navy of England.

THE MEMOIRS of Monſieur *du Guë Trouin*, Chief of a Squadron of the Royal Navy of France, and Great Croſs of the Military Order of S. Lewis; containing all his Sea-Actions with the Engliſh, Dutch, and Portugueſe, in the late Wars of King William and Queen Anne.

Tranſlated from the French by a *Sea-Officer*.

Printed for J. Batley, at the Dove, in Pater-noſter Row,

Where may be had,

The TRADITIONS of the CLERGY no way Deſtructive of Religion: A Sermon preach'd at Bingley-Church, on Sunday September 12th, 1731.

By IS. SMITH,

Miniſter of Haworth, near Kighley, Yorkſhire.

A L S O,

I. The Religion of Nature conſidered. To which is added a Poſtſcript, containing Reflections on Mr. Chubb's Diſcourſe concerning Reaſon, &c ſo far as it reſpects this Subject.

II. Some Thoughts concerning Virtue and Happineſs, in a Letter to a Clergyman.

This Day is publiſhed,

STOWE, the *Gardens* of the Right Honourable Richard Lord Viſcount Cobham.

Addreſs'd to Mr. POPE.

Devenere locos lætos, & amœna Vireta
Fortunatorum nemorum, ſedeſque beatas. Virg.

Printed for L. Gilliver, at Homer's-Head, over againſt S. Dunſtan's Church in Fleet-ſtreet.

Where may be had,

Of FALSE TASTE, the third Edition, with an additional Letter. By Mr. POPE.

ATHELWOLD: A Tragedy. By A. Hill, Eſq; as it is acted at the Theatre Royal in Drury-Lane.

A Collection of PIECES in PROSE and VERSE, which have been publiſhed on occaſion of the Dunciad. Together with Epigrams in Laud and Praiſe of the Gentlemen of the Dunciad, and completes all former Editions of the ſaid Book.

This Day is publiſhed,

THE *Preſent State of Europe*: Or, *The Hiſtorical and Political Monthly Mercury*; giving an Account of all the publick and private Occurrences, Civil, Eccleſiaſtical, and Military, that are moſt conſiderable in every Court; with a more particular Account of the Affairs of Great Britain, &c.

For the Month of *February*, 1732.

With political Reflections upon every State. Vol. XLIV.

Continued Monthly from the Originals publiſhed at the *Hague*, by the Authority of the States of Holland and Weſt-Frieſland, &c.

Printed for the Aſſigns of the Executors of H. Rhodes and Eliz. Harris; and ſold by J. Roberts in Warwick-Lane.

Where are to be had,

The whole Forty Three Volumes, beginning *November*, 1688. (Or ſingle Ones, from *July*, 1690, to this Time)

S. PALMER, Printer, near the Church in Bartholomew-Cloſe, being oblig'd, thro' an ill State of Health to remove his Buſineſs a little way out of Town (and his Partner, J. Huggonſon, intending to remove elſewhere) his Apartment and his Printing Room, which is 65 Foot long and 27 Foot wide, with glaz'd Lights all round, and very ſtrong and airy, is to be Lett, being very fit for any Tradeſman that requires a great deal of Light and Room.

N. B. If the Apartment is not big enough, there is more Room to be had on reaſonable Terms.

WHEREAS other *Coffee-Houſes*, and other *Publick Houſes*, take of their Cuſtomers 8 s. for a Quart of Arrack, and 6 s. for a Quart of Rum or Brandy made into *Punch*, ſo that it is now become the ſettled Price throughout the Town, and ſeldom leſs than a Bowl of 1 s. 6 d. is to be had: Therefore, for the better accommodating all Gentlemen, that are Lovers of *Punch*,

This is to give Notice,

That I have opened on Ludgate-hill, the *London-Coffee-Houſe* and *Punch Houſe*, (Two *Punch-Bowls* on Iron Pedeſtals before my Door,)

Where the fineſt and beſt old Batavia Arrack, Jamaica Rum, and French Brandy, are made into *Punch*, with the fineſt Ingredients, viz.

A Quart of Arrack made into *Punch* for 6 s. and ſo in Proportion to the ſmalleſt quantity, which is half a Quartern for four Pence Half-penny.

A Quart of Rum or Brandy made into *Punch* for 4 s and ſo in Proportion to the ſmalleſt Quantity, which is half a Quartern for 3 d. And Gentlemen may have it as ſoon made, as a Gill of Wine can be drawn; with the beſt of Eating, Attendance, and Accommodation.

This Undertaking has occaſion'd many, whoſe *Intereſt* it is to poſſeſs Gentlemen with ſuch an Opinion, that the Liquors by me uſed are not good: The Publick is hereby aſſured, that I buy my Goods on the Keys, and at the beſt Hand, with Ready Money, and am at this Time provided with as well-choſen Brandies, Rum [illegible] k, as any in Town, and will at all times procure [illegible] that is imported: But what may convince Gentlemen of the Truth hereof, is, (not only by the Encouragement I meet with) that the Sherbet is always brought by itſelf, and the Brandy, Rum, or Arrack in the Meaſure, ſo there can be no Impoſition, either in Quantity or Quality; for the Proof whereof I appeal to all Gentlemen who have done me the Honour to call at my Houſe.

James Aſhley.

THE Great and Wonderful Cures daily perform'd by Dr. *Bateman*'s Pectoral Drops, in the following Diſtempers, have gain'd them ſo indiſputable a Character, that few Families who have ever heard, or experienced the Virtues thereof, care to be without them in their own Houſes, viz. the Gout, Rheumatiſm, Jaundice, Stone, Gravel, Aſthma's and Cholicks, of what Kind or Nature ſoever, whether proceeding from Wind, Cold, or Hesterick Affection. Beſides which, there is no one Secret in the whole Art of Phyſick of that ſurpriſing and (were it not under the Confirmation of continual Experience) almoſt incredible Effects in Colds, Agues, Fevers, and thoſe endemic Evils which appear in moſt Constitutions at Spring and Fall. The Price of each Bottle, in which are three moderate Doſes, is but one Shilling, and may (by Vertue of the King's Letters Patents) be had at the Printing-Office, Bow-Church-Yard, Cheapſide, and no where elſe within three Quarters of a Mile from thence.

N. B. A Book of the Virtues thereof, with Teſtimonials of ſome hundred Cures perform'd thereby, under the Hands of Perſons of known Worth and Credit, may be had gratis with the ſaid Bottles.

Note alſo, Shopkeepers, &c. in any Town, where they are not already ſold, may be ſupply'd with the above Drops, (and good Allowance) to ſell again, by directing to Wm. Dicey, or Tho. Cobb and Comp. at Dr. Bateman's Wholeſale Warehouſe in Bow-Church-Yard, London.

LONDON: Printed by S. PALMER and J. HUGGONSON, in *Bartholomew-Cloſe*, for Captain GULLIVER, near the *Temple*, where Letters and Advertiſements are taken in: As alſo at the *Rainbow Coffee-Houſe* in *Cornhill*, and *John's Coffee-Houſe* in *Sheer-Lane*, near *Temple-Bar*. [Price Two Pence.]

The Grub-ſtreet Journal.

NUMB. 117

Thurſday, *MARCH* 30, 1732.

'Tis the too bold improbability,
That makes ridiculous the labour'd lye.
Mr. Wycherley to Mr. Dryden.

SIR,

THE favourable reception *The Modern Huſband* has met with from the Town, having given me ſome occaſion to doubt of the juſtneſs of the judgment I had framed of that Piece, from ſeeing it the firſt night of its repreſentation, I reſolved to give it a careful and unprejudiced reading. You know, Mr. BAVIUS, tho' it be poſſible to form a pretty tolerable idea of the goodneſs or badneſs of a Play from ſeeing it acted once; it is certainly the ſurer way to judge rightly of it, to examine it carefully in one's cloſet. An Author may, indeed, fare worſe from this examination, than from an immediate ſentence delivered from the benches in the Boxes or Pit. The good humour with which the Play houſe generally inſpires one; the beautiful appearance of the Ladies, who never fail to croud at a firſt night; the action of the Players; their cloaths, ſcenes, and other theatrical decorations, help very much a good, as well as a bad Play; and contribute not a little to byaſs us in our opinions. The tryal of the Play is, when we ſee it diveſted of all theſe exterior helps; and take it, as we would a fine woman, naked of all its ornamental drapery; then it is either really beautiful or not.

Having examined *The Modern Huſband* in this manner, without ſeeing any reaſon to alter my firſt judgment, I ſhall, with your good leave, Mr. BAVIUS, lay before you ſuch reflections as occurred to me during this examination. You muſt not expect a formal piece of criticiſm from me, deduced with method and order; all that I pretend to, is only to give you my reaſons for diſliking a performance that had been ſo cried up, both within and without the Houſe, before its appearance in print.

The deſign and end of Comedy, Mr. BAVIUS, is, as I take it, to divert and inſtruct mankind. We may then lay down as a maxim, That no Comedy that wants this fundamental point can be good. Now, I preſume, it will not be thought, that the diverting of mankind is properly done by the jokes of a Pickled-herring, the grimaces of a Scaramouch, or the agility of a Tumbler: at leaſt it muſt be allowed, that theſe methods of diverting mankind come not within the province of Comedy; nay, that they are even below Farce. What then does come within that province? To divert mankind, *Comedy chuſes ſuch characters, as having nothing abſolutely ill in them, render themſelves nevertheleſs ridiculous by their follies.* This then we may lay down as a general rule in this point.

As to the inſtruction of mankind, the ſecond end of Comedy, this may be done either by drawing characters that may ſerve for models for our conduct in life; or elſe by ſhewing the inconveniencies, under which the vicious bring themſelves, and opening a gate for them to eſcape. People that find themſelves in the circumſtances of ſuch a Drama, are by this means inſtructed, and very often reformed.

Thus Comedy, Mr. BAVIUS, may be either ſerious, or merry, or both. Our beſt Comedies are thoſe that mix the ſerious and merry together: of this kind are *The Careleſs Huſband*, *The Conſcious Lovers*, *The Journey to London*, &c. The decency of polite life is preſerved in theſe pieces; and the whole interſperſed with characters that enliven the ſcene, and feaſt the mind with an agreeable mixture of light and ſolid meats. The Fable likewiſe ought to be ſuch, as ſuits with theſe two ends; and this will neceſſarily exclude characters not ſeen in common life, or at leaſt very rarely. For no Poet ought to rake into human nature, and compound characters from the exceſſes of each of our paſſions, or the intemperance of ſome of our humours, in order to entertain his Audience with ſomething new; which would rather prove an inlet to vice and folly than an excluſion of either. Such a thing were ſcarce allowable, even if there were not follies and vices enow practiſed by the polite part of both ſexes, that require an immediate cure. A Poet therefore that neglects theſe, to expoſe others that as yet are only theoretic, and are introduced into life by his prolific brain, does a very abſurd thing, and falls very ſhort of the true end and deſign of Comedy. But to come to the Play now before me.

The Author of *The Modern Huſband* does not appear to have had a true notion of Comedy. He ſeems to have thought, that the aſſembling of a certain number of characters together, under the titles of Huſbands and Wives, Sons and Daughters, is ſufficient to preſerve the relation that ought to be kept up between the perſons of the Drama; and that the making of them talk together, is enough to form the dialogue part of it. Thus with the addition of a popular ſcene or two, ſuch as a great man's levee, which he thought could not fail of pleaſing, and therefore clapt it in without enquiring whether it was neceſſary to the Play or not, and ſome other accidental chit-chat, which filled up a certain quantity of paper, having artfully tacked the whole together, he calls this motly compoſition a Comedy.

Now if half the perſons of the Drama, and the converſation that paſſes between them, might all be entirely left out, without hurting the main action of the Play, all good judges will condemn the performance; unleſs there is ſomething exceeding beautiful and entertaining in the converſations of theſe perſons, that may juſtify their unaccountable introduction. I would fain aſk this Author, what buſineſs Capt BELLAMANT and EMILIA, Mr GAYWIT and LADY CHARLOTTE have with the main deſign of the Play? What buſineſs Lord RICHLY and his levee have? What is there in their converſation to juſtify their introduction? What variety is there in their characters? Mr. GAYWIT is only EMILIA dreſt in mens cloaths; and EMILIA, GAYWIT in womens. Capt. BELLAMANT and Lady CHARLOTTE need only change cloaths to appear each the other, we have the Captain's word for it.

Capt BELLAMANT. You dear agreeable creature! Sure never were two people ſo like one another as you and I are; we think alike, we act alike, and ſome people think we are very much alike in the face P. 64.

But what are their characters? Never was any thing more impertinent than Lady CHARLOTTE, or more ſilly than her converſation. She is ſuppoſed to be a young Lady of great life and vivacity, whoſe ſallies are to be both witty and agreeable Hear her ſpeak.

Lady CHARLOTTE. Oh! dear MODERN, I wiſh you had ſeen EMILIA's dreſſing-box; ſuch japanning, ——— he! he! he! — ſhe hath varniſhed over a window till ſeveral times, before ſhe diſcover'd ſhe had placed the wrong ſide upwards. P. 26.

Mrs. MODERN anſwers her in the ſame ſtyle. Oh! my Dear, I have had juſt ſuch another misfortune; I have laid out thirty pounds on a cheſt, and now I diſlike it of all things.

Wonderful indeed! But ſhe has not done yet.

But you have not heard half my misfortune; for when I ſent my cheſt to be ſold, what do you think I was offer'd for my thirty pounds worth of work? P. 27.

Lady CHARLOTTE. I don't know; fifty guineas, perhaps.

Mrs. MODERN. Twenty ſhillings, as I live.

Lady CHARLOTTE. Oh! intolerable! Oh! inſufferable!

Intolerable, inſufferable indeed! — After the Hazard they re-enter, and Lady CHARLOTTE is as bright as ever.

Lady CHARLOTTE. Oh, my Dear, you never ſaw the like. ——— MODERN has held in nine thouſand mains in one hand, and won all the world. P. 29

Oh heaven and earth! but this is wonderful!

Lady CHARLOTTE [ſpeaking of GAYWIT in a rallying way] Oh! the moſt agreeable creature in the world. — He has more wit than any body: he has made me laugh five hundred hours together. P. 30.

Gods! is't poſſible! ſure ſhe exaggarates: Oh BAVIUS! Oh! CONUNDRUM! Can this be true? The 5th, 6th, 7th and 8th ſcenes of the third Act are full of the ſame redundancies of wit, too numerous to point out here: but I cannot omit ſome ſtrokes of fire in the 5th Act.

Capt. BELLAMANT. Siſter, good-morrow; Lady CHARLOTTE abroad ſo early! P. 63.

Lady CHARLOTTE. You may well be ſurpriz'd: I have not been out at this hour theſe fifty years. P. 64. — Smart indeed!

Lady CHARLOTTE [Speaking of the Capt.] Well, he has ſuch an exceſſive aſſurance, that I am not really ſure whether he is not agreeable. Let me dye, if I am not under ſome ſort of ſuſpence about it; ——— and yet I am not neither; ——— for to be ſure I don't like the thing; —— and yet methinks I do too; —— and yet I do not know what I ſhould do with him neither. —— Hi! hi! hi! — This is the fooliſheſt circumſtance that ever I knew in my life. P. 72.

Hi! hi! hi! thou art the fooliſheſt creature I ever ſaw in my life.

Lady CHARLOTTE. What can the creature mean? I know not what to think of him. Sure it can't be true! but if it ſhould be true — I can't believe it true; — and yet it may be true too. P. 75. — Lack a-day, lack-a-day.

But to be a little ſerious. Either Lady CHARLOTTE's character is deſigned as a model for young Ladies of faſhion to imitate, or quite the reverſe; and ſhe is ſome impertinent character the Author intended to ridicule. Which of the the two he meant, I really can't tell. If it be an original of his own invention, which he has compoſed out of the intemperance of female vivacity, he has been led away by that falſe notion ſo prevalent among modern Poets, of ſhewing ſomething new; and, as I obſerved before, fallen very ſhort of the true end and deſign of Comedy. If he had any particular perſon in his eye, whoſe folly he intended to expoſe, in order to prevent other young Ladies from falling into the ſame errors; he has indeed ſucceeded in expreſſing that character, but will will hardly cure either that perſon, or ſave any others of the like turn. For as throughout the whole Play, Lady CHARLOTTE does not ſhew one grain of underſtanding, the real Lady CHARLOTTES that tread the grand Theatre of the world (if ſuch there be, which I much queſtion) muſt be ſuppoſed as void of underſtanding (for if they had any, they would not be what they are) and if they are void of underſtanding, what hopes of amendment or cure? Lady CHARLOTTE's vivacity ariſes from her want of underſtanding. Had he therefore given this Lady a little underſtanding, to temper this immoderate vivacity of her nature; he would have drawn a better character, and a more uſeful one.

As to EMILIA and GAYWIT, they are but faint ſketches after Lady GRACE and Mr. MANLY in *The Journey to London*; as Mr. and Mrs. BELLAMANT, are of Lord and Lady EASY in *The Careleſs Huſband*, with an alteration of ſome few circumſtances.

I know not why he has made Lord RICHLY a great man, unleſs it be for the ſake of deſcribing a levee; nor why this great man ſhould be the greateſt rogue that ever lived: I don't conceive but that the Play had gone on full as well without it. The making of a great man abſolutely and totally bad, both in his public and private ſtation, in his morals and behaviour, is ſo poor, ſo ſcandalous, ſo vulgar, and ſo mean a piece of ſatire, that (fools, malicious or diſcontented perſons, may indeed laugh, but) all good and wiſe men will deſpiſe the odious picture.

As to the *Modern Huſband* and his Lady, they are ſuch wretches, that they are as much below Comedy, as they are our pity: he calls them, very juſtly, in the *Prologue*, a pair of monſters *moſt entirely new*.

To night (yet ſtrangers to the ſcene) you'll view
A pair of monſters moſt entirely new!
Two characters ſcarce ever found in life,
A willing Cuckold ——— ſells his *willing Wife!*

Thus the affectation and inordinate deſire of ſaying ſomething new, has made our Author draw ſome of the vileſt characters that ever yet entered into Comedy, and honour them with the title of *Modern*; implying (in contradiction to what the *Prologue* ſays) by that title, not only, that there are ſuch characters, but that they are common too: for what can the *Modern Huſband* mean, but a character actually come into faſhion? elſe it is theoretic, as obſerved above, and introduced into life only by his prolific brain. But what inſtruction or pleaſure can be gathered from this heap of abſurdity? thoſe parts from which inſtruction may be reaped, (viz.) the reformation of Mr. BELLAMANT, the prudent conduct of his Wife; and the marriage of GAYWIT and EMILIA, being imitations from much better Plays than this; and thoſe parts from which we are to expect pleaſure, being a moſt monſtrous kind of wit, conſiſting in an affected invention of ridiculous names, ſuch as the *Dutcheſs of* SIMPLETON *Lady Betty* SHUTTLECOCK; Mrs. SQUABBLE, Mis. WITLESS, Lady BARBARA PAWNJEWELS, &c. and a more affected choice of very extraordinary ſimilies and ſurpriſing chit-chat.

Theſe, Mr BAVIUS, are the reflections that occurred to me in reading the *Modern Huſband*. I found indeed here and there, but very ſparingly ſcattered, a touch that implied good ſenſe and reflection; but, like an April ſun, it only ſhews itſelf, and away; bad weather returns, and we have a great deal of filth to ſtruggle through. I am,

Mr. BAVIUS,

March 7, 173½. Your unknown friend and admirer

DRAMATICUS

P. S. The Author having mentioned in the Prologue, hat he *feared no Critick that can read*; and ſaid in one part of his Play, that this ſelling one's Wiſe was quite †*unknown to the Ancients*; I deſire to know how I muſt underſtand this paſſage in *Horace*, Book III. Ode 6.

Mox juniores quærit adulteros
Inter mariti vina: neque eligit
Cui donet impermiſſa raptim
Gaudia luminibus remotis:
Sed juſſa coram non ſine conſcio
Surgit marito, *ſeu vocat inſtiſtor,*
Seu navis Hiſpanæ magiſter,
Dedecorum pretioſus emptor.

† This is not ſaid in any Part of the Play. GAYWIT ſays indeed, P. 23. 'It is a modern trade, *unknown to our 'Anceſtors.*' For it does not appear, that they were ſo much debauched as theſe Romans. BAVIUS.

DOMESTIC NEWS.

C. *Courant.*	E P. *Evening Poſt.*
P. *Poſt-Boy.*	S J. *S. James's Evening Poſt.*
D P. *Daily Poſt.*	WE. *Whitehall Evening P.*
D J. *Daily Journal.*	LE. *London Evening Poſt.*

THURSDAY, *March* 23.

Yeſterday the Rev. Mr. Bundy preach'd in the Chappel Royal at S. James's, before her Majeſty, his Royal Highneſs the Duke, and the 5 Princeſſes. *C.* ——— The R. Hon. the L. Wilmington, Preſident of the Council, was pleaſed to appoint Mr. Cha Dickinſon to be a Chamber-keeper to the Council-Office, in the room of his father deceaſed. *P.*

This morning his Excellency Geo. Woodward, Eſq; his Majeſty's Envoy Extraordinary to the Court of Poland, ſet out. *P.* ——— This morning he will ſet out. *D P. Mar.* 24. —Yeſterday morning he ſet out. *P. Mar.* 25.

On tueſday Dr. Clarke was unanimouſly choſen Phyſician for Guy's Hoſpital, in the room of Dr. Jurin, who hath reſigned. *C. D P.* —— A fine braſs ſtatue is going to be made of Mr. Guy, to be ſet on a pedeſtal, with iron rails round it, in the Court of the ſaid Hoſpital. *D P.*

The account publiſhed yeſterday, under the title of *An extract of a letter from* Briſtol, relating to the taking of the Biddy Snow by the Spaniards) (if underſtood to be a late tranſaction) is a groſs impoſition; the ſubſtance thereof was publiſhed in the *D. Journal*, Sept. 6; the Snow having been taken in April. *C.* — *Were this* tranſaction *either* formerly *or* lately, *it was* a groſs impoſition *upon us* by the Spaniards.

Yeſterday the R. Hon. the L. Mayor, with ſeveral of the Aldermen, went in the L. Mayor's barge to Weſtminſter, and held a Court for conſervation of the river Thames, commonly called Swan hopping, &c. *S J.*

We are aſſured that a method is newly found out to prevent infallibly the ſmoaking of chimneys, let their former ſituation be where or what it will. *S J.* —— *Mr.* TH - *reads* their form or ſituation, &c.

M. de Chavigny, who arrived here ſome months ſince from Paris, hath not as yet taken upon him a publick character. *L E.*

The Vicarage of Wandſworth in the County of Surrey, is in the gift of Mr. Ackworth, an unfortunate Gentleman, now priſoner in the King's Bench, and is reputed worth 400 l. per ann. *WE.*

They write from Glouceſter, that on monday ſe'nnight two Brothers in law, in a ſmall boat, endeavouring to paſs through one of the arches at Over's-bridge, it overſet, and they were both drowned. ——— On ſaturday ſe'nnight one Owner Pearce's paſſage boat bound from Briſtol to Newnham, ſtruck upon the ſands within 2 miles of Newnham, and ſunk immediately; by which accident 8 or 10 perſons loſt their lives. *D P.*

On tueſday laſt died at his houſe in Eſſex, after a tedious indiſpoſition, Capt. Winter, an old Commander in the Eaſt India Company's ſervice. *D P. C.* —— Yeſterday died of an apoplexy, at his houſe in Chancery-lane, Mr. Jabez Collier, an eminent Solicitor in the Court of Chancery. *D P.*

Chipping Campden, Glouceſterſhire, Mar. 20. The Office of High Steward of this Corporation being vacant by the death of the late L. Conway, the R. Hon. the E. of Gainſborough, and Will. Taylor of the Inner-Temple, Eſq, were put in nomination for that Office, and the latter duly elected. *P.*

Laſt night, between 11 and 12, one Sam. Slow, who keeps a Pamphlet ſhop without Temple-Bar, was committed by 6 Juſtices to Newgate, for publiſhing a Pamphlet called, *Vanella, or, the fair Concubine.* And we hear by the interceſſion of ſeveral eminent Jews, there are Warrants out againſt the Publiſhers of a Pamphlet called, *An Hiſtorical and Law Treatiſe againſt* Jews *and* Judaiſm. *W E.* ——— Yeſterday the Publiſhers of a ſcandalous, fooliſh Pamphlet were taken up; and one committed to Newgate. *D P. Mar.* 24.

The ſtory of the Warrants, *I dare ſay, is not true,*
But put in as a puff by the pyratical crew,
Whoſe Authors *ſeem* Turks, *and their* Printer *a* Jew.

N. B. *Inſtead of* Law Treatiſe *the falſe Title page has* Law-Treaties. *I take it to be nothing but a* Treatiſe *printed in two* Poſt boys *ſome time ago.*

FRIDAY, *March* 24.

Yeſterday his Majeſty, after walking in the Mall with the Envoys of Holland, Sardinia and Sweden, went in his chair to the Meuſe, and there view'd the ſtabling, &c. and gave a handſome preſent to the Workmen. *D P.* Ten guineas. *P.* —— On monday his Majeſty ſign'd a commiſſion, appointing Will. Simpſon, Gent. Lieut. in the Hon. Major Gen. Tatton's Regiment of foot, &c. *P.*

On wedneſday in the evening his Royal Highneſs the Prince gave an handſome entertainment at the Hay-market, to ſeveral perſons of diſtinction, of both ſexes. *C.* — Laſt night there was an aſſembly at the Opera houſe in the Hay-market. &c. *P.*

Yeſterday the Hon. John Roberts, Eſq; and Mr. Gray, a young Gentleman belonging to the Navy Office, Author of *A treatiſe on gunnery*, were admitted Fellows of the Royal Society. *C.*

Laſt week died at his ſeat of Penn in Buckinghamſhire, John Penn, Eſq; aged about 90, by whoſe death near 2000 l. per ann. falls to his Grandſon, Sir Nath. Curzon, Bar. *D P.* ——— On ſaturday died Eaſtland Hawksmore, Eſq; at his ſeat near Gainſborough in Lincolnſhire. *C.* At Gainſborough. *D P.* —On wedneſday died at his houſe in Lime-ſtreet, Mr. Tho. Grainger, Chief Clerk to the Committee of accounts of the Eaſt India Company. *D J.* At his lodgings at Iſlington. *P.* ——— Yeſterday Mrs. Haddock, a maiden Gentlewoman, daughter of Sir Richard, as ſhe was drinking a diſh of tea, at her lodgings near Golden-ſquare, was taken with an apoplectick fit, and died with the diſh in her hand. *P.*

The Small-pox has raged very much at Queenſborough, for 2 or 3 months, and been very fatal, having carried off many, both old and young. *D J.*

SATURDAY, *March* 25.

Yeſterday the Rev. Dr. Lockyer, Dean of Peterborough, preached before their Majeſties and the Royal Family at S. James's. *C.* —— Mr. Burroughs, lately Chamber-keeper at the Secretary's Office, is appointed one of the poor Knights of Windſor; and Mr. Winn, a Domeſtick of the R. Hon. the L. Harrington, is appointed to ſucceed him as Chamber-keeper. *C. D P.* Mr. Will. Gwyn. *P.*

On thurſday the Directors of the Bank, for the more ready diſpatch of buſineſs, appointed two additional Caſhiers, viz. Capt. Gregory and Mr. Caruthers. *C.* There are now 6 Caſhiers. *D J.*

Yeſterday the R. Hon. the Lord Mayor, attended with ſeveral of the Aldermen, went to Stratford to hold a Court of Conſervacy, according to annual cuſtom, and afterwards croſſed the river to Greenwich, where they were entertained at dinner in a very elegant manner. *D P.*

Yeſterday a General Court of the York Buildings Company was held at their houſe in Wincheſter-ſtreet, when Sir Bibye Lake and Sol. Aſhley, Eſq; were choſen Aſſiſtants, in the room of Mr. Squire and Mr. Townley. The accounts of the Company were laid before the Court by the Governor, to the great ſatisfaction of the Proprietors. *D J.*

Dover, Mar. 23. Yeſterday two Sons of the Lord Waldgrave embarqued here for Calais, in their way to Paris. *P.*

Yeſterday a General Court was held of the South Sea Company, at their Houſe in Threadneedle-ſtreet, when the Sub-Governor acquainted them, that the Court of Directors had conſidered of what was referr'd to them at the laſt General Court, about putting their affairs under a better regulation; and after ſeveral ſpeeches made, *pro* and *con*, a motion was made, and carried in the affirmative, that 600,000 l. Bonds in the Company's hands ſhould be forthwith cancell'd. And then, in order to prevent the Company running farther in debt, they reſolved that no Bonds ſhould for the future be iſſued without the conſent of a General Court called for that purpoſe ſpecially; and that when money ſhall be appropriated for paying any of the Company's Bonds, the ſame to be apply'd to all thoſe now outſtanding in equal proportions, the preſent amount being 1,967,850 l. Alſo that the Bonds hereafter iſſued ſhall be enter'd in a regiſter Book kept for that purpoſe, which may be inſpected by any Proprietor of 3000 l. Stock; and when any be paid off, to be done numerically. Likewiſe that the Court of Directors frame a ſcheme, built upon the plan then preſented by Mr. Woodford, to divide the Stock, viz. ¾ into an annuity free from all incumbrances, and ¼ into trading Stock charged with all the Company's Bonds; and to have the effects in trade, and all the benefits and advantages ariſing thereby; ſubject alſo to any, and all accidents that may happen therein; and that they print the ſaid ſcheme for the deliberation of the Proprietors. The debates about what is to be done with the million expected at Michaelmas, from the ſinking fund, was adjourn'd, the ſame not being yet appropriated by Parliament: after which the Sub Governor adjourn'd the Court *ſine die.* *D P.*

MONDAY, *March* 27.

Yeſterday the R. Rev. the L. Biſhop of Glouceſter preached before their Majeſties and the Royal Family, in the Chappel Royal at S. James's. *C.* —— Mr. Elliſon is made Enſign in Lieutenant Gen. Tatton's Regiment of Foot, in the room of Enſign Cole. *D P.*

On ſaturday, Mr. Chavigny, who lately arrived here as Reſident from the Court of France, went to reſide at the houſe of John Chetwynd, Eſq; Repreſentative in Parliament for Stockbridge in Hants, in Greek ſtreet, Soho. *P.*

On friday died the Lady of Sir Will. Humfreys, Bar at his ſeat at Jenkins in Eſſex. *P.* On ſaturday morning. *C. D P.* On friday died in Lincoln's-Inn-Fields, the Lady Stoughton, Wife of Counſellor Turner. *D P.* — We hear that Mr. Leaſe, belonging to the Charitable Corporation, who was diſcharged out of Newgate, died on friday laſt. *P.*

Wedneſday laſt Sam. Slow was committed to Newgate, by 6 of his Majeſty's Juſtices, for publiſhing a Pamphlet, in which were contained ſeveral leud and ſcandalous paragraphs, or paſſages, full of the moſt obſcene ribaldry, the ſpreading whereof has a tendency to corrupt the minds and manners of the youth, and others, of both ſexes of this kingdom. Warrants are granted by the ſaid Magiſtrates againſt others for the like offence. *C.*

Not for the Hiſtorical Treatiſe againſt the Jews;
But for vile bawdy Books, *fit only for the ſtews.*
And 'twould be for the benefit of the whole nation,
If themſelves, as well as Jews, *were to ſuffer caſtration.*

TUESDAY, *March* 28.

On thurſday Capt. Beresford, Commander of the Prince William, in the Eaſt India Company's ſervice, was married to Miſs Silveſter of the Tower a young Lady of great beauty and merit, with a fortune 10,000 l. *C.* ———
If this Lady's beauty *is as* great *as her* merit.

On ſunday, the High Conſtable of the Tower Diviſion, took up 19 vagrants, &c. in and about the pariſh of Shoreditch, 5 of whom were committed to Bridewell, and the reſt diſcharged on giving ſecurity. *C.*

Yeſterday died at his Chambers in Lincoln's Inn [at his houſe near Lincoln's-Inn. *D P.*] Ric. Foley, Eſq; Member of Parl. for Droitwich in Worceſterſhire, *one of the* Prothonotaries of the Court of Common-Pleas, and Brother to the R. Hon. the Lord Foley. *D J.* ——— On friday night died at Lincoln, the Rev. and Learned Mr. James Gardiner, M. A. Sub Dean of that Cathedral, &c. *L E.*

Yeſterday the Printer and Publiſhers of Fogg's Journal of ſaturday laſt, were taken into cuſtody of Meſſengers for the ſaid Paper. *L E.*

Of Poſtills *thy modeſt* Advertiſer, *Friend* Fog,
Declares, I am to'd, that thou'rt an impudent dog,
Who, to keep thee from biting, ſhould'ſt wear a
large plog.

WEDNESDAY, *March* 29.

On thurſday his Excellency the Earl of Cheſterfield made a preſent to the Queen of the picture of the Prince of Naſſau Frieſland; and we hear his Highneſs will ſhortly come over to England. *D J. P.*

Mr. Tho. Murray is appointed by the Duke of Argyle, to be Deputy Store-keeper at Woolwich. *P.*

Yeſterday was married at Hampton-Court by the Rev. Dr. Skirrit, Zachary Chambers of Chelſea, Eſq; to the Widow Lomax, (Mother of the late Caleb Lomax, Eſq; Member of Parliament for St. Alban's) a Lady of 12,000 l. fortune. *D P.*

On ſunday laſt, about ten in the morning, the woods lying near the Spaniard's by Hampſtead-Heath, were ſet on fire by ſome ill deſigning people; when the ſame (being very dry) burnt with great fury for about two hours; but was happily extinguiſhed, after having much damaged about ten acres. *Ibid.* —— *The* Spaniard *is a bad neighbour.*

Guildford, Mar. 27. This day the tryal of Mrs. Dorothy Longley came on here for the murder of her husband John Longley, by giving him Poiſon, called liquid *Laudanum*, on the 28th of Auguſt laſt. It appeared by the evidence of Mr. Seddell the Apothecary, who attended him, that he died a very ſudden and unaccountable death; and he did believe he was poiſoned with *Laudanum*; that at the opening of the body, ſome part of the ſtomach was mortified; and that when they give a Dog a wine glaſs full of liquor which came out of his ſtomach, the dog was preſently taking with ſleeping, and loſt the uſe of his hind parts, and continued ſo for ſeven hours, and then died. This was confirmed by ſeveral ſurgeons. It was alſo proved, that ſhe ſent for two half ounces of *Laudanum*, one on Saturday, the other on Sunday. She in her defence proved, that he was a groſs man, and was given to ſleeping, and had been a hard drinker; and as to her ſending for *Laudanum*, ſhe took it herſelf for a bleed[illegible]

at the nose: she brought several persons to her Reputation. The Counsel for the King then brought evidence to prove as to her character, that she had no good one in the neighbourhood. Upon the whole, after a tryal which lasted from 9 o'clock in the morning to 12 at night, there being no matters of fact proved against her, only circumstances, the Jury, after staying out about three quarters of an hour, brought her in *Not Guilty*. P.——*It would be a hard case upon the women, if they might ast and then poison their husbands, as well as husbands starve their wives, without being hanged.*

From the PEGASUS in Grub-street.

A Scotch Member acquainted the Society, that by a private letter from Edinburgh he had received advice, that at the late Funeral of one FRANCIS ——RIST, there having been a great hurricane, the populace were of opinion, the Devil had carry'd away the body, as well as the soul; and about three thousand assembled in the streets, crying, it was a *sham funeral*: they seized the leaden coffin, opened it, and beat it flat, then punched it full of holes, and lastly threw it into the grave, with six *dead dogs* after it. He added that he expected other particulars, in a post or two, which he would communicate when received.

Say, envious GRUBS, why thus is H —y blam'd,
For *Elocution* and for *Action* fam'd?
You see, he daily challenges his Foes:
None dares the Champion face to face oppose.
Nor wonder, since his voice, and limbs, and mien
Are terrible to all, when heard, or seen.
While ancient *Elocution* he restores,
Ation reviv'd inforces what he roars.
And should his lungs, or voice, or visage fail,
His brawny brandish'd arm must needs prevail.
Triumphant he would end the whole dispute,
And with one knock-down argument confute. MÆVIUS.

FOREIGN NEWS.

THURSDAY, *March* 23.
Yesterday arrived the Mail from France.
Paris, Mar. 29. Madam Magot, a country Farmer's wife 3 leagues from Versailles, is pitch'd upon to be nurse to Madame the fourth. C. P.
Carthagena, Jan. 12. We have received advice of a ship bound from Peru, Port Callao, with 1,500,000 pieces of eight for Panama, which was to have been employ'd in purchasing goods left by the last galleons, being intirely lost in her passage, which, with the ill success in the last fair, puts the Galleonista's at Panama in the greatest distress. D J.

FRIDAY, *March* 24.
Brussels, Mar. 24. On thursday last, the Count de Kinski, lately the Emperor's Ambassador in France, arrived here from Paris. C.
Hamburg, Mar. 21. We have received advice, that his Prussian Majesty has declared to the Roman Catholic Clergy of his dominions, that in case an immediate stop be not put to the unjust persecution that is carrying on against the Protestants of Salzburg, he will order all the Roman Catholic Churches to be shut up, and all the Clergy to depart the Country, &c. C.
Amsterdam, Mar. 28. Letters from Parma of the 8th take notice, that the levies are continued in that Dutchy, for raising 2 new regiments for the service of the Emperor, which is thought something extraordinary. D P.

SATURDAY, *March* 25.
Mantua, Mar. 14. On sunday at 4 in the afternoon the Infante Don Carlos arrived at Florence. The Electrice Palatine met him at Court, and complimented him. After a conversation of about an hour, she went into her apartment, where she received the visit of the Prince, and conducted him to the Great Duke's Chamber, who received him on his bed with extraordinary marks of friendship, and embrac'd him thrice with a great deal of tenderness. P.

MONDAY, *March* 27.
On saturday arrived the Mail from Holland.
Seville, Mar. 7. The Count de Mortemar, nominated General and Commander in Chief of the Forces that are assembling in Catalonia, purposes to set out the beginning of next week. C
Vienna, Mar. 19. We are assured, that at the breaking up of a great Council of war, which was held some days ago at Prince Eugene of Savoy's, orders were sent to the Italians which were to return to Germany from Italy, to remain there, and to others, which were marched, but were yet within call, to return back. C. D P.
Hague, Mar. 30. Letters from Leipsick advise, that the Duke of Saxe Gotha is dead, leaving issue seven Princes, and two Princesses. C. P.

TUESDAY, *March* 28.
Yesterday arrived the Mail from France.
Paris, Mar. 28. The execution of the gang of Robbers

at the Greve is continued: on wednesday last the *Grand Catin* (as she was called) was hanged there, to the great chagrin of the compassionate populace. She was one of the finest women in Paris; and having been debauched by a Person of Quality some years ago, she has had intrigues with several since, who however did not dream of her being a thief, and a harbourer of such people; she flatter'd herself 'till her tryal was ready to come on, that some of them would get her pardon; but when she found herself mistaken, she prepar'd for her exit, and died like a heroine. She was about 24 years old, and her body was carried to the Amphitheatre of S. Cosme to be dissected. P.
——*This was better, than to walk the streets of London, after such an adventure with Persons of Quality.*
Schaffhausen, Mar. 22. According to some letters from Milan, 8000 Imperialists are actually on their march for Corsica, where will be an army of 15,000 effective men, to act against the Malecontents. D P.
Paris, April 2. On monday the King made a considerable alteration in the Ministry, by associating the Keeper of the Seals in the Office of Prime Minister with the Cardinal de Fleury. P. DP. The Actions still continue at 1705 livres. D P.
This day arrived the Mail from Holland.
Rome, Mar. 15. On thursday evening arrived the Duke de St. Aignan, Ambassador of France. W E.
Leghorn, Mar. 15. They work hard repairing and augmenting the fortifications of this place, and new levies are making with great diligence. —— They write from Corsica, that 2000 Malecontents have burnt and plunder'd the province of Olmia, for having submitted to the Republick. L E. The Country of Olmia W E. —— The Rebels having sacked the Town of Olmia, there marched against them a party of the garrison of Ajaccio, who put the inhabitants of Palestina to flight, burnt the Rebels granaries there, and returned with a booty of 1000 beasts. S J. 100 cattle. D J. *Mar.* 29.

WEDNESDAY, *March* 29.
Genoa, Mar. 15. On monday 1000 German recruits arrived at San Pietro d'Arena, to embark for Corsica. C D J.
Hague, April 4. N. S. 'Our Ambassador Mynheer Van
'Hoey's, Master of the horse, is just arrived express from
'Paris. It is since reported, that the Cardinal Minister
'was retired, and had left the Keeper of the Seals in
'his room. His Eminency's retreat is looked upon here
'as an alarm to war, and as a declaration of the harmony
'between France and Spain in the enterprize the Spanish
'Fleet is going upon. P.

Books and Pamphlets published since our last.
23. The Genuine Works in verse and prose of the R. Hon. George Granville, Lord Lansdown.
Observations on Mr. Chubb's Discourse concerning Reason: by Anthony Bliss, A. M.
A Letter to the Proprietors of South-Sea Stock.
24. A Critique on Milton's Paradise Regain'd.
A Letter to Achitophel Bouteseu, &c. Price 6 d.
25. A Sermon on occasion of the death of Mrs. Mary Wilks: by James Foster. Price 6 d.
The Progress of Love, in four Eclogues.
The Lillian Compendium, &c. by Will. Baily.
Modern History: by Mr. Salmon. No. 93.
27. The Feasts and Fasts of the Church of England.
Taste. An Essay. Pr. 1 s.
Milton Restor'd. No. II. Pr. 6d.
A Letter to the Author of the Defence of the Bishop of Chichester's Sermon.
28. A new Treatise of Geography: by Edw. Hatton.
The Foundation of moral Virtue consider'd, in a Sermon, by Tho. Mole. Pr. 6 d.
Love in all shapes, &c. Pr. 1 s.
Universal Benevolence, or a Demonstration of the goodness of Reveal'd Religion in the Scripture account of Charity. Pr. 2s.
29. A short History of the Charitable Corporation, &c. Pr. 1 s.
Ecclesiastical Memoirs translated from M. Tillemont. No. III.
A Sermon occasioned by the death of Mr. Edw. Chamberlen: by Sam. Wilson. Pr. 6 d.
Present State of the Republick of Letters.

On Tuesday Stocks were
SouthSea Stock 98 1 qr. 98 3 8ths, 98 1 qr. 98 3 8ths. South Sea Annuity 109 7 8ths, to 110, for the Opening. Bank 150 1 half, for ditto. New Bank Circulation 7 l. Premium. India 176, 175 3 qrs. 176 1 qr. 176, for the Opening. Three per Cent. Annuity 97. Royal Exchange Assurance 99. London Assurance 13 3 8ths, to 1 half, for the Openining. York Buildings 7 3 qrs. African 42. English Copper 2 l. 10 s. Welch ditto 1 l. 16 s. South Sea Bonds 3 l. 10 s. Premium. India ditto 5 l. 15 s. ditto. Blanks 7 l. 7 s. 3 d. 20 l. Prizes 19 l. 12 s. 6 d.

This Day is published,

(With his Lordship's Effigies curiously engraved by Baron)

Written by EUSTACE BUDGELL, Esq;

MEMOIRS of the *Life* and *Character* of the late Earl of Orrery, and the Family of the *Boyles*. Containing several curious *Facts* and *Pieces of History*, from the Reign of Queen *Elizabeth* to the present Times: Extracted from *Original Papers* and *Manuscripts*, never yet printed. With a short Account of the Controversy between the late Earl of *Orrery*, and the Reverend Dr. *Bentley*, and some *sel. Letters* of Phalaris, the famous *Sicilian* Tyrant, translated from the *Greek*.

—— Te. animo repetentem exempla tuorum,
Et *Pater* ÆNEAS & *Avunculus* excite HECTOR. Virg.

Printed for W. Meares at the Lamb in the Old Bailey.

This day is published,

INTEREST at one View calculated to a Farthing, at 3, 4, 5, 6, 7 and 8 per Cent. from 1000 l. to 1 l. for one Day to 96 Days; and for 1, 2, 3, 4, 5, 6, 7, 8, 9, 10, 11, and 12 Months: With Rules and Examples to cast up Interest at any other Rates by the said Tables. To which is added, A Table for the more speedy casting up of Salaries and Wages, from one Million to one Pound per Year. Besides many other Tables of great Use in receiving and paying of Monies. The Whole being calculated, examined and corrected, and afterwards re-examined from the Press.

By RICHARD HAYES.

Printed for W. Meadows, at the Angel in Cornhill.

Where may be had, by the same Author,

1. The Purchaser's Pocket Companion, shewing at Sight what Interest is made by Money laid out in the Companies Stocks, or other publick Funds.

2. The Negotiator's Magazine of Monies and Exchanges, with a compleat Treatise of Arbitrations of Exchanges.

3. The Ship and Supercargo Book Keeper, shewing the Manner of the Masters settling Accounts with their Owners, the Privilege of Merchants, and Duty of Officers, with Supercargo's Accompts after the Italian Method of Double Entry.

4. An Estimate of Places for Life, calculated on the Chances of Lives in general, with an Account of Places in the Disposal of the City of London, and their Value.

This Day is published,

A VOYAGE to Arabia Fœlix through the Eastern Ocean and the Streights of the Red-Sea, being the first made by the French in the Years 1708, 1709, and 1710. Together with a particular Account of a Journey from Mocha to Muab, or Mawahib, the Court of the King of Yaman, in their second Expedition, in the Years 1711, 1712, and 1713. Also a Narrative concerning the Tree and Fruit of COFFEE, collected from the Observations of those who made the last Voyage; and an Historical Treatise of the Original and Progress of COFFEE, both in Asia and Europe; with curious Draughts, of several Parts of the Coffee-Tree, on Copper Plates; 1. Of the Tree in full Proportion; 2. Of its Branch with its Flowers and Fruit; 3. Of its Leaves; all drawn in *Arabia* according to Nature. Translated from the French. To which is added, An Account of the Captivity of Sir *Henry Middleton* at Mokha, by the *Turks*, in the Year 1612; and his Journey from thence to Zenan, or Sanaa, the Capital of the Kingdom of Yaman, with some Additions, particularly relating to that Country and the Red-Sea. Printed for E. Symon, over-against the Royal-Exchange, in Cornhill.

This Day is Published,

M. J. JUSTINI ex Trogi Pompeii Historiis Externis Libri XLIV. quam diligentissime ex variorum exemplorum collatione recensiti & castigati.

To which are added,

The WORKS of JUSTIN, disposed in a Grammatical or Natural Order, in one Column, so as to answer, as near as can be, Word for Word, to an English Version, as literal as possible in the other. Design'd for the easy and expeditious learning of JUSTIN, by those of the meanest Capacity, with Pleasure to the Learner, and without Fatigue to the Teacher. With Chronological Tables accommodated to JUSTIN's History; and also an Index of Words, Phrases, and most remarkable Things. For the Use of Schools. By *N. Bailey*.

Printed for J. Brotherton; J. Hazard; W. Meadows; T. Cox; W. Hinchliffe; W. Bickerton; T. Astley; S. Austen; L. Gilliver, and R. Willock.

Of whom may be had,

I. Fundamenta Grammatices: Or, a Foundation of the Latin Tongue. By N. Farmborough, Schoolmaster of Watford. The Seventh Edition, revised by Mr. N. Bailey, price 2 s.

II. The Rational Grammar; with easy Rules in English to learn Latin. Compared with the best Authors in most Languages, on this Subject. Written for the Use of his Royal Highness Prince William. By J. T. Phillips, Preceptor to his Royal Highness. The Second Edition, in 12mo. Price 2 s.

This Day was published,

REMARKS on the four Volumes of the Lives of Saints; published in English, and printed at London Anno 1729. Or four Appendexes to be bound up with the said four Volumes, to remedy and prevent Mistakes.

By THEOPHILUS EUPISTINUS.

Printed for T. Osborne in Grays Inn; price 2 s.

This Day is published,

HISTORIA LITTERARIA: Or, An Exact and Early Account of the most valuable Books published in Europe. In this Number are contained the following Extracts, viz. The Life and Actions of the famous Saladine: Part 3. Boerhaave's Chymistry: Part 1. Life of the Emperor Justinian, and the Empress Theodora, and of [illegible]. History of the Island of Hispaniola or San Domingo: Part 2. With the present State of Learning; or, the Books now printing or published in the Places following, viz.

[illegible], Rome, Milan, Florence, Padua, Venice, Lucca, Leipsick, Nuremberg, [illegible], Hamburg, Bourdeaux, Paris, Montpelier, Dijon, [illegible], Amsterdam, Franeker, Hague, and London. Printed for N. P[illegible] against South[amp]ton-Street in the Strand. [illegible] [illegible]ill; and sold by T. Payne in [illegible] [illegible]-Row [illegible] 1 s.

[illegible] had,

The two first Volumes [illegible] Litteraria, containing 12 Numbers, [illegible] single Numbers.

March 25, 1732.

PROPOSALS for Printing by Subscription, PANARETON: [illegible] Treatise of all Virtue: Or, the Pandects of Christianity. Being the [illegible] Will of God, and Duty of Man, methodically laid down, according to [illegible] the Law of immediate Obedience, and [illegible] Innocency, otherwise called the *Law of Nature*, and the *Moral Law*, contained in Ten Commandments. The Second the Law of Faith, and Love in Christ Jesus, wherein all that is to be known, believed and practised, in order to Salvation, is briefly comprehended. With *Prayers* and *Private Devotions* for most of the Concerns of Life. By THOMAS ALLEN, Rector of Kettering in Northamptonshire, Author of *The Practice of an Holy Life*; or, *The Christian's Daily Exercise*, and late of Wadham-College, Oxon. Subscriptions are taken in by B. [illegible], at the Red Bull in Ave-Mary-Lane, Ludgate-Street, near St. Paul's, who will deliver each Number as soon as printed, whereof Notice will be given in the *St. James's Evening Post*.

PROPOSALS.

I. The whole Work will make about fourscore Sheets which is designed to make two Volumes in Octavo. II. The Author, for the Ease of such Gentlemen and Ladies as are willing to encourage this Undertaking, proposes to publish every Month 8 Sheets, until the whole Work is compleated, for which they are to pay at Delivery only one Shilling; so that in about ten Months the whole will be compleated. III. Those who subscribe for Six, shall have a Seventh *Gratis*.

N. B. The Work will be put to the Press as soon as Two Hundred and Fifty are subscribed for.

This Day is published,

The Seventh Edition, of

OGILBY and MORGAN's Pocket-Book of ROADS, with their Computed and Measured Distances, and the Distinction of Market and Post Towns. To which are added several ROADS, and above five hundred Market Towns; a TABLE for the ready finding any Road, City, or Market Town, and their Distance from London; A SHEET MAP of England, fitted to bind up with the Book, and an exact Account of all the FAIRS, both fixed and moveable, in Alphabetical Order, shewing the Days on which they are held. By W. MORGAN, Cosmographer to his Majesty.

Printed for J. Brotherton, W. Meadows, T. Cox, W. Hinchliffe, R. Willock, in Cornhill; J. Hazard, over-against Stationers-Hall; W. Bickerton, without Temple-Bar; T. Astley, and S. Austen in St. Paul's Church-Yard; and L. Gilliver in Fleet-street; price 1 s. 6 d.

Lately published,

THE HISTORY of ENGLAND, as well Ecclesiastical as Civil, from the Invasion of the Romans, to the End of the Reign of King James the Second. By M. de Rapin Thoyras. Done into English from the French, with large and useful Notes, by N. Tyndal, A. M. Vicar of Great Waltham in Essex. Illustrated with the Heads of the Kings and Queens, engraven by Mr. Vertue, and with several Maps and Genealogical Tables on Copper Plates, in 15 Vols. 8vo.

Printed for James and John Knapton, at the Crown in St. Paul's Church-Yard.

Where may be had,

ACTA REGIA; or, An Historical Account of the Records and Acts in Rymer's Fœdera, on which Mr. Rapin has grounded his History of England, from the Reign of King Henry the First, to that of King Charles the First. Translated from the French of M. Rapin Thoyras, in 4 Vols. 8vo.

Publick Notice is hereby given,

[*For the Information of all* Gentlemen *and* Ladies]

THAT *Charles Lyon, Grecian*, Maker of the Jerusalem Washballs, otherwise called Grecian Washballs, so universally esteem'd by all the Quality, who, for many Years, have made use of no other, being removed from Ironmonger-Lane, where he had carried on his Business about 40 years, to the House of *Edward Hubbard*, over against Serjeant's-Inn, Chancery-Lane, where they may at any Time be furnished therewith, by sending a Letter to the said *Edward Hubbard*, who has, for ten Years past, assisted Mr. *Lyon* in making them, being the only Person intrusted with the true Method of preparing them, and to whom alone the Receipt will be communicated upon the Decease of the said Mr. *Lyon*.

N. B. At the following Places is sold an incomparable Tooth-Powder, which makes the Teeth as white as Ivory, and preserves them from Rotting or Decaying. It effectually cures the Scurvy in the Gums. Price one Shilling each Box.

Also a delicate Lip-Salve, that cures any rough and chopp'd Lips, and makes them of a fine lively red. Price one Shilling each Pot, viz. Cocoa-Tree Chocolate-House, Pall-Mall; Will's Coffee-House, Scotland-Yard, Charing-Cross; Guildhall Coffee-House, by Guildhall; Sword-Blade Coffee House, Birchin-Lane; and the East-India Coffee-House Leadenhall-Street.

FOREIGN BOOKS

Just Imported by John NOURSE, *at the* Lamb, *without* Temple Bar.

CHEF d'Oeuvre d'un Inconnu, 12°, 2 Vol. 1732.

2. Histoire du Theatre Italien, 8vo. *Par.* 1730.

3. Il Pastor Fido del Signo Cavalier Guarini. Edizione Nuova, Arricchita di curiose, ed utili Annotazioni, 4°, *Amsterdam.* 1732.

4. Histoire des Perses & des Grecs par Rollin, 12°, Tom. III. *Amst.* 1732.

5. Theatre de le Grand, 4 Vol. *Par.* 1732.

6. Memoires des Hommes illustres, 12°, 17 Vol. *Par.* 1732.

7. Cassandre, 12°, 10 Vol. *Par.* 1732.

8. Traite general du Commerce, 4°, par Ricard 5me Edition, Augmentee par Nicolas St[illegible], 1732.

9. Les Metamorphoses d'Ovide, traduits par M. L'Abbe Banier. Ouvrage enrichi de figures en Taille douce.

10. Terentius, cum Interpretatione Donati & Calphurnii & Commentario perpetuo. Curavit. Ant. Henr. Westerhovius, 2 Vol. 8°, *Hagæ—Comitum*, 1732.

11. Histoire des Rois de Chypre, 12°, *Par.* 1732.

12. Lettres de Mongon qui roulent sur les Negotiations, dont il a echarge 12°, *Amst.* 1732.

At the same Shop may be had,

A new Edition of Thucydides, in Fol. Mr. Le Clerc's Commentaries on the Bible, 4 Vol. or the 3d and 4th Volumes alone.

This Day is published,

(Price Two Shillings and Six Pence)

THE GENTLEMAN FARRIER: Containing Instruction for the Choice and Direction in the Management of Horses, either for Draught or Pleasure, on for a Journey, or in the Stable. With an Account of their Distempers, and Receipts for the Cure of them.

To which is added,

An Appendix concerning Dogs, either for the Field or the Lap: Wherein their Diseases are described, and the Means to Cure them. The Horse Receipt, by the D. of Devonshire, E. of Orrery, Ld. Carleton, Sir John Packington, Gen. Seymour, Portman Seymour, James Nicholson, Esqs; Thornton E. of Broxham, and published by Direction of a Person of Quality.

Printed for F. Cogan, at the Middle-Temple Gate; and H. Lintot, at the Cross-Keys in Fleet-Street.

Books printed for J. Batley, at the *Dove* in *Pater-Noster-Row*.

1. MIscellaneous Essays, viz. 1. Of Company and Conversation. 2. Of Solitariness and Retirement. 3. Of Nobility. 4. Of Contentment. 5. Of Women. 6. Of the Knowledge of God, and against Atheism. 7. Of Religion. 8. Of Kings, Princes, and the Education of a Prince. 9. Of Greatness of Mind. 10. Of the Education of Children. 11. Of Law. 12. Of Man. 13. Of old Age; with the Life and Conversion of St. Mary Magdalen, and some Reflections upon the Conversion of the good Thief. Also the Life and Conversion of St. Paul, by Sir Richard Bulstrode, Kt. Envoy at the Court of Brussels from King Charles II. and King James II. Published with a Preface, by his Son Whitlock Bulstrode, Esq; The second Edition. Price 4 s. 6 d.

2. The memorable Things of Socrates. Written by *Xenophon*, in five Books. Translated into English. The second Edition. To which are prefixed, the Life of Socrates from the French of Monsieur Charpentier, a Member of the French Academy. And the Life of Xenophon, collected from several Authors; with some Account of his Writings. Also compleat Tables are added by *Edward Bysshe*, Gent. price 5 s.

LONDON: Printed by S. Palmer and J. Huggonson, in *Bartholomew-Close*, for Captain Gulliver, near the *Temple*, where Letters and Advertisements are taken in: As also at the *Rainbow Coffee-House* in *Cornhill*, and *John's Coffee-House* in *Sheer-Lane*, near *Temple-Bar*. [Price Two Pence.]

The Grub-ſtreet Journal.

NUMB. 118

Thurſday, *APRIL* 6, 1732.

IN our 108th, 113h, and 116th Journals, an examination of Doctor B's. *Preface* to his MILTON's *Paradiſe Loſt* was publiſhed, as an introduction to a particular examination of the Doctor's alterations of that Poem. And tho' all the moſt material things in that Preface have been already anſwered; it may not be amiſs to take ſome notice of two or three particulars of leſs conſequence, and thereby compleat the whole animadverſion.

In P. 3. the Doctor ſays, that the Copy 'was purchaſed 'for ten pounds, and (if a ſecond edition follow'd) for 'five pounds more.' From which Mr. FENTON's account varies a little, who † tells us, that 'the payment of the 'fiveteen pounds depended on the ſale of three nume-'rous impreſſions.' Which I hope, for the honour of the Bookſellers, is a leſs true account than the Doctor's.

At P. 6. The Doctor declares 'I wonder not ſo much 'at the Poem itſelf, tho' worthy of all wonder; as that 'the Author, ... confin'd in a narrow and to him a 'dark chamber, ſurrounded with cares and fears, could 'ſpatiate at large through the compaſs of the whole Uni-'verſe, &c.' To a perſon who was blind, I imagine, that, with reſpect to contemplation, there could be no manner of difference betwixt a *broad* or a *narrow chamber*; ſince both *to him* muſt be equally *dark*: he might not indeed breathe, but he might think as freely in one, as in the other. And as to the circumſtance of his blindneſs, this is ſo far from increaſing my *wonder* at the unbounded range of his imagination, that it really leſſens it very much. And in this ſentiment I find Mr. FENTON, a Gentleman at leaſt as famous for his poetical genius as Doctor B. He, reaſoning a little upon this matter, tells us, that MILTON ‡ 'having treaſured up ſuch immenſe 'ſtores of ſcience, perhaps the faculties of his ſoul grew '*more vigorous after he was deprived of his ſight:* '*and his imagination* (naturally ſublime, and inlarg'd by '*reading Romances*, of which he was much inamour'd '*in his youth*) when it was wholly abſtracted from ma-'terial objects, was more at liberty to make ſuch amazing 'excurſions into the ideal world, when in compoſing his 'Divine work he was tempted to range

Beyond the viſible diurnal ſphere.

But how contrary ſoever this *Preface* hitherto has appeared to the opinion of the Learned, they will not be altogether ſo averſe to the concluſion of it. P. 6, 7. 'Had 'theſe very Notes been written forty years ago; it would 'then have been prudence to have ſuppreſs'd them, for 'fear of injuring one's riſing fortune.' The *prudence* of *ſuppreſſing* ſuch *notes then*, would not I believe have been queſtioned by any Reader, even tho' the reaſon aſſigned for their publication now, which immediately follows, had been omitted. 'But now when ſeventy years *jam-'dudum memorem monuerunt*, and ſpoke loudly in my ears, '*Mitte leves ſpes & certamina divitiarum*; I made the 'notes *extempore*, and put them to the preſs as ſoon as 'made, without any apprehenſion of growing leaner by 'cenſures, or plumper by commendations.' The truth of this matter of fact, no body who reads theſe Notes can diſpute; but the *prudence* of this conduct, in a perſon of ſo advanced an age, will not be ſo univerſally acknowledged. Had theſe *notes* been made *extempore*, by a young man, and publiſhed immediately; the heat, inconſiderateneſs, and ſelf-conceit natural to our youthful years, might have been pleaded in excuſe of ſo raſh a proceeding. Or had they been written by any one even of the Doctor's age, and only handed about in Manuſcript, the haſtineſs of the compoſition might have a little excuſed the oddneſs of it. Or if ſuch a ſtrange deſign had been put in execution only upon ſome leſs conſiderable Author; the world would not have had the ſame reaſon to reſent this uſage in ſo ſevere a manner. But for a perſon, who, tho' allowed to be a very learned Critic, was never imagined to be a Poet, to pour out in extemporary effuſions, crude and indigeſted criticiſms, upon the compleateſt Poem in the Engliſh language; to pretend to alter and correct it in every page; to ſtrike out great numbers of verſes; and to put in many of his own; this juſtly raiſes the wonder, ſcorn, and indignation of all that hear it. This is to act more like a Pedagogue than a Critic; and to treat the Heroic Poem of the Great MILTON, like the exerciſe of a School-boy. A proceeding ſo extravagant, that it would be even incredible, did not the Doctor himſelf aſſure us of the truth of it, and the notes themſelves ſtrongly confirm it. This infinitely exceeds the undertaking of ZOILUS in his animadverſions upon HOMER: of whom it is not even ſuſpected, that he had the audaciouſneſs to make them *extempore*; and much leſs, that he had the vanity, folly, and frenzy to declare that he did.

Every part of this *Preface* has been now carefully conſidered; and thereby the main foundation ſubverted, upon which much the greater part of the Doctor's alterations are built. Before we enter upon a particular examination of which, I ſhall beg leave to preſent to the Public the following Paper, which evidently ſhews, that if the Doctor's Art of Criticiſm be allowed, thoſe parts of this Poem, which he has left untouched, as needing no correction, are as liable to alterations, as thoſe which he has criticized. From hence it will likewiſe follow, that not only *Paradiſe regain'd*, and *Samſon Agoniſtes*, which he declares to be *without faults*, but alſo any Poem of any other Author whatſoever, may be amended after the ſame manner. And as this Paper is written, not only in the Doctor's manner, but likewiſe in his very expreſſions, it is no extravagant piece of banter, nor does it ſet his *Notes* in a light at all more ridiculous, than he himſelf has placed them.

BAVIUS.

† FENTON's *Life of Milton*, prefixed to an edition of *Paradiſe Loſt*, in 1730. P. 23.

‡ *Life of Milton*, P. 27, 28, Mr. FENTON ſays, P. 14. that MILTON left no more than 1500 l. behind him for the ſupport of his family.

To BAVIUS, Secretary of the Society of Grubſtreet.

BAVIUS,

IN the 4th Book of MILTON's *Paradiſe loſt*, v. 677. begins this paſſage.

Millions of ſpiritual Creatures walk the Earth
Unſeen, both when we wake, and when we ſleep:
All theſe with ceaſeleſs praiſe, his Works behold
Both day and night: how often from the ſteep
Of echoing Hill or Thicket have we heard
Celeſtial voices to the midnight air,
Sole or reſponſive each to others note,
Singing their great Creator: oft in bands
While they keep watch, or nightly rounding walk,
With Heav'nly touch of inſtrumental ſounds
In full harmonic number join'd, their ſongs
Divide the night, and lift our thoughts to Heaven.

In my late Edition you will find, that I have made no alteration in theſe verſes, except in v. 684 *Hymning* inſtead of *Singing*, juſt to keep my hand in uſe. While they were under conſideration, I was in a good humour, and a little drowſy: but now upon a reviſal, I find them polluted with ſuch monſtrous faults, ſuch a Defoedation in all the parts, as could proceed from no body but the ignorant and pragmatical Editor, whom I have had ſo much to do with. It will be a difficult task amidſt this heap of rubbiſh, to find out the native beauty, which the Author inſtincted through it: but let us try what can be done.

V. 677. Millions *of ſpiritual Creatures walk the Earth.*] Indeed! *Millions!* ſo many could not walk together in Paradiſe, which the Author muſt mean by *Earth*, unleſs *Gods met Gods and juſtled in the dark.* Beſides, ſo many ſingers would either quite deafen ADAM and EVE, or elſe deprive them of all ſleep, and diſtract them. Read it therefore, as the Author gave it *Several.*

Spiritual Creatures.] Here *ſpiritual*, which is properly four ſyllables, is by violence contracted into two. Whereas MILTON never makes it leſs than three: as *v.* 406. Spiritual *may of pureſt Spirits be found.* Here *ſpirit* — part of the firſt word is made two ſyllables, tho' *ſpirits*, in the ſame verſe is only one. By *ſpiritual Creatures* are certainly meant *Angels*, and ſo it came from MILTON without any affectation.

Walk the Earth.] What Language is that? *Walk* is never uſed in a tranſitive ſenſe, but a neuter; as in this very paſſage, v. 685, and III. 440.

So on this windy Sea of Land, the Fiend
Walk'd *up and down alone.*

Indeed in III. 200, we read,

Ye that in waters glide, and ye that walk
The Earth.

But I have plainly ſhewed in my note upon that place, that the Author was there guilty of *an overſight*. In the place before us read *walk upon the earth*; which is perſpicuous and intelligible: but when this vile Editor foiſted in *Spiritual Creatures* for *Angels*, he was forced to leave out the Prepoſition *upon*; and ſo for the ſake of the meaſure gave us nonſenſe.

V. 678. Unſeen, *both when we wake and when we ſleep.* Pray where's the wonder, that ADAM and EVE ſhould not *ſee* theſe Angels while they were *aſleep?* and what is it to the purpoſe, that the Angels were *unſeen?* A ſlight variation makes it good ſenſe; *And ſee. Think not*, ſays ADAM, *that Heaven wants ſpectators*, for the Angels *ſee, whether we wake or ſleep.*

V. 679. *And theſe with* ceaſeleſs *praiſe his Works behold.*] He adds, *Both day and night* in the next line; therefore *ceaſeleſs* is ſuperfluous and redundant. I perſuade myſelf our Poet gave it *celſeſt*, higheſt, from the Latin *celſus:* the ſenſe is unexceptionable; and who knows not MILTON's inclination to coin new words. See my note on I. 167.

Behold *with praiſe.*] This does not come up to the Poet's uſual exactneſs. They might *behold the works with* mental, internal *praiſe:* here ſhould be ſome word to ſhew that they expreſſed their praiſes. MILTON gave it *extoll*; as in this book, *v.* 436. *But let us ever* praiſe *him, and* extoll *His bounty*. And *v.* 164. *Join all ye Creatures to* extoll *him firſt.*

V. 680. *Both day and night.*] A manifeſt imitation of VIRGIL, *noctes atque dies.*

Ibid. How often from the ſteep.] *Steep* makes a rime to the penultimal verſe, which is carefully to be avoided. Better therefore *from the tip*; or if *tip* approaches too near to rime, it may be *top.*

V. 681. *From the* ſteep *Of eccboing hill or thicket.*] At firſt reading this ſtrikes one, as if it was *the ſteep of thicket* (ſee my note on I. 393.) whereas a *thicket* rather implies a low ſituation as IX. 179. *Through each* thicket *dank or dry, Like a black miſt* low *creeping.* The Author, who rather aims at ſtrong expreſſion, than ſmooth and flowing numbers (ſee note III. 145) muſt have given it thus. *How often from the top Of ecboing hill, or* from *thicket have we' heard:* the *e* in *we* is cut off in the pronunciation, as uſual before a vowel; for *h* is no letter. See *The Accidence.*

V. 682. *Celeſtial voices* to *the midnight* air.] The Author is not ſpeaking of the *air*, but the time, which was at midnight, as v. 687. *their ſongs Divide the night.* Therefore it muſt be here, *at the midnight* hour. He would have ſaid, *celeſtial voices* juſt at twelve a clock; but he prudently conſidered, that *clocks* were not then invented. You may ſee *noontide air* falſly put for *noontide hour* again, II. 309. as I have proved in my note there.

V. 689. *Sole* or reſponſive *each to others note.*] The Printer here has beſtowed upon the Poet abſolute nonſenſe: if each Angel by himſelf anſwered the note of another, he muſt ſing *ſole*; and there can be no place for the disjunctive particle *or*. If it was neceſſary to keep up an oppoſition, it ſhould be thus, *Jointly or reſponſive each to*, &c. but with the addition of but one ſingle letter to the preſent text, the Author undoubtedly ſaid, *Sole*, correſponſive *each to others note.* This *correſponſive* was an hard word, which the Printer did not underſtand; ſo he left out the firſt element, and ſplit the word into two.

V. 684. Singing *their great Creator.*] I have already ſaid in my Edition, that it ſhould be *Hymning:* and ſo it ſhall be: but *their Creator* is ſpurious. The Angels did not *hymn* God as being *their* Creator, but as the Creator of *thoſe works*, which they are deſcribed beholding. Reſtore the true reading thus, *Hymning the great Creator.* I have not yet done with this ſentence, tho' I have nothing more to ſay againſt the Amanuenſis, Editor, or Printer about it; but it muſt be laid to the Author's charge, tho' he may fairly plead not guilty. There is a diſagreeable identity of ſound in *great*, and the former part of the word *Creator*, which MILTON, had he not loſt his eye-ſight, would infallibly have diſcovered. Among ſeveral ways of changing it, this will not be found abſurd, or diſagreeing from the Miltonian character; *Hymning* GOD *the Greator*, as I. v. 369. *to forſake God their Creator.*

V. 685. *While they keep watch, or nightly rounding walk.*] *Nightly* is implied in the precedent phraſe, *While they keep watch.* I at firſt ſuſpected it ſhould be *nighly*; as I have proved *night* to be corruptedly put for *nigh*, I. 204. but when I conſider that the angelic guards went from the eaſtern gate to the weſtern point, part of them by the north, and part by the ſouth, as deſcribed, v. 782. I am poſitive the Author gave it, *or* while half *rounding walk:* as v. 862. *where thoſe* half *rounding guards Juſt met.*

V. 686. *With* heav'nly *touch of inſtrumental ſounds.*]

We have had *celeſtial*, which is exactly the ſame, but four lines before. Here it ſhould be *delicate*. *Touch of ſounds* is vicious, and could not come from MILTON but thus, of *inſtruments, with ſounds*.

V. 687. *In full* harmonic *number join'd*.] This *harmonic* is an harſh *unharmonious* word. Our Author, well ſkilled in Muſic, could not be guilty of any thing ſo abſoneus, (ſee my note. IV. 472.) It came from him, And *numbers full of* harmony.

V. 688. *And* liſt *our thoughts to Heaven*.] Poor Poet, in ſubiection to a ſaucy Editor, and ignorant Printer! *Songs* lifting *thoughts* is an incongruous metaphor; it gives us the idea of a Porter *lifting* his burden; it could not come ſo from MILTON. We have no way to retrieve his own word, as no manuſcript exiſts, but by ſagacity and happy conjecture. Among other words that offer themſelves, *waft*, or *blow* our thoughts may be proper for *ſongs*, which are made of air; but I am perſuaded the Author gave it *wing*; as III. 87. *He* wings *his way, Not far off Heaven*.

Thus at length I have got through this traſh, this ſtuff, this outrageous nonſenſe; which yet has been repreſented as a celebrated paſſage. (See alſo my note I. 590.) I flatter myſelf, that I have reſtored the Poet's own words; and that all good judges will allow this place, with theſe emendations, to be wrought up to all poſſible perfection. The whole now ſtands thus:

Several Angels walk *upon* the earth,
And ſee, both when we wake, and when we ſleep.
All theſe with *celeſtial* praiſe his works *extoll*
Both day and night: how often from the *top*
Of echoing hill, or *ſtern* thicket have *we* heard
Celeſtial voices *at* the midnight *hour*
Sole, correſponſive each to other's note
Hymning God the Creator: oft in bands
While they keep watch, or *while half* rounding walk,
With *delicate* touch of inſtruments, *with* ſounds,
And numbers full of *harmony*, their ſongs
Divide the night, and *wing* our thoughts to Heaven.

BAVIUS, I require you to publiſh this inſtantly, as a ſhort Appendix to my new Edition.

Imprimatur, *Id. Feb.* ZOILUS.

On the Firſt of April.

NAture is riſing from the dead:
Froſts and Scythian ſnows are fled;
Boreas to his cavern creeps,
And, tir'd with winter-bluſt'ring, ſleeps:
Soft Zephyrs from the ocean move,
The birth-place of the Queen of Love;
And o'er the meadows, hills, and dales
Play with their ſweet reviving gales;
Chaſing all diſcontent, and care,
And every ſadneſs but deſpair.
Ah! CHLOE, when, my charming Fair?

PHILO-VERIS.

DOMESTIC NEWS.

C. *Courant.*	E P. *Evening Poſt.*
P. *Poſt-Boy.*	S J. *S. James's Evening Poſt.*
D P. *Daily Poſt.*	WE. *Whitehall Evening P.*
D J. *Daily Journal.*	LE. *London Evening Poſt.*

Puffs of cold Hyp—o critic-oratorical March wind.

The Oratory ſubjects next ſunday morning will be, &c. *D J. Mar.* 3. —— Mr. P. having compar'd himſelf, &c. Maſter Iſaac, To-morrow, in his Hyp-Doctor, &c. *DJ*. 5. —— The Oratory ſubject next ſunday morning will be, &c. *D J*. 10. —— The Hyp-Doctor will, in his To-morrow's Paper, &c *D J*. 13. —— The ſunday's Diſcourſes of the Oratory are engaged to be, &c. *DJ*. 17. —— In To-morrow's Hyp-Doctor, we are inform'd from my Lady C——'s, &c. *D J*. 20. —— In To-morrow's Hyp-Doctor will be a Letter, &c. *D J*. 27. —— The Hyp-Doctor has ſatyrically anſwered Fog's laſt Journal, &c. *D J*. 31.

Beſides theſe ſhort Puffs, there were fourteen long-winded Blaſts: ſeven Oratorical; and ſeven Hypochondriacal. Of the former, four were in Fog's Journals, and three in the *S J*. and of the latter three in the *S J*. and four in the *D J*. —— Of Puffs and Blaſts ſum total in March, Twenty two. —— *An ill wind that blows no body any good.*

THURSDAY, *March* 30.

Yeſterday the Rev. Dr. Foulks preached before their Majeſties, and the Royal Family in the Chappel Royal at S. James's. *C.*

The R. Hon. the E. of Exeter, who hath lately been much indiſpoſed with the Small pox, is in a very fair way of recovery. *C.* —— Laſt night he was ſo dangerouſly ill, that there was but little hopes of his recovery. *P.* —— He is ſo well recovered, that yeſterday he ſaw company. *LE. Ap* 4.

On ſaturday at the Aſſizes at Exeter, Steph. Woone, Benj. Crews, and John Woone, received ſentence of death, for barbarouſly murdering Mr. John Pike, Tide Surveyor of the cuſtoms in the Port of Plymouth, in the execution of his duty. *C. P. D P.*

The ſhip Moor, from Dieppe, arrived yeſterd. in the river, having on board the corpſe of Dr. Atterbury, late Biſhop of Rocheſter. *D J.* —— Will. Morrice, Eſq; is not yet returned, that Gentleman meeting (as we are informed) with great difficulties in removing the perſonal eſtate of the ſaid Prelate to another kingdom. *D P. Mar.* 31.

A ſervant of Mr. Nickols, a Shop-keeper at Ongar, riding to town on tueſday laſt with 300 and odd pounds, was robbed near Snarebrook. As this robbery was committed about 11 o' clock in the forenoon, Mr. Nicholls we hear will ſue the Hundred. *C.* —— A ſervant to Mr. Parſons: 313l. *D J.*

On ſunday in the forenoon the Dutcheſs of Mancheſter's woman was robbed of a gold watch, in S. Clement's Church, during the time of divine ſervice. *D J.*

If Mrs. Nab *at pray'rs had leſs affected the* Dutcheſs,
Her gold watch *had been ſafe from the* Pick-pocket's *clutches.*

Lynn Regis, Mar. 27. On the 24th Mr. John Child, Dep. Collector, ſeized out of the Providence, lately arrived from Rotterdam, 150 gall. of brandy, 150 of compound waters, 14 of rum, all in bottles, 43 pounds of tea, and ſome coffee. *P.*

Dover, Mar. 26. Our Cuſtom-houſe boat brought in laſt week near 200 half anchors of brandy; and on friday they brought in the boat, in which they found 45 half anchors. *S J. LE.*

This day the Aſſizes for the County of Surrey ended, when 6 perſons received ſentence of death. *S J.*

On ſaturday laſt, of City Youths the Society,
At S. Mary Overs rang a compleat peal of *great variety*
5040 Tripples, plain bob method, which *then*,
They compleated in 3 hours 32 minutes with 9 men. *S J.*

FRIDAY, *March* 31.

Yeſterday was held a Court of Honour at the College of Arms at Doctors Commons, at which the R. Hon. the Earl of Effingham, Dep. Earl Marſhal of England, ſat as judge, attended by Blance Anſtis, Eſq; King at Arms, and Knox Ward, Eſq; Clarencieux King at Arms. The Court was moved againſt Mrs. Radborn; but being overruled, was deferred to the next Court, which is to be held Ap. 25. The Court was alſo moved againſt Sir John Blunt, for bearing a Coat of Arms ſuppoſed not to belong to that family; alſo againſt Mr. Ladbrook's Executor, for hanging up an Atchievement, and uſing ornaments at his funeral, that did not belong to the ſaid Mr. Ladbrook. *P.* —— Dr. Henchman, the King's Advocate, moved the Court againſt a perſon who had ſet up Banners in Ryegate Church, with eſcutcheons, &c. and alſo againſt others for aſſuming arms they had no right to; and a citation was granted againſt them: then one of the Heralds acquainted the Court, that the holding theſe Courts of Honour was reported to be for their profit and lucre only; and deſired the Judge would acquaint the E. Marſhal, that their intentions were *All honour*, and entirely free from ſelf-intereſt. *D P.*

Dover, Mar. 29. The Smugglers called the Mayfield gang, were in this town and neighbourhood on ſunday, having (as we hear) ſent an orderly man to Calais, where their veſſel lay loaded with tea and dry goods, to bring them to S. Margaret's bay. The cuſtom-houſe Officers having ſome notice, were upon their guard or duty, when the gang and boat appeared. The gang conſiſting of about 20 men and 25 horſes, ſeized 2 of the Officers, and put them into an Alehouſe, and ſet a guard upon them, when the boats of Deal and ſome others came up; and they alſo endeavouring to do their duty, Rich. Hill was ſhot into the back of his neck and out at his mouth, and had a very large wound on his head to the ſcull; and Tho. Low was wounded in the head. Hill died immediately. We hear that the gang went by Uphill of Folkſtone yeſterday morning with their drawn ſwords. They are extremely well armed, and their Heads or Captains (as we hear) are Gilb. Tomkins, and one Toms, Outlaws. *P.*

On the 26th died ſuddenly at his ſeat in Devonſhire, the R. Hon. the L. Clifford of Chudleigh: he was born in 1687, and ſucceeded his father in honour and eſtate, Oct. 13, 1730. *D P.* —— On monday died at his houſe in Aldermanbury, in the 91ſt year of his age, Tho. Uvedale, Eſq; a noted Turky Merchant. *D P.* —— Yeſterday in the afternoon died at her habitation near the Broad-way, Weſtminſter, Mrs. Martha Williams, reputed to be worth 40,000l. *D J.*

On tueſday a Weaver, up the top of a tree having got,
To ſee an exerciſe at arms, fell down, *as if he had been ſhot*;
(*Twas* in White-chappel fields) and died on the ſpot. *C.*

SATURDAY, *April* 1.

Yeſterday the Rev. Dr. Clarke, Dean of Sarum, preach'd before their Majeſties, &c. *C.* —— Mr. Betteridge, Gentleman to the Earl of Hallifax, ſucceeds Mr. Milward, deceas'd, as Meſſenger to the Auditor's Office in his Majeſty's Exchequer, a place worth about 300 l. per ann. *D J.*

On thurſday laſt Prince Cantimir de Valachie, Miniſter from the Czarina, arrived here from the Hague, and has taken up his reſidence in Park-Place, S. James's. *D P.*

Dennis Bond, Eſq; and Baron Birch, are both expelled the Houſe of Commons, on account of the ſale of the late Earl of Derwentwater's eſtate. *P.*

Yeſterday was held a veſtry of the Pariſh of S. George Hanover-ſquare, for the choice of a Lecturer, to ſucceed Dr. Smith, who lately reſigned: the Candidates were the Rev. Dr. Savage, and the Rev. Mr. Medlicot, and the votes were as follow: for Dr. Savage 42: for Mr. Medlicot 31. That veſtry conſiſts of 101 Gentlemen, and 28 were abſent. *D J.*

Yeſterday at a Court at Bridewell, Will. Gore, Eſq; took his charge as Governor, and the following Gentlemen were confirmed Governors of that and Bethlehem Hoſpital, viz.

Mr. Step. Harvey.	Mr. Will. Cooper.
John Strange, Eſq; Counſellor at Law.	Mr. Allen Webb.
Sir George Wynne, Bar.	Mr. Tho. Skipp.
Malachi Hawkyne, Eſq;	Mr. Will. Newland, Attertorney at Law.
Tho. Hardy, Eſq;	Mr. John Deeton,
Mr. Walt. Barnard.	Mr. Nevill Leman.
Mr. John Cooke.	

DP.

Yeſterday Counſellor Edwards of Chancery-lane, was ſworn in before the R. Hon. the L. Chancellor, one of the Maſters in Chancery, in the room of Mr. Tottle, who has reſigned. *P.*

Yeſterday morning died at Bromley in Kent, the Rev. Dr. Blomer, Miniſter of Allhallow's Lombard-ſtreet. *DP.*

MONDAY, *April* 3.

Yeſterday the R. Rev. the L. Biſhop of Wincheſter preach'd before their Majeſties, &c. *C. P.* —— We hear that her Majeſty will be appointed Regent in the abſence of his Majeſty, during his ſtay in viſiting his German dominions; and that her Majeſty will keep her Court at Kenſington. *P.* And likewiſe that his Majeſty will ſet out the latter end of next month. *D J.* —— We hear his Majeſty deſigns to ſet out the 7th of May. *P.*

On ſaturday laſt a new barge, built for his Royal Highneſs the Prince of Wales, was launch'd over-againſt Hungerford-market, and was immediately rowed, by his Royal Highneſs's 12 Watermen, to Whitehall ſtairs, where ſeveral perſons of diſtinction took water in her, and went up the river. *D J.*

We hear the R. Hon. the E. of Litchfield has been offer'd 10,000 l. for the Prothonotary's place, &c. the ſaid place bringing in about 1300 or 1400 l. per ann. *D P.* —— Rob. Warner of Lincoln's Inn, Eſq; is made one of the Prothonotaries of his Majeſty's Court of Common-Pleas, in the room of Rich. Foley, Eſq; deceaſed. *P.*

On friday laſt began the Horſe-races at New market with a match between the D. of Bolton's *Fearnought* and Mr. Coke's *Hobgoblin*, 4 miles for 500 guineas, which was won by the former; and we hear that above 10,000l. was won and loſt by the ſaid match. *D J.* Won by 2 lengths. *P.*

Yeſterday morning the Princeſs Amelia, Capt. Hen. Fiſher, and the Mermaid, Capt. Butler, in the Service of the South-Sea Company, ſailed from Graveſend, with a fair Wind, for the Downs, in order to proceed on their voyage to Buenos Ayres. *C.*

On Thurſday the Lords of the Council confirm'd the election of Mr. Halfpenny, as Town Clerk of Monmouth; the ſame being before their Lordſhips on petition of Mr. Catchmay, claiming a Right thereto. *D P.*

Yeſterday morning died the relict of the R. Rev. Rich. Fowler, late Biſhop of Gloceſter, &c. *P.*

TUESDAY, *April* 4.

Yeſterday his Majeſty went to the Houſe of Lords, and gave the Royal aſſent to the Land-Tax Act; to an Act for reviving the duty on ſalt; an Act for importing from America directly into Ireland, goods not enumerated in any Act of Parliament, &c. an Act for providing a recompence to Sir Tho. Lombe, for diſcovering and introducing the art of making and working the 3 capital Italian engines for making organzine ſilk; as alſo to ſeveral private Acts. *P. DJ.*

Yeſterday Geo. Robinſon, Eſq; late Treaſurer of the Charitable Corporation, was expelled the Houſe of Commons, and a new writ was ordered to be iſſued out for electing a new Member for Great Marlow in Buckinghamſhire. *D J.* —— A new writ was alſo ordered for Pool in Dorſetſhire [for an election of a Member] in the room of Dennis Bond, Eſq; who was expelled the Houſe, &c. *P. D J.*

We hear that a great prize of 20,000 guilders, drawn lately againſt No. 21, 17, in the 5th claſs of the Utrecht lottery, is fallen between 4 working men, ſervants to Sugar-bakers in this City, who received the money for it this week, &c. *D J.*

We hear that Rich. Foley, Eſq; has left the chief part of his eſtate (which was very conſiderable) to his younger Brother Edw. Foley, of Lincolns Inn, Eſq; ordering 100 l. per ann. out of it, to be paid quarterly, Tax-free, to Will. Shippen, Eſq; for eminent ſervices done to his Country. *DP.*

Letters from Norwich of the 1ſt inſt. ſay, that a few days ago ſome men at work in a ditch near Colton in Norfolk, found there the bones of a man buried with his

face downwards; and a rusty blade of a razor sticking in his neck-bone, by which it is evident he was murdered, and buried in that ditch; the bones were very dry, and lid for many years there, &c. *D P.*

Taunton in Somersetshire, Ap. 1. At the Assizes here, Jonathan Hakins received sentence of death for the murder of George Gast, and Mary his daughter. Gast was an antient man, and Mary his daughter was the only person who lived with him: Hakins was indebted to Gast 20 l. by bond, and having been threatned to be sued, declared he would soon prevent the law-suit, which he did in the following inhuman manner: On Nov. 19, in the evening, he went to Gast's house at a little village call'd Mark, and persuaded him to drink cyder and brandy 'till he was drunk, then help'd the daughter to put him to bed, and roll'd him in the bed-cloaths; after this he persuaded the daughter to drink with him some little time, and then murder'd her, then murder'd the old man, and set the house on fire by thrusting a burning coal into the thatch, lock'd the door, and threw away the key, (after using 25 s out of the girl's pocket): the house was burnt, but by the providence of God the bodies were found, and thrown out of the house before it was consum'd, and many marks of violence being found upon them, and the prisoner having been seen to go into the house the night before, was charg'd upon suspicion, and confess'd the fact: he pretended to make love to the poor girl, who was about 20 years of age, and esteem'd the handsomest lass in the parish. *D P.*

Yesterday came on a hearing before the R. Hon. the L. Chancellor, relating to the petition of several Constables, &c. complaining of the illegal practices of one of his Majesty's Justices for the County of Middlesex, in freeing disorderly persons taken up in the night, &c. and his Lordship was pleased to suspend the said Justice. *D P.* — Jack Catch could suspend him more effectually.

Dennis Bond, Esq; stands again for Wareham in Dorsetshire, as does Mr. Baron Birch, for Wotly, and 'tis believed will both be re-elected without opposition. *S J.* — Dennis Bond, Esq; Recorder of Pool and of Wareham in Dorsetshire, Carrier of all his Majesties letters between his Court or Palace of residence, and the first Postage or Post-Office. — John Birch Esq; Serjeant at Law, Cursitor Baron of the Exchequer. *L E.*

The Hyp-Doctor on K. William's character is much applauded, as a compleat Answer to the objections to K. William and his memory. *D J.* — Teste meipso Hypo-doctore.

What truth can you hear on Good Friday?
What doctrine divine upon Sundays?
If each Tuesday and Saturday's lie-day;
The other must sure be all fun-days.

WEDNESDAY, April 5.
We hear that a fine picture of the Princess Royal of Denmark has been lately sent over hither to this Court; and that Mr. Gervase is painting the picture of his Royal Highness the Prince of Wales, to be sent over to the Court of Denmark. *D P.*

From the PEGASUS in Grub-street.

To Mr WALKER, upon his Choice of ALEXANDER the Great, for his Benefit, on Monday next.

MACKHEATH, that petty Robber, once you feign'd,
And all the Town's deserv'd applause obtain'd:
Now, the great Robber of the World you aim,
To crown your action, and confirm your fame.
But, tell me, WALKER, is it chance or choice?
Say, does your heart, in vicious parts, rejoyce?
—Whate'er the case, beware of the event—
Let not example, your good morals taint,
Lest, by degrees corrupted, you appear
A very villain, void of grace and fear —
Take to the Road — an arrant Ruffian be,
And swing, at last, on TYBURN's triple Tree.
To mimick thunder bold Salmoneus try'd;
But, by a burst of real thunder, dy'd.
Perhaps, you hope, by growing great in sin,
To 'scape the gallows, and preferment win —
The Times are alter'd, Sir; for Rognes disguis'd,
E'en by the Great, begin to be despis'd.
The British Senate, with impartial care,
To the wide world lays lurking Knavery bare;
And, in proportion to its various ways,
Arrears of vengeance to the guilty pays.
This for your Caution. — But what cause to fear?
Your steed is honest, open, and sincere.
Improve and prosper, my brave Lad: and may
Approaching Monday prove an happy day;
A well-fill'd house your annual toil reward,
I glad your heart joy to meet the Town's regard.
                                    M. DRAMATICUS.

FOREIGN NEWS.
THURSDAY, March 30.
Yesterday arrived the Mail due from France.
Paris, Apr. 5. N. S. Our last letters from Constanti-

---

nople, by the way of Marseilles, advise, that the Prime Vizir had furnished the French Monks settled there gratis, with all materials necessary for rebuilding the 3 Churches they had in the suburb of Pera, which were destroyed by the late fire. *C. &c.* ——— The King has not granted the title of Prime Minister to the Keeper of the Seals; having only declared, that he shall do business with him, jointly with the Cardinal. *C. P.* ——— The King has named the Sieur Chicoineau his first Physician. *D P.*

Rome, Mar. 15. They write from Civita Vecchia, that the Turks having made a descent on the Island of Corsica, near Bastia, carried off a whole Convent of Monks prisoners. *D P.*

FRIDAY, March 31.
Milan, Mar. 15. His Royal Highness Don Carlos is to reside 6 months at Parma, to commence from the beginning of May next, and the other 6 at Florence. *D P.*

SATURDAY, Ap. 1.
Yesterday arrived the Mail from Holland.
Seville, Mar. 14. N. S. The Gen. Count de Mortemar is to set out on monday, to put himself at the head of the army in Catalonia: He will have under him 2 Lieut. Generals, 8 Major Generals, and 8 Brigadiers. The army consisting of 32 battalions of 700 men each, and 24 squadrons of 120 men each, a company of workmen, and 33 Engineers, is actually marching to Valencia, to go on board the squadron, which is composed of 12 men of war, and 2 bomb-galliots, besides gallies and transports: the train of artillery is to consist of 50 cannon, 8 mortars for throwing bombs, and 4 for throwing stones. — Letters from the camp before Gibraltar advise, that the wall of the line, and the 2 principal forts were entirely finished; and that they were now building a 3d fort. *C. P. D J.*

Schaffhausen, Mar. 30. It is written from Toulon, that the squadron which was fitting out there, consists of 6 men of war, 2 frigates, 3 bomb galliots, 2 other galliots, and several flat bottom'd vessels and transports. *C.*

MONDAY, April 3.
On saturday arrived the Mail from Flanders, and yesterday one from France.
Paris, Ap. 9. N. S. The Count de Maurepas has been nominated Superintendant of the Royal garden of plants; and M. du Fay of the Royal Academy of sciences, is made Intendant of the said garden, under the direction of the Count de Maurepas, with a salary of 3000 livres a year. *C. P. DP.* ——— We learn from Meaux, that there is an epidemical distemper in 2 villages near that city, which they call the sweating sickness, whereof 65 persons have died in 2 days, those who are seized dying in 24 hours; and 'tis pretended, that this sickness was occasion'd by the bursting of a cloud over those two villages, with much thunder and hail. *D J.*

TUESDAY, April 4.
Hague, Ap. 8. N. S. 'How uncertain still are all the ' dispositions of earthly Princes and Politicians! It is but ' very lately, that we could congratulate one another up- ' on the accession of this State to the Treaty of Vienna; ' and we are already apprehensive, that the King of ' Spain will explain that Treaty in such a manner, that ' fresh troubles may ensue. We are put in mind also of ' the position laid down in the French Pamphlet, pre- ' tended to be written by a German Patriot against the ' Pragmatick Sanction, wherein it is said, that the Crown ' of France has great pretensions upon some Imperial ' Countries and Provinces. *P.*'

This Day arrived the Mail from Holland.
Vienna, Mar. 29. The Emperor has named the D. of Lorrain Viceroy, or Vicar Gen. of Hungary and the Provinces depending, as Transilvania, Servia, Tamesmaer, and part of Wallachia: His Royal Highness is expected about the 23d of next Month, and his Marriage with one of the Archdutchesses will be declared shortly. *L E.*

WEDNESDAY, April 5.
Extract of a private letter from Vienna. ——— The Duke de Ripperda is got into a scrape, out of which he will have enough to do to extricate himself, if the last letters from Barbary may be relied upon; for they say positively, that he and all his Retinue have been seized and cast into a dungeon, as Traitors to Holland their Country, and to the King of Spain their Benefactor. *P.*

Books and Pamphlets published since our last.
30. Philosophical Transactions, No. 421. for October, November, and December, 1731.
Remarks on the occurrences of the years 1720 and 1721; relating to the South Sea scheme. Pr. 6 d.
Annotations on the book of Job, and the Psalms; collected by Tho. Fenton, M. A. Pr. 5 s. 6 d.
A Physico-mechanical Essay on improving the Corpuscular Philosophy, &c. Pr. 1 s.
Apparatus ad linguam Græcam ordine novo ac facili digestus, &c. Auctore Geo. Thompson, E. A. P.
Some Observations for improvement of trade, by establishing the fishery, &c. By Mr. Peck. Pr. 1 s.

Lately publiſhed,

The two following BOOKS,

I. PRactical Diſcourſes on the ſeveral Parts and Offices of the *Liturgy* of the Church of England: Wherein are laid open the Harmony, Excellency, and Uſefulneſs of its Compoſure. In four Volumes. By *Matthew Hole*, D. D. late Rector of Exeter College in Oxford. Vol. I. Containing 58 Diſcourſes on all the Parts of Morning and Evening Prayer, including the Creed of St. Athanaſius. Vol. II. and III. Containing 55 Diſcourſes on the Litany, and the Prayers and Thankſgiving that follow it. Vol. IV. Containing 174 Diſcourſes (in 3 large Parts) on all the Collects, Epiſtles and Goſpels, to be uſed throughout the Year. The Second Edition.

II. A practical Expoſition of the CHURCH-CATECHISM. In two Volumes. By the ſame Author. The Third Edition, with the Addition of two Diſcourſes; one on the Duty of confeſſing Chriſt, the other on the Danger of denying him; both preach'd at St. Mary's in Oxford.

Sold by J. and J. Knapton, and C. Rivington in St. Paul's Church-Yard; A. Betteſworth and C. Hitch in Pater-Noſter-Row; and S. Birt in Avemary-Lane.

This day is publiſhed,

INTEREST at one View calculated to a Farthing, at 3, 4, 5, 6, 7 and 8 per Cent. from 1000 l. to 1 l. for one Day to 96 Days; and for 1, 2, 3, 4, 5, 6, 7, 8, 9, 10, 11, and 12 Months: With Rules and Examples to caſt up Intereſt at any other Rates by the ſaid Tables. To which is added, A Table for the more ſpeedy caſting up of Salaries and Wages, from one Million to one Pound per Year. Beſides many other Tables of great Uſe in receiving and paying of Monies. The Whole being calculated, examined and corrected, and afterwards re-examined from the Preſs.

By RICHARD HAYES.

Printed for W. MEADOWS, at the Angel in Cornhill.

Where may be had, by the ſame Author,

1. The Purchaſer's Pocket Companion; ſhewing at Sight what Intereſt is made by Money laid out in the Companies Stocks, or other publick Funds.

2. The Negotiator's Magazine of Monies and Exchanges, with a compleat Treatiſe of Arbitrations of Exchanges.

3. The Ship and Supercargo Book-Keeper, ſhewing the Manner of the Maſters ſettling Accounts with their Owners, the Privilege of Merchants, and Duty of Officers; with Supercargo's Accompts after the Italian Method of Double Entry.

4. An Eſtimate of Places for Life, calculated on the Chances of Lives in general, with an Account of Places in the Diſpoſal of the City of London, and their Value.

Juſt publiſhed,

Dedicated to the Gentlemen of the Navy of England,

THE MEMOIRS of Monſieur *du Gué Trouin*, Chief of a Squadron of the Royal Navy of France, and Great Croſs of the Military Order of S. Lewis; containing all his Sea-Actions with the Engliſh, Dutch, and Portugueſe, in the late Wars of King William and Queen Anne.

Tranſlated from the French by a *Sea-Officer*.

Printed for J. Batley, at the Dove, in Pater-noſter Row,

This day is publiſhed, Price 6 d.

THE GENTLEMAN'S MAGAZINE: Or, *Monthly Intelligencer*.

No. XV. for MARCH, 1732.

Being the THIRD of VOL. II. Containing,

I. A View of the Weekly Eſſays, viz. On Players; Gratitude, Punning, Study; War with Prieſtcraft; Ambition; Of *Theatrical* Plays; Common Senſe; Liberty of Conſcience: Devotion, Country Wits; Dramatick Poets; Footmen a Nuſance; Milton's Failings

II. Political Points, viz. Dr. Swift of the Conteſts between the Nobles and Commons; Mr. Trenchard and Ld. Hallifax of Standing Armies, ſeconded by D'Anyers, Osborne and Walſingham; Advice to the Athenians; Caveat againſt Bubbles; the Neceſſity of the preſent Forces; the Expectations of the Jacobites; Legal and Arbitrary Governments differenced; the Tree of Corruption; Fog and Dr. Clarke on January 30; Fog and Biſhop Burnet on King William's Family and Actions; Fog's Crime; Hue and Cry after the Charitable Corporation Money; how the Pretender was to have been brought in; Balloting commended; a Blundering Club; Oliver Cromwell's Policy.

III. Poetry: Deſcription of the Spring in Maryland; Verſes on No Biſhop No King; Epigrams.

IV. Domeſtick Occurrences, Births, Deaths, Marriages, Promotions, &c. Mrs. Longley's Trial, Aſſize News.

V. Price of Goods, Grain, Stocks.

VI. Foreign Affairs.

VII. Books and Pamphlets.

VIII A Table of Contents.

By *SYLVANUS URBAN*, Gent.

Printed and ſold at St. John's Gate; by F. Jefferies in Ludgate-Street, and the Bookſellers in Town and Country.

Where may be had all the former Numbers.

Note, A few are printed on fine Royal Paper, large Margin, For the Curious.

This Day was publiſhed,

PHILOSOPHICAL TRANSACTIONS, N° 421. for the Months of October, November, and December, 1731. Containing, *inter alia*, A Propoſal of a Method for finding the *Longitude* at *Sea*, within a Degree, or twenty Leagues, by Dr EDMUND HALLEY, *Aſtr. Reg.* Vice-Preſident of the *Royal Society*. With an Account of the Progreſs he hath made therein, by a continued Series of accurate *Obſervations* of the *Moon*, taken by himſelf at the *Royal Obſervatory at Greenwich*.

Printed for William Innys, at the Weſt End of S. Paul's.

Where may be had,

1. A Compleat Set of the Philoſophical Tranſactions, in 36 Vols. in 4to.

2. An Abridgment of them, to the Year 1720, by Mr. Lowthorp and Mr. Jones, in 5 Vols. 4to.

WHEREAS other *Coffee-Houſes*, and other *Publick Houſes*, take of their Cuſtomers 8 s. for a Quart of Arrack, and 6 s. for a Quart of Rum or Brandy made into *Punch*, ſo that it is now become the ſettled Price throughout the Town, and ſeldom leſs than a Bowl of 1 s. 6 d. is to be had: Therefore, for the better accommodating all Gentlemen, that are Lovers of *Punch*,

This is to give Notice,

That I have opened on Ludgate-hill, the *London-Coffee-Houſe* and *Punch-Houſe*, (Two *Punch-Bowls* on Iron Pedeſtals before my Door,)

Where the fineſt and beſt old Batavia Arrack, Jamaica Rum, and French Brandy, are made into *Punch*, with the fineſt Ingredients, viz.

A Quart of Arrack made into *Punch* for 6 s. and ſo in Proportion to the ſmalleſt quantity, which is half a Quartern for four Pence Half-penny.

A Quart of Rum or Brandy made into *Punch* for 4 s and ſo in Proportion to the ſmalleſt Quantity, which is half a Quartern for 3 d. And Gentlemen may have it as ſoon made, as a Gill of Wine can be drawn; with the beſt of Eating, Attendance, and Accommodation.

This Undertaking has occaſion'd many, whoſe *Intereſt* it is to poſſeſs Gentlemen with ſuch an Opinion, that the Liquors by me uſed are not good: The Publick is hereby aſſured, that I buy my Goods on the Keys, and at the beſt Hand, with Ready Money, and am at this Time provided with as well-choſen Brandies, Rum and Arrack, as any in Town, and will at all times procure the beſt that is imported: But what may convince Gentlemen of the Truth hereof, is, (not only by the Encouragement I meet with) that the Sherbet is always brought by itſelf, and the Brandy, Rum, or Arrack in the Meaſure, ſo there can be no Impoſition, either in Quantity or Quality; for the Proof whereof I appeal to all Gentlemen who have done me the Honour to call at my Houſe.

James Aſhley.

This Day is publiſhed,

For the Uſe of Families, (beautifully printed in 2 Vols. 8vo.) *adorn'd with* 34 Plates, *engraven by Mr.* Sturt,

DUPIN's Evangelical Hiſtory; or, The Records of the Son of God, and their Veracity demonſtrated. In the Life and Acts of our bleſſed Lord and Saviour Jeſus Chriſt, and his Holy Apoſtles. Wherein,

I. The Life of the Bleſſed JESUS is related in all its Circumſtances, according to the Order of Time, in a pathetic Style and practical Method, thereby compoſing a perfect Harmony of the Goſpels.

II. Proofs from his Sermons and Diſcourſes of thoſe eſſential and important Truths, which all Chriſtians are oblig'd to know and practiſe, in order to their eternal Salvation.

III. His Parables, Miracles, and Sufferings, ſet in a clear Light, and defended fro . all the Oppoſitions of wicked and deſigning Men.

IV. An Application to the Whole to the reſpective Uſes of Chriſtians, with regular Devotions conformable to the ſeveral Periods of the Holy Hiſtory; and Directions how we may read the Life of Jeſus Chriſt to Advantage. Printed for R. Ware, at the Bible and Sun in Amen-Corner, near Pater-Noſter-Row; price 8 s. Where may be had,

1. The large Houſe Bibles, Folio, with the ſix Maps of ſacred Geography, and a brief Concordance for the more eaſy finding out of the Places therein contained. By J. Downame, B. D. Bound in Calf Leather at 1 l. 7 s. per Book. And with M. Sturt's Cuts, at 2 l. 5 s. ditto. On a fine Paper with Cuts 3 l. 3 s. ditto.

2. The Impartial Churchman; or, A fair and candid Repreſentation of the Excellency and Beauty of the Church of England. Together with an earneſt and affectionate Addreſs to the Proteſtent Diſſenters. By Robert Warren, D. D. Price 3 s. 6 d.

3. The Whole Duty of Man. Part II. Teaching a Chriſtian, 1. How to grow in Grace. 2. How to demean himſelf in Sickneſs. 3. How to prepare himſelf for a happy Death. Together with Advice how Viſitants and Attendants ſhould carry it toward the Sick; and ſome general Conſiderations that may induce Relations and Friends to take his Death patiently. By the Rev. and Learned Dr. John Williams, late Lord Biſhop of Chicheſter; price 3 s 6 d.

Where likewiſe may be had,

A curious Field's Bible, Folio, with very fine Cuts, two Volumes, bound in Turkey Leather; price 20 l.

And on Imperial Paper, three Volumes ditto, 30 l

This Day is publiſhed,

A VOYAGE to Arabia Fœlix through the Eaſtern Ocean and the Streights of the Red-Sea, being the firſt made by the French in the Years 1708, 1709, and 1710. Together with a particular Account of a Journey from Mocha to Muab, or Mowahib, the Court of the King of Yaman, in their ſecond Expedition, in the Years 1711, 1712, and 1713. Alſo a Narrative concerning the Tree and Fruit of COFFEE, collected from the Obſervations of thoſe who made the laſt Voyage; and an Hiſtorical Treatiſe of the Original and Progreſs of COFFEE, both in Aſia and Europe; with curious Draughts, of ſeveral Parts of the Coffee-Tree, on Copper Plates; 1. Of the Tree in full Proportion; 2. Of its Branch with its Flowers and Fruit; 3. Of its Leaves; all drawn in *Arabia* according to Nature. Tranſlated from the French. To which is added, An Account of the Captivity of Sir *Henry Middleton* at Mokha, by the *Turks*, in the Year 1612; and his Journey from thence to Zenan, or Sanaa, the Capital of the Kingdom of Yaman, with ſome Additions, particularly relating to that Country and the Red-Sea. Printed for E. Symon, over-againſt the Royal-Exchange, in Cornhill.

This Day is Publiſhed,

(Price Two Shillings and Six Pence.)

THE GENTLEMAN FARRIER: Containing Inſtructions for the Choice and Directions in the Management of Horſes, either for Draught or Pleaſure, on for a Journey, or in the Stable. With an Account of their Diſtempers, and Receipts for the Cure of them.

To which is added,

An APPENDIX concerning Dogs, either for the Field or the Lap: Wherein their Diſeaſes are deſcribed, and the Means to Cure them. The Horſe Receipts, by the D. of Devonſhire, E. of Orrery, Ld. Carleton, Sir John Packington, Gen. Seymour, Portman Seymour, James Nicholſon, Eſqs; —— Thornton Eſq; of Bloxham, and publiſhed by Direction of a Perſon of Quality.

Printed for F. Cogan, at the Middle-Temple Gate; and H. Lintot, at the Croſs-Keys in Fleet-Street.

This Day is publiſhed, *Price* 1 s.

The Second Edition of

THE PROGRESS of LOVE, in Four ECLOGUES.

I. *Uncertainty*, to Mr. Pope.	III. *Jealouſy*, to Edward Walpole, Eſq;
II. *Hope*, to the Honourable George Doddington, Eſq;	IV. *Poſſeſſion*, to the Right Hon. the Ld. Viſc. Cobham.

Printed for L. Gilliver, at Homer's-Head, over againſt S. Dunſtan's Church in Fleet-ſtreet. *Likewiſe*,

STOWE, the GARDENS of the Right Hon. *Richard*, Lord Viſcount *Cobham*. Addreſs'd to Mr. POPE.

Devenere locos lætos, & amœna Vireta
Fortunatorum nemorum, ſedeſque beatas. Virg.

SPEAKING FANS, Genteel and Cheap,

SOLD at one Shilling each Mount, by Mrs. Upton, near Golden-Square; Mrs. Guerrier againſt Will's Coffee-Houſe, Lincoln's-Inn Back-Gate; and Mr. Brooker, at the Sun and Fan, the Corner of St. Paul's Church-Yard At which Places all other Shop-Keepers may be ſupply'd

At the Printing-Office in Bow Church-Yard, London, is juſt publiſhed, Pr. bound 1s. 6d.

SENTENTIÆ SELECTÆ: Or, A Collection of miſcellaneous Sentences, Divine, Moral, and Hiſtorical. In Proſe and Verſe. Engliſh and Latin. Excerpted from the Works of many learned and judicious Authors, and digeſted into alphabetical Order. By *Edward Curray*. To which are added, various Forms for inditing Letters. The Characters, Places, and Significations of all Sorts of Stops, Points, Pauſes and Marks uſed both in Writing and Printing, with their Explanations. A Table of the moſt common Abbreviations, or Contractions of Words Pertinent Directions for fair and exact Writing; with Rules for making and managing the Pen, &c. The beſt approv'd Receipts for making Ink of many Colours. An ingenious Diſcourſe and Poem on the unſpeakable Advantages of Reading and Writing: Alſo Inſtructions and Rules for Behaviour; with many other uſeful and profitable Particulars.

Alſo a curious Book of ſelect Fables, and other ſhort Poems, &c. finely engrav'd on 32 Copper Plates, for the Amuſement of young Gentlemen and Ladies. To which are added, The moſt uſeful and ornamental Hands for their Improvement in the Art of *Writing*. Price 1 s 6 d. And a new Cyphering Book for the Uſe of Schools, being the beſt of the Kind ever yet extant. Engrav'd by *George Bickham*, Sen. Price 1 s. 6 d. Likewiſe the Third Edition of

The *Modern Muſick Maſter*: Or, The Univerſal Muſician; conſiſting of Inſtructions to Singing, and Directions to play on the Common Flute, German Flute, Hautboy, Violin, Harpſicord, or Organ: with a brief Hiſtory of Muſick to this preſent Time; in which Volume is included many other valuable Pieces. Engrav'd on above 320 Plates. Price 7 s. 6 d.

Books of Inſtructions for any ſingle Inſtrument. Pr. 1 s. 6 d.

N. B. At the abovesaid Printing-Office, Shop-Keepers Bills are engraved and printed, either at the Letter or Rolling-Preſs, at the loweſt Rates.

LONDON: Printed by S. PALMER and J. HUGGONSON, in *Bartholomew-Cloſe*, for Captain GULLIVER, near the *Temple*, where Letters and Advertiſements are taken in: As alſo at the *Rainbow Coffee-Houſe* in *Cornhill*, and *John's Coffee-Houſe* in *Sheer-Lane*, near *Temple-Bar*. [Price Two Pence.]

The Grub-ſtreet Journal.

NUMB. 119

Thurſday, *APRIL* 13, 1732.

I would know how it can be pretended, that the Churches are miſapplied? Where are more appointments and rendezvouzes of gallantry? Where more care to appear in the foremoſt box, with greater advantage of dreſs? Where more meetings for buſineſs? Where more bargains driven of all ſorts? And where ſo many conveniences or incitements to ſleep?

Swift's and Pope's Miſcell. Vol. I. p. 115.

To Mr. BAVIUS, Secretary to the Society of Grubſtreet.

SIR,

NOtwithſtanding the reflections, which a late Writer hath maliciouſly caſt on the laudable practice of going to Church, I am informed, by very good Phyſicians, that his theory of the piles is falſe; and that there is no more, (if ſo much) danger of getting that diſtemper at Church, than at a Play-houſe, eſpecially if ſoft primitive velvet cuſhions can be had to ſit upon: therefore people may venture to join in our communion, without endangering their bodily healths, contrary to the opinion of the Author I have in view.

I confeſs indeed, ſome regulations may be neceſſary for quieting of the tender conſciences of thoſe Diſſenters paſsing under no denomination, (which are far the greater number of Diſſenters) and for inducing them once in a week, at leaſt, to increaſe our congregations. And I am in great hopes, this heavenly work is in good forwardneſs, ſince, as a former Correſpondent of yours hath obſerved, the uſe of *Lillobolero*, *Jumping Joan*, and many other entertaining tunes, is moſt reaſonably permitted. —— I am heartily glad this work is begun. —— 'Tis every honeſt man's duty, with his utmoſt endeavours to promote it: and therefore 'tis, that I give you this trouble, humbly propoſing, that between the ſervices on Sundays and Holydays, we may be entertained with ſome elaborate performances; ſometimes a new minuet, ſometimes a rigadoon, but above all, a reviving jig after the ſermon. The inſtrument now uſed, I think, is an Organ, and ſometimes we meet with a Baſſoon: but why are we reſtrained from the Violin, Hautboy, Trumpet, French-horn, Flute, or any other pleaſing inſtrument? For my part, I can ſee no reaſon, why the *Gom Gom* of the *Hottentotts*, or their *Pot Drums*, may not for variety be introduced. Pray what divinity is there in an Organ, more than in any other inſtrument? none that I can perceive: tho' it will be well, if this peculiar honour done to the Organ doth not lead vulgar minds into ſome ſtrange ſuperſtitious notions about it: whereas it is a modern muſic, when compared with ſome others. For

——— long ago,
E'er heaving bellows learn'd to blow,
While organs yet were mute;
TIMOTHEUS, *with his breathing flute,*
And ſounding lyre
Could ſwell the ſoul to rage, or kindle ſoft deſire.

DRYDEN's Ode on S. Cæcilia's day.

Not but that Organs have been of antient ſtanding in the Church: as, to look no farther, we may find in DAN CHAUCER's *ſecond Nonne's Tale*, where we are informed that the heavenly maid *Sainct Cecily ſang in her herte*
Whiles that the Organs made melodie.

But what I argue for, is the liberty of taking other muſical inſtruments into the Church, if it ſo liketh us. *Right womanly, I trow, did* PEG *withſain her Brother* JOHN, *who tofore had taunted her with ſounding at the ſound of an Organ, and right merrily dauncing to Bagpipes. 'What is that to thee, Gundy Guts? ſaid* PEG: *every body is to chuſe their own muſick.* I think, Mr. BAVIUS, this depriving us of other melodious inſtruments is a very great impoſition on Chriſtian conſciences; and I am perſuaded the Act of Toleration loſes half the benefits, by wanting a clauſe for the free and unreſtrained exerciſe of *the Flute, Harp, Sackbut, Pſaltery, Dulcimer, and all other kinds of muſic.* But indeed, were the inſtruments never ſo various, and the hands never ſo fine, it will avail but little towards the accompliſhment of this great end, ſo long as a bawling Clerk, and an unſkilful booriſh congregation of hoarſe mechanics, are permitted to drown muſic's ſweet charms with the odious ſtuff of STERNHOLD and HOPKINS. I would therefore further propoſe, that we may have no vocal muſic in Churches, unleſs Italian Eunuchs might be imported for that purpoſe; and one, or more, placed in every pariſh to ſing a favourite ſong from ſome of our beſt Operas. 'Till this can be effected, which I hope the elegant Mr. H—— D—— R in time will have intereſt enough to do; I would have, by way of interlude, a minuet or rigadoon in London, York, and all other Cities; and a jig, or an horn-pipe in all other pariſhes, danced by ſome proper perſons in the broad ſpaces, which may be conſiderably inlarged for that purpoſe. Nor is this to be accounted an unreaſonable or irreligious propoſal, ſince we know DAVID often danced out of a ſpirit of devotion; and has more than once directed us not only to ſing, but to dance out our thankſgivings. I am very certain, if my method be complied with, a great many people will be brought to hear divine ſervice, upon the proſpect of ſeeing it at the ſame time; who at preſent don't know what the inſide of a Church is like: and leſt baſhfulneſs ſhould be any obſtruction to their reformation, I fancy it may be neceſſary to allow people of Quality to come in maſquerade.

I agree with moſt other cuſtoms of the Church, as it now is eſtabliſhed: but the Sermon, I think, ſhould be in the manner of that very Reverend Divine, Mr. H — LY. The Prayers may be, as they now are: for you know no body of faſhion hath leiſure to attend them. Whilſt they are reading, we Gentlemen are diſplaying our ſnuff-boxes, rings, &c. and the Ladies are employed in adjuſting their dreſſes. Both ſexes require no ſmall part of that time in paying and receiving reciprocal compliments, enquiring after abſent acquaintance, relating our fortunes the night before at Quadrille, appointing new meetings, and twenty other ſuch neceſſary amuſements.

I know very great attempts have been made to take away from us this freedom, as well as that of coming into, and going out of the Church, at our pleaſures; on pretence of its hindering well diſpoſed people from purſuing their devotions. —— Poor ſilly creatures! if they were to have their ways, I ſuppoſe, we muſt not be allowed to go to above one Church in a morning; whereas, with good management, we may now pay viſits to four or five before dinner, beſides ſhort compliments to the Chapels and Tabernacles that are in our ways; and, if occaſion be, to two or three Meeting-houſes.

Others, equally impertinent, would have us in our devotions turn all our faces one way, forſooth, towards the *Eaſt I trow*; becauſe, ſay they, it makes a congregation ſeem uniform and decent. —— Good Mr. BAVIUS, what will this world come to? —— This is hanging out *Popiſh colours* with a vengeance. ——— *Uniform* quotha! —— Why *Uniformity*, Sir, is downright *Popery* and *Jacobitiſm*, the very image of the ſcarlet whore, and of Antichriſt. —— And I appeal to the Ladies, the beſt judges of decency, whether it be decent for Gentlemen to turn their moſt diſhonourable and uncomely parts towards the moſt honourable and comely part of the Creation? —— Was this project to take place, I believe the *Vicar of S. N.* might preach to a very uniform congregation: for none, I dare ſay, would there be in his Church, but a pack of poor ſilly enthuſiaſtic tradeſmen and mechanics, as uniform in their education, as in their rank and quality. For can it be expected, that we, who know better, will be deprived of the pleaſure of paying our cuſtomary addreſſes to the Fair, to pleaſe an empty-headed Vicar? Do you think we will reſign ogling, dumb ſhews, and ſigns, for the ſake of introducing *uniformity*? No, no, Mr. BAVIUS, no other *uniformity* for me, than ſuch as is produced according to the Italian proverb.

Un diſordine fà un ordine.

Thanks to our ſtars, I am not the only advocate for liberty in this caſe! we have a better judge of decency and uniformity, than is this fore-mentioned Vicar, on our ſides; and, what I moſt admire at, one of the ſame cloth. I am ſure, was the purple in my gift, that excellent man ſhould no longer ſubſiſt upon tythe eggs and apples. —— But enough of this at the preſent.

And now I ſuppoſe, the grave dull ſots of the nation will ſay, that I am no friend to the Church; that I am for altering 'till nothing is left, and for pulling down every thing that is ſacred; will call me heathen, rake, &c. alledging, that *the aſſembling ourſelves together* in Churches is for ſpiritual improvement, and not for ſenſual recreation; that our minds ſhould there be intent on our devotions, which ſhould be ſolemn and ſteady; and ſo in ſhort make religion to be totally neglected by all Belles and Beaux. Whereas they don't conſider, *A man may lo'e the Kirk well enow, and not ride o' the riggen o't.* We may be good Churchmen, without being enthuſiaſts. And, I am certain, if the Divines will come into my ſcheme, their Churches will be filled with the moſt polite people, and their Aſſemblies be accounted as entertaining and genteel, as any others, not excepting even Maſquerades and Operas.

I hope, Mr. BAVIUS, as this Epiſtle is plainly calculated for the good of this nation in general; and as I have, with my moſt ſincere endeavours, aimed at the promotion of freedom and liberty in religion, as well as thoſe reverend Authors W———N, T—D—L, H-N—Y, B—N—N, and ASS——N, you will not refuſe me the honour of a fellowſhip in your Society; thereby advancing me to the converſation of thoſe charming witty men whom ignorant people indeed brand with the names of Atheiſts, &c. &c. &c. So ſhall I be taken from amongſt thoſe on the other ſide of the queſtion, juſtly 'titled *Papiſts, Non-jurors, High-flyers*, &c. who are *worſe Subjects, worſe Chriſtians, and worſe Men.*

I am, Sir, your moſt humble ſervant,

A FREE BRITON.

SIR,

FInding, that my Letter publiſhed in your Paper No. 112, has occaſioned ſome little noiſe in the world; and that in particular it has made one perſon uneaſy, whom it was intended indeed to cenſure, but in ſo good natured and gentleman-like a manner as neither to ſhock, nor expoſe him; I muſt beg once more, Mr. BAVIUS, you would allow me a little room in your Paper, that I may ſet that matter right, and juſtify myſelf.

I ſhall begin by aſſuring Mr. W. that the perſon that recommended my Play to him, was ſo far from having any hand in, or knowing any thing of that Letter, that he reſented it very highly, and thought I had uſed him very ill. I differed in opinion with him then, and do ſtill. The affair relating only to a private converſation about bringing a Play on the Stage, and reflecting, in no wiſe, on any body's character; I can by no means agree, that that converſation had any thing in it, ſo ſacred, as not to be revealed, without breach of friendſhip or honour, violation of good nature, or good manners. — It may indeed be objected, that Mr. W. having deſired he might not make himſelf an enemy, by giving his impartial opinion, he may perhaps fancy he has made one of me. I do declare, he has not made himſelf one enemy more, ſince this affair, than he had before, as I know of. That, as to myſelf, I look upon him with the ſame eye of admiration I ever did; receive as much pleaſure from his incomparable acting, and think the Stage will ſuffer an irreparable loſs, whenever it ſhall be deprived of him. But that I thought my Play improperly rejected is as true, as that I think ſo ſtill; and that ſuch a reaſon for rejecting it ought to be expoſed, was my ſentiment then, and is ſo now. It is true, Mr. BAVIUS, I was weak, or vain enough, to truſt to the merits of my Piece, for its being received; and to my friend's acquaintance with Mr. W. to introduce it to the houſe, without applying to more powerful ones, whom Mr. W. perhaps would not have refuſed, had the Play been no more *ſenſible* and *pretty*, than it was *theatrical*. And in this I committed a capital fault. But as I am no Author, who draws his ſubſiſtance from his pen, and lives only by his wits; I did not care to trouble any conſiderable perſons about it, or make ſtrong intereſt for a thing, the miſcarriage of which will not make me wear one ſuit the leſs in the year, or eat one coarſer meal, than I ſhould have done, had I had as many benefits as the Author of the *Modern Husband*. As to the Play it ſelf, if I had not thought it a very proper entertainment for the Town, much properer, I think I may ſay without vanity, than what they have had this winter, no conſideration on earth ſhould have made me offer it to the houſe. But to come to the point.

I have been accuſed of uſing Mr. W. ill, by expoſing in a ludicrous manner what he ſaid in ſerious confidence; and wilfully miſunderſtanding the word *theatrical*. I confeſs, I did enquire in a ludicrous manner into the meaning of the word *theatrical*, and offered ſome conjectures about it; which I think ſhewed more mirth than ſpleen, more good humour than ill nature. As to the breach of confidence complained of, if the thing made a confidence of is ridiculous in itſelf, it has, I think a greater right to be expoſed, than if it was not: but as it was an indifferent matter, and touched no body's character, there could, as I ſaid before, be no violation of good nature or good manners, friendſhip or honour.

I have been likewiſe accuſed of having made Mr. W. a compliment upon the genteel manner of his refuſal,

which looked more like a sneer, than sober truth. I don't know why it has been interpreted so; unless it was imagined, that it was impossible for me to think any behaviour civil, that contained a refusal of that kind. And indeed, Mr. BAVIUS, it is no very absurd imagination. A Poet, that finds all his pains in a moment frustrated by one person, without any satisfactory reason, is in no very fit disposition for complimenting that person: it goes very much against the grain, it must be confest. But I protest, I was very serious; and thought the manner of his refusal as civil, as the reason for it seemed to me ridiculous. I am as frank in owning one, as the other: both were my real opinions then; and I see no reason to retract either of them at present.

I shall now, Mr. BAVIUS, with your good leave, offer some more plausible reasons, why my Play was rejected, than its want of *theatricality*. but these are only conjectures of my own, founded upon my not thinking the reason alledged for rejecting it sufficient. 1st. It is possible Mr. W. tho' otherwise very willing to oblige my friend, might not think him of consequence enough to accept a Play upon his bare recommendation. 2dly. The season being pretty far advanced, and there being at that time two new Plays on the stocks, it might be too much to undertake a third. 3dly. There being a pretty large part, which would naturally fall to Mr. W's share, he might think the trouble too great at that time of the year. Whether any of these were the true reason for rejecting my Play, is out of the case at present. It was necessary to give a reason; and Mr. W. thought want of *theatricality* a better one than any of these; I suppose, because it not only contained an immediate and positive rejection, but prevented any future application. I shall therefore, without any design or view of shocking Mr. W. observe, that, if instead of rejecting absolutely a Play, which he allowed to be *sensible* and *pretty*, (which I must suppose was his real and impartial opinion, else he would not have made so much difficulty to give it) he had acquainted the Gentleman that spoke to him about it, what defects there were in the Play; how they might be remedied; what was wanting to suit it to the taste of the Town; and had gone so far as to tell him, that as the summer was coming on, and there was time enough before-hand, if the Author would take the trouble to revise his Play and correct it in such and such a manner, he should be very glad to receive it the next winter in the House; I say, if Mr. W. had done so, he had never heard of DRAMATICUS, nor had he been accused in the evening of his life, of having given a ridiculous reason to justify a ridiculous thing; that is, for I'll not mince the matter, of having rejected a Play, which he allowed to be a *sensible* and *pretty performance*, because it was not *theatrical*.

I cannot conclude, without returning my Brother C—— J——n thanks for his kind Epistle to me; but I must beg he would not take amiss my not accepting the communication he offers me. He tacks such conditions to it, that I should be too great a looser by it, and can't in conscience accept of them.

I must now beg leave, Mr. BAVIUS, to put one question to you, and likewise to desire the Society's opinion about it; and that is, whether since the intrinsic goodness of a Play is no more a reason for accepting, than its absolute badness is for rejecting it, and that a Play is received according to the degree of favour the Author stands in with the Managers, and the interest he has from without, I have not (as well as any other man) a natural right to applaud or discommend impartially any Play, according to the manner used time out of mind, in the Play-house, in expressing approbation or dislike? I may perhaps carry the point a little further; and as you seem to be full of health and vigour, and there is no symptom of a decay in you, become a Correspondent of yours next winter, in the way of Censor of theatrical performances. But this whole paragraph, as well as the prosecution of my design, I refer intirely to the consideration of the Society, and am,

Mr. BAVIUS, your unknown friend and admirer,

March 28, 1732. DRAMATICUS.

Honest Mr. CONUNDRUM,

IF you'll be pleased to put the following Epigram on the wings of your Pegasus, you will much oblige an aspiring young Fellow, who is a great admirer of your Society, and vastly ambitious to see some of his performances in your Journal.

On young Maister K—t's holding forth in the Diocese of H——d.

A preachment late was made by Parson K—t,
To vye with BOWMAN, that learn'd, pious Wight.
Him bravely born of hardy iron-breed,
With Ostrich stomach fit on Church to feed,
To qualify to guide and fleece a Flock,
Dad's golden keys the Church's door unlock.
With doctrine stoln from *Independent Whig*,
This ign'rant, raw, conceited, Reverend Prig,
To brook his name, would darken Scripture's light;
For take away the K, and all is NIGHT.

DOMESTIC NEWS.

C. *Courant.*	E P. *Evening Post.*
P. *Post-Boy.*	S J. *S. James's Evening Post.*
D P. *Daily Post.*	WE. *Whitehall Evening P.*
D J. *Daily Journal.*	LE. *London Evening Post.*

THURSDAY, *April* 6.

Yesterday the Rev. Dr. Terry preached before their Majesties, and the rest of the Royal Family, at the Chappel Royal at S. James's. *C.* —— Her Majesty has receiv'd a present of a fine easy chair, of a new invention from the King of Poland. *S J.*

The R. Hon. the L. Andover, Son to the R. Hon. the E. of Berkshire, who was taken ill of the Small-pox, is in a fair way of recovery. *P.*

On monday last a match was run at Newmarket between the E. of Hallifax's *Justice*, and the E. of Portmore's *Daffadil*, for 200 guineas, which was won by the E. of Hallifax. —— On tuesday the stakes of 500 guineas were run for by horses belonging to the Dukes of Devonshire, Bridgewater, and Ancaster, and the L. Lonsdale, and won by the D. of Bridgewater. *D J.*

Last tuesday, *Ap.* 4, the day fix'd upon by Act of Parliament for Mess. Robinson and Thompson to surrender themselves to the Commissioners in the Commission of the Bankruptcy issued out against them, they are, upon their not complying, declared felons convict. *S J.* —— It is written from Genoa the 1st inst. N. S. That Mr. Thompson having been seen in that city, the Consul applied to the Senate for power to seize him, but that through their dilatoriness, 'twas supposed he got notice of it, for at the writing the letter he had quitted the place. Two British Men of war were then in Port, on board one of which it was intended to have put him. *D J.* ——*I fear, he was born, neither to be* hanged, *nor* drowned.

This day being Maunday Thursday, his Grace the Archbishop of York, Lord High Almoner, according to ancient custom, distributed his Majesty's Royal bounty, in the Chappel at Whitehall, to a certain number of decayed Housekeepers. *L E. S J. Repeated in* D J. *Ap.* 7. —— The Rev. Dr. Gilbert, Dean of Exeter, and Sub-Almoner, preached an excellent sermon, in the absence of the Lord Archbishop of York, and washed the feet of 49 poor men and women, being the number of the King's years, and delivered to [each of] them cloth, shoes and stockings, and a purse with as many silver pennies as the King was years old; also one with shillings, and bread and fish in a basket. *P. Ap.* 7.

On saturday some unknown person generously put into the common box at Ludgate 5 guineas, which was equally divided among the poor prisoners. *D P.*

William Pulteney, Esq; who was taken ill in the House of Commons on monday last, and went out, is now very well recover'd from his indisposition. *L E.*

We hear that the corpse of the late Bishop Atterbury is not expected here from France 'till Whitsontide. *S J.* — *The* D J. *of Mar.* 30. *brought his* corpse *into the river the day before: which account was repeated by the* S J. *and* L E.

Mr. Arthur Rawlinson, Oilman in Pall-Mall, is appointed High-Constable for the City of West-minster. *D P.*

A woman intending to be married at the Fleet, and going last tuesday into an Alehouse with her Bridegroom, in order to send for a Minister, accidentally met the husband there smoaking his pipe, to whom she had been married upwards of 18 years, not having seen him for these 7 years past; both were over-joy'd to see each other, but the intended husband march'd off in the utmost surprize and confusion. *S J.*

Here is certainly some mistake of my Brother:
They could not be so over-joy'd to see each other.
They might all be surpriz'd, *and think it delusion*:
But the husband and wife *were* most in confusion.

FRIDAY, *April* 7.

Yesterday, by virtue of a Commission issuing out of the High Court of Chancery, a Jury was impanell'd to enquire of the lunacy of a noble Lord, and brought in their verdict that he was a Lunatick. *C.*

A brief account of Sir Tho. Lombe's *Machine for working Italian Organzine silk, erected at* Derby. —— It contains 26,586 wheels, and 97,746 movements, which works 73,726 yards of silk thread every time the water wheel goes round, which is thrice in one minute, and 318,504,960 yards in one day and night; one water wheel gives motion to all the rest of the wheels and movements, of which any one may be stopt separately; one fire engine conveys warm air to every individual part of the machine, and one regulator governs the whole work. *D P.*

On wednesday began the Gen. Quarter Sessions of the Peace for the Royalty of the Tower, which Sir John Gonson of the Inner Temple opened with a very learned and excellent charge to the grand Jury. *D P.*

Yesterday morning about 4 there happen'd a violent storm of rain, attended with thunder and lightning, which did considerable damage to a new built house at Hamersmith, where it broke through, set fire to the bed and window curtains, and split in pieces some pier glasses that were in the room; but we do not hear that a[ny] person was hurt. *D P.*

There is advice that the America, Capt. Will. Bell, o[f] South Carolina, was lost coming over the Bar, &c. *D*[*P.*] —— The Katherine, Will. Bell, Master, was lately l[ost] on Long Island, which probably occasioned the rep[ort] foregoing. *D J.*

We hear that the Books of the Oratory are under t[he] judgment of a very learned Writer in order to the a[n]swering of them. *D J.* —— We hear, *that this* puff *co[mes] from* Mr. Auditor H——Y.

Cambridge, Ap. 3. The Grace about Dr. Middleto[n] has been a 3d time stopt in the Caput; the terms of the last Grace were to take away his Place of Library-Keeper, because it was useless and burthensome to the University. *D J.*

Christned, Males, 188; Females, 145; in all 233.
Buried, Males, 212; Females, 214; in all 426.
Decreased in the burials, 7. *P.*

SATURDAY, *April* 8.

Yesterday being Good Friday, the R. Rev. the L. Bishop of Rochester preached before their Majesties and the Royal Family, at the Chappel Royal at S. James's. C. — The Bishop of Glocester. *P.*

On wednesday his Excellency Prince Kantimir, Ambassador from the Czarina, had his first audience of his Majesty, &c. —— On thursday he was introduced to his R. Highness the Prince, &c. *P.* —— This day he is to have his first private audience of their Majesties. *D P.*

On wednesday last the D. of Bridgewater's *Hazard* won the 500 guineas. —— And the E. of Hallifax's *Justice* beat the E. of Portmore's *Daffadil*, for 300 guineas. P.

We hear that the late D. of Ormond is speedily expected here. *P.*

A new Writ is order'd for electing a Burgess for Minehead in the room of Fran. Whitworth, Esq; whose seat was vacated by his accepting the Office of Surveyor Gen. of all his Majesty's woods on the north and south sides of the river Trent. *D J.*

On monday dy'd at his house at Wandsworth, Mr. Will. Green, formerly a Pawn-broker, said to be worth upwards of 10,000 l. which he had acquir'd by *charitably assisting industrious poor*. *D P.* — On tuesday dy'd John Ellis, lately condemned for Pyracy, and pardoned. *C. D P.* —— *Some of my Brethren, who have suffered by* Pawn-brokers, *say, a* Sea pyrate *is a more generous adversary than a* Land one.

An Epitaph on Mr. Aikman, a Painter, who surviv'd his only son but a very short time, and *lies buried* in the same grave with him: by the Author of *Eurydice*.

Dear to the wise and good, disprais'd by none,
Here sleep in peace the Father, and the Son:
By virtue, as by nature, close ally'd,
The Painter's genius, but without the pride;
Worth unambitious, wit afraid to shine,
Honour's clear light, and friendship's warmth divine.
The Son, fair-rising, knew too short a date;
But oh! how more severe the Parent's fate?
He saw him torn, untimely, from his side,
Felt all a Father's anguish, wept —— and dy'd. *WE.*

We hear that a marriage is on foot between his Royal Highness the Prince of Wales, and the Princess Royal of Denmark. *S J. L E.*

A son of the Hon. Cha. Radcliffe, Esq; brother to James late E. of Derwentwater, is newly arrived here from France. *L E.*

A warrant hath been impressed from the Treasury to the Exchequer, for the sum of 14,000 l. to be paid to Sir Tho. Lombe, Knt. pursuant to a late Act of Parliament, as a recompence for his extraordinary art of working the engine for making organzine silk. *S J. L E.* — 4000 l. *C. Ap.* 10.

On tuesday night last Mr. Arth. Gould, who keeps the Hague Lottery Office at Charing-Cross) and his wife, were set upon in Leicester-fields, by 5 street-robbers, but he drew his sword and defended himself in a very gallant manner, as did also his wife, who seized one of them, who proved too sturdy for her; but several persons coming by at that instant, the villains made off without any booty, whereby Mr. Gould sav'd his gold watch, 50 l. in money, besides some bank notes, &c. *S J.* —— *By this account it is plain she wore a* sword *too.*

Yesterday morn in Shug-lane, some villains *in haste*
Against Mr. Wood's *sign-post* a ladder *had plac'd*;
But by Watch-men surpriz'd *ran away in great fear*,
Leaving *no* SIGN but the ladder, *to shew they had been there.* D J.

MONDAY, *April* 10.

Yesterday the Rev. Dr. Gilbert, Dean of Rochester, preach'd before their Majesties, &c. *C. D P.* In the absence of the L. Archbishop of York. *D J.* The Prince and the 3 eldest Princesses received the Communion. *C.* Administer'd to them by the L. Bishop of London, Dean of the Chapel, assisted by the Bishops of Winchester, and of Bath and Wells. *D J.* ——The same day the Rev. Dr. Terry preach'd before his Royal Highness the Duke, &c. C.

Mr. Rob. Hargrove is appointed Meſſenger to the Commiſſioners of the Victualling-Office, in the room of Mr. Kelloway, deceas'd. *D P.*

Sir Archibald Grant, Bar. is admitted to bail, himſelf and two ſureties in 4000 l. to appear when call'd for by the Committee to enquire into the affairs of the Charitable Corporation. *D P.*

Saturday laſt came on the election of a Member for Great Marlow in Buckinghamſhire, in the room of Geo. Robinſon, Eſq; late Treaſurer of the Charitable Corporation: the Candidates were the L. Sidney Beauclerc, and Sir Tho. Hoby, Bar. and on cloſing the poll, the numbers were, for Tho. Hoby 72, for L. Beauclerc 67. Whereupon the former was declared duly elected. *D J.*

Two Nephews of the Hon. Sir Tho. Lyttleton, one of the Lords of the Admiralty, were lately inoculated for the Small-pox; and on friday laſt the eldeſt of them, aged about 20, died; the other is in a fair way of recovery, the pox having broke out in a kindly way. *P.*

Tueſday, April 11.

On ſaturday laſt his Majeſty was pleaſed to declare, in the drawing-room, his Royal intention to viſit his German Dominions this ſummer; and we hear the 10th of next month is the day fixt for his departure. *P.*

Yeſterday morning the ſpital Sermon was preached at S. Bride's Church, before the R. Hon. the L. Mayor, Aldermen, and Sheriffs, by the R. Rev. the L. Biſhop of Durham; and afterwards they went to dinner to Goldſmith's Hall. *P.*

The R. Hon. the L. Malton having preſented the Rev. Mr. Ric. Goodwin, D. D. Prebend of York, and Rector of Tanterly in Yorkſhire, to the Rectory of Preſtwhich in Lancaſhire, worth 500 l. per ann. laſt week a diſpenſation paſs'd the Great Seal. *D J.*

Dover, *Ap. 2.* The D. of Montroſe's ſon embarqued yeſterday for Calais, on his travels. *P.*

Yeſterday morning between 5 and 6, Mrs. Smith, ſiſter to Mr. Smith in Laurence-lane, fell from the top of his houſe, ſuppoſed to be diſordered in her ſenſes, and died ſoon after. *P.* Flung herſelf out of a window 3 ſtories high. *C.*

We hear from Falmouth, that the Cuſtom houſe Officers there have made a large ſeizure of jewels, to the amount of 80,000 l. *S J.*

Wedneſday, April 12.

Yeſterday Count Naſſau, lately arrived from Holland, was at Court, and waited on their Majeſties. *P.*

Yeſterday the Rev. Dr. Gooch, Archdeacon of Eſſex, preach'd the ſpital Sermon before the R. Hon. the L. Mayor. *C.* —— This day the Rev. Dr. Knight is to preach the ſpital Sermon, &c. *P.*

Yeſterday morning died at her houſe in Blackmore-ſtreet, near Lincoln's-Inn-fields, Mrs. Roberts, a rich Widow, ſaid to be worth 20,000 l. *DP.* 30,000 l. *C.*

From the PEGASUS in Grub-ſtreet.

An Anſwer to a Copy of verſes in our 117th Journal.

'Tis not the Champion's voice, or limbs, or mein,
That makes him terrible, when heard, or ſeen.
But 'tis the ſacred place, in which he ſtands,
Alternate brandiſhing his holy hands:
The ſhining Altar, and the gilded Tub,
That hoarſely loud reſounds with myſtic dub:
Theſe ſtrike at once my wond'ring eyes and ears,
And fill my mind with ſuperſtitious fears.
Let him deſcend one ſingle pair of ſtairs,
And in his Coffee-houſe diſplay his airs;
His match he probably will meet; and then,
Like Samſon ſhorn, be found like other men.
This once he try'd, when boaſting of his might,
He dar'd a Grub-ſtreet Brother to the fight:
This tall, Corinthian Pillar, buttock croſt,
Prov'd but a *Poſtill* in the *Morning Poſt.*

POPPY.

FOREIGN NEWS.

Thurſday, April 6.

Yeſterday arrived the Mail from France.

Paris, *Ap. 12.* The differences with the Republick of Genoa being amicably adjuſted, the Marqueſs Doria, Envoy Extraordinary from that Republick, had his publick audience of the King, on the 8th inſtant, and was afterwards ſumptuouſly entertain'd at dinner by the Officers of State. *C. D P.* —— The Actions are now at 1735.

Liſbon, *Mar. 6.* The King of Portugal has offered the Eaſt India Company newly erected at Stockholm, his protection towards the ſucceſs of their undertaking, and the port of Goa for the ſecurity of their ſhips, with permiſſion to build warehouſes there for their goods and merchandiſes. *P.*

Friday, April 7.

Hambourg, *Ap. 4.* The Magiſtrates of Altena have acquainted the Roman Catholick Clergy, that in caſe the Archbiſhop of Saltzbourg did not ceaſe his perſecution of

the Proteſtant ſubjects, they ſhould be obliged to uſe repriſals, by ſhutting up their Churches, and ſequeſtring their effects. The ſame declaration has been made at Copenhagen, and all the principal Towns of Denmark. *D P.*

Monday, April 10.

Vienna, *Ap. 2.* M. Thalman, the Imperial Reſident at Conſtantinople, has ſent advice to Court, that the horſetail has been ſet up there againſt the Chriſtians, which was believed to be deſigned againſt the Ruſſians. *D J. D P.*

Tueſday, April 11.

Yeſterday arrived the Mail from Holland.

Rome, *Mar. 29.* Some letters from Corſica adviſe, that Don Lewis Giaſſeri, General of the Malecontents, had publiſhed a proclamation, ſummoning all the abſent Corſicans fit to bear arms, to repair to his ſtandard before May-day, upon very ſevere penalties. They add, that that General had coined gold and ſilver ſpecies to the amount of 400,000 Crowns, having on one ſide a crowned Tyger, and on the reverſe this motto, *Tandem ſuperata libertas. P. C.* Having diſpoſed of oil, corn, &c. to the French, to the amount of 400,000 Crowns, &c. *D P.*

Halle, *Ap. 10.* On March 18th, died at Wettin Mynheer Barth. Von Groſchky, the King's Inſpector of the mines and minerals there, aged 113 years. He had by 2 wives 15 children, his younger daughter being born when he was 104 years old. He had no complaint till the laſt year, being always freſh and healthy. *P.*

Wedneſday, April 12.

By private letters from the Hague we are aſſured, that a treaty of marriage is concluded between his moſt Serene Highneſs Don Carlos and a Lady of the blood Royal of France: Hereupon the Politicians at the Hague are under great conſternation about the ſudden marriage of the two Crowns; to confirm which, we are aſſured the Imperialiſts judge the great armament of Spain deſigned for Corſica, and are reſolved to ſupport the Genoeſe in the Government thereof. *D P.*

Books and Pamphlets publiſhed ſince Mar. 29.

Dolæus upon the cure of the gout by Milk-diet. **By Will. Stephens, M. D. F. R. S.**

A Paraphraſe and Notes on S. Paul's 2d Epiſtle to the Theſſalonians: in imitation of Mr. Locke's manner.

Lukewarmneſs in Religion repreſented and reproved in 2 Sermons: by W. Harris, D. D. Pr. 1 s.

Memoirs of the Life and Character of the late Earl of Oſſery, and the family of the Boyles, &c. By Euſtace Budgell, Eſq;

31. The Feaſts and Faſts of the Church of England. Pr. 5 s.

The Hiſtorical Regiſter, No. 65:

Ap. 1. An examination of the facts and reaſonings in the L. Biſhop of Chicheſter's Sermon, Jan. 31. Pr. 1 s.

The married Philoſopher, a Comedy. Pr. 1 s. 6 d.

3. Longford's Glyn: a true Hiſtory tranſlated from the Iriſh. Pr. 6 d.

4. The monthly Catalogue of Books for March.
The monthly Catalogue in 8vo. No. 3. for March.
Memoirs of Love and Gallantry, &c. Pr. 1 s.

5. Mr. Taſte, the Poetical Fop, &c. Pr. 1 s. 6 d. Reyner. Grub.

The Roman Antiquities of Britain: by John Horſely, M. A. and F. R. S.

The intrigueing Courtiers: a Comedy. Pr. 1 s. 6 d.

The moral obligation to the poſitive appointments in Religion, chiefly as to the Sacraments. Pr. 4 d.

A third Conference in anſwer to *Chriſtianity as old,* &c. by Tho. Burnet, D. D. Pr. 1 s. 6 d.

8. Oldmixon's Reply to Dr. Atterbury's Vindication of Biſhop Smallridge, &c. Pr. 1 s.

The monthly Chronicle for March.

10. The Gentleman's Magazine, No. 15. for March.

A pocket Companion for young Gentlemen. Pr. 6 d.

A Detection of ſeveral miſrepreſentations of Facts in Oldcaſtle's Remarks on the Engliſh Hiſtory, &c. Pr. 6 d.

A Letter to a Country Gentleman on the revival of the Salt Duty.

The omniſcience of God ſtated and vindicated, &c. by D. Millar, A. M.

12. Some Remarks on a Reply to the Defence of the Letter to Dr. Waterland, &c. Pr. 1 s.

On Tueſday Stocks were

SouthSea Stock 98 7 8ths, 98 3 qrs. South Sea Annuity 110 3 qrs. for the Opening. Bank 151 1 half, for ditto. New Bank Circulation 7 l. 5 s. Premium. India 177 3 qrs. 178 to 1 8th, for the Opening. Three per Cent. Annuity 97 1 8th. Royal Exchange Aſſurance 99 1 half. London Aſſurance 13 3 8ths, to 1 half, for the Opening. York Buildings 7 1 half. African 42. Engliſh Copper 2 l. 10 s. Welch ditto 1 l. 15 s. South Sea Bonds 3 l. 2 s. Premium. India ditto 6 l. 2 s. ditto. Blanks 7 l. 7 s. 6 d. 20 l. Prizes 19 l. 13 s. 6 d.

This Day is Publiſhed,

In One Volume Octavo,

ANNOTATIONS on the Book of

JOB and the *PSALMS*.

Collected from ſeveral COMMENTATORS, and Methodized and Improved by THOMAS FENTON, M. A. Rector of Nately-ſcures in Hampſhire, and ſome Time Student of Chriſt-Church in *Oxford*.

Printed for *C. Rivington*, at the Bible and Crown in St. Paul's Church-Yard. *Where may be had, the 2d Edition, of*

An EXPOSITION on the *Thirty Nine Articles* of the *Church of England*: Founded on the Holy Scriptures, and the Fathers of the Three Firſt Centuries. In Two Vols. By J. VENNER, Rector of St. Andrew's in Chicheſter.

Juſt publiſhed, [Price 2 s. 6 d.]

(To be continued.)

NUMBER III. of

ECCLESIATICAL MEMOIRS of the Firſt SIX CENTURIES, made good by Citations from Original Authors: With a CHRONOLOGICAL TABLE, containing an Abridgment of the principal Things, placed according to the Order of Time; and with Notes, clearing the Difficulties of Facts and Chronology. Tranſlated from the French of *Lewis Sebaſtian Le Nain De Tillemont*.

Nothing eſcapes Mr. TILLEMONT'S *Exactneſs; and there is no Fact ſo obſcure and perplext, but his Criticiſm diſpels the Miſt, and diſentangles the Difficulties. Theſe Works of Mr.* TILLEMONT *are the Product of a prodigious Labour, and almoſt infinite Induſtry, and are compoſed with all poſſible Exactneſs. He is modeſt in his Expreſſions, juſt in his Citations, cautious in his Deciſions, pious and judicious in his Obſervations. The World may gain a great deal of Improvement from this Work, which is calculated both for the Inſtruction and the Edification of Mankind.*

Du Pin's Bibliotheque, Tom. 18.

Printed for the Author; and ſold by Charles Rivington at the Bible and Crown in St. Paul's Church-Yard; and William Clayton, Bookſeller in Mancheſter.

WHEREAS other *Coffee-Houſes*, and other *Publick Houſes*, take of their Cuſtomers 8 s. for a Quart of Arrack, and 6 s. for a Quart of Rum or Brandy made into *Punch*, ſo that it is now become the ſettled Price throughout the Town, and ſeldom leſs than a Bowl of 1 s. 6 d. is to be had: Therefore, for the better accommodating all Gentlemen, that are Lovers of *Punch*,

This is to give Notice,

That I have opened on Ludgate-hill, the *London-Coffee-Houſe* and *Punch-Houſe*, (Two *Punch-Bowls* on Iron Pedeſtals before my Door.)

Where the fineſt and beſt old Batavia Arrack, Jamaica Rum, and French Brandy, are made into *Punch*, with the fineſt Ingredients, viz.

A Quart of Arrack made into *Punch* for 6 s. and ſo in Proportion to the ſmalleſt quantity, which is half a Quartern for four Pence Half-penny.

A Quart of Rum or Brandy made into *Punch* for 4 s. and ſo in Proportion to the ſmalleſt Quantity, which is half a Quartern for 3 d. And Gentlemen may have it as ſoon made, as a Gill of Wine can be drawn; with the beſt of Eating, Attendance, and Accommodation.

This Undertaking has occaſion'd many, whoſe *Intereſt* it is to poſſeſs Gentlemen with ſuch an Opinion, that the Liquors by me uſed are not good: The Publick is hereby aſſured, that I buy my Goods on the Keys, and at the beſt Hand, with Ready Money, and am at this Time provided with as well-choſen Brandies, Rum and Arrack, as any in Town, and will at all times procure the beſt that is imported: But what may convince Gentlemen of the Truth hereof, is, (not only by the Encouragement I meet with) that the Sherbet is always brought by itſelf, and the Brandy, Rum, or Arrack in the Meaſure, ſo there can be no Impoſition, either in Quantity or Quality; for the Proof whereof I appeal to all Gentlemen who have done me the Honour to call at my Houſe.

James Aſhley.

The moſt Sovereign CEPHALICK SNUFF,

PRepared by *John Thirkell*, Tobacconiſt, at the Highlander, in Smock-Alley, Spittle-fields, (and communicated to him by an eminent Phyſician) is good againſt all Pains of the Head and Brain, that come by a cold Cauſe; and quickens the Underſtanding, helps the Memory, prevents Giddineſs and Drowſineſs; dries up the Rheum that often falls on the Stomach, and cauſes Conſumptions; prevents the Noiſe and Pain in the Ears; is good for the Eyes, and helps the Sight.

Alſo another moſt excellent Cephalick Snuff, for removing those Diſtempers of the Head and Brain, proceeding from a hot Cauſe; as Frenzineſs, want of Sleep, hot cholerick Humours, Intoxications of ſtrong Liquors, even rectifying the Underſtanding, and taking away the Pains in the Heads of thoſe ſo diſordered; dries up the Rheum that diſtils into the Eyes, Gums, and Teeth, which often cauſes Inflammation and Pains in them; cures the Dizzineſs of the Head, Ulcers and Stench of the Noſe, that come by taking too much Spaniſh Snuff, or otherwiſe.

N. B. They far exceed any yet made, as well in Colour as Beauty and Flavour; and the Preparer doubts not, but that thoſe that try, will experience great Benefit by them. He alſo makes Right *Scotch*, Fine *Spaniſh*, and *Rapeé* Snuffs.

This day is publiſhed,

INTEREST at one View calculated to a Farthing. at 3, 4, 5, 6, 7 and 8 per Cent. from 1000 l. to 1 l. for one Day to 96 Days; and for 1, 2, 3, 4, 5, 6, 7, 8, 9, 10, 11, and 12 Months: With Rules and Examples to caſt up Intereſt at any other Rates by the ſaid Tables. To which is added, A Table for the more ſpeedy caſting up of Salaries and Wages, from one Million to one Pound per Year. Beſides many other Tables of great Uſe in receiving and paying of Monies. The Whole being calculated, examined and corrected, and afterwards re-examined, from the Preſs.

By RICHARD HAYES.

Printed for W MEADOWS, at the Angel in Cornhill.

Where may be had, by the ſame Author,

1 The Purchaſer's Pocket Companion; ſhewing at Sight what Intereſt is made by Money laid out in the Companies Stocks, or other publick Funds.

2. The Negotiator's Magazine of Monies and Exchanges, with a compleat Treatiſe of Arbitrations of Exchanges.

3. The Ship and Supercargo Book-Keeper, ſhewing the Manner of the Maſters ſettling Accounts with their Owners, the Privilege of Merchants, and Duty of Officers; with Supercargo's Accompts after the Italian Method of Double Entry.

4. An Eſtimate of Places for Life, calculated on the Chances of Lives in general, with an Account of Places in the Diſpoſal of the City of London, and their Value.

This Day is publiſhed,

Beautifully Printed in 8vo. with his Effigies, engrav'd from an original Picture, by Mr. Vandergucht, and a Map,

THE HISTORY of CHARLES XII. King of Sweden, by M. de VOLTAIRE. Tranſlated from the French Original. The Second Edition corrected.

Printed for C. Davis, in Pater-Noſter-Row; and A. Lyon, in Ruſſel-Street, Covent-Garden.

Where may be had, lately publiſhed, in 8vo.

1. Hiſtoire de Charles XII. Roi de Suede, par M. de Voltaire. Seconde Edition. revue & corrigee par l'Auteur. 2. Dr. Lobbe's Treatiſe of the Small-Pox. In Two Parts. 3 Houghton's Collections for the Improvement of Trade and Husbandry, 4 Vol. 4. Pere Regnault's Philoſophical Converſations, with 89 Copper Plates. Tranſlated and illuſtrated with Notes, by T. Dale, M. D. 3 Vol. 5. Ariſticis Orationes, Gr. Lat. per S. Jebb, M. D. 2 Vol. 4to. 6. Somner's Treatiſe of Gavelkind, with his Life, by the Lord Biſhop of Peterborough, 4to. 7. Vertot's Hiſtory of the Knights of Malta, with 71 Heads, 2 Vols. Folio. 8. Kempfer's Hiſt. of Japan and Siam, with Variety of Cuts, 2 Vols. Folio. 9. Dr. Harris's Hiſt. of Kent, with Variety of Cuts, in ſmall and large Paper, Folio. 10. Hiſt. Mariæ Scot. Reg per S. Jebb, M. D. 2 Vols. Fol. 11. Gianone's Civil Hiſt. of Naples, tranſlated by Captain Ogilvie, 2 Vols. Folio

This Day is publiſhed

For the Uſe of Families, (beautifully printed in 2 Vols. 8vo.) adorn'd with 34 Plates, engraven by Mr. Sturt,

DUPIN's Evangelical Hiſtory; or, The Records of the Son of God, and their Veracity demonſtrated. In the Life and Acts of our bleſſed Lord and Saviour Jeſus Chriſt, and his Holy Apoſtles. Wherein,

I. The Life of the Bleſſed JESUS is related in all its Circumſtances, according to the Order of Time, in a pathetic Style and practical Method, thereby compoſing a perfect Harmony of the Goſpels.

II. Proofs from his Sermons and Diſcourſes of thoſe eſſential and important Truths, which all Chriſtians are oblig'd to know and practiſe, in order to their eternal Salvation.

III. His Parables, Miracles, and Sufferings, ſet in a clear Light, and defended from all the Oppoſitions of wicked and deſigning Men.

IV. An Application to the Whole to the reſpective Uſes of Chriſtians, with regular Devotions conformable to the ſeveral Periods of the Holy Hiſtory; and Directions how we may read the Life of Jeſus Chriſt to Advantage. Printed for R. Ware, at the Bible and Sun in Amen-Corner, near Pater-Noſter-Row; price 8 s. Where may be had,

1. The large Houſe Bibles, Folio, with the ſix Maps of ſacred Geography, and a brief Concordance for the more eaſy finding out of the Places therein contained. By J. Downame, B. D. Bound in Calf Leather at 1 l. 7 s. per Book. And with Mr. Sturt's Cuts, at 2 l. 5 s. ditto. On a fine Paper with Cuts 3 l. 3 s. ditto.

2. The Impartial Churchman; or, A fair and candid Repreſentation of the Excellency and Beauty of the Church of England. Together with an earneſt and affectionate Addreſs to the Proteſtant Diſſenters. By Robert Warren, D. D. Price 3 s. 6d.

3. The Whole Duty of Man. Part II. Teaching a Chriſtian, 1. How to grow in Grace. 2 How to demean himſelf in Sickneſs. 3. How to prepare himſelf for a happy Death. Together with Advice how Viſitants and Attendants ſhould carry it toward the Sick; and ſome general Conſiderations that may induce Relations and Friends to take his Death patiently. By the Rev. and Learned Dr. John Williams, late Lord Biſhop of Chicheſter; price 3 s 6 d.

Where likewiſe may be had,

A curious Field's Bible, Folio, with very fine Cuts, two Volumes, bound in Turkey Leather; price 20 l.

And on Imperial Paper, three Volumes ditto, 30 l

This day is publiſhed, Price 6 d.

THE GENTLEMAN'S MAGAZINE: Or, *Monthly Intelligencer*.

No. XV. for MARCH, 1732.

Being the THIRD of VOL. II. Containing,

I. A View of the weekly Eſſays, viz On Players; Gratitude, Punning, Study; War with Prieſtcraft; Ambition; Of *Theatrical* Plays; Common Senſe; Liberty of Conſcience: Devotion, Country Wits; Dramatick Poets; Footmen a Nuſance; Milton's Failings

II. Political Points, viz. Dr. Swift of the Conteſts between the Nobles and Commons; Mr. Trenchard and Ld. Hallifax of Standing Armies, ſeconded by D'Anvers, Osborne and Walſingham; Advice to the Athenians; Caveat againſt Bubbles; the Neceſſity of the preſent Forces; the Expectations of the Jacobites; Legal and Arbitrary Governments differenced; the Tree of Corruption; Fog and Dr. Clarke on January 30; Fog and Biſhop Burnet on King William's Family and Actions; Fog's Crime; Hue and Cry after the Charitable Corporation Money; how the Pretender was to have been brought in; Balloting commended; a Blundering Club; Oliver Cromwell's Policy

III. Poetry: Deſcription of the Spring in Maryland; Verſes on No Biſhop No King; Epigrams.

IV. Domeſtick Occurrences, Births, Deaths, Marriages, Promotions, &c. Mrs. Longley's Trial, Aſſize News.

V. Price of Goods, Grain, Stocks.

VI. Foreign Affairs.

VII. Books and Pamphlets.

VIII. A Table of Contents.

By *SYLVANUS URBAN*, Gent.

Printed and ſold at St. John's Gate; by F. Jefferies in Ludgate-Street, and the Bookſellers in Town and Country.

Where may be had all the former Numbers.

Note, A few are printed on fine Royal Paper, large Margin, for the Curious.

THE Great and Wonderful Cures daily perform'd by Dr. *Bateman's* Pectoral Drops, in the following Diſtempers, have gain'd them ſo indiſputable a Character, that few Families who have ever heard, or experienced the Virtues thereof, care to be without them in their own Houſes, viz. the Gout, Rheumatiſm, Jaundice, Stone, Gravel, Aſthma's and Cholicks, of what Kind or Nature ſoever, whether proceeding from Wind, Cold, or Heſterick Affection. Beſides which, there is no one Secret in the whole Art of Phyſick of that ſurpriſing and (were it not under the Confirmation of continual Experience) almoſt incredible Effects in Colds, Agues, Fevers, and thoſe endemic Evils which appear in moſt Conſtitutions at Spring and Fall The Price of each Bottle, in which are three moderate Doſes, is but one Shilling, and may (by Vertue of the King's Letters Patents) be had at the Printing-Office, Bow-Church-Yard, Cheapſide, and no where elſe within three Quarters of a Mile from thence.

N. B. A Book of the Virtues thereof, with Teſtimonies of ſome hundred Cures perform'd thereby, under the Hands of Perſons of known Worth and Credit, may be had gratis with the ſaid Bottles.

Note alſo, Shopkeepers, &c. in any Town, where they are not already ſold, may be ſupply'd with the above Drops, (on a good Allowance) to ſell again, by directing to Wm. Dicey, or Tho. Cobb and Comp at Dr. Bateman's Wholeſale Warehouſe in Bow-Church-Yard, London.

The *Cœleſtial Anodyne Tincture*: Or, The *Great Pain-Eaſing Medicine*,

FAm'd and approv'd of for its wonderful and never-failing Succeſs, in giving immediate Eaſe and Relief in all manner of pains, either inward or outward, and is the moſt certain Remedy in the World for a ſure and ſpeedy Cure of the Cholick, and expelling Wind, Gripes and pains in the Stomach, the Pleuriſy, ſtitches or pains in the ſide, back, loins, or any other parts; Rheumatick Ailments, which cauſe pain and dolor. It hath given eaſe to a Miracle, when all other Remedies have fail'd. In the Gravel and Stone in the Kidneys, it gives eaſe forthwith, and brings them away to Admiration. It alſo facilitates and cauſes a ſpeedy Delivery in Child-birth 'Tis no Quack trifling thing to allure the World with, but a real and well-experienced Medicine, not acting by Stupefaction (as Opiates) but by a friendly, balſamick, and ſubtile Nature, pacifying the moſt ſevere and terrible racking pains, and carries off the Cauſe, not by purging, but by Tranſpiration, by Urine, or breaking Wind. No Family ought to be without it. And uſed outwardly, it cures Swellings, Aches, pains, Numbneſs, or Weakneſs of the Joints: 'tis excellent far Cramps, and all other aged Infirmities, effecting Wonders in Agues, Fevers, Small-pox. &c. No Family ought to be without it.

It is ſold only by Mr. *PARKER*, Printer, at his Houſe in Salisbury-Court, or by ſuch perſons as he ſhall depute, viz at Mr. *Parker's*, a Printer, in Bull-Head Court, Jewin-ſtreet: at the Five Gallon Pot, a Chandler's Shop in Bandy-Leg-Walk, Southwark, and at Mr. Neal's, a Toy-ſhop over againſt the White Hart Inn in the Borough, at Eighteen pence a bottle, with printed Directions: and, if requeſted, will be brought to any Perſon, by the Hawker, who ſells his Penny-poſt. Sealed as above.

LONDON: Printed by S. PALMER and J. HUGGONSON; *in Bartholomew-Cloſe*, for Captain GULLIVER; near the *Temple* where Letters and Advertiſements are taken in: As alſo at the *Rainbow Coffee-Houſe* in *Cornhill*, and *John's Coffee-Houſe* in *Sheer-Lane*, near *Temple-Bar*. [Price Two Pence.]

The Grub-street Journal.

NUMB. 120

Thursday, APRIL 20, 1732.

We've cheated the Parson, we'll cheat him agen:
For why should a block-head have one in ten? Old Song.

THE following Treatise, occasioned by a report that the Tythe-Bill would be revived this Sessions, was sent from an unknown person, by the post, to our Bookseller, who soon communicated it to the Society. When it had been read, a great very majority declared for its publication: which, it is hoped, will intirely clear us of an aspersion, as if we were favourers of Priestcraft; an aspersion cast upon us by some of our renegado Members, vexed at the ill reception the world gives their daily or weekly Lucubrations, and inflamed with envy at the great success of ours.

HIS WORSHIP *holding the* PARSON'*s Tythe-pig by the tail: or* Five arguments *most humbly offered to the Public, and more particularly addressed to many Members of the Honourable House of Commons; setting forth, and shewing the great reason there is for passing the Tythe-Bill (as it is commonly called) which was brought before the Parliament the last Sessions, tho' unfortunately not ordered a second reading.*

Courteous Reader.

I Look upon it as one of the chief causes of the decay of primitive Christianity, that there is any set of men particularly appointed to attend upon the affairs of religion. We should certainly do much better without them, than with them; and be able to find a way to make their revenues more serviceable to the good of the Nation, and turn to a much better account than they do at present. If religion is a personal thing between God and a man's own conscience, (as without all doubt it must be) it then follows from the reason and nature of things, and is demonstratively proved by the *Independent Whig*, that there cannot be the least occasion for a PARSON; and that every man ought to be a spiritual guide unto himself: for which the country-men, and day-labourers of England seem at present to be extremely well qualified, they being most of them able, as I have been credibly informed, to read English.

As for the Clergy, it must be acknowledged, that they have hitherto tolerably well maintained their ground. But how have they maintained it? or why have they been able to maintain it? Why, not by their own great learning and abilities; not by the exemplariness of their lives, or the prudence of their behaviour; but by a constant fatal mismanagement in the worthy Gentlemen who have opposed them: who, by laying their arguments in too loose, indigested and incoherent a way, and by being more intent upon exposing the follies, weaknesses, or wickednesses of particular persons, than upon the grand point of showing the uselessness of the Order itself, have ever given the soberer, and more rational part of the Clergy some room for reclamation and triumph. I must say for my present performance, (and I hope that it will not be thought to have the least tendency towards vanity) that I have carefully avoided this method. I argue close; I keep to the point; and do not let my Reader lose sight of the subject, as is commonly done by most Writers: and tho' I have purposely insisted only upon five arguments, when I could very well have produced treble the number; yet, I hope, these five are so well managed, and set in so clear a light, that the *Reverends*, and the *Right Reverends*, will find themselves held to hard diet, and have a very troublesome and difficult bone to pick.

Fare thee well, live, and grow wiser.

BEfore I proceed to lay my arguments for passing the Tythe Bill before my Reader, I must beg leave, by way of introduction, to premise, and very solemnly to assure him, that I have set myself with the utmost impartiality, and without the least biass on my mind of interest, prejudice, or passion, to examine the subject. I can safely say, that I have not, nay that I never had, any private quarrel, or misunderstanding, with any Clergyman whatsoever; but on the contrary, have lived, and do even now live with many of them, in a very great freedom and familiarity; and have no possible objection against very many among them, as to their manners, or their morals, or indeed, in any other respect, than as they wear the gown and cassock.

As to my being prejudiced against them; it may rather, and with a greater shew of reasoning, be objected by a Layman, that I am prejudiced for them; because in fact I was bred up a Member of the Church of England, and still continue to profess myself a Member of it; and am not ashamed of confessing, that if we must have a Church (for which I hope no one will think me ignorant enough to believe, that there is any occasion) I really, and strictly speaking, consider the Church of England as the best constituted, and the freest from pedantry, morosensess, and superstition of any Church in the whole world.

And lastly, as to my being interested in the affair, this can surely only be urged by those, who are not acquainted with me, or my circumstances. For I here protest, and I can, if there is the least scruple remaining, bring sufficient evidence to the truth of what I say, that I do not pay tythe for a single foot of land in his Majesty's whole dominions; that little fortune that I have consisting chiefly in money, together with two or three copperas works, for which there was never any thing demanded, or so much as pretended to be demanded, by the neighbouring Minister.

I say thus much to obviate any unjust reflections, or loud-mouthed clamours, which may very probably come from the Clergy quarter, on account of my not being a competent judge, and writing with partiality on the subject: and I likewise say it, to dispose the Laity to attend to the following arguments (which by the way, ought to be in every one of their hands, from the highest to the lowest) with the same candour and disinterestedness, with which they were at first drawn up, and are now sent into the world by me.

And first, let me take notice, that the passing of this Bill, would in a great measure tend to lessen the exorbitant incomes, and overgrown revenues of the rural Clergy; who are generally observed, by those who are acquainted with their last wills and testaments (and particularly by the very learned and facetious Author of a late *London Journal*,) to die immensly rich, and to leave vast fortunes to their daughters. Taking the livings of England at a medium, I dare say, that they will even amount to near fourscore and ten pounds a year; and I am not ignorant, that some persons will pretend to carry the computation higher. And whether this is not an extravagant allowance for only getting up in the pulpit once a week, and reading an old sermon, when many an honest man labours in his lawful vocation of hedging, or mud-wall-making the whole year, for the fourth part of the income, I must leave to the consideration of every rational and understanding Englishman.

A second reason for passing this Bill is, that it would make Pork and Bacon plentiful, (which by the way, may be looked on as the staple diet of the nation) and of consequence it would render labour cheap, and save the Government a vast deal of money in victualling out their fleet, the next time they are obliged to make an expedition at such a great distance from us as Spithead. 'Tis no secret to the whole Nation, and even in the mouth of every Apprentice, provided he has any right turn to ingenuity and free thinking, that the Clergy are great lovers of roasting pigs. Now, upon a very moderate computation, and not to carry the thing higher than it will well bear, supposing that there are ten thousand Clergymen in England (I exclude the London Readers, and Country Curates, because they are Jewishly inclined, and have most of them scruples of conscience against this sort of diet, unless at a Christning;) and allowing to every Clergyman three roasting pigs, (which is as low as we can put it; without all doubt many of the dignified Clergy eat five or six;) and farther supposing, that two parts in three of these pigs are sows (and we cannot well imagine, that there should be fewer females, since these are generally made choice of by the Tyther, as best agreeing with the Parson's liquorish tooth,) and allowing that these sow pigs would, one with another, if not killed young, have five more at a litter, and two litters in a year, (which is a very reasonable reckoning;) why then it follows, that the Clergy are the cause of lessening the stock of pigs yearly in the nation to the amount of two hundred thousand; besides the ten thousand boar-pigs, and besides what they devour of brawn, hams, and flitch bacon. And whether this is not an insupportable charge upon our country, and the great cause of the decay of our trade, will be well worth my worthy friend Mr. H— inlarging upon, the next time he makes another polite speech before the Honourable &c.

A third reason for passing the Bill against the Clergy is, that they are very consi[...] [...]esigners of the King's revenues, by being a con[...] [...]g upon the consu[...]tion of our own home commodities, and by their [...] and officious impertinence in preaching against [...]ty and good fellowship, which are so well known [...]ment his Majesty's duties upon mum, cyder, pe[...] brandy, and that reviving liquor, commonly disti[...] by the name of gin. Not but that, to do the Clergy justice, there are many among them very good commonwealths-men in these respects: and I believe (was there any occasion for it, and would the good deeds of some of them make amends for the faults of others) proper vouchers might be produced of some hundreds among them, who are very pains-taking Gentlemen; and who almost every night of their lives give demonstrative proofs of their firm and inviolable attachment to the true interests of their King and Country on the former account. But some hundreds are very inconsiderable, when we speak of the bulk of the Clergy; who are well known both to preach up, and to practise such unprofitable commodities, as temperance and sobriety; and to talk a deal of idle stuff against many of the social virtues, such as profuseness and prodigality; and impertinently to busy themselves, and to make a mighty stir against erecting ale-houses, and brandy shops. And of consequence, (I insist upon it as the justest reasoning, and which may be made out beyond contradiction) they are direct enemies (for I cannot well use a milder term) to their King and Country, by annually sinking the taxes: and their conduct very visibly and plainly affects the landed interest (which is a good hint by the by, to make the Country Squires look about them) by lowering the price of barley.

A fourth argument for passing the Bill, and which indeed is of full as much importance as any of the former, is, that the Clergy are constant and unwearied enemies to all regularity, order, and good government in every Society. I don't mean by this to charge them with being in a foreign interest, or to insinuate as if they had any designs directly against his Majesty King George (no, the fellows are devilish cunning, and love the protestant religion too well for this) but what I mean is, that they are for ever disturbing his Majesty's Country Justices of the peace in the execution of their office; impudently making parties in their several parishes against them; and drawing in all the poor, honest, sober, and most industrious part of the neighbours to go to Church, and side with them against the Justice.—What a goodly and pleasant thing would it be, and how near would it approach to the original standard of Government, to see the Country Squires of Great Britain (who are generally men of great humanity and good breeding, of sound morals, and unquestionable learning) acting without the least controul or molestation in every one of their parishes! — sending one man to goal for not standing still when his worship was so kind as to beat him; — another to the stocks for swearing, because his Worship condescended to be a little too familiar with the fellow's wife; — ordering a writ of ejectment against a third, for not breeding up a couple of young hounds for his Worship's recreation; — and assigning a fourth to the whipping-post for sauciness and ill language, when his Worship did him the honour of riding over his corn, and breaking his hedges. —— I say, what a goodly thing would it be to behold all this; and to see the eastern polite method of governing by Bashaws, take place in our western part of the world! And this in fact would be the case in most parishes, as it is already in some, did not those forward fellows the Parsons thrust themselves into other persons affairs, and often impudently take upon them to understand some of the laws of the land, in opposition to his Worship's way of explaining them; and did they not prate a deal of idle stuff about reason, justice, and equity; and make a horrid noise and pother about oppression, violence, and grinding the faces of the poor, to the no small obstruction of their Worships laudable proceedings.

Besides, these fellows, more ways than one, disturb the peace of the Society; —— they will not suffer their Worships to sleep in peace at Church; —— they will not let them kiss their Tenants daughters in peace; — they will not let them get drunk, and play at cards on a sunday in peace: —— and to add to all their other offences, they will often even have the consummate i[...]e to apply to the Court of Exchequer for the Tyt[...] [...] his Worship's estate, when his Worship, out of his better judgment, and from his great knowledge in the law, thinks fit to detain them.

and when all theſe things are weighed together, they are ſurely ſufficient to engage all their Worſhips to uſe their utmoſt intereſt with their repreſentatives, that this Bill may paſs.

The laſt argument which I ſhall make uſe of, for paſſing this Bill againſt the Clergy is this, that notwithſtanding all their loud talk about mortification, abſtinence, and ſelf denial, yet upon a ſtrict examination, and upon conſulting the beſt authorities, we cannot but be perſuaded that they eat and drink; that they ſleep, they ſmoke, they wear ſhirts, and lye in ſheets; that they marry wives, live in houſes, get children, and do all the offices of life, after the ſame manner that Laymen do them. I have been very credibly informed, nay I make not the leaſt doubt of the truth of it (becauſe, as Biſhop B—N T well obſerves, I had it from a perſon of undoubted reputation, who aſſured me, that he had it from one, who had it from a very conſiderable Lady's woman's midwife, who had it from the Gentlewoman's own mouth,) who affirmed, 'that 'once at a chriſtening dinner ſhe ſaw the Parſon of the 'pariſh eat a very large ſlice of roaſt beef, two cuts of a 'marrow pudding, a conſiderable deal of the breaſt of a 'turkey, and after all, concluded with a mince pie.' — Now if this account be true (and there is not the leaſt room to call it in queſtion,) pray how can any one, after this, have the face to ſay one word for the Parſons; or ſo much as pretend to offer any thing in defence of a body of men, who are ſuch an intollerable and inſupportable charge upon a trading nation? Shall we not all immediately give our votes, that their houſes ſhould be pulled down, and their parſonages applied to the relief of the Sinking Fund?—That the fellows themſelves ſhould be ſent forthwith to the Plantations, and their wives and children be provided for in work houſes; —— that every maſter of a family ſhould be obliged to ſupply the place of a Parſon under his own roof; —— and that in caſe his Worſhip ſhould not have a facility in reading Engliſh, he ſhould have a toleration to provide himſelf with an able huntſman, who hath been brought up to learning, and is qualified to ſupply his place. — Tho' this way of proceeding with them ſeems extremely equitable, and not one bit or jot beyond what the Parſons very richly deſerve, yet I muſt moſt humbly beg leave to diſſent from it; and this (I aſſure you) not out of the leaſt love or kindneſs to the Parſons, or any tenderneſs towards their wives and children, but becauſe I think that there is a method full as effectual to undo them, and which will anſwer the end full as well, and at the ſame time make leſs noiſe in the world, and give leſs offence to very many ſilly, and well diſpoſed Chriſtians; (who, by the way, cannot at once get over the prejudices of their youth, and loſe all regard for a ſet of men, who have inſtructed them in the faith of that Saviour, from whom they expect eternal happineſs) and the method is this, to ſtarve them by degrees, and to let them die inch by inch. Let the Tythe Bill paſs, ſay I; —— let the whole *onus probandi* in recovering of Tythes lye upon the Country Vicars; —— let them not be able to get a few of his Worſhip's apples to make pies for their children, or a little milk to make them a pudding, without being at forty pound charge; —— let their Worſhips not only teeze and worry them themſelves, but let them likewiſe ſet on all the purſe-proud farmers in their ſeveral pariſhes to do the ſame thing; —— let their Worſhips make new improvements, and not pay the leaſt conſideration for them, becauſe there was never any thing payed before; — and let the patrons of livings take effectual care to make conſiderable reſervations of the glebe lands, when they lye contiguous to their own eſtates; —— let the capital farm in his Worſhip's manor be exempted from all demands, on pretence of belonging to ſome Abbey; and let the poor Vicar be once oppreſſed and overborne by a powerful adverſary; and a law be immediately trumped up, that his ſucceſſors ſhould acquieſce, and patiently and contentedly bear the oppreſſion for ever after it. —— I ſay, let the Tythe Bill paſs, and let theſe methods be regularly and conſtantly followed for one twenty or thirty years; and I make not the leaſt doubt (provided no extraordinary thing happen) but the Clergy will be as poor, as miſerable, as contemptible, and as uncapable of doing any good in a Society, and of interrupting the repoſe of our Country Squires, as their utmoſt enemies could wiſh them.

And laſtly, let me farther add, that when the Tythe Bill is paſſed, and another Bill, full as reaſonable, relating to the game, (and brought upon the ſtage at the ſame time with the other) by which the whole monopoly of woodcocks was to be aſcertained to their Worſhips and their heirs male; and no perſons (under a ſevere penalty) beſides the Country Squires and their eldeſt ſons, impowered to lay ſpringes for them for the future; — I ſay let this Bill paſs, as well as the other Bill, and let not only moſt of the Parſons be debarred from that heinous and unpardonable crime of killing a hare, but alſo the greateſt part of the Attorneys, the Counſellors, the Phyſicians, the Surgeons, the wealthy Tradeſmen, the Merchants, and his Majeſty's Officers in the army; and I dare promiſe my country-men glorious times, and that hounds and horſes, huntſmen and grooms, ſetters and ſpaniels, hares and partridges, woodcocks, wild ducks, and widgin, foxes, badgers, and Country Squires, would bear an unlimited and uncontroulable ſway, to the eternal praiſe and honour of old England.

P. S. Before I could perſuade myſelf to ſend this performance abroad in the world, which I am very ſenſible muſt raiſe up a terrible ſpirit among the Clergy, I prevailed with a friend (under the ſtricteſt ſecrecy) to ſhow it in manuſcript to ſome neighbours, whom he looked upon to have the beſt judgments; and who would candidly and impartially deliver to him their ſenſe of the thing; and what reception they thought it would meet with from the Laity, for whoſe ſakes it was ſolely written.

The firſt perſon he conſulted was a very near neighbour to him, a Gentleman farmer; who immediately declared, that he never read any thing ſo good in his whole life: 'By goles, ſays he, h'as maul'd the Parſons;' and then called out, with the utmoſt tranſport, to his wife, 'NANNY, ſays he, 'ſbud we have got the right pig by 'the ear; be ſure you don't let the ſpotted ſow go to 'brim before you know whether the Tythe Bill will paſs.'

The next he adviſed with was one of his Majeſty's Juſtices of the *Quorum*, and indeed a very able and learned man he was: and his Worſhip was ſo good to ſay ſo many kind things, and to expreſs himſelf ſo much to the advantage of the Author, that he cannot but think himſelf (out of modeſty) obliged to conceal the whole diſcourſe.

The laſt perſon conſulted was a very eminent and judicious Free-thinker, who ſeemed, as my friend told me, not to read the thing with the leaſt pleaſure, or any ſign of joy on his countenance: but after having gone over it twice, and made ſome marks with his pencil, he in a very grave and ſolemn manner delivered him the paper, and expreſſed himſelf, as near as I can remember in theſe words: —'Here, ſays he, give my humble ſervice to the 'worthy Author, and thank him from me, in the behalf 'of all the Free-thinkers of England. - - - And then he added, 'Take my word, ſays he, the thing will do; 'the right method of overturning religion, is firſt to be'gin with the Clergy: let us once get well rid of theſe 'fellows, and I make not the leaſt queſtion, but that all the 'abſurd doctrines about good and evil; about a reſurrecti'on, and a future judgment; hell and heaven; God and 'the Devil, will together go along with them.'

THE perſon who wrote the fore-going diſcourſe being a very publick ſpirited Gentleman, and deſiring to give all due encouragement to a work of this nature, which may be of ſuch great benefit to the world; deſired his Printer to give notice, that if any Country Squire has a mind to do good among his neighbours and tenants, by putting this little Treatiſe into their hands, he may be ſupplied with what number he has a mind to take, at 3 s. and 6 d. a dozen, ſent to him, carriage free, in any part of England.

DOMESTIC NEWS.

C. *Courant.*	E P. *Evening Poſt.*
P. *Poſt-Boy.*	S J. *S. James's Evening Poſt.*
D P. *Daily Poſt.*	WE. *Whitehall Evening P.*
D J. *Daily Journal.*	LE. *London Evening Poſt.*

THURSDAY, *April* 13.

Yeſterday the Gen. Quarter Seſſions was held at the Court of King's Bench, for the City and Liberties of Weſtminſter; when Sir John Gonſon, the Chairman, gave an elegant and learned charge to the Grand Jury. C. An excellent and learned charge. P.

The ſame day Mr. Alderman Perry made a declaration on the ſcrutiny for a Common Council Man for the Ward of Aldgate; the numbers were, for Mr. Smith 123; Mr. Fludyer 118. Whereupon the former was declared duly elected. C. Mr. Smith 125. *DP.*

On the 2d of laſt month was plowed up in the lands of Tho. Maſters of Cirenceſter in Glouceſterſhire, Eſq; a curious ſtatue of Corinthian braſs, being in length about 15 inches, and weighing upwards of 9 pounds; the poſture of it is erect, with one arm extended upwards, having held ſomething in the hand, but broke out; and the other deſcending, with one hand clinched, which holds part (as ſome term it) of a ſtaff of honour; it has a Majeſtick face and eye-lids of ſilver, its head is adorned with flowing hair in dropping ringlets, with a double parting on the crown; one leg extends itſelf backwards, and the fingers and toes (except 3) are compleat; ſome affirm it ſtood on a pedeſtal, which will be ſought after when the ſeed is off the ground. It is now ſent to Oxford, from whence it will be carried to the Royal Society, to have their opinions thereof. *D P.* —— *I preſume it will at laſt be brought to ours, as the dernier reſort.*

We hear that his Majeſty has been graciouſly pleaſed to offer a reward of 50 l. to any perſon who ſhall diſcover any of the perſons concerned in the murder of Ric. Hill, one of the Cuſtom-houſe Boatmen, at Deal, &c. *S J. WE.*

On monday the 3d, was executed at Chelmsford, one Tho. Doe, a Carpenter, for ſeveral robberies. It is remarkable, that 35 indictments were found againſt him. *LE.*

A petition, complaining of an undue election for Great Marlow in Bucks, is prepared by Lord Sidney Beauclerk. We hear, the Mayor of the ſaid Borough propoſed a double return, which was rejected by Lord Sidney. Chickens ſold at the ſaid Borough laſt week at one guinea each. *L E.*

We hear from Amſterdam, that the ingenious Capt. Buſhel, who was ſo uſeful to the French lately in drawing the piles, and clearing the harbour of Dunkirk, has undertaken to fiſh up the treaſure out of a Dutch Eaſt India man on that coaſt; and as a previous proof of his ſkill, has weigh'd up a piece of marble of 20,000 lb. weight, that was dropt by ſome accident into ſeveral fathom water. *L E.*

We hear that a marriage is treating between his Highneſs Prince Naſſau of Orange, and her Royal Highneſs the Princeſs Royal. *S J.*

We hear that the Parliament will riſe towards the 5th or 6th of next month. *W E.*

On friday laſt dy'd at King's college in Cambridge, of the Small-pox, which he contracted by inoculation, Mr. Weſt, a young Gentleman of about 20 years old, a near relation to the Lord Delawar. *L E*

Bath, Ap. 4. The Workmen who have been a long time employ'd in erecting a new ſquare in Barton Grounds, on ſaturday laid the firſt ſtone of the Chapel, in the preſence of many perſons of diſtinction, who contributed largely towards the ſaid work, which, with that of the ſquare, goes on with all expedition, and the latter will far exceed any public building of that kind in England, and outdo every thing in Bath both for air and ſituation. *D P.*

Ragley for ſhooting of his wife was hang'd,
At Maidſtone; where he thus the Mob harangu'd:
You here, Good People, I'm concern'd to ſee:
But pray take warning all by wretched me.
And, for God's ſake, of two things moſt beware;
Of loaded guns, and womens tongues take care. *S. J.*

FRIDAY, *April* 14.

The R. Hon. the Lord Harrington is to attend his Majeſty to Hanover, as Principal Secretary of State. —— Yeſterday the L. Malpas, received an expreſs, with an account of the Corpſe of his Lady (who lately died abroad) 2 footmen, and baggage of a conſiderable value, being loſt in an Engliſh ſhip bound for London, which was ſtranded on the coaſt of France. *D J.*

Yeſterday advice came to town of the death of the Lady Joliffe in Bedfordſhire. —— On ſunday died at his houſe in S. James's-ſtreet, Joſ. Hancock, Eſq; belonging to the Great Wardrobe. *D P.*

Chriſtned Males 168. Females 145. In all 313. *Buried* Males 220. Females 210. In all 430. Increaſed in the burials this week 4. *P.*

SATURDAY, *April* 15.

Yeſterday her Majeſty was ſuddenly taken ill in the Drawing-room, and withdrew; but being recovered laſt night, was pleaſed to appear again for a ſhort time. *P.* — Orders have been given for fitting up the apartments at Somerſet-Houſe, for the reception of his Royal Highneſs the Prince of Naſſau Orange, who is ſhortly expected at this Court. *DP.*

On thurſday the King's plate of 100 guineas was run for at Newmarket, and was won by the Gardener's Mare; this being the 6th plate that Mare has won this year. *P.*

The Dean and Prebendaries of Windſor have agreed with an eminent Painter to clean and beautify the repreſentation of the Lord's ſupper over the altar in the Cathedral of Windſor, which curious painting received much damage by being buried in the earth during Cromwell's tyranny and uſurpation. *D P.*

On ſunday laſt —— Bridges, Eſq; was married to Mrs. Knight, a widow Gentlewoman of fine accompliſhments, with a fortune of 10,000 l. *C.* —— *This is tautology, 10,000 l. are ſuch.*

This day being the birth day of his Royal Highneſs Prince William, who enter'd into the 12th year of his age, there was a drawing room at S. James's, in which their Majeſties and the Royal Family received the compliments of the Nobility and Gentry. *S J. WE. LE.*

The New-market Bank has won every match this meeting; it may now divide 43 per cent, out of the profits of this meeting, without leſſening their capital. It is to be wiſh'd that the Charitable Corporation could do the ſame. *S J.* —— *Tho' they can't, it muſt be own'd, they have as good Jockeys among them, as any at* New-market.

Laſt ſunday the Counteſs of Dyſart, daughter to the R. Hon. the L. Carteret, was brought to bed of a daughter, to the great joy of that noble family. *LE.*

Yeſterday morning died at his houſe in S. James's Place, Sir Will. Willis, Member of Bedwin in Wiltſhire. *WE. DJ. Ap.* 17. Of Stone, at Hutton-Hall, near Brentwood in Eſſex, Sir Will. Willys, of Ditton in Cambridgeſhire, Bar. His father was Will. Willys, Eſq; 4th ſon of Sir Thomas, the firſt Baronet of the family: Sir William died unmarried. *D P. Ap.* 17.

MONDAY, *April* 17.

Yeſterday the Rev. Dr. Holcomb preached before their Majeſties, &c. *C.* We hear that at the Right Hon. the L.

Visc. Torrington is appointed to command the squadron of men of war that are to wait on his Majesty into Holland. D P. —— Major Lumcanier is appointed Yeoman to the Robes, under Col. Schutz, a place worth 300 l. per ann. P.

A Case stated for the opinion of Counsel learned in the law. —— Part of the oath and ceremony used at the installation of Knights of the Bath. ' You shall defend ' Maidens, Widows, and Orphans in their rights, and ' shall suffer no *extortion*, as far as you may prevent it, &c.' —— After the installation, the King's Master Cook attended at the west door of Westminster Abbey, having a linnen apron and a chopping knife in his hand; and as soon as passed by him in their return from the Abbey, he severally said to each Knight, ' Sir, you know ' what great oath you have taken, which if you keep, it ' will be of great honour to you; but if you break it, I ' shall be compelled by my Office to hack off your spurs ' from your heels.' *Query*, Whether breach of trust in the management of the affairs of the *Charitable Corporation* will not be judged a breach of the oath above recited?

—*Query*, Whether in case such breach of trust and of oath should appear, his Majesty's *Master Cook* ought not to perform the functions of his office. *P.*

On saturday last a man was committed to Newgate, for attempting to hang his wife, having tied her up to a post in her chamber; but some neighbours coming in, she was cut down, and by proper means she was brought to herself, and is like to do well. *C. D P.*

Is flaring, or banging, an exit more easy?
I'll swear I can't tell. —— Go, and ask Mrs. Vezey.

On friday the Lady of the R. Hon. the Lord Guildford was safely brought to bed of a son and heir, at his Lordship's house in Albemarle-street. *P.*

Tuesday, April 18.

Yesterday the R. Hon. the E. of Essex had his audience of leave of his Majesty, &c. *P.* —All the Royal yatchts are entirely fitted and compleat for service, against his Majesty shall embark for Holland, and are fallen down to their proper moorings at Greenwich. *D P.*

On thursday came on the election at Weobly in Herefordshire, &c. *D P.* —— On friday; the numbers on the poll were, for James Cornwall, Esq; 55; Mr. Baron Birch 26; Paul Foley, Esq; 4. *DJ.*

On saturday at Droitwich, the Hon. Edw. Foley, Esq; brother to the L. Foley, and the late Member, was unanimously chosen. *Dj.*

The fine well in the Tower call'd Julius Cæsar's well, being broke up, there is a fine warehouse building to hold Salt petre, and other combustible stores. —— A fine magazine is also building at Woolwich for powder. *P.*

Yesterday died at his house in Norfolk-street, Dr. Goldsmith, an eminent Physician. *P.* A young Physician coming into vast practice. *D P.* —— On friday night died, —— Wardegates, Esq; son to the late Sir Rich. Wardegates, in Tufton street, Westminster. *P.*

This wardegates true name was Newdegate.

This morning a Bookbinder and his wife were found hanging in their house in Blackmoor-street, Southwark. They had a child about a year and a half old, which was likewise found dead, having been shot by a pistol. The man and his wife (who was big with child) were been this morning looking out at the window. *WE.* —— One Smith, &c.&c. Next door to the Yorkshire Grey. *P. DJ. Ap.* 19.

Hanging within a quarter of a yard of each other. *C. DJ.* About a yard. *P.* They hang'd themselves. *P.* Smith having been troubled for money lent him by an old woman, a relation to his wife, got out of his bed in a great passion, and hang'd her to one of the feet bed-posts in her shirt; and afterwards with a pistol shot his child in a cradle by the bed-side, and then hang'd himself to the other feet bed-post. *D P.* 19. —— My Brother *gives a punctual an account, as if he had been present.*

Wednesday, April 19.

At last Derby Assizes were condemned, and since executed, John Hewet and Rosamond Olerenshaw, for poisoning Hannah the wife of John Hewet; when under condemnation, they confess'd the fact, and charg'd another as a principal in the said murder, at whose house the unfortunate woman was poison'd: Olerenshaw was servant to the person they charg'd, who often had criminal conversation with Hewet, which occasion'd such differences betwixt them and the wife of Hewet, that at last ended in the death of three of them. The fourth is since committed to prison on suspicion of murder and felony; and at the next Assizes it is expected such a scene of villainy, debauchery and murder will be brought to light as will be shocking out to the present age: for the condemn'd woman discover'd all the intrigues of Hewet; so that a great many persons with whom she kept a wicked correspondence, have been examined, and much wickedness discover'd; particularly the bones of a child of about seven months growth, was found, having been privately buried in the garden belonging to the person taken up. *D P.*

Edinburgh, Ap. 10. A woman at Haddington was committed last week for the murther of her bastard child; which it is said, she put into a large peat fire, in order to consume it to ashes, but was happily discovered. Three women are to be try'd at Perth for the same unnatural crime. *C. P. Ap.* 18.

Dublin, Ap. 8. Last tuesday a man at Ratoath murdered 3 of his children as they lay in their bed, viz a daughter of 19, a son of 16, and a daughter of 9; he attempted to murder his wife and another child also, but they escaped, there is no account of the cause of this monstrous cruelty; but the villain is committed to the goal of Trim. *C.* John Gallagher at Raloath. *D P.* Gallogher, a poor labourer, about 4 years ago became lunatic, and cut his throat to the wind-pipe. Early on tuesday morning he rose, and got a wooden clandestick, and knock'd out their brains. *P.* At Ratooth. He cut their throats as they were asleep in bed. *DJ. Ap.* 15.

From the PEGASUS in Grub-street.

The *Daily Courant* of monday was read, in which there is an imitation of *Horace*, B. 1. Ode 3. which the ingenious Author has turned against Matrimony; one of the consequences whereof he makes to be the *Pox*. This puzzled the whole Society a while, which thought that distemper to be the product of fornication, rather than of marriage. But one of our Members, more sagacious than the rest, assured us, that the Author either hinted at the propagation of the *Small pox* by inoculation upon children, or that he wrote like a child himself.

The ingenious Gentleman, who sent us the *Pastoral* and the *Song* in blank verse, was mistaken in imagining, *that no enterprising Genius had undertaken to free the lesser parts of Poetry from that barbarous and Gothic tyrant rhyme.* The learned Mr. RALPH undertook this, some time ago, in his *Muses Address to the King*, an incomparable Pindaric ode in blank verse, of which proper notice has been taken in our Journal. The success of which specimen of this new species of Poetry was so great, that no person has presumed to imitate it.

FOREIGN NEWS.

Friday, *April* 14.

Paris, Mar. 19. Some days ago the King went incognito, accompanied by the Count de Chevrolois, and 2 or 3 Lords, to Issy, the country seat of the Cardinal de Fleury. His Majesty pretended to be a Gentleman in the neighbourhood, who was come to ask a favour; and being conducted to the Cardinal, his Eminency was agreeably surprized to see the King, who told him the favour he came to ask, was principally curiosity to see whether his house was so delightfully pleasant as fame would have it. His Majesty walk'd with the Cardinal in his gardens and groves; the Cardinal gave him an excellent collation; after which his Majesty return'd to Versailles. *C.*

Saturday, *April* 15.

Yesterday arrived the Mail from Holland.

Seville, Mar. 28. The works before Gibraltar are to be entirely finish'd before the end of May, and furnish'd with cannon. *C. &c.*

Cleves, Ap. 19. Francis Lewis Archbishop and Elector of Mentz, Arch-Chancellor of the Empire, Great Master of the Teutonick Order, and Bishop of Breslau and Worms, died at Breslau of an apoplexy, the 8th, in his 68th year. *C. P. DP.*

Ratisbon, Ap. 14. The resolution which the Evangelick Body has taken in the affair of Saltzburg, and which has been sent to all the Protestant Electors, &c. imports, ' That the best and most moderate expedient would be to ' shut up all the Roman Catholick Churches, and to se-' quester the Estates of the Clergy in the Lutheran Coun-' tries, 'till the satisfaction so justly demanded can be ob-' tained. *C. D P. DJ.*

Tuesday, *April* 11.

This Day arrived the Mail from Holland.

Genoa, Ap. 5 Yesterday the great Convoy sailed for Corsica, with the remainder of the auxiliary forces to the number of 6400 men. *W E.*

Vienna, Ap. 12 An express from Temesfwaer has brought advice, that the Grand Vizier had been deposed and murdered, with several other of the Grand Seignior's Ministers. *W E. S J. LE.*

On Tuesday Stocks were

South Sea Stock 98 7 8ths, 98 1 qr. 99 1 8th, to 1 qr. South Sea Annuity 110 1 8th, for the Opening. Bank 151 1 half, Books open. New Bank Circulation 7 l. 5s. Premium. India 177 7 8ths, 177 3 qrs. 178 1 qr. Three per Cent. Annuity 97 3 8ths. Royal Exchange Assurance 09 3 qrs. to 100. London Assurance 13 1 half, for the Opening. York Buildings 7 1 half. African 42. English Copper 2 l. 6 s. without the dividend. Welch ditto 1 l. 15 s. South Sea Bonds 2 l. 13 s. Premium. India ditto 6 l. 6 s. ditto. Blanks 7 l. 7 s. 9 d. 20 l. Prizes 19 l. 14 s. 6 d.

Now selling, and all next Month, the Libraries of the Rev. Robert Kilborn, *L'L. D. the Rev.* John Marshal, *L. L. D. and* Stephen Hall, *M. D. Physician to the Royal Hospital at* Greenwich, *all lately deceas'd, will continue to be sold very cheap (the Price fix'd in each Book) at* Tho. Osborne's *Shop in* Gray's-Inn. *Among near ten thousand Vols. are the following Books, viz.*

FOLIO, *Gr. Lat. &c.*

Monast. Ang. per Dugd. 3 v.
Fr. Baconi Opera, 4 vol
Codemi Anglica-Normannorum
Du Chesne Hist. Normannorum
Rymeri Fœdera, 18 volumes
Whartoni Anglia sacra, 2 vol. Charta magni
Buchanani Opera, 2 volumes
Livii Historiæ, Vener. 1498
Thucydidet, Gr. ib. 1502
J. Vaillant Numismata
Hippocrates Opera, Gr. ap. Aldum, 1526
Euripides Tragediæ, J. Barns
Plinii Historia Naturalis, Notis Harduini, 3 v. Charta maxima
Ciceronis Lambini, 2 volumes
Virgilii, 2 volumes
Opera, 2 vol. Chart. maxima Lond.
Aristotelis Opera, 2 vol. du Val Charta maxima
Josephus Hudsoni, 2 volumes
Quintilienus Oppr. on. C. M.
Athisophanes Kusteri, Ch. max.
Thucydid., Hudsoni, Ch. max.
Dion. Cassius Leunclavii
Strabonis Geographia, 2 volumes
Quintilianus per R. Steph.
Lucanus Bourdelotii
Livii Historiæ Sigonii
idem Liber, apud Fugger
idem Liber, apud Aldum
idem Liber, 1482
D. Halicarnass. Opera Hudsoni, 2 volumes
Suidæ Lexicon, 2 vol. Ch. max.
Stephani Thesaurus Ling. Lat. 2 volumes. Curio Rule.
Thef. Ling. Græc. 5 vol
Suiceri Thesaurus, 2 volumes
Hickerii Thesaurus, 2 volumes
Spelmanni Glossaria
Du Fresne Glossar. Gr. Lat. 5 v.
Cooperi Thesaurus
Lexicon Milit. C. de Aquino, 2 v.
Constantini Lexicon
Scapulæ Lexicon
Skinneri Etymologicum, Ch. max.
Somneri Dictionarium
Hispania illustrata, 4 volumes
Rerum Ital. Scriptores, 10 vol
Spencer & Legatis
Marmora Arundelliana, cum Commentt. Maittaire
Concil. Coll. Ch. Harduini, 12 vol
Hickelii Thesaurus, Ch. max.
N.Testament. Gr. J. Millii, Ch. max. Corio Turcico
Brabantia illustrata
D. Petavii Opera, 6 Tom. 3 vol
Thucydides Hist. J. Wassi
Hist. Cælestis Flamsteddio, 3 vol
G. Bidloo Anatomia, Ch. max.
idem Lib. C. Minori
Johnstoni Hist. d: Quadrup. &c.
M. Listeri Hist. Conchyl. 2 vol
Raii Hist. Plantarum, 2 volumes
Musæum Wormianum
F. Willughbei Hist. Piscium
Bochartii Hist. de Animal. 2 vol
Salviani Hist. Aquatilium
Palæographia Gr. B. Montfaucon
Mabilon de Re Diplomatica
Montfaucon Biblioth. Coisiniana
Hospiniani Opera, 6 volumes
Ciceil Hist. Literaria, 2 volumes
Jamblichus de Myst. Th. Gale
Fazelius de Rebus Siculis
Ripamontii Hist. Patriæ, 5 vol
Bembi Hist. Veneta, ap. Aldum
S. Byzantinus de Urbibus
strada de Bello Belg. 2 vol Romæ
Thuani Historia, 5 volumes
Æmilius de Rebus Gestis Franc.
Aristotelis Opera, Gr. ap. Aldum
Horat. cum Com. XL. Gramat.
A. de la Chausse Thesaur. Antiq.
Fabrettus de Columna Trajana
Inscriptiones Antiquarum
Lambecius de Auguft. Bibliotheca Cæsarea, 6 volumes
Cantabrigia & Oxonia illustratæ, per D. Loggan, 2 volumes
Theatrum Basilicæ Pisanæ
De Chalcis Cursus Mathemat. 3 v.
J. Wallis Opera Mathth. 3 vol.
Veteres Mathematici, Typ. Regia

Livres François, FOLIO.

Corps de l'Universel Diplomat. 16 v.
Œuvres Diverses de M.Boyle, 4 v.
Chronique de Froissart, 2 volumes
Bibliothèque du Croix du Maine
Biblioth. que Hist. de la France, gr. Pap.
Hist. de Bretagne, par Lobineau, 2 volumes
de France, par le Gendre, 3 v.
Etat de la France, par Boulainvilliers, 3 volumes
Chroniques de Monstrelet, 2 vol
Hist. de France, par Mezeray, 3 v.
Récit du Traité des Paix, 4 v.
Œuvres de Plutarque, par Amyot, 2 volumes
Bibliothèque de Verdire
Memoires d'Estat, pa Ribier, 2 v.
Memoires de Sulley, 2 volumes
Hist. Naturel de l'Or, gr. Pap.
Physique de la Mer, par Marsilly
Diction. de la Bible par Calmet, 4 volumes
de Morery, 4 volumes
de Richelet, 3 volumes
Universelle, par Fuset. 4 v.
de l'Academ. Franc. 2 vol
Geograph. par Baudrand
de Bayle, 4 volumes
Architect. de Palladio, par Leoni
de Vitruve, par Perrault
Cours d'Architect. par Blondel, 2 v.
Architecture de Scammozzi
Hist. de Louis le Grand, par Med.
Battailes de Prince Eugene
De l'Isle's Maps
Voyage au Levant, par le Brun
de Chardin
de Mandelslo
d'Olearius
Lts Loix Civile, par Domat, 2 vol
L'Antiq. Expliq. par Montfaucon, 15 volumes
Theatre de la Gr. Bretagne, 4 vol
Figures des Hist. de la Bible
Med. de Louis le Gr. en Marqu.
Descript. de l'Hospital des Inval.
Hist. du Vieux & N. Testam. par Martin
Discours sur la Bible, par Saurin, 2 volumes
Chroniq. de France, par Belleforest. gr. pap.
La Sainte Bible, par Def. 2 vol
Traita de la Police, 4 volumes
Storia Fiorentina de Vecchi
Hist. du Giulio Cesare di Angeloni
Bibliotec Nopolitana
Felicità di Padoua dl Portenari
Li Gierusalemme di Torq. Tasso
Fatti Veneti, 2 volumes
Hist. del Emper. Car. V. 2 vol
Descript. del Monart. de S. Lorenzo
Hist. Univ. del Mondo, par Pinedi, 6 volumes
Coronico del Rey Alonso
Vidas de los todos Pontifices, 2 vol
Obras di Ant. Herrera, 8 volumes

Hist. de Espana, par Mariana, 2 v.
Annales d'Arragon, 7 volumes
Vocabolario della Crusca, 3 vol
Architettura di Vitruvio
di Serlio
di Labacco
di Alberti
di Vignola
Materie Ferrariana de P. Pedrusi, 4 volumes
Hist. Naturale di Plinio 1476
di Josepho 1493

English Books in FOLIO.

Bayle's Dictionary, 4 volumes
Collier's Dictionary, with Supplement and Appendix, 4 volumes
Chambers's Dictionary, 2 volumes
S. Ambrosii Opera, 2 volumes
babani Annales Ecclesiast. 4 vol
Euclid Præp. at. Evang. ap. P. Steph.
Cypriani Opera, per Deduellum, 2 volumes
Forbesii Opera, 2 volumes
Ussii Annales, 2 volumes
Eusebii, Evagrii & Hist. H. Valesius, 3 volumes
Biblia Polyglotta, cum Castelli Lexicon, 8 volumes
Justini Mart. Op. Thirlby, C. M.
Corpus Juris Civilis, cum Gothofredi Notis, 2 volumes
Justelli Bibliotheca Juris, 2 vol
Lindenbrogii Codex Legum Ant.
Digestum Vetus, 6 volumes
D.Wilkins Leges Anglo-Sax.C.m.
Gaffendi Opera, 6 volumes
Sibaldi Scotia illustrata
Grafton's Chronicle
Devoe's Journal of Parliaments
Dugdale's Warwickshire, 2 vol
Dart's Antiquities of Canterbury
Chauncy's Hartfordshire
Peck's Antiquities of Stamford
Harris's Hist. of Kent, large Paper
Wright's Rutland
Plot's Oxfordshire
Gunton's Peterborough
Burton's Leicestershire
Rushworth's Collect on 8 volumes large and small Paper
Kennet's History of England, 3 vol, large and small Paper
Speed's Maps
State Tracts, 3 volumes
Brandt's Civil Wars of England
Burton's Comment on Antoninus Itinerary
Fox's Book of Martyrs, 3 volumes, large and small Paper
Camden's Britannia, by Gibson, 2 vols, large and small Paper
Winwood's Memorials, 3 volumes, large and small Paper
L'Epitome's Observations, 2 vol
Leslie's Rehearsals, 2 volumes
Dugdale's History of St. Paul's
Wood's Athenæ Oxon. 2 volumes
Sandford's Coronat. of K. James
Cambell's Vitruvius Britannicus, 3 vol, large and small Paper
Alberti's Architecture by Leoni
Flamsteed's Atlas Cælestis
Selden's Works, 6 volumes
Vertue's Hist. of Knights of Malta, 2 v. large and small Paper
L'Estrange's Josephus, 2 vol. L. P.
Brandt's History of the Reformation, 2 volumes, large Paper
Spelman's Eng. Works, large Pap.
Dryden's Virgil, large Paper
Langley's Pomona, large and f. P.
Davila's Civil Wars of France
Willughby of Birds
Shakespear's Plays
Pope's Homer, 6 volumes
Mariana's History of Spain
Giannone's History of Naples
Gordon's Tacitus, 2 volumes
L'Estrange's Josephus
Collier's Ecclesiast. Hist. 2 vol
De la Mortraye's Travels, 2 vol
Kempfer's Hist. of Japan, 2 vol
Heckluy's Voyages, 2 volumes
Purchas's Pilgrimage, 5 volumes
Atlas Maritimus
New General Atlas
Tillotson's Works, 3 volumes
Scot's Christian Life
Prideaux's Connection, 2 volumes
Lightfoot's Works, 2 volumes
Whitby on N. Testam. 2 volume
Religious Ceremonies, 3 volumes
Charnock's Works, 2 volumes
Blackall's Works, 2 volumes
Holy Bible bound in Turkey, Oxford, 1717.
Leslie's Theological Works, l. Pa.
Bedford's Scripture Chronology,

large paper

Blome's History of the Bible
Beveridge's Works, 2 volumes
Du Pin's Ecclesiast. Hist. 8 vol
Hammond on the New Testam.
Cambridge Concordance
Barrow's Works, 4 volumes
Kettlewell's Works, 2 volumes
Hammond's Works, 4 volumes
Salmon's English Herbal
Parkinson's Herbal
Domat's Civ. Law, 2 vol. large Pa.
Gerhard's Herbal, by Johnson
Cooper's Anatomy, best Edition
Montfaucon's Antiquities, with the Supplement, 7 volumes
Dart's Antiq. of Westm. 2 vol
Whitby, Patrick, and Lowth's Comment. 6 volumes
Harris's Collect. of Voyages
Sir W. Temple's Works, 2 vol
Bingham's works, 2 volumes
Brady's Hist. of England, 3 vol.
Locke's Works, 3 volumes
Stebbing's Pol. tical Tracts
Stackhouse's Body of Divinity, large and small Paper
Town's Travels, 2 volumes
Stillingfleet's Works, 6 volumes

Law, FOLIO.

Littleton, 2 vols French
Same, English by Nelson
Snower, 2 vol. English
Keble, 3 vols English
Siauer, 2 vol. Fr. and Eng.
Cathew's, English
Modern, 5 vols English
Plowden's
Dyer's
Bulstrode's, English
Sir T. More's, large and small Paper
Salk ld's, 3 vol English
Third volume fold down
Coke's 5 Parts. best Edition
Hobart's, English
Crok's, English
Owen's, English
Popham's, English
Yelverton's
Davis's
Hutton's, English
Wynche's, English
Savil's
Anderson's
Vaughan's, English
Levintz, French and Eng.
Leonard's, 2 volumes Eng.
Bulstrode's, English
Cumberbatch, English
Sir William Jones, English
Sir T. Jones, Fr. and Eng.
Rolle's, 2 volumes
Ventris's, English
Finch's, English
Syderfin's
Lilly's
Kellway
Styles's, En. large and fm. Pa.
Bendloe and Dallison
Maynard's Edward the IId.
Tables to all the Cases in the Books of Reports
Modern Cases, 2 Parts
Cases in Chancery, 2 Parts
Lilly's Practical Register, 2 vol
Danver's, 2 vol
Nelson's, 3 vol } Abridgments
Rolle's
Lilley's Conveyancer, 2 volumes
Bird's Practising Scrivener
Bridgman's Conveyances, 2 vol
Hawkin's Pleas of the Crown, 2 v.
Wood's Institutes of the Common Law
of the Civil Law
Jacob's Law Dictionary
Cowell's Interpreter
Swinburne of Wills
Maxims of Equity
Watson's Clergyman's Law
Dalton's Country Justice
Treman's Pleas of the Crown
Clift's
Rastal's
Cooke's } Entries
Hanford's
Registrum Brevium
Pynn's Records, 2 volumes
Domat's Civil Law, 2 volumes
Cotton's Records, large and f. Pa.
Dugdale's Origines Juridiciales
Summons to Parliament

QUARTO.

Tesoro Britannico per Haym, 2 v. large and small Paper

Ovidii Opera Brumanni, 4 vol
in Usum Delph. 4 vol
Livii Hist. in Usum Delph. 6 v.
Plutarchi Opera, 5 volumes
Homeri Opera, J. Barnes
Acta Eruditorum, 69 volumes
Hist. de France par Dan. 10 v.
Methode pour Etudier l'Hist. 4 v.
Hist. Ecclesiaft. par Fleury, 30 v.
Les Œuvres del C. Marot, 4 vol
Tournefort's Voyages, 2 volumes
Wright's Travels, 2 volumes
Albin's Hist. Insects, coloured
Tournefort's Inst. Rei. Herb. 4 v.
History of Harwich and Dover Court, large and small Paper
Anderson's Collections, 4 vol

With several Thousands of other Books in Folio, Quarto, and Octavo, in Greek, Latin, French, English, Italian, and Spanish ; containing a curious Collection relating to the History, Antiquities, Laws and Parliamentary Affairs of Great Britain and Ireland, as also of divers other Nations ; also a great many of the Classicks in Usum Delph. & cum Notis Variorum ; likewise many printed by Colinæus, Gioletto, Aldus, Juntæ, Rob. Char. and Hen. Stephens. Elzivir, and others the most celebrated Printers. Together with a curious Collection of Historians, Books of Architecture, Coins, Medals, Husbandry, Trade, Voyages, Travels, Mathematics ; Civil, Canon, and Common Law, Lexicographers, Natural History, Physick and Surgery, mostly gilt Backs, Letter'd, and many large Paper.

Catalogues *to be had at the Place of Sale, and Money for any Library of Books.*

LONDON: Printed by S. PALMER and J. HUGGONSON, in *Bartholomew-Close*, for Captain GULLIVER, near the *Temple*, where Letters and Advertisements are taken in : As also at the *Rainbow Coffee-House* in *Cornhill*, and *John's Coffee-House* in *Sheer-Lane*, near *Temple-Bar*. [Price Two Pence.]

The Grub-street Journal. NUMB. 121.

Thursday, APRIL 27, 1732.

EXTRACT from *The Character of King* WILLIAM *vindicated*, in the *London Journal*, Saturday, April 15.

DR. B———t (tho' he was a very valuable man, and highly useful in the cause of liberty) is not to be depended on in his character of King WILLIAM : for the King never liked him, nor would ever receive him into his councils of confidence ; and we seldom like men, who don't like us.

To strengthen the truth of this mutual dislike, there are now in the hands of ———— *Memoirs of the M——— of* H———, who, says, ' Such a day ; Dr. B———t told me, ' that King WILLIAM was an obstinate conceited man, ' that would take no advice : and, such a day, King WIL- ' LIAM told me, that Dr. B———T was a troublesome im- ' pertinent man, whose company he could not endure.'— These, with many other circumstances which could be produced, shew, that the King and the B———p did not like one another ; and from prejudices we can't reasonably expect truth.

He owed the B————k of S ———— entirely to a promise which Queen MARY made him in Holland : so that when her Majesty asked the King to make the Doctor a Bishop, he refused it ; but when she let him know, that she had promised it in Holland, he submitted to save her honour ; but desired her to tell the Doctor from him, *That the B———k was owing to her promise, and not to the King's inclination.*

There is a Noble Peer now living, who is of opinion, that some Characters in the Bishop's *History* have a tincture of his own passions ; and that his liking, or disliking men, or being well, or ill received by them, might have some influence on his mind ; and instances in himself, who stood with a very ill grace in the History, 'till he had an opportunity put into his hands of obliging the Bishop, by granting a favour at Court, which could not be obtained without his consent : upon which the Bishop told a friend of his, within an hour, that *he was mistaken in such a Lord, and must go and alter his whole character* ; and so he happens to have a pretty good one.

F. OSBORNE.

Part of the character of King WILLIAM, *given by* Bishop BURNET *in his* History *of his own Times*, Book IV. Page 689, 690.

THE Prince had been much neglected in his education : for all his life long he hated constraint. He spoke little. He put on some appearance of application : but he hated business of all sorts. Yet he hated talking, and all house games, more. This put him on a perpetual course of hunting, to which he seemed to give himself up, beyond any man I ever knew : But I looked on that always, as a flying from company and business. The depression of France was the governing passion of his whole life. He had no vice, but of one sort, in which he was very cautious and secret. —— He had a way that was affable and obliging to the *Dutch*. But he could not bring himself to comply enough with the temper of the *English*, his coldness and slowness being contrary to the genius of the Nation.

To Mr. BAVIUS. *London, Ap. 9, 1732.*
SIR,

IF you insert the following Epistle in your Journal, you will save me the trouble of enquiring for the place of the person's residence to whom it is directed, and him the postage of a Letter, from, Sir,
Your humble servant, A. H.

To the Author of the Preface to *Alkibla*, Part 2d.
Reverend Sir,

IN your *Preface* to the second Part of *Alkibla*, you have taken the liberty to say, * ' that you was given ' to understand, that not one of this high order (meaning ' the Bishops) did express any particular zeal for the point ' opposed (viz. *Eastward adoration*) or had given the ' least encouragement (whatever might be pretended) for ' its defence ; that the practice was rather imposed by

* Pag. 2.

EXTRACT from a *Letter to Mr.* OSBORNE in the *Daily Journal*, Saturday, April 22.

THERE are letters extant from King WILLIAM, the Duke of SHREWSBURY, the Earls of ROCHESTER, NOTTING-HAM, SUNDERLAND, and Lord SOMERS, as well as from Archbishop TILLOTSON and TENNISON, by which it should seem unquestionable, that Dr. BURNET was both personally acceptable to the King, and highly trusted by him.

You mention indeed an idle Extract out of *Memoirs*, which no body knows of, which are in the hands of no body knows who: but were the Extract you quote a real entry made by the Marquis of HALLIFAX in his *Diary*, would it prove any more than that Dr. BURNET had given advice to the King, which he was displeased at, and perhaps at the time out of humour with him for ? Does this shew a settled dislike of a man ? No ! that must be collected from actions, not from hasty words, set down in a ludicrous light, by a man of wit. Had King WIL-LIAM disliked Dr. BURNET, why did he choose him, to accompany him to England in 1688, as his Chaplain, or afterwards to attend him as his Clerk of the Closet, both which employments necessarily brought him near his Royal Person ? If King WILLIAM had no confidence in him, why did he appoint him Preceptor to the Duke of GLO-CESTER ? and when the Bishop earnestly declined that task, why did he insist upon his accepting it, as being the only man in whom he could place so great a trust, as the education of that Prince ?

He [Dr. B.] was so far from thinking of any promise in Holland (which is a mere fiction) that, when the Bishoprick of Salisbury became vacant, he went to sollicit his Majesty for it, in behalf of his friend Dr. LLOYD, the Bishop of St. Asaph : the King coldly answer'd, *he design'd it for another person* ; and the next day Dr. BUR-NET himself was nominated to that See. Of this there are two unexceptionable vouchers, one in writing, the other a person, who has pass'd through some of the highest employments with credit and honour.

Mr. OSBORNE is pleased to give us another Anecdote, of a most scandalous nature. ..... Sure the absurdity of this tale is in itself a sufficient confutation of it. I dare appeal to the greatest enemy he ever had, if he can conceive so meanly of Dr. BURNET's understanding, as to believe that he would expose his own character in so foolish a manner. — I cannot easily apprehend why Mr. OSBORNE is at present employed to vilify and asperse the memory of a man, to whom the present happy establishment is in a great measure owing. He is a Ministerial Writer, as some would insinuate ; but I shall scarce believe that he has directions to second the ill treatment, which Bishop BURNET's family has met with from a certain quarter, with an insult upon his memory, which I shall ever think myself, as a Whig and a Protestant, bound to vindicate. S. T.

' custom, than observed by choice ; and that their Lord- ' ships probably would not be displeased to find themselves ' freed from the imposition.' I think, Sir, with submission ' to that judgment which you are so very fond of, whoever *gave you to understand* this, did cast a very high reflection upon their Lordships the Bishops ; who are here represented as complying with an illegal custom, the practice of which is dangerous to the † Church and State ; a custom of an idolatrous nature, and contrary to reason and sense, (for such you have represented it to be) only for the sake of being in the mode ; a fine reason for the Bishops to give ! of which, I am sure, the women, nay, the weakest of their sex, would be ashamed ! and yet you are not abashed to say this, or however, make some *old friend* of yours say this, for their Lordships. How great is the indignity offered by this paragraph, when you farther say, ' the Prelates of the Church would not be displeased to ' be freed from the imposition ? *From the imposition of*

† Page 104, & passim.

---

what ? Why, of a custom, which you say is neither or-dained by the laws of the land, the canons of the Church, nor the rubric of the Common Prayer, but imposed by the practice of those, to whom the Bishops are dictators and guides : nay, a custom which you have (in your opi-nion, I suppose) proved to be directly contrary to the laws of the land, and the Articles of religion. How then can, the Bishops want any body to free them from *the imposition of a custom, which the laws of the land, rea-son, and conscience oblige them not to practise ?* Fye, fye, Sir, you must ask public pardon for this offence, which you have so publicly given to your Governors in the Church, or be reputed to be hardened against reproof.

I observed, in the first place, that you have been given *to understand, that not one of this high Order have given the least encouragement for the defence of eastward ado-ration.* Now, Sir, I conceive, one at least of that *high Order has given some small encouragement for its defence* ; I mean, that most Reverend and Learned Prelate, † a part of whose Sermon you have quoted in your *Postscript* to this last work. Which Sermon, altho' wrote in a former capa-city, remains still unretracted ; and therefore is, notwith-standing your shuffling, for any thing that yet appears, the opinion of a Bishop ; and consequently some small encourage-*ment* has, and still is *given for the defence* of the point you oppose, and by one of *that high Order*. And if up-on second thoughts, his Lordship may be of another opi-nion, as you intimate, yet will that be no excuse to your false representation in your Preface, which is antecedent to any retractation. I am, Sir,
Your humble servant, *A. H.*

† Lord Bishop of Litchfield and Coventry. See the *Postscript* to *Alkibla*, Part the second, pag. 138.

The following Copy of Verses was spoken lately at the Tripos in Cambridge.

ONE night, as home I tripp'd alone,
  Between the hours of twelve and one,
Wrapt in my virtue and my Gown ;
(The hour it matters not a groat,
Whether canonical or not)   5
Tho' Laymen, who at midnight roam,
We may suppose, go reeling home ;
Yet upon blasphemy it borders,
Thus to asperse a man in Orders.
The Moon, who saw what was design'd,   10
Just reach'd a cloud, and popp'd behind ;
Nor deign'd to lend one single spark
To give a light to deeds so dark.
What could I see without a light ;
When not a man o'th' sharpest sight ?   15
The case is not so strange ; you know,
'Twas Sir JOHN FALSTAFF's long ago.
Besides, Sir, I in answer thereto ;
Saw them both well enough to swear to.
Tho' I suspected much their air,   20
Yet forward I resolv'd to bear ;
Pluck'd up my little heart, and then,
Essay'd to pass these Buckram-men :
For I suppos'd they wou'd be loth,
Abandon'd rogues, to rob the cloth.   25
This, through good nature, I believ'd :
But man is born to be deceiv'd.
Then up stept *that young graceless lad* ;
That youth should dare to be so bad !
But in this place, 'tis my intention,   30
The band of Providence to mention ;
Which, whilst this rogue to Newgate goes,
And, to disguise him, shifts his cloaths,
So plainly did my cause espouse.
For whilst the crafty villain thought   35
To be secure in 's t'other coat,
He put on (it is strange, pray hear it)
The coat he robb'd in ; I aver it ;
To be the same, —— or somewhat near it.   40
And partner of his crime had none,
Yon fellow with the banging look ;
Who, in conjunction with the rest,
Held a clasp'd knife up to my breast ;
Which through similitude of look,   45
My fears for pistol then mistook ;
And in the sad affright I stood in,
I'd thought so, had it been *black pudding.*

Now selling, and all next Month, the Libraries of the Rev. Robert Kilborn, L'L.D. the Rev. John Marshal, L.L.D. and Stephen Hall, M.D. Physician to the Royal Hospital at Greenwich, all lately deceas'd, will continue to be sold very cheap (the Price fix'd in each Book) at Tho. Osborne's Shop in Gray's-Inn. Among near ten thousand Vols. are the following Books, viz.

FOLIO, Gr. Lat. &c.

Monast. Ang. per Dugd. 3 v.
Fr. Bacon Opera, 4 vol
Monumenti Anglica-Normannica
Du Chesne Hist. Normannorum
Hist. Franciorum, 5 vol
Rymeri Fœdera, 18 volumes
Whitoni Anglia sacra, 2 vol.
Charta magna
Buchanani Opera, 2 volumes
Livii Historia, Venet. 1498
Thucydides, Gr. ib. 1502
J. Vaillant Numismata
Hippocrates Opera, Gr. ap. Aldum, 1526
Euripides Tragœdiæ, J. Barns
Plinii Historia Naturalis, Notis Harduini, 3 v. Charta maxima
Ciceronis Lambini, 2 volumes
——— Verburgii, 2 volumes
——— Opera, 2 vol. Char. max-
xima Lond.
Aristotelis Opera, 2 vol. du Val
Charta maxima
Josephus Hudsoni, 2 volumes
Quintiliani Capperon. C.M.
Aristophanes Scaueri, Ch. max.
Thucydides Hudsoni, Ch. max.
Dion. Cassius Leunclavii
Strabonis Geographia, 2 volumes
Quintilianus per R. Steph.
Lucanus Bourdelotii
Livii Historia Sigonii
——— idem Liber, ap. Frobenium
——— idem Liber, apud Aldum
——— idem Liber, 1492

D. Halicarnass. Op. ar. Hudsoni, 2 volumes
Suidæ Lex cen. 2 vol. Ch. max.
Stephani Thesaurus Ling. Lat. 2 volumes. Cerio Ruic.
——— Thes. Ling. Græc. 5 vol
Suiceri Thesaurus, 2 volumes
Hickesii Thesaurus, 2 volumes
Spelmanni Glossaria
Du Fresne Glossar. Gr. Lat. 5 v.
Cooperi Thesaurus
Lexicon Milit. C. de Aquino, 2 v.
Constantini Lexicon
Scapulæ Lexicon
Skinneri Etymologicon, Ch. max.
Somneri Dictionarium
Hispania illustrata, 4 volumes
Rerum Ital. Scriptores, 10 vol
Spenceri de Legibus
Marmora Arundelliana, cum Comment. Mattaire
Concil. Collect. Harduini, 12 vol
Hickesii Thesaurus, Ch. max.
N.Testament. Gr. J. Millii, Ch. max. Corio Turcico
Brabantia illustrata
D. Petavii Opera, 6 Tom. 3 vol
Thucydides Hist. J. Wasse
Hist. Cœlestis Flamstedio, 3 vol
G. Budæo Anatomia, Ch. max.
——— Idem Lib. C. Minori
Johnstoni Hist. de Quadrup. &c.
M. Lisleri Hist. Conchyl. 2 vol
Raii Hist. Plantarum, 2 volumes
Museum Wormianum
F. Willughbei Hist. Piscium
Bochartii Hist. de Animal. 2 vol
Salviani Hist. Aquatilium
Palæographia Gr. B. Montfaucon
Mabillon de Re Diplomatica
Montfaucon Biblioth. Coisliniana
Hofpiniani Opera, 6 volumes
Cavei Hist. Literaria, 2 volumes
Jamblichus de Myst. Th. Gale
Eusebius de Rebus Siculis
Ripamontii Hist. Patriæ, 5 vol
Bembi Hist. Veneta, ap. Aldum
S. Byzantinus de Urbibus
Stradæ de Bello Belg. 2 vol Romæ
Thuani Historia, 5 volumes
Æmilius de Rebus Gestis Franc.
Aristotelis Opera, Gr. ap. Aldum
Horat. cum Com. XL. Gramat.
A. de la Chaussée Thesaur. Antiq.
Fabrettus de Columna Trojana
——— Inscriptiones Antiquarum
Lumbecius de August. Bibliothecæ Cæsarea, 6 volumes
Cantabrigia & Oxonia illustrata, per D. Loggan, 2 volumes
Theatrum Basilicæ Pisanæ
De Chalcis Cursus Mathemat. 3 v.
J. Wallis Opera, Math. 3 vol.
Veteres Mathematici, Typ. Regia

Jonsenii Novus Atlas, 4 volumes
Clerici Comment. 2 volumes
Tremner Concord. Biblio. 2 vol
J. Grebe Septuaginta, 2 volumes
Cau tu Lectionis Antiq. 4 vol
M. Poli Synopsis Criticorum, 5 vol
Critici Sacri, 9 volumes
S. Ambrosii Opera, 2 volumes
Sabarni Annales Ecclesiast. 4 vol
Edition Byzat. tot. Evangel. ap. P. Steph.
Cypriani Opera, per Dedwellum, 2 volumes
Fonsicini Opera, 2 volumes
Uffarii Annales, 2 volumes
Eusebii, Evagrii & Hist. H. Valesius, 3 volumes
Biblia Polyglotta, cum Castelli Lexicon, 8 volumes
Justini Mart. Op. Thirlby, C.M.
Corpus Juris Civilis, cum Gothofr. & Notis, 2 volumes
Justelli Bibliotheca Juris, 2 vol
Digestum Vetus, 6 tomi
D.Walkhius Leges Anglo-Sax.C.m.
Gesfandi Opera, 6 volumes
Sibaldi Scotia illustrata

Livres François, FOLIO.

Corps de Universel Diplomat. 16 v.
Oeuvres Diverses de M.Boyle, 4 v.
Critique de Froissart, 2 volumes
Bibliotheque du Croix du Maine
B.Bibliotheque Hist. de la France, gr. Po.
Hist. de Bretagne, par Lobineau, 2 volumes
——— de France, par le Gendre, 3v.
Etat de la France, par Boulainvilliers, 3 volumes
Chroniques de Monstrelet, 2 vol
Hist. de France, par Mezeray, 3 v.
Recueil des Trait. des Paix, 4 v.
Oeuvres de Pasquier, par Amyot, 2 volumes
Bibliothéque de Verdire
Memoires d'Estat, par Ribier, 2 v.
Memoires de Sulley, 2 volumes
Hist. Naturel de l'Or, gr. Pap.
——— Physique de la Mer, par Morslily
Diction. de la Bible par Calmet, 4 volumes
——— de Morery, 4 volumes
——— de Richelet, 3 volumes
——— Universelle, par Furet. 4v.
——— de l'Academ. Franc. 2 vol
——— Geograph. par Baudrand
——— de Bayle, 4 volumes
Architect. de Palladio, par Leoni
——— de Vitruve, par Perrault
Cours d'Architect. par Blondel, 4v.
Architecture de Scammozzi
Hist. de Louis le Grand, par Med.
Battailes de Prince Eugene
De l'Isle's Maps
Voyage au Levant, par le Brun
——— de Chardin
——— de Mandeslho
——— d'Olearius
Lts Loix Civile, par Domat, 2 vol
L'Antiq. Expliq. par Montfaucon, 15 volumes
Theatre de la Gr. Bretagne, 4 vol
Figures du Hist. de la Bible
Med. de Louis le Gr. en Maroq.
Descript. de l'Hospital des Inval.
Hist. du V. eux & N. Testam. par Martin
Discours sur la Bible, par Saurin, 2 volumes
Chronol. de France, par Belleferret. gr. pap.
La Sainte Bible, par Desf. 2 vol
Traita de la Police, 4 volumes
Storia Fiorentina de Vecchi
Hist. du Giulio Cesare di Angeloni
Bibliotec. Napolitana
Felicita di Paolo di Portenari
La Gierusalemme di Torq. Tasso
Fatti Veneti, 2 volumes
Hist. del Emper. Car. V. 2 vol
Descript. del Monasterio de S. Lorenzo
Hist. Univ. del Mondo, per Pineda, 6 volumes
Coronico del Rey Alonso
Vidas des de todos Pontifices, 2 vol
Obras di Ant. Herrera, 8 volumes

Hist. de España, par Mariani, 3 v.
Annales d'Arragon, 7 volumes
Vocabolario della Crusca, 3 vol
Architectura di Vitruvio
——— di Serlio
——— di Labacco
——— di Alberti
——— di Vignola
Museo Ferrneliana de P. Pedrusi, 4 volumes
Hist. Naturale di Plinio 1476
——— di Josepho 1493

English Books in FOLIO.

Bayle's Dictionary, 4 volumes
Collier's Dictionary, with Supplement and Appendix, 4 volumes
Chambers's Dictionary, 2 volumes
Harris's Lexicon, 2 volumes
Torriano's Italian Dictionary
Brodie's Family Dictionary, 2 v.
Phillips's Dictionary
State-Trials, 6 volumes, large and small Paper
Clarendon's History, 3 volumes
Stowe's Survey, by Strype, 2 vol
Whitlock's Memorials
Sandford's Genealogical History
Baker's Chronicle
Dugdale's Baronage, 2 vol
Ashmole's Order of the Garter, large Paper
Sir Lionel Jenkyns's Works, 2 vol
Burnet's Hist. Reformation, 3 vol
Hollingshead's Chronicle, 2 vol
Froissart's Chronicle
Hall's Chronicle
Polychronicon
Grafton's Chronicle
Dove's Journal of Parliaments
Dugdale's Warwickshire, 2 vol
Dart's Antiquities of Canterbury
Chauncy's Hertfordshire
Peck's Antiquities of Stamford
Harris's Hist. of Kent, large Pap.
Wright's Rutland
Plott's Oxfordshire
Gunton's Peterborough
Barton's Leicestershire
Rushworth's Collect ons 8 volumes, large and small Paper
Dugdale's History of St. Paul's
Wood's Athenæ Oxon. 2 volumes
Sandford's Coronat. of K. James
Cambell's Vitruvius Britannicus, 3 vol. large and small Paper
Alberti's Architecture by Leoni
Flamsteed's Atlas Cœlestis
Selden's Works, 6 volumes
Vertot's Hist. of Knights of Malta, 2 v. large and small Paper
L'Estrange's Josephus, 2 vol. L. P.
Brandt's History of the Reformation, 2 volumes, large Paper
Spelman's Eng. Works, large Pap.
Dryden's Virgil, large Paper
Langley's Pomona, large and f. P.
Davila's Civil Wars of France
Willughby of Birds
Shakespear's Plays
Pope's Homer, 6 volumes
Mariana's History of Spain
Giannone's History of Naples
Gordon's Tacitus, 2 volumes
L'Estrange's Josephus
Collier's Ecclesiast. Hist. 2 vol
De la Mortraye's Travels, 2 vol
Kempfer's Hist. of Japan, 2 vol
Hackluy's Voyages, 2 volumes
Purchas's Pilgrimage, 5 volumes
Atlas Maritimus
New General Atlas
Tillotson's Works, 3 volumes
Scot's Christian Life
Prideaux's Connection, 2 volumes
Lightfoot's Works, 2 volumes
Whitby on N. Testam. 2 volumes
Religious Ceremonies, 3 volumes
Charnock's Works, 2 volumes
Blackall's Works, 2 volumes
Holy Bible bound in Turkey, Oxford, 1717.
Leslie's Theological Works, 1. P.
Bedford's Scripture Chronology,

large paper
Blome's History of the Bible
Beveridge's Works, 2 volumes
Du Pin's Ecclesiast. Hist. 8 vol
Hammond on the New Testam.
Cambridge Concordance
Barrow's Works, 4 volumes
Kettlewell's Works, 2 volumes
Hammond's Works, 4 volumes
Salmon's English Herbal
Parkinson's Herbal
Domat's Civ. Law, 2 vol. large Pa.
Gerhard's Herbal, by Johnson
Cooper's Anatomy, best Edition
Montfaucon's Antiquitiey, with the Supplement, 4 volumes
Dart's Antiq. of Westm. 2 vol
Whitby, Patrick, and Lowth's Comment. 6 volumes
Harris's Collect. of Voyages
Sir W. Temple's Works, 2 vol
Bingham's works, 2 volumes
Brady's Hist. of England, 3 vol
Locke's Work, 3 volumes
Stebbing's Polemics. Tracts
Stackhouse's Body of Divinity, large and small Paper
Tcart's Travels, 2 volumes
Stillingfleet's Works, 6 volumes

Latin, FOLIO.

Lutwyche, 2 vols French
Same, English by Nelson
Snower, 2 vol. English
Kebb, 3 vols English
Saunder, 2 vols. 1st and Eng.
Cathew's, English
Modern, 5 vols English
Plowden's
Dyer's
Bridstrode's, English
Sir T. Raimi, large and small Paper
Salk le's, 3 vol English
Third volume sold alone
Coke's vol. Parts. 6 th Edition
Howard's, English
Cork, English
Owen's, English
Popham's, English
Yelverton's
Davis's
Hatton's, English
Wyeche's, English
Savill's
Anderson's
Vaughan's, English
Levintz, French and Eng.
Leonard's, 2 volumes Eng.
Bulstrode's, English
Comberbatch, English
Sir William Jones, English
Sir T. Jones, Fr. and Eng.
Rolle's, 2 volumes
Ventris's, English
Finch's, English
Syderfin's
Lilly's
Keilway
Style's, En. large and fm. Pa.
Bendloe and Dalifion
Maynard's Edward the IId.
Tables to all the Cases in the Books of Reports
Modern Cases, 2 Parts
Cases in Chancery, 2 Parts
Lilly's Practical Register, 2 vol
Danver's, 2 vol
Nelson's, 3 vol) Abridgments
Rolle's)
Lilley's Conveyancer, 2 volumes
Bird's Practising Scrivener
Bridgman's Conveyancer, 2 vol
Hawkin's Pleas of the Crown, 2v.
Wood's Institutes of the Common Law
——— of the Civil Law
Jacob's Law Dictionary
Cowell's Interpreter
Swinburne of Wills
Maxims of Equity
Watson's Clergyman's Law
Dalton's Country Justice
Treman's Pleas of the Crown
Clift's)
Rastal's)
Cooke's } Entries
Hanfard's)
Registrum Brevium
Pynn's Records, 2 volumes
Domat's Civil Law, 2 volumes
Cotton's Records, large and f. Pa.
Dugdale's Origines Juridiciales
——— Summons to Parliament

QUARTO.

Tesoro Britanico per Haym, 2 v. large and small Paper

Ovidii Opera Brumanni, 4 vol
——— in Usum Delph. 4 vol
Livii Hist. in Usum Delph. 6 v.
Plutarchi Opera, 5 volumes
Homeri Opera, J. Barnes
Acta Eruditorum, 69 volumes
Hist. de France par Dan. 10 v.
Methode pour Etudier l'Hist. 4 v.
Hist. Ecclésiast. par Fleury, 36 v.
Les Oeuvres del O. Marot, 4 vol
Tournefort's Voyages, 2 volumes
Wright's Travels, 2 volumes
Albin's Hist. Insects, coloured
Tournefort's Inst. Rei. Herb. 3 v.
History of Harwich and Dover Court, large and small Paper
Anderson's Collections, 4 vol

With several Thousands of other Books in Folio, Quarto, and Octavo, in Greek, Latin, French, English, Italian, and Spanish; containing a curious Collection relating to the History, Antiquities, Laws and Parliamentary Affairs of Great Britain and Ireland, as also of divers other Nations; also a great many of the Classicks in Usum Delph. & cum Notis Variorum; likewise many printed by Colinæus, Giolito, Aldus, Juntæ, Stephens, Rob. Char. and Hen. Stephens. Elzivir, and others the most celebrated Printers. Together with a curious Collection of Historians, Books of Architecture, Coins, Medals, Husbandry, Trade, Voyages, Travels, Mathematicks; Civil, Canon, and Common Law, Lexicographers, Natural History, Physick and Surgery, mostly gilt Backs, Letter'd, and many large Paper.

Catalogues to be had at the Place of Sale, and Money for any Library of Books.

LONDON: Printed by S. PALMER and J. HUGGONSON, in Bartholomew-Close, for Captain GULLIVER, near the Temple, where Letters and Advertisements are taken in: As also at the Rainbow Coffee-House in Cornhill, and John's Coffee-House in Sheer-Lane, near Temple-Bar. [Price Two Pence.]

From the PEGASUS in Grub-ſtreet.

The Gentleman, who ſent the Reflection upon the Tranſlation of the Ode of HORACE, which was inſerted in the Article from this place laſt week, fell into two miſ-takes. That Ode was not publiſhed in the Daily Courant of Monday, but in that of Friday, the 14th inſtant. And the Pix is not there made one of the conſequences of Ma-trimony, but of the opening of PANDORA's box, agreea-bly enough to the words of HORACE.

The fatal conſequences upon which he inſiſts, are the fears incident to that ſtate; the Spouſes fears of a numerous family, legitimate booved; and the Husbands fears of a ſpu-rious one. The firſt and laſt of which are as common in the ſtate of whoring, as of matrimony.

The Inſcription upon the Monument, which is now erect-ing in Weſtminſter Abbey, to the memory of the late Dr. WOODWARD.

M. S.

IOHANNIS WOODWARD,
Medici Celeberrimi,
Philoſophi Nobiliſſimi,
Cujus
Ingenium et Doctrinam,
Scripta per Terrarum ſerè orbem
Pervulgata ;
Liberalitatem verò, et Patriæ caritatem,
Academia Cantabrigienſis,
Munificentiâ ejus aucta,
Opibus ornata,
In perpetuum declarabit.
Natus Kal : Maii A. D. MDCLXV.
Obiit vii Kal : Maii MDCCXXVIII.
Richardus King,
Tribunus militum, Fabrûmq; Præſectus,
Amico optimè de ſe merito,
M. P.

Mr. BAVIUS,

Pleaſe to publiſh the following curious Extract, taken from the Play-bill of Drury-lane Theatre for tueſday the 25th of this inſtant, (for the honour of the Britiſh Stage) viz.

A Lapland Entertainment, call'd, Æſop's Conſort of Animals, being the firſt of the kind that ever was per-formed in England.

The Violins by three Cats.	French Horn by a Stagg.
Hautboy by a Dog.	With ſinging in Welſh by a
Harpſichord by a Monkey.	Goat.
Baſſoon by a Bear.	

The Curious, perhaps, may deſire to know, what Play-ers performed their extraordinary characters. Be it known then, that the parts were miraculouſly topp'd by the fol-lowing perſons, in which they out-did their uſual Out-doing.

The three Cats by three vertuous Actreſſes.
The Dog by every Manager in his turn.
The Bear by Father K—B—R.
The Monkey by the Son, bare-fac'd.
The Stagg by ditto, with a moſt illuſtrious frontiſpiece.
The part of the Goat and the Welſh ſong, performed and written by the Lapland Laureat, and deſigned as a compliment to the Welſh Nation.

Note, This Entertainment muſt be allowed to be ſenſible, pretty, and truly theatrical : excelling, if poſſible, the Epheſian Matron, acted laſt Friday at the above-named Theatre. —— Soon will be publiſhed, The Tears of the Muſes, in imitation of SPENCER, dedicated to the Mana-gers of the Theatre in Drury-lane, upon occaſion of their being conſtituted Emperors of Parnaſſus, and Patentees of the Royal Company of Comedians, to the great joy and comfort of the Dramatic Writers of the preſent age.

I am your, &c.   PHILO-DRAMATICUS.

Dublin, Ap. 15. Our Parliament is prorogued to Dec. 21. C. Ap. 22. —— On tueſday ſome people at Donne-brook ſetting a mark at a door to ſhoot at, the ball went through it, and ſhot a Coachman who ſat drinking there in through the breaſt, and the ball went out at his back, and lodged in a ſtone wall : the Coachman died inſtant-ly. C. P. 22.

FOREIGN NEWS.

THURSDAY. April 20.

Yeſterday arrived the Mails from France and Flanders.

Vienna, Ap. 9. N. S. A Royal road is making in Hun-gary, quite croſs Sclavonia and Croatia to Trieſte. This is one of the greateſt undertakings that has been attempted in Europe theſe two Centuries. P.

SATURDAY, April 22.

Paris, Ap. 20. We are to have 4 camps, more conſi-derable than have been formed in any of the preceding years, both horſe and foot ; the firſt is to be in Alſace, under the command of the Marq. de Nangis ; the 2d in Franche Comté, to be commanded by the D. de Levy :

---

the 3d at Metz, at the orders of the Count de Belliſle ; and the 4th in Flanders, with the Prince de Tingry at their head. P.

Yeſterday arrived the Mail from Holland.

Vienna, Ap. 16. Some will have it, that a treaty of mar-riage is on foot between the Infante Don Carlos, and the Princeſs Anne Charlotte of Lorrain, born May 4, 1714. P. C.

MONDAY, April 24.

Hague, Ap. 1. We have received advice from Barbary, that the D. de Ripperda has been made a ſlave ; and that the King of Morocco is taking meaſures to oblige him to draw out the money he has in the Bank of England, to purchaſe his liberty. —— The Infante Duke having writ-ten a letter to his Imperial Majeſty, directed To the Empe-ror my Brother, the Imperial Court could not help ſhew-ing ſome reſentment at it ; and it is believed it will be ſent back unanſwered. It is all the talk here, that that young Prince has formed the deſign to make himſelf King of Corſica, or of Lombardy. P.

Yeſterday arrived the Mail from France.

Paris, Ap. 30. On the 23d the Royal Academy of Sci-ences held their yearly general meeting after Eaſter ; when M. de Fontenelle read the Eulogium of the late Preſident de Maiſons : M. Donſonbray [Danſembray. P.] read a lec-ture upon a new machine, called the Metrometer, or mea-ſurer of time in muſic ; M. de Reaumur read another upon the hiſtory of the Teigne, a ſmall inſect, that eats the Pa-renchymous parts of the leaves of tree ; M. Du Fay read a ſecond Diſſertation upon the colours of the Cornelians, called Cornelians of the old rock : M. Buache read a lec-ture upon a Compaſs of a new invention, to determine with greater certainty the declination of the needle ; and M. du Hamel read another upon the different methods of making ſoluble Tartar, by mixing ſeveral ſorts of earth. C. P.

Books and Pamphlets publiſhed ſince April 13.

13. Sermons and diſcourſes by Rob. Moſs, D. D. 4 vol.
14. The bleſſedneſs of giving, above that of receiving : a Sermon at the Tabernacle at Blandford, by Geo. Con-way, M. A.
15. Reflections on the Letter to Dr. Waterland, and the Defence of it Price 6 d.
17. The Caſe of the Salt-duty and Land tax, &c. Pr. 6 d.
A Report from the Committee concerning the ſale of the late Earl of Derwentwater's eſtate, Price 1 s.
Animadverſions upon a Paper in the London Journal, Feb. 26. Price 4 d.
Remarques hiſtoriques & critiques ſur l'Hiſtoire de Charles XII. &c. par M. de la Motraye
The Political State of Great Britain : for March.
Deſiderata Curioſa : or, a Collection of ſcarce and curi-ous Pieces, &c. by Francis Peck, M. A. Price 15 s.
18. An Apology for the Church of England, &c. Pr. 1 s.
A Poem to his R. Highneſs the Duke on his Birth-day : by Stephen Duck.
An expoſtulatory-Letter to Mr. Dan. Neal, concerning his Hiſtory of the Puritans. Price 6 d.
Miſcellaneous Obſervations on Authors, No. 16.
A Letter to a Free-holder on the reduction of the Land-tax. Price 1 s.
20. A detection of the ſtate and ſituation of the Sugar Planters of Barbadoes, &c. Pr. 1 s.
The benefit of dying : a Sermon at New Woodſtock, Mar. 19 by Peter Du Bois.
21. The Charing-Croſs Medley. Pr. 1 s.
The Council of women. Pr. 1 s.
A Diſſertation concerning the canonical authority of the Goſpel according to Matthew, &c. Price 1 s.
A Letter to the mens-meeting of the People called Quakers, &c. Pr. 4 d.
The reigns of K. Edward II. and part of K. Edward III. by J. Adamſon.
The Whetſtone : a Propoſal of a new ſcheme of Gram-mar, &c. by Mr. Lowe. Pr. 6 d.
24. An Anſwer to Mr. Fog's ſham Propoſal for erecting a ſtatue, &c. Pr. 6 d.
The Progreſs of an Harlot. Pr. 1 s.
25. The preſent ſtate of the Republick of Letters, for March.
A Muſe in Livery : a collection of Poems. Pr. 1 s. 6 d.
Humo-Thumbo's Lucubratioas. Pr. 3 d.
The Hiſtory of the Abdication of Victor Amadeus, late King of Sardinia, &c. Pr. 1 s.

On Tueſday Stocks were

South Sea Stock 100, 99 ⅜ qrs. South Sea Annuity 107 7 8ths, Books open. Bank 148 1 half, without the Dividend. New Bank Circulation 7 l. 7 s. 6 d. Premium. India 177 3 qrs. 178 1 8th. Three per Cent. Annuity 97 5 8ths, to 3 qrs. Royal Exchange Aſſurance 101. Lon-don Aſſurance 13 1 half, for the Opening. York Buildings 7 1 half, to 3 qrs. African 42. Engliſh Copper 2 l. 6 s. Welch ditto 1 l. 15 s. South Sea Bonds 2 l. 16 s. Pre-nium. India ditto 6 l. 16 s. ditto. Blanks 7 l. 8 s. 6 d 20 l. Prizes 19 l. 16 s.

This Day is published,

INTEREST at one View, calculated to a Farthing, at 3, 4, 5, 6, 7 and 8 per Cent. from 1000 l. to 1 l. for one Day to 95 Days; and for 1, 2, 3, 4, 5, 6, 7, 8, 9, 10, 11, and 12 Months: With Rules and Examples to cast up Interest at any other Rates by the said Tables. To which is added, A Table for the more speedy casting up of Salaries and Wages, from one Million to one Pound per Year. Besides many other Tables of great Use in receiving and paying of Monies. The Whole being calculated, examined and corrected, and afterwards re-examined from the Press.

By RICHARD HAYES.

Printed for W. Meadows, at the Angel in Cornhill.

Where may be had, by the same Author,

1. The Purchaser's Pocket Companion; shewing at Sight what Interest is made by Money laid out in the Companies Stocks, or other publick Funds.

2. The Negotiator's Magazine of Monies and Exchanges, with a compleat Treatise of Arbitrations of Exchanges.

3. The Ship and Supercargo Book-Keeper, shewing the Manner of the Masters settling Accounts with their Owners, the Privilege of Merchants, and Duty of Officers; with Supercargo's Accompts after the Italian Method of Double-Entry.

4. An Estimate of Places for Life, calculated on the Chances of Lives in general, with an Account of Places in the Disposal of the City of London, and their Value.

WHEREAS other Coffee-Houses, and other Publick Houses, take on their Customers 8 s. for a Quart of Arrack, and 6 s. for a Quart of Rum or Brandy made into Punch, so that it is now become the settled Price throughout the Town, and seldom less than a Bowl of 1 s. 6 d. is to be had: Therefore, for the better accommodating all Gentlemen, that are Lovers of Punch,

This is to give Notice,

That I have opened on Ludgate-hill, the London-Coffee-House and Punch House, (Two Punch-Bowls on Iron Pedestals before my Door,)

Where the neat and best old Batavia Arrack, Jamaica Rum, and French Brandy, are made into Punch, with the finest Ingredients, v.z.

A Quart of Arrack made into Punch for 6 s. and so in Proportion to the smallest quantity, which is half a Quartern for four Pence Half-penny.

A Quart of Rum or Brandy made into Punch for 4 s. and so in Proportion to the smallest Quantity, which is half a Quartern for 3 d. And Gentlemen may have it as soon made, as a Gill of Wine can be drawn; with the best of Eating, Attendance, and Accommodation.

This Undertaking has occasion'd many, whose Interest it is to possess Gentlemen with such an Opinion, that the Liquors by me used are not good: The Publick is hereby assured, that I buy my Goods on the Keys, and at the best Hand, with Ready Money, and a w at this Time provided with as well-chosen Brandies, Rum and Arrack, as any in Town, and will at all times procure the best that is imported: But what may convince Gentlemen of the Truth hereof, is, (not only by the Encouragement I meet with) that the Sherbet is always brought by itself, and the Brandy, Rum, or Arrack in the Measure, so there can be no Imposition, either in Quantity or Quality; for the Proof whereof I appeal to all Gentlemen who have done me the Honour to call at my House.

James Ashley.

This Day is published, Price 1 s.

The Second Edition of

THE PROGRESS of LOVE, in Four Eclogues.

I. Uncertainty, to Mr. Pope.
II. Hope, to the Honourable George Doddington, Esq;
III. Jealousy, to Edward Walpole, Esq;
IV. Possession, to the Right Hon. the Ld. Visc. Cobham.

Printed for L. Gilliver, at Homer's-Head, over-against S. Dunstan's Church in Fleet-street.

L. Kt wise,

STOWE, the Gardens of the Right Hon. Richard, Lord Viscount Cobham. Address'd to Mr. POPE.

Devenere locos lætos, & amœna Vireta Fortunatorum nemorum, sedesque beatas. Virg.

Lately published,

And Sold by J. Brotherton at the Bible over-against the Royal-Exchange in Cornhill, A New Edition of

LES Aventures de Telemaque, Fils d'Ulysse. Par feu Messire Francois de Salignac de la Motte Fenelon, Precepteur de Messieurs les Enfans de France, & depuis Arche eque-Duc de Cambrai, Prince due Saint Empire, &c. Nouvelle Edition, conforme au Manuscript Original. Enrichie d'un grand Nombre de Figures en Taille Douce. Avec des Remarques pour l'eclaircissement de cet Ouvrage.

This new Edition is correctly printed, with a good Letter, upon a fine Paper, with 25 Cuts and a Map, all engrav'd by the best Hands, and is no way inferior to the Hamburgh Edition, and is sold 10 per Cent. cheaper than that Edition; and besides, in the Allowance will be made to all Gentlemen who rat Numbers to use in Schools.

N.B. This Edition has 12 Cuts more than that of Hamburgh.

At the Printing-Office in Bow Church-Yard, London, is just published, Pr. bound 1 s. 6 d.

SENTENTIÆ SELECTÆ: Or, A Collection of miscellaneous sentences, Divine, Moral, and Historical. In Prose and Verse. English and Latin. Excerpted from the Works of many learned and judicious Authors, and digested into alphabetical Order. By Edward Curney. To which are added, various Forms for Inditing Letters. The Characters, Places, and Significations of all Sorts of Stops, Points, Pauses and Marks used both in Writing and Printing, with their Explanations. A Table of the most common Abbreviations, or Contractions of Words. Pertinent Directions for fair and exact Writings, with Rules for making and managing the Pen, &c. The best approv'd Receipts for making Ink of many Colours. An ingenious Discourse and Poem on the unspeakable Advantages of Reading and Writing; Also Instructions and Rules for Behaviour; with many other useful and profitable Particulars.

Also a curious Book of select Fables, and other short Poems, &c. nicely engrav'd on 32 Copper Plates, for the Amusement of young Gentlemen and Ladies. To which are added, The most useful and ornamental Hands for their Improvement in the Art of Writing. Price 1 s. 6 d. And a new Cyphering Book for the Use of Schools, being the best of the Kind ever yet extant. Engrav'd by George Bickham, Sen. Price 1 s. 6 d. Likewise the Third Edition of The Modern Musick Master: Or, The Universal Musician; consisting of Instructions to Singing, and Directions to play on the Common Flute, German Flute, Hautboy, Violin, Harpsichord, or Organ, with a brief History of Musick to this present Time, in which Volume is included many other valuable Pieces. Engrav'd on above 320 Plates &c. 7 s. 6 d.

Books of Instructions for any single Instrument, 1 s. 6 d.

N.B. At the abovesaid Printing-Office, Shop-Keepers Bills are engraved and printed, either at the Letter or Rolling-Press, at the lowest Rates.

Books printed for J. BATLEY, at the Dove in Pater-Noster-Row.

1. A Compleat Introduction to the Reading the Holy Scriptures, intended chiefly for young Students in Divinity. In two Parts. Part I. Containing an account of several and religious State of the Jews, the Same itans, economics, Temple, Sacrifices, Synagogues, High-priests, sounds of Justice, particularly the Sanhedrin, Proselytes, Sects, Jewish Sects, Pharisees, Sadducees, Essenes, Proselytes of the Gate, Years, Months, Days, and Hours of the Jews, &c. Part II. Containing the Proofs of the Truth of the Christian Religion; Nature of the New Testament; the Hebrew Money, Weights and Measures; various Readings, Division into Chapters and Verses, Herein in the Apostles days, Versions of the New Testament, Ancient and Modern; To which are added the English ones, &c. Written originally in French by Messieurs De Beaufobre and Lenfant, with Order of the King of Prussia. Now first done into English with additional Notes.

2. A compleat Body of Divinity, consonant to the Doctrine of the Church of England. In Six Books. In Two Volumes. By N. Clark, Rector of Shatton St. James in Dorset. Price 9 s.

Next Thursday will be published, Price Six Pence,

Very proper for private Families, or to send into the Country, and Places abroad, where the English reside; being a compendious View of all our publick Papers:

THE GENTLEMAN's MAGAZINE: Or, Monthly Intelligencer.

No XVI. Containing more in Quantity, and greater Variety than any other Book of the Kind and Price, viz.

I. A View of the Weekly Essays, viz. Religion and Deism; Ambition and Avarice; Wit and Madness; Church Musick; Dr. Bentley's Manner of Criticism; Mischiefs of Bargains in Marriage; Liberty of Conscience; Arguments for the Tythe Bill; Libels; Coquetry; Friendship, &c

II. Political Points; viz. Remarks on the Reign of King Charles I, King William and Queen Mary's Characters; Paralel History; Orations of Demosthenes; the Revolution Vindicated; Considerations on the South Sea Affairs; Corruption, &c. Voltaire's History.

III. Poetical Pieces.

IV. Domestick Occurrences, Births, Deaths, Marriages, the melancholy Case of Richard and Bridget Smith, with their genuine Letters of Apology for Self-Murder; Executions at Derby, Exeter, &c.

V. Price of Goods, Grain, Stocks.

VI. Foreign Affairs.

VII. Books and Pamphlets.

VIII. A Table of Contents.

By SYLVANUS URBAN, Gent.

Printed and sold at St. John's Gate; by F. Jefferies in Ludgate-street, and the Booksellers in Town and Country.

Where may be had all the former Numbers.

Note, A few are printed on fine Royal Paper, large Margin, for the Curious.

Speedily will be published,

The Third and Fourth Volumes of

A General Collection of Treaties, Manifestoes, Declarations of War, and other publick Papers, from the Year 1640, to the present Time. In which will be inserted several remarkable Treaties made after the Death of King CHARLES I, and during the Protectorship of Oliver Cromwell in Ogho. Printed by J. Darby and T. Browne in Bartholomew-Close.

The First Volume of this Work, which has been some Years out of Print, will, at the same Time, be republished. Printed for J. and J. Knapton; J. Darby; D. Midwinter and A. Ward; A. Bettesworth and C. Hitch; E. Fayram and T. Hatchett; J. Pemberton; J. Osborn and T. Longman; C. Rivington; F. Clay; J. Batley, and R. Hett.

This Day is published,

For the Use of Families, (beautifully printed in 2 Vols. 8vo. adorn'd with 34 Plates, engraven by Mr. Sturt,

DUPIN's Evangelical History; or, The Records of the Son of God, and the Veracity demonstrated. In the Life and Acts of our blessed Lord and Saviour Jesus Christ, and his Holy Apostles. Wherein,

I. The Life of the Blessed Jesus is related in all its Circumstance, according to the Order of Time, in a pathetic Style and practical Method; thereby composing a perfect Harmony of the Gospels.

II. Points from his Sermons and Discourses of those essential and important Truths, which all Christians are oblig'd to know and practice, in order to their eternal Salvation.

III. His Parables, Miracles, and Sufferings, set in a clear Light, and defended from all the Oppositions of wicked and designing Men.

IV. An Application to the Whole to the respective Uses of Christians, with regular Devotions conformable to the Doctrines of the Holy History; and Directions how we may read the Life of Jesus Christ to Advantage. Printed for R. Ware, at the Bible and Sun in Amen-Corner, near Pater-Noster-Row; price 8 s. Where may be had,

1. The large House Bibles, Folio, with the six Maps of Sacred Geography, and a brief Concordance for the more easy finding out of the Places therein contained. By J. Downame, B.D. Bound in Calf Leather at 1 l. 7 s. per Book. And with M. Sturt's Cuts, at 1 l. 5 s. ditto. On a fine Paper with Cuts 2 l. 5 s. ditto.

2. The Impartial Churchman, or, A fair and candid Representation of the Excellency and Beauty of the Church of England, together with an earnest and affectionate Address to the Protestant Dissenters. By Robert Warren, D.D. Price 2 s. 6 d.

3. The Whole Duty of Man. Part II. Teaching a Christian, 1 How to grow in Grace. 2 How to demean himself in Sickness. 3 How to prepare himself for a happy Death. Together with Advice how Visitors and Attendants should carry it toward the Sick; and some general Considerations that may induce Relations and Friends to take his Death patiently. By the Rev. and Learned Dr. John Williams, late Lord Bishop of Chichester. price 3 s. 6 d.

Where likewise may be had,

A curious Field's Bible, Folio, with very fine Cuts, two Volumes, bound in Turkey Leather; price 30 l.

And on Imperial Paper, three Volumes ditto, 30 l.

The Cælestial Anodyne Tincture: Or, The Great Pain-easing Medicine,

FAm'd and approv'd of for its wonderful and never-failing Success, in giving immediate Ease and Relief in all manner of pains, either inward or outward, and is the most certain Remedy in the World for a sure and speedy Cure of the Cholick, and expelling Wind, Gripes and pains in the Stomach, the Pleurisy, stitches or pains in the side, back, loins, or any other parts; Rheumatick Ailments, which cause pain and dolor. It hath given ease to a Miracle, when all other Remedies have fail'd. In the Gravel and Stone in the Kidneys, it gives ease forthwith, and brings them away to Admiration. It also facilitates and causes a speedy Delivery in Child-birth. 'Tis no Quack trifling thing to allure the World with, but a real and well-experienced Medicine, not acting by Stupefaction (as Opiates) but by a friendly, balsamick, and subtile Nature, pacifying the most severe and terrible racking pains, and carries off the Cause, not by purging, but by Transpiration, by Urine, or breaking Wind. No Family ought to be without it. And used outwardly, it cures Swellings, Aches, pains, Numbness, or Weakness of the Joints, 'tis excellent for Cramps, and all other glad Infirmities, effecting Wonders in Agues, Fevers, Small-pox, &c. No Family ought to be without it.

It is sold only by Mr. PARKER, Printer, at his House in Salisbury-Court. or by such persons as he shall depute, viz. at Mr. Parker's, a Printer, in Bull-Head Court, Jewin-street; at the White Gallon Pot, a Chandler's Shop over against the White Hart Inn in the Borough, at Eighteen pence a bottle, with printed Directions; and, if requested, will be brought to any Person, by the Hawker who sells his Penny-post. Sealed as above.

LONDON: Printed by S. PALMER and J. HUGGONSON, in Bartholomew-Close, for Captain GULLIVER, near the Temple, where Letters and Advertisements are taken in; As also at the Rainbow Coffee-House in Cornhill, and John's Coffee-House in Sheer-Lane, near Temple-Bar. [Price Two Pence.]

The Grub-ſtreet Journal.

NUMB. 122

Thurſday, *MAY* 4, 1732.

Munditiis capimur: non ſint ſine lege capilli :
Admotæ formam dantque negantque manus.
　　　　　　Ovid. Art. Am. iii. 133.

To Mr. Bavius, Secretary of the Society of Grub-ſtreet.

§ I R,

Happened the other night into company with three or four Gentlemen at a tavern, when the converſation chiefly turned upon matrimony, and conjugal happineſs. There was but one married man among us; and he, it ſeems, was ſo far from being an advocate for the holy ſtate, that after a long diſpute, which was the moſt eligible, a ſingle one, or that, upon the company's appealing to his deciſion, he gave his judgment abſolutely in favour of the former.

This Gentleman I ſhall call Clorius : and, for the ſervice of the fair Sex, ſhall preſent his character to them, as well as the reaſon upon which he founded his opinion ; —Clorius is a perſon of great fortune, young, witty, and well bred ; his acquaintance love him, his tradeſmen reſpect him, and all the world allows him to be a fine Gentleman. In every part of life he has been remarkable for acting ſtrictly the man of honour. By this I do not mean, that he adheres in all things to the rules of a rigid virtue ; but that he is tenacious of his word, ſpeaks with ingenuity and candour, and deteſts any thing that has the leaſt appearance of diſſimulation or hypocriſy. And tho' for ſome years he has been, in the Town phraſe, a man of pleaſure ; yet he never could bring himſelf to ſuch a refinement in his vices, as either to debauch the wife, or the daughter of any man. He has always contented himſelf with ſuch as he found debauched to his hand : and whenever he parted from them, with a generoſity peculiar to good nature, he never failed to beſtow in ſuch a manner, as he judg'd moſt probable to render them ſecure from want all the reſt of their lives. *Such is the man who determined this important Queſtion.*

I ſhall now proceed to give the reaſon, upon which he grounded his reſolution : as near as I can recollect, the Gentleman's own words were as follow : —— Since the Company has done me the honour to declare a willing acquieſcence in whatever opinion I ſhall give ; in order therefore to canvas the matter with the greater accuracy, I think it neceſſary to premiſe to you the conſiderations, which at firſt determined me to a married ſtate. I had long and warily deliberated the inconveniencies of a ſingle life ; the irregularities which are often incident to it ; and the diſorders which are but too frequently the conſequences of an illicit commerce with the fair Sex.

And as I had likewiſe, on the other hand, often remarked, that there were more unhappy marriages proceeded from the avarice of mankind, than from any other ſource that I could diſcover ; this obſervation made me reſolve, that if my own fortune was ſufficient, not only for all the neceſſaries, but even the innocent pleaſures of a matrimonial condition, I would never object againſt a woman I liked, on account of her not having ſuch a portion, as in a fair way of bargaining, and in a mercantile nation (ſuch a one is) I might not only reaſonably expect, but had, it ſeems, a very good right to demand. Beſides, by this I was ſure of avoiding that ſcandalous practice of ſettling my whole eſtate on my firſt iſſue male. A practice materially injurious to Society, not only as it deſtroys that equality ſo eſſentially neceſſary in all well governed Commonwealths ; but as it has a direct tendency to the defrauding the induſtrious tradeſman of his juſt and due demands. I know nothing that is more monſtrous, than to hear parents talk of the love and impulſe of nature towards their progeny, and yet leave all their younger children beggars to enrich, in all probability, a prodigal extravagant heir. —— Having gained my point thus far, my next conſideration was, whether my temper was of that airy volatile nature, as that it would be impoſſible for me to confine it within the limits preſcribed by the nuptial appointment. This, after a ſevere ſcrutiny into myſelf, I was very well aſſured would be feaſible. Nothing then remained of further difficulty, but to find out ſome woman, whoſe perſon and education I could approve of ; and whoſe humour I could fix upon, as entirely correſpondent and agreeing with my own. —— A man of a great eſtate has always a large field to chuſe in. For my own part, to obtain what I wanted, I imagined a tour

into the country would be the propereſt expedient I could make uſe of. Women of Town-educations are but too generally either Prudes or Coquets, both which, tho' not equally entertaining, yet are equally to be avoided. —— But, not to be too minute in my narration, I muſt tell you, that at laſt I met with an honeſt Gentleman's daughter, whoſe perſon, temper and education I flattered myſelf were unexceptionable. Her I married ; and yet with her am I unhappy.

The Company upon this ſtaring earneſtly upon Clorius ; I don't wonder, Gentlemen, ſays he, at your ſurpriſe ; but your admiration will, I believe, be raiſed ſomewhat higher, when I aſſure you, that there is not that woman in the world, who has a diſpoſition more mild, gentle, or good-natured : and had not the one fault, (a fault, which upon enquiry, I find but too common a one,) I would not exchange her for all the pomp and luxury of the moſt voluptuous, eaſtern Monarch. What I mean is, that indecent diſregard, with which married women treat their own families, by neglecting at home thoſe advantages of dreſs and cleanlineſs, which ſeldom fail of engaging the affections of a ſenſible man. This, added he, is the moſt intolerable grievance to a man, who conſiders himſelf as obliged in honour and conſcience to be conſtant in his careſſes to only one woman, and to whom he has vowed an attachment in the moſt ſacred manner. To this cauſe may, in a great meaſure, be attributed the ſtraying of ſo many married men to lewd women of the Town ; and to this it is, that I muſt wholly impute the uneaſineſs which I at preſent labour under. —— Such is my objection againſt matrimony ; and ſo important a one I take it to be, that I muſt, and do declare my judgment abſolutely in favour of a ſingle life.

One of the Company (an old Batchelor) upon hearing the deciſion of the Queſtion, got up, and with a grave ſneer told us, That he thought a remedy might eaſily be found out for redreſſing the grievance upon which Clorius's judgment was built. —— Suppoſe, ſays he, that Huſbands were to treat their Wives like their Miſtreſſes, and bribe them into cleanlineſs, by a daily or weekly ſtipend for that purpoſe : or, if this ſhould be thought too expenſive a remedy, a general licence to the Ladies to receive their gallants at home in their own apartments, would, doubtleſs, be found a moſt effectual proviſion againſt this evil.

Upon retiring to my own lodgings, after the Company had broken up, I muſt own, it was not without a good deal of concern, that I apprehended there might be too much truth in Clorius's obſervation. However, I was by no means convinced, that the charge in general was juſt. To argue from a caſual abuſe to the entire diſuſe of any thing, is ſurely an unfair way of reaſoning. Human underſtanding is of ſo limited a nature, that at beſt we can only form ſchemes that are plauſible. No wiſe man will therefore conſider any condition in this world, but as a ſtate of imperfection. He that deviſes the moſt rational ſyſtem, and ſuch as is beſt connected with the happineſs of mankind, is undoubtedly our greateſt benefactor. But we muſt not expect, that our reaſon ſhould be infallible, whilſt our natures are corrupt. The beſt inſtitutions that ever were, have been debaſed to ſerve the vileſt purpoſes ; and the moſt holy of religions has been often a pretext for the perpetration of the blackeſt crimes. It is therefore no objection to the purity of any eſtabliſhment, that it does not always anſwer the ends for which it was at firſt intended. —— Whoever ſeriouſly conſiders the nature and deſign of marriage, will be ſoon convinced, that, as propagation is neceſſary for the ſupport of mankind, ſo marriage is truly wiſe and political, for the ſake of decency and order. If there are ſome women who come under the cenſure of being ſlattiſhly indolent, where they ought to endeavour to make themſelves moſt agreeable ; this, doubtleſs, can never be a juſt foundation for condemning in general what is indiſputably attended with ſo many important advantages. —— I muſt own, it's a ſhameful thing, that there ſhould be even one Lady in the kingdom of this character : however, 'tis by no means equitable to involve the innocent in the ſentence of the guilty ; eſpecially, when 'tis, I hope, no unreaſonable preſumption, that there is not one in a hundred who juſtly merits the reproach. —— Love is certainly a nice Deity, and will have no incenſe but the pureſt burned on his altar. The utmoſt delicacy is required to keep our paſſions alive. A ſollicitude for the decency of our perſon is, doubtleſs, an amiable and rational expedient

to anſwer this end. But this alone won't do ; there is beſides a neceſſity of baniſhing all obſcenity and looſe converſation from our intercourſe with the fair Sex.

　　Not, that warm thoughts of the tranſporting joy
　　Can ſhock the chaſteſt, or the niceſt coy ;
　　But obſcene words, too groſs to move deſire,
　　Like heaps of fuel, do but choak the fire.
　　　　Duke of Buckingham's Eſſay on Poetry.

'Tis impoſſible to preſerve a reſpect for any company we keep, without laying on ourſelves at leaſt the common reſtraints of good manners, and a virtuous decorum. Before I conclude this letter, I muſt beg leave to obviate a miſtake, which I find moſt Ladies are in. —— I have obſerved, that women generally caſt their eyes in company on the beſt dreſſed man ; men on the handſomeſt faced woman. The applauſe therefore, which the female Sex expect from the ſplendor of their attire, is rarely attained by them. Women are from their infancy bred up with notions of finery. Miſs, before ſhe can ſpeak, is arrayed out in ſomething very glaring ; the firſt word that is taught her, is Huſband : ſo that the ideas of finery and Huſband being the firſt that ſtrike upon her imagination, ſhe can ſeldom ſeparate them all her life time after. —— The education of Boys being ſo entirely different, we rarely find that women are ever diſtinguiſhed by the men for the luſtre of their dreſs. Indeed, among one another, their dreſs ſeldom fails of exciting, either contempt, or envy. But amongſt men, I have known the fineſt dreſſed Lady in an aſſembly paſſed by with leſs regard, than a tolerable pretty woman in plain bombazine. I am, Sir,

　　　　　　Your humble ſervant.

The Double Contest.

A Short, big-look'd man,
　Four foot and a ſpan,
I th' dreſs of his trade,
Attack'd a poor Maid :
　She'd fruit, brought from far, 　　　　　5
To tempt to her bar :
To cool was its uſe,
And ſweet was its juice.
Two ſnares, at one wheel,
He dar'd, and ſcap'd well, 　　　　　10
Tho' kind dice cou'd let her
Have, moſt times, the better.
　But fortune will beat
Down, little and great :
Another ſad day, 　　　　　15
Two wheels ſtood in way ;
The driver had name,
From what does enflame ;
Diſputings enſu'd,
The iſſue was rude ; 　　　　　20
The worthi'ſt the field,
At preſent muſt yield ;
(He ſooner might draw
A ſtubborn old law ;)
Go ſomething about, 　　　　　25
And through dirt, no doubt.
To ſoften his pain,
He borrows a cane;
Then his up lift arm,
Can reach to do harm ; 　　　　　30
Revenge makes it ſweet,
You'd admire the feat.
The man-mountain ſtay'd,
While little thing play'd ;
Then ſtretching one hand, 　　　　　35
Which ſoon fix'd his ſtand ;
He outs with a ſquirt,
To wipe off his dirt :
And leaſt the hot range
Shou'd make his fleſh change, 　　　　　40
Well ſoaks him in brine,
Which porter made ſhine :
To ſeaſon each lip,
The ſalts thither ſkip ;
And did they get through, 　　　　　45
They'd ſcour'd his teeth too :
Where malice may lurk,
His boſom next ſearch :

Leſt fear ſhould them miſs,
His breeches be-piſs:
Not breaking his ſhin,
Pour ſmart-water in:
At no time out dar'd,
O'er head it had rear'd;
And now, to be low,
Trickle down to's toe;
To harden our Squire,
'Gainſt he won'd ſeem high'r.
The well drench'd Poor Dear
Is looſ'd with a ſneer;
And innocent cane
Clean'd, and giv'n again.
  Now what law means evil,
To Collier ſo civil?
Who vanquiſh'd his foe,
Without word or blow;
And ſtiller than mob,
Pump'd proud, wrangling ſquab;
And ſent him well taught,
To ſtrive, where he ought.

P. S. A word to Mr. CONUNDRUM; Quære, Whether Dr. BENTLEY's *Paradiſe Loſt*, would not be MILTON's *Paradiſe Regained*. BAVIUS.

DOMESTIC NEWS.

C. *Courant.*	E P. *Evening Poſt.*
P. *Poſt-Boy.*	S J. *S. James's Evening Poſt.*
D P. *Daily Poſt.*	W E. *Whitehall Evening P.*
D J. *Daily Journal.*	L E. *London Evening Poſt.*

THURSDAY, *April* 27.

The King's journey to Hanover is ſuſpended,
For a longer time, we hear, than was intended. *S J.*

Laſt week a duel was fought between the Lord John Ruſſel and Capt. Janſſen, when the former retreating a little to have a more advantageous thruſt, had the misfortune to fall down; and the latter being too generous to take the advantage, the ſame happily ended without any miſchief. *S J. LE.* —— *I think* the ſame *was no* misfortune *at all.*

On tueſday at a hearing before the L. Chancellor, L. Chief Juſtice Raymond, and Baron Comyns, the Court unanimouſly agreed, that the Patent granted by his Majeſty to R. Wilks, C. Cibber, and Barton Booth, Eſqs; for the Play-houſe in Drury lane, was a lawful Grant; and it paſſed the Broad Seal accordingly. *D P.* ——— The Patent is for 21 years to the longer liver, and aſſignable. The Maſters have renewed their leaſe with his Grace the Duke of Bedford. *S J.*

Yeſterday being the firſt day of the Term, the Lord Chancellor, &c. went in the uſual ſtate to Weſtminſter-hall, &c. *S J.*

On monday at New-market the Duke of Bolton's horſe *Sterling* won the great ſtakes of 700 guineas; and Mr. Coke's *Bauble* beat the Earl of Portmore's *Miſs Eſſex*, for 200 guineas. *S J. WE. LE.*

We hear the learned Dr. Bentley of Cambridge, is reſolved to anſwer the Reflections Mr. Budgell has made upon him in his late celebrated Book, entitled, *Memoirs of the Life of the late Earl of Orrery, and of the Family of the Boyles. P.*

I think the Book-ſellers of Mr. Budgell,
For his, and their own reputation judge ill,
To blow his Works *about with* puff *on* puff;
As if they were Hyp-Oratory *ſtuff.*

John Hopkins, Eſq; appears to have died worth 300,000 l. He has left ſeveral legacies, 500 l. to S. Thomas's Hoſpital; 500 l. to the Incurable; 500 l. to be divided to poor houſe-keepers, 20 l. to each family: but the bulk of his great eſtate is limited to the heirs male of the daughters of a names ſake and kinſman, a Farmer in Eſſex or Suffolk, a ſon *of whoſe*, to whom this eſtate was deſign'd to be given died not long ſince *D J.*

A few days ſince died ſuddenly at Bath John Henley, of Abbots Wotton in Dorſetſhire, Member in the laſt Parliament for Lyme. *D P.* —— *This was* Mr. Orator Henley: Mr. Auditor Henley WE HEAR *is ſtill alive, tho' in a weak condition.*

FRIDAY, *April* 28.

We are aſſured, that the Parliament will not riſe before the 25th of next month; and that his Majeſty will not viſit his German Dominions, 'till towards the middle of June. *P.*

We hear the R. Hon. the Lord How will go as Governor of Barbadoes. *P.*

On wedneſday night the Lady of the Right Hon. Sir Will. Yonge was ſafely brought to bed of a ſon and heir. *P.* Yeſterday. *C. Who omits* Right Hon.

The Lord Viſc. Dunkeron, Mr. Kinneſley, and Mr. Stewart, being diſcharged the 14th inſt. from their confinement at Tours, are expected here daily. *D P.*

Yeſterday was a tryal in the Court of Exchequer, between the Rev. Mr. D'Oyly, Rect. of Fryering in Eſſex, Plaintiff, and Mr. Char. Hornby, Defendant, for with-holding of tythes, on a pretence of the barenneſs of land; which after a ſhort hearing was determined in favour of the Plaintiff. *D P.*

Laſt wedneſday was held a Lodge by its Maſter, at the Golden Spikes in Hampſtead, of the ancient and honourable Society of Free-Maſons, when the R. Hon. the Lord Tenham was elected Maſter of the Lodge, on the reſignation of the R. Hon. the Lord Viſc. Montacute. *D P.*

On monday John Garth, Eſq; Counſeller at Law, was unanimouſly elected Recorder of the Devizes, in the room of Serjeant Webb, deceaſed. *D J.*

On ſunday Mrs. Helen Andrews, 2d daughter of Sir Francis, renounced the errors of the Church of Rome, and received the ſacrament by the hands of the Rev. Dr. Warren, at the pariſh Church of Stratford le Bow. *P.*

Capt. How, who commanded the Lady Amelia, which arrived in the river on wedneſday, died at Jamaica by the following accident: A bull was given him, which deſigning to kill for his ſhip's uſe, he got dogs to bait it; and a dog, which had been hurt, faſtening on the calf of his leg, he fell down; and the bull running at him, with his horn ripped his belly up, ſo that he died on the ſpot. *D J.*

On wedneſday died, after a tedious indiſpoſition, at his houſe in Leiceſter fields, the Hon. Brigadier Gen. Pocock. *P.*

SATURDAY, *April* 29.

We hear the Parliament will break up on May 28th, and that his Majeſty will imbark for his German Dominions June 1. *D J.* ——— It was talk'd yeſterday at Court, as if his Majeſty's journey began to be doubted of. *D P.*

Yeſterday all the Gen. Officers met at Whitehall. *D P.*

On tueſday at New-market, the Earl of Hallifax's *Bay Colt* beat the Earl of Godolphin's *Shanks*, 4 miles, for 200 guineas, and the next day the Earl of Portmore's *Grey Colt* beat the Lord Londſdale's *Bay Colt*, for 300 guineas. *D J.*

On wedneſday Tho. Windham, Eſq; was unanimouſly choſen Member of Parliament for Pool in Dorſetſhire, in the room of Dennis Bond, Eſq; *D P.* —— Will. Wyndham, Eſq; *D J.*

Laſt ſunday Mr. Rich. Petit, Gardener to Sir Will. Leman, of Northall in Hertfordſhire, Bar. preſented a ripe Melon to his Majeſty, being the firſt that has been produced this year; and the next day made her Majeſty a preſent of another. *D P.*

Yeſterday a pacquet from Paris brought an account, that Mr. Morrand, one of his Majeſty's Meſſengers, had the misfortune to fall from his horſe on the road from Paris to Calais, and broke his neck. *P.*

Chriſtned Males 159. Females 175. In all 334. *Buried* Males 211. Females 220. In all 431. Decreaſed in the Burials this week 4. *P.*

Laſt night died at his houſe in Soho-ſquare, the R. Hon. Tho. Parker, Earl of Macclesfield, &c. in the 66th year of his age, and after he had had a ſuppreſſion of urine in his kidnies about 8 days. He left one ſon and one Daughter, George L. Viſc. Parker, and the Lady Elizabeth Heathcote, Wife of Will. Heathcote, Eſq; of Hurſley Lodge in Hampſhire. *L E.*

MONDAY, *May* .

Yeſterday the Rev. Dr. Maddox preached before their Majeſties, his Royal Highneſs the Prince of Wales, &c. —— The ſame day the Court went into mourning for 3 weeks, for the death of the Prince of Saxe and Elector of Mentz. *C.* His Majeſty has been pleaſed to appoint Col. Pet. Betteſworth, to be Lieut. Governor of the Iſland of Jerſey. —— And Rob. Clark, Advocate, one of the 4 Commiſſaries of Edinburgh. *D J. C. D P.*

Laſt ſaturday in the afternoon, Horatio Walpole, Eſq; was overturned in his Chariot, near Whitehall, but received no damage. *D J.* —The ſame day died his daughter Miſs Suſan Walpole. *D P.*

On thurſday at the horſe-races at Newmarket, the Earl of Hallifax's *Juſtice* beat the L. How's *Miſs Heyden*, for 100 guineas. —— On friday Mr. Coke's *Hobgoblin* beat Mr. Fleetwood's *Eaton* for 200 guineas. *D J.* For 500. *P.*

The ſame morning the corpſe of the late Biſhop Atterbury arrived at the Cuſtom-houſe. *D P. D J.* —— We hear the Officers examining the caſe, found in it 4 pieces of fine French ſilk brocaded with ſilver; which they ſeized. *C.* — *I ſuſpend my belief, 'till I have* examined this caſe.

On ſaturday the Lady of the R. Hon. the L. Viſc. Limerick of the Kingdom of Ireland, was delivered of a ſon. *P.*

TUESDAY, *May* 2.

We hear that the intended journey of his Majeſty is intirely laid aſide; and that the Parliament will not break up before the middle of June. *C.* —— The R. Hon. the L. Vere Beauclerck is made one of the Commiſſioners of the Navy, in the room of the R. Hon. Rob. Byng, Eſq; who hath reſign'd. *D P.* —— Of Alexander Cleveland, Eſq; *C.* 3.

Yeſterday the corpſe of the R. Hon. the E. of Macclesfield was opened by Mr. Chiſelden, according to his Lordſhip's own deſire, when 3 ſtones were taken out the bladder, and ſeveral out of the kidnies. *C.* Large ſtones. *D P.*

Sir Jam. Naſemith, Bar. is elected Knight of the Shire for Peebles in Scotland, in the room of the Hon. John Douglas, Eſq; deceaſed. *D P.*

Yeſterday the R. Hon. the L. Mayor, attended by the Sheriffs, held a Court Leet at the Crown-tavern in Dukes-place, according to annual cuſtom; each inhabitant paying one half-penny per head, as an acknowledgment of his Lordſhip's being Lord of the manor. *C.*

Aſcenſion-day being near, it is the requeſt of ſome ſerious people, that Miniſters and Church-wardens would take care to prevent thoſe riotous doings, which commonly happen in their Church and Church-yards upon the occaſion, contrary to their Homilies and Canons, as well as to common decency and modeſty. *D P.*

On ſaturday Francis Seymour, Eſq; 2d ſon of Sir Edward, who married the Lady Inchinbrook, was choſen Member of Parliament for Great Bedwin in the County of Wilts, unanimouſly without oppoſition. *P.* —— *It would have been more ſurpriſing news, if this had been* unanimouſly *with* oppoſition.

All the ſhips that have lately arrived in our Ports from the Coaſt of France, have been very ſtrictly ſearched; as alſo the paſſengers and ſeamen; but on what account we cannot yet learn. *P.*

Dover, Ap. 22. We hear from Boulogne, that 7 or 800 of the French Troops are ſuddenly expected there, to repair the roads, or make a pavement, where wanted, between each ſtage, from Paris to Calais. *P.* It is great pity our Troops are not employed in mending the Roads, which would not only eaſe the poor of the burden of Turn-pikes, prevent Treaſurers, &c. getting Eſtates, but alſo prevent the lazy idle Troopers from burdening the Pariſhes with Baſtard children. *L E.* —— *Tho' I like this propoſal, yet I don't apprehend, how the* Soldiers *turning* Highway-men *before they are disbanded, will prevent their getting of* Baſtards.

The E. of Waldegrave, his Majeſty's Embaſſador at the Court of France, is very ſpeedily to return home, and Mr. Robinſon, his Majeſty's Miniſter at the Court of Vienna, is to ſucceed him at Paris. *L E.*

We hear there is now living at Rome, the Hon. Will. Ratcliffe, Eſq; 4th ſon of the late E. of Derwentwater's great Grand father; being the younger Brother to the father of that Earl that was beheaded; and who was never attainted, and its ſaid is Heir to part of the Derwentwater Eſtate. *L E.* — *It is ſaid he keeps a Toy-ſhop there.*

Will. Morrice, Eſq; who had been taken into cuſtody of a Meſſenger upon his landing at Dover from Paris, was examined laſt night at the Cockpit, and diſcharged. *L E.*

Laſt ſaturday in the evening Mr. Teal, ſon of the late Apothecary General, ſhot himſelf at his houſe in Maſham-ſtreet, Weſtm. and on ſunday in the evening the Coroner and his Jury ſate upon him, and it appear'd very plain to them that he was lunatic. *L E.* —— *The circumſtances mentioned in the* S J. *are almoſt all falſe.*

WEDNESDAY, *May* 3.

Yeſterday a Man dwarf, who lately came from Denmark, and is not quite three foot high, was preſented to their Majeſties at S. James's, as alſo to the Royal Family, and was much admir'd. He ſtood under the arm of the D. of Cumberland, with which his Royal Highneſs was much pleaſed. *P.*

Yeſterday the R. Hon. the Earl of Albemarle took his leave of their Majeſties at S. James's, his Lordſhip intending to ſet out for his Regiment at Gibraltar to-morrow. *Ib.*

We hear that three Regiments on the Iriſh eſtabliſhment are order'd to reinforce the garriſons of Gibraltar and Port Mahon. *D P.*

We hear George Vernon, Eſq; hath petition'd his Majeſty for the Barony of Powis, as being the heir to Edward the laſt Lord, who died without iſſue; and that his petition is referr'd to the Attorney General; and it's believ'd it will ſpeedily come before the Houſe of Peers, and he be heard by Counſel againſt Mr. Kynaſton and Sir Nathaniel Curzon, Bar. who are alſo Claimants to the ſaid Barony. *D P.*

The affair between the Biſhop of Ely and Dr. Bentley, which was to have been heard at the Bar of the Houſe of Lords yeſterday, was by their Lordſhips put off till ſaturday next. *P.*

Yeſterday the Sheriffs of London and County of Middleſex went up with a petition to the Hon. Houſe of Commons, praying, That all actions for debt under the ſum of 20 l. within the City of London, ſhould be tried in their Court. *C.*

Laſt night the corpſe of the late Biſhop of Rocheſter was brought from on board a ſhip to Mr. Purdys, an Undertaker's in Clare ſtreet, Clare market. —— We hear that all the ſaid late Biſhop's papers were ſeized by Thomas Walker, Eſq; one of the Commiſſioners of the Cuſtoms, on board the veſſel that brought over his body. *D P.*

Yeſterday morning died Miſs Leiceſter, niece to Sir Nathaniel Curzon, in Brook ſtreet, Hanover-ſquare, an heir-

es of great fortune. —— In the afternoon, at Addington in Surrey, Sir John Leigh, after a long illness of a mortification in his leg. P.

On sunday last the Rev. Mr. Webb of Dorsetshire, was marry'd to Mrs. Phipps, youngest Daughter of the late Sir Constantine Phipps, Knt. formerly Lord Chancellor of Ireland. —— Yesterday morning the Rt. Hon. the Lord Petre was marry'd at S. Paul's Cathedral, to the Hon. Miss Ratcliff, a Daughter of the late Earl of Derwentwater, a Fortune of 30,000 l. after which his Lordship set out with a great retinue for his seat at Ingatestone in Essex, being attended by six coaches and six, a great number of his Tradesmen and Tenants on horseback, and upwards of twenty servants in liveries. D P. —— The C. of the 29th married his Lordship on Friday last.

On Thursday last, at a Court of Delegates held at Doctors Commons, an Appeal was lodged by Mr. Greenly, Proctor for Mrs. Katharine Weld, alias Aston, against her Husband Mr. Edward Weld, in a cause of insufficiency, and Mr. Boycott, Proctor for Mr. Weld, appeared for him by Proxy; and the Judges Delegates order'd an inhibition and monition against the Register of the Arches, to bring in the Process. P.

From the PEGASUS in Grub-street.

The Characters of King WILLIAM and of Bishop BURNET, as drawn by F. Osborne, Esq; F. G. S. in the London Journal of Saturday April 29.

In the world ne'er were seen two men more contrary :
The King cool, the Bishop was warm and unwary.
The one was both politic, close and reserved :
The other was passionate, open, unguarded.
A secret by the first, I say, never was told :
But a secret the last, 'tis known, never could hold.
The King ran for measures of keeping his crown,
Tho' with difficulties some, yet measures his own.
The Bishop for measures ; into which had be entered,
The King thought his crown too much would be ventured.
The Prince was still prudent, and spoke little and clever :
The Prelate impudent, and his tongue could hold never.
The King lov'd retirement when Hyp was upon him ;
The Bishop would always be breaking in on him ;
To take up his Time with whimsical schemes,
Which the King, still awake, always hated like dreams.

He knew he was credulous, one, whom a story on
War easily impos'd : yet an honest Historian.
Could two such men possibly agree ? — I think not :
The Prince was a Dutchman, and the Prelate a Scot.
MÆVIUS.

The Letters signed C. RUFINA, PHILANTHROPOS, PHILOSBUB, and several others, were received ; of which notice will be taken as opportunity shall serve.

Dublin, Ap. 22. We hear that the ship in which was the Corpse of the Lady Malpas, arrived here late this week; notwithstanding it was inserted in some of the English Papers, that the said ship was stranded on the Coast of France. C. P. 29.

Charles Town in South Carolina, Jan. 29. The Alice and Elizabeth, John Pain, Master, in her passage from Jamaica, Dec 9. about 3 in the morning, met with a small vessel off the Bahama banks. It being moon-light, the Capt. discover'd her at some distance ; but before he could hide any thing that was valuable, they came up with him, demanded his yawl out, in which Mr. Christ. French, the Mate, with 4 hands, went on board them, and found them to be Spaniards and French. At first they were saluted with the usual compliments of hanging, burning matches between their fingers, &c. But the Mate speaking French, had some talk with the Captain of the Sloop, who was somewhat less uncivil than the rest. The Sloop was mounted with 8 cannon, and mann'd with 70 hands. They carried the Alice and Elizabeth upon the banks, turned her hold upside down, took away money, sails, rum, sugar, and dry goods, to a considerable value, and having stripp'd the Captain, a Mate, and the men of all their cloaths and bedding, were so civil as to give them leave to proceed with their Snow, and what little they thought proper to leave in her, on their voyage to this place, where they were so facetious as to say, they design'd to make a visit, as soon as the cold weather should be over. P. Ap. 29

FOREIGN NEWS.
THURSDAY, April 27.
Paris, May 3. N. S. The King has given the Abbey of Chaumont la-Pitcine, in the Diocese of Reims to the ancient Bishop of Orange. C. P. —— The Royal Academy of Sciences having received no satisfactory answer to the Question proposed in 1730, have resolved to continue the same for the prize after Easter 1732, which will then amount to 5000 livres : the Question is, 'What is the cause of the inclination of the planets with regard to the plain [plane. C.] of the Equator, and the revolution of the Sun round its axis ; and whence comes it to pass, that the inclination of the said orbits differ one from another ? D P.

Vienna, Ap. 19. Two days since M. Robinson, the British Minister, who has lately held several conferences with Prince Eugene, on the present juncture of affairs, notify'd to the Court, that the King his Master had call'd a Council upon the arrival of an express from Spain, with some advices not very satisfactory, wherein it was resolv'd to fit out 28 men of war in all haste for the Mediterranean. D P.

Hague, Ap. 1. Private letters from Leghorn assure us, that the Spaniards have at least 12,000 men in Porto-Longone and that neighbourhood. L. E.

FRIDAY, April 28.
Leghorn, Ap. 12. By a Felucca from Aleria, we are inform'd, that the Prince of Wirtemberg was arrived at Calvi, with all the Gen. Officers and the Imperial troops : upon which the Malecontents call'd a Grand Council, and bound themselves by an oath, not to accept the amnesty of the Republick ; which resolution they all confirmed with a loud acclamation, Conquer or die. —— The Genoeze lately attack'd a French ship at Gnolato, kill'd several of her men, and dangerously wounded the Captain, only 3 of the French sailors having escap'd on shoar; after which they towed the ship from the land, and burnt her, leaving the Captain stark-naked upon a cliff, from which he was taken on board by another French ship which pass'd by accidentally. P.

SATURDAY, April 29.
Yesterday arrived the Mail from Holland.
Hamburgh, May 2. N. S. Some private letters from Petersburgh advise, that Baron Shaffiroff, the Czarina's Minister at Ispahan, on Feb. 1. concluded a Treaty with the Sophi's Ministers, whereby that Prince yields to Muscovy for ever, the Towns of Derbent, Andreoff, Baku, and some other places, formerly belonging to the Kingdom of Persia. C. DP.

Lisbon, Ap. 2. N. S. Our last advices from Santa Cruz in Barbary say, that King Muley Abdallah had, in a pitch'd battle within 2 days journey of Morocco, entirely defeated the forces of the rebellious Arabs, most of whom had since laid down their arms, and implored his Clemency ; that that Prince had afterwards made himself master of all Mount Atlas, which is what the late King his father could never do. C.

MONDAY, May 1.
Yesterday arrived the Mail from France.
Paris May 7. Card. Coscia having been ill of a cold, was obliged to stay some days at Cisterna ; but he arriv'd at Rome the 14th in the evening, and was set down at the Convent of Praxede. C. P.

Genoa, Ap. 21. Our last letters from Seville say, all is near ready for the African expedition, as they are pleased to call it, tho' the same letters insinuate as if the Court would not give final orders for sailing 'till the return of an express from Vienna, with the Imperial answer to some proposals made by his Catholick Majesty. D P.

Books and Pamphlets published since our last.

27. A Letter from Caleb D'Anvers to Mr. Shimei Troublewater, &c. Pr. 6 d.
Modern History, by Mr. Salmon, No. 94, 95.
The Comedian, No. 1. for April. Pr. 6 d.
Historical and Critical Remarks on the History of Charles XII. By M. A. de la Motraye. Pr. 1 s. 6 d.
Full Instructions for Country Gentlemen, Farmers, &c. Pr 1 s.
The nature of the Charitable Corporation, &c. Pr. 6 d.
The Harlot's Progress : in 6 Cintos. Pr. 1 s.
Revelation examin'd with candour, &c.
28. The Progress of Beauty : a Poem. Pr. 1 s.
The excellency and advantage of the Gospel Dispensation, &c. By Rob. Emmes. Pr. 1 s.
29. The Proceedings at the Sessions in the Old Bailey, &c. Pr. 6 d.
The History of Essex, No. 1. By N. Tindal. Pr. 1 s. 6 d.
May 2. The watchful Christian prepared for early death: a Sermon by T. Watts, D. D.
The Blazing Comet : a Play : By Mr. Johnson.
Some Remarks, &c. concerning the Amicable Society for a perpetual Assurance Office, &c. Pr. 6 d.
A Reply to a Letter to the Minister of Moffat, &c.
A Sermon preached at the Assizes at Guildford, Mar. 24. By Geo. Osborne, Vicar of Battersea.
3 The London Magazine, &c. for April. Pr. 6 d.
A sober and Charitable Disquisition concerning the importance of the Doctrine of the Trinity, &c. Pr. 1 s.

On Tuesday Stocks were
South Sea Stock was 98 1 half, 98 3 8ths. South Sea Annuity 108 1 qr. Bank 147 3 8ths. New Bank Circulation 7 l. 7 s. 6 d. Premium. India 177 1 half, 177 3 qrs. 177 1 half to 3 qrs. Three per Cent. Annuity 97 3 qrs. Royal Exchange Assurance 101. London Assurance 13 3 8ths without the Dividend. York Buildings 7 1 half. African 42. English Copper 2 l. 6 s. Welch ditto 1 l. 15 s. South Sea Bond. 2 l. 15 s. Premium. India ditto 6 l. 7 s. ditto. Blanks 7 l. 8 s. 6 d. 20 l. Prizes 19 l. 16 s.

This Day is publiſhed, (Price 6 d.)
By Mr. LOWE of Hammerſmith,

THE WHETSTONE: A Propoſal of a New Scheme of Grammar, and method of Inſtruction; by which the grounds of a language may be learned in a Few Hours, ſo as to read and write intelligibly. With a Specimen of the Eſſay in a ſyſtem of FRENCH Rudiments, containing a full account of the grounds of that language in Few Pages —— Sold by J. Noon in Cheapſide —— Where may be had GREEK, LATIN, ITALIAN Rudiments, on the ſame Plan, by the ſame Author —— with a Vocabulary and Sententiæ Pueriles, in a method entirely new; to a ſpeedy gaining a Copa of Words, Phraſes, Idioms, Apophthegms, Proverbs, and various other uſeful Peculiarities.

Lately publiſhed,
The two following BOOKS,

I. PRactical Diſcourſes on the ſeveral Parts and Offices of the Liturgy of the Church of England: Wherein are laid open the Harmony, Excellency, and Uſefulneſs of its Compoſure. In four Volumes. By Matthew Hole, D. D. late Rector of Exeter College in Oxford. Vol. I. Containing 58 Diſcourſes on all the Parts of Morning and Evening Prayer, including the Creed of St. Athanaſius. Vol. II. and III. Containing 55 Diſcourſes that follow it. Vol. IV. Containing 174 Diſcourſes on 3 large Parts on all the Collects, Epiſtles and Goſpels, to be uſed throughout the Year. The Second Edition.
II. A practical Expoſition of the Church-Catechiſm. In two Volumes By the ſame Author. The Third Edition, with the Addition of two Diſcourſes; one on the Duty of confeſſing Chriſt, the other on the Danger of denying him: both preach'd at St. Mary's in Oxford
Sold by J. and J. Knapton, and C. Rivington in St. Paul's Church-Yard; A. Bettesworth and C. Hitch in Pater-Noſter-Row; and S. Birt in Avemary-Lane.

This Day is publiſhed,

BRITANNIA ROMANA: Or, The Roman Antiquities of Britain In three Books. The
1. Contains the Hiſtory of all the Roman Tranſactions in Britain, with an Account of their Legionary and Auxiliary Forces employed here, and a Determination of the Stations per ineam valiis; alſo a large Deſcription of the Roman Walls, with Maps of the ſame, laid down from a Geometrical Survey.
2. Contains a compleat collection of the Roman Inſcriptions and Sculptures which have hitherto been diſcovered in Britain, with the Letters engrav'd in their proper Shape and proportionate ſize, and the reading plac'd under each; as alſo an Hiſtorical Account of them, with explanatory and critical Obſervations.
3. Contains the Roman Geography of Britain, in which are given the Originals of Ptolemy, Antonini Itinirarium, the Notitia, the annonymous Ravenna's and Peutinger's Table, ſo far as they relate to this Iſland; with particular Eſſays on each of theſe antient Authors, and the general Places in Britain mentioned by them. To which are added,
※ A Chronological Table and Indexes to the Inſcriptions and Sculptures, after the Manner of Gruter and Reineſius: alſo Geographical Indexes, both of the Latin and Engliſh Names of the Roman Places in Britain, and a general Index to the Work. The whole illuſtrated with above an Hundred Copper Plates By John Horſley, M A and F. R. S.
Printed for John Osborn and Thomas Longman at the Ship in Pater-Noſter-Row.
N. B. There is a conſiderable Number of curious Inſcriptions in this Collection which were never before publiſhed.
A few Copies are printed on the beſt ſuperfine Dutch Writing Medium.

Books printed for J. BATLEY, at the Dove in Pater-Noſter-Row.

1. A Compleat Introduction to the Reading the Holy Scriptures, intended chiefly for young Students in Divinity. In two Parts. Part I. Containing an Account of the civil and religious State of the Jews; the Samaritans, Ceremonies, Temples, Sacrifices, Synagogues, High-Prieſts, Courts of Juſtice; particularly the Sanhedrin, Prophets, Scribes, Jewiſh Sects, Phariſees, Sadducees, Eſſenes, Proſelytes of the Gate. Years, Months, Days, and Hours of the Jews. &c. Part II. Containing the Proofs of the Truth of the Chriſtian Religion; Nature of the New Teſtament Stile; the Chronology and Geography of the New Teſtament; the Hebrew Money, Weights and Meaſures; various Readings, Diviſion into Chapters and Verſes, Hereſies in the Apoſtles Days, Verſions of the New Teſtament, Antient and Modern: To which are added the Engliſh ones, &c. Written originally in French by Meſſieurs De Beauſobre and Lenfant. By the Order of the King of Pruſſia. Now firſt done into Engliſh, with additional Notes.
2. A compleat Body of Divinity, conſonant to the Doctrine of the Church of England. In Six Books. In Two Volumes. By N. Clark, Rector of Shaſton St. James in Dorſet. Price 9 s.

This Day was publiſhed,
Dedicated to the KING,

REVELATION Examin'd with CANDOUR.
OR, A FAIR

ENQUIRY into the SENSE and USE of the ſeveral REVELATIONS expreſly declared, or ſufficiently implied, to be given to Mankind from the Creation, as they are found in the BIBLE. By a Proof of ſaid Friend to an honeſt Freedom of Thought in Religious Enquiries. PART I. Containing DISSERTATIONS upon the ſeveral Revelations from the CREATION to the FLOOD, incluſive.
Printed for C. Rivington, at the Bible and Crown in St. Paul's Church-Yard.

This Day is publiſhed,

For the Uſe of Families, (beautifully printed in 2 Vols. 8vo. adorn'd with 34 Plates, engraven by Mr. Sturt,

DUPIN's Evangelical Hiſtory; or, The Records of the Son of God, and their Veracity demonſtrated. In the Life and Acts of our bleſſed Lord and Saviour Jeſus Chriſt, and his Holy Apoſtles. Wherein,
I. The Life of the Bleſſed Jeſus is related in all its Circumſtances, according to the Order of Time, in a pathetic Style and practical Method, thereby compoſing a perfect Harmony of the Goſpels.
II. Proofs from his Sermons and Diſcourſes of thoſe eſſential and important Truths, which all Chriſtians are oblig'd to know and practiſe, in order to their eternal Salvation.
III. His Parables, Miracles, and Sufferings, ſet in a clear Light, and defended too all the Oppoſitions of wicked and deſigning Men.
IV. An Application to the Whole to the reſpective Uſes of Chriſtians, with regular Devotions conformable to the ſive al Points of the Holy Hiſtory; and Directions how we may read the Life of Jeſus Chriſt to Advantage. Printed for R. Ware, at the Bible and Sun in Amen-Corner, near Pater-Noſter-Row; Price 8 s. Where may be had,
1. The large Bouti Bible, Folio, with the ſix Maps of ſacred Geography, and a brief Concordance for the more eaſy finding out of the Places herein contain'd. By J. Downame, B. D. Bound in Calf Leather at 1 l. 7 s. per Book. And with M. Stuit's Cuts, at 2 l. 5 s. ditto. On a fine Paper with Cuts 2 l. 3 s. ditto.
2. The Impartial Churchman; or, A fair and candid Repreſentation of the Excellency and Beauty of the Church of England. Together with an earneſt and affectionate Addreſs to the Proteſtant Diſſenters. By Robert Warren, D. D. Price 1 s. 6 d.
3. The Whole Duty of Man. Part II. Teaching a Chriſtian, 1. How to grow in Grace. 2. How to demean himſelf in Sickneſs. 3. How to prepare himſelf for a happy Death. Together with Advice how Viſitants and Attendants ſhould carry it toward the Sick; and ſome general Conſiderations that may induce Relations and Friends to take his Death patiently. By the Rev. and Learned Dr. John Williams, late Lord Biſhop of Chicheſter; price 3 s. 6 d.
Where likewiſe may be had,
A curious Field's Bible, Folio, with very fine Cuts, two Volumes, bound in Turkey Leather; price 2 0 l.
And on Imperial Paper, three Volumes ditto, 30 l.

This Day is publiſhed, Price 6 d.

THE GENTLEMAN's MAGAZINE: Or, Monthly Intelligencer. NUMBER XVI. Containing more in Quantity, and greater Variety than any other Book of the Kind and Price, viz.
I. A View of the Weekly Eſſays, viz. Religion and Deiſm; Ambition and Avarice; Wit and Madneſs; Church Muſick; Dr. Bentley's Manner of Criticiſm; Miſchiefs of Bargains in Marriage; Liberty of Conſcience; Arguments for the Tythe Bill; Female Piety; Coquettry; Friendſhip. &c
II. Political Points; viz. Remarks on the Reign of King Charles I. King William and Queen Mary's Characters; Parallel Hiſtory; Orations of Demoſthenes; the Revolution vindicated; Conſiderations on the South Sea Affairs; Corruption, &c. Voltaire's Hiſtory.
III. Poetical Pieces, viz Dean Swift in good Quarters; the Free Maſon; the Farmer's Daughter; Receipt for Courtſhip. IV. Domeſtick Occurrences, Births, Deaths, Marriages, the melancholy Caſe of Richard and Bridget Smith, with their genuine Letters of Apology for Self-Murder; Executions: Duke of Dorſet's dangerous Paſſage
V. Price of Goods, Grain, Stocks, &c. as the former.
※ N. B. The Cuſtomers to the GENTLEMAN's Magazine, or Monthly Intelligencer, are deſired to take Care that they are not deceived by a Book with a ſimilar Title, which will be offer'd them at ſome Shops, and as they have been ſo kind to encourage this uſeful Undertaking, it is hoped they will not, by any Arts, be miſled to favour an Attempt ſo unfair and ungenerous as the ſupplanting an Author in his whole Plan, Deſign, and even Title. A Practice which would be condemned by every Individual concerned in it, if their own Caſe. And the Public may be aſſur'd that whatever our Rivals may pretend, nothing ſhall exceed this Magazine.
Printed at St. John's Gate; and ſold by F. Jefferies in Ludgate-ſtreet, and all unprejudiced Bookſellers.
Where may be had all the former Numbers.
Note, A few are printed on fine Royal Paper. Price one Shil.

This Day is publiſhed,

INTEREST at one View calculated to a Farthing, at 3, 4, 5, 6, 7 and 8 per Cent. from 1000 l. to 1 l. for one Day to 96 Days; and for 1, 2, 3, 4, 5, 6, 7, 8, 9, 10, 11, and 12 Months: With Rules and Examples to caſt any Intereſt at any other Rates by the ſaid Tables. To which is added, A Table for the more ſpeedy caſting up of Salaries and Wages, from one Million to one Pound per Year. Beſides many other Tables of great Uſe in receiving and paying of Monies. The Whole being calculated, examined and corrected, and afterwards re-examined from the Preſs.
By RICHARD HAYES.
Printed for W. Meadows, at the Angel in Cornhill. Where may be had, by the ſame Author,
1. The Purchaſer's Pocket Companion; ſhewing at Sight what Intereſt is made by Money laid out in the Companies Stocks, or other publick Funds.
2. The Negotiator's Magazine of Monies and Exchanges, with a compleat Treatiſe of Arbitrations of Exchanges.
3. The Ship and Supercargo Book-Keeper; ſhewing the Manner of the Maſters ſetling Accounts with their Owners, the Privilege of Merchants, and Duty of Officers; with Supercargo's Accompts after the Italian Method of Double Entry.
4. An Eſtimate of Places for Life, calculated on the Chances of Lives in general, with an Account of Places in the Diſpoſal of the City of London, and their Value.

WHEREAS other Coffee-Houſes, and other Publick Houſes, take of their Cuſtomers 8 s. for a Quart of Arrack, and 6 s. for a Quart of Rum or Brandy made into Punch, to that it is now become the ſettled Price throughout the Town, and ſeldom leſs than a Quart for 1 s. 6 d. is to be had: Therefore, for the better accommodating all Gentlemen, that are Lovers of Punch,
This is to give Notice,
That I have opened on Ludgate-hill, the London-Coffee-Houſe and Punch Houſe, (Two Punch-Bowls on Iron Pedeſtals before my Door,)
Where the fineſt and beſt old Batavia Arrack, Jamaica Rum, and French Brandy, are made into Punch, with the fineſt Ingredients, viz.
A Quart of Arrack made into Punch for 6 s. and ſo in Proportion to the ſmalleſt quantity, which is half a Quartern for four Pence Half-penny.
A Quart of Rum or Brandy made into Punch for 4 s. and ſo in Proportion to the ſmalleſt Quantity, which is half a Quartern for 2 d. And Gentlemen may have it as ſoon made, as a Gill of Wine can be drawn; with the beſt of Eating, Attendance, and Accommodation.
This Undertaking has occaſion'd many, whoſe Intereſt it is to poſſeſs Gentlemen with ſuch an Opinion, that the Liquors by me uſed are not good: The Publick is hereby aſſured, that I buy my Goods on the Keys, and at the beſt Hand, with Ready Money, and am at this Time provided with as well-choſen Brandies, Rum and Arrack, as any in Town, and will at all times procure the beſt that is imported: But when may convince Gentlemen of the Truth hereof, is, (not only by the Encouragement I meet with) that the Sherbet is always brought by itſelf, and the Brandy, Rum, or Arrack in the Meaſure, ſo there can be no Impoſition, either in Quantity or Quality; for the Proof whereof I appeal to all Gentlemen who have done me the Honour to call at my Houſe.
James Aſhley.

Lately publiſhed,
And Sold by J. Brotherton at the Bible over-againſt the Royal-Exchange in Cornhill, A New Edition of

LES Aventures de Telemaque, Fils d'Ulyſſe. Par feu Meſſire Francois de Salignac de la Motte Fenelon, Precepteur de Meſſeigneurs les Enfans de France, & depuis Archeveque-Duc de Cambrai, Prince due Saint Empire, &c. Nouvelle Edition, conforme au Manuſcrit Original. Enrichie d'un grand Nombre de Figures en Taille Douce. Avec des Remarques pour l'eclairciſſement de cet Ouvrage.
This new Edition is correctly printed, with a good Letter, upon a fine Paper, with 25 Cuts and a Map, all engrav'd by the beſt Hands, and is no way inferior to the Hamburgh Edition, and is ſold 20 per Cent. cheaper than that Edition; and beſides, a fair Allowance will be made to all Gentlemen who take Numbers to uſe in Schools.
N. B. This Edition has 12 Cuts more than that of Hamburgh.

This Day is publiſhed, Price 1 s.
The Second Edition of

THE PROGRESS of LOVE, in Four Eclogues.
I. Uncertainty, to Mr. Pope.   III. Jealouſy, to Edward
II. Hope, to the Honourable   Walpole, Eſq;
George Doddington, Eſq;   IV. Poſſeſſion, to the Right
                                   Hon. the La. Viſc. Cobham.
Printed for L. Gilliver, at Homer's-Head, over againſt
S. Dunſtan's Church in Fleet-ſtreet.   Likewiſe,
STOWE, the Gardens of the Right Hon. Richard,
Lord Viſcount Cobham.   Addreſs'd to Mr. POPE.
    Devenere locos lætos, & amæna Vireta
    Fortunatorum nemorum, ſedeſque beatas. Virg.

LONDON: Printed by S. Palmer and J. Huggonson, in Bartholomew-Cloſe, for Captain Gulliver, near the Temple, where Letters and Advertiſements are taken in: As alſo at the Rainbow Coffee-Houſe in Cornhill, and John's Coffee-Houſe in Sheer-Lane, near Temple-Bar. [Price Two Pence.]

The Grub-ſtreet Journal.

NUMB. 123

Thurſday, *MAY* 11, 1732.

To Mr. BAVIUS, Secretary of the Society of Grub-ſtreet.

Mr. BAVIUS, *S. John's College, Cambrige, April* 29.

THE following is a true copy of a letter to a young Gentleman ſince dead: and as the matter therein contained may be applicable to others of the like character, I beg the favour to have it inſerted in your Paper.

Yours, SERIUS.

To SILVANUS.

YOU may, perhaps, think this letter a little unſeaſonable, both as a piece of advice, and as coming from an unknown hand. That we ought to caution one another (whenever there is juſt cauſe) is generally agreed on; but ſeldom put in practice, as it ought, through the fooliſh complaiſance of Intimates, and fear of giving offence: and the taſk is ſuch as ſtrangers (being not concerned for a man's welfare) are ſeldom willing to trouble themſelves with.

The reaſon why I thought proper to conceal my name, was a hint which I took from your friend TERENCE: who was very ſenſible, how much one man's venturing to reprimand another for his faults, expoſes the adviſer to diſlike; however ſincere the deſign, or neceſſary the admonition.

For my part, my being nameleſs ſecures me from the common effects of reſentment; nor need I dread the aſperſions, which are uſually beſtowed with great freedom on him who dares to ſerve a man againſt his will.

That you may not think I deal too hardly with you, and repreſent you at too great a diſadvantage, I ſhall ſet your good qualities in as fair a view as I can; and ſhew you how much they are obſcured by your bad ones.

The ſeveral verſes which go under your name, have to your friends, paſt for a kind of proof, that you were owner of a good underſtanding, and a mind well furniſhed: *but at the ſame time* your converſation and behaviour afford ſuch a frequent ſcene of childhood and folly, that you give too much cauſe for an enemy to argue, you are deſtitute of even common ſenſe. For God's ſake, behave like a perſon of ſuch accompliſhments, as you endeavour to make us believe you poſſeſs.

You ſeem to have no natural propenſity to ſpite or ill-nature; your very looks promiſe humanity and ſweetneſs of diſpoſition. But if your temper be naturally good, to what degree is it warped? and what pains muſt you have taken to extinguiſh almoſt every ſpark of good nature about you?

I appeal to yourſelf, if you do not find a great ſatisfaction at any thing which makes another uneaſy. When you are in company, how comes it to paſs, that one or other is generally the undeſerving mark of your ſenſeleſs and ill-natured laughter? Moreover, if you happen at any time to get the laugh on your ſide, either through the ſtupidity of ſome, who both equal and encourage your follies, or the paſſion of the affronted, you are ſure to congratulate yourſelf, (like ÆSOP's Fly on the chariot wheel) as if you had performed ſome worthy and laudable exploit.

Strange, but true, it is, that you ſcarce can ſuffer any man to paſs you in the ſtreets, without making ſome remark or other on his dreſs, his gate, or geſture. Nay, ſo much do you ſeem reſolved to gratify this fooliſh riſibility of yours, that you contract falſe friendſhips with perſons, on purpoſe that they may be the more off their guard, and ſo give you greater opportunities of deriding them: witneſs the uſage of your friend Sir ONKELON KIMCHI, a man whoſe ſolid ſenſe and good conduct one would think might have raiſed in you a noble emulation, and not an ungenerous attempt to ridicule him; had you not very ingenuouſly and wiſely confeſſed, that you deſired his acquaintance for no other purpoſe. You ſeem in this, as well as your other actions, to be compleatly maſter of the folly, tho' not the innocence of the dove; and of the baſe ſubtilty of the ſerpent, like him, ſtinging thoſe moſt, about whom you twine.

'Tis owned by all, that your cloaths are rich, and well made; and that you ſometimes appear in company with men of the beſt fortunes. But theſe being the effects of your riches, are (in my opinion) no more to be aſcribed to your perſonal merit, than the eſtate, which your father got for you, is to be imputed to your induſtry.

As acquaintance with the rich ſerves to gratify your pride, ſo are they ſecure from being ſneered at by you; nor do you offer to diſtort the muſcles of your face at a man of five hundred a year.

I beg leave to inform you, that endeavouring to raiſe the company's laughter at another's expence, is no proof of a generous and candid temper; nor does ſucceeding in the attempt diſcover the leaſt grain of wit. We may daily ſee the moſt impertinent ſilly fellow do the very ſame, if he chance to be *vultu fortis et ære minax:* and as people of this ſtamp are but rarely given to bluſh, or be ſenſible of affronts, they have great advantages in a phiz-warfare, over any who contend with them, and are unqualified in theſe reſpects.

I muſt likewiſe give you a ſhort admonition, for your effeminate carriage; and if you diſlike being nick named Miſs SILVANA, be ſure from henceforth not to deſerve the title.

I would not have you think you have no other faults. When you amend theſe, I ſhall inform you farther; I have otherwiſe ſaid too much already, who am

Your Well-wiſher, &c.

Friend BAVIUS,

THO' I would not willingly ſay any thing to the prejudice of the Book-ſellers, thoſe great retalers of knowledge; much leſs againſt their Maſters-that-ſhould-be, the body of Writers; yet they muſt expect, and, I dare ſay, you will permit me (for the benefit of the much greater majority of mankind, the readers) to enter a caveat, in the records of your Society, againſt ſuch performances at leaſt, as deſerve to be ſtigmatized for cheats. Such I reckon thoſe, which do not anſwer the character they bear in their title. Not that I am againſt an Author's ſetting off his works with all the advantages that are conſiſtent with decency; even an *exegi monumentum ære perennius* I can pardon, on ſome occaſions; nay almoſt excuſe the hyperbolical ſtyle of a Grammarian of ſome note, who has juſt publiſhed *A propoſal of a new ſcheme of Grammar, and method of inſtruction, by which the grounds of a language may be learned in a few hours, ſo as to read an author, and write intelligibly*; becauſe his pretences are ſupported by pretty ſtrong probabilities. But to be tricked out of one's money, beſide loſs of time and patience, by a ſpecious title, with an empty performance, is what, I think, I am obliged to reſent; and, if you judge it not unſerviceable, ſhall, from time to time, bear my teſtimony againſt.

The piece I ſhall begin with, is the laſt I purchaſed, viz. *Apparatus ad linguam Græcam, ordine novo & facili digeſtus; in quo defectus aliorum quam-plurimi ſupplentur, &c. auctore* GEO. THOMSON. The title, as you will obſerve, bade me expect a new method, and an eaſy way: what do you think then muſt be my ſurprize, when I found it, not only old and trite, but ſhamefully encumbered with the moſt trifling ſuperfluities, to the great embaraſſment of learners? Again, by the title I am drawn in with hopes of a large ſupplement of the defects of other Grammarians: and, after all, I find nothing new, but that the work is incomparably more defective than any of the ſame ſize, that was ever publiſhed in any nation; and that we have abundance more in (what is already in every body's hands) the excellent *Rudiments* of the great Dr. BUSBY.

This may ſuffice to have obſerved in general: but as ſomething more particular may be expected, to render this charge more probable; the importance of the occaſion, tho' the ſubject be unpopular, will, I hope, excuſe the addition of the following obſervations. Whatever Mr. THOMSON may pretend to in his title, I do not find that he piques himſelf particularly on any thing, at leaſt, ſo much, as on his *Tabella verborum compoſitorum*; which he gives us with this introduction: 'Since none of the 'Grammars I have met with has treated this ſubject as it 'ſhould, I have ſubjoined the following table, by which 'ſuch verbs may very eaſily be formed.' Now, what is this table? why, only a parcel of compound verbs, carried through the moods, tenſes, and voices, and diſpoſed in columns, without ſo much as hinting at the peculiarities they are deſigned to teach, or even ſignifying that they are patterns to others: ſo that a learner, far from being led thereby into a juſt notion of the matter, may drudge through 12 pages, and, at the end, be very little the wiſer. And yet all this, which takes up ſo many pages, and more than this, I find very plainly taught by others in leſs than half a page; nay, with all the evidence that can be deſired, in a matter of three hexameter verſes, by the aforementioned Dealer in Grammatical novelties, in a new method of his, which I was likewiſe, on that account, induced to buy about 12 or 13 years ago. In like manner, I find a like diſproportion in the reſt of the main articles, e. g. The doctrine of verbs and adjectives takes up in THOMSON, a matter of 110 pages; in LOWE, a little above 5, &c

But I fear I have already tranſgreſſed too far, and therefore ſhall only add a reflection, or two, on what perhaps may be alledged to invalidate what I have aſſerted.—*Obj.* Is not this work publiſhed by Mr. OSBORN, approved—of by Mr. MORLAND, Mr. PILGRIM, Mr. WARD, Mr. PATRICK; and dedicated to Prince WILLIAM, with a proſpect of his uſing it? *Anſw.* Yes, but what then?——The young Prince's Governors know better, than to ſacrifice his time at ſuch a rate. For my part, were I to adviſe, inſtead of diſheartening the little Hero with the ſight of 279 pages, he ſhould not be troubled with above 5 or 6; into which compaſs, I apprehend, one might reduce what is neceſſary for a due knowledge of the language.——As to the Bookſeller, if he knew nothing of the matter, he is innocent of the impoſition; and 'tis pity he ſhould ſuffer by it.——For the worthy Gentlemen, who, he ſays, approve of it; if he wrongs them, or they wrong themſelves, I cannot help it: but truth is truth; and

I am Yours,

DOWNRIGHT HONESTY.

N. B. *An* Anſwer *to this letter, if not too long, ſhall be inſerted in this* Paper; *if any of the Gentlemen concerned think fit to ſend one.*

The following Copy of verſes came incloſed in a letter ſigned PHILANTHROPOS, who aſſured us, that they were written by a Lad of twelve years old; which are here publiſhed, as an extraordinary performance for one of that age.

RICHARDUS YEO, duodecim annorum puer. GULIELMO CHESSELDEN Lithotomorum præſtantiſſimo, qui me iv. Id. Apr. 1731, calculo è veſica extracto, ad ſalutem reſtituit.

O Gratitude, do thou inſpire,
And warm me with poetic fire;
Bid thou the Muſe to ſtretch her wing;
And raiſe her infant voice to ſing.
Be CHESSELDEN thy theme of praiſe,
The ſubject of thy earlieſt lays.
By him reſtor'd from pain to eaſe,
My life again begins to pleaſe.
But I ſuch ceaſeleſs racks before,
And ſuch inteſtine tortures bore;
That e'en a child I wiſh'd to die,
Nor grow a man in miſery.
PROMETHEUS felt not ſharper pain,
Tho' all were true the Poets feign:
Tho' beaked vultures, as 'tis ſaid;
On his renewing vitals prey'd.
Oft I complain'd the time was ſlow,
And linger'd out my hours of woe:
Weary of day, I wiſh'd the light
Would haſten, and give way to night;
Impatient of the night I lay,
And wiſh'd again for riſing day:
Nor day, nor night, my torments ceas'd;
The growing evil, ſtill encreas'd:
'Till thou (that day be ever bleſt,)
Wer't call'd, great Artiſt, from the weſt.
The work was in a moment done,
If poſſible, without a groan:
So ſwift thy hand, I could not feel
The progreſs of the cutting ſteel.
ÆNEAS could not leſs endure,
Tho' VENUS did attend the cure:
Not her ſoft touch, nor hand divine,
Perform'd more tenderly than thine;
When by her help IAPIS own'd,
The barbed arrow left the wound.
For quicker e'en than ſenſe, or thought,
The latent ill to view was brought;
And I beheld, with raviſh'd eyes,
The cauſe of all my agonies.
Of CÆSAR's ſword we wonders hear;
ALCIDES' club, PELIDES' ſpear:

Hi. th:e let others celebrate,
T:: watleful inſtruments of fate.
Thy lancet merits more by far,
Than all the weapons us'd in war:
By wounds, and death, they glory gain;
Thou triumph'ſt over death, and pain.
This I, with thouſands, witneſs true;
Whilſt that we live, we live by you.
That I inſtruction can attend;
Enjoy the converſe of a friend;
Delight o'er fields and meads to ſtray,
And with my dear aſſociates play;
That now my thoughts with eaſe can flow;
All this to hee, to thee I owe.
Henceforth, if any time I live;
It any joy I ſhall perceive;
If any good hereafter do;
To thee my thanks for all is due.
O! could I reach the true ſublime,
With energy of thought in rhime;
My verſe ſhould fair inſcribe thy name,
In laſting monuments of fame.
Long as my life its courſe ſhall run,
Till all the fatal thread be ſpun;
Each morn, as duly as I riſe,
Each eve before I cloſe my eyes;
When I adore th' Unſeen above,
In whom I live, in whom I move,
And pay my reverential praiſe,
For all the bleſſings of my days:
Recounting all, from firſt to laſt,
As I from youth to age have paſt;
In this memorial firſt ſhall ſtand
His mercy by thy ſaving hand;
And above all the race of men,
I'll bleſs my GOD for CHESSELDEN.

DOMESTIC NEWS.

C. *Courant.*	E P. *Evening Poſt.*
P. *Poſt-Boy.*	S J. *S. James's Evening Poſt.*
D P. *Daily Poſt.*	WE. *Whitehall Evening P.*
D J. *Daily Journal.*	L E. *London Evening Poſt.*

Hyp-o critic-oratorical Advertiſements in April	10
Ditto Puffs ——— ———	5
Hypochondriacal Advertiſements. ———	8
Ditto Puffs ——— ———	4
Sum Total ——— ———	27

Deduct the 5 ſundays in April, and there will be more than a Puff or Advertiſement for every day in the month. We have therefore two *Daily Advertiſers.*

THURSDAY, *May* 4.

We hear that the Prince of Naſſau Orange, who is contracted to the Princeſs Royal of Great Britain, will be made Governor of Hanover. *D P.*

An order is paſſed for all Officers, Horſe and Foot to repair immediately to their reſpective poſts. *D P.* ——— At Gibraltar and Port Mahon. *C.* — Sir Char. Hotham, Bar. is ſet out for Ireland, to viſit his Regiment there. *D P.*

The Duke and Dutcheſs of Dorſet embark'd on ſaturday ſe'nnight, with a fair wind; and after a few hours ſail a gale of wind ſprung up full in [took them ſhort in *D P.*] their teeth, continuing with ſuch violence for 36 hours, that they lay under a riefed main-ſail; the ſeas ran ſo high, that they broke into the ſtate room, where their Graces were in bed; which obliged them to put back into Carricfergus; but the wind ſpringing up at N. W. they arrived ſafe at Park-gate in about 8 hours. *C.*

Yeſterday the Lord Petre gave a grand entertainment, at his ſeat at Ingateſtone, to all his neighbours and tenants, &c. his Lordſhip will keep open houſe for 3 weeks for all comers and goers. *C.* ——— The Lady Webb has given her houſe in S James's ſquare to the Lord and Lady Petre for their Town reſidence. *S J.*

Yeſterday came on a Trial in the Court of King's-Bench, between Rob. and Mary Proof, Suſ. and Amy Whithall, Plaintiffs; and Sir Geo. Saunders, Knt. Fleuellin Aſpley, Tho. Bullock, and James Coleby, Defendants; on an iſſue directed out of Chancery, to try whether the Plaintiffs were ſole heirs, or coheirs with Sir Geo. Saunders, &c. to Sir Tho. Colby, Bar. The Trial laſted from 10 'till after 8, when the ſpecial Jury, of which Sir Tho. Croſs was Foreman, gave their verdict, that they were coheirs. The eſtate in conteſt is about 1200 l. per ann. *D P.*

The Rev. Mr. Geo. Reynolds, L. L. D Archdeacon of Lincoln, was inſtall'd Sub-dean of that Minſter, Ap. 24. *P.*

Sir Rob. Sutton, and Sir Archibald Grant, are expelled the Houſe of Commons, on account of the Charitable Corporation. *P. D P*

The ſame morning Abraham Ambroſe, Eſq; 2d ſon of the late Sir Tho. Ambroſe, Knt. an eminent Brewer in Houndſditch, was married to a Niece of the late Counteſs Dowager of Coleraine, an agreeable young Lady, with a fortune of 20,000 l. *DP. P.* — A few days ſince the Lord Viſc. Cullen was marry'd to Mrs. Warren, Daughter of Borlace Warren, Eſq; Repreſentative for Nottingham. *L E.*

On monday Mr. Rouſe, one of the Collectors of the Land Tax for Felſted in Eſſex, going to make his payment to the Receiver General, was robbed within 2 miles of his own houſe of 180 l. and upwards. *L E.*

On wedneſday died of a dropſy at Standgate, Mr. Jeſſeries, formerly Keeper of the Gate-houſe, and late of the Poultry Compter: he was reckoned one of the beſt Sollicitors in England; and 'tis thought the fatigue he underwent in aſſiſting Mrs. Longley at her Tryal at Guildford, haſten'd his death. *L E.* — *He would have done more juſtice* —— *to himſelf, had he left her* unaſſiſted *to be hanged.*

FRIDAY, *May* 5.

Orders have been given for 3 ſets of horſes to come from Hanover to Holland, to be in readineſs to eſcort his Majeſty on his arrival. *C.* ——— On monday a Meſſenger was diſpatch'd from the Secretary's Office, with orders for ſeveral ſetts of horſes, &c. his Majeſty being expected to ſet out the 17th inſt. *P.*

The South-Sea Company have received a Schedule from Spain for ſending a ſhip to La Vera Cruz, and on wedneſday begun to ſhip goods in the Prince William, whoſe name is now changed to the Royal Caroline. *D J.*

Will. Morris, Eſq; waited yeſterday on the Commiſſioners of the Cuſtoms for the goods and effects of the late Biſhop of Rocheſter, and had them deliver'd to him. *D J.*

Mr. Francklin has receiv'd notice of Tryal for the Sittings after Term, for printing and publiſhing an Anſwer to one Part of a late infamous Libel, intitled, Remarks on the Craftſman's Vindication of his two honourable Patrons, in which the Character and conduct of Mr. P. is fully vindicated, &c. *D P.*

Chriſtned, Males 130: Females 150: in all 280. *Buried* Males 159: Females 157: in all 316. Decreaſed in the burials this week 115. *P.*

SATURDAY, *May* 6.

Yeſterday at the Admiralty, their Lordſhips gave Orders for his Majeſty's Yatchs to be in a readineſs for ſailing at an hour's warning. Sir George Saunders was ſworn in Commander, under the R. Hon. the L. Viſc. Torrington. *P.* — The R. Hon. the L. Harrington, one of the principal Secretaries of State, and the Hon. Bar. Hartop, prime Miniſter for Hanover, are appointed to attend his Majeſty to Hanover. *C.* — The Hon. Pattee Byng, Eſq; Treaſurer of the Navy, [eldeſt. *P.*] ſon of the R. Hon. the L. Viſc. Torrington, is appointed one of his Majeſty's moſt Hon. Privy Council. *C. D P. D J.* — Monday the 29th inſt. is the day fixed for her Majeſty's removal from St James's to Kenſington. *P.* — On thurſday the Hon. John Fitzwilliams, Eſq; Page of Honour to his Majeſty, kiſs'd the King's hand, for the Poſt of Cornet in the Royal Regiment of Horſe Guards, Blue. *D P. D J.* — His Majeſty has appointed the Lord How to be Governor of Barbados. *S J.*

Laſt night about 8 o' clock, his Grace the D. of Dorſet, and his Dutcheſs, arriv'd at their houſe at White hall. *D J. C.* He was met at Barnet by Gentlemen and Tradeſmen to the number of 100. *P.*

Soon after the Parliament is broke up, we hear, that ſeveral Men of War will be put into Commiſſion; ſome to be guard ſhips, and others to cruiſe on the coaſt. *P.*

The R. Hon. the E. of Albermarle, who was to have embarked this day for his Regiment at Gibraltar, is countermanded; and his Majeſty (we hear) has been pleaſed to appoint him Colonel of a Regiment of Dragoons on the Engliſh Eſtabliſhment, commanded by the late L. Carpenter. *P.* — To promiſe him a Regiment, &c. *D J.* 8.

Canterbury, Ap. 26. At the General Quarter Seſſions of the Peace held for the Eaſtern Diviſion of this County on Friday laſt, the Juſtices took into conſideration the many illegal practices uſed by ſervants in husbandry, in order to extort exceſſive wages from maſters, and thereupon, according to direction of the Act of Parliament in that caſe provided, ſettled and directed their wages as follows;

	l.	s.	d.
Head Ploughman, Waggoner, or Seedſman by the Year	8	0	0
His Mate not exceeding	4	0	0
Beſt Woman Servant not exceeding by the year	3	0	0
Second ſort not exceeding	2	0	0
Second Ploughman not exceeding by the year	6	0	0
His Mate not exceeding	3	0	0
Labourers by the day, in ſummer	0	1	2
In winter	0	1	0

And whereas ſervants often neglect or refuſe to be retained at the expiration of their terms, till they can extort illegal wages; the Juſtices of the Peace, to prevent ſuch practices, determine, within their ſeveral diviſions, to order, that all ſuch ſingle perſons as lay at their own hands, and are fit to go to ſervice, or who ſhall refuſe to take the wages as above ſettled, ſhall, from time to time be brought before them, in order to be ſent to the houſe of correction, or further puniſh'd, as the law in ſuch caſe ſhall direct. *D J.* —— It is hoped the Magiſtrates of other Counties will regulate the wages of ſervants according to the cheapneſs of the place; for at Canterbury it's almoſt as dear living as at London. *L E.*

Cambridge in *New-England, Dec.* 30, 1731. Some time ſince died here Mr. Matthew A——y, in a very advanced age: he had for a great number of years ſerved the College here, in the quality of bed maker and ſweeper. Having left no child, his wife inherits his whole eſtate, which he bequeathed to her by his laſt will and teſtament, as follows:

TO my dear wife,
My joy and life,
I freely now do give her
My whole eſtate,
With all my plate,
Being juſt about to leave her.

A tub of ſoap,
A long cart rope,
A frying pan and kettle,
An aſhen pail,
A thraſhing flail,
An iron wedge and beetle.

Two painted chairs,
Nine warden pears,
A large old dripping platter;
The bed of hay
On which I lay,
An old ſauce pan for butter.

A litle mug,
A two quart jug,
A bottle full of brandy,
A looking-glaſs
To ſee your face,
You'll find it very handy.

A musket true
As ever flew,
A pound of ſhot and wallet,
A leather ſaſh,
My calabaſh,
My powder-horn and bullets.

An old ſword blade,
A garden ſpade,
A hoe, a rake, a ladder,
A wooden can,
A cloſe-ſtool pan,
A clyſter-pipe and bladder.

A greaſy hat,
My old ram cat,
A yard and half of linnen,
A pot of greaſe,
A woollen fleece,
In order for your ſpinning.

A ſmall tooth-comb,
An aſhen broom,
A candleſtick and hatchet,
A coverlid
Striped down with red,
A bag of rags to patch it.

A ragged mat,
A tub of fat,
A book put out by *Bunyan,*
Another book
By *Robin Rook,*
A skain or two of ſpun-yarn.

An old black muff,
Some garden ſtuff,
A quantity of borrage,
Some devil's weed,
And burdock ſeed,
To ſeaſon well your porridge.

A chafing diſh,
With one ſalt fiſh,
If I am not miſtaken,
A leg of pork,
A broken fork,
And half a flitch of bacon

A ſpinning wheel,
One peck of meal,
A knife without a handle,
A ruſty lamp,
Two quarts of ſamp,
And half a tallow candle.

My pouch and pipes,
Two oxen tripes,
An oaken diſh well carved;
My little dog
And ſpotted hog, [ſtarved.
With two young pigs juſt

This is my ſtore,
I have no more,
I heartily do give it,
My years are ſpun,
My days are done,
And ſo I think to leave it. *P.*

— *I would adviſe my good Friend* Mr. Curle *to employ ſome of my Brethren, to turn the* laſt Wills and Teſtaments, *of thoſe* Great Men *whoſe* Lives *he has written, into rhime, according to the preceding pattern.*

MONDAY, *May* 8.

Yeſterday the Rev. Dr. Bernard preached before their Majeſties, &c. *C.* — On ſaturday his Excellency Count Kinski, the Emperor's Ambaſſador, and the Envoy from the King of Poland, had their Audiences of leave of his Majeſty, &c. *P.* —— His Majeſty has been pleaſed to appoint Capt. Edw. Falkingham, Commander of the Saliſbury, to be Governor of Newfoundland. *P.*

On ſaturday morning ſeveral Officers, &c. embarked for their Regiments at Gibraltar and Port Mahon. *C.* — Who were to have accompany'd the Earl of Albemarle. *D P.*

The late Brigadier Gen. Pocock did, by his will, leave to the pariſh church of S. Martin in the Fields, a ſilver diſh and cup of 400 l. value. *D P.*

The Patent granted in 730 to Rob. Hamblin for 14 years, for the ſole uſe and benefit of a new invention for diſtinguiſhing of Lights at ſea, &c. was ordered on thurſday laſt in Council to be cancell'd. *D P.* —— The ſame day an order paſſed at the Treaſury to pay all arrears due to the Penſioners belonging to the Cheſt at Chatham to Mar. 25, 1731. *D J.*

On friday dy'd at her houſe in Bloomsbury-ſquare the Lady Hatton, Wife to Sir Thomas of Long-ſtanton in Cambridgeſhire, Bar. *D P.*

TUESDAY, *May* 9.

Yeſterday a great part of his Majeſty's baggage was ſent to Deptford; his Majeſty being, we hear, to ſet out on monday ſe'nnight. *P.*

The Lords Commiſſioners of the Admiralty have put the Durſley-Galley, a 6th rate, into commiſſion, and appointed Tho. Smith Captain, and Will. Bouſflower Lieutenant. *P.* It is expected ſhe will be put into commiſſion this day. *D P.*

Laſt week Mr. Alderman Arnham was elected Mayor of the city of Norwich. *S J.*

We hear that Major St. Clair is to have Col. Coſby's Regiment of foot. *SJ. WE.*

His Grace the D. of Bedford, who has been dangerouſly ill at his Seat at Woodburn Abbey in Bedfordſhire is in a very fair way of recovery. *WE.* —— His Grace the D. of Bedford is relapſed, and lies dangerouſly ill, *P.* 10.

Laſt thurſday Mr. Wyke of Clerkenwell, an eminent Malt Diſtiller, was married to Miſs Hope, a young Gentlewoman of 10,000l. fortune. *SJ.* —— Mr. John Wilks jun. *C.* 10.

They write from Aberdeen, that Mr. George Gordon, Teacher of the Mathematicks and experimental Philoſophy, now in London, is lately made Maſter of Arts by the Mariſchal College there; and that his Diploma was order'd to be ſent him in a very handſome manner. *DJ.*

WEDNESDAY, *May* 11.

His Excellency Baron Sparr, Envoy from the Court of Sweden, and Mynheer Hop from Holland, will accompany his Majeſty. *C.* —— We hear that the Parliament will certainly break up tueſday next. *DP.* —— Col. Phipps, a native of New England, is appointed Lieutenant Governor of the Province of Maſſachuſett's Bay. *DJ.*

On monday the Houſe of Lords revers'd the Judgment that was given by the Court of King's Bench, in the Cauſe that has ſo long depended between the Lord Biſhop of Ely, and the famous Dr. Bentley. *C.* — *About* 20 *years.*

Yeſterday the Gibraltar, a 6th rate, was put into Commiſſion at Deptford, Capt. Medley, being appointed to command her. *C.*

We are inform'd, that Dennis Bond, Eſq; is removed from being Letter Carrier to the Government, a place worth about 400 l. a year. *DP.*

From the PEGASUS *in Grub-ſtreet.*

Quandoquidem aliquot abhinc dies, atrox & immane flagitium in Perſonas quorundam mortuorum commiſſum fuit, nobis hoc, noſtrâ animadverſione perdignum exiſtimantibus, viſum eſt ex hac tripode oppugnari. Nec, ut opinor, fas erit hic præterire quendam, tam pacis, quàm dignitatis Academiæ, indeſeſſum Cuſtodem.

A wight he is, whoſe very ſize
Speaks him pacific, grave, and wiſe;
Whoſe double chin, and full-fed face,
Shews Juſtice there had fixt her place.
His knowledge, true, he could not boaſt of;
* *But what he* had, he made the moſt of:
Cou'd Charters make, and Warrants draw,
With all the petty plagues of Law.
Cou'd deal his little All about,
And eke his inch of Juſtice out.

Cum talis tantuſque ſit, quid non de tali Juſtitiæ mole expectare licet? Haud ita pridem, cùm ope cujuſdam ÆSCULAPII mortuus quidam è ſepulchro reſurrexiſſet; ille, haud abſurdè putans, ſui eſſe officii, tam inter mortuos, quàm inter vivos, pacem cuſtodire, convocavit Cœtum popularem; & e manu ſilentium provocanti ſic tandem vox prorumpit.

Since by his Majeſty's permiſſion,
I hold a place in the Commiſſion;
And, by a worthy Member's bounty,
Am Sub-Lieutenant of the County;
Therefore I ought, ſo vile the fact is,
To ſtop this moſt inhuman practice.
If robbing thus the Dead endure,
No man alive can be ſecure.
If to kill living men be murther;
To cut up dead men's ſomething further.
T'aſſault a man beſide his ſenſes,
We all allow a great offence is:
What then's th' offence to hack and maul
A man that has no ſenſe at all?
'Tis very baſe and vile, you know,
To give a peaceful man a blow;
And ſurely none ſo peaceful prove,
As thoſe who cannot ſtir or move.
We all allow, that Phyſic Knaves,
Oft ſend good people to their graves:
But you'd eſteem it ſtrange, no doubt,
Theſe ſelf-ſame men ſhou'd fetch them out;
As tho' the Faculty had ſwore,
T'undo what they had done before.
I therefore, Neighbours, who am here
Plac'd in condition popular,
Shall puniſh this ſame poſthumous murther,
Upon our dear departed Brother;
Aſſert my office too, that by it
The Dead may enjoy their graves in quiet.
Let's in, and none ſhall dare to ſtop us,
Unleſs they ſhow their *Habeas Corpus*.
Take up your poſts then, all and ſome,
And beat up my militia drum,
To make it known to all the nation,
When Juſtice angry is, —— ſhe's in a paſſion.

Prante 10 *Cal. Mai.*

* He had lately ſold his Books.

Peebles, Ap. 28. This day came on the election of a Member of Parliament for this Shire, when Sir Alex. Murray of Stenhope, was choſen Commiſſioner by a majority of good votes, and in preſence of the meeting, required the the Sheriff to return him. —— Sir Jam. Naſmith of Poſſo was choſen by a plurality of voices, and returned by the Sheriff. *P.* 9.

Edinburgh, May 1. The Profeſſors of the Univerſity have choſe the Rev. Mr. Profeſſor Hamilton as their Repreſentative in the General Aſſembly. *C.* In the room of the Rev. Mr. Profeſſor Crawford, who has deſired to be excuſed. *P.* 9. —— We hear from Kirkaldy, that Marg. White, aged 87, who has been toothleſs for many years, has juſt got out 8 new and freſh teeth. Her huſband is in hopes ſhe may bring a new progeny, as ſhe recovered, with theſe new tuſks, a blooming and juvenile air. *P.* —— *Theſe hopes are vain; the upper end of* old Women *being much longer* prolific *than the lower.*

FOREIGN NEWS.

THURSDAY, *May* 4.

Yeſterday arrived the Mail from France.

Liſbon, Ap. 3. The 31ſt was celebrated at Court the anniverſary of the Birth-day of the Princeſs of Braſil, who then enter'd into the 15th year of her age; in the evening ſhe went to the apartment prepared in the palace for her, and the Prince of Brazil, her Conſort. *C.*

FRIDAY, *May* 5.

Extract of a private letter from Genoa. —— A ſquadron of 6 Spaniſh men of war came into this port, and ſent an officer on ſhore, to take on board the money which the Queen had in the Bank of S. George, which is ſaid to amount to ſeveral millions, which was immediately delivered. *P.*

SATURDAY, *May* 6.

Yeſterday arrived the Mail from Holland.

Hague, May 13. Letters from Seville of the 18th ſay, the late Duke of Ormond was preparing to return to Madrid, whence, it was reported he would take a tour to Paris. *P. C. DP.* —— Thoſe from Peterſburg of the 21ſt adviſe the death of the L Duffus, a Rear-Admiral in the Czarina's ſervice, which happen'd at Croonſtadt, the 12th of that month. *P. C. DJ.* — The Count de Gallowin, Rear Admiral, has been declared Vice-Admiral and Inſpector General of the fleet. *C. DJ.*

MONDAY, *May* 8.

Yeſterday arrived the Mails from France *and* Flanders.

Paris, May 14. N. S. Our laſt letters from Leghorn adviſe, that 3 Galley ſlaves of the Republick having made their eſcape to the Rebels of Corſica, they were well received by them, and ſent back to the Dey of Algiers, who thereupon wrote them a letter of thanks, offering to ſuccour them. He at the ſame time ſent their two Generals each of them a fine ſabre with a gold hilt, one ſet with diamonds, the other with pearls, and a piece of ſcarlet for each. *C. P. DP.*

TUESDAY, *May* 9.

Yeſterday arrived the Mail from Holland.

Hague, May 16. We have no certain news yet of the Spaniſh fleet: but ſome ſay, they departed from Alicant the 24th ult. and ſteered towards Sardinia. The Peace between the Turks and Perſia, and that between the Czarina and Perſia, are confirmed. *P.* —— The new Prime Vizir is depoſed, and the Baſhaw of Tauris appointed in his ſtead. —— The Emperor's forces conſiſt, if complete, of 143,395. *C.* &c.

Books and Pamphlets publiſhed ſince our laſt.

4. All are not ſheep that wear ſheeps cloathing, &c.

Homeri Ilias Græce & Latinè cum annotationibus Sam. Clarke, S. T. P. Vol. II.

Co-Adamitæ, &c. Pr. 1 s.

A Sermon at S. Mary le Bow, on S. Mark's day: by Hen. Stebbing, D. D.

The Ladies Law.

5. A Philoſophical Enquiry into the phyſical ſpring of human actions. Pr. 1 s.

A Letter to a Biſhop, concerning ſome important diſcoveries in Philoſophy and Theology. Pr 1 s.

6. The Progreſs of a Rake. Pr. 1 s.

8. Bœoticorum liber; or, A new Art of Poetry, in 2 Cantos. Pr. 6 d.

The Mountebank, No. III. for March.

A ſelect Collection of Moliere's Comedies in French and Engliſh. Vol. I. Pr. 2 s. 6 d.

9. The true Cauſe of Declenſions in Religion. Pr. 6 d.

An Epiſtle to the R. Hon. John Earl of Orrery: by L. Theobald. Pr. 6 d.

Salvation by Jeſus Chriſt alone, &c. in 2 Sermons before the Univerſity of Oxford, Jan. 2, 6 by Tho. Cockman, A. M. Maſter of Univerſity College. Pr. 1 s.

The Dramatic Poetaſter: a Viſion, 3 Cantos. Pr. 1 s.

The Political State of G. Britain: for April.

The Watchful Chriſtian: a funeral Sermon, Ap. 2. By J. Watts, D. D.

A Letter to the Author of The Examination of the facts and reaſonings in the L. B. of Chicheſter's Serm. &c. P. 6 d.

On Tueſday Stocks were

South Sea Stock was 98, 98 1 8th, to 1 qr. South Sea Annuity 108 1 8th. Bank 147. New Bank Circulation 7 l. 15 s. Premium. India 178, 177 1 8th. Three per Cent. Annuity 97 1 qr. to 3 8ths. Royal Exchange Aſſurance 101 1 half. London Aſſurance 13 1 qr. York Buildings 7 1 qr. African 40. Engliſh Copper 2 l. 6 s. Welch ditto 1 l. 15 s. South Sea Bonds 2 l. 8 s. Premium. India ditto 6 l. ditto. Blanks 7 l. 7 s. 9 d. 20 l. Prizes 19 l. 14 s. 6 d.

ADVERTISEMENTS.

Next Week will be publiſhed,

MArci Hieronymi Vidæ Cremonenſis Albæ Epiſcopi Poemata quæ extant omnia. Quibus nunc primùm adjiciuntur ejuſdem Dialogi de Reipublicæ Dignitate. Ex collatione optimarum editionum emendata, præcipuè verò ad Cremonenſis fidem expreſſa; & in II Partes, II Tomis comprehenſas, diſtributas: additis Indicibus accuratis: à RICHARDO RUSSEL, A. M.

Impenſis Lawtoni Gilliver, & Johannis Nourſe, Bibliopolarum.

This Day is publiſhed,

A Journey from ALEPPO to JERUSALEM at Eaſter, A. D. 1697. The Fifth Edition. To which is now added an Account of the Author's Journey to the Banks of Euphrates at Beer, and to the Country of Meſopotamia. By HEN. MAUNDRELL, M. A. late Fellow of Exeter College, and Chaplain to the Factory at Aleppo.

Printed for J. Brotherton; J. Hazard; W. Meadows; T. Cox; W. Hinchliffe; W. Bickerton; T. Aſtley; S. Auſtin; L. Gilliver, and R. Willock.

Juſt publiſhed,

(By the late ingenious Mrs. ASTEL,)

SOME Reflections upon MARRIAGE. The Fourth Edition with Additions.

Printed for W. PARKER, at the King's Head in St. Paul's Church-Yard.

Where may be had, by the ſame Author,

1. The Chriſtian Religion, as profeſs'd by a Daughter of the Church of England.

2. A ſerious Propoſal to the Ladies for the Advancement of their true and greateſt Intereſt. Wherein a Method is offer'd for the Improvement of their Minds. In two Parts. The Fourth Edition.

3. An Enquiry after Wit, in Anſwer to the late Earl of Shafrſbury's Letter concerning Enthuſiaſm.

This Day is Publiſhed,

A SERMON on 2 Kings vii. 2. latter Part: Printed on the Occaſion of a late unparallel'd Inſtance of Diſtruſt in Providence, ſhewn in the wilful Murders committed by R. SMITH on the Bodies of his Wife and Child.

Put thou thy Truſt in the Lord, and be doing Good: Dwell in the Land, and verily thou ſhalt be fed. Pſalm xxxvii 3.

By a Divine of the Church of ENGLAND.

Printed for J. Roberts in Warwick-Lane. Price 6 d.

May 4 **was publiſhed,** Price 6d.

THE GENTLEMAN's MAGAZINE: Or, *Monthly Intelligencer.* NUMB. XVI. for APRIL.

Containing more in Quantity, and greater Variety than any other Book of the Kind and Price, viz.

I. A View of the Weekly Eſſays, viz. Religion and Deiſm; Ambition and Avarice; Wit and Madneſs; Church Muſick; Dr. Bentley's Manner of Criticiſm, Miſchiefs of Bargains in Marriage; Liberty of Conſcience; Arguments for the Tythe Bill; Female Piety; Coquetry; Friendſhip &c.

II. Political Points; viz. Remarks on the Reign of King Charles I. King William and Queen Mary's Characters; Parallel Hiſtory; Orations of Demoſthenes; the Revolution vindicated; Conſiderations on the South Sea Affairs; Corruption, &c. Voltaire's Hiſtory.

III. Poetical Pieces, viz. Dean Swift in good Quarters; the Free Maſon; the Farmer's Daughter; Receipt to Courtſhip.

IV. Domeſtick Occurrences, Births, Deaths, Marriages, the melancholy Caſe of Richard and Bridget Smith, with their genuine Letters of Apology for Self Murder; Executions; Duke of Dorſet's dangerous Paſſage.

V. Prices of Goods, Grain, Stocks, &c. as the former.

*** N. B. *The Cuſtomers to the* GENTLEMAN's Magazine, *or* Monthly Intelligencer, *are deſired to take Care that they are not deceived by a Book with a ſimilar Title, which may be offer'd them at ſome Shops, and as they have been ſo kind to encourage this uſeful Undertaking, it is hoped they will not, by any Artifice, be miſled to favour an Attempt ſo unfair and ungenerous as the ſupplanting an Author in his whole Plan, Deſign, and even Title. A Practice which would be condemned by every Individual concerned in it, if their own Caſe. And the Public may be aſſur'd that, whatever our Rivals may pretend, nothing ſhall excell this Magazine.*

The above N. B. tho' entirely defenſive, has been rudely attack'd in ſome Advertiſements that are impertinent in every Reſpect, except ſubmitting to the Judgment of the Public, to which we freely agree.

It was on account of the Eſſays, ſeveral Occurrences, and the Elections of ſome Members of Parliament, being omitted, that we preſum'd to call a ſimilar Book *defective.*

Printed at St. John's Gate, and ſold by F. Jefferies in Ludgate-ſtreet, and all the Bookſellers.

Where may be had all the former Numbers.

This Day is published, (Price 6 d.)

By Mr. LOWE of Hamerſmith,

THE WHETSTONE: A Propoſal of a *New Scheme of Grammar, and Method of Inſtruction;* by which the grounds of a language may be learned in a Few Hours, ſo as to read an author and write intelligibly. — With a *Specimen of the Deſign* in a Syſtem of FRENCH *Rudiments,* containing a full account of the grounds of that language in Five Pages. — Sold by J. Noon in Cheapſide — Where may be had GREEK, LATIN, ITALIAN *Rudiments,* on the ſame Plan, by the ſame Author — with a VOCABULARY and SENTENTIÆ PUERILES, in a method entirely new, for a ſpeedy gaining a *Copia of Words, Phraſes, Idioms, Apophthegms, Proverbs,* and various other uſefull Peculiarities.

This Day is published,

A MUSE in LIVERY. A Collection of POEMS on various Subjects.

Written by a FOOTMAN.

Printed for John Noarſe at the Lamb without Temple-bar. Price 1 s. 6 d.

Juſt published,

(In 3 Vols. Octavo. Price 15 s.)

SEveral SERMONS, chiefly upon Practical Subjects, many of which were publiſhed before her preſent Majeſty when Princeſs of Wales. By her Chaplain in Ordinary, the late Reverend Nicholas Brady, D. D. Rector of Clapham, and Miniſter of Richmond in Surrey. Now firſt publiſhed from the Author's Manuſcripts.

Printed for Tho. Osborne, in Gray's-Inn.

Where may be had, juſt publiſhed, The Practical Conveyancer. In two Parts. Part 1ſt. Containing Rules and Inſtructions for drawing all Sorts of Conveyances or Eſtates and Intereſts, whether Real or Perſonal, in poſſeſſion or Expectancy: Alſo particular Rules for the Expoſition of Deeds, Wills, &c. and of Words uſed in Conveyances. Together with the Reſolutions of ſeveral Courts at Weſtminſter, in Caſes wherein Difficulties have ariſen touching the Words and Clauſes in Deeds, Deviſes, &c. The whole extracted, by way of Abridgment, from the Reports at large of the ſaid Caſes, and alphabetically digeſted under proper Heads. Part 2d. Being the firſt Part reduced into Practice, in a ſelect Collection of Precedents, viz. Marriage-Settlements; Bargains and Sales; Leaſes and Releaſes; Deeds of Copartnerſhip or Exchange; of Releaſe and Confirmation; Mortgages; Surrenders; Wills; Letters of Attorney; Aſſignments of Stocks; and Exchequer Annuities; Eccleſiaſtical Inſtruments, &c. By JOHN LILLY, Gent. The Second Edition corrected, and very much enlarged. To which are now added, Caſes in Chancery, under all the Titles of Conveyancing, digeſted by way of Common-Place, under alphabetical Heads.

To be RUN for.

ON the Common of MORFE near BRIDGNORTH, in the County of Salop, on the 13th and 14th Days of June next, will be run for two Plates, viz.

The Firſt, being a Purſe of Forty Guineas, by any Horſe, Mare or Gelding, carrying 12 Stone, the beſt of three Heats; every ſuch Horſe, Mare or Gelding, to be ſhewn and enter'd at the Market-houſe in the Town of Bridg-North, and to be kept in the ſaid Town ſeven Days before the Day of Running; and any Horſe, Mare or Gelding, which ſhall win the ſaid Purſe, is to be raffled for, if demanded, at Fifty Guineas, by the Subſcribers then preſent. Every Subſcriber who owns any Horſe, Mare or Gelding, which ſtarts for this Plate, ſhall pay one Guinea on the Day of entering to the Clerk of the Courſe; but the Perſon not being a Subſcriber, ſhall pay two Guineas, and one Guinea more in Caſe ſuch Horſe, &c. wins the Plate; all to be appropriated for the Benefit of the ſecond beſt Horſe.

The Second Plate is a Purſe of twelve Guineas, to be run for by any Galloways that never won the Value of above twenty Guineas, carrying nine Stone, if under Size, Weight for Inches.

N. B. There will be a Cocking.

Juſt Published, beautifully Printed,

SERMONS and Diſcourſes on Practical Subjects never before printed, by Robert Moſs, D. D. late Dean of Ely, and Preacher to the honourable Society of Gray's-Inn. Publiſhed from the Originals, at the Requeſt of the ſaid Society; with a Preface, giving ſome Account of the Author, by a learned Hand, in 4 Vols. 8vo.

Printed for Richard Williamſon, near Grays-Inn Gate, Holbourn; and William Thurlbourn, at Cambridge; and ſold by Thomas Osborne, near Grays-Inn Walks.

This Day was published,

Dedicated to the KING.

REVELATION *Examin'd with* CANDOUR.

OR, A FAIR

ENQUIRY into the SENSE and USE of the ſeveral REVELATIONS expreſsly declared, or ſufficiently implied, to be given to Mankind from the *Creation,* as they are found in the BIBLE. By a profeſs'd Friend to an honeſt Freedom of Thought in Religious Enquiries. PART I. Containing DISSERTATIONS upon the ſeveral Revelations from the CREATION to the FLOOD, incluſive.

Printed for C. Rivington, at the Bible and Crown in St Paul's Church-Yard.

This day is published,

INTEREST at one View calculated to a Farthing, at 3, 4, 5, 6, 7 and 8 per Cent. from 1000 l. to 1 l. for one Day to 96 Days; and for 1, 2, 3, 4, 5, 6, 7, 8, 9, 10, 11, and 12 Months: With Rules and Examples to caſt up Intereſt at any other Rates by the ſaid Tables. To which is added, A Table for the more ſpeedy caſting up of Salaries and Wages, from one Million to one Pound per Year. Beſides many other Tables of great Uſe in receiving and paying of Monies. The Whole being calculated, examined and corrected, and afterwards re-examined from the Preſs.

By RICHARD HAYES.

Printed for W. Meadows, at the Angel in Cornhill.

Where may be had, by the ſame Author,

1. The Purchaſer's Pocket Companion; ſhewing at Sight what Intereſt is made by Money laid out in the Companies Stocks, or other publick Funds.

2. The Negociator's Magazine of Monies and Exchanges, with a compleat Treatiſe of Arbitrations of Exchanges.

3. The Ship and Supercargo Book-Keeper, ſhewing the Manner of the Maſters ſettling Accounts with their Owners, the Privilege of Merchants, and Duty of Officers; with Supercargo's Accompts after the Italian Method of Double Entry.

4. An Eſtimate of Places for Life, calculated on the Chances of Lives in general, with an Account of Places in the Diſpoſal of the City of London, and their Value.

This Day is published,

AN ANSWER to Mr. FOGG'S Sham-Propoſal, for erecting a Statue to the Memory of King WILLIAM. In a Letter to a Gentleman in the Country.

Faithful are the Wounds of a Friend; but the Kiſſes of an Enemy are deceitful. Prov. xxvii. 6.

Printed for J. Roberts, at the Oxford-Arms in Warwick-Lane. Price Four Pence.

This Day is published,

[Price Six-Pence.]

BÆoticorum Liber: Or, A New Art of Poetry; containing the beſt Receipts for making all Sorts of Poems, according to the Modern Taſte. In Two Canto.

— *Verſus inopes rerum, nugæque canore Validus oblectant Populum.* Hor.

Te doceam tanere, & mea Te præcepta jervaiunt, Nunquam hinc, ne dubita, prorſum inconſultus abibis. Vida.

DUBLIN, printed: London, re-printed, and ſold by J. Roberts in Warwick-Lane.

Where may be had, juſt publiſh'd,

1. The Advantages propos'd by repealing the Sacramental Teſt, conſider'd.

2. City Cries, Inſtrumental and Vocal.

3. The Soldier and Scholar.

4. Scheme from Ireland.

5. Love and Ambition. A Tragedy.

6. The Nature and Conſequences of the Sacramental Teſt, conſider'd.

7. Conſiderations on two Iriſh Bills, relating to the Clergy. By Dr. SWIFT.

8. Longford's Givn. A true Hiſtory.

9 The Progreſs of Beauty. A POEM.

Lately published,

And Sold by J. Brotherton *at the* Bible *over-againſt the* Royal-Exchange *in* Cornhill, *A New Edition of*

LES Aventures de Telemaque, Fils d'Ulyſſe. Par feu Meſſire Francois de Salignac de la Motte Fenelon, Precepteur de Meſſeigneurs les Enfans de France, & depuis Archeveque-Duc de Cambrai, Prince due Saint Empire, &c. Nouvelle Edition, conforme au Manuſcript Original. Enrichie d'un grand Nombre de Figures en Taille Douce. Avec des Remarques pour l'eclairciſſement de cet Ouvrage.

This new Edition is correctly printed, with a good Letter, upon a fine Paper, with 25 Cuts and a Map, all engrav'd by the beſt Hands, and is no way inferior to the Hamburgh Edition, and is ſold 30 per Cent. cheaper than that Edition; and beſides, farther Allowance will be made to all Gentlemen who take Numbers to uſe in ſchools.

N. B. This Edition has 12 Cuts more than that of Hamburgh.

LONDON: Printed by S. PALMER and J. HUGGONSON, in *Bartholomew-Cloſe,* for Captain GULLIVER, near the *Temple,* where Letters and Advertiſements are taken in; As alſo at the *Rainbow Coffee-Houſe* in *Cornhill,* and *John's Coffee-Houſe* in *Sheer-Lane,* near *Temple-Bar.* [Price Two Pence.]

The Grub-street Journal.

Thursday, *MAY* 18, 1732.

Extract of a *Discourse relating to* King WILLIAM *and* Bishop BURNET; *in answer to a Letter in the* Daily Journal.—— Printed in the *London Journal,* Ap. 29.

YOU set out with asking me a Question, as a Casuist in Morality, 'Whether an Author, who publishes a fact tending to destroy the character of another, when that fact is positively contradicted, is not bound to produce either his *authority* or *proofs,* on pain of being branded as the inventor of the calumny?' No, for 'tis so far from being *moral,* that is, *reasonable,* to name the persons from whom I had the several facts, that it would be absolutely *immoral,* and breaking through the most *sacred ties* of private conversation and friendship, to name them without their consent.

Till I have their consent, which I'll endeavour to get, the facts following stand upon *my authority*; which, by all who know me, will be equal to any man's in the kingdom.

I do affirm, That Dr. BURNET's obtaining the Bishoprick of *Salisbury,* by virtue of a promise from the Queen, and not from King WILLIAM's inclinations, is attested by a Gentleman of undoubted integrity, who held a Post of great honour and trust under King WILLIAM, who was intimately acquainted with his Majesty, and had the story from the King himself.

You say, 'No person will imagine, that a promise 'made in *Holland* would have weight enough to promote 'an unacceptable man in *England.*' And can you think it improbable, that K. W. would in the infancy of his power, which he owed originally to his marriage with the Queen, refuse her Majesty such a favour, to a man who had done him service, tho' he did not like his qualities, nor approve of his mind, so far as to admit him into his confidence and councils?

You say further, 'That Dr. B. was so far from seek-'ing this Bishoprick for himself, 'that he went to sollicit 'in the behalf of his friend Dr. LLOYD.' If this is true, it weighs nothing against the probability of the other story: for at that time, which, I think, was before the Coronation, Dr. B. might imagine, that his merit and interest were great enough to put him at the head of the Church; and to make him Archbishop when SANCROFT resigned: but when the King gave the cold answer which you mention, *that he designed it for another person,* he might then go to the Q. plead her promise, and insist on it for himself.

I do also affirm, That another Gentleman of equal integrity, who hath read the *Memoirs* of the M——— of H——— told me those very words were in the *Memoirs.* 'Such a day Dr. BURNET told me, That King WILLIAM 'was an obstinate conceited man, that would take no ad-'vice. And such a day King WILLIAM told me, That 'Dr. BURNET was a troublesome impertinent man, whose 'company he could not endure.

And thirdly I affirm, That there is a Noble Peer now living, well known for his high sense of probity and ho-nour, and an inviolable attachment to the interests of his Country, who asserts the truth of that story about *altering his whole Character,* on his granting the Bishop a favour, which could not be obtained at Court without his consent. These three things I know to be true, and they rest, at present, upon my authority.

Extract of a *Letter to* Mr. OSBORNE, *occasioned by his* London Journal *of Saturday last,* Ap. 29.—— Printed in the *Daily Journal,* May 3.

NOW, Sir, I say, that a man who had either *pru-dence,* or any regard to the *moral obligation to truth,* or to his own reputation, would not have ventured positively to assert in print (for you do it not by way of hear say in the *Journal* of the 15th) a fact, which might very probably be disputed, without having first obtained *leave* of his Authors, in case of necessity, to vouch them; and if they refused him this *leave,* would give no credit to what they related.

Should an inquisitive reader ask, Who this OSBORNE is, that settles the characters of Kings, Princes, and Bishops that he never saw; has Anecdotes from Noble Peers and Great men that must be nameless; and whose *authority* (if you believe himself) would *be equal to any man's in the kingdom*; would not the Answer raise a laugh not un-mix'd with indignation?

Somehow the integrity you do not question, who had a Government, as you have been told, and who says is intimately acquainted with K. W.) has told you, that the K. told him that Dr. B &c. Do you not see, that it is not sufficient in this case to believe your *veracity,* as to the words related, but also we must adopt your *judgment* implicitly, as to the character of your Author, which perhaps some other people may be better acquainted with than yourself?

I might have added many other improbabilities, as that Q. MARY, if K. WILLIAM had a personal dislike to Dr. B. should be ignorant of it; or that, knowing it, she should engage to serve him; that she, who in all things a pattern of conjugal submission, should promise away Bishop-ricks without consulting her Husband; and this too at a time, when at best it was very doubtful if either of 'em would ever have a right or power to dispose of any.

Now I will appeal to any man of common sense, if it be imaginable, that Dr. B. (who, as you pretend, was so vigilant after his own interest, as even in Holland to sollicit and obtain the promise of a Bishoprick) should quite forget himself in England, when so good a Bishoprick as Salisbury was vacant, and should go to the K. and sollicit for a friend? Let us see then how you would evade this: even according to custom, by coining a piece of *secret History,* but which (not according to custom) you are honest enough to own you have *no authority* for. 'Dr. B. say you, *might* imagine his merit and interest '*might* make him Archbishop when SANCROFT *might* 'resign; but when the K. gave the cold answer, he '*might* go to the Queen, &c.' He might, and he might not. Was there ever such a way of answering a fact? Who, pray, informed you, that he ever had any desire of going to *Lambeth*? Does his great and uninterrupted friendship with Dr. TILLOTSON favour of a man who had been crossed in his views to the same Dignity? Would the taking *Salisbury* have been any hindrance to the Archbishoprick, when it should become vacant; or was there any certainty that it shortly would be so? Was it ever known that *Sancroft* would; or did he ever in fact resign? And when he had refused the oaths, did he not continue in his Dignity 'till 1691? Was it likely therefore that Dr. B. should neglect a present Preferment of 3000 l. a year, in hopes of a greater, which might not fall in his life-time, and to which his present promotion could be no hindrance?

To this I had said, 'That if this entry was a real one, it 'would prove no more, than that the Bishop had given ad-'vice, which the King at the time was out of humour with 'him for; and not a settled dislike of him?' But since this, like your former *Tale,* stands unattested, I am at liberty to call it a *Forgery,* especially as there are Letters and a Character of the Bishop, by the Marq. of Halifax, which no ways agree with your quotations.

One OSBORNE, a *Weekly Writer,* and as some say, a *Writer* in pay, affirms, upon his unquestionable credit, That a Noble Lord (who does not consent to be named) *told him,* That somebody else (who must too be nameless) had *told him,* that he stood with *an ill grace in the History,* (which, perhaps, neither the *nameless* Peer, nor his *name-less* Informer ever saw) 'till granting the Bishop a favour, he *told* another *nameless friend* of this Lord, (who *told* him again) *That he must go and alter his whole Character.*

Extract of an *Answer to a Letter in the* Daily Journal [May 3]——Printed in the *London Journal,* May 13.

I Do assure you, that I would never have produced my Vouchers *without leave,* because I count that *immoral,* and breaking upon *the laws* of private Conversation. You own: but know how tenderly *great Names* are to be used; how *rash,* and indeed *unsafe,* it would be to bring them into publick disputes.

Yes, indeed, a loud laugh against the Querist: for, I'll tell you, Sir, who this OSBORNE is; he is a man who spent the first part of his life in *study,* and the latter part in *conversation;* and who hath always so behaved, as to be well received in the company of Gentlemen of *integrity,* who understand *books* and *men*; and the highest cha-racter he pretends to, is that of an *honest man,* and an *agreeable companion;* who hath an equal right with you to ask in his turn, who is this S. T. or. pray, Sir, who are you? and what sort of understanding must you have, to think, That a Man who has *read good authors,* and keeps variety of *good company,* may not be as able to *judge* of, and *draw* the characters of Kings, Princes, Bishops, as a man with a *Title,* a *Ribban, Lawn-sleeves,* or a plentiful *estate* handed down from the conquest? As to my *authority's* being *equal* to any man's in the Kingdom, it is so *in this case* for there are no *degrees* of honesty, or sincerity, as there are of knowledge and power. All honest men are *equally* honest.

The Gentleman from whom I had the fact relating to the Bishoprick of *Salisbury,* is at the *Bath*; but as soon as he comes home, which will be in about a fortnight, you shall be entirely satisfied on what authority I rested: for men, tho' of the strictest honour and probity, don't care to have their names in publick Papers, 'nor to be en-gaged in personal disputes.

The King knew him [the Bishop] to be very credulous, and easy to be imposed upon; a great Harkner to stories, and a great retailer of them; that tho' he was a *good man,* hearnly in the Revolution, yet he was not a *wise man,* nor able to keep a secret, and therefore unfit for publick ma-nagement; so unfit, that when the 3 Commissioners came from K. JAMES to treat with the P. of ORANGE at Hun-gerford, he bid those about him *lock up* BURNET, *for he would blab and spoil all.*

What an unfortunate man are you, never to deviate into one just remark! For this supposition is not brought to answer your fact, but to reconcile the *two facts,* yours and mine. I affirm, mine is true; and, if yours is so too, (which in Civility I allow'd) then the supposition is rea-sonable; for Dr. B. had reason to expect SANCROFT would resign; or, at least, not take the oaths, and lose his Bishoprick; for at that time, Bishop KENNET says, he re-fused to consecrate Dr. BURNET: The Historian's words are, *His Grace the Archbishop of Canterbury began now to deny the legality of the new Government, &c.* What is become now of your triumphant Question, 'Was it ever 'known that SANCROFT would resign? with a hundred more of equal use to your argument?

The fact from the *Memoirs* of the M—— of H——— you can satisfy yourself about; for those *Memoirs* are pro-bably in the hands of one of the Noblemen, who married the Heiresses of the S——— family.

The Great Person referred to, is of the highest Quality, as well as of the highest Character; such a Character, as all men who know it, would immediately allow to decide in any point of debate: But, tho' I presume not to name him here, I hope I can give you full satisfaction, by referring you to Mr. *Woodward,* Bookseller in Fleet street, who can convince you, that, what I have said, I have said upon good authority; and the fact is stronger than I told it; for the Bishop came himself, and told the Noble Peer, *That he must go and alter his whole Character.*

Mr. OSBORNE's Letter in *London Journal*, Ap. 29.

Would the Biſhop, had he liked the King, as well as he did the Revolution, have ſaid of him, that he had a *ſecret vice*, which was thought too abominable to name? Would a man in the King's confidence and councils, highly eſteeming, and highly eſteemed by him, have affirmed in a *publick Hiſtory* of the King his Maſter, Benefactor, and Friend, that he had a vice, which could no way relate to the Publick, which the Publick was ignorant of, and which left the reader's imagination open to apprehend a vice the moſt unnatural, and moſt ſhocking to human minds?

Extract of a *Letter to* Mr. OSBORNE, *occaſioned by the* London Journal, May 13. Printed in the *Daily Journal. May* 16.

AS to your ribald aſperſions on the Biſhop's reputation, it were an injury to it, but to ſuppoſe they wanted an anſwer, any more than your new-coined ſtory at Hungerford. His character is placed as much above the reach of your Scandal, as it was of your Knowledge.

That *Letter Writer* ſays, That there was not an *angry* word in his letter, though there were many compaſſionate ones; that in it he did not complain of injuſtice done to himſelf, but to poor unhappy orphans, whoſe *Father's* ſervices and diſburſements merited another treatment; and that the injuſtice was and could be done only by the *Perſon*, to whom the letter was wrote; which, if he pleaſes, may be given you to print, and then the Publick will judge of it. —— * Fye for ſhame! if your Patrons, your Directors, your Pay-maſters can't prevail upon you not to print ſuch ſtuff, methinks your Bookſeller Mr. *Peele*, who is a ſenſible man, ſhould not ſuffer it. For my part, were Biſhop *Burnet's* character once reſcued from your dirty clutches, I would not be bound to read your *Journals*, for twice the penſion you have for writing them.

How do your three *facts* ſtand now? — The firſt, relating to Queen MARY's promiſe in Holland, ſtands with all its abſurdities about it, and no voucher yet to ſupport it, ſo that being a fatherleſs ſtory, like other ſpurious iſſue, it muſt lye at the door of the perſon who uſher'd it into the world, 'till you can find a father for it. —— The ſecond *fact* relates to a paſſage in *Memoirs* that are in the hands of a certain family. The paſſage is of no conſequence when it is proved; but hitherto nobody aſſerts, that they have ſeen it, and therefore nobody is bound to believe it. —— As to your third *fact*, If Mr. *Woodward*, the Bookſeller, has named the right perſon to a friend of mine, it is vouch'd by one, who can never be mentioned with terms of too much honour and *reſpect*. In what manner, with what intent, and upon what occaſion the Biſhop might ſay thoſe words, I muſt not preſume to inquire. But this the perſon, in whoſe cuſtody the Biſhop's *Hiſtory* now is, has authorized me to affirm, That whatſoever Dr. BURNET might *ſay*, he did not, nay he could not *go and alter his whole character*: for there is but one copy of the *Hiſtory* in the Biſhop's own hand-writing, (the other is a Copy from that by a ſervant) and there is no character of the Perſon (Mr. *Woodward* named) in the whole *Hiſtory*, unleſs the tranſient expreſſion of *very brave*, can be called a character. The Noble Perſon is mentioned but in five places of the *Hiſtory*, and in all theſe there is no razure, or word ſtruck out, nor is there any interlineation that alters the ſenſe. And for proof of this, the original manuſcript is ready to be produced, in the manner, which the Printer of this Paper will inform any proper Perſon that ſhall inquire.

S. T.

S. T's Letter in *Daily Journal*, May 3.

Like a very *honeſt man*, that has a great concern for the glorious memory of King WILLIAM, you are pleaſed to term [this] a vice *too abominable to name*, &c. Pray, why muſt this be ſo abominable a vice? Why muſt the Reader's imagination be as vile as Mr. OSBORNE's, and immediately apprehend the moſt *unnatural*? Is there any thing in the Biſhop's words to warrant ſuch a conſtruction? He ſays, 'That he had no vice but of one ſort, 'in which he was very cautious and ſecret?' Now if the Reader is pleaſed to conſider this Character, as drawn in the Life-time of Q. MARY, he will ſcarce let his imagination apprehend, that this vice muſt be the moſt ſhocking to human minds. ——— The Biſhop would not LYE for him [his Benefactor, Friend, and Patron] to poſterity, but ſaid he had *one vice*, and *but one*. Oh glorious Prince! Look through the Hiſtorians of all ages, and ſhew me ſuch another King! who had but *one vice*, and ſo far from being above the rules of decency, took care to conceal even that from giving offence, or ſetting an ill example.

I ſaid Mr. OSBORNE *is a miniſterial Writer, as ſome would inſinuate*; He is angry at this, and yet in the ſame breath owns, that Mr. D'ANVER's has called him ſo; which is all that I had advanced. Far be it from me to affirm him to be ſuch. It would be great ill manners to ſuſpect men of wiſdom, dignity, and power, of employing ſuch a Champion in their Cauſe. Tho' perhaps in a *bad one*, it might be policy to employ a *round Aſſerter*, who is not out of countenance when he is contradicted, and cannot maintain his aſſertions.

* *This relates particularly to the great character* Mr. OSBORNE *gives himſelf; which is printed in the ſecond paragraph of the third column on the other ſide.*

Mr. OSBORNE's Letter in *London Journal*, May 13.

The Biſhop's mentioning that *one vice*, which the King took ſo much care to keep *ſecret*, was not only the weakeſt thing in the world, but ſeemed to flow from reſentment: And Sir, in what Cell have you lived, not to know, that all the enemies to the Revolution and King WILLIAM, beſides a great many others, have conſtantly inſinuated, That had not that vice been too abominable to be named, the Biſhop would have named it? and have not the friends to K. WILLIAM been put to great difficulties to defend him againſt thoſe inſinuations?

But, you ſay, the Biſhop would not LYE; and who but *Higgons*, *Jacobites*, and *Nonjurors* ſay he would? But would he have been a *Lyar*, not to have mentioned a vice, which the world knew nothing of? What hath a Prince's private life to do in a publick Hiſtory? or would any man but an Enemy, or an Ideot have mentioned in an Hiſtory to be tranſmitted to poſterity, a vice of a Prince ſo private, that no body knew any thing of it, 'till he told it? What does this ſhew, love of truth, or love of tale bearing? Manly virtue, or childiſh folly? Affection to K. W. or contempt of his memory?

When you call me *Weekly Writer*, *Writer in pay*, &c. you become (as Mr. *D'Anvers* very well ſays, a *Male ſcold*, a mere *Mob-Writer*; you ſhow, that you are as ignorant of the character of the perſon you write to, as of the ſubject you write about; .... Mr. OSBORNE .... is neither *in pay*, nor does he *ever expect* to be paid; he wants nothing; and will always *ſo* live, as never to want: He has indeed been obliged to *One Gentleman* in power; and but *one* in his whole life. He aſk'd that Gentleman about the ill uſage of the *Burret* Family, who gave him leave to ſay, That a *certain perſon* wrote him an angry letter once, (I find that's his uſual way) but *that he never did him any injuſtice in his life*. As to other Gentlemen in power, I don't know them; nor have I any thing to ſay about them. I worſhip power no more than you.

DOMESTIC NEWS.

C. *Courant.*	E P. *Evening Poſt.*
P. *Poſt-Boy.*	S J. *S. James's Evening Poſt.*
D P. *Daily Poſt.*	WE. *Whitehall Evening P.*
D J. *Daily Journal.*	LE. *London Evening Poſt.*

THURSDAY, *May* 11.

The ſquadron of men of war, which conſiſt of 7 ſail, appointed to convoy his Majeſty to Holland, is order'd to the Nore, to be in readineſs to receive his Majeſty. *C.* Under the command of the L. Viſc. Torrington. *D P.* — Yeſterday their Majeſties went to ſee the Princeſſes Mary and Louiſa perform their exerciſes on horſeback, at the Riding-houſe at Kenſington: they are taught to ride by Mr. Backenſwantz, Clerk of her Majeſty's ſtables. *D P.* — His Majeſty's Chappel at Whitehall is now repairing and beautifying, and a new gallery is erecting for the reception of the Royal Family. *P.*

Yeſterday the Court of King's Bench was moved for an information againſt Mr. Oſborne, a Printer in the Minories, for printing and publiſhing a Libel, reflecting on the Jewiſh nation, charging ſome of thoſe people with committing a barbarous murder, in burning an infant that was begot by a Chriſtian on the body of a Jewiſh woman; by reaſon of which they were frequently inſulted by the populace. The Court granted a Rule for the Defendant to ſhew cauſe this term. *P.* — *I hope the* King's Bench *will be* moved *e'er long* for an information againſt *ſeveral* Printers for printing and publiſhing libels, reflecting on *all* Chriſtian nations, *for their folly and ſtupidity in being ſuch.*

They write from Mitchel-Dean in the County of Glouceſter, that on friday Ap. 28th, between 7 and 8 in the evening, as ſuppoſed, one Tho. Turbeville, Carpenter, was in a moſt barbarous and inhuman manner murder'd in his own ſhop, having his brains beat out, and his ſkull chopp'd to pieces with a broad axe: the deceaſed being a Widower, and having no child, liv'd alone, and was not found 'till ſaturday evening, when the axe was lying by him bloody. A Weaver of the ſaid Town is taken up on ſuſpicion, having been obſerved between the hours abovementioned, to follow the ſaid Turbeville into his houſe, and the deceaſed was not ſeen afterwards, 'till found in the manner aforeſaid; and when the ſuppoſed Murderer was on examination before the Coroner, a pair of ſtockings and a ſhirt were found upon him: upon which he was committed to Glouceſter Caſtle. *D P.*

Yeſterday the R. Hon. the L. Vere Beauclerk kiſs'd the King's Hand, on his being made one of the Commiſſioners of the navy. *D P.*

FRIDAY, *May* 12.

His Majeſty has been pleaſed to conſtitute his Royal Conſort, the Queen's moſt excellent Majeſty, Guardian of the Realm of Great Britain, and his Majeſty's Lieutenant within the ſame, during his Majeſty's abode in foreign parts; and a Commiſſion is paſſing the ſeals accordingly. *D J.*

We hear it will be propoſed to the Parliament, that the Proprietors of ſhares in the Charitable Corporation ſhall have an equal proportion out of the Directors and Aſſiſtants eſtates, with thoſe that are poſſeſs'd of bonds or notes of the ſaid Corporation. *D P.*

On wedneſday came on at the Court of Common Pleas at Weſtminſter, a tryal on an action brought by Dingley, Goodere, Eſq; (ſon of Sir Edward Goodere, Bar.) Plaintiff, againſt Sir Rob. Jaſon, Bar. for criminal converſation with his wife; when, after a long tryal, which laſted 'till about one yeſterday morning, the whole appear'd ſo plain, that the Jury gave 1000 l. damages. *D P. P.*

On wedneſday next, his Majeſty will go to the Houſe of Peers, and put an end to this Seſſion of Parliament. *P.* —— *My* Brother *ſpeaks, I believe,* with *greater* aſſurance, *than* truth.

Canterbury, May 10. We hear the Rev. and Hon. Mr. Dawney (ſon of the late L. Viſc. Downe of the Kingdom of Ireland) is made Prebendary of this Church, in the room of the Rev. Ralph Blomer, D. D. deceaſed. *D J.*

On monday the Town and Corporation of Henly upon Thames, made choice of George Earl of Macclesfield to be their high Steward, in the room of the late Earl his father. *S J.*

On tueſday there was a board of Admiralty held, at which the Hon. John Cockburn, Eſq; one of the Lords Commiſſioners did not aſſiſt: he having reſigned his ſaid poſt. *L E.* —— This report is entirely without foundation. *C.* 13.

We hear that the Earl of Eſſex, after having executed his Commiſſion at the Court of Turin, is to return to Vienna in a publick character. *L E.* — *Before he has been there at all.*

On thurſday laſt the Right Hon. the E. Cowper, and the Hon. the L. Strathnaver, ſon and heir of the R. Hon. the E. of Sutherland, were admitted Fellows of the Royal Society, at a numerous meeting of the Fellows at their houſe in Crane Courtt, Fleet-Street. *D P.*

Laſt thurſday morning a barber near S. John's-ſtreet Pound, undertook to let his wife blood (who was not very well) apprehending he had not performed the operation as it ought to be, ſurprized him ſo greatly, that he ſwooned away, and nobody being preſent, before he came to himſelf, his wife bled to death. *S J.* — *He ought to bring good proof, that he was really* gone away *from* himſelf.

On the 7th died at Lynn, Edm. Hill, Eſq; Land Surveyor of that port. *P.* —— On monday died the Lady Furneſe, mother of Sir Robert, at her houſe in Hanover-ſquare *S J. W E.*

Tueſday died Mr. Sam. Palmer, an eminent Printer of this City, who was compiling a Hiſtory of Printing, ſome parts of which are publiſhed. *D J.*

On tueſday next the corpſe of the late Dr. Atterbury, Biſhop of Rocheſter, is to be interr'd in Weſtminſter-Abbey, in a decent but private manner. *C.*

SATURDAY, *May* 13.

Laſt night the corpſe of the Rev. Dr. Atterbury, late Biſhop of Rocheſter, was remov'd (from Mr. Purdy's, an Undertaker) and interr'd, about 12 at night, in his vault in Weſtminſter-Abbey, (near Secretary Cragg's monument) in a decent private manner, attended only by Will. Morice, Eſq; his ſon in law, and his two Chaplains, the Rev. Dr. Savage and the Rev. Mr. Moore: on the urn which contain'd his bowels, &c. was inſcrib'd, *In hac urna depoſiti ſunt cineres Franciſci Atterburi Epiſcopi Roffenſis. DP.*

His Majeſty has been pleaſed to declare his Royal intentions of embarking for his German dominions on monday ſe'nnight. *C.* — *If this* declaration *was made to my* Brother, *he ſhould have ſaid ſo.*

Yeſterday Will. Burroughs, Eſq; belonging to the Charitable Corporation, was committed cloſe priſoner to the Fleet priſon, by order of the Hon. Houſe of Commons. *P.*

His Grace the L. Archbiſhop of Canterbury has been pleaſed to confer the degree of Doctor in Divinity upon the Rev. Rich. Bundy, formerly of Chriſt Church College in Oxford, in order to attend his Majeſty during his reſidence in his German dominions, as Chaplain in ordinary. *P.*

We hear from Dartford in Kent, that Ap. 26th, at a Farm called S. Margaret's near that place, in the occupation of Edw. Vickers, there was a large barn and cow-houſe conſumed by fire, with a large quantity of wheat, &c. The ſuddenneſs of the fire raiſed a ſuſpicion, that it was done with deſign, whereupon one Hen King, a boy about 12 years of age, and ſervant to Vickers, was taken up, and upon his examination confeſs'd, that he was employ'd by 2 men to ſet houſes and barns on fire, and

was to have a guinea for each; and that with a coal and
match he let fire to his Mafter's barn: but he could not be
brought to confefs who the men were. Being examined
before another Juftice, he faid he was fmoaking a piece of
wood-bine, which dropping among the ftraw, fet it on
fire: but he own'd he had ftole his Mafter's plough-irons,
and hid them in a chalk pit, where they were found;
and thereupon he was committed to Maidftone jail. P.

.MONDAY, May 15.

Yefterday the Rev. Dr. Crow preached before their Majefties, his Royal Highnefs the Prince of Wales, &c.
And the Rev. Dr. Holcomb before his Royal Highnefs the
Duke, &c. — His Majefty has been pleafed to appoint
John Cockfon, Efq; to be one of the Commiffioners for
licenfing Hackney coaches and chairs. — And John
Temple, Efq; to be Auditor of the Duties on Hydes, Cof-
fet, Tea, and Chocolate. C. DP. Dy. — Yefterday
the Court went out of mourning, on account of the Elector of Mentz. C. P. DP. — On faturday in the afternoon his Royal Highnefs the Duke's young Company of
Granadiers perform'd a handfome exercife at arms in the
Royal Gardens at S James's, when a fon of Major Kemp
was prefented to his Royal Highnefs as an Enfign of the
faid Company, and receiv'd his Trophies; after which he
had the honour to kifs his hand. DP.

On faturday the Lady of the R. Hon. the Lord Harvey
was fafely deliver'd of a fon, at her apartments in S. Jame's,
Palace; on which occafion his Majefty was moft gracioufly
pleafed to order the Guards to mount without beat of drum.
C. DP. About 6 o'clock in the morning. P.

On friday a General Court of the Honourable Turky
Company was held at Salters-hall, when Mr. Geo. Boding-
ton, their Conful at Smirna, was order'd to be recall'd, he
having refided there ever fince the year 1718. C. DP.

On faturday the Mails from Briftol and Gloucefter, containing 46 bags, lately taken from the Poft-Boy by a fingle
perfon on foot, were found in a wheat field, and brought
up the fame evening to the General Poft Office. All the
bags were entire and unopen'd, except the Briftol, the
feals of which were not broke, but it had been cut open,
and only one letter was found in it, which was directed to
a Gentleman in Bremen. D y.

On thurfday died at Oxford, in a very advanced age,
the Hon. Walt. Leather, Efq; for many years a Reprefentative in Parliament, and one of his Majefty's Juftices of
the peace for that City. P.

Orders have been given to thofe of his Majefty's livery and houfhold fervants who are to attend his Majefty
to Hanover, to hold themfelves in readinefs at an hour's
warning. C.

Yefterday the Houfe of Lords (who on monday was
fe'nnight revers'd the Judgment given by the Court of
King's-Bench in Trinity Term laft, in favour of Dr. Bentley againft the Lord Bifhop of Ely) granted a confultation,
i.e. liberty to proceed judicially as Vifitor againft the
Doctor, upon the article which relates to the Doctor's
keeping Chappel in his College. Ibid. — The Article, I
am affured, relates to the Doctor's not keeping Chappel.

TUESDAY, May 6.

Yefterday the L. Vere Beauclerk was unanimoufly re-
elected a Reprefentative for Windfor. LE. S y.

This morning the R. Hon. the E. of Sunderland was
married to the daughter of the R. Hon. the E. of Trevor;
a beautiful young Lady, and 20,000 l. fortune. The ceremony was performed by the R. rev. the L. Bifhop of S.
Davids. W E. — This evening the E. of Sunderland
will be married, &c. S y. — Laft night the E. of
Sunderland was married, &c. C. DP. 17.

Yefterday was married at the Charter-houfe Chapel, Mr.
Walcot, of Walcot in Shropfhire, a Gentleman of 4000 l.
per ann. to a daughter of Sir Fran. Dafhwood, and niece
to the faid mafter, a very agreeable Lady of 10000 l. fortune. S y.

Early this morning Mr. Pitt, Head Keeper of Newgate,
died at his houfe in Newgate-ftreet. W E.

WEDNESDAY, May 17.

A new Commiffion is paffing the feals, appointing Tho.
Sutton, John Philpot, and Francis Compton, Efqs; Com-
miffioners for licenfing and regulating Hackney-Coaches.
D y.

Yefterday Humphrey Parfons, Efq; Alderman, fet out
for Dover, to proceed from thence to Paris. D P.

The fame morning when the firft Regiment of foot were
firing in Platoons in Hyde-Park, a ball was difcharged
from a Piece, which graz'd on the brais-work of a foldi-
er's pouch, and went through the pouch of his left hand
man againft his thigh; but he having fome money in his
pocket, prevented the ball from entring, but was much
bruifed. C. It is thought it was defigned elfewhere. D P.
— The having money in ones pocket is the beft je-
cefity!

At the races on Epfom Downs on Saturday laft, for
the 30 guineas plate, three horfes ftarted, which were
entered at the poft, and the plate was won by a horfe
faid to belong to John Rich, Efq; D y.

The Mall in St. James's Park, by order of his Majefty's board of works, is now digging up; and is to be
levelled, ftrowed, and roll'd down with Cockel-fhells, and
repaired in a beautiful manner.

<hr>

From the PEGASUS in Grub-ftreet.

To CÆLIA, at the laft Affizes at —— 1732.

WHere Juftice all its pompous terror wears,
   Lo! CELIA in her pride of charms appears.
The Judge's frown no longer ftrikes with awe,
But all fubmit to beauty's fofter law.
ASTRÆA fure, we cry, is now reftor'd,
And leaves the fky to reaffume her fword:
Or elfe has mercy chofe that Angel face,
To footh the wonted rigour of the place,
To fhew where tender pity fhould prevail,
And fheathe the fword, and turn the equal fcale,
See! at the Bar appear a wretched throng,
Dragging their load of guilt and chains along:
See! from the fight the gentle CELIA turns,
With tendereft woe their defperate plight fhe mourns.
Their galling chains alone afflict the Fair:
Unmindful of the chains her captives wear,
She wonders at the Murd'rer's heart of ftone;
Shakes at his guilt, unconfcious of her own.

               PHILO GRUB.

<hr>

Dublin, May 9. Laft week died at Dollarftown, in the
County of Meath, Arth. Meredith, Efq; aged 112 years.
— On friday the Grave digger of S. Andrew's Church,
was committed to Newgate, for opening feveral graves,
and ftripping the corps. C. P. 16. And his Wife to Bridewell. P.

Edinburgh, May 5. This day the venerable General
Affembly fat down (after a Sermon preached by the Rev.
Mr. James Smith, Moderator of the laft Affembly) and
the Rev. Mr. Neil Campbell, Principal of the Univerfity
of Glafgow, was chofen Moderator. C. P. — Laft monday there was a great fall of fnow, and on tuefday the ice
was fo ftrong as to bear men and horfe, and feveral of the
young lambs were kill'd by the exceffive cold. P.

<hr>

FOREIGN NEWS.

TUESDAY, May 16.

Yefterday arrived the Mails from France and Holland.
Paris, May 21. N. S. Letters from Rome of the 1ft
inft. advife, that they had received a confirmation of a
battle fought in Corfica; wherein the Allies had 2500 men
killed upon the fpot, feveral Officers wounded, and among
them the Prince of Wirtemberg himfelf flightly. On
the 16th, the Chambers [of Parliament] met; when the
firft Prefident having acquainted them with the Kings orders, they retired without fpeaking a word, and have not
met fince. C. D P.

Venice, May 9. Our laft letters from Conftantinople fay,
the people are much diffatisfy'd, and murmur loudly
againft the conditions of the Peace concluded with Perfia; mean while his Sublime Highnefs has fent orders to
the Bafhaw of Tauris to furrender the place to the Perfians.
The fame letters confirm the depofition of the Prime Vizir, and his banifhment to Trebifonde; advifing that the
Tefterdar is nam'd to act in that quality 'till the arrival of
the Serafquier, who commands the Ottoman army in Perfia,
whom the Grand Signor has appointed his fucceffor. D P.

<hr>

Books and Pamphlets publifhed fince our laft.

11 The Roman Hiftory, No 17, 18, 19, tranflated
by Mr. Ozell.
An Account of the late dreadful fire at Tiverton, &c.
by Sam. Smith, M. A.
Acis and Galatea: an Englifh Paftoral Opera.
The Uncharitable Corporation. Pr. 6 d.
Ecclefiaftical Memoirs by M. de Tillemont. No. IV.
Select Comedies of Moliere in French and Englifh. Vol. I.
15. Celfus Triumphatus: or Mofes vindicated, &c. Pr. 1 s.
A Review of the Text of Milton's Paradife Loft. Part II.
16. The Examiner examined, or an Anfwer to the Examination of the facts and reafonings in the Bifhop of Chi-
chefter's fermon. Jan. 30.
A Defence of the Religion of Nature and the Chriftian
Revelation, &c. By Sim. Browne.
17. The ten thoufand Torments of a Termagant dif-
play'd, &c. Pr. 6 d.

On Tuefday Stocks were

South Sea Stock was 98, 1 qr. South Sea Annuity
108 3 8ths. Bank 147 1 half. New Bank Circulation
7 l. 15 s. Premium. India 177 1 half. Three per Cent.
Annuity 97 3 8ths. Royal Exchange Affurance 101
1 half. London Affurance 13. York Buildings 7 1 qr.
African 40. Englifh Copper 2 l. 9 s. Welch ditto 1 l.
15 s. South Sea Bonds 2 l. 11 s. Pre. cent. India ditto
6 l. 7 s. ditto. Blank 7 l. 8 s. 5 s. 20 l. Prizes 19 l.
15 s. 6 d.

ADVERTISEMENTS.

This Day is published,

Dedicated to the KING,

REVELATION *Examin'd with* CANDOUR.

OR, A FAIR

ENQUIRY into the SENSE and USE of the several REVELATIONS expresly declared, or sufficiently imply'd, to be given to Mankind from the *Creation*, as they are found in the BIBLE. By a profess'd Friend to an honest Freedom of Thought in Religious Enquiries. PART I. Containing DISSERTATIONS upon the several Revelations from the CREATION to the FLOOD, inclusive.

Printed for *C. Rivington*, at the Bible and Crown in St Paul's Church-Yard.

Lately published,

The two following BOOKS,

I. PRactical Discourses on the several Parts and Offices of the *Liturgy* of the Church of England: Wherein are shewn the Harmony, Excellency, and Usefulness of its Composition. In four Volumes. By *Matthew Hole*, D. D. late Rector of Exeter College in Oxford. Vol. I. Containing 58 Discourses on all the Parts of Morning and Evening Prayer, including the Creed of St. Athanasius. Vol. II. and III. Containing Discourses on the Litany, and the Prayers and Thanksgivings that follow it. Vol. IV. Containing 174 Discourses (in 2 large Parts) on all the Collects, Epistles and Gospels, to be used throughout the Year. 2d Edition.

II. A practical Exposition of the CHURCH-CATECHISM. 2 Volumes. By the same Author. The Third Edition, with the Addition of two Discourses; one on the Duty of owning Christ, the other on the Danger of denying him; preached at St. Mary's in Oxford.

Printed for J. and J. Knapton, and C. Rivington in St. Paul's Church-Yard; A. Bettesworth and C. Hitch in Paternoster-Row; and S. Birt in Avemary-Lane.

Just published,

(In 3 Vols. Octavo. Price 15 s.)

Several SERMONS, chiefly upon Practical Subjects, many of which were published before the present Queen, when Princess of Wales. By the Chaplain in Ordinary, the late Reverend *Nicholas Brady*, D. D. Rector of Clapham, and Minister of Richmond in Surrey. Now first published from the Author's Manuscripts.

Printed for Tho. Osborne, in Gray's-Inn.

Where may be had, just published,

The Practical Conveyancer. In two Parts. Part first, Containing Rules and Instructions for drawing all Sorts of Conveyances of Estates and Interests, whether Real or Personal, in Possession or Expectancy: Also particular Rules for the Exposition of Deeds, Wills, &c. and of Words used in Conveyances. Together with the Resolutions of several Courts at Westminster, in Cases wherein Difficulties have arisen touching the Words and Clauses in Deeds, Devises, &c. The whole extracted, by way of Abridgment, from the Reports at large of the said Cases, and alphabetically digested under proper Heads. Part 2, Being the first Part reduced into Practice in a select Collection of Precedents, viz. Marriage-Settlements; Bargains and Sales; Leases and Releases; Deeds of Copartnership of Exchange; of Release and Confirmation; Mortgages; Surrenders; Wills; Letters of Attorney; Assignments of Stocks; and Exchequer Annuities; Ecclesiastical Instruments, &c. By JOHN LILLY, Gent. The Second Edition corrected, and very much enlarged. To which are now added, Cases in Chancery, under all the Titles of Conveyancing, digested by way of Common-Place, under alphabetical Heads.

BOOKS printed for, and sold by J. Brotherton, at the Bible next the Fleece Tavern, in Cornhill.

Whitlock's Memorials	Telemachus, by Boyer.
Temple's Works, 2 Vol.	Ditto in Fol.
Bailey's Eng. Dict. Fol.	Guardians, 2 Vol.
Tillotson's Works, 3 Vol.	Langham's Duties.
Bates's Works, Fol.	Free Thoughts on Religion.
State of Britain, for 1732.	La Bell Assemble, 3 Vol.
Bailey's Justin.	Vanburgh's Plays, 2 Vol.
Origin of Honour.	Addison's Works, 4 Vol.
Ladies Conduct.	Spectators, 8 Vol.
Virgin unmask'd	Trapp's Virgil.
Hays's Ship and Supercargo Book-Keeper.	D'Urfey's Songs, 6 Vol.
Coke's Detection, 3 Vol.	Milton Lost and Regain'd.
Bohun's Law of Tythes.	D'Anois Tales, 3 Vol.
Feasts & Fasts of the Church.	De Retz Memoirs, 4 Vol.
Ecclesiastica	Tom Brown's Works, 4 Vol.
Life of Oliver Cromwell.	Farnborough's Grammar.
Life of the K. of Sweden.	Philips's Grammar.
Dampier's Journal to Madagascar.	Dorrington's Devotion.
Rapin's Hist. of England, 15 Vol.	Congreve's Plays, 3 Vol.
Arbuthnot of Ailments, com	Pope and Swift Mis. 3 Vol.
	Pope's Misc. 2 Vol.
	Turkish Spy, 8 Vol.

Yesterday was published, Price 6d.

Neatly printed on a fine Dutch *Paper*.

The SECOND EDITION of No XVI. for APRIL. To which is added, *A Register* of Books and Pamphlets, Titles at length, disposed under proper Heads, after the Manner of the Monthly Chronicle, which the Proprietors have discontinued,

THE GENTLEMAN's MAGAZINE: Or, *Monthly Intelligencer.*

Containing more in Quantity, and greater Variety than any other Book of the Kind and Price, viz.

I. A View of the Weekly Essays, viz. of Deism; Superstition; Ambition and Avarice; Wit and Madness; Church Musick; Dr. Bentley's Manner of Criticism; Mischiefs of forc'd Marriages; Liberty of Conscience; Moral Good and Evil; Arguments for the Tythe Bill; against Despair; of Love; Friendship; Poverty of Authors. The Case of Self-murder consider'd; Duty of a Kt. of the Bath; Religion vindicated; Success of Libels; Female Piety commended.

II. Political Points, viz. Remarks on the Reign of King Charles I. King William and Queen Mary's Characters; History of Faction; Parallel History; the Revolution vindicated; Remarks on Voltaire's History; Considerations on South Sea Company's Affairs; Corruption; Difficulty of speaking of dead Princes; Reply to Reprimand; Swedish Company.

III. Poetical Pieces, viz. the Free Mason; Dean Swift in good Quarters; Farmer's Daughter; Receipt for Courtship.

IV. Domestick Occurrences, Births, Deaths, Marriages, Promotions, &c. Duke of Dorset's dangerous Voyage; the tragical Catastrophe of Rich. and Bridget Smith, with their Letters, uncastrated as in the *London Magazine*.

V. Prices of Goods, Grain, Stocks.

VI. Foreign Affairs.

VII. Account of Criminals executed.

VIII. A Table of Contents.

Plurimum in parvo. *Prodesse & delectare.*

By SYLVANUS URBAN, *Gent.*

Printed by E. Cave, at St. John's Gate; and sold by Mrs. Nutt, Mrs Charlton, Mrs. Cook, Pamphlet Shops at the Royal Exchange; Mr. Batley, at the Dove in Pater-Noster-Row; Mr Midwinter, at the Three Crowns and Looking-Glass in St Paul's Church-Yard; F. Jefferies in Ludgate-street; the Pamphlet Shops in Fleet-Street, Pall Mall, the Strand; Mrs Dodd, at the Peacock, Mr. Bickerton, at Lord Bacon's Head without Temple-Bar; Mr. Chichley at Charing-Cross; Mr Stagg and Mr. King, in Westminster-Hall; Mr. Williamson in Holbourne; Mr. Mountague in Great Queen-street, and most other Booksellers in Town and Country.

*** N. B. *The Customers to the* GENTLEMAN's Magazine, *or* Monthly Intelligencer, *are desired to take Care that they are not deceived by a Book with a similar Title, which may be offer'd them at some Shops; and as they have been so kind to encourage this useful Undertaking, it is hoped they will not, by any Artifice, be misled to favour an Attempt so unfair and ungenerous as the supplanting an Author in his whole Plan, Design, and even Title. A Practice which would be condemned by every Individual concerned in it, if their own Case. And the Publick may be assur'd that, whatever our Rivals may pretend, nothing shall excell this* Magazine.

The above N. B. tho' entirely defensive, has been rudely attack'd in some Advertisements that are impertinent in every Respect, except submitting to the Judgment of the Public, to which we freely agree.

It was on account of 12 Essays, several Occurrences, and the Elections of some Members of Parliament, being omitted, that we presum'd to call a similar Book *defective*.

The said Omissions are pointed out in this Edition, and some frivolous Objections against us receive an answer; but we must ask the Reader's Pardon for two or three litteral Errors that escaped, thro' Haste, in part of the Impression.

The Publick may be sure of this Book being continued, tho' by a little Shift it is left out of the Monthly Catalogue *of Books, which is one Inducement to add the Register of Books, Titles at length, to ours.*

P S. The Essays in the *Gentleman's Magazine*, which are not in the *London*, are as follow:

Of Moral Good and Evil	p. 687	*Defence of Bp Burnet*	page 711
Of Liberty of Conscience	693	*Of Friendship* 701 *Footmen*	710
FOG quoting Demosthenes	695	*A Taste of Two Hyp Doctors*	714
Of Wit and Madness	700	*Of Heroick Friendship*	715
Two Essays on English History	692	*King of Sweden's Character*	715
Grubstreet J. on the Tyth-Bill	704	*A Reply to a Reprimand*	716
On the Success of Libels	707	*Advice to a desponding Director*	

This Day is published, *Price* 1 s.

The Second Edition of

THE PROGRESS of LOVE, in Four ECLOGUES.

I. *Uncertainty*, to Mr. Pope.
II. *Hope*, to the Honourable George Doddington, Esq;
III. *Jealousy*, to Edward Walpole, Esq;
IV. *Possession*, to the Right Hon. the Ld. Visc. Cobham.

Printed for L. Gilliver, at Homer's-Head, over against S. Dunstan's Church in Fleet-street. Likewise,

STOWE, the GARDENS of the Right Hon. *Richard* Lord Viscount *Cobham*. Address'd to Mr. POPE.

Devenere locos lætos, & amœna Vireta
Fortunatorum nemorum, sedesque beatas. Virg.

On Wednesday the 3d of May was published, beautifully printed on a fine Paper,

THE *London Magazine*, or *Gentleman's Monthly Intelligencer*, for *April* 1732. To be continued each Month. Pr. 6d. Containing greater Variety, and more in Quantity, than any Monthly Book extant.

1. A View of the Weekly Essays, viz. Of Religion and Superstition, a humourous Project to promote going to Church, unhappy Marriages, occasioned by Covetousness and Ambition of Parents, Love and Generosity, Mischief of kept Mistresses, Dr. Bentley's Notes on Milton burlesqued, Self-murder, Monuments, and Statues, Burlesque upon Authors.

2. Political Subjects, viz. The Revolution vindicated, Character of K. William and Q. Mary, Remarks on the Reign of K Charles I. on Voltaire, Parallel History, Faction, Causes of Corruption, K. William and Bp Burnet, Monopoly of Posts and Lands, Character of Lord Burleigh, Political Spectacles, Reduction of the Land Tax, Considerations on the S. S Company.

3. Poetry. A Knave at the Bottom, on the Death of a Friend, on Parson P——r, Kitty a Pastoral, a Miser on his Death-Bed, Epigrams.

4. Domestick Occurences, Promotions, Ecclesiastical, Civil and Military, Marriages, Births, Deaths, &c. Tragical Account of Mr. Smith, Bookbinder, and his Wife, with their genuine Letters; a remarkable Epitaph.

5. Prices of Goods, Grain, Stocks, Monthly Bill of Mortality.

6. Foreign Affairs.

7. A Catalogue of Books and Pamphlets, the Titles at large, with their Prices.

8. A Table of Contents. *Multum in Parvo.*

Printed by C. Ackers, in St John's-street, for J. Wilford, behind the Chapter-house near St. Paul's; and sold by W. Meadows, T. Cox, W. Hinchliffe, H Whitridge, and E. Nutt in Cornhill; J Clarke in Duck-lane; T. Astley, at the Rose against the North Door of St Paul's; A. Dodd, without Temple-bar; J. Stagg in Westminster-hall; J. Jackson in Pall-Mall; J. Brindley, and W. Shropshire in Bond-street.

To Mr. Edward Cave, *at St. John's Gate*:

SIR,

YOU being the Undertaker of the *Gentleman's Magazine*, we cannot help charging you with that scurrilous N.B. which follows the Advertisement of that Book. Your Assurance, we think, is very extraordinary, in reflecting upon us for compiling a Book of this Kind from the Publick Papers, in several of which we have a Property, when you have not the least Share in any one of them; which makes your Work little better than a downright *Piracy*. As to supplanting you in your Design, pray, Sir, who gave you (a Proprietor in no one Paper) a Right, exclusive of all others, even of Proprietors themselves, to a Design of this Nature? *In other* Cases, where Persons are upon a Level, (as you are *not* with us in this Case) one and the same Design lies open and free to Several, to execute in the best Manner they can. Is not this the Case of Manufactures, of Arts and Sciences, and of News Papers themselves? Whence else are there so many at this Time? But as the Publick is to judge which is the best Manufacture, or Book of the Kind, and which is the best News-Paper, so they must be the Judges which is the best Magazine, our *London*, or your *Gentleman's*. We fear not the Issue of their Judgments, notwithstanding your modestly charging us with being defective, for omitting some trifling Things, of little or no Use or Entertainment, when we can make it appear you have omitted Papers and Things of Importance, in that very *Magazine* you oppose to ours. We are willing ours should be compared with yours, Essay for Essay, and shall say no more, but submit the *London-Magazine*, both as to Compiling, Paper, and Letter, to the Judgment of the Publick, not doubting but they will encourage those most, by whom they are most agreeably entertained.

Tho. Cox.
John Wilford.
John Clarke.
Tho. Astley.
Charles Ackers

Books printed for J. BATLEY, at the *Dove* in *Pater-Noster-Row*.

1. A Compleat Introduction to the Reading the Holy Scriptures, intended chiefly for young Students in Divinity. In two Parts. Part I. Containing an Account of the civil and religious State of the Jews; the Samaritans, Ceremonies, Temples, Sacrifices, Synagogues, High-Priests, Courts of Justice; particularly the Sanhedrim, Prophets, Scribes, Jewish Sects, Pharisees, Sadducees, Essenes, Proselytes of the Gate. Years, Months, Days, and Hours of the Jews, &c. Part II. Containing the Proofs of the Truth of the Christian Religion; Nature of the New Testament Stile; the Chronology and Geography of the New Testament; the Hebrew Money, Weights and Measures; various Readings, Division into Chapters and Verses, Heresies in the Apostles Days, Versions of the New Testament, Antient and Modern: To which are added the English ones, &c. Written originally in French by Messieurs De Beausobre and Lenfant. By the Order of the King of Prussia. Now first done into English, with additional Notes.

2. A compleat Body of Divinity, consonant to the Doctrine of the Church of England. In Six Books. In Two Volumes. By N. Clark, Rector of Shaston St. James in Dorset. Price 9 s.

LONDON: Printed by J. HUGGONSON, in *Bartholomew-Close*, for Captain GULLIVER, near the *Temple*, where Letters and Advertisements are taken in: As also at the *Rainbow Coffee-House* in *Cornhill*, and *John's Coffee-House* in *Sheer-Lane*, near *Temple-Bar*. [Price Two Pence.]

The Grub-ſtreet Journal.

NUMB. 125

Thurſday, *MAY* 25, 1732.

Ὃς ῥ᾽ ἔπεα φρεσὶν ᾗσιν ἄκοσμά τε, πολλά τε ᾔδη. Hom. Il. B. 213.

To Mr. Bavius, Secretary of the Society of Grub-ſtreet.

SIR,

IN your *Journal*, No. 118. you accuſe Dr B of 'making his Notes on Milton '*extempore*, and putting them to the Preſs 'as ſoon as made.' I confeſs, you ſupport your accuſation pretty ſtrongly, both by the Dr's own confeſſion, pag 7. and the many ſigns of haſte in the performance itſelf But, I hope, you will give me leave to ſay ſomething in the Dr's Defence, and to clear him (if 'tis in my Power) from ſo extravagant a proceeding —Iſt, then, I think his own confeſſion ought to have very little weight with us, ſince he did not make it to take ſhame to himſelf, but glory. He never gives his opinion with any diſtruſt, but aſſerts poſitively, corrects boldly, and reflects with much ſelf-complacency on his wonderful work. Now if he could make the world believe, that he performed all this with a great deal of eaſe, and in a ſhort time, he knew it would very much enhaunce his praiſes His confeſſion therefore ſhould only be conſidered, as a bait laid for complements, or as the teſtimony of a man in his own cauſe. IIdly, with regard to the tokens of haſte in the Notes, it ſhould be conſidered, that ſome men are ſo obſtinately addicted to their own notions, that no length of time, no reflection can prevail on them to correct their firſt thoughts; to do which they think would be, tho' not an open acknowledgment, yet a tacit accuſation of themſelves, as having been once in the wrong Therefore the works of ſuch men, if reſerved in the deſk ten years, muſt carry with them the ſame marks of haſte, as if they were immediately printed off from the firſt draught · and that this is the caſe in the preſent inſtance, I have very good reaſon to be aſſured

It is now ſix years ago ſince Dr. Ashenhurst (whoſe great intimacy with Dr B was no ſecret) declared at Briſtol, that Dr B was then engaged in making Notes on Milton neither did he ſpeak of it as a work juſt then taken in hand, for he himſelf had then been detained by an ill ſtate of health at Bath and Briſtol two or three years, and had not ſeen Dr. B. in all that time So that it is not improbable, but that this work, which is given us as if made *extempore*, may have coſt the Author as many years labour, as even his Horace. He may perhaps imagine, that it highly concerns the world to be informed of the moſt minute particulars concerning himſelf: but why he ſhould pretend to have waſted ſo many years upon Horace, and to have beſtowed ſo little time on Milton, is to me unaccountable: for there can be no queſtion, but that he has an equally good opinion of both performances. The perſon who received the before-mentioned account from Dr Ashenhurst's own mouth, is ready to atteſt the truth of it with his name, whenever he ſhall be called upon ſo to do by the Gentleman concerned. In the mean time, we may look upon him as not guilty of mangling ſo noble a Poem, without deliberation and reflection; and upon his Notes, as the elaborate product of his riper years, and more confirmed judgment.

Mr. Bavius, there is ſtill one paſſage in the Dr's *Preface*, which I do not perceive to have been taken notice of by any one, and the meaning of which I really do not comprehend Speaking of the ſtrength of Milton's ſpirit, that under ſuch troubles *could ſpatiate at large* thro' the whole univerſe, he ſays, 'And it would almoſt ſeem 'to me to be peculiar to him; had not experience by 'others taught me, that there is that power in the human mind, ſupported with innocence and *conſcia virtus*, that can make it quite ſhake off all outward uneaſineſſes, and involve itſelf ſecure and pleaſed in its own 'integrity and entertainment.' At the firſt reading of this paſſage, I thought the Dr. had meant himſelf, and had ventured to compliment his own *innocence and conſcia virtus*, on which ſubject a great deal has been, and more may be ſaid. but then that odd dark expreſſion, *experience by others taught me*, may, for ought I know, mean any body, or any thing elſe

As for Milton, and the praiſes given him in this paragraph, I am as willing as any man to extol him for his poetical works; which will be an honour to our nation as long as his language can be underſtood. Let them attone for, and cover thoſe miſchiefs, which his tongue and pen committed in proſe. But the crude and undiſtinguiſhing encomiums, which this Editor has beſtowed on his innocence and morality, might provoke one to inquire into the juſtneſs of them; and with what view this Gentleman could ſo profuſely celebrate the memory of a man, who was ſo bitter an enemy to that Church and State, of whoſe revenues and favours this Editor has enjoyed ſo large a ſhare. The kindeſt excuſe I can make for him is, that he ſcatters both his cenſures and praiſes at random, and with a careleſs hand; that as he has heaped the moſt ſcurrilous reproaches on Milton's imaginary Editor, for imaginary faults, ſo he has dawbed Milton himſelf with the moſt fulſome panegyric for imaginary virtues: and thus in effect he has moſt injudiciouſly condemned Milton for his poetry, and praiſed him for his religious and civil principles. I am, Sir, your moſt humble ſervant,

April, 13, 1732. A Z.

SIR,

IT has puzzled many people to aſſign the reaſon, why Dr B in his edition of Milton's *Paradiſe Loſt*, ſhould embrace the whimſical notion of an Editor, who wilfully altered the text, and foiſted in his own verſes. Some think, that he is only in jeſt; that he is either deſirous of ſhowing how plauſibly he can defend paradoxes, or that this is one of his critical traps, laid to enſnare others into a belief of what he knows to be falſe, that he may afterwards divert himſelf with their credulity Others are apprehenſive, that the poor Gentleman is really ſerious; that this is one of the deformed births of a Critic's brain, which looks lovely in its parent's eye; that he is now drawn off to the laſt dregs, and doatingly takes his fancies and dreams for realities. I believe it will be difficult intirely to diſprove the laſt of theſe accounts. but there is a third, which ought not to be overlooked, and which may fall in with either of the other Some people have received from nature, or gained by practice, a particular talent for abuſive language, which muſt be exerted upon all occaſions

I remember in the Paper-war carried on in the year 1721, about Dr. Bentley's intended *new edition of the Greek Teſtament* His adverſaries extracted out of a Pamphlet written in the Dr's defence (the Author of which no one doubted of,) a moſt monſtrous catalogue of *Billingſgate* oratory, which was voted by the Vice-Chancellor and Heads of the Univerſity of *Cambridge*, to be 'moſt 'reproachful, infamous, and ignominious, and a moſt virulent and ſcandalous libel' The Author pointed this ribaldry at Dr Colbatch, a moſt innocent and worthy Gentleman, not only out of perſonal hatred to him, but becauſe his own genius was to be followed, and his budget of ſcandal diſcharged, whether he was provoked or not. As therefore on that occaſion Dr. Colbatch was to be pelted with dirt, for a work known to be written by Dr. Middleton, ſo it is in the preſent caſe Dr B. knew it would be very impolitic to exerciſe this talent againſt Milton, and therefore conjures up this apparition of an Editor, (or by the help of a ſtrong imagination perſuades himſelf, that there indeed was ſuch a one) whom he may brand with ſcurrilous names at pleaſure, give vent to his ſpleen, and raiſe the indignation of no man I do not pretend to equal the catalogue before ſpoken of; but conſidering the Dr. only fights with a ſhadow, or with one, who, if real, could never have given him any provocation, I think he has laid about him very ſmartly; as may be ſeen in the following collection of complements beſtowed by this Editor on his imaginary rival

'He vilely executed his truſt. The defœdation by a 'bad Printer, and a worſe Editor. *Preface*. Clogs and 'ſullies the Poem with romantic traſh, a heap of barbarous 'words, pedantry, and a ſilly boaſt of uſeleſs reading, 'Pag. 26. His rude hand, 34. His boldneſs and ſillineſs, 56. Silly and pedantical, 60. His traſh, his foul 'play, 61. His trivial and common chat, 62. His vile 'negligence, not to be endured, 66 His dirt, 70. Abominable, ſo very groſs, it would be penal in a ſchool-'boy of an inferior claſs, 74, 75. The ridiculous mark 'of his fiſt, his polluting hand, 78. The buſy Editor returns to his abſurd trade, 91. His impertinencies, ſilly 'interruption, 93. His ſilly dream, ſtrange ſhocking 'expreſſion, falſe ſenſe and ſyntax, 94 His frolick oſtentation, low and doggeril. The limbo of fools his fitteſt 'habitation, 95. His foul neglect, 96. His inſufferable 'pedantry and affectation, 99. His puerile fancy, his 'ſilly thought, ſillily conducted; his contemptible meanneſs of ſtile, his patches, 115, 116. His vitious diction, ſilly, ſuperfluous and ſpurious inſertion, 118. This 'pragmatical Editor, 132. Saucy Editor, 140 A covetous Carl, 146 His uſual abſurdneſs, ſtill blunders on 'through ſenſe and nonſenſe, 156 His rare trifling, 157. 'His ſilly inſertions, 160. Trifling remark, uſual blundering, 161. *Chœrilus*'s ſtuff raiſes my indignation, 170 Let 'him eat the ordure he has thrown in: his affected ſtuff, '171. An inſufferable mortal, 175 The bold Editor's 'groſs miſtake, ſilly queſtion, and ſenſeleſs wiſh, 185. His 'odious blunder, 194. Returns improved in dullneſs, nonſenſe and bungling. This idiot, 202. His mean, flat, 'ſuperfluous, cumberſome handiwork, 211'

All theſe rhetorical flowers are contained in the Notes on the 6 firſt Books: the other 6 are quite as well embelliſhed; but I believe the ſample will ſatisfy every Reader, and therefore I will waſh my hands. — But, Mr. Bavius, is this the proper dialect of a Scholar, a Royal Librarian, a Clergyman, a Dr. of Divinity, an Archdeacon, a Maſter of a College, and a *Regius Profeſſor*? Is it poſſible for any man, either to write or read ſuch ſtuff with pleaſure? And after all, if the ſuppoſal, which urged the Dr. to ſpit ſo much venom, is groundleſs, if all men will agree to protect Milton himſelf from theſe darts. and if Dr B. is the only Editor that ever changed Milton's text, and inſerted his own verſes, how eaſy is it to make a proper application of all the foregoing phraſes? Indeed I think the Dr juſtly deſerves to ſuffer the law of retaliation; but I dare aſſure him, that he will eſcape, ſince no Gentleman will condeſcend to be his executioner However, if he ſhall, upon this occaſion, find himſelf treated with any ſeverity of expreſſion, or rather with contempt, which is the propereſt puniſhment for him, I hope he will reflect upon his deſerts, and, tho' *he is under no apprehenſion of growing leaner by cenſures*, that he will ſuffer patiently, and in ſilence.

For my own part, I am free to allow him quarter; and moreover, to return him my hearty thanks, that with theſe extraordinary abilities and talents, he could keep his hands off from the Holy Scriptures, and content himſelf to ſpend his rage upon Milton May he never want a tub to toſs about, as long he will permit the ſhip to ride in ſafety. I am, Sir, your moſt obedient ſervant,

April, 28, 1732. A. Z.

That old Manuſcript lend me, to B—— y ſays B——l,
I'll collate, and return it, without the leaſt ſoyl.
No, I thank you, good Sir, cries the Doctor not pleas'd
When collated 'twill be like an Orange that's ſqueez'd.
At Aſhburnham Houſe this Book lately was toaſted;
And is now like an Orange, not ſqueezed, but roaſted.
But in turning the ſpit, there has been ſome miſtake:
For nor Orange, nor Doctor, a Biſhop will make.

DOMESTIC NEWS.

C *Courant*.	EP. *Evening Poſt*.
P *Poſt-Boy*	SJ. *S James's Evening Poſt*.
DP. *Daily Poſt*,	WE. *Whitehall Evening P*.
DJ. *Daily Journal*.	LE. *London Evening Poſt*.

Thursday, *May* 18.

His Royal Highneſs the Prince, has purchas'd the Lady Ayre's houſe at Kew-Green, and is to allow her 1000 l. for ſome improvements her Ladyſhip had made thereto *SJ*.

The affair which has been ſo long depending between the Biſhop of Ely and Dr. Bentley, is put off 'till the next Seſſion of Parliament. P. The firſt tueſday in the next Seſſion. *DP*.

We hear that Mr. Thompſon, late Warehouſe-keeper of the Charitable Corporation, is confined at Rome, which is confirm'd by ſeveral letters in town. —*It is hard, that a zealous* charitable Proteſtant *ſhould be thus perſecuted by* Papiſts.

Quæ tanta fuit Romam tibi cauſa videndi?

The latter end of laſt ſummer, ſome difference aroſe between the L Viſc Micklewaite, and Mr. Crowle, a Gentleman of the Temple, (whoſe Brother is Member for Hull with L. Micklewaite) about ſome expreſſions, the hi-

ter dropp'd, when arguing in a Cauſe where the ſaid Lord was concern'd ; But the ſame never being made up, and Mr. Crowle going yeſterday into the Court of Requeſts, ſnatch'd a cane out of a Gentleman's hand, and ſtruck the L. Micklewaite ſeveral blows, which he return'd ; but company coming up, parted them. *D R.* — Yeſterday, about 1 o' clock, &c. *P.* ——— About 3 in the afternoon a challenge was ſent to Mr. Crowle to fight the ſaid Lord ; and he went away directly, and they fought ; but neither were much hurt. *LE.* —— Mr. Crowle diſarm'd his Lordſhip without any wound given on either ſide, and their ſeconds parted them. *D.P.* 19. —— We are well inform'd that this is not true. *C. DP. DJ.* 20.

The Keeper of Newgate's place, reckon'd worth 5 or 6000 l. falls one third to the L. Mayor, one third to the City, and one third between the 2 Sheriffs. *D P. C.*

This being Aſcenſion-day, the Officers of the ſeveral Pariſhes in London and Weſtminſter, went to mark the bounds of their reſpective Pariſhes, and afterwards had very elegant dinners provided for them ; ſome few of which were paid out of their own pockets, but moſt out of the poor's money. *L E.* ——— *This is an odd reflection upon the many* Charitable Corporations *in theſe two Cities.*

Yeſterday the Election at Weſtminſter School determined, when the following Scholars were elected, viz.

To Oxford.		The following 8 were elected into College.	
Salter Captain ——	1ſt.	Newdigate ———	1ſt.
Ellis ———	2d.	Amyand ———	2d.
Thomas ——	3d.	Dickins —— ———	3d.
Hopton ———	4th.	Winnyat ——	4th.
To Cambridge.		Pickering ———	5th.
Gawton ——	1ſt.	Jeffreys —— ——	6th.
Williamſon ———	2d.	Yates ———	7th.
Brome ——	3d.	Vitaſſe ——	8th.
Bingham ———	4th.		*S J. WE.*

One Pearce was ſent to Newgate for inhumanly beating and dangerouſly wounding his wife, ſo that her life is deſpair'd of. ——— Tueſday a man was committed to Newgate for cutting his wife's ear off. *SJ.* — *He ſhould have* cut her head off. *He may now ſuffer upon the ſtatue againſt maiming.*

This morning Sam. Reynardſon of Bloomſbury-ſquare, Eſq; was marry'd at Ely Chapel to Mrs. Knipe, Daughter of the late Sir Randolph Knipe, Knt. an agreeable young Lady of 15,000 l. fortune. *LE.*

We hear that Mr. Gregory of the Bank of England, knows a Gentleman who hath in his poſſeſſion, to be diſpoſed of, one of the greateſt curioſities of antiquity in Europe, viz. a large fair medal of Otho, one of the 12 Cæſars, ſtruck in his life-time, and well preſerv'd. *C.*

FRIDAY, *May* 19.

The R. Hon. the L Tyrawley, his Majeſty's Envoy at Liſbon, has obtain'd leave to return home on his private affairs. *C.*

The King's Journey is put off for a week longer than was intended. —- Its talk'd as if there would be no inſtallation of the Knights of the Bath this year ; but that they would have a grant to wear the Enſigns of the Order, &c. the ſame as if inſtall'd. *D P.*

On tueſday laſt Will. Carbonnel, Eſq; was marry'd to Miſs Whaland, a very agreeable Lady, and a good fortune. *D P.*

Chriſtned, Males 163 : Females 147 : In all 310. — *Buried*, Males 203 : Females 188 : In all 391. Decreaſed in the burials this week 61. *P.*

SATURDAY, *May* 20.

Baron Sparre, Envoy of Sweden, and the Chevalier de Oſſorio, Envoy from the King of Sardinia, will go with his Majeſty to Hanover. *D P.* —— Thurſday next is fix'd for his Majeſty's going to the Houſe of Peers, &c. and on monday ſe'nnight his Majeſty will ſet out for his German Dominions. *P.*

We hear, that upon the Dutcheſs of Richmond's preſenting an humble Petition to her Majeſty, ſetting forth the moſt deplorable circumſtances of 6 daughters of the late Dr. Davenant (who were left quite deſtitute of all manner of ſubſiſtance, by their brother's leaving the Kingdom) her Majeſty, with great goodneſs, recommended their miſerable condition to the King ; and his Majeſty, out of his Royal bounty, was graciouſly pleaſed to order each of them a penſion of 50 l. a year. Sir Rob. Walpole ſhewed great humanity on this occaſion. *P.*

Yeſterday at a Board of Admiralty their Lordſhips were pleaſed to appoint Sir Chaloner Ogle Commander of the Edinburgh, a 3d rate, to be Commodore of the ſquadron lately ſailed to the Weſt Indies, in the room of Commodore Leſtock, who is recalled home : — Capt. Rob. Trevor to be Commander of the Edinburgh : ——— and Capt. Joſ. Laws to be Commander of the Exeter. *P.*

Yeſterday the Rev. Dr. Grey preſented to his Royal Highneſs the D. the 2d edition of his New method of artificial memory, was very graciouſly received, and had the honour to kiſs his Highneſs's hand. *C. D P.* — *It is to be wiſhed, that this* New Method of artificial Memory, *may teach ſome* Courtiers *to lay aſide the* Old Method of artificial Forgetfulneſs.

Laſt tueſday 400 l. was paid out of the Treaſury to the perſons concern'd in apprehending Tho. Beck and Edw. Wentland, to be executed on monday next ; Pet. Robinſon, condemn'd laſt Seſſions at the Old Baily, but repriev'd ; and one Hall, lately executed at Guildford. *D J.*

On tueſday evening ——- Bray, Eſq; of Barrington in Glouceſterſhire, being at play with Capt. Robinſon, brother of Sir Tho. Robinſon, Bar. at Epſom, a difference aroſe, and Mr. Bray threw a box at the Captain, which cut him on the head ; the company interpoſing, prevented any further miſchief at that time, and ſeveral Gentlemen, their mutual friends, endeavour'd to reconcile them. Capt. Robinſon, believing Mr. Bray might have been in liquor when he offer'd him this inſult, was willing to put it up, in caſe Mr. Bray would aſk his pardon before the ſaid company ; but he refuſing this, they met yeſterday morning, and fought, when Mr. Bray was killed on the ſpot. *D J.* —— This account is wrong, the Gentlemen having been reconciled. *W E.* Mr. Bray is in good health, not having fought. *L E.* ——— *We* News Writers *have the power of life and death, as well as* Phyſicians : *but in one reſpect excell them, bringing thoſe to life again, whom we have killed before their time ; which they never do.*

Yeſterday a private Centinel of the 1ſt Regiment of Foot guards, received 300 laſhes on the Parade in S. James's Park, and was afterwards drum'd out of the Regiment. His crime was for beating the Hon. Col. Pitt, when on duty. *D J.*

The notice of Mr. Francklyn's Tryal the ſittings after Term, for printing and publiſhing the Anſwer to one part of a late infamous Libel, &c. is countermanded. *D P.*

Yeſterday the Lady Lawley, who was lately concern'd in the affair with Japhet Crooke, was committed a priſoner to the King's Bench priſon, for being guilty of a contempt of that Court. *C.* For publiſhing a ſcandalous Libel, intitled, The true caſe of the Lady Lawley *DP. DJ.*

On wedneſday night died the Rev. Mr. Will. Lowth, Prebendary of Wincheſter, and Rector of Buriton, near Petersfield in Hampſhire, Author of thoſe excellent *Commentaries on the Prophets*, and other books in Divinity. *D P.*

On thurſday morning a man was found dead, hanging in the fields near Mile end ; the body was carried to the watch houſe, and he proved to be a Shop-keeper in Rag-fair. *DJ.*

Ruthyn in *Denbighſhire, May* 15. Laſt week, within 2 miles of this town, a man about 70 years of age, was married to a girl about 17 ; and what is more remarkable, when the Bridegroom on the wedding day went to aſk bleſſing of the Bride's father, mother, and grandmother, it was obſerved, that he was not only older than the ſaid father and mother, but ſome years older than the grandmother. *S J.*

The great cock match fought at Bath between the Hon. — Grevill, Eſq; and Mr. Segar, is ended, in which match battles and byes were 59 in number. The match was won by Mr. Grevill, by 2 battles. *S J.*

This morning it was currently reported, that Geo. Robinſon, Eſq; had been ſeiz'd at Paris, at the inſtances of the E. of Waldegrave. *S J. LE.* —— Thompſon *was ſafe* at Paris.

This day the R. Hon. the L. Abergavenny was marry'd to the Lady Rebecca Herbert, daughter to the R. Hon. the E. of Pembroke. *S J.* — And afterwards ſet out with his Lady for his ſeat near Eaſt Grinſtead in Suſſex. *L E.* — *C. DP. D J.* 22. — Early on ſunday morning : youngeſt daughter of the E. of Pembroke. *P.* 22.

MONDAY, *May* 22.

Yeſterday the Rev. Dr. Holcomb preach'd before their Majeſties, his Royal Highneſs the Prince, &c. and the Rev. Dr. Crow before his Royal Highneſs the Duke, &c. *C.* — — The Rev. Dr. Franks preached before their Majeſties, &c. *S J.* 23.

Yeſterday his Grace the D. of Richmond had his leg broke, by a vaſt piece of iron falling upon it of 900 weight, which was happily ſet by Mr. Medcalfe, Mr. Amyand, and 3 other eminent Surgeons ; and his Grace is thought to be in a fair way of recovery. *D P. D J.* By putting his foot on the upper bar of a ſtove, to have his ſpurs put on ; by which the iron back fell upon his leg, and occaſion'd the ſaid accident. *P.*

We hear that Mr. Morrice has attended the Secretary's Office, in order to receive the papers of the late moſt Rev. Biſhop Atterbury, amongſt which are ſeveral of great value, particularly an *Harmonia Evangelica*, drawn up in a new, clearer, and more exact method than any yet publiſh'd, much preferable to thoſe heavy *German* labours on that ſubject, which have ſo long loaded the preſs, and engroſs'd the leſs illuminated judgments of mankind. It is ſaid alſo, that the aforeſaid Prelate (eſteem'd a Critick in Latin and Engliſh poetry, as appears from his Latin tranſlation of Dryden's Abſalom and Achitophel, &c.) has tranſlated *Virgil's Georgicks*, which he ſent to a friend with the following lines prefix'd ; in which he ſeems to have diſcover'd a ſpirit of prophecy, as well as that fine eaſy diction and noble ſentiments, for which he was remarkable.

——————— *Hæc ego luſi*
Ad Sequanæ *ripas*, Tameſino *a flumine longe*
Jam ſenior, fractuſque, ſed ipſa morte meorum
Quos colui, patriæque memor, neque degener uſquam. DP.

On tueſday laſt a match was run between 2 horſes, one belonging to a Farmer, and the other a Butcher, of Lewis in Suſſex, for 100 guineas, each carrying 11 ſtone and 4 pounds ; to ſtart from Lewis to London, and back again, which is computed to be 100 miles, which was won by the Butcher's ; the Farmer's horſe, on his return, dropt down dead within 3 miles of Lewis, and the other was ſo bad, that it was thought he cannot recover. Several conſiderable wagers were likewiſe loſt on this match. *C.* — — *I fancy my* Brother *is miſtaken ; and that this* humane match *was between two* Butchers.

Laſt friday died Nich. Reaves, Eſq; Examiner in the London Brewery, belonging to his Majeſty's Exciſe ; a place worth between 3 and 400 l. per ann. *D J.*

TUESDAY, *May* 23.

The King's ſetting out for Hanover will not be theſe 3 weeks, on occaſion of the ſitting of the Parliament. —— His Majeſty has been pleaſed to grant his Royal licence for the E. of Lincoln to continue in France with his mother 3 years longer. *D P.*

On ſaturday the Officers of his Majeſty's Cuſtoms made a large ſeizure of 9 horſes loaded with coffee, tea, &c. and other prohibited goods, at the half-way houſe between Putney and Kenſington, which was brought to the Cuſtom-houſe under a ſtrong guard of ſoldiers. *C. D P.*

The ſame day came on a Cauſe at the Court of Delegates at Serjeants Inn, between the Rev. Dr. Hawkins, Appellant, and Mr. Mitchel Appellee, concerning the Doctor's non-reſidence at a living in the County of Eſſex ; and after ſeveral learned debates on both ſides, it was determined in favour of the Doctor. *P. D J.*

The ſame day the Rev. Mr. Moriſon, a Minor Canon of S. Paul's, and Lecturer of S. Bennet's Fink, was preſented by the Dean and Chapter of S. Paul's to a living of 200 l. per ann. in Eſſex. *DP. C*

Yeſterday being the laſt day of Term, ſeveral Printers and Publiſhers appear'd on their recognizances, ſome of whom were diſcharged, and others continued. *D J. D P.* ——— The Court of King's Bench was moved for Mr. Oſborn, a Printer in the Minories, upon a rule of the ſaid Court obtained againſt him, for printing a pamphlet reflecting on the Jewiſh people, and after a ſhort hearing, the Court thought fit to diſcharge the ſaid rule. *P.* — — The Court deferr'd giving judgment on the Lady Lawley 'till next Term. *D J.*

The ſame day Tho. Beck and Edw. Wentland, convicted the laſt Seſſions at the Old Baily, for ſeveral ſtreet and highway robberies, were executed at Tyburn. *P.* Both for ſtreet robberies. *D P.* —— Both their bodies were deliver'd to the Surgeons. *C.*

WEDNESDAY, *May* 24.

The Hon. John Verney, Eſq; Brother to the L. Willoughby de Broke, being in an ill ſtate of health, has reſign'd his place of Judge of Brecknock, Glamorgan, and Radnorſhire ; and is ſucceeded by Mr. Proctor, Steward and Dean of the Chapter of S. Paul's. *D P.* — Yeſterday the Commiſſioners of his Majeſty's Navy appointed Mr. Jam Hatter to ſucceed Mr. Reeves, as Examiner in the London Brewery. *C.*

Dover, May 21. Mr. Alderman Parſons embarqued here on friday, with his Lady for Calais. *P.*

Yeſterday there was a Tryal in the Court of King's Bench at Weſtm. between Mr. Warwick and Mr. Smith, Sheriffs Officers, Plaintiffs, and Mr. Figg, the famous Prize-fighter, the Jury gave the Plaintiffs 100 l. damage. —— Afterwards a Tryal was had, in which the ſaid Mr. Figg was Plaintiff, and the ſaid Warwick and Smith, Defendants, for a treſpaſs, in unlawfully entering his houſe ; in which Caſe the Jury gave Mr. Figg 100 l. damage. *DP.* —— *The famous* Hero *and his* Antagoniſts *fought the* prize *for the ſole benefit of the* Lawyers.

Yeſterday morning the R. Hon. the E. of Sunderland was married to Miſs Trevor, daughter to the late L. Trevor, an agreeable young Lady with 20,000 l. fortune. The ceremony was perform'd at his Lordſhip's houſe in Piccadilly, &c. *P.* — — At the L. Trevor's ſeat at Eaſt Barnet. *D P.* —— *The* W E. *of May* 16 *married this honourable couple that* morning : *The* SJ. *the* ſame evening : *which was confirmed by the* C. *and* DP. of *May* 17.

On monday died John Metcalfe, Eſq; a Bencher of Gray's Inn. *C. D P.* ——— At his lodgings at Kenſington Gravel pits died Col. How, an old experienced in the army. *C.*

From the PEGASUS *in Grub-ſtreet.*

SIR,

YOU having already obliged the Town with Extracts out of the Letters of F. OSBORNE, and S. T's Letter a

to compleat the whole, it seems neceffary you should add that of Mr. OSBORNE's laft, which I here send you: not doubting your regard for fo compleat a Graduate in your Society.

An Extract of Mr. OSBORNE's wit and politenefs, taken out of his Poftfcript in the London Journal of faturday, May 20th.

BE it known unto all men, that I, F. OSBORNE, late dealer in birch and books, but at prefent fet up to be as honeft a man as any in England (there being no degrees of honefty,) and likewife an agreeable companion, do now defire in this my Poftfcript, that I have roundly afferted thefe things as real facts: one of which, I fuppofe, muft not be queftioned; the fecond I am at a ftand to bring ready vouchers for; and the third muft vouch for itfelf. ——Which, a forry fellow, one S. T. has thought fit to difpute the veracity of, whereby my confummate honefty and agreeable companion-fhip, have been much vilified and difparaged. Now I think it high time to give over correfponding with a perfon, who writes without COMMON SENSE or COMMON DECENCY, who hath NOT HONESTY enough to acknowledge my honefty, and honeftly afk my pardon for abufing him and his friend's memory; NOR UNDERSTANDING enough to difcern where the ftrefs of my argument has all along lain; who is not able or willing to diftinguifh between the ufeful and agreeable (which indeed are both my talents;) nor able to fee, that a man may be REGARDED and NEGLECTED both at the fame time.

Now after I had probably proved my round affertions, I might reafonably expect an acknowledgment from an honeft man. —— But the Letter-writer does not feem capable of fo much integrity as to acknowledge things that he does not underftand. —— Inftead of that, he writes on in the fame fcurrilous manner, and wittily fays, he abufes No-body, —— as if forfooth, I was No BODY, —— when every BODY, who fees me, can plainly perceive, that I am SOME-BODY. —— How often muft I tell this Jack Straw (I fuppofe S. T. ftands for Straw) that I am an honeft man, and an agreeable companion. And pray, is not an honeft man fomebody? Is an agreeable companion who CAN print every thing he hears in company —— NOBODY? Befides, how can Nobody write letters to Nobody? That would be fine correfpondence indeed.

Now I'll SUPPOSE —— But what fignify fuppofitions! —— Be they true or falfe, it is nothing to me. —— Tis S. T's bufinefs to anfwer fuppofitions: —— And how does he do it? —— Why he calls one of my fuppofed facts, a fatherlefs ftory, which, like other fpurious iffue, muft lye at the door of the perfon who uthered it into the world. Here he downright lays a baftard to me. —— But I'll be even with him prefently, with his beautiful fimile of fpurious iffue: for can any thing be more ridiculoufly unjuft, than to call that a fatherlefs ftory, for which I am ready to produce a father, as foon as I can get one. —— But this man having once IMPUDENT-LY afferted, that I invented three falfe facts, can't bear the producing my authorities, even before I have produced them; and feems more angry at my APPEARING HONEST, than afhamed at his own appearing a —— Ads bobs, my WIT here had like to have run away with my politenefs.

As to the fact from the Memoirs of the M. of H. tho' I don't know Mr. S. T. yet I know that he knows who I mean by the M. of H. and that he can fatisfy himfelf (and probably has done, but has not grace to own it); for he may find them in the hands of one of the Noble Peers, who married the heirefles of the S—s family. He may probably be acquainted with this family, and they may probably fhow the manufcript to any one that afks it. And therefore he certainly has feen it, tho' he has not the grace to own it.

Now what is the reply to this? Why, the paffage is of no confequence, and NOBODY affents they have feen it. —— A POX on THIS NOBODY. —— But, I fay, the paffage is of the highest confequence to my point; and therefore 'tis abfolutely falfe to fay, NOBODY affents they have feen it : For I, if he will allow me to be SOMEBODY, (and I think I have fairly proved myfelf to be SOMEBODY) have feen perfons that have feen others, who affert, they have feen the Memoirs, and feen thofe words.

Till I hear from Mr. S. T. again, I have nothing more to fay, but that he fhould have left his filthy words, fuch as dirty flutcher, &c. to porters, and his pretty phrafes of, Fie, for fhame, to little Miffes and fchool boys; and learn good language of me, as I am; and ought to know, that 'tis no fhame for a perfon (who is not Nobody) to fay of himfelf, that he pretends to the higheft character, which is that of an honeft man, and an agreeable companion

And tho' I have NOTHING MORE to fay, I can't conclude without SAYING ONE THING MORE, and that is, I was as well acquainted with Julius Cæfar, as I was with Bp. Burnet; and I think Julius Cæfar was full as great a Man as the Bifhop, tho' probably he was not quite fo good a Chriftian.

This Letter-writer may blufter, and labour to refcue the Bifhop's character out of my hands, but that's impoffible; fo that he may go on, and ring as many changes as the College-Youths. He may alfo produce letters, even from the greateft perfonages of the Bifhop's own time; and tho' I know not one word of their contents, yet I here roundly affert, that they can be nothing to the purpofe, againft what I have advanced. —— We (our felf) know him better than any of his Contemporaries could know him; and when I examine fome of his characters, I will carry it to a demonftration, that the Bifhop was not fo agreeable a companion as ourfelf. —— But that I referve to the next opportunity. —— For I find I can write full as well as FIGG or SUTTON ; fo am refolved to fight it out to the laft, for the diverfion of the Town.

F. OSBORNE.

FOREIGN NEWS.

THURSDAY, May 18.
Yefterday arrived the Mail from France.

Paris, May 24. The Sieur Prauli is printing an Analyfis of the military Hiftory of France, fince the beginning of the Monarchy to this time, in form of Chronological Tables with the names of all the Princes and great men who have ferved in the battles, fieges, &c. it will make one volume in folio. D P. Monf. Prault. P.

MONDAY, May 22.
On faturday arrived the Mail from Flanders.

Hague, May 27. The States General refolved yefterday to form an encampment this fummer, of a body of Troops in the neighbourhood of Nimeguen or Breda. C. DP. DJ.

WEDNESDAY, May 24.
The Holland Mail which came in on monday, brought advice from Turky, by the way of Venice, of new infurrection at Conftantinople, wherein the new Sultan was depofed, and the old one fet again upon the throne; for the truth of which we muft refer to our next letters from thence. P.

On Tuefday Stocks were

South Sea Stock was 98 3 8ths, 98 1 qr. to 3 8ths. South Sea Annuity 108 1 qr. Bank 147 1 qr. to 3 8ths. New Bank Circulation 7 l. 15 s. Premium. India 178 1 8th, 178 1 qr. 178, 178 1 qr. 178 1 8th. Three per Cent. Annuity 97 7 8ths. Royal Exchange Affurance 101 1 qr. London Affurance 13. York Buildings 7. African 40. Englifh Copper 2 l. 6 s. Welch ditto 1 l. 15 s. South Sea Bonds 2 l. 13 s. Premium. India ditto 6 l. 10 s. ditto. Blanks 7 l. 8 s. 3 d. to 6 d. 20 l. Prizes 19 l. 16 s.

Books and Pamphlets publifhed fince our laft.

18. An Effay on generofity and greatnefs of Spirit : by Hen. Mills, A. M.

Mifcellaneous Obfervations on Authors, ancient and modern, No. XVII.

A Defence of Reveal'd Religion, &c. by John Conybeare, D. D.

Chriftianity diftinct from the Religion of Nature, &c. Part I. by Tho. Braughton, A. M. Price 1 s.

An Analytical Inquiry into the fpecifick property of Mercury, &c. Price 6 d.

The Hiftory of Scotland, in two Volumes.

A Letter to the R. Hon. Sir Rob. Walpole, &c. by Char. Foreman, Efq; Price 1 s.

An Enquiry into the grounds and reafons of 2 Anniverfary folemnities, Jan. 30. and Nov. 5. by Tho. Chubb. Price 1 s.

A Report from the Committee concerning the Lifts of the Officers in the feveral Courts in Weftminfter, and their Fees.

Select Letters taken from Fog's Weekly Journal, in 2 Volumes.

An Appeal to the Publick : or the remarkable Cafe of Mr. Ifaac Broderick, &c. Price 1 s.

The Fine Gentleman, or the compleat education of a young Nobleman : by Mr. Cofteker. Price 1 s.

20. A Hymn to the Chair. Price 6 d.

A Sermon on 2 Kings vii. 2. Printed on occafion of a late unparallel'd inftance of diftruft in providence, &c. Price 3 s. 6 d.

22. Secret Memoirs of the late Duncan Campbell, &c.

23. A Letter to the Author of the London Journal, wherein the fentiments of Mr. Fog, as to K. W. are fully vindicated. Price 6 d.

The Englifh Lawyer, &c. By Will. Bohun, Efq;

24. A Letter to a Gentlewoman concerning Baptifm, &c. P1. 1 s.

Just published,

(By a Member of the College of Physicians,)
The Second Edition of,

THE FAMILY COMPANION for HEALTH: Or, Plain, easy, and certain Rules, which being punctually observ'd and follow'd, will keep Families free from *Diseases*, and procure them a LONG LIFE. Designed for the Direction of all charitable House-keepers, in administring *Kitchen Physick* in their *Families*.

Printed for F. Fayram and T. Hatchett, under the Royal-Exchange; and J. Leake, Bookseller in Bath. Price Five Shillings.

Where also may be had,

The PRACTICAL PHYSICIAN for Travellers, whether by Sea or Land.

To which is annex'd,

Dr. RADCLIFF's Letter to the late Duke of ORMONDE, concerning his HEALTH, and Medicine, prescribed from him conducive thereto, &c. Price 3s. 6d.

This Day is published,

THE Muse in Livery. A Collection of Poems. Containing, 1. An Entertainment design'd for her Majesty's Birth-day. 2. An Epistle to Stephen Duck. 3. The Wish. 4. The Footman. 5. Religion, a Simile. 6. The Guardian-Angel. 7. The Advice. 8. Sir Amorous Whimsy: Or, the desperate Lover, a true Tale. 9. Kitty, a Pastoral. 10. The Expectation. 11. The Petition. 12. The Enquiry, a Fable. 13. An Entertainment design'd for the Wedding of Governor Lowther and Miss Pennington. 14. A Dream. To which is added, The List of Subscribers. The Second Edition. By R. DODSLEY, a Footman to a Person of Quality at Whitehall. Printed for T. Osborn, Gray's-Inn; and John Nourse, without Temple-Bar.

B O O K S.

Catalogus Librorum in omnibus Facultatibus & Linguis præstantissimorum:

O R, A

CATALOGUE of Books in all Faculties and Languages, which will be sold very cheap this Day, the 25th of this Instant May, 1732, beginning at 9 o'Clock in the Morning, the Price mark'd on each Book, at

NICOLAS PREVOST's *Warehouse, at the Sign of the Ship in the Savoy,*

Turning down the Great Savoy-Gate, where is a commodious Place for Coaches to stand and turn:

Among which are the following,

F O L I O.

Chronique Martienne
Chronique de Froissard, 2 vol.
Laur. Valensis Hist. Ferdinandi Regum Aragoniæ
Thesaurus Italiæ, 45 vol. l. p.
Muratorii Rerum Italicarum Script. 20 vol.
Montfaucon Antiquites Expliques, 15 vol. 1 Edit.
Historia Byzantina, 37 vol.
Museo Farnese, 10 vol.
Marsili Opus Danubiale, 6 v.
Atlas Blavianus, 11 vol.
Theatre de Savoye, 2 vol.
Theatre d'Italie, 4 vol.
Atlas de De Witt, 2 vol.
——— de Sanson, 2 vol.
Ciacconius de Vitis Pontif. Romanor. 4 vol.
Anastasius de Vitis Pontif. Romanor. 3 vol.
Ughelli Italia Sacra, 10 vol.
Gallia Christiana, 4 vol.
Sanderi Chronographia Brabant. 3 vol. l. and sm. p.
Banagii Annales, 3 vol. l. p.
Pagii in Baronii Annales, 4 v.
Histoire Sacree de la Providence, with 500 Copper-Plates
Joan. Matth. & Ph. Villani Historia, 2 vol
Sirmondi Opera, 5 vol. l. p.
Medailles de Louis XIV. 1st Edition, avec la preface tres bien ecrite & proprement enchalsée dans des bordures; Comme aussi le Testament de Louis XIV. & la Proces verbal de ce qui s'est passé au Parlement le 2d 7bre. 171?, que l'on a ajouté a la fin.
Saraponis Practica Medicena Arab. Lat.
Ant. Nattæ de Pulchro.

Q U A R T O.

Autores Classici ad usum Delphini, 61 vol. *compleat, and all bound uniform*
Les Hexaples ou Histoire de la Constitution, 8 vol.
Bibliotheques des Predicateurs, 20 vol.
Histoire Romiane, 16 vol.
Fleury Histoire Ecclesiastique 30 vol. g. & p. p.
Le Polybe de Folard, 6 vol.
Gemme Antiche de Maffei, 4 vol.
Les Vies de Plutarque, par Dacier, 8 vol. l. p.
Histoire de Constantinople, Romaine & de l'Eglise, par Cousin
——Militaire de Louis XIV. 7 vol. fig.
Orlando furioso di Porro
Apollonii Rhodii Argonautica, Gr. cum Majusculis Litteris
Coppin Bouclier de l'Europe
Ammianus Marcellinus Valesii
Casp. Bauhini Pinax Theatri Botanici

O C T A V O.

Plutarchii Opera, Gr. Lat. Hen. Steph. 13 vol.
Les Oeuvres de Plutarque, 13 vol. chez Vascosan
Homelies de St. Chrysostome, avec ses Lettres, traduites en Francois, 19 vol.
Oeuvres de M. Fouquet, 16 v.
Ciceronis Opera, 9 vol. R. Steph.
——idem 10 vol. Seb Gryph.
——idem 16 vol Elzivir
——idem 18 vol. cum Notis Græ ii
——idem 16 vol. Verburgii
ONE HUNDRED Volumes of curious and scarce Hebrew Books
500 Volumes of the best Spanish and French Romances.

This Day was published,

(Being the most useful Work of its Kind yet Extant, to all Sorts of Tradesmen, as well the Old and Experienc'd, as the Young Beginners,)
The THIRD EDITION, of

THE COMPLEAT ENGLISH TRADESMAN: In familiar Letters, directing him in all the several Parts and Progressions of TRADE. In two Volumes:

Vol. I: Treating of the several Points necessary to be known by the YOUNGER TRADESMAN, as well in his Apprenticeship, as on his first Entring upon Business; with regard to Diligence, Over-Trading, Expensive Living, Too-Early Marrying, Diversions, Credit, Partnerships, Compounding, Trading-Frauds, Punctuality, and many other material Subjects. With a Supplement, containing brief and plain Specimens of BOOK-KEEPING, &c.

Vol. II. Containing, 1. Needful Instructions to the MORE EXPPERIENC'D TRADESMAN; with regard to Projects, being Bound one for another, Engrossing, Underselling, Combinations, Leaving of Business, Litigiousness, Dangerous Adventures, Reasons why Tradesmens Differences should, if possible, be ended by Arbitration. 2. Useful Generals in Trade, describing the Principles and Foundations of the Home Trade of Great Britain, with large Tables of the British Manufactures, Product, Shipping, Land-Carriage, Importation, Home Consumption, &c.

Printed for *C. Rivington*, at the Bible and Crown in St. Paul's Church-Yard. Price 11s.

Where may be had,

A PLAN of the English COMMERCE: Being a compleat Prospect of the Trade of all this Nation, as well the Home Trade as the Foreign. The Second Edition. Pr. 5s. 6d.

May 16, was published, Price 6d.

Neatly printed on a fine Dutch *Paper.*

The SECOND EDITION of Nº XVI. for APRIL.

THE GENTLEMAN's MAGAZINE: Or, *Monthly Intelligencer.*

Containing more in Quantity, and greater Variety than any other Book of the Kind and Price.

Printed at St John's Gate, and sold by F. Jefferies in Ludgate-street, at which Places may be had all the former Numbers, except two or three in the first Vol which are re-printing.

IN answer to some invidious Advertisements we reply, That we did not take the full Liberty we had Permission for in using the Names of some WORTHY *Booksellers*, nor said any Thing but the TRUTH (not deny'd us or others, to advertise Country Traders where they might be faithfully served, which we had strong Reason to think they wou'd not be in *some* Places.

What Proof do our *Antagonists* want of their being impertinent? Is it not so, or worse, to pretend that half a dozen Men have a Right to publish Abridgements, and a less Number intitled to the same Privileges, shall be excluded such a Right? Do they pretend to any Title or Qualification better than that of FREE STATIONERS? But if they value themselves on being Booksellers, and have taken this Step to assert the Rights of Booksellers, against a Printer, as some have given out, why do they bring *C. Akers* Printer in Swan-Alley into their Undertaking, and lugg him from the Place where his Sign hangs out, into St. *John's Street*? If a Plea of such Right was any thing but Pretence, why do some of them hug *Non Freemen* in Partnerships with them, and let 'em into the Mysteries of the Trade and Company? nay *Non Freemen* in POSTS, tho' they are so inveterate against a FREEMAN in *such*

We submit the Decency of our Advertisements to the Publick. Their Charge of Scurrility will not make our Work *confused* or *defective*; that theirs is so, we shall prove. If they had put on their SPECTACLES they might have seen the *Ratification of the Treaty*, the *King's intended Tour*, and other Things in ours, which they roundly charge to be omitted. If they leave out some Pieces to be fuller in others, what becomes of their Pretensions to GREATER VARIETY, Words they purloin'd from our Title.

The *Craftsman Extraordinary* was out of Time, as the Publisher acknowledg'd, was calculated only for the Day it was publish'd on, and had no Effect on the Ballot for the S. Sea Affairs, on which we had been sufficiently large.

Can those who have made Applications to the Venders of our Book in Town and Country, and hinder our Advertising in some Papers, with any Colour of Justice blame us for making a proper Defence in another Manner? They talk of Opportunities of sending Advertisements into the Country, and of making mean Applications to Gentlemen. They have sent Advertisements into the Country, and have had Applications made for them to Post-boys and Carriers.

As to a Right to the publick Papers, did not some of our Rivals use it uncontroll'd in their *Monthly Chronicle*? But now nothing will serve their *Purpose* less than our *Plan, Method,* and *almost Title.* There might be a Reason indeed for that; Orders and Messages came indiscriminately for THE MAGAZINE, and any thing with that Name might be put off to the unwary, instead of the GENTLEMAN's. Of this we thought proper to give a Caution; and have rais'd a Storm upon it. —— We would ask their Pardon for our calling their Attempt *ungenerous*, and *unfair*, was it not generally call'd so, or worse, by Persons in Trade. However we beg leave to give Our Reason for it; *viz.* Because in setting out the *Gentleman's Magazine*, we publish'd our Design a Month before; and took care not in the least to clash or interfere with the Title, Method, Form or Plan of any Book in being, that it might have no Dependance but its own Worth, and stand, unassisted with the modern way of Reflecting on others. We never mentioned any Names. How furiously do they lay about them! Their Case may require the extraordinary Assistance of spiteful Insinuations, and the Pen of the noted Advertiser and Title-page-Man; but the World will excuse us, if we use no *Cavilism*, and only insist on Facts. For tho' we were not aware of any Competition secretly manag'd against us, we have accepted the challeng'd Comparison, and shall give it the Publick at our own Expence. Those who do not meet with the GENTLEMAN's MAGAZINE *compar'd and defended*, at the Coffee houses, may have it of Mr. *Jefferies*, Bookseller in Ludgate Street, *Gratis*.

This Day is published,

MArci Hieronymi Vidæ Cremonensis Albæ Episcopi Poemata quæ extant omnia. Quibus nunc primùm adjiciuntur ejusdem Dialogi de Rei-publicæ Dignitate. Ex collatione optimarum editionum emendata, præcipuè verò ad Cremonensis fidem expressa; & in iv Partes, II Tomis comprehensas, distributa: additis Indicibus accuratis: à RICHARDO RUSSEL, A. M.

Impensis Lawtoni Gilliver, & Johannis Nourse, Bibliopolarum.

Went away from his Master,

ON Sunday the 30th of April last, a Negro-BOY, Named SCIPIO, and has not been heard of since. He had on a blue Livery, a small Sleeve to his Coat, turn'd up with yellow Plush, trim'd with white Metal Buttons; his Coat double-breasted to the Waste; the Buttons of his Breeches plain and flat, made of white Metal. He is a strong made Boy, talks bad English, and is about thirteen or fourteen Years old. Whoever takes the said Boy, and brings him to Mr. *Andrew Smith*, Attorney in *King-Street*, near *Guild-Hall*, shall have *Two Guineas* Reward, and all reasonable Charges paid.

BOOKS printed for, and sold by J. Brotherton, at the Bible next the Fleece Tavern, in Cornhill.

Whitlock's Memorials.
Temple's Works, 2 Vol.
Bailey's Eng. Dict. Fol.
Tillotson's Works, 3 Vol.
Bates's Works, Fol.
State of Britain, for 1731.
Bailey's Justin.
Origin of Honour.
Ladies Conduct.
Virgin unmask'd.
Hays's Ship and Supercargo Book-Keeper.
Coke's Detection, 3 Vol.
Bohun's Law of Tythes.
Feasts & Fasts of the Church.
Erasmii Ecclesiastica.
Life of Oliver Cromwell.
Life of the K. of Sweden.
Dampier's Journal to Madagascar.
Rapin's Hist. of England, 15 Vol.
Arbuthnot of Ailments, com.
Telemachus, in French.
Ditto in Fol.
Guardians, 2 Vol.
Langham's Duties.
Free Thoughts on Religion.
La Bell Assemble, 3 Vol.
Vanburgh's Plays, 2 Vol.
Addison's Works, 4 Vol.
Spectators, 8 Vol.
Trapp's Virgil.
D'Urfey's Songs, 6 Vol.
Milton Lost and Regain'd.
D'Anois Tales, 3 Vol.
De Retz Memoirs, 4 Vol
Tom Brown's Works, 4 Vol.
Farnborough's Grammar.
Philips's Grammar.
Dorrington's Devotion.
Congreve's Plays, 3 Vol.
Pope and Swift Misc. 3 Vol.
Pope's Misc. 2 Vol.
Turkish Spy, 8 Vol.

BOOKS *lately printed for* J. Clarke *at the* Golden-Ball *in* Duck-Lane, *near* Little-Britain.

FAbulæ Æsopi Selectæ, or select Fables of Æsop, with an English Translation, more literal than any yet extant; designed for the readier Introduction of Beginners in the Latin Tongue. By H. CLARKE, Master of the publick Grammar School at Islington.

Corderii Colloquiorum Centuria selecta. With a literal Translation. Fourth Edition.

Cornelii Nepotis vitæ excellentium imperatorum, &c. or Cornelius Nepos's Lives of the excellant Commanders: With an English Translation as literal as possible, with English Notes, and a large Index: Third Edition. Both by J. CLARKE, Master of the publick Grammar School in Hull.

The Greek Grammar construed (very proper to be bound up with the Greek Grammar) for the Help of young Beginners. Second Edition, revised and carefully corrected: For the Use of Eton School.

BOOKS printed for J. BATLEY, at the *Dove* in *Pater-Noster-Row.*

1. A Compleat Introduction to the Reading the Holy Scriptures, intended chiefly for young Students in Divinity. In two Parts. Part I. Containing an Account of the civil and religious State of the Jews; the Samaritans, Ceremonies, Temples, Sacrifices, Synagogues, High-Priests, Courts of Justice; particularly the Sanhedrim, Prophets, Scribes, Jewish Sects, Pharisees, Sadducees, Essenes, Proselytes of the Gate. Years, Months, Days, and Hours of the Jews, &c. Part II. Containing the Proofs of the Truth of the Christian Religion; Nature of the New Testament Stile; the Chronology and Geography of the New Testament; the Hebrew Money, Weights and Measures; various Readings, Division into Chapters and Verses, Heresies in the Apostles Days, Versions of the New Testament, Antient and Modern: To which are added the English ones, &c Written originally in French by Messieurs De Beausobre and Lenfant. By the Order of the King of Prussia. Now first done into English, with additional Notes.

2. A compleat Body of Divinity, consonant to the Doctrine of the Church of England. In Six Books. In Two Volumes. By N. Clark, Rector of Shaston St. James in Dorset. Price 9s.

LONDON: Printed by J. HUGGONSON, in *Bartholomew-Close*, for Captain GULLIVER, near the *Temple*, where Letters and Advertisements are taken in: As also at the *Rainbow Coffee-House* in *Cornhill*, and *John's Coffee-House* in *Sheer-Lane*, near *Temple-Bar*. [Price Two Pence.]

The Grub-ſtreet Journal.

NUMB. 126

Thurſday, JUNE 1, 1732.

Penſylvania in *America*,
12*th month*, 1731-2.

To BAVIUS, *Reader of Controverſies to the moſt illuſtrious Society of* GRUB-STREET.

FRIEND,

AS, no doubt, it is thy more peculiar province, ſince thy induction into this Society, to lay before them all papers of the like kind with the following, I have the rather directed it to thee, that thou may'ſt firſt peruſe it; and then, if thou ſhalt think it worthy, (becauſe, I believe, their time is too precious to be ſpent about trifles) commit it to their hearing at the firſt opportunity; with this deſire, that I ſhould rather chuſe to have it meet my brethren at their next Annual Meeting at *London*. But it may not be amiſs if I give thee a hint of what incouraged me to ſend this ſo far to you, which was, the publication of my brother AMINADAB's Epiſtle in your 92d Journal; in which, as he ſet an *example of imparţiality, (in not inſiſting ſo much on his own principles, as the manifeſting, that Parſon BOWMAN's *memory* was full as bad as his *reaſoning*) ſo your Society ſhewed their generoſity, and unprejudiced minds, in not throwing aſide that Epiſtle, becauſe it appeared to have come from a *Quaker*. So much for your Society: now for my Title.

Conſiderations on Parſon SMITH's Preſervative againſt *Quakeriſm*: Or,
The Quakers *proved no* Deiſts, Enthuſiaſts, Hereticks, *or* Schiſmaticks, (*but* True Believers *in* GOD, *in* CHRIST, *and* of HIS Church) *from ſundry of the Parſon's own pretended Quotations from* their Works.

Which I deſire leave to introduce with this Text, by way of Motto.

Surely, the ſerpent will bite without enchantment, and a babler is no better, Eccleſ. x. 11. *The words of a wiſe man's mouth are gracious: but the lips of a fool will ſwallow up himſelf*, Ver. 12. *The beginning of the words of his mouth are fooliſhneſs: and the end of his talk is miſchievous madneſs*, Ver. 13.

NOW it is proper to advertiſe the readers, (becauſe it is very likely that this may fall into more hands than his *Preſervative*) that the Parſon having uſed a new way of quoting from authors, (*viz.* without diſtinguiſhing their words, either by different characters, or inverted comma's) I am obliged to make uſe of a double diſtinction for quoted matter: the firſt, for what is cited out of the *Preſervative*, and which he ſeems to put for my brethren's words, in the Roman print with inverted comma's: the ſecond, for the real words out of the works of one of my brethren, not only with inverted comma's, but encloſed between Brackets. And further, that I have not here attempted a regular, formal Anſwer to his numerous abſurd Aſſertions, and falſe Charges, (becauſe that would ſwell beyond the bounds of ſeveral of ſuch Letters as are generally publiſhed in the Journal, and) for that, I hope, ſome of my brethren in *England* will find time and a readier pen to do that work, but only taken notice of ſuch paſſages hinted at by him, in the works of only one of our authors; which, however, I believe will prove ſufficient to ſhew the diſingenuouſneſs of the Man. Then, to proceed:

1. *Preſervative*, p. 4. '— And will not allow any 'knowledge or faith of Chriſt's outward coming in the 'fleſh, to be eſſential to Chriſtianity; but ſay, he that 'believeth in the *light within*, believeth in Chriſt, and is 'a Chriſtian, and his religion Chriſtianity.' Againſt which, in the margin, is, R. BARCLAY's *Collect.* p. 895. whoſe words are theſe:

1. ['Firſt then; That is falſly ſuppoſed, that the eſ'ſence of the Chriſtian religion conſiſts in the hiſtorical 'faith and knowledge of the birth, death, life, reſur'rection and aſcenſion of Chriſt. That faith and 'hiſtorical knowledge is, indeed, a part of the Chriſtian 'religion; but not ſuch an eſſential part, as that without 'which the Chriſtian religion cannot conſiſt; but an in'tegral part, which goes to the compleating of the Chriſti'an religion: as the hands or feet of a man are integral 'parts of a man, without which, nevertheleſs, a man may 'exiſt, but not an entire and compleat man.'] And again, in the ſame page, ['— the inward revelation or 'illumination of God, proceeding from the divine Sun, 'doth ſhine into the eye of the Mind, and by its in'fluence moves the mind to aſſent unto the hiſtorical 'truth of Chriſt's Birth, Life, &c. in the reading or 'hearing the Scripture, or meditating therein.'] From which it is evident, that my friend BARCLAY is ſo far from ſaying, He that *believes only in the Light within is a Chriſtian*, (as, P. SMITH, has aſſerted) that he affirms, The *divine illumination*, or light within, *moves the mind to aſſent to the hiſtorical truth of Chriſt's* coming in the Fleſh, &c.

2. *Preſerv.* p. 10. '— Who (Mankind) have not (as 'the *Quakers* themſelves own,) the outward knowledge 'of Chriſt, or of Chriſt's *outward* Manhood, and out'ward Birth, and Death, and Sufferings in the Fleſh; 'but from the Scripture, and outward teaching.' ROBERT BARCLAY's *Coll. of his Works*, p. 895.

2. ['Secondly, If by an immediate revelation be un'derſtood ſuch a revelation of God, as begets in our 'Souls an hiſtorical Faith and Knowledge of the birth 'of Chriſt in the Fleſh, without the means of the holy 'Scripture, we do not contend for ſuch a revelation, as '*commonly* given, or to be expected by us, or any 'other Chriſtians.'] Again,

'2 ['Thirdly, Nevertheleſs we do firmly aſſert, that 'God can moſt eaſily, clearly and certainly manifeſt to 'our minds the hiſtorical Truths of Chriſt's Birth, &c. 'when it ſo pleaſeth him, even without the Scripture, or 'any other outward mean.'] With this the Parſon himſelf agrees, who ſays, at the top of p. 10.

3. 'For tho' Chriſt the Word, is by his divine eſ'ſence every where, in all things, and in all men, and 'ſufficient or able in an *extraordinary way*, inwardly to 'teach men all the eſſentials of Chriſtianity, without 'any outward teaching; —'

Therefore, I hope, here is no *Deiſm, Enthuſiaſm, Hereſy*, or *Schiſm*. Nay, I have a good mind to drop my Pen; for the Man has in this one poſition expreſſed the ſubſtance of our Doctrine, *viz.* That *Chriſt is in all men*, (and conſequently in thoſe that have not the means of outward teaching) *teaching them the eſſentials of Chriſtianity*: For what? Why, that they might know them, and obey them; and receive Salvation for ſo doing. And, that this is an *extraordinary*, and not the *ordinary way*, by which the *hiſtorical knowledge of Chriſt in the fleſh*, (as my friend BARCLAY phraſes it) or of his *outward manhood*, &c. (as P. SMITH terms it) *is commonly manifeſted to us*, they both ſeem to agree in: Then what foundation was there for the Parſon's vile imputation on us?

4. *Preſerv.* p. 14. '*Queſt.* Does not the Apoſtle to 'the *Coloſſians* ſay, That the *Goſpel was preached then 'to every creature under heaven?* or, as ſome ſay the 'word may be rendered, *in every creature?* And how 'could this be, if every individual man had it not in'wardly preached to him by the *light within* him? *Col.* 'i. 23.' *R. B*'s *Apol.* p. 132, 133.

['Thirdly, That God, in and by this light and ſeed, '*(or ſpirit)* invites, calls, exhorts, and ſtrives with every 'man, in order to ſave him; which, as it is received, 'and not reſiſted, works the ſalvation of all, even of 'thoſe who are ignorant of the death and ſufferings of 'Chriſt, and of *Adam*'s fall, both by bringing them to a 'ſenſe of their own miſery, and to be ſharers in the ſuf'ferings of Chriſt inwardly, and by making them partakers 'of his reſurrection, in becoming holy, pure and righte'ous, and recovered out of their ſins. By which alſo are 'ſaved they that have the knowledge of Chriſt outwardly, 'in that it opens their underſtanding, rightly to uſe and 'apply the things delivered in the Scripture, and to re'ceive the ſaving uſe of them.'] To which I will here add another:

4. ['Sect. XXIII. Thirdly, This ſaving ſpiritual light 'is the Goſpel, which the Apoſtle ſaith expreſly, is '*preached in every creature under Heaven*; even that very 'goſpel, whereof PAUL *was made a Miniſter*, Col i 23. 'For the goſpel is not a meer declaration of good things, 'being *the power of God unto ſalvation, to all thoſe 'that believe*, Rom. i. 16. Though the outward de'claration of the goſpel be taken ſometimes for the goſ'pel; yet it is but figuratively, and by a metonymy: 'For to ſpeak properly, the goſpel is this inward power 'and life, which preacheth glad tidings in the hearts of 'all men, offering ſalvation unto them, and ſeeking to 'redeem them from their iniquities; and therefore it 'is ſaid to be *preached in every creature under heaven*; 'whereas there are many thouſands of men and wo'men, to whom the outward goſpel was never preach'ed.'] Page 167, 168.

Now, if Parſon SMITH has gain-ſaid any of this, he muſt have contradicted his own poſition, in p. 10. before quoted, Parag. 3. For what is the *goſpel*, but the *eſſentials of Chriſtianity?* (as he terms it.) To whom taught? To men; (as he ſays.) How? Inwardly; (as he owns.) And, inaſmuch as, in this quotation from my friend BARCLAY, not only this inward goſpel (or *Chriſt the power of God*, 1 Cor. i. 24) is inſiſted on; and the outward declaration (or glad tidings of *His* being come as a Saviour) is acknowledged; and both according to Scripture, ſurely there can be no *Deiſm, Enthuſiaſm, Hereſy*, or *Schiſm* truly charged on us, the People called *Quakers*, for believing accordingly.

5. *Preſerv.* p. 18, 19. '*Queſt.* What will be the con'ſequence of ſaying, That the *light within every* man 'coming into the world, is ſufficient to teach him all the 'eſſentials of Chriſtianity, without the Scripture, or any 'outward teaching; *(ſee the top of his 10th page men'tioned before)* and yet, that it does not teach them 'any thing of Chriſt's outward birth, and death, and 'ſufferings in the fleſh, and the other hiſtorical truths 'and matter of fact concerning him, recorded in the 'ſcriptures, without the ſcripture, and outward teach'ing?' Who has aſſerted this? Why Parſon SMITH himſelf: for R. BARCLAY (in the very page mentioned by him, 895th of his *Coll.* and the firſt line of the following) has declared the direct contrary; as may be ſeen in the latter part of the ſecond quotation before cited: ſo that if there is any *Deiſm*, &c. here, it is of the Parſon's own making.

6. *Preſerv.* p. 19. '*Queſt.* Do not they ſay, that though 'the *light within* does not teach them any thing of 'Chriſt's outward birth and ſuffering in the fleſh; *(the 'contrary to this has been ſhewn already,)* yet it teaches 'them many other evangelical truths without the Scrip'ture.' *R. B*'s *Coll.* p. 895. See his own Words:

6. ['For albeit many other evangelical Truths be ma'nifeſted to us by the immediate manifeſtation of God, 'not uſing the Scriptures as the means; yet the hiſtori'cal knowledge of Chriſt is not *commonly* manifeſted to 'us, nor to any others, but by the holy Scripture, as 'the means, and that by way of a material Object.'] Again,

7. *Preſerv.* ib. '*Anſ.* Yes: they ſay ſo, and that is all, 'without having ever given us any proof that the *light 'within* teaches them any of the peculiar truths of the 'goſpel without the Scripture.' Pray obſerve,

7. ['But firſt thou may'ſt mind, that the Prophets, who 'fortold Chriſt's coming in the fleſh, and being to be 'born of a virgin, and afterwards to ſuffer death, did 'know theſe truths of fact by the inward Inſpiration 'of God without outward means: for which, ſee 1 *Pet.* 'i. 10, 11. Now that which hath been, may be.'] BARCLAY, ib. p. 896.

I apprehend every one will readily conclude, what a man this Parſon is; and, that they, who believe this doctrine of *R B*'s, are not *Deiſts, Enthuſiaſts, Hereticks*, or *Schiſmaticks*.

8. *Preſerv.* p. 20. '*Queſt.* Is not the *goſpel*, ſpeaking 'properly, the inward power and life of the *light within*, 'which preacheth glad tidings in the hearts of men; 'and not the outward declaration of the doctrine of Chriſt 'in the Scripture, which is ſometimes called the goſpel, 'but only figuratively? *R. B*'s *Apol.* p. 167, 168.

For the true ſenſe of this Queſtion, *R. B*'s own words before cited, Parag. 4. Sect. XXIII. and what follows in Parag. 9. quoted from him.

9. *Preſerv.* p. 21. '*Queſt.* Is not *the word that was 'nigh to the Romans, in their mouth, and in their 'heart*, and which the Apoſtle directed them to, the 'inward powerful word or goſpel, preached inwardly 'in the hearts of all, by the *light within*; Rom. x. 8?' *R. B*'s *Ap.* p. 170.

9. ['But the Apoſtle Paul opens and illuſtrates this 'matter yet more, *Rom.* x. where he declares, *That the 'word, which he preached*, (now the *word* which he 'preached, and the *goſpel* which he preached, and where'of he was a Miniſter, is one and the ſame) *is not far off, 'but nigh, in the heart, and in the mouth*; which done, 'he frameth as it were the objection of our adverſaries, in

the 14th and 15th verſes, *How ſhall they believe in him, of whom they have not heard? And how ſhall they hear without a Preacher?* This he anſwers in the 18th verſe, ſaying; *But* (*I ſay*) *have they not heard? Yes, verily,* ‘*their ſound went into all the earth, and their words unto the ends of the world*; inſinuating, that this divine preacher hath ſounded in the ears and hearts of *all men*; for of the *outward Apoſtles*, that ſaying was not true, neither then, nor many hundred years after; yea, for ought we know, there may be yet great and ſpacious nations and kingdoms, that never have heard of *Chriſt* nor his *Apoſtles*, as outwardly.’]

If I had ſtood at P. Smith's elbow, when he dictated theſe Queſtions, I would have adviſed him to have phraſed one of them thus:

Is not the *Light within*, the powerful *Light within*, preached by the *Light within?*

Which he might as well have done, as to have pretended, that he had given either the words or ſenſe of our authors: for then he would have had his darling words (*the Light within*) of ridicule, as he ſeems to uſe them, lugg'd in oftner, in order to have embelliſhed his ſtyle more.

10. *Preſerv.* p. 23. ‘*Queſt.* Is it not enough that the *Quakers* own, they are bound to believe the hiſtorical truths, and matters of fact concerning Chriſt's outward birth, and death, and reſurrection recorded in the Scripture, when they are made known to them, by the Scriptures?’ (R. B's Apol. p. 275.) ‘*Anſ.* No, It is not enough, but they muſt own them as *eſſential* truths of Chriſtianity; tho' they are not made known to them by the *Light within*, but by the Scripture.’ So far for *Patrick*, now for *Robert*:

10 [To be a *Member* of a particular *Church of Chriſt*, as this inward work is indiſpenſibly neceſſary, ſo is alſo the *outward profeſſion* of, and *belief in Jeſus Chriſt*, and thoſe *holy truths* delivered by his Spirit in the Scriptures; ſeeing the teſtimony of the Spirit recorded in the Scriptures, doth anſwer the teſtimony of the ſame Spirit in the heart, even *as face anſwereth face in a glaſs*. Hence it follows, that the inward work of holineſs, and forſaking iniquity, is neceſſary in every reſpect to the being a member in the *Church of Chriſt*; and that the *outward profeſſion* is neceſſary to be a member of a particular gathered *Church*, but not to the being a member of the *Catholick Church*; yet it is abſolutely neceſſary, where God affords the opportunity of knowing it: and the *outward teſtimony* is to be believed, where it is preſented and revealed; the ſum whereof hath, upon other occaſions, been already proved.’]

Having, in the compaſs of only theſe *ten* quotations, had matter enough to make evident, to them who have eyes to ſee, and ſenſe to underſtand, the aſſertion in my title, *viz.* That we (the *Quakers*) are *Believers in God, in Chriſt, and of his Church*, and ſo conſequently not *Deiſts, Enthuſiaſts, Hereticks*, or *Schiſmaticks*, as Patrick Smith, Vicar of *Great Paxton* in *Huntingtonſhire*, has fally and maliciouſly endeavoured to prove: therefore now, Bavius, I ſhall conclude, greeting thee in love, and bid thee farewel, who am

Thy ſincere Friend,

OBADIAH.

DOMESTIC NEWS.

C. *Courant.*	E P. *Evening Poſt.*
P. *Poſt-Boy.*	S J. *S. James's Evening Poſt.*
D P. *Daily Poſt.*	WE. *Whitehall Evening P.*
D J. *Daily Journal.*	LE. *London Evening Poſt.*

Hyp-Oratorical Puffs and Advertiſements in the month of May.

Hyp Advertiſements 6. Oratorical Ditto 5. In all, 11.
—— Hyp. Puffs 5. Oratorical 3. In all, 8.
—— Decreaſed in the Advertiſements this month, 7.
—— Decreaſed in the Puffs, 3.

Thursday, *May* 25.

A ſtatue of his Royal Highneſs the Duke on horſeback, done by a ſkilful Artiſt, is placed at Major Foubert's in King-ſtreet near Golden-ſquare, to be there view'd by his Majeſty. *D P.*

Cardiganſhire, May 15. In the Pariſh of Kilkening, one Edwards, a Sadler, coming home about 12 or 1 a clock in the morning drunk, made his maid get out of bed, and carry his horſe into the field; and he went after her, and in the morning ſhe was found dead in the field. The Jury brought him in guilty of *Wilful murder*, and he was committed to our jail; he ſays the horſe kicked her on the head. *P.* —— *Glouceſter, May* 20. On tueſday one Farmer Townſhend and his ſervant coming through a clover ground belonging to a Butcher, accidentally broke the gate, which ſo enraged the owner, that he went after them, and (notwithſtanding all they could ſay to pacify him) fell violently on the ſervant, and broke his ſcull, ſo that he died in a few hours: the Coroner's inqueſt brought in their verdict Wilful murder. *D P.*

This morning Col. Coſby, his Lady and 2 daughters, embark'd in the River for New York. *L E.*

On thurſday ſe'nnight Mrs. Wyvill, ſiſter of Sir Marmaduke Wyvil of Conſtable-Burton in Yorkſhire, Bar. was marry'd to the Rev. Mr. Gee, who has a living of 500 l. per ann. in that County. *D P.* ——Sir Marmaduke's daughter. *P.*

Bath, May 18. Yeſterday dy'd here Sir Hen. Aſhurſt of Water-ſtoke in Oxfordſhire, Bar. *D P.*

This day a Pad belonging to the Earl of Tilney being frighten'd at the flirting of a Coachman's whip, ran away with the rider, and in her career fell; bruiſed the groom, broke her own neck, and dy'd on the ſpot: the mare was valued at 100 guineas. *D P.* —— *The death of ſo celebrated a* Mare *makes almoſt as good a paragraph in a News-Paper, as that of ſome celebrated* Lady.

Friday, *May* 26.

On ſaturday a full length picture of his preſent Majeſty, painted by Mr. Lucy of S. Martin's-lane, was ſhipp'd off for Edinburgh, to be ſet up in the Town-Council Chamber of that City. *D P.*

Yeſterday the R. Hon. the L. Wilmington, Lord Preſident of his Majeſty's Privy Council, was elected a Governor of the Charter houſe. *C. D P.*

We hear that the Earl of Sunderland preſented his Bride with a diamond necklace of 3000 l. value, the day of her Marriage. *D P.*

On wedneſday was heard at Doctor's Commons, a cauſe between Rich. and Char. Devon. The Queſtion was, Whether a teſtamentary Schedule wrote with the deceaſed's own hand could, with circumſtances attending it, deſtroy a Will executed in the preſence of 3 witneſſes. The ſame was learnedly argued; and Dr. Betteſworth gave ſentence for the validity of the Will, which was upwards of 10,000 l. *P.*

The latter end of laſt week died the Rev. Mr. John Laurence, Rector of Biſhop's-Weremouth in the Biſhoprick of Durham, and Prebendary of Sarum. He was remarkable for his extraordinary writings on *Chriſtian Morals*, and the *Art of Gardening*. His living was near 500 l. per ann. and is in the gift of the L. Biſhop of Durham. *C. D P.* —— Yeſterday died Mr. Edw. Goſlin ſenior, Carver to the R. Hon the L. Mayor. *P.* ſenior Carver to the R. Hon. the L. Mayor. *D P.* — *Obſerve how* different *the ſenſe is made, only by the* different *place of a ſingle* comma! *And yet ſome Learned Members of our Society are ridiculed by the illiterate for their exactneſs in theſe niceties.*

Yeſterday morning a Glover at Stratford in Eſſex ſtabb'd his Apprentice with a knife in the breaſt, ſo that he died on the ſpot: the boy was his own brother's ſon. *D P.*

Chriſtened Males 168. Females 155. In all 323. *Buried* Males 192. Females 192. In all 384. Decreaſed in the Burials this week 7. *P.*

Saturday, *May* 27.

Yeſterday the Letter from Sig. John Angelo Belloni at Rome directed to the Committee to whom the Petition of the Proprietors of the Charitable Corporation, &c. is referred; or if they did not ſubſiſt, to Sir Rob. Sutton, Sir John Shadwell, Dr. John Mowbray, or any of them, was burnt by the hands of the Common Hangman, at the Royal Exchange, the Sheriffs of London and Middleſex being preſent. *D P.* The Letter &c. *P.* — The infamous Libel contained in a letter from Signior Angelo Belloni, the Pretender's Banker at Rome, &c. amidſt a great croud of ſpectators, who ſignified their ſatisfaction by repeated Huzza's; and it was no ſmall pleaſure to honeſt men to hear the 12 bells at S. Michael's ring at the ſame time. *C.* A moſt audacious Libel. *D J.* —— *A Member, who had been bit by* the Charitable Corporation, *obſerves, that tho' the taking notice of the* bells *with ſo much* ſatisfaction *might be a token of the* honeſty *of theſe* honeſt men, *it was none of their* wit: *for*, As the bell-clinketh, &c.

Yeſterday morning Mrs. Man, wife to Mr. John Man, a Surgeon, in Wych-ſtreet, S. Clements-Danes, having been ill of a fever, and as is ſuppoſed delirious, being in bed with her huſband, found an opportunity when he was aſleep, to take a Lancet out of his pocket, and therewith ſtabb'd herſelf in the throat, ſo that ſhe died a few hours after. *D P.*

Extract of a Letter in the Daily Journal. —— The following paragraph is extracted from a little book, with a very *unfaſhionable* title for the times, viz. *The Practice of Piety*, which ſo little a while ago, as when the preſent generation was in hanging ſleeves, who now, with great ſelf ſufficiency, ſtalk about in their Fool's coat, and an honeſter and more religious ſet of people, tho' *leſs illuminated*, were *in eſſe*, was in ſo great vogue, that there was hardly a family in the Kingdom without it, as the more than forty large impreſſions, it had run thro', teſtify. 'Tis true, it is written in the exploded ſtrain of Judgments; but perhaps ſome of your Readers will forgive the *Bigotry* of the writer, for the ſake of the *honeſt intention*, who, having lived an *age ago*, believed one part of the world might be warn'd and amended by the misfortunes of the other.— ‘Tiverton in Devonſhire (whoſe remembrance makes my heart bleed) was oftentimes admoniſhed by her godly Preacher, that God would bring ſome heavy judgment on the Town, for their horrible profanation of the Lord's day, occaſion'd chiefly by their market on the day following. Not long after his death, on the 3d of April 1598, God (in leſs than half an hour) conſum'd with a ſudden and fearful fire the whole Town, except only the Church, the Court-houſe, and the Alms-houſes, or a few poor peoples dwellings, where a man might have ſeen 400 dwelling houſes all at once on fire, and above 50 perſons conſum'd with the flame. And again, on the 5th of Auguſt 1612 (14 years ſince the former fire) the whole Town was again fir'd and conſum'd, except ſome 30 houſes of poor people, with the School-houſe and Alms-houſes. *Practice of Piety*, 8vo. p. 247.’

Payne, of the Inner Temple, Eſq; is appointed one of his Majeſty's Council in the Dutchy Court of Lancaſter, in the room of John Finch, Eſq; who hath reſign'd. *S J.*

On monday died Miſs Orme, in New Bond ſtreet, daughter to an eminent Merchant in Dublin, and a fortune of 10,000 l. *S J.* —— *There come, it ſeems*, Fortunes, *as well as* Fortune-hunters, *from* Ireland.

N.B. The Defence of the Oratory, which has been ſome time publiſhed, and is directly applicable to the Controverſies now on foot, is to be had there, with the other books, but 210 being left of ſeveral thouſands which were printed. *Fog's Journal.* —— *The tacking theſe* Defences *to the* Lectures concerning Miſs Cadieres raptures, *and putting them off upon the buyer as new pieces, has ſucceeded wonderfully, according to this account: we may therefore ſoon expect a* fourth-firſt Edition.

On thurſday died at the India Warehouſe, Mr. John Gilbert, Auctioneer and Warehouſe-keeper to the Eaſt-India Company, and father of the preſent worthy Dean of Exeter. *S J. WE. L E.*

Laſt night Edm. Cheeſeborough, who was yeſterday capitally convicted, hang'd himſelf in his cell, with the packthread which ty'd up his irons. *S J.*

Monday, *May* 29.

Yeſterday the R. Rev. the L. Biſhop of Litchfield and Coventry preach'd before their Majeſties, his Royal Highneſs the Prince of Wales, &c. *C. D P.* —— And the Rev. Dr. Franks before his Royal Highneſs *the Duke*, &c. — It being the anniverſary of the birth of *his late Majeſty* King George the firſt, of glorious memory, the ſame was obſerved throughout the Cities of London and Weſtminſter, by ringing of bells, and all other demonſtrations of joy. *C.*

Yeſterday morning, Mr. Will. Peſtel, one of the Fellows of S. John's College, Oxford, and ſon to Mr. Tho. Peſtel, an eminent Jeweller, was found dead in his bed, at his father's houſe in Coleman ſtreet, having voided a large quantity of blood. *C. D P.*

Tuesday, *May* 30.

Yeſterday being the Anniverſary of the Reſtoration of King Charles II. the ſame was obſerved throughout the cities of London and Weſtminſter with the uſual rejoicings, as ringing of bells, firing the great guns at the Park and at the Tower, and the evening concluded with bonfires and other illuminations. —The Rev. Dr. George, preached before the honourable Houſe of Commons, at St. Margaret Weſtminſter: and the Rev. Dr. Simpſon before the Right Honourable the Lord Mayor, &c. at St. Paul's. *C. P. D P.*

We hear that Sir George Cooke, Knt. has ſurrender'd the Office of chief Prothonotary of the court of Common Pleas to his ſon, George Cooke of the Inner Temple, Eſq; and that Richard Thompſon, Eſq; one of the Secondaries of that Court, has purchas'd the Office of ſecond Prothonotary of — Warner, Eſq; who lately ſucceeded Richard Foley, Eſq; deceaſed. *D P.* ——Mr. Higgs, Clerk of the Indictments at Hicks's-Hall, ſucceeds Mr. John Rolfe as Deputy-Clerk of the Peace for the city and liberty of Weſtminſter, lately deceaſed. *P.*

Yeſterday the Seſſions ended at the Old-Baily, when the nine following perſons receiv'd ſentence of death, *viz.* John Osborn, Edward Paul, alias Spaw, [alias Shaw, *D J.*] and Michael Shaw for Street-Robberies; Robert Robinſon, John Wakeling, and John Dunſtan, for Burglary; Henry Barns, William Woolcott, and John Longman, [Longmore, *D J. C.*] for the Highway. Three were burnt in the hand, and twenty-ſeven order'd for tranſportation. *D P.*

On ſaturday morning George Chamberlayne, Eſq; Member of Parliament for Buckingham, was married at St. James's Church to Miſs Hardey, a daughter of Sir Thomas Hardey, a beautiful young Lady, with a Fortune of 10,000 l. *D P.*

This day being the birth-day of her Royal Highneſs the Princeſs Amelia, 2d daughter to their Majeſties, when ſhe enter'd into the 22d year of her age; and alſo of her Royal Highneſs the Princeſs Carolina, third daughter to

their Majesties, when she enter'd into the 19th year of her age; there was a great appearance of Nobility, and their Royal Highnesses received the Compliments usual on such occasions. *S J. WE.*

On Saturday died Mr. Argus of St. Margaret's West-minster, near 90 years of age; he was Church-warden when great Tom, was told, which is now at St. Paul's. *J.*

There is a Puff Letter, in commendation of the Wit, Learning, and Style of the *Hyp-Doctor,* which seems to be published 2 days too soon, speaking of the *Hyp-Doctor* of May 30, as past. *The contradiction of expelling, &c.* shews it to be the Doctor's own composition, and that he is - - - - - -VERUS.

O Doctor, *leave off fruitless puffing. Why in VERUS name wilt thou presume to lye?*

WEDNESDAY, May 31.

Yesterday his Majesty was pleased to make the following promotions in the Army, viz. Major General Honeywood to be Commander of the Regiment of Dragoons, lately the L. Carpenter's. The L. Mark Kerr to succeed Honeywood. ——Col. John Middleton to succeed L. Kerr. ——And the E. of Rothes to succeed Col. Middleton. *DP.* ——To morrow his Majesty will go to the house of Peers, and put an end to the present Session of Parliament. And it is thought his Majesty will embark for Holland, in his way to Hanover, on Saturday next. *DJ. P.* —— Gen. Deimer will attend his Majesty. *C.* We hear that his Majesty designs to return the latter end of August. *DP.*

Yesterday John Trevor, Esq; son of the L. Trevor, was married to Miss Steele, only daughter of the late Sir Rich. Steele, Knt. a young Lady of fine Accomplishment, and a good fortune. *C. DP.*

On Sunday next the new Chappel in Spring gardens will be opened by the Rev. Dr. Pearce of S. Martin's; the Rev. Mr. Lamplugh being appointed morning Preacher, and the Rev. Mr. Freeman in the Afternoon. *C. P.*

From the PEGASUS in Grub-street.

SIR,

YOU are desired to publish the following lines in the next *Grub-street Journal,* which were written about two months before that Paper was first published. By so doing you will give a woman's longing; you will prevent their being printed in any other Paper; you will shew your own impartiality, and regard to truth, more than interest; and you will very much oblige a great number of Ladies, who are real admirers of the unparallel'd stupidity of that *Journal,* and in particular, your humble servant,

CLAUDIA RUFINA.

To the ingenious Author of the *Grub-street Journal.*

At first, your *Journal,* to elude the shame
It fear'd, by owning its true parents name,
Stole that of matchless POPE, to give it fame.
But soon the cheat appear'd; for now we see,
'Tis *Grub-street* all, without an irony;
Its future merit you yourself knew best,
So nam'd it *Grub,* and spoke the truth in jest.

This being read, Mr. POPPY declared, that in his opinion a particular regard ought to be paid to a fair Lady, especially in the condition here mentioned, and something done effectually to *save her longing.* ——To which Mr. DACTYL answered, that he questioned very much both the fairness of the Lady, and the reality of her longing. For as to the first, he could not suppose, that when she was charging others with *stealing* a false name, she would subscribe a false one herself: and if the had subscribed her true name, she was certainly both lame and bad-hair'd. And as to the second, he could not believe, that any Lady, either fair or foul, big with a poetical company, could contain herself for two years and two months together, in a longing condition. —— Mr. SPONDEE rejoined, that he believed there was good proof of the truth of what Mr. DACTYL had suggested. The two years ago as the last Autumnal Equinox, a little Brat appeared in the world with a Label in its mouth—*Cinna vult videri pauper, & est pauper:* and the following verses in its breast,

Cinna affects to wear a Beggars cloaths;
And is the very beggar that he shows:
So *Grub-street Journalists* are found in fact
To be the Dunces they'd be thought to act.
This little creature was at first owned by the *Register of Grub-street,* who being not able to support him, it is probable this Lady picked him up, and charitably cloathed him in her own livery.—To this Mr. MÆVIUS added, that the Lady might be very charitable, but she seemed to be bolder than some concerned in the Charitable Corporation. For she had charged the Society with a thing which was absolutely false, viz. the *stealing* Mr. POPE's *name,* to make their *Journal* sell. But the time she had fixed upon for the discovery of the cheat, *two months after it was first*

published, was very much to our advantage. For from that very time, notwithstanding the tricks of some Booksellers, Printers, and Hawkers, it has risen gradually 'till this; when five times the number are sold which were then. This is certainly owing to the *unparallel'd stupidity* of it, of which this Lady and *a great number of her Sex are real admirers.* It is this which gives it such a pre-eminence, while *parallel'd,* vulgar *stupidity,* such as that of —no body will buy; no body will read, but those who are payed for doing it. Our Motto is *Crescit sub pondere virtus.*

Dublin, May, 23. We hear from Birr, *alias* Parson's Town, in the King's County, that they have near that place such quantities of locusts, that there is scarce any riding in the evening, and they destroy all greens, except ash, which they do not touch. *P. 30.*

Edinburgh, May 18. The General Assembly rose last tuesday, and appointed the next Assembly to meet the first thursday of May, 1733.——This week died Barnaby Barrow, Esq; General Comptroller of the excise in Scotland, a place reckoned worth 400 l. a year. *C. DP.*

Edinburgh, May 23. Friday last died Mrs. Miller, a Quaker, famous for her industry and improvements in home manufactures. It is said she employed 6 or 700 poor people at spinning, &c. which makes her death much regretted. She was yesterday interred in the Quakers burying place; where friend Erskine gave the word of exhortation to a very numerous auditory. *DJ 30.*

✦✦✦✦✦✦✦✦✦✦✦✦✦ ✦✦✦✦✦✦✦✦✦✦✦✦✦

FOREIGN NEWS.

THURSDAY, May 25.

Bologna, May 3. Yesterday in the afternoon the famous Laura Bassi, being accompanied with the chief Ladies of this City, went to the College of Philosophers, where she was very strictly examin'd in several points of Philosophy, to which the answer'd with such uncommon learning, that the won universal applause. She was thence conducted by our L. Chief Justice and Senators, &c. to the Palace; where she was promoted to the degree of Doctor of Philosophy with the usual formalities, in the presence of the Cardinal Legate, the Cardinal Archbishop, &c. *S J. LE.*

Paris, May 31. On the 29th, the Abbot Terrasson, of the Royal Academy of Sciences, was received in the French Academy, &c. *C. P.* Author of *The Life of Sethos. WE.* —— On the 26th, the Parliament received Letters Patents from the King, enjoining them to go upon the publick business; and on the 27th the chambers met and agreed to register the Letters Patents; and afterwards they began to plead as usual. *C. P. DP.*

FRIDAY, May 26.

Leghorn, May 10. By a letter from Marseilles, we have advice, that they had receiv'd orders from the Court of France to fit out in all haste 6 galleys and 6 galleots, to be sent to Toulon, to join 6 men of war that are equipping in that port, where it is said 12 more men of war are expected from Brest. *C.*

Hague, May 30. Private letters from Berlin insinuate, that the Prince Royal's marriage with the Princess of Beveren is put off till May, 1733; that is to say, 'till Latter Lammas.—— That their Britannick and Prussian Majesties will have an interview with the Emperor at Carelsbad, where those 2 Princes will not only be reconcil'd, &c. *P.* *Hamburgh, May 23.* Letters from Berlin of the 20th mention, as if the accommodation between Great Britain and that Court it not so far advanc'd as was imagin'd. *D. P.*

SATURDAY, May 27.

Hamburgh, May 23. We learn from Berlin, of the 20th, that negotiations are on foot for an accommodation between that Court and that of London. *D 7.*

Madrid, May 13. 'Tis assur'd from the Camp before Gibraltar, that the works will infallibly be compleated and mounted with Artillery before the end of this month. *D P.*

Extract of a letter from Paris. There is no wine to expected from Bosne, Mulfau, Volnay, Pornard, Diffeneau, and other adjacent places, there remaining little less than rocks, occasioned by a most terrible hurricane, which swept away most of the earth, with the roots of the Vines; and also the Cattle which were feeding thereabouts, and likewise threw down several Houses. *S 7.*

MONDAY, May 29.

On Saturday arrived the Mail from Holland, yesterday one from France, and another from Flanders.

Lisbon, Ap. 22. The King has publish'd an edict, setting forth, That his Majesty having been informed, that the great number of young women brought into this Kingdom from Brazil, under the pretence of going into Nunneries, is one of the chief causes why that Country is not so well peopled as it might be; and having heard

that many, who might be married, are brought hither against their wills, and forced into Convents, where they lead a melancholy life; his Majesty has thought fit to forbid any women or maidens being brought over hither, until his Majesty has given consent thereto. *C.*

TUESDAY, May 30.

Rome, May, 17. On tuesday morning the Chevalier de S. George took leave of his Holiness, designing to go and pass the summer at Albano: we understand this Comfort has lately received from Prince James Sobieski (her Father) in Poland, several jewels of great price, together with a sabre, the hilt whereof is set with a ruby and large diamonds, for the Chevalier her Husband; also a large topaz for her eldest son, and a bandelier covered with diamonds for the youngest; all which rarities King John took from the Turks, when he beat them, and made them raise the siege of Vienna. *P.*

Venice, May, 24. We have received advice from Jannina, that another conspiracy having been discovered at Constantinople, for deposing the Grand Seignior, restoring the old Sultan Achmet, the same had cost a bundance of people their lives. —— *Paris, May 30* Our last letters from Constantinople, by the way of Marienne, confirm the deposition of the Prime Vizir Osman Bassan. *P.*

WEDNESDAY, May 30.

Leghorn, May, 17. Our last advices from Corsica confirm, that the Malecontents of that Island had accepted the general pardon offered them by the Prince of Wirtemberg, in the name, and under the Guaranty of the Emperor. *P.*

Hague, May, 9. Notwithstanding all the menaces and motions of our Merchants to deter the swedish East-India-Company from accepting of the King of Sweden's Charter, that Company will be established, and possibly the Ostenders will jumble in with them, the King of Portugal having offered them the use of the City Goa, with liberty to build what warehouses they please there, for the entire security of the commerce. *P.*

On Tuesday Stocks were

South Sea Stock was 98 1 half. South Sea Annuity 108 3 qrs. Bank 147 5 8ths. to 3 qrs. New Bank Circulation 8 l. Prem. cm. India 177 3 qrs. 178, 177 7 8ths. Three per Cent Annuity 97 7 8th, to 98. Royal Exchange Assurance 101 1 qr. London Assurance 13 to 1 8th. York Buildings 1 l. 9 s. African 40. English Copper 2 l. 6 s. Welch ditto 1 l. 15 s. South Sea Bonds 2 l. 18 s. to 19 s. Premium. India ditto 6 l. 11 s. ditto. Blanks 7 l. 8 s. 9 d. 20 l. Prizes 19 l. 16 s. 6 d. to 17 s.

ADVERTISEMENTS

This Day is published,

In Two Volumes, Octavo, on a Superfine Genoa Paper,

A Treatise of Architecture, with Remarks and Observations: By that excellent Master thereof *Sebastian Serlio*, Knight of the Empire, Designer and Engraver to his Majesty of the French King, Member of the Academy of Arts and Science, necessary for young People who would apply to that noble Art. Engraved in 200 Copper Plates, by John Sturt. Translated by Mr. Charbers. Price 10 s. 6 d. Printed for R. Ware, at the Bible and Sun in Amen-Corner, near Pater-Noster-Row.

Also may be had, just published, at the same Place,

1. An Historical Narration of the whole Bible. In two Parts. The first treating of the Old Testament, with the various Histories of the Lives and Travels of our Blessed Saviour and his Apostles: With a Summary of the Matter, Doctrine, Scope and Divine Authority of all the Canonical Epistles; and an Explanation of several chief Heads in that mysterious Book of St. John's Revelation. By J. Hammond, D. D. and curiously adorn'd with Cuts, engrav'd by John Sturt, at 4 s. 6 d.

2. English and Latin Exercises for School-Boys. Comprizing all the Rules of Syntax, with Explanations, and other necessary Observations on each Rule, and shewing the Genitive Case, and Gender of Nouns and Pronouns: as also the Preterperfect Tense, Supine, and Conjugation of Verbs. Answering perfectly to the Design of Mr Garretson, and Hermes Romanus, in bringing on Learners most gradually and expeditiously to the translating of English into Latin. By J. Bailey, School-Master The 8th Edition corrected. Pr. 1 s.

3. Emblems for the Entertainment and Improvement of Youth, containing hieroglyphical and enigmatical Devices relating to all Parts and Stations of Life. Together with Explanations and Proverbs in French, Spanish, Italian and Latin, alluding to them, and translated into English. The Whole curiously engrav'd on 62 Copper Plates. Pr. 2 s. 6 d.

4. The Compleat Constable, directing Constables, Headboroughs, Tything-Men, Church-Wardens, Overseers of the Poor, Surveyors of the Highway, and Scavengers, in the Duty of their Office, according to the Power allowed them by the Laws. Price 1 s.

This Day is published,

INTEREST at one View calculated to a Farthing, at 3, 4, 5, 6, 7 and 8 per Cent. from 1000 l. to 1 l. for one Day to 96 Days; and for 1, 2, 3, 4, 5, 6, 7, 8, 9, 10, 11, and 12 Months: With Rules and Examples to cast up Interest at any other Rates by the said Tables. To which is added, A Table for the more speedy casting up of Salaries and Wages, from one Million to one Pound per Year. Besides many other Tables of great Use in receiving and paying of Monies. The Whole being calculated, examined and corrected, and afterwards re-examined from the Press.

By RICHARD HAYES.

Printed for W. Meadows, at the Angel in Cornhill.

Where may be had, by the same Author,

1. The Purchaser's Pocket Companion; shewing at Sight what Interest is made by Money laid out in the Companies Stocks, or other publick Funds.

2. The Negotiator's Magazine of Monies and Exchanges, with a compleat Treatise of Arbitrations of Exchanges.

3. The Ship and Supercargo Book-Keeper, shewing the Manner of the Masters settling Accounts with their Owners, the Privilege of Merchants, and Duty of Officers; with Supercargo's Accompts after the Italian Method of Double Entry.

4. An Estimate of Places for Life, calculated on the Chances of Lives in general, with an Account of Places in the Disposal of the City of London, and their Value.

BOOKS printed for, and sold by J. Brotherton, at the Bible next the Fleece Tavern, in Cornhill.

Whitlock's Memorials.	Telemachus, in French.
Temple's Works, 2 Vol.	Ditto in Fol.
Bailey's Eng. Dict. Fol.	Guardians, 2 Vol.
Tillotson's Works, 3 Vol.	Langham's Duties.
Bates's Works, Fol.	Free Thoughts on Religion
State of Britain, for 1732.	La Bell Assemble, 3 Vol.
Bailey's Justin.	Vanburgh's Plays, 2 Vol.
Origin of Honour.	Addison's Works, 4 Vol.
Ladies Conduct.	Spectators, 8 Vol.
Virgin unmask'd	Trapp's Virgil.
Hays's Ship and Supercargo Book-Keeper.	D'Urfey's Songs, 6 Vol.
Coke's Detection, 3 Vol.	Milton Lost and Regain'd.
Bohun's Law of Tythes.	D'Anois Tales, 3 Vol.
Feasts & Fasts of the Church.	De Retz Memoirs, 4 Vol
Erasmii Ecclesiastica	Tom Brown's Works, 4 Vol
Life of Oliver Cromwell.	Farnborough's Grammar.
Life of the K. of Sweden.	Philips's Grammar.
Dampier's Journal to Madagascar.	Dorrington's Devotion.
	Congreve's Plays, 2 Vol.
Rapin's Hist. of England, 15 Vol.	Pope and Swift Misc 3 Vol.
	Pope's Misc. 2 Vol.
Arbuthnot of Ailments, com	Turkish Spy, 8 Vol.

This is to give Notice to all Persons,

THAT there is a SALE of Plate, Watches, and Jewellery Works, which is to be disposed of by Subscriptions, at one Shilling each, up two Pair of Stairs, at the Door between the Chandler's-Shop and Snuff-Shop, facing the Play-House in New Street, Covent-Garden There are 6000 Subscriptions, whereof 750 are conceited, which makes just Seven to One; and, for the better Encouragement of all Purchasers, the first and last Number which shall come up, it is happens not to be beneficial, shall be intitled to a Thirty Shilling Benefit, which is over and above the Sum total of the Sale.

N. B. If any Person shall be willing to take a Number of Subscriptions, they may have Twenty Two allow'd to the Score, in order to dispatch it sooner, tho' it is already very forward.

This Day is Published,

(By a Member of the College of Physicians,)
The Second Edition of,

THE FAMILY COMPANION for HEALTH. Or, Plain, easy, and certain Rules, which being punctually observ'd and follow'd, will keep Families free from Diseases, and procure them a LONG LIFE. Designed for the Direction of all charitable House-keepers, in administring Kitchen Physick in their Families.

Printed for F. Fayram and T Hatchett, under the Royal-Exchange; and J. Leake, Bookseller in Bath Price Five Shillings.

Where also may be had,

THE PRACTICAL PHYSICIAN for Travellers, whether by Sea or Land.

To which is annex'd,

Dr. RADCLIFF's Letter to the late Duke of Ormonde, concerning his Health, and Medicine, prescribed from him corductive thereto, &c. Price 3 s. 6 d.

BOOKS.

Catalogus Librorum in omnibus Facultatibus & Linguis praestantissimorum:

OR, A

CATALOGUE of Books in all Faculties and Languages, which will be sold very cheap this Day, the 25th of this Instant-May, 1732, beginning at 9 o'Clock in the Morning, the Price mark'd on each Book, at

NICOLAS PREVOST's Warehouse, at the Sign of the Ship in the Savoy,

Turning down the Great Savoy-Gate, where is a commodious Place for Coaches to stand and turn:

Among which are the following,

FOLIO.

Chronique Martienne	phini, 61 vol. compleat, and all bound uniform
Chronique de Froissard, 2 vol.	Les Hexaples ou Histoire de
Laur. Valensis Hist. Ferdinandi Regum Aragoniæ	la Constitution, 8 vol.
Thesaurus Italiæ, 45 vol. l. p.	Bibliotheques des Predicateurs, 20 vol.
Muratori Rerum Italicarum Script. 20 vol.	Histoire Romaine, 16 vol.
Montfaucon Antiquitez Expliquees, 15 vol 4 Edit.	Fleury Histoire Ecclesiastique 30 vol. g. & p p.
Historia Byzantina, 37 vol.	Le Polybe de Folard, 6 vol.
Museo Farnese, 10 vol.	Gemme Antiche de Maffei, 4 vol.
Marsili Opus Danubiale, 6 v.	Les Vies de Plutarque, par
Atlas Blavianus, 11 vol.	Dacier, 8 vol. l. p.
Theatre de Savoye, 2 vol.	Histoire de Constantinople,
Theatre d'Italie, 4 vol.	Romaine & de l'Eglise, par
Atlas de De Witt, 2 vol.	Cousin
— de Sanson, 2 vol.	— Militaire de Louis XIV. 7 vol. fig.
Ciaconius de Vitis Pontif. Romanor. 4 vol.	Orlando furioso di Porro
Anastasius de Vitis Pontif. Romanor. 3 vol.	Apollonii Rhodii Argonautica, Gr. cum Majusculis
Ughelli Italia Sacra, 10 vol.	Litteris
Gallia Christ ana, 2 vol.	Coppin Bouclier de l'Europe.
Sanderi Chronographia Brabant. 3 vol. l. and fin. p.	Ammianus Marcellinus Valesii
Banagii Annales, 3 vol. l. p.	Casp. Bauhini Pinax Theatri Botanici
Pagii in Baronii Annales, 4 v.	
Histoire Sacree de la Providence, with 500 Copper-Plates	OCTAVO.
	Plutarchii Opera, Gr. Lat. Hen. Steph. 13 vol.
Joan. Matth. & Ph. Villani Historia, 2 vol	Les Oeuvres de Plutarque, 13 vol. chez Vascofan
Sirmondi Opera, 5 vol. l. p.	Homelies de St. Chrysostome,
Medailles de Louis XIV. 1st Edition, avec la preface tres bien ecrite & proprement enchasée dans des bordures; Comme aussi le Testament de Louis XIV. & la Proces verbal de ce qui s'est passé au Parlement le 2d 7bre. 1715, que l'on a ajouté a la fin.	avec ses Lettres, traduites en Francois, 10 vol
	Oeuvres de M. Fouquet, 16 v.
	Ciceronis Opera, 9 vol. R. Steph.
	— idem 12 vol. Seb. Gryph.
	— idem 16 vol Elzivir
	— idem 18 vol. cum Notis Græ ii
Saraponis Practica Medicena Arab. Lat.	— idem 16 vol. Verburgii
Ant. Nattæ de Pulchro.	ONE HUNDRED Volumes of curious and scarce Hebrew Books
QUARTO.	500 Volumes of the best Spanish and French Romances
Autores Classici ad usum Del-	

This Day was published,

(Being the most useful Work of its Kind yet Extant, to all Sorts of Tradesmen, as well the Old and Experienc'd, as the Young Beginners,)
The THIRD EDITION, of

THE COMPLEAT ENGLISH TRADESMAN: In familiar Letters, directing him in all the several Parts and Progressions of TRADE. In two Volumes. Vol. I. Treating of the several Points necessary to be known by the YOUNGER TRADESMAN, as well in his Apprenticeship, as on his first Entring upon Business, with regard to Diligence, Over-Trading, Expensive Living, Too early Marrying, Diversions, Credit, Partnerships, Corresponding, Tradesmen's Hands, Punctuality, and many other plain Specimens of BOOK-KEEPING, &c.

Vol. II. Containing, 1. Needful Instructions to the MORE EXPERIENC'D TRADESMAN: with regard to Frauds, being Forearm'd for another, Ingrossing, Underselling, Combinations, Leaving off Business, Litigiousness, Dangerous Adventures, Reasons why Tradesmen Differ, &c. should, if possible, be traded by Arbitration. 2. Useful Generals in Trade, describing the Principles and Foundations of the Home Trade of Great Britain; with large Tables of the British Manufactures, Produce, Shipping, Land-Carriage, Importation, Home Consumption, &c.

Printed for C. Rivington, at the Bible and Crown in St. Paul's Church-Yard.

Where may be had,

A PLAN of the English COMMERCE: Being a compleat Prospect of the Trade of all this Nation, as well the Home Trade as the Foreign. The Second Edition. Pr. 5 s. 6 d.

This Day is published, Price 1 s.

The Second Edition of

THE PROGRESS of LOVE, in Four Eclogues.

I. Uncertainty, to Mr. Pope.	III. Jealousy, to Edward Walpole, Esq;
II. Hope, to the Honourable George Doddington, Esq;	IV. Possession, to the Right Hon. the Ld. Visc. Cobham

Printed for L. Gilliver, at Homer's-Head, over against S. Dunstan's Church in Fleet-street. Likewise, STOWE, the Gardens of the Right Hon. Richard Lord Viscount Cobham. Address'd to Mr. POPE.

Devenere locos laetos, & amoena Vireta
Fortunatorum nemorum, sedesque beatas. Virg.

BOOKS *lately printed for* J. Clarke *at the Golden-Ball in Duck-Lane, near Little-Britain.*

FABULÆ Æsopi Selectæ, or select Fables of Æsop, with an English Translation, more literal than any yet extant; designed for the readiest Introduction of Beginners to the Latin Tongue. By H. CLARKE, Master of the publick Grammar School at Islington.

Corderii Colloquiorum Centuria selecta. With a literal Translation Fourth Edition.

Cornelii Nepotis vitæ excellentium imperatorum, &c. or Cornelius Nepos's Lives of the excellent Commanders: With an English Translation as literal as possible, with English Notes, and a large Index: Third Edition. By J. CLARKE, Master of the publick Grammar School in Hull.

The Greek Grammar construed (very proper to be bound up with the Greek Grammar) for the Help of young Beginners. Second Edition, revised and carefully corrected: For the Use of Eton School.

Books printed for J. BATLEY, at the Dove in Pater-Noster-Row.

1. A Compleat Introduction to the Reading the Holy Scriptures, intended chiefly for young Students in Divinity. In two Parts. Part I. Containing an Account of the civil and religious State of the Jews; the Samaritans, Canonies, Temples, Sacrifices, Synagogues, High-Priests, Courts of Justice; particularly the Sanhedrim, Prophets, Scribes, Jewish Sects, Pharisees, Sadducees, Essenes, Proselytes of the Gate. Years, Months, Days, and Hours of the Jews, &c. Part II. Containing the Proofs of the Truth of the Christian Religion; Nature of the New Testament Stile; the Chronology and Geography of the New Testament; the Hebrew Money, Weights and Measures; various Readings; Division into Chapters and Verses, Heresies in the Apostles Days; Versions of the New Testament, Antient and Modern: To which are added the English ones, &c Written originally in French by Messieurs De Beaufobre and Lenfant, by the Order of the King of Prussia. Now first done into English, with additional Notes.

2. A compleat Body of Divinity, consonant to the Doctrine of the Church of England. In Six Books. In Two Volumes. By N. Clark, Rector of Shafton St. James in Dorset. Price 9 s.

LONDON: Printed by J. HUGGONSON, in Bartholomew-Close, for Captain GULLIVER, near the Temple, where Letters and Advertisements are taken in: As also at the Rainbow Coffee-House in Cornhill, and John's Coffee-House in Sheer-Lane, near Temple-Bar. [Price Two Pence]

The Grub-street Journal.

NUMB. 127

Thursday, *JUNE* 8, 1732

On est un grand menteur. French Proverb.

THE Letter of Signor BELLONI, Banker at Rome, being at present the chief subject of conversation, the world is, no doubt, in expectation to hear something from our Society upon this extraordinary occasion. To satisfy which, I was ordered to draw up the substance of what past in our last meeting upon the reading *The Hyp-Doctor* of tuesday, and *The Courant* and *The Free Briton* of thursday last; in which this wonderful *Phanomenon* has been treated with great variety of learning, argument, wit, and language. —— The Society was much surprized at the second of those *Papers*, in which the Author pretending to have *obtained a true copy of a Declaration or Letter lately transmitted hither from Rome*, gives us a Paper signed BELLONI, in which there is not one sentence the same with any contained in BELLONI's Letter printed in the *Free Briton* of the same day. This seemed to them *an extraordinary artifice and contrivance, a meer forgery, an idle scheme*, designed *to disguise this affair, by turning it into ridicule*; and which might tend to lessen the *contempt*, with which all persons ought *to treat the Person of the Pretender, and his wicked Accomplices*; who, being found to be falsely charged with writing a sham Letter, may not, perhaps, meet with that abhorrence and detestation which they justly deserve on the account of that Letter, which they did really send. It was therefore thought proper, in the first place, to exhibit true copies, both of the original Letter in French, and of the translation of it in English, as published by the Author of the *Free Briton*. But since the French, as printed in the *Free Briton*, was scarcely intelligible *by reason of a feverish illness, under which the Author laboured on wednesday last*, it is here transcribed from *a perfect copy, given* by him in the *Whitehall Evening-Post* of saturday last: and for the greater ease of the reader, in comparing the French and the English together, to each sentence in the former, the translation in the latter is here subjoined.

Messieurs, *à Rome le 4me May*, 1732.

C'Est avec beaucoup de plaisir que je profite d'une occasion, qui s'est presentée pour montrer mon estime, & mon affection pour la Nation Angloise, en contribuant à l'avantage de plusieurs Particuliers de ce Royaume, & par consequent à la satisfaction du Parlement, & de la Nation même.

Rome, the *4th of May*, } 1732.
Gentlemen, *23d of* April, }

'It is with much pleasure, that *I* embrace an opportunity, which hath presented itself, to shew *my* esteem 'and *my* affection for the *English Nation*, in contributing to the advantage of many persons of the said Kingdom; and consequently to the satisfaction of the Parliament, and of the Nation itself.

Comme les frau des, qui ont eté commises dans l'Administration de la Compagnie Charitable, ont fait beaucoup de bruit par tout, On a eté icy *vivement touché des maux dont elles ont eté la cause*, & on *a senti l'intéret que la Nation avoit d'y remedier, ce qui ne pouvoit être effectué qu'en se saisissant de la personne, des papiers, des livres, & des effects du Sieur* Thompson, *à quoy le Parlement n'avoit pas encore pu parvenir.* —— 'As the frauds which 'have been committed in the management of the Charitable Corporation, have made much noise every where, '*we have here* been touched in a lively manner with the 'evils which they have occasioned; and *we are sensible* 'of the interest that the Nation hath in their remedy, 'which could not be effected, but by seizing of the person, the Papers, the books and effects of the Sieur *Thomson*, to which the Parliament had not as yet been able to 'attain.

A cet effet comme on avoit eu avis, que le dit Thomson *pourroit venir à* Rome *sous un Nom emprunté, on a pris les mesures necessaires, pour l'arr ter quand il y seroit arrivé, ce qui a eté executé.* —— 'To this purpose, as *We* 'had received advice, that the said *Thomson* might come 'to *Rome*, under a borrowed name, *we have taken* the 'necessary measures to arrest him when he should arrive, 'which hath been executed.

On s'est saisi en même temps de ses papiers, des lettres qu'il a reçu d'Angleterre depuis qu'il en etoit parti, des copies de lettres qu'il a écrites à ses confidens, & des notes de ses affaires les plus secretes. —— '*We have seized* at the same 'time his Papers, the letters which he hath received from '*England* since his departure from thence, the copies of 'letters which he hath written to his correspondents, and 'the *memorandums* of his most secret affairs.

Il est à present luy même dans le Château de St. Ange; & a eté mis de cette façon dans une espece de necessité de decouvrir tout le mistere de cette affaire; ce qu'il a fait amplement, en decouvrant non seulement les livres & les effets de la Compagnie, mais aussi les siens propres. —— 'He himself is at present in the *Castle of St. Angelo*; and by this means is at present under a kind of 'necessity to discover the whole mystery of this affair, 'which he hath amply done, by discovering not only the 'Corporation's books and effects, but also his own.

Cela etant fait, on m'a chargé *de communiquer cette importante decouverte à qui & où il conviendroit pour le bien & l'avantage de la Nation.* —— 'This having been 'done, *I have it in charge* to communicate this important discovery to whom, and where, it may be proper 'for the good and advantage of the nation.

C'est pourquoy je depêche, *sans delay, un Courier à un de mes correspondens à* Paris, *avec tous les Papiers qui ont rapport à cette affaire, afin qu'il trouve les moyens de vous les faire remettre.* —— 'Tis on this account that *I dispatch* a Courier to one of my Correspondents at *Paris*, 'with all the Papers which have relation to this affair; 'to the end that he may find the means of putting them 'into your hands.

Mais comme l'Equité exige *que les Proprietaires de la Compagnie Charitable (qui tireront un si grand avantage de cette decouverte) se prêtent à de certaines conditions, avant que les Papiers & les ecrits vous soient remis; j'ay ordonné à mon Correspondent d'insister que ces conditions soient prealablement accordées, & de regarder, en attendant, ces ecrits comme un simple depôt entre ses mains, sans les en laisser sortir jusqu' à ce que cela soit fait;* & Je *ne doute point que cette precau ion aussi bien que les conditions ne paroissent justes & raisonnables à tous ceux qui sont interessez dans cette affaire.* —— 'But as EQUITY *demands*, that 'the Proprietors of the Charitable Corporation (who will 'reap so great an advantage from this discovery) should 'yield to certain conditions, before that the Papers and 'writings be delivered to you, I have ordered my correspondent to *insist*, that these conditions be previously 'agreed to: and in the mean time to look upon these 'writings *meerly as a pledge in his hands*, without suffering them to pass from him, untill this be done. 'And I doubt not, that this precaution, as well as the 'conditions, does appear just and reasonable to all who are 'interested in this affair.

M'etant ainsi acquitté de ma Commission *il ne me reste qu' à vous prier d'être persuadé de mon respect pour la Nation, & de l'envie que j'auray toujours de contribuer à son avantage. J'ay l'honneur d'etre,*

Messieurs, Vôtres très humble, & très Obeissant serviteur,
JEAN ANGE BELLONI.

'Having thus *acquitted myself of my commission*, nothing 'remains for me, but to intreat you to be persuaded of my '*respect for the Nation*, and the *ambition which I shall always have to contribute to its advantage*. I have the 'honour to be, Gentlemen,

'Your most humble, and most obedient servant,
'JOHN ANGELO BELLONI.

A Messieurs, Messieurs du Committé du Parlement d'Angleterre etabli sur les affaires de la Corporation Charitable; ou si le dit Committé ne subsiste plus, à Messieurs le Chevalier Robert Sutton, *le Chevalier* Jean Shadwell, Walter Molesworth, *Docteur* Jean Mowbray, *ou à quelqu'un d'eux, à Londres.*

'To the Gentlemen of the Committee of the Parliament of England, appointed for the affairs of the Charitable Corporation, or if the said Committee does not 'subsist, to Sir *Robert Sutton*, Sir *John Shadwell*, *Walter Molesworth*, Doctor *John Mowbray*, or to any one of 'them, at London.

Concerning the Particle *On*, and the translation of it by *We*, the learned Mr. WALSINGHAM has added the following observations. 'In the Translation the Particle *On* '(which makes a great figure, and is a *Gentleman of no small importance*, through the whole letter) is rendered 'in the *first person*, though equivocal, and though it may be 'used either in the *first*, or *third*, or for *people in general*. 'RICHELET's Dictionary, the Folio edition of 1728, 'hath this observation concerning this Particle, *viz.* On is "used in a modern sense in the first Person, *I*; for, instead of saying, JE SONGERAI A VOS INTERETS, *I will* "*take care of your interests*; I may very well say, in "writing or speaking familiarly, *On songera a vos interets.* "*On aura soin de vous*; which, if not thus used for the "*first* person, would be understood in the *third*, or in a "more general sense, *Your interests will be taken care of.*" Pag. 2. Col. 2. —— 'I may remark upon this Translation, that the Letter is divided into *two parts*, the *first* 'of which runs in the Particle *On*, and is in the style of 'great authority; for which reason *On* hath been rendred 'in the *first person plural*, or the *style Royal*. The 'second part uses the Particle *Je*, or *I*, *the first person singular*, and is writ in the style and character of a *private Banker* at *Rome*. Pag. 3. Col. 1.'

Mr. SPONDEE stood up first, and said, Mr. President, This is the first Letter in which ON ever *made a great figure*, and appeared as *a Gentleman of no small importance*. In all other places where I have ever seen him, which I have done above five thousand times, he always seemed to be no more than a personal indeterminate Pronoun. As to his Family it is indeed very ancient, his name being derived from *Homme*, which by a corruption, to which all names are subject, has been changed into *On*. In ancient times the public Criers begun their proclamations by HOM *fait sçavoir*, instead of ON *fait sçavoir*. He afterwards gained the force of a collective noun, representing several uncertain and indefinite persons, either in the first or third person plural. I have often thought it very probable, that the English Phrase in the singular number, *One cannot imagine*, and the like, were derived from the French *On ne peut imaginer*, &c. but however, this is certain, that the phrases so much in vogue among my learned Brethren the News Writers, *They write*, *They advise*, and the HYP-ORATORICAL Phrase, *We hear*, which appears constantly in the Daily Papers, are most properly translated into French by *On*. So that it is certain, that the Particle *On* may be used for the *first* or the *third* person plural. —— And it is as certain, that it may likewise be used for the *first person* singular; of which the authority of RICHELET, produced by my Brother WALSINGHAM, is a full proof. But then he has produced it in such a manner, that it is justly to be suspected, that he had it at second hand from One who understood but little of the French Language. RICHELET's words are, ON *se met en un sens nouveau* pour *la premiere personne* Je, &c. which is here falsly translated, ON *is used in a modern sense* IN *the first person* I, &c. instead of FOR *the first person*. And whereas Mr. WALSINGHAM says just before, that *it may be used, either* IN *the first or third*, &c. (which by the way shews this mistake to be no error of the press) it is absolutely false: for ON is never [illegible] the *first* person, but is always joined to a verb of the *third* person singular. —— But not to insist any longer on this mistake, I beg leave to observe, that when M. RICHELET affirms, that ON *is used for the first person* singular, he immediately adds this restriction, *in writing or speaking familiarly*; and that Father BUFIER asserts, that it is never so used but *en riant*, or out of modesty: all which, tho' consistent enough with *the style and character of a private Banker*, are altogether inconsistent with *the style of great authority*. And therefore it is something strange, that in the Translation, '*On* hath been rendered in the *first Person Plural*, or the *style Royal*': and stranger, that M. RICHELET's authority has been brought to support it. He says, ON *is used for the first person singular*: the inference is, Therefore it is used for the first person plural, or the *style Royal*.— I allow indeed, that it is used for the first person plural, and may be translated by *We*: but then this *We* must signify several uncertain and indefinite persons, and never one certain person as in any authority. Marshal TURENNE first introduced Monsieur ON at the French Court: where tho' this *Gentleman* was well received, yet the King never gave him any Commission to represent his person. That was always done by Monsieur *Nous*, as the King here in England is by Mr. WE: and I challenge my learned Brother WALSINGHAM to produce one instance, where Monsieur ON ever appeared *as the style of great* authority, and declaring the Royal Pleasure of the Grand Monarch.

[*To be continued.*]

Gentlemen,

Of esteem and affection this fallacious pretence
Our loyalty attacks; this Proposal, common sense.
Much should we be wanting to ourselves, did we not show
A proper resentment; and let *all* the World know,

That, tho' of our property most notoriously *fobb'd*,
Of understanding and principles we have not been robb'd.
I know not, *nor care*, what *things* may be in the Trunk;
But as it comes from the hands of the Babylonish Punk,
I think, if we take it, we shall soon be Pœnitentes:
For my part, Timeo Danaos & dona ferentes.
This Trunk may *probably* be a *new* Pandora's box,
Full of Pestilence, Popery, Pretender, and Pox.

Let us shew the Rogues at Rome, that we English men *at* London
Are honest and loyal, tho' we're *ruin'd and* undone.

BAVIUS.

DOMESTIC NEWS.

C. *Courant.*	E P. *Evening Post.*
P. *Post-Boy.*	S J. *S. James's Evening Post.*
D P. *Daily Post.*	WE. *Whitehall Evening P.*
D J. *Daily Journal.*	LE. *London Evening Post.*

THURSDAY, *June* 1.

They write from Roan in France, that Geo. Cammock, Esq; the English Major General, who serv'd in that quality his Catholic Majesty for several years, and came from Spain with his Lady and his family about a twelvemonth ago to France, died in that city, June 3, N. S. as it is believed of grief, from the ill treatment he had met with. He was by all allow'd a brave and most experienced Sea Officer. *D P.*

On tuesday last his Majesty's plate of 100 guineas was run for at Guildford in Surrey, when 7 [horses] started, which was won by Mr. Kettle's Barrowshedges. *P.*

Their Royal Highnesses the Princess Amelia and Carolina have been taken ill with the chicken pox. *S J.*

Yesterday the report of the 9 Malefactors, condemn'd the last Sessions at the Old Bailey was made to his Majesty. *S J.* -- To morrow it is expected the report of the Malefactors, &c. will be made to his Majesty. *W E.*

By a letter from Nottingham, dated May 29, we are advis'd, that Will. Levins of Grove, Esq; and Tho. Bennett of Nottingham, Esq; were that day chose Members of Parliament without opposition, in the room of L. How and Sir Rob. Sutton. *S J.*

They write from Sunderland, that by a Master of a ship arrived from London, they had received the following particulars, that 5 light Collier ships coming from London, were cast away on the coast of Yorkshire; that he saw 2 of them with their bottoms beat out against the rocks. *D P.*

Some evenings ago about 9 o' clock Mr. Ockell, an Apothecary in Pater-noster-row, was robb'd by a person on foot, as he was coming from Holloway, where he had been to visit a patient. He was attack'd within a quarter of a mile of the house where he had been. The rogue took from him his cloak, coat, hat and wig, and the buckles out of his shoes, with what money he had in his pocket. Mr. Ockell pleaded hard for a medicine in the pocket of his coat, he being in a very ill state of health, which the rogue denied him, saying, he might have occasion for it himself. *P.* — *I should have thought he would rather have forc'd him to take it immediately.*

Last week one Stephen Biss, a Baker of Painswick in Gloucestershire, pull'd off his cloaths, and jump'd into a well and drown'd himself; there were 10 or 15 pounds found, which he had laid by the side of the well: he was worth 6 or 700 l. and generally thought to be lunatic for the greater part of his life. *D P.*

On friday last died Mr. Tho. Bryquett, Tobacconist in Friday-street, who, after leaving several handsome legacies, devised his whole estate (computed at 30,000 l.) to his nephew John Bryquett, Esq; a Gentleman of the Law. *D P.* —— On monday died Miss Jackson, a rich Heiress at Horsham in Sussex. *C.*

FRIDAY, *June* 2.

Yesterday his Majesty went to the House of Peers, and made a most gracious speech to both Houses of Parliament, and gave the Royal assent to several public and private acts. *D J.* —— To 24 public, and 28 private Bills. *D P.* —— And prorogued the Parliament to Thursday July 27. *C.* &c. —— His Majesty has been pleased to appoint Tho. Clutterbuck, Esq; to be one of the Lords of the Admiralty, in the room of John Cockburne, Esq; who has resigned. *P.*

On wednesday last the Treasurer of the public Infirmary in Chappel-street, Westminster, received from a worthy Benefactor, who desired to have his name concealed, a bank bill of 100 l. for the use of that charity. *C.*

On wednesday Mr. Watson of S. Margaret's, Westminster, was chosen Clerk of the Company of Gardeners. *P.*

Yesterday was marry'd, at S. Paul's Church John Walton, Esq; to Mrs. Jacobson, daughter of Sir Jacob Jacobson, and Grand-daughter of Sir Gilbert Heathcote, a Lady of good fortune and great merit. *D P.* — Great fortune and great merit *sounds better.*

Christened Males 157. Females 137. In all 294.—*Buried* Males 176. Females 173. In all 349. Decreased in the burials this week, 35. *P.*

SATURDAY, *June* 3.

Yesterday his Majesty held a Chapter of the most ancient order of the Thistle, when he was pleased to give to the R. Hon. the E. of Portmore, the green Ribbon, late the E. of Loudon's. —— His Majesty has been pleased to appoint Sam. Tuffnell, Esq; Member of Parliament for Colchester, to be his Majesty's Commissioner at Antwerp. *P.* —— Major Ric. Harwood is appointed Lieut. Col. to Maj. Gen. Bisset's Regiment of foot, in the room of Lieut. Col. Pet. Bettesworth, lately made Deputy Governor of the Island of Jersey. *D P.*

Yesterday the R. Hon. the L. Chancellor, the L. Raymond, the Speaker of the House of Commons, Sir John Hinde Cotton, and Mr. Hanbury, Trustees of the Cotton Library, order'd the said Library to be removed from the new Dormitory at Westminster, into the old Dormitory (which is fitting up for that purpose) to be there reposited till a new edifice shall be erected for the reception thereof; which we hear will be very speedily begun, pursuant to the address of the House of Commons. *C.*

On wednesday his Excellency Count Kirski, his Imperial Majesty's Ambassador at this Court, set out on his return home, with a great retinue. *P.*

Last night the new Comedy call'd, *The Old Debauchees*, and *The Covent-Garden Tragedy*, were acted for the first time, at the Theatre Royal in Drury-lane, with universal applause. *D P.* —— We were partly misinform'd as to the reception of the two Pieces play'd on thursday night last, at the Theatre Royal in Drury lane: we are assur'd the Comedy call'd, *The Old Debauchees*, did meet with universal applause; but the *Covent Garden Tragedy* will be acted no more, both the Author and the Actors, being unwilling to continue any Piece contrary to the opinion of the Town. *D P. June* 5. *For* unwilling *read* unable.

Yesterday Major Gen. Russel kiss'd the King's hand on his being appointed Dep. Governor of Berwick, and of Holy Island. *S J. L E.*

A few days since died the Rev. Will. Owens, M. A. Rector of Warden, and Vicar of Leysdown in the diocese of Canterbury; the former is in the gift of the heirs of Admiral Hosier, and the latter in that of the L. Archbishop of Canterbury. *S J. W E. L E.*

On sunday last died the R. Worshipful Tho. Allen, L. L. D. Dean of Chester, Archdeacon of Stafford, &c. —— On thursday, at his house in Old Palace-yard, Westm. the learned and Rev. Edmund Calamy, D. D. —— Yesterday morning, about 10, Mr. Wingfield, a Quaker, walking on the Royal-Exchange, fell down dead in an apoplectic fit. *D P.*

On tuesday dy'd at Chelsea, in the 81st year of his age, Dr. John King, Minister of the Church there. —— Yesterday morning, at Highgate, Mr. Norris, formerly a Bookseller on London-Bridge, reckon'd to have dy'd worth 10,000 l. the chief of which was acquir'd by —— and lending out his money.—*L E.*—*Did he* acquire *it* by *worse ways than all other Book-sellers, that he is thus* double dash'd?

MONDAY, *June* 5.

On saturday about 1, his Majesty, attended by several of the Nobility, went in his chair to Whitehall, [to the Lord Herbert's. *D J.*] where he crost the water to Lambeth in one of the Royal Barges, and proceeded from thence in his open chaise, [in his coach. *D J*] to Greenwich, escorted by a detachment of the Life Guards: His Majesty immediately embarked on board the Carolina Yacht, where a sumptuous [elegant. *D P.*] dinner was provided. At his going on board, his Majesty was saluted by all the Royal Yachts and ships at Greenwich; and there was a very great appearance of the Nobility and other Persons of distinction, to take their leaves of his Majesty. Before 6 they were all under sail; [at 20 minutes after 6. *P.*] but there being but little wind, they were tow'd by the boats as far as Woolwich. *C.* —— On saturday in the afternoon her Majesty, his Royal Highness the Duke, and the Princess Royal, and the Princesses Mary and Louisa, set out for Richmond; and the same evening his Royal Highness the Prince of Wales set out for Kew. *C. D P. D J.* —— The Princesses Amelia and Carolina being indispos'd, their Royal Highnesses stay at S. James's 'till their health will permit them to remove. *P.*

His Majesty has been pleas'd to appoint the Rev. Mr. Dawney, A M. son to the R. Hon. the L. Downs, to be one of the Prebendaries of Canterbury, void by the death of the last incumbent. *P.* — John Wainright of Lincoln's-Inn, Esq; is made one of the Justices of the Court of Common-Pleas in Ireland. *D P.* —— On wednesday Sam. Clarke, Esq; of West-Bromwich in the County of Stafford, was sworn one of the Gentlemen of his Majesty's most Hon. Privy-Chamber. *D J.*

A few days since, Sir Rowland Hill, Bar. a young Gentleman of 8000 l. a year, was married to Miss Broughton, only daughter of the late Sir Bryan Broughton, Bar. of Broughton in the County of Stafford, a young Lady of great virtue, beauty, and merit, worth 30,000 l. fortune. *D J.*

TUESDAY, *June* 6.

Her Majesty will continue at Kew Green 'till she h[as] advice of the King's being arriv'd in Holland. *C.* —— Yesterday advice came of the safe arrival of his Majesty and all the Royal Yatchts at the Nore, [his Majesty went] to sea about 2 on sunday in the afternoon, tho' they were oblig'd to tow most part to the Buoy. *P.*] where his Majesty was saluted with 21 guns by all the men of war under the command of the L. Visc Torrington; and likewise saluted with 21 guns from the garrison of Sheerness. *D P.*

On sunday last, a Lady of distinction, much talk'd of lately about S. James's, was safely deliver'd of a son. *P.*— Yesterday morning. *L E.*

We hear that soon after the arrival of the R. Hon. the L. Torrington from Holland, several ships of war will be put into commission. *C.*

On saturday night, about 10. *C. P. D P.* On sunday night, about 10, Capt. Rob. Saunders, Commander of the Ruby, was attack'd about 200 yards on this side of New Cross, by 2 Foot-pads, who came out of a ditch, one of whom swore, and at the same instant fir'd at him; the ball entered the side of his right breast, and grazed on the bone, went out near the pit of his stomach; when a third [footpad *I suppose*] came on the other side the horse, and seized the bridle, and then they knock'd him off, and dragged him up a lane which leads to Peckham, where they rifled him: they staid by him till they had recharged, and commanded him to sit there till he heard them whistle: but in half a quarter of an hour they came back to him, and one of them taking pity on him, prevailed on the rest to let him go, giving him a shilling for a coach. The Captain getting to the Half way house found his horse again, and having had some refreshment, he mounted, and coming to his brother's (a Distiller in Thames-street) Mr. Girle, an eminent Surgeon, was sent for (who dressing the wound, found a piece of his coat and waistcoat in it) and yesterday he was in a fair way of recovery. *D J.* They robbed him of 2 guineas, some silver and his watch. *P.* Of his money and a gold Watch valued at 30 guineas. *C. D P.* And afterwards shot him in the thigh. *D P.*

Yesterday the 9 Malefactors condemned at the last Sessions at the Old Bailey were executed at Tyburn; and two of their bodies were delivered to the Surgeons. *C. D P.* —— One was delivered to the Surgeons, and the other lay under the gallows for some time, and was afterwards buried by the mob in a ditch in Acton road. *D J.*

Yesterday 2 Drums belonging to the first Regiment of Foot-guards, were whipt on the Parade in S. James's Park, for going about a begging with their drums on weddings, contrary to the rules of the Army. *P.*—*This account of the* 2 Drums, *that went* about with their Drums, *seems to be given by a* Hum-Drum.

On saturday Col. Inwood, of Stanmore in Middlesex, was marry'd to Miss Bridges, Niece to the D. of Chandos, at his Grace's house in S. James's square. *D P.*

York, May 29. This evening a little before 10, the grave of Will. de Melton, Archbishop of York, was open'd; it was near the Font, a vault cover'd with 6 large stones, when one of them was lifted up from over the breast a most beautiful large silver chalice appeared, upon which was curiously engraved a crucifix: he had first been put in a lead coffin, and then in one made of wood, both of which were much decayed. *D P.*

On wednesday last a lad, son of Mr. Barnardiston, a wholesale Linnen-draper, lately deceased, was killed by a blow on his ear which he received accidentally with a [illegible] pin bowl at Chislehurst in Sussex. *D P.* In Kent. *C.*

On saturday dy'd Dr. Francis Meade, in the 64th year of his age. —— Yesterday morning at his lodgings in Wich-street, Tho. Leigh, Esq; a Gentleman of a very plentiful estate in Somersetshire. *P.*

The Rev. Mr. John Swinton, A. M. Fellow of Wadham College, Oxon. and F. R. S. was lately appointed by his Majesty Chaplain to the British Factory at Leghorn, &c. *S J.*

This day came an account of his Majesty being put into Sheerness, waiting for a wind. *S J.*

WEDNESDAY, *June* 7.

His Majesty has been pleased to appoint Lieut. Gen. Wade to be Governor of the town of Berwick upon Tweed, and of Holy Island. —— Major Gen. Russel to be Lieut. Governor. —— Col. Tho. Howard to be Aide de Camp to his Majesty. —— The Rev. Mr. Tho. Brooke, M. A. to be Dean of Chester: And the Rev. Cha. Meredith, to be Dean of Ardsert in the Kingdom of Ireland. *C.* —— Ardfert. *P. D P.* — A Commission has passed the Great Seal, constituting Col. Kane Governor of Minorca. *C.*

There has lately arrived from Genoa 50 land tortoises, as a present to her Majesty. *C.*

Yesterday Mr. Alderman Barber was translated from the Company of Stationers to that of the Goldsmiths. *P. D*

7

From the PEGASUS *in Grub-street.*

In our laſt, in the Article from this place, *line* 27. read her lodging: *Hiſ ſo read no-honeſter,*
It is reported that the late Earl of Marr is dead.

S I R,

AS Dramatical-performances come under the cognizance of your Society, I hope, without any apology, you'll give this letter a place in your next.

The depravity of modern taſte has been long-complained of ; and ſeveral Dramatic performances have been inſtanced in to prove that depravity. I thought this only the bi-gotted opinion of ſome peeviſh old Gentlemen, who com-mend every thing of the laſt age, and condemn every thing of the preſent. I entered into a diſpute on this ſubject the other evening with a Gentleman of the Temple, who eſteems it a more amiable Character to be a man of wit and pleaſure, than a great Lawyer. After I had urged all the common arguments againſt our preſent theatrical taſte, and he had ſpoken as ſtrenuouſly in the defence of it. Sir, ſays he, there is a fine burleſque Piece to be played to night at Drury-lane ; which, for pointed ſatire, true humour, and mock heroick, will exceed any thing that ever appeared on the ſtage. It is founded on as good a ſubject as the *Beggars Opera* ; and I aſſure you, the mo-ral is as inſtructive. In ſhort, he urged our theatrical taſte was rather improved than depraved ; and engaged me to go with him to ſee it the next evening.

But, Mr. BAVIUS, how was I ſurprized to ſee the moſt notorious Bawds, Pimps, and Whores, brought on the ſtage to pleaſe as polite an audience as I ever ſaw for the time of the year. My Man of pleaſure was not only very buſy in explaining the beauties of the language, but the ſecret hiſto-ry, the reality of the characters, and ſome perſonal ſcan-dal. I obſerved there were ſeveral young fellows in the pit and boxes ſmiling, and mightily pleaſed at ſome paſ-ſages ; which, tho' they knew the meaning of them, were entirely miſunderſtood by three parts of the audience. It gave me ſome ſatiſfaction to ſee ſo many too ignorant to reliſh the archneſs of the Poet, and dull enough not to ap-plaud the wit they did not underſtand.

After an *Epilogue* entirely adapted to the Play, and liſtening to ſome different whiſpers in the pit, of Critics, Wits, Men of pleaſure, &c. as my companion and I were returning to his Chambers, coming along the Play-houſe paſſage, a Lady of his acquaintance trip'd out of an ad-joining Coffee-houſe, and clapping him on the ſhoulder, accoſted him with two lines of this new Piece. He re-plied in two others, which, tho' I've forgot, were in the character of LOVEGIRLO ; and then they very lovingly hur-ried into the Roſe.

I had ſeen too much in the Play-houſe to follow them, and went to a Coffee-houſe to examine, whether there was any thing in this *Covent Garden Tragedy,* that could lay the leaſt claim to wit, or deſerve any encouragement from the Town. I muſt ſubmit it to all men of ſenſe, whether that can paſs for humour, which is only the dull repreſentation of the moſt obſcene characters in life ; and humour is the only thing the Poet can pretend to boaſt. Were it ſo, I doubt not but every Drury-lane Bully might make a humourous Poet : for ſurely he could very natu-rally deſcribe a ſcene of life in which he was always con-verſant ; nor is there the moſt ſtupid wretch but might paſs for a Wit, would he gain that name at the expence of all decency, as well as innocence.

Where is the humour of the Bawdy-houſe ſcene to any but a Rake ? Or that of HACKABOUTA and STORMANDRA to any women, but thoſe of the Town ? Theſe indeed, may ſmile to ſee how naturally the Poet enters into their cha-racters ; but the joke is entirely loſt to all others. — As to the mock Heroic, the lines are bad, nor any thing to recommend the numerous ſimilies. The ſucceſs of this Piece will determine whether the age is fallen to the loweſt ebb ; for I ſhould entertain but a bad opinion of the intellects of that Man, or chaſtity of that Woman, who would give the leaſt encouragement to the moſt dull ob-ſcene Piece, that I may venture to ſay, ever appeared on any public ſtage.

Tom's Coffee-houſe, Covent-Gardens, June 3.   PROSAICUS.

Grub-ſtreet Verſes for the tenth of June.

On this bleſt day, as Jacobites recite,
S. GEORGE'S CHEVALIER firſt view'd the light :
But Whigs declare, that not one lucid ſpark
——— Then ſhone ; but all was acted in the dark.

Some ſay, the Queens no breeding qualms perceiv'd,
But o'er her belly plac'd a cuſhion heav'd :
Some, that tho' pregnant, yet abortive pain
Made all her hopes of living Offspring vain.
Others affirm, that after 9 months paſt,
A Female Infant came in mighty haſte :
For which, a Male, in warming-pan convey'd,
By artful hand in Royal bed was lay'd.

This Boy, as ſome believ'd, ſoon after dy'd :
But one as greatly born his place ſupply'd.
At Richmond this expir'd, ſaid common Fame ;
A Third ſucceeds, another, yet the ſame.

Of all the tales, which up and down were toſt,
The Boy in velvet warming-pan took moſt.
Of Lady OGLETHORP, this Lad, ſome ſay,
Was born ; but ſome affirm of Miſtreſs GRAY :
To each one perſon equal witneſs bore :
This, Mr. FULLER, that Miſs SHAFTOE ſwore.
If at one time, you'll ſay, as Papiſts tell,
One body may in different places dwell,
Why, from a fruitful, tho' a different womb,
Of two fair Mothers, may'nt one Off-ſpring come ?
Such miracles let Papiſts ſtill deceive :
I'm a ſtanch Proteſtant, and can't believe.
A private man, I own, or Prince has had
Sometimes a double, or a treble Dad :
But I'll be hang'd, before I'll own that ſham,
That e'er one Child can have a double Dam.

                                                    MÆVIUS.

Extract of a letter from Barbadoes, dated Ap. 5. ——— Many of our inhabitants are on the ſpur, ſome going off with their families, and others talking of going every day ; which undoubtedly will very much leſſen the num-ber of our inhabitants, never ſo thin in my memory, as at this time. *P.* 2.

❀❀❀❀❀❀❀❀❀❀❀❀❀❀❀❀❀❀❀❀❀❀❀❀

F O R E I G N   N E W S.

THURSDAY, *June* 1.

Extract of a letter from Algier, *Ap.* 18. O. S. — A Dutch Galliot arrived here a few days ago with hemp, which theſe people work up into very good cordage, by the help of ſome Renegadoes, and being taught by them, the Dey is determined to make all his cordage here for the future, and improve his ſubjects in whatever concerns their navigation. ——— The French, by the indolence of other nations, have now prevail'd on the Dey to grant them the monopoly of all the trade on the coaſt, from about 20 leagues eaſtward of this City, as far as Tunis, which comprehends the moſt fertile and richeſt part of this Kingdom, abounding with wheat, barley, honey, wax, oil, wool, hides, tallow, coral, &c. and by this grant the French are impower'd to ſeize and confiscate all they find trading in that diſtrict, without their licence ; and they have goods of all ſorts there for near two thirds leſs than can be pur-chaſed here of the Dey ; ſo that the trade of this King-dom muſt in a little time be entirely in their hands. *DY.*

Books and Pamphlets publiſhed ſince our laſt.

25. Marci Hieronymi Vidæ Opera : in II Vol.
A Collection of New State Songs, &c. Part I. Pr. 6 d.
The Reſtoration of K. Charles II. &c. an Hiſtori-Tragi-Comi-Ballad Opera. Pr. 1 s. 6 d.
Mr. Oldmixon's Reply to Biſhop Atterbury examined. Pr. 6 d.
Two new and curious Eſſays : 1. Concerning pruning of fruit-trees. 2. Concerning Potatoes. Pr. 1 s.
The Principles of the leading Quakers truly repreſented as in inconſiſtent with the fundamental doctrines of the Chriſtian Religion, &c.
Chiron to Achilles : a Poem. Pr. 6 d.
The Coquet's Surrender : or, The Humorous Punſter. A Comedy.
26. The Merry Compaign : &c. Pr. 6 d.
27. A Letter to Dion ; occaſion'd by his Book call'd Al-ciphron, or the minute Philoſopher.
A Diſſertation on the Eclipſe mention'd by Phlegon, &c. By Arthur Aſhley Sykes, D. D.
31. Some important Conſiderations on the Standing Ar-my. Pr. 1 s.
The Principles and Facts of the L. Bp. of Chicheſter's Sermon further examined
The Touch-ſtone : or Paradoxes brought to the Teſt of a rigorous and fair examination, &c. Pr. 6 d.
A Defence of Dr. Clark's Demonſtration of the Being and Attributes of God, &c. Pr. 2 s.
The delightful Adventures of honeſt John Cole, &c.
June 1. The Life, Conduct, &c. of Philip late Duke of Wharton, in 2 volumes. Pr. 10 s.
2. A Sermon before the Houſe of Commons. By Will. George, D. D.
3. An Ode to his Grace the D. of Newcaſtle. Pr. 6 d.
The Tenets and Principles of the Church of Rome, &c. Pr. 6 d.
5. The Proceedings at the Seſſions Houſe in the Old Baily, &c.
The caſe of the revival of the Salt Duty, &c. Pr. 1 s.

On Tueſday Stocks were
South Sea Stock was 98 3 qrs. 98 1 half, 98 5-8ths. South Sea Annuity. 108 7 8ths. Bank 148 1 8th. New Bank Circulation 8 l. Premium. India 177 1 qr. 176 1 half, 176 7 8ths, to 177. Three per Cent. Annuity 98 1 8th. Royal Exchange Aſſurance 101 1 qr. London Aſſurance 13 to 1 8th. York Buildings 7 1 half to 3 qrs. Africain 40. Engliſh Copper 2 l. 6 s. Welch ditto 1 l. 15 s. South Sea Bonds 2 l. 19 s. Premium. In-dia ditto 6 l. 13 s. ditto. Blanks 7 l. 9 s. 3 d. 20 l. Prizes 19 l. 18 s.

This Day is publiſhed,

THE Youth's Inſtructor in the ENGLISH Tongue: or, a ſparing-Book, containing more Words, and a greater Variety of very uſeful Collections, than any Book o this Kind and Bigneſs: With two Copper-Plates, curiouſly engrav'd. The firſt, Mathematically demonſtrating at on. View, the exact Proportion each Letter ought to bear to the reſt in Writing; to which is annex'd a full Explanation of the ſame. The ſecond, is a Specimen of the moſt uſual Hands for Buſineſs; with plain Directions and Copies for Writing. To which is added, a Compendious Grammar of the Engliſh Tongue. Firſt deſign'd for the Author's own Scholars, and now made publick for a general Benefit.

By J. OWEN, Schoolmaſter.

Printed for J. Oſwald, at the Roſe and Crown, in Little-Britain; and J Hughotton, Printer, in Bartholomew-Cloſe. [Price One Shilling and Six Pence.]

This Day is publiſhed,

Price SEVEN SHILLINGS.

Printed for L. Gilliver, at Homer's Head againſt St. Dunſtan's Church; and J. Nourſe at the Lamb near Temple-Bar, in two Volumes, on an Elzevir Letter, a beautiful and correct Edition of,

MArci Hieronymi Vidæ Cremonenſis Albæ Epiſcopi Poëmata quæ extant omnia. Quibus nunc primum adjiciuntur quædam Dialogi de Rei-publicæ Dignitate. Ex collatione optimorum exemplarium emendatis: Additis Indicibus accuratis. A RICHARDO RUSSEL, A. M.

The Edition in 8vo of SS. Patrum Apoſtolicorum Barnabæ, Clementis, Hermæ, Ignatii, Polycarpi, vera Opera cum verſionibus, & ſelectis Variorum Notis, undertaken by the ſame Perſon, but which has been retarded by ſome Obſtacles, is now going forward with Expedition; and as the greateſt Part of it has been printed off ſome Time, the Remainder, will be finiſhed without Interruption, ſo as certainly to be publiſh'd the next Winter.

June 3, **was publiſhed,** Price 6d.
[To be Continued.]

Neatly printed on a fine Paper.
Very proper for private Families, or to ſend into the Country (and Places Abroad, where the Engliſh refuſe) being a compendious View of all our Publick Papers.

THE GENTLEMAN's MAGAZINE: Or, Monthly Intelligencer.

No XVII. for May, 1732. being the Fifth of Volume II

Containing more in Quantity, and greater Variety than any Book of the Kind and Price.

I. Views of the Weekly Eſſays, viz. Conveniencies and Inconveniencies in a Married and Single Life; of Common and Kept Women; new Reaſons of Divorce; Negligence of Dreſs; Lover of Gold; Friendſhip; Deſcription of Scarborough; Advice to Silvanus; Tane of Plays; Mr. Thompſon's Greek Grammar; of Education; Uſage of Beaſts; Vampyres; Caſe in Love; old Pair; Wife of Quality; Paſſis; Pantomime Entertainments; Dr. B.

II. Political Points, viz. Diſputes on the Reduction of the Land-Tax, and reviving the Salt Tax; the Lords Proteſt thereon; Hyp-Doctor and Fog; K. Wm and the Revolution; Voltaire, and his Hiſtory of the late K. of Sweden; Letter concerning Bp. Barnet, Miniſterial Power; the Whigs Monopolizers; Cromwell a Fortunate Fool; Ballance of Power, Oxon ne burleſqu'd; Poetical Vampyres; Chairs and Stools; Charitable Corporation Affairs; Boloni's Letter, (French and Engliſh) burnt by the Hangman; Account of Bills paſſed.

III. Poetical Pieces, viz. Elegiac Song on Edw. Bell, Eſq; the Grateful Patient; a Humorous Will; Epigrams.

IV. Domeſtic Occurrences, Births, Deaths, Marriages, Promotions, &c.

V. Prices of Goods, Grain, Stocks. London Monthly Bill of Mortality.

VI. Foreign Affairs.

Together with a Table of Contents, and a Regiſter of Books and Pamphlets.

By SYLVANUS URBAN, Gent.

Printed at St John's Gate, for Fr. Jeffeis in Ludgate-Street, and ſold by E. Midwinter, at the Three Crowns and Looking-Glaſs in St Paul's Church-Yard; J. Baſies, at the Dove in Pater-Noſter-Row; R. Williamſon, in Holbourn; S. Harding, in St. Martin's-Lane; W. Bickerton, at Lord Bacon's Head, without Temple-Bar; R. Mountaine, in Great Queen-ſtreet; B. Dickinſon, in the Strand; A. Chapman in Pall-Mall; J. Stagg and C. King, in Weſtminſter-Hall; A. Dodd, E. Nutt, and all Pamphlet Shops.

N. B. At the firſt Places may be had, the ſecond Edition of No XVI. for April; the third Edition of No I and II. the ſecond Edition of No III, IV V VI. X. XI. The other Numbers of Vol. I. being out of Print again. compleat Sets at preſent cannot be had, but may in about a Month's Time; when the whole Sett will be done on Royal Paper, large Margin, for the Curious.

This Day is publiſhed, Price 6d.

Dedicated to John White, Eſq; of Walting Wells,

THE TOUCH-STONE: Or, Paradoxes brought to the Teſt of a rigorous and fair Examination, for the ſettling of dubious Points to the Satisfaction of the Curious and Contentious.

Part I. LORD'S SUPPER ought to be adminiſter'd to Children. —— WASHING one anothers feet, a Sacrament inſtituted by Chriſt. —— BODY has no Exiſtence but in the Mind. STEALING in the Air, not impracticable. DELUGE occaſion'd by the Sons of God marrying the Daughters of Men.

By an Honeſt FREE THINKER.

Quod verum atque Decens, Curo, & Rogo; & omnis in hoc ſum. Hor.

Printed for J. Noon, at the White-Hart, near Mercers Chapel, Cheapſide.

Whereinmay be had,
I. JESUS CHRIST the Mediator between GOD and MEN; an Advocate for us with the Father; and a Propitiation for the Sins of the World: Containing an Anſwer to M. Chubb's Objections, with ſome Remarks on Mr. Foſter's Account or Repreſentation of this Doctrine, &c.
II. The Second Part of the Plea for Human Reaſon: In Anſwer to a Letter written to the Author of the Plea for Human Reaſon, under the Name of John Bowman, Curate of Richmond, &c. In which Anſwer is particularly and fully conſider'd, the Scripture Doctrine of the Sacrifice or the Death of Chriſt for Sin; on which the Right Knowledge of the Chriſtian Religion intirely depends. Price 1s.

This Day is publiſhed,

In Two Volumes, Octavo, on a Superfine Genoa Paper,

A Treatiſe of Architecture, with Remarks and Obſervations: By that excellent Maſter thereof Sebaſtian le Clerc, Knight of the Empire, Deſigner and Engraver to the Cabinet of the French King, and Member of the Academy of Arts and Sciences, neceſſary to young People who would apply to that noble Art. Engraved in 200 Copper Plates, by John Sturt. Tranſlated by Mr. Chambers. Price 10s. 6d. Printed for R. Ware, at the Bible and Sun in Amen-Corner, near Pater-Noſter-Row.

Alſo may be had, juſt publiſhed, at the ſame Place,
1. An Hiſtorical Narration of the whole Bible. In two Parts. The firſt treating of the Old Teſtament, with the various Hiſtories of the Lives and Travels of our Bleſſed Saviour and his Apoſtles: With a Summary of the Matter, Doctrine, Scope and Divine Authority of all the Canonical Epiſtles; and an Explanation of ſeveral chief Heads in that myſterious Book or St. John's Revelation. By J. Hammond, D. D and curiouſly adorn'd with Cuts, engrav'd by John Sturt, at 4s. 6d.
2. Engliſh and Latin Exerciſes for School-Boys. Compoſing all the Rules of Syntaxis, with Explanations, and other neceſſary Obſervations on each Rule, and ſhewing the Genitive Caſe, and Gender of Nouns and Pronouns; as alſo the Preterperfect Tenſe, Supine, and Conjugation of Verbs. Anſwering perfectly in the Deſign of Mr Garretſon, and Hermes Romanus, in bringing up Learners moſt gradually and expeditiouſly to the tranſlating of Engliſh into Latin. By J. Bailey, School-Maſter. The 8th Edition corrected. Pr. 1s.
3. Emblems for the Entertainment and Improvement of Youth, containing hieroglyphical and enigmatical Devices relating to all Parts and Stations of Life. Together with Explanations and Proverbs in French, Spaniſh, Italian and Latin, alluding to them, and tranſlated into Engliſh. The Whole curiouſly engrav'd on 62 Copper Plates. Pr. 2s. 6d.
4. The Compleat Conſtable, directing Conſtables, Headboroughs, Tything-Men, Church-Wardens, Overſeers of the Poor, Surveyors of the Highway, and Scavengers, in the Duty of their Office, according to the Power allowed them by the Laws. Price 1s.

BOOKS lately printed for J. Clarke at the Golden Ball in Duck-Lane, near Little-Britain.

FAbulæ Æſopi Selectæ, or ſelect Fables of Æſop, with an Engliſh Tranſlation, more literal than any yet extant; deſigned for the readieſt Introduction of Beginners in the Latin Tongue. By H. CLARKE, Maſter of the publick Grammar School at Iſlington.

Cordelii Colloquiorum Centuria ſelecta. With a literal Tranſlation Fourth Edition.

Cornelii Nepos vitæ excellentium imperatorum, &c. or Cornelius Nepos's Lives of the excellent Commanders: With an Engliſh Tranſlation as literal as poſſible, with Engliſh Notes, and a large Index; Third Edition, Forth by J. CLARKE, Maſter of the publick Grammar School in Hull.

The Greek Grammar conſtrued (very proper to be bound up with the Greek Grammar) for the Help of young Beginners, Second Edition, reviſed and carefully corrected. For the Uſe of Eton-School.

BOOKS printed for, and ſold by J. Brotherton, at the Bible next the Fleece Tavern, in Cornhill.

Whitlock's Memorials.	Telemachus, in French.
Temple's Works, 2 Vol.	Ditto in Fol.
Bailey's Eng. Dict. Fol.	Guardians, 2 Vol.
Tillotſon's Works, 3 Vol.	Langham's Duties.
Bates's Works, Fol.	Free Thoughts on Religion.
State of Britain, for 1732.	La Bell Aſſemblé, 3 Vol.
Bailey's Juſtin.	Vanburgh's Plays, 2 Vol.
Origin of Honour.	Addiſon's Works, 4 Vol.
L di s Cond. &c.	Spectators, 8 Vol.
Virgin unmaſk'd	Trapp's Virgil.
Hale's Ship and Supercargo	D'Urfey's Songs, 6 Vol.
Book-Keeper.	Milton Loſt and Regain'd.
Coke's Detect on, 2 Vol.	D'Anois Tales, 3 Vol.
Bohun's Law of Tythes.	De Retz Memoirs, 4 Vol.
Feſtis & Faſts of the Church.	Tom Brown's Works, 4 Vol.
Eraſmi Eccleſiaſtica.	Farnborough's Grammar.
Life of Oliver Cromwell.	Philips's Grammar.
Life of the K. of Sweden.	Dorrington's Devotion.
Dampier's Journal to Madagaſcar.	Congreve's Plays, 3 Vol.
Rapin's Hiſt. of England, 15 Vol.	Popeand Swift Miſc. 3 Vol.
Arbuthnot of Ailments, com	Pope's Miſc. 2 Vol.
	Turkiſh Spy, 8 Vol.

This Day was publiſhed,

AN ODE, to his Grace the Duke of Newcaſtle, Written on the preſent Tranquillity of Europe, eſtabliſh'd by the Influence of the Britiſh Power.

Nibil habet aut Fortuna tua majus, quàm ut poſſis, aut Natura tua melius, quàm, ut velis, quàm plurimis conſervare. Cic.

Printed for J. Batley, at the Dove in Pater-Noſter-Row. Price 6 d.

Where may had, juſt publiſhed,
Dedicated to the Gentlemen of the Navy of England, The Memoirs of Monſieur DU GUE TROUIN, Chief of a Squadron of the Royal Navy of France, and Great Croſs of the Military Order of S. Lewis; containing all his Actions with the Engliſh, Dutch, and Portugueſe, in the late Wars of King William and Queen Anne.
Tranſlated from the French by a Sea-Officer.

This Day is publiſhed, Price 1s.

The Second Edition of

THE PROGRESS of LOVE. In Four Eclogues.

I. Uncertainty, to Mr. Pope.	III. Jealouſy, to Edward
II. Hope, to the Honourable	Walpole, Eſq;
George Doddington, Eſq;	IV. Poſſeſſion, to the Right
	Hon. the Ld. Viſc. Cobham.

Printed for L. Gilliver, at Homer's Head, over againſt S. Dunſtan's Church in Fleet-ſtreet. Likewiſe, STOWE, the GARDENS of the Right Hon. Richard Lord Viſcount Cobham. Addreſs'd to Mr. POPE.

Devenere locos lætos, & amæna Vireta Fortunatorum nemorum, ſedeſque beatæ. Virg.

The Cœleſtial Anodyne Tincture: Or, The Great Pain-Eaſing Medicine.

FAm'd and approv'd of for its wonderful and never-failing Succeſs, in giving immediate Eaſe and Relief in all manner of pains, either inward or outward, and is the moſt certain Remedy in the World for a ſure and ſpeedy Cure of the Cholick, and expelling Wind, Gripes, and pains in the Stomach, the Pleuriſy, ſtitches or pains in the ſide, back, loins, or any other parts. Rheumatick Ailments, which cauſe pain and dolor. It hath given eaſe to a Miracle, when all other Remedies have fail'd. In the Gravel and Stone in the Kidneys, it gives eaſe forthwith, and brings them away to Admiration. It alſo facilitates and cauſes a ſpeedy Delivery in Child-birth. Tis no Quack trifling thing to abuſe the World with, but a real and well-experienced Medicine, acting by Stupefaction (as Opiates) but by a friendly, balſamick, and ſubtile Nature, pacifying the moſt ſevere and terrible racking pains, and carries off the Cauſe, not by purging, but by Tranſpiration, by Urine, or breaking Wind. No Family ought to be without it. And uſed outwardly, it cures Swellings, Aches, pains, Numbneſs, or Weakneſs of the Joints; tis excellent for Cramps, and all other and Infirm ſtiff, effecting Wonders in Agues, Fevers, Small-pix, &c. No Family ought to be without it.

It is ſold only by Mr. PARKER, Printer, at his Houſe in Saliſbury-Court; or by ſuch perſons as he ſhall depute, viz. at Mr. Parker's, a Printer, in Bull-Head-Court, Jewin-ſtreet; at the White Gallon Pot, a Chandler's Shop in Bandy-Leg-Walk, Southwark, and at Mr. Neal's, a Toy-ſhop over againſt the White Hart Inn in the Borough, at Eighteen pence, a bottle, with printed Directions; and, if requeſted, will be brought to any Perſon, by the Hawker who ſells his Penny-poſt. Sealed as above.

LONDON: Printed by J. HUGGONSON, in Bartholomew-Cloſe, for Captain GULLIVER, near the Temple. where Letters and Advertiſements are taken in: As alſo at the Rainbow Coffee-Houſe in Cornhill, and John's Coffee-Houſe in Sheer-Lane, near Temple-Bar. [Price Two Pence]

The Grub-ſtreet Journal.

NUMB. 128

Thurſday, *JUNE* 15, 1732.

On eſt un grand menteur. French Proverb.

MR. Blunderbuss, Hiſtoriographer to the Society, roſe up next; —— Mr. President, the learned Gentleman who ſpoke laſt, has given ſo full an account of that *high and incomparable Perſonage*, Monſieur On, that I ſhall not preſume to add any thing thereto. But with ſubmiſſion, Mr. Preſident, I think he has not ſet Mr. Walsingham's great ſkill in the French language in ſo clear a light as he ought to have done. And therefore, Mr. Preſident, to do juſtice to this learned Gentleman, I beg leave to repeat his quotation from M. Richelet, and to make an obſervation or two upon it. His words, Mr. Preſident, are 'On is uſed in 'a modern ſenſe IN the firſt perſon, *I:* for inſtead of ſay-'ing, Je songerai *a vos interets, I will take care of 'your intereſts*, I may very well ſay, in writing or ſpeak-'ing familiarly, On songerai *a vos interets.*' As to the former part of this quotation, Mr. Spondee very well obſerved, that IN *the firſt perſon* was a falſe tranſlation of M Richelet's words POUR *la premiere perſonne*; but he took no notice of the reaſon aſſigned for the aſſertion, that On *is uſed* in *the firſt perſon*, namely, becauſe, inſtead of *Je ſongerai*, one might very well ſay, *On ſongerai.* Were this true, Mr. Preſident, it would undeniably prove the aſſertion: but it unfortunately happens, that *On ſongera* is a ſort of French, invented either by Mr. Walsingham, or his Printer. In the *Whitehall Evening Poſt* of ſaturday June 3. the former has charged this miſtake upon the latter: for which reaſon, I ſuppoſe, Mr. Spondee paſſed it by in ſilence. But to me it is very plain, Mr. Preſident, that the Author gave it at firſt On *ſongerai*; a direct inſtance, as he thought, to prove, that On was uſed *in the firſt perſon ſingular*, inſtead of Je: but being afterwards informed, that *On* was always joined to a verb of the third perſon ſingular, he corrected it to On *ſongera*, not conſidering, that this alteration, which mended the French, would marr the Argument, which now ſtands thus: On is uſed in the firſt perſon ſingular, becauſe it is uſed in the third. Let this Gentleman therefore take his choice, Whether we ſhall account him a bad *French-man*, or a downright blundering *Briton*.

I have inſiſted longer upon this, Mr. Preſident, than I at firſt intended; and ſhall now paſs directly from this criticiſm in Grammar, to a ſubject of much greater importance, to a Caſe in Law: with the Forms of which, tho' I own, this Gentleman has had great opportunities of acquainting himſelf, yet as to the Matter, I think I may without vanity affirm, that the opportunities of information which I have had have been ſuperiour. —— He tells us, *Pag.* 3. *Col.* 2. 'It appears, that the perſon, 'whom I, by authority of the Laws, call the Pretender, 'and whom *Fog*, with greater complaiſance, ſtiles the 'the *Chevalier*, this worthy perſon hath actually turned 'Thief-Broker, hath taken up the profeſſion of *Jonathan Wild*, and hath engaged in the *compoſition of felony*, for which I do inſiſt, he ought to ſuffer death as a 'Felon, even *though he had not been attainted as a* Traitor; and that the ſame Law, by which *Jonathan Wild* 'was convicted, would be ſufficient to execute him even 'as a *common Malefactor*. For, by the Statute made 'againſt *Thief-Broking*, whoever undertakes to reſtore '*ſtolen goods* or *effects*, without bringing him who ſtole 'them to *condign Puniſhment*, ſuch perſon is *guilty of 'Felony*, without *benefit of Clergy*, and on conviction of 'the crime is *to ſuffer death* accordingly.' —— Now ſuppoſing all this, Mr. Preſident, to be exactly according to Law, and that whoever 'hath engaged in the *compoſi-'tion of* [meaning *for*] *Felony*, and undertaken to reſtore '*ſtolen goods*, without bringing him who ſtole them to '*condign puniſhment*, ought to ſuffer death as a *Felon*,' yet the *Statute* upon which this is founded, tho' conceived in terms the moſt general, includes only private perſons, and cannot poſſibly extend to Legiſlators themſelves. Theſe may make what *compoſition* they pleaſe for Felony; theſe may '*indemnifie* a Felon from the penalties of all 'his crimes; theſe may entitle him to the *quiet poſſeſſion* 'of all property in his hands, and to the enjoyment of 'that property even in his *native Country*.' All this, Mr. Preſident, the Parliament actually did, with reſpect both to Thomson and Robinson, as Mr. Walsingham himſelf aſſures us, *Pag.* 1. *Col.* 2. —Nay, Mr. Preſident, I will be bold to averr, that even a private perſon who *hath engaged* in a treaty with a Felon, in order to make a *compoſition* for Felony, and lays that treaty before the Parliament for their approbation, does not come within the penalties of the Statute. If he have *taken* no *money directly or indirectly, under pretence of helping any perſon to ſtolen goods*, he is ſecure from the Statute; notwithſtanding any correſpondence he may have held, in order to the recovery of ſuch goods; this is evident from the words of the Statute, Mr. Preſident, which I ſhall preſently have occaſion to recite. Thus far therefore, Mr. Preſident, I think Monſieur On, or 'the Pretender, whom (as Mr. Walsingham ſe-'verely remarks) Fog, with greater complaiſance, ſtiles 'the *Chevalier*,' has evaded this Statute: for it does not appear, that he hath taken any money, &c. and he hath layed before the Parliament an account of his tranſactions with Thomson. —— But how then, Mr. Preſident, doth That *appear*, which Mr. Walsingham ſo poſitively and confidently aſſerts, 'That this worthy perſon hav-'ing actually turned Thief-Broker, ought to ſuffer 'death as a Felon, even *though he had not been attainted 'as a* Traitor?' Why, Mr. Preſident, this Gentleman '*inſiſts*, that the ſame Law, by which Jonathan Wild 'was convicted, would be ſufficient to execute him even 'as a *common Malefactor*. For, continues he, by the Sta-'tute made againſt *Thief-Broking*, whoever undertakes to 'reſtore *ſtolen goods* or *effects*, without bringing him who 'ſtole them to *condign puniſhment*, ſuch perſon is de-'clared *guilty of Felony*, without the *benefit of Clergy*, 'and on conviction of the crime is *to ſuffer death ac-'cordingly*.' I wiſh, Mr. Preſident, this Gentleman, inſtead of giving us the ſenſe of this Law in his own words, had given the words of the Law itſelf, and referred us to it in the Statute-book. For my part, Mr. Preſident, I freely own, I have never read this Statute; tho', with all humility I ſpeak it, I believe I have *read*, tho' not *written*, ſo much as this Gentleman. —— *The Law by which* Jonathan Wild *was convicted*, I take to be a Statute of the 4th of George I. part of which, Mr. Preſident, I beg leave to recite. In Chap. xi. Sect 4. it is enacted, 'That if any perſon taketh money or reward, 'directly or indirectly, under pretence of helping any 'perſon to ſtolen goods, he ſhall (unleſs he apprehends 'the Felon, and cauſes him to be brought to Trial, and 'gives evidence againſt him) be guilty of Felony, and ſuf-'fer the penalties, according to the nature of the Felony 'committed in ſtealing ſuch goods, and in the ſame man-'ner as if he had ſtolen them himſelf.' —— I beg leave, Mr. Preſident, to compare the Statute of the 3d of the Free Briton, with this of the 4th of George I. and to make two or three obſervations upon them as I go along. In the former it is ſaid, *Whoever undertakes to reſtore ſtolen goods.* Pray, Mr. Preſident, what is meant by this dubious word *undertake*; and how ſhall ſuch an *under taking* be proved? The words of the latter are much plainer, *If any perſon taketh money or reward, directly or indirectly, under pretence of helping any perſon to ſtolen goods.* The *taking* of *money* is an act which is capable of ſeveral kinds of proof: but, as my Brother Mr. Conundrum ſaid very well on this occaſion, it is impoſſible to prove an *under-taking* to be an *overt-act.* —— The exception in the one Statute is, *Without bringing him who ſtole* the goods *to condign puniſhment*. This is an exception, Mr. Preſident, which can be of no ſervice to any private perſon, being grounded on a condition which it is not in the power of any ſuch to perform. *Condign puniſhment* muſt neceſſarily be preceded by two things, a ſentence of condemnation paſſed by a Court of Judicature, and a Warrant for Execution ſigned by the ſovereign Power: and therefore he only, who can ſecure both theſe, can certainly *bring* a Felon to *condign puniſhment*. But the exception in the other Statute contains a condition which may be eaſily accompliſhed by any one, viz. *unleſs he apprehends the Felon, and cauſes him to be brought to Trial, and gives evidence againſt him.* —— In the laſt place, Mr. Walsingham's ſevere Statute declares *ſuch perſon guilty of Felony, without the benefit of Clergy*, and that he ſhall *ſuffer death accordingly*. But King George's Statute is much gentler, declaring only that he ſhall *ſuffer the penalties, according to the nature of the felony committed in ſtealing ſuch goods*, which may happen to be no more than Tranſportation; under which Monſieur On has lain above theſe forty years. — From theſe obſervations, Mr. Preſident, I humbly preſume it evidently appears, that there is a very great difference betwixt a Statute drawn up in a Garret in Chancery-lane, or Grub-ſtreet, and interpreted at a Coffee-houſe, and a Statute paſſed in the Parliament-houſe, and expounded in Weſtminſter Hall.

As ſoon as Mr. Blunderbuss was ſate down, Mr. Orthodoxo ſtood up and ſaid, —— Mr. Preſident, the learned Mr. Spondee and Mr. Blunderbuss have fully manifeſted Mr Walsingham's great learning and knowledge, with reſpect to the French language, and the Engliſh Laws. I beg your attention upon a ſubject of a very different nature, which I ſhall diſpatch with brevity; and for the greater perſpicuity ſhall reduce my diſcourſe under theſe three general heads. i. Mr. Walsingham's method of arguing. ii. The poignancy of his Wit. iii. The fineneſs of his Language. —— i. As to his method of arguing. He aſſerts, that the *Pretender*, under pretence of impriſoning Thomson, deſigned only to protect him, and to ſhare with him in the plunder of the *Charitable Corporation*. This he endeavours to prove by the following arguments, 1. 'It ever was notorious, that Thomson was a '*Jacobite*, *Pag.* 1. *Col.* 2. 2. This became more noto-'rious, when he was received into the protection of 'Lieutenant General Dillon and Abbe Dun, Principal 'Miniſters to the Pretender in France. *Ibid.* 3. But 'what gives ſtronger light to this affair, the late *Biſhop of 'Rocheſter*, who lived at open variance with the Iriſh Fac-'tion, died with a public Declaration that *Robinſon* and '*Thomſon* had plundered the *Charitable Corporation* for 'the benefit of the *Jacobites*; but that he abhorred and 'deteſted ſo vile, ſo infamous a practice to promote their 'intereſt. *Pag.* 2. *Col.* 1. 4. David Avery, who 'went to France by leave of the Houſe of Commons, 'informed them at his return, that *Thomſon*, as he had 'heard, had offered 100,000 l. to the Pretender for 'his protection; which he had refuſed with the higheſt 'indignation, declaring that he would never give his pro-'tection to one who had betrayed and injured a Peo-'ple, whom he was pleaſed to call his loving Subjects. '*ibid.* 5. The Government have had undoubted intel-'ligence, that the Pretender's Eldest Son, and '*hopeful Heir apparent*, went to viſit Thomson on 'his arrival in Rome, that he was in conference with him 'full two hours; that Murray and Hay, the titular 'Lords of Dunbar and Inverness, Principal Miniſters 'to the Pretender, went to confer with him every day: 'of ſo great importance was this man thought to be to 'the Jacobite Cauſe, and with ſo great diſtinction was he 'received at Rome.' *Pag.* 4. *Col.* 1. Theſe are five facts which he aſſerts, and upon which he reaſons in the following manner. 'Was it natural or probable, that a man 'who had offered ſuch a price, and been refuſed with 'ſcorn, ſhould leave a place where he was undoubtedly 'ſafe, and take a journey to Rome, to the very reſidence 'of that Perſon, from whom he muſt expect danger and 'confinement? Was it not much more natural, that Lieu-'tenant Gen. Dillon and the Abbe Dun, who ſo gene-'rouſly protected him in France, and who being the 'Pretender's Miniſters, dared not give him that pro-'tection without his permiſſion, did likewiſe recommend 'him to their Friends at Rome, and *ſtipulate with* the 'Pretender for his kind reception? . . . Does it not 'appear to a Demonſtration, that as he was well received 'by the Pretender's Miniſters at Paris, they recom-'mended him to the Pretender himſelf at Rome? '*Pag.* 2. *Col.* 1. —— In anſwer to the facts here aſſerted, as to the 1ſt. It is denied, that it was notorious that Thomson was a Jacobite: I never heard of it before, but have been aſſured, that he was a Scotch Presbyterian. As to the 2d and 5th it is likewiſe denied, that Dillon and Dun, Murray and Hay, are the Pretender's *principal Miniſters* in France, and at Rome. As to the 3d, if the Biſhop made uſe of the very words alledged, which is very uncertain, it is moſt likely he meant, that this villany was only conſequentially, but not originally deſigned, *for the benefit of the Jacobites*; amongſt whom Thomson might hope for a refuge. As to the 4th Mr. Walsingham himſelf endeavours to invalidate it in his two next paragraphs: but he does not mention the time when, and the place where the *offer* of 100,000 l. was ſaid to be made; by which two circumſtances the ſtrength or weakneſs of his following arguments would evidently appear. —— In one of which he inſiſts, 'that Dillon and Dun dared not give Thom-'son protection without permiſſion from the Preten-'der.' Pray, what *protection* could they give him in France? Was converſing with him, when neither Engliſh nor Scotch Jacobites would, *protection?* And might

not that converſation be antecedent to any *permiſſion* from the PRETENDER? If they had his *permiſſion*, what occaſion was there for their *ſtipulating with the Pretender for his kind reception at Rome?* Why ſhould they *recommend a perſon to the* PRETENDER, whom he had juſt before recommended to them, by giving them his *permiſſion* to entertain and protect him? May I not therefore, Mr. Preſident, with greater reaſon, make uſe of Mr. WALSINGHAM'S words, *Does it not appear to Demonſtration*, either that the PRETENDER gave no permiſſion for protecting THOMSON to DILLON and DUN, or that they made no ſtipulation, gave no recommendation in his favour to the PRETENDER?

DOMESTIC NEWS.

C. *Courant.*	E P. *Evening Poſt.*
P. *Poſt-Boy.*	S J. *S. James's Evening Poſt.*
D P. *Daily Poſt.*	WE. *Whitehall Evening P.*
D J. *Daily Journal.*	LE. *London Evening Poſt.*

THURSDAY, *June* 8.

They write from York of May 29, that the friday before the workmen having taken up in the York Minſter a long ſpotted marble in the great Iſle, but a little weſt of the Lantern, or great Tower, perceiv'd the top of a ſtone coffin 2 yards and ſome inches long, about a foot from the ſurface of the earth: upon lifting up the cover, appear'd a little coffin of lead, in which they found the bones of a man, carefully wrapt up in ſilk, which, by thoſe Gentlemen preſent, who underſtood the Records of the Church, were ſtrongly preſum'd to be thoſe of S. William, once related to King Stephen, Archbiſhop of this See from the year 1141 to 1147, and who dy'd 1154. *S J.*

We have an account from Wellington in Somerſetſhire, that on thurſday laſt, about 3 o' clock in the afternoon, there fell ſuch a prodigious quantity of rain, attended with thunder, between Glouceſter and Taunton, that there was no travelling for ſome hours; and one Lyppincott, a Carrier, had the miſfortune to have 3 horſes drowned about a mile from Taunton. *D P.*

Laſt week a moſt curious piece of furniture, being a large and magnificent lanthorn, in imitation of that of Norfolk, was hung up at Henry Smith's, Eſq; near Reading in Berks. *D P.*

Yeſterday the Court of Directors of the Hon. Eaſt India Company appointed Mr. Robins their Warehouſe keeper, in the room of Mr. Gilbert, deceaſed. *C.*

Weymouth, June 5. Laſt week put in here the Eagle ſloop, belonging to Sir Char. Wager, Capt. Evans, bound to the weſtward to dive on ſome wreck'd veſſels; and being inform'd by ſome old Fiſhermen, that the Pembroke man of war was ſunk about 3 miles to the eaſtward of this harbour near 70 years ſince, Capt. Evans went on friday laſt on it, and this day has brought aſhear from the wreck one of her anchors, about 17,00 weight; and he is apprehenſive by ſome tokens that her guns are braſs: he is now going to purſue his intended expedition, the wind being fair. *P. D J.* —— *June* 10. On thurſday he brought on ſhore a large anchor and 2 iron guns. *P.* 13. — *The* Captain *is now become leſs* apprehenſive.

Laſt night was the *Ridotto al' Freſco* at Spring-Gardens. Vaux-Hall; there were about 100 ſoldiers planted at the outward doors and along the avenues to the houſe, to prevent any diſturbance: the chief of the company went in between 9 and 11; and the dreſſes, for the moſt part, were Dominees and Lawyers gowns; tho' one third of the Company had no dreſſes or maſks: it is reckon'd there were about 400 people there, and about 10 men to 1 woman. The Company broke up between 3 and 4 this morning. There was no diſturbance, but the whole conducted with good order. His Royal Highneſs, attended by ſeveral Noblemen and Gentlemen, &c. went in about 10, and ſtaid about 2 hours. A pick-pocket well dreſs'd was taken picking a watch out of a Maſquerader's pocket; (he having got the Gentleman's purſe, with about 50 guineas before, and convey'd it away) but he was committed priſoner 'till to day to be examined. *LE.* —— Yeſterday a man was committed to the new jail in Southwark, for picking a Gentleman's pocket at the *Ridotto*, of a green purſe, in which were 60 guineas. *P.* 9. —— We hear that a certain Middleſex Juſtice of the peace offered to make oath, that his pocket was picked of fourſcore guineas. *This happened by wandering out of his own Liberties.* C. 9.

This day the Hon. George Doddington, one of the Lords Commiſſioners of the Treaſury, ſet out for Paris, from whence he will proceed to Rome, and return home from thence about Michaelmas next. *S J.* —— He hath orders to purchaſe ſeveral books and other curioſities for her Majeſty. *P.*

On ſaturday died George Jacob, Eſq. at Martin in Surrey, reputed worth 30,000 l. *P.*

Yeſterday Iſaac Iſrael was committed to Newgate, for feloniouſly ſtealing 40 diamond rings, ſome ſilver hafted knives and forks, &c. from divers perſons. *P.*

Plymouth, June 4. The Vicarage of S. Andrews here is void; probation ſermons are frequently preached, and any Clergyman of merit may enter himſelf a Candidate. It is worth between 3 and 400 l. per ann. the election will come on about the end of Auguſt; and is in the gift of the Mayor and Aldermen, who will beſtow it on the moſt meritorious. *S J.* —— *In lungs, or in learning.*

Yeſterday the remains of the Cottonian Library were removed from the new Dormitory of Weſtminſter ſchool to the old one. And the Gentlemen of the College lay laſt night in the new Dormitory for the firſt time. *S J.*

FRIDAY, *June* 9.

Hen. Barns, Eſq; hath purchaſed the place of Secondary of the Court of Common Pleas (to Prothonotary Borrett) of Rich. Thompſon, Eſq; *P. D P.* —— Will. Criſtrele, Eſq; a relation of the Speaker of the Houſe of Commons, is appointed Huſband of the 4 and half *per Cent.* Duty, in the room of Tho. Scott, Eſq; deceas'd, a place worth 300 l. per ann. *C.* Mr. Will. Creſwell: 4 and half Plantation Duty. *C.* 10. Mr. Ric. Creſſwell, upper Clerk of the Roaſting Houſe in Fetter-lane, a King's Huſband at the Port of London. *D P. S J. LE.* 10. Mr. Will. Creſswell. *WE.* 10. —— *I hope this Wife's fortune is not as uncertain as her name, and that of her* Huſband.

Canterbury, June 7. Laſt thurſday came on before the worſhipful Geo. Lee, L. L. D. Surrogate, a Cauſe between the Church-wardens of New Romney and the Rev. Mr. O Neale, concerning ſeveral immoralities, ſaid to be committed by him: and after a hearing of near 4 hours, the Surrogate declared, that Mr. O Neale ought to be diſmiſſed, and on monday laſt he gave ſentence accordingly. *D J.*

Laſt week Sir Tho. Peyton of Doddington in the Iſle of Ely, Bar. was marry'd to Mrs. Skeffington, a Leiceſterſhire Lady of 20,000 l. fortune. *D P.*

Chriſtned Males 140, Females 136: in all 276.
Buried Males 181, Females 191: in all 372.
Increaſed in the Burials this week, 23.

SATURDAY, *June* 10.

Yeſterday being the firſt day in Trinity Term, the R. Hon. the Lord Chancellor and Judges went in the uſual ſtate to Weſtminſter-Hall, &c. *C. D J.*

The Carolina Yacht, &c. anchored in ſight of Harwich at 7 o' clock on thurſday morning, where they continu'd when the Poſt came away. *D J.* —— Yeſterday one of his Majeſty's Meſſengers brought an account that they put to ſea about 5 on thurſday evening. *D P.*

His Majeſty before he left London, was graciouſly pleaſed to ſign the engroſſed Bill incorporating Truſtees for eſtabliſhing the Colony of Georgia in America; ſo that the Charter is now entirely paſſed through the Secretary of State's Office; and his Grace the Duke of Newcaſtle, moſt generouſly refuſed to accept the fees due to him, which are conſiderable. *D P.* Since they were to come out of money appropriated to the aſſiſtance of the unfortunate. *D J.* —— His Grace *ſcorned to received any advantage himſelf from this truly* Charitable Corporation.

Yeſterday Mr. Allen, Purſer of the Eaton, Capt. Upton, from Buenos-Ayres, belonging to the South Sea Company, brought an account of her ſafe arrival at Falmouth; her cargoe chiefly conſiſts of hides, gold duſt, ſome ſilver, and other rich goods: ſhe failed from England June 5, 1730. *D P.* — From Buenos Ayres, Mar. 14. *D J.*

The ſame day there was a meeting of ſeveral Knights of the Bath, at his Grace the D. of Montague's, Grand Maſter of the ſaid Order, and afterwards [they] went to K. Henry VIIths Chapel, Houſe of Lords, and Court of Requeſts. And we hear the time fix'd for the inſtallation of the 4 new Knights will be on the 30th Inſt. and that the Grand Entertainment will be in the Court of Requeſts; and orders are ſent to all the Knights to be preſent on that day, with their Squires. *D J.* —— It is fix'd for the 31. *S J.*

On tueſday at the races at Saliſbury, Sir Michael Newton's gray Horſe won the King's Plate of 100 l. *D P.*

On wedneſday evening the Rev. Mr. Beſſomber was attack'd by a ſingle Highwayman, near Stamford Hill, who took from him ſome ſilver, and a pair of ſilver buckles. *C. D P.*

Letters yeſterday from Paris ſay, that the late Earl of Mar dy'd of a dropſy at Aix la Chappelle, a few days ſince; and that his ſon, the Lord Ereſkine, was going to be marry'd to a German Lady, with 200,000 Florins down, and as much more at her mother's death. *D P.*

On tueſday dy'd as the boarding ſchool at Black Lands by Chelſea, Miſs Sweetapple, Grand-daughter to the late Dr. Lewis Atterbury of Highgate, aged about 8 years. By her death, an eſtate of 400 *l. per ann.* falls to Aubrey Atterbury, Eſq; only ſon of the late Biſhop of Rocheſter, who is juſt arrived in the Cæſar from the Eaſt-Indies. *P.* —— Yeſterday dy'd of a looſeneſs and vomiting Mrs. Anne Sandford, a Gentlewoman of prodigious prudence, piety, and patience. *D J.*

On wedneſday laſt Tho. Clutterbuck, Eſq; was unanimouſly re-elected Member of Parliament for the Borough of Leſkard in Cornwall. *LE. S J.*

Yeſterday morning dy'd Fran. Blunt, Eſq; formerly an eminent Attorney of New Inn, at Kentiſh Town, after a tedious indiſpoſition. —— The ſame evening the Rev. Mr. Jackman, formerly Chaplain to the late E. of Carnarvon, in Piccadilly, in the 92d year of his age. *S J.*

MONDAY, *June* 12.

On ſaturday in the evening her Majeſty, and the Royal family, removed from Richmond to Kenſington, where they will reſide 'till the King returns from his German Dominions. *C. D P. D J.* At 9 o' clock. *P.* — Yeſterday being the anniverſary of his Majeſty's inauguration, when he enter'd into the 6th year of his reign, the ſame was obſerved with the uſual rejoicings. *C.* &c.

Yeſterday being the firſt ſunday in Trinity Term, the R. Hon. the L. Mayor, the Judges, &c. went with the uſual ſtate to S. Paul's Church, and heard a ſermon preach'd by the Rev. Dr. Middleton, Chaplain to his Lordſhip, and returned to an elegant dinner provided by Mr. Sheriff Pindar, at Haberdaſhers Hall. *C. P. D P.*

On thurſday 400 l. was paid to the perſons concern'd in apprehending John Oſborn. John Longmore, Will. Woolcot, and Hen. Barns, executed laſt monday. *D J.*

We hear there is a very merry Allegorico-Botanico-Badinical piece handed about, entitled the natural Hiſtory of *Arbor Vitæ*, or *The Tree of life.* *P.*

On friday died at his lodgings at Newington-Green, after a tedious indiſpoſition, Monſ. Salle, a celebrated Dancer belonging to Lincolns-Inn Fields Playhouſe. *D P.*

TUESDAY, *June* 13.

Yeſterday morning about 3, Mr. Over, one of his Majeſty's Meſſengers, arrived at Kenſington, with the agreeable news of his Majeſty's ſafe landing at Helvoetſluys in Holland on ſaturday laſt, at 3 in the afternoon, being in good health. *D P.* &c. —— The Princeſs Mary, youngeſt daughter to their Majeſties, has the chicken pox at Kenſington. *D P.*

The ſame morning about 10, was held a Council at the Cockpit, Whitehall, and laſt night about 7, was held another, on ſome important affairs. *P.* —— On account of the Papers belonging to John Thomſon, ſent over by Mr. Arbuthnot, Banker at Paris. And we hear that Mr. Woodcraft, an Attorney, was taken into cuſtody upon that occaſion. *C.* — After examination he was diſcharged. *C.* 14.

A fellow was yeſterday taken up and committed to Tothill fields Bridewell, for hawking and ſelling about the ſtreets a lewd and obſcene Pamphlet, entitled *Vanella.* C.

Laſt ſaturday were perform'd ſeveral exerciſes in Latin and Greek, proſe and verſe, by the 8 ſenior ſcholars of Merchant Taylors ſchool, before the Preſident and Examiner of S. John's College in Oxford, &c. and a numerous audience, when the young lads gain'd great applauſe, and the next day the Company met and filled up four vacancies in S. John's College with Abel Moyſey, John Spier, Edw. Bridges Blackett, and James Weedon, the four ſenior ſcholars. *D P.*

On friday laſt a Tyger at Deptford, on board the Cadogan, from the Eaſt Indies, broke his chain, which obliged moſt of the ſailors on board to get out of his way, the boys being on ſhore that uſed to feed him, while he jump'd from ſhip to ſhip, and cleared all before him, 'till a Sawyer belonging to the King's-yard, knock'd him down with a handſpike, and kill'd him on the ſpot. *C.*

Yeſterday the Livery of the Salter's Company unanimouſly concurr'd with their Court of Aſſiſtants recommendation, to elect Mr. Sheriff Pindar, Maſter of their Company for the year enſuing. *C.*

Yeſterday came advice, by way of Holland, of Edw. Carteret, Eſq; only ſon of the Hon. Edw. Carteret, Eſq; (one of the Commiſſioners for executing the Office of Poſt-Maſter-General) being dead at Bengall, of which Factory he was in November laſt appointed one of the Council. *D J.*

This day the noted John Waller ſtood in the Pillory at the Seven Dials for wilful and corrupt perjury, in ſwearing a robbery on the highway againſt ſeveral perſons whereby they had been convicted. The populace was ſo exaſperated againſt him, that they broke in upon the Peace officers, got upon the pillory, and beat him in ſuch a violent manner, that in leſs than 5 minutes he was taken down for dead, and carried to the Round houſe, and from thence to Newgate, where he lies in a dangerous condition. *S J.* —— He was very ſeverely handled. *WE.* —— The mob pelted him ſo ſeverely, that he was knock'd on the head, and dropt off the pillory dead. *LE. D P.* 14. —— They ſtripp'd him naked, and beat the pillory flat to the ground, then ſtamp'd upon him and terribly bruiſed him, he was carried to S. Giles's Round-houſe, and a Surgeon ſent for to bleed him, but before he got to Newgate he expired. *D J.* 14. —— He had not ſtood above 8 minutes, before they pulled him down, by which his ſkull was fractured in ſuch a manner that he died on the ſpot: his body was brought back to Newgate in a coach, where he remained about 3 hours before the Keeper would receive him, 'till an order came from the Sheriffs. *C.*

WEDNESDAY, June 14.

Kinfington, June 13. The King's Commiffion appoint-ing her moft excellent Majefty the Queen Regent over this Kingdom was opened and read; after which his Royal Highnefs the Prince of Wales, and all the Lords and others of the Council who were prefent, had the honour to kifs her Majefty's hand. *C. &c.*

Her Grace the Dutchefs of Buckingham, hath lately fet out for France. —— Laft week the Lady of Sir Cha. Blackwell, Bar. was fafely delivered of a fon. *D P.*

Yefterday at a Court of Aldermen —— Reed, Efq; was appointed Keeper of Newgate, which place, we hear, he purchafed for 3000 l. —— Marriot, Efq; was ap-pointed to be Auditor of the City and Bridge-works ac-compts. *C. D P.*

Counfellor Folkes of the Temple is appointed Regifter of the Alienation Office, in the room of Mr. Serjeant Webb, deceafed. *D P.*

Yefterday the Lady Lawley was by rule of Court of King's Bench, brought up into the faid Court to hear her judgment, who having fatisfied the Profecutor his cofts, the Court was pleafed to impofe on her a fine of 5 marks. *P. 8.*

From the PEGASUS *in Grub-ftreet.*

S I R,

I Did not think I fhould have troubled you before next winter, as Cenfor of theatrical performances, little dreaming I fhould have been call'd upon to exercife that Office fooner. But the horrible profanation of the Stage at prefent is fuch, that unlefs fome ftop be put to it, no man of any tafte, or woman of common modefty muft dare henceforward to appear there.

For the truth of this, Mr. BAVIUS, I appeal to laft night's new Entertainment, and particularly to that part of it, called, The Common Garden Tragedy, written, as is faid, by the Author of The Modern Husband. Such a fcene of infamous lewdnefs, was never brought, I believe, before on any Stage whatfoever ! For my part, if I had any intereft in the prefent young Managers, who copy, but too well, the old in their choice of (I prefume) theatrical Pieces, I would advife them, inftead of acting this Play again, to invite the audience to fome noted Bawdy-houfe in Drury-lane, giving the old Lady timely notice to have her Whores, Bullies, Cullies, &c. in readinefs. There would be no difference in the Entertainment I affure you. Sir John Gonson might indeed interrupt the action there, and fend the Actors to Bridewell, which he cannot fo well do, where the thing is theatrically reprefented. In every refpect elfe it would do full as well.

If this, Mr. BAVIUS, be theatrical Pieces; thefe the only fit Entertainments for the Town; thefe fuch only as can be undertaken to be acted; I defpair indeed of ever making mine fit for the Stage, or feeing it there. God forbid I fhould ever attempt it.

It would be ridiculous to aim at any fort of criticifm upon fo fhameful a Piece; for which reafon I fhall drop it, and only add, that if I had not a greater regard for the pub-lic, than I have for my own felf, I fhould be overjoyed to fee fuch monftrous Pieces received in a Houfe where mine had been rejected; which certainly muft be the moft con-folatory thing that could happen to me, as it neceffarily implies, that the true reafon for rejecting mine, was be-caufe it was not bad enough for the Stage.

If any body fhould be foolifh enough to alledge in jufti-fication of fuch proceedings, that this being a dead time of the year, moft of the Company being either gone, or going out of Town, any Play will go down; I will go fo far as to agree, that the beft Plays ought indeed to be kept for the beft Company, and the beft time of the year: but no Company, nor any time of the year can juf-tify the turning the Stage into a rank Bawdy-houfe, and the Actors into arrant Bawds, Pimps, Whores, Rogues, Rakes, and Cullies. I am, Mr. BAVIUS,

Your admirer, and old correfpondent,

Friday, June 2, 1732. DRAMATICUS.

A Ballad on the RIDOTTO AL FRESCO.

I.

YE Nymphs and Swains, who love the fport,
And value *reputation*,
Come boldly all to VENUS Court,
Where no prim Juftices refort ——
Or none for *reformation.*

2.

Yor now fo pious are we grown,
A girl that's *common* civil
Dares hardly fhew her face in Town,
But ftiulks in corners up and down,
As if her *deeds* were evil.

3.

Then thanks to thofe of generous foul,
Who, prompted by *good reafon,*

Have found a way, without controul,
The ardor of the blood to *cool*
So heighten'd by the feafon.

4.

But ftill the vertue of the age
Appears e'en in our lewdnefs;
For, tutor'd by the modeft Stage,
At leaft we keep from bare-fac'd rage,
Becaufe 'tis reckon'd rudenefs.

5.

In Town this trick has long got ground
Of amorous mafquerading:
And reafon good, for all around
Was nought but mafquerading found,
In every other trading.

6.

Nay, this is not the firft, they fay,
Has been beyond the water;
For there, fame tells us, every day
Some mafques are feen, tho' not fo gay,
And of more CANTING nature.

7.

Then you, who *wifely* right and wrong
By fafhion always meafure,
To fave your credit join the throng;
And you, who for that fame may-long,
Come for the fake of pleafure.

8.

Of fomething new you can't here fail,
If you'll defy all dangers;
For tho' perhaps the face be ftale,
A man find his Spoufes *tail*
As new, as any ftranger's.

9.

So on the bowers of Ida JOVE
Once met his wife and fifter
In mafquerade; and tho' her love
Had long fince ceas'd his heart to move,
He could not then refift her.

10.

O ftate of blifs, by laws not chain'd !
Which all the world had fhar'd in,
Had EVE but from the fruit refrain'd :
But now 'tis to th' Elect reftrain'd,
That wander in this garden.

FOREIGN NEWS.

THURSDAY, *June 8.*

Yefterday arrived the Mails from France *and* Flanders.

Hague, June 4. The States of Friefland have written to the Provinces of Zeland, Utrecht, Overyffel and Holland, to prevail upon them to admit the Prince de Naffau Dietz in their Council of State, in quality of Stadtholder of their Province, of Guelderland, Groningen and Ommelands; but all the inftances they could make were unavailable, the Province of Holland having peremptorily refufed to give their confent. *D P.*

Vienna, May 31. Private advices from Turky fay, that the Count de Bonneval dy'd lately at Conftantinople of a natural death; and that the Turkifh Conful who refided laft in this City, was beheaded at Niffa. *D P.*

FRIDAY, *June 9.*

Extract of a private letter from Paris. —— The Card. de Fleury has fent a pofitive order from the King to Mon-fieur de Vaugrenan, his Ambaffador at Turin, to demand the immediate liberty of King Victor-Amadeus, whom they fay, his moft Chriftian Majefty is defirous of feeing at his Court, that he may pay him the duty of a Grand-fon; and in cafe of a refufal we are told, he is to talk of troops fufficient to releafe him from his imprifonment, and what not. *P.*

Alicant, May 28. We have advice from Oran, that the Moors making the oppofing the Spaniards a common caufe, they would have an army of above 100,000 men, in the neighbourhood of Oran, ready to receive them, in cafe they fhould attempt to make a defcent.

SATURDAY, *June 10.*

Yefterday arrived the Mail from Holland.

Seville, May 23. The preparations which are con-tinued in all the Ports of this Kingdom, for the projected expedition, far exceed thofe which were made fome years ago for that of Sicily : there are fhipped off, befides the ufual arms and ammunition, a vaft number of faddles, &c. 20,500 fhovels, &c. 18 field ovens; 60,000 fafcines, moft of them 18 foot long; 81,000 wool-facks; 17,220 ga-bions; above 80,000 of Granadoes, &c. 125,000 pound of gunpowder; 21 millions of rations for man and horfe; 24,000 bufhels of water, wine, &c. And at Port S. Mary they are getting ready 80,000 Arroba's of ftraw, each being a quarter of a hundred. *C. &c.*

MONDAY, *June 12.*

Yefterday arrived the Mail from France.

Paris, June 18. Letters from Barcelona of 1ft inftant, inform us, that all the men of war and tranfports, which had laiin in that Port, put to fea the 31ft of May, to join

---

the reft of the fleet at Alicant; from which place they write, that all the fhips expected were arrived there. *C. P. D P.*

Vienna, June 4. There was lately brought to the fifh market from Hugary, a Sturgeon taken in the Danube, 5 ells long, and 2 ½ broad : the roe was 88 lb. weight, the entrails 74, and the body 805, in all 967 lb. *D Y.*

On Tuefday Stocks were
South Sea Stock was 98 5 8ths, to 3 qrs. South Sea Annuity 109 1 half. Bank 148 to 1 qr. New Bank Cir-culation 8 l. 2 s. 6 d. Premium. India 174 1 half, 174 1 8th. Three per Cent. Annuity 98 1 qr. Royal Ex-change Affurance 102. London Affurance 13 1 8th. York Buildings 7. African 40. Englifh Copper 2 l. 6 s. Welch ditto 1 l. 15 s. South Sea Bonds 2 l. 5 s. Premium. India ditto 6 l. 12 s. to 13 s. ditto. Blanks 7 l. 9 s. 6 d. 20 l. Prizes 19 l. 18 s. 6 d.

HIS MAJESTY

HAving been pleaſed to grant to WALTER CHURCHMAN *Letters Patent* for his new Invention of making Chocolate without FIRE, to greater Perfection, in all Reſpects, than by the common Method, as will appear on Trial, by its immediate Diſſolving, full Flavour Smoothneſs on the Palate, and intimate Union with Liquids: And as it is much finer than any other Sort, ſo it will go farther, and is leſs offenſive to weak Digeſtions, being by this Method made clean, and free from the uſual Grit and groſs Particles ſo much diſliked, which is referred to the fair and impartial Experiment; ſuch the Patentee propoſeth for his common Standard; which is now ſold at 4 s 9 d. per Pound, with Vanello's 5 s 9 d.

N. B. The Curious may be ſupply'd with his Superfine Chocolate, which is as many Degrees finer than the above Standard, as that exceeds the fineſt ſold by other Makers, plain at 6 s. with Vanello's at 7 s.

To be ſold only for Ready Money,
At CHURCHMAN's Chocolate Warehouſe,
at Mr. John Young's in St. Paul's Church-Yard;
Where Perſons in Town or Country may be ſupply'd with any Quantities, with Encouragement to Venders, who ſhall be Licensed under the Hand and Seal of the Patentee, and their Places of Sale advertis'd, if requir'd.

This Day is publiſhed, Price 6 d.

Dedicated to John White, Eſq; of Walting Wells,

THE TOUCH-STONE: Or, *Paradoxes* brought to the Teſt of a rigorous and fair Examination, for the ſettling of dubious Points to the Satisfaction of the Curious and Conſcientious.

Part I. LORD'S SUPPER ought to be adminiſter'd to Children.—— WASHING one anothers feet, a Sacrament inſtituted by Chriſt.—— BODY has no Exiſtence but in the Mind. SAILING in the Air, not impracticable. DELUGE occaſion'd by the Sons of God marrying the Daughters of Men.

By an Honeſt FREE THINKER.

Quod verum atque Decens, Curo, & Rogo; & omnis in hoc ſum. Hor.

Printed for J. Noon, at the White-Hart, near Mercers Chapel, Cheapſide

Where may be had,

I. JESUS CHRIST the Mediator between GOD and MEN; an Advocate for us with the Father; and a Propitiation for the Sins of the World. Containing an Anſwer to Mr. Chubb's Objections, with ſome Remarks on Mr. Foſter's Account or Repreſentation of this Doctrine, &c.

II. The Second Part of the Plea for Human Reaſon: In Anſwer to a Letter written to the Author of the Plea for Human Reaſon, under the Name of John Browne, Curate of Richmond, &c. In which Anſwer is particularly and fully conſider'd, the Scripture Doctrine of the Sacrifice of the Death of Chriſt for Sin; on which the Right Knowledge of the Chriſtian Religion intirely depends. Price 1 s.

This Day is publiſhed,

Beautifully printed in one large Quarto Volume. Price Twelve Shillings.

The Second Edition of

THE Hiſtory and Antiquities of Harwich and Dovercourt in the County of Eſſex. By *Silas Taylor*, Gent. To which is added, a large Appendix, containing the Natural Hiſtory of the Sea-Coaſt and Country about Harwich, particularly the Cliff, the Foſſils, Plants, Trees, Birds, Fiſhes, &c. illuſtrated with Variety of Copper Plates By Samuel Dale, Author of the Pharmacologia.

Printed for C. Davis, in Pater-Noſter-Row; T. Osborn, in Gray's-Inn; and H. Lintot at the Croſs-Keys, againſt St. Dunſtan's Church, in Fleet-Street.

N. B. There are a few Copies printed on a Superfine Royal Paper.

This Day is publiſhed,

(Dedicated to, and approved by the Ingenious Mr. SHIPTON, Surgeon,)

The Second Edition, in a neat Pocket Volume. Price Two Shillings.

Proſodia Chirurgica: Or, a *Memoria Technica*, Calculated for the Uſe of Old Practitioners, as well as Young Students in Surgery. Being a Lexicon; wherein all Terms of Art are accounted for, their moſt received Senſe given, and an exact Definition of them from the beſt *Greek* Authors: Alſo their Pronunciation, as to Quantity determined by proper Marks over each Syllable.

Printed for CHARLES CORBETT, at Addiſon's Head, and RICHARD CHANDLER, at the Flower de Luce, without Temple-Bar.

On Saturday *June* 3, was publiſhed,

Beautifully Printed on a fine Paper,

The LONDON MAGAZINE:

Or, GENTLEMAN'S *Monthly Intelligencer.*

NUMB. II. For MAY, 1732.

To be Continued. (*Price Sixpence each Month.*)

CONTAINING,

(*Greater Variety, and more in Quantity, than any* MONTHLY BOOK *extant.*)

I. A *View* of the WEEKLY ESSAYS, *viz.* Several relating to Marriage; Education; different Taſtes; Coquets; Cruelty to Animals; Affectation and Scurrility; extravagant Itch of Building; Character of a Miſer; Power of Gold; Eloquence; Puffs; Credibility; Dr. Bentley's Milton; Deſcription of Scarborough.

II. Political Subjects, viz. Remarks on Osborne's Revolution Principles; the Whig Intereſt conſider'd; bad Miniſters; Diſſertation on Chairs; Political Vampyres; Craftsmans Manner of Writing; a Caudle for Caleb; Governing by a Party; Reduction of the Land-Tax; Balance of Power; Corruption; Remarks on Voltaire; Earls of Godolphin and Oxford; Dr. Atterbury and Mrs. Oldfield; ſeveral Letters relating to Bp. Burnet, &c

III. Poetry: Eſther, a ſacred Drama; to Sir H—— S—— on Raitiſes, a humourous Epiſtle; on being cut for the Stone, to Mr. Cheſelden; two Wills; on the Duke of Dorſet's dangerous Paſſage; Lady with long Nails; Osborne's Characters; Epigrams.

IV. Domeſtick Occurrences, Promotions, Eccleſiaſtical, Civil and Military; Marriages and Births, Deaths, &c. Belloni's Letter; Speaker's Reprimand, and the Reply; King's Speech

V. Foreign Affairs.

VI. Price of Goods, Grain, Stocks, Monthly Bill of Mortality.

VII. A Table of Contents

To which is added, A Catalogue of Books and Pamphlets, with their Prices, publiſhed by the Proprietors of the *Monthly Chronicle*, now diſcontinued.

MULTUM IN PARVO.

LONDON: Printed by *C. Ackers* in *St. John's-Street*, For J. Wilford behind the Chapter-houſe near St. Paul's; and ſold by W. Meadows, T. Cox, W. Hinchliffe, W. Whitridge, R. Willock, and E. Nutt in Cornhill; J. Clarke in Duck-lane; T. Aſtley, in St. Paul's Church-Yard; A. Dodd without Temple-Bar; J. Stagg in Weſtminſter-hall; J. Jackſon in Pall-Mall; J. Jolliffe in St. James's-ſtreet; J. Brindley and W. Shropſhire in Bond-ſtreet, and all Bookſellers both in Town and Country.

BOOKS printed for, and ſold by J. Brotherton, at the Bible next the Fleece Tavern, in Cornhill.

Whitlock's Memorials.
Temple's Works, 2 Vol.
Bailey's Eng. Dict. Fol.
Tillotſon's Works, 3 Vol.
Bates's Works, Fol.
State of Britain, for 1732.
Bailey's Juſtin.
Origin of Honour.
Ladies Conduct.
Virgin unmask'd
Hays's Ship and Supercargo Book-Keeper.
Coke's Detection, 3 Vol.
Bohun's Law of Tythes.
Feaſts & Faſts of the Church.
Eraſmii Eccleſiaſtica.
Life of Oliver Cromwell.
Life of the K. of Sweden.
Dampier's Journal to Madagaſcar.
Rapin's Hiſt. of England, 15 Vol.
Arbuthnot of Ailments, com

Telemachus, in French.
Ditto in Fol.
Guardians, 2 Vol.
Langham's Duties.
Free Thoughts on Religion.
La Bell Aſſemble, 3 Vol.
Vanburgh's Plays, 2 Vol.
Addiſon's Works, 4 Vol.
Spectators, 8 Vol.
Trapp's Virgil.
D'Urfey's Songs, 6 Vol.
Milton Loſt and Regain'd.
D'Anois Tales, 3 Vol.
De Retz Memoirs, 4 Vol
Tom Brown's Works, 4 Vol
Farnborough's Grammar.
Philips's Grammar.
Dorrington's Devotion.
Congreve's Plays, 3 Vol.
Pope and Swift Miſ. 3 Vol.
Pope's Miſ. 2 Vol.
Turkiſh Spy, 8 Vol.

This Day was publiſhed,

AN ODE to his Grace the Duke of Newcaſtle. Written on the preſent Tranquillity of Europe, eſtabliſh'd by the Influence of the Britiſh Power.

Nihil habet aut Fortuna tua majus, quàm ut poſſis, aut Natura tua melius, quàm, ut velis, quàm plurimos conſervare. Cic.

Printed for J. Batley, at the Dove in Pater-Noſter-Row. Price 6 d.

Where may had, juſt publiſhed,
Dedicated to the Gentlemen of the Navy of England,
The Memoirs of Monſieur DU GUE TROUIN, Chief of a Squadron of the Royal Navy of France, and Great Croſs of the Military Order of S. Lewis; containing all his Sea-Actions with the Engliſh, Dutch, and Portugueſe, in the late Wars of King William and Queen Anne.
Tranſlated from the French by a *Sea-Officer*.

June 3, was publiſhed, Price 6d.

[*To be Continued.*]

Neatly printed on a fine Paper.
Very proper for private Families, or to ſend into the Country (and Places Abroad, where the Engliſh reſide) being a compendious View of all our Publick Papers.

THE GENTLEMAN'S MAGAZINE: Or, *Monthly Intelligencer.*

Nº XVII. for May, 1732. being the Fifth of Volume II.

Containing more in Quantity, and greater Variety than any Book of the Kind and Price.

I. Views of the Weekly Eſſays, viz. Conveniencies and Inconveniencies in a Married and Single Life, of Common and Kept Women; new Reaſons of Divorce; Negligence of Dreſs; Power of Gold; Friendſhip; Deſcription of Scarborough; Advice to Silvanus; Taſte of Plays; Mr. Thompſon's Greek Grammar; of Education; Uſage of Beaſts; Vampyres; Caſe in Love; old Pair; Wife of Quality; Puffs; Pantomine Entertainments; Dr. B.

II. Political Points, viz. Diſputes on the Reduction of the Land-Tax, and reviving the Salt Tax; the Lords Proteſt thereon; Hyp-Doctor and Fog; K. Wm. and the Revolution; Voltaire, and his Hiſtory of the late K. of Sweden; Letter concerning Bp. Burnet, Miniſterial Power; the Whiggs Monopolizers; Cromwell a Fortunate Fool; Ballance of Power, Osborne burleſqu'd; Political Vampyres; Chairs and Stools; Charitable Corporation Affairs; Belloni's Letter, (French and Engliſh) burnt by the Hangman; Account of Bills paſſed.

III. Poetical Pieces, viz. Elegiac Song on Edw. Bell, Eſq; the Grateful Patient; a Humorous Will, Epigrams.

IV. Domeſtic Occurrences, Births, Deaths, Marriages, Promotions, &c.

V. Prices of Goods, Grain, Stocks. London Monthly Bill of Mortality.

VI. Foreign Affairs.

Together with a Table of Contents, and a Regiſter of Books and Pamphlets.

By SYLVANUS URBAN, *Gent.*

Printed at St John's Gate, for Fr. Jefferies in Ludgate-Street, and ſold by E. Midwinter, at the Three Crowns and Looking-Glaſs in St. Paul's Church-Yard; J. Batley, at the Dove in Pater-Noſter-Row; R. Williamſon, in Holbourn; S. Harding, in St. Martin's-Lane; W. Bickerton, at Lord Bacon's Head, without Temple-Bar; R. Mountague, in Great Queen-ſtreet; B. Dickinſon, in the Strand; A. Chapman in Pall-Mall; J. Stagg and C. King, in Weſtminſter-Hall; A. Dodd, E. Nutt, and all Pamphlet Shops.

N. B. At the firſt Places may be had, the ſecond Edition of Nº XVI. for April; the third Edition of Nº I. and II. the ſecond Edition of Nº III. IV. V. VI. X. XI. The other Numbers of Vol. I. being out of Print again, *compleat Setts* at preſent cannot be had, but may in about a *Month's Time*; when the whole Sett will be done on Royal Paper, large Margin, for the Curious.

This Day is publiſhed,

In Two Volumes, Octavo, on a Superfine Genoa Paper,

A Treatiſe of Architecture, with Remarks and Obſervations: By that excellent Maſter thereof *Sebaſtian le Clerc*, Knight of the Empire, Deſigner and Engraver to the Cabinet of the French King, and Member of the Academy of Arts and Sciences, neceſſary for young People who would apply to that noble Art. Engraved in 200 Copper Plates, by John Sturt. Tranſlated by Mr. Chambers. Price 10 s. 6d. Printed for R. Ware, at the Bible and Sun in Amen-Corner, near Pater-Noſter-Row.

Alſo may be had, juſt publiſhed, at the ſame Place,

1. An Hiſtorical Narration of the whole Bible. In two Parts. The firſt treating of the Old Teſtament, with the various Hiſtories of the Lives and Travels of our Bleſſed Saviour and his Apoſtles: With a Summary of the Matter, Doctrine, Scope and Divine Authority of all the Canonical Epiſtles; and an Explanation of ſeveral chief Heads in that myſterious Book of St. John's Revelation. By *J. Hammond*, D. D. and curiouſly adorn'd with Cuts, engrav'd by John Sturt, at 4 s. 6 d.

2. Engliſh and Latin Exerciſes for School-Boys. Compriſing all the Rules of Syntaxis, with Explanations, and other neceſſary Obſervations on each Rule, and ſhewing the Genitive Caſe, and Gender of Nouns and Pronouns; as alſo the Preterperfect Tenſe, Supine, and Conjugation of Verbs. Anſwering perfectly to the Deſign of Mr Garretſon, and Hermes Romanus, in bringing on Learners moſt gradually and expeditiouſly to the tranſlating of Engliſh into Latin. By *J. Bailey*, School-Maſter The 8th Edition corrected. Pr. 1 s.

3. Emblems for the Entertainment and Improvement of Youth, containing hieroglyphical and enigmatical Devices relating to all Parts and Stations of Life. Together with Explanations and Proverbs in French, Spaniſh, Italian and Latin, alluding to them, and tranſlated into Engliſh. The Whole curiouſly engrav'd on 62 Copper Plates. Pr. 2 s. 6 d.

4. The Compleat Conſtable, directing Conſtables, Headboroughs, Tything-Men, Church-Wardens, Overſeers of the Poor, Surveyors of the Highway, and Scavengers, in the Duty of their Office, according to the Power allowed them by the Laws. Price 1 s.

LONDON: Printed by J. HUGGONSON, in *Bartholomew-Cloſe*, for Captain GULLIVER, near the *Temple*, where Letters and Advertiſements are taken in; As alſo at the *Rainbow Coffee-Houſe* in *Cornhill*, and *John's Coffee-Houſe* in *Sheer-Lane*, near *Temple-Bar*. [Price Two Pence.]

The Grub-street Journal.

NUMB. 129

Thursday, *JUNE* 22, 1732.

On est un grand menteur. French Proverb.

WHILE Mr. WALSINGHAM is proving, that the PRETENDER, under pretence of imprisoning THOMSON, designed to protect him, and to share with him in the plunder of the *Charitable Corporation*, he informs us, that 'when THOMSON took refuge in France, he was received into the protection of the most *considerable Jacobites* there.' And then immediately adds, 'that Lieut. General DILLON, and Abbe DUN, the Heads of the Faction in France, and Principal Ministers to the Pretender, were the only persons with whom he dared entrust himself.' *Pag.* 1. *Col.* 2. Where, by the *most considerable Jacobites*, one would naturally imagine, he meant all the most considerable Jacobites; and by the *Faction*, the whole *Jacobite Faction*, including English and Scotch, as well as Irish. But will this Gentleman affirm, that DILLON and DUN are the *Heads* of this whole Faction? Does he not in the very next sentence mention the *Irish Faction*, as a part only of the Jacobite Faction? Now if the English and Scotch parts of this Faction had likewise some *Heads*, were not those *Heads* some of the *most considerable Jacobites*? If so, How was THOMSON received into the protection of all the most considerable Jacobites, when DILLON and DUN, the Heads of the *Irish Faction*, were the *only persons* with whom he dared intrust himself? —— But DILLON and DUN, it seems, had the greatest interest with the PRETENDER; and, according to Mr. WALSINGHAM's way of *Demonstration*, 'it appears, that they not only recommended THOMSON to him, but even *stipulated* with him for the kind reception of this charitable Warehouse keeper.' I have just now observed, how inconsistent this recommendation and stipulation were with that *permission* which Mr. WALSINGHAM likewise asserts the PRETENDER gave them to protect THOMSON in France. I shall now shew the improbality of such a successful recommendation and stipulation upon another account. This Gentleman assures us, 'that ATTERBURY, the late Bishop of Rochester, who lived at open variance with the *Irish Faction*, died with a publick Declaration, abhorring and detesting this vile and infamous practice to promote the interest of the Jacobites.' This by the way represents the late Bishop, as a *considerable Jacobite*, and the Head of the English Faction. Give me leave therefore, upon this foundation, to suppose, that the Bishop transmitted his own sentiments to Rome, and advised the Pretender to get THOMSON seized and confined. It is agreed on all hands, that he was actually seized there, with all his Papers; and that he is now in the Castle of S. Angelo. The question then between Mr. WALSINGHAM and me is this, Whether he is there, as in a place of rigorous confinement, or of favourable protection; in a prison, or in *an apartment* fitted up for his lodgings; in consequence of the advice of the late Bishop, or of the recommendation of DILLON and DUN. Now, for my part, were not the appearance of severe imprisonment in this case so evident, I should be apt to think, that the *Head* of the *English Faction* had greater influence at Rome, than the *Heads* of the *Irish Faction*. And had THOMSON even appeared publickly without any restraint among the PRETENDER's adherents at Rome, by the same way of arguing which Mr. WALSINGHAM uses, I might have *demonstrated*, that he was under confinement. For if strict confinement be a proof of the favour and protection of a person at whose instance a man is confined; then free conversation among the adherents of that person may be a proof of his resentment, and of his detaining a man under confinement who is actually in full liberty. —— But Mr. WALSINGHAM, as a further confirmation of the PRETENDER's *protection* of THOMSON, asserts, that 'THOMSON was received with great distinction at Rome.' In proof of which he says 'The Government have had undoubted intelligence, that the PRETENDER's *Eldest Son*, and *hopeful Heir Apparent*, went to visit Thomson on his arrival in Rome, that he was in conference with him full two hours. *Pag.* 4. *Col.* 1.' Had this Gentleman acquainted us with the Ceremonial observed at this *conference*, we might have formed some judgment of the *great distinction* with which these eminent Personages *received* each other. But as he is altogether silent upon this head, the chief thing here proved is the *hopefulness* of the PRETENDER's *Eldest Son* and *Heir apparent*; who must needs be a very *hopeful* Lad to be able at twelve years of age to manage a *conference* of *full two hours* with so cunning a Plenipotentiary as Mr. THOMSON.

But as a clearer proof still of the good understanding betwixt the PRETENDER and Mr. THOMSON, this Gentleman adds, 'MURRAY and HAY, the titular Lords of *Dunbar* and *Inverness*, principal Ministers to the PRETENDER, went to confer with THOMSON every day.' Should I here be so ill-natured to deny, which I might very justly do, that MURRAY and HAY are either *principal Ministers*, or any *Ministers* at all, to the PRETENDER, or are indeed resident at Rome; how would this Gentleman prove either of these circumstances? But supposing, tho' not granting, that they are true, did these *titular Lords* visit THOMSON *every day*, before, or after his confinement? If after, the circumstance will be too late to shew the *distinction* with which he was *received*. If before, it may be asked how many days intervened between his arrival at Rome, and his confinement? A true answer to which may perhaps reduce this *every day* to one single day; if THOMSON, as there is reason to believe, was arrested immediately upon his arrival. —— But suppose all the circumstances here mentioned are true; how will the double consequence follow which Mr. WALSINGHAM draws from them? 'Of so great importance was this man thought to be to the *Jacobite Cause*, and with so great distinction was he received at *Rome*.' The Jacobites there might indeed think *this man* of *great importance* to their cause, in discovering the persons principally concerned in the villainies of the Charitable Corporation; and these conferences, which were in order to that discovery, may be a proof of the belief of that *importance*; but they prove not one tittle of the main point undertaken to be proved, the *great distinction with which he was received*. There is indeed one thing, I own, sufficiently proves it, which is just mentioned by Mr. WALSINGHAM. *Pag.* 2. *Col.* 1. 'The fitting-up an apartment for Mr. THOMSON's lodgings in the *Castle of St. Angelo*.' To which if I could add an account of the Ceremonial used in conducting him to that *apartment*, and placing him in it, it would most evidently appear, that he was *received* with very *great distinction*: perhaps with as great as was shewn to Mr. KELLY, or even to Bishop ATTERBURY, when they went to the *apartments fitted up* for them in the Tower of London. —— That which I have said on this occasion has manifested, I presume, Mr. WALSINGHAM's inconclusive way of reasoning; and in some degree cleared Monsieur ON from the charge he has brought against him, of designing to protect THOMSON under pretence of imprisoning him, and to share with him in the plunder of the Charitable Corporation. And as I was induced to undertake this vindication by that proverbial Rule of Equity, that *We ought to give even the Devil his due*, which Mr. W. will not deny to include both the POPE and the PRETENDER: so I find myself justified in applying this Rule to the latter by Mr. WALSINGHAM himself, who at the end of his learned Dissertation informs us, that Monsieur ON was *allowed* by an honourable Gentleman in the House of Commons, to be *in very truth the* PRETENDER, *the Devil with cloven feet*. I thought the censure passed upon Monsieur ON's Letter by that Honourable House sufficient to render it odious to the whole Nation. They voted it, among other things, to be 'an insolent and audacious Libel, attempting to impose upon the Parliament and British Nation, and to amuse the unhappy Sufferers with vain and deceitful hopes of relief; and the whole transaction to be a scandalous artifice, calculated purely to delude the unhappy, and to disguise and conceal the wicked practices of the professed enemies to his Majesty's person, crown, and dignity:' and as such they ordered it to be burned by the hands of the Common Hang-man. They did not so much as allow the fact contained in the Letter to be true, viz. the seizure of the person and papers of THOMSON, and only said, that he is therein 'represented to have been arrested and detained in safe custody.' This vote Mr. WALSINGHAM declares to be *the most perfect description of the thing itself*; and yet he pretends to give us a more perfect one, by adding several historical circumstances, which depend solely upon his own authority. —— Before I dismiss this head, I cannot but observe, that Mr. WALSINGHAM, in his ingenious Comment upon the Letter, has done in some measure the very same thing, for which this is chiefly censured, as 'amusing the unhappy sufferers with vain and deceitful hopes of relief.' For the fourth paragraph in the first Column consists of these comfortable words. 'Amidst the horrors of this scene of distress, the most terrible and most affecting that ever any people have seen or suffered, we have joyfully seen the justice of the nation exerted in the relief of the unhappy, and in the punishment of the oppressors. Both Houses of Parliament gave their attention to the redress of this grievance, and made it a National enquiry. They proceeded with vigour, unanimity, and impartiality. The suffering Proprietors, and their wretched families, have been restored to life and comfort by the publick proceedings. The Offenders, even to the greatest, have been pursued with exemplary justice, compelled to answer in the severest manner, and to render ample satisfaction to the injured.' But that this is only a vain amusement Mr. WALSINGHAM plainly shews in the next column, where he says, 'Indeed it must be lamented, that, in the present instance, neither the Justice of the King, the Enquiries of Parliament, or the fidelity of his Majesty's Ministers, could effectually procure this Nation the full demands of Justice, or discover the whole iniquity. The Plunderers, and the acting Managers had withdrawn themselves from the power of the Laws, and had taken refuge in other countries. The books, the papers and effects of the Corporation were also withdrawn or secreted. The persons who had been the deepest concerned, and the evidence of their dark iniquity, could not be pursued or overtaken. The publick enquiry was in a great measure defeated, and the Nation deprived of light, when secret villainy, when the hidden springs, and most concealed workings of these infamous oppressors, ought to have been laid open; without which light, redress became deficient, a plundered Corporation without the just satisfaction, and the Criminals without the *righteous measure* both of shame and punishment.

But tho' this Gentleman has thus actually *amused the unhappy sufferers*, yet I must own, I believe he did not designedly *attempt* to do it, and that this apparent contradiction proceeded solely from the shortness of his memory. —— Which naturally brings me to take some notice of the greatness and poignancy of his Wit, which was the iid thing to which I proposed to speak: but of this very briefly, being not able to discover, after the most laborious search, above two instances of wit in the whole Paper; but those indeed are extremely poignant. The first is *Pag.* 3. *Col.* 1. 'But what are the CONDITIONS which he hath in charge to stipulate for *Thomson*? Why they are a CHARTE BLANCHE filled up by *Thomson*'s own hand.' The other is in *Pag* 4. *Col.* 1. 'In the first Part of this honest Composition, *Thomson*, Equity, and the Pretender; alas! *poor* EQUITY, crucified like *Jesus Christ*, between two *Thieves*.' The *Charte Blanche* intirely *filled up* is certainly a new thought, and comes properly under the article of Wit: but the *crucifixion of poor Equity* depending upon the placing it between the words THOMSON and the PRETENDER, and the joke terminating in calling them *thieves*, might more properly perhaps have been deferred to my iiid general head, The fineness and politeness of his language, to which I now proceed. —— And here I might be as large upon this head as I was upon my first; but the time will not permit. And therefore I shall only give you two or three instances of the hyperbolical and onomastical style, in which this Gentleman greatly delights, tho' his chief excellence lyes in the Battological or tautological; which shines through all his compositions, and makes it as needless, as it would be endless, to produce particular instances. In the very first sentence there is a noble Hyperbole, 'The late management of the Charitable Corporation is agreed *by all mankind*, to have been the *most unheard* of villainy that *ever* was projected or perpetrated in *any* Country.' This is followed at a little distance by another 'This scene of distress [not only] the most terrible [but also] and most affecting that *ever any* People have seen or suffered.' I shall mention but one more which is near the end of his Paper, 'This .... will make the name of W. P. Esq; amiable to *all* good men *in the World*.' We are it seems grown famous of late to *all mankind*, for our villainies; and some of us will be so to all *the World* for our virtues. — In the onomastical style this Gentleman has far outdone the [illegible] DOCTOR. For whereas the latter, with his usual con[illegible]cy, calls Signor BELLONI first A *Son of* A *Whore of* [illegible]*l*...*n*, and then *Pimp master General to* THE *Whore* [illegible]

byon, Mr. WALSINGHAM calls him Monſieur ON, who who is the ſame perſon with Signor BELLONI, *a moſt high and incomparable perſonage, a ſilly inſolent thing, a Broker, a wretched ridiculous Impoſtor, a Cheat, the Guardian of a Bankrupt, a Thief, a Thief-Broker,* and *a Felon.*

It is now time to draw to a Concluſion; and I think none can be more proper than to take particular notice of a remarkable inſtance of Mr. WALSINGHAM's veracity and impartiality. For as I have been obliged, for the ſake of truth, to mention in this diſcourſe ſome miſtakes of this Gentleman, I am bound in conſcience to act by him, in the ſame manner that he has acted towards *the late Biſhop of Rocheſter*, to whom he has done a ſignal piece of Juſtice. For by him we are informed, as more particularly mentioned above, that the *Biſhop* expreſſed the greateſt abhorrence of THOMSON's offer to divide his plunder among the Jacobites, This action will appear the more extraordinary, if we conſider it as done by a perſon in exile, and at the head of a poor diſaffected Party; and compare it with the rapacity of ſome who lived in affluence here, who profeſſed the greateſt attachment to the preſent happy eſtabliſhment, who were Members of the Honourable Houſe of Commons, who were Privy Counſellors, who were, &c. and yet combined with a ſet of inferiour Villains to rob and pillage their Fellow Subjects under the pretence of Charity. Let this laſt action of his life caſt a veil upon his errors in ſentiment or conduct, and induce us to think as favourably of them as we can; ſince it is a proof of his title, in ſome degree, at leaſt, to the character he gave of himſelf in thoſe lines prefixed to his Tranſlation of VIRGIL's GEORGICS, which were lately publiſhed in moſt of the News Papers. With theſe I ſhall conclude my diſcourſe; adding two tranſlations, one literal in blank verſe, and the other paraphraſtical in rhime, communicated to our Society by one of our ingenious Correſpondents.

——————— *Hæc ego luſi*
Ad Sequanæ ripas, Thameſino à flumine longè,
Jam ſenior, fractuſque, ſed ipsâ morte, meorum,
Quis colui, patriæque memor, neque degener uſquam.

———— ————Thus on the banks of Seine,
Far from my native home I paſs my hours,
Broken with years and pain; yet my firm heart
Regards my Friends and Country e'en in death.

Thus, where the Seine through realms of ſlavery ſtrays,
With ſportive verſe I wing my tedious days;
Far from Britannia's happy climate torn,
Bow'd down with age, and with diſeaſes worn:
Yet e'en in death I act a ſteddy part,
And ſtill my Friends and Country ſhare my heart.

BAVIUS.

DOMESTIC NEWS.

C. *Courant.*	E P. *Evening Poſt.*
P. *Poſt-Boy.*	SJ. *S. James's Evening Poſt.*
D P. *Daily Poſt.*	WE. *Whitehall Evening P.*
D J. *Daily Journal.*	LE. *London Evening Poſt.*

THURSDAY, *June* 15.

The Hon. Mrs. Vane is ill of a dropſical diſorder in S. James's-ſtreet, attended by Dr. Hollings, Dr. Douglas, and other Phyſicians. *D P.*

This being his Majeſty's Proclamation day, her Majeſty received the compliments of the Nobility and Gentry on that occaſion, &c. *S J. W E.* —— Yeſterday James Stamford, Eſq; being appointed a Captain in the foot Guards, kiſſed her Majeſty's hand. *D J.* —— On monday Capt. Franc. Danſeys was appointed Captain of the Lyme man of war. *D P.* —— Yeſterday morning the R. Hon. the E. of Albemarle ſet out for Falmouth, to embark for Gibraltar, to take on him the command of his Regiment. *P.* —— This morning at 9. *L E.* —— His Lordſhip is embarked on board a ſhip in the River for Gibraltar. *D J.*

This morning the E. and Counteſs of Thanet, the E. and Counteſs of Winchelſea and Nottingham, and the Lady Betty Fielding, ſet out together for Dover, on their way to the German Spaw. *S J. L E.* —— Capt. Berkley, ſon to the L. Berkley of Stratton, ſet out this morning for Portſmouth, to ſail for Guiney, to protect the trade on the Gold coaſt, in the room of the Hon. Capt. Lee daily expected home. *L E.* —— *Dover*, June 13. The Dutcheſs of Buckingham this morning embarqued for Calais. *P.*

We hear the Secretary of a certain great Company lately threatned to knock down a Clerk in his Office, for doing his duty. *P.*

We hear Mr. Rob. Arbuthnot has been ſent for hither from Paris. *LE.*

An extraordinary inſtance, almoſt preternatural has lately happened to one Mrs. Page at the Royal Oak in Barnaby-ſtreet, who tho' 90 years of age, nor has had a tooth in her head theſe 20 years, has lately cut 6 teeth in her upper jaw, and by the ſymptoms of the lower jaw, ſhe will ſhortly cut more there; ſhe appears to be as peeviſh and diſorder'd as a young child under thoſe circumſtances. *S J.* —— *This* almoſt preternatural inſtance *is publiſhed, I ſuppoſe, as a* natural *way to* ſell ale.

There is an account that Sir Will. Keith, Bar. is elected Knight of the Shire for Aberdeen, in the room of Sir Archibald Grant, Bar. *D P.*

The Rev. Mr. Ayleſmore, a relation of Sir Hans Sloan, Bar. is preſented by Sir Hans to the Living of Chelſea, worth about 400 l. per ann. *D P.*

Lewes in Suſſex, June 11. A quarrel happened here laſt week at a Fair, between 2 noted Farmers; they this day unhappily met in this Town, and getting two ſwords, they fought; but before any perſon could part them the one kill'd the other on the ſpot, by running him through the body: the other was ſecured and committed to gaol. *W E.* —— *If* Farmers *fight* duels, *it is to be hoped* Gentlemen *will leave them off. But the ſtory is falſe.*

We hear from the Devizes, of a duel fought May 31ſt, between 2 perſons, one above 80, and the other about 70, for a young woman. After a long combat the battle was won by the former with great victory. *S J.* — *People often* fight *about* ſome-thing, *which is really* no-thing *to them.*

Yeſterday the Coroner's Jury ſat on the body of Waller, who was killed in the Pillory laſt tueſday at the Seven Dials; but did not agree in their Verdict. *W E.* —— And brought in their Verdict Wilful murder with unlawful weapons by perſons unknown. *S J.* —— Yeſterday a relation of Waller's made an information againſt a Chimney Sweeper and one Dalton, who are both abſconded. *D J.* 16.

Yeſterday the Lords of the Admiralty ordered all the Guardſhips, to the number of 14, to be with their full compliments of men, they being to be fitted out for the ſea-ſervice with all expedition; and we hear they are all to have 6 months proviſion laid on board. *P.*

FRIDAY, *June* 16.

Yeſterday the Hon. Artillery Company appeared in arms, and performed a handſome exerciſe in honour of the day, and waited on the R. Hon. the L. Mayor, who entertained them in a handſome manner at Goldſmith's Hall. *C. D P. D J.* —— A handſome exerciſe *deſerved* a handſome *entertainment; at which I hear they* performed *a ſecond* handſome-exerciſe.

Yeſterday there was a General Court of the Charitable Corporation, at their houſe in Spring-Garden, when the following Gentlemen were choſen Directors, viz. Dr. John Mowbray, Clifford Will. Phillips, Will. Wilkinſon, Andrew Dautevite, Cha. Staples, Jam. Gaſtine, and Step. de la Creuze. Eſq; *D J.* —— Seven Committee men for the year enſuing. *P.*

Yeſterday the R. Hon. the L. Viſc. Weymouth ſet out for Dover in order to embarque for Calais, in his way to Paris, on his travels. *P.*

Yeſterday come on a farther hearing before the Barons of the Exchequer in Weſtminſter Hall, in a Cauſe long depending between the R. Rev. the Biſhop of Hereford, Plaintiff, and his brother the D. of Bridgewater, Defendant in relation to tythes which the Biſhop lays claim to, at Whitchurch, &c. in the County of Salop, and after a long hearing, an iſſue was granted for the ſame to be tried at the next Aſſizes in that County. *P.*

The *Old Debauchees* has met with great applauſe from the Town, &c. *D P.* — *This* great applauſe *was* univerſal *in the* D P. *of June 2. and affirmed in the ſame Paper to have been given to the* damn'd Common or Covent-Garden Tragedy. *We hear they were both* illuminated *by* Mr. Hint, Candle-Snuffer, *who finding the latter fit only to be acted in* the Dark, ſnuff'd *out the candles. Hence, it has only* ſtunk, *but has not been* ſeen *ſince. This Gentleman has written a learned Defence of both, in which it is evident, that ſome* ſad Comi-Tragical Grubean *had both* a finger *and* thumb.

Chriſtned Males 172. Females 169. In all 341. —— *Buried* Males 232. Females 201. In all 433. Increaſed in the burials this week 61.

Yeſterday one Brown, a Milkman in Old-ſtreet, cut his throat in a dangerous manner, that it is thought he cannot live; and being aſked the reaſon for ſo doing, ſaid, That he met the Devil in the fields that morning, who adviſed him to it. *C.* —— He expired yeſterday morning. *S J.* 17.

It being agreed that the cleareſt and fulleſt account of all Queſtions in Divinity is the Oratory, &c. *D J.* —— *This* agreement *was made privately between* Mr. Orator *and* Mr. Hyp-Doctor, *and is now made public for the benefit of both.*

SATURDAY, *June* 17.

His Grace the Duke of Montagu, Great Maſter of the moſt Hon. Order of the Bath, hath ſent circular letters to all the Knights Companions, requiring their attendance on friday the 30th, in the Prince's Chamber at Weſtminſter, &c. *D P.*

Yeſterday the R. Hon. the Earl of Eſſex ſet out for Dover, to embark for Calais, &c. *P.* —— The Earl of Eſſex's departure for the Court of Turin is put off for ſome time. *D P.* —— Yeſterday his Lordſhip ſet out for Dover, &c. *D P.* 19.

We hear that a great many Papers relating to the Charitable Corporation, belonging to Thompſon, have been lately been deliver'd up by Mr. Arbuthnot in France; and its ſaid make great diſcoveries into that iniquitous undertaking. *D P.* —— Mr. Walſingham *calls them a* Cargo of Waſte-Paper.

Yeſterday there was a General Court of the South Sea Company, when they came to the following Reſolutions: That the million payable to this Company at Michaelmas next, be applied to the Bond Creditors, by payment of 50 per cent. of the principal debt due to them, and be taken as a reduction of ſo much of the trading Capital. —— That a Committee be appointed to inſpect and examine the Accompts, and that they make their report with all the diſpatch they conveniently can. —— That the ſaid Committee conſiſt of 15 perſons, whereof 7 be a Quorum. —— That the qualification of each be 2000 l. ſtock in his own name and right. —— That no perſon who has been in the Direction ſince 1720 ſhall be choſen. —— That after Midſummer next Liſts of the names of all Proprietors poſſeſſed of 2000 l. ſtock and upwards, ſhall be printed. —— That 10 days notice be given for the holding of a General Court in order to balloting for the ſaid Committee. —— That the Court of Directors are hereby empower'd to receive any Propoſals from Spain made under ſufficient authority, for giving a compenſation to the Company for their yielding up of their annual Ship. *D J.*

We hear that Rev. Mr. Spateman, Rect. of S. Bartholomew's the Great, is appointed Chaplain to the R. Rev. the L. Biſhop of Chicheſter. *C.* Mr. Spackman. *D P.*

Her Majeſty ſince her reſidence at Kenſington, has been pleaſed to order the mount in the gardens, on which is a handſom ſeat, to be raiſed 18 foot higher than it is now, in order to have a proſpect of the Thames. *S J.* —— Her Majeſty hath been pleaſed to grant a licence of leave under her Royal ſign manual, for Major Gen. Ric. Sutton, to go to the German Spaw for the recovery of his health. *S J. L E.*

Its affirm'd by good authority, that his Excellency Mr. Robinſon, his Majeſty's Miniſter at Vienna, is certainly ſet out from that Court on his return home. *S J.*

Yeſterday a Gentleman well dreſs'd was arreſted by 3 Bailiffs in S. Margaret's Church yard, *Weſtminſter*, whoſe ſword they broke all to pieces while they were ſtruggling with him to get him into a coach, which they were not able to accompliſh. This occaſioned the Mobb to gather together in great numbers, when ſome of them, no doubt their beſt friends, cry'd out, ſend for the Scholars, wherewith they were ſo terribly frighted, they took to their heels, to avoid the ſmart of a rod, and gave the Gentleman a fair opportunity to provide alſo for his own ſafety. *S J.* —— Weſtminſter Scholars *hate all* Knaves *of* Juſtice.

MONDAY, *June* 19.

His Majeſty has been pleaſed to confer the dignity of a Baronet of Great Britain, upon Mark Stuart Plydell of Coleſhill in the County of Berks: — and to grant unto Tho. Robe and Cha. Peter, Eſqs; the Office of Clerk of the Market of his Majeſty's Houſhold, as well within the Liberties as without. *D P. D J.* —— Francis Clarke, Eſq; one of the Gentlemen daily Waiters to her Majeſty, is appointed Gentleman-Uſher to his Majeſty. *P.*

Her Majeſty will keep every ſunday as a publick day at Kenſington, during the King's ſtay beyond ſea. *D P.* — On ſaturday laſt, a Patent paſſed the Great Seal, creating the Rev. Mr. Tho. Brooke, M. A. to be Dean of Cheſter, in the room of the Rev. Mr. Tho. Allen, deceaſed. *P.*

TUESDAY, *June* 20.

On ſunday in the afternoon one of his Majeſty's Meſſengers brought an account, that his Majeſty was in good health, and arrived ſafely at Hanover on wedneſday laſt. *C.*

Several preſs warrants having been iſſued out for impreſſing ſeamen into his Majeſty's ſervice, yeſterday they began to preſs at the Nore, and at other places below, when they preſſed a great number of able ſeamen out of homeward bound ſhips, and put them on board his Majeſty's ſhips lying at the Nore. *P.*

On ſunday morning died, after a long indiſpoſition, Mr. Sedgwicke, an eminent Hamburgh Merchant of this city. *D P.*

Her Grace the Dutcheſs Dowager of Marlborough made a preſent of 1000 l. to Cha. Hanbury Williams, Eſq; to purchaſe a ſet of plate upon his marriage with the Lady Frances Coningſby, youngeſt daughter to the late Earl. *S J.*

Laſt ſunday the Rev. Dr. Knight, preach'd before her Majeſty, the Prince of Wales, &c. *S J.*

On wedneſday Sam. Borlace, Eſq; was married to Miſs Jarvis, a beautiful young Lady of great merit and fortune. *S J.*

Laſt week there came advice from Paris, that the R. Hon. Cha. Boyle, Lord Viſc. Bleſſington of the King-

dom of Ireland, died near that City on the 2d; by whose death an estate of 3000 l. per ann. descends to his Lordship's sister the Right Hon. Lady Viscountess Mountjoy. *S.J.*

WEDNESDAY, *June* 21.

They are beating up for volunteer seamen in the suburbs of this City, and great diligence is used in equipping a strong squadron of men of war; for what service is not yet publickly known. *D.P.*

The Lord Erskine, now Earl of Mar, is not in the French service, but has been a Captain in the service of Great Britain several years, and a Member of the present House of Commons. *P.*

On Saturday night the new-born son of a certain Lady, much talked of about S. James's, was baptized at her house in S. James's street; when the Hon. Harry V—ne, Esqr. and the R. Hon. the L. Bal——re stood Godfathers. We hear the ceremony was performed by the Rev. Dr. Sn—we. *P.*

High words pass'd yesterday in a Coffee-house by S. James's, between an hon. Gentleman of the House of Commons and Mr. Henley, on charging him with paragraphs in some of the Hyp-Doctors. *D.J.* —— *These high words were on'y puffs of wind.*

From the PEGASUS in Grub-street.
To DRAMATICUS.

SIR,

NOT having heard any thing of you, in our Brother Bavius's lucubrations, since your letter published in the Paper marked No. 119, I imagined, that sensible of your former folly (forgive my freedom) in expecting to carry your point *l'epee à la main*, you had secretly recanted, and made your submission to Mr. W. The consequence of which, for your sake, I supposed, was his engaging to act your Play next winter. Whether I have made a right guess, or no, I can't tell; but the discontinuance of so brisk an attack, seems naturally to imply as much. If you have not, you may take the hint from one, who, tho' unknown to you, is the admirer of your mirth and good humour, and has therefore sent you a proper form of a Palinody or Recantation long; which he advises you to sing the first opportunity, being

Your hearty Well-wisher and humble Servant,
May 19, 1732. POETICUS.

Horace, Lib. I. Ode XVIth. imitated.

To Mr. W.

O thou who managest the Stage,
Late subject of my *Grub-street* rage;
To flames, or seas, or any where,
O W—those hated papers bear.

Not PHOEBUS from the secret shrine,
Not CYBELE, nor God of wine,
Their Priests with half the fury fill,
That anger in a moment will.

Anger, which nothing can restrain,
Not the drawn sword, nor wrecking main;
Nor furious fire, nor mighty JOVE
Rushing with tumult from above.

'Tis said, when first PROMETHEUS bold
Compos'd of clay the human mould;
Something he took from every beast,
And fir'd with Lion's rage our breast.

Anger THYESTES murd'rous made,
And stately towns in ashes laid;
Drew o'er their walls the hostile plow,
Mark of their total overthrow.

Then calm thy mind. My boiling heat
Made me prudential thoughts forget;
While disappointment and quick ire
Inflam'd me with *Grubean* fire.

Now gentler methods I pursue,
Renouncing all I said of you.
Then friends once more we'll be to day;
Act but my *Un-theatric* Play.

Books and Pamphlets published since June 7.

8. See and seem blind: or a critical Dissertation on the public Diversions, &c.

The Political State of Great Britain, for May. Pr. 1s. 6d.

The method of learning to draw in Perspective, &c.

The Lords Protest in the late Session of Parliament. P.6d.

10. Remarks on a Sermon preached by the Rev. Mr. Tho. Mole, &c. Pr. 8d.

The Speaker's Thanks to the R. Hon. the L. Visc. Gage, &c. Pr. 3d.

12. Vanella in the straw: a Poem. Pr. 6d.

The Lives of the Roman Poets: by L. Crusius. Vol. 2d.

Poems on Divine subjects, original and translated from Vida, by Tho. Morell, A.M. Pr. 5s.

13. The natural History of the Arbor vitæ, &c. Pr. 6d.

Christianity neither false, nor useless, &c. Pr. 1s.

The Old Debauchees, a Comedy: by the Author of the Modern Husband. Pr. 1s.

---

13. A Sermon at the Funeral of Mr. Ben. Tomkins by Peter Belbin. Pr. 6d.

15. A Collection of Voyages and Travels, in 6 vol. fol. Miscellaneous Observations on Authors, &c. No. XVIII. Pr. 6d.

17. The natural History of the Arbor Vitæ, versify'd. Pr. 6d.

A true state of the South Sea scheme. Pr. 1s.

A Sermon on the reasonableness of submission under afflictive Dispensations, &c. by J. Partington.

The present Government of England in Church and State asserted, against the Oppugners of the L. Bp. of Chichester's Sermon, &c. Pr. 1s.

The Lady's Dressing Room, &c. 6d.

The Character of the Times delineated. Pr. 6d.

A Sermon before the Corporation of the City of Oxford, May 29. by Tipping Silvester, M.A. Fellow of Pembrook College.

Edinburgh, June 8. Yesterday Mr. Will. Dalrympl Writer to the Signet, had dined in perfect health, but was seized with a violent cholick, which instantly carried him off. He never in his life tasted wine, or spirits, or malt liquor. *P.* 15.

Dublin, June 6. By letters from Tullow near Carlow, we have an account of a rape, committed on the body of a young Gentlewoman, by 8 Fellows, belonging to a mill; their usage was so barbarous as not fit to mention. The Magistrates have caused several of the Villains to be secured. *C.P.* 15. —— Col. K——walking along the side of the Liffey, where were 2 young Women, the foot of one slipped, and she pulled the other with her into the river, which carried them some way; but the Colonel leaped in, and catching hold of their petticoats in his mouth, by fair swimming brought them both to shore. *C.P. D.J.* 15. —— Within a mile of Belfast on the 1st, there fell a hail which lay 8 inches deep; all the hailstones were as big as common nuts. Near Athlone the greatest part were as big as wallnuts. *P.* 15.

FOREIGN NEWS.

THURSDAY, *June* 15.
Yesterday arrived the Mail from France.

Paris, June 21. M. Le Bart, Secretary to the King, &c. going home a few days ago, met 3 persons, who all stabbed him with their swords; and he died of his wounds the 10th. *C.P. D.P.* Le Boit. *D.J.* —— The Comedians have presented a new Comedy, intitled, *The Progress of the Senses*, which has been well received. *D.R.* —— *The Process of the senses.* C. 16.

FRIDAY, *June* 16.
Lisbon, May 15. On the 11th in the afternoon, her Czarian Majesty took the diversion of hunting in some lands belonging to the Marq. de Fonteira. *C.* —— Her Czarian Majesty *went a long voyage on purpose* to hunt.

Paris, June 21. A mould is making at Compiegne for new casting the great bell of the Royal parish of S. James; and 'tis thought the King will stand Godfather, and one of the Princesses of the blood Godmother, to that bell. *C.* — *This will be* a most Christian Bell.

Venice, June 7. The Great Council having met, as usual, 3 days successively, chose the 41 Electors, who shut themselves up in the Ducal Palace on sunday, and on monday morning elected the Chevalier Carlo Ruzzini, Procurator of S. Mark, to be Doge of Venice. *P.*

TUESDAY, *June* 20.
This day arrived the Mails from Holland and Flanders.

Leghorn, June 7. Several vessels from Corsica bring word, that 4 Chiefs of the Malecontents are put under close confinement in the Castle of Bastia. *S.J. WE. LE.*

Francfort, June 22. On the 17th the Archbishop and Elector of Triers were elected Bishop of Worms. *LE.*

WEDNESDAY, *June* 21.
Yesterday arrived the Mail due from Holland.

Hague, June 27. N.S. All our advices from France, the Netherlands, and even from Spain, assure us, that the Spanish fleet is bound to Sicily, where the Court of Spain has a party; as has been discovered by a letter from the Prince de Resultano, Prætor of Palermo, to Don Joseph Patinho, which was intercepted. —— Yesterday an an Express from Mynheer Assendelst, their High Mightinesses Resident at Brussels, brought the surprizing News, that the Offenders had taken, and carried into their Port, a ship belonging to our West-India Company, by way of reprizal for their East-India Ship, which the Vessels belonging to the English and Dutch East-India Companies took and sunk at the mouth of the Ganges about two years ago; and, that having complained thereof to the Court of Brussels, he was answered, that it was done by the Emperor's Order. *Of which more another time. P.*

Rome, June 7. N.S. The Chevalier de S. George has hired the palace of Galoppi, near the four Fountains, for a lodging for the little Duke of Ormonde, who (we are told) is expected here from Spain with a certain secret Commission.

Printed by J. HUGGONSON, in Bartholomew-Close, for Captain GULLIVER, near the Temple. [Price Two Pence.]

The Grub-ſtreet Journal.

NUMB. 130

Thursday, *JUNE* 29, 1732.

This is thy Province, this thy wondrous way,
New humours to invent for each new Play:
This is that boaſted byaſs of thy mind,
By which one way to dulneſs 'tis inclin'd.

DRYDEN's Mac Flecknoe.

SIR,

AS ſome obſervations on our Dramatic performances may be uſeful, as well as entertaining, eſpecially to your Readers in the Country, I intend to ſend you ſome remarks on each new Piece, as it ſhall appear, during this ſummer ſeaſon at Drury-lane. I undertake not this office, as inſtituting myſelf ſole Critic, and invading the known liberties of the Pit; but rather as a taſk impoſed on me by a young Templar, whom I have lately had occaſion to mention, to give him an account of the progreſs of theatrical poetry in his abſence. How far he may agree with my ſentiments, I know not; but he is very well aſſured, that I ſhall not be biaſſed by partiality or prejudice. He was the more earneſt to engage me in this correſpondence, as he had been aſſured, that the Manager of the young Company had ſeveral good Pieces, which were every way *theatrical.* — *Theatricality* is ſure ſomething of which the Drury-lane Managers only can form an idea. There have been ſo many expoſitions of its ſenſe, that it ſeems to me almoſt impoſſible accurately to define it. But whatever it be, this I have obſerved, that thoſe Pieces, which were ſaid to be moſt theatrical, were leaſt conſiſtent with the rules of Dramatic writing. I could prove the truth of this aſſertion in an examen of the *Modern Husband:* but as Mr. DRAMATICUS hath given already a critique on it in your 117th *Journal,* I ſhall at preſent only obſerve, that there is ſcarce a ſcene in the whole, but what betrays want of judgment, or, to uſe ſofter terms, manifeſts at leaſt the Author's haſty way of writing. The latter I believe, he himſelf will moſt readily own, as thinking it a ſufficient plea for whatever his moſt fertile Muſe may produce. But I muſt beg leave to diſſent from him: no haſty productions ſhould be impoſed upon the Town; a conſtant flow of which is no better proof of a fruitful brain, than a numerous, ſickly, ſhort-liv'd off ſpring is of a fruitful womb. In either caſe, ſuch a courſe of barren fruitfulneſs is but one degree beyond frequent abortion. —— Beſides, this Gentleman has the leaſt excuſe for haſty writing of any Author. The vaſt encouragement he met with laſt winter, might ſure have enabled him to take due time to finiſh any Piece he intended to bring on the Stage ſince; unleſs he has agreed with the Managers to furniſh them with ſo many annual Pieces. Beſides his *Lottery* and *Modern Husband* in the winter, he has produced two more, his *Covent Garden Tragedy* and *Old Debauchees* within four months after. But the former of theſe twins being in a dying condition under the juſt cenſure of the Town, he publicly made a ſort of a voluntary ſacrifice of it to their reſentment, in order to preſerve the life of the latter. This was a fairer piece of policy, than that, which perhaps may by cuſtom become truly THEATRICAL; I mean an endeavour to puff a favourite Piece of a favourite Author into reputation; ſo that its character is not to depend on the reception the Town gives it at the Theatre, but on the figure it makes in a *theatrical* paragraph in a *Daily Poſt.* In that Paper, of June 2, and 5. *The Old Debauchees* was ſaid to have met with *univerſal applauſe;* and tho' the 3d night's audience on June 13th was diſmiſſed, as not being ſufficient to pay half the charges, yet in the *Daily Poſt* of the 16th a paragraph was inſerted, affirming that it had *met with great applauſe.* The Author, I dare ſay, had no hand in any of theſe Puffs; he has been two well approved by the Town to endeavour to delude them into an approbation of any Piece of his, by deſcending to as low and mean artifices as Mr. Orator and Hyp Doctor almoſt daily ſtoops. —— But leſt he may think himſelf any way injured by my general cenſure of *The Old Debauchees,* I will next week ſend you ſome obſervations on it; and continue the ſame courſe on all the new productions at Drury-lane, in letters to my Friend of the Temple: not that I am reſolved to condemn every thing, but to examine impartially, and give promiſcuouſly the praiſe or cenſure they may deſerve. One thing before I conclude, I would adviſe the Manager of the young Players, that, as he ſeems to ſtand in favour with the Town at preſent, he would not foiſt that on them which they may not be willing to receive; but if he finds one thing not go off well (as he has ſuch variety of new Pieces) to bring on another. By this conduct, he can't fail of conſiderable ſucceſs this ſummer vacation, and may prepare the way for ſomething more diverting and inſtuctive the enſuing winter.

Tom's Coffee-Houſe, *June* 17.

I am, Mr. BAVIUS, yours,

PROSAICUS.

Mr. BAVIUS,

AS *in this age there needs no great apology for commencing Author,* I hope you'll give this a kind reception, tho' it is dated from a place, where I believe you have but few correſpondents. As to my character, let it ſuffice, that I have been a conſtant ſpectator at Drury-lane Playhouſe theſe 10 years, and am well known in this place for keeping up a decorum, and being an impartial Critic. I think, Sir, from ſo long an attendance, I may be as good a judge of Dramatical performances as Mr. HINT the *Candle-ſnuffer*; whoſe letter in the *London Evening Poſt* of laſt night I have now before me, and on which I ſend you theſe obſervations.

In the ſecond paragraph Mr. HINT alledges in vindication of Mr. F. from the charge of indecency, that *Bullies, Bawds, Rakes, Whores, are in themſelves characters not improper to be ſhewn on the ſtage, if they were, you muſt quarrel with half our Plays, and particularly with the Beggars Opera.* I own, thoſe characters have been brought on the Engliſh ſtage: nay I'll go farther, and give a ſanction to it by the example of TERENCE. This is certainly allowable, as to the characters in *themſelves:* but then, Mr. BAVIUS, is a Poet to have nothing in his Play but ſuch characters? Is he in drawing ſuch a character to pick out the moſt profligate wretches in it? Is he to correct lewdneſs by almoſt ſhewing the commiſſion of it? Did TERENCE to ridicule the tricks of a *Whore,* exhibit to a Roman audience a brothel? No, he could repreſent the vices in low characters of life in a language not unbecoming the Roman dignity, nor offending againſt the rules of decency. I don't doubt but he might have found in Rome among the dregs of the people, characters as vicious as thoſe of our modern Author; but his *Thais's* and *Lenones* betray their ſeveral artifices in a pleaſing inoffenſive humour. I know not whether in reality they were more decent than the HACKABOUTA's and BILKUM's of the preſent age; but this I affirm, that the Roman Pagan was far more modeſt than our Engliſh Chriſtian.

Neither *envy,* nor *malice,* nor *provocation* has *inhumanly animated* me againſt the Author, or Theatre; I am diſintereſted and impartial, I have no enmity to the man, but to his Tragedy: no *exclamation* from a *Bawd* to a *Poete* has given me any diſturbance: nor indeed can I ſee that thoſe againſt whom the little ſatyrical line was levelled, have any occaſion to complain; for however keen the rage of the Author might be, his wit was too dull to wound. Mr. HINT in the next paragraph declares, he thinks *it is incumbent on every man who affirms a Play to be bad, indecent, and infamous to give ſome quotations from it, or mention ſome particular ſcene or incident which are ſo.* It cannot be ſuppoſed, that quotations could be given from the action only; and it was unneceſſary to mention any *particular ſcene,* when there was not one ſcene through the whole but would make the accuſation good; which will be obvious to every one, if the Author proceeds to print his incomparable Piece, faithfully as it was acted.

The reſt of this letter is a retort on DRAMATICUS's Play and your *Journal.* As to the firſt, I know nothing of it, nor will I pretend to vindicate any thing on hearſay only. As to the latter, you are the beſt judge, what anſwer to give to it. I am now impatiently waiting to ſee another production of the Author of the *Covent Garden Tragedy,* tranſlated from MOLIERE; and to ſhew my envy to the Poet, I only wiſh he has kept up to the ſpirit of the original.

Theatre Royal in Drury-lane: Firſt row in the upper Gallery. Friday, June 23.

I am, Mr BAVIUS,
Yours,
A. B.

To Mr. WM. HINT, Candle-ſnuffer.

Saturday, June the 24th, 1732.

SIR,

I Have received your favour ſent in the *Daily Poſt* of the 21ſt, and repeated in the *London Evening Poſt* of the 22d inſt. for which I return you as many thanks as you deſerve. I have called at the Theatre Royal Alehouſe ſince, in order to drink a pot of beer with you, and ſettle our differences in an amicable way; but I was told, they knew no ſuch perſon. Upon which, I immediately imagined you had taken this name upon you, as I did that of DRAMATICUS, (it having ſome relation to the ſubject I treated upon,) and that there was no ſuch perſon as Mr. WM. HINT. But upon ſecond thoughts, recollecting that the character of a *Candle-ſnuffer* could not poſſibly give you any right to talk of any thing above the ſnuffing of candles, and that it would therefore be very ſenſleſs to perſonate a character in order to talk in a much higher ſtrain, than ſuch character could allow; I am come, at laſt, to this concluſion, that there is really ſuch a perſon as Mr. WM. HINT, and that he really wrote this letter, for certainly none above the degree of an aſpiring *Candle-ſnuffer* could have written it. I ſhall therefore, in the courſe of my anſwer, conſider you in the light of as arrant a Candle-ſnuffer as ever trod the ſtage; but at the ſame time, would adviſe you, as a friend, to dawb your fingers more with tallow for the future, and leſs with ink.

I agree with you, that an *apology for commencing Author* would be needleſs in you, ſince you can never make one, that can juſtify your laying aſide your uſual vocation, for the ſake of becoming an *aſinus ad lyram.*

As to your complaint that a *ſett of ſcribblers pretend to give laws to our Theatres,* you therein do an honour to the Gentlemen you ſtrike at, this very appellation having been conſtantly beſtowed by the Candle-ſnuffers of wit upon the Authors of the wittieſt Papers, from the *Tatlers, Spectators,* &c. down to the *Grub ſtreet Journal.* And had you been as converſant upon the ſtage of the world, as upon that in Drury-lane, you muſt have obſerved, that the Writers of all ſuch Papers, have ever thought the ſtage a proper ſubject for their notice, and have as freely cenſured what is bad, as commended what is good. It were to be wiſhed the Gentlemen concerned in the management of the Theatre would afford half the ſubject for praiſe, which they do for cenſure. But, alas! I much fear you will ſnuff the candles next winter to more bad than good Plays, to more *Modern Husbands, Old Debauchees, Covent Garden Tragedies,* &c.

You are groſly miſtaken as to the perſon of DRAMATICUS. He never ſollicited, and conſequently never could have been refuſed *a place* in the Houſe. He has indeed had a *Play rejected.* But he fancies, if he had not thought fit to conceal his name from the Manager in queſtion at firſt, his Play had never been refuſed. But his modeſty happened to be greater than his judgment at that time; as well as his mirth afterwards, upon his refuſal, ſtronger than his reſentment. What reception his Papers have met with from the Town, he will not pretend to declare; what he has caſually heard in Coffee-houſes, has not diſpleaſed him.

If you had read the date of my laſt letter (but perhaps you cannot read figures, for I find no date to your) you would have diſcovered before now, that it was written the morning after the exhibition of this notable performance, and its being given out for a ſecond repreſentation; that is, before the knowledge of the *Author's deference to the opinion of the Town,* could have reached any body but himſelf. But ſuppoſing it had, I am not the only one of opinion, that ſuch a ſhameleſs and obſcene performance could not be too early, or too warmly expoſed.

I have no *Dictionaries* by me, but thoſe individual ones I uſed when I went to ſchool, ſo that this ſtroke of ſecret ſatyr does not touch DRAMATICUS; neither have I conſulted them on this occaſion, or want their help, *to wreſt one word of this* Covent Garden Tragedy *into an indecent meaning.* It need only be publiſhed to convince mankind, that it would be infinitely a more difficult taſk, *to wreſt one word of it into* a decent *meaning.* But I ſuppoſe Mr. HINT is of opinion, that unleſs every thing is named by its proper name, it cannot be called *indecent.*

Indeed, Sir, *Bawds, Whores, Rakes, Bullies,* &c. are very improper to be ſhewn on the ſtage in the rankeſt dreſs of lewdneſs they can poſſibly wear. The inſide of a Bawdy-houſe, and the private management and behaviour of a Bawd, are very unfit repreſentations for any but the inhabitants, or frequenters of Drury lane. And I believe even *The Beggar's Opera* owed its ſucceſs more to the novelty of the thing, and ſome other concurring circumſtances, than to its intrinſic worth; tho' I make an infinite difference in every reſpect between that Opera, (which has all the advantages of wit to excuſe what may be vicious in) and this Tragedy.

[illegible] assure you, Sir, it was neither *envy*, nor *malice*, that made me attack the *successful* Play, called *The Modern Husband*; neither was the Bawd's smart accusation of the Porter *the real occasion of my falling thus inhumanly on this poor little Farce.* My reason for falling on both these Pieces was, because I thought them both exceeding bad, and think so still,

If *The Covent Garden Tragedy* had been published, I should have accompanied my letter with *Quotations* from every Page, and every Scene; but indeed my memory was not sufficient to contain enough of it to quote.

I am likewise, Sir, better satisfied with the opinion the Town may form of my *capacity* for *writing a Play*, from the little I have published concerning Plays, than apprehensive they should form any against it, from what you are pleased to say of me. But this is wide of my purpose at present, and it is time (don't be witty upon this expression) I should draw to a conclusion.

I shall therefore only add, that I fear you have gone beyond your commission, and in the heat of passion, have blabbed out some secrets you ought to have concealed. Sure Mr. W. did not shew you my Play? and yet these words, *But I shall not proceed to criticise on what will, I dare swear, never be acted at all*, seem to imply as if you had seen it; else how can you *proceed to criticise* upon it? If such heads, as that which Mr. Wm. Hint carries upon his shoulders, were consulted about my Play, I am not surprised it was refused. But recollect, that the Head of your house did not refuse it, as a bad piece, but dismissed it as a *sensible and pretty performance*, only *not theatrical*, the meaning of which has been already explained.

And now, Mr. Hint, give me leave to tell you, tho' you burst, that this Paper, this *Grub street Journal*, you exclaim so much against, is, in the opinion of the Town, a Paper that contains much real wit and humour; and that it will be rendered henceforward, even more useful, by constantly animadverting upon the enormities that are daily introduced upon the Stage. I am, Sir,

Your very good friend and admirer,

Dramaticus.

P. S. I had the honour last night to see your pretended new Entertainment. I shall defer my thoughts of it to another opportunity, tho' I can't help whispering you, 'Tis miserable stuff.

DOMESTIC NEWS.

C. *Courant.*	E P. *Evening Post.*
P. *Post-Boy.*	S J. *S. James's Evening Post.*
D P. *Daily Post.*	W E. *Whitehall Evening P.*
D J. *Daily Journal.*	L E. *London Evening Post.*

Thursday, *June 22.*

Last week her Majesty was pleased to order 200 l. to be paid out of the Treasury, to James Hammond, Esq; who some time since brought the express of the States General acceeding to the Treaty of Seville. *D J.*

Yesterday the R. Hon. Sir Rob. Walpole sate in the Court of Exchequer, as Chancellor of the said Court, being the first time he sate on hearing causes since his being Chancellor. There was a plea lodged to the title of the estate of Sir Will. Althrop, deceased, by Sir Tho. Althrop, Bar. and Mrs. Althrop. On arguing the merits of the plea, the L. Chief Baron and Mr. Baron Comyns were of opinion, that the plea was not a good one; Mr. Baron Carter and Mr. Baron Thompson were of the contrary opinion: so the Chancellor was obliged to decide it. After hearing the merits over again, he made a very learned speech, and afterwards agreed with the L. Chief Baron and Mr. Baron Comyns; so the plea was set aside. *P.* A cause between Mr. Trollop, Plaintiff, and Sir Tho. Trollop, Defendant. There has not a Chancellor sat for many years before. *D J.*

A Gentleman at Richmond, who had his papers seized by warrant from his Grace the D. of Newcastle, on suspicion of having had some concern in Signor Belloni and Mr. Rob. Arbuthnot's correspondence, hath had them restored to him again. *D P.*

A few days since her Grace the Dutchess Dowager of Marlborough subscribed 300,000 l. on the salt duty. *D P.* —— We hear from Boulogne, that the Dutchess of Buckingham was taken very ill, and remains so there. *P.* —— *I hear her Grace went abroad for her health, to prevent being* taken ill.

We hear the Fleet of men of war that is now fitting out, will be commanded by the R. Hon. Sir Char. Wager; who will hoist his flag on board his Majesty's ship the Namur, a second rate of 90 guns. *C. D P.* —— Yesterday there was an account that about 1700 seamen had been impressed since monday last. *D P.*

Yesterday the Court of Directors of the South Sea Company appointed Factors for their ship the Assiento, Cap. Pearce, for Buenos Ayres, viz. Mr. Spackman, 1st, Mr. Ford, 2d, and Mr. Fran. Eyles, 3d, and Writer. *C. D P.* They determined to have no more than 2 Factors at that place for the future, and Mr. Spackman and Mr. Faure were elected. *D J.*

Yesterday the Rev. Mr. Bayes was elected one of the 6 preachers of the Merchants Lecture at Salters Hall, in the room of the Rev. Dr. Calamy, deceased. He had 47 votes, and Mr. Mayo 25. *D J.*

The law to prevent Watermen working on the Thames on sundays without licence is of late less regarded than ever, and 'twas remarkable that there never were seen so many licentious Watermen rowing up and down the river as on sunday last, which 'tis to be hoped will soon be put a stop to by those who are impowered by law to do it. *C.* —— *I wish* those who are impowered *would begin a reformation with the* licentious Land-men, *who are continually* running up and down on sundays.

Yesterday Lieut. Col. Robinson, Chamberlain of this City, was so well recovered, that his *Death* is despaired of. *P.*

The Hon. Benedict-Leonard Calvert, Esq; Brother to the R. Hon. the L. Baltimore, Proprietor of Maryland, who had for some time been Governor of that Province, under his Lordship, finding himself in an ill state of health, and resigning that post, imbarked for England, and sailed the 18th of May, but died in the passage the 1st of June, and was buried at sea. *D J.*

On monday died the Relict of the late Sir Theophilus Oglethorpe, Knt. Mother to James Oglethorpe, Esq; Representative in Parliament for Haslemere in Surrey. *W E.* —— Yesterday died at Edmonton, in the 60th year of her age, the Lady Monson, Mother to the R. Hon. John L. Monson. *L E.*

Friday, *June 23.*

On wednesday night at the *Ridotto al Fresco*, at Vaux Hall, there was not half the Company as was expected, being no more than 203 persons, amongst whom were several persons of distinction, but more Ladies than Gentlemen; and the whole was managed with great order and decency, a detachment of 100 of the Foot guards being posted round the garden: a Waiter belonging to the house having got drunk, put on a dress and went to *Fresco*, with the rest of the company; but being discovered, he was immediately turned out of doors. *C.* —— His Royal Highness the Prince, the E. of Scarborough, the L. Gage, &c. were present, and the whole affair was managed with decency and good order: about 2 o' clock his Royal Highness went away, but the greatest part of the company staid 'till 5 in the morning. *D P.*

Five servants belonging to Mr. Selby, a Whitster at Mitcham, having been bit by a mad dog, some time ago, 4 of them were dipt in salt water, and are like to do well; but the other, to whom his Master had lent a horse to go to Gravesend, in order to be dipt, went another way in the Country, and neglected the same; and on monday he died in a raving condition. *C.* —— Mr. Conundrum *says he only* went another way to Graves-end.

Yesterday the Court of King's Bench was moved for an information against a Justice of the Peace for Middlesex and Westminster, alledging that several persons were brought before him, for robbing the Lady Crew some time ago, at S. James's, of a considerable sum of money, and he admitted them to bail, and the persons and bail are since fled; and the Court ordered him to shew cause why an information should not pass against him. *D J.*

Christned Males 153, Females 132; in all 285. *Buried* Males 174, Females 170; in all 344. Increased in the burials this week 11. *P.* —— *The* P. *of June* 16, *copied from the* Weekly Bill *of the* 13th, *gave us* Buried in all 433. *Instead therefore of* Increased in the Burials this week, 11, *it should be,* Decreased 89. *It is of bad consequence, to represent the City in a worse state of health than it really is.*

Saturday, *June 24.*

Only the Esquires of the 4 last new Knights of the Bath are to attend at the installation on friday next. *D P.*

Yesterday they began to press for seamen above bridge up to Fulham, when we hear they impressed near 200 able men. *P.* About 400 Watermen. *D J.* —— A press-gang went into a Glass-house in White-fryars, in order to press some of the men at work; but they were no sooner got in, but the mettal was flung about them, and happy was he that could get out first, and in hurrying out they ran over their Officer, who was almost scalded to death. *D J.*

Yesterday was brought forth at the Tower, a young Lion, produced from the English Lion and Lioness, which brought forth 2 the last year, &c. *S J.*

In the West-riding of the County of York, in the township of Sourby and parish of Hallifax, one Jos. Ryley, had a field of corn (very good to look at) that was in less than 2 nights time by some small insects reduced to nothing; there was not so much as one pile of grass or corn, only about a quarter of one third of an acre left in the same field standing undevoured or seemingly touched then, the rest was devoured or eat up, so that the earth was as bare as a garden bed prepared to sow seeds. *S J.* —— *If there be no more truth than sence, in this paragraph, it is certainly false.*

The great house that the Earl of Marchmonte lately resided in at the corner of Arlington-street, is hired for the Hon. Mrs. Mary Vane. *S J.*

Monday, *June 22.*

On saturday her Majesty walked from Kensington to Chelsea, and having view'd the Royal Hospital, she return'd to Kensington to dinner. *D P.* —— Made a visit to the E. of Ranelaugh, and breakfasted. *C.*

On saturday last came on the election of Sheriffs for this City and County of Middlesex for the year ensuing; when Rob. Alsop, Esq; and Henry Hankey, Esq; Aldermen and Haberdashers, where chosen by so great a majority, that no poll was demanded. It was very observable, that the friends of the abovesaid Gentlemen heard the declaration with all the temper and quiet imaginable, without using the least insult to their losing opponents. *C. D P. D J.* —— *This* was very observable, *because* unusual, *when they had a* Hank *upon their opponents.*

Mr. Will. Rous, Deputy of Vintry Ward, and Mr. John Lequesne, Deputy of Broad-street Ward, were chose Auditors of the City and Bridge accounts, in the room of Mr. Sisson and Mr. Pitt, who went out in course, having served two years. *D J.*

Yesterday morning all the Royal yachts that attended his Majesty to Holland arrived at Greenwich, having on board the Lord de la War, and several other persons of distinction. *C.*

On friday Mr. Cholmondeley, Publisher in Holbourn, was taken into custody, for publishing the picture of the late L. Bishop of Rochester, Dr. Atterbury. *D P.* —— And upon examination discharged.

The new Comedy of the *Old Debauchees*, and the new Farce of the *Mock Doctor*, were both acted on Friday last, at the Theatre-Royal in Drury-Lane, to a full House, with great applause. *Le Medicin malgre Lui*, of Moliere, from whence the *Mock Doctor* is taken, bears the greatest reputation of any petit Piece in the French language; and many good Judges allow the English Farce is no way inferior to the Original. *D P.* —— *L E.* 27. *These* good Judges *are certainly Members of our Society; and I hope the world will take their words, that the* Author is no way inferior *to* Moliere.

Tuesday, *June 27.*

Christopher Rhodes, Esq; is appointed Comptroller of the excise in Scotland, with a salary of 500 l. per ann. for himself and Clerks. —— And Mr. Elstob and Mr. Watson joint receivers of the rents and profits of the estate of the late E. of Derwentwater. —— Sir Rob. Walpole sets out for his seat in Norfolk on saturday next. *C.*

It is written from Falmouth, that on Thursday the E. of Albemarle embarqued on board the Prince Frederick Pacquet, who sailed the same day for Lisbon. *P.*

The 2 hon. Societies of the Temple have presented the Rev. Mr. Broughton (Reader of the Temple church) with 40 guineas for his 3 discourses, intitled, *Christianity distinct from the religion of Nature*, in answer to, *Christianity as old as the creation.* P

There is a hot press at Yarmouth, for seamen to man the guard ships which are fitting out. *D P. D J.*

Mr. Gery has obtained a rule of court for upwards of 240 l. N. B. Some persons are taken ill and cannot be spoken withal, and others do not see company. *P.*

This morning the R. Hon. the E. Cowper was married to the second daughter of the E. of Grantham, Vice-chamberlain to the Queen. *P.* —— This evening at 12 he is to be married, &c. *D P.* —— *This* Vice-Chamberlain *is* Lord Chamberlain.

Wednesday, *June 28.*

Yesterday [late at night. *D J.*] the R. Hon. the Earl Cowper was married, &c. at his Lordship's [E. of Grantham's] house in Albemarle-street. Afterward his Lordship set out with his new-married Lady for his seat at Hertingford-Berry in Hertfordshire. *P.* —— This day they will set out. *D J.* —— Letters from Manchester say, that Lady Egerton, Relict of Sir Holland Egerton of Heaton in Lancashire, Bar. was lately married married to John Brooke, Esq; youngest Son of Sir Thomas, Bar. *D P.*

Lionel Vane, Esq; is made Clerk of the Council to his Royal Highness the Prince. —— The Rev. Mr. Bourne is appointed by the R. Rev. the Bishop of Winchester, one of the Prebendaries of that Cathedral. *D P.*

On monday night a Cause was heard before the L. Raymond at Westminster, wherein his Grace the D. of Richmond was Plaintiff, and a Grazier of Sussex, Defendant, upon the statute of *Scandalum Magnatum*, for scandalous and defamatory words, which being fully proved, the Jury gave a verdict for his Grace with very considerable damages. *D P.*

On monday night, about 9, Lieut. Smith, with his press-gang, belonging to the Edinburgh man of war, went on board some Norway ships lying in Hanover-hole, being Danes, Swedes, &c. in order to press some of the men, several of whom were English; but all the ships crews in the teer gathered together, and got their handspikes, iron

crows, hatchets (with which they cut wood in their Country) and other weapons, and as fast as the press-gang got up the sides of the ship they knock'd them into the Thames; but the press-gang still persisted, and got into the ship, but being over-power'd, their adversaries got the Lieutenant, and was going to cut his head off with one of the hatchets, and would certainly have done it, had not a stout fellow knock'd the person down as he was going to strike the blow, and at the same time took the Lieutenant in his arms and flung him over-board, by which means he saved his life: after the press gang was got into their boat, some with broken arms, others with their ribs broke, the ships crews flung into the boat at them several handspikes, hatchets, and other desperate weapons, all which were brought into the publick hall of the Admiralty, and a complaint was likewise made to their Lordships yesterday, but what the consequence will be must be referred to another opportunity. *D J.* —— The same day a Lieutenant going to press a sailor with his gang, out of an Ale house in Hungerford Market, the Watermen and Butchers rose and beat them terribly, and were so outrageous as to drag the commanding Officer in the kennel, and rescued the man. *P.*

Fleet-Prison, June 26th, 1732.

To the Gentlemen Prisoners, &c. in his Majesty's prison of the Fleet. The memorial of Mr. *J. W.* a Prisoner in the said prison.

IN the beginning of January, 173½, so soon as the Parliament had met, the said Mr. *J. W.* drew up a petition and case in behalf of the Prisoners of the Fleet, copies of which he laid upon the table in the upper Coffee-room for their inspection, proposing to have the first presented to both Houses, and the other put into the hands of every respective Member thereof. These papers were generally approved by the said Prisoners; and Mr. *J. W.* had the favour to be thanked by several of the most considerable of them on that occasion, who promised to raise, by a collection, a fund to defray the charge of printing both the case and petition; the first for the purpose aforementioned, and the latter to be sent to every prison of the kingdom, as a form, to the end that they might be all unanimous in their requests. Upon these grounds Mr. *J. W.* at his own proper expence, by and with the universal consent of the Prisoners of the Fleet, printed off a sufficient number of petitions and cases for the said uses; as also some *small precatory* letters to be given to the Members the same day the petition was delivered: and in every thing else he spared no pains, time, nor cost, as far as he was able, to render himself serviceable to his fellow sufferers in general throughout the kingdom, tho', at the same time, he did not apprehend, that an Act of Insolvency would be of any benefit to himself.

A collection was soon after made in the Fleet, which did not reimburse Mr. *J. W.* half the money he had laid out, as appears by the accounts laid on the table in the said upper Coffee-room. There was, indeed, a guinea sent for him from the prison of WEST-CHESTER; but, he says, the person who brought him this intelligence, and promised to come again, after he had made enquiry, with a fuller information to whose hands it was remitted, failed in the performance; so that it cannot sure be expected he should place that money to account, no part of which he ever received: however, the Gentlemen at WEST-CHESTER have his thanks for their good intentions towards him.

'Tis not unlikely that other prisons may also have been as grateful as WEST-CHESTER, and the same fraud committed by their agents, tho' not yet discovered; for which reason this memorial is printed, that knavery may be detected, and the persons punished, by law, as well as made to refund, who could possibly be guilty of so mean a felony as to rob a poor Prisoner.

Notwithstanding the collection fell so short of his disbursements, Mr. *J. W.* still zealous for the common good of Prisoners, tho' he could reap no benefit himself from his labours, was aiding and assisting in writing a large pamphlet for the press, addressed by way of letter to a Member of Parliament, wherein most or all the material arguments in behalf of Debtors, both confined and at large, were comprised. In short, day and night, during the whole session of Parliament, he chearfully exerted his whole vigour for the common cause, and refused several advantageous offers of employment, purely that he might devote more of his time to its service: yet he does not require any satisfaction for all the care and pains he has taken, as well as loss of time and hinderance of his business; all that he desires is, only that by a general subscription you would be pleased to pay him the balance of his account current which he actually laid out; and not suffer him to be so a great loser by his good will, in breach of all the promises that were made him; especially since it is evident, that he had no other end in view than the advantage of all Debtors confined in general, and that of his fellow Prisoners in particular.

From the PEGASUS *in Grub-street.*

On saturday last the corpse of the Lady Oglethorpe was, pursuant to her will, privately interred in the same grave with her Husband, Sir Theophilus, and her Son Lewis Oglethorpe, near the altar in S. James's Church. The pall was supported by the R. Hon. the Earl of Arran, the R. Hon. the Lords Muskerry, Kingsale, and Carpenter, Sir Robert Sutton and Rogers Holland, Esq; She has left issue Eleanor, Widow to the Marquess de Mezciers; Charlotte, Wife to the Marquess des Marches; Anne unmarried, and James, her only surviving Son and sole executor. She was Daughter and heir to Richard Walle, Esq; of Rathkenny in the County of Tipperary, in the Kingdom of Ireland. The first of which family was Richard Seigneur De Val Dery, called by the English Waile, who, as appears from Hollingshead, came over with William the Conqueror. One of his descendants was Sir Thomas De Val or Walle, Knight of the Garter in the reign of King Edward the Third. He was the first of the founders whose stall became void, into which succeeded Reginald, Lord Cobham. Sir Edward De Val or Walle, a descendant of the same Lord De Val Dery, settled in Ireland upon lands conquered there, and which were granted him by Henry the Second, and left seven Sons, from the eldest of whom came the three families of Walles of Kilcash, Rathkenny and Calnemuck. The latter still continues in the family, and is possessed by William Walle, Esq; Member of Parliament for Cashal; the other two families are now extinct.

The body of the Lady Oglethorpe, Relict of Sir Theophilus Oglethorpe, was on saturday last privately buried in S. James's Church. She died in the 80th year of her age, and was very conversant with state affairs in the end of King Charles the Second and King James's Reign, and was acquainted with the first springs and motives of the principal transactions of those and the succeeding times. At the Revolution Sir Theophilus, who was then Major General, Colonel of a Regiment and Gentleman of the Horse, resigning his employments; she, tho' bred in all the gayety of a Court, was not only contented, but even pleased with the putting down their equipage, and living in the most frugal and retired manner. She was severe to herself, human to others, and contemned all kind of delicacy and shew. She was a Woman of excellent memory and address, piercing wit, and solid judgment, and indefatigable in serving her friends. She had courage and learning superior to her sex: the latter of which she strove to conceal; and was far from being vain of the former, but used it as a support in the various accidents of life. To her last hour she kept her chearfulness, tho' three months bed-rid and dead on one side with the palsy. The very day before her death, tho' she knew she could not outlive the morrow, she in a pleasant and easy way rallied the Physician, spent the evening as usually in prayer, and died in a calm, christian, and heroic manner.

Mr. BAVIUS read an Answer to a Letter printed in the *D P.* June 21st and *L E.* June 22, which being too long to be inserted in our *Journal* this week, was ordered to be deferred 'till the next. —— He then read the following Certificate.

Whereas it is reported, that I WM. HINT, Candle-snuffer at the Theatre-Royal, Drury-lane, have by the joint assistance of the learned Mr. C— Jun. and Mr. F—— written a letter in vindication of Mr. F——'s Farces, I the said WM. HINT do hereby certify, that I was not in the least concerned in the said letter: having always thought from my long experience and observations on the Stage, that the said Mr. F——'s writings were either above my apprehension, or below my notice. And I do hereby farther affirm, that the aforesaid Mr. C——and Mr. F—— were the sole authors and contrivers of that letter; that they were shut up in consultation at Mrs. ——ld——m's for the space of 3 hours, where their surprizing heads produced that wonderful letter. This I testify, from a sincere love of truth, and in vindication of my own character, being not willing to have my mean parts put in competition with theirs, or to rob them of the least share of the glory they have obtained by the said letter.

Done behind the Scenes at the Theatre Royal *in* Drury-lane, *Friday, June* 23.

Witness my hand,
The mark H of WM. HINT,
Candle-snuffer.

Witnesses,
D. DASH Secretary.
P. PUFF Prompter.

A debate having risen concerning the genuineness of this Certificate, the majority were of opinion that it was forged: because the Letter in question was written with much more spirit, than the Letters Dedicatory of the two Gentlemen *hinted* at; and it was not probable, that they would write better in the name of a Candle-snuffer, than in their own.

Mr. SPONDEE informed the Society, that he had cursorily read over *The Covent Garden Tragedy*, alias, *The Humours of a Bawdy-house*, which did not answer the expectations he had conceived of it, from the character given it by DRAMATICUS and PROSAICUS: that if he might be permitted to imitate the witticisms of the Author, there was a great deal too little ribaldry for a shilling: that he therefore thought it incumbent upon those two Critical Gentlemen, to write a Comment upon it, and *wrest* every part of it *to an indecent meaning*; otherwise, he was apprehensive, that the Ladies *of the first modesty* in Drury-lane, who were highly pleased with it in the action on the Stage, would think it too dear a purchase to entertain them in their closets.

FOREIGN NEWS.

THURSDAY, *June* 22.

Vienna, June 14. The Pope has sent a letter to his Imperial Majesty, signifying, that whereas the supreme dominion of the holy See over the Dutchies of Parma and Placentia incontestably belong to his Holiness, 'tis hoped the Emperor will not oppose the investiture he designs to grant thereof to the serene Infant Don Carlos. *D P.*

Petersburg, June 7. Our land forces amount in time of war to 242,180 men, and 10,000 less in peace. *D J.*

FRIDAY, *June* 23.

Extract of a letter from Alicant, June 11. N. S. — The whole fleet in 2 or 3 days may probably put to sea, consisting of about 500 sail, whereof 20 are line of battle ships, 2 fire ships, 2 bomb ketches, and 7 gallies, having on board about 5000 horse, and 20,000 foot, the choicest soldiers belonging to Spain. *D J.*

SATURDAY, *June* 24.

Hague, June 20. N. S. Some will have it, that the rumour of a secret Treaty between the Emperor and the King of Prussia has occasioned a sort of lukewarmness between the Courts of Vienna and London. It is certain, the Court of France begins to take off the mask with regard to the views of the House of Austria in the *Pragmatick Sanction*; and that they are resolved to make use of force, if necessary, to hinder the Election of a King of the Romans, as long as the present Emperor lives. P.

Petersburgh, May 27. Her Imperial Majesty has appointed Admiral Gordon to be Chief Commander in her fleet. *D J.*

MONDAY, *June* 26.

On saturday arrived the mail from Holland, *and yesterday those from* France and Flanders.

Mentz, June 24. We hear the Emperor [illegible] to erect a tenth Electorate in favour of the Duke [illegible]rain, *C. P.*

Paris, July 2. By letters from Marseilles we [illegible] that the Spanish Fleet had been seen off the Islands of Yvica and Formentera. *C. P. D J.*

TUESDAY, *June* 27.

Yesterday arrived the Mail due from Holland.

Paris, June 27. We have advice from Spain, that the great Armada put to sea the 15th and 16th instant, and steered towards Majorca, where the orders and instructions concerning the expedition were to be opened. *P.*

Rome, June 11. N. S. The late D. of Ormond came into this neighbourhood *incognito* from Spain, and went directly to Albano, without passing through this city; and having had a long private conference with the Chevalier de S. George, he set out (as we are told) on his return to Spain, by the way of France, in order to go on board the great Armada. P.

Vienna, June 21. His Imperial Majesty has sent the Order of the Golden Fleece to the young Prince of Schwartzenburg belonging to his late Father, and has also conferred on him the office of Grand Master of the Horse, and made it hereditary in his family. *D J.*

ADVERTISEMENTS.

Lately published,

The Second Edition, corrected,

The LAW of TITHES:

SHewing their Nature, Kinds, Properties, Incidents, by whom, when, and in what Manner payable; how, and in what Courts to be sued for and recovered; what Things, Lands, or Persons are charged with, or exempted therefrom. With the Nature, Incidents, and Effects of Customs, Prescriptions, Real Compositions, Modus Decimandi, Libels, Suggestions, Prohibitions, Consultations, Custom of London, &c. Wherein all the Statutes and adjudged Cases, relative to the Subject, are introduced and considered. By *William Bohun* of the Middle Temple, Esq;

Also, Just published, by the same Author,

A TITHING TABLE: Shewing (by way of Analysis) of what Things Tythes are or are not due, either by Common Law, Custom, or Prescription. Price 1 s.

N. B. These two may be had bound together, or separate. Printed for J. Brotherton, W. Meadows, T. Cox, W. Hinchliffe, and R. Willock, in Cornhill; J. Hazard, near Stationers Hall; W. Bickerton, without Temple-Bar; T. Astley, and S. Austen, in St. Paul's Church-yard; and L. Gilliver, in Fleet-street.

June 12, 1732.

By PERMISSION of

The Right Honourable the Lord Chancellor.
The Right Honourable the Lord Raymond, Lord Chief Justice of his Majesty's Court of King's Bench
The Right Honourable Arthur Onslow, Esq; Speaker of the House of Commons.
The Honourable Sir John Hind Cotton, Bart.
Francis Annesley, Esq;
Samuel Burroughs, Esq; one of the Masters of the High Court of Chancery.
John Hanbury, Esq;
Trustees of the Cottonian Library.

IT is propos'd by *John Pine*, to Engrave, by Subscription, a Correct Copy of King JOHN's *Great Charter*, taken from the Original now remaining in the *Cottonian* Library; which, being a Recognition of the Rights and Liberties of the People, it is presumed the Publick will encourage a Design to perpetuate a Record of such Dignity and importance.

It will be contained in one Imperial Sheet of Paper, and engraved in the same Form and Character with the Original, and adorned with proper Decorations.

The Price to Subscribers will be Half a Guinea; to be paid on the Delivery, which will be about Christmas next.

Those Gentlemen, who are willing to encourage this Subscription, are desired to send their Names and Places of Abode as soon as possible, which will entitle them to the first Impressions.

N. B. Those who subscribe for Six, shall have a Seventh gratis.

Subscriptions are taken in by C. King, in Westminster-Hall; N. Prevost, in the Strand; R. Gosling, B. Motte, T. Woodward, near the Temple, Fleet-Street; W. Innys, C. Rivington, S. Austen, in St. Paul's Church-Yard; A. Bettesworth and C. Hitch, J. Batley, in Pater-Noster-Row; W. Hinchliffe, E. Symons, at the Royal-Exchange; J. Stendley, in New Bond-street; J. Clark, Print-seller in Grays-Inn; and J. Pine, Engraver, over-against Little-Britain, in Aldersgate-Street.

This Day was published,

The Fifth Edition, of

A Journey from ALEPPO to Jerusalem, at Easter, A. D. 1697. To which is added, An Account of the Author's Journey to the Banks of Euphrates and the Peer, and to the Country of Mesopotamia. By *Henry Maundrel*, M. A. late Fellow of Exeter-College, and Chaplain to the Factory at Aleppo.

Oxford, printed at the Theatre for Anthony Peisly; and sold by J. Brotherton, W. Meadows, T. Cox, W. Hinchliffe, and R. Willock, in Cornhill; J. Hazard, near Stationers Hall; W. Bickerton, without Temple-Bar; T. Astley, and S. Austin, in St. Paul's Church-yard; and L. Gilliver in Fleet-street.

Of whom may be had,

Dr. TRAPP's Sermons at Lady *Moyer's* Lecture on the Doctrine of the TRINITY, with the Objections against it answered in a summary View of the whole Controversy. To which are added, Discourses on the Parable of Dives and Lazarus; setting forth the deplorable Corruption, Immorality and Infidelity of the present Age: Shewing the absolute Necessity of a Holy Life; demonstrating the Certainty of a Future state, and the Truth of the Christian Religion.

This Day is published,

A new Edition (with all the Alterations supply'd, and the Places of Abode,)

AN Exact LIST of the Lords Spiritual and Temporal; shewing by distinct Marks the Knights of the Garter; Knights of the Bath; the Peers of Scotland; Knights of the Thistle, those *under Age*; Who *don't sit in the House*; Lords of the Treasury; of the Admiralty; Privy Counsellors; Governors of the Charter-House; Protesters. Also a compleat Alphabetical double LIST of 1. The Counties, Cities, and Boroughs, with their Representatives against each. 2. The Names of the Knights, Citizens, and Burgesses of the Present Parliament of Great Britain; shewing, (1.) The Places they represent; (2.) The new Members; (3.) How many Parliaments the Others have serv'd in; and (4.) The Gentlemen of the last not chose again in this. With Blank Pages for Alterations; and may be had in Broad Sheets for Publick Offices or Coffee Rooms.

Printed at St John's Gate; sold by A. Dodd, and W. Bickerton, without Temple-Bar; J. Stagg, and C. King in Westminster-Hall; and E. Nutt at the Royal-Exchange.

Where may be had, publish'd every Month, at 6 d. each.

The GENTLEMAN's MAGAZINE; or, MONTHLY INTELLIGENCER. Containing a compendious View of all our Public News-Papers, and other Collections in Prose and Verse, in such a Method as hath occasion'd many of the Numbers to pass two, and some three Editions. No. XVII. for May 1732, was publish'd the 3d Instant. Those Numbers which were wanted of last Year are in the Press again, in order to compleat Gentleman's Setts; and will be done in about a Month's time.

This Day is published,

[Price Six-Pence.]

THE PRESENT STATE of LEARNING, RELIGION, and INFIDELITY in *Great Britain*. Wherein the Causes of the present Degeneracy of Taste, and Increase of Infidelity, are inquir'd into, and accounted for. Published by a sincere Friend to Cause of RELIGION and VIRTUE. With a View to awaken the Secure, to stimulate the Lukewarm, to chastise the Profligate, and to animate the Professors of Christianity, to do their Duty, maugre all Discouragements.

To whom shall I speak and give warning, that they may hear? Behold, their ear is uncircumcised, and they cannot hearken: behold the word of the Lord is unto them a reproach: they have no delight in it, Jer. vi. 10.

Printed for *C. Rivington*, at the Bible and Crown in St Paul's Church-Yard.

This Day was published,

(Beautifully printed in One Volume, Octavo,)

A Treatise of Continual FEVERS, in four Parts. To which are added, *Medicinal Observations*, in Three Books; wherein are enumerated, the Diagnosticks, Prognosticks, and Events of the several Diseases incident to Human Bodies. By JODOCUS LOMMIUS.

Translated from the Latin by THOMAS DALE, M. D.

Printed for J. Brotherton, W. Meadows, T. Cox, W. Hinchliffe, and R. Willock, in Cornhill; J. Hazard near Stationers-Hall; W. Bickerton without Temple-Bar; T. Astley and S. Austin in St. Paul's Church-Yard; and L. Gilliver in Fleet-Street.

This Day was published,

A General Abridgment of Cases in Equity argued and adjudged in the High Court of Chancery, &c. With several Cases never before published, alphabetically digested under proper Titles, with Notes and References to the Whole; and Three Tables: The First of the Names of the Cases. The Second of the several Titles, with their Divisions and Subdivisions; and the Third of the Matter under General Heads.

By a Gentleman of the Middle-Temple.

Printed for Henry Lintot, at the Cross Keys against St. Dunstan's Church, Fleet-Street.

This Day is Published,

The COMEDIAN, *or Philosophical Enquirer*. Numb. III. June. 1732.

COntaining, 1. A farther Enquiry into the Being of GOD, *&c.* 2. Reflections on some modern Plays. 3. An Epistle to Sir *Robert Walpole*. 4. The History of the Times, *&c.*

Printed for J. Roberts, at the Oxford-Arms in Warwick-Lane. Price 6 d.

Where may be had,

Numb. I. Containing, 1. The Design of the *Comedian*. 2. Of Custom. 3. Of Philosophy, History, Poetry, and Oratory. 4. A Song. 5. The History of the Times, *&c.* And

Numb. II. Containing, 1. An Enquiry into the Origin and Constitution of Man, the Powers of Matter, and the Being of a GOD, with a View to prove that GOD requires no more of us than Nature requires. 2. A Letter in Prose to Mr. *Alexander Pope*, occasioned by his Epistle in Verse to the Earl of *Burlington*. 3. Some Thoughts on Painting and Painters. 4. *London*, an Ode. 5. The History of the Times, *&c.*

BOOKS printed for, and sold by J. Brotherton, at the Bible next the Fleece Tavern, in Cornhill.

Whitlock's Memorials.	Telemachus, in French.
Temple's Works, 2 Vol.	Ditto in Fol.
Bailey's Eng. Dict. Fol.	Guardians, 2 Vol.
Tillotson's Works, 3 Vol.	Langham's Duties.
Bates's Works, Fol.	Free Thoughts on Religion.
State of Britain, for 1732.	La Bell Assemble, 3 Vol.
Bailey's Justin.	Vanburgh's Plays, 2 Vol.
Origin of Honour.	Addison's Works, 4 Vol.
Ladies Conduct.	Spectators, 8 Vol.
Virgin unmask'd.	Trapp's Virgil.
Hays's Ship and Supercargo Book-Keeper.	D'Urfey's Songs, 6 Vol.
Coke's Detection, 3 Vol.	Milton Lost and Regain'd.
Bohun's Law of Tythes.	D'Anois Tales, 2 Vol.
Feasts & Fasts of the Church.	De Retz Memoirs, 4 Vol.
Erasmii Ecclesiastica	Tom Brown's Works, 4 V
Life of Oliver Cromwell.	Farnborough's Grammar.
Life of the K. of Sweden.	Philips's Grammar.
Dampier's Journal to Madagascar.	Dorrington's Devotion.
Rapin's Hist. of England, 15 Vol.	Congreve's Plays, 3 Vol.
Arbuthnot of Ailments, com	Pope and Swift Misc. 3 Vol.
	Pope's Misc. 2 Vol.
	Turkish Spy, 8 Vol.

This Day was published,

AN ODE to his Grace the Duke of Newcastle. Written on the present Tranquillity of Europe, establish'd by the Influence of the British Power.

Nihil habet aut Fortuna tua majus, quàm ut possis, aut Natura tua melius, quàm, ut velis, quàm plurimos conservare. Cic.

Printed for J. Batley, at the Dove in Pater-Noster-Row. Price 6 d.

Where may be had, just published,

Dedicated to the Gentlemen of the Navy of England,

The Memoirs of Monsieur DU GUE TROUIN, Chief of a Squadron of the Royal Navy of France, and Great Cross of the Military Order of St. Lewis; containing all his Sea Actions with the English, Dutch, and Portuguese, in the late Wars of King William and Queen Anne.

Translated from the French by a *Sea-Officer*.

At the Printing-Office in Bow Church-Yard, London, is just published, Pr. bound 1s. 6d.

SENTENTIÆ SELECTÆ: Or, A Collection of miscellaneous Sentences, Divine, Moral, and Historical. In Prose and Verse, English and Latin. Excerpted from the Works of many learned and judicious Authors and digested into alphabetical Order. By *Edward Cocker*. To which are added, various Forms for indicting Letters. The Characters, Places, and Significations of all Sorts of Stops, Points, Pauses and Marks used both in Writing and Printing, with their Explanations. A Table of the most common Abbreviations, or Contractions of Words. Pertinent Directions for fair and exact Writing; with Rules for making and managing the Pen, &c. The best approv'd Receipts for making Ink of many Colours. An ingenious Discourse and Poem on the unspeakable Advantages of Reading and Writing: Also Instructions and Rules for Behaviour; with many other useful and profitable Particulars.

Also a curious Book of select Fables, and other short Poems, &c. finely engrav'd on 32 Copper Plates, for the Amusement of young Gentlemen and Ladies. To which are added, The most useful and ornamental Hands for their Improvement in the Art of *Writing*. Price 1 s 6 d. And a new Ciphering Book for the Use of Schools, being the best of the Kind ever yet extant. Engrav'd by *George Bickham*, Sen. Price 1 s. 6d. Likewise the Third Edition of The *Modern Musick Master*: Or, The Universal Musician; consisting of Instructions to Singing, and Directions to play on the Common Flute, German Flute, Hautboy, Violin, Harpsicord, or Organ: with a brief History of Musick to this present Time: in which Volume is included many other valuable Pieces. Engrav'd on above 200 Plates. Price 7 s. 6d.

Books of Instructions for any single Instrument. Pr. 1 s 6 d.

N. B. At the abovesaid Printing-Office, Shop-Keepers Bills are engraved and printed, either at the Letter or Rolling-Press, at the lowest Rates.

This Day was published,

In One Volume in Quarto,

THE Genuine WORKS in PROSE and VERSE, of the Right Hon. GEORGE GRANVILLE, LORD LANSDOWNE.

Printed for L. Gilliver, at Homer's-Head, over against St. Dunstan's Church, Fleet-street.

Where may be had, just published,

1. A New and Beautiful Edition of the DUNCIAD, 8vo. with some Additional Notes and Epigrams.
2. A Collection of Pieces in Prose and Verse, publish'd on Occasion of the Dunciad.
3. The Progress of Love, in four Eclogues, 1. *Uncertainty*, 2. *Hope*, 3. *Jealousy*, 4. *Possession*.
4. STOWE, the GARDENS of the Right Hon. the Lord *Cobham*.
5. Of FALSE TASTE, the 3d Edition, dedicated to the Right Hon. the Earl of Burlington.

By Mr POPE.

BOOKS *lately printed for* J. Clarke *at the* Golden Ball *in* Duck-Lane, *near* Little-Britain.

FAbulæ Æsopi Selectæ, or select Fables of Æsop, with an English Translation, more literal than any yet extant; design'd for the readier Introduction of Beginners in the Latin Tongue. By H. CLARKE, Master of the publick Grammar School in Islington.

Corderii Colloquiorum Centuria selecta. With a literal Translation. Fourth Edition.

Cornelii Nepotis vitae excellentium imperatorum, &c. or Cornelius Nepos's Lives of the excellent Commanders: With an English Translation as literal as possible, with English Notes, and a large Index: Third Edition. Both by J. CLARKE, Master of the publick Grammar School in Hull.

The Greek Grammar construed (very proper to be bound up with the Greek Grammar) For the Help of young Beginners. Second Edition, revised and carefully corrected: For the Use of Eton School.

LONDON: Printed by J. HUGGONSON, in *Bartholomew-Close*, for Captain GULLIVER, near the *Temple*, where Letters and Advertisements are taken in: As also at the *Rainbow Coffee-House* in *Cornhill*, and *John's Coffee-House* in *Sheer-Lane*, near *Temple-Bar*. [Price Two Pence.]

The Grub-ſtreet Journal.

NUMB. 131

Thurſday, JULY 6, 1732.

IN the following examination of Dr. B.'s alterations of MILTON's *Paradiſe Loſt*, it is intended to conſider thoſe in the firſt place, by which he pretends to correct the errors, either of the Amanuenſis, to whom the verſes were at firſt dictated, or of the Printers who printed the three firſt editions. As a ſimilitude of ſound in different words might occaſion ſeveral miſtakes of the former kind: ſo many of the latter proceeded, no doubt, from a ſimilitude in the letters and a wrong poſition of the ſtops, which muſt neceſſarily change the ſenſe. As theſe are the moſt ſolid, if not the only juſt, foundations for altering the preſent text, the alterations which are built upon theſe juſtly demand the firſt place in our examination.

Book I. Ver. 6. —— *that on the* ſecret *top*
Of Horeb or of Sinai didſt inſpire
That ſhepherd, &c.

The Dr, as if he had ſtood at the blind Poet's elbow, tells us poſitively, that he dictated *ſacred*; for which he gives the following reaſons. 1. It is ſaid to MOSES concerning *Horeb*, Ex. iii. 5. *The place whereon thou ſtandeſt is holy ground.* 2. *Sacred* is an epithet frequently applied by the Poets to a mountain. 3. *Secret* cannot agree to the *top* of one viſible ſeveral leagues off; and which being in the dry deſert of Arabia is not probably often covered with a cloudy cap like the European hills. 4. But if it be, the epithet is common to all mountains; whereas *Horeb, the mountain of God*, deſerves a peculiar epithet, which in the judgment of the beſt Poets is always preferable to a general one. —— To this it has been anſwered, by a very learned and ingenious * Gentleman, 1. That tho' that part of *Horeb* on which MOSES ſtood was holy, it does not follow that the *top* of it was then holy too; and if it were, by the rules of good poetry, allowed by the Dr. himſelf, the epithet ought to be peculiar to the *top*, of which only the poet here ſpeaks. 2. That the frequent application of *ſacred* to mountains is an argument againſt it in this place, even according to the Dr's own words almoſt immediately following. 3. That *Horeb* and *Sinai* are two ſeveral eminencies of one and the ſame mountain; of the latter of which JOSEPHUS in his *Jewiſh Antiquities* ſays, B. iii. C. 5. *That the top of it cannot be ſeen without ſtraining the eyes.* Agreeably to which the Poet expreſſes his doubt, which name to give to that mountain, on *the top* of which MOSES received his inſpiration. 4. That *ſecret* is the moſt *peculiar* epithet that could have been uſed; becauſe when God gave the Law to MOSES, *the top of Sinai* was covered with *a thick cloud* and *ſmoke*, Ex. xix. 16, 18. and thereby made *ſecret* in ſuch a *peculiar* manner as diſtinguiſhed it from all other mountains in the world. And the very ſame thing ſeems intended by another epithet, xii. 227.

God from the mount of Sinai, whoſe gray top
Shall tremble, he deſcending, &c.

Since therefore the Dr. allows, that 'a *proper* epithet is always preferable to a *general* one,' *ſecret* muſt neceſſarily here have the preference to *ſacred*. —— It is very ſtrange, that the Dr, while he was writing this note, did not conſult the ſeveral places of Scripture, where the circumſtances of giving the Law are recorded. In one of which Ex. xxiv. 16, 18. it is ſaid, *the cloud covered mount Sinai ſix days; and on the ſeventh, Moſes went into the midſt of the cloud, and was in the mount forty days and forty nights.*

The *top* of that mountain muſt certainly be very *ſecret*, on which MOSES, *that ſhepherd* here pointed out by the Poet, remained concealed for ſo long a time from ſuch a multitude of people. If the Dr. did conſult theſe places, I fear the frequent mention of *ſmoke, darkneſs, clouds, and thick darkneſs* in them, had raiſed very diſmal ideas in his mind, and darkened his underſtanding: for he ſeems, as if ſurrounded with *darkneſs viſible*, to grope in the dark, and has certainly ſtumbled at the very threſhold of the book, which is a very bad beginning, and

ſeems to caſt
Ominous conjecture on the whole ſucceſs

VER. 15. —— *while* it purſues.

* *Review of the Text of* MILTON: Part 1. *pag.* 1, &c.

'The Author, I believe, gave it *while* I purſue, as iii. 15.' ſays our Critic. But this place is not parallel to the former, for here the firſt perſon is uſed all along, whereas there the perſon is changed. And whether we read *ſong* according to MILTON in VER. 13. or *wing* according to the Dr, it is very unneceſſary to change the third perſon for the firſt, ſince either of thoſe words may as well be ſayed to *purſue* things, as the former of them is ſayed to *tell of deeds*, in the *faultleſs* edition of *Paradiſe Regain'd*, i. 11.

VER. 36. The *mother of mankind*.

The Dr. believes the Author ſpoke it to EVE, Thee, *mother of mankind*, which he ſays will *raiſe* the ſenſe. It may ſo in the Dr's opinion; but to me it ſeems a ſenſeleſs and unnatural affectation, in the midſt of a narration, which ought to be plain and ſimple. And ſince the beginning of an Epic poem ought to be ſo too, if this could *raiſe* the ſenſe, 'it would raiſe it in a place where it ought 'not to be raiſed, if we may judge from the practice of 'the beſt Poets,' as is well obſerved by the Author of the *Review*, &c.

VER. 42. *With hideous ruin and* combuſtion *down*.

Flaming being mentioned in the preceding verſe, the Dr. ſays, that *combuſtion* is ſuperfluouſly added, and doubts not, that MILTON gave it *confuſion*. If this ſuperfluity be a ſufficient reaſon for alterations, many more places ſhould have been altered, which the Dr. has left untouched: Such as Ver. 69. *ever burning ſulphur unconſum'd. Ver.* 87 *with tranſcendent brightneſs didſt outſhine.* iii. 306. *enjoying Godlike fruition:* and an hundred parallel inſtances. From whence it is evident, that the Dr's brain was in ſome *confuſion* when it was at work upon this place, which occaſioned him to put in this word; which is as ſuperfluous after *ruin*, as *combuſtion* after *flaming*; and in one reſpect more ſo, becauſe placed much nearer to the word comprehending the ſame idea. It has been well remarked, that *combuſtion* is the better word, as being more nervous and forcible in this place, repreſenting at once to the mind the ideas of *burning* and *confuſion* too.

VER. 54. —— *for now the* thought
Both of loſt happineſs and laſting pain
Torments *him*.

Our Critic ſays 'it is probable, MILTON gave it in 'the plural, *the thoughts torment him:* becauſe the thought 'of happineſs, and the thought of pain, are not one, but 'two.' To which the Author of the *Review* anſwers very juſtly, that by *the thought* MILTON undoubtedly meant *the thinking on*, which intirely removes the Dr's objection. Beſides, the expreſſion in the ſingular number is more poetical than that in the plural.

VER. 72. *In* utter *darkneſs*.

This expreſſion is likewiſe uſed in the Argument of this Book, and in iii. 16. in all which places the Dr. ſubſtitutes *outer*, becauſe he ſays *utter darkneſs* is abſolute darkneſs. —— Yes, ſo it is, and for this very reaſon becauſe it is *outer* darkneſs; both words ſignifying the ſame thing, and being only differently ſpelt. Thus, in the next verſe but one, *utmoſt* ſignifies the ſame with *uttermoſt* or *outmoſt*. From this criticiſm it is evident that the Dr. is an *utter* Critic, in his own ſenſe of the word. But there are a multitude of the like nature, with which he has pelted MILTON, his Amanuenſis, his Editor, and his Printer;

And laid about as hot and brain-ſick
As th' UTTER Barriſter *of* Swanſwick. *Hud.* P. iii. C. 2.

Which appellation of *utter Barriſter* is uſed in contradiſtinction to *inner Barriſter*; and applied to perſons on the account of their ſitting *uttermoſt* on a form.

VER. 127. —— *Anſwer'd ſoon his* bold *compeer*.

The Dr. does not think the following ſpeech *bold* enough to juſtify the epithet, and therefore changes it to *old*. But the high ſtation of BEELZEBUB, who was next in power to SATAN, his actions in battle, and even the blaſphemy in this ſpeech, are either of them ſufficient to juſtify the epithet. So that there is almoſt as much reaſon to call this *old* companion of Satan *his bold compeer*, as to call the Dr. himſelf a *bold*, as well as an *old*, *Critic*.

VER. 129. *That* led *th' embattel'd Seraphim to war*
Under thy conduct, and in dreadful deeds
Fearleſs endanger'd *heav'n's perpetual King*;
And put *to proof his high ſupremacy*,

The Dr. rejects *led, endanger'd*, and *put*, becauſe, if retained, he ſays 'BEELZEBUB commends himſelf and 'other thrones for what SATAN had made his own ſole 'glory.' To this it has been well anſwered, in the *Review*, that he attributes as much to SATAN as he could wiſh, by adding *under thy conduct:* which words are very unneceſſary if we read *led'ſt*, becauſe the verb implies them. To this I may add, that tho' BEELZEBUB does indeed covertly commend himſelf and other thrones for their prowesſ, yet he ſufficiently diſtinguiſhes the ſuperiour dignity and prowesſ of SATAN, by giving him the title of *chief*, and aſſerting all to have been done *under his conduct*. If their courage and conduct were ſo eminent in that dreadful day, what muſt his be, who had the ſupreme command over all thoſe *throned pow'rs!* —— To juſtify the ſubſtitution of *led'ſt, endanger'dſt, put'ſt*, he produces inſtances of *Laugh'ſt* from v. 737, and of *Reject'ſt, Storm'ſt*, and *Hold'ſt* from the 4th book of *Paradiſe Regain'd*. But not one of theſe inſtances is exactly parallel, they being all in the preſent tenſe, and ſounding ſofter than *endanger'dſt*. But were they exactly parallel, the uſe of them in caſes of neceſſity where the verſe required it, can never juſtify the alteration of verſes, where the ſenſe is very good and the ſound very harmonious, into worſe ſound, tho' into ſomewhat better ſenſe: much leſs can it juſtify a change into worſe ſenſe, tautological expreſſion, and the moſt harſh and ungrateful ſound. Nay I ſhall venture to affirm, that theſe abbreviated words ought to be uſed as ſeldom as poſſible in poetry, and never in proſe; the introduction of which from the former into the latter, in the opinion of one of the moſt celebrated Writers of the age, has had a very bad effect upon the Engliſh language. His charge againſt many of our moſt eminent Authors, tho' very ſevere, is certainly very juſt, which I ſhall therefore here repeat in his own words. 'There is another ſet of men who have contributed very much to the 'ſpoiling of the Engliſh Tongue; I mean the Poets, from 'the time of the Reſtoration: Theſe Gentlemen, although 'they could not be inſenſible how much our language was 'already overſtocked with monoſyllables, yet to ſave time 'and pains, introduced that barbarous cuſtom of abbreviating words, to fit them to the meaſure of their verſes: 'And this they have frequently done, ſo very injudiciouſly, 'as to form ſuch harſh unharmonious ſounds, that none 'but a northern ear could endure: they have joined the 'moſt obdurate conſonants without one intervening vowel, 'only to ſhorten a ſyllable: and their taſte in time became 'ſo depraved, that what was at firſt a poetical licence, 'not to be juſtified, they made their choice, alledging, 'that the Words pronounced at length, ſounded faint and 'languid, This was a Pretence to take up the ſame cuſtom 'in proſe; ſo that moſt of the books we ſee now a-days, 'are full of thoſe manglings and abbreviations. Inſtances 'of this abuſe are innumerable: what does your Lordſhip 'think of the words, *drudg'd, diſturb'd, rebuk'd, fledg'd*, 'and a thouſand others, every where to be met with in 'proſe as well as verſe? Where by leaving out a vowel to 'ſave a ſyllable, we form ſo jarring a ſound, and ſo difficult to utter, that I have often wondered how it could 'ever obtain.' Dr. SWIFT's *Letter to the Earl of Oxford* SWIFT's *and* POPE's *Miſcellanies, Vol.* I. *pag.* 239. —— See here how theſe two learned Doctors differ, both of them great Poets, one in his own, and the other in the opinion of the world: the former would unneceſſarily uſe theſe abbreviated words in poetry, perhaps on account of their harmonious ſound, the uſe of which, by reaſon of their barbarous roughneſs, the latter thinks not allowable even in proſe.

Againſt the epithet *fearleſs* in VER. 131. our Critic objects, that if it be right, 'then the *dreadful deeds* muſt 'be thoſe of MICHAEL and the good Angels; but it's 'plain they are here meant of SATAN's crew; for ſo ii. '549. *Others ſing Their own* heroic deeds, *but hapleſs 'fall.* The Author therefore gave it *Peerleſs*.' The anſwer given to this has been, That *dreadful deeds* may here mean ſuch in general, without any particular reſpect to thoſe either of the good Angels, or of SATAN's Crew, and without conſidering who is frighted by them; and then *fearleſs* will ſtand very well, meaning without fear in the midſt of terrible deeds. But it may be further obſerved, that the Dr's way of proof is very odd, to pretend to aſcertain the exact meaning of *dreadful deeds* in this firſt book, by *heroic deeds* in the ſecond. May not SATAN's crew ſing their own *heroic deeds* in the latter, and yet BEELZEBUB in the former extoll their *fearleſſneſs* amidſt the *dreadful deeds* of MICHAEL and the

good Angels? The Dr instead of proving SATAN here to
be a *Peerless* Commander, has proved himself to be both
a *fearless* and a *peerless* Critic.

> ZOILUS, tir'd with conning o'er
> Dull Indexes, a precious store,
> Foresee to Chapel took his way,
> Resolv'd to take a knap, — or pray:
> Proceeding flow in solemn state
> Forward he marches to his seat:
> But oh! the lock, long since difus'd,
> T'admit the holy Man refus'd.
> The Virger tugs with fruitless pains;
> The rust invincible remains.
> Who can describe his woful plight,
> Plac'd thus to view in fulleft light,
> A spectacle of mirth, expos'd
> Tu'sneering friends and gigling foes?
> Then first, as 'tis from same receiv'd,
> (But fame can't always be believ'd,)
> A blush, the sign of new-born grace,
> Gleam'd through the horrors of his face.
> He held it shameful to retreat,
> And worse to take a lower seat.
> The Virger soon with nimble bound
> At once vaults o'er the wooden mound,
> And gives the door a furious knock,
> Which forc'd the disobedient lock.
> Then ZOILUS ent'ring in confusion,
> His elbows placing on the cushion,
> Devoutly loll'd, in musing deep,
> Unable now to pray, or sleep;
> Some words imperfect mumbled o'er:
> The wicked Sophs declar'd he swore,
> That none should e'er for sev'n years space
> Again behold him in that place.
> What then? — 'Tis plain with strictest troth,
> Religiously he kept his oath.

DOMESTIC NEWS.

C. *Courant.* E.P. *Evening Poſt.*
P. *Poſt-Boy.* S.J. *S. James's Evening Poſt.*
D.P. *Daily Poſt.* W.E. *Whitehall Evening P.*
D.J. *Daily Journal.* L.E. *London Evening Poſt.*

THURSDAY, June 29.

Yesterday the Rt. Hon. the E. Cowper and his Lady
received the compliments of great numbers of the Nobility and Quality, upon their nuptials, at the E. of Grantham's house in Albemarle-street. *D P.*

On monday a Matter was heard before the Rt. Hon.
the Lords of the Treasury, relating to the Royal Mines
in Scotland, between his Grace the D. of Argyle and Sir
Alex. Murray, Bar. which was determined in favour of
the latter. *D P.* — Yesterday being the last day of Term
several persons appeared on their recognizances, at the
King's Bench Bar, &c. *D P., D J.* — The Attorney General acquainted the Court, that he had an information
against the Printer and two of the Publishers of Fog's
Journal, for the letter on K William. *D J.* — The
Court discharged the Rule, with costs which was made
for Justice De Veil to shew cause why an information
should not be granted against him, for taking bail of some
persons committed to the Gate-house, on suspicion of
felony, in picking the Lady Crew's pocket of 12 guineas. *D J, D P.*

Yesterday the Duke and Dutchess of Dorset set out
with a handsome retinue for his Grace's seat at Knowl in
Kent. — *I met his Grace in the Park this day at two.*

The same day her Grace the Dutchess Dowager of
Marlborough set out with a grand retinue, from her house
at S. James's for Scarborough. *C D P.* — The Dutchess
and Major Hanbury will set out together next Sunday. *S J.*

Mr. Lewis Elliot, and Mr. John Watson, are made Receivers of the Rents of the late E. of Derwentwater's estates
for the use of the public. *S J.*

2000 l. damages were given on monday, to the Duke
of Richmond against a Grazier of Chichester for scandalous and defamatory words. *L E.* One Farmer Ho-
baldson. *S J.*

We hear that his Royal Highness the Prince hath lately recovered (received. *S J.*) 20,000 l. of rents due to
his Royal Highness from the Dutchy of Cornwall. *L E.*

One Mr. Hamilton, a Scotch Gentleman, having proposed a machine for causing a ship of what burthen soever to sail against wind and tide, has been presented by
the E. of Selkirk to several of the Lords of the Council
and others, for an experiment to be made of so useful
an invention. *L E., S J.* — *This is a strange invention
for a Scotch Gentleman.*

On monday night the Lady Grace Vane, wife to the

Hon. Hen. Vane, Esq; eldest son of Lord Barnard was
brought to bed of a son. *S J., L E.*

Last thursday Edw. Warren, Esq; was married to Miss
Holt of Norfolk-street in the Strand, a beautiful young
Lady of 10,000 l. *S J.* — This morning Cha. Hanbury Williams, Esq; 3d son of Major Hanbury, was married
to the Lady Frances Coningby, &c. *W E.* — He was
married on Saturday-morning. *C July 3.*

We hear from Rumsey in Hampshire, that a man going by a plot of beans, a cat came out and seized on his
leg; he could not disengage himself, but calling for help
those who came to his assistance cut off her legs and head,
and was [were] forced to wrench open the jaws; the
man was carried to the sea, fearing the cat was bitten by
a mad dog. *C.* — At Clipton in Oxfordshire, one Mrs
Clever having laid a child (about a year old) asleep on
bed, a hog eat the nose, one eye, and a side of the face
and head. — Two youths apprentices, one to a Coache-
maker in Long-Acre, the other to a Frame-maker in Gies-
Queen-street, having some words, agreed to fight it out;
and beat one another to such a degree, that the former
dy'd on tuesday, and the latter remains speechless. *S J.*

FRIDAY, June 30.

The Hon. Sir Cha. Wager, Rear Admiral of the Red,
is appointed Admiral of the Blue; and Sir Geo. Saunders, Rear Admiral of the White — the former will hoist
his flag on board the Namur, and the latter on board
the Edinburgh. *P.*

Yesterday Will. Dunstar, Esq; was chosen Governor;
John Phillips, Esq; Sub governor; and Ric. Lockwood,
Esq; Deputy-governor of the Royal Exchange Assurance
Company. *C D P.*

The Rev. Mr. Price, of Newington, is presented to the
Living of S. Ethelburga within Bishopgate. *D P., C.*

Yesterday a Sessions of Admiralty was held at the Old
Bailey, when John Tatum, Andrew Dove, Tho. Perkins,
Elias Parry, and Tho. Hill, were tried for Piracy, com-
mitted near Portugal in April, in the Duke of Cambridge,
Capt. Wilson, for endeavouring to seize and carry away
the ship, and confining the captain for half an hour; and
after a long hearing they were brought in not guilty. *C.,
D P.* — Andrew Tuff, Abel Perkins, Elias Berreel *P.*
— It appeared to be a malicious prosecution, the Court
ordered them a copy of their indictment. *C. D P., D J.*
— Their irons were knock'd off in Court, and they
were ordered to be discharged without fees. *P.* —
Capt. Sam. Nailer, Commander of the Hunter Galley,
was tried for the murder of his Boatswain, and acquitted.
C. D P., D J.

Yesterday began the Gen. Quarter Sessions of the Peace
for the City and Liberty of Westminster, and Sir John
Gonson, the Chairman, gave a very learned and ingenious charge to the Grand Jury, which was very much
commended by several Gentlemen of the Long Robe
who heard the same. *D P.*

Christen'd	Males	171		312			Between 40 and 50	26
	Fem.	141					50 and 60	20
Bury'd	Males	159		328			60 and 70	23
	Fem.	169					70 and 80	13
Decreased in burials 16.							80 and 90	7
Died under 2 years old 116							90 and 100	2
Between 2 and	5	24			Choaked with a cherry	1.		
	5 and 10	18			Drowned 2. Drinking	1.		
	10 and 20	12			Overlaid 3. Aged 23. Con-			
	20 and 30	29			vulsions 104. Fever	37.		
	30 and 40	38			Small-pox 11.			

Dover, June 27. N. S. This morning Monſ. S. Andre
and his Lady embarqued for Calais; and the Lady of Mr.
Harvey of Comb with her Brother. *P.*

SATURDAY, July 1.

Matthew Concanen, Esq; Barrister at Laws, of the Inner Temple, is appointed his Majesty's Attorney-General
to the Island of Jamaica, in the room of Alexander Hen-
derson, Esq; deceased. *P.*

On wednesday the Court of King's Bench gave judgment against Knox Ward, Esq; on the action brought by
Miss Holt, for a contract of marriage, on the trial whereof the Jury gave 2000 l. damages: but on Serj. Chapple's
moving for a new trial, on the account of the excessive
damages, the Court made a rule, that the Plaintiff should
shew cause next Term, why such new trial should not
be had. *D J.*

Yesterday was held a General Court of the South Sea
Company, when it was resolved to pay off the 50 l. per
cent. immediately on their bonds, with interest to Michaelmas, as the million is expected in a day or two to be paid
to the said Company by the Government. *C.*

Yesterday there was an installation of the four new
Knights of the Bath, viz. the Right Hon. the Marquis of
Carnarvon, the Lord Bateman, Sir Charles Gunter Nichols,
and Sir George Downing, and they, with the several
Knights Companions, having apparelled themselves in
their surcoats and mantles, and having the great collars of
the Order and white hats, met in the Prince's Chamber,
from whence a solemn procession was made to the west door

of the Abbey-Church, Westminster, in the following manner, viz. — The drums and trumpets of his Majesty's
houshold. — Twelve Alms-men of the Church of Westminster, two and two, in the gowns, uncovered. —
The Messenger of the Order, in his proper habit and
badge, cover'd. — The Esquires in their proper habits,
three and three, uncovered. — The Prebends of Westminster, two and two, in their habits, cover'd with
square caps. — The Pursuivant, Heralds, and King at
Arms, in their tabars, collars, and badges, all cover'd. —
Then the four new Knights nominated proceeded two and
two, all in their surcoats, carrying in their hands the
white hat and plume of feathers, and followed by the rest
of the Knights Companions in their surcoats, with the
white hat and plume of feathers, cover'd. — Then the
Register of the Order, having the Secretary on his right,
and the Gentleman-Usher on his left hand, each in his
mantle and surcoat, with his proper badge pendant to a
gold chain, and all of them with their bonnets on their
heads. — Then Garter Principal King at Arms, in his
tabart, collar, and badge, cover'd, having on his right
hand and on his left two other Kings at Arms, in their
mantles, with their bonnets on. — The Dean of
the Order, in his mantle, &c. with the form of the Oaths
to be given to the Knights, and cover'd with a square
cap. — Then the Great Master in his full habit,
with his collar, cover'd with a white hat, and adorn'd
with a plume of feathers. — Then his Roy-
al Highness the Duke, in the full robes of the Order.
— In this form they proceeded to the Chapel of Henry
the VIIth; and after the Ceremony was over, which was
perform'd by the Right Rev. the Bishop of Rochester,
Dean of the said Order, which was ended about three
o'clock, they returned back in the same order, as before-
mentioned, and a grand Entertainment was prepared for
them in the Courts of Requests. — His Royal Highness
the Prince of Wales, the Princess Royal, and the two young
Princesses, sat on a throne erected at the west door of
the choir, and saw the procession. — About 20 centinels
of the Foot-guards were sent to the Savoy, for molest-
ing people if they would not give them money; and they
are to be try'd by a Court-martial. *D J.*

The occasion of his Royal Highness the Duke's not
staying to dine with the Knights of the Bath was, that
being taken with a great bleeding at the nose in the
Prince's Chamber at Westminster, he was carried back to
Kensington as soon as the procession was ended. *S J.*

Yesterday Ensign Jones, of the Foot-guards, upon duty
in S. Margaret's Church-yard, had his pocket pick'd of a
gold watch. *S J.*

This day the Queen with the Princess Royal, Princesses Amelia and Carolina came from Kensington to Somer-
set-house, and viewed the several apartments there for
some hours. *S J.* — Her Majesty is indisposed at Kensington, having taken a great cold. *L E.*

This morning the notorious Moll Harvey, alias Mach-
eig, &c. &c. was by the Bench of Justices, at Westminster sessions, committed to the Gate-house. *S J.*
For beating a Constable. *D J.* — *Either she was not
a man, or far more than woman.*

MONDAY, July 3.

On saturday came on a cause at the Common Pleas
Court Westm. wherein Jos. Green was Plaintiff, and Jos.
Molineux, Defendant. The action was for 500 l. for criminal conversation with the Plaintiff's wife. The Plaintiff's evidence proved the fact, but the Defendant's evidence proved, that the Plaintiff's house was a reputed bawdy-house, and that some of them had carnal knowledge of
the wife and 2 of his daughters. So the Jury acquitted
the Defendant. *C.*

The same day Sir Rob. Walpole set out for his seat in
Norfolk. *C.*

TUESDAY, July 4.

On sunday his Excellency Count Degenfeldt, Envoy
from his Prussian Majesty, had his audience of leave of
his Majesty, &c. being on his return home. *C D P.*

On saturday Sir Tho. Hatton of Cambridgeshire, Bar.
was married to Mrs. Henrietta Astry, youngest daughter
of the late Sir James Astry of Bedfordshire, Knt. *P.*

Complaints having been made to the Lords Commissioners of the Admiralty of the several abuses that the
Lieutenants and their gangs received in impressing of men,
on saturday last they were pleased to send several warrants to Waterman's Hall, commanding them [the Hall]
to impress their complement. *C.* — Upon which a
great number of Watermen have retired into the country
to make hay. *C.*

We are credibly inform'd, that the estate of the late D.
of Wharton at Wooburn, is not sold, as industriously given
out; but that any fair bidder may still become a purchaser, upon offering a sufficient sum more than 24,100 l. already bid by Mr. Fonnereau. *D P.*

Last saturday night ended the Quarter Sessions for the
city and liberty of Westminster, at which Mary Millicent,
indicted for a common scold, pleaded guilty, and submitted to the mercy of the Court, who, in regard to her

having been in priſon above 10 weeks, fined her one ſhilling, and ordered her to be diſcharged. *D P.*

The Juſtices unanimouſly deſired Sir John Gonſon to continue their Chairman another year, thanked him for his very learned and excellent Charge, and deſired him for the public good to permit the ſame to be printed *D P.*

On friday Mr. Cook, walking in his warren at Northall, found 3 ſervants of a neighbouring Gentleman, who had ſhot 3 rabbits and one hare. And aſking the reaſon why they uſed him in ſuch a manner, one of them ſhot him in the thigh, ſo that his life is deſpair'd of; but being purſued, they were taken and committed to S. Alban's jail. *P.*

On ſunday died the Lady Rochley, relict of the late Lord, at her houſe in Pall-Mall. *P. DP.* — Yeſterday in the 69th year of his age, at his houſe in Great Marlborough ſtreet, Tho. Woodſtock, Eſq; firſt Commiſſioner for the duties on ſalt, ever ſince the acceſſion of K. George I. *DJ.*

The Truſtees for the Colony of Georgia are appointed in order to relieve ſuch Britiſh ſubjects as are by misfortunes rendered incapable of ſupporting themſelves and families here, and to give a ſafe and comfortable retreat to foreigners perſecuted for conſcience ſake, and to augment the number of the ſubjects of Great Britain, by preſerving of the firſt and drawing over the latter. Every perſon preſerv'd from periſhing by want, is a ſubject gain'd, as well as every foreigner, who is allur'd to ſettle in the Britiſh Dominions. The Truſtees are to facilitate the ſettling theſe people in Georgia, under a regular form of government, to grant lands there to them and their heirs for ever, to have them inſtructed and encouraged in the raiſing of raw ſilk, wine, flax, hemp, and ſuch other groſs materials as may be uſeful to the trade of England, and to prevent them from making any manufactures that may interfere with it. One and twenty noblemen and gentlemen are nam'd by the Charter as truſtees, and their number is to be augmented in March, by the addition of ſeveral others, of very great rank and diſtinction, and none of the truſtees are to have any advantage whatſoever by this deſign, except that of relieving he miſerable. *D. J.*

Laſt Thurſday John Guiſe, Eſq; Son of Sir John Guiſe, was married to Miſs Saunders, an heireſs of 40,000 l.—— On Sunday Sam. Gower, Eſq; to Miſs Anne Blake, of Soho-Square, an heireſs of 7000 l. *S J.*

Letters from Dublin ſay, that Sir Tho. Smyth of Redcliffe in Buckinghamſhire Bar. Ranger of the Park, died *there June 20. by* whoſe deceaſe an Eſtate of 300 l. per *ann. with the* dignity of a Baronet, deſcends to Sir Will. Smyth of Warden in Bedfordſhire. *S E.*

WEDNESDAY, *July* 5.

On Sunday ſe'nnight the E. of Eſſex arrived at Paris on his way to the Court of Turin, his Excellency having received great Honours thro' all the places he paſs'd.—— We hear that her grace the Dutcheſs of Buckingham hath hired a houſe for two years at Paris. *D P.*

Yeſterday about 5 in the afternoon, Mr. Abr. Fernandes Nunes, an eminent Jew of New-Broad-ſtreet, went to the Ship Tavern behind the Royal exchange, and call'd for a flaſk of French claret, intimating that he expected Company: in a quarter of an hour he rang the bell, and the Drawer found him all bloody, having ſhot himſelf with a piſtol; the ball had grazed behind his ear, and lodged in his ſhoulder, Phyſicians and Surgeons were immediately ſent for, and his wound being dreſt, he walked into his chariot and was carried home, and there are hopes of his doing well. *D J.* ——— The ſon of an eminent Jew in Billiter Square. *C.* ——— A ſon of Mr. Nunes. *DP.*

On Monday laſt a Cauſe was try'd at Doctors-Commons, concerning a Marriage pretended to be ſolemnized at an Alehouſe, between Mr. Luff, a Brewer at Weſtminſter, and a Woman with whom he was intimate; although a Fleet Clergyman ſwore he marry'd them, and a Woman depos'd ſhe was preſent, yet upon circumſtances, and conſidering the little Credit given at Law to Fleet Marriages, the ſame, upon a full and long hearing, was ſet aſide by the Judge, as ſeveral have been before. *D P.*

From the PEGASUS *in Grub-ſtreet.*

Sir,

Notwithſtanding the many curious and uſeful Memoirs which have been from time to time inſerted in your Journal, to the immortal honour of the great Mr. H—, I believe the following lines (containing a true relation) will, if you pleaſe to publiſh them, convey his name to poſterity in a light very different from any it has yet appeared in. I mean that of a Conjurer, or, as the vulgar phraſe it, A Cunning Man.

One day at a Coffee-houſe two were diſputing,
On quibbling, haranging, oppoſing, confuting,
When one of them mentioned Sir HYP-DOCTOR H—,
Affirming no Mortal did either ſo cleanly —
Says t'other, Why, faith I ſhould like him, but oft' I
Have heard, that his learning has made him ſo lofty,
He'll ſcarce condeſcend to inſtruct a poor Lay-man.
Replies Sir HYP's Friend, Never mind what they ſay man,
He anſwers — Nor is he confin'd to your ſmall ſorts,
No Sir — *He reſolves lawful Queſtions of all ſorts.*

What a glory, Mr. BAVIUS, muſt a *Reſtorer of antient Elocution*, an Univerſal Scholar, and a great Reformer of Church and State, reflect on a Science which has been ſo long diſeſteemed by the learned, tho' miſtaken part of mankind! — For my part, I ſhall from this time expect to hear of many extraordinary events before they happen, and to ſee the Papers ſtuffed with accounts of the return of ſtrayed ſilver ſpoons and porringers. Yours

DE RIPIS.

Edinburgh, June 22. This day the Lords of Juſticiary ſentenc'd Foulden, the Tobacconiſt, for an attempt to raviſh Agnes Donaldſon, to ſtand in the Pillory at Jedburgh, with a paper on his brow expreſſing his crime; after that to be whipt through the ſaid town, and baniſh'd out of the ſame for ever. *D P.* 29.

Edinburgh, June 27. We hear from Old Deer in Buchanſhire, that one Joan Johnſton, of that place, aged about 80, was lately married to her 4th huſband, a young man of 19, and after bound him Apprentice to a Wheelwright. *C. July* 4. —— She ſeems exceeding well pleaſed with him. Says, that had it not been for the many changes of huſbands ſhe has been bleſs'd with, ſhe had been long dead; and is even hopeful to get the better of this too, and try a 5th ſpouſe. *P. July* 4.

FOREIGN NEWS.

SATURDAY, *July* 1.

Yeſterday arrived the Mail from Holland.

Seville, June 13. The King has at laſt declared, that the Grand Fleet was deſigned againſt the Coaſt of Barbary; and his Majeſty has ſent the following order to the Preſident of Caſtile, viz. My intention being to retake the places in Africa which formerly belong'd to my Crown, I order you, that you cauſe public prayers to be put up in all the Churches of this Capital, to beſeech God to give good ſucceſs to this enterprize, and to ſhower down his bleſſing upon my arms. *C. P.*

MONDAY, *July* 3.

Yeſterday arrived the Mail from France.

On the 3d an extraordinary Courier arrived at Verſailles, with advice, that the Emperor had had an apoplectic fit at Carelsbad; but we hope to hear it is gone of again. *P. DJ.*

ADVERTISEMENTS.

London, July 5, 1732.

On Monday next will be publiſh'd in Folio (Tranſlated by JOHN KELLY *of the Inner Temple, Eſq;) No. 6. of*

MR. RAPIN de THOYRAS's Hiſtory of England, with Critical and Explanatory Notes; Chronological and Genealogical Tables. The Subſtance of the Propoſals a e, 1. That the Work will contain about 400 Sheets, and be finiſh'd in near two years. 2. That 4 Sheets, ſtitch'd together, be deliver'd every week at the place appointed by Subſcribers, if in Town, at the price of 6 d. Any Perſon living in the Country (by ſending a Letter, Poſt paid) may have the Sheets ſent weekly or monthly to the Carriers.

Directions are taken by J. MECHELL, Printer, at the King's Arms near Red Lion Street, High Holborn; at Joe's Coffee-houſe Mitre Court, Fleetſtreet, &c. where Propoſals at large may be had gratis. J. MECHELL.

N. B. The Demand for the Sheets already publiſh'd has been ſo great, that the firſt Impreſſion is ſold off. The reprinting them will be compleated next Week, when any Perſon may be furniſhed from the Beginning.

Note, If any Gentleman, &c has a mind to compare Mr. Knapton's *compleat* Work with what I publiſh, they may ſee both at the Printing Office as above.

WHEREAS Meſſrs John and James Knapton have aſſerted, That I have falſely computed what number of Sheets this Work will contain, and that by this means I have *drawn Gentlemen in by a ſpecious Pretence as to the Time of compleating it*, I here again ſay, That my Calculation (upon a ſecond Examination of the French Edition printed in Holland) is as near as may be; and I do ſincerely believe, was Mr. RAPIN's Hiſtory to be printed, without the Tranſlator's Notes (which cannot ſwell it to many Sheets more) it wou'd be compriz'd in the Number ſpecified. It ſhall be my conſtant Endeavour, throughout the whole, to merit the Encouragement already gain'd, and not to deviate in the leaſt from the Propoſals.

They alſo tacitly own, in the ſame Advertiſement, to have over-reach'd ſome Thouſands, by making them pay five Guineas, or more, for the very ſame Hiſtory they can now, as they ſay, afford for two: How they can anſwer this to thoſe who have already bought the Compleat 15 Vols. I know not.

Lately publiſhed,

The Second Edition, corrected,

The LAW of TITHES:

SHewing their Nature, Kinds, Properties, Incidents, by whom, when, and in what Manner payable; how, and in what Courts to be ſued for and recovered; what Things, Lands, or Perſons are charged with, or exempted therefrom. With the Nature, Incidents, and Effects of Cuſtoms, Preſcriptions, Real Compoſitions, Modus Decimandi, Libels, Suggeſtions, Prohibitions, Conſultations, Cuſtom of London, &c. Wherein all the Statutes and adjudged Caſes, relative to the Subject, are introduced and conſidered. By *William Bohun* of the Middle Temple, Eſq;

Alſo, Juſt publiſhed, by the ſame Author,

A TITHING TABLE: Shewing (by way of Analyſis) of what Things Tythes are or are not due, either by Common Law, Cuſtom, or Preſcription. Price 1 s.

N. B. Theſe two may be had bound together, or ſeparate.

Printed for J. Brotherton, W. Meadows, T. Cox, W. Hinchliffe, and R. Willock, in Cornhill; J. Hazard, near Stationers Hall; W. Bickerton, without Temple-Bar; T. Aſtley, and S. Auſten, in St. Paul's Church-yard; and L. Gilliver, in Fleet-ſtreet.

This Day was publiſhed,

THE EXAMINER examin'd: Or, An Anſwer to the Examination of the Facts and Reaſonings in the Biſhop of Chicheſter's Sermon. Part II. By a Friend to Monarchy and Epiſcopacy.

Printed for J. Roberts in Warwick-Lane. Price 1 s.

Where may be had,

The Second Edition of the Firſt Part. The Reader is deſired to correct the following Miſtake, P 44. inſtead of, *In the 4th of King James the 1ſt, the Canons, &c* Read, *In the 4th of King James the 1ſt, the Court decreed, that the Canons.*

In a few days will be publiſhed,

THE MOCK DOCTOR, or, the DUMB LADY cur'd. A Comedy. Done from *Moliere*. As it is acted at the Theatre Royal in Drury-Lane By his Majeſty's Servants Printed for J. Watts, and ſold by J. Roberts in Warwick-Lane Of whom may be had, juſt publiſhed,

The *Covent Garden Tragedy*. As it is acted at the Theatre-Royal in Drury-Lane. By his Majeſty's Servants.

The *Old Debauchees*. A Comedy. As it is acted at the Theatre-Royal in Drury-Lane

Amelia. A new Engliſh Opera. As it is perform'd at the new Theatre in the Hay-Market, after the Italian Manner. Set to Muſick by Mr. John Frederick Lampe

Acis and *Galatea*. An Engliſh Paſtoral Opera in three Acts. Set to Muſick by Mr. Handal. Price 6 d. And,

Chiron to *Achilles*. A Poem By Hildebrand Jacob, Eſq; *Res eſt ſevera Voluptas*. Price 6 d.

This Day is Publiſhed,

For the Uſe of all private Families,

THE ancient PHYSICIAN'S LEGACY to his *Country*. Being what he has collected himſelf in Forty Nine Years Practice: Or an Account of the ſeveral Diſeaſes incident to Mankind, deſcribed in ſo plain a Manner, that any Perſon may know the Nature of his own Diſeaſe Together with the ſeveral Remedies for each Diſtemper, faithfully ſet down.

Homines ad Deos, nulla in re propius accedunt, quam ſalutem hominibus dando. Cic

By THOMAS DOVER, M B.

Printed for the Author: and ſold by A Bettesworth and C. Hitch, in Pater-Noſter-Row; W. Mears at the Lamb in the Old Baily; and L. Gilliver, at Homer's Head over againſt St Dunſtan's-Church, Fleet Street.

Next Saturday will be publiſhed,

Printed on the ſame Size and Letter,

(Price Six Pence.)

AN Appendix to Bibliotheca Legum: Or, a Liſt of ſuch *Law Books* as were either omitted, or have been ſince publiſhed, giving an Account of ſeveral ſcarce and uncommon Law Tracts. Many of which were publiſhed between the Years 1450 and 1660 with their Dates and Price. To which is added, uſeful to Practiſers of the Law, a new and compleat Liſt of all the Law Books extant (from Mag. Cha. to Trinity Term 1732.) wherein is contain'd many ENGLISH Precedents, giving an Account of their different Editions, Dates and Price.

Compil'd by JOHN WORRAL, and ſold by him at the Dove in Bell-yard near Lincoln's Inn.

Of whom may be had lately purchaſed, and will be ſold cheap, Statutes at large, 5 Vols. curiouſly bound in Ruſſia. ——— Statutes as publiſhed in Seſſions for the 9th, 10th, 11th, 12, 13th, of King George I. and 1ſt, 2d, 3d, 4th, and 5th of King George II Large Paper compleat.——— Year-Books with Maynard's Edward II compleat beſt Edition.— Rolle's and Danver's Abridgments.— Anderſon's, Carthew's, Croke's, Hardreſs's, Hobarts, Jones's, (Sir William and Sir Thomas) Keble's, Leving's, Lutwyche's, Plowden's, Shower's Reports, beſt Editions.

Bird's and Bridgman's Conveyances. Brownlow's, Hanvard's, Leving's, Raſtal's, Violiar's, Winch's, and other Entries. ——— Coke's Inſtitutes beſt. Alſo a great Number of ſcarce Miſcellanies, and all new Law-Books as ſoon as publiſhed.

THE GRUB-STREET JOURNAL, 131, p. 4

June 12, 1732.

By PERMISSION of

The Right Honourable the Lord Chancellor.
The Right Honourable the Lord Raymond, Lord Chief Justice on his Majesty's Court of King's Bench.
The Right Honourable Arthur Onslow, Esq; Speaker of the House of Commons.
The Honourable Sir John Hind Cotton, Bart.
Francis Annesley, Esq;
Samuel Burroughs, Esq; one of the Masters of the High Court of Chancery.
John Hanbury, Esq;

Trustees of the Cottonian Library.

IT is proposed by *John Pine*, to Engrave, by Subscription, a Correct Copy of King JOHN's *Great Charter*, taken from the Original now remaining in the *Cottonian* library; which, being a Recognition of the Rights and Liberties of the people, it is presumed the Publick will encourage a Design to perpetuate a Record of such Dignity and Importance.

It will be contained in one Imperial Sheet of Paper, and engraved in the same Form and Character with the Original, and adorned with proper Decorations.

The Price to Subscribers will be Half a Guinea; to be paid on the Delivery, which will be about Christmas next.

Those Gentlemen, who are willing to encourage this Subscription, are desired to send their Names and Places of Abode as soon as possible, which will entitle them to the first Impressions.

N. B. Those who subscribe for Six, shall have a Seventh *gratis*.

Subscriptions are taken in by C. King, in Westminster-Hall; N. Prevost, in the Strand; R. Gosling, B. Motte, T. Woodward, near the Temple, Fleet-street; W. Innys, C. Rivington, S. Austen, in St. Paul's Church-Yard; A. Bettesworth and C. Hitch J. Batley, in Pater-Noster-Row; W. Hinchliffe, E. Symons, at the Royal-Exchange; J. Brindley, in New Bond-Street; J. Clark, Print-seller in Gray's-Inn; and J. Pine, Engraver, over-against Little-Britain, in Aldersgate-Street.

This Day was published,
The Fifth Edition, of

A Journey from ALEPPO to Jerusalem, at Easter, A. D. 1697. To which is added, An Account of the Author's Journey to the Banks of Euphrates and the Peer, and to the County of Mesopotamia By *Henry Maundrel*, M. A. late Fellow of Exeter-College, and Chaplain o the Factory at Aleppo.

Oxford, printed at the Theatre for Anthony Peisly; and sold by J. Brotherton, W Meadows, T. Cox, W. Hinchliffe, and R. Willock, in Cornhill; J. Hazard, near station is Hall; W. Bickerton, without Temple-Bar; I. Astley, and S. Austen, in St. Paul's Church-yard; and L. Gilliver in Fleet-street.

Of whom may be had,
Dr. TRAPP's Sermons at Lady Moyer's Lecture on the Doctrine of the TRINITY, with the Objections against it answered in a summary View of the whole Controversy. To which are added, Discourses on the Parable of Dives and Lazarus; setting forth the deplorable Corruption, Immorality and Infidelity of the present Age: Shewing the absolute Necessity of a Holy Life; demonstrating the Certainty of a Future State, and the Truth of the Christian Religion.

July 6. 1732.
Lately publish'd the First Volume, and this Day is publish'd,

THE Second Volume of a select Collection of MOLIERE's Comedies, in French and English. This Collection will consist of eight Pocket-Volumes; one Volume to be publish'd every Month, till the Collection be completed.

The Translation is entirely new, and was undertaken by several Gentlemen, who all join'd and consulted together about every Part of it. Particular Care has been had to keep as close as possible to the Original, and to observe the very Words of the Author as well as his Sense, so far as was consistent with giving a spirited and easy Comick Stile, in order to make it the more serviceable to those of our own Nation who are Learners of the French Language; as likewise to Foreigners who desire to be acquainted with our so: To whom the Method we have taken of placing the French and English opposite to each other, will be of no small Benefit. The Work will be printed in a very beautiful manner, and adorn'd with new Frontispieces, design'd by Mr. HOGARTH. Price of each Volume, done up in blue Covers, will be Two Shillings and Six-pence. Printed for and sold by J Watts at the Printing-Office in Wild-Court, near Lincoln's-Inn Fields: And J. Brotherton in Cornhill; A. Bettesworth and C. Hitch in Pater-noster-row; J. Roberts in Warwick-lane; J Pemberton, and T Worral, in Fleet-street; P Dunoyer in the Strand; J Stagg in Westminster-Hall; and J. Brindley in New Bond-street.

N. B. The Third Volume will be publish'd on Wednesday the 19th Day of this Instant July, and the Fourth Volume on Thursday the 10th Day of August next; and the Collection will be compleated with all convenient Speed.

On Monday last was published,
The LONDON MAGAZINE:
Or, GENTLEMAN's *Monthly Intelligencer.*
NUMB. III. For JUNE, 1732.
To be Continued. *(Price Sixpence each Month.)*
CONTAINING,

(Greater Variety, and more in Quantity, than any MONTHLY BOOK extant.)

I. A View of the WEEKLY ESSAYS, *viz.* On Poetry; Painting; Modern Taste; scheme to prevent Marriage Complaints; two Sorts of Avarice; a Vision, occasion'd by the Ridotto al Fresco; true Spirit of Popery; a Rebuke to those who villify the Germans; the just Monarch; Vindication of Lord Shaftsbury; Character of Horatio Walpole, Esq; English Queens.

II. Political Subjects, viz. the Use and Abuse of Power; Excellency of Knowledge in a State; Sir William Temple on popular Discontents; Practices of the Pretender and his Agents in relation to the Charitable Corporation, and Remarks on the Free Briton upon that Subject; State of the Pretender's Hopes and Interest here; Reflections on the Examiner of Bp. Hare's Sermon; Craftsman's Sketch of bad Ministers, and Memorandums to him thereupon; Mr. Osbourne censur'd of governing by one Minister; good Ministers; Disputes on the Salt-Tax, Land-Tax, and a general Excise; the least burdensome Way of raising Taxes; the Lord's Protests; State of the National Debt; Speaker's Thanks to Lord Gage; and Reply, &c.

III. Poetry: The Queen Regent; Description of Love; Description of Anger; Lady's Dressing-Room, by D. S——t; Epigrams.

IV. Domestick Occurrences: Promotions Ecclesiastical, Civil and Military; Marriages and Births; Deaths; Acts pass'd; Affairs of the S—— Company; King's going Abroad, &c.

V. Foreign Affairs.

VI. Price of Goods, Grain, Stocks, Monthly Bill of Mortality.

VII. A Table of Contents
To which is added, A Catalogue of Books and Pamphlets, with their Prices, published by the Proprietors of the *Monthly Chronicle*, now dis-continued.

MULTUM IN PARVO.

LONDON: Printed for C Ackers in St. John's-Street, For J. Wilford behind the Chapter-house near St. Paul's; and sold by S. Madowe, T. Cox, W Hinchliffe, W. Whitridge, R. Willock, and E Nutt in Cornhill; J Clarke in Duck-lane; T Astley in St. John's Church-Yard; A. Dodd without Temp'-Bar; J. Stagg in Westminster-hall; J. Jackson in Pall-Mall; J. Brindley in St. Shropshire in Cornhill; and J. Milan in the Admiralty-Office.

Where may be had, the former Numbers.

BOOKS printed for, and sold by J. Brotherton, at the Bible next the Fleece Tavern, in Cornhill.

Whitock's Memorials Temple's Works, 2 Vol.	Telemachus, by Boyer. Ditto in French.
Bailey's Eng Dict, Fol	Guardians, 2 Vol.
Tillotson's Works, 3 Vol.	Langham's Duties.
Bates's Works, Fol.	Free Thoughts on Religion
State of Britain, for 1732.	Ia Bell Assemble, 3 Vol.
Bailey's Justin.	Vanburgh's Plays, 2 Vol.
Origin of Honour.	Addison's Works, 4 Vol.
Ladies Conduct.	Spectators, 8 Vol.
Virgin unmask'd	Trapp's Virgil.
Hays's Ship and Supercargo	D'Urfey's Songs, 6 Vol.
Boyle's K eper.	Milton Lost and Regain'd
Coke's Detection, 3 Vol.	D'Anois Tales, 1 Vol.
Bohun's Law of Tythes.	De Retz Memoirs, 4 Vol
Feasts & Fasts of the Church.	Tom Brown's Works, 4 Vol.
Erasmii Ecclesiastica	Farnborough's Grammar.
Life of Oliver Cromwell.	Philips's Grammar.
Life of the K. of Sweden	Derrington's D votion.
Dampier's Journal to Madagascar.	Congreve's Plays, 2 Vol.
Rapin's Hist. of England, 15 Vol.	Pope and Swift Misc. Vol. Pope's Misc. 2 Vol.
Arbuthnot of Aliments, com	Turkish Spy, 8 Vol.

This Day was published,

AN ODE to his Grace the Duke of Newcastle. Written on the present Tranquillity of Europe, establish'd by the Influence of the British Power.

Nihil habet aut Fortuna tua majus, quàm ut possis, aut Natura tua melius, quàm, ut velis, quàm plurimos conservare. Cic.

Printed for J. Batley, at the Dove in Pater-Noster-Row. Price 6 d.

Where may had, just published,
Dedicated to the Gentlemen of the Navy of England,
The Memoirs of Monsieur DU GUE TROUIN, Chief of a Squadron of the Royal Navy of France, and Great Cross of the Military Order of St. Lewis; containing all his Sea-Actions with the English, Dutch, and Portuguese, in the late Wars of King William and Queen Anne.

Translated from the French by a *Sea-Officer*.

July 3, was published, Price 6 d.
Neatly printed on a fine Dutch Paper.

THE GENTLEMAN's MAGAZINE: Or, *Monthly Intelligencer.*

No XVIII. for June, 1732. being the Sixth of Volume II. Containing more in Quantity, and greater Variety than any Book of the Kind and Price.

I. Views of the Weekly Essays, viz. The Quaker's Plea; a critique on Poetry and Painting; Ridotto al Fresco, humorously and satyrically described; Bp. Hare and Lord Shaftsbury vindicated; Deism and Christianity; a Remedy for conjugal Unhappiness and popular Discontents; Observations on Trade and Masquerades; the Mischiefs of Dancing; K. of Sweden's Life; of Restitution; Antiquities at York

II. Political Points, viz. The Affair of Belloni (or the Pretender and his Agents) Thomson's Proposals; Mr. Arbuthnot's Letters, and Remarks on the Whole; Of Ministers, Councils, &c. Disputes on the Salt and Land-Tax; King William's Statue; King's Speech; Lords Protests; State of the National Debts; Speaker's Thanks to Lord Gage, his Lordship's Answer, &c.

III. Political Pieces, viz. The Ladies Dressing-Room, and Poor Parson's Prayer, b. Dr. Swift; Verses on the 10th of June; from New-England, Spring Gardens, &c.

IV. Domestic Occurrences, Births, Deaths, Marriages, Promotions, Proceedings of the S Sea Gen. Court, &c.

V. Prices of Goods, Grain, Stocks, Monthly Bill of Mortality.

VI. Foreign Affairs.

VII. A Table of Contents.
With a Register of Books and Pamphlets.

By SYLVANUS URBAN, *Gent.*

Note, a few are printed on a fine Royal Paper, large Margin, for the Curious.

Printed and sold at St. John's Gate, by Fr. Jefferies in Ludgate-Street, and the Booksellers in Town and Country. (Price 6 d.) Where may be had the former Numbers, from January last, that being now reprinted, as well as Numb. XVI. for April last. The 6 Numbers which were wanting of the first Volume, are in the Press again (some a third time) and will speedily be publish'd to compleat Gentlemen's Setts.

An exact List of Parliament as it now stands, with the proper Distinctions, and a curious Table of the Bishops, shewing their Promotions, Successions and Translations, at one View.

This Day was published,
(Beautifully printed in One Volume, Octavo.)

A Treatise of continual FEVERS, in four Parts. To which are added, Medicinal Observations, in Three Books; wherein are enumerated, the Diagnosticks, Prognosticks, and Events of the several Diseases incident to Human Bodies. By JODOCUS LOMMIUS.

Translated from the Latin by THOMAS DALE, M.D.
Printed for J. Brotherton, W Meadows, T. Cox, W. Hinchliffe, and R. Willock, in Cornhill; J. Hazard near Stationers-Hall; W. Bickerton without Temple-Bar; T. Astley and S. Austen in St. Paul's Church-Yard; and L. Gilliver in Fleet-Street.

The Celestial Anodyne Tincture: Or, The Great Pain-Easing Medicine,

LONDON: Printed by J. HUGGONSON, in Bartholomew-Close, for Captain GULLIVER, near the Temple, where Letters and Advertisements are taken in: As also at the Rainbow Coffee-House in Cornhill, and John's Coffee-House in Sheer-Lane, near Temple-Bar. [Price Two Pence.]

The Grub-ſtreet Journal.

NUMB. 132

Thurſday, *JULY* 13, 1732.

Shall we, you cry, learn writing ill by Rule;
And have we need to ſtudy to be dull?
Harlequin-Horace, pag. 35.

To Mr. BAVIUS, Secretary of the Society of Grub ſtreet.
Monday, June the 26th, 1732.

SIR,

I HAVE juſt dipt into a monthly *thing* called The *Comedian*, or *Philoſophical Enquirer*: in which the Author, who ſeems very deſirous to be thought an *acquaintance of perſons of ſuperior rank*, as well as a man of a conſiderable ſhare of underſtanding, has attacked me for ſome reflections on *The Modern Husband*.

As I never publiſh any thing but what I think right, (not having any view of intereſt to anſwer which might oblige me to write) I was rather ſurprized, than concerned, at an attack from ſo unexpected a quarter. And indeed, were it not for the contempt, which from the height of his underſtanding, he inſolently beſtows on those he quarrels with, I ſhould have taken no manner of notice of him, nor drawn him from the peaceful ſtate of obſcurity, in which he lies, from one month to another, by placing him in ſo conſpicuous a light, as he will henceforth appear in, by being known to be an oppoſer of the GRUBEANS.

Under an article which he calls † *Reflections on ſome modern Plays*, he tells us, he made a viſit lately to a Yorkſhire Gentleman juſt come to town, who told him, that ſome perſons, who lived in the Country, and himſelf among the reſt, could not believe, that ſeveral Plays printed within theſe 3 years, had ever been really acted; and therefore they looked upon them to be no other than impoſitions of the Bookſellers upon their cuſtomers in the country. He inſtanced in *Timoleon, Periander, Medea, George Barnwell, Injured Innocence, Sylvia* or *The Country Burial, The Devil to pay*, and a long catalogue of rubbiſh. (This, by the way, I conceive is what he means by *Reflections on ſome modern Plays*; for I don't find in the whole article any other *reflection* on them: nay, our Author expreſly declares he had been *neither a ſpectator nor reader of any of them*.) Upon this our *Comedian* mentioned *The Modern Husband*, as not liable to the cenſure which our Yorkſhire Critic had paſſed upon the reſt. This Comedy, the Gentleman owns, ‡ 'gave him pleaſure, tho' 'it is not entirely conformable to the rules of the Drama.'

From the mention of the rules of the Drama, our Philoſophical Critic takes an opportunity to talk in the following moſt profound, unintelligible manner about Plays, and the rules for writing them. 'By the rules of the 'Drama, ſays I, you mean, I preſume, the rules of Critics, who have no right to impoſe rules: the antient 'writers of Tragedy and Comedy divided their Plays into five Acts, in which we have generally followed their 'example; and I know no other ſtated rule to be obſerved, and that may be departed from ſometimes without any diſadvantage.' —— Thus, Mr. BAVIUS, there is no rule to be obſerved in writing of Plays, but to divide them into five Acts, and even that rule may be departed from: ſo that in fact there is no rule at all abſolutely neceſſary to be obſerved. What direction then is a Poet to follow in compoſing a Dramatical Piece? Why, —'Unerring reaſon is the only guide in Tragedy and 'Comedy, tho' a man, who is merely a reaſonable man, 'and no more, is not qualified to write either, particular 'talents being requiſite for both, under the conduct of 'reaſon; and that Poet who wants any other rule, beſides nature or reaſon, miſtakes his province when he 'attempts to write.' If *unerring reaſon is the only guide in Tragedy and Comedy*, it is no wonder that we have ſo many bad ones: nay, I fear it is impoſſible that there ſhould be a good one, of either kind. For what Poet ever had this guide; which muſt make him as infallible in poetry, as the old Gentleman at Rome pretends to be in religion? But it ſeems a merely *reaſonable man and no more*, tho' he has this *unerring reaſon, is not qualified to write*, becauſe *particular talents are requiſite under the conduct of* [this unerring] *reaſon*. By theſe *talents*, I ſuppoſe, he means invention, wit, humour, &c. which a man who wants cannot write a Play: but no other rule is neceſſary beſides nature or [unerring] reaſon: ſo that nature and *unerring reaſon* are the ſame. Now the whole meaning of this ſublime period, if it has any, is no more than this, That a man of good ſenſe without a genius cannot write a Play; and that *nature or reaſon* is the only guide which a Dramatic Poet is to follow. But how does this ſet aſide the rules of the Critics? which I affirm are agreeable to nature or reaſon, and conſequently, according to this Author's own conceſſion, ought to be obſerved.

He then goes on: '*The Modern Husband* I acknow'ledge to have ſome ſcenes independent on the main buſineſs of the Play, and ſome expreſſions, the omiſſion of 'which would be no detriment to the work; yet it has 'wit, humour, ſatire, and moral reflections in it, not un'worthy the pen of the beſt Stoic. If indeed the Author 'had made every ſcene conducive to the principal deſign, 'to the plot of the Play, and as dependent one on the 'other as every link in a chain, and every expreſſion as 'neceſſary as every ſcene, he would have produced a 'more perfect piece than it now is: and I doubt not but 'that he who is capable of writing ſo entertaining a Play 'as it now * is, is ingenuous enough to confeſs theſe truths, 'and to acknowledge that his intent was to expoſe par'ticular vices and follys, to make theſe ridiculous, and 'thoſe odious, to give his audience pleaſure, and himſelf 'profit, and that he had not leiſure to make it other'wiſe than it now is, and that he laughs without anger 'at thoſe who expoſe themſelves by a truitleſs endeavour 'to expoſe him.' This is to ſay, *The Modern Husband* is defective in the principal conſtituents of a good Play, but has ſome very entertaining things in it, (at leaſt the Comedian tells us ſo) which make amends for the want of the reſt: ſo that all things conſidered, the Author's *want of leiſure*, not ability, to make it better; *his intent* of giving *pleaſure to his audience* and *profit to himſelf*; his *ingenuity to confeſs theſe truths, his intent to expoſe particular vices and follys, in order to make theſe ridiculous and thoſe odious*; all this put together plainly proves, what the *Philoſophical Comedian* undertook, which was to ſhew, that this Play *was not liable to the cenſure*, which his Yorkſhire friend had *paſſed upon the reſt*, which he owns he himſelf had neither ſeen, nor read, and conſequently muſt be a very proper perſon to make *reflections upon modern Plays*, and to give one the preference before all the others. As to the Author's *laughing without anger at thoſe who expoſe themſelves by a fruitleſs endeavour to expoſe him*, I have received an account of a tranſaction at a certain Bookſeller's ſhop near Temple-bar, which directly contradicts this: for there two celebrated Captains quarrelled about this affair, and were likely to have come to blows; at which it was thought the Bookſeller, as uſual, would have had the advantage of the Tragedian.

Upon the whole, I think, Mr. BAVIUS, till this *Philoſophical Comedian*, or *Comical Philoſopher*, or his friend the Author of *The Modern Husband*, or Mr. *Wm. Hirt*, the Candle ſnuffer, ſhall be more explicit in their juſtification of this Play, I may even ſit down without anger, and content myſelf with referring them once more to *the Grub-ſtreet Journal*, No. 117. without giving myſelf any further trouble to defend a Paper which has been ſo lamely attacked by this Dramatical *Enquirer*.

This Gentleman, who has ſo ſhort a memory that he could not, or was ſo ill natured that he would not, tell his country friend the name of that *paultry weekly Journal* he mentioned to him, concludes very affirmatively that 'The *ignorant thing*, viz. DRAMATICUS, diſcovered 'himſelf to have no notion of humour, and that his con'verſation was not among perſons of ſuperior rank, eſpe'cially the Ladies.' But how has he made this diſcovery of himſelf? Why, becauſe he had queſtioned whether there are any real Lady CHARLOTTES in the world; and therefore he *can't be ſuppoſed to have any notion of humour*, or *converſation with Ladies of ſuperior rank*. A pretty genteel compliment, upon my word, for which the *Ladies of ſuperior rank* he frequents, are infinitely obliged to him. Inſtead of anſwering ſuch a ridiculous ſurmiſe, or giving him a liſt of the Ladies of my acquaintance, I muſt once more beg leave to ſay, that I both believe and hope, that there is no ſuch character among the Ladies as Lady CHARLOTTE; and as for the *Comedian's young Lady that came in* while he was in converſation with his Yorkſhire friend, if ſhe is a real perſon, ſhe clearly proves the truth of what I advanced in that Paper about Lady CHARLOTTE, viz. *that ſuch Ladies as anſwer this character can never be cured*. I am, Mr. BAVIUS, your moſt humble ſervant,

DRAMATICUS.

† *Numb.* 111. *Pag.* 11, 12. ‡ *Pag.* 13

* *Pag.* 14.

THE preceding letter occaſioned me to look into the monthly Pamphlet to which it relates; and in the firſt place I read the Article intitled *Reflections upon ſome modern Plays*: which I found to conſiſt only of one general *reflection* upon ſeven (which our *Comedian* had neither ſeen nor read,) as being *ſtuff, indigeſted traſh*, and *nonſenſe*, and of a few lines in defence of *The Modern Husband*. In the very beginning of theſe learned Reflections I ſtopped at theſe words, 'I wonder why the ma'nagers of the Theatres will ſuffer themſelves to be abu'ſed, in ſuch a manner, by the *chicane* of the book'ſellers' I caſt my eye back, to ſee in what manner the book-ſellers had employed this chicane; and found them charged with putting in the title pages of Plays, *As it is acted at the Theatre Royal*, &c. when no ſuch Play had been ever acted. I always took *chicane* to ſignify originally any captious ſubtlety or quirk made uſe of to delay the determination of a ſuit at law: from whence it has been applied to a ſophiſtical way of diſputing merely for diſputation's ſake. That book-ſellers may uſe *chicane*, as well as perſons of any other profeſſion, is certainly very true; but, I believe, this is the firſt time that the inſerting of a lye in a title page, (a thing very frequently done) has been called *chicane* by a learned Critic. However two things may be layed in his vindication. He puts this word in the mouth of a *Yorkſhire Gentleman juſt come to Town*, perhaps about a tedious law-ſuit; who might either not know the meaning of it, or might ſtrike the Lawyers obliquely, while he levelled directly at the bookſellers. But I rather think our COMEDIAN uſed this word thus, as a proof of his *converſation among perſons of ſuperior rank, eſpecially the Ladies*, ſome of whom, it is probable, might apply it in this manner, ſince he expreſly tells us, he *has met with ſome who partake of a volubility of talking nonſenſe*.

When I had gone through the Critical Article, I turned back to the Philoſophical, which is the firſt: wherein I found this Philoſopher as dogmatical in *laying down rules to diſtinguiſh truth from falſehood* in Theology, as in Poetry. He there places himſelf *in cathedra*, and from the infallibility of his own *unerring Reaſon* delivers the following oracle * 'When we are told of wonder-wo'rking men, performing miracles contrary to the nature 'of things, to the known ſyſtem of creation, and of the 'reſurrection of others from the dead, and their aſcenſion 'into heaven, the reports deſtroy the credit of the firſt 'reporters in the opinion of all reaſonable men [meaning 'ſuch only, who having *unerring Reaſon* think as he 'does] and when we are told of cruel, partial, penitent, 'fickle, ſuffering, and bleeding Gods, the wiſe, the honeſt, 'and pious man, [which none can be in his opinion un'leſs he think like him] is like to weep for the ſins of the 'impoſtors, while he ſmiles at the credulity of weak be'lievers. In whatever books, and by whatever men, 'tales of theſe kinds are told, they ſhould be regarded as 'impious and abominable fictions, and derogatory from 'the honour of God. *Page* 10'

To atone for this blaſphemous ſatire upon Jeſus Chriſt and his religion, he gives us in the third article a fulſome panegyric upon a Great man and his adminiſtration: which that honourable Gentleman will no doubt ſcorn to receive from his pen, if he knows it to have been drawn againſt that Divine Perſon, whom, at his entrance upon his many high employments, he has ſo often acknowledged in the moſt ſolemn act of religious worſhip

BAVIUS.

SIR,

AN ingenious and learned Writer has lately informed us, 'that both in Athens and Rome the Stage was 'an engine of the State; that the wiſeſt Stateſmen have 'eſteemed it of admirable uſe in amuſing the people, and 'keeping them from too ſtrict an enquiry into Politics and 'Religion; and that formerly if ever Players meddled 'with Politics it was in favour of the power governing.' He then complains, 'that ſome pragmatical Players of the 'preſent age, forgetting both their duty and intereſt, 'have under pretext of declaiming at vice in general ex'hibited ſtate lampoons;' but, in the concluſion, aſſures us, that 'the conduct of thoſe in Drury-lane has been as 'decent as the general licentiouſneſs of the age would ad'mit of.' In confirmation of the *decent conduct* of thoſe

* See *Daily Courant* of *May* 9.

Gentlemen, I think it will be of ſome ſervice, Mr. BAVIUS, to produce a famous inſtance of a Comedy, or rather a Farce, lately acted ſeveral times by them, called the *O'd Debauchees*.

The ſtory of Father GIRARD and Miſs CADIERE had been treated with great variety, both in proſe and verſe; and yielded a comfortable ſubſiſtence to ſeveral of your Members during the laſt winter. At the ſame time the Drawers and Engravers went to work upon it, and exhibited ſeveral lively pictures to the view of all perſons who paſſed the ſtreets. When the ſubject ſeemed quite exhauſted, and the diſcourſe about it was almoſt ceaſed, a Gentleman of a ſurprizing genius wrought it into a Play, under the title mentioned above, and brought it upon the Stage with ſucceſs. I may take another opportunity to point out the ſeveral beauties of this Piece; at preſent I ſhall only take notice of the principal deſign, and ſhew how happily it has been executed. — The principal deſign is to expoſe the Clergy: and, ſince in opinion of all wiſe and honeſt men, they are the teachers of ſuch doctrines as tend to introduce popery and arbitrary power, can there poſſibly be a more juſtifiable deſign? —— Nor has the manner of executing it been liable to the leaſt cenſure, the Author having employed no other weapon againſt them but the keeneſt wit, and treated them with all the good manners and politeneſs imaginable: of which the following inſtances are an evident demonſtration.

O'd LAROON, before he knows any thing of the villainy of *Father* MARTIN, ſays to him, 'It were happy for ſuch 'Raſcals as you, Sirrah, &c.' *pag.* 23. calls him 'a roguiſh 'Prieſt.' *p.* 34. 'a raſcal. *p.* 35. ſays he has ſeen 'a 'damn'd rogue of a Prieſt riding an old honeſt whore-'maſter to the Devil.' *p.* 10. and under a curſe declares, 'I'll carbonade the villain: I'll make a ragout for the De-'vil's ſupper of him. *ibid.*'

JORDAIN ſays, 'I once committed a Prieſt to New-'gate for picking pockets.' *p.* 12.

All this indeed particularly relates to one Prieſt; but that which follows ſtrikes in general at the whole order. *Old* LAROON ſays, 'Peace cannot ſtay long in any place 'where a Prieſt comes. *p.* 5. Judgment cannot be far 'off when a Prieſt is near. *p.* 23. I no more rely on 'what a Woman ſays out of a Church, than on what a 'Prieſt ſays in. *p.* 10.' To *Father* MARTIN, 'Exert 'thy ſelf in thy proper office, and hold the door. *p.* 23. 'Thou art the Devil's footman, and weareſt his proper 'livery. *p.* 22. Death and the Devil, another Prieſt. *p.* 16. 'You are poſſeſſed with a Prieſt, and that's worſe:' [than being poſſeſs'd with the Devil.] *p.* 21. The Prieſts in general are called, wild beaſts. *p.* 36. a ſet of dirty Prieſts. '*p.* 2. of greaſy Prieſts. *p.* 25. of raſcally Prieſts *p.* 4. of 'black locuſts. *p.* 23. and a regiment of black guards. *p.* 10.

You may imagine perhaps, Mr. BAVIUS, that much the greateſt part of this fine language being ſpoken by *Old* LAROON, a vicious character, and only of the Popiſh Clergy, it can have but very little efficacy in expoſing ours. But there are two maxims which you are to take as a key to the whole: That whatever ſcandalous thing is ſaid of a Prieſt, you are to regard only what is ſpoken, and not the perſon who ſpeaks it: and That

Prieſts of all religions are the ſame.

Yours MISO-CLEROS.

EPIGRAM.

To young K— quoth F——, I pity thy caſe,
On the Stage oft obliged to wear a falſe face.
In poor BARNWELL's repentance don't ſtrain on a mask:
Be LOVEGIRLO thy much more agreeable task:
Follow nature: and never by Parſons be flamm'd:
Thou know'ſt, as LOVEGIRLO, what 'tis to be damn'd.

D.V.

DOMESTIC NEWS.

C. *Courant.*	E P. *Evening Poſt.*
P. *Poſt-Boy.*	S J. *S. James's Evening Poſt.*
D P. *Daily Poſt.*	WE. *Whitehall Evening P.*
D J. *Daily Journal.*	LE. *London Evening Poſt.*

Important Articles omitted in our laſt.

Hyp-Oratorical Puffs and Advertiſements in the month of June.

Hyp Advertiſements 4. Oratorical ditto 5. In all 9.
Hyp Puffs 7. Oratorical ditto 3. In all 10.
Decreaſed in the Advertiſements this month 2.
Increaſed in the Puffs 2.

We hear the laſt Hyp-Doctor is thought unanſwerable, and of greater ſervice than any thing written for the Government. *D J. June* 14.

This Puff was put in by the Hyp-Doctor We Hear,
For double front famous, and double character.

THURSDAY, *July* 6.

Yeſterday his Excellency Count Degenſeldt, Envoy from the King of Pruſſia, ſet out for Hanover. *C.* —— Yeſterday his Lady was ſafely deliver'd of a ſon, the Count has deferr'd his departure for a few days. *P.*

A Patent is paſſing for Sir James Thornhill to be Serjeant Painter to his Majeſty of all his Royal Palaces and edifices, ſhips of war, &c. *D J.* —— This Patent was granted to his ſon. *D J.* 8.

We hear from Hockley in Hampſhire, that Mrs. Hawkley of that place, aged 103, having been blind 11 years, after ſhe was turned of 100, recover'd her ſight in a moſt miraculous manner; that ſhe can now read without the help of ſpectacles, is in good health, and can walk for 2 or 3 miles together, which exerciſe ſhe daily uſes after dinner. *C.* —— *This* Engliſh *Gentlewoman has a more real* ſecond ſight *than any* Scotch.

Mr. Nunes who ſhot himſelf died yeſterday. *C.* —— The Surgeons have hopes of his recovery. *D P.* Is in a fair way of recovery. *D. P.* 12.

Mr. Rob. Manning is made Secretary to the Commiſſioners for the Land-tax. *LE.* — We hear that there are 11 Candidates for the place of Commiſſioner for the ſalt duties, in the room of Tho. Woodcock, Eſq; deceaſed. *S J. L E.*—Some ſay 3 times that number. *Craftſman*, 8.

Cambridge, July 4. Commencers this day: 8 Doctors, and 86 Maſters of Arts — Dr. Gretton of Trin. College, Dr. Webſter of Caius, Dr. Gouge of Katharine Hall, Doctors of Divinity. —— Dr. Brook of Queen's, Doctor of Civil Law. —— Dr. Sunber of Caius, Dr. Bateman of Queen's, Dr. Reeve of Emanuel, Dr. Brent of Katherine Hall, Doctors of Phyſic. *P.*

On ſaturday died at Abbots Langley, in Hertfordſhire, in his 54th year, Nath. Sheppard, Eſq; one of the chief Projectors of the late Sir Rich. Steel's Fiſh pool ſcheme. *S J.*

FRIDAY, *July* 7.

Several artificers are daily employed in repairing and beautifying the late Count Bothmar's houſe, near the Treaſury Office in S. James's Park, for the reception of R. Hon. Sir Rob. Walpole, which his Majeſty made him a preſent of ſome time ſince. *P.*

Yeſterday the Royal Society m[illegible] according to cuſtom, and adjourned their further meeting [illegible] 26th of October next. *P.*

A magnificent chair of ſtate, of [illegible] gilt with gold, for the throne of the Empreſs of Ruſſia, is juſt finiſhed, by a German artiſt, and ſo richly chaſed, that the workmanſhip is not much leſs expenſive than the ſilver, which amounts to 1900 ounces. On the top of the chair is an Imperial crown, and on the back part a ſpread eagle holding a ſceptre, and other emblems. *D J.*

Laſt week the Rev. Dr. Croxall was preferr'd to the Archdeaconry of Salop. *D J.*

Laſt night was interr'd at Chelſea Church Narciſſus Luttrell, Eſq; he was well known to the Curious for his large and valuable collection of books, now remaining in that very ſtudy where the late Earl of Shaftſbury and Mr. Locke compoſed many of their learned productions. *D P.*

Dover, July 5. Her Grace the Dutcheſs of Buckingham is pretty well recover'd at Boulogne; her ſon the Duke is with her, and we expect them both very ſoon. *P.*

On June 28, Nic. Philpot, Eſq; formerly Member of Parl. for Weobly in Herefordſhire, was found ſhot dead thro' the temples in his own gardens at Newton Hall near Hereford; he lay ſtretched on his back, with his arms extended, and a piſtol in his right hand: the Coroners Inqueſt brought in their verdict, *Lunacy. C.*

On wedneſday died Mr. Dav. Boſanquet, Sen. a Turky merchant, reputed worth upwards of 100,000 l. *C. D P.* Near 100,000 l. *D J.* —— Yeſterday at the Lord Bruce's ſeat at Tottenham Foreſt, within 2 miles of Marlborough, the R. Hon. Earl of Cardigan: he has left 2 ſons and 2 daughters. *D P.*

Chriſten'd { M. 157. F. 172. }	329.	Between 40 and 50	26
Bury'd { M. 157.		50 and 60	30
Incr. B. 31 { F. 172. }	359.	60 and 70	22
Died under 2 years old	146	70 and 80	13
Between 2 and 5	21	80 and 90	3
5 and 10	16	90 and 100	7
10 and 20	12	Drowned 1 in a ditch, and 2 in the Thames. Drinking 2. Aged 23. Convulſ. 109. Fever 33. Small pox 25. *P.*	
20 and 30	26		
30 and 40	37		

Yeſterday a ſoldier was whipt on the parade,
For *exerciſing in private the plundering trade.* DJ.

SATURDAY, *July* 8.

The Daniſh Dwarf, ſo much admir'd at Court, is taken into the ſervice of his R. Highneſs the Prince, who has put him in the dreſs of a Polander. *D P.*

On wedneſday his Majeſty's plate of 100 l. guineas was won at Nottingham by a horſe of Watkins Williams Wynne, Eſq; *P.*

The Court of Aldermen have not admitted any perſon into the place of Keeper of Newgate, and we are aſſured they will not ſuffer any perſon to hold it longer than his conduct ſhall render him agreeable to them. *D J.* —— *This is a proper way* of keeping the keepers.

On thurſday at a general Court of the York Buildings Company, it was reſolved, that no new bonds be created but by the conſent of a general Court; that 3 Gentlemen of the Proprietors be joined with the Governor and Directors as Truſtees for the cuſtody of the ſeal; and then they adjourned to the 19th. *C.*

On wedneſday night one Allen, a Poulterer at Tottenham Court, dreaming that he was purſued by robbers, unfortunately got out of bed, and jump'd out of his window 2 ſtories high in his ſleep, by which one of his legs was broke, and his body much bruiſed. *D P.* —— *I think he* jump'd *very* fortunately, *ſince he did not* break his neck.

Sir Char. Wager, Vice Admiral of the Red, is made Admiral of the Blue. —— Sir Geo. Walton Vice Admiral of the Red. —— Salmon Morris, Eſq; Vice Admiral of the White. —— Philip Cavendiſh, Eſq; Vice Admiral of the Blue. —— John Balchen, Eſq; Rear Admiral of the Red. —— Charles Stuart, Eſq; Rear Admiral of the White. —— Sir George Saunders, Rear Admiral of the Blue. *WE.* — Solomon Morris. Phil. Cavendiſh Rear Admiral of the Red. John Balchin Vice Admiral of the Blue. *P.*

MONDAY, *July* 10.

On ſaturday the Seſſions ended at the Old Bailey, when 9 Malefactors received ſentence of death, viz. John Gladman, for horſe ſtealing; Dan. Tipping, for the highway; Rob. Ellymant, for felony and burglary; John Gillet, for a ſtreet-robbery; Rich. Dangerfield, Hen. Barrett, Joſ. Charly, Valentine Robins and John Robins, 2 brothers, for robbing a Gentleman in a field near Pancras. —— The opinion of the Court was aſked by the Jury, in relation to the laſt 5 youths, whether they might not be acquitted of the robbery, and found guilty of ſingle felony only; to which Mr. Dep. Recorder anſwered, that if they were of opinion that the perſon was robbed without being put in corporal fear, they might acquit them of the robbery; but it appearing the reverſe on the trial, they having preſented a piſtol to him, they were found guilty. *D J. P.* —— 30 were caſt for tranſportation, 2 burnt in the hand, and 1 ordered to be whipt. *P.* 27 caſt for tranſportation. *D P.* — *Is a man the leſs* robbed *of his money, for being leſs* fearful *about his carcaſe?*

A few days ſince —— Knightly, Eſq; of Fawſley in Northamptonſhire, was married to Miſs Adams of that County, a young Lady of great merit, and a fortune of 12 000. *C.* —— On ſaturday John Rogers, of Milk-ſtreet, Eſq; to a Widow of 10,000 l. *D P.* — My Brother *either forgot this Lady's* merit, *or thought it included in the* 10,000 fortune.

Yeſterday morning about 4, 9 fiſh-women going in a boat from Weſtminſter to Billingſgate, ran againſt a barge near Whitehall, which ſunk the boat, and one woman was drowned. *C. D J.* —— It was ſunk by the riſing of one of the women. *P.* —— Being moſtly overcome with liquor; one of them, a man, was drowned. *D P.* — *I am aſſured the poor* woman *who* was drowned, *was* overcome with *no* liquor *but water.*

TUESDAY, *July* 11.

On tueſday his Majeſty's purſe of 100 guineas was won at Ipſwich by Mr. Shepherd's bay horſe Daſhwood. *D P.*

Laſt week the Lord Jedburgh, ſon and heir to the Marq. of Lothian, arrived here from Rome, having been 3 years upon his travels, and immediately ſet out for Nottingham to viſit his mother. *D P.*

Laſt ſaturday a coach glaſs grinder, carrying 2 glaſſes along S. Martin's Church-yard, ſlipped down by treading on a bean ſhell, broke both the glaſſes, cut one of his eyes quite out, and a piece of glaſs ſtuck in his ſkull. *D J.*

WEDNESDAY, *July* 12.

Yeſterday began the Gen. Quarter Seſſions for the Royalty of the Tower, &c. when Sir John Gonſon, being unanimouſly choſen Chairman, gave a very learned and ingenious Charge *as uſual* to the Grand Jury. *D P.*

On monday Mr. Cotton, Mercer in Grace-church-ſtreet, was unanimouſly elected Common-Council-man for Biſhopſgate Ward. *D P.*

From the PEGASUS *in Grub-ſtreet.*

The Charter appointing Truſtees for eſtabliſhing the Colony of Georgia in America is paſſed the Broad Seal. The Right Honourable Lord Viſcount Percival is appointed Preſident by the Charter, and as ſuch, on friday laſt took an oath for the faithful execution of his truſt before the Right Honourable the Lord Chief Baron of his Majeſty's Court of Exchequer.

Sir,

You are deſired, for a particular reaſon, to inſert in your next Journal the following tranſlation of a few lines in VIRGIL's *Æneis*, which were done by a young Gentleman under 20, who was bred up to the Law; in whoſe *Virgil* they were found after his deceaſe.

Æn. X. 62, &c. —— *Tum regia Juno*
Acta furore gravi: Quid me alta ſilentia cogis
Rumpere, & obductum verbis vulgare dolorem?
Ænean hominum quiſquam Divûmque ſubegit
Bella ſequi, aut hoſtem regi ſe inferre Latino?

To whom with haughty pride,
Fir'd with diſdain, the Queen of heav'n reply'd;
Why my deep ſilence muſt I break, renew
My former woes? why bleed my wounds anew?
Tell me, what man below; or God above,
Far froth his native home Æneas drove;
With wars to ravage diſtant climes, and bring
Preſumptuous arms on Latiums peaceful King?

SIR,

Mr. WALSINGHAM having at laſt gained a complete victory over the enemies of the Adminiſtration, intends after the manner of the Roman Conquerors, to paſs through the city in triumph; that is to ſay, in the modern phraſe, he is to come out next week with a moſt flaming chariot. I had an inclination to contribute my mite upon this occaſion; and as I have learnt to deſign in the true Grubean ſtile, I reſolved to furniſh our hero with a ſigniſicant coat of arms: but the late proceedings in the Court of Honour have clipt the wings of all the genius's in heraldry. All therefore I can do at preſent is, to ſend him a Motto, which I intended at firſt to take out of one of our own Authors; but I recollect he will appear more glorious, adorned with the ſpoils of one of our moſt bitter enemies. So I give him the choice of two out of HORACE, viz.

— Inſani præmia SCRIBÆ;
ſignifying, that he owes his advancement intirely to his extraordinary knack of writing like mad in all ſenſes. And

—Satis eſt EQVITEM mihi plaudere;
ſhewing his noble contempt of the cenſures of the Town, as long as he enjoys the applauſe and encouragement of his patron. I am, worthy Sir,
Your affectionate Fellow-labourer,

From my ſtudy upon the
rails in Lincolns-Inn Fields,
June the 28th, 1732.

CLUVIENUS.

EPIGRAM.

Being aſk'd, If our Members, abus'd in a ſatire,
Would not this week return ſpatter for ſpatter?
No, I hope not, crys I, that it e'er will be ſaid,
That they anſwer'd a Paper which no-body read.
Why, I've read it my ſelf, ſays my Friend. — I reply'd,
Prithee, tell me its name then, and where it did hide.
'Tis call'd, anſwers he, — no — 'tis call'd The Re-hearſal,
Intitled, tho' ſcarce ſeen before, Univerſal:
'Tis as vinegar ſharp, and as biteing as muſtard:
Od Fleet-bridge it lay under a tart and a cuſtard.

MÆVIUS.

Edinburgh, June 29. Some time ago a conſiderable quantity of Papers belonging to John Thompſon were ſeized here in a friend's houſe, and are to be ſent to London. The Commiſſioners of the Cuſtom-houſe have received a letter from an unknown hand with a Bank note for 50l. incloſed; the writer declares he had wronged the King in Duties of that ſum, and could not be eaſy, 'till he had made reſtitution. C. &c. 6. — It would have been better, if Thompſon and his Country-man had exchanged conſciences.

Iriſh news from Dublin June 27. in heroic verſe.
A Cooper in College-ſtreet upon laſt ſaturday,
Belonging to Mr. Burleigh was run over by a dray,
As he was endeavouring to ſave ſome children that ſtood
in the way.
Laſt ſaturday a poor man near Aſton's key was found;
But it is not known who he is, nor when he was drown'd.
The ſame day a woman, going along Bolton-ſtreet,
Being big with child, a rude fellow chanc'd to meet:
Who aſk'd her to go with him, in which ſhe being ſlack,
With a pen-knife he barb'rouſly cut her down the back.
Mrs. Griſſel Martin, about ſeventy years old,
Was married to a youth who but eighteen had told. P. 7.
Near Montown, a young fellow met a girl of threeſcore,
In the fields; and moſt rudely attack'd her before.
She caſt her eyes round, and could ſee no aſſiſtance;
So wiſely lay ſtill, and made little reſiſtance.
At laſt, on the caſtle ſhe looking upright,
Spy'd ſome Gentlemen laughing at the comical ſight:
Then hideouſly ſcream'd out, A rape, A rape, A rape!
The fellow run for his life, and made his eſcape. C. P. 11.

FOREIGN NEWS.

THURSDAY, July 6.

Yeſterday arrived the Mail from France.
Paris, July 11. On tueſday the Firſt Preſident of the Parliament, with the Preſidents à mortier, &c. went to Verſailles. His Majeſty received them very graciouſly, and told them, it was more agreeable to him to pardon than to puniſh; recommended it to them to continue the functions of their offices, and not abuſe his clemency. On wedneſday they gave an account to the Gentlemen of the Enquetes and Requetes of what had paſſed, who having withdrawn their reſignation, all met the next day in the great Chamber, and reſolved to make remonſtrances to the King. C. &c.

FRIDAY, July 7.

Hague, June 24. ' It is not the Emperor's deſign at preſent to raiſe the Duke of Lorrain to the dignity of ' King of the Romans, but his eldeſt ſon when he comes ' to be 8 or 10 years old; becauſe it is not impoſſible but ' his Imperial Majeſty may have male iſſue. — The ' Biſhop of Soiſſons perform'd the ceremony of bleſſing ' the great bell at Compiegne, at which the Marq. d'O ' ſtood Godfather, as Proxy for their Majeſties; the ' King preſented the Lady her firſt ſmock, which was ' put on upon this occaſion, containing 45 ells of fine ' Holland. P.' — Mr. Conundrum ſays, That by her ſmock it is plain this Lady was a Good Belle. ' Monſieur de Voltaire has compos'd up in 3 weeks time a ' fine theatrical piece, entitled Zaire and Oroonan Zaire ' is a Princeſs of the houſe of Luſignan, and Oroonan, ' ſon of the famous Saladin. Thoſe who have read this ' Play, aſſure us, that it is extremely moving, and full of ' the nobleſt ſentiments both of religion and heroiſm, ' which we hope will not be the leſs inſtructive or exem- ' plary, becauſe our Author has had the handling of ' the characters. P.' — He has writ it ſeems repreſented his own morals in his characters; and his piece is eſteemed theatrical in France, tho' full of ſentiments of religion.

MONDAY, July 10.

Yeſterday arrived the Mails from France and Holland.
Paris, June 16. Laſt thurſday the Cardinal de Polignac returned hither from Italy. C. &c.

TUESDAY, July 11.

Yeſterday arrived the Mail from Holland.
Berlin, July 10. The King has received the agreeable news of the ratifications of the treaty of accommodation between his Majeſty and the Prince de Naſſau Orange being exchanged, and by conſequence the difference touching the ſucceſſion of the late King William III. happily determined. D P.

Paris, July 11. At length the affairs of Parliament are determined, tho' within an ace of being further embroil'd, ſeveral Chambers being of opinion they ought to diſavow the conduct of the Firſt Preſident, who without their conſent had aſk'd the King pardon in their name. The voice of one young Counſellor is ſaid to have turn'd the ſcale in favour of compliance with the Court. Yeſterday the Parliament did nothing but order Remonſtrances to be drawn up to be preſented to his Majeſty. D P.

ADVERTISEMENTS.

To be Lett,

A SHOP in Ludgate-ſtreet. Enquire at the Oxford-Arms Tavern in the ſaid Street.

To be Lett, or the Leaſe to be Sold,

O F a very good convenient Houſe in Warwick-Court in Warwick Lane, near Newgate-Street, lately in in the Poſſeſſion of Mr. Crompton, Attorney at Law, being in a very good Repair, which may be entered upon immediately. Enquire at Mr. Merryfields, Upholſterer, at the three Chairs and Crown at the Ditch ſide, near Fleet ſtreet.
N. B. There is 18 Years of the Leaſe to come.

This Day was publiſhed,
The POLITICAL STATE
OF
GREAT BRITAIN
For the Month of June, 1732.

CONTAINING,

1. A Journal of the Proceedings and Debates of laſt Seſſions of Parliament, particularly the ſeveral Speeches that were made upon the Occaſion of the Addreſs of Thanks to his Majeſty — 2. An Account how the laſt Year's Money was diſpoſed of — 3. Tryals at the Old Baily. — 4. The noble Behaviour of a Proteſtant Martyr in France. — 5. A full Account of the Diſpute between the French King and his Parliament. — 6. A Portugueze Edict in Favour of Matrimony. — 7. The Roman Cuſtom of keeping Concubines. — 8. Conditions on which the Corſicans have ſurrendred. — 9. A Lady made a Doctor in Philoſophy. — 10. A curious Treatiſe againſt the Pragmatick Sanct on, which was never publiſhed — 11 Sir John Eyles's Speech to the South Sea Company. — 12. Marriages. — 13. A Bill of Mortality. — 14. Imports and Exports
Printed for T. Warner at the Black Boy in Pater-Noſter-Row, where may be had the former Months.
N. B. The Debates in Parliament are not in any other Monthly Account, and we ſhall oblige our Readers with a Continuation of them in our ſucceeding Numbers until the whole are finiſhed.

June 12, 1732.

By PERMISSION of

The Right Honourable the Lord Chancellor.
The Right Honourable the Lord Raymond, Lord Chief
Justice of his Majesty's Court of King's Bench.
The Right Honourable Arthur Onslow, Esq; Speaker of
the House of Commons.
The Honourable Sr John Hind Cotton, Bart.
Francis Annesley, Esq.
Samuel Burroughs, Esq; one of the Masters of the High
Court of Chancery.
John Hanbury, Esq;
Trustees of the Cottonian Library.

IT is proposed by *John Pine*, to Engrave, by Subscription, a Correct Copy of King JOHN's *Great
Charter*, taken from the Original now remaining in the *Cottonian Library*; which, being a Recognition of the Rights
and Liberties of the People, it is presumed the Publick will
encourage a Design to perpetuate a Record of such Dignity and Importance.

It will be contained in one Imperial Sheet of Paper, and
engraved in the same Form and Character with the Original, and adorned with proper Decorations.

The Price to Subscribers will be Half a Guinea: to be
paid on the Delivery, which will be about Christmas next.

Those Gentlemen, who are willing to encourage this Subscription, are desired to send their Names and Places of
Abode as soon as possible, which will entitle them to the
first Impressions.

N. B. Those who subscribe for Six, shall have a Seventh
gratis.

Subscriptions are taken by C. King, in Westminster-
Hall; N. Prevost, in the Strand; R. Gosling, B. Motte,
T. Woodward, near the Temple, Fleet-Street; W. Innys,
C. Rivington, S. Austen, in St. Pauls Church-yard;
A. Bettesworth and C. Hitch, J. Batley, in Pater-Noster-
Row; W. Hinchliffe, E. Symons, at the Royal-Exchange;
J. Brindley, in New Bond-Street; J. Clark, Pall-Mall; r in
Gray's-Inn; and J. Pine, Engraver, over-against Little-
Britain, in Aldersgate-Street.

This Day was published,

(Beautifully printed in One Volume, Octavo,)

A Treatise of continual FEVERS, in four Parts.
To which are added, *Medicinal Observations*, in Three
Books; written are enumerated, the Diagnosticks, Prog-
nosticks, and Events of the several Diseases incident to Hu-
man Bodies. By JODOCUS LOMMIUS.
Translated from the Latin by THOMAS DALE, M.D.
Printed for J. Brotherton, W. Meadows, T. Cox, J. Hinch-
liffe, and R. Willock, in Cornhill; J. Hazard near Stationers-
Hall; W. Bickerton without Temple-Bar; T. Astley and
S. Austen in St. Paul's Church-Yard; and L. Gilliver in
Fleet-Street.

This Day was published,

*For the Use of Families, beautifully printed in Two Vols.
8vo. adorn'd with 34 Plates, Engraven by Mr. Sturt,*

DUPIN's EVANGELICAL HISTORY: Or the Records of the SON of GOD, and their Veracity demonstrated, in the Life and Acts of our Blessed Lord and
Saviour Jesus Christ, and the Holy Apostles. Wherein 1.
The Life of our Blessed Saviour Jesus Christ is related in
all its Circumstances, according to the Order of Time, in
a pathetick and practical Method, thereby composing a perfect Harmony of the Gospels. 2. Proofs from his Sermons
and Discourses of these Essential and Important Truths,
which all Christians are obliged to know and practise, in
order to their Eternal Salvation. 2. His Parables, Miracles,
and Sufferings, set in a just Light, and defended from all
the Oppositions of wicked and designing Men. 4. An Application of the Whole to the respective Uses of Christians,
with regular Devotions conformable to the several Periods
of the Holy History; and Directions how he may read the
Life of Jesus Christ to Advantage.
Printed for R. Ware, at the Bible and Sun in Amen-
Corner, near Pater-Noster-Row. Price 8 s.
Also may be had at the same Place,
1. The large House-Bibles, Folio, with the six Maps of
sacred Geography, and a brief Concordance for the more
easy finding out of the Places therein contained. By
J. Downame, B. D.
Bound in Calf Leather   1 l 3 s. per Book.
And with Mr Sturt's Cuts at 2 l. 5 s. ditto.
On a fine Paper with Cuts   2 l. 3 s. ditto.
2 Impartial Churchman; or, A fair and candid Representation of the Excellency and Beauty of the Church of England. Together with an earnest and affectionate Address
to the Protestant Dissenters. By Robert Warren, D. D.
Price 3 s. 6 d.
3 A Description of 300 Animals, viz. Beasts, Birds,
Fishes, Serpents and Insects. With a particular Account of
the Whale-Fishery. Extracted out of the best Authors, and
adapted to the Use of all Capacities, especially to allure
Children to read. Illustrated with Copper Plates, whereon
is curiously engraven every Beast, Bird, Fish, Serpent and
Insect described in this whole Book. Price 3 s. 2 d.
4. Tradesman's Guide. Containing a List of all the Stage
Coaches and Carriers, with an Account of all the Market
Towns in England. Price 1 s.

On Monday last was published,
The LONDON MAGAZINE:
Or, GENTLEMAN's *Monthly Intelligencer.*

NUMB. III. For JUNE, 1732.
To be Continued. *(Price Sixpence each Month.)*

CONTAINING,

*(Greater Variety, and more in Quantity, than any MONTH-
LY* BOOK *extant.)*

I. A *View* of the WEEKLY ESSAYS. viz. On Poetry;
Painting; Modern charge come to prevent sacri-
fice; Complaints; two Sorts of Avarice; Vition, occasioned by the Ridicule of Felony; true Spirit or oppress'd
Rome to the worthy the Germans; the just Monarch;
Vindication of our Industry; Crueelty of Horatio Wal-
pole; English Queens.
II. various Subjects, viz. the Use and abuse of Power;
Folly of Knavishness in a State; William the pious
on popular Discontents; Undress of the Presbyterian;
his Arms in relation to a Continual Coronation, and
Remarks on the Free Briton upon the Suspect State of
the Pretender's Hopes in action concern'd Reflections on the
Extract of Bp. Hare's Sermon; C. Hingman's Sketch of
bad Manners, and Memorandum't hint concerning Mr.
Osborne; Cost of Government under one Minister; good
Ministers; Disputes on the Salt Tax, and Excise, and Hue
and Cry; the Lords Protest; State of the National Debt; Remarks
to the Lords; Thanks to Lord Gage; and Robert, &c.
III. Poetry: The Queen Regent; Description of Love;
Description of Anger; Lady's Dressing-Room, by D. S——t;
Epigrams.
IV. Domestick Occurrences: Promotions Ecclesiastical, Ci-
vil and Military; Marriages and Births; Deaths; Acts pass'd;
Affairs of the S. Company; King's going Abroad, &c.
V. Foreign Affairs.
VI. Price of Goods, Grain, Stocks, Monthly Bill of Mor-
tality.
VII. A Table of Contents.
To which is added, A Catalogue of Books and Pamphlets,
with their Prices, published by the Proprietors of the
Monthly Chronicle, now dissontinued.

MULTUM IN PARVO.

LONDON: Printed by C. Ackers in St. John's-Street,
For J. Wilford behind the Chapter-house near St. Paul's;
and sold by A. Meadows, T. Cox, W. Hinchliffe, A. Wim-
sidge, R. Willock, and E. Nutt in Cornhill; J. Clarke in
Duck-lane; T. Astley, in St. Paul's Church-Yard; J. Dodd
without Temple-Bar; J. Stagg in Westminster-Hall; J. Jackson
in Pall-Mall; J. Brindley and W. Shropshire in Bond-
Street; and J. Millan near th. Admiralty-Office.
Where may be had, the former Numbers.

This Day was published,
The Fifth Edition, of

A Journey from ALEPPO to Jerusalem, at Easter,
A.D. 1697. To which is added, An Account of the
Author's Journey to the Banks of Euphrates and the Peer,
and to the Country of Mesopotamia. By *Henry Maundrel*,
M.A. late Fellow of Exeter-College, and Chaplain to the
Factory at Aleppo.
Oxford, printed at the Theatre for Anthony Peisly; and
sold by J. Brotherton, W. Meadows, T. Cox, W. Hinchliffe,
and R. Willock, in Cornhill; J. Hazard, near Station-
Hall; W. Bickerton, without Temple-Bar; T. Astley, and
S. Austen, in St. Paul's Church-yard; and L. Gilliver in
Fleet-street.
Of whom may be had,
Dr. TRAPP's Sermons at Lady Moyer's Lecture on the
Doctrine of the TRINITY, with the Objections against it
answered in a summary View of the whole Controversy.
To which are added, Discourses on the Parable of Dives
and Lazarus; setting forth the deplorable Corruption, Im-
morality and Infidelity of the present Age: Shewing the
absolute Necessity of a Holy Life; demonstrating the Cer-
tainty of a Future State, and the Truth of the Christian
Religion.

This Day was published,

AN ODE to his Grace the Duke of Newcastle.
Written on the present Tranquillity of Europe, establish'd by the Influence of the British Power.

*Nihil habet aut Fortuna tua majus, quàm ut possis, aut
Natura tua melius, quàm, ut velis, quàm plurimes
conservare.*   Cic.

Printed for J. Batley, at the Dove in Pater-Noster-
Row. Price 6 d.
Where may had, just published,
Dedicated to the Gentlemen of the Navy of England,
The Memoirs of Monsieur DU GUE TROUIN, Chief
of a Squadron of the Royal Navy of France, and Great
Cross of the Military Order of S. Lewis; containing all his
Sea Actions with the English, Dutch, and Portuguese, in
the late Wars of King William and Queen Anne.
Translated from the French by a *Sea-Officer*.

July 3, was published, Price 6d.
Neatly printed on a fine Dutch Paper.
THE GENTLEMAN's MAGAZINE:
Or, *Monthly Intelligencer.*

No XVIII. for JUNE, 1732. being the Sixth of Vol. II.
Containing more in Quantity, and greater Variety than
any Book of the Kind and Price. Also some Pieces not
printed elsewhere.
I. Views of the Weekly Essays, viz. The Quaker's Plea;
a critique on Poetry and Painting; Ridotto al Fresco, hu-
morously and satyrically described; Bp. Hare and Lord
Shaftsbury vindicated; Deism and Christianity; a Reme-
dy for conjugal Unhappiness and popular Discontents;
Observations on Trade and Masquerade; Dancing; King of
Sweden's Life; or Restitution; Antiquities at York.
II. Political Points, viz. The Affair of Belloni (of the Pre-
tender and his Agents) Thomson's Proposals; Mr. Arbuth-
not's Letters, and Remarks on the Whole; Of Ministers,
Councils, &c. Disputes on the Salt and Land-Tax; King
William's Statue; King's Speech; Lords Protests; stated
ta: National Debts; Speaker's Thanks to Lord Gage; his
Lordship's Answer, &c.
III. Poetical Pieces, viz. The Ladies Dressing-Room, and
Poor Pasquin's Prayer, by Dr. Swift; Verses on the 10th of
June, from New-England; Spring Gardens, &c.
IV. Domestick Occurrences, Births, Deaths, Marriages,
Promotions, Proceedings of the Sea Gen. Court, &c.
V. Prices of Goods, Stocks, Monthly Bill of Mortality.
VI. Foreign Affairs.
VII. A Table of Contents.
With a Register of new Books and Pamphlets.
By SYLVANUS URBAN, Gent.
Note, a few are printed on a fine Royal Paper, large
Margin, for the Curious.
Printed and sold at St. John's Gate, by Fr. Jefferies in
Ludgate-Street; also, Mrs. Nutt; Mr. Charlton; Mrs.
Cox, at the Royal-Exchange; M. Batley, in Pater-Noster-
Row; Mr. Midwinter, in St. Paul's Church-Yard; A. Chap-
man, in Pall-Mall; M.s Dodd and Mr. Bickerton with-
out Temple-Bar; Mr. Crichley, at Charing-Cross; Mr.
Stagg, and M. King, in Westminster-Hall; Mr. Robinson
in Holbourn; Mr. Harding, in S. Martin's Lane; Mr.
Montague, in Great Queens-street; and all unprejudiced
Booksellers in Town and Country. (Price 6 d.) Where may
be had the new Numbers, from January last, that being
now reprinted, as well as Numb. XVI. for April last. The
Numbers which were wanting of this Volume, are in
the Press again (done a third time) and will speedily be
publish'd to complete Gentlemen's Setts.

Lately published,
The Second Edition, corrected,
The LAW of TITHES:

SHewing their Nature, Kinds, Properties, Incidents;
by whom, when, and in what Manner payable; how,
and in what Courts to be sued for and recovered; what
Things, Lands, or Persons are charged with, or exempted
therefrom. With the Nature, Incidents, and Effects of
Customs, Prescriptions, Real Compositions, Modus Decl-
mandi, Libels, Suggestions, Prohibitions, Consultations,
Custom of London, &c. Wherein all the Statutes and adjudged Cases, relative to the Subject, are introduced and
considered. By *William Bohun* of the Middle Temple, Esq;
Also, just published, by the same Author,
A TITHING TABLE: Shewing (by way of Ana-
lysis) of what Things Tythes are or are not due, either by
Common Law, Custom, or Prescription. Price 1 s.
N. B. These two may be had bound together, or separate.
Printed for J. Brotherton, W. Meadows, T. Cox, W. Hinchliffe, and R. Willock, in Cornhill; J. Hazard, near Stationers Hall; W. Bickerton, without Temple-Bar; T. Astley,
and S. Austen, in St. Paul's Church-yard; and L. Gilliver,
in Fleet-street.

LONDON: Printed by J. HUGGONSON, in Bartholomew-Close, for Captain GULLIVER, near the Temple. where Letters and Advertisements are taken
in: As also at the Rainbow Coffee-House in Cornhill, and John's Coffee-House in Shear-Lane, near Temple-Bar.   [Price Two Pence.]

The Grub-ſtreet Journal.

NUMB. 133

Thurſday, *JULY* 20, 1732.

'Tis then, and then alone, the point you gain,
If no one precept in your works remain,
But ribaldry, *and* ſcandal, *lawleſs reign.*
Thus ſhall all Drury *in your praiſe combine,*
And diſtant Goodman's Fields *their Peans join :*
So far Barbadoes *ſhall reſound your fame,*
And ev'n tranſported Felons *know your name*

HARLEQ. HOR. p 46

To Mr BAVIUS.

SIR,

As in my younger days I was a great frequenter of Dramatic Entertainments, ſo I have been ever ſince a ſtrenuous advocate for the Stage I have been always particularly warm againſt any who declared for a total demolition of it ; and looked on them as perſons employed to introduce popery and arbitrary power, as many other honeſt people have thought I uſed to offer in its behalf, that, however it might be perverted in particulars, it was ſtill wholeſome in the general ; that from thence our youth might not only acquire a good addreſs, and juſt elocution, but likewiſe, by ſeeing vice puniſhed, and folly corrected, the particularities of caprice and affectation expoſed, and honour and honeſty come off triumphant, they might be induced to chuſe the good, and refuſe the evil This, and much more, Mr BAVIUS, have I hitherto urged againſt the enemies of the ſock and buſkin But, alas, I can now ſtand my ground no longer; for, as the Stage is at preſent directed by the *Drury-Lane-Managers*, and ſupply'd by their *Farce-Writers*, I muſt acknowledge it to be ſo far from being uſeful, that 'tis not tolerable ; and that the extirpation of it is more neceſſary, and would be of more publick ſervice, than of *night-cellars*, *brothels*, and common *gaming-tables* Surely the *Maſters* of that houſe procured the renewal of their *Patent*, with a deſign of inſulting the common ſenſe, and common modeſty, of mankind ; and they have very happily pitched on *Authors*, who were fit to execute ſuch a deſign I think the firſt new Entertainment they gave us, after the confirmation of their *Grant*, was a *concert* of *cats*, *dogs*, *monkeys*, *goats*, &c and the firſt new Plays were the *Covent-Garden Tragedy*, and the *Old Debauchees* The two laſt performances, Mr BAVIUS, having meritoriouſly met with the *univerſal deteſtation* of the Town (inſtead of their *univerſal applauſe*, as ſome of our pander News-writers had impudence enough to aſſert,) I was excited to look into them, that I might ſee what grounds there were for ſuch a general outcry ; when I was ſoon convinced, that they were ſo far improper for an *Engliſh Stage*, or to be exhibited to a *polite*, an *honeſt*, and a *chriſtian* people, that, (unleſs Sodom and Gomorrah had been now undeſtroyed) they were only fit for the hangman's flames. But, notwithſtanding the juſt abhorrence the Town has ſhewed to this impoſition, theſe performances were too good, it ſeems, in the opinion of their promoters, to be given up ; a formal defence of them has been publiſhed in the papers, and a challenge to their oppoſers to produce a ſingle paſſage which can be wreſted into *indecency* or *profaneneſs*. This challenge, however diſagreeable, I accept ; holding myſelf obliged to do a little dirty work, rather than ſuffer others to be ſuffocated with the mire.

To begin then with the Tragedy. The ſcene of this Piece lies in a *bawdy-houſe*, and the characters of it, as the Author informed us in his Prologue, are *bullies*, *bawds*, *ſots*, *rakes*, and *whores* ; a very pretty collection to entertain the Boxes ; tho', to their honour be it told, many that were there had neither ſo much taſte, nor ſo little modeſty, as to be able to ſit it out, but quitted their places in the middle of the performance. But, to come to particulars, (and yet I'm aſhamed to come to them too) obſerve the following ſpeech of LOVEGIRLO, Page 13.

Oh! I am all on fire, thou lovely wench ;
Torrents of joy my burning ſoul muſt quench,
Reiterated joys!
Thus, burning from the fire, the waſher lifts
The red hot iron to make ſmooth her ſhifts ;
With arm impetuous rubs her ſhift amain,
And rubs, and rubs, and rubs it o'er again ;
Nor ſooner does her rubbing arm withhold,
'Till ſhe grows warm, and the hot iron cold.

Abominable! ſure a man muſt wreſt with all his might to make any thing elſe of this but the moſt groſs obſcenity. I don't know whether the impudence or the naſtineſs of another ſpeech in the ſame ſcene is moſt to be wondered at

LOVEG. *Who but a fool would marry that can keep?*
Sounds leſs the ſcolding of a vertuous tongue?
Or who remembers, to increaſe his joy,
In the laſt moments of exceſſive bliſs,
The ring, the licence, Parſon, or his Clerk?
Beſides, whene'er my miſtreſs plays me foul,
I caſt her like a dirty ſhirt away.
But oh! a wife ſticks like a plaſter faſt,
Like a perpetual bliſter to the pole.

Here's inſtruction! here's delicacy! a dirty ſhirt, and a bliſter, are moſt entertaining images! why this turns my ſtomach, as well as ſhocks my underſtanding. This is language more groſs than even goats and monkeys, if they could ſpeak, would expreſs their brutality in And as this writer, in the foregoing quotations, expoſes matrimony and recommends whoredom, ſo, in the next, he is as ſtrong an advocate for *drunkenneſs*

And were it not for wine, I would not be ;
Wine makes a Cobler greater than a King ;
Wine gives mankind the preference to beaſts, &c

Here the end of a man's being, and the excellency of his nature, are placed in debauchery ; and, leſt the audience ſhould forget to league lewdneſs and intemperance together, the writer joins and enforces them in the following reflection

BILK *Wine is a good, and ſo is woman too,*
But which the greater good, I cannot tell
Either to other to prefer I'm loth,
But he does wiſeſt who takes moſt of both

The wit and burleſque of this Piece is likewiſe very uncommon, the following lines I ſuppoſe are meant for ridicule.

Oh! I am mad, methinks I ſwim in air,
In ſeas of ſulphur, and eternal fire
Methinks I'm mad, mad as a wild march-hare ;
My muddy brain is addled like an egg,
My teeth, like Magpies, chatter in my head ;
My reeling head! which akes like any mad

It muſt be an *addled brain* indeed that ſuch ſtuff as this could come from Is this *burleſque?* Where is the ſimilitude? Where is the point? No, 'tis downright toothleſs, taſteleſs, *original nonſenſe* ; there never was any thing like it, and, I hope, never will be Methinks the writer tho' might as well have left *ſeas of ſulphur*, and *eternal fire* out of the mad joke, for fear he ſhould meet with them in ſober ſadneſs

And now, Mr BAVIUS, I muſt beg pardon for ſoiling your paper with ſuch ſmut, and loading it with the language of Billingſgate and the ſtews ; but, as I told you before, 'tis by abſolute force, much againſt ſtomach or inclination But, that we may get out of the kennel as ſoon as poſſible, we'll take a ſkip at once as far as the Epilogue, not doubting but the Reader has got enough of the Play Now this bravely carries on the buſineſs of the Piece, and clenches its *moral* ; here the Author leaves fiction and the Stage, and addreſſes himſelf in *propria perſona* to the Boxes. What had been ſaid before by the different characters, might poſſibly have been miſtaken : the audience might have looked on it as falſe and ridiculous when it came from ſuch ſpeakers ; but, to prevent this, the Poet appears in the *Epilogue*, and informs us, that 'tis nothing but ſolemn truth. Pray obſerve him.

The Prieſt makes all the difference in the caſe,
Kiſſinda*'s always ready to embrace,*
And Iſabel *ſtays only to ſay grace*
For ſeveral prices ready both to treat,
This takes a guinea, that your whole eſtate
For prudes may cant of vertues, and of vices ;
But, faith, we only differ in our prices

A very decent complement to the Boxes, in truth, and the Ladies will, I hope, reward him for it his next benefit night He tells them, without any ceremony, that there's no difference betwixt the beſt of them, and the *bawdy-houſe trulls* they had been ſeeing on the Stage ; and that, pretend what they would, they were all a parcel of *downright arrant whores*. Here is reſpect and decency with a vengeance, a moſt elegant deſſert to regale the Ladies at the cloſe of the Entertainment ; we are mightily obliged to him for the good opinion he has of our wives and daughters ; and, in good truth, were we to ſuffer them to frequent his Entertainments, the opinion might ſoon become juſt enough too.

But now, Mr. BAVIUS, let us take a ſlight look on the other of theſe performances, and have done ; for I'm both tir'd and ſick of the employment. The *Old Debauchees* is the Author's favourite, it ſeems ; for, in the preface to a piece of MOLIERE's, which he has moſt *execrably murdered*, he modeſtly compares it with the *Miſanthrope* of that Author. This writer then makes no diſtinction between the moſt chaſte, moral, witty performance, and the moſt coarſe, vicious, inſipid trumpery that ever was hatched. Juſt ſo much difference is there between the *Miſanthrope* of MOLIERE, and the *Old Debauchees*. However, it muſt be ſaid for the writer, that in this piece he has made moſt violent attempts to be witty ; and how he has ſucceeded may be beſt ſeen by ſetting a few of his flowers to view. Old LAROON ſays, P. 3. *I remember the time when I could have taken a hop, ſtep, and jump over the ſteeple of Notre Dame.* To which the fine Lady ingeniouſly makes anſwer, *I fancy the ſparks of your age had wings, Sir.* Which anſwer was contrived, I ſuppoſe, to introduce the following wonderful witty reply. O. LAR. *Wings, you little baggage, no, but they had limbs like elephants, and as ſtrong they were as Sampſon, and as ſwift as* ——— *Why, I have myſelf run down a ſtag in a fair chace, and eat him afterwards for dinner.* Certainly, when the Poet penn'd this ſpeech, his *brains were* in a *wild gooſe chace* after wit, and the Reader's ſtomach muſt be as coarſe as the writer's fancy, that can digeſt this *ſtag* But he kindles, you'll find, as he runs, and grows wittier and wittier. O. LAROON adviſes the young Lady, *not to let a ſett of raſcally Prieſts put ſtrange notions in her head, for that there are no raptures worth a* LOUSE, *but thoſe in the arms of a briſk young Cavalier.* He ſays to his ſon, *At your Devotions! Nay, then you are no ſon of mine ; I believe you are the ſon of ſome travelling Engliſh Alderman, and muſt have come into the world with a cuſtard in your mouth* Here's wit! here's imagery! was ever any thing like this ſpoke out of a ſculler? but this is decent to what follows in almoſt every page; obſerve the next. O. LAROON ſays, *The Devil is a great lover of Muſick: I have known half a dozen Devils dance out of a man's mouth at the tuning of a Violin, then preſent the company with a Hornpipe, and ſo dance a Jig through the key-hole.* MARTIN very juſtly makes anſwer, *Thou art the Devil's ſon.* To which the other replies, *Thou art the Devil's Footman, and weareſt his proper Livery.*

This is delightful jeſting indeed! could the Writer imagine, that any above Draymen and Scavengers would laugh at this? But we have more of ſuch pleaſantry. O. LAROON aſſures JOURDAIN, *That Purgatory is a very warm place, for he had called there to take lodgings for him, that 'twas not above a mile and a half there, and every ſtep of the way down hill.* JOURDAIN *ſays, Is it poſſible that you can have ſeen the dreadful horrors of that place.* O. LAROON *Seen 'em, Ay, ay, I have ſeen 'em, and a pretty tragical ſort of a ſight they are ; if it was not for the confounded heat of the air* ——— *Then there's ſuch a fine conſort of groans, you would think your ſelf at an Opera, ſome ſpirits are ſhut up in ovens, ſome are chained to ſpits, ſome are ſcattered in frying-pans* ——— *And I have taken up a place for you on a gridiron.* The Scripture has given us too frightful a deſcription it ſeems of Hell, and painted the Devil and his Angels in too formidable colours ; our Poet therefore, in order to prevent any ill effect ſuch diſmal ideas might have on the mind, is perpetually drolling throughout this piece upon Hell and Damnation, and repreſenting the *Devil* as a *Bugbear* fit only to fright children. This muſt be an admirable entertainment for the Ladies, as well as excellent inſtruction to our youth. When ſuch things as theſe are ſuffer'd on the Stage, 'tis no wonder there are ſo many *Whores* and *Pickpockets* in the ſtreets. And now, ſince he makes ſo free with the Bible, no wonder if the Prieſts are ſplaſhed with his mud. I'll give you, Mr. BAVIUS, one or two of his genteel reflections upon them, and ſo waſh my hands, and meddle with him no more.

The fine Gentleman of the Play ſays, That *if you once attack a hornet, or a Prieſt, the whole neſt of hornets, and the whole regiment of black guards, are ſure to be upon you.* O LAROON, being asked the cauſe of his mirth, anſwers, *'Tis the ſight of an old honeſt whore-maſter in a fit of deſpair, and a damn'd rogue of a Prieſt riding him to the Devil* Two ſpeeches after he ſays, *Well, I have never tapp'd a Prieſt yet ; but if I don't let out ſome reverend blood before the ſun ſets,*——*I'll make a ragout for the Devil's ſupper of him.* ——— 'Tis a pity but the Poet was to ſerve for *ſauce* then, tho' 'twould be very

Insipid. But he goes on, *I no more rely on what a woman says out of a Church, than on what a Priest says in it.* —— *Hearkee, old Gentleman, set the young couple together, and they'll sacrifice their first fruits to the Church. What the Devil are you possessed with? — I am possess'd with the Devil.* —— *You are possess'd with a Priest, and that's worse,* —— *I'll disband such a sett of black locusts,* —— *wild beasts* — *rascally Priest,* — *greasy Priests, &c. &c. &c.* ——He compliments *England* *upon every man's believing what religion he pleases, and must be leaving none at all.* His belief of the last is indeed the only apology he can make for his way of entertaining them; but then he ought to have taken away their modesty too. And this he really does in the character of his fine Lady in the two last lines of the Play, where she concludes the piece with the following chaste and instructive moral. *The fears of a lover are very unreasonable, when he is once assured of the sincerity of his mistress:*

For when a woman sets herself about it,
Nor Priest, nor Devil, can make her go without it.

Soh! — I've done, which the Reader, I dare say, will be glad of as well as myself. This writer can't accuse me of wresting any thing, since I have done little more than quoted from him; and this can't offend him, because 'tis what he demanded. If I had either leisure, or inclination, I could go a little farther with him; and make it appear, from all his performances, that his pen is not only void of *wit, manners,* and *modesty,* but likewise of the most common *rules* of *Poetry,* and even *Grammar.* But this, Mr. BAVIUS, I leave to you, and your correspondents; I shall only observe at present, that the *managers* of the *Theatre* are more in blame than the writers, by giving encouragement to such writings, and such Authors, and to none but such. I am, Sir, your most obedient,

PUBLICUS.

P. S. I would advise this writer, that, if he does any thing more from MOLIERE, as he threatens us, he would forbear to *adulterate* it with any thing of his own, or to mix it with such *Debauchee-Songs,* and *Covent-Garden Ribaldry,* as he has done in the *Forc'd Physician* of that Author; which he has mangled and misunderstood from the very *Title-Page* to *Finis.* He might as well have translated, *Medecin ma gre lui,* the *Mock-Poet,* as the *Mock-Doctor,* nay, better; for that had been applicable to the Translator, if not to the Piece; but the other suits nothing but the Person to whom he dedicates it.

EPIGRAM.

'Tis strange, you say, in this refined age,
That brothels, bawds, and whores adorn the stage.
I think 'tis not. They justly lay the scene:
Don't Drury Play-house stand in Drury Lane?
And own you must; tho' void of wit, or art,
They naturally write, and act their part. F. N.

DOMESTIC NEWS.

C. *Courant.*	EP. *Evening Post.*
P. *Post-Boy.*	SJ. *S. James's Evening Post.*
DP. *Daily Post.*	WE. *Whitehall Evening P.*
DJ. *Daily Journal.*	LE. *London Evening Post.*

THURSDAY, *July* 13.

Mr. Booth of Drury lane Play-house hath sold his share and interest in the stock and management to John Highmore of Hampton Court, Esq; *C.*

Christ. Rhodes, Esq; is appointed Comptroller of the new duties of Excise, &c. in Scotland with a salary of 900 l. per ann. *DJ.*

The Rev Mr. Lane succeeds Dr. Croxal as Treasurer of the Cathedral Church of Hereford. *P.*

On June 13, the Sheriffs presented John Read, Esq; to the Court of Aldermen, in order to his being admitted Keeper of Newgate; but a debate arising concerning the form of his admission, the affair was deferred till the 20th. The only question was, Whether Mr. Read should be admitted during good behaviour, or only during pleasure. The Council for the Sheriffs insisted, that the former was supported by all the Precedents of admissions down to the present time. Upon which an order was made for the searching of Precedents: and tho' there was not a single instance of admission during pleasure, the Court made an order July 4. 'That for the future no 'person shall be admitted Keeper of Newgate, but only 'during the pleasure of the Court.' And it was referred to a Committee of 6 Aldermen and 12 Commoners to consider what may be a proper satisfaction to the L. Mayor and Sheriff, and how the place shall for the future be disposed of. *DJ.* *This worthy Court could not think that the many Precedents of the oppressions of Jailors at all justified them.*

Her Grace the Dutchess of Buckingham is gone from Bologn to Paris to a house she has hired there. *LE.*

The Council Office at the Cockpit, Whitehall, is pulling down in order to be rebuilt. *LE*

On sunday morning Sam. Wilt. Terry, Esq; was married to Miss Brimley of Banbury, a young Lady of great merit, and 16,000 l. fortune. *SJ.*

Mr. Weeks, a noted Mercer on Ludgate Hill, going lately on a party of pleasure on the water, by the furling of a sail, was thrown overboard and drowned on monday last. *DP.* In his passage between Portsmouth and the Isle of Wight. *P.*

We hear the whole performance of the Beggar's Opera (which was acted last tuesday for the first time at the Theatre-Royal in Drury-lane by the summer Company) met with great applause: there was a very handsome audience, &c. *DP.* —— *This puffing was not occasioned by the* great applause, *nor by the crouding of the* Audience, *which might be* very handsome, *tho' not* very numerous.

Christen'd	M. 186.	352.	Bury'd	M. 180.	374.
	F. 166.			F. 194.	

SJ. LE.

Increased in the burials, 15 —— *Diseases:* Aged 25. Consumption 55. Convulsion 128. Dropsy 17. Fever 46. Small pox 17. Stillborn 12. Teeth 20 *LE.* *Casualties:* Shot himself, 1. Cut her throat, 1. Died suddenly in the street, 1. Drowned 3. Excessive drinking, 1. Kill'd accidentally, 2 by falls from horses, and 1 by a cart. Murdered, 1. Overlaid, 1. *SJ. LE.*

FRIDAY, *July* 14.

Yesterday morning Count Degenfeldt, Envoy from the King of Prussia, set out for Hanover; his Lady and family remain here. *C. DP.* The same morning the wind was so prodigious high, that the ferry-boat at Westminster (when the R. H L Visc Falmouth was in it, in his coach and 6) was driven down as far as Somerset house, and forced on shore on the sand bank: several of the ferry boats were drove as far as Standgate, and were forced to get 5 pair of oars to each to tow them back again. —— Several trees were blown down in S James's Park. *DJ.* —— *These* several ferry boats *could be but 4, there being but 3 in all.*

SATURDAY, *July* 15

Col. Sam Robinson, Chamberlain of this City, being relapsed, at his house at Enfield, is attended by 3 physicians. *C.*

We hear, that the bills relating to the feast at the late installment having been delivered, the whole charge of the dinner amounts to 1250 l. *DP.*

We hear that the effigies of the late ingenious Will Congreve, Esq; in wax-work, at the expence of 200 l. which was kept at a person of quality's house in S James's, was broke to pieces by the carelessness of a servant in bringing it down stairs last monday night *DP.*

Dover, July 13. Yesterday my Lord Glenorchy embarqued here for Ostend, in order for Aix la Chapelle. *P.*

On thursday morning an Irish Ballad singer, who frequently cries and sings about streets very scandalous songs and ballads, and thereby raises mobs and riots in the streets, as well as occasions the picking of pockets, &c. was committed to Tothill fields Bridewell to beat hemp, by Sir John Gonson, &c. *DP.*

On wednesday a faculty passed the seal for the solemnization of matrimony between Columbine-Lee Carré of Cork, Esq; and Mrs. Eliz. Julia Bavand of S Anne's West. a young Lady of 10,000 l. fortune, and the ceremony was performed the same day. *P.*

On wednesday about 11 at night [thursday morning about 1. *P. DJ.*] Mr. Seger one of the Clerks belonging to the Treasury, came to the Feathers tavern in Castle-street, and desired he might lodge there, called for half a pint of red wine, desired the key to lock himself in, and bid the drawer call him at 8, [saying if he did not, it would be at least 10 l. out of his pocket. *DJ.*] The drawer called at the time, but no body answered, [he heard him groan. *P DJ*] and the door being broken open, they found him almost expiring: his head was swelled very much, [and his face black. *DJ*] about noon he expir'd. *C.* His place is worth 60 l. per ann. *DJ.* 100 l. *P.* He has left a wife and 2 children. *P. DJ.* He had all the symptoms of poison. The Surgeons having viewed his body, were of opinion, that he died a natural death. *P.* —— *This was an odd* opinion, *if he* had all the symptoms of poison.

The latter end of last week died at Cirencester, Mr. Bouchier, a relation to the Duke of Chandois. *C.* Mrs. Bouchier. *DP.*

Yesterday morning a man in Old-street, for a trifling wager drank a quart of Geneva, and died in about 3 hours. *C.*

MONDAY, *July* 17.

Yesterday the Right Hon. Sir Rob. Walpole came to his house at Chelsea, from his seat at Norfolk; and afterwards waited on her Majesty at Kensington. *DJ.*

A new Commission of the Peace for the County of Middlesex and Liberty of Westminster is passing the seals. *P.*

Yesterday the two Envoys from the Government of Algiers dined with Sir Cha. Wager at his house on Parsons Green, and had their own Cook to kill and dress for them. *DP.*

On saturday morning an unhappy accident happened at Mr. Rogers's in Chandos-street, Covent-garden. Mr. Rogers, who was going out of town, came back to his house for a paper, when hearing one of his children cry, he ask'd what was the matter, and was told by the child and another person, who was present, that the maid had on purpose swept some dust into the child's eyes; whereupon he insisted that she should immediately go out of his house, having caused some disturbances before, which she refused to do; upon which he went to push her out of the house, but she resisted, and fell upon the pit of her stomach against a chair, and afterwards with her temple against an iron grate, whereby she was so much bruised that she did not live above an hour afterwards, tho' all possible means were used for her recovery; but in vain. The said Mr. Rogers is committed to the Gatehouse. *DP.* — The Coroner's Inquest brought in their verdict *man slaughter. C. P. DJ.*

Cambridge, July 14. About a fortnight since the Rev. Dr. Hacket, of Trinity College, resigned the Vicarage of Enfield in Hertfordshire, before a publick Notary, in the presence of the 16 senior Fellows of the said College; and thereupon his presentation to the Rectory of Pakenham in Norfolk, worth 300 l. per ann. was sealed, in consideration of his peculiar merits and abilities. —— The workmen are pulling down the stair-case leading to the old Regent house, in order to join that room to what was the Physick schools, for the more advantageous placing the magnificent collection of books, purchased of Bp. Moore's Executors, by his late Majesty King George I. *LJ.*

TUESDAY, *July* 18.

On sunday last the new born son of the Hon. Hen. Vane, Esq; eldest son and heir to the R. Hon. the Lord Barnard, was baptized by the name of Frederick, his Royal Highness the Prince of Wales in person, his Grace the Duke of Cleveland, and the Hon. Mrs. Anne Vane, lately maid of honour to her Majesty, being Godfathers and Godmother. *DP.*

On saturday between 6 and 7 in the evening, a country Inn-keeper was robbed by a highwayman in the cross road between the lower-street, Islington, and Kingsland, of 500 l. 10 s. for the recovery of which it is said he will sue the county. *P.*

There having been no sufficient purchasers for the late Earl of Ranelagh's fine house at Chelsea, the same is going to be let in tenements, after the manner of Canbury-house near Islington. *DP.*

A few days since died the Rev. Mr Copley, Rector of Thornhill in Yorkshire, a living said to be worth 500 l. per ann. and in the gift of Sir Geo. Savile, Bar. *C. DP.*

On wednesday at his seat at Eaton Hall in Cheshire, Sir Ric. Grosvenor, Bar. leaving no issue: so the dignity and great estate descend to his 2d brother, now Sir Thomas, Representative for Chester. *C. DP. DJ.* —— Yesterday morning died at her house in Lisle-street, Mrs. Tolhurst, a maiden Gentlewoman, possessed of a fortune of 20,000 l. left her by the Lady Cheney, lately deceased; which we hear she has bequeathed to the R. Hon. Lord Gower. *DP.*

Last week a private Centinel plac'd the butt end of his firelock against a step, and put the muzzle to his left breast, and with the rammer pushed the trigger, shot himself, and expired immediately. *DJ.*

Dartmouth, July 11. Yesterday came in the Anne of Weymouth; on the 1st she met with a French ship, who sent his men aboard, and plundered out of her a silver watch, 6 silver spoons, half a hogshead of wine, &c. to the value of 15 l. *C. DJ.* — *A French Guarde de costa.*

On saturday last a Fleet Parson was convicted before Sir Ric. Brocas, of 43 oaths (on the information of a Plyer for weddings there) for which a Warrant was granted to levy 4 l. 6 s. on the goods of the said Parson; but upon application to his Worship he was pleased to remit 1 s. per oath; upon which the Plyer swore he would swear no more against any man upon the like occasion, finding he could get nothing by it. *SJ.* — *This was hard upon the* Parson, *and the* Plyer: *upon the former, to make his wit and politeness sense; upon the latter, to make him swear* for nothing.

Last week Mr. Angel of Isleworth, formerly an eminent Taylor, aged upwards of 70, was marry'd to Miss Lyne, an agreeable young Lady of the same place, of about 22. *LE.* —— *I hope he is more than the ninth part of a man at this age, otherwise I fear he will live the life of a dog.*

On saturday died suddenly the Hon. Col. Egerton, Brother to his Grace the Duke of Bridgewater. *WE.* Last sunday as he was walking in his gardens. *C. 19.*

WEDNESDAY, *July* 19.

Rob. Paunceford, Esq; is appointed Steward to his Royal Highness the Prince, in his manor of Kennington. *DJ.*

Charles Hardy, Esq; Capt. of the yatch Carolina, was a few days ago chosen one of the Directors of Greenwich hospital. *DJ.*

On sunday evening a Cornet of the Duke of Bolton's Blue Guards, and another Gentleman, coming from Kew in a chair, were attack'd by 2 highway men on Barnes Common, who robb'd them of their gold watches and some silver. *DP.*

The same day dy'd at Bromfield in Essex, the R. Hon. Countess of Donnegal. *DP.*

From the PEGASUS *in Grub-street.*

In our last, Pag. 2. *col.* 2. *l.* 30. *after* rascal, p. 35. *Read* the Devil's son. p. 25.
Line 62. *after* Epigram *read* occasioned by the damning of the *Covent-Garden Tragedy*.

We are impatient here to learn the particulars of the Charter for establishing the new Colony in GEORGIA. We can only yet gather in general, that it is calculated for the relief of the unfortunate, that all who go are to be free, to have Lands given them, and to be settled under a regular form of Government, with the rights and privileges of *Englishmen*; that there will be attempts made for raising Raw Silk, Vines, Olives, and other things, which succeed very well there, and do not grow well in *England*; and the people will be incouraged in bringing Raw Silk, Wine, and Oil to perfection, and be prohibited from making any Manufactures which may interfere with *Great Britain*. It is generally believed, that this Matter will, in a few years, considerably lessen the poor's tax, by relieving great numbers of unfortunate people, and by giving employment to the Manufacturers in *England*, for furnishing them with all kind of necessaries.

SIR, *Eastbourn, July* 10, 1732.

I here send an account of the water spout, word for word, as I had it from Mr. HURST, who was an eye witness of it, and is a man of credit. On June 16, 1732, about half an hour after 8 in the morning, about two miles from the shore in Pevensey Bay, there appeared a very thick dark cloud, and from which descended a very large tube or spout, which gradually sunk within 6 or 8 foot of the surface of the sea, which made the water all in a ferment and motion. The water did not ascend in a continued body, but sometimes the Horizon might be seen through it; and in about half an hour the spout seemed to draw up into the cloud again, and so disappeared, it being very calm fine weather. See *Philosoph T ans* abrid. vol. ii. pag. 104. concerning the water spout at Topsham, near Exeter. —— 'At other times these pipes and funnels are 'observed to come from the clouds, and suck up the water with great violence, p. 104. The water that was 'nearest seemed to fly hither and thither, as tho' it 'would fain have made its escape from it.' p. 105.

The RETIREMENT.

1.
ALL hail, ye fields, where constant peace attends;
 All hail, ye sacred solitary groves;
All hail, ye books, my true, my lasting friends,
 Whose conversation pleases and improves.

2.
Could one, who studies your sublimer rules,
 Become so mad to seek for joys abroad?
To run to towns, to herd with knaves and fools,
 And undistinguish'd pass among the crowd?

3.
To wild ambition many there a prey
 Think happiness in great preferment lyes;
Nor fear for that their Country to betray,
 Gaz'd at by fools, and laugh'd at by the wise.

4.
More still, whom eager hopes of wealth bewitch,
 Their precious time consume, t'increase their gain;
And fancying wretched all that are not rich,
 Neglect the end of life to get the name.

5.
But most of all soft pleasures charms invite
 In one gay scene of sensual joys to live,
Who vainly hope to find that long delight
 In vice, which virtue's charms alone can give.

6.
But how perplex'd, alas, is humane fate!
 I, whom nor sordid pelf, nor pleasures move,
Who view with scorn the trophies of the Great,
 Am made myself a wretched slave to love.

7.
If this dire passion never will be gone,
 If beauty always must my heart inthrall,
O! rather let me be confin'd to one,
 Than madly thus become a prey to all.

8.
One, who has early known the pomp of state,
 (For things unknown 'tis ignorance to condemn)
And after having view'd the gawdy bait,
 Can boldly say, The trifle I contemn.

9.
In her blest arms contented could I live,
 Contented could I dye. —— But, O my mind
Imaginary scenes of bliss deceive,
 With hopes of things impossible to find.

10.
In woman how can sense and beauty meet?
 The wisest men their youth in folly spend:
The best is he, who earliest knows the cheat,
 And finds his error, while there's time to mend.

STREPHON.

Edinburgh, July 11. This morning died his Excellency Brigadier Gen. Di Bourgay, an Officer of great conduct and experience. *C. P.* 18.

Important news from Ireland *in heroic verse*, Dublin, *July* 8.
On wednesday a young man, who was swimming was drown'd.
Last thursday —— Tennison, Esq; marry'd a Lady of ten thousand pound. *P. DJ.*
On wednesday Farrel and Riley to the gallows were tied,
But both denied the fact for which by hemp they died.
The Journeymen Shoemakers and Taylors on both these days
Were valiantly ingag'd in two most bloody frays,
In which the Gentle Craft won double glorious bays.
C. DP. DJ.

New York, May 22. On wednesday last a woman of this City had liberty to go into a garden to gather a mess of green herbs, and in gathering them, she took hold of the top of a raddish, and pulling it up, found that the stem of the raddish grew out of the appearance of a child's hand and fingers; which being surprizingly strange, it was carried before a Magistrate, who ordered it to be put into some spirits to preserve it: the spirits became thick and ruddy, like blood and water, and did stink; whereupon they put it into fresh spirits, and it continues in the shape and colour of an human hand and 5 fingers, with sinews and joints, which open and shut. —— It is to be seen at Serjeant Tingles in this City, and abundance of people resort daily to see it. Some are of opinion, that an infant has been buried there, and the seed of the raddish to have taken root in the wrist of the child's hand, and the vegetative quality of the raddish to have preserved the flesh from putrifying, or at least to retain the colour and appearance of a hand and fingers of human flesh, it being hard and very tough, like flesh. *DJ.* 17.

FOREIGN NEWS.

THURSDAY, *July* 13.

Hague, July 1. N.S. The late Duke of Ormonde's being at Rome and Albano cannot be true; for by these letters we find him upon the road between Madrid and Barcelona. *P.*

Hambourg, July 12. A few days since the Magistrates annulled the ancient law touching majority; and enacted, that no male shall be accounted a major at 18, but at 22; nor any female as before at 14, but at 18. *DP. DJ.*

FRIDAY, *July* 14.

Paris, July 1. N.S. Extract of the French King's answer to the Duke of Lorrain's letter, notifying his advancement to the dignity of Vice-roy of Hungary. ——
'Whatever opposition the times may have raised between 'my interests and those of the Imperial house, I hope the 'place you are in will not give me any occasion to change 'my sentiments with regard to your family.' *P.*

The late Prince of Schwartzemberg had such a misgiving of some accident in his journey to Prague, that having spoke of it to several intimate friends, he made his will the day before he set out, which he signed with these words in his mouth, That he should never see Vienna again. *P.* — *Let our* Free-thinkers *account for this* misgiving, *upon their own principles, if they can.*

SATURDAY, *July* 15.

This day arrived the Mails from Holland *and* Flanders.

Vienna, July 9. They write from Constantinople, that the Grand Seignior had declared to the English Ambassador, that if the King of Spain should attack the Republicks of Barbary under the protection of the Porte, he must support them with all his might. *WE. LE.*

TUESDAY, *July* 18.

Yesterday arrived the Mail from Holland.

Extract of a letter from Seville, *dated July* 8. N. S. — The Spanish troops landed near Oran the 29. The next day the King's army, and that of the Moors, consisting of about 20,000 men, came to an action, wherein the latter were defeated. The Spaniards had 30 men killed and 170 wounded. On the 1st they entered Oran. The enemy's army was to have been reinforced with 10,000 Moors, and 6000 Turks from Algiers: but these hearing of the defeat made the best of their way back. There were found in the town and castles of Oran, 80 brass cannon, 50 iron, 12 field pieces, a great quantity of ammunition, grain in abundance, a great number of sheep, oxen, and poultry, a vast quantity of wool, provisions for 3 months. *C. P. DJ.* — — *I cannot accede to* my Brother DP.'*s opinion, that these* poultry *had no* cocks, *nor* chicken *among them; and fear he was a little mistaken in translating the french word by* pullets.

The Beak Galley arrived in the river, came from Cadiz the 29th ult. she brings advice that the Spaniards lost 4000 men, 2 entire regiments, one Irish and the other French, with a Major General, having been cut off by an ambuscade, which loss they ascribed to false intelligence received from the French Consul, of the Town being deserted. The Moors are said to have lost 7000 men. *DJ.*

On Tuesday Stocks were

South Sea Stock was 98 1 qr. 98 3 8ths to 1 half, for the Opening. South Sea Annuity 110 3 8ths, to 1 half Bank 149 1 half. New Bank Circulation 8 l. 10 s. Premium. India 167, 167 1 half, for the Opening. Three per Cent. Annuity 98 7 8ths to 99, for ditto. Royal Exchange Assurance 100, without the Dividend. London Assurance 13 3 8ths, to 1 half. York Buildings 4 1 half, to 5. African 40. English Copper 2 l. 6 s. Welch ditto 1 l. 15 s. South Sea Bonds 3 l. 17 s. to 18 s. Premium. India ditto 6 l. 19 s. to 7 l. ditto. Blanks 7 l. 10 s. 20 l. Prize 20 l.

ADVERTISEMENTS.

To all Gentlemen, Builders, and others,
ALEXANDER EMERTON,
Colour Man, *at the* Bell *over-against* Arundel-Street, *in the* Strand, LONDON,

SELLS all Sorts of COLOURS ready prepared (at the lowest Prices) that any Gentleman, Builder, &c. may set their Servants or Labourers to paint their Houses only by the Help of a printed Direction, which he gives with his Colours.

N. B. Five Pounds Worth of Colours will paint as much Work as a House-Painter will do for Twenty Pounds.

He likewise sells (to the Ladies) all Sorts of Water-Colours and Varnish, with every Thing necessary for the New Japanning, and gives a printed Direction, for the doing of it to the greatest Perfection, to those that buy Colours. —— Also Italian Powder for cleaning Pictures.

He dealls only for Ready Money.

PROPOSALS
For Printing by SUBRCRIPTION,

THE HISTORY of the Grand Controversy between the Secular and Regular Clergy of the Church of *Rome*, from the Year 162[illegible] to 1634, concerning the Usurpation of RICHARD SMITH, Titular Bishop of *Chalcedon*, who pretended to be sole Ordinary Bishop of all *England* and *Scotland*. Wrote in *Latin* by the President of the *English* Benedictine Monks, RUDISINDUS BARLO, and faithfully done into *English* from the Original, for the Entertainment of the Curious, especially Divines and Lawyers, both Ecclesiastick and Civil, of what Religion soever.

With the Remonstrances of the *Roman* Catholick Laity made to the said Bishop, and also to his Excellency *Carolo Coloma*, Embassador Extraordinary of the Most Catholick Majesty, and to the Marquis *Fontany*, Embassador of the Most Christian King, *&c.* taken also from the *Latin* Originals: All which Treatises have been hitherto suppress, by the *Papists*, for Political Reasons given therein.

As also the famous Bull of Pope URBAN VIII. called PLANTATA, necessary for the right understanding of the Whole, which was never before any where printed.

To which will be added,

A LETTER concerning the Disputes that have happen'd among the Benedictine Monks since the Year 1700 to this present Time. Shewing how even they themselves have varied from their original Principles. By one who was a Member of that Body, and concerned therein.

By JOHN WILLIAMS

PROPOSALS may be had of (and SUBSCRIPTIONS taken for the Author by) W. Meadows, at the Angel, in Cornhill; T. Astley, at the Rose, and S. Austen, at the Angel and Bible, St. Paul's Church-Yard; C. Davis, Pater-Noster-Row; T. Woodward, at the Half-Moon, L. Gilliver, at Homer's Head, and J. Stephens, at the Hand and Star, between the Two Temple-Gates; B. Motte, at the Middle Temple-Gate; T. Worral, at Judge Coke's Head, H. Walthoe, next Door to the Rainbow Coffee-House, W. Reason, in Flower-de-Luce-Court, J. Isted, at the Golden-Ball, near Chancery-Lane, Fleet-Street; F. Gyles, against Gray's-Inn-Gate, Holborn; O. Payne, in Round-Court, T. Game, at the Bible, by the New Church, in the Strand; T. Green, Charing-Cross; J. Jackson, in Pallmall; J. J[illegible] at the Bible, in St. James's-Street; J. Brindley, at the King's Arms, and W. Shropshire, opposite to the Duke of Grafton's, New Bond Street; and J. Stagg, Westminster-Hall, Booksellers: J. Hug[illegible] in Bartholomew-Close, and T. Gover, by Fleet-Ditch, Black-[illegible] Printers.

Lately published,
The Second Edition, corrected,
The LAW of TITHES:

SHewing their Nature, Kinds, Properties, Incidents, by whom, when, and in what Manner payable, [illegible] and in what Courts to be sued for and recovered; what Things, Lands, or Persons are charged with, or exempt therefrom. With the Nature, Incidents, and Effects of Customs, Prescriptions, Real Compositions, Modus decimandi, Libels, Suggestions, Prohibitions, Consultations, Custom of London, &c. Wherein all the Statutes and adjudged Cases, relative to the Subject, are introduced and considered. By *William Bohun* of the Middle Temple [illegible]

Also, Just published, by the same Author,

A TITHING TABLE: Shewing (by way of Analysis) of what Things Tythes are or are not due, [illegible] Common Law, Custom, or Prescription. Price 1 s.

N. B. These two may be had bound together or separate. Printed for J. Brotherton, W. Meadows, T. Cox, [illegible] liffe, and R. Willock, in Cornhill; J. Hazard, near Stationers Hall; W. Bickerton, without Temple-Bar; T. [illegible] and S. Austen, in St. Paul's Church-yard; and L. G[illegible] in Fleet-street.

To be Lett,

A SHOP in Judgate-Street. Enquire at the Oxford-Arms in the said Street.

NOTICE is hereby given, to all Encouragers of Mr. PALMER's
HISTORY of PRINTING,
That the Remainder of it will be finished from his own Manuscript, and published in about a Fortnight.

N. B. This last Number, containing a greater number of Sheets than any of the former, will finish the first Volume, which relates to the Historical Part.

June 12, 1732.

By PERMISSION of
The Right Honourable the Lord Chancellor.
The Right Honourable the Lord Raymond, Lord Chief Justice of his Majesty's Court of King's Bench.
The Right Honourable Arthur Onslow, Esq; Speaker of the House of Commons.
The Honourable Sir John Hind Cotton, Bart.
Francis Annesly, Esq.
Samuel Burroughs, Esq; one of the Masters of the High Court of Chancery.
John Hanbury, Esq.
Trustees of the Cottonian Library.

IT is proposed by John Pine, to Engrave, by Subscription, a Correct Copy of King JOHN's Great Charter relating to the Original now remaining in the Cottonian Library; which, being a Recognition of the Rights and Liberties of the People, it is presumed the Publick will encourage a Design to perpetuate a Record of such Dignity and Importance.

It will be contained in one Imperial Sheet of Paper, and engraved in the finest manner and Character with the Original, and adorn'd with proper Decorations.

The Price to Subscribers will be Half a Guinea to be paid on the Delivery, which will be about Christmas next.

Those Gentlemen, who are willing to honour this Subscription, are desired to send their Names and Places of Abode as soon as possible, with will entitle them to the first Impressions.

N. B. Those who subscribe for Six, shall have a Seventh gratis.

Subscriptions are taken in by C. King, in Westminster-Hall; N. Prevost, in the Strand; R. Gosling, B. Motte, T. Woodward, near the Temple, Fleet-Street; W. Innys, C. Rivington, S. Austen, in St. Paul's Church-Yard; A. Bettesworth and C. Hitch; J. Batley, in Pater-Noster-Row; W. Hinchliffe, E. Symons, at the Royal-Exchange; J. Brindley, in New Bond-Street; J. Clark, Print-seller in Gray's-Inn; and J. Pine, Engraver, over-against Little-Britain, in Alderfgate-Street.

This Day was published,

The Fifth Edition, of

A Journey from ALEPPO to Jerusalem, at Easter, A. D. 1697. To which is added, An Account of the Author's Journey to the Banks of Euphrates and Pair, and to the Country of Mesopotamia. By Henry Maundrell, M. A. late Fellow of Exeter-College, and Chaplain to the Factory at Aleppo.

Oxford, printed at the Theatre for Anthony Peisley; and sold by J. Brotherton, W. Meadows, T. Cox, W. Hinchliffe, and R. Willock, in Cornhill; J. Hazard, near Stationers-Hall; W. Bickerton, without Temple-Bar; T. Astley, and S. Austen, in St. Paul's Church-yard; and L. Gilliver in Fleet-street.

Of whom may be had,
Dr. TRAPP's Sermons at Lady Moyer's Lecture on the Doctrine of the Trinity, with the Objections against it answered in a summary View of the whole Controversy. To which are added, Discourses on the Parable of Dives and Lazarus; setting forth the deplorable Corruption, Immorality and Infidelity of the present Age: Shewing the absolute Necessity of a Holy Life, demonstrating the Certainty of a Future State, and the Truth of the Christian Religion.

This Day is published,

[Price One Shilling.]
The Second Edition corrected, of

A Practical GRAMMAR of the English TONGUE In two Parts. Containing, I. Instructions for the true Spelling, Reading and Writing of English. II. The Principles of Arithmetick, Geography, and Chronology, explained and suited to the meanest Capacities. For the Use of Schools.

By THO. DYCHE, late School-Master at Stratford Bow.

Printed for J. Clarke, at the Golden-Ball in Duck-Lane, near West-Smithfield.

This Day is published,

THE Youth's Instructor in the ENGLISH Tongue: or, a Spelling-Book, containing more Words, and a greater Variety of very useful Collections, than any Book of this Kind and Bigness: Written, with two Copper-Plates, curiously engrav'd. The first, Mathematically demonstrating at one View, the exact Proportion each Letter ought to bear to the rest in Writing: to which is annex'd a full Explanation of the same. The Second, is a Specimen of the most useful Hands for Business, with plain Directions and Copies for Writing. To which is added, a Compendious Grammar of the English Tongue. First design'd for the Author's own Scholars, and now made publick for a general Benefit.

By J. OWEN, Σχολάρχης.

Printed for J. Oswald, at the Rose and Crown, in Little-Britain; and J. Hughson, Printer, in Bartholomew-Close. [Price One Shilling and Six Pence.]

There is now in the Press, and will speedily be publish'd A SECOND EDITION, in two Volumes in Folio, of

RAPIN THOYRAS's History of ENGLAND. By N. Tindal, M. A. Vicar of Great Waltham in Essex, with the following Improvements: 1. The Translation is thoroughly revised. 2. All the Errors and Mistakes of the Original are corrected. 3. Several Hundred of Marginal References, accidentally omitted by the Author, are supply'd with additional Notes.

Whereas there is I say set on Foot the Project of a new Translation, in Weekly Pamphlets of four Sheets for Six Pence; and whereas it is affirmed by the Undertaker, that the Whole will be compriz'd in 400 Sheets, it is evident, on the contrary, by comparing the first Week's Performance with the Original, that the Number of Sheets will amount to 600; wherefore, that Gentlemen may not be drawn in by such specious Pretences, while the abovemention'd Volumes are printing, there will be publish'd every Week, beginning in a fortnight ten Days, five Sheets for 6 d. in such a Manner as to contain six of the projected new Translation; so that what is proposed by the Undertaker for 1s. 6d. will be sold for 1s. and the Whole visibly reduced to 300 Sheets, at the Price of two Guineas, including the Maps and Tables, engraven on Copper Plates, for which nothing more will be demand'd to the Buyer; and both Volumes will be publish'd in the Space of a Year, which is but a Quarter of the Time that it can be new done, as it ought, by any one Hand.

Proposals, with a Specimen, will be publish'd this Week by James at John Knapton, at the Crown in St. Paul's Church-Yard.

Where may be had, the History compleat, in 15 Volumes in Octavo.

This Day was published,

For the Use of Families, beautifully printed in Two Vols. 8vo. adorn'd with 34 Plates, Engraven by Mr. Sturt,

DUPIN's EVANGELICAL HISTORY: Or the Records of the SON of GOD, and their Veracity demonstrated, in the Life and Acts of our Blessed Lord and Saviour Jesus Christ, and the Holy Apostles. Wherein 1. The Life of our Blessed Saviour Jesus Christ is related in all its Circumstances, according to the Order of Time, in a pathetick and practical Method, thereby composing a perfect Harmony of the Gospels. 2. Proofs from his Sermons and Discourses of these Essential and Important Truths, which all Christians are obliged to know and practise, in order to their Eternal Salvation. 3. His Parables, Miracles, and Sufferings, set in a just Light, and defended from all the Oppositions of wicked and designing Men. 4. An Application of the Whole to the respective Uses of Christians, with regular Devotions conformable to the several Periods of the Holy History; and Directions how he may read the Life of Jesus Christ to Advantage.

Printed for R. Ware, at the Bible and Sun in Amen-Corner, near Pater-Noster-Row. Price 8 s.

Also may be had at the same Pace,

1. The large House-Bibles, Folio, with the six Maps of sacred Geography, and a brief Concordance for the more easy finding out of the Places therein contained. By J. Downame, B. D.
Bound in Calf Leather — 1 l. 8 s. per Book.
And with Mr. Sturt's Cuts at 1. 19. ditto.
On a fine Paper with Cuts — 1. 9 s. ditto.
2. Impartial Churchman; or, A fair and candid Representation of the Excellency and Beauty of the Church of England. Together with an earnest and affectionate Address to the Protestant Dissenters. By Robert Warren, D. D. Price 3 s 6 d.
3. A Description of 300 Animals, viz. Beasts, Birds, Fishes, Serpents and Insects. With a particular Account of the Whale-Fishery. Extracted out of the best Authors, and adapted to the Use of all Capacities, especially to allure Children to read. Illustrated with Copper Plates, wherein is curiously engraven every Beast, Bird, Fish, Serpent and Insect described in the whole Book. Price 3 s 6 d.
4. Tradesman's Guide. Containing a List of all the Stage Coaches and Carriages; with an Account of all the Market Towns in England. Price 1 s.

This Day was published.

(Beautifully printed in One Volume, Octavo,)

A Treatise of continual FEVERS, in four Parts. Books; wherein are enumerated, the Diagnosticks, Prognosticks, and Events of the several Diseases incident to Human Bodies. By JODOCUS LOMMIUS. Translated from the Latin by THOMAS DALE, M. D. Printed for J. Brotherton, W. Meadows, T. Cox, W. Hinchliffe, and R. Willock, in Cornhill; J. Hazard, near Stationers-Hall; W. Bickerton without Temple-Bar; T. Astley and S. Austen in St. Paul's Church-Yard; and L. Gilliver in Fleet-Street.

BOOKS printed for, and sold by J. Brotherton, at the Bible next the Fleece Tavern, in Cornhill.

Whitlock's Memorials.	Telemachus, by Boyer.
Temple's Works, 2 Vol.	Ditto in French.
Bailey's Eng. Dict. Fol.	Guardians, 2 Vol.
Tillotson's Works, 3 Vol.	Langham's Duties.
Bates's Works, Fol.	Free Thoughts on Religion
State of Britain, for 1732.	La Belle Assemble, 3 Vol.
Bailey's Justin.	Vanburgh's Plays, 2 Vol.
Origin of Honour.	Addison's Works, 4 Vol.
Indias Conduct.	Spectators, 8 Vol.
Virgin unmask'd.	Trapp's Virgil.
Hays's Ship and Supercargo	D'Urfey's Songs, 6 Vol.
Book-Keeper.	Milton Lost and Regain'd.
Cole's Detection, 3 Vol.	D'Anois Tales, 3 Vol.
Bohun's Law of Tythes.	De Retz Memoirs, 4 Vol.
Feasts & Fasts of the Church.	Tom Brown's Works, 4 Vol.
Enfield Freeholdship.	Farnborough's Grammar.
Life of Oliver Cromwell.	Phillips's Grammar.
Life of the K. of Sweden.	Donnington's Devotion.
Dampier's Journal to Madagascar.	Congreve's Plays, 2 Vol.
Rapin's Hist. of England, 15 Vol.	Pope's and Swift's Misc; Vol.
Arbuthnot of Ailment's, com.	Pope's Misc. 4 Vol.
	Turkish Spy, 8 Vol.

This Day was published,

AN ODE to his Grace the Duke of Newcastle, Written on the present Tranquillity of Europe, establish'd by the Influence of the British Power.

Nihil habet aut Fortuna tua majus, quàm ut possis, aut Natura tua melius, quàm, ut velis, quàm plurimis conservare. Cic.

Printed for J. Batley, at the Dove in Pater-Noster-Row. Price 6 d.

Where may had, just published,
Dedicated to the Gentlemen of the Navy of England, The Memoirs of Monsieur DU GUE TROUIN, Chief of a Squadron of the Royal Navy of France, and Great Cross of the Military Order of S. Lewis; containing all his Sea-Actions with the English, Dutch, and Portuguese, in the late Wars of King William and Queen Anne.
Translated from the French by a Sea-Officer.

The Cælestial Anodyne Tincture: Or, The Great Pain-Easing Medicine,

FAm'd and approv'd of for its wonderful and never-failing Success, in giving immediate Ease and Relief in all manner of pains, either inward or outward, and is the most certain Remedy in the World for a sure and speedy Cure of the Cholick, and expelling Wind, Gripes and pains in the Stomach, Pleurisy, stitches or pains in the side, back, loins, or any other part; Rheumatick Ailments, which cause pain and dolor. It hath given ease to a Miracle, when all other Remedies have fail'd. In the Gravel and Stone in the Kidneys, it gives ease forthwith, and brings them away to Admiration. It also facilitates and causes a speedy Delivery in Child-birth. 'Tis no Quack trifling thing to allure the World with, but a real and well-experienced Medicine, not acting by Stupefaction (as Opiates) but by a friendly, balfamick, and subtile Nature, pacifying the most severe and terrible racking pains, and carries off the Cause, not by purging, but by Transpiration, by Urine, or breaking Wind. No Family ought to be without it. And, used outwardly, it cures Swellings, Aches, pains, Numbness, or Weakness of the Joints; 'tis excellent for Cramps, and all other aged Infirmities, effecting Wonders in Agues, Fevers, Small-pox, &c. No Family ought to be without it.
It is sold only by Mr. PARKER, Printer, at his House in Salisbury-Court, or by such persons as he shall depute, viz. at Mr. Parker's, a Printer, in Bull-Head Court, Jewin-street; at the White Gallon Pot, a Chandler's Shop in Bandy-Leg-Walk, Southwark, and at Mr. Neal's, a Toy-shop over against the White-Hart Inn in the Borough, at Eighteen pence a bottle, with printed Directions; and, if requested, will be brought to any Person, by the Hawker who sells his Penny-post. Sealed as above.

The Grub-ſtreet Journal.

NUMB. 134

Thurſday, *JULY* 27, 1732.

Thy throne is darkneſs in th' abyſs of light,
A blaze of glory that forbids the ſight.
DRYDEN's *Hind and Panther*, Part I.

Mr. BAVIUS,

NO doubt you have obſerved, that the attention of Divines and good inquiſitive Chriſtians has of late been greatly engaged about a celebrated controverſy concerning *God's preſcience, man's free-will, &c.* The champions in this cauſe are Mr. FANCOURT, Mr MILLAR, Mr. NORMAN, Mr. BLISS, &c. worthy gentlemen all. But, unhappily, the diſpute has ſwelled into ſo many volumes, that no head can compaſs it: even the diſputants themſelves have now almoſt loſt ſight of their original deſign; the zeal of their hearts having tranſported them ſo far, as to uſe one another a little unkindly. In ſhort, the combuſtion of their paſſions breaks-out with ſo much fury, that it would be a piece of charity to part them. The only expedient, I can think-of, is to ſtate the matter in the cleareſt light; and to pray them, for Chriſtianity's ſake, to forbear their altercations a while, till they have obliged the public with their animadverſions on the following abſtract; when, it is to be hoped, they will grow cool enough to condemn, each man himſelf; and to pardon one another. So will they be at quiet, and the church better edifyed. —— Pray, conjure them to be ſhort; and not to ſay one word beſide the purpoſe.

AN ABSRACT *of a lately revived diſpute concerning* Liberty, Preſcience, *&c. by way of ſupplement to* Mr. Chamber's Dictionary.

PRESCIENCE (paragr. 2. dele the reſt, and add] To reconcile the preſcience of god with the free-agency of man, has long been looked-upon as an inſuperable difficulty: inſomuch that ſome, to eſtabliſh free-will, have denied preſcience; and others, to ſet-up predeſtination, have brought-in a fatal neceſſity. —— But, if the matter be well weighed, without prejudice or partiality, neither is our freedom to be given-up, nor God's preſcience denied; of both which we have the greateſt aſſurance (V. Liberty, Omniſcience, Prediction) nor yet will it be found ſo difficult to reconcile them upon the principles of reaſon, as that we ſhould have recourſe to that ſtanding principle of Divines, as Mr. BAYLE invidiouſly ſuggeſts, of captivating the underſtanding to the obedience of faith.

It is, indeed, pretended, that all things muſt neceſſarily be, becauſe certainly foreſeen. ——— The argument, in its ſtrongeſt light, is this: God can foreknow the certain exiſtence of things, either only as that exiſtence is the effect of his decree, or as it depends on its own cauſes. If he foreknows that exiſtence, as it is the effect of his decree; his decree makes that exiſtence neceſſary: for, it implies a contradiction, for an all-powerful being to decree any thing, which ſhall not neceſſarily come to paſs. If he foreknows that exiſtence, as it depends on its own cauſes, that exiſtence is no leſs neceſſary: for, it no leſs implies a contradiction, that cauſes ſhould not produce their effects (cauſes and effects having a neceſſary relation to, and dependance on each other) than that an event ſhould not come-to-paſs, which is decreed by God. —— Anſwer (1) As to the decrees of God, it may well be ſaid with Moſes (Deut. xxix. 29) that *Secret things belong unto the Lord*; and therefore are not the proper objects of our enquirys: but, as for thoſe things which are revealed, which belong to us; we do not find any ſuch repreſentations of them, as would induce us to look-upon ourſelves under a fatal neceſſity in all our actions (V. Predeſtination). (2.) As to the preſcience of God, If, upon other accounts, there be no impoſſibility, but that the actions of men may be free; the bare certainty of the divine fore-knowledge can never be proved to deſtroy that freedom, or make any alteration in the nature of mens actions. For it is certain, that bare foreknowledge has no influence at all, in any reſpect; nor affects, in any meaſure, the manner of the exiſtence of any thing.

All, that the greateſt oppoſers of liberty have ever urged, or can urge, upon this head, amounts only to this; that "fore-knowledge implies certainty, and certainty implies neceſſity." But neither is it true, that certainty implies neceſſity; nor does fore knowledge imply any other certainty, than ſuch a certainty only as would be equally in things, tho' there was no fore-knowledge. —— For (firſt) the certainty of fore-knowledge does not cauſe the certainty of things; but is it ſelf founded on the reality of their exiſtence. Whatever now is, 'tis certain that it is; and it was yeſterday, and from eternity, as certainly true, that the thing would be to day, as it is now certain that it is. And this certainty of event is equally the ſame, whether it is ſuppoſed that the thing could be fore known, or not. For, whatever at any time is; it was certainly true from eternity, as to the event, that that thing would be: and this certain truth of every future event, would not at all have been the leſs, tho' there had been no ſuch thing as fore-knowledge. Bare preſcience, therefore, has no influence, at all, upon any thing; nor contributes, in the leaſt, towards making it neceſſary, any more than the ſimple knowledge of it, when it is done; both theſe kinds of knowledge, implying plainly a certainty only of the event; which would be the ſame, tho' there were no ſuch knowledge; and not-at-all any neceſſity of the thing. —— 'Tis true; the manner how God can foreſee future things, without a chain of neceſſary cauſes, is impoſſible for us to explain diſtinctly. We have but finite faculties and meaſures, which bear no proportion to infinite powers and objects. Could we explain the manner how infinite knowledge knows things, we ſhould be like God in knowledge: our underſtandings would be infinite like his: and, in this eſpecially, it becomes us to put-on the modeſty of creatures, and to remember that we are finite and limited. —— There are indeed thoſe, who undertake to explain the particular manner: ſome ſay, that God ſees future events *in ſpeculo voluntatis*: others ſay, that the eternity of God is actually commenſurate to all duration, as his immenſity to all ſpace; and that God does not ſo properly fore-ſee and fore-know, as ſee and know future things by the preſentiality and exiſtence of all things in eternity: for, ſay they, future things are actually preſent and exiſting to God, tho' not *in menſura propria*, yet *in menſura aliena*. But this is but to darken difficulties with a ſhow of knowledge. In finite underſtandings it is mere vanity to pretend to explain all the ways of infinite knowledge. —— (Secondly) Certainty of event does not, in any ſort, imply neceſſity. For, let a fataliſt ſuppoſe, that there was in man a power of beginning motion, that is, of acting freely; and let him ſuppoſe further, if he pleaſe, that thoſe actions could not-poſſibly be fore known: will there not yet, nothwithſtanding this ſuppoſition, be, in the nature of things, the ſame certainty of event, in any one of the man's actions, as if they were never ſo fatal and neceſſary? For inſtance, ſuppoſe the man, by an internal principle of motion, and an abſolute freedom of will, without any external cauſe or impulſe at all, does ſome particular action to day; and ſuppoſe it was not poſſible that this action ſhould have been fore ſeen yeſterday? was there not, nevertheleſs, the ſame certainty of event, as if it had been foreſeen: that is, would it not, notwithſtanding the ſuppoſed freedom, have been as certain a truth yeſterday, and from eternity, that this action was in event to be performed to day, tho' ſuppoſed ever ſo impoſſible to have been fore known, as it is, now, a certain and infallible truth that it is performed?

Wherefore (1.) mere certainty of events does not, in any meaſure, imply neceſſity: (2.) and conſequently fore-knowledge, however difficult to be explained as to the manner of it, yet, ſince 'tis evident it implies no other certainty, but only that certainty of event, which the thing would equally have without being fore-known, 'tis evident, that it alſo implies no neceſſity.

S I R, *July* 16, 1732.

AUthors in general (and in particular Dramatic) may be divided into two claſſes, the Venal, and the Gentlemen-Writers. The firſt of theſe have a very numerous offspring, and contrary to all other parents, inſtead of feeding, are fed by them; if any one of their children fail of procuring this end, let them think it never ſo hopeful and promiſing; nay, tho' it be the parents favourite brat, they'll knock it on the head, to ſave another, for which they may not have ſo much fondneſs. An inſtance of this has been lately ſeen in the *Covent Garden Tragedy*; which, tho' a favourite child, was cruelly abandoned by its daddy, to ſave a twin-brother, that happened not to be ſo obnoxious to the town.

There is another very remarkable circumſtance attending theſe venal parents, and that is, tho' they may make ſome diſtinction among their children, they are not really anxious, whether they are good for any thing or no, but only whether they will bring any thing in. From hence it is, that when any of theſe half-begotten children are attacked in public, their parents, inſtead of defending them, ungratefully give them up; or if they do offer at a juſtification, are aſhamed to do it in their own names, but have recourſe to thoſe of the loweſt orders of men, *viz.* Candle Snuffers and Prize-Fighters. A low joke, a Bear Garden flouriſh, is all they can muſter up. By this indeed they evade pleading guilty, at the ſame time that they dare not ſtand a tryal. It were to be wiſhed ſome invention could be found out to oblige them to plead one way or other. In civil, and criminal matters, the law has wiſely proceeded againſt *contumacy*: and I think the town has equal right, in matters of Entertainment, to inſiſt upon the Poet's juſtification of himſelf, or acknowledgment of his accuſation. I ſhall not pretend to preſcribe the nature or degree of puniſhment, to which I would ſubject theſe *Contumaces*; but I think the moſt effectual way to reſtore the Stage to its former decency and dignity, would be for the town to join, never to admit on the Theatre a ſecond production of an Author, who ſhall have refuſed to vindicate his firſt. Such a reſolution as this, would not only be the occaſion of having better Plays taken into the houſe, but would likewiſe gradually be that of the total excluſion of bad ones. For a Poet that ſhould find he muſt have regard to ſomething more, than his meer profit, would endeavour to cultivate his genius, and depend more upon that, than the intereſt he may have in a ſett of managers, whoſe favour he may have abſolutely ſecured to himſelf by arts, either unknown to, or unbecoming a gentleman.

Now that, I am upon this topic, I cannot help wiſhing the Gentlemen concerned in the management of the houſe, would ſeriouſly reflect on the ſpirit and indignation the town ſhewed laſt winter, when they attempted to force a moſt abſurd and ridiculous * Play upon them; and likewiſe how unanimous every body has ſince been in all private companies, in condemning † another Play, altho' it was ſuffered to be acted ſeveral nights ſucceſſively. I fancy the ſpirit of the town will not be leſs next winter than it was the laſt, if they ſee the ſame tyrannical impoſition of bad Plays on them. It may perhaps be carried higher, if they find (as poſſibly they may in one ſhape or other) a real good Play has been rejected, becauſe it was only *ſenſible*, and *pretty*, but not *theatrical*.

Another thing that I would recommend to the ſerious conſideration of the Managers, is, not to refuſe a Play, becauſe it is written by a Gentleman, whom a natural genius that way, and ſome little leiſure may prompt to write. I am inclin'd to think better Pieces may be expected from ſuch a quarter, than from any venal Poet, that lives only by the numerous productions of his too-often-drained brains.

I have been led into theſe few reflections, Mr. BAVIUS, by an advertiſement in the Bear-Garden ſtile, publiſhed in the *Daily Poſt* of the 14th inſtant; on which I ſhall only make this remark, that it looks as if the Author of it was deſirous to divert the town from examining into the criticiſms lately formed againſt his poetical off-ſpring, by endeavouring, like a Hockley-in-the-Hole-Merry-Andrew, to make them laugh, tho' by jeſts adapted to an audience fit only to appear there. I am, Mr. BAVIUS,

Not you yourſelf, but your humble ſervant,

DRAMATICUS.

* *The Modiſh Couple.* † *The Modern Husband.*

Mr. BAVIUS,

AS the following verſes ſeem to be written ſomewhat in the ſpirit of the Ancients, I believe, they will be acceptable to you, and your readers. They came into my hands very accidentally: I was told they were written on a certain Arch-deacon, who uſed on all occaſions, in his charges, to ſet the Clergy and people agape by citeing fathers, councils, canons, &c. As they may be ſerviceable to ridicule this falſe ſhew of learning, you will beſt judge what uſe to make of them.

Neſcit vox miſſa reverti.

E ſede nuper, Clericis adſtantibus,
Mediam, ſonorâ voce dicens *Abbates*,
Jus faſque contra, ſyllabam brevem dedit
Notus Sacerdos, ——— qui nomen trahit;
Epiſcopo ſecundus, vel potiùs prior;
Largoque circa collum ſerico tumens;
Doctoris idem titulo adornatus gravi;

Tonare suetus, bruta factu fulmina
[illegible] a pecore tuul tradit em
PERICLES [illegible] lter, [illegible] quatiens forum
At d[illegible] cat [illegible] [illegible] mentitum
Sint [illegible] regulas protede e,
Vocemque [illegible] continere spiritu:
Ut, si qui Graeca forte verba proferat
Sub [illegible] rectius possit loqui;
Nec, dum Chronistis, quos nunquam legit, citat,
Offendat aures graviter audientium.

DOMESTIC NEWS.

C. *Courant.*	E P. *Evening Post.*
P. *Post-Boy.*	S J. *S. James's Evening Post.*
D P. *Daily Post.*	WE. *Whitehall Evening P.*
D J. *Daily Journal.*	LE. *London Evening Post.*

THURSDAY, *July* 20.

On tuesday a great match was play'd at Tennis, for 500 guineas, between the R. Hon. the L. James Cavendish and Mr. Bladen, at the King's Tennis Court in the Haymarket; but the same being equal, is to be play'd over again. *C.*

This morning the R. Hon. the Lady Gage, accompany'd by Mrs. Osborn, daughter to the L. Visc. Torrington, set out for Paris for 6 weeks, to visit her daughter, who lies ill there. *D P.*

Dover, July 16. Yesterday the R. Hon. Lord Arundel of Wardour, and some of his children landed here, as did also the Lord Herbert from Calais. *WE. LE.*

Tho. Beasly, Esq; is made Collector of his Majesty's Customs in Pensilvania, in the room of William-Erdman Fox, Esq; deceased. *D J.*

Yesterday a Court of Directors was held at the Bank of England, when Mr. Hunt, who had disqualify'd himself some time since, was re-chosen a Director. *D P.*

On tuesday night, about 10, a person very well dress'd, came to the white horse inn in Fleet-street, to lodge, pretending he had just come off a journey; he had a tit-bit for supper, and having regal'd himself with a bottle of wine, retir'd to his chamber, and made off in the morning before any of the family were stirring, taking the sheets and pillow biers with him. *S J.*

On tuesday morning Mr. Farrow, an eminent Apothecary in Newgate market, was married to Mrs. Davis, a rich widow Gentlewoman, with a fortune of 600 l. per ann. *D P.* —— *Yesterday morning* —— Hollyer, Esq; was married to Miss Caswell of Hatton garden, a young Lady of 16,000 l. fortune. *S J.*

On saturday died of the Small-pox, Mr. John Sawyer, Keeper of the King's little or home park at Windsor; and her Grace the junior Dutchess of Marlborough, as Ranger, has been pleased to bestow that employment on his son. *D P.* —— Yesterday morning John Fellows, Esq; at his house in Red-lion-square. *P. D J.* Martin Fellows. *D P.*

FRIDAY, *July* 21.

Yesterday his Grace the D. of Newcastle gave a grand entertainment at his house at Kensington to several persons of distinction. *C. P.* An elegant entertainment. *D P.*

Mr. Morffet is by the Serjeant at Arms attending the House of Commons made Door-keeper to the said house, in the room of his father lately deceased. *D P.*

Sir Arthur Forbes, of Cragievar, is chosen Member of Parliament for the County of Aberdeen, in the room of Sir Arch. Grant, Bar. expelled the house. *D J.*

On wednesday a large quantity of gold was seized by the King's Officers on board the ship Hertford at Woolwich, lately arrived from China, and said to belong to a Gentleman, who came home in that ship. *D P.*

Yesterday 2 boys were committed to the Gatehouse, Westminster, for robbing a child in the street of a gold chain and locket. *D J.*

Cambridge, July 15. Last week, at the Commencement, Dr. Ric. Grey, Author of the *Abridgment of the Bishop of London's Codex*, and *Memoria Technica*, came to this University, and they presented him with a Doctor's degree, as the University of Oxford had done before, for his writing the said books. *C.*

On monday at a Florists feast at Hammersmith, was the greatest shew of flowers that has been seen this 10 years. Mr. Heater, Gardener of Barns, by producing 6 very large seedlings, won the large prize of a silver cup: the 4 other prizes were won by several Gardeners of Hammersmith. There was a Sermon preached by the Rev. Mr. Hall to the Society of Gardeners, at their Parish Church; after which they dined at the Swan, which dinner consisted of above 50 dishes. *P.*

A few days since died of a tedious indisposition that had long prey'd upon his spirits, occasioned by too close an application to his studies, the Rev. Mr. Roger Laurence, celebrated for his labours on Lay-Baptism, for which he was created Master of Arts by the University of Oxford, and on tuesday his corpse was carried out of town to be interr'd at Springrove in Kent. *D P.* —— He is in a very good state of health, and is endeavouring to detect the forgers of that falshood. *D P.* 26 —— *Mr* Brother *the* D P. *proves his power superior to that of* Physicians.

The Oratory is new painting and beautifying within and without; the Doctor's people have presented him with a handsome clock, for his chimes of the times, and the week days orations will be soon revived. *D J.* — *This* Doctor *I take to be the* Hyp Doctor; *whose* chimes *repeat the same tune over and over again.*

On July 18, about 2, two men rode through Southwark armed, one with a short gun in his hand, and the other with a pistol, who by reason of their extraordinary posture, [which ought to have been mentioned as some thing extraordinary] were suspected to be Highwaymen, and therefore were soon taken, tho' not without great resistance; being brought before Sir John Lade, Bar. and searched, there were found in the pocket of one of them, who goes by the name of Moses, alias Will. Johnson (besides the gun, which was loaded with slugs) [which it seems was found in his pocket too] 2 pistols loaded with bullets, 2 butcher's knives, and some deer's fat; and in the other man's pocket, who goes by the name of Rob. Hill, a pistol loaded with a bullet, which before he surrender'd [not afterwards] he divers times endeavour'd to fire. They appear to be Deer stealers, and had that morning stole out of Beddington park, 2 fat bucks. The number of this gang is about 9. These 2 were committed to the County gaol. *D J.*

SATURDAY, *July* 22.

We hear that on friday se'nnight the R. Hon. Sir R. Walpole made a present of bills for 10,000 l. to his eldest son, the L. Walpole, whose Lady was [illegible] that day from Devonshire to his Lordship's seat in Norfolk. *D.*

Last wednesday, at the Buck feast at S. Thomas's Hospital, Mr. John Serocold, Merchant, was unanimously chosen a Governor of the said Hospital. *C.*

Last night was closed the ballot at the York Buildings house, by which it was determined, That a call of one *half per cent.* be made on the capital stock, to be paid between the first and last of August, to discharge the emergencies of the Company, and to carry on their works; and that interest at the rate of 5 *per ann.* be allowed from the day of payment to the last day of August. Yeas 265, Noes 129. *C. D J.*

Yesterday —— Barnardiston of Brightwell-Hall in Suffolk, Esq; was married to Miss Jennings, a young Lady of great accomplishments and fortune. *D P.*

We have assurances, that in the Oratory to morrow, the discourses will be on, &c. *D J.* —— *No wonder:* the Oratory *is an Assurance Office.*

Yesterday was held a General Council at Kensington, when the Parliament was by her Majesty prorogued to Octob. 12. *WE.*

Christoph. Wyvill, Esq; one of the Commissioners for Hawkers and Pedlars hath obtain'd a promise to succeed Tho. Woodcocke, Esq; deceased, as one of the Commissioners of the Salt duties. *L E.*

On thursday Francis Annesley of the Inner Temple, Esq; was married to Mrs. Gumbleton, (Relict of Mr. Gumbleton, a very rich Jeweller) of Red Lyon-square, a widow Lady of great fortune. *L E.*

MONDAY, *July* 24.

On saturday morning her Majesty in her chaise, his Royal Highness the Prince, the Duke, and Princesses Royal, Amelia, and Caroline, &c. hunted the stag in the New Park at Richmond, which gave them very good diversion for about two hours, &c. *C. D P.* —— It was run down and killed in an hour's time. *P.* —— It afforded but little diversion being killed in half an hour. *D J.*

On friday Col. Hamilton kissed her Majesty's hand for the Regiment on the Irish establishment late Col. Egerton's. *P.*

Tho. Woodcock, Esq; late one of the Commissioners for the Salt-duty, did by his last will bequeath 200 l. to the girls of the Charity school of S. James's, being one of the select vestry. *D P.*

On thursday James Borthwick, late book-keeper to Mess. Tho. and Ric. Jeffreys, was taken, in company with his brother David, a Journeyman Tallow-chandler, at the cock and coach in Chelmsford, with the bank notes, and most of the cash, 3 gold rings, a silver watch, a snuff box, &c. upon David were found one of the cases of pistols, and a silver-hilted sword. They were taken by the industry of Mr. Swain, a Perriwig-maker in Brentwood, who followed them all night through bye ways to Chelmsford, where they had hired horses to go for Colchester: James Borthwick made an ample confession, but would fain have excused his brother. *D J.*

Last friday Tho. Jennings, Esq; was married to Mrs. Anne Canso, a widow Lady of 16,000 l. fortune. *D J.*

We hear, that in To morrow's Hyp-Doctor, will be a proof that Fog and Caleb, &c. *D J.* —— *We not only* hear, *but* see, *that this is* a *standing* lye.

TUESDAY, *July* 25.

Sir Adolphus Oughton, Bar. and Major Sinclaire, are nominated to succeed to the command of the 2 Regiments of foot on the Irish establishment, vacant by the deaths of Major Gen. Dubourgay and Col. Egerton. *D P.*

Yesterday the R. Hon. the E. of Rothes, set out for Falmouth, in order to embark for Lisbon in his way to Gibraltar, to take on him the command of his regiment. *P. D J.* —— Yesterday his Grace the Duke of Buckinghamshire went to Oxford to begin his studies. *D P.* —— Yesterday morning about 11. *P.* 26.

Rob. Hill, one of the 2 persons committed last week to the New Prison, Southwark, for Deer-stealing, made himself an evidence, and has impeach'd about 15 of his gang, who are not yet taken. *C.*

Yesterday morning 2 coaches going for Dover with some French Gentlemen, were stopt near Blackheath by a single Highwayman, who took out of their Portmanteaus about 80 l. the neighbourhood was soon alarmed, and he was traced into Deptford, but there lost. *D J.* —— Yesterday morning about 5, Mr. Lawrence, Cook to the R. Hon. the E. of Litchfield, coming to town, was set upon by 2 Highwaymen well dressed and mounted, on Stoken Church Hill; he drew his hanger and engaged them, who fired 2 pistols at him, but missed him: he gave one of them such a cut cross his scull and face, as broke the edge of the hanger; upon which they made off. When he came to Wickham he was seized for a highwayman, having his cloaths torne, and being all bloody; but making affidavit of his case, several persons set out to take the highwaymen, and he was discharged; and before he left the town, he heard, that one of the rogues, who was cut, was taken up for dead, and carried to a neighbouring place to have his wound dressed. *P.*

On thursday the Assizes ended at Winchester, when only one person was capitally convicted. *P. D J.*

On sunday last Edw. Perkins, of Pilston in the County of Monmouth, Esq; was married to Mrs. Winterbourn, a maiden Lady, (Niece to the Countess of Abercorne) and above 20 000 l. fortune. *D P.*

Yesterday died John Lane, Esq; at his house near Lincoln's-Inn Fields; 'tis said, he died worth 200,000 l. his daughter was married to the late E. of Macclesfield. *D J.*

Norwich, July 22. On tuesday a famous Frenchman slew off from the top of S. Giles's steeple into the broad street, and then went up the same way he came down, performing several surprizing things *on the rope as he went*: and on thursday he flew from the same steeple again, being the highest tower in the city, to the surprize of thousands of spectators. *P.*

They write from Blandford in Dorsetshire, that the Sufferers by the late dreadful fire there, had received 2 s. in the pound from the charities received, and were soon to be paid 1 s. and 10 d. more in the pound; and that several collections were not yet paid in, particularly that of the Parish of S. James's at Westminster. *LE. S J.*

In the garden of Walter Pettyward, Esq; at Enfield, the large American Aloe is now blowing; the height of it is 16 foot, and 12 inches at the crown of the plant, it being much stronger and finer, than the plant that blowed at Mr. Cowel's some time ago, which was copper-plated with the two torch thistles. *S J.*

On sunday last died Miss Gallway, Daughter to the R. Hon. the L. Gallway. *LE.*

WEDNESDAY, *July* 26.

Yesterday a Proclamation was published prohibiting his Majesty's subjects from trading to the East Indies, contrary to the liberties and privileges granted to the English East India Company; and from being unlawfully concerned in any foreign Company or Society trading to the East Indies. *C. D J.*

The Society of Apothecaries having resolv'd to erect a magnificent Green House and hot houses in the Physick-garden at Chelsea, several designs were made and presented to them by persons skill'd in building, and those made by Mr. Edward Oakley, Architect (Author of the Magazine, &c.) were approv'd of, and he was unanimously chosen Surveyor; and the Committee of the said Society contracted on monday last, with Mr. Lambeth a Bricklayer, for building the same. *D P.*

On monday John Bates, Esq; was married to Miss Calvering of St. Alban's, a young lady of great merit and fortune. *D P.*

Last saturday night died at the Bath, Mrs. Sloane, Wife to Will. Sloane, Esq; *D J.*

On thursday last one Will. Wardell, a Heel-maker at Hull, stabbed his wife in the breast in two places, with a knife, of which she immediately died, and he was committed to Goal, and put in irons. *D J.*

Sunday morning Mr. Ennys, a Peruke-maker, who had the misfortune to be bit by a mad dog about 6 weeks ago, died raving-mad, at his house in Brewer-street, notwithstanding the best advice, and other proper medicaments for his recovery. *S J.* —— The best advice *is but an* improper Medicament.

From the PEGASUS *in Grub street.*

It is thought neceſſary to inform our kind and ingenious Correſpondents of two things. The firſt is, that their letters, &c. cannot be conveniently inſerted in any particular Journal, unleſs they are ſent a week before its publication. The other, that it will be in vain to ſend us lampoons, containing ſcandalous reflections on private perſons; in publiſhing of which, we are determined not to gratify the private malice of any one. Upon this account we have rejected abundance of Pieces, particularly one laſt week, which was afterwards publiſhed in the *Foſt-Boy* and *St. James's Weekly Packet* of July 22. If ſuch perſons indeed have either endeavoured to corrupt the age by their lewd and wicked writings, or have treated the learned or virtuous in a vile opprobrious manner: in endeavouring to ſet ſuch in a true light, we think we ſhall do a good action; and not an unjuſtifiable one, in now and then expoſing a public remarkable folly of perſons, tho' not ſo obnoxious on either of thoſe accounts. And if the whole ſeries of our Papers be examined with this diſtinction, the world will clear us from the imputation of malice and detraction, caſt upon us by the renegado members of our Society, who deal in nothing but the groſſeſt calumny, or ſtupidity.

A paraphraſe of four lines and a half of HORACE, inſcribed to the Honourable Mr. — — an imperfect copy of which was printed ſome time ago in *The Whitehall Evening Poſt.*

(1) *Abſentem qui rodit amicum:*
(2) *Qui non defendit a io culpante.* (3) *Solutos Qui captat riſus hominum, famamque dicacii:*
(4) *Fingere qui non viſa poteſt:* (5) *Commiſſa tacere Qui nequit: hic niger eſt: bunc tu Romane caveto.*

(1) The Fop, whoſe pride affects a *Patron's* name,
Yet abſent, wounds an Author's honeſt fame:
(2) That more abuſive fool, who calls me friend,
Yet wants the honour, i'jur'd to defend:
(3) Who ſpreads a *Tale,* a *Libel* hands about,
Enjoys the jeſt, and copies ſcandal out:
(4) Who to the *Dean* and ſilver *Bell* can ſwear,
And ſees at *Caxton's* what was never there:
(5) Who tells you all I *mean,* and all I *ſay*;
And, if he has not, muſt at leaſt *betray:*
'Tis not the ſober Satyreſt you ſhould dread,
But ſuch a babbling Coxcomb in his ſtead.

Edinburgh, July 13. There are a great many letters in town which mention the ſhock of an earthquake to have been felt at Glaſgow, and ſeveral other places in that neighbourhood, on tueſday laſt between 2 and 3 in the afternoon, and which laſted about a ſecond, but mention no harm done by it. Theſe letters add, that the plates and cups were heard and obſerved to move on the ſhelves. C. P. 10 P. 20. — On tueſday morning died Brigadier Gen. Dubourgay. D. P. 20. ——July 17. On ſaturday his Majeſty's plate of 100 guineas was run for on the ſands of Leith, and won by a bay horſe belonging to Hon. Fletcher, Eſq; P. 25. Mr. Fletcher a Yeoman of York. P. 25. —— Yeſterday died her Grace Elizabeth ſenior Dutcheſs Dowager of Gordon. P. D P. 25.

Dublin, July 11. We hear that laſt week a man was waſhing himſelf in the river about 10 at night, when he eſpied a woman paſſing along Batchelors Walk Key, whom he followed naked as he was, and raviſhed her. C. P. 20. ——July 15. Laſt night, a bark from Newry, with 9 paſſengers, viz. 3 men and 6 women founder'd and ſunk in our bay: all periſh'd except the maſter and 1 paſſenger. C. 22.

By a Dutch ſhip lately arrived at Amſterdam from the Bay of Honduras, we have advice, that the Spaniards had viſited that Bay once more; and had taken ſeveral veſſels. He ſays that he narrowly eſcaped being taken, that all the Bay men were gone, except 8 or 9. who hide in the woods till they can get an opportunity of tranſporting themſelves to ſome other place more ſecure. The Spaniards declare, that they will frequently viſit the ſaid Bay, to prevent all other Nations from cutting the Logwood there, and likewiſe will condemn all ſhips which they ſhall ſeize in that clandeſtine trade. P. 21.

FOREIGN NEWS.
FRIDAY, *July* 11.
Naples, July 1. Some days ago a German ſoldier was executed here, for the murder of another ſoldier, by ſhooting him with his muſket without any manner of provocation. Being aſked what could induce him to commit ſo vile an action, he anſwer'd, that being weary of ſo miſerable a life as that of a ſoldier, he killed his comrade, that he might die by the hands of juſtice, and was ſure he could not expect if he were to die in the field. C.
Peterſbourg, July 1. 'Tis obſerv'd, that in the prayers of the Church, the title of Imperial Highneſs is given to the Princeſs of Mecklembourg. D P. D J.

SATURDAY, *July* 22.
Yeſterday arrived the Mail from Holland.
Vienna, July 16 N S A Courier from Conſtantinople brings advice (as we are informed) that the Ottoman Porte was in great confuſion upon the news they had received by a Courier from Perſia, that Schach Thamas had not only broke the peace lately concluded with the Grand Seignior, but was advanced with an army of 60,000 men, and had taken the city of Erivan by ſurprize. C. &c.
Se ilia, July 9. A Spaniſh Serjeant, the day of the Debarkation, having been detached with 16 Soldiers to take a certain poſt, was immediately ſurrounded by 300 Turkiſh Cavaliers; but the Serjeant and his little Troop defended themſelves with ſuch valour, and changed the enemy ſo dexterouſly, that they at laſt carry'd the Poſt, and obliged the Turks to retire. D J.
Yeſterday arrived the Mails from France and Flanders.
Vienna, July 16. We learn from Conſtantinople, that the new Prime Vizir, upon the unlucky turn of affairs at that Court, has been depoſed, contrary to all expectation, and his Predeceſſor reinſtated in his room; who no ſooner enter'd on his poſt, but he cauſed 200 perſons to be ſtrangled in one night, who had been inſtrumental in his diſgrace. D P. D J.
Paris, July 30. Our laſt letters from Seville confirm the victory of the Spaniards, and the taking of Oran; adding, that Bigoligio [Bigotigio. C. P. D J.] the Governor, who is above 80 years of age, went off the night before the battle with 217 camels laden with effects, to Marequin, a Town about 14 leagues from Oran: that the Spaniards found in Oran 138 pieces of cannon, whereof 87 were of braſs, 7 mortar-pieces, with a vaſt quantity of leſſer arms, and a few Brigantines: the ſame letters add, the Duke de Riperda is return'd from Mequinez to Tetuin, where he is to make his reſidence. D P.
Hamburgh, July 25. Letters from Peterſburgh advize, that there has been a great fire at Croſslot, which had conſumed above 100 houſes. C. ——The D J. 22. ſays 400.
THURSDAY, *July* 25.
Amſterdam, Aug. 1. They write from Rome of the 12th inſt that Card. Colcia had been thrice examin'd, ſeveral hours each time, and the laſt he was obſerv'd with tears in his eyes to pray the Cardinals to have pity on him. A guard of 24 ſoldiers is placed before his apartment, two of them in his ſight, who are order'd not to ſuffer him to talk or write to any perſon. D J. C. D P.

On Tueſday Stocks were
South Sea Stock was 98 1 half, 98 1 half to 5 8ths for the Opening. South Sea Annuity 110 5 8ths, to 3 qrs. Bank 149 3 qrs.to 150. New Bank Circulation 8 l. 10 s. Premium. India 163, 3 qrs. 163 1 qr. without the Dividend. Three per Cent. Annuity 91 1 half, for the Opening. Royal Exchange Aſſurance 100. London Aſſurance 13 3 8ths. York Buildings 4 3 qrs. to 5. African 40 Engliſh Copper 2 l. 4s. Welch ditto 1 l. 15 s. South Sea Bonds 3 l. 19s. to 4 l. Premium. India ditto 7 l. 1 s. ditto.

Books and Pamphlets publiſhed from June 22 to July 4.
21 Philoſophical Tranſactions, No. 422, for January, February, and March, 1732
A Letter to the Merchants of G. Britain, or a proper Reply to the London Journal, &c. Pr 1 s. 6 d.
A Funeral Sermon occaſioned by the death of Edm. Calamy, D. D. By Daniel Mayo, M. A.
The Life and infamous actions of J. Waller, &c. Pr. 6 d.
Eccleſiaſtical Memoirs: by M. Tillemont, No. V.
The 2d Volume of Revelation examined with candour.
Chriſtianity diſtinct from the Religion of Nature: Parts 2d and 3d. By Tho. Broughton, A. M.
22 Zara: an Elegiac Paſtoral on the death of Mrs. Sarah Abney: by Sayer Rudd. Pr. 6 d.
23. Ridotto al' Freſco. Pr. 4 d.
A Treatiſe of the Animal Oeconomy: by Dr. Bryan Robinſon.
24. The Royal Guardian: a Poem. Pr. 6 d.
The City Liberties: or the rights and privileges of Freemen, &c. Pr. 3 s. 6 d.
27. The preſent ſtate of learning, religion, and infidelity, in Great Britain, &c. Pr. 6 d
The Conſideration of God as our Father in heaven, a powerful engagement to early religion: a Sermon by John Oakes.
The Comedian, or Philoſophical Enquirer, No. 3.
28. Modern Hiſtory, No. 96, 97. By Mr. Salmon.
29. Alexis's Paradiſe: a Comedy, by James Newton, Eſq;
A Vindication of the Goſpel of S. Matthew: by Leonard Twells. Pr. 1 s. 6 d.
30. The hope of a good man in the view of death: a funeral Sermon, by Jeremiah Tidcombe.
July 1. Diſſertationes duæ de viribus medicata olei animalis in epilepſia, &c. Pr. 1 s. 6 d.
An Eſſay on the ſeveral Diſpenſations of God to mankind.

3. The Gentleman's Magazine, Numb. 18.
The London Magazine, Numb 3.

This Day is published.

AN Account of the Eight Parts of Speech, so far as is necessary for Children to understand them before they proceed to Propria Quæ Maribus, and the other Parts of the Latin Grammar. For the Use of Merchant-Taylor's School. The Eleventh Edition, corrected. Printed for J. and J. Bonwicke, at the Red-Lyon in St. Paul's Church-Yard. Where may be had (for the Use of the said School) the three following Books.

1. Compendium Syntaxis Erasmianæ: Or, a Compendium of Erasmus's Syntax; with an English Explication and Resolution of the Rules, according to both antient and modern Grammarians and Criticks. The Fifth Edition, corrected.

2. Catechismus cum ordine Confirmationis, Græce & Latine.

3. ΞΕΝΟΦΩΝΤΟΣ ΣΩΚΡΑΤΟΥΣ ΑΠΟΜΟΝΙΑ ΤΟΥ ΑΥΤΟΥ ΑΠΟΜΝΗΜΟΝΕΥΜΑΤΩΝ ΒΙΒΛΑ Δ Calci cujusque Paginæ subjecta est accuratissima Sol. et a Leunclavii annotationi Interpretatio Latina directa sunt a Henrico Stephani, Johannis Leunclavii, & Æmilii Porti Notæ integræ. Accessit ΣΤΑΧΥΟΛΟΓΙΑ Spicilegium: sive Nova quorundam Græcorum Epigrammatum Collectio, Variorum Locorum, & Necessariis Notis Explicata, cum Indice cum Verborum tum Rerum. Editio Tertia Emendatior. In Usum Scholæ Fertilodinensis, Com. Essexiæ S. Lydiat, Quondam Gymnasiarcho.

PROPOSALS

For Printing by SUBSCRIPTION,

THE HISTORY of the Grand Controversy between the Secular and Regular Clergy of the Church of Rome, from the Year 1602 to 1604, concerning the Usurpation of RICHARD SMITH, Titular Bishop of Chalcedon, who pretended to be sole Ordinary Bishop of all England and Scotland. Wrote in Latin by the President of the English Benedictine Monks, RUDESINDUS BARLO, and faithfully done into English from the Original, for the Entertainment of the Curious, especially Divines and Lawyers, both Ecclesiastick and Civil, or what Religion soever.

With the Remonstrances of the Roman Catholick Laity made to the said Bishop, and also to his Excellency Carolo Coloma, Embassador Extraordinary of the Most Catholick Majesty, and to the Marquis Fontany, Embassador of the Most Christian King, &c. taken also from the Latin Originals: All which Treaties have been hitherto suppress'd, by the Papists, for Political Reasons given therein.

As also the famous Bull of Pope URBAN VIII. called PLANTATA, necessary for the right Understanding of the Whole, which was never before any where printed.

To which will be added,

A LETTER concerning the Disputes that have happen'd among the Benedictine Monks since the Year 1700 to this present Time: Shewing how even they themselves have varied from their original Principles. By one who was a Member of that Body, and concerned therein.

By JOHN WILLIAMS.

PROPOSALS may be had of (and SUBSCRIPTIONS taken in for the Author by) W. Meadows, at the Angel, in Cornhill; T. Astley, at the Rose, and S. Austen, at the Angel and Bible in St. Paul's Church-Yard; C. Davis, Pater-Noster-Row; T. Woodward, at the Half-Moon, L. Gulliver, at Homer's Head, and J. Stephens, at the Hand and Star, between the Two Temple-Gates; B. Motte, at the Middle Temple-Gate; T. Worral, at Judge Coke's Head, H. Walthoe, next Door to the Rainbow Coffee-House, W. Reason, in Flower-de-Luce-Court, J. Isted, at the Golden-Ball, near Chancery-Lane, Fleet-Street; F. Cyles, over-against Gray's-Inn-Gate, Holborn; O. Payne, in Round-Court, and T. Game, at the Bible, by the New Church, in the Strand; T. Green, Charing-Cross; J. Jackson, in Pallmall; J. Jolliffe, at the Bible, in St. James's-Street; J. Brindley, at the King's Arms, and W. Shropshire, opposite to the Duke of Grafton's, New Bond-Street; and J. Stagg, Westminster-Hall, Booksellers: J. Huggonson, in Bartholomew-Close, and T. Gover, by Fleet-Ditch, Black-Fryars, Printers.

This Day is published,

In Octavo (from the Folio Edition) Price Six Pence.

THE PROGRESS of LOVE, in four Eclogues, I. UNCERTAINTY, to Mr. Pope. 2. HOPE, to the Honourable George Doddington, Esq; 3. JEALOUSY, to Edw. Walpole, Esq; 4. POSSESSION, to the Right Honourable Lord Viscount COBHAM.

Printed for Lawton Gilliver at Homer's Head in Fleet-Street. Where may be had,

1. An Epistle to Mr. Pope, from a young Gentleman at Rome. By the same Author.

2. The Art of POLITICKS, with a curious Frontispiece. Rusum teneatis Amici. Price 1 s.

3. Two Epistles to Mr. Pope, concerning the Authors of the Age. By the Author of the Universal Passion. Price 1 s. and may be bound with the said Satyrs.

4. A new and correct Edition of the Dunciad Variorum, in 8vo. with some additional Notes and Epigrams.

5. A Collection of Pieces relating to the Dunciad. By several Hands.

6. Of FALSE TASTE, to Richard Earl of Burlington. By Mr. Pope. Price 1 s.

7. STOW: The Gardens of the Right Honourable the Lord Cobham. Price 1 s.

There is now in the Press, and will speedily be published, A SECOND EDITION, in two Volumes in Folio, of

RAPIN THOYRAS's History of ENGLAND. By N. Tindal, M. A. Vicar of Great Waltham in Essex, with the following Improvements: 1. The Translation is thoroughly revised. 2. All the Errors and Mistakes of the Original are corrected. 3. Several Hundred of Marginal References, accidentally omitted by the Author, are supply'd with additional Notes.

Whereas there is lately set on Foot the Project of a new Translation, in Weekly Pamphlets of four Sheets for Six Pence; and whereas it is affirmed by the Undertaker, that the Whole will be comprised in 400 Sheets, it is evident, on the contrary, by comparing the first Week's Performance with the Original, that the Number of Sheets will amount to 600; wherefore, that Gentlemen may not be drawn in by such specious Pretences, whilst the abovemention'd Volumes are printing, there will be publish'd every Week, beginning in about fourteen Days, five Sheets for 6 d. in such a Manner as to contain six of the projected new Translation; so that what is propos'd by the Undertaker for 1 s. 6 d. will be sold for 1 s. and the Whole visibly reduced to 400 Sheets, at the Price of two Guineas, including the Maps and Tables, engraven on Copper Plates, so which is nothing more will be reckon'd to the Buyer; and both Volumes will be publish'd in the Space of a Year, which is but a Quarter of the Time that it can be new done, as it ought, by any one Hand.

Proposals, with a Specimen, will be publish'd this Week by James and John Knapton, at the Crown in St. Paul's Church-Yard. Where may be had, the History compleat in 15 Volumes in Octavo.

Just published,

For the Use of Families, beautifully printed in two Volumes Octavo, adorn'd with 34 Plates, Engraven by Mr. STURT.

DUPIN'S EVANGELICAL HISTORY: Or, the Records of the SON of GOD, and their Veracity demonstrated, in the Life and Acts of our Blessed Lord and Saviour Jesus Christ, and the Holy Apostles. Wherein, 1. The Life of our Blessed Saviour Jesus Christ is related in all its Circumstances, according to the Order of Time, in a pathetick and practical Method, thereby composing a perfect Harmony of the Gospels. 2. Proofs from his Sermons and Discourses of these Essential and Important Truths, which all Christians are obliged to know and practise, in order to their Eternal Salvation. 3. His Parables, Miracles, and Sufferings, set in a just Light, and defended from all the Oppositions of wicked and designing Men. 4. An Application of the Whole to the respective Uses of Christians, with regular Devotion conformable to the several Periods of the Holy History; and Directions how he may read the Life of Jesus Christ to Advantage.

Printed for R. Ware, at the Bible and Sun in Amen-Corner, near Pater-Noster-Row. Price 8 s.

Also may be had at the same Place,

1. The large House-Bibles, Folio, with the six Maps of sacred Geography, and a brief Concordance for the more easy finding out of the Places therein contained. By J. DOWNAME, B.D.
Bound in Calf Leather 11. 8 s. per Book.
And with Mr. Sturt's Cuts at 2 l. 5 s. ditto.
On a fine Paper with Cuts 3 l. 5 s. ditto.

2. Impartial Churchman; or, A fair and candid Representation of the Excellency and Beauty of the Church of England. Together with an earnest and affectionate Address to the Protestant Dissenters. By ROBERT WARREN, D.D. Price 3 s. 6 d.

3. A Description of 300 Animals, viz. Beasts, Birds, Fishes, Serpents and Insects. With a particular Account of the Whale-Fishery. Extracted out of the best Authors, and adapted to the Use of all Capacities, especially to allure Children to read. Illustrated with Copper Plates, whereon is curiously engraven every Beast, Bird, Fish, Serpent and Insect described in the whole Book. Price 2 s. 6 d.

4. Tradesman's Guide. Containing a List of all the Stage Coaches and Carriers; with an Account of all the Market Towns in England. Price 1 s.

This Day is published,

Printed for J. Brotherton, at the Bible, next the Fleece Tavern in Cornhill,

AN Enquiry into the Origin of Honour, and the Usefulness of Christianity in War.

By the Author of the FABLE of the BEES.

Where may be had,

1. A Letter to Dion, being an Answer to a Book call'd Alciphron, or the Minute Philosopher.

2. The present State of Great Britain and Ireland, for the Year 1731.

3. Traditions of the Jews.

4. Dampier's Journal to Madagascar.

5. Religious Courtship.

6. Life of OLIVER CROMWELL, Lord Protector of the Commonwealth.

7. Receipts in Cookery and Surgery, by John Keetilby.

To all Gentlemen, Builders, and others, ALEXANDER EMERTON, Colour Man, at the Bell over-against Arundel Street, in the Strand, LONDON,

SELLS all Sorts of COLOURS ready prepared (at the lowest Prices) that any Gentleman, Builder, &c. may set their Servants or Labourers to paint their Houses, only by the Help of a printed Direction, which he gives with his Colours.

N.B. Five Pounds Worth of Colours will paint as much Work, as a House-Painter will do for Twenty Pounds.

He likewise sells (to the Ladies) all Sorts of Water Colours and Varnish, with every Thing necessary for the New Japanning, and gives a printed Direction, for the doing of it to the greatest Perfection, to those that buy Colours. — Also Italian Powder for cleaning Pictures.

He deals only for Ready Money.

HIS MAJESTY

HAving been pleased to grant to WALTER CHURCHMAN Letters Patent for his new Invention of making Chocolate without Fire, to greater Perfection, in all Respects, than by the common Method, as will appear on Trial; being its immediate Dissolving, full Flavour, Smoothness on the Palate, and intimate Union with Liquids: And as it is much finer than any other Sort, so it will go farther, and is less offensive to weak Digestions, being by this Method made clean, and free from the usual Grit and gross Particles, so much disliked, which is referr'd to the fair and impartial Experiment; such the Patentee proposes for his common Standard, which is now sold at 4 s. 9 d. per Pound, with Vanello's 5 s. 9 d.

N.B. The Curious may be supply'd with his Superfine Chocolate, which is as many Degrees finer than the above Standard, as that exceeds the finest sold by other Makers, plain at 6 s. with Vanello at 7 s.

To be sold only for Ready Money,

At CHURCHMAN'S Chocolate Warehouse, at Mr. John Young's in St. Paul's Church-Yard; Where Persons in Town or Country may be supply'd with any Quantities, with Encouragement to Venders, who shall be licens'd under the Hand and Seal of the Patentee, and their Places of Sale advertis'd, if requir'd.

Just published,

The Fourteenth Edition, of,

THE Benefit of FARTING explain'd; or the Fundament-All Cause of the Distempers of the Fair Sex inquir'd into, proving a Posteriori most of the Disorders intail'd on them, are owing to Flatulencies not seasonably vented. Wrote in Spanish by Don Fart-in-hando Puff-indorft, Professor of Bombast in the University of Craccow, and translated into English at the Request, and for the Use of the Lady Damp-fart, of Herfart-shire. To which is annex'd, a Certificate of the Virtue of Farting, from the Court of the Princess Arsemini. Together with some Verses on Mrs. V——ne's Fart, in the Phillipic Strain; and a Squire Nump's Fart, in the Brewers Strain. Also a Meditation on T——d, wrote in a Place of Ease. Printed for F. Jefferis in Ludgate-Street.

Where may be had,

1. TEA, a Poem, or Ladies into China Cups, a Metamorphosis. Price 6 d.

2. A General History of Executions, for the Year 1730. Containing the Lives, &c. of 60 Highwaymen, and other Malefactors. Price bound 2 s. 6 d.

3. A new Method of Tanning without Bark. Price 6 d.

4. The Batchelor's Recantation. Price 6 d.

This Day was published,

AN ODE to his Grace the Duke of New-castle. Written on the present Tranquillity of Europe, establish'd by the Influence of the British Power.

Nihil habeat aut Fortuna tua majus, quàm ut possit, aut Natura tua melius, quàm, ut velis, quàm plurimis conservare. Cic.

Printed for J. Batley, at the Dove in Pater-Noster-Row. Price 6 d.

Where may be had, just published,

Dedicated to the Gentlemen of the Navy of England, The Memoirs of Monsieur DU GUE TROUIN, Chief of a Squadron of the Royal Navy of France, and Great Cross of the Military Order of S. Lewis; containing all his Sea-Actions with the English, Dutch, and Portuguese, in the late Wars of King William and Queen Anne.

Translated from the French by a SEA-OFFICER.

This Day is published,

[Price One Shilling.]

The Second Edition corrected, of

A Practical GRAMMAR of the English TONGUE. In two Parts. Containing, I. Instructions for the true Spelling, Reading and Writing of English. II. The Principles of Arithmetick, Geography and Chronology, explained and suited to the meanest Capacities. For the Use of Schools.

By THO. DYCHE, late School-Master, at Stratford Bow.

Printed for J. Clarke, at the Golden-Ball in Duck-Lane, near West-Smithfield.

LONDON: Printed by J. HUGGONSON, in Bartholomew-Close, for Capt. GULLIVER, near the Temple, where Letters and Advertisements are taken in: As also at the Rainbow Coffee-House in Cornhill, and John's Coffee-House in Sheer-Lane, Temple-Bar. [Price Two Pence.]

The Grub-ſtreet Journal.

NUMB. 135

Thurſday, *AUGUST* 3, 1732.

SIR,

I WAS in company the other evening with ſome Gentlemen and Ladies, who were lamenting the preſent want of taſte, and inquiring among themſelves what could be the occaſion of it. Various, Mr. BAVIUS, were the reaſons aſſigned. Some imputed it to our bringing into the world too ſoon the young ones of either ſex. The want of a ſufficient foundation in our youths, before they are let looſe to acquire, by the commerce of the world, the knowledge of it, and a behaviour proper for all parts of life, was (according to them) the occaſion of ſuch numbers of raw boys of 25 and 30 years, that infeſt all public and private places, and are incapable of converſation, and conſequently of improvement. As to the youthful part of the other ſex, they were of opinion, that their too early acquaintance with ours, made them too ſoon acquainted with their own beauty; which being repreſented to them as their diſtinguiſhing characteriſtic, they were thereby induced to apply their chief care to the cultivation of that, and almoſt entirely to neglect, as a thing altogether unneceſſary, the requirement of intellectual qualifications.

A Gentleman of a ſplenetic turn of mind, who had liſtened a good while without ſpeaking, at laſt broke ſilence, by telling us, that tho' he entirely agreed with us, yet ſince empires, as well as arts and ſciences, had their riſe and declenſion, he rather thought our period was come; and that henceforward there was little to be expected but a gradual decreaſe of every thing that was good: for which reaſon he had reſolved to keep leſs and leſs company, and to live more within himſelf. We did not care to put him upon proving his aſſertion, by ſhewing the ſymptoms of this fatal period, but contented ourſelves, with telling him, that we hoped things were not ſo bad, but that a cure might be found out. He ſhook his head, and made no anſwer.

My opinion, Mr. BAVIUS, being then aſked, I told them, that I thought there muſt be more than one reaſon for this want of taſte; and that ſo great a depravation could not ariſe from any one ſingle cauſe. That as to myſelf, I did really believe, that the preſent degeneracy of the Stage was one principal occaſion of that of our taſte. For as in former times the Stage was looked upon as the ſchool of riper youth (and indeed ſo it ought to be) from whence they were to copy their manners, and gather their knowledge of the world in ſome degree; ſo the young people of both ſexes were ſtill taught the ſame doctrine, and frequented plays with the good will of their parents, in this very view. And therefore it is no wonder, when ridiculous, ſtupid, obſcene, and infamous Pieces are repreſented, that ridiculous, ſtupid, obſcene, and infamous characters are formed by both ſexes, and ſeen ſo often, and in ſuch numbers on the theatre of the world.

This notion appeared ſo juſt to moſt of the company, that we immediately dropped all further enquiry into this matter, and turned our thoughts to the remedying of this diſorder of the ſtage. Many ſchemes were propoſed for this effect, and many objections raiſed. At laſt one of the company, a moſt inveterate enemy to any thing that tends to debaſe the underſtanding, or corrupt the morals, after having in a ſuccinct manner, by ſhort quotations from every Piece that has been acted ſince the beginning of laſt winter, ſhewn that they were either ſilly, lewd, or immoral, and expreſt his utter deteſtation of them, went on in the following manner. ——— I have liſtened (ſaid he) with great attention to the ſeveral ſchemes you have propoſed, for reſtoring the Stage to its former ſtate; but I think none of them goes to the root of the evil. For my part, I know none ſo likely to be effectual, as taking the management of the Stage out of the hands of thoſe, that now conduct it. I don't mean either the oeconomical, or the profitable part of it; I mean only that the receiving, or rejecting of Plays ſhould not lye in the breaſt of the managing-actors. I would propoſe, that a Committee of three, or five perſons, Gentlemen, if poſſible, of rank and figure, and men of known wit and learning, ſhould be appointed to ſit at certain times weekly, and receive all Plays that ſhall be offered, without reſpect of perſons, favour, or intereſt. Theſe Gentlemen, if three, ſhould have a ſalary of 300 l. per ann. if five, but of 200 l. the majority ſhould determine which Plays ſhould be received, and which rejected; and the Houſe ſhould be obliged to act ſo many every ſeaſon as had been approved. This would not only excite a much greater number of Gentlemen to write, becauſe they would not be obliged to pay ſervile court to perſons beneath themſelves, but likewiſe prevent the increaſe of bad Poets, who would have no hopes at all of getting their Plays acted.

There were but two difficulties raiſed againſt this ſcheme; the firſt was the finding out a fund for the payment of this theatrical commiſſion; and the ſecond, that as the managers were to ſtand to the expence of acting new Plays, it ſeemed hard not to let them have the choice of what Plays they were to act. It was replied to this by the ſame Gentleman, that he believed the yearly profits of the managers were ſo conſiderable, that there would be no very great hardſhip in ſubjecting them to act what much better judges than themſelves ſhould think proper; and that they would run much leſs rique then, than they do now. As to the finding out a fund, he would propoſe no other method, than the raiſing the boxes a ſhilling, and the pit ſix pence, which he computed would produce ſufficient to pay the ſalaries and an officer or two more to ſuperviſe the collection; and this he believed the town would readily come into, for the ſake of being more decently, agreeably, and ſenſibly entertained.

How you, Mr. BAVIUS, will approve this ſcheme, I don't know; I was deſired by the company to communicate it to you for your ſentiments of it; which having done, I beg leave to ſubſcribe myſelf,

July 27, 1732. Your moſt humble ſervant,

THEATRICUS.

DRAMATICUS to another DRAMATICUS, *alias* DRAMATICUS Senior, in the *Daily Courant* of July 29.

SIR,

ALtho' I think it very hard, that you ſhould take up the cudgels againſt a near relation (at leaſt a name ſake) in behalf of the *Comedian*, one whom you ſolemnly declare you do not know, no more than you do me, I ſhall not refuſe to enter the liſts with you, tho' I do it very unwillingly, and ſhould have been very glad to have been excuſed. But before I proceed I muſt beg your attention to two things.

The firſt is, that thoſe who unprovoked and unjuſtly begin an attack are generally in the wrong, and anſwerable for all that follows. I neither attacked the *Comedian*, nor you, till both of you fell unexpectedly upon me, the *Comedian* in a moſt dogmatical, contemptuous manner, and you, Sir, in a leſs ſhocking indeed, but more ſevere one, becauſe you attempt to reaſon.

The ſecond thing is, that I am ſorry you choſe the *Courant* to publiſh your thoughts in, that paper being dedicated to political facts, written in anſwer to the Enemies of the Government, and I, one of their moſt zealous friends, have therefore ſome ſcruple in my conſcience, whether I ſhould draw my pen againſt any perſon that appears in a paper ſacred to that uſe. For which reaſon, if you ſhould think fit to honour me with any further notice, I muſt beg you would chuſe ſome other paper, or elſe not look upon my future ſilence as a mark of your victory; and I hope the managers of the *Courant*, who have not admitted your letter this time without ſome difficulty, will be more obdurate another.

I come now, Sir, to the conſideration of the letter itſelf, and firſt I remark, that the Witticiſm you are pleaſed to beſtow on Sir JOHN FALSTAFF and me turns very much to my advantage. ——— You do me the honour to ſay, *I think I reaſon*, while I only *wrangle*. If *I think I reaſon*, ſurely I am more juſtifiable in writing, than if *I thought I did not*. I do not then endeavour to impoſe upon others what I am conſcious is wrong myſelf. I then deceive myſelf firſt. *Humanum eſt errare.* You may think *I wrangle*; *I*, that you *reaſon*. We are both equally ingenuous and candid in confeſſing it, and neither of us ought to be dealt too hardly with, ſuppoſing we are both miſtaken in our opinions, that is ſuppoſing, I really *reaſon*, and you only *wrangle*, which, after all, may be the truth.

But how do you make out that *I wrangle*? becauſe I don't think that what is ſaid in the *Comedian* about Plays anſwers the title of the diſcourſe, which is really the caſe; tho' you rather than not juſtify that author, are forced to have recourſe to the loweſt degree of *wrangling*, viz downright *quibbling*, as I ſhall make appear in a very few words.

Here is a Gentleman, who ſtiles himſelf the *Comedian*, and promiſes the town in his bill of fare, *ſome reflections on modern Plays*. Inſtead of which, at firſt ſetting out, he declares himſelf totally ignorant of thoſe mentioned in the article, having neither *ſeen*, nor *read them*, and reſolving *never to read them*; but not to baulk us quite, he makes another perſon call them *ſtuff*, *a long catalogue of rubbiſh*, *indigeſted traſh*, *and nonſenſe*. It is poſſible moſt of the there mention'd pieces may deſerve theſe appellations. I don't diſagree in the cenſure paſs'd on them in the main, but I think *ſtuff*, *rubbiſh*, *traſh* and *nonſenſe*, are moſt improperly call'd *reflections*, which ſeem to imply ſomething more. But this remark of mine was made only *en paſſant*, and not much dwelt upon, and therefore ought not to have been ſo waſpiſhly ſnapp'd at. Beſides, is it not a moſt injudicious, not to ſay abſurd thing, for one who ſets up for a reflecter on modern Plays, to declare himſelf profoundly ignorant of them? where was the neceſſity for this? why muſt he bring a country Gentleman to town on purpoſe to call them names to ſave his credit? That there are ſuch things I'll very readily grant you, as *general reflections*, and *pieces*, which *are beneath criticiſm*. But then, either all the pieces mention'd, and the reſt tacitly referr'd to were ſuch, which ſurely cannot be ſaid of all; or elſe it was incumbent on this Gentleman, or his friend, to have given ſome few *reflections* on them: which might have been entertaining, as well as inſtructive, and juſtify'd, without your laboured quibbling, the title of the diſcourſe. But he had unfortunately, by the ſcene he layed, tyed up his own hands: and to chuſe a country Gentleman for a critic *en detail*, would have been a little abſurd, many other characters being preferably to be choſen for that end. It helps your very little to ſay † *an unprejudiced reader* would not underſtand by the *Comedian*'s words, that he really had neither *read*, nor *ſeen* thoſe pieces: for, if we are to ſuppoſe he had both *read* and *ſeen* them, the abſurdity, as well as ſtupidity of the ſcene laid becomes more flagrant, and the execution of his plan more ridiculous. Upon the whole, Sir, your juſtification of the *Comedian* in this particular ſeems to carry more of the *wrangling* or *quibbling* genius in it, than my condemnation of him; and ſo I leave it to the opinion of the town.

The next thing in which you are pleaſed to become an advocate for the *Comedian* is, where he pompouſly aſſerts, ‡ that *unerring reaſon is the only guide, and no other rule neceſſary to be obſerved in writing Plays*, tho' he ſays in the ſame breath, *other talents are requiſite under the conduct of this only guide*; and that *a meer reaſonable man*, that is, a *man that has only this guide*, *cannot write a Play*. I thought I had given the moſt favourable conſtruction of this ſublime period, when I ſaid, I thought it meant that *a man of ſenſe could not write a Play without a genius*. I'm ſure, if you conſtrue it literally, it will turn out abſolute *nonſenſe*. Neither do I find, that you declare yourſelf any where of his opinion. You endeavour indeed to juſtify the *Comedian* by miſ-ſtating what I ſay. You make me very unfairly diſapprove of *reaſon* and *nature* as a *guide*; which I believe you'll be puzzled to find in any part of my letter: and then moſt ridiculouſly aſk me, What I will ſubſtitute in its place? *Erring reaſon? or that which is not reaſon.* Oh ſilly! poor DRAMATICUS *ſenior*, thou doteſt! or elſe art naturally very *quarrelſome*.

I come, now, Sir, to the laſt point of your juſtification of the *Comedian*, and your unfairneſs to me; and for once agree with you, that this Gentleman having ſeen or read the *Modern Husband*, may poſſibly *be a judge, whether it was liable to the cenſure paſſed on the reſt*, without *having ſeen them*, that is, may *poſſibly* be a judge whether it was *ſtuff*, *rubbiſh*, *traſh* and *nonſenſe*: but I cannot go ſo far as to think him *a proper perſon to make reflections on Plays, he had neither read, nor ſeen, or to give one the preference before all the others*: which, Sir, if you'll be pleaſed to turn to my letter, you'll find is all I ſay, and is ſomewhat different from what you are ſo juſt as to put in my mouth: ſo that the *folly* complained of, by only changing the epithet, muſt lye at your door.

I am very glad you think the reſt of my remarks too *confuſedly made*, and *conclusions* too *void of meaning to admit of any obſervations on them*: for, as I have purſued you ſtep by ſtep, in caſe you had done ſo by me, I ſhould have had more trouble than I really care for.

I now take my leave of you, and *ſolemnly declare I neither know who* the COMEDIAN is, *nor who* DRAMATICUS *ſenior*; *and I am, without partiality, unleſs attachment to truth is partiality, a well-wiſher* to him, as well as to you.

London, July the 31, 1732. DRAMATICUS.

Column 1

To all Gentlemen, Builders, and others,

ALEXANDER EMERTON,
Colour Man, *at the* Bell *over-against* Arundel
Street, *in the* Strand, LONDON,

SELLS all Sorts of COLOURS ready
prepared (at the lowest Prices) that any Gentlemen, Builders, &c. may set their Servants or Labourers to paint their Houses,
only by the Help of a printed Direction, which he gives with his
Colours.

N.B. Five Pounds Worth of Colours will paint as much Work,
as a Hand-Painter will do for Twenty Pounds.

He likewise sells (to the Ladies) all Sorts of Water-Colours and
Varnish, with every Thing necessary for the New Japanning, and
gives a printed Direction, for the doing of it to the greatest Perfection, to those that buy Colours. — Also Italian Powder for
cleaning Pictures.

He deals only for Ready Money.

Just published,

*For the Use of Families, beautifully printed in
two Volumes Octavo, adorn'd with 3½ Plates,
Engraven by Mr.* STURT,

DUPIN's EVANGELICAL HISTORY : Or, the
Records of the SON of GOD, and their Veracity demonstrated, in the Life and Acts of our Blessed Lord and Saviour Jesus
Christ, and the Holy Apostles. Wherein, 1. The Life of our Blessed saviour Jesus Christ is related in all its Circumstances, according
to the Order of Time, in a pathetick and practical Method, thereby comprising a perfect Harmony of the Gospels. 2. Proofs from
h.S. to assure the Doctrines of the Essential and Important Truth,
which all Christians are obliged to know and practise, in order to
their Eternal Salvation. 3. His Parables, Miracles, and Sufferings,
setting in a Light, and defended from all the Oppositions of wicked and
designing Men. 4. An Application of the Whole to the respective
Uses of Christians, with regular Devotions conformable to the several Periods of the Holy History ; and Directions how he may read
the Life of J. Christ to Advantage.

Printed for R. Ware, at the Bible and Sun in Amen-Corner,
near Pater-noster-Row. Price 8s.

A few may be had at the same Place,

1. The large Hebr. Bible, Folio, with the six Maps of sacred
Geography, and a Leaf Cemented in, for the more easy finding out
of the Places therein contained. By J. DOWNAME, D.D.

Bound in Calf Leather 11. 8s. per Book.
And with Mr. Sturt's Cuts at 2l. 5s. ditto.
On a finer Paper with Cuts 2l. 3s. ditto.

2. Impartial Churchman ; or, A fair and candid Representation
of the Excellency and Beauty of the Church of England. Together
with an earnest and affectionate Address to the Protestant Dissenters.
By ROBERT WARREN, D.D. Price 3s. 6d.

3. A Description of 300 Animals, viz. Beasts, Birds, Fishes, Ser-
pents and insects. With a particular Account of the Whale-Fishery.
Extracted out of the best Authors, and adapted to the Use of all
Capacities, especially to allure Children to read. Illustrated with
Copper Plates, wherein is curiously engraven every Beast, Bird, Fish,
Serpent and Insect described in the whole Book. Price 2s. 6d.

4. Tradesman's Guide. Containing a List of all the Stage Coaches
and Carriers ; with an Account of all the Market Towns in England. Price 1s.

This Day is published,

Printed for *J. Brotherton*, at the *Bible*, next
the Fleece Tavern in Cornhill,

AN Enquiry into the Origin of Honour,
and the Usefulness of Christianity in War.

By the Author of the FABLE of the BEES.

Where may be had,

1. A Letter to Dion, being an Answer to a Book call'd *Alciphron*,
or the *Minute Philosopher*.

2. The present State of Great Britain and Ireland, for the Year
1731.

3. Tradition of the Jews.

4. Dampier's Journal to Madagascar.

5. Religious Courtship.

6. Life of OLIVER CROMWELL, Lord Protector of the Commonwealth.

7. Receipts in Cookery and Surgery, by John Keetilby.

This Day is published,
[Price Six Pence.]

AN Epistle humbly address'd to the Hon.
Mrs. ELIZABETH TREVOR, Daughter of the late Sir
RICHARD STEELE, upon her Marriage with the Hon. JOHN
TREVOR, Esq; Son to the Rt. Hon. THOMAS late Lord TREVOR.
By ROBERT DYER.

Hail, wedded Love!
Perpetual Fountain of Domestick Sweets!
Here, Love his Golden Shafts employs ; here Lights
His constant Lamp, and waves his Purple Wings. MILTON.
Felices ter & amplius
Quos irrupta tenet copula ; nec malis
Divulsus querimoniis,
Suprema citius solvet Amor Die. HOR.

Printed for Lawton Gulliver, at Homer's Head, against St. Dunstan's Church in Fleet-Street.

Column 2

Aug. 3. **This Day is published**, Pr. 6d.

*Very proper for private Families, or to send into the Coun-
try (and Places abroad where the English reside) being
a compendious View of all our Publick Papers.*

The GENTLEMAN's MAGAZINE:
Or, Monthly Intelligencer.
NUMBER XIX. for JULY, 1732.
Being the SEVENTH *of* VOLUME II.
CONTAINING,
[More in Quantity, and greater Variety, than any Book of
the Kind and Price.]

I. Views of the WEEKLY ESSAYS, viz. On
Bribes ; Will of John Hopkins, Esq; True Greatness ; Mo-
ney no Equivalent for unequal Marriages ; Style and Elocution ;
Ruling the Passions ; Propagating Opinions ; Panegyrick on Cowardice ;
On the Quaker Philosophy ; Criticism of the Grub-street
Journal, Dr. Bentley, the Country, and two Plays ; Female Ex-
travagance ; Rake's Fortune ; Idle Curiosity ; Humane Nature ;
Love and Philosophy ; Instruction ; Wit ; Trust in Providence,
Necessity and Free Will ; Religion, &c.

II. POLITICAL POINTS, Proceedings and Debates of the English and French Parliaments, Remarks on both ; British Discontents ; Treatment of Church ; Battle of Contradictions ; Magna
Charta, the Fruits of Bad Ministers ; Improvements of Ireland ;
Blunderers, Struggles for Liberty.

III. POETRY, York Lottery ; Cornbuiton Fair ; Lady and Caterpillar ; the prudent Damsel ; Croydon Workhouse ; The Blind Puppies ; Love and Reputation ; The Grotto, Tales, Fables, Epigrams.

IV. Domestick Occurrences, &c. Births, Deaths, Marriages, Promotions, &c.

V. Prices of Gold, Grain, Stocks ; London Monthly Bill of
Mortality.

VI. Foreign Affairs.

VII. A Table of Contents.

— By SYLVANUS URBAN, Gent.

London : Printed, and sold at St. John's Gate ; by F. Jefferies
in Ludgate-Street ; Mrs. Nutt, Mrs. Charlton, Mrs. Cook, at the
Royal-Exchange ; Mr. Bathy in Pater-Noster-Row ; Mr. Midwinter, in St. Paul's Church-Yard ; A. Chapman, in Pall-Mall,
Mrs. Dodd, and Mr. Bickerton, without Temple-Bar ; Mr. Crichley, at Charing-Cross ; Mr. Stagg, and Mr King, in Westminster-
Hall ; Mr. Williamson in Holbourn ; Mr. Montague, in Great
Queen-Street ; Mr. Harding, in St. Martin's-Lane ; and all unprejudiced Booksellers in Town and Country.

Note, a few are printed on a fine Royal Paper, large Margin, for
the Curious.

Note. The great Demand for the GENTLEMAN's MAGAZINE
these 18 Months last past, has occasion'd most of the Numbers to
be out of Print several times. At present Setts can only be had for
the Year 1732. Having been obliged unexpectedly to reprint our
last for June ; and also to put No. I. and No. II. a 4th time in the
Press, we have not been able to get the first ready, as promis'd, in
August ; but Gentlemen may depend on compleat Setts in September.

PROPOSALS
For Printing by SUBSCRIPTION,

THE HISTORY of the Grand Con-
troversy between the Secular and Regular Clergy of the
Church of Rome, from the Year 1625 to 1634, concerning the
Usurpation of RICHARD SMITH, Titular Bishop of Chalcedon,
who pretended to be sole Ordinary Bishop of all England and Scotland. Wrote in Latin by the President of the English Benedictine
Monks, RODULPHUS BARLO, and faithfully done into English
from the Original, for the Entertainment of the Curious, especially Divines and Lawyers, both Ecclesiastical and Civil, of what
Religion soever.

With the Remonstrances of the Roman Catholick Laity made to
the said Bishop, and also to his Excellency Carolo Colonna, Embassador
Extraordinary of the Most Catholick Majesty, and to the Marquis
Fontenay, Embassador of the Most Christian King, &c. taken also
from the Latin Originals : All which Treatises have been hitherto
to suppress'd, by the Papists, for Political Reasons given therein.

As also the famous Bull of Pope URBAN VIII. called PLAN-
TATA, necessary for the right Understanding of the Whole, which
was never before any where printed.

To which will be added,

A LETTER concerning the Disputes that have happen'd among
the Benedictine Monks since the Year 1700 to this present Time :
Shewing how even they themselves have varied from their original Principles. By one who was a Member of that Body, and
concern'd therein.

By JOHN WILLIAMS.

PROPOSALS may be had of (and SUBSCRIPTIONS taken in
for the Author by) W. Meadows, at the Angel, in Cornhill ;
T. Astley, at the Rose, and S. Austen, at the Angel and Bible in
St. Paul's Church-Yard ; C. Davis, Pater-Noster-Row ; T. Wood-
ward, at the Half-Moon, L. Gulliver, at Homer's Head, and J. Ste-
phens, at the Hand and Star, between the Two Temple-Gates ;
B. Motte, at the Middle Temple-Gate ; T. Worrall, at Judge
Coke's Head, H. Walthoe, next Door to the Rainbow Coffee-
House, W. Reason, in Flower-de-Luce-Court, J. Isted, at the
Golden-Ball, near Chancery-Lane, Fleet-Street ; F. Gyles, over-
against Gray's-Inn-Gate, Holborn ; O. Payne, in Round-Court, and
T. Game, at the Bible, by the New Church, in the Strand ;
T. Green, Charing-Cross ; J. Jackson, in Pallmall ; J. Jolliffe,
at the Bible, in St. James's-Street ; J. Brindley, at the King's Arms,
and W. Shropshire, opposite to the Duke of Grafton's, New Bond-
Street ; and J. Stagg, Westminster-Hall, Booksellers : J. Huggonson,
in Bartholomew-Close, and T. Cover, by Fleet-Ditch, Black-Fryars,
Print ers.

Column 3

This Day is published,

The LONDON MAGAZINE:
Or, GENTLEMAN's Monthly Intelligencer.
NUMB. IV. for JULY, 1732.
To be Continued. (Price Sixpence each Month.)
CONTAINING

(*Greater Variety, and more in Quantity, than any* MONTH-
LY *Book extant.*)

I. A View of the WEEKLY ESSAYS, viz. Of
marrying purely for Interest ; Causes of Unhappiness in
Marriage ; Story of Conatus ; ill Effect of Curiosity ; a Censure on
the Ladies ; Self-Government ; Vanity of Titles ; Inconstancy and
Fickleness ; Resignation to the Will of God ; Comparison of the
Distressed ; Peaknence and Free-Will ; Unreasonableness of Imposition ; Wit ; Philosophy ; Style ; the Writer and Orator ; Play-
house Writers ; Dr. B——ly's Notes on Milton examin'd ; Praise
of Cowardice ; Education, and the Power of Love.

II. POLITICAL Subjects, viz. Slavery and Liberty ; true Greatness ; Liberty and Property ; Struggles for Liberty ; Fog and Ob-
servers of the Church and State ; Craftsmen on the last Session of
Parliament, and Remarks upon him, &c. Parliament of Paris ;
Ministerial Writers ; the Genuine Minister ; Great Britain's Interest in Ireland ; Advantages from bad Ministers ; Marks of such ;
of bad Kings making and Ministers, &c.

III. POETRY : Carpholeon Fair ; the Retirement ; Love and Reputation ; to a Militia Captain ; Panegyrick on Cuckoldom ; Craftsmen always in the same Story ; Epigrams, &c.

IV. DOMESTICK Occurrences : Promotions Ecclesiastical, Civil
and Military ; Marriages and Births ; Deaths ; Sessions at the Old
Baily ; Task Buildings Company, &c.

V. FOREIGN AFFAIRS.

VI. Price of Goods, Grain, Stocks ; Monthly Bill of Mortality.

VII. A TABLE of Contents.

To which is added, a Catalogue of Books and Pamphlets, with
their Prices, published by the Proprietors of the Monthly Chronicle,
now discontinu'd.

MULTUM IN PARVO.

LONDON : Printed for C. Ackers in St. John-Street ; for J. Wil-
ford, behind the Chapter-House, near St. Paul's : And sold by
W. Meadows, T. Cox, W. Hinchliffe, W. Whitridge, R. Willock,
and E. Nutt, in Cornhill ; J. Clarke in Duck-Lane ; T. Astley in
St. Paul's-Church-Yard ; A. Dodd without Temple-Bar ; J. Stagg
in Westminster-Hall ; J. Jackson in Pall-Mall ; J. Brindley and
W. Shropshire in Bond-Street ; and J. Millan near the Admiralty-
Office. Where may be had the former Numbers.

PROPOSALS
For Printing by SUBSCRIPTION,

A Second Edition of the Translation of
Mr. RAPIN DE THOYRAS his History of ENGLAND. In
two Volumes in Folio. By N TINDAL, M.A. of Great Waltham in Essex. With the following Improvements.

I. The Translation is thoroughly revised and corrected.

II. The many Errors and Mistakes of the Original are carefully
rectified.

III. Several Hundred of Marginal References, accidentally omitted
by the Author, are supplied.

IV. Additional Notes throughout, with Maps, and Genealogical
Tables.

As the chief Intent of this Edition is to render RAPIN's History as universal as useful, it will be publish'd in the following Manner.

I. The Whole will be comprized in four hundred Sheets, and
printed in a new Letter, and on a fine Genoa Paper.

II. The Price to the Subscribers (including Cutts, Maps and
Tables,) will be two Guineas in Sheets ; one Guinea to be paid
down, and other at the Delivery of the second Volume.

III. It is design'd, (whilst the Two Volumes are printing) to
publish every Week Six Sheets for Six-pence, the first Number to be published on Saturday the fifth of August. The Reason
of this, is, to prevent Gentlemen from being drawn in by the
specious Pretences of one, who has lately set on Foot the Project of a new Translation to be published in weekly Pamphlets
of four Sheets only for Six-pence, and pretends the Whole will be
contain'd in four hundred Sheets. When it is evident, (by comparing
what is already publish'd with the Original) that the Number of
Sheets will amount to between five and six hundred ; consequently
the Price will be almost double of this second Edition, considering
the great Expence of engraving the Maps and Tables.

N.B. The five Sheets to be published weekly, will contain above
six of the new projected Translation.

IV. Such as take the weekly Numbers will be reckon'd as Subscribers, that is, shall pay but two Guineas, tho' the Number of Sheets
should happen to exceed four hundred.

V. The first Volume will be ready to be delivered to the Subscribers soon after Christmas next, and the second by Michaelmas following, which is but one quarter of the Time wherein a new Translation can be done as it ought by any one Hand.

Subscriptions are taken in by James, John and Paul Knapton,
removed from St. Paul's Church-Yard, to the Crown in Ludgate-
Street, near the West-End of St. Paul's.

Where may be had this History compleat in Fifteen Volumes in
Octavo.

N.B. The Translator having a few Copies of this Edition to dispose of, all such Gentlemen as are willing to give him Encouragement, are desired to declare, at the Place above-named, that they
subscribe for his Benefit, or to pay the Subscription-Money to any
of his Friends, that shall apply to them for that purpose.

LONDON: Printed by J. HUGGONSON, *in Bartholomew-Close*, for Capt. GULLIVER, near the *Temple*, where Letters and Advertisements
are taken in : As also at the *Rainbow Coffee-House in Cornhill*, and *John's Coffee-House in Sheer-Lane, Temple-Bar*. [Price Two Pence.]

And after this, Mr. BAVIUS, what does the letter writer do, in what he calls an *answer* to all that has been written against the performances of a *Gentleman to whom the town has ow'd so much diversion*? Why truly, not attempt to answer one single objection, or defend one single passage that has been quoted against him ; only by the *trite* and general complaint that PUBLICUS had *tore out several passages* without inserting the *whole speeches*. It this had been fact, why did not he quote those *speeches* entire, shew the misrepresentation, and justify the writer? Oh no, they were by no means fit to appear any more ; he knew the more they were stirr'd the more they would —— and therefore, instead of vindicating the writings, he gives us a *full and true account of the birth, parentage, and education of the writer*. This is a merry evasion enough; 'tis like the fool in the Play —— *If you talk of wit, and fine sense, and all that, 'gad; pray what d'ye say to this feather in my hat*? Surely, Mr. BAVIUS, an author's high birth is as poor an excuse for the low scurrility in his writings, as his having been *mounted* at Eaton school is for the false English in them. If the *Letter-writer* and *Farce-writer* be the same person, (as I believe no one will doubt, since no other person could attempt a vindication of such performances, but he that could write them,) then we need go no farther than the *Daily Post* before us, to prove this *high-born, high-bred Gentleman* as incapable of writing one page of good English, as one scene of good sense. In the first column he says, that the *Debauchees was reciv'd with as great applause, as was ever given* ON *the Theatre*, instead of *in a Theatre*. In the next column you meet with *human wish*, instead of *humane wish*, which is absolute nonsense.

● ● ● ● ● ● ●
● ● ● ● ● ● ●

So much for this author at present : I shall take another opportunity to make good what I asserted, that his *pen is not only void of wit, modesty, and good manners, and the most common rules of poetry, but even Grammar*, and that too in every sheet of his productions.

I am, Mr. BAVIUS,
Your very humble servant,
PUBLICUS.

P. S. As to the reception the *mock Doctor* has met with from the town, I must inform him, that 'tis not owing the poet, but to the player : every one agreeing, that 'tis as ill written, as 'till well acted.

EPIGRAM.

Charg'd with writing of bawdy, this was F——'s reply:
Tis what DRYDEN and CONGREVE have done as well as I.
Tis true — but they did it with this good pretence,
With an ounce of rank bawdy went a pound of good sense:
But thou hast proportion'd, in thy judgment profound,
Of good sense scarce an ounce, and of bawdy a pound.
MÆVIUS

Dublin, July 22. At the Assizes at Wicklow, Samuel Ewart, a soldier was condemned for the murder of one Keightly, a Smith in Bray, whom in a quarrel he stabbed, so that he died on the spot. *C. P. D'J.* ——This week one Rose Neal, between 9 and 10 years old, who lived in a cellar, was searched by several good women, on account of her being abused by a wicked wretch, and many of them declare they believe her to be pregnant, having symptoms like persons in that condition. The fellow accused made off. *P. D'J.* ——*July 25.* Last saturday died of a violent fever Tho. Elrington, Esq; the famous Tragadian, Deputy Master of the revels, Steward of the Commons [Inns. P.] and chief of his Majesty's Company of Comedians. *C. D'J.* —— An account of the Taylors feast this day : 10 dozen of chickens, 37 rumps of beef, 49 legs of mutton, 46 gibelet-pyes, 2 waggons loaded with turneps and carrots, 1 ditto loaded with provocatives of pickling. *P.*— N. B. *They had too much cabbage at home, to eat any with their rumps of beef abroad.*

FOREIGN NEWS.

TUESDAY, July 27.

Extract of a letter from Alicant, *July* 16. N. S. — It seems the Spaniards are contented with the taking of Oran, having ordered all their forces back, except 8000 ; which they leave to garrison that place ; so that their Barbary expedition it quite at an end. *P.*

FRIDAY, July 28.

Rome, July 12. On the 6th some workmen, digging in a field belonging to the Chapter of S. John de Lateran, found 4 statutes, a pillar of Jasper, several urns, lamps, and medals of Roman Emperors. *DP. D'J.*

SATURDAY, July 29.

Paris, Aug. 1. The Duke of Ormond is arrived with a numerous equipage at Valencia, where he rests some time, and then sets out for Barcelona. A good part of

his heavy baggage is sent before him to Avignon. The Marq. de Pomponne, long afflicted with the gout and rheumatism, has found an easy, tho' a very odd cure, from a sympathetic Doctor, one Pezzuas : the operation was thus, he put a kind of powder into the urine of the patient, which put him into a sweat, and perhaps into a fright, and this was the malignity was discharged. *P.*

This day arrived the Mail from Holland.

Seville, July 11. The French squadron, which had been at Genoa and Leghorn, is arrived in the road of Algiers. *W. E.* To demand satisfaction for the insult committed on the flag of France. *DP.* 31.

MONDAY, July 30.

Yesterday arrived the Mail from France.

Paris, Aug 1. N. S. They write from Genoa, that the inhabitants of Corsica, being uneasy to see their chiefs in prison, begin to excite new commotions, and had put to the sword several soldiers and sbirri that came to carry some of them to prison. The Prince of Wirtemberg, not accustomed to little republican arts, insists upon a fair, open, and punctual performance of all the conditions stipulated with those unfortunate people, once their masters, now by German arms made their slaves, and by their own credulity their prisoners. *P.*

Books and Pamphlets published from July 4. to July 20.

6. A Sermon at S. Paul's before the Hon. L Mayor, &c. May 29 by Will Sympson, D. D.
The Court Gossips : the Christening, a satyrical Poem. Pr. 1s.
Remains of the late Dr. Will. King. Pr. 5s.
The present state of Europe, for May.
A seasonable Preservative against Popish delusions, translated from the Latin of Dr. Will. Whitaker, by Tho. Dawson, D. D.
The greatness of the Divine love farther vindicated, &c. by Sam. Fancourt.
The History of Essex, No. II. Pr. 1s. 6d.
Ora io de novo Phytologiæ explicandæ munere, &c. à Conyers Middleton, S T P.
7. The Divine authority of the Christian Religion, &c. in 8 Sermons at L. Moyer's Lecture: by John Browne, M. A.
A Letter to a Lady, in defence of the Gospel of S. Matthew. Pr. 1s. 6d.
8. An Appendix to Bibliotheca legum. Pr. 6d.
Remarks on a Sermon preach'd by Mr. Tho. Mole. Pr. 6d.
10. The Political state of Great Britain : for June.
The hope of a good man in the view of death : a funeral Sermon, by Jer. Tidcombe.
11. A Supplement to the Lords Protest.
The Mock Doctor : or The dumb Lady cur'd. A Comedy ; done from Moliere.
Miscellaneous observations on authors, No. xix.
15. The Romish doctrine of Transubstantiation impartially consider'd, &c. by R. Cornthwaite. Pr. 6d.
17. The natural probability of a lasting peace in Europe, &c. Pr. 6d.
The historical, political, and poetical works of Geo. Waldron, Gent. &c.
The proceedings at the Sessions in the Old Bailey, July 5, 6, 7, 8, &c.
18. A vindication of the Quakers : or an answer to the Bishop of L——d's charge against them.
The present state of the Republick of letters, for June.
The progress of Divine Love, a Poem : by a young Lady of 15. Pr. 6d.
Henriade : an Epick Poem: translated from the French of Mons. Voltaire, into English blank verse.
20. An Epistle to the Hon. Miss Trevor, daughter to Sir Ric. Steele, upon her marriage, &c. By Rog. Dyer. P.6d.

To al. Gentlemen, Builders, and others,
ALEXANDER EMERTON,
Colour Man, *at the* Bell *over-against* Arundel-
Street, *in the* Strand, LONDON,

SELLS all Sorts of COLOURS ready
prepared (at the lowest Prices) that any Gentlemen, Builders, may set their Servants or Labourers to paint their Houses,
only by the Help of a printed Direction, which he gives with his
Colours.

N. B. Five Pounds Worth of Colours will paint as much Work,
as a House-Painter will do for Twenty Pounds.

He likewise sells (to the Ladies) all Sorts of Water-Colours and
Varnish, with every Thing necessary for the New Japanning, and
gives a printed Direction, for the doing of it to the greatest Perfection, to those that buy Colours. —— Also Italian Powder for
cleaning Pictures.

He deals only for Ready Money.

Just published,

*For the Use of Families, beautifully printed in
two Volumes Octavo, adorn'd with 34 Plates,
Engraven by Mr. STURT,*

DUpin's EVANGELICAL HISTORY : Or, the
Records of the SON of GOD, and their Veracity demonstrated, in the Life and Acts of our Blessed Lord and Saviour Jesus
Christ, and the Holy Apostles. Wherein, 1. The Life of our Blessed Saviour Jesus Christ is related in all its Circumstances, according
to the Order of Time, in a pathetick and practical Method, thereby composing a perfect Harmony of the Gospels. 2. Proofs from
his Sermons and Discourses of these Essential and Important Truths,
which all Christians are obliged to know and practise, in order to
their Eternal Salvation. 3. His Parables, Miracles, and Sufferings,
set in a just Light, and defended from all the Oppositions of wicked and
designing Men. 4. An Application of the Whole to the respective
Uses of Christians, with regular Devotions conformable to the several Periods of the Holy History; and Directions how he may read
the Life of Jesus Christ to Advantage.

Printed for R. Ware, at the Bible and Sun in Amen-Corner,
near Pater-Noster-Row. Price 8 s.

Also may be had at the same Place,
1. The large House-Bibles, Folio, with the six Maps of sacred
Geography, and a brief Concordance for the more easy finding out
of the Places therein contained. By J. Downame, B. D.
Bound in Calf Leather   1 l. 8 s. per Book.
And with Mr. Sturt's Cuts added   1 l. 5 s. ditto.
On a fine Paper with Cuts   3 l. 3 s. ditto.
2. Impartial Churchman; or, A fair and candid Representation
of the Excellency and Beauty of the Church of England. Together
with an earnest and affectionate Address to the Protestant Dissenters.
By ROBERT WARREN, D. D. Price 3 s. 6 d.
3. A Description of 300 Animals, viz. Beasts, Birds, Fishes, Serpents and Insects. With a particular Account of the Whale-Fishery.
Extracted out of the best Authors, and adapted to the Use of all
Capacities, especially to allure Children to read. Illustrated with
Copper Plates, whereon is curiously engraven every Beast, Bird, Fish,
Serpent and Insect described in the whole Book. Price 2 s. 6 d.
4. Tradesman's Guide. Containing a List of all the Stage Coaches
and Carriers; with an Account of all the Market Towns in England. Price 2 s.

This Day is published,

Printed for *J. Brotherton*, at the *Bible*, next
the Fleece Tavern in Cornhill,

AN Enquiry into the Origin of Honour,
and the Usefulness of Christianity in War.

By the Author of a FABLE of the BEES.

Where may be had,
1. A Letter to Dion, being an Answer to a Book call'd *Alciphron*,
or the *Minute Philosopher*.
2. The present State of Great Britain and Ireland, for the Year
1731.
3. Traditions of the Jews.
4. Dampier's Journal to Madagascar.
5. Religious Courtship.
6. Life of OLIVER CROMWELL, Lord Protector of the Commonwealth.
7. Receipts in Cookery and Surgery, by John Keetilby.

This Day is published,

[Price Six Pence.]

AN Epistle humbly address'd to the Hon.
Mrs. ELIZABETH TREVOR, Daughter of the late Sir
RICHARD STEELE, upon her Marriage with the Hon. JOHN
TREVOR, Esq; son to the Rt. Hon. THOMAS late Lord TREVOR.
By ROBERT DYER.

Hail, wedded Love!
Perpetual Fountain of Domestick Sweets!
Here, Love his Golden Shafts employs; here lights
His constant Lamp, and waves his Purple Wings. MILTON.
Far鸡er ter & amplius
Quos irrupta tenet copula; nec malis
Divulsus querimoniis,
Suprema citius solvet Amor Die. HOR.

Printed for Lawton Gilliver, at Homer's Head, against St. Dunstan's Church in Fleet-Street.

Aug. 3. **This Day is published**, Pr. 6 d.
*Very proper for private Families, or to send into the Coun-
try (and Places abroad where the English reside) being
a compendious View of all our Publick Papers.*

The GENTLEMAN's MAGAZINE:

Or, MONTHLY INTELLIGENCER.
NUMBER XIX. for JULY, 1732.
Being the SEVENTH *of* VOLUME II.
CONTAINING,
[More in Quantity, and greater Variety, than any Book of
the Kind and Price.]

I. Views of the WEEKLY ESSAYS, viz. On
Beds; Will of John Hopkins, Esq; True Greatness; Mo-
ney no Equivalent for unequal Marriages; Style and Elocution;
Ruling the Passions; Propagating Opinions; Panegyric on Coward-
ice; On the Quakers, Philosophy; Criticisms of the Grub-street
Journal, Dr. Bentley, the Comedian, and two Plays; Female Ex-
travagance; Rake's Fortune; idle Curiosity; Humane Nature;
Love and Philosophy; Irresolution; Wit; Trust in Providence;
Necessity and Free Will; Religion, &c.
II. POLITICAL POINTS, Proceedings and Debates of the Eng-
lish and French Parliaments, Remarks on both; British Discon-
tents; Treatment of Charles I. Battle of Contradictions; Magna
Charta, the Fruits of Bad Ministers; Improvements of Ireland;
Blunderers, Struggles for Liberty.
III. POETRY, York Ladies; Carshalton Fair; Lady and Cater-
pillar; the prudent Damsel; Croydon Workhouse; The Blind Pup-
pies; Lore and Reputation; The Grotto, Tales, Fables, Epigrams.
IV. DOMESTIC OCCURRENCES, &c. Births, Deaths, Marri-
ages, Promotions, &c.
V. Prices of Goods, Grain, Stocks; London Monthly Bill of
Mortality.
VI. FOREIGN AFFAIRS.
VII. A Table of CONTENTS.
With a Register of Books and Pamphlets.

By SYLVANUS URBAN, Gent.

London: Printed, and sold at St. John's Gate; by F. Jefferies
in Ludgate-Street; Mrs. Nutt, Mrs. Charlton, Mrs. Cook, at the
Royal-Exchange; Mr. Batley in Pater-Noster-Row; Mr. Midwinter, in St. Paul's Church-Yard; A. Chapman, in Pall-Mall,
Mrs. Dodd, and Mr. Bickerton, without Temple-Bar; Mr. Crichley, at Charing-Cross; Mr. Stagg, and Mr. King, in Westminster-
Hall; Mr. Williamson in Holborn; Mr. Montague, in Great
Queen-Street; Mr. Harding, in St. Martin's-Lane; and all unprejudic'd Booksellers in Town and Country.
Note, a few are printed on a fine Royal Paper, large Margin, for
the Curious.
Note, The great Demand for the GENTLEMAN'S MAGAZINE
these 18 Months last past, has occasion'd most of the Numbers to
be out of Print several times. At present Setts can only be had for
the Year 1732. Having been obliged unexpectedly to reprint our
last for June; and also to put No. I. and No. II. a 4th time in the
Press, we have not been able to get the first ready, as promis'd, in
August; but Gentlemen may depend on compleat Setts in September.

PROPOSALS
For Printing by SUBSCRIPTION,

THE HISTORY of the Grand Con-
troversy between the Secular and Regular Clergy of the
Church of Rome, from the Year 1625 to 1634. concerning the
Usurpation of RICHARD SMITH, Titular Bishop of Chalcedon,
who pretended to be sole Ordinary Bishop of all England and Scot-
land. Wrote in Latin by the President of the English Benedictine
Monks, RUDESINDUS BARLO, and faithfully done into English
from the Original, for the Entertainment of the Curious, especially Divines and Lawyers, both Ecclesiastick and Civil, of what
Religion soever.
With the Remonstrances of the Roman Catholick Laity made to
the said Bishop, and also to his Excellency Carolo Coloma, Embassador
Extraordinary of the Most Catholick Majesty, and to the Marquis
Fontany, Embassador of the Most Christian King, &c. taken also
from the Latin Originals; All which Treatises have been hitherto suppress'd, by the Papists, for Political Reasons given therein.
As also the famous Bull of Pope URBAN VIII. called PLAN-
TATA, necessary for the right Understanding of the Whole; which
was never before any where printed.
To which will be added,
A LETTER concerning the Disputes that have happen'd among
the Benedictine Monks since the Year 1700 to this present Time:
Shewing how even they themselves have varied from their original Principles. By one who was a Member of that Body, and
concerned therein.

By JOHN WILLIAMS.

PROPOSALS may be had of (and SUBSCRIPTIONS taken in
for the Author by) W. Meadows, at the Angel, in Cornhill;
T. Astley, at the Rose, and S. Austen, at the Angel and Bible in
St. Paul's Church-Yard; C. Davis, Pater-Noster-Row; T. Wood-
ward, at the Half-Moon, L. Gilliver, at Homer's Head, and J. Ste-
phens, at the Hand and Star, between the Two Temple-Gates;
B. Motte, at the Middle Temple-Gate; T. Worral, at Judge
Coke's Head, H. Whitbone, next Door to the Rainbow Coffee-
House, W. Reason, in Fleuve-de-Luce-Court, J. Illed, at the
Golden-Ball, near Chancery-Lane, Fleet-Street; F. Gyles, over-
against Gray's-Inn-Gate, Holborn; O. Payne, in Round-Court, and
T. Game, at the Bible, by the New Church, in the Strand;
T. Green, Charing-Cross; J. Jackson, in Pallmall; J. Jolliffe,
at the Bible, in St. James's-Street; J. Brindley, at the King's Arms,
and W. Shropshire, opposite to the Duke of Grafton's, New Bond-
Street; and J. Stagg Westminster-Hall, Booksellers: J. Huggonson,
in Bartholomew-Close, and T. Cover, by Fleet-Ditch, Black-Fryers,
Print ers.

This Day is published,
The LONDON MAGAZINE:
Or, GENTLEMAN's *Monthly Intelligencer.*
NUMB. IV. For JULY, 1732.
To be Continued. (Price Sixpence each Month.)
CONTAINING
(*Greater Variety, and more in Quantity, than any* MONTH-
LY BOOK *extant.*)

I. A View of the WEEKLY ESSAYS, viz. Of
marrying purely for Interest; Causes of Unhappiness in
Marriage; Story of Caruto; ill Effect of Curiosity; a Censure on
the Ladies; Self-Government; Vanity of Titles; Inconstancy and
Fickleness; Resignation to the Will of God; Compassion to the
Distressed; Prescience and Free-Will; Unreasonableness of Imposition; Wit; Philosophy; Style; the Writer and Orator; Play-
house Writers; Dr. B—y's Notes on Milton examin'd; Praise
of Cowardice; Education, and the Power of Love.
II. POLITICAL Subjects, viz. Slavery and Liberty; true Greatness; Liberty and Property; Struggles for Liberty; Fog and Osborne of the Church and State; Craftsman on the last Session of
Parliament, and Remarks upon him, &c. Parliament of Paris;
Ministerial Writers; the Genuine Blunderer; Great Britain's Interest in Ireland; Advantages from bad Ministers; Marks of such
of bad Kings making bad Ministers, &c.
III. POETRY; Carshalton Fair; the Retirement; Love and Re-
putation; to a Militia Captain; Panegyrick on Cuckoldom; Craftsman always in the same Story; Epigrams.
IV. DOMESTICK Occurrences: Promotions Ecclesiastical, Civil
and Military; Marriages and Births; Deaths; Sessions at the Old
Baily; York Buildings Company, &c.
V. FOREIGN AFFAIRS.
VI. Price of Goods, Grain, Stocks; Monthly Bill of Mortality.
VII. A TABLE of Contents.
To which is added, a Catalogue of Books and Pamphlets, with
their Prices, published by the Proprietors of the Monthly Chronicle,
now discontinu'd.

MULTUM IN PARVO.

LONDON: Printed for C. Ackers in St. John-Street; for J. Wil-
ford, behind the Chapter-House, near St. Paul's: And sold by
W. Meadows, T. Cox, W. Hinchliffe, W. Whiridge, R. Willock,
and J. Nutt, in Cornhill; J. Clarke in Duck-Lane; T. Astley in
St. Paul's Church-Yard; A. Dodd without Temple-Bar; J. Stagg
in Westminster-Hall; J. Jackson in Pall-Mall; J. Brindley and
W. Shropshire in Bond-Street; and J. Millan near the Admiralty-
Office. Where may be had the former Numbers.

PROPOSALS
For Printing by SUBSCRIPTION,

A Second Edition of the Translation of
Mr RAPIN DE THOYRAS his History of ENGLAND. In
two Volumes in Folio. By N. TINDAL, M. A. of Great Wal-
tham in Essex. With the following Improvements.
I. The Translation is thoroughly revised and corrected.
II. The many Errors and Mistakes of the Original are carefully
rectified.
III. Several Hundred of Marginal References, accidentally omitted
by the Author, are supplied.
IV. Additional Notes throughout, with Maps, and Genealogical
Tables.

As the chief Intent of this Edition is to render RAPIN's History as universal as useful, it will be publish'd in the following Manner.
I. The Whole will be compacted in four hundred Sheets, and
printed in a new Letter, and on a fine Genoa Paper.
II. The Subscribers (including Cutts, Maps and
Tables) will be two Guineas in Sheets; one Guinea to be paid
down, and other at the Delivery of the second Volume.
III. It is design'd, (with the Two Volumes are printing) to
publish every Week Six Sheets for Six-pence, the first Number to be published on Saturday the fifth of August. The Reason
of this, is to prevent Gentlemen from being drawn in by the
specious Pretences of one, who has lately set on Foot the Project of a new Translation to be published in weekly Pamphlets
of four Sheets only for Six-pence, and pretends the Whole will be
contain'd in four hundred Sheets. When it is evident, (by comparing
what is already publish'd with the Original) that the Number of
Sheets will amount to between five and six hundred; consequently
the Price will be almost double of this second Edition, considering
the great Expence of engraving the Maps and Tables.
N. B. The five Sheets to be published weekly, will contain above
fix of the new projected Translation.
IV. Such as take the weekly Numbers will be reckon'd as Subscribers, that is, shall pay but two Guineas, tho' the Number of Sheets
should happen to exceed four hundred.
V. The first Volume will be ready to be delivered to the Subscribers soon after Christmas next; and the second by Michaelmas following, which is but one quarter of the Time wherein a new Translation can be done as it ought by any one Hand.
Subscriptions are taken in by James, John and Paul Knapton,
removed from St. Paul's Church-Yard, to the Crown in Ludgate-
Street, near the West-End of St. Paul's.
Where may be had this History compleat in Fifteen Volume in
Octavo.
N. B. The Translator, having a few Copies of this Edition to dispose of, all such Gentlemen as are willing to give him Encouragement, are desired to declare, at the Place above-named, that they
subscribe for his Benefit, or to pay the Subscription-Money to any
of his Friends, that shall apply to them for that purpose.

The Grub-street Journal.

NUMB. 136

Thursday, AUGUST 10, 1732.

——————— *reason'd high*
Of providence, fore-knowledge, will, and fate;
Fix'd fate, free will, fore-knowledge absolute:
And found no end, in wandring mazes lost.
Paradise Lost, B. II. 558, &c.

Mr. BAVIUS,

I HAVE seen your 134th *Journal*, dated July 27th, 1732, and find by it, that subjects of the nicest importance are sometimes allowed a place in your paper. Having since received some *Remarks* upon that part of it, intitled, *An abstract of a lately revived dispute concerning liberty and prescience*, I must desire you, if possible, to insert them in your next.

Sir,

The *Abstract* which you was so kind as to send me I have carefully read. It relates, I see, to that celebrated controversy concerning *God's prescience*, and *Man's free-will*. As the author writes with temper, and like a sincere enquirer after truth, I have, according to his own desire, made a few animadversions upon it. If you think they may be of any service in the cause of *liberty*, (without which we seem to be no better than conscious machines, capable neither of virtue nor vice, praise nor blame, rewards nor punishments;) you have my free consent to publish them, when, and in what manner you please.

This Gentleman *conjures* his opponents *to be short, and not to say one word beside the purpose*. I shall therefore, without any further introduction observe, 1st. That Mr. FANCOURT (as is obvious to every unprejudiced and impartial reader) has allowed from the very beginning, that *what was ever certain, was ever foreknown*. What he denies, is, *that our free actions were ever certain*; or, *that actions, which were ever certain, can be free*. His reason is short and plain; because free actions, by the confession of both parties, either may, or may not be. But when one side is certain, the other side is impossible, and cannot be; no more than what is certain can be false.

Therefore, 2dly, tho' 'the certainty of fore-knowledge 'does not cause the certainty of things, but is itself found'ed on the reality of their [*future*] existence;' yet *fore-knowledge*, with him, *implies* a *certainty* in things; and *certainty* implies *necessity*, and *necessity* destroys *free-agency*.

So that, 3dly, when the Author of the *Abstract* contends, that 'tho' foreknowledge *implies* a certainty in things, 'yet it is no other than such a certainty only, as would 'be equally in things, tho' there was no fore-knowledge;' this, I conceive, is saying nothing towards removing the grand difficulty; and seems calculated, not so much to establish *prescience*, as to destroy *liberty*; not so much to evince God's *fore knowledge* of our free actions, as that there are no *free actions* to be foreknown. Which must, I am pretty confident, be the real case, was his argument in the next paragraph just and conclusive, viz. 'What'ever now is, 'tis certain that it is; and [therefore] it was 'yesterday, and from eternity, as certainly true, that 'the thing would be to day, as it is now certain that it 'is.' Whereas the present or past existence of a thing is an argument, indeed, that it was *ever possible* before, not that it was *ever certain*. ——— Let us suppose this Gentleman's *Abstract* to have been a contingent or free performance; what, upon the whole, he either might, or might not have made. What Mr. F. asserts is, whilst it remained free and contingent, it was at that time neither *certain* that he would, nor *certain* that he would not write it; but only in his power, as a free agent, to have made *either* certain. For when his writing becomes *certain*, his not writing becomes *impossible*; because, what will be, must be, and cannot but be.

This, I apprehend, is set in a very easy and convincing light in the *Appendix* to his *letter to Mr.* NORMAN. Where, in the compass of a two-penny pamphlet, that has undergone a third impression, you have (as I conceive) a clear and decisive view of the present controversy. 'I would ask, says Mr. F. why can't 'we recall what is past? But because to recall it, is to 'make it not past; and so it would be both past and not 'past. Why can't we hinder what is? But because to 'hinder it, is to make that it is not; and so it would be 'true that it is, and yet true that it is not. Why can't 'we do the thing that is impossible? But because to do it, 'is to prove that it is possible; and so it would be both 'possible and impossible. For the same reason it is, that 'none can prevent what will be; because to prevent it, 'is to make that it will not be; and so true, and not true, 'that it will be.' *Page* 12. —— I durst undertake for him, that he shall venture the whole controversy upon this single point, *Whether whatever is now certain, was ever certain?* And if our Author can fairly demonstrate the affirmative, Mr. F. shall yield him, that what we call free actions were *ever certain*, and certainly *foreknown from eternity*: tho' here to prove they were *ever free* also, and what we might have prevented, will be the question.

4thly, 'Bare prescience, we'll grant him, has no in'fluence at all, upon any thing; nor contributes, in the 'least, towards making it necessary, any more than the 'simple knowledge of it, when it is done.' But still the difficulty continues in its full strength, how it came to be true [of sin, for instance,] that it was *ever certain*, which God's fore-knowledge always supposes. To say, it was made so by an act of the divine will, stains the divine purity: to say, it was certain, antecedently to any act of the divine will, is to make it in its own nature necessary, and to establish a fatal necessity of all that we call sin: and in both cases the free agency of the creature is gone.

5thly. As to what he adds, ''tis true; the manner how 'God can foresee future things, without a chain of ne'cessary causes, is impossible for us to explain distinctly;' I answer, if he can solidly prove, that all our free actions were always future or *ever certain*, we'll allow they were *ever foreseen*, without giving him the trouble of explaining it at all, and much less of *explaining* it *distinctly*. Let them be foreseen in the *glass of the divine will*, or by means of God's *eternity being actually commensurate to all duration*, and to by the *presentiality and existence of all things in eternity*, or any other way he pleases, we will not contend with him; tho' this (as our Author himself justly observes) is but to *darken difficulties with a shew of knowledge*. However, in the mean time, he would do well to *explain* a little more *distinctly*, the consistency of what follows, viz. that 'certainty of event does not, in any sort, imply necessity.' Since, by his own confession, the event that's *certain*, must be; else it is beyond me to understand his meaning, when he asks, 'Will 'there not yet, ——in the nature of things, be the same '*certainty* of event, in any one of our actions, as if they 'were never so *fatal* and *necessary*?' To conclude: what God infallibly foreknows, will be; the actions of free agents, whilst contingent, only may be: and therefore are no more the objects of such a *fore knowledge*, than to square a circle is an object of power. He that can *foreknow* the one, I presume, may do the other.

Aug. 2d, 1732. I am, Sir, your &c.

FROM the time that the memoirs of our Society have been published weekly, they have been attaqued by persons who were formerly members, but for private reasons deserted us; and to disguise and palliate that desertion, have professed an open enmity to our whole Body. All these Gentlemen may be reduced to two classes: being either persons, who by their ignorance and immorality, were a a scandal to our Society; or such, who by the greatness of their genius and their learning, were ornaments thereto. Tho' the former have frequently fallen upon us in obscure News Papers, endeavouring to draw us into a dispute, in order to promote the sale of them: yet we have always despised such adversaries, and either taken no notice at all of them, or in that contemptuous manner which they deserved. But when any of the latter have appeared against us, we have payed a proper respect to them, and treated them with all the decency which was due to such learned and well-bred persons. This has been more especially manifested by two controversies, in which we have been ingaged for some time; one of which is with a famous ACTOR at the Theatre at the corner of Lincoln's-Inn-fields, near Clare-market; the other with as famous a DRAMATIC WRITER belonging to the Theatre in Drury-lane. And because the last of these disputes has been particularly favoured with the attention of the Public, being concerning points of great consequence, we shall give a short but exact account of the occasion and state of this important controversy.

A weekly Journal is published by Mr. BAVIUS, to whom several ingenious and learned persons, generally unknown to him, communicate pieces from time to time. These pieces are published sometimes with, and sometimes without alterations, according as they are approved by some other persons who are consulted. Neither Mr. BAVIUS, nor his Colleagues are obliged to defend any of these pieces which come from other hands, unless they have expresly declared them to be agreeable to their own sentiments. In other cases, they are only to be looked upon as merely publishers; and, as such, have frequently assured the public, that any person who thinks himself unjustly attacqued in this Journal, shall have an opportunity of defending himself in the same; than which offer they cannot imagine any thing fairer and more impartial.

About four months ago, a Gentleman under the name of DRAMATICUS sent us a criticism upon *The Modern Husband*, which was printed in Number 117. To which the Author, HENRY FIELDING, Esq; instead of returning any answer, thought it sufficient to inveigh bitterly among his acquaintance against the *Grub street Journal*, representing the Authors of it as a set of paltry, ill natured, and ignorant scribblers. About two months ago he brought upon the stage a Comedy of three Acts, called *The Old Debauchees*; to which he added a Farce of two, representing the humours of a bawdy-house, and intitled the *Covent garden Tragedy*, which was damned the first night. In the first scene of which he introduces the Bawd saying to her Porter,

The Grub street Journal *thou hast known to write,*
Thou art a judge.

Some reflections upon this tragical Farce, in two letters, one from PROSAICUS, and the other from DRAMATICUS, were published in our 127th and 128th Journals. To which an answer was printed in the *Daily Post* of June 21. under the name of *Mr.* WM. HINT, *Candle-snuffer*, directed to DRAMATICUS, *alias* PROSAICUS, *alias* BAVIUS, &c. This answer consisted of two parts, a general defence of the *Covent garden Tragedy*, and an invective against the *Grub-street Journal*. To the former DRAMATICUS sent a reply, printed in number 130: and to the latter another reply was drawn up; which, tho' approved by our Society June 29, and ordered to be published the first convenient opportunity, yet being pretty long has been postponed from time to time, to leave room for things of greater importance, and will perhaps now never see the light in its original form.

But since this great Author by a fresh invective against our Society, published in the *Daily Post* of July 31, seems resolved to have a controversy with us concerning the design and nature of our Journal, we are willing to join issue with him upon that point. And to shew ourselves fair adversaries, we shall here republish *verbatim* all that he has alledged against us, under the name of *Mr.* WM. HINT *Candle-snuffer*; subjoining a short answer to every article.

'When a set of *Scribblers*, who very justly stile them'selves of *Grub street*, pretend to give laws to our The'atres, the Press is surely open to any pen.'— *Scribblers* is a term, which, in every learned controversy, the authors on either side claim a right, by immemorial custom, to apply to their adversaries; but it belongs only to the public to fix it, which is generally done with strict justice. *The set of Scriblers* here pointed at do not *pretend to give* new *laws to our Theatres*, but to revive the old laws of the Drama, intirely consonant to the laws of nature; against *a set of Scriblers*, who either have not genius and learning sufficient to furnish a rational and moral entertainment, or else basely suppress their talents in compliance with the vicious taste of the age. But, whether we had *pretended* to do this, or not, *the press is surely* enough *open to any pen*, otherwise it would not be employed in blotting paper with such ribaldry as is to be seen in the *Old Debauchees, Covent-garden Tragedy*, and *Mock Doctor*.

'But, I fancy, however envy and malice may animate 'you against a successful Play, you had not (*unprovok'd*) 'fallen thus inhumanly on one the Town dislik'd, and 'the Author gave up without appealing to a second trial.' — The success of the *Modern Husband* was not great enough to excite the *envy* and malice of any good Dramatic Writer; and if it had, that *envy* must have been soon allayed by the opinion the world entertained of this piece upon its publication. And the Bookseller is really obliged to our Journal for the republication of it; otherwise it might have lain as quietly in the shop as *The Modish Couple*. *To fall on one the Town disliked*, alias, hissed off

the ſtage, was no otherwiſe *inhuman*, than as it might ſeem to be a *falling on*, or abuſing of the dead: but *The Covent-garden Tragedy*, tho' dead, was not buried, but ſtunk in the noſtrils of the audience; and there was a report that it would even be revived by the ſkill of a certain MOCK-DOCTOR. As this, we believe, *provoked* PROSAICUS to write the firſt letter about it: ſo, we are certain, this only *provoked* us to contribute to its interment, by printing his letter; in doing which, we think, we performed, not an *inhuman*, but an *human* office.

'I fancy the real occaſion of all your exclamations may 'be found in one little line, where the Bawd tells her 'Porter (not much, I think, to his honour) that he is one 'of the Authors of the *Grub ſtreet Journal*.' —— I do aſſure you, that when PROSAICUS's firſt letter was publiſhed June 8, in our 127th *Journal*, we did not know that there was any ſuch *little line*, as you juſtly call it, in that tragical Farce. And when we did know it, it *provoked* us only to laughter, at a poor Poet, who could imagine that he could ridicule us in a line, which was ſo improbable that no one could believe one ſyllable of the imputation. That it is not *much*, nay not at all, *to* the *honour* of a *Porter* to a bawdy houſe, to be *one of the Authors* of our *Journal*, we intirely agree; becauſe, acting in the latter capacity would be detrimental to his former. But to aſſiſt a venal and venereal Poet, in writing lewd dramatical entertainments, would be very *honourable* for ſuch a perſon; as being not only conſiſtent with his other profeſſion, but tending very much to promote the intereſt of it. And that this may have been the caſe in relation to the pieces before us, is highly probable: for there is nothing in the *Old Debauchees*, or *Covent-garden Tragedy*, but what a Drurian Porter might, and ſome things, which, one would imagine, none but one as converſant with ſtrumpets, could have written.

'You mention the depravity of our taſte, but the 'ſucceſs of ſuch a Paper (if it had any) would be a 'ſtronger inſtance of that depravity than the ſucceſs of 'Hurlothrumbo was;' —— Tho' *Mr.* HINT ſeems here to queſtion *the ſucceſs of* our *Paper*, yet his brother PHILALETHES expreſsly acknowledges it, and pretends to account for it, but how truely we ſhall hereafter examine. At preſent, we muſt tell *Mr.* HINT, that the ſucceſs of it was never owing to daily or weekly puffs in the News-Papers, giving an account how it was read to *a great audience with univerſal applauſe*, &c. The *applauſe* it has met with came from other hands than thoſe which applauded either HURLO-THRUMBO, or HURLO-THUMBO, the ſucceſs of both which afforded *inſtances* equally *ſtrong of the depravity of taſte*.

'A Paper which any perſon of common ſenſe ought to 'be more aſham'd of reading, than women of the firſt 'modeſty to ſee any Performance ever yet exhibited.' — The perſon here introduced as a learned Critic upon Plays and Grub-ſtreet Journals; as a great judge of decorum, what is proper for *perſons of common ſenſe*, and *women of the firſt modeſty* to decline; and as a great enemy to the ſuppoſed compoſitions of his brother the Drury-lane Porter, is *Mr.* WM. HINT, *Candle-ſnuffer*. This ſhews how able the real Author of this letter is to write in character, when he endeavours it. But then it muſt be acknowledged, that he is very happy in ſucceeding, directly contrary to his endeavours, in characters the moſt different. For, as when he deſigned to mimic a *Candle-ſnuffer*, he wrote like a Critic: ſo, when he would fain appear as a Dramatic Poet, he made only the figure of his pretended Grubean Author, a mere Drury-lane Porter and Pimp.

I ſhall add no more at preſent, than that I have the greateſt reaſon to believe, that PROSAICUS and DRAMATICUS are different perſons, their letters being written in very different hands and ſtyles: but I neither know, nor can I gueſs, who either of them is. It is much eaſier to gueſs at Mr. *Wm.* HINT and PHILALETHES, who perhaps are likewiſe two different perſons, a Player and a Poet; of both whom either letter is perhaps the joint compoſition: and we don't doubt, that we ſhall make it evident to the world, before we have done with them, that, in the way of literature, the one is fit only for a *Candle-ſnuffer* to our Society, and the other for a *Porter* to carry about our lucubrations.

BAVIUS.

DOMESTIC NEWS.

C. *Courant.*	E P. *Evening Poſt.*
P. *Poſt-Boy.*	S J. *S. James's Evening Poſt.*
D P. *Daily Poſt.*	W E. *Whitehall Evening P.*
D J. *Daily Journal.*	L E. *London Evening Poſt.*

Omitted in our laſt.

It being owned by the Hyp Doctor's enemies, that his Paper is an Inſurance againſt, &c. D J. July 31. — *The* Doctor *is miſtaken: it was not* Inſurance *but* Aſſurance, *that was predicated of* his Paper.

THURSDAY, *Auguſt* 3.

Yeſterday Mr. Wiggs, one of his Majeſty's Meſſengers in ordinary arrived from the Earl of Waldegrave, and has, as we hear, brought ſome diſpatches relating to the affairs of the Charitable Corporation. *D P.*

On ſaturday a Gentleman near Epſom ſent his ſervant to receive 160 l. which was put up in his boots; but meeting with ſome ſharpers in returning, he went to gaming, and loſt 60 l. telling his Maſter, that he had been robb'd; and to make his ſtory gain credit, cut his boot, and made a large wound in his leg. *D P.* —— Mr. Conundrum *ſays, this fellow play'd* booty.

On monday one Mr. Wood, a chain maker, was attack'd by 3 footpads near Pancras, who beat him in a cruel manner, and robb'd him of a ſilver watch, &c. *D P.* —— A chair maker. *S J.*

The Rev. Dr. Delany, Chancellor of S. Patrick's in Dublin, juſtly celebrated for his excellent writings in defence of Chriſtianity, was married to Mrs. Tenison, a widow Lady of 2000 l. per ann. and 20,000 l. in caſh. *D J. S J. L E.* —— 1500 l. per ann. *W E.*

This day ſe'nnight there was a great Cricket match at Kew, where his Royal Highneſs the Prince was preſent; at the ſame time Mrs. Lindſay, who keeps the new great room at Bath, was introduced to his Royal Highneſs by Col. Schutz, who expreſs'd the higheſt pleaſure in ſpeaking of the Bath, which he promis'd to honour with his preſence; and, as a mark of his favour, was pleaſed to ſalute Mrs. Lindſay, who conducts with ſo much elegancy the diverſions of that place. *W E.* —— My Brother *has expreſſed himſelf in ſuch a* manner, *that it is uncertain, whether* his Royal Highneſs, or Col. Schutz ſaluted *this Lady.*

Glouceſter, July 29 On thurſday died Rayton Jones, Eſq; one of the Verdurers of the Foreſt of Dean. *D J.*

FRIDAY, *Auguſt* 4.

Yeſterday a Board of Treaſury was held at Sir Rob. Walpole's houſe in Arlington-ſtreet: upon which ſome people flatter themſelves, that Mr. Pulteney is not at ſuch a diſtance from the board as has been imagined. *C.* —— Will. Pulteney, Eſq; being returned from Oxford, is gone to his retirement at May-place, near Dartford in Kent, to paſs the remainder of the ſeaſon. *D J.*

Yeſterday about one, the Governor, Sub-Governor, &c. of the Bank came to their new building in Threadneedle-ſtreet, to ſee the firſt ſtone laid, &c. *D J.* —— *'Tis ſtrange, that this* new building, *before* the firſt ſtone *was* laid, *ſhould ſtand* in Thread needle ſtreet.

On wedneſday came advice from Gibraltar, that the Earl of Albemarle was arrived, after a very dangerous paſſage; that his Lordſhip and the Officers were once obliged to take to the ſhip's boat in a violent ſtorm, and had in all probability periſh'd if a ſhip had not taken them on board that came accidentally by; and that his Lordſhip had not heard of his ſervants and baggage. *D P.*

At the Aſſizes at Durham 3 perſons received ſentence of death. *D P.*

SATURDAY, *Auguſt* 5.

Yeſterday her Majeſty and all the Royal Family, attended by many perſons of diſtinction, went to Mr. Jervis's the Queen's limner [his Majeſty's painter. *C.*] in Cleaveland Court, and view'd his collection of pictures, then went to the E. of Tankervile's houſe in S James's-ſquare, and ſaw the fine ſtair caſe, [painted by Sir James Thornhill. *D P.*] and his collection of pictures, &c. and return'd to Kenſington to dinner. *P. D J.*

An order has paſſed his Majeſty's board of works for rebuilding the Treaſury Office at the Cockpit, Whitehall, during which time their Lordſhips will tranſact all buſineſs at the Lottery Office, which is now preparing for their reception. *C. D P.*

Mr. Tho. Oakes (late Coachman to the Hon. Col. Schutz) is appointed to be body Coachman to his Majeſty, in the room of Mr. Hooffe, deceaſed. *D J.* Tho. Oates. *P.*

On thurſday the ſilver arrow, value 3 l. was ſhot for at Harrow on the Hill, by 6 youths of that ſchool, and won by the ſon of Mr. Marton of Warwick-court, Holbourn: there was a very great appearance of Gentry. *D P.*

Yeſterday in the afternoon, after an hour's ſearch in his Chambers in the Middle-Temple, Mr. Crawford, an Attorney, was found in a hole under his deſk, and taken from thence by one of his Majeſty's Meſſengers, aſſiſted by a file of Muſqueteers, and carried to Weſtminſter, in order to be examined, being ſuſpected to be the author of Fog's Journal about King William, for which the Printer and Publiſher were ſome time ſince taken into cuſtody, and informations fil'd againſt them. *D P.* —— He is admitted to bail. *L E.* 8.

Yeſterday Hen. Catten, one of the perſons taken up for ſodomitical practices, was by Juſtice De Veil committed to the Gatehouſe; and Geo. Cadogan, alias Beho, was alſo taken up, and admitted to bail by Juſt. Bere of Hammerſmith, &c. *D P.* He is ſince committed likewiſe to the Gatehouſe. — *By the names* Cadogan and Catten, *this ſeems to be* Iriſh *unnatural* caterwauling.

The wiſe of an eminent Tradeſman of the City of Weſtminſter will ſet out very ſpeedily on her journey to Portſmouth, to be will dipt in the ſalt water, having been lately grievouſly afflicted with a diſtemper call'd the ſpleen, and 'tis hop'd ſhe will return free from that deplorable malady. *D P.*

We hear from Dover, that one of the Mayfield gang, who was preſent when Hill the Deal Officer was kill'd, has impeach'd ſeveral of the parties; and that 2 of them are now in priſon at Maidſtone; but that the perſon who actualy ſhot him, is in Boulogne, diſtracted. *P.*

On thurſday night died at his lodgings in Pall-Mall, the Rev. Dr. Aſpingwall, Sub-dean of his Majeſty's Chapel, and one of the Prebendaries of Weſtminſter. *D P.*

On ſaturday died John Stephens of Gray's Inn, Eſq; in his 80th year, ſaid to be worth 100,000 l. *S J.*

MONDAY, *Aug.* 7.

Yeſterday the Rev. Dr. Waterland preach'd before her Majeſty, his Royal Highneſs the Duke, and the 5 Princeſſes at the Chappel Royal at Kenſington. *C.*

At the Aſſizes at Launceſton, for the County of Cornwall, 4 malefactors received ſentence of death. —— At the Aſſizes at Stafford. 2. —— And at the Aſſizes at Maidſtone 2. *D J.*

On ſaturday there was a general Court of Directors of the Charitable Corporation, when they inſpected into the ſeveral pledges in their Warehouſe, and compared them with the entry-book of their Office; alſo the Commiſſioners received ſeveral claims according to the Act of Parliament, of ſuch perſons who had neglected to give them in by the 1ſt inſtant, purſuant to the ſaid Act. *P.*

A few days ſince the 2d and 3d ſons of Col. Meyrick, were married, one to Miſs Lucy Pitt, a Lady of 14 years, and 10,000 l. and the other to a Daughter of Char. Cholmondeley of Vale-royal, Eſq; a Lady of 17, and a great fortune. *D P.*

Laſt friday died at the Bath General Roſs. *C.*

TUESDAY, *Aug* 8.

On friday laſt Mr. James Vernon, Robert Hucks, and George Heathcote, Eſqs; paid 300 l. into the Bank of England for the uſe of the Truſtees for eſtabliſhing the Colony of Georgia in America.

We hear her Majeſty is about purchaſing the fine houſe and gardens, call'd Campden-houſe at Kenſington; together with ſome lands that lie contiguous to the ſame, for his Royal Highneſs the Duke. *C.* Near Kenſington Gravel-pits. *D P.* —— We hear from Folk-ſtone in Kent, that at the Floweriſts feaſt, there on *the 1ſt inſt.* there was a great appearance of Gentlemen, &c. *where Mr.* Will. Hammond of the ſaid town produced a flower call'd the Duke of Cumberland, meaſuring 5 inches and 3 quarters under the great ſtem, and crowned anſwerable to it, which carried the firſt prize of a ſilver punch ladle; and the ſecond prize, being a China bowl, was carried by a flower called the Princeſs, produced by Mr. Saile of the ſaid place. *C.*

Dover, Aug. 5. The Right Hon. the Lady Petre embarqued here on friday on board one of our pacquets for Calais. —— Laſt night came into our harbour from Amſterdam, the Experiment of London, with about 180 Palatines for New York. *P.*

On friday laſt the Wanſtead ſtage-coach with 2 Gentlemen, 2 Ladies, and a child, being near the E. of Tilney's, the horſes making to the water, and the coachman unable to command them, they went down a precipice into a pit, one of the Gentlemen leaped out of the coach into the pit, which was deep in water, and carried out the child and Ladies, without much more damage than the very great fright the Ladies ſuſtained thereby. *C.*

On friday laſt, a foreign Gentleman, who took lodgings at the German Coffee-houſe in S. James's-ſtreet, died ſuddenly. The maſter of the Coffee-houſe was in a concern how to bury him, and was about applying to the pariſh; but telling a Gentleman the caſe, who was drinking the night before with the deceaſed, the Gentlemen told the Landlord, he heard the deceaſed ſay, that whenever he died, there was ſomething in a ſpinnet that he uſed to play on, that would bury him; upon which they took it to pieces, and found therein about 100 guineas, which afforded him a handſome burial. *P.*

They write from Scarborough, thar a plan of buildings for improving the Town had been laid before her Grace the Dutcheſs Dowager of Marlborough, who ſeemed to approve of the ſame, and deſigned to give directions for its being put in execution. *S J. L E.*

The Hon. Mrs. Anne Vane is gone to paſs ſome time at the L. Baltimore's houſe near Epſom in Surrey. *L E.*

WEDNESDAY, *Augt* 9.

The Hon. Mrs. Fox, daughter of the late L. Bingly, and wife to Geo. Fox Eſq; was lately delivered of a ſon and heir. The bulk of L. Bingley's eſtate goes to that Lady and her heirs male. *C.*

His Grace the D. of Bedford lies dangerouſly ill at his ſeat near Wooburn Abbey in Bedfordſhire. *D P.* Attended by 4 Phyſicians. *C.*

Her Majeſty having built a fine grotto or hermitage at

Richmond, and adorned it with the Buſtoes of Mr. Locke, Sir Iſaac Newton, Mr. Woolaſton (Author of *The religion of nature delineated*) and the late Dr. Clarke ; it has been recommended to all the fine Genii of the two Univerſities, of the ſchools at Eaton and Weſtminſter, and all the learned whatſoever, to compoſe ſome Latin inſcription proper to the place, the furniture, and the foundreſs. Whatever is thought beſt, will be engrav'd on the building ; and the Author will thereby render himſelf worthy of her Majeſty's patronage. Accordingly ſeveral ingenious things have been already written, tho' not preſented, abounding with elegant and ſuitable encomiums on the taſte of her Majeſty, the beauty of her *Muſæum*, and the accompliſhments of thoſe Engliſh ſages whoſe buſtoes adorn it. C.

From the PEGASUS in Grub-ſtreet.

Mr. Bavius,

I Think you are juſtly to be blamed in publiſhing ſo many ſevere reflections upon the *Old Debauchees*, and *Covent-Garden Tragedy*. Your Correſpondents ſeem unwilling to allow, that there is any thing good in either of them. Sure you muſt needs have received ſomething in vindication of ſome part of them at leaſt, and thought fit to ſuppreſs it. To try, whether my conjecture is right, I have ſent you a plain narration of the plot and whole management in the laſt of thoſe pieces, adding a few of the fineſt thoughts and expreſſions: from which the reader may form a proper judgment of the great genius and good deſign of the Poet ; and diſcover how injuriouſly he has been treated, by Prosaicus, Dramaticus, and Publicus.

The Scene is an antichamber, or rather back-parlour in *Mother Punchbowl's* houſe.

Act. I. Sc. 1. *Mother Punchbowl* a bawd, complains to *Leatherſides* her porter, and two of her whores *Nonparel* and *Induſtrious Jenny* of the badneſs of her trade ; and of the loſs of a bill due from a Poet, whoſe Play *Nonparel* had juſt now diſcovered to be damned. — Sc. 2. *Leatherſides* and the two whores being retired, *Capt. Bilkum* the Bully and a Chairman enter, quarelling about his fare ; without which the latter is forced to go off. — Sc. 3. *Mother Punchbowl* rebukes the Captain for making ſuch a noiſe ; who deſires her to get him a wench, and lend him half a crown. — Sc. 4. *Leatherſides* enters to inform *Mother Punchbowl*, that a porter was juſt come from *Lovegirlo* to beſpeak a whore. — Sc. 5. He re-enters immediately, to beſpeak a fat whore for the Squire, and a lean one for *my Lord*. — Sc. 6. *Capt. Bilkum*, in a ſoliloquy, laments his inadvertency in not having ſearched *Hecatiſſa's* pockets, and then goes off. — Sc. 7. *Lovegirlo* and *Gallone*, two Cullies, diſpute which is preferable woman or wine. — Sc. 8. *Capt. Bilkum* recommends both. — Sc. 9. *Lovegirlo* and *Kiſſinda* expreſs a violent paſſion for each other in a lewd ſtrain.

Act II. Sc. 1. *Stormandra* a whore and *Capt. Bilkum* diſpute about paying before-hand. — Sc. 2. *Mother Punchbowl*, after hearing them upbraid each other, ſends the Captain to bed, promiſing that *Stormandra* ſhall ſoon follow. — Sc. 3. Accordingly adviſes her to go to bed to him. — Sc. 4. *Stormandra* in a ſoliloquy wiſhes for *Lovegirlo* whoſe ghoſt ſhe imagines ſhe ſees. — Sc. 5. *Lovegirlo* and the upbraid each other with their falſhood. — Sc. 6. *Kiſſinda* enters to them ; when ſhe and *Stormandra* quarrel about *Lovegirlo*, who prefers *Kiſſinda* to her. — Sc. 7. *Stormandra* goes to *Bilkum*, and inſiſts upon his fighting *Lovegirlo*. — Sc. 8. She in a ſoliloquy, reſolves to go and hang herſelf. — Sc. 9. *Mother Punchbowl* adviſes *Nonparel* and *Kiſſinda* to have no regard to any thing but money. — Sc. 10. *Leatherſides* informs them that *Capt. Bilkum* had killed *Lovegirlo*. — Sc. 11. *Gallone* rails at *Mother Punchbowl*, as the cauſe of his friend *Lovegirlo's* fate. — Sc. 12. *Capt. Bilkum* and *Mother Punchbowl* lament *Stormandra* as having hanged herſelf ; and *Kiſſinda* and *Gallone* lament *Lovegirlo*. — Sc. 13. *Lovegirlo* and *Stormandra* enter : the former tells them, he was only run through the coat ; and the latter, that ſhe hanged up her gown, inſtead of herſelf.

From out thy empty head, I'd knock thy brains. p. 3.
Requir'd the *unready Ready* to come down. p. 14.
Truſt me to-night, and never truſt me more,
If I do not *come down* when I *get up*. p. 15.
For if he were not *dead*,
How could his *living* Ghoſt be walking here? *p.* 19.
Man without woman is a ſingle boot,
Is half a pair of ſheers. p. 8.
Skin of [oſt] your fleſh, and bite away your eyes ;
Lug out your heart, and dry it in your hands ;
Grind it to powder, make it into pills,
And take it down your throat. *p.* 29.
Then when a hole within thy ſtocking's ſeen,
(For ſtockings will have holes) I'll darn it for thee,
With my own hands I'll waſh thy ſoapen'd ſhirt,
And make the bed I have unmade with thee. *p.* 12.

Your &c. B. B.

FOREIGN NEWS.

Thursday, Auguſt 1.

Extract of a letter from Alicant, July 3. N. S. — The Moors have had ſeveral ſmart ſkirmiſhes with the Spaniards, ſince they deſerted Oran : and in a late one 200 Spaniſh horſe were cut off, and the Duke de S. Blaſ, a Colonel, and 7 Captains were killed. *D J.*

Yeſterday arrived the Mail from France.

Lisbon, July 3. N. S. Letters from Braga tell us, that ſome men, at work on the foundation of the Church of S. Martin de Dume, found the veſtiges of a temple dedicated to Jupiter, on one of the columns of which was this inſcription, *Jovi Expulſori de mia Luſſina ex voto poſuit.* They moreover diſcovered near the column, a tomb of white marble, 11 palms in circumference, and 3 palms in breadth, wherein were found the bones of a human body, which the learned of that country take to be that of Theadomir, one of the Kings of the Sweths that reigned in Portugal, who died in 570, and was founder of the Monaſtery of S. Martino de Dume. As the Goths ruined the edifices of the Romans, ſo the Arabs or Saracens deſtroy'd thoſe of the Goths. P.

Friday, Aug 4.

Yeſterday arrived the Mail from Flanders.

Rome, July 19. M. Sardini is condemned to 10 years impriſonment in the caſtle of S. Angelo, and degraded from his prelacy. ——— The jewels belonging to the Charitable Corporation, taken lately from an Engliſhman, were eſtimated in the preſence of the Governor of Rome at 22,000 crowns. D P.

Amſterdam, Aug. 10. Some advices from Alſace ſay, that the French will ſhortly have an army there of 40,000 men. D P.

Hague, July 25. Letters from Grenoble tell us, that a gang of ſmugglers having been attacked by the Archers, 3 or 4 were taken and hanged at Grenoble. Their accomplices were indefatigably vigilant 'till they took 3 of the Archers, whom they tried and formally condemned to be hanged ; and condemned the Intendant and firſt Preſident of Grenoble to be hanged in effigie for contempt. P. ——— *Theſe Smugglers have all the forms of Juſtice among them, and ſeem to want only numbers to give them a right to exerciſe them.*

Saturday, Aug. 5.

Amſterdam, Aug. 2. They write from Seville of the 18th, that the tranſports which are at Alicant, &c. are to tranſport ſuddenly 7000 men from thence, but whether for Africa, or any other part was not known ; however it appear'd that the Court had ſome great deſign in view, which was kept ſecret. D J. &c.

Weſel, Aug. 9. The King of Pruſſia was on the 30th received by their Imperial Majeſties with the higheſt tokens of friendſhip, 4 leagues from Prague, and the next day the 3 illuſtrious perſonages enter'd that City, &c. D P.

Yeſterday arrived the Mail from France.

Monday, Aug. 7.

Paris, Aug. 13. By letters from Marſeilles we are adviſed, that the Count de Montemar having ſent a great detachment to attack the Infidels in the mountains, the Spaniards had about 400 men kill'd, and were forc'd to retire. ——— The Hollanders make a great noiſe about the Charter granted by the King of Spain to the new Company erected at Cadiz, to carry on a commerce to the Philippine Iſlands. They have engaged the King of Great Britain, France, and Portugal to make repreſentations againſt it ; and in caſe thoſe repreſentations have not the deſired effect, they would have thoſe Powers to enter into a league with them to conſtrain his Catholick Majeſty to ſuppreſs that Company ; but 'tis very much queſtion'd whether they will comply therewith, being perſuaded, that his Catholick Majeſty is Maſter, and may do what he pleaſes in his own dominions. C. P. &c.

Tuesday, Aug. 8.

Yeſterday arrived the Mail from Holland.

Florence, July 26. At the inſtance of the Britiſh Reſident, a certain Engliſhman was taken up a few days ſince, and after examination ſent to the Caſtle of S. John Baptiſt, together with his wife and all his baggage, ſaid to be one of thoſe that robb'd the Charitable Corporation at London : we learn from Rome, that another accomplice is lately ſhut up in Caſtle Angelo. D P. ——— At the requeſt of the Engliſh Reſident. P. ——— *Who is this Engliſh Reſident?*

Books and Pamphlets publiſhed from July 20. to July 26.
The canonical authority of S. Matthew's Goſpel defended, &c.
A Sermon preached at Halesworth in Suffolk, June 11, by Tho. Anguiſh, M. A.
25. The eternal obligation of natural Religion, &c. by Phil-orthos. Pr. 6d.
The excellency of the Conſtitution of the Church of England : a ſermon by Hen. Stebbing, D. D.
26. The antiquity, innocence, and pleaſure of gardening : a ſermon at Malpas, Ap. 18. by W. Harper.

NOTICE is hereby given, to all Encouragers of Mr. PALMER's

HISTORY of PRINTING,

That the Remainder of it will be finished from his own Manuscript, and published in about a Week.

To all Gentlemen, Builders, and others,

ALEXANDER EMERTON,

Colour Man, *at the Bell over-against* Arundel-Street, *in the* Strand, LONDON,

SELLS all Sorts of COLOURS ready prepared (at the lowest Prices) that any Gentlemen, Builders, &c. may set their Servants or Labourers to paint their Houses, only by the Help of a printed Direction, which he gives with his Colours.

N. B. Five Pounds Worth of Colours will paint as much Work, as a House-Painter will do for Twenty Pounds.

He likewise sells (to the Ladies) all Sorts of Water-Colours and Varnish, with every Thing necessary for the New Japanning, and gives a printed Direction, for the doing of it to the greatest Perfection, to those that buy Colours. —— Also Italian Powder for cleaning Pictures.

He deals only for Ready Money.

Last Saturday was published,

No I. (*containing five Sheets, with a Map of Britannia Romana*) *at the Price of* 6 d. of

THE HISTORY of ENGLAND.

By Mr. RAPIN THOYRAS. Translated by N. TINDAL, M. A. Vicar of Great Waltham in Essex. The 2d Edition. With the following Improvements:

1. The Translation is thoroughly revised and corrected.
2. The many Errors and Mistakes of the Original are rectified.
3. Several Hundred of Marginal References, accidentally omitted by the Author, are supplied.
4. Additional Notes throughout, with Cuts, Maps and Genealogical Tables, on Copper Plates.

Printed for James, John and Paul Knapton, removed from St. Paul's Church-Yard, to the Crown in Ludgate-Street, near the West-End of St. Paul's.

N. B. The Whole will be comprised in 2 Volumes, in Folio, containing 400 Sheets, at the Price of 2 l. 2 s. in Sheets, including the Copper Plates. Five Sheets of the Work will be published every Saturday 'till the Whole is completed, at the Price of 6 d. and the said Sheets will be delivered every Week at the Houses of the Gentlemen who are pleased to order them.

Proposals at large, with a Specimen of the Work, may be had gratis.

No. II. Containing 5 Sheets and a Map of Britannia Saxonica, will be published next Saturday.

PROPOSALS

For Printing by SUBSCRIPTION,

THE HISTORY of the Grand Controversy between the Secular and Regular Clergy of the Church of Rome, from the Year 1625 to 1634, concerning the Usurpation of RICHARD SMITH, Titular Bishop of Chalcedon, who pretended to be sole Ordinary Bishop of all England and Scotland. Wrote in Latin by the President of the English Benedictine Monks, RUDISINDUS BARLO, and faithfully done into English from the Original, for the Entertainment of the Curious, especially Divines and Lawyers, both Ecclesiastical and Civil, of what Religion soever.

With the Remonstrances of the Roman Catholick Laity made to the said Bishop, and also to his Excellency Carolo Cosima, Embassador Extraordinary of the Most Catholick Majesty, and to the Marquis Fontenay, Embassador of the Most Christian King, &c. taken also from the Latin Originals: All which Treatises have been hitherto suppress'd, by the Papists, for Political Reasons given therein.

As also the famous Bull of Pope URBAN VIII. called PLANTATA, necessary for the right Understanding of the Whole, which was never before any where printed.

To which will be added,

A LETTER concerning the Disputes that have happen'd among the Benedictine Monks since the Year 1700 to this present Time: Shewing how even they themselves have varied from their original Principles. By one who was a Member of that Body, and concerned therein.

By JOHN WILLIAMS.

PROPOSALS may be had of (and SUBSCRIPTIONS taken in for the Author by) W. Meadows, at the Angel, in Cornhill; T. Astley, at the Rose, and S. Austen, at the Angel and Bible in St. Paul's Church-Yard; C. Davis, Pater-Noster-Row; T. Woodward, at the Half-Moon, J. Gilliver, at Homer's Head, and J. Stephens, at the Hand and Star, between the Two Temple-Gates; B. Motte, at the Middle Temple-Gate; T. Worral, at Judge Coke's Head, H. Walthoe, next Door to the Rainbow Coffee-House, W. Reason, in Flower-de-Luce-Court, J. Jolliffe, at the Golden-Ball, near Chancery-Lane, Fleet-Street; F. Cogan, over-against Gray's-Inn-Gate, Holborn; O. Payne, in Round-Court, and T. Game, at the Bible, by the New Church, in the Strand; T. Green, Charing-Cross; J. Jackson, in Pallmall; J. Jolliffe, at the Bible, in St. James's-Street; J. Brindley, at the King's Arms, and W. Shropshire, opposite to the Duke of Grafton's, New Bond-Street; and J. Stagg, Westminster-Hall, Booksellers; J. Huggonson, in Bartholomew-Close, and T. Gover, by Fleet-Ditch, Black Fryers, Printers.

This Day is published,

The LONDON MAGAZINE:

Or, GENTLEMAN's Monthly Intelligencer.

NUMB. IV. For JULY, 1732.

To be Continued. (*Price Sixpence each Month.*)

CONTAINING,

(*Greater Variety, and more in Quantity, than any MONTHLY BOOK extant.*)

I. A View of the WEEKLY ESSAYS, viz. Of marrying purely for Interest; Causes of Unhappiness in Marriage; Story of Conento; ill Effect of Curiosity; a Censure on the Ladies; Self-Government; Vanity of Titles; Inconstancy and Fickleness; Resignation to the Will of God; Comparison to the Distress'd; Presidence and Free-Will; Unreasonableness of Imposition; Wit; Philosophy; Style; the Writer and Orator; Playhouse Writers; Dr. B——ly's Sermon Milton examin'd; Praise of Cowardice; Education, and the Power of Love.

II. POLITICAL Subjects, viz. Slavery and Liberty; true Greatness; Liberty and Property; Struggles for Liberty; Fig and Oak, &c.

III. POETRY, Confutation Fair; the Retirement; Love and Reputation; to a Man a Captive; &c.

IV. DOMESTICK Occurrences; Promotions Ecclesiastical, Civil and Military; Marriages and Births; Deaths; Sessions at the Old Bailey; Buildings Company, &c.

V. FOREIGN AFFAIRS.

VI. Price of Goods, Grain, Stocks; Monthly Bill of Mortality.

VII. A TABLE of Contents.

To which is added, a Catalogue of Books and Pamphlets, with their Prices, published by the Proprietors of the Monthly Chronicle, now discontinued.

MULTUM IN PARVO.

LONDON: Printed for C. Ackers in St. John-Street; for J. Wilford, behind the Chapter-House, near St. Paul's: And sold by W. Meadows, T. Cox, W. Hinchliffe, W. Whitridge, R. Wellock, and E. Nutt, in Cornhill; J. Clarke in Duck-Lane; T. Astley in St. Paul's Church-Yard; A. Dodd without Temple-Bar; J. Stagg in Westminster-Hall; J. Jackson in Pall-Mall; J. Brindley and W. Shropshire in Bond-Street; and J. Millan near the Admiralty-Office. Where may be had the former Numbers.

This Day is published,

[Price Six Pence.]

AN Epistle humbly address'd to the Hon. Mrs. ELIZABETH TREVOR, Daughter of the late Sir RICHARD STEELE, upon her Marriage with the Hon. JOHN TREVOR, Esq; Son to the Rt. Hon. THOMAS late Lord TREVOR.

By ROBERT DYER.

Hail, wedded Love!
Perpetual Fountain of Domestick Sweets!
Here, Love his Gold a-shaftes employs; here lights
His constant Lamp, and waves his Purple Wing. MILTON.

Fœlices ter & amplius
Quos irrupta tenet copula; nec malis
Divulsus querimoniis
Suprema citiùs solvet Amor Die. HOR.

Printed for Lawton Gilliver, at Homer's Head, against St. Dunstan's Church in Fleet-Street.

The Cœlestial Anodyne Tincture: Or, The Great Pain-Easing Medicine,

FAm'd and approv'd of for its wonderful and never-failing Success, in giving immediate Ease and Relief in all manner of Pains, either inward or outward, and is the most certain Remedy in the World for a sure and speedy Cure of the Cholick, and expelling Wind, Gripes and Pains in the Stomach, the Pleurisy, Stitches or Pains in the Side, Back, Loins, or any other Part; Rheumatick Ailments, which cause Pain and Dolor. It hath given Ease to a Miracle, when all other Remedies have fail'd. In the Gravel and Stone in the Kidneys, it gives Ease forthwith, and brings them away to Admiration. It also facilitates and causes a speedy Delivery in Child-Birth. 'Tis no Quack trifling Thing to allure the World with, but a real and well-experienced Medicine, not subject to Stupefaction (as Opiates) but by a friendly, balsamick and subtle Nature, pacifying the most severe and terrible racking Pains, and carries off the Cause, not by purging, but by Transpiration, by Urine, or breathing Wind. No Family ought to be without it. And used outwardly, it cures Swellings, Aches, Pains, Numbness, or Weakness of the Joints; 'tis excellent for Cramps, and all other aged Infirmities, effecting Wonders in Agues, Fevers, Small-Pox, &c. No Family ought to be without it.

It is sold only by Mr. PARKER, Printer, at his House in Salisbury-Court, or by such Persons as he shall depute, viz. at Mr. Parker's, a Printer, in Bull-Head Court in Jewin-Street; at the White Gally-Pot, a Chandler's Shop in Bandy-Leg-Walk, Southwark, and at Mr. Neal's, a Toyshop over-against the White Hart Inn in the Borough, at Eighteen Pence a Bottle, with printed Directions; and if requested, will be brought to any Person, by the Hawker who sells his Penny-Post. Sealed as above.

Aug. 3. This Day is published, Pr. 6 d.

Very proper for private Families, or to send into the Country (and Places abroad where the English reside) being a compendious View of all our Publick Papers.

The GENTLEMAN's MAGAZINE:

Or, MONTHLY INTELLIGENCER.

NUMBER XIX. for JULY, 1732.

Being the SEVENTH of VOLUME II.

CONTAINING,

[*More in Quantity, and greater Variety, than any Book of the Kind and Price.*]

I. Views of the WEEKLY ESSAYS, viz. On Beds; Will of John Hopkins, Esq; True Greatness; Money no Equivalent for unequal Marriages; Style and Education; On the Quakers, Philosophy; Criticism of the Grub-Street Journal, Dr. Bentley, the Comedian, and two Plays; Female Extravagance; Rake's Fortune; Idle Curiosity; Humane Nature; Love and Philosophy; Irresolution; Wit; Trust in Providence; Necessity and Free Will; Religion, &c.

II. POLITICAL POINTS, Proceedings and Debates of the English and French Parliaments, Remarks on both; British Discontents; Treatment of Chichester; Battle of Contradictions; Magna Charta, the Fruits of Bad Ministers; Improvements of Ireland; Blunderers, Struggles for Liberty.

III. POETRY, York Ladies; Carshalton Fair; Lady and Caterpillar; the prudent Damsel; Croydon Workhouse; The Blind Puppies; Love and Reputation; The Grotto, Tales, Fables, Epigrams.

IV. DOMESTIC OCCURRENCES, viz. Births, Deaths, Marriages, Promotions, &c.

V. Prices of Goods, Grain, Stocks; London Monthly Bill of Mortality.

VI. FOREIGN AFFAIRS.

VII. A TABLE of CONTENTS.

With a Register of Books and Pamphlets.

By SYLVANUS URBAN, Gent.

London: Printed, and sold at St. John's Gate; by F. Jefferies in Ludgate-Street; Mrs. Nutt, Mrs. Charlton, Mrs. Cook, at the Royal-Exchange; Mr. Batley in Pater-Noster-Row; Mr. Midwinter, in St. Paul's Church-Yard; A. Chapman, in Pall-Mall, Mrs. Dodd, and Mrs. Bickerton, without Temple-Bar; Mr. Crichley, at Charing-Cross; Mr. Stagg, and Mr. King, in Westminster-Hall; Mr. Wilhamson in Holborn; Mr. Montague, in Great Queen-Street; Mr. Harding, in St. Martin's-Lane; and all unprejudic'd Booksellers in Town and Country.

Note, a few are printed on a fine Royal Paper, large Margin, for the Curious.

Note, The great Demand for the GENTLEMAN's MAGAZINE these 18 Months last past, has occasion'd most of the Numbers to be out of Print several times. At present Setts can only be had for the Year 1732. Having been obliged unexpectedly to reprint our last for June; and also to put No. I. and No. II. a 4th time in the Press, we have not been able to give the first Volume ready, as promis'd, in August; but Gentlemen may depend on compleat Setts in September.

Just imported, and sold by JER. BATLEY, at the Dove in Pater-Noster-Row.

HISTOIRE des Papes depuis St. Pierre jusqu' à Benoit XIII. inclusivement en Deux Volumes 4to, à la Haye, chez Henri Scheurleer, 1732.

Lately published, and sold by J. BATLEY,

Philosophiæ Mathematicæ Newtonianæ Illustratæ. Tomi Duo. Quorum, prior tradit Elementa Matheseos ad comprehendendam demonstrationem hujus Philosophiæ scitu necessaria: Posterior continet 1) Definitiones & Leges motus generaliores; 2) Leges virium centripetarum & Theorium attractionis seu gravitationis cœptarum in se mutuò; 3) Mundi Systema.

A GEORGIO PETRO DOMCKIO.

HIS MAJESTY

HAving been pleased to grant to WALTER CHURCHMAN Letters Patent for his new Invention of making Chocolate without Fire, to greater Perfection, in all Respects, than by the common Method, as will appear on Trial, by its immediate Dissolving, full Flavour, Smoothness on the Palate, and intimate Union with Liquids: And as it is much finer than any other Sort, so it will go farther, and is less offensive to weak Digestions, being by this Method made clean, and free from the usual Grit and gross Particles, so much disliked, which is return'd to the fair and impartial Experiment; such the Perfection propos'd for his common Standard, which is now sold at 4 s. 9 d. per Pound, with Vanello's 5 s. 9 d.

N. B. The Curious may be supply'd with his Superfine Chocolate, which is as many Degrees finer than the above Standard, as that exceeds the finest sold by other Makers, plain at 6 s. with Vanello's the finest sold by other Makers, plain at 6 s. with Vanello's at 7 s.

To be sold only for Ready Money,

At CHURCHMAN's Chocolate Warehouse,

At Mr. John Yeung's in St. Paul's Church-Yard;

Where Persons in Town or Country may be supply'd with any Quantities, with Encouragement to Venders, who shall be licens'd under the Hand and Seal of the Patentee, and their Places of Sale advertis'd, if requir'd.

LONDON: Printed by J. HUGGONSON, *in* Bartholomew-Close, *for* Capt. GULLIVER, *near the* Temple, *where* Letters *and* Advertisements are taken in : *As also at the* Rainbow Coffee-House *in* Cornhill, *and* John's Coffee-House *in* Sheer-Lane, Temple-Bar. [Price Two Pence.]

The Grub-ſtreet Journal.

NUMB. 137

Thurſday, *AUGUST* 17, 1732.

Mr BAVIUS,

NOtwithſtanding the ſcurrility of ſome reflexions, that are caſt on you by perſons, whoſe paſſions are engaged againſt you; the unprejudiced, I think, muſt allow that you give fair play to the combatants on your Theatre on which, tho' you now and then exhibit a trial of ſkill between two vixens with all the ſpirit of Billingſgate; yet you refuſe not ſometimes to admit even a couple of grave Philoſophers, to debate a point with all the decorum that belongs to their character If you will give me leave, I ſhall be proud to enter the liſts in your laſt match about preſcience, &c as a ſecond to the author of the *Abſtract*, publiſhed in your 134th *Journal* in vindication of whoſe repreſentation, pleaſe to forward the encloſed.

To Mr FANCOURT'*s friend*,

SIR,

BY your candor and good conſideration, the controverſy about liberty and preſcience (as it lies between the *Abſtracter* and Mr FANCOURT) is brought into ſuch a compaſs, that, notwithſtanding the abſtruſeneſs of the point, a man may pretty well ſee where he is; and almoſt hope to come to a reſolution

You are pleaſed to undertake for Mr FANCOURT, that he ſhall venture the whole controverſy on this ſingle point: *Whether whatever is now certain, was ever certain* The affirmative is what the ABSTRACTER aſſerts, and has endeavoured to demonſtrate in the latter end of the third paragraph But, ſince what he has ſaid is not ſatisfactory, I will try to add, only by way of elucidation, what perhaps may ſet the matter in ſuch a light, as will carry conviction Be pleaſed therefore, to review the third paragraph, and go on with what follows.

To be more particular, let us ſuppoſe a future poſſible action, for inſtance *Mr.* FANCOURT'*s anſwering theſe reflections*; which we will conceive as free and contingent, viz that it may, or may not be. Of ſuch a performance, however, may it not be ſaid, that it is now certain that it will, or that it will not be? And, whether-ſoever ſhall happen, may it not be ſaid that it was, ever, as certain that it would happen (tho' the contrary, there being no antecedent neceſſity, might have happened; and then the caſe would be the ſame, only inverted) as it will be, after it ſhall happen, that it did happen? And, as its having happened, after it ſhall happen, will be no argument that it was neceſſary it ſhould happen: ſo, neither ought the certainty of its being to happen, before it ſhall happen, to be looked upon as, at all, implying any neceſſity, or deſtroying free agency Whatever therefore will be, will certainly be, tho' not neceſſarily · and, conſequently, Whatever is now certain, was ever certain. Q. E. D.

This is all that I have to offer at preſent, on what we are not agreed about If I ſhould not have expreſſed my mind clearly or warily enough, you will, I dare ſay, take no advantage from any overſight · but, being honeſt in the queſt of truth, will make the beſt uſe of what you find I aim at; that you may, with the greater ſatisfaction, adhere to whatſoever ſhall come with the cleareſt evidence I expect your thoughts thereupon, and am,

Sir, your obliged humble ſervant,

Auguſt 12, 1732. ELIOT.

Animadverſions on Dr BENTLEY'*s* Edition of *Paradiſe Loſt*, continued

BOOK, I. VER 147 Strongly *to ſuffer and ſupport our pains?*

Dr B' ſays poſitively 'the ſenſe plainly requires, and 'therefore the Author gave it *ſtronglier*' This poſitive aſſertion, without aſſigning any reaſon for it, has been denied, and that denial ſupported by reaſon. The preceding words are not, *What if our conqueror has* given us MORE *ſtrength?* which would have required in the following part of the ſentence, MORE *ſtrongly to ſuffer*, &c But, as the former part of it now runs, *What if he have left us this our ſtrength entire*, the latter is much more proper in the poſitive degree, *ſtrongly to ſuffer*. ——Beſides, there is no ſuch word as *ſtronglier* · and tho' the Author might be allowed to coin a new word, yet this liberty is not to be taken by an Editor.

VER 204 ————night-*founder'd ſkiff*] '*Foundering*, 'ſays the Dr. is *ſinking* by a leak; ſo that *night* alone 'can never founder; which word is likewiſe ſuperfluous, 'becauſe mentioned in the cloſe of this compariſon The 'Poet therefore gave it *nigh-founder'd* or almoſt founder'd, 'as ii 940, ſpeaking of SATAN, *nigh-founder'd on he 'fares*'. To this it has been ingeniouſly anſwered, if *foundering* is *ſinking*, it would be of little uſe to fix an anchor any where, which could not prevent the ſinking of a leaky ſkiff. *Night-founder'd* therefore means, overtaken by night, and at a loſs which way to ſail Which very word MILTON, in his poem called the *Mask*, publiſhed when he was very young, puts into the mouth of one of the brothers who had loſt their way in the wood, *ſome one, like us*, night founder'd *here* —— Neither, as the Dr urges, 'is night here ſuperfluous, becauſe *while night inveſts the ſea* follows ſo ſoon;' for by that is denoted the time this *ſkiff* continued *moored by* the whale's *ſide* Mr CONUNDRUM was here a little arch in his way upon the Dr, ſaying, the Critic was in this place certainly *nigh-founder'd*, if not *night-founder'd*

VER 329. *Transfix us to the bottom of this gulf* The Dr 'believes the Poet gave it FAST *fix*, becauſe 'to *transfix* is to pierce quite through the body, and its 'ſignification is there bounded and cloſed ſo that to '*transfix to* a thing, or *on* a thing cannot be juſtly ſaid' ——MILTON has ſaid both: and where, I pray, is the impropriety? If he took the greater liberty of coining new words, ſurely he might take the leſs of adding a new ſenſe to an old word, and thereby make it doubly ſignificant. There is nothing more beautiful in poetry than ſuch bold comprehenſive expreſſions; for which VIRGIL is particularly admired. If theſe *linked thunderbolts* had *pierced quite through* SATAN'*s* ſubſtance, and fixed him *to the bottom of this gulf*, they might very properly be ſaid to have *transfixed* him *to* it This reading is confirmed by ii 180 *Shall be hurl'd Each on his rock* transfix'd. To take off the force of which, the Dr. either would have the conſtruction to be, *Hurl'd on his rock*, not *Transfix'd on his rock*, (which conſtruction I own is agreeable enough to the place) · or elſe would ſubſtitute *infix'd*; But this word neceſſarily relating to *on the rock* requires the common conſtruction, and conſequently juſtifies the common reading *transfix'd*

VER. 347. '*Till, as a ſignal giv'n, th' uplifted ſpear*, &c 'The *uplifted ſpear* was not AS *a ſignal*, but the ſignal 'itſelf: the Author gave it AT' The learned *Reviewer of* MILTON'*s Text* has ingeniouſly obſerved, that if MILTON had deſigned *at*, he would have ſaid, *at* THE *ſignal*, as in i 776 and ii. 56. And therefore he very rightly includes part of the 3 lines in a parentheſis, reading them thus,

'Till (as a ſignal given, th' uplifted ſpear
Of their great Sultan waving to direct
Their courſe) in even ballance down they light, &c.

But this Gentleman ſeems to be a little miſtaken in aſſerting, that '*th' uplifted ſpear* was not *the ſignal* it'ſelf it was deſign'd, by its *waving to direct their courſe*, 'tho' it ſerv'd at the ſame time *as a ſignal for them to* 'begin to move.' *Its waving* then was certainly *the ſignal for them to move* to a certain place for they were not now *to begin to move*, having been all put in motion before by SATAN'*s* ſpeech as we are told VER 331 *They heard, and were abaſh'd, and up they ſprung Upon the wing*

VER 421. *Ægypt from Syrian* ground] 'I believe he 'dictated *bound*,' ſays the Dr 'This is wrong, ſays the '*Reviewer*, for the *brook* was itſelf the *bound*, becauſe it 'parted them' And conſequently, ſay I, as much the *Ægyptian*, as the *Syrian*, bound

VER 465] *Of warriors old*] As the Dr. in VER 127 had ſtrook out *bold* to make room for *old* ſo to make *old* amends, he here takes its part, and thruſts out *bold* His reaſon is, becauſe 'We had a little before VER 552 '*Heroes old*' To which the *Reviewer* anſwers, that it was 13 verſes before, and therefore might have been uſed here again, tho' in the ſame ſenſe; but that it ſeems to be uſed in a different ſenſe, and to mean long-experienced warriors, as in *Sampſon Agoniſtes*, V. 140. old warriors *turn'd Their plated backs under his heel*

VER 636. *If counſels* different.] The Dr alters this to *counſels* E'ER DIFFER'D by which it is plain he means DEFERR'D from the explication which follows, '*If counſels*, publickly reſolv'd on, were ever *delay'd* by my 'ſloth' He rejects the common reading, becauſe 'there's 'no hint in all the Poem, that SATAN differs from all the 'Council, or acted without their conſent.' ——If there had been any ſuch hint, I am ſure, it would have been a good argument againſt the common reading, unleſs we are neceſſarily to ſuppoſe, that the Devil always lyes; and could never ſpeak any truth, even to his *old compeers*, or *bold warriors*; and likewiſe that he would be ſo impudent as to appeal to them for the truth of a fact, which they all knew to be falſe. Beſides, as the Author of the *Review* has obſerved, the Dr's reaſon is equally ſtrong againſt his own emendation, there being likewiſe *no hint* of SATAN'*s* having ever *deferr'd* counſels publicly reſolv'd on, and is indeed the very foundation, upon which the common reading is to be juſtifyed To which I ſhall add, that ſuppoſing both readings ſtood upon equal authority, *different* would be more probable than *deferr'd*: becauſe it is much more credible, that SATAN ſhould have *differed* in opinion from the reſt, than that through ſloth or fear he ſhould have *delayed* to execute public reſolutions.

VER. 647.—*That* he no leſs] The Dr ſays, '*No leſs* 'is in an unuſual ſenſe here, if in any I with the ſame 'letters propoſe a different word, in a new ſenſe, and read '*That* LESSON he.' This *new ſenſe* the *Reviewer* proves to be none, by obſerving, that if the Dr's alteration be admitted we muſt read *This leſſon*; becauſe *This* properly refers to what follows, *That* to what went before *No leſs*, neantmoins, nevertheleſs. —— That *no leſs* is here uſed not only in ſome ſenſe, but likewiſe in a very *uſual*, and conſequently a very good ſenſe, is evident to me from the whole reaſoning taken together SATAN could not talk ſo abſurdly as to pretend to teach God a leſſon He owns in the preceding lines, that they were not a match for *th' Almighty*, and that they *know* his ſtrength therefore, continues he, we muſt *work by fraud, that he* NO LESS *from us may find*, than we have found from him, that we are but half overcome we have *found* him ſuperior in force; He may at length *no leſs find* from us, that we can ſtill oppoſe him by fraud But tho' I hope I have cleared MILTON from the charge of writeing *unuſual ſenſe* in this place; yet I cannot pretend to clear the Dr's alteration from the imputation of *unuſual nonſenſe*: *That* leſſon he *At length from us may* find Of this the Dr was a little ſuſpicious; and, I ſuppoſe, well remembering from the time he went to ſchool, (as I believe all good and bad ſcholars do) the great difference betwixt *finding* and *learning* a leſſon, would fain ſubſtitute *learn* inſtead of *find*, upon no other foundation than 'Perhaps 'for *find* it was given *learn*, as vi. 717 *There let them learn, as likes them, to deſpiſe*' MILTON has in one place ſayed *learn to deſpiſe*, therefore he here ſays *learn a leſſon* Since *Perhaps* is imagined to be a word of ſuch force, I ſhall venture here to make a conjecture myſelf; *Perhaps* MILTON gave it *take* · which word I preſume I can prove to be not only as Miltonic, but likewiſe more proper in this place than *learn*, as being both more pedagogical, and more poetical

Having thus ſhewn from the obſervations of others, and from my own, that ſeveral of the Dr's alterations of the firſt Book of *Paradiſe Loſt*, have no good foundation; I ſhall now as readily give ſome inſtances of his conjectures, which either probably ſeem to be, or certainly are, well grounded

VER. 52.———*Rolling* in *the fiery gulf* VER. 324. ——*Rolling* in *the flood*] In both theſe places, according to the Dr 'the Poet gave it *rolling* on' As he has proved that MILTON has uſed ON in the *Argument* of this Book, and in VER 195, 210, 266, 280. ſo IN may be juſtified by VER 76 where the Poet expreſly tells us, that theſe rebellious angels were *overwhelm'd with floods and whirlwinds of tempeſtuous fire* But tho' it be of little conſequence, whether IN or ON be read in the two verſes under conſideration; yet, I believe, if any one ſhall nicely examine all the places where either of theſe two words is uſed in relation to this matter, he will be apt to think, that one has a greater propriety in each particular place than the other could have had.

VER 167 ————————*And* diſturb
His inmoſt counſels from their deſtin'd aim.

The Dr's objection againſt this place, is only that it 'does 'not reach up to our Poet's uſual exactneſs.' He therefore changes it to *diſturn*, a word he ſays 'uſed by CHAU'CER in *Troilus and Creſſida*, iii 719. tho' in two other 'places, his copies, perhaps erroneouſly, now have *miſturn*. '*Diſtornare*, a vulgar word Italic; as Gallic, *detourner*. 'And who knows not MILTON'*s* inclination to revive old 'words, or even coin new ones, eſpecially with the In-

[illegible] ' Allowing this conjecture to be probable, yet we may defend the common reading, if we have more regard to the derivation of the word, than to its vulgar use; for that will justify the sense requisite in this place: and M. Du Cange derives even the French word [illegible] from the Latin *disturbare*, which he says signifies the same thing.

Ver. 663. ——— *From the* books *of life*] The Dr. rightly conjectures, that 'the Author spoke it *book of life*, according to the Scriptures.'

Ver. 669. *Hurling defiance tow'rd the* vault *of heaven.* Against this reading the Dr. argues very strongly. '*Heaven*, 'the habitation of God and angels, was never described 'as *vaulted*, nor once so hinted by Milton. To our visible heaven Spenser assigns the orb of stars for a *vault*: 'but to the heaven where angels reside he attributes an *illimitable hight*. But allowing these heavens were *vaulted*, yet if the Devils *hurl'd toward* that *vault*, they 'hurl'd quite beyond the mark: for their enemies did 'not reside in the vaults, but on the plains of heaven. 'Therefore Milton must have given it walls of heaven.' This emendation he confirms by two places ii. 343. vi. 860: to which the Author of the *Review* has added three more, ii. 1035. iii. 71. 503

Ver. 703. *With wondrous art* found out *the massy ore.* The ore was *found out* before at *ver.* 688: and therefore the Dr. justly rejects this erroneous reading, and restores the true one, in the first edition, *founded*, or melted, from *fundere*: which was communicated to the public in our 25th Journal, June 25, 1730.

These are all the places in the first book, in which the Dr. imagines any errors to have been occasioned, by the mistakes, either of the Amanuensis, or of the Printer: which are certainly the most solid, if not the only just, foundation for any alterations of the present text.

Bavius.

Mr Bavius,

I Believe you have not guessed at the true reason why Dr B. preferred *old* to *bold* in *Paradise Lost*, B. I. 127. where he reads, instead of bold *compeer*, old *compeer*. This I imagine he did in opposition to his *quondam* antagonist the learned Johnstonus; who in his criticisms upon the *Ode of* Tom Bostock, hath given the preference to, *bold*, and instead of *old* Tom Bostock, reads *bold* Tom Bostock.

Give me leave to propose an emendation in the Bentleian manner of the famous song called *Chevy Chace*. In the common editions we read,

A bow he had bent in his hand
Made of a trusty tree:
An arrow of a cloth yard long
Full to the head drew he.

This corrupt reading leaves us to seek of what wood the *bow* was made, only informing us it was of a *tree*; and it makes the rime not *bold* enough. Read therefore on my authority,

—— made of a trusty yew
An arrow of a cloth yard long
Full to the head he drew.

What an easy alteration is this? none but a dull wooden-headed blunderbuss of an Editor could suppose the Poet wrote otherwise. The bows were generally, if not always, made of *yew*; for which see Robin Hood's *Songs*, and *The Life of* Johnny Armstrong.

I am your humble servant,

July 31, 1732. Philo-Bent.

DOMESTIC NEWS.

C. *Courant.*	E P. *Evening Post.*
P. *Post-Boy.*	SJ. *S. James's Evening Post.*
D P. *Daily Post.*	WE. *Whitehall Evening P.*
D J. *Daily Journal.*	LE. *London Evening Post.*

Thursday, *August* 10.

Yesterday Daniel Tipping, condemn'd at the last Sessions in the Old Bailey (and whose sentence was respited for 14 days) was executed at Tyburn. *D P.* Reprieved for 14 days. *C. P. DP.*

We hear that the Rev. Mr. Barnard, Chaplain to his Majesty, and to his Grace the D. of Newcastle, will be made one of the Prebendaries of Westminster, vacant by the death of Dr. Aspinwall. *P. SJ.* —— Is appointed one of the Prebends. *C.* Prebendaries. *DP. WE. LE.*

Yesterday was held a Gen. Court of the East-India Company, when Sir Mat. Decker acquainted them with the state of their affairs in relation to their trade, and of the bad return for their European goods: an enquiry was made into the conduct of their servants at Bengail, when it was agreed that a Court of Directors be impower'd to proceed therein, and make a report thereof at the next Gen. Court. *DP.*

By letters from Dewsbury we hear, that the Rev. Mr. Will. Bowman has finished his defence of himself and his sermon, from the many several pamphlets that have been put out against him, which is now printing. He has also added, a letter to the English Laity, which, he says, is design'd as a preservative against the principles and practices of the Clergy. *SJ. WE* ——— We *do not* hear, *but we* hope, *that this* Rev. Gentleman *has written* his Defence of himself *in English*; *a language, which he seemed to be learning, when he wrote* his sermon.

On tuesday the Lord Charles Cavendish arrived here with his Lady from Rome, where they have been about 2 years. *SJ.* ——— Lord James Cavendish. *C.* 11.

On tuesday night died of a fever in her 17th year, at Tunbridge in Kent, the Hon. Miss Ashburnham, only Daughter to the R. Hon. the E. of Ashburnham. *SJ.* —— The Lady Harriot. *P.* 11. Lady Ann. *DP.* —— By his 2d Lady, widow of the E. of Anglesey. *DP.* 11.

Friday, *August* 11.

Yesterday at a Court of Common Council held at Guildhall, the Bill relating to the disposal of the place of Keeper of Newgate was read twice; and the question being put, whether it should be read the 3d time the next Court, it was carried in the negative. *P.* ——— Yea's 76, No's 85. *DP. DJ.* ——— It is very surprising that the Court should refuse making satisfaction to the L. Mayor and Sheriffs for sinking the said place; when in the Mayoralty of Sir Ric. Brocas the place of Apothecary to the Pest house became vacant, when they voted the place useless, and order'd the full value of the said place to be paid out of the Chamber of London to Sir Ric. Brocas, and an annuity of 10 l. per ann. to all succeeding L. Mayors in lieu thereof. *D P.*

Yesterday a Court of Directors was held of the India Company, when they resolved to send no ships to China this year, &c. *C. P. DP.*

We hear that Will. Mittins, Esq; brother to John Mittins, Esq; a Gentleman of 4000 l. per ann. in Shropshire, is appointed Secretary to the L. How, Governor of Barbadoes. *C. DP.*

Saturday, *Aug.* 12.

On thursday her Majesty was pleased to appoint the Rev. Mr. Carleton, one of the King's Chaplains, to be Sub-dean of the Chappel Royal at S. James's, in the room of the Rev. Dr. Aspinwall, deceased. *C. DP.*

The 8 new sloops which are building in his Majesty's yards, are (we hear) to carry 80 men each, and 8 swivel guns; and it is said 3 of them are to go to the West-Indies, and the other 5 to be on the Irish station. *P. DJ.*

We are inform'd that Mr. Crawford, who was taken into custody, is not an Attorney; and that when the Messenger, &c. enter'd his Chambers, he immediately came out of his study, and surrender'd. *DP.*

On monday last a Reaper found, in a field behind the Bell at Coal Harbour, near Stockwell, a man who had been hang'd, but the rope was broke, and he had lain on the ground a considerable time, his throat being eaten away by maggots. The Coroner having summoned a Jury, they were of opinion he destroy'd himself, being *non compos mentis.* DJ

Canterbury, Aug. 9. We hear from Marden, that one George Usborn being at Horsenden Fair, near Goudhurst, laid a wager of 50 l. with a man of Maidstone, that he would be married the next day before noon, tho' he then had held no conversation with any woman on that head. The Maidstone man, to make sure of his wager, put a stop in the Court there; but the other took horse and went to a Miser that night, and ask'd him for his daughter, who giving him a slight answer, he turn'd away and went to another, and they were married the next day, just 3 minutes within the time: it seems too he met with a good bargain, for she has 700 l. to her portion. However, his antagonist disputes paying the 50 l. because they were not bedded also within the time. *SJ.* —— *In my opinion, he both won the wager, and deserves it, for acting so courageously in defiance of the proverb.*

Monday, *Aug.* 14.

The Hon. Will. Finch, Esq; next brother to the E. of Winchelsea, is appointed his Majesty's Envoy Extraordinary to the Court of Spain. — Mr. Howarth, son to Sir Humph. Howarth, Knt. Representative in Parliament for the shire of Radnor, is appointed one of the Clerks of the Treasury. *DP.* —— The Lords of the Treasury have appointed Steph. Crowch of Tetherington, in the County of Wilts, Esq; who had been Receiver Gen. of the land-tax for one part of that County for many years, to be Receiver for the whole, Hen. Flower, Esq; being removed. *C.*

Yesterday morning Mr. Brown, one of his Majesty's Messengers, arrived with dispatches from his Majesty, by which we hear that his Majesty will return to England about the middle of next month. *P.*

By the Amelia arrived at Dover we hear, that Sir Chaloner Ogle was arrived, and had taken on him the command of his Majesty's squadron of men of war in those parts; and that Commodore Lestock was preparing to return home. *D P. C.* ——— This formal story is absolutely wrong. *D J.* 15.

The Ockham was attack'd by 10 of Angria's Gallivats, out of whom she kill'd 75 men, and wounded 30, not having one man on board her hurt. *D J.* —— 13 Grabes and Callevats, with upwards of 1800 men: the Ockham having no more than 67 men, tacking about fell in amongst the whole fleet, and then could give them a broadside, which she follow'd closely; but the night coming on she lay by for the morning, when the Pyrates seemed to give sign of battle; whereupon the Ockham standing to with a fair wind, prepared for engaging them afresh, when Angria's fleet ran away, with the loss of 70 men killed, and 30 wounded, whom Angria, when they got into Callaby, burnt as a sacrifice; and a few days after, putting out to sea, they fell in with the Rose Galley, Capt. Thorp, whom they took, and made them all prisoners. *D P.* —— The Ockham had in company the London, the Sovereign, and another country ship: Angria 'tis said lost near 200 men. *C.*

On saturday the Assizes ended at Kingston, when 4 persons received sentence of death. —— Jam. Bradshaw, a Quaker, was try'd for wilful and corrupt perjury, and also for subornation of perjury, and acquitted: but is to be removed to Newgate, in order to be try'd at the Old Bailey, on an indictment for wilful and corrupt perjury. *DJ.* ——— *How can a* Quaker, *who never* swear, *be guilty of* perjury?

There was a trial at the same Assizes, between one Diner a Wheeler of Eshare, Plaintiff, and Mr. Harvest a Brewer of Kingston, Defendant. The case was thus: Mr. Harvest going home to Kingston, the Plaintiff being drunk, came up to him on horseback, and would drink with him; but Mr. Harvest bid him desist, and go about his business, which he refusing, Mr. Harvest order'd his man to cut him or shoot him. It was try'd by a special Jury of Gentlemen, who brought in a verdict of 400 l. for the Plaintiff. P.

Tuesday, *Aug.* 15.

On saturday the horse races ended at Lewes in Sussex. The King's plate of 100 guineas was won by a horse named Diamond, and 50 l. plate by Mr. Rich's Merry Tom. *DJ. P.* —— His Grace the D. of Newcastle keeps open house during his stay in that country. *DJ.*

We are informed, that, as the Commissioners for Putney-bridge continue to keep up their pontage for a one horse chaise to 1 s. the Proprietors *of the Ferry* at Kew and Richmond have lowered their price *to 8 d. and intend* shortly to reduce them to 6 d. *C.*

A woman belonging to a gang who for some time have made it their practice to cheat people, by pawning or selling to them false plate, viz. spoons, tankards, mugs, &c. of brass silver'd over, was yesterday detected as she was offering two of those sorts of spoons (not worth 2s.) to pawn for 15 s. to one Mr. Christ. Reynolds in Hart-street, Covent-garden; and being carry'd before Sir John Gonson was committed to Tothill-fields Bridewell. *DP.*

On sunday morning the Rev. Mr. Richardson, who keeps a school at Lewisham, going to preach at Woolwich, was robbed by a foot-pad, in Hanging Wood, of a guinea. *DJ.* —*Both the person and the place were ominous.*

On saturday dy'd, aged near 100, Mr. Cotsworth, formerly a watch-maker in Fleet-street, the oldest inhabitant in S. Dunstan's parish. *D P.*

On sunday, during the time of the service at St. Margaret's Church, at Westminster, when the Minister was praying for his Majesty King George, a man called out King James, which put the congregation into a great consternation. Upon examination the person appear'd to be distracted. *SJ.* – *The* LE. *says it was only* a great surprize; *which is most* probable. —— This morning a man, supposed to be disorder'd in his senses, came to S. James's house, and proclaimed the Pretender as King of England, by the name of King James the third, which made a great deal of disturbance: the Officer on duty sent him to the Savoy. *SJ.*

Wednesday, *Aug.* 16.

A great number of workmen are employed in repairing and beautifying the Royal palace at Hampton-Court, for the reception of the Royal family. *C. DP.* Upwards of 200. *P.* —— We hear from Windsor, that upwards of 200 workmen are employ'd in repairing and beautifying his Majesty's Castle there. *DJ.*

A fine monument is erecting in Westminster Abbey, in memory of the late E. of Stanhope. *DJ. C.*

J. Mechell says he *got* one (Advertisement) into this Journal, "but *we* refuse to print more, notwithstanding "the Printer received for three." It's true, *he* did *get* one in, but it was when I was absent: And he paid for two more at the same time; but he was offer'd his Money again; or, on his thinking it a Hardship, to have two more Advertisements inserted: But now he refuses both, unless we will advertise for him as long as he pleases; which plainly shews him to be a Man wanting both Truth and Understanding.

J. H.

From the PEGASUS *in Grub-ſtreet.*

SIR,

AS you are engaged in the cauſe of virtue, and chaſtiſe your writing Brethren, whenever they preſume to be guilty of nonſenſe or immorality, I take the liberty to deſire you to animadvert a little upon the following paragraph, inſerted in the *Daily Poſt-Boy* of the 12th of *Aug.* 1732.

Calais, Aug. 20. N. S. 'This day was ſhipped on 'board of two Engliſh ſhips for the new world, a great 'number of ragged Chriſtians from Germany for the 'Weſt-Indies. They ſay they are to people a new Colo'ny, and alſo to plant a new religion there, which is ex'treamly well calculated for the eaſe of tender conſci'ences, a plan whereof now lyes before the Com——rs 'for their approbation.'

As that Paper is reputed to come from a Chriſtian of the Church of *England*, it ſeems very odd, that he ſhould treat the being perſecuted for religion as a jeſt; I therefore am perſwaded, that he printed this paragraph juſt as it came to hand from his foreign correſpondent, without conſidering it himſelf. I am ſure he could not think, that the adding the word *ragged* to *Chriſtians* could convey an idea of ridicule. If raggedneſs were in itſelf ridiculous, the Stoicks, the primitive Chriſtians, the Janſeniſts in France, the Roman Catholicks in Ireland, and the Nonjurors in England, would be liable to ridicule as well as the perſecuted German Proteſtants. Sickneſs, miſery, and poverty, more eſpecially when voluntarily ſubmitted to in defence of virtue and religion, are objects of compaſſion and eſteem, not of contempt. But a Coxcomb, and one who pretends to be witty without genius, and upon improper ſubjects, is a real object of ridicule. As to the new religion mentioned in the paragraph, it is no newer than that of the *Church of England*, to which theſe poor people are reconciled, both in diſcipline and doctrine. Their Miniſter, Mr. Bigniong, came to London on purpoſe, received ordination, returned to them again, and is now failed with his little flock, to begin the new Colony on the Savanah river.

THE controverſy lately ariſen betwixt the Societies of Grub-ſtreet and of Drury-lane, which had lived ſo long in the greateſt harmony, was brought down by me, in our laſt Journal, to the middle of the laſt month: about which time, a Farce intitled *The Covent-Garden Tragedy* was publiſhed. To which the learned Author has prefixed *Prolegomena,* containing two pieces: a *Letter from a fine Gentleman*; and a *Crititiſm* on that *Tragedy, originally intended for the Grub-ſtreet Journal*. In the latter he has given a freſh inſtance of his ability to write in character: making his perſonating Critic ſay, *pag.* 7. 'How reading 'Play-bills, and writing *Grub-ſtreet* Papers can qualify 'him [the Drury-lane Porter] to be a judge of Plays, I 'confeſs, I cannot tell'. As *Grub-ſtreet Papers* can here mean no other than *Grub ſtreet Journals*; this pretended member of our Club, caſts this general reflection upon them all. This is probability and propriety.

In the *Letter*, the fine Gentleman tells his friend, 'I 'have applied my ſelf pretty much to my books; I have, 'beſides the *Craftſman* and *Grub-ſtreet Journals*, read a 'good deal in Mr. POPE's *Rape of the Lock*, and ſeveral 'pages in the *Hiſtory of the King of Sweden*'. pag. 2.

That this could not be deſigned as a ſatire only upon the firſt, third, and fourth of the pieces mentioned, is indiſputable: and therefore it muſt be levelled either againſt the *Grub-ſtreet Journal* alone, or againſt all four together. If againſt the Journal alone, it muſt ſuppoſe the other pieces very bad in the opinion of the world, and worſe than the *Journal*, rather than otherwiſe. If it was aimed againſt all four, it muſt ſuppoſe their merits to be pretty near equal. So that let either be choſen, it is a fine complement to our Lucubrations, repreſenting them as ſuperior, or at leaſt equal, to the moſt celebrated pieces that have been publiſhed of late years.

But the Author deſigned no ſuch complement: for he has expreſly declared, *pag.* 2. the Authors of our Journal to be a 'Club, which hath determin'd to inſtruct the 'world in arts and ſciences, without underſtanding any; 'who

With leſs learning than makes felons ſcape,
Leſs human genius than God gives an ape.
are reſolv'd ——— ——— —— *in ſpite*
Of nature, and their ſtars to write.

This is a ſevere quotation upon us; but as it ſeems to include the CRAFTSMAN, Monſieur VOLTAIRE, and even Mr. POPE himſelf, the Author of the two firſt lines, we ſhall be very eaſy in ſuch good company. However, as this Gentleman has been guilty of an act of inſincerity, in joyning the words of two different Authors, as if they were the ſame; and in following the example of moſt controverſial writers, who produce only one part of a ſentence, which ſeems to be on their ſide, and leave out the other which makes againſt them; I ſhall here give the whole paſſage, as it is in the *Dunciad*, B. i. 335, &c. From whence it will evidently appear, that theſe lines are not at all applicable to the Authors of our Journal, but only to thoſe Dramatical renegado Members of our Society, againſt whom they were originally intended.

How, with leſs reading than makes felons 'ſcape,
Leſs human genius than God gives an ape,
Small thanks to France, and none to Rome or Greece,
A paſt, vamp'd, future, old, reviv'd, new piece,
'Twixt Plautus, Fletcher, Congreve, and Corneille,
Can make a Cibber, Johnſon, or Ozell.

See *Temple Beau, Tom Thumb, Modern Husband, Old Debauchees, Covent garden Tragedy,* and *Mock Doctor.*

BAVIUS.

To Miſs RAFTOR, on her ſucceſs in acting *Polly Peachum.*

By HINT and KEYBER form'd to pleaſe the age,
See little RAFTOR mount the Drury ſtage;
FENTON outdone, with her no more compares,
Than GAY's beſt ſongs with HINT's *Mock Doctor* airs.
Lament, O RICH: thy labours all are vain:
HINT writes, and RAFTOR acts in Drury-lane.

Dublin, Aug. 1. At a hurling match on the 25th, being S. James's day, near Clenard Bridge, many quarrels and riots enſuing, one Mr. White endeavouring to appeaſe the mob, was himſelf ſtoned to death. An odd proceeding this; when the Reverence which his profeſſion claimed from them (moſt of them being Papiſts) and a ſtrict Act, could not protect him from their violence. *C. P. D J.* 10. —— *Aug.* 5. 'Tis reported, that Cork Goal being almoſt full of criminals, they broke out, and upwards of 40 got clear off. *D J.*

FOREIGN NEWS.

THURSDAY, *Auguſt* 10.

Yeſterday arrived the Mail from France.

Prague, Aug. 13. This day his Pruſſian Majeſty and the Prince Royal, having taken leave of their Imperial Majeſties, ſet out for Berlin. *D P.*

FRIDAY, *Aug.* 11.

Rome, July 23. The effects which were ſeized at Mr. John Thompſon's, Caſhier of the Charitable Corporation in London, have been ſent to the Count de Giraud, in order to be delivered to the Directors of the Company. *C.*

It is written from Cadiz, the 29th, N. S. That a perſon was brought there in irons from Ceuta, and ſent to Seville to be examined. The Moors had brought an army before Ceuta, from which this perſon deſerted into the town, but being ſuſpected of being a ſpy, they examined him there, and diſcovered that he was Secretary to the D. de Riperda, who was in the Mooriſh army: they ſent him to Spain, for farther examination. *D J.*

SATURDAY, *Aug.* 12.

Hague, Aug. 4. N. S. The Miniſter of Bavaria's ſudden retreat from the Imperial Court, and the orders publiſhed in that Electorate for the augmentation of the army, occaſion many reflexions, and make us fearful that the affairs between the 2 Courts will take a turn productive of freſh broils. *P.*

MONDAY, *Aug.* 14.

Yeſterday arrived the Mails from France *and* Holland.

Seville, July 26. The E of Albemarle, who was receiv'd here with the higheſt marks of diſtinction, is gone for his regiment at Gibraltar. 'Tis ſaid his Excellency, after ſome ſtay there, will return again to Great Britain, by the way of Italy, France, and Holland. *D P.*

Paris, Aug. 20. Laſt week the Gens du Roy went to Verſailles, to receive an anſwer from the King to their Remonſtrances; but his Majeſty was pleaſed to ſuſpend his anſwer once more for a few days. *D P.*

Geneva, Aug. 8. They write from Turin, that that Court has ſeized 5 fiefs of the holy See in Piedmont; and that the affairs between the 2 Courts are more embroiled than ever, upon the account of Senior Sardini. *P.*

Baſil, Aug. 10. The French Troops in Alſace begin to leave their quarters, in order to form the camp on that ſide, and in the Dutchy of Bar the French are making ſome ſuſpicious motions. *P.*

TUESDAY, *Aug.* 15.

Yeſterday arrived the Mail from Holland.

Hague, Aug. 22. Our laſt letters from Corſica, by the way of Leghorn, ſay the Malecontents of that Iſland begin to gather again; and that they have actually committed ſome diſorder in the open Country. This news is not at all ſurpriſing here, conſidering how unaccountably their leaders have been betray'd into the towsr of Genoa, whence they will hardly ever come out, unleſs it be to loſe their heads. *P.*

Florence, Aug 2. They are hard at work on the new road mark'd out by the famous M. Galilei, in a direct line to Parma. *D P. D J.*

Rome, Aug. 2. On monday the Cardinals, Chiefs of orders, interrogated the Cardinal the 8th time, for 4 hours, upon which his Eminency fell into a ſwoon: this frightened his Examiners, and broke off further proceedings for that bout. *D P.*

WEDNESDAY, *Aug.* 16.

Berlin, Aug. 16. The King left Prague the 5th, and returned the 14th to Potſdam in perfect health. *D J. C.*

Paris, Aug. 15. The firſt Preſident received a letter de cachet from the King on the 11th at night, containing his Majeſty's anſwer to their remonſtrances: all the Chambers met thereon the next day; but neither the contents of the anſwer, nor the reſult of the conferences held upon it, are yet known. *D P.*

Books and Pamphlets publiſhed from July 26. to Aug. 3.

27. Reflections hiſtorical and political, occaſioned by a vindication of General Monk and Sir Ric. Granville. Pr. 1s.

28. Hiſtoria Literaria. No. 17. Pr. 1 s.

A Defence of ſome important doctrines of the Goſpel: in 26 ſermons preach'd in Lime ſtreet by ſeveral Miniſters.

Modern Hiſtory, &c. by Mr. Salmon No. 98, 99.

29. The fruit garden diſplay'd, &c. for June. Pr. 1 s.

31. Liberty and Property, &c. by Euſtace Budgell, Eſq; Pr. 18 d.

The Comedian or Philoſophical Enquiry, Numb. IV. for July.

Aug. 1. The certain and unchangeable difference betwixt moral good and evil: a Sermon at Salter's-hall, July 3 by W. Wiſhart, D. D.

The political ſtate of G. Britain for July.

A Defence of Quakeriſm, in anſwer to Pat. Smith, M. A.

Mr. Whiſton's vindication of the teſtimony of Phlegon againſt Dr. Sykes. Pr. 1 s.

The ſervants Plea. Pr. 6 d.

2. Chriſtianity diſtinct from the religion of nature in anſwer to Chriſtianity as old, &c. Parts 2d and 3d. by Tho. Broughton, A. M.

The preſent ſtate of Europe, &c. for June.

3. The London Magazine, No. 4. for July.

The Gentleman's Magazine, No. 19.

On Tueſday Stocks were

South Sea neat Stock was 103 7 8ths, 103 5 8ths. South Sea Annuity 111 3 qrs. Bank 151 3 qrs. New Bank Circulation 4 l. Premium. India 157 1 qr. 156 1 8th, 156 3 8ths, 156. Three per Cent. Annuity 99. Royal Exchange Aſſurance 102. London Aſſurance 13 1 half. York Buildings 6. African 40. Engliſh Copper 2 l. 4 s. Welch ditto 1 l. 15 s. South Sea Bonds 3 l. 16 s. Premium. India ditto 5 l. 16 s. ditto.

ADVERTISEMENTS.

PROPOSALS

For Printing by SUBSCRIPTION,

THE HISTORY of the Grand Controverſy between the Secular and Regular Clergy of the Church of *Rome*, from the Year 1625 to 1634, concerning the Uſurpation of RICHARD SMITH, Titular Biſhop of *Chalcedon*. who pretended to be ſole Ordinary Biſhop of all *England* and *Scotland*. Wrote in *Latin* by the Preſident of the *Engliſh* Benedictine Monks, RUDISINDUS BARLO, and faithfully done into *Engliſh* from the Original, for the Entertainment of the Curious, eſpecially Divines and Lawyers, both Eccleſiaſtick and Civil, of what Religion ſoever.

With the Remonſtrances of the *Roman* Catholick Laity made to the ſaid Biſhop, and alſo to his Excellency *Carolo Coloma*, Embaſſador Extraordinary of the Moſt Catholick Majeſty, and to the Marquis *Fontany*, Embaſſador of the Moſt Chriſtian King, *&c.* taken alſo from the *Latin* Originals: All which Treatiſes have been hitherto ſuppreſt, by the *Papiſts*, for Political Reaſons given therein.

As alſo the famous Bull of Pope URBAN VIII. called PLANTATA, neceſſary for the right Underſtanding of the Whole, which was never before any where printed.

To which will be added,

A LETTER concerning the Diſputes that have happen'd among the Benedictine Monks ſince the Year 1700 to this preſent Time: Shewing how even they themſelves have varied from their original Principles. By one who was a Member of that Body, and concerned therein.

By *JOHN WILLIAMS.*

PROPOSALS may be had of (and SUBSCRIPTIONS taken in for the Author by) W. Meadows, at the Angel, in Cornhill; T. Aſtley, at the Roſe, and S. Auſten, at the Angel and Bible in St. Paul's Church-Yard; C. Davis, Pater-Noſter-Row; T. Woodward, at the Half-Moon, L. Gilliver, at Homer's Head, and J. Stephens, at the Hand and Star, between the Two Temple-Gates B. Motte, at the Middle Temple-Gate; T. Worral, at Judge Coke's Head, H. Walthoe, next Door to the Rainbow Coffee-Houſe, W. Reaſon, in Flower-de-Luce-Court, J. Iſted, at the Golden-Ball, near Chancery-Lane, Fleet-Street; F. Gyles, over-againſt Gray's-Inn-Gate, Holborn; O. Payne, in Round-Court, and T. Game, at the Bible, by the New Church, in the Strand; T. Green, Charing-Croſs; J. Jackſon, in Pallmall; J. Jolliffe, at the Bible, in St. James's-Street; J. Brindley, at the King's Arms, and W. Shropſhire, oppoſite to the Duke of Grafton's, New Bond-Street; and J. Stagg, Weſtminſter-Hall, Bookſellers: J. Huggonſon, in Bartholomew-Cloſe, and T. Gover, by Fleet-Ditch, Black-Fryers, Printers.

NOTICE is hereby given, to all Encouragers of Mr. PALMER's

HISTORY *of* PRINTING,

That the Remainder of it is finished from his own Manuscript, and will be published on Monday next.

This Day is published,

THE Historical, Political, and Poetical Works of GEORGE WALDRON, Gent. late of Queen's College, Oxon; particularly his Description of the Isle of Man.

Printed on a fine Paper in Folio; and sold by J. OSBORN, at St. Saviour's Dock-Head, and by the Booksellers of London and Westminster, at half a Guinea bound.

Where may be had,

Morgan's History of Algiers and Oran, in 4to, complete.
Moliere's Plays in English, 6 Vols. 12mo complete.
Montfaucon's Travels to Italy, in English, Folio.
Archbishop Wake's State of the Church, in Folio.
Ephrem Syrus, in Greek, printed at Oxford.
Bradley's Works of Nature, 4to.
Robert's Voyages.
Sir Tho. More's and the Earl of Leicester's Lives.
Revolutions in Spain, 5 Vols.

This Day is published,

The Second Edition of

A PAMPHLET highly necessary to be read by every *Englishman*, who has the least Regard for those Two *Invaluable Blessings*. Containing several *Curious Stories* and *Matters of Fact*, with *Original Letters* and other *Papers*. And some Observations upon the Present *State of the Nation*.

The Whole in a Letter to a Member of the House of Commons.

By EUSTACE BUDGELL, *Esq*;

Qui uni nocet, omnibus minatur.
——— *Jam proximus ardet*
Ucalegon. ——— VIRG.

Printed for *W. Mears*, at the *Lamb* in the *Old Bailey*; and Sold by the Booksellers of *London* and *Westminster*. Price stitched *Eighteen Pence*.

Note, *As I have Published this* Pamphlet *with a sincere Design to do my Country Service; and as there are some* Facts *in it, which I think it highly proper all my Fellow-Subjects shou'd be acquainted with, I have made it the* Cheapest Eighteen Penny Pamphlet *that I believe was* ever *printed. It contains no less than* Eleven Sheets *in no* large Character.

E. BUDGELL.

Last Saturday was published,

No. II. *(containing five Sheets, with a Map of* Britannia Saxonica) *at the Price of* 6 *d. of*

THE HISTORY of *ENGLAND*. By Mr. RAPIN DE THOYRAS. Translated by N. TINDAL, M. A. Vicar of Great Waltham in Essex. The 2d Edition. With the following Improvements:

1. The Translation is thoroughly revised and corrected.
2. The many Errors and Mistakes of the Original are rectified.
3. Several Hundred of Marginal References, accidentally omitted by the Author, are supplied.
4. Additional Notes throughout, with Cuts, Maps and Genealogical Tables, on Copper Plates.

Printed for James, John and Paul Knapton, removed from St. Paul's Church-Yard, to the Crown in Ludgate-Street, near the West-End of St, Paul's.

Where may be had,

No. I. Containing 5 Sheets and a Map of Britannia Romana; price 6 d.

N. B. The Whole will be comprised in 2 Volumes, in Folio, containing 400 Sheets, at the Price of 2 l. 2 s. in Sheets, including the Copper Plates. Five Sheets of the Work will be published every Saturday 'till the Whole is compleated, at the Price of 6 d. and the said Sheets will be delivered every Week at the Houses of Gentlemen who are pleased to order them.

Proposals at large, with a Specimen of the Work, may be had gratis.

This Day is published,

Printed for *J. Brotherton*, at the *Bible*, next the Fleece Tavern in Cornhill,

AN Enquiry into the Origin of Honour, and the Usefulness of Christianity in War.

By the Author of the FABLE of the BEES.

Where may be had,

1. A Letter to Dion, being an Answer to a Book call'd *Alciphron*, or the *Minute Philosopher*.
2. The present State of Great Britain and Ireland, for the Year 1731.
3. Traditions of the Jews.
4. Dury's Journal to Madagascar.
5. Religious Courtship.
6. Life of OLIVER CROMWELL, Lord Protector of the Commonwealth.
7. Receipts in Cookery and Surgery, by John Keetilby.

This Day is published,

The LONDON MAGAZINE:
Or, GENTLEMAN's *Monthly Intelligencer*.

NUMB. IV. For JULY, 1732.
To be Continued. (*Price Sixpence each Month.*)

CONTAINING,

(*Greater Variety, and more in Quantity, than any* MONTHLY BOOK *extant.*)

I. A *View* of the WEEKLY ESSAYS, *viz.* Of marrying purely for Interest; Causes of Unhappiness in Marriage; Story of *Cornuto*; ill Effect of Curiosity; a Censure on the Ladies; Self-Government; Vanity of Titles; Inconstancy and Fickleness; Resignation to the Will of God; Compassion to the Distressed; Præscience and Free-Will; Unreasonableness of Imposition; Wit; Philosophy; Style; the Writer and Orator; Playhouse Writers; Dr. *B——ly*'s Notes on *Milton* examin'd; Praise of Cowardice; Education, and the Power of Love.

II. POLITICAL *Subjects*, viz. Slavery and Liberty; true Greatness; Liberty and Property; Struggles for Liberty; *Fog* and *Osborne* of the Church and State; *Craftsman* on the last Session of Parliament, and Remarks upon him, &c. Parliament of *Paris*; Ministerial Writers, the Genuine Blunderer; *Great Britain*'s Interest in *Ireland*; Advantages from bad Ministers; Marks of such; of bad Kings making bad Ministers, &c.

III. POETRY: *Carshalton* Fair; the Retirement; Love and Reputation; to a *Militia* Captain; Panegyrick on Cuckoldom; *Craftsman* always in the same Story; Epigrams.

IV. DOMESTICK *Occurrences*: Promotions Ecclesiastical, Civil and Military; Marriages and Births; Deaths; Sessions at the *Old Baily*; *York Buildings* Company, &c.

V. FOREIGN AFFAIRS.

VI. Price of Goods, Grain, Stocks; Monthly Bill of Mortality.

VII. A TABLE of Contents.

To which is added, a *Catalogue of Books* and *Pamphlets*, with their Prices, published by the Proprietors of the *Monthly Chronicle*, now discontinu'd.

MULTUM IN PARVO.

LONDON: Printed for C. Ackers in St. John-Street; for J. Wilford, behind the Chapter-House near St. Paul's: And sold by W. Meadows, T. Cox, W. H[illegible] [illegible] Whitridge, R. Willock, and E. Nutt, in Cornhill; J. [illegible] near Birch-Lane; T. Astley in St. Paul's Church-Yard; A. [illegible] without Temple-Bar; J. Stagg in Westminster-Hall; J. Jackson in Pall-Mall; J. Brindley and W. Shropshire in Bond-Street; and [illegible] Milan near the Admiralty-Office. Where may be had the former Numbers.

Just published,

In Octavo, Price bound 4 s 6 d.

A General History of the World, from the Creation to the Destruction of Jerusalem by Nebuchadnezzar: Being the Period with which the Old Testament conclud[e]s. Wherein the sacred and profane History is connected, the Septuagint and Hebrew Chronology compar'd and adjusted to the Years before Christ.

By THOMAS BRETT, L. L. D.

Printed for FLETCHER GYLES, over-against Grays-Inn, in Holborn.

Where may be had, by the same Author, and fit to bind with it.

1. A Chronological Essay on the sacred History, from the Creation to the Birth of Christ: *And an Essay on the Confusion of Languages*; price 1 s. 6 d.
2. VERTOT's History of the Knights of Malta, with fine Cuts, 2 Vol. Folio; price 2 l. 12 s. 6 d.
3. LAMBARDE's Topographical and Historical Dictionary of England and Wales, 4to; price 1 l. 1 l.
4. SOMNER's Treatise of Gavelkind, with a curious Account of his Life, by Bp. Kennet, 4to; price 12 s.
5. Dr. THO. SHORT's Dissertation upon Tea, 4to; price 2 s. 6 d.
6. A Rational Catechism, 12mo; price 1 s. 6 d.

This Day is published,

[Price Two Shillings and Six Pence,]

(*To be continued,*)

NUMBER VI. *of*

ECCLESIASTICAL MEMOIRS of the First SIX CENTURIES, made good by Citations from Original Authors: With a Chronological Table, containing an Abridgment of the principal Things, placed according to the Order of Time; and with Notes clearing the Difficulties of Facts and Chronology. Translated from the French of LEWIS SEBASTIAN LE NAIN DE TILLEMONT.

N. B. Monsieur TILLEMONT has not only an extraordinary Character given him by the famous *Du Pin*, but is likewise cited with the utmost Esteem by numberless Authors of eminent Learning and Judgment, both English and Foreign.

The Translator having some Years ago published a small Part of this Noble Work (*The History of the* Arians) as a Specimen of the Whole, the Great Dr. *Waterland* was pleased to recommend it in the following Words: "TILLEMONT's *History of the* "Arians, a Book which I would *particularly* commend to the "Perusal of the English Readers, to give them a *just* Notion "both of the ancient and modern Arianism." WATERLAND's *second Defence of some Queries, p.* 302. 2*d Edition.*

Printed for the Author; and sold by J. Wilford at the Three Flower de Luces in St. Paul's Church-yard, and W. Clayton, Bookseller, in Manchester.

At which Places Subscriptions are taken in.

Aug. 3. **This Day is published**, Pr. 6d.

Very proper for private Families, or to send into the Country (and Places abroad where the English *reside) being a compendious View of all our Publick Papers.*

The GENTLEMAN's MAGAZINE:
Or, MONTHLY INTELLIGENCER.

NUMBER XIX. for JULY, 1732.
Being the SEVENTH *of* VOLUME II.

CONTAINING,

[*More in Quantity, and greater Variety, than any Book of the Kind and Price.*]

I. VIews of the WEEKLY ESSAYS, viz. On Beds; Will of John Hopkins, Esq; True Greatness; Money no Equivalent for unequal Marriages; Style and Elocution; Ruling the Passions; Propagating Opinions; Panegyric on Cowardice; On the Quakers, Philosophy; Criticisms of the Grub-street Journal, Dr. Bentley, the Comedian, and two Plays; Female Extravagance; Rake's Fortune; Idle Curiosity; Humane Nature; Love and Philosophy; Irresolution; Wit; Trust in Providence; Necessity and Free Will; Religion, &c.

II. POLITICAL POINTS, Proceedings and Debates of the English and French Parliaments, Remarks on both; British Discontents; Treatment of Charles I. Battle of Contradictions; Magna Charta, the Fruits of Bad Ministers; Improvements of Ireland; Blunderers, Struggles for Liberty.

III. POETRY, York Ladies; Carshalton Fair; Lady and Caterpillar; the prudent Damsel; Croydon Workhouse; The Blind Puppies; Love and Reputation; The Grotto, Tales, Fables, Epigrams.

IV. DOMESTIC OCCURRENCES, &c. Births, Deaths, Marriages, Promotions, &c.

V. PRICES of Goods, Grain, Stocks; London Monthly Bill of Mortality.

VI. FOREIGN AFFAIRS.

VII. A Table of CONTENTS.

With a Register of Books and Pamphlets.

By *SYLVANUS URBAN*, Gent.

London: Printed, and sold at St. John's Gate; by F. Jefferies in Ludgate-Street; Mrs. Nutt, Mrs. Charlton, Mrs. Cook, at the Royal-Exchange; Mr. Batley in Pater-Noster-Row; Mr. Midwinter, in St. Paul's Church-Yard; A. Chapman, in Pall-Mall, Mrs. Dodd, and Mr. Bickerton, without Temple-Bar; Mr. Crichley, at Charing-Cross; Mr. Stagg, and Mr. King, in Westminster-Hall; Mr. Williamson in Holbourn; Mr. Montague, in Great Queen-Street; Mr. Harding, in St. Martin's-Lane; and all unprejudic'd Booksellers in Town and Country.

Note, a few are printed on a fine Royal Paper, large Margin, for the Curious.

Note, The great Demand for the GENTLEMAN's MAGAZINE these 18 Months last past, has occasion'd most of the Numbers to be out of Print several times. At present Setts can *only* be had for the Year 1732. Having been obliged *unexpectedly* to *reprint* our last for June; and also to put No. I. and No. II. a 4th time in the Press, we have not been able to get the first Volume ready, as promis'd, in August; but Gentlemen may depend on compleat Setts in September.

Just imported, and sold by JER. BATLEY, *at the Dove in Pater-Noster-Row.*

HIstoire des Papes depuis St. Pierre jusqu' a Benoit XIII. inclusivement en Deux Volumes 4to, a la Haye, chez Henri Scheurleer, 1732.

Lately published, and sold by J. BATLEY,

Philosophiæ Mathematicæ Newtonianæ Illustratæ. Tomi Duo. Quorum prior tradit Elementa Matheseos ad comprehendendam demonstrationem hujus Philosophiæ scitu necessaria: Posterior continet 1) Definitiones & Leges motus generaliores; 2) Leges virium centripetarum & Theoriam attractionis seu gravitationis corporum in se mutuo; 3) Mundi Systema.

A GEORGIO PETRO DOMCKIO.

This Day is published,

In Octavo (from the Folio Edition)
Price Six Pence.

THE PROGRESS of LOVE, in four Eclogues, 1. UNCERTAINTY, to Mr. Pope. 2. HOPE, to the Honourable George Doddington, Esq; 3. JEALOUSY, to Edw. Walpole, Esq; 4. POSSESSION, to the Right Honourable Lord Viscount COBHAM.

Printed for Lawton Gilliver at Homer's Head in Fleet-Street.

Where may be had,

1. An Epistle to Mr. Pope, from a young Gentleman at Rome. *By the same Author.*
2. The Art of POLITICKS, with a curious Frontispiece. *Risum teneatis Amici.* Price 1 s.
3. Two Epistles to Mr. Pope, concerning the Authors of the Age. By the Author of the Universal Passion. Price 1 s. and may be bound with the said Satyrs.
4. A new and correct Edition of the Dunciad Variorum, in 8vo. with some additional Notes and Epigrams.
5. A Collection of Pieces relating to the Dunciad. By several Hands.
6. Of FALSE TASTE, to Richard Earl of Burlington. By Mr. Pope. Price 1 s.
7. STOW: The Gardens of the Right Honourable the Lord Cobham. Price 1 s.

LONDON: Printed by J. HUGGONSON, *in Bartholomew-Close*, for Capt. GULLIVER, near the *Temple*, where Letters and Advertisements are taken in: As also at the *Rainbow Coffee-House* in *Cornhill*, and *John's Coffee-House* in *Sheer-Lane*, *Temple-Bar*. [Price Two Pence.]

The Grub-street Journal.

NUMB. 138

Thursday, AUGUST 24, 1732.

Dear NED,

THE province you assigned me of giving you an account of our Dramatical Poetry, is more irksome than I at first imagined. And as a paper war seems to be commenced between the favourite Poet of Drury-lane and the Grub-street Journal, I should upon no account enter the lists, but to gratify your unaccountable whim, and keep my promise. There is much more pleasure to be found in rural than theatrical scenes: and I envy you the natural and innocent amusements you have in Salop, whilst I am doing penance, in seeing those, which are opposites to nature and innocence at Drury-lane. My Remarks upon *The Old Debauchees* and *Covent-Garden Tragedy* will be very short, several having been already published by others. The Author from his first appearance in the world as a Poet, has always aimed at humour: which, if founded on a right basis, is the chief support and life of all comic writing. But as that basis is nature only, he has often succeeded ill, when he had great hopes of pleasing well. Humour, when embellished by the assistance of wit, still grows more diverting; and hence it is, that CONGREVE is generally more admired than JOHNSON; a great deal of the humour of the latter being found in the former, with that charming additional beauty of wit, of which JOHNSON was not a master. This assertion may not be so readily agreed to by many; but a further defence of it here is foreign to my subject.

There runs through *the Old Debauchees* a continued conatus both at wit and humour: but the Poet, like TANTALUS in the fable, is ever aiming at what is ever deceiving him. His wit is nothing but a few forced common-place strokes against Priestcraft; and the whole character of *Father* MARTIN is but DRYDEN's GOMEZ and SHADWELL's *Teague o' Divelly* curtailed, and divested of their native *beauties. I accuse* him not for having said any thing *against Priestcraft*, but for having said nothing new. The characters of old JORDAIN and LAROON are as far from being humorous, as they are from being natural; they might have passed in a Farce; but are altogether inconsistent with Comedy. 'Tis true, there are such things as Priest-ridden and debauched old men; but the Poet has not drawn them with a just humour. The superstition of the one consists chiefly in a deep groan; and the ranting of the other in the natural rodomontadoes and descriptions, such as *leaping over Notre Dame Steeple, and an Opera in purgatory, an Opera of groans, &c.* If this is what he is pleased to call his *ridiculum acre*, I must ingenuously confess it is stronger than any I have ever met with among the antients or moderns; and is much beyond my taste.

As to the *Covent-Garden Tragedy*, I shall pass by the moral part, which has been attacked by other hands; and consider it only in the Author's own way, whether 'tis a piece of just humour; and as such to be tolerated on the stage. I should not have entered on this subject, since the Author so prudently gave this Piece up the first night, had not his defence of it since (which shews his submission to the Town was not voluntary) required it. As I layed it down before, that nature must be the basis of humour, Mr. F— may say this is just humour, as being a just imitation of nature; and that the characters are drawn from known realities.. But humour is to represent the foibles of nature, not its most shocking deformities; and when any thing becomes indecent, it is no longer humour, but ribaldry. BEN JOHNSON, the greatest humourist, I believe, of any age, never makes any infringement on morals or good manners: That would be only to pretend to an excellence in which a Poet might be equalled if not excelled, by any rake or bawdy house bully.

These observations were not occasioned by spleen or malice; I am ignorant of Mr. F —, even as to his person, nor do I envy him his interest with the Managers at Drury-lane. I am not of a party against him, nor the same with DRAMATICUS, PUBLICUS, &c. I have not used any scurrility, but have censured his writings, not him: I pay a deference to his birth, but cannot think it a title to wit, any more than it is to a fortune; nor that every man who has had the honour of being scourged at Eaton or Westminster is a man of sense: this I mention only that I would have no Poet pique himself on his family or his school.

I should now give you some account of the *Mock Doctor*, about which you are so very earnest. 'Tis done from MOLIERE by Mr. F—g. The Town has receiv'd it well; but some Critics say, he has not done justice to the French Poet, nay, that he has translated the very title itself wrong. As I am ignorant of the original, I shall not pretend to pass my judgment upon the Translation: but here, to show my freedom from all prejudice against Mr. F—g, I must confess, that I think it an entertaining Farcical Piece; but whether the pleasure is owing to him, or MOLIERE, I know not. Some say it is owing only to *young* CIBBER's playing his part so well: but tho' a Player may set off and give life to a part, yet action only would not divert, where there was not some original pleasantry.

There was a thing acted last night called, *Rural Love*, or *The Merry Shepherd*: I can compare it to nothing but that extraordinary Piece of C— y C— r, Esq; called *Love in a Riddle*, its likeness to which, I suppose, might be the occasion of its appearance on the stage: for tho' it is neither tragic, comic, pastoral, nor farcical, yet it seems it is theatrical, which is the *primum mobile* of Drury-lane. I must add, the young company are now rehearsing a farcical ballad Opera of the *Devil of a Duke*, altered from *A Duke and No Duke*, which is their last production for the summer season. As the original Farce is void of wit and just humour, the few additional tunes make no other alteration in it than to make it appear more ridiculous, and to seem even below the hopes of pleasing the upper gallery. I should not have been able to have passed any censure on it before its representation, but from hearing one of the performers out of the joy of his heart, repeat some of its beauties in a publick Coffee-room. This seemed to intimate in what esteem young C— their present Manager held it; and that the beauties the young player pointed out were such as Mr. C— had commended at the rehearsal. I shall not in justice here censure them, but leave them to the fate of the other beautiful pieces of this summer's production.

It has been said *young C— was esteemed a judge of something besides acting*: but his management this vacation has not increased his reputation as a judge. If I am not misinformed he apes his father, and must not only judge, but correct. Whatever pretensions the father has to such a liberty, I am sure the son can have none as yet. And even his judgment has been called in question for bringing the *Covent-Garden Tragedy* on the stage, and afterwards pretending to defend it in a public Paper. I am glad, Dear NED, that Bartholomew Fair relieves me from my engagement; tho' I might as well have promised to have sent you an account of the Drolls there, as of those at Drury-lane.

I am, Dear NED, yours,
PROSAICUS.

To Mr. BAVIUS, Secretary to the Grubean Society.

SIR,

THere is not any reflection which occurs so often in RAPIN's *History of England*, as that concerning divine judgments: wherever a wicked man happens to suffer, he never fails remarking how rarely Providence permits criminals to escape without a judgment. The numerous repetitions of this observation induced me to examine into the truth of it. In order to which, it was necessary to know, what our Author might mean, when he made use of the word judgment. A judgment then I take to be a punishment inflicted by God in this world, upon account of such actions, as render the agent a proper object of that treatment.

Arguments against judgments.

Argument 1. With a view to shew the falsity of the supposition, it is allowed, that judgments are sometimes exercised upon the wicked. Accordingly we observe, if this be so, then it follows, that every wicked man since the creation of ADAM has undergone a penalty for the sake of his transgressions. For if this hath been the case sometimes, the motive, God acted upon, must have been, that those delinquents had made themselves suitable marks for his resentment. Now since all delinquents are alike suitable marks for his resentment, therefore all delinquents that have lived since ADAM, must have felt the effects of that resentment. These two propositions therefore, That judgments have been exerted upon some sinners, and, That they have been exerted upon all sinners, rest upon the same bottom, and must stand or fall together. Whence it appears, that, as punishments have not overtaken all offenders in this world, so they cannot have overtaken any offender, — *Answer*. It is presumed in the foregoing argument, that God Almighty in his determinations concerning the punishment of sinners in this world, takes in nothing but their guiltiness; (that is to say) it is presumed that he only examines, whether they be guilty or not, and according as he finds the one or the other to be true, punishes or does not punish. But this, I think, is only taking a point for granted and not proving it: so that, for what has yet been shewn to the contrary, there may be abundance of inducing considerations to the great mind for the punishment of sinners; consequently there may be reasons for doing it in one case, which reasons may not subsist in another case, or it is possible that it is right for God to take vengeance upon some offenders, and yet it may be even wrong to do the same with respect to others. Nothing conclusive has therefore been offered to make appear the establishment of the two propositions in question upon the same bottom: and consequently the argument about the impunity of some bad men, does not conclude against judgments poured down upon others, that is, it does not answer the purpose for which it was alledged.

Argument 2. 'Tis plain, that wicked men could never have been punished in this world for their misdeeds, because the good have been plunged in calamities as grievous as the bad. Now it can never be thought, that good men have suffered for their crimes (for this were to suppose them at the same time to be both good and bad) from whence 'tis evident that the misfortunes of the wicked likewise ought not to be imputed to their wrong conduct. We are very sensible it may be urged, that we are uncapable of knowing who is good, and that therefore we cannot be certain of any oppressions of virtue: but, this conclusion is obviously unsound, for tho' we cannot infallibly determine, whether this or that particular man be good or no, yet we have good reason to believe that a few upright men at least have lived in the world, and very sure we are that those few must have been racked with pains and troubles, which is sufficient for our purpose. — *Answer*. 'Tis allowed that the good participate in their share of the anxieties and vexations of human life, but it does not follow from thence (as it is asserted in the preceeding argument) that the burdens under which the wicked labour, are not put upon them for the sake of their demerits: I say, this by no means follows: for as right actions render the agent a proper object of reward, so opposite actions produce an opposite effect: if therefore any one be motleyed with a mixture of both these, in part he deserves the divine favour, and partly the divine displeasure: this I take to be the case of every righteous man, (for it is only the preponderancy of good actions which procure him that denomination) every righteous man then is worthy of punishment; from whence it follows, that even the good may bring down the wrath of God upon them by their crooked behaviour, and if the good may do so, this argument about the pains of the good is so far from proving that the wicked cannot suffer here, that it clearly evidences, how well they may. — No, (says the argument) to say this of the good, is to suppose them both good and bad. To which I answer, that if by good and bad men, the argument means, those, whose just conduct prevails, but who nevertheless are not faultless, I must confess my position to suppose the same man both good and bad, but then there is nothing absurd in the supposition: but if by the words good and bad, the argument means, those, whose conduct of each kind exceeds or predominates, then I allow it to be absurd to say, that the same man may be both good and bad; but in that sense, what I have said no way supposes it, and cannot therefore be in any manner affected by it; so that if the words good and bad be taken in either of these two meanings, it will still be nothing to the purpose to object, that my propositions imply the same man to be both good and bad.

Argument 3. It must necessarily be false, that the wicked ever call down the anger of their Creator upon themselves in this world, because the contrary supposition would infallibly exclude his future indignation: for it would be highly unjust in God, to punish in both these ways; now the Scripture expresly declares, that he will do it in the latter; since therefore the two opinions in debate are inconsistent, and either the one or the other must be given up, surely it is much preferable, to recede from that, which is not delivered in Scripture, than from that which is: it is much more likely to believe, that the immoral come off with impunity in this life, than that they

ſhould avoid the torments of a future ſtate. —— *Anſwer.* Matters are not come to that deſperate iſſue, as that there ſhould be a neceſſity of retracting either of the two points mentioned in the argument. It is there (in the argument) ſaid to be contrary to the juſtice of God, that the impious ſhould bear the weight of their folly both here and hereafter likewiſe. How ſo? Juſtice is the diſtribution of rewards and puniſhments, in exact proportion to the degree of merit or demerit: injuſtice then is failing in ſuch a diſtribution: what therefore has the ſuppoſition of puniſhment in this world, and the ſtate ſucceeding this, to do with injuſtice? There ſeems to be no manner of connexion between them: for the ſame degree of puniſhment may be as well inflicted at different times, as at the ſame time: admit for example, that the degree of puniſhment be equal to eight, it is ſtill no more than eight, tho' you divide it into two equal ſeparate payments. Injuſtice then conſiſts in too great a quantity of pain given, for the quantity of tranſgreſſion, not in its being given at different times. Now ſince no concluſion can be juſt which is drawn from wrong premiſes, it follows that the inference in the foregoing argument, which is founded on ſo miſtaken a principle, cannot remain firm and unſhaken. Upon the whole,

Nothing as yet appears deſtructive of the doctrine of judgments, either from the conſequence ſuppoſed to follow from thence, that they muſt have been exerciſed upon all wicked men, (which is argument the 1ſt) or from the oppreſſions of virtue, (which is argument the 2d) or from the excluſion of a future ſtate, (which is argument the 3d and laſt) If you let me know, whether you think this worth inſerting in your Journal, poſſibly you may hear again upon the ſame ſubject, from,

Sir, your humble ſervant, &c.

DOMESTIC NEWS.

C. *Courant.*	E P. *Evening Poſt.*
P. *Poſt-Boy.*	S J. *S. James's Evening Poſt.*
D P. *Daily Poſt.*	W E. *Whitehall Evening P.*
D J. *Daily Journal.*	L E. *London Evening Poſt.*

THURSDAY, *Auguſt* 17.

Laſt week Edw. Stephens, Eſq; was appointed, by the Royal African Company, Governor and Chief of Cape-Coaſt Caſtle, and all the Engliſh ſettlements on the coaſt of Africa. *D P.*

On monday in the evening a Gentleman going for Dover was attacked by a ſingle Highwayman on Shooter's hill, who robbed him of about 130 l. in money, &c. *C. P. D P.*

Yeſterday morning died at Hampſtead, after a long indiſpoſition, Sir Tho. Hardy, Bar. *D P.* He commanded the Pembroke, a 4th rate of 60 guns, with Sir Geo. Rooke, when they took the Spaniſh galleons, and was the perſon who brought the news of their being in Vigo to the Admiral; for which he was knighted. He commanded the Bedford in the memorable Spaniſh engagement 1718. *P.* He was Rear Admiral of the Red that year in the Mediterranean. *C.* He was Firſt Commiſſioner of the Sewers. *D J.*

Glouceſter, Aug 12. About 20 years ago was found near Rodborough in this county, and is now in the hands of a perſon in this city, a Roman coin, with the following inſcription, viz. IMP. OTHO. CASAR. AUG. TRI. POT. on the reverſe, PAX ORBIS TERRARUM. *W E.*

This day John Evelin, Eſq; one of the Equerries to his Royal Highneſs the Prince, Son of Sir John Evelin, was married to a daughter of the L. Viſc. Falmouth, a young Lady of great beauty and merit, with a fortune of 10,000 l. *L E.* — At S. Margaret's Church. *P.* 18. In K. Hen. VIIth's Chapel. *D J.* 18. —— Hen. Belaſyſſe, Eſq; was married at the Royal Chapel of S. James's, to Miſs Billingſly of Pall Mall, Daughter of the late Capt. Billingſly. *L E.* ——— An heireſs of 30,000 l. fortune. *P.* 18.

This day her Majeſty, with his Royal Highneſs the Prince, his Highneſs the Duke, and the 3 eldeſt Princeſſes, went about 12 o'clock to Chelſea, and were elegantly entertained at dinner by Sir Rob. Walpole. *W E.* ——— They dined in the Green-houſe, which upon this occaſion was adorned with the fineſt pictures in Europe. *C.* 18. —— The deſert was ſaid to be the moſt magnificent that has been ſeen in this Kingdom. *D P.* 18. — *This* deſert *was* the moſt magnificent *as the* deſert *of the* Prime Miniſter, *for the time, is always the greateſt.* -------- 'Tis reported that the entertainment coſt 2000 l. *D J.* 18.

On thurſday Sir Marmaduke Greſham, Bar. and Char. Hoſier, Eſq; ſet out on a wager for 100 l. to try who could travel fartheſt in a day; Sir Marmaduke rode a horſe, and the other drove a chaiſe with 2 mares. They ſet out from Godſtow, came through London, and got as far as Colcheſter, where they both gave out, and drew ſtakes, being utterly unable to proceed any farther. *S J.* —— *It is pity* horſes *and* mares *ſhould be employed in determining ſuch a wager: which was moſt proper for* aſſes.

FRIDAY, *Auguſt* 18.

Yeſterday the Orange Regiment of foot Militia, belonging to this City, commanded by Sir Gerrard Conyers, marched from Holborn, by way of Fleet-ſtreet, to the Royal-Exchange, and from thence to the Artillery ground; they made a fine appearance, and performed a good exerciſe before they were muſter'd. *C.*

Yeſterday Dr. Guy Rouſſignac, a Phyſician in Gough-ſquare, Fleet-ſtreet, was unanimouſly choſen Lecturer of Anatomy at Surgeons hall, in the room of Dr. Goldſmith, deceaſed. *P.*

Farmer Heberdeen, who was lately caſt in an action of 2000 l. damages, for ſcandalous words ſpoken againſt the D. of Richmond, has agreed to pay 150 l to the poor of the City of Chicheſter, being one part of the agreement between his Grace and the ſaid Heberdeen. *D P.*

We hear from Bath, that on monday died Miſs Fletcher of Glouceſterſhire, a young Lady of 5000 l. fortune. *C.* A beautiful young Lady. *D P.*

SATURDAY, *Aug.* 19

On thurſday night there was a ball at the R. Hon. Sir Rob. Walpole's houſe at Chelſea, which laſted till 2 in the morning: it was twelve before her Majeſty and the Royal family departed. *C.* The Prince, Duke, and all the Princeſſes danced country dances, and her Majeſty played at Quadrille. *D P.*

The Rev. Dr. Bundy, Rector of Barnet in Hertfordſhire, and one of his Majeſty's Chaplains, is made Prebend of Weſtminſter, in the room of Dr. Aſpingwell, deceaſed. *C.* Who is now abroad with his Majeſty. *P.*

On thurſday the R. Hon. the Lady Albemarle received advice by a private letter from Gibraltar, that his Lordſhip's ſervants and baggage were ſafely landed there; but that his Lordſhip was not arrived when the letter came away. *P.*

On monday his Majeſty's purſe of 100 guineas was run for at York, by 4 horſes, and won by Mr. Bathurſt's cheſnut horſe Diamond. *D P.*

We have an account from Speengreen in the Pariſh of Aſtbury in Cheſhire, that on the 9th a cow was killed there, belonging to one Sam. Yarwood of that place, who had no leſs than 74 ſtones in her belly. *D P.*

On thurſday in the evening a man was taken in Grub-ſtreet, being charged with robbing a Surgeon on the highway near Tottenham-court, and taking from him a caſe of inſtruments, a watch, and ſome money; and committed to Newgate. *D P.* —— N. B. *This* man *was not* of, *but only* taken in Grub-ſtreet.

On wedneſday night a fire broke out in a ſtack of hay, at a great farm near Slough in Bucks, occaſioned by its being put up too green; it conſumed the rick it broke out in, and 2 or 3 others, and a ſtack of wheat, wherein was 140 load; the whole damage is computed at 1500 l. the farm is rented of the Dutcheſs Dowager of Marlborough. *L E.*

On thurſday was held a Gen. Court of the York-buildings Company, where it was reſolved, That all ſtock on which the call has not been paid, ſhall not be transferr'd till the call is paid: That all the monies received and to be received upon the call of 11 half per cent. already made, and upon all future calls, be paid into the Governor and Court of Aſſiſtants, and the 5 following Proprietors, viz. the Hon. Will. Chetwynde, Eſq; Sir And. Chadwick, Rich. Farwell, Eſq; the Rev. Mr. Sam. Grove, and John Neale, Eſq; and the ſame not to be applied without the conſent of at leaſt 2 of the above named Gentlemen concurring with the Governor and Court of Aſſiſtants.—A motion was made, that a Committee of 9 perſons ſhould be appointed for inſpecting the Company's affairs and accounts; but the previous queſtion being put, it was carried in the negative. *C.*

MONDAY, *Aug.* 21.

By letters from Hanover, we hear that his Majeſty will return on thurſday next from the Gore, one of his hunting ſeats, for Hanover, and that after 3 weeks ſtay his Majeſty will ſet out for Holland, in oder to embark for England. *C*

Letters from Rome make mention of the death of Sir Will. Ellis, an old ſervant of the Chevalier de S. George. He was deſcended of a good family in England, and had, by ſeveral creditable employments, which he exerciſed before the revolution, acquired a very conſiderable eſtate in the Kingdom of Ireland. This he afterwards thought fit to abandon, and follow the fortune of the late King James. He was employed, and truſted by that Prince, whilſt he lived, and more ſince by the Chevalier, who with an entire confidence placed in his hands the whole management of his domeſtick affairs, and the old Gentleman always acquitted himſelf of it to his maſter's ſatisfaction. He was much reſpected for his integrity by all that had any dealings with him, and was, as far as his circumſtances would allow it, very compaſſionate and charitable to the poor. He liv'd to upwards of 90 years of age, and as he had always formerly adhered to the Proteſtant religion, as profeſſed by the Church of England, ſo he died in it, and was attended to the laſt by a Clergyman of the ſame communion, and interred at Rome according to the rites and ceremonies of the Engliſh Church. —— The ſame letters adviſe, that Mr. Thompſon was diſcharged out of priſon, and ordered to depart Rome in 24 hours, and the Eccleſiaſtical ſtate in 10 days. *P.*

On ſaturday the Solebay man of war was paid off at Woolwich, when 3 men who had received 40 l. a piece, took a boat, with all their cheſts and bedding, in order to go to Greenwich; ſoon after they had put off a light Collier coming down, with all the ſail ſhe could make, ran foul of them and ſunk the boat immediately, and all of them periſh'd, except one of the ſeamen: the Waterman's name was Oliver Leonard. *C.* The boat ran under her head, and was ſplit in two: 2 of the ſeamen were drowned, and one ſaved by a pair of oars. *P. D P.*

The R. Hon. the Lords Commiſſioners of his Majeſty's Treaſury have adjourned for 3 weeks. *D J.*

They write from Cheſter, that the mobbing continues there to ſuch a degree, on account of their future elections of a Mayor and Member of Parliament, that 50 l. will ſcarce repair the windows broke in one night by both parties. 'Tis added that Capt. Perrey, the famous Engineer, who ſo ſkilfully and ſucceſsfully repaired Dagenham breach in the river Thames, was arrived there from Lincolnſhire, in order to inſpect and repair the harbour there, which, 'tis talked, 2 great men conteſt who ſhall do it; and that the freemen begin to drink free-coſt at the inns in that City. *D J.*

On friday a large copper gridiron, made by Mr. Tomlinſon, Blackſmith, near Honey-lane Market, was ſet up on the top of S. Laurence's ſteeple, in imitation of a fane, to the great ſatisfaction of the Gentlemen of that pariſh; and it is allow'd by all artiſts who have viewed it, to be the beſt in London: it weighs upwards of 100 pounds, and moves with the ſmalleſt breeze. *D P.*

TUESDAY, *Aug.* 22.

Yeſterday his Royal Highneſs the Prince entertained her Majeſty, his Royal Highneſs the Duke, and the 5 Princeſſes at dinner in a moſt ſumptuous manner at Kew. *C. D J.* In a magnificent manner. *D P.* Attended by the Dukes of Grafton, and Newcaſtle, the R. Hon. the E. of Pomfret, and Sir Rob. Walpole, &c. where they were elegantly entertained. *P.*

On friday a lodge of the antient and honourable Society of free and accepted Maſons was conſtituted at Mr. Bodley's at the Rummer tavern, Charing-croſs, (in the abſence of the R. Hon. the L. Viſc. Montacute, Grand Maſter) by Tho. Batſon, Eſq; Dep. Grand Maſter, *the reſt* of the Grand Officers, Secretary, &c. attending. *D P.*

On ſaturday morning ſeveral Officers belonging to the train of Artillery went down to Woolwich in the Tower barge, and made a proof of 70 pieces of large cannon at the Warren, after which there was an elegant entertainment on that occaſion for all the Officers, &c. *D P. C.*

Sir Roger Butler, who was a Lieutenant of the Namur man of war, is made Commander of one of the Sloops now building at Deptford. *D P.* —— Which is to be called the Bonetta. *P.*

Thurſday laſt the Hon. Col. Norton, Lieut. Governor of Chelſea-College, one of the Repreſentatives in Parliament for the Borough of Bury S. Edmond's, and one of the Burgeſſes of that Corporation, was unanimouſly elected their Chief Magiſtrate for the enſuing year. *C.* Tho. Norton, Eſq; *D P.*

Yeſterday the Juſtices of the Peace for the city and liberty of Weſtminſter met, when ſeveral perſons appeared on their recognizances and were diſcharged, and others continued. *D J.*

On wedneſday the Aſſizes ended at Hereford; but no perſon was capitally convicted. *C. D J.*

Yeſterday morning died the Rev. Mr. Evans, ſenior Prebendary of Weſtminſter, and Vicar of S. Brides in Fleet-ſtreet. He was made a Prebendary of that Church by Queen Anne in the year 1702. *P. D J.* Yeſterday morning about 2, in his 88th year. *C.* Between 3 and 4. He was near fourſcore years of age, dy'd a Batchelor, and reckon'd to have dy'd worth 40,000 l. He was not much eſteem'd as a Preacher, but a man of great humanity and charity. 'Tis ſaid he will be ſucceeded as Prebendary by the Rev. Mr. Barnard, one of the Chaplains at Chelſea College. *D P.*

A diſpenſation is paſſing the ſeals to enable the Rev. Mr. John Webb, Clerk, M. A. of Univerſity College in Oxford, and Chaplain to the R. Hon. Robert E. of Ker, to hold the Rectory of Great Riſſington in the County and Dioceſe of Glouceſter, together with the vicarage of Arlingham. *L E. S J. W E.*

On ſaturday laſt the R. Hon. the E. of Radnor arrived at his houſe in Jermyn-ſtreet, S. James's, from his travels, where he has been about 6 years. *W E.*

WEDNESDAY, *Aug.* 23.

Yeſterday a Board of Admiralty was held; when orders were ſent for the Royal yatchts to be in readineſs for ſailing to Holland on the firſt notice, in order to wait his Majeſty's arrival. *D P. C.* Lieut. Cha. Smith is appointed Capt. of one of the new Sloops now building at Cha-

them. *P. D J.* And Lieut. Fowkes to be Lieutenant of his Majesty's Sloop the Terrible. *P.*

At the said Board Matthew Concanen, of the Inner Temple, Esq; Barrister at law and Attorney-General of Jamaica, took the oaths before the Lords Commissioners, as Advocate Gen. in the Admiralty Court of that Island. *D J.*

Yesterday in the afternoon the Dutchess of Kent was brought to bed of a son and heir at his Grace's house in S. James's-square. *P.* He is stiled Lord Harold. *D J.*

The same day the R. Hon. the Lady Clifford, relict of the late Lord Clifford, was safely brought to bed of a son, at his Grace the D. of Norfolk's house in the said square. *D J. P.*

Yesterday in the morning died at his habitation near Greenwich in Kent, John Storer, Esq; formerly in the Commission of the Peace. *P.*

From the PEGASUS in Grub-street.

Errata, in the Remarks on prescience, in our Journal, No. 136. Col. 2. l. 11. read, for *tho' here*, tho' how. l. 52. read, for *to square a circle*, a square circle.

Mr. BAVIUS, *Aug.* 17, 1732.

I Am a great overgrown boy, at a country free-school, where for this twelvemonth past, instead of earning a goat a day at Harrow, (with which my industrious Mother continually reproaches me) have I been scratching this poor head, over the rugged pages of JUVENAL and PERSIUS. As a specimen of my capacity for the authors, I here send you a translation of the prologue to PERSIUS. It was an exercise appointed me against the usual visitation of our school; as something applicable to my own condition, and to recommend myself to the notice of the Governors, some honest tradesmen of the town, who are great judges of these matters. As it has received their sage approbation, I cannot make any doubt of yours. If my dealing in this crabbed author (I must confess an old enemy to your illustrious Society) does not raise too great a prejudice against me, at the venerable board at the Pegasus, I make no doubt but you will find me, in all other points, as duly qualified for a Member, as the renowned Mr. D is for President of your Society. That you, Mr. BAVIUS, would be pleased to make a motion, at your next meeting, to matriculate an aspiring lad is the ambitious petition

Of your humble admirer,
HOBBINOL LUBBIN.

I don't know whether you have yet admitted my lucky kinsman Mr. STEPHEN DUCK.

The Prologue to PERSIUS translated.

I never dipp'd my lips, not I,
In learned Heliconian streams;
Parnassus top I ne'er was nigh,
Nor the fantastick Poets dreams;

The Muses and their mountains too,
I leave to VIRGIL, and the rest;
Who far from us poor GRUBS below.
Those airy seats have long possess'd.

I, a dull Swain, have left my plough,
Without their help to try the bays;
Nor need you wonder much to know,
What cou'd possess my head with lays:

What taught poor POL for sack to call?
What did the PYE to language guide?
Ingenious want can teach us all,
What sparing nature has deny'd.

Fill then my purse, and I will try,
T'exert my supernat'ral knack;
My brains inspir'd shall mount as high,
As noble BAY's fir'd with sack;

My mouth shall flow with Poetry,
As natural to me and COL;
As language to the chattering PYE;
Or human sense to *pretty* POL.

FOREIGN NEWS.

THURSDAY, *August* 17.
Yesterday arrived the Mail due from France.

Paris, Aug. 23. On the 13th inst. the French Company of Comedians acted for the first time M. Voltaire's new Tragedy called *Zaire*, which met with a general applause. *C.* — On the 19th at 6, the Chambers of Parliament assembled, and at half an hour after 7 their Deputies set out for Marly. The King delivered to them a Declaration sealed up, and ordered them to register it. 'The Chambers assembled again the next morning to know the answer; but broke up without doing any thing, only resolved that the King should be supplicated to withdraw that Declaration. *C.*

Carthagena, July 28. 'Tis said that the Duke de Riperda is turn'd Mahometan, and engaged in the service of

the Emperor of Morocco. *D P.* The King of Mequinez. *D J.* — *I hope he has now some* religion; *while he was a* Christian, *I fear, he had* none.

Gibraltar, July 8. We are often insulted by the Spaniards advances, who pretend the ground without the town is theirs, and that they may do as they please with it. The great cry made some time ago, that the Spanish works were to be demolished (only intended the old ones raised during the siege) is not yet begun. It was agreed what they should do, and what we were to do, but they will not begin, nor suffer us to do any thing. till approbation comes from Seville. Those works grow harder, and are better than ever, in case they should have occasion to make use of them. *D J.* — *How could this* great cry be made some time ago, *since it is not yet* begun?

SATURDAY, *Aug.* 19.
Yesterday arrived the Mail from Flanders.
Leghorn, Aug. 1. The master of a vessel which arrived last from Alicant reports, that part of the transports which returned thither from Oran have been retaken into service and new freighted with provisions for the Spanish army. *LE.*

MONDAY, *Aug.* 21.
Yesterday arrived the Mail from France.
Paris, Aug. 27. On the 22d the Gens du Roy went to Marli, to know of the King when his Majesty will be pleased to receive their remonstrances upon the declaration. The King told them, that the Parliament should have no audience till they resumed their functions. — On the 23d the Gens du Roy made a report to the Chambers in Parliament of the King's answer, who, after mature deliberation, declared they could not re-enter on their functions before the King had withdrawn his declaration, and charg'd the Gens du Roy to return again to Marli. *D P.* &c.

Ratisbon, Aug. 18. 'Tis said the 2 armies which the French are going to form at [in] Alsace and upon the Moselle, will amount to near 80,000 men. *D P.*

Extract of a letter from Tetuan, July 28. — We hear that the Governor of Oran, on his arrival at Algier, was beheaded, for his cowardly deserting that town. *D J.*

Yesterday arrived the Mail due from Holland.
Paris, Aug. 25. We hear from Spain that the Count de Montemar having received orders from the Court to return to the Ports of Spain, and disarm his Fleet and Army, had left in Oran 8 Battallions, under the command of the Marquis de Santa Cruz the Governor, and was departed thence accordingly. *P.*

Florence, Aug. 9. They write from Genoa, that the Spanish Minister has deliver'd a new memorial to the Regency, to demand satisfaction for the insult committed on the person of his Catholic Majesty's Consul at Bastia. *D P.*

Vienna, Aug. 16. We have received letters from Constantinople of the 10th past, importing, that the plague makes great ravages there. *D J. C.*

Books and Pamphlets published from July 26. to Aug. 17.

Fino-Godol : a poem, in two cantos. Pr. 1 s.

5. The reports from the Committee appointed to inquire into the Charitable Corporation. Pr. 5 s.

Christianity vindicated against infidelity : a second Charge to the Clergy of Middlesex, by Dan. Waterland, D. D.

8. Observations on the Bishop of Bangor's Dissertation iv. Christ's entry into Jerusalem. Pr 6 d.

10. Ecclesiastical Memoirs, by M. Tilemont, No. VI. The happy unfortunate, a novel : by Mrs Eliz. Boyd.

A Collection of Poems, &c. by John Whaley, Fellow of King's College, Cambridge.

12. A select collection of novels : in 2 volumes.

15. The Per-juror, or Country Justice : a Farce. Pr. 6 d. The Fruit-garden displayed : for July. Price 1 s.

Miscellaneous observations on Authors: No. XX.

A select collection of Moliere's Comedies, in French and English : Vol. 4th.

17. The Spanish Conquest; or, a Journal of their late expedition. Price 6 d.

Divine Inspiration : or, a Collection of manifestations to make known the Visitation of the Lord, &c.

Modern History, No. 100. By Mr. Salmon.

Miscellaneous Observations on Authors, antient and modern, No. 20.

On Tuesday Stocks were

South Sea neat Stock was 104 3 8ths, 104 5 8ths, to 3 qrs. for the Opening. South Sea Annuity 111 3 qrs. Bank 151 1 half, to 3 qrs. New Bank Circulation 4 1. 5 s. Premium. India 157 1 qr. 157 3 qrs. 157 1 half, 158 1 half, 158 1 qr. 158 3 qrs. Three per Cent. Annuity 99 5 8ths, to 3 qrs. Royal Exchange Assurance 103. London Assurance 13 1 half to 5 8ths. York Buildings 6. African 38. English Copper 2 l. 2 s. Welch ditto 1 l. 15 s. South Sea Bonds 3 l. 15 s. Premium. India ditto 5 l. 16 s. ditto.

This Day is published,

The Third Edition of

LIBERTY *and* PROPERTY,

A PAMPHLET highly necessary to be read by every *Englishman*, who has the least Regard for those Two *Invaluable Blessings*. Containing several *Curious Stories* and *Matters of Fact*, with *Original Letters* and other *Papers*. And some Observations upon the Present *State of the Nation*.

The Whole in a Letter to a Member of the House of Commons.

By EUSTACE BUDGELL, *Esq;*

Qui uni nocet, omnibus minatur.
——— *Jam proximus ardet*
Ucalegon. ——— VIRG.

Printed for *W. Mears*, at the *Lamb* in the *Old Bailey*; and Sold by the Booksellers of *London* and *Westminster*. Price stitched *Eighteen Pence*.

Note, *As I have Published this* Pamphlet *with a sincere Design to do my Country Service; and as there are some* Facts *in it, which I think it highly proper* all *my Fellow-Subjects should be acquainted with, I have made it the* Cheapest Eighteen Penny Pamphlet *that I believe was ever printed. It contains no less than* Eleven Sheets *in no large* Character.

E. BUDGELL.

Last Saturday was published,

No III. (*containing five Sheets*) *at the Price of 6 d. of*

THE HISTORY of *ENGLAND*.

By Mr. RAPIN DE THOYRAS. Translated by N. TINDAL, M. A. Vicar of Great Waltham in Essex. The 2d Edition. With the following Improvements:

1. The Translation is thoroughly revised and corrected.
2. The many Errors and Mistakes of the Original are rectified.
3. Several Hundred of Marginal References, accidentally omitted by the Author, are supplied.
4. Additional Notes throughout, with Cuts, Maps and Genealogical Tables, on Copper Plates.

Printed for James, John and Paul Knapton, removed from St. Paul's Church-Yard, to the Crown in Ludgate-Street, near the West-End of St. Paul's.

Where may be had,
No. I. and II.

N. B. The Whole will be comprised in 2 Volumes, in Folio, containing 400 Sheets, at the Price of 2 l. 2 s. in Sheets, including the Copper Plates. Five Sheets of the Work will be published every Saturday 'till the Whole is compleated, at the Price of 6 d. and the said Sheets will be delivered every Week at the Houses of Gentlemen who are pleased to order them.

Proposals at large, with a Specimen of the Work, may be had gratis.

PROPOSALS

For Printing by SUBSCRIPTION,

THE HISTORY of the Grand Controversy between the Secular and Regular Clergy of the Church of *Rome*, from the Year 1625 to 1634, concerning the Usurpation of RICHARD SMITH, Titular Bishop of *Chalcedon*. who pretended to be sole Ordinary Bishop of all *England* and *Scotland*. Wrote in *Latin* by the President of the *English* Benedictine Monks, RUDISINDUS BARLO, and faithfully done into *English* from the Original, for the Entertainment of the Curious, especially Divines and Lawyers, both Ecclesiastick and Civil, of what Religion soever.

With the Remonstrances of the *Roman* Catholick Laity made to the said Bishop, and also to his Excellency *Carolo Coloma*, Embassador Extraordinary of the Most Catholick Majesty, and to the Marquis *Fontany*, Embassador of the Most Christian King, *&c.* taken also from the *Latin* Originals: All which Treatises have been hitherto suppress, by the *Papists*, for Political Reasons given therein.

As also the famous Bull of Pope URBAN VIII. called PLANTATA, necessary for the right Understanding of the Whole, which was never before any where printed.

To which will be added,

A LETTER concerning the Disputes that have happen'd among the Benedictine Monks since the Year 1700 to this present Time: Shewing how even they themselves have varied from their original Principles. By one who was a Member of that Body, and concerned therein.

By *JOHN WILLIAMS*.

PROPOSALS may be had of (and SUBSCRIPTIONS taken in for the Author by) W. Meadows, at the Angel, in Cornhill; T. Astley, at the Rose, and S. Austen, at the Angel and Bible in St. Paul's Church-Yard; C. Davis, Pater-Noster-Row; T. Woodward, at the Half-Moon, L. Gilliver, at Homer's Head, and J. Stephens, at the Hand and Star, between the Two Temple-Gates B. Motte, at the Middle Temple-Gate; T. Worral, at Judge Coke's Head, H. Walthoe, next Door to the Rainbow Coffee-House, W. Reason, in Flower-de-Luce-Court, J. Isted, at the Golden-Ball, near Chancery-Lane, Fleet-Street; F. Gyles, over-against Gray's-Inn-Gate, Holborn; O. Payne, in Round-Court, and T. Game, at the Bible, by the New Church, in the Strand; T. Green, Charing-Cross; J. Jackson, in Pallmall; J. Jolliffe, at the Bible, in St. James's-Street; J. Brindley, at the King's Arms, and W. Shropshire, opposite to the Duke of Grafton's, New Bond-Street; and J. Stagg, Westminster-Hall, Booksellers: J. Huggonson, in Bartholomew-Close, and T. Gover, by Fleet-Ditch, Black-Fryers, Printers.

Just published,

The FOURTH VOLUME *of*

A SELECT COLLECTION *of* MOLIERE's COMEDIES, *in* French *and* English,

neatly Printed on a Fine Paper, with a Curious Frontispiece to each Comedy.

This Fourth Volume contains,

L'Ecole des Maris. The School for Husbands.	*Dedicated to the Right Hon. The Lady* Harriot Campbell.
L'Ecole des Femmes. The School for Wives.	*Dedicated to the Right Hon.* *Sir* Wm. Yong, *Knt. of the* Bath.

The Collection will consist of EIGHT POCKET VOLUMES; one Volume to be publish'd every Month, 'till the Collection be compleated. Printed for and sold by J. Watts at the Printing-Office in Wild-Court, near Lincoln's-Inn Fields: And J. Brotherton in Cornhill; J. Clarke in Duck-Lane; A. Bettesworth and C. Hitch, J. Osborne and T. Longman, and J. Batley in Pater-Noster-Row; J. Roberts in Warwick-Lane; J. Pemberton, L. Gilliver and T. Worral in Fleet-Street; F. Clay and R. Wellington without Temple-Bar; A. Millar and P. Dunoyer in the Strand; J. Batson in Little Ormond-Street; J. Stagg in Westminster-Hall; and J. Brindley in New Bond-Street. Of whom may be had, just publish'd, with a curious Frontispiece to each Comedy.

Vol. I. containing,

A General PREFACE to the whole Work.

L'AVARE. The MISER.	*Dedicated to* His Royal Highness the Prince of Wales.
Sganarelle ou le Cocu Imaginaire. The Cuckold in Conceit.	*Dedicated to Miss* Wolstenholme.

Vol. II. containing,

Le Bourgeois Gentilhomme. The Cit turn'd Gentleman.	*Dedicated to* His Royal Highness the DUKE.
Le Medicin Malgre Lui. A Doctor and No Doctor.	*Dedicated to Dr.* MEAD.

Vol. III. containing,

L'Etourdi ou les Contre Tems. The Blunderer: Or the Counter Plots.	*Dedicated to the Right Honourable* Philip *Earl of* Chesterfield.
Precieuses Ridicules. The Conceited Ladies.	*Dedicated to Miss* Le Bass.

The Translation is entirely New, and was undertaken by several Gentlemen, who all join'd and consulted together about every Part of it. Particular Care has been had to keep as close as possible to the Original, and to observe the very Words of the Author as well as his Sense, so far as was consistent with giving it a spirited and easy Comick Stile, in order to make it the more serviceable to those of our own Nation, who are Learners of the French Language; as likewise to Foreigners who desire to be acquainted with ours: To whom the Method we have taken of placing the French and English opposite to each other, will be of no small Benefit. The Work will be printed in a very beautiful Manner, and adorn'd with new Frontispieces, design'd by Mons. COYPEL, Mr. HOGARTH, Mr. DANDRIDGE, Mr. HAMILTON, &c. Price of each Volume, done up in blue Covers, will be 2 s. 6 d.

N. B. The FIFTH VOLUME will be publish'd on Wednesday the 6th of September; and the Collection will be compleated in October next.

In the Press, and will be published with all convenient Speed, beautifully printed in three Pocket Volumes, the Types *being all* New.

A new Translation of HOMER's ILIAD: As this Translation was undertaken by Gentlemen who understand GREEK, the Reader may be sure he has the Sense of the AUTHOR; and as they have avoided the Fault of other Translators, who leave their Original meerly for the sake of Versification and Gingle, he will generally have his very Words likewise. To this EDITION will be added some Remarks both on the Beauties and Imperfections of the Author, after the Manner of Mr. ADDISON's REMARKS upon MILTON. Printed by and for John Watts at the Printing-Office in Wild-Court near Lincoln's-Inn Fields.

N. B. The ODYSSEY will be printed in the same Manner in three more Pocket Volumes.

Just imported, and sold by JER. BATLEY, *at the Dove in Pater-Noster-Row.*

HIstoire des Papes depuis St. Pierre jusqu'a Benoit XIII. inclusivement en Deux Volumes 4to, a la Haye, chez Henri Scheurleer, 1732.

Lately published, and sold by J. BATLEY,

Philosophiæ Mathematicæ Newtonianæ Illustratæ. Tomi Duo. Quorum prior tradit Elementa Matheseos ad comprehendendam demonstrationem hujus Philosophiæ scitu necessaria: Posterior continet 1) Definitiones & Leges motus generaliores; 2) Leges virium centripetarum & Theoriam attractionis seu gravitationis corporum in se mutuo; 3) Mundi Systema.

A GEORGIO PETRO DOMCKIO.

This Day is published,

[Price One Shilling.]

The Second Edition corrected, of

A Practical GRAMMAR of the English TONGUE. In two Parts. Containing, I. Instructions for the true Spelling, Reading and Writing of English. II. The Principles of Arithmetick, Geography and Chronology, explained and suited to the meanest Capacities. For the Use of Schools.

By THO. DYCHE, late School-Master, at Stratford Bow.

Printed for J. Clarke, at the Golden-Ball in Duck-Lane, near West-Smithfield.

Just published,

In Octavo, Price bound 4 s. 6 d.

A General History of the World, from the Creation to the Destruction of Jerusalem by Nebuchadnezzar: Being the Period with which the Old Testament concludes. Wherein the sacred and profane History is connected, the Septuagint and Hebrew Chronology compar'd and adjusted to the Years before Christ.

By THOMAS BRETT, L. L. D.

Printed for FLETCHER GYLES, over-against Grays-Inn, in Holborn.

Where may be had, by the same Author, and fit to bind with it.

1. A Chronological Essay on the sacred History, from the Creation to the Birth of Christ: *And an Essay on the Confusion of Languages*; price 1 s. 6 d.
2. VERTOT's History of the Knights of Malta, with fine Cuts, 2 Vol. Folio; price 2 l. 12 s. 6 d.
3. LAMBARDE's Topographical and Historical Dictionary of England and Wales, 4to; price 1 l. 1 l.
4. SOMNER's Treatise of Gavelkind, with a curious Account of his Life, by Bp. Kennet, 4to; price 12 s.
5. Dr. THO. SHORT's Dissertation upon Tea, 4to; price 2 s. 6 d.
6. A Rational Catechism, 12mo; price 1 s. 6 d.

This Day is published,

In Octavo (from the Folio Edition) Price Six Pence.

THE PROGRESS of LOVE, in four Eclogues, 1. UNCERTAINTY, to Mr. Pope. 2. HOPE, to the Honourable George Doddington, Esq; 3. JEALOUSY, to Edw. Walpole, Esq; 4. POSSESSION, to the Right Honourable Lord Viscount COBHAM.

Printed for Lawton Gilliver at Homer's Head in Fleet-Street.

Where may be had,

1. An Epistle to Mr. Pope, from a young Gentleman at Rome. *By the same Author.*
2. The Art of POLITICKS, with a curious Frontispiece. *Risum teneatis Amici.* Price 1 s.
3. Two Epistles to Mr. Pope, concerning the Authors of the Age. By the Author of the Universal Passion. Price 1 s. and may be bound with the said Satyrs.
4. A new and correct Edition of the Dunciad Variorum, in 8vo. with some additional Notes and Epigrams.
5. A Collection of Pieces relating to the Dunciad. By several Hands.
6. Of FALSE TASTE, to Richard Earl of Burlington. By Mr. Pope. Price 1 s.
7. STOW: The Gardens of the Right Honourable the Lord Cobham. Price 1 s.

This Day is published,

Printed for *J. Brotherton*, at the *Bible*, next the Fleece Tavern in Cornhill,

AN Enquiry into the Origin of Honour, and the Usefulness of Christianity in War.

By the Author of the FABLE of the BEES.

Where may be had,

1. A Letter to Dion, being an Answer to a Book call'd *Alciphron*, or the *Minute Philosopher*.
2. The present State of Great Britain and Ireland, for the Year 1731.
3. Traditions of the Jews.
4. Dury's Journal to Madagascar.
5. Religious Courtship.
6. Life of OLIVER CROMWELL, Lord Protector of the Commonwealth.
7. Receipts in Cookery and Surgery, by John Keetilby.

The Cœlestial Anodyne Tincture: *Or*, *The* Great Pain-Easing Medicine,

F*Am'd and approv'd of for its wonderful and never-failing Success, in giving immediate Ease and Relief in all manner of Pains, either inward or outward, and is the most certain Remedy in the World for a sure and speedy Cure of the Cholick, and expelling Wind, Gripes and Pains in the Stomach, the Pleurisy, Stitches or Pains in the Side, Back, Loins, or any other Part; Rheumatick Ailments, which cause Pain and Dolor. It hath given Ease to a Miracle, when all other Remedies have fail'd. In the Gravel and Stone in the Kidneys, it gives Ease forthwith, and brings them away to Admiration. It also facilitates and causes a speedy Delivery in Child-Birth. 'Tis no Quack trifling Thing to allure the World with, but a real and well-experienced Medicine, not acting by Stupefaction (as Opiates) but by a friendly, balsamick and subtle Nature, pacifying the most severe and terrible racking Pains, and carries off the Cause, not by purging, but by Transpiration, by Urine, or breaking Wind. No Family ought to be without it. And used outwardly, it cures Swellings, Aches, Pains, Numbness, or Weakness of the Joints; 'tis excellent for Cramps, and all other aged Infirmities, effecting Wonders in Agues, Fevers, Small-Pox, &c. No Family ought to be without it.*

It is sold only by Mr. PARKER, *Printer, at his House in Salisbury-Court, or by such Persons as he shall depute, viz. at Mr. Parker's, a Printer, in Bull-Head Court in Jewin-Street; at the White Gally-Pot, a Chandler's Shop in Bandy-Leg-Walk, Southwark, and at Mr. Neal's, a Toyshop over-against the White Hart Inn in the Borough, at Eighteen Pence a Bottle, with printed Directions; and if requested, will be brought to any Person, by the Hawker who sells his Penny-Post. Sealed as above.*

LONDON: Printed by J. HUGGONSON, *in Bartholomow-Close*, for Capt. GULLIVER, near the *Temple*, where Letters and Advertisements are taken in: As also at the *Rainbow Coffee-House* in *Cornhill*, and *John*'s *Coffee-House* in *Sheer-Lane, Temple-Bar*. [Price Two Pence.]

The Grub-ſtreet Journal.

NUMB. 139

Thurſday, AUGUST 31, 1732.

—— *Et* RESPONDERE *parati.*

To Mr. BAVIUS.

THIS *diſputing age* having carried *controverſy* about almoſt *every thing* to ſo great perfection, that in a little time we may expect to ſee it made a queſtion, whether the ſun ſhines by day, or the moon by night; I have been thinking, Mr. BAVIUS, that a diſſertation upon *anſwering* books, pamphlets, and papers, may not be at preſent unſeaſonable. I am ſenſible, that if what I advance ſhall have any conſiderable weight; it may prove prejudicial to the venders of weekly ſheets and half ſheets in general, and to your Society in particular; by leſſening the number of writers, and conſequently of advertiſements. But I know, you, and your brethren are Gentlemen of ſo publick a ſpirit, that you will encourage any thing which tends to the common good, tho' contrary to your own private intereſt.

Here is a book ſuppoſe, which, being in truth *unanſwerable*, makes a deep impreſſion upon a certain perſon. He mentions it to his friend, who is of different principles. O, *anſwers* he, *That book's anſwered*. Thus the Papiſts in defence of their ridiculous abſurdities in reaſon, and groſs falſhoods in fact, and the Preſbyterians and other Proteſtant Diſſenters, in juſtification of their ſenſeleſs and wicked ſchiſm, have this reply always ready at hand. Every thing they have urged, and do, or can urge, has been *unanſwerably anſwered* a thouſand times over, and their cauſe demonſtrated to be indefenſible: yet becauſe they have written innumerable books on their own ſide, they think it ſufficient to ſay, that all thoſe on ours are *anſwered*. They will ſay, no doubt, that this is not true of *them*, but of *us*: and I own the bare aſſertion is no argument for either. However, that ſo it is on one ſide or other, will be granted on both; in all controverſies whatſoever; whether philoſophical, theological, or political; whether in point of reaſon, of religion, or of fact. To explain myſelf, Mr. BAVIUS, and to avoid the repetitions of *ſays he*, and *ſays he*, and *ſays ſuch a one*; I will throw the ſubſtance of what I mean into two ſhort dialogues.

DIAL. I.

A. That book's *anſwered*; thoſe papers and pamphlets are *anſwered*. There are ſix or ſeven *anſwers* to them.

B. Ay, but all thoſe *anſwers* are fully *anſwered*.

A. By whom, pray?

B. Why by Mr. *W.* by Dr. *S.* by *J. T.* Eſq; by my Lord *W.* and by three or four without names.

DIAL. II.

A. That book was *never anſwered*.

B. True; becauſe it is not *worth anſwering*.

A. That's eaſily ſaid; but the real reaſon is, becauſe 'tis *unanſwerable*: the man would anſwer it if he could, but he can't.

B. I tell thee, 'tis not becauſe he can't, but becauſe he won't. 'Tis not worth his while; it does not deſerve an *anſwer*, and ought to be *anſwered* only with ſilence and contempt.

C. Gentlemen you are both miſtaken. That book is *anſwered*: I have ſeen and read an *anſwer* to it.

A. That's impoſſible, I am ſure. The *anſwer* is *no anſwer* at all. The book may be *written againſt*, if you pleaſe; but it can't be *anſwered*.

Thus ſhall they go on for an hour together, and upon the ſame foot might go on for ever, contradicting one another, begging the queſtion on both ſides, and ſaying nothing. I will therefore endeavour to adjuſt theſe matters, and ſettle that flutter of thought, under which my Countrymen ſeem to labour, upon the ſubject of *anſwering* and *not anſwering* books. And here in the firſt place, I deſire them not to argue, as multitudes ſeem to do, that there's no *certainty* in *any thing*, becauſe in *theſe times* there's ſo much *diſputing* about *every thing*. It does not follow, that becauſe there's much ignorance, impudence, folly, knavery, impertinence, lying, obſtinacy and perverſeneſs, W—M, and O—N, HENLEY, and BOWMAN in the world; therefore there's no truth. There are many truths for all that; and many of them are plain and eaſy. Some fools will cavil for ever, and about every thing; always wrangling, never convinced. *Anſwers* (as they have been called) have been written to various books, demonſtrating from the plaineſt facts, the truth of the Chriſtian religion. And ſo an *anſwer* may be written to EUCLID'S elements. Indeed I wonder there has been none. It would be a work worthy the genious of this learned and ſagacious age and nation, in which we have the honour and happineſs to live. Were that book a defence of Chriſtianity, it would undoubtedly have been *anſwered* before this time. I will from the very firſt line give a ſpecimen how it may be done. *A point is that which has no parts.* That? What? Is it a body, or a ſpirit? A ſubſtance, or an accident? If it has no parts, 'tis nothing. As for ſpirit, that's nonſenſe. An incorporeal ſubſtance is the ſame as an incorporeal body. And if it be body, it muſt have parts. This is *myſtery* with a witneſs; that is, a *contradiction*, as all myſteries are. We cannot *comprehend* it; and therefore it cannot be *true*. The word *point* in EUCLID is as ridiculous as the word *perſon*, which the Parſons make ſuch a clutter about in their contradictious doctrine of the Trinity. There is no *clear, diſtinct, adequate idea* annexed to either: and therefore we cannot *know*, or *believe* any thing about them. I have repreſented this in their own cant; to ſhew that they may argue againſt *Mathematicks*, in the ſame language, and upon the ſame principles, as they argue againſt *Chriſtianity*. I would have it further obſerved, that in all controverſies the *worſt cauſe* has generally the *laſt word*; becauſe the maintainers of it have the moſt obſtinacy; and what is wanting in argument is made out in confidence. But ſpeaking, or writing laſt, ſignifies nothing. In trials at the bar the accuſers and the plaintiffs have the *reply*, or the *laſt word*; but for all that the accuſed and the defendants often carry their cauſe, and that before the moſt learned, and uncorrupt judges. But to go on, Mr. BAVIUS,

I obſerve (as was well hinted in the 2d dialogue above) that every thing is not properly an *anſwer* which is called ſo. For inſtance, not a heap of ſpiteful perſonal reflections foreign to the purpoſe. This is not *anſwering*, but *railing*: nor repeating the ſame arguments which have been fully *anſwered* by one's antagoniſt, without taking notice of thoſe *anſwers*, or adding any thing new. This is not *anſwering*, but *tautology, fraud, teiſing*, and *impertinence*. Nor wilfully miſtating the queſtion; repreſenting that as a man's own opinion, which was by him mentioned as another's; falſe quotations and falſe facts: this is not *anſwering*, but *lying*. But then, as to the firſt, let it be noted by way of caution, that in ſome certain caſes and circumſtances, a man cannot be uſed too roughly, and no language can be too ſevere for him. Should a Clergyman, for example, whether a P—— e or a plain Presbyter, not only be guilty of the greateſt falſhoods both in reaſoning and fact, and propagate principles deſtructive of human happineſs in this world, and the next; but maliciouſly calumniate the Church and Clergy, and vilify thoſe perſons and things, which he is by his ſacred profeſſion, and ſolemn promiſe, obliged to defend; he ſhould be not barely *anſwered* (if at all *anſwered*) but to the laſt degree *expoſed*. Becauſe the man would be directly INFAMOUS; and ought to be *ſtigmatized* accordingly. Imagine ſuch a one to exiſt *in rerum naturâ*: if what he ſays be true, why does he not reſign his rich B——, or other eccleſiaſtical preferments, and renounce his holy orders? I appeal to all men of honour, particularly the Gentlemen of the army, whether they would not declare that Officer INFAMOUS, who ſhould defame, and labour to render odious, or contemptible, that Prince, or General, under whom he ſerves, and from whom he received his commiſſion? nay, whether he would not deſerve to be drummed out of the regiment, for making it his buſineſs, and conſtant practice to ſpeak ill of him, tho' never ſo truly? Whatever therefore becomes of the poor Church, Clergy and Chriſtianity; and whatever opinions be entertained concerning them: ſurely if there be any ſuch thing as common honour, and common honeſty yet remaining among us, *ſuch men as theſe* at leaſt will be *deteſted* and *deſpiſed*; and all ingenuous perſons of what perſuaſion ſoever, will (to uſe K. Charles I's words in one of his *anſwers* to the rebels) brand them, and their doctrine, with the marks of their perpetual ſcorn and indignation.

But what really deſerves the name of an *anſwer*, is 1ſt, Talking to the purpoſe, and reaſoning clearly, and ſtrongly; tho' not with truth on one's ſide. This is *an anſwer*, tho' not *full anſwer*. 2dly, Proving one's point, and demonſtrating that truth is on one's ſide. This is not only an *anſwer* but a *confutation*. Ay, but you'll ſay, the man *won't* be confuted. That is, ſay I, he won't *own* he is confuted: and neither you, nor I can help that. In ſhort, the difference between *merely writing againſt* a book, and *anſwering* it, is plainly this: the one is *nominally* anſwering; the other is *really* anſwering.

But muſt *every* book, pamphlet and paper be *anſwered*? Or every *anſwer* (as it may be called) *re-anſwered*, or *replied to*? No. Some are true, and *unanſwerable*; and therefore no body ſhould pretend to *anſwer* them. Others are too ridiculous, impertinent, and abſurd, to deſerve an *anſwer*. As thoſe which are themſelves called *anſwers*, but really are not; of which above. And the ſame may be ſaid of *any* ridiculous impertinent books, papers, or pamphlets; tho' they are not called *anſwers*. Thoſe which have any thing ſolid in them, or even a fair and plauſible appearance of truth, which has not been ſubſtantially *anſwered* already, (I mean in the ſame controverſy) ought to be *anſwered*. But for the reſt, I ſay as I did before. If I find a book all over impertinent, tautological, impudent and abſurd, written againſt me; I will not *anſwer* it, but *ſcorn* it. O! but ſome will ſay, 'tis becauſe I *can't* anſwer it. Let 'em: nobody of judgment and honeſty will ſay ſo; and I will venture my reputation with the world. I myſelf, Mr. BAVIUS, have had eleven pamphlets written againſt me, which I never took the leaſt notice of; tho' I have *anſwered* others. Beſides, with regard to diſputes about *religion*, do people think the Clergy here in *London* eſpecially, have nothing elſe to do with their *time*, but to *anſwer* all the traſh and trumpery which every unlettered, half-witted pettifogger in controverſy is pleaſed to ſcrawl out againſt Jeſus Chriſt, without underſtanding one word of the ſubject he is upon? *Thoſe* of the Clergy who have both *will* and *abilities* to *defend Chriſtianity*, and actually *do* defend it, are, 'tis well known, (except two, or three) very *buſy*, becauſe very *poor*, having enough to do to *get bread*. For *preferments*, and the conſequents of them, *quiet* and *leiſure*, were, to be ſure, never intended for ———. But I forbear, Mr. BAVIUS; that is a *nice ſubject*, and deſerves to be conſidered by itſelf.

But you will ſay, at this rate thoſe *little vermin* will eſcape the puniſhment they deſerve, merely *becauſe* of their being *little*; which is not juſt; ſince they are as *malicious* as *impotent*, and as *odious* as *contemptible*. I *anſwer*, tho' they ought not to be *anſwered*, they ought to be *chaſtiſed*; to be, in a *few* words, and a *ſhort* reflection upon them, *ſhewn*, for *deſpicable wretches*, who *would* do miſchief if they *could*. And this, Mr. BAVIUS, is one end and deſign of YOUR honourable Society. To the good influence of which it were well, if a law were added, that *theſe creatures*, being duly convicted, ſhould be delivered over to the *King's Scholars*, and undergo the ſame diſcipline as CURLL did at *Weſtminſter*.

In *anſwering*, or *not anſwering*, it much alters the caſe whether the book or pamphlet be publiſhed with, or without a *name*. I will *anſwer* any thing *well* written, tho' *without* a name; but I will not *anſwer* anonymous ignorance, dullneſs, and ſcurrility. Then again if *with* a name; the character, quality, and ſtation of the perſon, are material circumſtances. I will (if I can, if I cannot, I will ſubmit) anſwer a man of known parts, learning and great abilities, as a S—K, or a H—E; if I differ from him in any material point: tho' in this particular book he writes much below himſelf. I will anſwer one of a quite contrary character, as a S—K—S, or a J—K—N, if he writes well now, tho' he never did ſo before: but he deſerves not to be anſwered, if he writes as he uſually does. I ſay *deſerves not*; for it does not therefore *follow* that he *ſhould* not. I will *anſwer ſuch*, or *ſuch* a one running down all eccleſiaſtical *authority*, and all *revealed religion*; becauſe he is a B—— (I ſpeak, as I did juſt now, upon ſuppoſition there was ſuch a perſon) and ſo much reſpect is due to his L——'s quality, that he *muſt* be anſwered. But I am not obliged to anſwer BOWMAN writing upon the ſame ſubject, and in the ſame manner; becauſe he is my equal, or perhaps inferior; and infidelity, malice againſt the Church, and a ſolemn pompous ſhow of reaſon and argumentation, with nothing but ignorance, and illiterate ſophiſtry at the bottom, have not in *him* a right to be complemented with the ſame ceremony.

Very often the doubt and difficulty is this. If a book, or pamphlet *be* anſwered, it will do the author too much honour, and make his crudities taken notice of, which otherwiſe they never would have been, but would have died of themſelves. If it be *not*; it will be ſaid it is *unanſwerable*, and the ſcribler will triumph in his adverſaries ſilence. This, I confeſs, is a difficult point, and hard

... determined. We must judge, as well as we can, ... prudent considerations, and comparing of circumstances. There is a kind of middle way between answering and not answering. I mean answering, so as directly not to answer: utterly overthrowing the principles of him you are engaged with; yet treating him and his work with neglect and contempt, and answering him without appearing to be in earnest, tho' you really are. How many books were written by the most learned men against the trifles of Hobbs? yet the ingenious Eachard, by disguising his solid reasonings with ludicrous wit, inimitable in its kind, did more to the mortification of that solemn dogmatical coxcomb, than all the rest of his answerers put together. It was indeed right to answer so philosophical and voluminous an atheist, both ways; seriously, as many did; and comically, as Eachard did. T—d L, the Hobbs of this age, has been abundantly answered in the former way; it would be well if he were a-nswered in the latter. His Christianity as old as the Creation, in which there is not a word of truth, or sound reasoning, is as good a subject of ridicule, as any age has produced.

But it will be asked, who are in the right, and who are in the wrong, in answering, and not answering, according to the measures here laid down? Who is impertinent, tautological, impudent, absurd, fraudulent, &c. and who not? And who shall be judge? The resolution is easy. The writers in the dispute must judge as well as they can; and others must judge of them as well as they can. But let both take care they be diligent, unprejudiced, and impartial. For if they make an ill use of the reason which God has given them, in judging about answering, and not answering; they must one day severely answer for it. Pray, Mr. Bavius, give my service to Mr. Conundrum; and tell him I do not by those words intend to invade his Province. I am very grave; and my meaning is only this; that those who think, talk, and write perversely about answering in the one sense, would do well seriously to consider it in the other.

Aug. 26, 1732.   I am, &c.

✠✠✦◊◊✦ ✦✦✦✦✦✦✦✦✦✦✦ ✦✦✦✦✦✦✦✦✦✦

DOMESTIC NEWS.

C. Courant.
P. Post-Boy.
DP. Daily Post.
DJ. Daily Journal.

EP. Evening Post.
SJ. S. James's Evening Post.
WE. Whitehall Evening P.
LE. London Evening Post.

Thursday, August 24.

Yesterday the R. Hon. the L. Torrington, accompanied by several persons of distinction, went in the Admiralty barge from Whitehall to Greenwich, and hoisted his flag on board the William and Mary yacht, in which he will sail for Holland to convoy his Majesty to England. P. DJ.

Yesterday a Court of Aldermen was held at Guildhall; and from thence the R. Hon. the L. Mayor, accompanied by several of the Aldermen, &c. went to Smithfield and proclaimed Bartholomew-fair; and his Lordship stopt at Newgate, where the Keeper presented him with a cool tankard, of which his Lordship drank and returned. C. DJ. P.

The same day the Directors of the East-India Company received tenders from 15 Captains and owners of several ships to be taken into their service this year. C.

Yesterday came on the election of a Clerk to the Vintners Company, worth about 300 l. per ann. The election lay between Mr. Wilcox of Thavies Inn, and Mr. Willis; and the former carried it by 4 votes. DP. There were 3 Candidates, viz. Mr. Wilcox, Mr. Willis, and Mr. Bedell. DJ.

It is said Dr. Broderick, one of the Prebendaries of Westminster, will succeed Mr. Evans, deceased, as Vicar of S. Bride's in Fleet-street. DP.

We hear from Reading, that on thursday last a hay rick belonging to one Farmer Mason, a Tenant to the Dutchess of Marlborough took fire, and fir'd 8 more stacks of corn and hay; and the damage is computed at 1000 l. DJ. On saturday the Assizes ended at Monmouth, which proved a maiden one. P. DJ.

Friday, August 25.

Yesterday a Gen Council was held at Kensington, at the breaking up of which one of his Majesty's Messengers was dispatch'd for Hanover. DP. C. From whence his Majesty intends to set out for Great Britain the 10th or 11th of next month. P.

The same day his Grace the D. of Newcastle gave an entertainment at his house at Kensington, at which were present the Dukes of Grafton and Dorset, the Earls of Scarborough and Godolphin, Sir Rob. Walpole, and several other persons of distinction. P. An elegant entertainment. DP. A grand. C.

Yesterday the board of Green cloth gave orders to his Majesty's Cooks, &c. to go to Somerset house this day,

and to send on board the Royal yachts all necessary provisions, &c. P. DP. Who [which] are ordered to sail for Holland on sunday next. C.

This day the 3 new sloops building at Deptford will be launched there, and their names will [we hear] be the Shark, Cruizer, and Trial, being the names of 3 of his Majesty's sloops that were lately sold as unfit for service; and next week the said sloops will be commission'd, and the command of one of them will be given to Lieut. Compton, first Lieutenant of the Namur: and the command of another to Lieut. Pocock, 2d Lieutenant of the said ship. P.

Yesterday lay in state in the Jerusalem Chamber, the corpse of Sir Tho. Hardy; and last night was interr'd in great pomp in the middle isle, near the entry into the Choir of Westminster Abbey. C. DJ. Last night about 9. P.

They write from Hereford, that so soon as the Assizes ended for that City, the mob rose and pull'd down all the turnpikes leading thereto. DP.

Christned Males 205, Females 149, in all 354.—Buried Males 204, Females 211, in all 415. Increased in the burials this week 48.

Saturday, August 26.

Her Majesty has been pleased to send to Berlin 12 pair of shoes and 12 pair of slippers of the most exquisite workmanship, made by a shoe-maker in S James's street, as a present to the Queen of Prussia. DP.

We hear that his Royal Highness the Prince of Wales, and the L. Visc. Limerick, will stand Godfathers to the new born son of his Grace the D. of Kent, and the Princess Royal Godmother. P.

The Hon. Mrs. Anne Vane has purchased the house next to the L. Bishop of Salisbury's in Grosvenor-square for 3000 l. DP.

Yesterday was held a General Court of the South Sea Company, for taking the ballot, pursuant to resolutions of the General Courts held the 16th and 30th of June last, for choosing a Committee of 15 of the Proprietors, qualified according to the resolutions of the said General Courts, to inspect and examine the several accounts prepared by the Accomptant, and laid before them; when we hear the following Gentlemen were chosen the said Committee, viz. Mr. Joseph Beachcroft, Charles Colborne, Esq; Mr. William Colebrooke, Mr. Jonathan Collyer, Mr. Richard Coope, Jeremiah Dummer, Esq; Mr. Michael Garnault, Mr. Robert Henley, Philip Hollingworth, Esq; Mr. Benjamin James, jun. Mr. Samuel Lessingham, Mr. Patrick Macky, Mr. Nathaniel Newnham, jun. Samuel Wright, Esq; Mr. William Wilkins. C.

We hear that Thomas Walker, Esq; one of the Commissioners of the Customs, will be appointed Surveyor General of the land revenue, in the room of Dr. Sayer, deceased. C.

On thursday evening about 6, and not before, his Grace the D. of Bedford came from his seat at Woburn Abbey in Bedfordshire, to his house in Bloomsbury-square, from whence he will set out in a few days for Lisbon, for the recovery of his health. P.

Yesterday the Hon. Court of Directors of the East India Company received the agreeable news of the safe arrival of their ship Middlesex, Capt. John Pilley, who sailed from the Downs, Dec. 13, 1730, having buried but 13 men in her whole voyage. Governor Dean, late Governor of Fort William, is arrived in the Middlesex. DP. DJ. P.

Monday, Aug. 28.

Last saturday Mr. Bowey, one of his Majesty's Messengers arrived express at Whitehall, with dispatches from his Majesty, whereby we understand that his Majesty is expected at the Hague in less than 10 days. C.

A dispensation is lately passed the great seals to enable the Rev. Mr. Humphrys of Trinity College in Cambridge, to hold the Vicarage of Ware in the County of Hertford and Diocese of London, together with that of Thundridge. P.

Tho. Killback, Esq; is made an Ensign in the first regiment of foot-guards, commanded by Sir Cha. Wills. DJ.
——And Mr. Rich. Graydon, lately belonging to the first troop of horse-guards, an Ensign in Sir Cha. Hotham's regiment of foot at Port Mahon. P.

On saturday at a Board of Admiralty, their Lordships were pleased to appoint Capt Edw. Smith of Dover, to be Commander of the new sloop building at Chatham, which is named the Spy; and Lieut. Will. Fielding to be Lieutenant of the said sloop. P.——The same day their Lordships received advice of the safe arrival of his Majesty's ship the Pearl, from the West-Indies at the Nore. L. DP.

We hear that Mr. Tho. Salway, lately belonging to the Theatre Royal in Lincoln's-Inn fields, is admitted one of the Gentlemen belonging to the Choir of the Cathedral Church at Salisbury. DP. C.

Last saturday morning 2 Bricklayers, that were at work in Mr. Shepherd's buildings in Grosvenor-street, happening to quarrel at the Royal Oak, one of them dart-

ed his trowel at the other's breast, which run into his body, so that he died on the spot. G.

On saturday morning died at his house in Crutched-Fryars, John Hanbury, Esq; Deputy Governor of the South Sea Company. DP. C. P. Of a paraletick illness, which seized him 7 days before: Governor of the Company of Merchant Adventurers of England (i. e. Hamburgh Merchants.) DJ.——On thursday morning died, at his seat at Swindon in Wiltshire, Ric. Goddard, Esq; he died a Batchelor, and his estate reputed near 3000 l. per ann. descends to his brother Pleydell Goddard, Esq; Merchant of this city. DJ.

Tuesday, Aug. 29.

We hear that Lee and Harper intend to play at their two great Booths on the Bowling-Green, behind the Marshalsea in Southwark, during the time of the fair; at one the celebrated Droll of Whittington, that has given such a general satisfaction to all spectators: and at the other, a new Droll never acted before, called Female Innocence; or, a School for a wife, with the comical humours of Captain Blusterr, and his man Didimo. And, for the further entertainment of the audience, they are getting up a very diverting new entertainment.

Yesterday morning the Prince, the Princess Royal, and the Princess Emilia, went to the Tower and viewed the Armory there; and in the evening went to Bartholomew-fair, and saw Mr. Pinchbeck's curious entertainment, with which they were highly delighted. DP.

A fine engine or spinning wheel of curious workmanship has lately been sent hither from Ireland, which is to be made a present to her Majesty. P.

We hear from Copenhagen, that on the 26th, the K. of Denmark at Fredericksburgh in full Court acknowledg'd the Empress of Russia by the title of Empress, and that the same should be given to her for ever, both by the King of Denmark and his States. DJ.

We hear that Mr. Corbet of the Navy Office will succeed John Hanbury, Esq; deceased, as one of the Directors of Greenwich Hospital. DP. C.

On wednesday last came on at Plymouth the election of a Vicar of S. Andrew's Parish, which has been upwards of 500 l. per ann. and is at present upwards of 900 l. which terminated in favour of Mr. Mudge: the Candidates were 9; but the stress of the dispute lay between Mr. Mudge, and one Dr. Berned, who went thither about a fortnight before the election; he was so acceptable to the Gentry, that they prevailed with all the other Candidates, besides Mr. Mudge, to desist and throw their interest on him; and notwithstanding he found a great number of the electors engaged before he came, yet he lost the election only by one. DP.

On wednesday last at Norwich Mr. John Brown, a Grocer in Market-street place, was by the Court of Aldermen chosen one of the Sheriffs of that City for the ensuing year. DP. DJ.

By letters from S. Thomas on the coast of Africa, dated June 6, by a Dutch ship, we learn, that the S. Andrew, Capt. Nic. Webb, from London, who was arrived there, was dead, and all his men except 4; and that the ship had been seized by the Portugueze; but according to the Captain's desire, 4 days before his death, she was delivered to an English ship, Capt. Blizard, who carried the said ship directly to Barbadoes. C. DP. About 6 or 7 of her hands, which remained alive, carried her into the Island of Princes, where the Portugueze would have taken possession of her, but through the good conduct of Capt. Hogg she was preserved, and enabled to prosecute her voyage. DJ.
——By these letters we learn also that Fort Jaquin was destroyed by the King of the country, and all the people cut off. DP. C.

On sunday morning last two Farmers and two labouring men went to a fish-pond by Lambone Church, near Aybridge in Essex, belonging to Mr. Moore, who having frequently suffered by the taking fish out of it, happened at the same time to be so near it, as that only a hedge was between; one of the men, who went in first, being deceived in the depth, sunk; the other then went to assist him, but shared the same fate; and Farmer Meredith, endeavouring to recover them, was near drowning; but his neighbour, with much difficulty, fortunately saved him by the help of Mr. Moore, who, seeing the Tragedy, came to their relief. This affair being soon rumoured in the church, the people went out to see the unhappy men that were drowned; so that the prayers being ended, and the congregation gone, the Parson reserved his sermon to another opportunity. DJ.

Yesterday morning, about 3, dy'd at his habitation at Mile end, of the gout in his stomach, aged 74, Major Stuart, a half-pay Officer, who was in the commission of the peace for the Tower-hamlets in the reign of Queen Anne: he was a brother to the late Gen. Stuart. DP. P.
——Yesterday in the afternoon at his house in S. Martin's lane, Major Bembow, who formerly belonged to the first troop of Life-guards. DJ.

Wednesday, Aug. 30.

Yesterday at a Board of Admiralty, their Lordship,

were pleased to appoint Mr. John Douglas first Lieutenant of his Majesty's ship the Hector, and Mr. Will. Huet 2d Lieutenant; and Mr. Webber, late Boatswain, and Mr. Molding, Carpenter of the sloop Cruizer, to be Officers of his Majesty's sloop the Spy. *C. D J.*

Yesterday the Prince and Princesses went to Bartholomew-fair, and saw Mr. Feilding's celebrated Droll, call'd, the Earl of Essex and the Forc'd Physician, and were so well pleased as to stay to see it twice perform'd. *D P.*

Extract of a letter from Calcutta in the East Indies, dated Jan. 5. Two days since a party of Gentlemen were hunting Jackalls about 6 miles from this town, it being a custom so to do two or three times a week at this season of the year, who were met by about 100 Peons belonging to a petty Jemmidar, and assaulted in a violent manner, many arrows being shot at them, for no other provocation than riding over their grounds; the Gentlemen, having no arms to defend themselves, narrowly escaped with their lives, and immediately went and represented the case to our Governor, who ordered about 50 soldiers, a Captain and an Ensign to go and demand the Jemmidar's person, to answer for the affront done to the English, with orders, in case of refusal, to burn his fort and town; which was accordingly done, and about 4 of the Peons kill'd in the attack: how this may terminate we know not. *D P.*

We learn from Jamaica, by letters of the 26th of June, that the hulks, &c. were removed from Kingston, &c. to Port Antonio, at the east end of the island, which new town encreased daily, and Kingston and Port Royal visibly decreased. This port is very safe, and commodiously situated for the windward passage; and being encouraged by the Government, it is believed will soon be the most flourishing in that island. Many persons who were settled near it, had planted Coffee, and were using their utmost endeavours to bring it to perfection. *D J.*

The South Sea Company's ships employ'd this year in the whale fishery, are now all safely arrived back in the river, consisting of 21 sail, 14 of which came from Greenland, and 7 from Davis's Streights, bringing among them twenty four Whales and a half, several of which are very large, and the rest are good sizeable fish. *Ibid.*

Yesterday in the afternoon a melancholy accident happen'd a little below the bridge, where 9 women crossing the river from Billingsgate, the boat running upon an iron chain which serv'd to moor ships by, overset so suddenly, that 3 of 'em (one big with Child) were drown'd, and the other 6 were with much difficulty saved, notwithstanding the immediate assistance which came to their relief. *Ib.*

A few days since Tomkin the smuggler, who lately turn'd evidence against some of his gang, was seiz'd at Riverhead in Kent, by a party of his former comrades (but what they have done with him is not yet known; tho' their intention was (as they declared) to put him in a sack, and drown him in the sea. *D P.*

From the PEGASUS in Grub-street.

The following copy of verses, sent to the Society some time since, is now published, not as containing their sentiments, but those of the unknown Author, whom they are willing to oblige.

While Drurian Actors, RICH, with envious eyes
In Bow-street see th'aspiring fabric rise;
That great success thy great design may crown,
Employs the wishes of th'impartial Town.
Too long indulgent to one House alone   5
With brighten'd rays their partial favour shone:
Now streaks of ruddy light, like early morn,
With kind presage thy rising pile adorn.
No more shall crowds in Drury-lane be seen,
While half-fill'd boxes found at Lincolns-Inn.   10
W——ks shall no more our eyes and ears ingage,
Or B——tn with steps majestic tread the stage.
Poets no longer shall submit their Plays
To learned C——r's gilded wither'd bays;
To such a Judge the labour'd scene present,   15
Whom *sensible* and *pretty* won't content.
But to thy Theatre with pleasure bear
The comic laughter and the tragic tear.
Let that great Actor, who so oft has shown
All Nature's graces heighten'd by his own,   20
As age increases, and his strength decays,
Willing retire, grown old in wealth and praise.
As for the rest, none e'er will rise so high,
But vainly with thy noble Actors vie.
Let thy *Othello* roar, or bid *King Lear*   25
Rage in wild frenzy, and they'll disappear.
Form on thy stage thy *Lady Townley* call,
And H——n a victim shall to Y——c fall.
Improving C——p—n such applause will gain,
That C——a-k's both shall act and write in vain.   30
Nor Sire, nor Son, so witty, pert, and gay
Can humour e'er like H——p——y display.

Be cautious H——L—— M lest you soar too high,
And by attempting to match R——— n dye.
Let B——c—R no more act *Hotspur's* rage,   35
While W——K—R lives to shake the trembling Stage.
Nor jigging M—— L strive to force a tear,
While H——L——r; G'oster ravishes our ear.
Let but B——cH—n *Desdemona* play
And conscious TH——R D must resign to day;   40
Or *Lady Grace* with reading blind her eyes,
And Madam C——B—R tacitly complys.
Tho' last, not least in worth, let M——D come
To strike young M——n with grief and wonder dumb.
With such experienc'd forces take the field,   45
And make these antiquated tyrants yield.
Despotic arbitrary pow'r they claim:
But legal rule alone is all your aim.
Proud, insolent, and vain, applause they'd seize:
Whilst you endeavour modestly to please.   50
Go on, and prosper: to the ravish'd eye
May thy vast art new wondrous scenes supply:
And when thou hast art forc'd to quit the Stage;
Another RICH arise to please the age.

Dublin, Aug. 22. We are informed that some days ago a blast of whirlwind carried a great hay-cock of Mr. James Dunn, at the Cross-Gans in Castleknock, and Clerk of the said Parish, a great height into the air, where it continued, as it is said, above an hour, and at last fell entire, as it formerly stood, in a field of corn at a great distance from the place it was taken from. *P.*

Charlestown in Carolina, June 24. Wednesday night we had a violent storm of thunder and lightning, which did considerable damage in the house of Dr. Tho. Smith. in Broad street; having passed through most of the rooms, melted the blade of a sword in a scabbard, and the muzzle of a gun, and shattered the whole house in a terrible manner. *P.*

FOREIGN NEWS.

THURSDAY, *August* 24.

Yesterday arrived the Mail due from France.

Milan, Aug. 9. Above 8000 workmen are said to be actually employed in the new fortifications of Alexandria de la Paille in Savoy, and that by the Emperor's consent, by virtue of a treaty concluded between the Courts of Vienna and Sardinia. *D P.*

Petersburgh, July 30. N. S. By a Courier dispatched by the Czarina's Resident Neplies at Constantinople, we hear, that he met on this side of Adrianople several detachments of Albanian troops marching towards the Hellespont: That the Horse-tail was erected before the gates of the Seraglio the 6th inst. and war publickly proclaimed against the Sophi of Persia: That above 80,000 men of the European troops were going by the way of the black Sea: that the troops were still assembling in all parts of Asia, and that in 2 months at farthest the Grand Seignior proposed to have an army in Persia of 300,000 men. *D P.*

Paris, Aug. 30. The same day the Gens du Roy reported to the Chambers assembled, that the King would not hear them. Upon it was resolved, that they should return again to Marli, and humbly beseech his Majesty to hear his Parliament. *D P.*

FRIDAY, *Aug.* 25.

Yesterday arrived the Mail from Flanders.

Moscow, July 30. The Express dispatched from General Lewaschau at Derbent brings word, that all things go in favour of the Sophy; that all the Provinces of that great Kingdom have sent their Deputies to Ispahan, to thank his Majesty for the step he has taken, &c. for which reason they were unanimously resolved to exert themselves, and raise a sufficient number of horse and foot, to extend the limits of the kingdom as far as they were in the glorious reign of the Great Chack Abbas his Ancestor: 'tis added, that all the cities in Persia are in arms, and no person that is capable exempted from service. *D P.*

Hague, Aug. 5. N. S. The Duke of Ripperda (we hear) is to civilize the kingdom of Morocco, wherein he has made a considerable progress; and to give him a sort of authority, they talk of a match between him and the Queen-mother, who was a Christian slave, and some say a native of England: but be that as it will, she has a great influence over her son King Abdallah. If this match goes forward, the Duke will carry his point at Court, and do what good or harm he pleases there, the King being a very easy and good-natured Prince. *P.*

Milan, Aug. 6. We have received advice, that the great rains which fell last week, having swelled several streams and rivers to an extraordinary degree, which came down from the neighbouring mountains, had done an incre-

dible deal of damage in the country; that the borough of Gallerata, among others were entirely overflowed; that all the houses were borne down by the rapidity of the torrent; and that a great number of men, women and children were drowned, together with all the cattle that were in the meadows. They add, that the castle of the Marquis de Maganda was entirely destroyed by lightning. *C.*

Parma, Aug. 9. Bigotilius late Governor of Oran appears to be the same person who took Oran from the Spaniards in 1708, and was ever held in high esteem amongst the Moors. Many remarkable things are told of him, (now known under the name of Mustapha) in praise of his valour, good sense, and integrity; amongst others, that being bred a Mason in his youth, he has constantly employed his leisure hours that way, not to forget the condition from whence he rose. *D P.*

WEDNESDAY *Aug.* 30.

Ratisbon. Aug. 28. N. S. A Prussian officer, who went from hence some days ago with some recruits, passing thro' the territories of Bavaria, was attacked by a detachment of Bavarian troops, who fired upon him; but the Prussian officer nimbly repassing the Danube, had the good luck to escape, and returned hither.——We see here a Memorial which has been communicated to the publick dictature on the part of the Emigrants of Saltzburgh; whereby it appears, That those poor people are forced to leave their country, without giving them time to provide themselves with money or other necessaries for a journey: That they still suffer all manner of injuries: That in the very passports which are granted them, several of them are treated like rebels, and that in spite to their religion: That they are forbid to return into that country, upon pain of being used with the utmost severity: That several of their children are detained by force: That among others, a boy of 10 years of age, being locked up to prevent his going with his parents, jumped out of a window 3 stories high in the night, without coming to any harm, and overtook his parents at Augsburg: That several who have considerable estates were not permitted to carry any thing away with them: And that they had kept back 10 *per Cent.* of what the others brought away, &c. *C.*

Books and Pamphlets published from Aug. 19. to Aug. 30.

19. A Report from the Committee appointed to view the Cottonian Library, &c. Pr. 5 s.

The Cases of Polygamy, &c. Price 2 s. 6d.

22. Sermons on religious education of children. By P. Doddridge.

The natural probability of a lasting peace in Europe. P. 6d.

The eternal Obligation of natural Religion, or the foundation of morality of God and man. Price 6 d.

24. The antient Physician's legacy to his country. By THO. DOVER, M. B. Price stitch'd 5 s.

The Historical Register, No. LXVI.

25. A defence of Dr. Clarke's demonstrations of the being and attributes of God. Price 2 s.

A Sermon on the reasonableness of a quiet submission under afflictive dispensations of providence. Price 9 d.

26. The History of England, No. IV. Price 6 d. (containing 5 sheets.)

The true-born Englishman. A satire. Price 1 s.

Interest at one view calculated to a farthing, &c.

A vindication of the Gospel of S. Matthew, &c. By LEONARD TWELLS, Vicar of S. Mary's in Marlborough. Price 1 s. 6d.

28. An epistle from Mr. Savage to the R. Hon. Sir Rob. Walpole. Price 1 s.

A discourse on self-murder. Price 4 d.

Remarks on a sermon preached by the Rev. Mr. THO. MOLE, &c.

29. Advice of a mother to a son and daughter. Pr. 1 s.

Charity and sincerity defended. Price 1 s.

29. De morbo Gallico: a treatise of the French disease, &c. Price 1 s. 6d.

30. An historical, critical, geographical, chronological, and etymological Dictionary of the Holy Bible. In 3 Vol. folio.

Mr. Morgan's compleat History of the seat of the war in Africa, between the Spaniards and Algerines.

On Tuesday Stocks were

South Sea next Stock was 104 5 8ths, 104 3 qrs. 104 5 8ths, to 3 qrs. Books open. South Sea Annuity 111, 7 8ths, to 112. Bank 152 3 8ths. New Bank Circulation 5 l. 4 s. Premium. India 157 1 qr. 158, 157 3 qrs. 158 1 qr. 157 3 qrs. 158 1 qr. 157 1 qr. to 1 half. Three per Cent. Annuity 99 3 qrs. Royal Exchange Assurance 103. London Assurance 13 1 half to 5 8ths. York Buildings 5 3 qrs. to 6. African 38 English Copper 2 l. 2 s. Welch ditto 11. 15 s. South Sea Bonds 3 l. 15 s. Premium. India ditto 5 l. 16 s. ditto.

LONDON: Printed by J. HUGGONSON, in Bartholomew-Cloſe, for Capt. GULLIVER, near the Temple, where Letters and Advertiſements are taken in: As alſo at the Rainbow Coffee-Houſe in Cornhill, and John's Coffee-Houſe in Sheer-Lane, Temple-Bar. [Price Two Pence.]

THE GRUB-STREET JOURNAL, 140, p. 1

The Grub-ſtreet Journal.

Thurſday, *SEPTEMBER* 7, 1732.

O ſatisfy the importunity and expectation of ſeveral of our Correſpondents, who are apt to think themſelves neglected, if their pieces do not ſoon appear in our Paper, the following are here publiſhed together, tho' they have no relation to one another.

SIR,

YOUR ſo vigorouſly attacking the profane poetic rubbiſh, with which the Town has of late been ſo much peſtered, encourages me to deſire a place in your Paper for the following Ode. It was written by a young Gentleman of a private ſchool, not far from London, for an evening's exerciſe, juſt before his going for the Univerſity. That ſpirit of piety and devotion which runs through the whole, (a thing ſo rare in youth) would be a ſufficient plea in any leſs degenerate age for its publication ; and, were they not paſt conviction, muſt put thoſe Gentlemen to the bluſh, who have endeavoured by their late impious productions, (the Dramatic eſpecially) to make degeneracy itſelf degenerate.

Your conſtant reader, &c. M. B.

On Divine Poetry.

Poeta a natura ipſa valet, & mentis viribus excitatur, & quaſi divino quodam ſpiritu afflatur.
Cic. pro Arch. poeta.

1.
If nothing but celeſtial fire
Can the true Poet's breaſt inſpire,
And if the Muſe be heav'nly born ;
A ſubject ſtill he ought to chuſe
As heav'nly as his ſacred Muſe,
And make his theam his lines adorn.

2.
Ambitious Pegaſus wou'd fly
In tranſports wrapt above the ſky ;
But impious Poets clip his wings :
Their groveling fancy dreads ſuch heights,
They baſely check his daring flights,
And force him down to earthly things.

3.
Sublime the theam, ſublime the lays,
When in the great JEHOVAH's praiſe
We happily our breath imploy ;
When him who gave us breath we ſing,
Such ſonnets to his altar bring,
As vanquiſh'd death ſhall ne'er deſtroy.

4.
What ſhame the ſacred Nine to ſee
Diſgrac'd in CUPID's livery ?
Stars far outſhine bright CLOE's eyes :
Their God the roſe and lilly ſpeak,
And far excell the wanton's cheek ;
Which ſoon like them too fades and dies.

5.
No! Lord, thy works in ſolemn verſe
I moſt devoutly will rehearſe :
Thou ſpak'ſt the word, and all obey'd.
Let Nature then in praiſe conſpire,
All beings make one ſacred choir :
For him all things, which are, were made.

6.
Beneath the ſubject angels faint,
Nor can their hymns his glories paint,
Tho' they are plac'd ſo high above.
By us below are beſt expreſt
Th' ecſtatic tranſport of the bleſt,
When thee, dear Lord, we ſing and love.

7.
Sweet JESUS come ; my ſoul inſpire,
And touch my lips with hallow'd fire ;
Teach me thy wond'rous love to praiſe :
May glory round my temples ſhine,
And all my numbers, Lord, be thine ;
Let him who will enjoy the bays.

8.
Thus, happy in our ſacred mirth,
We may a heav'n enjoy on earth ;
Each lifening angel will rejoyce :
And God himſelf approve our ſong,
Till we amidſt th'angelic throng
With Seraphs ſhall unite our voice,

Mr. BAVIUS,

I Have been thinking whether this new method of printing lately ſet on foot, may not turn to the advantage of literature. It will not only lower the extravagant prices of Books, but perhaps in time we may ſee the Claſſics and other valuable Authors delivered from the bondage of incorrect editions, vile paper, and worſe types, to which the avarice of ſome Bookſellers have ſo long condemned them. — By this means alſo Authors of merit, who could not ſubmit to the oppreſſive meaſures of the Bookſellers, may find an opportunity of publiſhing their works, and meeting with a reward adequate to their labours. — On the other hand, haſty productions will find no encouragement. Bubbles will come to nothing before they can do any hurt ; and the generous Subſcriber avoid a great impoſition by the loſs of a few pence at moſt.

'Tis true, ſome Authors of theſe ſeem already to take advantage of the firſt run of the preſent humour : they are known by propoſals with glaring titles, big and general promiſes, without a plan, or ſometimes any determinate meaning. Amongſt the reſt, there is one ſtiled *The univerſal traveller, or a complete account of the moſt remarkable voyages and travels of the eminent men of our own or other nations, to the preſent time, &c.* Something ſeems to be promiſed here, but it is impoſſible to find out by the whole propoſal what the Author intends : in all likelihood he has not reſolved himſelf ; out of ſuch a title he has many ſubjects in his election. It may ſerve for a Hiſtory, a book of Geography, either by way of ſyſtem or dictionary ; the lives of the old Philoſophers, or modern Miſſionaries, a weekly medly, or any work wherein ſome account of voyages and countries may be introduced. It is a policy perhaps of the undertaker to tye himſelf to no ſubject yet, 'till he has tried what will be moſt agreeable to the public, or eaſy to himſelf. ——— All that can with certainty be inferred from the propoſal is, that it cannot be intended for a complete collection of voyages and travels, as has been inſinuated. For the work is ſpecified to be no more than an extract ; and beſides, 200 ſheets of paper, printed on a large character are to contain the whole : perhaps the Author's ſpecimen, when it is publiſhed, may give us ſome light into his ſcheme.

A complete collection of travels is a work which would well deſerve the encouragement of the public: nor does it ſeem impracticable to comprize the ſubſtance of all the valuable Authors on that ſubject within a reaſonable compaſs, by incorporating them according to the plan, which I have met with in an anonymous Author, publiſhed ſome time ago. But to perform ſuch a deſign in any tolerable degree, would require more than ordinary ſkill both in the hiſtory and geography of foreign Countries, with ſome knowledge of the principal languages ; the Authors ought to be carefully compared, their differences adjuſted, errors in orthography as well as facts corrected, and their chief deficiencies ſupplied : but all this is not to be done at a week's warning ; a much leſs taſk might be the buſineſs of many years. In ſhort, to be capable of ſuch an undertaking, a man ſhould have made it his particular ſtudy, and be provided of a large apparatus, before he ſits down to write ; and after all, he ſhould allow himſelf proper time for digeſting his materials.

What has been ſaid with regard to a collection of travels, will extend in proportion to all other compoſitions. A bare Tranſlator would have enough to do to keep up with the preſs in the way of publiſhing by weekly portions ; and to ſay the truth, it ſeems to be fit for none but Editors, who have all their copy finiſhed before-hand. However, it is in the power of theſe alſo to abuſe the public: to prevent which, a calculation might be made of the ſeveral rates of printed copy proportioned to the ſort of paper and print, ſize of page and letter, whereby the Subſcriber would know, upon ſight of the work, whether he ought to pay at the rate of two pence, three half-pence, a penny, or no more than a half-penny per ſheet. This, Mr. BAVIUS, may be the ſubject of another letter from
Your humble ſervant,
THE INSPECTOR.

SIR,

THE underwritten verſes are the laments of a true lover for the death of a Lady, who, as you will obſerve from them, had ſuffered in her character on his ac-

count. If Mr. BAVIUS thinks them worth a place in your Paper, your inſerting them will be very acceptable to
Your moſt humble ſervant,
PASTOR PLORANS.

In death's cold arms my fair ARDELIA lies.
Whom none could once behold without ſurprize ;
No more muſt my fond eyes ſurvey that face,
Whilſt raptures follow'd each reſiſtleſs grace.
Yet, faireſt of thy ſex, we ne'er ſhall part,
Fix'd is thy form for ever in my heart :
There ſhall thy lov'd idea ever reign,
And death but ſpeak my paſſion in my pain.

For oh ! how vainly ſhould I hope to find
So fair a body, and ſo bright a mind,
Where ev'ry charm with ev'ry vertue ſtrove,
Refin'd by friendſhip, and improv'd by love.
With thee, bright Maid, for ever muſt expire
Each ſoſter hope, and elegant deſire.

What tho' the buſy world, to ſcandal prone,
On thy fair name have foul reproaches thrown !
Think not, bright ſhade, that vulgar breath can move,
A ſoul like mine, inform'd with truth and love.
Let the mean cenſure blame the Lover's part,
I hug the dear remembrance in my heart ;
It ſtirs the grateful ardour of my breaſt,
And all thy gen'rous kindneſs ſtands confeſt.

Ye ven'mous tongues that would profane my Fair,
With ſcorn I give your malice to the air ;
Love ſtands the guardian of ARDELIA's fame:
Love joins with beauty to aſſert my flame.
But oh ! ye very few, who right can tell
What vaſt diſtreſs I feel, who love ſo well,
Bring each his cypreſs wreath; *with me bemoan,*
The charming dear ARDELIA *dead and gone :*
So may your flames more laſting union prove,
While my ſad ſhade bemoans my ſhort-liv'd Love.

A begging Epiſtle in rhime from a poor Poet.

SIR,

1.
YOUR friendſhip I court
For a timely ſupport ;
My guts are grown wond'rous limber :
My belly complains
Of the want of my brains,
Which us'd to ſupply it with timber.

2.
May I ſwing like a dog
If I have a hog,
A ſmelt, a George, or a teaſter :
But here am I pent
To keep a ſad lent,
Without any hopes of an Eaſter.

3.
I've ſent to my betters
Circular letters,
Of this my diſmal condition :
But you, Sir, I'm ſure
My diſtemper will cure ;
Or a halter muſt be the Phyſician.

4.
'Tis the firſt time that I,
E'er at Rayming did try :
In which if I had any Skill ;
In a more elegant Way,
As I ought I would ſay,
Your obliged Servant RA. ARGILL.

P.S.
I hope you'll excuſe,
My unpolite Muſe:
Did Bacchus my fancy inſpire,
Addreſs you I wou'd,
In Verſes as good,
As any of POPE or of PRIOR.

DOMESTIC NEWS.

C. *Courant.*	E P. *Evening Post.*
P. *Post Boy.*	S J. *S. James's Evening Post.*
D P. *Daily Post.*	WE. *Whitehall Evening P.*
D J. *Daily Journal.*	LE. *London Evening Post.*

Important Articles omitted in our last.

Next sunday evening the Oratory-Lecture will be new, and last near an hour, &c. *D J.* 24. --- We hear, the Lecture of the Oratory to-morrow at six in the evening will be new entirely, and last an hour, &c. *D J.* 26. *This latter* Puff, *tho' almost word for word the same with the former, is, in the manner of the* ORATORY, entirely new, by *having the word* entirely *inserted in it.*

Hyp-Oratorical Puffs and Advertisements in the month of August.

Hyp Advertisements, 8. Oratorical ditto, 4. In all 12.
— Hyp Puffs, 5. Oratorical ditto, 6. In all 11.
Increased in the Advertisements this month, 2. Increased in the Puffs, 2.

THURSDAY, *August* 31.

On tuesday last the Prince, Princess Royal, and Princess Emilia, went to the top of the monument, to take a view of the neighbouring country. *D P.* — — Neighbouring *to the* Monument.

On sunday last the Hon. Cha. Hervey, A.M. of Queen's College in Cambridge, 3d son of the R Hon. the E. of Bristol, was ordained a Deacon, at Bugden, by the very Rev the Bishop of Lincoln. *D J.*

Yesterday Capt. Purvis was unanimously elected an Elder Brother of Trinity-house, in the room of Sir Tho. Hardy. C. – Geo. Purvis, Esq; one of the Representatives in Parlament for Aldborough in Suffolk. *D J.*

We have an account from Preston in Lancashire, that a merry wedding was celebrated there a few days since, between 2 beggars, whose ages made 160 together; they were ushered from the Church to Walton, about a mile from that place, by about 30 of the same fraternity, most with crutches; among them were 7 Bag-pipers, and one who played on a bladder marine. A dinner was provided for the guests of roast mutton, with 30 pounds of potatoe and a large salmon, 30 pounds of cheese, and 8 pounds of butter for the 2d course, with bread in proportion, and a gallon of strong beer each; and 100 yards of ribbon were distributed in favours. The whole was carried on with a great deal of mirth and jollity, the cripples throwing away their crutches, 'till the beer got into their heads, when they went to fighting, but parted without further loss of limbs. The marriage was consummated in a barn, by the side of an hay-mow, which in the night fell on the new married couple, who calling out for assistance, a person went in, removed the hay, and took them out naked, and almost smothered. *D J.*

Yesterday se'nnight the Assizes ended at Gloucester, when Ely Hatton received sentence of death, for the murder of Tho. Turbevile. *DP. D J.*

Lady Harriot, wife to the R Hon. John E of Orrery, and youngest daughter to Geo. E. of Orkney, died a few days since of a mortification in her bowels, at his Lordships seat in the County of Cork in the Kingdom of Ireland. *L E.*

On tuesday one Oates, a Plyer for and Clerk to weddings at the Bull and Garter by the Fleet gate, was bound over to appear at the next Sessions, for hiring one John Funnell, a poor boy, for half a guinea, that sells fruit on Fleet-bridge, to personate one John Todd, and to marry a woman in his name, which he accordingly did; and the better to accomplish this piece of villainy, the said Oates provided a blind parson for that purpose. *S J.* —— *Our learned* Dr. T—d—l *says, it would have been more difficult to have* provided *one that* could see.

Yesterday being the day appointed for the Committee to meet, who were lately chose to inspect the affairs of the South Sea Company, a large room was provided for their reception, and only the 5 following Gentlemen were present, viz. Mr. Will. Colebrooke, Mr. Colborne, Mr. Henley, Mr. Hollingsworth, and Mr. Macky; which being two less than the number required to make a Committee, they could not proceed to business. *P.* —— We hear they adjourned *sine die. D J.* —— *I hope the* inspection *will not be* sine die.

The same day a fine spring wheel of curious workmanship, that lately came from Ireland, was presented to her Majesty; at which she was pleased to express great satisfaction. *C.* —— Dr. B. *by an easy mutation, for* spring wheel *reads* spinning wheel.

Lyme Regis, Aug. 28. John Rodbard, Esq; son in law to the Hon. Col. Henley, one of the Gentlemen Ushers of his Majesty's Privy Chamber) was this day elected Mayor. *DP.*

FRIDAY, *Sept.* 1.

Holland Wilson, Esq; is appointed by her Majesty Capt. Lieutenant of a Company in the regiment, commanded by Col. Peirce Kirke. *P.*

Yesterday the Rev Mr. Tho. Davis was presented by the R. Rev. the L. Bishop of S. David's, to the Vicarage of Llandyfriog in Cardiganshire. *C. P.*

We hear that Mr. Talbot, Brother to the Attorney General, will be made a Commissioner in the Salt Duty, in the room of Tho. Woodcock, Esq; deceased. *C.*

Last night was closed the Ballot taken at the York-buildings house, upon the question, Whether a Committee of inspection be now appointed or not? When there appeared for the question 142 votes, against it 346. *C. D J.* —— A Committee of superinspection *is more proper for great Companies than a* Committee of inspection.

We hear from Dunkirk, that on wednesday the 23d past, there was a most terrible storm of thunder and lightning, which untiled several houses, and did incredible damage to the Churches, the like not having been known in the memory of man. *D J.*

On wednesday night Mr. Tracy, son to the late Judge Tracy, who has been ill for a long time, with a violent pain in his stomach, having sent his man out on an errand, it is supposed fell a vomiting, and burst something within him; for when the servant return'd, he was found dead on the floor, and a thick clod of blood coming out of his mouth. *D P.*

Yesterday a Countryman had his pocket picked in Smithfield, of a leathern purse, in which were 4 broad pieces, 10 shillings, &c. upon missing it, he cry'd out he was robb'd, and challenging several people with the fact, occasion'd a great mob; so that he was oblig'd to make off. *P.*

The same day dy'd at her house in Salisbury-court, Mrs. Daffy, the preparer of the Elixir. *D J.*

SATURDAY, *Sept.* 2.

Yesterday at noon a General Council was held at Kensington, where the R Hon. the L. Chancellor assisted; at the breaking up of which a Messenger was sent to his Majesty at Hanover. *C*

Yesterday the Rev. Mr. Will. Parry was presented by the R Hon. the L. Chancellor to the Vicarage of Stangene, in Greenness, in the County of Salop. *P.* — Stinginess *in Divinity is, in the opinion of some, alias* Greediness; *and the one is sometimes a step to the other. Vide* Dissenters and discouragements, &c.

Yesterday at a Board of Admiralty their Lordships were pleased to appoint Capt. Symonds to the command of the Shark sloop, and Mr. Dennis a Lieutenant: And Mr. Slaughter to the command of one of the sloops building at Deptford. *C.* &c.

Mr Jones of Jesus College, Oxon, who formerly killed Mr. Price in a duel at Bath, and fled beyond sea, is now at Hanover, being admitted a Cadet in the Regiment commanded by the Prince of Orange, and designs to come over hither in his Majesty's retinue, to take his tryal for killing the said Gentleman. *D J.*

On thursday last died, at his house at Thistleworth, after a long illness Mr. Wilks, one of the masters of the old Play-house in Drury-lane. *P S J. WE.* —— This report is entirely false: he has been indisposed for a day or two at his house in Bow street. *LE.*

On friday last week, one Gadbury, a prisoner in the Fleet, being charg'd in execution with large sums, made his escape thence in a great chest, which was fetched away by 2 persons like seamen, who pretended they were to carry it on shipboard. *DP.* —— He did not escape in a chest. *DP.* 4.

We are informed that his Majesty designed to set out from Hanover as yesterday for Holland. *C.* As this day: *D P.* —— We hear he will not set out 'till a Messenger arrives at Hanover. *WE.* —— Yesterday morning about 5, the R. Hon. the Visc. Torrington sailed from Greenwich in the William and Mary yacht for Holland. *D J. P.* —— Yesterday a party of Life-guards marched into Kent and Essex to escort his Majesty. *D J.*

His Grace the D. of Bedford is relapsed at his house in Bloomsbury-square. *D J. WE.* ——— His Grace will imbark on board his Majesty's ship the Torrington. *C.*

We hear there are about 800 shares in the Charitable Corporation not claimed before the Commissioners, and that some of those that are claimed its thought will not be allowed. *LE.*

This day being the anniversary fast for the great fire, in the year 1666, when 13,200 houses were burnt in London, the same was observed in this city with great solemnity. *S J.* ——— *It should be* with usual solemnity.

On thursday dy'd, at his house at Thistleworth, after a long illness, Mr. Wilks, one of the Masters of the Old Play-house in Drury-lane. *S J. WE.* --- This report is entirely false: he has been indispos'd for a day or two at his house in Bow-street. *L E.*

MONDAY, *Sept.* 4.

According to our last advices from Hanover his Majesty had fixed his departure from thence for England, for this day se'nnight, the 11th instant. *P.*

On thursday a patent passed the Great Seal, to enable the Rev. Ric. Bundy, D. D. to be one of Prebendaries of Westminster.

On saturday in the evening Mr. Alderman Parsons, Alderman Salter, Alderman Champion, and several other worthy Gentlemen, [persons of distinction. *DP.*] landed at Dover from Paris, and last night arrived safe in town. *C.*

Last week the Hon. Ric. Arundell, Esq; Surveyor General of his Majesty's works, &c. was married to the Lady Susan Manners, sister to the Duke of Rutland. *DP.*

On friday dy'd at his seat at Enfield, Isaac Beddington, Esq; an eminent Turky Merchant, and Husband to that Company many years, &c. *C.*—For that Company. *DP.*

On saturday night dy'd Sir Edw. Becher, Knt. Alderman of Bishopsgate Ward within. *C. P.*

TUESDAY, *Sept.* 5.

Yesterday advice came that the R. Hon. the L. Torrington, on board the William and Mary yacht, was safe at an anchor at Gravesend; the wind blowing easterly. *C.*

We hear that Will. Kent, Esq; is made Architect to his Royal Highness the Prince of Wales. *D P.* —— The Hon. Miss Vane is gone to reside at the L. Baltimore's seat near Epsom in Surry for some time. *P.*

Yesterday the noted Moll Harvey was committed to the Gatehouse, for keeping a disorderly house in the Hay-market. *P. D J.* —— And also for insulting Justice Lambert, in the execution of his office. *D P.*

His Grace the D. of Montague's house in Great Russel-street, is taken for the Count of Monteio, his Catholic Majesty's Embassador to this Court, who is expected in 2 or 3 weeks. *P. D P.*

Norwich, Sept 2. Last tuesday came on the election of the other Sheriff of this city, when Mr. Balderstone was elected. The poll stood thus, Mr. Alderman Churchman 596, Mr. Barth. Balderstone 793.

Canterbury, Sept. 2. His Grace the L. Archbishop has chosen the Rev Mr. John Head, Vicar of Selinge, to be one of the 10 Vicars of this Diocese, who receive a yearly augmentation, according to Act of Parliament. —— The Rev. Will Egerton, L L. D. one of the Prebendaries of Christ Church, Canterbury, is presented by the R. Rev. the Dean and Chapter, to the Rectory of All Hallows in Lombard-street, London. *DP. D J.*

They write from the Devizes in Wiltshire, that on friday morning died, in the prime of life, the worthy Dr. Matthews, &c. *D J.* ——— On sunday evening, in his 80th year, Will. Taylor, Esq; Usher of the Long-room in the Custom-house, a patent-place, which he enjoyed many years. Sir John Norris has a grant of the *place*, which is worth at least 500l. per ann. *P. DP.*

Last saturday Tho. Merrick, Esq; was married to Miss Rebecca South, an agreeable young Lady of 12,000l. *S J.* —— Yesterday morning was married at Cripplegate, a man near 90 years of age to a widow of about 40. *S J. WE.* ——— Cripple-gate *was the properest place for such a marriage.*

On saturday evening were baptized in Barbican, 2 sons and one daughter, all born at one birth that morning about 7, and very likely to live. *S J. WE.*

On saturday last died John Sanby, Esq; chief Clerk under the R. Hon. Hen Pelham, Esq; Pay Master Gen. of his Majesty's forces. *S J.*

His Majesty's yacht the Carolina, in falling down the river, ran foul of a Collier, by which she received much damage. *S J.* ——— *I think the* Collier *rather* ran foul of *the* Carolina.

Norton in the Bishoprick of *Durham, Sept.* 1. In a piece of ground in this parish, call'd South Meadow, belonging to Mr. Kitching, they are now making the 2d crop of hay: it was eat bare 'till May last, according to the custom of this country, so that it will undoubtedly bear 2 crops every season. The like was never known in these parts before. I really believe there is 30 load on about 16 acres. *LE.*

Yesterday morning Pet. Buck, a prisoner in Newgate, threw a pot at his sister, who went to see him, and cut her nose off; she is dangerously ill of the same. *S J.* —— viz. the same nose.

WEDNESDAY, *Sept.* 6.

On sunday his Majesty's ship the Gibraltar and the Sea Nymph, with the R. Hon. the L. Baltimore and his Lady and family, sailed from Portsmouth with a fair wind for Maryland. *DP. C. P.*

Yesterday Rob. Godschall, Esq; Citizen and Ironmonger, was chosen Alderman of Bishopsgate Ward, in the room of Sir Edw. Becher, deceased. *DP.* —— Richard Godschall. *C,* —— An eminent Portugal Merchant. *DJ.* —— without any opposition *P.*

Barington in *Cambridgeshire, Aug.* 31. Yesterday about 12 at night, a fire broke out in the Parsonage barn belonging to —— Calverd, Esq; which intirely consumed the barn, and all the out-houses, with all the corn, &c. the Vicarage-house belonging to Trinisy College, with all the out-houses, barns, &c. were likewise consumed. The Parsonage-house stood on one side the Church, and the Vicarage house on the other, so that the Church was with

much difficulty faved ; and we may fay, without offence, that it never was in fo much danger. C.

Yefterday died Mrs. Williams, at her houfe near New Palace-yard, Welini. She had the care of his Majefty's mufick for many years, being a woman of great piety and charity. P. —— The fame day dy'd, in an advanced age, John Rufton, Efq; one of his Majefty's Juftices of the Peace for the City of Weftminfter, which commiffion he held near 40 years. C. —— upwards of 40 years. By his death a place of about 200 l. per ann. become vacant in the Exchequer, in the gift of the R. Hon. the E. of Halifax. D7. —— of 500 l. per ann. D7.

From the PEGASUS in Grub-ftreet.

Tho' we do not think it at all improper, that accounts of books which are foon to be publifhed fhould appear in News Papers ; yet we have frequently declared our intimated our averfion to all recommendatory accounts of them after publication, vulgarly called Puffs. Thefe are generally no other than impofitions on the Public, in order to promote the fale of pieces which have no run ; and as fuch we have often refufed to infert them, even upon advantageous offers. We hope therefore, that the Gentleman, who fent us one about a fortnight ago, will not take our refufal amifs. But if he do, we defire him to call to mind the obligations he layed upon him in two or three remarkable inftances ; and his own repeated promife of making us fome return, which he never yet performed.

The fame notion of Puffs will, we prefume, excufe us for having not publifhed fome pieces, in which the Authors have either artfully introduced quotations from book, or pamphlets little known in the world, or have referred the reader to them, as extraordinary performances.

The Letter figned PHILO GRUB was received ; and the contents fhall be concealed, and well confidered. To one part of them, however, it is neceffary to give this immediate anfwer. —— The Compofitor was ordered to print the two unpublifhed advertifements of Mr MECHELL, in order to a punctual performance of the agreement made with him, thro' unknown to our Printer, for the publication of three. But Mr. M. would not confent to it, without a promife, that his advertifements fhould be taken into our Paper, as often as he fhould think fit to fend them. This was a promife very unreafonably demanded, and not in the power either of our Compofitor, or of our Printer, to make : for we look upon ourfelves to be the fole judges, what advertifements fhall be either inferted, or excluded every week. Had Mr. M. agreed to the offer of our Printer; it is highly probable, his third advertifement would not have been his laft.

On the new Attorney General.

COME, Dunciad Authors, come to dinner all,
C————'s made Attorney General.
Think not his honour a mere Act of Grace ;
His noble talents juftly claim'd the place :
For all Attorney Generals, 'till of late,
Were ever fam'd for legal Billingfgate ;
And he that us'd the turn-coat Lord of Dawley
In the fame ftile that COKE of old did RAWLEY,
Goes to reftore, in Climes from Britain far,
The ancient elocution of the Bar.

FOREIGN NEWS.

THURSDAY, Auguft 31.

Extract of a letter from Oran. —— I believe it may be computed, that we have loft, what with the fword, what with ficknefs, from 6 to 8000 men. P.

Perpignan, Aug. 20. Yefterday was conducted into this town, in the Intendant's coach, his Excellency (as he is here called) the late Duke of Ormonde. He was received on our frontiers by the Count de Partons, Governor of Bellegarde, entertained at dinner at the houfe of the Intendant, and lay there ; but his coaches and equipage were fent forward. —— Montpelier, Aug. 25. On the 22d arrived here with a great retinue, the late Duke of Ormonde. He was received with all poffible marks of refpect and diftinction, and lodged in the Intendant's houfe, whither all perfons of diftinction went to pay him their compliments. The next night a Comedy was acted for his entertainment. LE.

FRIDAY, Sept. 1.

Yefterday arrived the Mail from France.

Paris, Sept. 6. On the 3d the Parliament arrived about 10 at Verfailles. The King came from Marly and held his bed of juftice ; and caufed to be enregifter'd the Declarations of the 3d and 18th : both which enrollments were figned by the Parliament, in prefence of all the

Princes of the blood, foreign Minifters, and Lords of the Court. At the end the King gave orders to his Parliament touching the execution of juftice in their refpective Chambers. C. &c. - - Mr. Conundrum afked, if this bed of juftice was a bed on which fhe ufed to fleep.

MONDAY, Sept. 4.

Yefterday arrived the Mail from France.

Paris, Sept 10. N.S. On the 4th the Parliament met, when it was refolved, That a verbal procefs fhould be taken of all that was faid and done, at the bottom of which fhould be added, That confidering the place where the feat of juftice was held, and the defect in not communication any of the matters to be tranfacted therein, th'y neither could, nor ought, nor intended to give their advice there. That as to the declaration of Aug. 18th, they fhall not ceafe to reprefent the impoffibility they lie under of executing it. And as for the repeated remonftrance concerning the return of the members abfent, the Chancers fhall continue affembled, till the King fhall be pleafed to give an anfwer to the faid remonftrances. C. &c. —— In the night between the 6th and 7th all the members of the Enquetes and Requetes received Lettres de cachet, ordering them into confinement, and allowing them but 24 hours to determine. C. 24 hours for their departure. D. D7.

Vienna, Aug. 27. The Imperial Minifters have given the Marq. Palavicini, the Genoefe Envoy, to underftand, that his principals would do well to releafe the 4 chiefs of the malecontents out of hand ; elfe his Imperial Majefty fhall take other meafures. D.P.

TUESDAY, Sept 5.

Yefterday arrived the Mail from Holland.

Rome, Aug 23. Card. Colcia was interrogated laft funday for the 4th time. D7. DP. —— The Englifh Gentleman imprifoned in the Caftle S. Angelo, at the requeft of the Chevalier de S George, is fet at liberty. P.

Hamburgh, Sept. 9. The Oftend fhip Svren, or Merman, is at laft arrived in the Elbe, under French colours from Cadiz. P.

Books and Pamphlets publifhed fince our laft.

31. Modern Hiftory, by Mr. Salmon. No. 101.

L'Avare : The Mifer : a Comedy in French and Englifh, tranflated by Mr Ozell. Pr. 1 s.

Sept. 2. The prefent ftate of Europe : for July.

The Gentleman's Magazine : for Auguft. No. 20.

The London Magazine : for Auguft.

A Letter from the Rev. Dr. Jofiah Woodward to the late Archbifhop of Canterbury, &c. Pr. 4 d.

4. The Comedian, or Philofophical Enquirer. No. 5.

The Political ftate of Great Britain : for Auguft.

5. Mr Winflow's Anatomy in Englifh : by G. Douglas, M. D.

Univerfal Hiftory : Numb. VI. Pr. 3 s. 6 d.

5. Count Piers's packet, &c. Pr. 1 s.

On Tuefday Stocks were

South Sea Stock was 104 7 8ths. South Sea Annuity 111 7 8ths, to 112. Bank 153. New Bank Circulation 4 l. 7 s. 6 d. Premium. India 157 1 qr. 157 3 qrs. 157 1 half, 157 3 qrs. Three per Cent. Annuity 99 7 8ths. to 100. Royal Exchange Affurance 105 to 106. London Affurance 13 5 8ths. York Buildings 5 7 8ths. African 38. English Copper 2 l. 2 s. Welch ditto 1 l. 15 s. South Sea Bonds 3 l. 18 s. Premium. India ditto 6 l. ditto.

ADVERTISEMENTS.

This Day is publifhed,

NUMBER VI. of

AN UNIVERSAL HISTORY, from the earlieft Account of Time to the prefent : Which comprifes not only the General Hiftory of the World, but alfo that of every particular Empire, Kingdom and State, from its firft Foundation to its Diffolution, or to the prefent Time ; with an exact Account of the Migrations and Conquefts of every People, the Succeffions and Reigns of their perfpective Princes, their Religions and Governments, Cuftoms, Learning, &c.

The whole immediately extracted from the Original Authors, and illuftrated with neceffary Maps, Cuts, Chronological and other Tables. To be continued.

Printed for J. Batley, in Pater-Nofter-Row ; E. Symon, overagainft the Royal-Exchange in Cornhil ; N. Prevoft, againft Southampton-Street in the Strand ; T. Ofborne, at Gray's-inn ; J. Crokatt, at the Golden Key in Fleet-Street ; and fold by T. Payne, at the Crown in Pater-Nofter-Row.

N. B. This Work has met with very favourable Reception ; and feveral learned Authors having pleas'd in their Writings, not only to refer to, and give it an extraordinary Character, but earneftly to defire a Completion of it : The Authors are determin'd to proceed with all Expedition, which a juft Execution of the Undertaking requires ; and they fo affure, that they are fo forward with their Copy, as to be able to publifh it regularly for the future.

NOTICE is hereby given, to all En-couragers of Mr. PARMER's

HISTORY of PRINTING,

That the Remainder of the 1ſt Vol. is now publiſhed, having been finiſhed from his Manuſcript ; and, containing Sixteen Sheets and Half, (ſeven Sheets and Half more than any of the former Numbers, ſold at 2 s. 6 d.) the Price is Four Shillings.

Sold by his Widow at his late Printing-Houſe in Bartholomew-Cloſe : Alſo by J. Roberts in Warwick-Lane, and by moſt Book-ſellers in Town and Country.

On Thurſday, Aug. 31. was publiſhed,

The COMEDIAN, *or Phiſophical En-quirer,* Numb. V. Auguſt. 1732.

CONTAINING, I. An Enquiry into the Im-mortality of the Soul, with a Confutation of the Doctrine of Immateriality, and an Examination into the Difference betwixt the Souls of Men and Beaſts.

II. A Letter to the Biſhop of Litchfield and Coventry concern-ing the Principles of the Quakers, and ſome late Charges againſt them.

III. Obſervations on Government, the Liberty of the Preſs, News-papers, and Party-writers.

IV. An Epiſtle to Mr. Ellys the Painter.

V. The Hiſtory of the Times, containing a Continuation of the Account of the Spaniſh Expedition in Barbary, of the French Par-liament, of the Inſurrection in Corſica, with Occurrences from South-Carolina, and London, with the Deaths and Characters of eminent Perſons.

Printed for J. Roberts, at the Oxford-Arms in Warwick-Lane. *(Price Six Pence.)*

Where may be had,

Number I. for *April.* II. for *May.* III. for *June.* IV. for *July.*

PROPOSALS
For Printing by SUBSCRIPTION,

THE HISTORY of the Grand Con-troverſy betwixt the Secular and Regular Clergy of the Church of Rome, from the Year 1621 to 1634, concerning the Uſurpation of RICHARD SMITH, Titular Biſhop of Chalcedon, who pretended to be ſole Ordinary Biſhop of all England and Scot-land. Wrote in Latin by the Preſident of the Engliſh Benedictine Monks, RUDESINOUS BARLO, and faithfully done into Engliſh from the Original, for the Entertainment of the Curious, eſpe-cially Divines and Lawyers, both Eccleſiaſtick and Civil, of what Religion ſoever.

With the Remonſtrances of the Roman Catholick Laity made to the ſaid Biſhop, and alſo to his Excellency Caroie Coloma, Embaſſador Extraordinary of the Moſt Catholick Majeſty, and to the Marquis Fontony, Embaſſador of the Moſt Chriſtian King, &c. taken alſo from the Latin Originals : All which Treatiſes have been hither-to ſupport, by the Papiſts, for Political Reaſons given therein.

As alſo the famous Bull of Pope URBAN VIII. called PLAN-TATA, neceſſary for the right Underſtanding of the Whole, which was never before any where printed.

To which will be added,

A LETTER concerning the Diſputes that have happen'd among the Benedictine Monks ſince the Year 1700 to this preſent Time : Shewing how even they themſelves have varied from their origi-nal Principles. By one who was a Member of that Body, and concerned therein.

By JOHN WILLIAMS.

PROPOSALS may be had of (and SUBSCRIPTIONS taken in for the Author by) W. Meadows, at the Angel, in Cornhill ; T. Aſtley, at the Roſe, and S. Auſten, at the Angel and Bible in St. Paul's Church-Yard ; C. Davis, Pater-Noſter-Row ; T. Wood-ward, at the Half-Moon, L. Gilliver, at Homer's Head, and J. Ste-ward, at the Hand and Star, between the Two Temple-Gates B. Motte, at the Middle Temple-Gate ; T. Worral, at Judge Coke's Head, H. Walthoe, next Door to the Rainbow Coffee-Houſe, W. Reaſon, in Flower-de-Luce-Court, J. Iſted, at the Golden-Ball, near Chancery-Lane, Fleet-Street ; F. Gyles; over-againſt Gray's-Inn-Gate, Holborn ; O. Payne, in Round-Court, and T. Game, at the Bible, by the New Church, in the Strand ; T. Green, Charing-Croſs ; J. Jackſon, in Pallmall ; J. Jolliffe, at the Bible, in St. James's-Street ; J. Brindley, at the King's Arms, and W. Shropſhire, oppoſite to the Duke of Grafton's, New Bond-Street ; and J. Stagg, weſtminſter, Bookſellers : J. Huggonſon, in Bartholomew-Cloſe, and T. Gover, by Fleet-Ditch, Black-Fryers, Printers.

Juſt imported, and ſold by JER. BATLEY, *at the Dove in Pater-Noſter-Row.*

HIſtoire des Papes depuis St. Pierre juſqu' à Benoît XIII. incluſivement en Deux Volumes 4to, à la Haye, chez Henri Scheurleer, 1732.

Lately publiſhed, and ſold by J. BATLEY,

Philoſophiæ Mathematica Newtonianæ Illuſtratæ. Tomi Duo. Quorum prior tradit Elementa Matheſeos ad comprehendendam demonſtrationem hujus Philoſophiæ ſcitu neceſſaria : Poſterior con-tinet 1) Definitiones & Leges motus generaliores; 2) Leges virium centripetarum & Theoriam attrachonis ſeu gravitationis corporum in ſe mutuo; 3) Mundi Syſtema.

A GEORGIO PETRO DOMCKIO.

On Saturday, Sept. 2, was publiſhed,
[Beautifully printed on a fine Paper.]

The LONDON MAGAZINE:
Or, GENTLEMAN's *Monthly Intelligencer.*

NUMB. V. For AUGUST, 1732.
To be Continued. *(Price Sixpence each Month.)*
CONTAINING,
(Greater Variety, and more in Quantity, than any MONTH-LY BOOK *extant.)*

I. A *View of the* WEEKLY ESSAYS, *viz.* Rea-ſons of the preſent want of Taſte ; Plan of Education for a young Prince ; Summum Bonum, or the chief Good of Man ; Preſcience and Free-Will ; Benevolence and publick Spirit ; Blef-ſings of Plenty ; Variety of Wit ; Royal Example ; Diſcourſe in Honour of the Queen ; Ethicks ; Divine Judgments of anſwering Books ; Slander ; Foppery in Dreſs ; Self-Murder ; antient Mytho-logy ; Animadverſions on Dr. Bentley's Milton.

II. POLITICAL Subjects, viz. Remarks on the natural Probability of a laſting Peace; Deſigns of the Truſtees for the Colony of Geo-gia ; a Royal Britiſh Fiſhery ; Reflections on Oſborne's Principles ; Craftſman's Manner of Writing ; Thoughts on King William ; Caſe of the Renuntiation of Gibraltar ; Juſtices of the Peace ; Se-cretaries of State and Meſſengers ; Atticus ; Minibus Capitolinus ; Anarchy, Tyranny, and Hereditary Right ; Political Pedantry ; Laws and Courts of Juſtice ; Dangers to Liberty ; 'of the Legi-ſlative and Executive Powers; Uſe of Faction, or the Good of ill Writers; Proceedings and Debates in Parliament; Account of Money diſpoſ'd of, &c.

III. POETRY : A new Simile for the Ladies ; the Merry Mo-narch ; the Roſe Bud, a Song ; a humorous Love-Letter ; Mock Heroes ; the Vicar's Race ; Epigrams.

IV. DOMESTICK Occurrences ; Promotions Eccleſiaſtical, Civil and Military ; Marriages and Births ; Deaths, &c.

V. FOREIGN AFFAIRS.

VI. Price of Goods, Grain, Stocks ; Monthly Bill of Mortality.

VII. A TABLE of Contents.

To which is added, a *Catalogue of Books and Pamphlets,* with their Prices, publiſhed by the Proprietors of the *Monthly Chronicle,* now diſcontinu'd.

MULTUM IN PARVO.

LONDON : Printed for C. Ackers in St. John-Street ; for J. Wil-ford, behind the Chapter-Houſe, near St. Paul's : And ſold by W. Meadows, T. Cox, W. Hinchliffe, H. Whitridge, R. Willock, and E. Nutt, in Cornhill ; J. Clarke in Duck-Lane ; T. Aſtley in St. Paul's Church-Yard ; A. Dodd without Temple-Bar ; J. Stagg in Weſtminſter-Hill ; J. Jackſon in Pall-Mall ; J. Jollyfe in St. James's-Street ; J. Brindley and W. Shropſhire in Bond-Street ; and J. Millan near the Admiralty-Office.

Where may be had the former Numbers.

Notice is hereby given, That

THE Great and Wonder-ful Cures daily performed by Dr. Bate-min's *Pectoral Drops,* in the following Diſtempers, have gain'd them ſo indiſpu-table a Character, that few Families who have ever heard, or experienc'd the Virtues thereof, care to be without them in their own Houſes, viz. the Gout, Rheumatiſm, Jaun-dice, Flux, Stone, Gravel, Aſthmas and Cholicks, of what Kind or Nature ſoever, whether proceeding from Wind, Co'd, or Hoſterick Affection. Beſides which, there is no Secret in the whole Art of Phyſick ſo ſurpriſing and (were it not under the Confirmation of continual Experience) almoſt incre-dible Effects in Colds, Agues, Fevers, and thoſe endemic Evils which appear in moſt Conſtitutions at Spring and Fall. The Price of each Bottle, in which are three moderate Doſes, is but one Shilling, and may (by Vertue of the King's Letters Patents granted to Benjamin Okell, and Company) be had at the Printing-Office, Bow-Church-Yard, Cheapſide, and no where elſe within three Quarters of a Mile from thence.

N. B. *A Book of the Virtues thereof, with Teſtimonies of ſome hun-dred Cures perform'd thereby, under the Hands of Perſons of known Worth and Credit, may be had gratis with the ſaid Bottles.*

Note alſo, *That Shopkeepers, &c. in any Town, where they are not already ſold, may be ſupply'd with the above Drops, (and good Allowance) to ſell again, by directing to Wm. Dicey, or Tho. Cobb and Company, at Dr. Bateman's Wholeſale Warehouſe in Bow Church-Yard, London.*

This Day is publiſhed,
Printed for J. Brotherton, at the Bible, next the Fleece Tavern in Cornhill,

AN Enquiry into the Origin of Honour, and the Uſefulneſs of Chriſtianity in War. By the Author of the FABLE of the BEES.
Where may be had,

1. A Letter to Dion, being an Anſwer to a Book call'd Alciphron, or the Minute Philoſopher.

2. The preſent State of Great Britain and Ireland, for the Year 1731.

3. Traditions of the Jews.

4. Dairy's Journal to Madagaſcar.

5. Religious Courtſhip.

6. Life of OLIVER CROMWELL, Lord Protector of the Common-wealth.

7. Receipts in Cookery and Surgery, by John Keetilby.

Saturday, Sep. 2. was publiſhed, Pr. 6d.
[Neatly Printed on a fine Paper.]

The GENTLEMAN's MAGAZINE:
Or, MONTHLY INTELLIGENCER.
NUMBER XX. for AUGUST, 1732.
CONTAINING,
[More in Quantity, and greater Variety, than any Book of the Kind and Price.]

I. Views of the WEEKLY ESSAYS, viz. De-generacy of Taſte ; Improvement of the Stage; Princely Education ; Poetry, Painting, Dancing ; Muſick and Hiſtory. Of Liberty and Preſcience ; Benevolence ; Engliſh Fiſhery ; Fops ; Cri-ticiſms : Summum Bonum, or Chief Good ; Divine Judgments; Royal Example.

II. Colony of Georgia, the Truſtees, Deſign of their Charter, and Account of Carolina ; Mr. Pury's Account of the Town to be built, his Propoſals to 400 Swiſs to go with him to build his Town of Purryſburg ; now firſt tranſlated from the French.

III. POLITICAL POINTS : Debates in Parliament concerning a ſtanding Army ; The Peace laſting ; queſtioned ; Partition-Trea-ty ; Pragmatic Sanction ; Trading Juſtices; Of Multiplicity of Laws the Evil ; Political Pedantry, and Honeſty ; Conſcience ; Steps to Tyranny ; State Principles, and Ethicks ; Uſe of Faction, and ill Writers ; Grants of Money for 1731 and 1732.

IV. POETRY, A Winter's Journey to preach ; Lady's Pattern ; the Merry Monarch ; Zoilus at Church ; Woman a Cloud ; and a Bliſs that will not tire ; The Queen's Hermitage ; Epigrams.

V. DOMESTIC OCCURRENCES, &c. Deaths, Births, Marri-ages ; Promotions, Prices of Goods, Bill of Mortality in London, &c.

VI. FOREIGN AFFAIRS.

VII. A Remarkable Trial of a Woman at Derby, &c. &c.

By SYLVANUS URBAN, Gent.

London : Printed, and ſold at St. John's Gate; by F. Jefferies in Ludgate-Street ; Mrs. Nutt, Mrs. Charlton, Mrs. Cook, in the Royal-Exchange; Mr. Batley in Pater-Noſter-Row ; Mr. Mid-winter, in St. Paul's Church-Yard ; A. Chapman, in Pall-Mall, Mrs. Dodd, and Mrs. Bickerton, without Temple-Bar ; Mr. Crichley, at Charing-Croſs ; Mr. Stagg, and Mr. King, in Weſtminſter-Hall ; Mr. Wil-liamſon in Holborn ; Mr. Montague, in Great Queen-Street; Mr. Harding, in St. Martin's-Lane.

Note, a few are printed on a fine Royal Paper, large Margin, for the Curious.

This Day is publiſhed,
For the Uſe of all private Families,

THE ancient PHYSICIAN'S LEGACY to his Country. Being what he has collected himſelf in Forty Nine Years Practice : Or, an Account of the ſeveral Diſeaſes incident to Mankind, deſcribed in ſo plain a Manner, that any Perſon may know the Nature of his own Diſeaſe. Together with the ſeveral Remedies for each Diſtemper, faithfully ſet down.

Homines ad Deos, nulla in re propriùs accedunt, quam ſalutem hominibus dando.

By THOMAS DOVER, M.B.

Printed for the Author : And ſold by A. Bettesworth and C. Hitch, in Pater-Noſter-Row ; W. Mears, at the Lamb in the Old Baily ; L. Gilliver, at Homer's Head over-againſt St. Dunſtan's Church, Fleet-Street ; and James Brotherton, at the Bible in Cornhill.

The Cœleſtial Anodyne Tincture: *Or,*
The Great Pain-Eaſing Medicine,

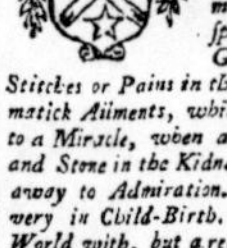

FAm'd and approv'd of for its wonderful and never-failing Succeſs, in giving immediate Eaſe and Relief in all manner of Pains, either inward or outward, and is its moſt certain Remedy in the World for a ſure and ſpeedy Cure of the Cholick, and expelling Wind, Gripes and Pains in the Stomach, the Pleuriſy, Stitches or Pains in the Side, Back, Loins, or any other Part ; Rheu-matick Ailments, which cauſe Pain and Dolor. It hath given Eaſe to a Miracle, when all other Remedies have fail'd. In the Gravel and Stone in the Kidneys, it gives Eaſe forthwith, and brings them away to Admiration. It alſo facilitates and comforts a ſpeedy De-livery in Child-Birth. 'Tis no Quack trifling Thing to impoſe on the World with, but a real and well-experienced Medicine, not acting by Stupefaction (as Opiates) but by a friendly, balſamick and ſubtile Na-ture, pacifying the moſt ſevere and terrible racking Pains, and car-ries off the Cauſe, not by purging, but by Tranſpiration, by Urine, or breaking Wind. No Family ought to be without it. In Womens di-ſorderly, it cures Swellings, Aches, Pains, Numbneſs, or Weakneſs of the Joints ; 'tis excellent for Cramps, and all other aged Infirmities, effecting Wonders in Agues, Fevers, Small-Pox, &c. No Family ought to be without it.

It is ſold only by Mr. PARKER, Printer, at his Houſe in Salis-bury-Court, or by ſuch Perſons as he ſhall depute, viz. at Mr. Parker's, a Printer, in Bull-Head Court in Jewin-Street; at the White Gelly-Pot, a Chandler's Shop in Bandy-Leg-Walk, South-wark, and at Mr. Neal's, a Toyſhop over-againſt the White Hart Inn in the Borough, at Eighteen Pence a Bottle, with printed Di-rections ; and if required, will be brought to any Perſon, by the Hawker who ſells his Penny-Poſt. Sealed as above.

LONDON : Printed by J. HUGGONSON, *in Bartholomew-Cloſe, for Capt.* GULLIVER, *near the* Temple, *where Letters and Advertiſements are taken in : As alſo at the* Rainbow Coffee-Houſe *in* Cornhill, *and* John's Coffee-Houſe *in* Sheer-Lane, Temple-Bar. [Price Two Pence.]

The Grub-ſtreet Journal.

NUMB. 141

Thurſday, SEPTEMBER 14, 1732.

THE many falſe and ſcandalous accounts given of us and of our Paper, from time to time, in an obſcure Weekly Journal, we have generally paſſed by with that ſilence and contempt which they deſerved. For tho' they were printed indeed, yet they could not properly be ſayed to be publiſhed, in a Paper, which ſo few perſons read: and we were unwilling to oblige our apoſtatizing brethren by a publication of their Journal in ours. But when two eminent members now of the Society in Drury-lane, which has of late flouriſhed ſo much by the productions of our Society, thought fit to attaque us with two letters, in ſo famous a Paper as the *Daily Poſt*, we thought ſo much deference due to the Writers, as to return a particular anſwer to each letter. The provocation we gave was by publiſhing two or three letters containing criticiſms upon ſome pieces lately acted at the Old Houſe. And tho' we declared, that we did not know from whom thoſe letters came, and that we would publiſh anſwers to them, if communicated to us; yet this gave no ſatisfaction, nor could ſoften the reſentment of the Poet and the Player. Had they ſhewn this reſentment only by endeavouring to ridicule us in a ludicrous way, we ſhould have defended ourſelves in no other: but as they have fallen upon us ſeriouſly and in earneſt, it is proper that our defence ſhould be made in the ſame manner.

In our 136th Journal an anſwer was publiſhed to every thing alleged againſt our Paper, in a letter written by Mr. C——, or Mr. F——, or by both conjointly, under the name of Mr. WM. HINT, and printed in the *Daily Poſt*, June 21. As we therein took no notice of a challenge from Mr. HINT to Mr. BAVIUS, with his acceptance of it, printed in the *Daily Poſt* of July 24. our ſilence was a tacit acknowledgment of Mr. C——'s ſuperiority in the ſtyle of the Bear-garden, to which it is generally ſayed he has had the honour to be Secretary for a conſiderable time. But Mr. HINT having in his letter of June 21. 'defied his antagoniſts to wreſt one word of 'the *Covent-Garden Tragedy* into an indecent meaning,' Mr. PUBLICUS produced ſeveral quotations from it; which it ſeemed impoſſible to *wreſt* into a *decent* one; and added ſome from the *Old Debauchees*, to ſhew the ſtupidity, profaneneſs, and abuſe of the Prieſthood in general, in that Farce. To this letter of PUBLICUS, printed in our 133d Journal, an anſwer appeared in the *Daily Poſt*, July 31, under the name of PHILALETHES; wherein the Author, inſtead of vindicating the paſſages quoted from the Farces, made a few exceptions againſt ſome parts of the letter, ſayed two or three general things in his own defence, and railed at the Grub-ſtreet Journal. PUBLICUS replied in our 136th, to that part of the letter which related to himſelf; in our 137th an attaque made upon us in the *Prolegomena* to the *Covent-Garden Tragedy* was repelled: and in our 138th a few more obſervations upon that and the *Old Debauchees* were made by PROSAICUS. This is a ſhort account of the whole controverſy; which we hope now intirely to finiſh by the following anſwer to that part of PHILALETHES's letter which is levelled againſt our Journal.

'I have read, with the deteſtation it deſerves, an in'famous Paper called *The Grub-ſtreet Journal:*' — *Infamous Paper* and *infamous libel* are terms of art, which controverſial writers on either ſide, generally apply to the productions of their antagoniſts. But why is *infamous* applied to this Paper? Has any whole order or profeſſion of men been abuſed in it? Has any truth of religion been ridiculed? Has profane ſwearing and curſing been exhibited as a genteel accompliſhment? Or has lewdneſs been propagated, by looſe deſcriptions and ſimiles, and vile repreſentations of the tranſactions in a bawdy-houſe? If it has been ſubſervient to any of theſe purpoſes, I muſt own it to be an *infamous Paper*, and to *deſerve* univerſal *deteſtation*.

'A Paper written by a ſet of obſcure ſcriblers,' —— Does PHILALETHES know the perſons by whom this *Paper is written?* If he does, how comes he to be at a loſs to *determine*, whether DRAMATICUS, PROSAICUS, PUBLICUS, &c. are the ſame? If he does not know them, why does he call them *obſcure ſcriblers*: ſince poſſibly ſome of them, under their real names, may be as famous authors, as Mr. F——G, or even Mr. C——R himſelf? He gives them this appellation therefore, either becauſe their real names are obſcured under feigned ones, or becauſe their writings, even under theſe, are obſcure, and little taken notice of by the world. If on the former account, his reaſon is too extenſive, and will include under the title of *obſcure ſcriblers* ſome of the moſt eminent writers of the preſent age, Mr. OSBORNE, Mr. WALSINGHAM, &c. and even PHILALETHES himſelf. If on the latter, he contradicts himſelf immediately by acknowledging the ſucceſs of the GRUBEANS, and pretending to account for it.

'In the true ſtyle and ſpirit of Billingſgate,' —— Tho' this Gentleman's great ſkill in *the ſtyle of Billingſgate* cannot be queſtioned, by any one who has read the quotations from his Farces, printed in our 117th, 132d, and 133d Journals, or who reads only this or his former letter; yet we have juſt reaſon to queſtion his integrity in doing us this honour; which we ſhall therefore decline, 'till he ſhall produce ſome paſſages from our lucubrations, to prove our title to it as clear and indiſputable, as we have proved his.

'Without either learning, wit, decency, or often com'mon ſenſe.' —— General aſſertions without particular proof are nothing at all to the purpoſe. Several inſtances of ignorance, ſtupidity, indecency, and nonſenſe, in the writings of this Gentleman, have been actually already given, to which many more may eaſily be added. When ſome of the ſame kind are produced from any pieces compoſed by any of our Society, it will be time enough either to acknowledge, or to refell the charge.

'And deſign'd to vilify and defame the writings of 'every Author, except a few, whoſe reputation is too 'well eſtabliſh'd for their attacks.' —— Since this Gentleman ſeems to be intirely ignorant of the chief deſign of our Paper, I will inform him in plain words: It is to ridicule and expoſe the writings of thoſe Authors, who, by their ignorance, or immorality, are continually endeavouring to debauch either the taſte, or the manners of perſons; and to cheat them of their money, which they imprudently part with, in exchange for ſuch corrupt traſh and vile trumpery, as was never permitted to be ſold publicly before in any other country in the world.

'The characters of whom they have, in the opinion of 'all wiſe men, blacken'd more with their applauſe, than 'they have the others with their cenſures.' —— By *all wiſe men* PHILALETHES means only thoſe of his own ſtandard of learning and wiſdom.

'The love of ſcandal is ſo general an appetite, that no 'one can wonder at the ſucceſs of any nonſenſe and ri'baldry which hath that to recommend it:' —— Here PHILALETHES owns the *ſucceſs* of our Paper, which his brother HINT, or rather he himſelf, under that name, ſeemed to call in queſtion. But he would do well to produce ſome inſtances of *nonſenſe and ribaldry*, from our writings, in return for thoſe many inſtances of both, which have been produced from his.

'To this all the infamous ſcriblers of the age owe a 'very comfortable maintenance;' —— Here PHILALETHES ſeems unmindful of his name, and is fallen (through inadvertency I hope) into two miſtakes. For it is certain, that *all the infamous ſcriblers of the age* have not *a very comfortable maintenance*; and that all thoſe who have, do not *owe* it to *the love of ſcandal*. I appeal to this Gentleman himſelf, whether he does not know ſome of his ſcribling brethren to be in a *very uncomfortable* condition; and whether, of thoſe who are in a *very comfortable* one, ſome do not owe it more to the love of ſomething elſe, than of ſcandal.

'And to this, and this only, the *Grub-ſtreet Journal* 'owes its being.' —— Tho', with the ſtricteſt truth and juſtice, I might here retort ſome of this Gentleman's fine language in this letter, and tell him, that this is *a moſt infamous lye*; yet I ſhall rather call it a miſtake, and attribute it to the miſinformation of ſome of our renegado members of this Gentleman's acquaintance. And as to the general objection of ſcandal and defamation, which theſe have ſo often made againſt our Journal, no other anſwer can be given to it but a direct denial. Let ſome inſtances be produced of our attempts to defame any truely great, or good men, or to expoſe any learned or unlearned perſons whatſoever, who have not by their writeings or actions given juſt cauſe of offence to the public. When ſuch inſtances are alleged, we ſhall either endeavour to clear ourſelves, or to make all the ſatisfaction in our power.

'I believe every man of good ſenſe and good nature 'hath view'd with abhorrence' [whoever hath not, he modeſtly *believes* wants both] 'the ſcandalous undeſerv'd 'attacks, which THEY have lately ſo often repeated on a 'Gentleman',—According to grammatical conſtruction, THEY ſhould refer to *all the infamous ſcriblers of the age*, who are the perſons ſpokn of laſt: but according to this Gentleman's *good ſenſe*, the authors of our Journal are to be underſtood. Whoſe *attacks* upon him are as certainly *ſcandalous*, if *undeſerved*, as they were juſtly deſerved, if drawn upon him by his *ſcandalous attacks* upon good ſenſe, good manners, and good men.

'To whom the Town hath owed ſo much diverſion, 'and to whoſe productions it has been ſo very favoura'ble': —— If the Town has been *ſo very favourable* to his productions, it hath not *owed* ſo much diverſion to him, their favour being always accompanied with ready money: and if they have payed him well for their *diverſion*, they cannot be ſayed to *owe* it to him.

'An attack which the favour of the Town, and the 'good reception he hath met with from the Players, hath 'drawn on him'.—— What motives induced DRAMATICUS, PROSAICUS, THEATRICUS, or PUBLICUS to *attack* this Gentleman, I know no more than he himſelf does, being as much in the dark as he is, as to their perſons. But this I can aſſure him, that neither of the motives aſſigned induced us to print their letters.

'This torrent of ribaldry hath come abroad under ſe'veral names'.—— I have conſulted my Brother BAILEY's *Etymological Dictionary* (which I would adviſe PHILALETHES likewiſe to conſult before he writes another letter,) and there I find under the word 'RIBALDRY [*Ribaude* F. a whore] Debauchery or obſcene talk. *Ital*'. Though I do not here intirely agree with my learned brother in every particular; yet I will venture to aſſert, that the moſt proper ſignification of *ribaldry* is *bawdry* or *obſcene talk*. And therefore I defy PHILALETHES to produce any other inſtances of *ribaldry* from the letters of DRAMATICUS, &c. than thoſe which have been quoted from the Farces againſt which they are written.

'I muſt tell our Critick, there is a vein of good hu'mour and pleaſantry which runs through all the works of 'this Author, and will make him and them amiable to a 'good-natured and ſenſible reader, when the low, ſpite'ful, falſe criticiſms of a *Grub-ſtreet Journal* will be for'gotten'. —— Since this Gentleman here tells what it is impoſſible for him to know, he is no more to be regarded than a common Fortune-teller. Let the *criticiſms* in the *Grub-ſtreet Journal* be not only as *ſpiteful*, but likewiſe as *low* and *falſe*, as he would have them thought; yet by venting his ſpite againſt the authors of the *Journal*, who did not write the *Criticiſms*, inſtead of vindicating his works againſt them, he has plainly ſhewn the world, that thoſe *Criticiſms* are too high, and too true, for him to anſwer.

BAVIUS.

On a Poet's pleading the example of CONGREVE, WYCHERLY, &c. for writeing of bawdry.

A Fop of old ambitious once to pay
His court, by mimicking his Prince's way,
Unable in his mind, or mien, to trace
His inward virtues, or external grace,
To imitate ſome little oddneſs try'd,
And held affectedly his head aſide.
The Monarch, vex'd at this fantaſtic Wight,
Set with one box of th'ear his block upright.
Thus modern Poetaſter fain would hit
The ſenſe of WYCHERLY, or CONGREVE's wit;
But finding ſoon his labour all in vain,
He imitates alone their ſmutty ſtrain.
O BAVIUS, may the ſtrokes thy hand diſpenſe,
Beat out the ribald thought, and beat in ſenſe.

MÆVIUS.

DOMESTIC NEWS.

C. *Courant.*	EP. *Evening Poſt.*
P. *Poſt-Boy.*	SJ. *S. James's Evening Poſt.*
DP. *Daily Poſt.*	WE. *Whitehall Evening P.*
DJ. *Daily Journal.*	LE. *London Evening Poſt.*

THURSDAY, *Sept.* 7.

Lincoln, Sept. 4. This day the King's plate of 100 guineas was run for by 5 horſes, and won by Mr. Griſewood's Cheſnut horſe. *DP.*

Yeſterday the 3 new ſloops, built in Deptford-yard, to cruiſe on the Iriſh coaſt, were launched. *DJ.* ——— The Hound, the Tryal, and the Cruizer. *C. P. DP.*

Laſt thurſday Benj. Bathurſt, Eſq; was (at Mitchel Dean in Glouceſterſhire) elected Verdurer of his Majeſty's foreſt of Dean, in the room of Raynon Jones, Eſq; deceaſed. *DP.* —— —— Norris, Eſq; is appointed Uſher of the Long-room in the Cuſtom-houſe, which place is worth upwards of 500 l. per ann. in the room of Will. Taylor, Eſq; deceaſed. *P.* —— John Norris, Eſq; eldeſt ſon to Sir John Norris, Knt. in purſuance of reverſionary grant. *SJ. LE.*

On tueſday dy'd at her houſe in Albemarle-ſtreet, the Hon. Mrs. Bennet, great Aunt to the R Hon. the E. of Saliſbury, &c. *DP.* Yeſterday the Lady Bennet, &c. *DJ.* —— The ſame day, about 9 in the morning dy'd at Mitcham in Surry, the Hon. Gen. Harvey, brother of Will. Harvey, Eſq; of Comb-Park. *C. P. DJ.* ——— Major-General Harvy. *DP.* —— The ſame day Will. Bridges of Nelmes, in Hornchurch pariſh, Eſq; was at the Veſtry there, and being a little faint, call'd for a glaſs of water, but before the taking of it dy'd. *LE.*

Yeſterday morning the body of a man well dreſs'd was found in a ditch in the fields near the half way houſe between Rotherhith and Deptford; he had a watch and and ſome money in his pocket, and is ſuppoſed to have been in liquor, and fell in by accident. *C. DP.*

On ſaturday the Aſſizes ended at Briſtol, when one man was capitally convicted, and Ric. Baggs, who aſſaulted a young man, with intent to commit ſodomy, was fined 200 l. order'd to ſtand in the pillory, and to be impriſon'd for 6 months. *DP.*

Laſt week Mr. Cheſelden, the Surgeon, ſet out for the academy at Paris, having received an invitation from the ſame *SJ.*

On tueſday night, a lodge of Free and accepted Maſons was held at the Royal Vineyard in S. James's Park, at which we hear a Clergyman of the Church of England, 2 diſſenting Miniſters, and 2 Officers of Dragoons were admitted into that Society. *LE.*

On tueſday laſt a waggon loaded with 3 pipes of wine and ſeveral paſſengers, was overturned by the horſes taking a flight, whereby one woman paſſenger was kill'd upon the ſpot, and others very much bruiſed. *SJ.*

We hear that 2 dozen of Engliſh maſtiffs have been commiſſion'd by the Spaniſh father of the redemption in Morocco, deſigned for a preſent to King Muley Abdallah; and that a butcher's lad is to go over with them to Morocco, at the allowance of 12 d. per day for himſelf, and the ſame for the maintenance of each dog. *LE.*

In Lemon-ſtreet laſt tueſday, it is ſaid,
Whilſt a keen Barber ſhav'd a perſon's head,
One jogg'd his elbow coming up too cloſe;
Down ſlipp'd the razor, and ſhav'd off his noſe. *SJ.*

FRIDAY, *Sept.* 8.

Yeſterday the Veſtry of S. Martin's in the fields made choice of Mr. Ric. Downs, Hoſier to the young Princeſſes, who formerly kept a ſhop in the Strand, to be Clerk and Sexton of the ſaid pariſh, a place worth about 200 l. per ann. in the room of Mr. Young deceas'd. *DP.*

Early yeſterday morning a quarrel happened in the Mint, Southwark, between a man and his wife, and his wife's brother; in the fray the huſband received a wound in the body with a penknife, that he died on the ſpot; and yeſterday the woman and her brother were committed to the new goal by Sir John Lade, Bar. *C.* —— All being much in liquor. *DP.*

Cambridge, Sept. 4. Yeſterday a ſtack of hay taking fire at a farm of —— Pemberton, Eſq; of Trumpington, burnt all the barns and out-houſes, &c. the loſs is computed at 1500 l. *C.*

The Lecture of the Oratory on ſunday evening next, we hear will be new, and laſt an hour, &c. Proof that ſpiritual pigs are carnal, and not jure divino, &c. *DJ.*

The Hyp Orats of old, who were uſed to ſlam well,
Would ſtrain at a gnat, and ſwallow a camel:
Our modern Hyp-Orat in the ſame track does jog,
Scruples taking a *pig*, and yet ſeizes a *hog*.

SATURDAY, *Sept.* 9.

Yeſterday at a General Court of the South Sea Company it being reported, that ſeveral Gentlemen of the Committee for inſpecting the Company's accounts had declined acting, and that no more than 5 had ever met, whereas 7 were requiſite to make a Quorum; it was reſolved that the Quorum be reduced to 5. —— A ſtate of the bonds was then read and delivered to the Court, wherein it appeared, that upwards of 700,000 l. had been paid off, and 200,000 l. were not brought in, but that when they were would be paid. *DJ.*

Yeſterday the R. Hon. the L. Mayor, &c. preceded by the city muſick, went with the uſual ſtate and proclaimed the Fair of Southwark, and afterwards his Lordſhip was entertained in a very elegant manner at dinner by the Bridge-maſters, at the Bridge-houſe. *C. DP.*

Yeſterday at the Old Bailey was try'd Will. Holmes, for robbing Barth. Harnet, an Iriſhman. The proſecutor ſwore, that on Jul. 19th, about 8 at night, he met the priſoner at the Iron-gate near the Tower, of whom he enquired the way to Biſhopſgate-ſtreet: the priſoner offered to ſhew him, and carried him through many ſtreets and allies into Moorfields; when giving a whiſtle, an accomplice came up, clapt his piſtol to his breaſt, and demanded his money, which he gave him, being 5 s. 9 d. Afterwards they took one of his buckles out of his ſhoes, and were about to take the other, when hearing people, they made off. The next night the proſecutor with a Conſtable and another man, took the priſoner at the ring in Moorfields: which man ſwore, that the proſecutor told him that the priſoner had the buckle upon him. Accordingly the buckle was found upon him, and he was committed to Newgate. Five evidences ſwore, that on Jul. 19, the priſoner was at ſupper at his brother in law's from 8 to 11. It appearing to be a villainous proſecution, the Jury brought him in, *not guilty*, and the Court diſcharg'd him immediately, without paying any fees: directing the priſoner to proceed againſt the proſecutor for wilful and corrupt perjury, and ordering him into the cuſtody of the Keeper of Newgate. *C.* —— The irons were knocked off from the priſoner, and put on his proſecutor. *DJ.*

On wedneſday laſt, died, at his ſeat at Haſlemere in Surrey, Will. Broughton, Eſq; *C.* —— And on thurſday, at his houſe at Bethnal Green, —— Okey, Eſq; *C. DP.*

Horatio Walpole, Eſq; is ill of a high fever at his lodgings at Kenſington. *DP. WE. LE.* —— The Hon. Horatio Walpole, Eſq; is in good health, and has not been ill. *C.* 11.

On thurſday at 6 in the evening 2 Gentlemen on horſeback, and a Lady in a chaiſe, were robb'd by one highwayman and one footpad, on the road near Black-health leading to Charlton. The highwayman ſtopt the chaiſe, and one of the Gentlemen turning back, he with the aſſiſtance of the footpad, robb'd him and Lady of a gold watch and ſome money. The other Gentleman ſpurring his horſe to the aſſiſtance of the Lady and his friend, was knock'd off his horſe by the footpad, who mounted the ſame, and made off. *SJ.*

On wedneſday as the Canterbury coach,
At night did tow'rds London Town approach,
In which ſix Gentlemen with ſwords did ride,
And eke two braces of piſtols beſide;
Two highwaymen them robb'd like fearful Ninnies,
Of watches five, and alſo fifty guineas. *SJ.*

MONDAY, *Sept.* 11.

Laſt night the new born ſon and heir of his Grace the Duke of Kent was baptized by the name of George: their Majeſties, his Royal Highneſs the Prince, and the Princeſs Royal ſtood Godfathers and Godmothers by proxy, &c. *C. P. DJ.*

Peregrine Fury, Eſq; of the War Office, is appointed to ſucceed Hatch Moody, Eſq; as one of the Clerks in the Pay-Maſter General's Office, who was preferred to the place of Accomptant General, in the room of Rob. Sambre, Eſq; deceaſed. *P.* —— Squire Fury *ſeems to be the propereſt perſon* to ſucceed Squire Moody, in the War Office.

Mr. Jonathan Waller, jun. Alderman of Northampton, will ſucced Tho. Railton, Eſq lately deceaſed, as Clerk in the Examiner's Office in the Exchequer, a place worth upwards of 200 l. per ann. *DJ.* ——— Is appointed to ſucceed. *P.*

Sir Rob. Sutton, Knight of the Bath, Sir Archibald Grant, Bar. Dennis Bond, Will. Burroughs, Eſqs; Mr. Ric. Woolley, and Mr. Tho. Warren, are preparing inventories of all and ſingular their lands, tenements, hereditaments, of their real and perſonal eſtates, to be delivered to the Barons of the Exchequer before the 29th inſt. purſuant to a late Act of Parliament. *P.* —— *One would be apt to infer from this article, that* lands, tenements, hereditaments, *are neither* real *nor* perſonal eſtates.

We hear from Birmingham in Warwickſhire, that a certain tradeſman's wife of that place dying on a tueſday, her huſband buried her on the wedneſday, married again on the thurſday, his new wife was brought to bed on friday, and he hanged himſelf on the ſaturday. A rare week's work. —— How happy a theme for the modern *drama! Tragico-comical*, and *Comico tragical*, following cloſe upon the heels of one another! Pity it were that the three *ſacred Unities* muſt be broke to repreſent it in one night! But they may eaſily be as much reſpected here as in Shakeſpear's Henry IV. *C.*

On ſaturday laſt dy'd at his lodge at Swinley in Windſor foreſt, Francis Negus, Eſq; of Dallingoe in Suffolk, Eſq; Repreſentative in Parliament for the Town of Ipſwich, Avener and Clerk Martial to his Majeſty, Maſter of his Majeſty's buckhounds, Ranger of Swinly chace, Lieutenant and Deputy Warden of Windſor foreſt, and one of the Commiſſioners of the Lieutenancy for the County of Middleſex and liberty of Weſtminſter. He is ſucceeded as Ranger of Swinley chace by his only ſon, who had a reverſion of it ſome years ago. *DP.* Of a lethargy. *DJ.*

Yeſterday morn, we hear, in Stepney ground,
Call'd fields, the body of a man was found,
Cut was his throat, and almoſt naked ſtript,
(So ſays my Author, but I think he ſlipt)
By which it is believed, and well may be,
That baſely robb'd and murdered was he. *DP.*

TUESDAY, *Sept.* 12.

Laſt week Mr. How of New Windſor, who had occaſionally officiated in his Majeſty's free Chapel of S. George, was ſworn one of the Gentlemen of the chapel Royal, in the room of the late Sub-Dean Aſpinwall, who held that, together with his other Eccleſiaſtical employments, to the day of his death. *DP.*

On friday the workmen began to meaſure out the piece of ground and dig a foundation for a vault at Marybone, for a burial ground belonging to the new chapel there, which the Earl of Oxford made a preſent of for that purpoſe. *P.*

Yeſterday the Seſſions ended at the Old Baily; when 19 perſons received ſentence of death; 2 were burnt in the hand, 22 ordered for tranſportation, and 3 to be whipt. *C. DP.* ——— 1 was burnt in the hand, and 4 ordered to be whipt. *P.* —— About 30 ordered for tranſportation. *P. DJ.*

Yeſterday John Ward of Hackney, Eſq; ſurrender'd himſelf to the Commiſſioners of Bankruptcy, who were ſitting at Guildhall, in order to give an account of his eſtate and effects. *DP.*

A few days ſince Brigadier General Ruſſel was married to Mrs. Franklin, Relect of Dr Franklin. *C.* —— The Hon. General Ruſſell, to Mrs. Frankland. *P.*

On wedneſday dy'd at Norwich, Henry Bedingfield, Eſq; a youth of about 9 years of age, eldeſt ſon of Sir Hen. Bedingfield of Oxburgh in Norfolk, Bar. *DP.* — This family has enjoy'd the honour of knighthood above 700 years: they have been either Knights or Baronets by the name of Henry, ever ſince the reign of Queen Mary. *DP.* —— On ſaturday died at Kenſington Tho. Sutton, Eſq; *C. DJ.*

Laſt night the corpſe of Tho. Railton, Eſq; was interr'd in S. Margaret's Church, Weſtminſter, in great pomp and ſolemnity. *DJ. WE.* —— This morning at 3 was privately interr'd, purſuant to his requeſt. *SJ. LE.*

A ſoldier at Dublin, condemn'd to be whipt,
Took brandy and gun-powder e'er he was ſtript,
To make him inſenſible of the ſmart pain:
He was ſo: for he dy'd, by gun-powder ſlain. *SJ.*

WEDNESDAY, *Sept.* 13.

Yeſterday ſeveral ſervants belonging to the R. Hon. the L. Harrington, arrived here from Holland; by whom we learn, that his Majeſty was expected in Holland as this day; and that he would immediately embarque on board the Carolina yacht. *P.*

John Ward, Eſq; late of Hackney, was under the examination of the Commiſſioners of Bankruptcy on monday from 3 in the afternoon 'till 3 the next morning; and was by them committed a priſoner to the Fleet. *C. DP.*

Yeſterday Sam. Kent, Eſq; late High Sheriff of the County of Surrey, ſet out for Ipſwich, to offer himſelf as a Candidate to repreſent that town in Parliament, in the room of the Hon. Francis Negus, Eſq; deceaſed. *DJ.*

Two High Dutch Jews, who lately took bills at Amſterdam on London, to the amount of 2180 l. retired from thence without paying the value of them; and we hear the moſt, if not all, were accepted, before the manner by which they were obtained, was known to the acceptors. *DJ.*

The latter end of laſt week, the Rev. Dr. John Wilcox was collated to one of the Prebends of the Cathedral Church of S. Paul's. *P.*

On ſunday laſt died at Camberwell, aged about 83, Capt. Ric. Diamond, who was Commander of the firſt ſhip which arrived in Carolina from London. —— Yeſterday died at her ſon's in Sherbourn-lane, Mrs. Suſ. Behrens, a native of the Palatinate (but of Jewiſh parents) aged 106. Her mother lived to 108 years, and her ſon is now 74. *DJ.*

At Mancheſter races the thirty pound purſe
Was won by Mr. Watkin Williams Wynne's bay horſe. *DP.*
The rhime I muſt acknowledge is not very pat:
But the truth and importance makes amends for that.

From the PEGASUS *in Grub-ſtreet.*

The *Regiſter* of *Grub-ſtreet* is hereby forbidden to reprint any more of the verſes which have been publiſhed in this *Journal*, unleſs he gets them illuſtrated with annotations. *The Epiſtle from* ROBIN *the Butler to* KITTY *the Cooks daughter*, which he printed in his laſt, as a new piece, was publiſhed in our 83d *Journal, Aug.* 5, 1731. He might well fall his Journal to three half pence, when he barely tranſcribes much the greateſt part of his copy from other Papers, and that without mentioning one.

Verſes occaſioned by the late Advertiſements from Drury-lane and Smithfield, concerning the acting of the ſame piece of MOLIERE, *Le Medecin malgre ſui*, under the different titles of the *Mock Doctor*, and the *Forc'd Phyſician*.

By ſome I'm told, *Mock Doctor* cannot be
A verſion juſt of *Medicin malgré lui*.
They ſay the *Forc'd Phyſician* is much patter,
Tho' Drury gave the firſt, Smithfield the latter.
Nor is it ſtrange, one Play'r ſhould ſhade his brother,
Or Smithfield F—— G ſhine beyond the other:
For Grub-ſtreet ſtands, of modern Wit the bane,
To Smithfield nearer than to Drury-lane.

POPPY.

FOREIGN NEWS.

THURSDAY, *Sept.* 7.

Yeſterday arrived the Mail from France.

Paris, Sept. 13. N. S. All the Preſidents and Counſellors of the Chambers of the *Enquetes* and *Requetes* of the *Palais*, to the number of 142, who received *lettres de cachet* in the night between the 6th and 7th ſet out within the 24 hours allowed them, for the reſpective places of their exile. ——— In the night between the 8th and 9th, each Member of the Great Chamber likewiſe received a letter *de cachet*, ordering them to go the next day to the *Palais*, and ſign a Commiſſion for eſtabliſhing a Chamber of vacations; and they went accordingly, and nominated the whole Great Chamber. *C.* &c.

Petersbourgh, Aug. 13. The new manufactory new ſettled at Moſcow, ſucceeds to admiration, ſo that 'tis thought a prohibition will be iſſued next year, from the wear of foreign cloth. *D P.*

MONDAY, *Sept.* 11.

On ſaturday arrived the Mail from Holland, *and yeſterday thoſe from* France *and* Flanders.

Hamburgh, Sept. 12. N. S. There has been a clean piece of legerdemain played here. A ſhip under French colours came into the Elbe ſome days ago, but did not care to paſs by Staden, becauſe it was given out that ſhe was the Syren, an Eaſt-India ſhip belonging to the Oſtend Company. However by the blowing of ſome good blaſt, this veſſel was metamorphoſed into the good French ſhip named the Mary Armande, juſt come from Cadiz, with part of the cargo of the Syren, or Phœnix, or ſome other Oſtend ſhip, which ſhe is actually unloading here. *P.*

Paris, Sept. 17. N. S. The laſt letters from Seville inform us, that one Jacob, an Engineer, and natural ſon to the Duke de Ripperda, who was ſeized ſome time ago at Ceuta, whither he went to take a plan of that place, and to debauch ſome Officers of the Garriſon, for which purpoſe he carried jewels with him to a conſiderable value, having been put to the rack, confeſſed all he knew of the matter, and declared, that it was owing to the intrigues of a certain Court, that the Emperor of Morocco had reſolved to undertake the ſiege of Centa. *C.* &c. ——— The Count de Montijo, Ambaſſador Extraordinary from the King of Spain to the Court of England arrived here the 13th with his Lady; he has ſent ſome of his domeſticks by ſea to London, but 'tis not believed he will go thither very ſoon. *C. P. D P.*

TUESDAY, *Sept.* 12.

Duſſeldorp, Sept. 12. We are aſſured from the frontiers, that about 6000 French troops are arrived near Thionville, a like number is actually marching to the frontiers of Bar, and that the garriſon of Landau marched out the 27th to join the troops on the Sambre. *D P.*

WEDNESDAY, *Sept.* 13.

Paris, Sept. 12. We have now the favour of Mr. Thompſon's company, a Gentleman of *charitable* memory, who was lately caſt out of the territories of the *Church*. He keeps himſelf as yet very private, ſees but few friends, to whom he complains much of the *protection* and *encouragement* found at Rome. For ſix days, he ſays, he was depoſited in a dungeon, and the otherwiſe rigorous confinement he ſuffered, brought on him a violent fit of ſickneſs, but hopes now to be in a way to do well. An agent from his acquaintance in London has juſt ſpoke with him, who had been alſo upon an Embaſſy 15 days before in Scotland. He turns poſt for England to morrow; but Mr. Thompſon, he purpoſes, as far as we can hear, to ſtay ſome time longer abroad, for the benefit of his recovery. — By letters from Rome, of the 27th of Auguſt, we learn that certain Engliſh Gentlemen, and with them two Ladies, arrived there ſome days before, and are already preparing to depart. It was ſuppoſed, that one among them had been ſent by another certain perſon, not proper to be named, to ſpeak with Mr. Thompſon; but he was gone for France; ſo if that was their errand, loſt is their labour. But perhaps he may be viſible at their return home. Thompſon in his ſickneſs told the Phyſician that attended him in the Caſtle of S. Angelo, that he had cleared his breaſt of that iniquitous affair; therefore we may expect in due time to ſee ſome ſecrets brought into light, that now lie in a little ſhade. *P.*

Books and Pamphlets publiſhed ſince our laſt.

7. Miſcell. Obſervations on Authors, No. 21. Pr. 6d.
The Devil of a Duke: a ballad Opera. Pr. 6d.
8. A letter to the Rector of Fryerning, &c. Pr. 6d.
A ſelect Collection of Moliere's Comedies, Vol. 5th.
The great tribunal: an Aſſize Sermon at Northampton, Aug. 2 By Ric. Grey, D. D.
9. The preſent State of the Republick of letters, for Auguſt.
12. Caſtle-Howard: a Poem. Pr 1 s.
A ſecond defence of Dr. Clarke's Demonſtration of the being and attributes of God, &c.
13. The Beau Ideal: tranſlated from the French.
The hiſtory of the Popes; from the French, No I.

On Tueſday Stocks were

South Sea Stock was 104 7 8ths to 105. South Sea Annuity 112 1 qr. to 38ths. Bank 152 3 qrs. for the Opening. Bank Circulation 4 l. 10 s. Premium. India 157, 157 1 qr. 157, 157 1 qr. Three per Cent. Annuity 99 7 8ths. Royal Exchange Aſſurance 105. London Aſſurance 13 5 8ths. York Buildings 6 1 8th, to 1 qr. African 38. Engliſh Copper 2 l. 2 s. Welch ditto 1 l. 15 s. South Sea Bonds 3 l. 14 s. to 15 s. Premium. India ditto 5 l. 16 s. to 17 s. ditto.

ADVERTISEMENTS.

Juſt publiſhed,

The GREAT TRIBUNAL.

A SERMON preached at the Aſſizes held at Northampton on Auguſt 2, 1732. Before the Honourable the Lord Chief Juſtice Eyre, and the Honourable Mr. Juſtice Price.

By RICHARD GREY, D. D.

Rector of Hinton in Northamptonſhire.

Publiſhed at the Requeſt of the High-Sheriff and Gentlemen of the Grand Jury.

Printed for C. King, in Weſtminſter-Hall; J. Batley at the Dove in Pater-Noſter-Row; J. Fowler, Bookſeller in Northampton; and J. Wilmot of Oxford.

Juſt publiſhed

With a handſome Frontiſpiece,

THE BLASING COMET; the MAD LOVER: Or, the BEAUTIES of the POETS. A Play. As it is acted at the New Theatre in the Hay-Market. Mr. JOHNSON, Author of HURLOTHRUMBO.

Sold by John Oſborn, at the Dock-Head, near Horſley-down; and by the Bookſellers of London and Weſtminſter; price 6 d. With Variety of other Plays and Novels, at the ſame Price.

Where may be had, in Octavo,

The Fortunate Miſtreſs	Glanville on Witches
The Life of Col. Jack	Wilſon's Chymiſtry
Mandey's Mathematicks	Daniel's Hiſt. of France, 5 V.
A Voyage round the World	Bradley's New Improvements in Husbandry and Gardening
Youth's Emblems, with Cuts	His General Treatiſe of Husbandry.
Hartcliffe's Moral Virtues	
Mandeville's Travels	

The following in Twelves,

John Gulliver, 2 V.	Creech's Horace, Latin and Engliſh, 2 V.
Perſian and Turkiſh Tales, 2 V.	Chineſe Tales, 2 V.

On the 1ſt of September was publiſhed,

The POLITICAL STATE OF GREAT BRITAIN

For the Month of July, 1732.

Containing in particular,

I. PRoceedings as to the Diſpoſal of the Keeper of Newgate's Place. —— II. Affairs of the York-Buildings Company.— III. Proclamation againſt Foreign Eaſt-India Companies. — IV. Parade of the Royal Archers at Edinburgh. — V. Aſſociation againſt Smuggling in Ireland. —— VI. Meaſures taken againſt the Spaniards in the Weſt-Indies. —— VII. Account of the Company for ſettling the Colony of Georgia. —— VIII. Journal of the Proceedings and Debates of laſt Seſſion of Parliament. Containing,

1. Sir Tho. Lombe's Petition, with ſeveral Speeches for and againſt it. —— 2. Motion as to Chelſea Hoſpital. —— 3. Mr. P——y's Speech thereupon. ——— 4. Sir W——m S——d's Speech. —— 5. Sir J——n R——t's Speech. ——— 6. Mr. P——m's Speech. ——— 7. Sir R——t W——'s Speech. ——— 8. Petition of the Charitable Corporation. ——— 9. Several Speeches, and Diviſion thereupon. ——— 10. Repreſentation from the Commiſſioners for Trade relating to our Settlements in the Weſt-Indies.

IX. Meaſures taken as to the Dutch Ship lately ſeized at Oſtend. —— X. Cargoes of the Dutch Eaſt-India Ships lately arrived. —— XI. Cargoes of French Eaſt-India Ships lately arrived —— XII. A full and diſtinct Account of the Proceedings relating to the Diſpute between the King of France and his Parliament of Paris. —— XIII. Marriages, &c. —— XIV. Bill of Mortality. —— XV. Imports and Exports.

Printed for T. Warner, at the Black-Boy in Pater-Noſter-Row; and A. Rocayrol, in Green-Street, near Leiceſter-Fields; pr. 1 s. 6 d.

Of whom may be had,

The Political States for June and July, in which are contain'd, the Debates in the laſt Seſſions of Parliament.

N. B. *No other Monthly Account but the Debates in Parliament.*

This Day is publiſhed,

The FIFTH VOLUME *of*

A SELECT COLLECTION *of* MOLIERE's COMEDIES, *in* French *and* Engliſh, *neatly Printed on a Fine Paper, with a Curious Frontiſpiece to each Comedy.*

This Fifth Volume contains,

Tartuffe, ou L'Impoſteur. The Impoſtor. *George Dandin, ou le Mari Confondu.*	*Dedicated to Mr.* Wyndham *of* Clowes-Wall, *in* Glouceſterſhire.
George Dandin, or the Husband Defeated.	*Dedicated to the Right Honourable the Lady*, ***

The Collection will conſiſt of EIGHT POCKET VOLUMES; one Volume to be publiſh'd every Month, 'till the Collection be compleated. Printed for and ſold by J. Watts at the Printing-Office in Wild-Court near Lincoln's-Inn Fields: And J. Brotherton, in Cornhill; J. Clarke in Duck-Lane; A. Bettelworth and C. Hitch, J. Oſborne and T. Longman, and J. Batley in Pater-Noſter-Row; J. Roberts in Warwick-Lane; J. Pemberton, L. Gilliver and T. Woral in Fleet-Street; F. Clay and R. Wellington without Temple-Bar; A. Millar and P. Dunoyer in the Strand; J. Batſon in Little Ormond-Street; J. Stagg in Weſtminſter-Hall; and J. Brindley in New Bond-Street. Of whom may be had, juſt publiſh'd, with a Curious Frontiſpiece to each Comedy,

Vol. I. containing,

A General PREFACE to the Whole WORK.

L'AVARE. The MISER.	*Dedicated to* His Royal Highneſs the Prince of Wales.
Sganarelle ou le Cocu Imaginaire. The Cuckold in Conceit.	*Dedicated to Miſs* Wolſtenholme.

Vol. II. containing,

Le Bourgeois Gentilhomme. The Cit turn'd Gentleman.	*Dedicated to* His Royal Highneſs the DUKE.
Le Medicin Malgre Lui. A Doctor and No Doctor.	*Dedicated to Dr.* MEAD.

Vol. III. containing,

L'Etourdi ou les Contre-Tems. The Blunderer: Or the Counter-Plots.	*Dedicated to the Right Honourable* Philip *Earl of* Cheſterfield.
Precieuſes Ridicules, The Conceited Ladies.	*Dedicated to Miſs* Le Bas.

Vol. IV. containing,

L'Ecole des Maris. The School for Husbands.	*Dedicated to the Right Hon. the Lady* Harriot Campbell.
L'Ecole des Femmes. The School for Wives.	*Dedicated to the Right Hon. Sir* Will. Yong, *Knight of the* Bath.

The Tranſlation is intirely New, and was undertaken by ſeveral Gentlemen, who all join'd and conſulted together about every Part of it. Particular Care has been had to keep as cloſe as poſſible to the Original, and to obſerve the very Words of the Author as well as his Senſe, ſo far as was conſiſtent with giving it a ſpirited and eaſy Comick Stile, in order to make it the more ſerviceable to thoſe of our own Nation, who are Learners of the French Language; as likewiſe to Foreigners who deſire to be acquainted with ours: To whom the Method we have taken of placing the French and Engliſh oppoſite to each other, will be of no ſmall Benefit. The Work will be printed in a very beautiful Manner, and adorn'd with new Frontiſpieces deſign'd by Monſ. COYPEL, Mr. HOGARTH, Mr. DANDRIDGE, Mr. HAMILTON, &c. Price of each Volume, done up in blue Covers, will be Two Shillings and Six-pence.

N. B. The SIXTH VOLUME will be publiſh'd on Saturday the Thirtieth of this Inſtant September; and the Collection will be compleated in October next.

In the Preſs, and will be publiſh'd with all convenient Speed, Beautifully Printed in Three Pocket Volumes, the Types *being all* NEW,

*** A NEW TRANSLATION of HOMER's ILIAD: As this Tranſlation was undertaken by Gentlemen who UNDERSTAND GREEK, the Reader may be ſure he has the SENSE of the AUTHOR; and as they have avoided the Fault of other Tranſlators, who leave their Original meerly for the ſake of Verſification and Gingle, he will generally have his very Words likewiſe. To this EDITION will be added ſome Remarks both on the Beauties and Imperfections of the Author, after the Manner of Mr. ADDISON's REMARKS upon MILTON. Printed by and for John Watts at the Printing-Office in Wild-Court near Lincoln's-Inn Fields.

N. B. The ODYSSEY will be printed in the ſame Manner in three more pocket Volumes.

Laſt Saturday was publiſhed,

No. VI. (*containing five Sheets) at the Price of* 6 d. *of*

THE HISTORY *of* ENGLAND.

By Mr. RAPIN DE THOYRAS. Tranſlated by N. TINDAL, M. A. Vicar of Great Waltham in Eſſex. The 2d Edition. With the following Improvements:

1. The Tranſlation is thoroughly reviſed and corrected.
2. The many Errors and Miſtakes of the Original are rectified.
3. Several Hundred of Marginal References, accidentally omitted by the Author, are ſupplied.
4. Additional Notes throughout, with Cuts, Maps and Genealogical Tables, on Copper Plates.

Printed for James, John and Paul Knapton, removed from St. Paul's Church-Yard, to the Crown in Ludgate-Street, near the Weſt-End of St. Paul's.

Where may be had,

No. I. II. III. IV. and V.

N. B. The Whole will be compriſed in 2 Volumes, in Folio, containing 400 Sheets, at the Price of 2 l. 2 s. in Sheets, including the Copper Plates. Five Sheets of the Work will be publiſhed every Saturday 'till the Whole is compleated, at the Price of 6 d. and the ſaid Sheets will be delivered every Week at the Houſes of Gentlemen who are pleaſed to order them.

Propoſals at large, with a Specimen of the Work, may be had gratis.

Saturday, Sep. 2. was published, Pr. 6 d.
[*Neatly Printed on a fine Paper.*]

The GENTLEMAN's MAGAZINE:
Or, MONTHLY INTELLIGENCER.
NUMBER XX. for AUGUST, 1732.
CONTAINING,
[*More in Quantity, and greater Variety, than any Book of the Kind and Price.*]

I. Views of the WEEKLY ESSAYS, viz. Degeneracy of Taste ; Improvement of the Stage ; Princely Education ; Poetry, Painting, Dancing ; Musick and History. Of Liberty and Prescience ; Benevolence ; English Fishery ; Fops ; Criticisms ; Summum Bonum, or Chief Good ; Divine Judgments ; Royal Example ; Hyp-Doctor's Flight.

II. Colony of Georgia, the Trustees, Design of their Charter, and Account of Carolina ; Mr. Parry's Account of the Towns to be built, his Proposals to 400 Swiss to go with him to build his Town of Purrysburg ; now first translated from the French.

III. POLITICAL POINTS: Debates in Parliament concerning a standing Army ; The Peace lasting ; questioned ; Partition-Treaty ; Pragmatic Sanction ; Trading Justices ; Of Multiplicity of Laws the Evil ; Political Pedantry, Honesty and Conscience ; Steps to Tyranny ; State Principles, and Ethicks ; Use of Faction, and ill Writers ; Grants of Money for 1731 and 1732 compar'd.

IV. POETRY, A Winter's Journey to preach ; Lady's Pattern ; the Merry Monarch ; Zealus at Church ; Woman a Cloud ; and a Bliss that will not tire ; The Queen's Hermitage ; Epigrams.

V. DOMESTIC OCCURRENCES, &c. Deaths, Births, Marriages ; Promotions, Price of Goods, Bill of Mortality in London, &c.

VI. FOREIGN AFFAIRS.

VII. A Remarkable Trial of a Woman at Derby, &c. &c.

By SYLVANUS URBAN, Gent.

London : Printed, and sold at St. John's Gate ; by F. Jefferies in Ludgate-street ; Mrs. Nutt, Mrs. Cook, at the Royal-Exchange ; Mr. Bailey in Pater-Noster-Row ; Mr. Midwinter, in St. Paul's Church-Yard ; A. Chapman, in Pall-Mall, Mrs. Dodd, and Mr. Bickerton, without Temple-Bar ; Mr. Crichley, at Charing-Cross ; Mr. Gee, and Mr. King, in Westminster-Hall ; Mr. Wilson in Holbourn ; Mr. Montague, in Great Queen-street ; Mr. Barrow, in St. Martin's-Lane.

Note. *The increasing Demand for the* GENTLEMAN's MAGAZINE *these twenty Months last past, has occasion'd most of the Numbers to be out of Print several times. At present Sets can only be had for the Year 1731 ; for, having been sold of unexpectedly to reprint some of our last, and also to print No. I. and No. II. a fourth time in the Press, we have not been able to get the first Volume ready, as promis'd, in August ; but Gentlemen who have hitherto been disappointed, may depend on compleat Sets by the 30th Inst. and following the future Numbers early each Month.*

PROPOSALS
For Printing by SUBSCRIPTION,

THE HISTORY of the Grand Controversy between the Secular and Regular Clergy of the Church of Rome, from the Year 1625 to 1634, concerning the Usurpation of RICHARD SMITH, Titular Bishop of Chalcedon, who pretended to be sole Ordinary Bishop of all England and Scotland. Wrote in Latin by the President of the English Benedictine Monks, RUDESINDUS BARLO, and faithfully done into English from the Original, for the Entertainment of the Curious, especially Divines and Lawyers, both Ecclesiastick and Civil, of what Religion soever.

With the Remonstrances of the Roman Catholick Laity made to the said Bishop, and also to his Excellency Carolo Coloma, Embassador Extraordinary of the Most Catholick Majesty, and to the Marquis Fontany, Embassador of the Most Christian King, &c. taken also from the Latin Originals: All which Treatises have been hitherto suppress'd, by the Papists, for Political Reasons given therein.

As also the famous Bull of Pope URBAN VIII. called PLANTATA, necessary for the right Understanding of the Whole, which was never before any where printed.

To which will be added,

A LETTER concerning the Disputes that have happen'd among the Benedictine Monks since the Year 1700 to this present Time : Shewing how even they themselves have varied from their original Principles. By one who was a Member of that Body, and concerned therein.

By JOHN WILLIAMS.

PROPOSALS may be had of (and SUBSCRIPTIONS taken in for the Author by) W. Meadows, at the Angel, in Cornhill ; T. Astley, at the Rose, and S. Austen, at the Angel and Bible in St. Paul's Church-Yard ; C. Davis, Pater-Noster-Row ; T. Woodward, at the Half-Moon, L. Gilliver, at Homer's Head, and J. Stephens, at the Hand and Star, between the Two Temple-Gates B. Motte, at the Middle Temple-Gate ; T. Worral, at Judge Coke's Head, H. Walthoe, next Door to the Rainbow Coffee-House, W. Reason, in Flower-de-Luce-Court, J. Isted, at the Golden-Ball, near Chancery-Lane, Fleet-Street ; F. Gyles, over-against Gray's-Inn-Gate, Holborn ; O. Payne, in Round-Court, and T. Game, at the Bible, by the New Church, in the Strand ; T. Green, Charing-Cross ; J. Jackson, in Pallmall ; J. Jolliffe, at the Bible, in St. James's-Street ; J. Brindley, at the King's Arms, and W. Shropshire, opposite to the Duke of Grafton's, New Bond-Street ; and J. Stagg, Westminster-Hall, Booksellers : J. Huggonson, in Bartholomew-Close, and T. Gover, by Fleet-Ditch, Black-Fryers, Printers.

On **Saturday,** Sept. 2. was published,
[*Beautifully printed on a fine Paper.*]

The LONDON MAGAZINE:
Or, GENTLEMAN's *Monthly Intelligencer.*
NUMB. V. For AUGUST, 1732.
To be Continued. (*Price Sixpence each Month.*)
CONTAINING,
(*Greater Variety, and more in Quantity, than any MONTHLY BOOK extant.*)

I. A *View of the* WEEKLY ESSAYS, viz. Reasons of the present want of Taste ; Plan of Education for a young Prince ; Summum Bonum, or the chief Good of Man ; Prescience and Free-Will ; Benevolence and publick Spirit ; Blessings of Plenty ; Variety of Wit ; Royal Example ; Discourse in Honour of the Queen ; Ethicks ; Divine Judgments of answering Books ; Slander ; Foppery in Dress ; Self-Murder ; antient Mythology ; Animadversions on Dr. Bentley's Milton.

II. POLITICAL *Subjects, viz:* Remarks on the natural Probability of a lasting Peace ; Designs of the Trustees for the Colony of Georgia ; a Royal British Fishery ; Reflections on Osborne's Principles ; Craftsman's Manner of Writing ; Thoughts on King William ; Case of the Remonstration of Gibraltar ; Justices of the Peace ; Secretaries of State and Messengers ; Atticus ; Manlius Capitolinus ; Anarchy, Tyranny, and Hereditary Right ; Political Pedantry ; Laws and Courts of Justice ; Dangers to Liberty ; of the Legislative and Executive Powers ; Use of Faction, or the Good of all Writers ; Proceedings and Debates in Parliament ; Account of Money dispos'd of, &c.

III. POETRY : A new Simile for the Ladies ; the Merry Monarch ; the Rose-Bud, a Song ; a humorous Love-Letter ; Mock Heroes ; the Vicar's Race ; Epigrams.

IV. DOMESTICK *Occurrences :* Promotions Ecclesiastical, Civil and Military ; Marriages and Births ; Deaths, &c.

V. FOREIGN AFFAIRS.

VI. Price of Goods, Grain, Stocks ; Monthly Bill of Mortality.

VII. A TABLE of Contents.

To which is added, a *Catalogue of Books and Pamphlets,* with their Prices, published by the Proprietors of the *Monthly Chronicle,* now discontinu'd.

MULTUM IN PARVO.

LONDON : Printed for C. Ackers in St. John-Street ; for J. Wilford, behind the Chapter-House, near St. Paul's : And sold by W. Meadows, T. Cox, W. Hinchliffe, H. Whitridge, R. Willock, and E. Nutt, in Cornhill ; J. Clark, in Duck-Lane ; T. Astley in St. Paul's Church-Yard ; A. Dodd without Temple-Bar ; J. Stagg in Westminster-Hall ; J. Jackson in Pall-Mall ; J. Jolliffe in St. James's-Street ; J. Brindley and W. Shropshire in Bond-Street ; and J. Milan near the Admiralty-Office.

Where may be had the former Numbers.

Just published,

Carefully translated from the *French* Original, to compleat Gentlemen's Setts,

THE VOYAGES and TRAVELS of A. De La Motraye, Vol. III. in several Provinces and Places of the Kingdoms and Dukedoms of Prussia, Russia, Poland, &c. Containing, A Treatise of the divers Orders of Knighthood ; many curious Particulars concerning the Insurrection of Thorn ; of the Diet of Grodno ; of the Life of Peter the First, Emperour of Russia ; and of Catherine, his Empress ; as also of General Le Fort, and Prince Menzikoff. With Remarks Geographical, Topographical, Historical and Political, on the Provinces and other Countries through which the Author travelled ; as Mecklembourg, Pomerania, Courland, Livonia, Estonia, the Principalities of Pleskow and Novogrod, the Lake Ladoga, the Dutchies of Carelie, Ingria, Silesia, Brandenbourg, &c. over some Parts of France, of Flanders, of England, and of Ireland. Drawn not only from his own Observations, but also from the Memoirs that have been communicated to him by Persons of Honour and Credit ; and the Whole embellished with Plans and Cuts, and curiously engraved on Copper-Plates.

Printed for E. Symon, in Cornhill ; J. Newton, and J. Oswald, in Little-Britain ; L. Gilliver, over-against St. Dunstan's Church in Fleet-Street ; J. Nourse, without Temple-Bar ; and T. Payne, in Pater-Noster-Row.

N. B. In this Vol. the History of the several Orders of Knighthood in the different Kingdoms of Europe, and other material Occurrences, began in the two former Vols. of this Author's Travel, are concluded.

This Day is published,

Printed for J. Brotherton, at the *Bible,* next the Fleece Tavern in Cornhill,

AN Enquiry into the Origin of Honour, and the Usefulness of Christianity in War.
By the Author of the FABLE of the BEES.

Where may be had,

1. A Letter to Dion, being an Answer to a Book call'd *Alciphron,* or the *Minute Philosopher.*

2. The present State of Great Britain and Ireland, for the Year 1731.

3. Traditions of the Jews.

4. Dury's Journal to Madagascar.

5. Religious Courtship.

6. Life of OLIVER CROMWELL, Lord Protector of the Commonwealth.

7. Receipts in Cookery and Surgery, by John Keetilby.

This Day is published,
Price Two Shillings and Six Pence bound,
The Second Edition of

THE GENTLEMAN FARRIER. Containing Instructions for the Choice, and Directions in the Management of HORSES, either for Draught or Pleasure, on a Journey, or in the Stable ; with an Account of their Distempers, and Receipts for the cure of them. To which is added an Appendix concerning Dogs, either for the Field or the Lap, wherein their Distempers are describ'd, and the Means to cure them. The Horse-Receipts by his late Grace of Devonshire, Earl of Orrery, Lord Carleton, Sir John Packington, General Seymour, Portman Seymour, Esq; James Nicholson, Esq; —— Thoreson, Esq; of Blandon, &c. Published by the Direction of a Person of Quality. Printed for F. Cogan, at the Middle-Temple Gate, Fleet-Street.

N. B. This Book contains above 300 Pages, and 30 Receipts more than Captain Burdon's.

This Day is published,

For the Use of FAMILIES, or PRIVATE PERSONS, (With a PREFACE giving some Account of the Life, Writings, and most exemplary Character of the Author, now first printed, and his Effigies very neatly engraven by Mr. Vertue,)

THE Whole WORKS of the Most Rev. Father in God Sir WILLIAM DAWES, Bart. late Lord Archbishop of York, Primate of England, and Metropolitan.

In Three large Volumes in Octavo ; price 15 s.

Printed for J. Wilford, behind the Chapter-House, near S. Paul's Where may be had,

Sir WILLIAM DAWES's Duties of the Closet. Being an earnest Exhortation to private Devotion. The 7th Edit. Printed on a much larger Character, and a finer Paper, than any of the former Edit ons. To which is now added, (by way of Supplement) a regular Course of Devotions, both fitted and occasional, as they are referr'd to by Sir Wm. Dawes ; price 2 s. 6 d.

His Great Duty of Communicating, explain'd and enforc'd : The Objections against it answer'd, and the necessary Preparations for it stated. With Devotions before, at, and after the Lord's Supper. The Ninth Edition ; price 3 d. or 20 s. a Hundred, to those who are so well disposed as to give them away.

His Anatomy of Atheism. A Poem. Dedicated to the Hon. Sir George Darcy, Bart. The 4th Edition ; price 6 d.

N. B. A very neat and large Picture of Archbishop Dawes, engraven by Mr. Vertue, may be had of J. WILFORD, as aforesaid ; price 2 s. or 3 s. ready fram'd, with a Glass.

This Day is published,

In Octavo (from the Folio Edition) Price Six Pence.

THE PROGRESS of LOVE, in four Eclogues, 1. UNCERTAINTY, to Mr. Pope. 2. HOPE, to the Honourable George Doddington, Esq; 3. JEALOUSY, to Edw. Walpole, Esq; 4. POSSESSION, to the Right Honourable Lord Viscount COBHAM.

Printed for Lawton Gilliver at Homer's Head in Fleet-Street.

Where may be had,

1. An Epistle to Mr. Pope, from a young Gentleman at Rome. By the same Author.

2. The Art of POLITICKS, with a curious Frontispiece. Risum teneatis Amici. Price 1 s.

3. Two Epistles to Mr. Pope, concerning the Authers of the Age. By the Author of the Universal Passion. Price 1 s. and, may be bound with the first Satyrs.

4. A new and correct Edition of the Dunciad Variorum, in 8vo with some additional Notes and Epigrams.

5. A Collection of Pieces relating to the Dunciad. By several Hands.

6. Of FALSE TASTE, to Richard Earl of Burlington. By Mr. Pope. Price 1 s.

7. STOW : The Gardens of the Right Honourable the Lord Cobham. Price 1 s.

LONDON: Printed by J. HUGGONSON, in *Bartholomew-Close,* for Capt. GULLIVER, near the *Temple,* where Letters and Advertisements are taken in : As also at the *Rainbow Coffee-House* in *Cornhill,* and *John's Coffee-House* in *Sheer-Lane, Temple-Bar,* [*Price Two Pence.*]

The Grub-street Journal.

NUMB. 142.

Thursday, SEPTEMBER 21, 1732.

From these their Politicks our Quidnuncs *seek,*
And Saturday's the learning of the week.

Dr. Young's 1st Ep. to Mr. Pope.

Mr. BAVIUS,

COffee-houses are the places to which the generality of persons resort in this great city, either for the dispatch of business, or for their diversion after the fatigue of it. This diversion arises principally from hearing the sentiments of others, and freely delivering their own, upon all subjects whatsoever. A dayly instance this of the liberty of Britons, a blessing injoyed in such full extent by no other people in the world. This alleviates the weight of those many heavy taxes raised upon them for above these forty years; which otherwise might have been thought an intolerable burthen, tho' absolutely necessary to keep out popery and arbitrary power.

Since the present and future happiness of mankind depends upon government and religion, it is necessary that all persons should entertain right notions of these two things. And these notions are to be acquired only two ways, by reading and conversation. The many excellent political discourses written since the Revolution concerning the rights of sovereigns and subjects, have explained the matter of government in a very full and clear manner. And the obligation of taking the oaths, under which persons of all degrees either were layed, or imagined themselves to be layed, about ten years ago, put them upon carefully reading those pieces, that they might swear with judgment, as well as with truth, and with righteousness.

I am sensible, that it has been suggested by some, that much the greater part of these persons, especially of the female sex, being incapable of rightly informing themselves in this matter, took the oaths implicitly, in obedience solely to the commands of their superiors. But this I look upon as a false and scandalous reflection, both upon those who injoined, and upon those who took the oaths. The former were such declared enemies to all implicit blind obedience, that they would never have imposed the belief of two political points, one positive, and the other negative, upon persons who were incapable of forming a right judgment concerning them. This would have rendered an Abjuration-oath too much like an Athanasian creed, consisting of terms that were unintelligible; and the injunction of the former might have been justly looked upon as unreasonable a piece of lay-craft in politics, as that of the latter is by some of priest-craft in religion. Nay there are two circumstances to the advantage of the latter case, in which a declaration and subscription is required only of the clergy; whereas in the former, the laity, as well as the clergy, are comprehended, and the subscription of the belief of both is accompanied with the solemnity of an oath.

But the good people of Great Britain had too much understanding and honesty, to act in such a blind manner, as solemnly to repeat words without ideas, and to swear that they *believed in their consciences* things of which they had a very confused, if any notion at all. And I have been well assured, that several persons of mean fortune and education, and some even of the female sex, both young and old, were very inquisitive in this affair, and satisfied themselves concerning it, by reading some of the ingenious and learned pieces published in defence of the oaths, which fully explain the nature of our constitution, as placed upon a new basis at the Revolution. And therefore it has been frequently matter of wonder to me, that some persons, who pretend to be the greatest friends to our excellent constitution, should blame this inquisitive temper of our people, and censure them for meddling with matters relating to government; since they were formerly, and many of them are still, obliged either to swear with their eyes shut (like those who strain to swallow something too large for their throats) or else to inquire into the rights of princes; and consequently, either to become formally perjured, or to become politicians.

To the exact inquiries made at that general time of swearing I cannot but attribute the foundation of that great skill in politics, to which the generality of persons have now attained. Which is so very extensive, that it is amazing to hear them talk with the nicest exactness, concerning the titles and interests of foreign princes, as well as of their own, of the natural rights and liberties of subjects, and of the reciprocal duties of the one and of the other. But tho', I think, I ascribe the foundation of this consummate knowledge to a true cause; yet I must own the superstructure is chiefly owing to those weekly letters and dissertations, which furnish our Coffee-houses still with a fresh supply of political pieces, and at one and the same place, and time, afford the most agreeable and useful subject of study and conversation.

Nor are points of government alone debated and settled in these places of assembly, but likewise the abstrusest points of religion are here clearly determined: which was the other thing, mentioned at the beginning of this letter, concerning which it is necessary that all persons should have just apprehensions. Several long, laborious, and learned books, as well as many short, ingenious, and satirical pamphlets, have for forty years been written against priest-craft; the knavery of which has been effectually exposed in a great variety of ways. Natural religion has been advanced to that just superiority it ought to have above all pretended revelations; the inconsistency, and consequently the falseness, of which has been evidently demonstrated. The most eminent of those which were written a pretty many years ago, are *The rights of the Christian Church, A Discourse of free-thinking*, and *The independent Whig*. The last of these came out in weekly papers; which, tho' taken almost intirely from the first were recommended to the public by many additional strokes of satire upon the Parsons, and by a stile and manner peculiar to the author, and not to be imitated. So happily did he execute his undertaking, that a Gentleman, to whom he was personally unknown, left him by will a good estate, as a just reward for the merit of that performance. A remarkable instance this of the charity and generosity of a Free-thinker; and not to be parallelled by any charitable or generous act of any bigotted High church man whatsoever, towards any defender of priest-craft and arbitrary power. From these two books the reverend Mr. BOWMAN, not long since, made a short extract, in which he was so faithful, as to represent the same thoughts in almost the very same expressions; and by an extraordinary piece of christian fortitude preached it as a Visitation-sermon to his superstitious brethren; of which the public impatiently expects his defence against some trifling objections which have been made thereto.

The most celebrated books against Revelation, which have appeared of later years, are *A discourse of the grounds and reasons of the christian religion*, and *Christianity as old as the creation*. The former of these was generally thought to be written by the author of the *discourse of free thinking*: against whom it has been objected, that tho' this *discourse* was fully answered by PHILELEUTHERUS LIPSIENSIS, and the ignorance of the writer exposed to all the world, in so much that he was frequently called *the idiot evangelist*, yet he neither defended, nor retracted that *discourse*; one of which he ought to have done, before he presumed to publish another *discourse* in pursuance of the same subject ——To this it may be answered, that as no name was put to either of the *discourses*, it is not certain, that both were written by one and the same person, but that if they were, the prosecution of the same subject, in the latter, may justly be looked upon as a defence of the former in the main; tho' the author have neglected to vindicate himself from some small mistakes in translating a few Latin or Greek passages, which an ill-natured Pedant may have discovered.

But the last, and most glorious book of all, is *Christianity as old as the creation*; the strength and force of which is plainly manifested by the many fruitless endeavours of its adversaries to answer it. And it is one great objection against the *answers* to this, as well as against those to the fore-mentioned books, that they are almost all of them written by persons prejudiced in favour of Revelation, and obliged by their profession and interest to support and maintain it, because it supports and maintains them. *Sirs, ye know, that by this craft they have their wealth*, is an unanswerable reply to all those pretended *answers*; and sufficient, I hope, to keep the honest laity from reading, or at least from regarding them. To such I would recommend a constant and careful perusal of those admirable observations concerning religion and government, extracted chiefly from the books of which I have been speaking, and published weekly in the *Free-Briton* and *London Journal*. With these, as with the rays of the sun united in a burning-glass, they may kindle such a flame, as may both inlighten and warm themselves, and at the same time dazle and scorch their adversaries. This will certainly be the consequence, if Mr. OSBORNE perform the promise which he very lately made, to set * *these subjects in so clear a light, that it will be* IMPOSSIBLE *to mistake them*. When he has done this, of which I do not in the least doubt, it will prove to demonstration the truth of that which I have had chiefly in view throughout this short essay, That just notions both of government and religion are best to be acquired in a Coffee-house.

I am, Mr. BAVIUS,

Your humble Servant,

D. D

* See *London Journal, Sept. 9. 1732.*

Mr. A—— F——s Letter to his Curate at C—— N versifyed.

LEST Curates proud should make a stir,
I will begin with *Reverend Sir*,
Without a compliment I send
These lines, to tell you I intend
To send of flowers a basket down,
By friday's coach to A——FORD town,
To you directed at the Swan;
For which I'd have you send your man
To fetch 'em saturday by noon,
And plant them all before the moon.
Let all your care to this be given;
And pray for me to gracious heaven,
To put them forward in their bloom,
When I to C——N shall come.
Curates may rub the winter o'er:
I come at spring, and not before.
Watch W——KS my servant day by day,
And see he earns what I shall pay.
Write every thing about my garden:
I leave the church to the church-warden.
Has N—L—D made his promise good,
And *gratis* fetch'd my stock of wood?
If he in this has kept his word,
Say what the sort, how many cord.
If malt proves good, and casks don't stink,
I hope you soon will brew my drink.
If the good malster looks askew,
Pray tell him, that for me you brew,
And then perhaps, he'll trust on you.
I wonder, and am much confounded,
Since corn of late has so abounded,
That all my tenants, griping elves,
Should keep their money to themselves;
When as they know their rent is due,
And they may have receipts from you.
Pray travel up, and travel down,
And talk, and vaunt, as 'twere your own.
The tardy N—L—D ever teaze,
Nor let JOHN H—L—R sleep in peace;
If sober admonition fail,
Put them in mind there is a jail.
When every due is duly pay'd,
And ballance is to ballance lay'd,
Forthwith to W——R repair,
'Twill do you good to take the air.
There Mr. H—K—R you may see,
Receiver-General is he.
The sacred Idol don't detain,
Nor with unhallow'd hands prophane;
To him the weighty trust consign,
And bid him write a golden line;
For every hundred pounds (oh! oh!)
Five shillings in return must go.
But let the Bills that he shall write
Be after date, not after sight:
Not after sight; for tell me who
Would cash it twice, when once will do?
If to your self you have respect,
My interest you'll not neglect,
If you in my behalf would stout it,
And write about it, and about it,
H—L—R from K—PS—N would descend,
And N—L—D with his rent attend:
Then G—W—N would the call obey,
Nor whining P—P—R longer stay.
I then expect you send me word,
Put under cover to my Lord,
And when I see in this you're true,
I'll find you something else to do.
Pray ask JOHN H—L—R sunday next,
And mind it, as you mind your text,
If Mrs. R——GE will hold the tythe
At the new rent of ninety five.

Perhaps she may not like the ground,
Because I've rais'd the odd five pounds.
Tell him I soon would know her mind,
That if she be not well inclin'd,
I may some other tenant find.
In all these premisses don't fail ye:
As you're my curate, you're my bailey.
Thus I appoint you my attorney,
And am your servant, R—— F——.

DOMESTIC NEWS.

C. *Courant.*	E P. *Evening Post.*
P. *Post-Boy.*	S J. *St. James's Evening Post.*
D P. *Daily Post.*	W E. *Whitehall Evening Post.*
D J. *Daily Journal.*	L E. *London Evening Post.*

THURSDAY, *Sept.* 14.

Yesterday her Majesty, and the Princesses Royal and Carolina, attended with several of the Nobility, were at Major Foubart's, Riding-Master to his Royal Highness the Duke perform the exercise of riding the great Horse; which he performed with great judgment, dexterity, and courage. *C.*

The Phoenix, supposed to belong to Ostend, arrived at Cadiz, from whence her cargoe was sent, one third in one French Ship, and two in another, to Hamburgh. And from Lisbon the 10th past, N.S. it is written, that a Ship under the same suspicion was that day arrived there from East India. — *I was in hopes the* Ostend Trade *had been at an end.*

The Commissioners of the Treasury have ordered 300 *l.* to be paid to the persons concerned in the apprehending Tho Loveday, convicted last Sessions of sending a threatning Letter. *S J.*

Reading, Sept. 11. On tuesday last a Scotchman rose in a dream, and went out of a window one pair of stairs into the Street, and walk'd near 100 yards before he waked, and received but little hurt. *S J.*

We hear that her Grace the Duchess of Buckinghamshire is relaps'd, and lies dangerously ill at Boulogn in France *S J.*

On saturday Anth. Luthire, Esq of Dodenhurst, near Brentwood, being disorder'd in his senses, shot himself, and died in a few hours. *D P.* —— On monday died at the seat of the Lord Cobham in Buckinghamshire, his Excellency Abraham Stanyan, late Ambassador to the Ottoman Porte. *C.* —— At his seat in Oxfordshire. *D J.* —— Yesterday advice came from Oxford of his death. *P.*

FRIDAY, *Sept.* 15.

It is the opinion of persons learned in the laws, That, from the time *the act* for qualifying justices of the peace takes place, no clergyman can act as such, unless his benefice is rated at 100 *l.* in the King's Book (the authentick record of its value, and against which there is no averring) or unless he has a real temporal estate of 100 *l.* a year, or an estate of that nature sufficient to make up, what he is rated at in the King's book, 100 *l.* a year. *C.*

Yesterday the Bank declared a dividend of 2 3 4ths per cent for the half year, ending at Michaelmas next; the warrants to be payable October 12, and the books to open Octob. 10. *P. D P.*

Yesterday the Lord Mayor and Court of Aldermen heard the Masters and Journeymen of the Clothworkers; when his Lordship proposed, That the hours of work should be the same as before, from 5 in the morning till 7 at night, and the wages the same; but that the Masters should pay 3d for every hour's work done above the said time, allowing 2 hours for breakfast and dinner. *C.* — *I am glad they have so much work upon Cloths, as to quarrel about it.*

We hear the Justices of the Peace of the Committee appointed at Westminster Sessions for suppressing night-houses, &c. have agreed to meet weekly, it appearing by the trials last week at the Old Baily, that several persons have gone from those places to rob in the streets, &c. *D P.*

On monday 2 gentlemen were stopped between Esher and Kingston by a single Highwayman on a black mare. They gave him a wound in his back with a hanger; upon which he fired 3 times at them, and the last shot one of their horses dead; but finding he could not manage them, he rode off. They had received near 200 *l.* that morning at Guildford. The rogue had a mask on. *P.*

SATURDAY, *Sept.* 16.

We hear from Yorkshire, that the Tower of Bibbe's Abbey, near Hemsley, was lately blown down by a violent high wind; by which accident 2 men, who were at work underneath, were killed. *C.* ——Ribbis — Abbey. *D P.*

On wednesday his Royal Highness the Prince of Wales was at Mrs. Lee's booth in Southwark Fair, to see the entertainment called Female Innocence: or, A school for a wife. *D. J.*

Yesterday, about 5 in the evening (notwithstanding the wind was high) a sailor flew from the top of the monument to the upper Three-tun Tavern in Grace-church-street, which he did in less than half a minute. —— In the morning, when the rope was tied round the monument, a waterman's boy, paid for going up; but in his return finding the stairs crouded, he thought the quickest way down again would be by the rope, and accordingly swung down upon it as it hung loose. *D J.* —— Last night Mr. Heard, who kept the Glass-house in Old Bedlam, returning from Gracechurch-street, where he had been to see the sailor fly from the top of the monument: he had no sooner got home, but he dropt down dead. 'Tis said with the surprise of the same. *W. E.*

Yesterday a messenger arrived here from his majesty at Helvoet-sluys; by whom we hear he continues in a perfect state of health, but is detained by contrary winds *P. S J. WE. L E.* —— We are well assured that there has no messenger arrived from Holland for this week past. *C.*

Mr. Blunt has 34 sets of horses at 40 s per diem, waiting at Harwich and Margate for his Majesty's landing. *L E. S J.*

On saturday her Majesty and the Princess Carolina, accompanied by several persons of distinction, came to the Meuse at Charing-Cross, and viewed the new Stables, at which her Majesty expressed her intire satisfaction, and ordered a handsome donation to the workmen. *C.* —— Her Majesty and the two youngest Princesses. *P.* —— Attended by several ladies, *&c.* and was pleased to order money for the workmen. *D. P.*

The rev. Mr. Barnard, one of his Majesty's chaplins, and chaplin to the Duke of Newcastle, is appointed one of the Prebendaries of Westminster. *D P.*

On thursday night his Grace the Duke of Bedford arrived at Portsmouth, having been 4 days going thither. *D P.* —— He went immediately on board the Torrington for Lisbon. *D J.*

At the Oratory, the corner of Lincoln's-Inn Fields, &c. to morrow at eleven, &c. 2. There will be a *New* Oration, &c. At *six* there will be a *New* Theological lecture, &c. *Fog's Journal.* —— The rainbow, &c. will be the subject of a *new* oration, &c. *D J.* -- At Mr. Pinchbeck jun. &c. great Theatrical Booth, &c. He has several *tricks* entirely *new*, which were never done by any other person but himself. *D P.*

MONDAY, *Sept.* 18.

A few days ago Mr. Brigin, an eminent wine-merchant, coming by Stratford, was robbed by 2 highway men, who took his money and gold watch, which he desired them to let him have again; assuring them, upon his word and honour, that he would give them more than they could make of it, which was 10 guineas; accordingly they came with him to the man in the moon tavern in Whitechapel, and delivered him his watch, upon his word, till he went home, and sent his servant with 10 guineas *D J.* ——*This was no* robbery, *but a fair bargain betwixt men of* honour.

On saturday 18 fine horses were landed at the Tower for the use of the Spanish Ambassador; which with those landed before, make 36, and are said to be exceeding fine. *P.*

The national debt as it stood Dec. 31, 1730,	49 301,555	05	01 ½
Increased betwe n Dec. 31. 1730, and Dec. 1731.	1,200,000	00	00
Paid off within the said time.	1,516,416	13	04
Amount of the National debt, Dec. 31. 1731.	48 985,438	12	09 ½

They write from Cambridge, that Sturbridge Fair has proved very good this year, and plenty of all sorts of commodities; hops were sold at 7 l. 5 s. per hundred, and Gloucester and Warwickshire cheese at 1 l. 2 s. per hundred. *D P.*

TUESDAY, *Sept.* 19.

Will. Woolliston, of Great Finborough in Suffolk, Esq; has declared to stand a Candidate to represent the said Borough, in the room of Col. Negus, deceased. *D P.*-- We hear that Will. Negus Esq; only son of Col. Negus, will also stand a candidate. *P.*

On sunday night, Admiral Stuart arrived in the Rye man of war in the Downs; and yesterday he was at Kensington, and waited on her Majesty. *P.*

The late Abraham Stanyan, Esq; dying a Batchelor, hath left the gross of his estate to Temple Stanyan, Esq; his brother. *D P.*

Folkstone, Sept. 16. The Ship which lately came on shoar here, was from Gottemburgh, and bound for Lisbon: of her cargo which was iron, deals &c. very little was saved, the country and towns people having carry'd off abundance. She had 14 hands and a boy on board, of whom 9 and the boy were lost, and 5 saved; among the former was the master, who was safe on shoar, and attempting to save his child, was lost, and when taken up had him fast folded in his arms. *P.*

Six new houses are ordered to be built at the Meuse at Charing-Cross for his Majesty's Equerries, viz: Edmund-Charles Blomberg Esq; Thomas Panton Esq; Couthorpe Clayton Esq; the Hon. Henry Berkeley Esq; Henry Pulteney Esq; and Philip Lloyd Esq; *L E.*

The large American Aloe is in bloom at Walter Pettyward's Esq; at Enfield in Essex, where it may be seen; it being much finer than that which blowed at Hoxton, or any that ever blowed in England before; the bunches of flowers being a foot diameter, and thirty bunches upon the stem, placed in a very regular pyramid. *S J.*

A curious monument is erecting at Crayford in Kent in memory of the Lady Shovell, relict of Sir Cloudesley Shovell, who some years ago was cast away on the Rocks of Scilly. *S J. WE. L E.* —— *I hope it will be a more* curious one *than that in Westminster Abbey* in memory of Sir Cloudesly.

One day last week two young women at Lewes in Sussex going to bed, spied a young man under the bed; one of them took up a pot to throw at him; which he perceiving, jumped out of the window, three pair of stairs, and broke his neck *S J.* ——. *He had better have ventured the* breaking *of* his head *with* the piss-pot: *but I believe, they are safe.*

The march of the Regiments of Westminster Train'd Bands is appointed for the 27th, 28th, and 29th Instant; councils of war have in the mean time been held at several Taverns, for concerting measures for the opening of this short campaign; and we hear that the Siege of Oran, in Tothill-Fields, has been resolved upon: The town to be attacked by the Spaniards of St. Martin's in the Fields, and defended by the Infidels of St. James's. *S J.*—*I fear many of these* Spaniards *are* Infidels, *or at least incumcised.*

WEDNESDAY, *Sept.* 20. 1731.

Mr. Evelin, second son to Sir John Evelin, was married last thursday to miss Prideaux, a Devonshire young lady of 40 000l. fortune. *C.*

Yesterday there was a court of aldermen at Guildhall, when Robert Godschall Esq; was sworn in Alderman of Bishopgate Ward; and the Court was pleased to order 40 Freedoms to the Right Honourable the Lord Mayor and the two Sheriffs, in lieu of the sale of the place of Keeper of Newgate *P.*

Last monday night a man in Farmer-street near Ratcliff-Highway, having had some words with his wife, hanged himself. Being discovered by some neighbours, he was cut down; when they found some life in him; but he expired soon after. *C.* — He swore he would be reveng'd of her. *D J.* —— *I suppose he did not doubt, that she would marry a worse husband.*

Between forty and fifty beds are fitting up at the three houses hired in Jermyn-Street, St. James's, for his Excellency the Marquis de Montejo, Embassador from his Catholick Majesty. His Excellency brings with him his lady and children, and two chaplains, and a vast retinue. *D P.*

From the PEGASUS *in Grub-street.*

As we do not know the subject of the following lines, they are published solely to oblige the Gentleman who sent us two copies of them.

See mad MARIA plunge the lifted knife,
A Fury turn'd, because not made a wife!
The amazed guests the murd'rous deed detest,
And grief and horror trouble all the feast:
Mad she exults aloud, and thinks too slow
The vow'd revenge, and aimes a second blow;
And thus, she crys, Thus may all traitors prove
The rage of jealousy and slighted love.

A letter published in Mr. Fog's last Journal was read, containing some severe reflections upon our Society, for printing in our 140th Journal an Epigram in a different manner from that in which it was sent. Upon which Mr. BAVIUS stood up and sayed, that as he was principally concerned in making the alteration in that Epigram, he thought himself obliged to vindicate them and himself.

The Gentleman, who wrote the letter, says, *The epigram was sent word for word,* as it is now printed in Mr. Fog's Paper. This is not true: for instead of the R—— in one line, and the C—— s in two other, there were names at length in all three places —— He affirms, that it was published by us *most scandalously altered, quite contrary to his purpose and meaning.* The latter of which I own may be true: but I deny the former, for reasons which will appear presently. —— By this proceeding, he says, we have *proved* ourselves TRUE TURNCOATS; *and he wishes a certain person joy of his new Allies.* And as a confirmation of this, adds, that he has *some reason to suspect that the Hero of the Epigram, may be the person who altered it into a panegyrick upon* himself. All this falls to the ground, if the point of the Epigram is the same, and is directed at the same person in our Journal, at whom it is directed in Fog's. As he does not mention the

faw either of his strange *suspicion* about. *the Hero*, or of his strange opinion, that the Epigram has been turned into a *Panegyrick*, no other answer can be given, but that there is not the least foundation for either. — One end of writing this letter the Gentleman *far I*, to shew others *who may amuse themselves with writing what they may expect from the* GRUB JOURNAL. To shew them this the more plainly, I shall give some reasons for the alteration of this Epigram. The two first lines were in a different measure from the other eight, which I thought very odd in this sort of poetry. The second and third

Nor think Sir R —— did him grace,
C——s faltness claim'd a Place.

did not seem to me to be sense: for tho' a man's *talents* may justly claim a Place as their due reward, yet he may very well be sayed to be graced or adorned by it. *Common far*, in the ninth verse, I took to be very harsh English, if it be English at all. As to the additional lines which has given this Gentleman so much offence, I shall leave that to every readers impartial consideration. Upon the whole, I am persuaded, that the alterations are all emendations, which have made the Epigram more poetical, and truer in all respects than it was before but this is submitted to the judgment of the town. I could make some observations upon the stile of this letter but I omit them, because, when a person is angry, it is not natural for him to talk grammatically. — I shall only add a few words more for the satisfaction of those whom this Gentleman would deter from becoming our Correspondents. That if any of them send any piece with a real name, we will publish it without alteration, it we publish it at all. But whatsoever comes without any name, or under a feigned one, we shall take the liberty to alter it, if we think there is occasion, as being the proposed judges what may be convenient or inconvenient for us to publish.

Poeta nascitur, non fit.

Thistles are Asses food, we're told
By learn'd Philosophers of old,
Parnassus mount afforcs a crop,
Which spring up far beneath its top
Of these same Asses having heard,
Their course about the mountain steer'd,
They clamber'd till their heads turn'd round,
At last, the prickly plant they found,
Loud hideous brays their joys rehearse,
And what is more, they bray'd in verse,
If not in verse, at least, in rhime,
For Ass to Ass return'd a Chime :
At their own sound in great surprize
They danc'd, but cou'd no higher rise
From Critics now they Bards commence,
Toning out sound instead of sense
The Chardon juice had made them hope
They soon might be a match for Pope
But e'er they left th' inchanted place,
They proper thought to ask a Grace
Since from thy face a genial ray
'Hus kindled in us a fire latent,
'O grant us a poetic patent,
'And that our ears, which now so long
'Expose us to the vulgar throng,
'May not extend so high upright,
'Or be with laurel hid from sight.
He, who was with the Muses quaffing,
Could scarcely answer them for laughing :
'Go to my Clarks, quoth He, and see 'em,
'Your ears they'll place, that you shan't see 'em.
'Twas thus, if fame be not a fibber,
He serv'd our Poet L——— C———
They went ———— 'twas done ——— In discord join'd
They sing, and to their ears are blind
And tho' one's bray his friend's surpasses,
They're all a consort fit of Asses.

Letters from New-York, dated Aug 4. advise, that their new governor, Col. Cosby, arrived there 2 days before. D F 15 ——— New-York, July 26 Last thursday morning, a creature of an uncommon size and shape was believed to break through a window of a store-house in this city, and jumped into the street, where was suddenly a number of spectators, who followed it, till it passed over several high fences, and at last stuck between two houses, where they shot at. It was 7 foot long, and some think it is a Panther P. 18
Philadelphia, June 1. On sunday last a thunder-clap struck into the house of the widow Mifflin, about three into the city. It first struck the chimney, and split it down several feet, tore and shattered part of the roof of the house. Split a rafter, and it broke off in two places.

FOREIGN NEWS.

THURSDAY, Sept. 14.

Petersburg, Aug. 26. N. S. Our last advices from Derbent and Persia say, That Schach Thamas, having gathered the greatest parts of his troops together into one army, was marched with all speed towards Babylon, to lay siege to that important place, before the Turks can assemble an army to relieve it. C. D P. D F.

FRIDAY, Sept. 15.

Ratisbon, Sept 11 It is observable, that in 1683 and 1684, many in the country of Saltzburg declared for the Protestant religion, and retired to other Parts, some of which returned afterwards with such books, as 'tis believed, laid the foundation for the present propagation of that religion. D F.

SATURDAY, Sept 16.

Extract of a letter from a Merchant of Turin, dated Sept. 6, 1732. N S. *to his Correspondent at Leeds in Yorkshire.*
We are here under the greatest consternation, on account of an order from our Consulado or Council of commerce, to all the merchants dealing in English manufactures, to take large quantities of mean woollen goods made in this country (in proportion to their imports from England) at a very low price, upon pain of having their effects seized ——— As our repeated complaints to that board have procured us no relief, we must give over ordering cloth from your parts, or any other in England, the loss attending the goods they impose upon us here at their own rates, in order to force a consumption of them, running away with more than the profit the English goods can possibly yield , and consequently that branch of trade, which hath been computed some years to take off to the value of 400,000 l. of English manufactures, will be entirely lost. B P.
Hague, Aug 19 N S It is confirmed, that the Most Christian King has written to the duke of Lorrain, exhorting him not to be longer absent from his Dutchy, which gives his Royal Highness a great deal of uneasiness. ——— One of the secret articles, or the treaty between the Emperor, the Czarina of Muscovy, and the King of Denmark, relates to the Duke of Holstein's succession to the throne of Sweden, which is consistent with the law made by the states of that kingdom, when they abolished the monarchy and hereditary right, wherein they declare, that they will always have regard to the Royal Family , though it is sure to meet with oppression from the King and Queen, who would fain get the crown settled upon the family of Hesse-Cassel ——— It is reported, that the French Court has sent orders to Dunkirk, to forbid the engineers of any foreign nation whatever to take surveys of the canal and harbour there , the ministry being so tired, they say, with the continual complaints upon that subject, that they do not care to hear any more But for the truth of this report we will not be answerable D P

TUESDAY, Sept. 19

Hague, Sept 5 N S According to our last Advices from Italy, every thing seems ripe for a new revolt in Corsica, where the minds of the people are more exasperated than ever against the Genoese, who without regard to treaty or amnesty, seize some or other of the Malecontents every day, find out a pretence for prosecuting them, and then put them to death by the hands of the common Hangman But whenever the war in that island breaks out again, the republick of Genoa will find it a very difficult matter to put an end to it there being no likelihood of the Emperor's assisting them a second time, after having seen so much perfidy and ter-giversation in a treaty brought about by his imperial Majesty's generals, and secured (as one would think) by his guaranty. P.

WEDNESDAY, Sept. 20.

Hague, Sept. 15. N. S. It is certain that there is a treaty concluded between the courts of Saxony and Bavaria,

In a lower room it struck off the Plaistering, and part of the brick-wall, broke the window-glass, and melted the lead. Another story lower, several splinters of a window-frame were broke off, some of the glass broke, and lead melted ; it also struck down a lad that stood in a porch near the said window, and burnt him badly in a streak about the breadth of a hand, from the side of his face down to the calf of his leg, but no ways hurt his cloaths, he is also very much hurt by the fall There were four or five children sitting in the house near to the lad, who were very much surprized and stunned by the thunder, and almost suffocated with the Smoak and sulphurous Smell that filled the Room. It also split a large tree near the house S F, 19.

for the maintenance of their respective rights and pretensions, which implies a plain contradiction to the execution of the Austrian *Pragmatick Sanction*, from which those two courts have appealed. This cannot but give the Emperor a great deal of uneasiness; and the more, because his Imperial Majesty well knows, from what quarter this blow comes, and that every thing is now conducted in those two courts by the compass of the intrigues of France, by whom a Pamphlet was lately published at Ratisbon, the author whereof pretends to prove the Most Christian King's right to several hereditary counties of the House of Austria, in case the present Emperor should happen to die without Issue-Male.

BOOKS and PAMPHLETS published since our last.

14 Modern History, &c by Mr Salmon, No. 102.
Knowledge and charity considered separate and united, in a sermon at Nottingham, July 16. by Sam. Wright, D.D.
The political state of Great Britain, for August.
16 The works of Mr Joseph Stennett, in 4 vol.
19. An essay on the freedom of will, &c Pr. 1 s. 6d.
An essay toward the proof of a separate state of souls, between death and the resurrection, &c. Price 1 s.
All future free actions, future contingences, &c. By David Millar. Pr. 1 s 6 d.
20. The proceedings at the Old Bailey, Sept. 6th, 7th. 8th. 9th, and 11th.

On Tuesday Stocks were
South Sea Stock was 104 3 qrs 104 7 8ths. 104 3 qrs to 7 8ths. South Sea Annuity 3 qrs. to 7 8ths Bank 152 to 1 qr for the Opening. Bank Circulation 4 l 10 s. Premium. India 158 Three per Cent Annuity 99 7 8ths. Royal Exchange Assurance 10 s. London Assurance 13 5 8ths. to 3 qrs. York Buildings 6. Bookselhut African 38 English Copper 2 l 2 s. Welch ditto 1 l 15 s South Sea Bonds 2 l. 13 s. to 14 s. Premium India ditto 41 5 s. ditto.

On Saturday, Sept. 2. was published,
(*Beautifully printed on a fine Paper,*)
The LONDON MAGAZINE:
Or, GENTLEMAN'S *Monthly Intelligencer.*
NUMB. V. For AUGUST, 1732.
To be Continued. [*Price Sixpence each Month.*]
CONTAINING.
[*Greater Variety, and more in Quantity, than any*
Monthly Book extant.]

I. A *View of the* WEEKLY ESSAYS, *viz.*
Reasons on the present Want of Taste; Plan of Education for a young Prince; Summum Bonum, or the Chief Good of Man; Prescience and Free-Will; Benevolence and publick Spirit; Blessings of Plenty, Variety of Wit; Royal Example; Discourse in Honour of the Queen; Ethicks; Divine Judgments; of answering Books; Slander; Foppery in Dress; Self-Murder; antient Mythology; Animadversions on Dr. Bentley's Milton.

II. POLITICAL SUBJECTS, *viz.* Remarks on the natural Probability of a lasting Peace; Designs of the Trustees for the Colony of Georgia; a Royal British Fishery; Reflections on Osborne's Principles; Craftsman's Manner of writing; Thoughts on King-William; Case of the Renunciation of Gibraltar; Justices of the Peace; Secretaries of State and Messengers; Atticus; Manlius Capitolinus; Anarchy, Tyranny, and Hereditary Right; Political Pedantry; Laws and Courts of Justice; Dangers to Liberty; of the Legislative and Executive Powers; Use of Faction, or the Good of ill Writers; Proceedings and Debates in Parliament; Account of Money dispos'd of, &c.

III. POETRY: A new Simile for the Ladies; the Merry Monarch; the Rose-Bud, a Song; a humorous Love-Letter; Mock Heroes; the Vicar's Race; Epigrams.

IV. DOMESTICK OCCURRENCES: Promotions Ecclesiastical, Civil and Military; Marriages and Births; Deaths, &c.

V. FOREIGN AFFAIRS.

VI. Price of Goods, Grain, Stocks; Monthly Bill of Mortality.

VII. A TABLE of Contents.

To which is added, a Catalogue of Books and Pamphlets, with their Prices, published by the Proprietors of the Monthly Chronicle, now discontinu'd.

MULTUM IN PARVO.

LONDON: Printed for C. Ackers in St. John-Street; for J. Wilford, behind the Chapter-House, near St. Paul's: And sold by W. Meadows, T. Cox, W. Hinchliffe, H. Whitridge, R. Willock, and E. Nutt, in Cornhill; J. Clarke in Duck-Lane; T. Astley in St. Paul's Church-Yard; A. Dodd without Temple-Bar; J. Stagg in Westminster-Hall; J. Jackson in Pall-Mall; J. Jolliffe in St. James's-Street; J. Brindley and W. Shropshire in Bond-Street; and J. Millan near the Admiralty-Office.
Where may be had the former Numbers.

Just published,
With a handsome Frontispiece,
THE BLAZING COMET, the MAD
LOVER: Or, The BEAUTIES of the POETS. A Play.
As it is acted at the New Theatre in the Hay-Market. By Mr. JOHNSON, Author of HURLOTHRUMBO.

Sold by John Osborn, at the Dock Head, near Horsly-Down; and by the Booksellers of London and Westminster, Price 6 d. With Variety of other Plays and Novels at the same Price.
Where may be had in Octavo.

The Fortunate Mistress	Glanville on Witches
The Life of Col. Jack	Wilson's Chymistry
Mauley's Mathematicks	Daniel's History of France, 5 Vols.
A Voyage round the World	Bradley's New Improvements in
Youth's Emblems, with Cuts	Husbandry and Gardening.
Hartcliffe's Moral Virtues	His General Treatise of Husbandry
Mandeville's Travels	

The following in Twelves.

John Gulliver, 4 V.	Creech's Horace, Lat. & Eng. 2V.
Persian and Turkish Tales, 2 V.	Chinese Tales, 2 V.

This Day is published,
(*Designed for the Use of all Private Families,*)
THE Ancient Physician's LEGACY to
his Country, being what he has collected himself in 49 Years Practice; Or, An Account of the several Diseases incident to Mankind, described in so plain a Manner, that any Person may know the Nature of his own Disease. Together with the several Remedies for each Distemper, faithfully set down.

Hominet ad Deos nulla in re propius accedunt, quàm Salutem Hominibus dando. Cic.

By THOMAS DOVER, M.B.

Printed for the Author, and sold by J. Brotherton at the Bible in Cornhill; A. Bettesworth and C. Hitch, in Pater-noster Row; W. Mears at the Lamb in the Old Baily; and L. Gilliver at Homer's-Head, over-against St. Dunstan's Church in Fleet-Street. Price Stitch'd Five Shillings.

Note, The Doctor is to be heard of, or spoke with, at the Jerusalem Coffee-House in Exchange-Alley.

Just imported, and sold by JER. BATLEY, at the Dove in Pater-Noster-Row.

HIstoire des Papes depuis St. Pierre jusqu'à Benoît XIII. inclusivement en Deux Volumes 4to. à la Haye, chez Henri Scheurleer, 1732.

Lately published, and sold by J. BATLEY.

Philosophiae Mathematicae Newtonianae Illustratae Tomi Duo. Quorum prior tradit Elementa Mathesea ad comprehendendam demonstrationem hujus Philosophiae scitu necessaria; Posterior continet 1) Definitiones & Leges motûs generaliores; 2) Legesvirium compositarum & Theoriam attractionis seu gravitationis corporum in se mutuo; 3) Mundi Systema.

à GEORGIO PETRO DOMCKIO.

Saturday, Sept. 2. was published, Pr. 6 d.
[*Neatly Printed on a fine Paper:*]
The GENTLEMAN's MAGAZINE:
Or, MONTHLY INTELLIGENCER.
NUMBER XX. for AUGUST, 1732.
CONTAINING.
[*More in Quantity, and greater Variety, than any Book of*
the Kind and Price.]

I. VIews of the WEEKLY ESSAYS, viz.
Degeneracy of Taste; Improvement of the Stage; Princely Education; Poetry, Painting, Dancing, Musick, and History. Of Liberty and Prescience; Benevolence; English Fishery; Fops; Criticisms; Summum Bonum, or Chief Good; Divine Judgments; Royal Example; Hyp-Doctor's Flights.

II. Colony of Georgia, the Trustees, Design of their Charter, and Account of Carolina: Mr. Purry's Account of the Towns to be built; his Proposals to four hundred Swiss to go with him to build his Town of Purysburgh. Now first translated from the French.

III. POLITICAL POINTS. Debates in Parliament concerning a Standing Army: The Peace lasting; questioned; Partition Treaty; Pragmatic Sanction; Trading Justices; Of Multiplicity of Laws, the Evil; Political Pedantry; Honesty and Conscience; Steps to Tyranny; State Principles, and Ethicks; Use of Faction, and ill Writers; Grants of Money for 1731 and 1732 compar'd.

IV. POETRY, A Winter's Journey to preach: Lady's Pattern: The Merry Monarch: Zoilus at Church; Woman, a Cloud, and a Bliss that will not tire: The Queen's Hermitage: Epigrams.

V. DOMESTIC OCCURRENCES, &c. Deaths, Births, Marriages; Promotions, Prices of Goods, Bill of Mortality in London, &c.

VI. FOREIGN AFFAIRS.

VII. A Remarkable Trial of a Woman at Derby, &c. &c.

By *SYLVANUS URBAN*, Gent.

London: Printed, and sold at St. John's-Gate, by F. Jefferies in Ludgate-Street; Mrs. Nutt, Mrs. Charlton, Mrs. Cook, at the Royal Exchange; Mr. Batley in Pater Noster-Row; Mr. Midwinter, in St. Paul's Churchyard, A. Chapman, in Pall-Mall; Mr. Dodd, and Mr. Bickerton without Temple-Bar; Mr. Gilchley, at Charing-Cross; Mr. Stagg, and Mr. King, in Westminster-Hall; Mr. Williamson, in Holborn; Mr. Montague, in Great Queen-Street; Mr. Harding, in St. Martin's-Lane.

Note, The increasing Demand for the GENTLEMAN's MAGAZINE these Twenty Months last past, has occasion'd most of the Numbers to be out of Print several Times. At present Sets can only be had for the Year 1732 for having been obliged unexpectedly to reprint Some of our last, and also to put No. I. and No. II. a fourth Time in the Press, we have not been able to get the First Volume ready, as promis'd, in August; but Gentlemen, who have hitherto been disappointed, may expect a compleat Set by the 30th Instant, and of having the future Numbers early each Month.

Last Saturday was published,
No. VII. (*containing five Sheets*) at the Price of 6 d. of

THE HISTORY of ENGLAND.
By Mr. RAPIN de THOYRAS. Translated by N. TINDAL, M. A. Vicar of Great Waltham in Essex. The 2d Edition.
With the following Improvements:
1. The Translation is thoroughly revised and corrected.
2. The many Errors and Mistakes of the Original are rectified.
3. Several Hundred of Marginal References, accidentally omitted by the Author, are supplied.
4. Additional Notes throughout, with Cuts, Maps, and Genealogical Tables on Copper Plates.

Printed for James, John, and Paul Knapton, removed from St. Paul's Church-Yard, to the Crown in Ludgate-Street, near the West-End of St. Paul's.
Where may be had,
No. I. II. III. IV. V. and VI.

N. B. The Whole will be comprised in 2 Volumes, in Folio, containing 400 Sheets, at the Price of 1 l. 2 s. in Sheets, including the Copper Plates. Five Sheets of the Work will be published every Saturday, 'till the Whole is compleated, at the Price of 6 d. and the said Sheets will be delivered every Week at the Houses of Gentlemen who are pleased to order them.
Proposals at large, with a Specimen of the Work, may be had gratis.

This Day is Published,
Printed for J. Brotherton, at the *Bible*, next the Fleece-Tavern in Cornhill,

AN Enquiry into the Origin of Honour, and the Usefulness of Christianity in War.
By the Author of the FABLE of the BEES.
Where may be had,
1. A Letter to Dion: Being an Answer to a Book, call'd, Alciphron: Or, the Minute Philosopher.
2. The present State of Great Britain and Ireland, for the Year 1731.
3. Traditions of the Jews.
4. Dury's Journal to Madagascar.
5. Religious Courtship.
6. Life of OLIVER CROMWELL, Lord Protector of the Commonwealth.
7. Receipts in Cookery and Surgery. By John Keetilby.

This Day is published,
In Octavo (from the Folio Edition)
Price Six-Pence.

THE PROGRESS of LOVE in four Eclogues. 1. UNCERTAINTY, to Mr. FILOUSY, to the Honourable George Doddington Esq; 2. JEALOUSY, to Edward Walpole Esq; 3. POSSESSION, to the Right Honourable Lord Viscount COBHAM.
Printed for Lawton Gilliver, at Homer's Head, in Fleet-Street.
Where may be had,
1. An Epistle to Mr. Pope from a Young Gentleman at Rome. By the same Author.
2. The Art of POLITICKS, with a curious Frontispiece. *Risum teneatis, Amici.* Price 1 s.
3. Two Epistles to Mr. Pope, concerning the Use of Reason in the Age. By the Author of the Universal Passion. Price 1 s. May be bound with the said Satyrs.
4. A new and correct Edition of the Dunciad Variorum, in 8vo. With some additional Notes and Epigrams.
5. A Collection of Pieces relating to the Dunciad. By Samuel Hands.
6. Of FALSE TASTE, to Richard Earl of Burlington. By Mr. POPE. Price One Shilling.
7. STOW: The Gardens of the Right Honourable the Lord Cobham. Price 1 s.

PROPOSALS
For Printing by SUBSCRIPTION,
THE HISTORY of the Grand Controversy between the Secular and Regular Clergy of the Church of Rome, from the Year 1625 to 1631, concerning the Usurpation of RICHARD SMITH, Titular Bishop of Chalcedon, who pretended to be sole Ordinary Bishop of all England and Scotland. Wrote in Latin by the President of the English Benedictine Monks, RUDISINDUS BARLO, and faithfully done into English from the Original, for the Entertainment of the Curious, especially Divines and Lawyers, both Ecclesiastick and Civil, of what Religion soever.

With the Rest utterances of the Roman Catholick Laity made to the said Bishop, and also to his Excellency Carolo Colonni, Embassador Extraordinary of this most Catholick Majesty, and to the Marquis Fontany, Ambassador of the most Christian King, &c. than also from the Latin Originals; but which Treatises have been hitherto suppress'd by the Papists, for Political Reasons given herein.

As also the famous Bull of Pope URBAN VIII. called PLANTATA, necessary to the right Understanding of the Whole, which was never before any where printed.

To which will be added,

A LETTER concerning the Disputes that have happen'd among the Benedictine Monks since the Year 1700, to this present Time. Shewing how even they themselves have varied from their original Principles. By one who was a Member of that Body, and concerned therein.

By JOHN WILLIAMS.

PROPOSALS may be had of (and SUBSCRIPTIONS taken in for the Author by) W. Meadows, at the Angel in Cornhill; T. Astley, at the Rose, and S. Austen, at the Angel and Bible in St. Paul's Church-Yard; C. Davis in Pater-noster Row; T. Woodward, at the Half-Moon, L. Gilliver, at Homer's Head, and J. Stephens, at the Hand and Star between the Two Temple-Gates; J. Motte, at the Middle-Temple-Gate; T. Worrall, at Judge Coke's Head; H. Walthoe, next Door to the Rainbow Coffee-House; W. Reston, in Flower-de-Luce-Court; J. Isted, at the Golden-Ball, near Chancery-Lane, Fleet-Street; F. Gyles, over-against Gray's-Inn-Gate, Holborn; G. Payne, in Round-Court; and T. Gunn, at the Bible, by the New Church, in the Strand; T. Green, Charing-Cross; J. Jackson, in Pallmall; J. Jolliffe, at the Bible, in St. James's-Street; J. Brindley, at the King's Arms, and W. Shropshire, opposite to the Duke of Grafton's, New Bond-Street; and J. Stagg, Westminster-Hall, Booksellers: J. Huggonson, in Bartholomew-Close, and T. Gover, by Fleet-Ditch, Black-Fryers, Printers.

The Cœlestial Anodyne Tincture: Or, The Great Pain-easing Medicine.

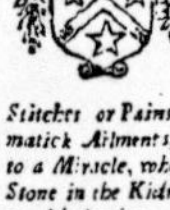

FAm'd and Approv'd of for its wonderful and never-failing Success in giving immediate Ease and Relief in almost all Pains, either inward or outward, and is the most certain Remedy in the World for a sure and speedy Cure of the Cholick, and expelling Wind, Gripes and Pains in the Stomach, the Front-Stitches or Pains in the Side, Back, Loins, or other Part; Rheumatick Ailments, which cause Pain and Dolor. It hath proved to a Miracle, when all other Remedies have failed. In the Stone in the Kidneys, it gives Ease forthwith, and brings them to Admiration. It also facilitates and causes a speedy Delivery in Child-Birth. 'Tis no Quack trifling Thing, to abate the symptom but a tried and well-experienced Medicine, not acting by simple Nature, purging Opiates, but by a friendly, balsamick, and active Virtue, curing the most severe and terrible racking Pains, and cures of the Cholick not by purging, but by Transpiration. No Family ought to be without it, and used outwardly, instant heat. No Family ought to be without it. The surprizing, Aches, Pains, Numbness, or Weakness of the Joints. The excellent for Cramps, and all other aged Infirmities, effecting Wonders in Agues Fevers, Small-Pox, &c. No Family ought to be without it.

It is Sold only by Mr. PARKER Printer, at his House in Salisbury-Court, or by such Persons at he shall depute, viz. at Mrs. Parker's Printer, in Bull Head-Court in Jewin-Street; at the White-Lyon Printer, in Bull Head-Court in Jewin-Street; at the White-Lyon a Chandler's Shop in Sandy-Leg Walk, Southwark; and at Mr. Hold's Toy-Shop over-against the White-Hart Inn in the Borough, at Eighteen Pence a Bottle, with printed Directions; and if required, will be brought to any Person by the Hawker who sells his Papers, stated at above.

The Grub-street Journal.

NUMB. 143.

Thursday, SEPTEMBER 28 1732.

As diversion was not the sole design of this Paper, we have frequently inserted in it short Pieces upon very important points, written in a very serious manner. Being fully persuaded of the usefulness of this conduct, which is approved by all who read in order to instruction, we shall not change it, in compliance with those, whose sole end in reading is diversion. Having in our 138th Journal presented to the Public some arguments in relation to *Divine judgments*, which we received in a letter from a person unknown, and having since received a second letter from him, we think proper to publish it now, both because we would willingly go through every subject which has been begun in this paper, and likewise exhibit the latter part of any piece, as soon as possible, after the former. —— Our dropping of the controversy about the *Divine Prescience*, &c. may perhaps be objected to us: to which objection we give the following answer. Mr. F——'s *Reply* to Mr. ELIOT's letter in our 137th Journal, concluded with a long quotation out of a pamphlet: which looking so much like a design to puff that pamphlet, we insisted, that the book-seller, who communicated to us the *Reply*, should take a certain number of our Journals: but he refusing, we would not publish it; which we had certainly done, had it come without that quotation. As we have frequently either intimated, or declared our aversion to Puffs, and have refused several advantageous offers in relation to them, we shall take care not to be drawn in, by artful management, to insert them in our Paper, without any advantage to ourselves at all.

Mr. BAVIUS,

I proceed in my inquiry concerning judgements, and shall here pursue the same method which I observed in my letter to you upon that subject, namely, to give my opinion on neither side of the question under consideration, but only to state such arguments as may be brought in *proof of the negative*, and then subjoin answers (in my poor *conception*) conclusive against them.

A Continuation of the Arguments against Judgments.

ARGUMENT 4. We cannot help dissenting from the asserters of Judgements, because it appears to us, That the great Sovereign of the universe never punishes at all. For punishments relating only to actions already committed, and it being impossible to recall these, they can serve no end or purpose in the world, and of consequence must be highly wrong: but as right and wrong is ever the rule of action to the supreme judge, 'tis clear it must be so in the case before us, that is to say, the wrongness of punishments will influence the Creator to a merciful treatment of his creatures in that respect. —— *Answer*, It is not just reasoning to argue, that God will lay aside rigour, because the use of it tends to no purpose: for the severity we are speaking of, may be right in itself, tho' it may not be so upon account of any design it is subservient to. Thus, for instance the relief of the distressed is an action proper in its own nature, whether it hath any further tendency, or not: this last consideration needs not at all to be taken into the question. I know very well, there are some men who deduce moral obligation from the will of God only: these people will be ready to assert, in this place, that the assistance of the needy is not good upon its own account, but on account of its agreeableness to the divine inclinations. But I would gladly have them resolve me, why I am to do that which best pleases my Creator? They will say, perhaps, because he gave me existence. And then I ask further, Why is gratitude my duty? for this is what you plainly suppose, either it has some intrinsic worth in it, or it takes that character from something else: if you allow the former, you give up what I am contending for; if you maintain the latter, the same question returns upon you as before, viz. Why am I to regard that something else? In like manner, if you always insist upon the same answer, the same query will be eternally arising, and never resolved. In short, a search after one's duty, upon this scheme, is an exact resemblance of a man's hunting his own shadow, which perpetually flies from him, as fast as he pursues it. And let the dispute regard any point of duty whatsoever, precisely the same reasoning may be fitly applied to it. So that, if the philosophy I am opposing should be admitted to take place, then 'tis impossible we can come to any final decision in relation to our duty; then all moral obligation entirely falls to the ground. — Now the question springing from hence is, Whether we shall adhere to the notion of these Gentlemen, thus repugnant to the existence of moral obligation? or whether we shall grant ourselves bound to the practice of virtue, and reject this notion, which would supplant it? And here, the determination lies clearly on the side of moral obligation; which, if true, we may safely conclude, from what has been said, that some things must have a native underived perfection inhering in them; and this, notwithstanding they may not in the least advance any view or design whatsoever: and consequently it is far from being just reasoning, to argue the wrongness of divine punishments, from their unfitness to promote any end or purpose: which was the very thing I undertook to make good. — It may perhaps be objected, that I have gone upon the absurd supposition of an infinity of entities or things existing, because I said, that if the rightness of any thing depended upon some thing beyond it self, then we could never arrive at a determination of what was, or was not our duty, seeing it would be a doubt, to all eternity, suggesting it self, what obligation I lie under to act in conformity to this something beyond. To which I answer, that I have not built upon the supposition mentioned in the objection, but only shewed it to be a consequence, necessarily resulting from the doctrine I was endeavouring to subvert: and therefore it is quite beside the purpose to urge the falsity of that position, my argument being not at all invalidated, but on the contrary confirmed by means of it: for if an infinity of entities, or things existing, be a tenet unquestionably absurd; and this undeniably follows, from affirming that every thing right and proper owes its value to something beyond it self; this latter opinion cannot possibly be true, because no proposition can be just, which leads to an absurdity.

I now pass over to what is contained against divine judgements in ARGUMENT 5. It was urged by the late Mr. TRENCHARD against the appearance of spirits, that it was much better for the great architect, so to contrive the plan of our system, as that any purpose he should have in view might flow from a train of natural causes, than that he should make use of the assistance of spirits to the attainment of his end. As this is much better, says Mr. TRENCHARD, so it furnishes us with a good reason for thinking it to be really the case: because the contrary supposition would highly reflect upon the character of that Being who always projects every thing for the best. This artillery of Mr. TRENCHARD's we beg leave to turn against divine judgements: and accordingly we observe it to be much better, that God annex misery to sin, so that the one may be the constant attendant of the other, than for him to effect the same thing, by his immediate interposition. Just as it needs a quicker invention in a mechanic to form a watch, which will always discover the time of the day of its own accord, and by its own motions, than to make one requiring frequent helps of winding up to compass the same point. It may be said indeed, that if God be supposed to have disposed matters in our method, viz. that vice should of necessity produce unhappiness; this would be a weighty proof in behalf of Judgements, instead of oppugning them; because this would be inflicting penalties upon the wicked in this world on account of their misconduct; which is the very definition at first given of the term Judgement. But this difficulty will vanish, if we consider, the distinction between Judgments, and punishments in our way inflicted. Upon our principles, irreligion in general is the object of punishment to the supreme Judge; whereas when God is affirmed to exercise a judgment, the wickedness of some particular person is supposed to be his motive in so doing; this is clear from the latter part of the definition referred to. —— ANSWER, I shall not deny the validity of your distinction, but fix upon another part of your argument. You lay it down, that because the method of punishment you prescribe is better than that of Judgements, therefore God hath put the former in execution. Very well; pray give me leave to carry on the argument; To make all the parts of the creation corresponding to more numerous purposes, is preferable to the adapting of them only to those uses which they serve at present, therefore this is really the case; that is to say, the several parts of the creation correspond to a certain determinate number of purposes, and yet they correspond to more. It may here be alleged, that in fact God has acted congruously to the rule above specified, consequently it must be wisest and best so to do, namely, to link vice and wretchedness together by an inseparable connexion. And to this I reply: Let us suppose it absolutely requisite, that the wicked should go through some chastisement or other; let us further imagine it to be a matter of indifference, whether their correction be brought about by the natural course of things, or by the extraordinary operation of the divine hand; let us picture to ourselves in the third place, that God Almighty makes choice of the former way: certainly all these may happen; and consequently it does not follow from God's preferring to act in one way, rather than in the other, that therefore the way he prefers is wisest and best, according to our apprehensions.

The sum of all is, that Judgments are secure of any danger from the efforts of argument the 4th, to prove that God never punishes at all; or from the attempt, in argument the 5th, to establish a better method of punishment.

I am, Sir, your most humble servant, &c.

SIR,

WHEN a man has once publicly found fault with any writings, I think, in justice, it is incumbent on him to defend the censure: otherwise, he shews himself fond of the name of a Critic, and may well be suspected to have more ill-nature than good-judgment. —— The censure I passed in a letter published in your 138th Journal, on a piece then in rehearsal, called, *The Deal of a Duke*, has given occasion at Drury-lane to say, that that censure was as malicious as ill-grounded; and that they doubt not of that piece's taking a run equal to its merit. That the censure was strictly just, I hope this letter will demonstrate: and I sincerely wish, the town may suffer it to have such a run, and such only, as is equal to its merit.

The *original piece*, I sayed, *was void of wit and just humour*: but the just defence of that proposition would be mere trifling; since the whole is suited only to the capacities of the upper gallery. What then would the managers at Drury-lane value this farce for? —— The songs. —— The songs, in which the two Messieurs, Senior and Junior, are both sayed to have had a hand. — A criticism on farcical songs, is such a thing, that I I should not attempt to trouble the public with it, was I not accused both of malice, and want of judgment.

Mr. PHILIPS says, in his *Essay on song-writing*, that Songs, like Epigrams, should turn on a point of wit. Such are those in the *Beggars Opera*, which are mostly Epigrams; and which, with their poignancy, give a pleasure without the aid of music. But in this farcical-ballad Opera, I can find none turned in this manner: and I think the author, be he who he will, would have been more prudent, had he learned the rules of Syntax, before he had attempted to entertain a British audience.

Lest this should seem my *ipse dixit*, I shall have recourse to quotations, which will shew my impartiality, tho' it should betray my judgment. It would take up too much of your paper to examine all the songs; I shall only point out the peculiar beauties in some, which may shew the *merit* of the whole.

AIR III. *Young damsels were formerly won*
By a pimp's application to Mother ——

Mother who? That is to be understood *Mother* PUNCH-BOWL in the *Covent Garden Tragedy*, or &c. —— This is an instance of sense.

AIR XI. *Since in every degree of men,*
Sergeants follow their masters,

What follows from that? Why that

Kirkers-like, what Elders pen,
High zealots mitred Pastors.

If any one can find sense or meaning in this stanza, I must confess he has a happier discernment than I have.

In AIR XII. *Transport appears* in its *gaudy array*, is admirable; and nothing could equal this happiness of stile, but in AIR XV.

The bird whom Fate oppressing,
Had coop'd within a grate.

AIR XVI. *Wine expert will prompt desire*, demonstrates the Author's judgment in his choice of epithets.

AIR XVII. *Pleasure can never come sincere,*
While power is obey'd.

Why not? The reason the author wisely reserves to employ the imagination of the audience.

The sudden glooms dark nights disclose,
Will justle with the morn.

This is a ſtyle worthy the approbation of Father and Son.

In AIR XX. a woman is moſt ingeniouſly compared both to tea and coffee. Firſt, ſhe is like tea:

A woman like the liquid tea,
Can yield no true repaſt;
'Till by a man ſhe ſweeten'd be,
And ſuited to the taſte.

This admirable compariſon is built upon this indiſputable ſuppoſition, that *liquid tea can yield a true repaſt*, or meal.

But then ſecondly, ſhe is like coffee.

Like coffee ſinks the ſingle Dame,
To the bottom of the cup,
'Till man exciting Cupid's *flame,*
Boils inclination up.

I could not comprehend how *the ſingle dame ſinks to the bottom of the cup*; and was much ſurprized at this new way of making *coffee*; which is here ſuppoſed to be poured into a *cup*, before it is *boiled*; and to have the grounds raiſed by *boiling*, which generally cauſes them to ſubſide. To make this a little better ſenſe, I humbly offer the following emendation in the Bentleian manner.

Like coffee, ſinks the ſingle Dame,
To the bottom of the pot,
'Till man exciting Cupid's *flame,*
Boils inclination hot.

Now let the reader determine, whether I wrongfully cenſur'd this favourite piece, which ſeems to me to be very incoherent, low, dull buffoonry. If the Town ſhould ſuffer ſuch to be impos'd on them, they will have little reaſon to expect to be ever entertained better.

Sept. 22. 1732. I am, Sir, yours,

PROSAICUS.

DOMESTIC NEWS.

C. *Courant.*	E P. *Evening Poſt.*
P. *Poſt-boy.*	S J. *St. James's Evening Poſt.*
D P. *Daily Poſt.*	W E. *Whitehall Evening Poſt.*
D J. *Daily Journal.*	L E. *London Evening Poſt.*

THURSDAY, *Sept.* 21.

The Hon. Mrs. Anne Vane is indiſpoſed at her houſe in St. James's Street. *D P.*

Yeſterday the 4 Companies of Grenadiers paraded in Bloomsbury-Square, and afterwards marched into Tothill-fields, where they performed a fine exerciſe, and then beſieged the 5 chimneys, which they took without the loſs of one man. *D J.*

On tueſday night a loaded Collier, at anchor near the North-fleet reach, was run foul on by an empty one, and ſunk: the men were all ſaved; but the maſter endeavouring to ſave his niece, by carrying her up to the ſhrowds, the water flowed ſo faſt, he was obliged, for his own preſervation to let her drop, whereby ſhe periſhed. —— At the ſame time, another empty Collier ran foul on a Merchant-man, and carried away her fore-maſt, and broke her head ſhear off: the Merchant-man was laden, and coming up for London. *D J.*

Northampton, Sept. 18. On wedneſday the widow *Biſhop*, whoſe husband was ſome time ſince killed by the fall of the caſtle-wall, and whoſe ſon died raving mad, was run over by a waggon, and died in a few minutes. *C. D J.*

When the Lady Dolin and her daughter were robbed laſt monday, after the highway-man was going off, Miſs called to him to take her ſnuff-box; which when he had got, finding it to be a wooden one (Tunbridge) he curſed her, and flung it back to her. *D J.* —— *He took ſnuff, tho' not the* box.

Robberies near London are now very frequent: it is ſaid, that 2 perſons returned from tranſportation have committed ſeveral of late, from which it is plain, that ſaving perſons from the gallows, is of no ſervice; and this laſt ſeſſion 2 were try'd, and one capitally convicted, who were evidences the Seſſions before, and ſaved their lives by hanging their comrades. *L E.*

The 40 poor widows of the city and liberty of Weſtminſter, in a great meaſure ſupported by the beef, bread, and money, given once a week, the legacy of the lady Margaret, mother to Henry VII. have loſt 13 s. 4 d. per week, by the death of the late Rev. Mr. Mich. Evans, who made an addition to that charity of 4 d per week to each of them, during his life-time. *S J.* —— *This loſs, no doubt, will be made up to them, by ſome of the* Prebendaries.

Laſt monday a pedlar was found murder'd in a field between Hampton-court and Shepperton, his throat being cut from ear to ear, and his pack rifled. *S J.*

Mr. Evelin, ſecond ſon to Sir John, was married laſt thurſday to Miſs Prideaux, a devonſhire young Lady of 40,000 l. fortune. *S J.*

FRIDAY, *Sept.* 21.

Yeſterday, being St. Matthew's day, the Right Hon. the Lord Mayor, accompanied by the Governors of St Bartholomew's, Chriſt Church, Bethlehem, and Bridewell Hoſpital, went, according to cuſtom, to Chriſt Church; where an excellent ſermon was preached by the Rev. Mr. Ferriby, in praiſe of the ſeveral donors of the ſaid Hoſpitals. —— After divine ſervice the Lord Mayor, &c. went and heard a Latin and Engliſh oration, ſpoken by two lads belonging to the Grammar School of Chriſt-Church Hoſpital. *D J.* —— The Latin by John Dutton, and the Engliſh by Thomas Potter. *C* —— Mr. Ferebee received thanks for his ſermon, and was deſired to print the ſame. *P.*

On wedneſday morning a Gentleman run round S. James's Park for 50 guineas: he had 20 minutes allowed him to do it, and performed the ſame in 15 and a half. Several conſiderable wagers were alſo depending, and great odds were laid againſt him. *D P.* —— *This Gentleman was* Mr. Clark, belonging to the Peacock brewhouſe in Whitecroſs-ſtreet. *C.*

On ſunday, about two in the afternoon, was held a lodge of free and accepted Maſons at the Roſe tavern in Cheapſide; where, in the preſence of ſeveral brethren of diſtinction, as well Jews as Chriſtians, Mr. Edw. Roſe was admitted of the fraternity by Mr. Dan. Delvalle, an eminent Jew Snuff Merchant, the Maſter, Capt. Wilmot, &c. who were entertained very handſomely; and the evening was ſpent in a manner not infringing on the morality of the Chriſtian ſabbath. *D P.* —— *Theſe* Jews, *I fear, entertained no very favourable notion of this* manner *of keeping the* Chriſtian ſabbath.

Yeſterday the Rev. Mr. Wells was choſen, by ballot, Lecturer of the united pariſhes of S. Swithin and S. Mary Bothaw. *D J.*

Yeſterday, in the afternoon, a duel was fought at the old Royal African Coffee-houſe in Leadenhall-ſtreet, between 2 Gentlemen, who had formerly been abroad in the African Company's ſervice; and a Gentleman who interfered in the ſaid quarrel, was dangerouſly wounded. *D J.*—*This* duel *was only begun to be* fought, *according to the following account of another my brethren:* They drew, and made a paſs at each other; another Gentleman interpoſing betwixt them was very much wounded. *C.*

Cambridge, Sept. 16. The 9th inſt. a man flew down from the top of S. Mary's ſteeple upon the ſhambles, and up again with great dexterity, firing 2 piſtols, and toſſed his flags when he was midway, and hung by his feet, and acted the Taylor and Shoemaker, to the great admiration of the ſpectators. —— On the 16th he fixed his rope to the top of Cheſterton ſteeple, and had like to have pulled part of it down; ſo they would not let him proceed. *D J.*

Laſt monday the Jews obſerved, in a very ſtrict manner, their annual feaſt in memory of the deſtruction of Jeruſalem. *D P.*

SATURDAY, *Sept.* 23.

Yeſterday the committee appointed to inſpect and examine the South-ſea company's accompts, met at the South ſea houſe, and choſe Mr. John Adlam, Clerk of the Weaver's company, to be their ſecretary and accomptant. We hear they will ſit 3 days a week, holidays excepted. *C. D J.*

On thurſday night, an eminent Spaniſh merchant, coming from a tavern, in his way home, fell into the hands of a woman of the town, who carried him to a diſorderly houſe in Finch-lane, where he loſt upwards of 30 guineas; ſince which, all the perſons of the ſaid houſe are fled. *P.*—*This* Spaniſh merchant *loſt his money in the way* of trade, *by making uſe of* a leaky bottom.

Yeſterday morning Sir Tho. Groſvenor croſs'd the water from his houſe at Milbank, Weſtm. in order to proceed on his intended journey for Montpellier, to drink the waters for the recovery of his health. *D J.*

A yacht is ordered to be got ready to carry the Earl of Iſlay, Dr. Edm. Halley, and Mr. Hadley to Sea, to make ſome obſervations upon Mr. Hadley's Scheme for diſcovering the longitude. *S J. L E.*

John Bury Eſq; ſenior, is appointed Receiver-general of the taxes of the County of Nottingham, in the room of John Bury, of Nottingham, Eſq, who ſome time ago fell from his horſe, and broke one of his legs, whereof he died. —— Laſt tueſday John Cooper, Eſq, Receiver-general of the taxes for the County of Nottingham, had the misfortune to fall from his horſe, and died on the ſpot. *S J.*

Letters from Bourn, in Lincolnſhire, dated Aug. 30. ſay, that about 20 years ago a miller, after he had been marry'd about two years, took a diſlike to his wife, and left her; who has been maintained by the pariſh of Bourn for near 18 years: during which time the miller went to Colcheſter in Eſſex, where he marry'd another woman, and lived in good circumſtances and credit. The beginning of laſt month a millwright informed the inhabitants of Bourn where the ſaid miller was Whereupon they ſent over two perſons, who apprehended him at Glouceſter; who preſently agreed to pay 20 l. down, and gave ſecurity for payment of 30 l more, for the charges the pariſh of Bourn had been at in maintaining his wife, and promis'd to take her from thence in a little time. Accordingly, on the 22d of Auguſt, he came to Bourn; where he bought a new pillion; and on the 24th took her from thence behind him. The next morning a woman was found dead in a ditch, ſtrangled with a ſmall cord, that would ſcarce meet round her neck, with a pillion ſome diſtance from her, in a place call'd Pillgate-Field, in the pariſh of Barnac in Northamptonſhire, about 8 miles from Bourn. She was ſoon diſcover'd to be the miller's wife: whereupon he was purſued by 2 perſons, who apprehended him at Glouceſter. He was ſent to Clemsford Goal; from whence he is to be removed to Northampton, to take his tryal at the next Aſſizes. The coroner's inqueſt have brought in their verdict *Wilful Murder*, and ſuppos'd to be done by the ſaid miller. *L E.*

Yeſterday died Mr. Herman Moll, a noted Geographer, at his houſe near Temple bar. *P. D J.* —— Laſt night died of a fever, Will. Holmes, a Sawyer, who was tried at the laſt Seſſions at the Old Baily, for robbing one Barth. Harnet of 5 s. 9 d. and a ſilver buckle, ſaid to have been committed on the 19th of July in Moorfields: Upon which trial a horid ſcene of villany was diſcovered againſt the priſoner's life, for the ſake of the reward of 140 l. But he he was honourably acquitted, a copy of his indictment granted him, and directed by the Court to proſecute the ſaid Harnet at the next Seſſions for wilful and corrupt perjury. He has left a wife and two ſmall children, all unprovided for; but his friends are reſolved to aſſiſt her in carrying on the proſecution againſt Harnet, who is now in Newgate, with the utmoſt rigour of the law. *W E.*—*This ſort of* perjury *deſerves to be made* capital.

MONDAY, *Sept.* 25.

His Excellency James Earl Waldegrave, his Majeſty's Ambaſſador at the Court of France, is declared Governor of the Iſland of Guernſey, in the room of Lieut. Gen. Harvey, deceaſed, his Excellency having obtained a reverſionary grant thereof in the late reign. *D P.*

By private letters from Seville we hear, that the Spaniards at Oran are in a very ſickly condition; and the Moors, who preſs down upon them, give them great uneaſineſs, and have entirely blocked them up. *C. D P.*—*This does not intirely agree with an article in the foreign news of* ſaturday.

Laſt night a man was ſecured by the centry at S. James's, for aſſaulting a Clergyman belonging to the chapel, and for curſing the King, the Queen, and all the royal family. *D J.* —— He was committed to Tothill-fields Bridewell. *D J.* 26.

A few days ago a marriage was conſummated between Will. Vaughan Eſq; *cuſtos rotulorum* for the county of Merioneth, and Mrs. Kath. Nanney, a lady of great merit, and a fortune of 1500 l. per ann. *P.*

TUESDAY, *Sept.* 26.

Mr. Pennington, ſon of Sir Joſeph, is made one of the clerks of the Treaſury, a place of 100l. per ann. *D. J.*—We hear that Mr. Warner, ſon of Alderman Warner, of Northampton, is appointed Receiver-general of the land tax for that county. *P.*

The Hon. Col. Tho. Herbert, 3d ſon to the Earl of Pembroke, is choſen mayor of the corporation of Wilton in Lincolnſhire. —— Yeſterday ſe'nnight the Hon. Edw. Trelawney Eſq; a commiſſioner of the Victualling Office, was unanimouſly choſen mayor of the corporation of Looe. *D P.*

They write from Gibraltar, that the Right Hon. the Earl of Rothes arrived there Aug. 17. to take upon him the command of a regiment. *P.*

Lewis De Vic and Paul Cray, under ſentence of death in Newgate, are both ſo ill, that their lives are deſpaired of: they are attended by 2 phyſicians and an apothecary: their irons have been taken off, and they removed from the cells into an appartment in the Preſs-yard. *C. D P.*

On friday died at Nottingham, in a very advanced age, Paul Jervice Eſq; *C. D P.* —— The ſame day, at his ſeat in Norfolk, Sir Ralph Hare: —— On ſaturday the Hon. Col Godolphin, at his houſe near Kingſton. —— Laſt week, in her 84th year, Mrs. Crequet, wife of the Rev. Mr. Crequet, miniſter of the Lutheran church in the Savoy. He was married to her about 3 months, with whom he had a fortune of upwards of 7000 l. *P.*—*He was well payed for his* three months *kindneſs.*

WEDNESDAY, *Sept.* 27.

On ſunday laſt, between ſix and ſeven in the morning, his Majeſty, with his retinue, embarked on board the Carolina yatcht at Helvoetſluys, and, in about an hour and half more, all the yatchts and men of war were under ſail. After ſeveral becalmings and anchorings, his Majeſty landed yeſterday about two in the afternoon at Graveſend, in good health, where, being received in her Majeſty's body coach, in which were the Earl of Scarborough, Lord Delawar, and Lord Herbert, he arrived at Kenſington between five and ſix in the evening, having paſſed thro' the City. *D P.*

Yeſterday was taken at the India Houſe the general ballot for reducing the bonds to three per Cent. and a debate aroſe, Whether the Gentlemen that were the Inſpectors ſhould declare the ballot laſt night, or to the General C

this day; and it was carried for the declaration last night; which was as follows, 185 for the question, 147 against it. *D. P.*

The Committee of City lands have agreed with a Gardener for planting 231 elm-trees round the quarters in Moorfields, 1 s. 6 d. per tree; and on saturday a view was taken of the same, and the ground marked out: the walks are likewise all ordered to be neatly gravel'd; and all those people who sit with fruits, ballads, &c. will not be suffered to sit there any longer, they being accounted as common nusances. *C. P.*

From the PEGASUS *in Grub-street.*

SIR,

IN the *Miscellaneous observations on Authors*, &c. *for August*, we meet with a few curious corrections of some passages in SHAKESPEAR from the learned and never-enough-admired Mr. L. T. For my part, I cannot join with this sagacious gentleman in all his alterations; and therefore hope you will give me leave to propose my reasons for dissenting from two of them more especially, in the Poem called VENUS *and* ADONIS, *Stanz.* 142.

> *For who hath she to spend the night withall*
> *But idle sounds, resembling parasites?*
> *Like shrill tongu'd tapsters, answ'ring ev'ry call,*
> *Soothing the humour of fantastick Wits.*

To suit this *Idea* as well as to close the *Rhyme* more fully, he says, that he is persuaded the Poet wrote

> *Soothing the humour of fantastick Wights:*

Now, Mr. BAVIUS, if we prove this Stanza rhyme and reason, as it now stands, there will be no room to suppose the Author wrote otherwise. The Rhyme is undoubtedly as just as near an hundred places in the same author; which will be obvious to every reader, and their numbers save me the trouble of quoting them. And even Mr. T's own word *Wights* requires an unjustifiable strong pronunciation of the last syllable in *parasites*, to make a just rhyme, therefore on the account of rhyme, *Wits* may be as well supposed to be the poets word, as *Wights*. But it seems the sense is not so good, because the exercise of this fantastic humour is not the character of *Wits*, but of persons of a wild and jocular extravagance of temper. To which I answer, These persons, of a wild and *jocular* extravagance of temper, do very well suit with the character our poet *jocoursely gives* them of *fantastick Wits*, tho' not of *true or real Wits*. The best reason I can have for assenting to this alteration, is that which Mr. CONUNDRUM gives, who says, *Good Wits jump*, and consequently supposes L. T. may be the best judge of what SHAKESPEAR wote.

In *Titus Andronicus* (Act the 2d, Scene the last) MARCUS says to LAVINIA,

> *Speak*, gentle neice, *what stern ungentle hands*
> *Have lopp'd and hew'd, and made thy body bare*
> *Of her two branches, those sweet ornaments,*
> *Whose circling shadows kings have sought to sleep in,*
> *And might not gain so great an happiness,*
> *As half thy love.*

Instead of *half thy love*, which is very good sense, the critic reads *have thy love*, which is very obscure nonsense. And for what reason? Why because *Kings* would not be contented *with half her love* —— That might be; but they were forced to be *content* with less; for as little happiness as Mr. T. thinks half LAVINIA's Love might be to *Kings*, SHAKESPEAR has thought it too great for them, and makes MARCUS say, very elegantly, that *Kings* themselves had *fought to sleep in* her arms, could not obtain so great an happiness as even *half her love*. Pray, Mr. BAVIUS, where is the impropriety of this expression; is it not sense? is it not SHAKESPEAR's manner? How then is this alteration to be justified? Why, by no other reason, but because the sharp-sighted Mr. T. has discovered that these two words have erroneously usurped upon one another in several other places. And by the same authority I may read, instead of

> —— *kings* have *fought*
> —— *kings* half *fought*

And say, that it is to be supposed, if such great men as kings had fully *fought* to sleep in LAVINIA's arms, she must not in good manners have refused them. Upon mentioning these two emendations to Mr. CONUNDRUM, he said, he feared Mr. T. was but a *half-witted* Critic, and immediately repeated two lines from *Harlequin Horace*.

At more leisure, I perhaps may examine this Emendator a little further: at present (to use his own words) upon a careful perusal (of his criticisms) I dare warrant, that any person of moderate sagacity may furnish out a large crop of errors.

Sept. 19. 1732.

I am, Sir, your most humble servant,
A. H.

> ONce W—— to th' Aonian mountain came,
> And thus asserted his pretence to fame.
> As PHILIPS with immortal MARO —— I
> With celebrated FLACCUS justly vye:
> O PHOEBUS! him I've imitated well,
> And modern Poets I by far excell:
> Whom former ages knew, and present see.
> Britons are barb'rous, if compar'd with me:
> By fit examples I the means dispense,
> To smooth their numbers, and refine their sense,
> With utmost purity of word and thought;
> Style is by me to full perfection brought:
> With equal worth and modesty I aim,
> Mark, O LATONA's son, my double claim!
> Let, son of JOVE, my title be allow'd,
> Who gain abhor, and ne'er to falshood bow'd.
> The bold pretension grave APOLLO mov'd
> To wrath —— and thus the trifler he reprov'd:
> FLACCUS I know, and his desert allow,
> Some moderns too commend---- but what art thou?
> Can'st thou, can'st thou, to lasting fame aspire,
> Devoid of sense, or elegance, or fire?
> O mortal! thou hast little art, or grace,
> Or any thing —— but a Corinthian face.
> Pragmatic Bard! far other practice try,
> And title bring, e'er thou presume so high;
> Take my advice to modulize thy strain,
> (Tho' much I fear my council is in vain)
> Never, fond Bard! from nature's rules depart;
> Chuse those, altho' thou slight'st the rules of art.
> Rough be thy satire, arm'd with scourge, or sting,
> And do not softly, as to CELIA sing;
> On ev'ry subject be concise and clear,
> Aim more to move the soul, than charm the ear:
> Thy sentiments from partial blindness free.
> From affectation let thy diction be:
> Let justice lead thee, let not interest guide,
> Court plain desert, nor flatter pamper'd pride;
> In worth's true cause majestically flow,
> Nor tell in frothy Cant a tale too low:
> With curious search find out the path to fame;
> By truly-worthy precedent reclaim,
> And this way bring misguided men to shame.
> But LEONARD, glowing with disdainful thought,
> (Enrag'd and startled to be check'd and taught,
> Out of all patience, —— in a furious haste
> Withdrew —— and swore—— APOLLO had no Taste.

P. B.

FOREIGN NEWS.

THURSDAY, *Sept.* 21.

Hague, Sept. 9 N. S. The Court of France are at last come to the resolution to make vigorous representations, concerning the succession to the Dutchy of Deuxponts, once more to the general dyet of the Empire, and to let them know, That this was the last time his Most Christian Majesty would recommend the interests of the prince of Birkenfeldt, and that the dyet would do well to call to mind the dismal consequences which the affairs of Furstemberg formerly brought upon the Roman Empire.—— We are told, that it is out of all doubt, that France underhand favours the new East India company erected at Cadiz. *P.*

FRIDAY, *Sept.* 22.

Yesterday arrived three Mails from France, *and three from* Flanders.

Paris, Sept. 20. N. S. On the 16th the Duke of Orleans, and the Queen Dowager of Spain, his sister, stood Godfather and Godmother to one of the great bells lately cast for the abbey of St. Genevieve. —— On the 17th another bell was baptized, the Duke de Noailles standing Godfather. *C.*

Paris, Sept. 27. Some of the banished counsellors of the parliament have changed the places of their exile; others have leave to go to their country seats, and some few to return to Paris. *C.* —— Mr. Chiselden, an English Surgeon, having been presented to the King at Fontainebleau, his Majesty sent a letter to the new Academy of Surgeons, commanding them to chuse him immediately a member, without any regard to forms, no foreigner having yet been chosen. *P.*

SATURDAY, *Sept.* 23.

Rome, Sept. 3. They write from Naples, that a new college is just opened there for teaching young clergymen the eastern languages, who are to be sent to the Indies as missionaries, to oppose the progress made in those countries by the Lutheran and Calvinistical missionaries, sent thither by the English and Danes.—— The King of Sardinia has seized the revenues of the abbey of St. Agatha in Savoy, which takes in 5 fiefs that till now have been reckoned to depend on the holy see. *C. DP.*

Letters from Vienna, of Sept. 13. N. S. say, that the Jews of Wurtzbourg have committed a barbarous murder in a village of the Bailywick of Sternberg; where 5 of their tribe persuaded a young peasant, of 21 years of age, to bring into the wood a poor young beggar of 11 years, promising him a recompence of 300 crowns. The peasant having comply'd with it, and the Jews having got the young beggar into their hands, they hung him upon a tree by his feet, cut his belly in the form of a cross, and scourg'd him afterwards in this posture to death. The peasant having been seen to go out of the city in company with the young beggar, the bailiff of Sternberg caus'd him to be taken up, and strictly examined, who denounc'd the 5 Jews guilty of this most execrable murder: they were immediately seized; and tho' they offer'd 10000 florins, he committed them to prison, and sent them to Konigshoffen, where they undergo a rigorous examination. 'Tis said that the peasant has been confronted with them; but that they persist tenaciously in the denial of the commission of that horrible fact. *S J.*

This day arrived three Mails from Holland.

Seville, Aug. 30. They talk of a numerous fleet to be equipped against next spring, wherein will be embarked about 40 000 men, on some expedition yet unknown. *L E* —— *Sept.* 5. An express from Oran has brought advice, that the old Bey had twice attacked the fort of S. Andrew with 10 or 12000 men; but was beat off, and left 4000 of his men behind him. *W E.*

TUESDAY, *Sept.* 26.

Hague, Sept. 16 N. S. All our advices from Seville [illegible] Court of Spain is making preparations to [illegible] greater expedition in the month of April [illegible] to Africa, and many people are apt to [illegible] that they will then undertake the siege of Gibraltar. *P.*

Paris, Sept. 26 N. It appears by letters from Rome, that the process of Cardinal Coscia is drawing to an end. If one may judge of his crimes by the length of the proceeding, by the sums with which he has offer'd to buy himself off, or by the complaints of the Roman people, then is he a rogue of an enormous size. And yet for all that, there is no appearance that his eminency will reach the gallows. It rather looks as if it was designed only to make this mitred criminal, this ministerial robber, compound for all his felonies, and refund only part of the great wealth he has scraped together. If this should be the case, and after that he should be absolved, and his conscience scour'd clean, we may live to see Coscia sovereign pontiff, and then he may go over his old rogueries *cum privilegio*. Let Coscia possess himself once of the keys, and what thieves in purple shall we behold locked into the sacred college? *Marche à Terre* may then be a cardinal, and our bishops chosen out of the *Charitable Corporation*. —— Here has been dispersed in France, as well as in Holland, a letter from the chevalier Belloni at Rome to an English Lord, upon the subject of a judicial burning of a former letter written by him to the parliament of England. In the second letter signior Belloni compares the affair of the *Charitable Corporation*, and the escape of Thompson, to the case of the Directors of the South Sea Company, and the flight of the Cashire Knight. He insinuates as if there was some mystery of iniquity in both these events, which he could reveal; but contents himself with justifying his own conduct. He suggests some suspicions, indeed, which do no honour to the persons they are applied to; yet he keeps his pen to terms of civility and good-breeding. In short, the letter, as my Dutch correspondent words it, is *very delicately*, or, if you will, *very artificially* written. *P.*

WEDNESDAY, *Sept.* 27.

Leghorn, Sept. 13. They write from Genoa, that the State has received the Emperor's final resolution on the affairs of Corsica, whereby they are given to understand, that without any further tergiversation they must release the four chiefs, and send them to Milan, as well as send home the hostages which the commissaries of the republick received at Bastia, and, in short, conform in all things to the treaty concluded under the guaranty of the imperial Court. *D. P.*

On Tuesday Stocks were

South Sea Stock was 104 3 qrs. South Sea Annuity 111 5 8ths, to 3 qrs. Bank 152 to 1 qr. for the Opening. Bank Circulation 4 l. 10 s. Premium. India 157 3 qrs, 158 1 qr, 158 Three per Cent. Annuity 99 7 8ths, to 100. Royal Exchange Assurance 105. London Assurance 13 5 8ths. to 3 qrs. York Buildings 6, for the Opening. African 38. English Copper 2 l. 2 s. Welch ditto 1 l. 15 s. South-Sea Bonds 2 l. 6 s. Premium. India ditto 3 l. ditto.

Now in the Press, and shortly will be published,

THE ADVOCATE. A Defence of the B. of Lichfield and Coventry, from the Charge of being the Author of a Pamphlet called, The Principles of the Leading Quakers. Including some Remarks on the Writings of the late Mr. CHARLES LESLIE. In a Letter to his Lordship. By E. B.

Printed by J. Hugonson, in Bartholomew-Close, for J. Roberts, at the Oxford-Arms in Warwick-Lane. [Price One Shilling.]

LONDON: Printed by P. SANDERS, in Crown-Court, Butcher-Row, without Temple-Bar; where Letters and Advertisements are taken in, and by Capt. GULLIVER, near the Temple; also at the Rainbow Coffee-House in Cornhill, and John's Coffee-House in Sheer-Lane, near Temple-Bar. [Price Twopence.]

The Grub-ſtreet Journal.

NUMB. 144.

Thurſday, OCTOBER 5. 1732.

Great Wits to madneſs ſure are near ally'd.
DRYDEN's Abſolom and Achitophel.

IT is now above two years ſince our bookſeller delivered into my hands a manuſcript containing about ſeven or eight ſheets of paper, which he found upon removing ſome of his books. He cou'd not call to mind from whom he had received it, or that any perſon had ever been with him to inquire after any ſuch copy. He deſired it might be communicated to our Society, and their opinion taken, whether it was divided into chapters which had no dependance upon one another, it might not be proper to publiſh now and then one in our Journal? They approved of the propoſal; but thought the execution ought to be delayed for ſome conſiderable time; in which the author might probably be diſcovered, and his conſent obtained to the publication in this manner. But after two years fruitleſs enquiry, concluding that he is dead, either corporally, or at leaſt legally; and that this ingenious and learned piece will not now ſee the light in a more advantageous manner; they have at laſt given me orders to publiſh it.

I ſhall not pretend to give any account of the nature and deſign of a work, a very great part of which was not underſtood when read in our Society. As it is a greater compliment to the underſtanding of every ſagacious reader to leave him to form his own conjectures concerning a compoſition ſo much above the reach of vulgar apprehention: ſo I dare affirm, that its being unintelligible will not render it at all leſs agreeable to a very great number of curious and inquiſitive perſons. As to the author, I think it is very plain, that he was a member of our Society; and I believe a writer of Political Pamphlets at the proper ſeaſon of the year. Whether the great or little ſucceſs of his writings, his gaining or his miſſing of penſion or preferment according to his deſerts, turned his brains, is now perhaps impoſſible to be known. But it appears evidently enough, that when he compoſed this laſt work his head was a little touched. And the work itſelf is indeed a manifeſt imitation of an *Eſſay towards the theory of the intelligible world intuitively conſidered*; written about twenty years ago, by one Mr GREGORY, of Chriſt-church in Oxford, under the name of GABRIEL JOHN, and whom every body, but himſelf, thought to be mad. However, it muſt be confeſſed, that the copy (a thing which very ſeldom happens) infinitely exceeds the original. It has no title prefixed to it, but begins with

A POSTSCRIPT *by way of* PROLEGOMENA.

THE words *Advertiſement to the Reader*, *Introduction*, *Preamble*, *Preface*, *Prelude*, *Proem*, &c. have from time immemorial, one or other of them, been preferred to the firſt place, in all thoſe inſtructions, which the clan of ſcribblers, at the importunity, either of their friends, or of their own wants, is continually obtruding on the public. Upon this account, they claimed the ſame place of diſtinction in the enſuing Treatiſe, and preſented a petition in form to the learned and judicious committee in my brains. But this committee, being reſolved to ſhake off all old-faſhioned, foppiſh ceremonies, which have no real ſignificancy, and to free me from the ſlaviſh and ponderous burthen of forms and rules, which ſtint the ſpirit, and depreſs the towering imagination, the bill was rejected *nemine contradicente*. I have likewiſe carefully avoided all ſmooth metaphors, gloſſy paraphraſes, and tautological excurſions; the ſole end and deſign of which, is to dazle the eyes of the reader by falſe lights, and to draw him into the mazes of error. Nature is a perfect beauty, and wants not the aſſiſtance of artificial ornaments to ſet her off. Would you form a true idea of her charms, you muſt view her naked. It is thus the following Treatiſe preſents itſelf to your contemplation. Would you ſee a modern lady (the proper emblem of a modern book) in all her ſplendor, view her painted and patched, as ſhe comes from her morning devotion at her toilet, or as ſhe is going to receive that of the evening in the Park, or at the Playhouſe: but never hope to ſee her true face, 'till ſhe is married; nor even then, unleſs in the husband's company.— Would you make a right judgment of any Great Man, attend his levee; obſerve what paſſes between him and his paraſites; the promiſes on one ſide, and the profeſſions on the other: as nothing is meant by either, ſo nothing is the conſequence; for *ex nihilo nihil fit*. But you may negatively conclude ſomething from this diverting farce: and by ſeeing what theſe gentlemen are not, in ſome meaſure diſcover what they really are.

In order to which, I JOHN GABRIEL, patruelian adopted ſon of GABRIEL JOHN of ſupermortal fame, and heir apparent to all the grounds of wit, and tenements of humour, ſituate, lying, and being in Grub-ſtreet and Moorfields, the bicipital ſummits of the Britiſh mount Parnaſſus, now in the poſſeſſion of my honoured Uncle aforeſaid, and in the occupation of his under-tenants, do hereby authorize and impower the following four of them, viz. JAMES FROTH, JEREMY FLIGHTS, THOMAS FUSTIAN, and NATHAN BOMBAST, all, or any of them, *conjunctim*, *diviſim*, *diſtinctim*, *ſeparatim*, *or ſeorſim*, to write in large capitals, THIS IS THE POSTSCRIPT.

But tho' I am conſcious, that the ſame anti-melancholic juice flows from my pen as well as that the ſame hypomaſtic honourable blood flows in my veins, which once flowed from and in thoſe of my great and good Uncle; yet I don't indulge myſelf in ſo much vanity as to think, that my inelaborate lucubrations will, like his, immediately meet with univerſal applauſe. No — I don't expect they will be attended with ſuch applauſe, 'till, like thoſe of HORACE and VIRGIL, they have received the ſanction of near two thouſand years, having eſcaped ſtill more pure from the fiery ordeal of the Critics.

What means this mighty tumult in my ſoul?
Somewhat prodigious labours in my breaſt.
Hah! who art thou? — The flatt'ring mirror lies,
Or elſe there's madneſs rolling in that eye.
'Tis ſo — the films that dimm'd my viſual ray
Scatter like hail-ſtones at the ſight of thunder.

The ſphere of my breaſt is expanded, my ſoul walks upon ſtilts, or has got a fit of the cholic. Lo, before my eyes a pile, of which the baſe is founded on proſe, and the middle curiouſly carved with verſe; but the top cannot be ſeen, it riſes higher than Teneriff, and *caput inter nubila condit*. It ſhines like a ſtatue of gold: on the pedeſtal I read engraved VIRO IMMORTALI JOHANNI GABRIELI. But it will be more durable than braſs, and defy the teeth of devouring time. So great is its firmneſs and ſolidity, that it can be melted down by nothing but the laſt conflagration.

But ha! whence this ebb of extaſy! Off, off, thou greaſy fiend, nor tear me from a proſpect of ſuch tranſport.— Ah! 'tis in vain! I am tumbled from the higheſt orb of exalted fancy, whence I looked down with contempt upon a vile race of tellurigenous mortals. I am now ſo near them, that I plainly ſee whatever they are doing: ſome are employed at land in undermining their country, while they are enriching themſelves with the precious ore which they dig out of her bowels. Others are embarqued at ſea in a leaky bottom, laden with Britiſh gold, which they are conveying abroad to foreign climes, where Britiſh iron formerly had a much greater influence. But ſee, the winds ariſe, the waves run high, and the ſhattered veſſel is made the ſport of both.

Appendix to the POSTCRIPT.

Cedite Romani ſcriptores, cedite Graii,

Avaunt, ye muckworms of old Greece and Rome,
Vaniſh ye fantoms, let JOHN GABRIEL come.

Talk no more of your HORACE's *Exegi monumentum*, 'twas a mere bauble; and your OVID's *Jamque opus exegi* was no more than a dirt-pie, that might be taken and demoliſhed by the puny buff-coats that ſtrut in Tothill-fields. As for VIRGIL, poh! ——The Leviathan! the great Leviathan! ſounds not this more terrible, than his *fortemque Gyan, fortemque Cloanthum*? What is his
Bronteſque, Steropeſque, & nudus membra Pyracmon, to
Coſtarum gardæ, Dunkirka, Mahona, Gibraltar,
Fundi, Bull-doggique, & Stock-jobbero—Britannus.

As the words are noble, ſo is the ſubject; and I don't queſtion but you are already convinced, that I have handled it with a becoming dignity of ſentiments and language. ——— Give me leave, Gentlemen, to obſerve, that you have in this ſmall Treatiſe, whatever has been written upon this occaſion; which therefore you may wonder how I could reduce within ſo narrow a compaſs. But by the advantage of a political preſs, I have been enabled to condenſe the ſubſtance of a whole Tract into a few lines, nay, ſometimes into a ſingle word, which may very often be done with leſs difficulty than you imagine. I have likewiſe invented a very valuable menſtruum, in which any Piece, being ſteeped a few minutes, is converted into a fluid, the finer parts whereof aſcend, as the groſſer fœtid matter ſubſides. I chuſe not to ſpeak in the language of the Chymiſts, becauſe I would willingly be underſtood. The ſpirituous part appears in colour like *Mercurius ſublimatus*; which, being fixed upon white paper, immediately forms itſelf into words, containing the quinteſſence of the Tract. I have made an infinite number of experiments in both ways; and having generally found them anſwer, I take them to be as infallible as the Pope's Bulls. Neither of theſe methods I muſt own, has had the ſame ſucceſs upon ſome weekly political Papers; out of which neither my preſs cou'd ſqueeze one ſenſible word, nor my menſtruum produce any ſpirituous liquor.—But my book-ſeller calls aloud upon me, and ſays, there is too much for a *Poſtſcript* already; and, I hope, my reader is of the ſame opinion. For my own part, I am almoſt tired, and find myſelf on the flats. Therefore to oblige all three. I have ordered my Amanuenſis to write,. *Here endeth the* POSTSCRIPT.

To my worthy friend Mr. John Gabriel on his excellent Treatiſe, entitled, *The ſtate of the nation*.

I mmortal GABRIEL, hail, immortal ſon,
O f thy immortal uncle, GABRIEL JOHN!
H ow haſt thou opened our politic eyes,
N ow hovering low, now towering to the skies!

G reat are the myſteries which thou deign'ſt t'unfold,
A nd in ſuch language worthy to be told.
B ritain inſtructed by each nervous line,
R ound the vaſt globe ſhall ſound thy praiſe divine.
I n ancient ſplendor ſhe ſhall raiſe her fame:
E nrich'd by thy advice, let her proclaim,
L ong live JOHN GABRIEL on the banks of Thame.

Another by an unknown hand.

LET PHILIPS his *Chimeras dire* rehearſe,
Or *Galligaskins* in Miltonian verſe;
Thoſe Galligaskins, which had long withſtood
The rough incroaching froſt, and wintry flood.
Altho' the Bard's, both lofty and ſerene,
The numbers noble, yet the theme is mean.
Let Rhimers ſputter forth ——— praiſe,
A wretched ſubject in more wretched lays:
Let hireling ſcribblers fulſome proſe diſplay,
In praiſe of debts and beggary, for pay.
Thou, thou, my friend, doſt nobler themes purſue,
Thy native Britains good thy only view.
Thy ſyſtem, GABRIEL, ſo much judgment ſhows,
So ſtrong thy ſatire, yet ſo ſmooth it flows,
That nought thy verſe can equal but thy proſe.
Nature, bright Goddeſs, guides th' inſtructive pen,
Unheard, unſeen, by deaf and purblind men.
Hail, mighty Patriot, to thy native ſoil,
To pleaſe, inſtruct, and dignify our Iſle.
† So the pure radiant God to Delian plains
Deſcending, cheers his wandring kindred ſwains:
Improves their genius, mends their viſual ray,
And pours into their eye-balls new-born day.

There were twelve lines more, which I choſe to leave out, the compliments being greater than I could bear. The ingenious author, I hope, will excuſe this freedom; which, I dare ſay, the reader will commend, as an inſtance of modeſty rarely to be found among the writers of the preſent learned age.

† N. B. Theſe lines are the author's own; but he hopes the authority of ſome modern poets will excuſe this additional compariſon.

Mr. BAVIUS, *Middle-Temple, October 2d, 1732.*

THE death of that celebrated actor Mr. WILKS has (theſe few days paſt) been the ſubject of our News-papers, in ſeveral ſhapes. I believe the Town in general is of opinion, that his loſs is irreparable: but what may be the ſentiments of thoſe actors who are endeavouring to ſucceed him, I won't pretend to ſay.

The ſurviving managers are now, in my opinion, reduced to the neceſſity of ſhewing the utmoſt of their skill in theatrical affairs, if they intend, as I humbly preſume they do, to make the ſtage turn to their uſual advantage. I will ſubmit the proper meaſures to do this, to their own inventions; and ſhall here only obſerve to them, that they propoſe to proceed in letting the moſt unqualified of their actors and actreſſes wretchedly ſupply the place

their late predecessors, they will find themselves very much mistaken.

I was last week a spectator at the Tragedy of *Macbeth*, where I found the character of the late tall, manly MACDUFF, performed by an actor, in every particular less than man; and consequently, unfit for an ancient heroe. The part of MACDUFF is of importance, particularly in a scene in the close of the fourth act, in which there is admirable distress; and which, for the fineness of the writing, would be greatly applauded from the mouth of any actor that could speak to be understood —— His remarkable little strut in this scene, put me in mind of the fly in the fable, who, sitting upon the spoke of a chariot-wheel, said to herself, *What a dust do I raise!* In this light, no doubt, all men appear, who are vainly fond of shewing themselves in characters, to which they are unequal.—But Mr. BAVIUS, I should think myself guilty of an unpardonable injustice, if I concluded, without allowing this actor to have a genius well adapted to the stage. —— In the *Mock-Doctor*, in the *Busy-Body*, and in several parts in comedy, he promises very fairly, and has a just title to encouragement; in that walk, he is very capable of giving pleasure; but when he is so mistaken as to attempt to personate the heroe, he does prejudice to himself, and affronts the audience. I am, Mr. BAVIUS,

Your humble servant,

PHILO-DRAMATICUS.

N. B. There are actors who have stature to personate the heroe, without any other essential; and who, by their vain attempts, are proper subjects for ridicule —— You may occasionally hear from me again on his head.

To the author of the copy of verses in the Grub-street Journal, Number 139.

An EPIGRAM.

IN vain with glowing heart, and smiling eyes,
RICH sees his theatre in Bow-street rise;.
In vain with expectation fills the Town,
Whilst thou at random knock'st his actors down:
Thy executing pen, dear scribbler, sheathe;
Already thou hast prais'd thy friends to death.

DOMESTIC NEWS.

C. *Courant.*	E P. *Evening Post.*
P. *Post-Boy.*	S J. *St. James's Evening Post.*
D P. *Daily Post.*	W E. *Whitehall Evening Post.*
D J. *Daily Journal.*	L E. *London Evening Post.*

THURSDAY, *Sept.* 28.

Yesterday a general court of the East-India Company unanimously agreed to the reducement of their bonds at 3 per cent. *C. DP.* —— The East-India company's four per cent bonds are generally reckoned to be near 3,000,000. every one of which becomes due at Lady-day next. .... The lame manner in which the 400,000 l has been pick'd up, to make this push, gives a glorious prospect of success, when a subscription shall be opened for 3,000,000 l. *DP.* *Octob.* 3, 4.

We hear from Shealing, in Berkshire, that on the 10th inst. the wife of John Seedwell was deliver'd of three boys, who were next day baptized by the names of *Abraham*, *Isaac*, and *Jacob*, and are all like to live. —— And on monday last, the wife of Will. Harvey, of Chipping Sodbury, was delivered of three girls, who were christen'd the next day by the names of Love, Peace, and Unity. *D J.* — John Seedwell *brooked his name.* Abraham, Isaac and Jacob, *I hope, may live to marry* Love, Peace, and Unity.

Yesterday a woman was committed to Newgate for having three husbands. *D J.* —— *Had this* woman *had* three children *at a birth, it had not been so strange.*

The Rt. Hon. the Lord Mayor and Aldermen have agreed, that the procession on the next Lord's Mayor's day shall be performed on horseback through the city, which has not been for above twenty years, the whole being to be performed in a very grand manner. *WE.*

Oreford, Sept. 25. This day Mr. Rob. Duffin, in the interest of the country gentlemen, was elected, he and his electors well deserving the title granted by Queen Elizabeth in her charter, wherein her majesty was pleased to call the number then, Her *honest men of Oreford.* *L E.*

Yesterday morning died, at his house in Bow-street Covent-garden, Mr. Wilks, that celebrated comedian,* belonging to the Theatre Royal in Drury-Lane. *C.* — Between nine and ten, *P. DP.* —— Rob. Wilks Esq; one of the Masters, &c. *P.* —— One of the patentees and managers: the reputation the English theatre has had, was very much owing to his indefatigable care, and regular conducting of the whole. *DP.* —— It may be truly said, that his death is the greatest loss the English State [Stage *I suppose*] has ever sustained. *P.*

They write from Marlborough in Wilts, that one day last week the batchelors there collected among themselves (some say) 9 l. for entertaining all the maids in town, of 30 years of age and upwards: and we hear that 5 l. 10 s. was given to Mr. Middleton's company of comedians, for diverting the antique virgins with the play of the Old Batchelor, (to which none of the sex under that age were admitted; and a certain maid that wanted but a month thereof, being, to her great mortification, denied entrance) and that the remainder of the money was expended in treating of the ladies with biskets and wine. 'Tis said there were present above 40 batchelors, and 120 old Maids; but, we hope, the publication of this frolick will contribute towards lessening their number. *S J.* —— *I think these* 40 batchelors, *by way of penance, should be obliged to marry* 3 *of these* old maids *apiece: and so take off the whole number: but I fear, in this case, the latter would think the greatest penance unjustly layed upon themselves.*

On tuesday the flying man attempted to fly from Greenwich church; but the rope not being drawn tort enough, it waved with him, and occasioned his hitting his foot against a chimney, and threw him off the same [chimney *according to my grammar, but* rope *according to my author's*] to the ground; whereby he broke his wrist, and bruised his head and body in such a desperate manner, that 'tis thought he cannot recover. *D J.* —— On saturday he died. *C. DP. Oct.* 3.

FRIDAY, *Sept.* 21.

His Majesty was pleased, before he left the Carolina yatcht, to confer the honour of knighthood on Capt. Charles Hardy, commander. *P.*

Yesterday at Guildhall Rob. Alsop and Hen Hankey Esqs were sworn in Sheriffs —— Afterwards the Lord Mayor in his coach of state drawn by six horses, accompanied the Aldermen, &c. went to Kensington, to wait upon his Majesty: Sir William Thomson, Recorder, made their compliments to his majesty upon his happy return to his kingdoms, in an elegant speech [a very pathetick speech. *C.*] To which his Majesty was pleased to return a most gracious answer, and to confer the honour of knighthood on the Lord Mayor, John Bernard Esq; and Hen. Hankey Esq; C. &c.

The rev. Dr. Bundy is presented to the rectory of S. Bridget, *alias* S. Brides, in Fleetstreet, in the room of Mr. Evans deceased. *C. P. D J.* —— Yesterday Mr. Cradwick, an eminent surgeon, was chosen surgeon of Guy's hospital, in the room of Mr. Cooper deceased. *C. D J.* — The candidates were Mr. Cradock, Mr. Anbury, and Mr. Sharp. *D P.*

On sunday Mr. Carr, being disordered in his senses, drowned himself in a pond near Epsom. —— On wednesday Mr. Coston, a young gentleman of a plentiful fortune shot himself at his lodgings near Mark-lane, being disordered in his senses. *C.*

SATURDAY, *Sept.* 23.

Yesterday, at Guildhall, John Barber Esq; and Sir Will. Billers Knt. were return'd by the Common-hall to the court of Aldermen, who made choice of the former, he being the senior Alderman, and was accordingly declared duly elected, on which occasion he made a handsome speech, &c. *D P.*

Yesterday, at a general court of the York-buildings company, the Hon. Col. Sam. Horsey was chosen governor; Nat. Blackerby, Alex. Burham, Ric. Farwell, Jer. Horsey, Andr. Meare, Will. Stephens Esqrs, Assistants. *D J.* —— Alex. Barham, And. Mecere. *C.*

His Grace the Duke of S. Albans, Constable of his Majesty's castle of Windsor, &c. has appointed Ric. Aldworth Esq. his Lieutenant and Deputy-warden. *P.*

Mr. Jam. Johnson, book-keeper to Mr. Alderman Perry is chosen chief Clerk to the Committee for inspecting the accounts of the South-sea company. *D J.*

On wednesday last one hundred and fifty freemen were shipped for Chester, to give their votes at the ensuing election of a Mayor. *D P.* —— *It is not usual, for* freemen *to be* transported.

Last thursday was proclaimed, by the Lord of the manor, a fair at Mile-end old town, which has not been near this hundred year: it began this day, and will hold three days. *S J.* —— Yesterday a fair was opened at Mile-end old town, by John King Esq; Coroner of the City of London, and proprietor of the court of Whitechappel, by vertue of a patent granted by King Charles II. *W E.*

We hear that a patent will shortly pass the Great Seal, for creating the Rt. Hon. Sir Fran. Child Knight, Lord Mayor, a Baron of these realms. *C.* —— This is notoriously false. *L E.* —— *I suppose, that* my Brother *means,* is *made* notoriously false *by this contradiction.*

Yesterday morning died at Cambridge, Mr. Harper, a Barrister of the Temple, eldest son of Miles Harper Esq; of S. James's, Westminster: he was a young gentleman of a good education and genius, and distinguished himself in a most remarkable manner, in the great cause between the Bishop of Ely and Dr. Bentley, at the bar of the House of Lords in the last Session of Parliament, by which he got great reputation; he was of council for the Bishop. *D P.*

Last tuesday morning a gentleman, who liv'd at Hays near Bromley in Kent, possessed of a plentiful income, went to London, and after, being return'd that evening, went immediately into his chamber, and shot out his brains, to the great surprize and grief of his family, there not appearing in the least any discontent of mind in his behaviour, or other cause for committing so desperate an action. *S J.*

Exeter, Sept. 27. On monday last Mr. Ric. Vivian was chosen mayor. It was observable, that one John Drew, who hath been a freeman near seventy years, and born in 1626, went to the Guildhall without any one's assistance, and gave his vote. *L E.*

MONDAY, *Oct.* 2.

Kensington, *Sept.* 28. His Majesty in council was pleased to order, that the Parliament, which stands prorogued to Oct. 12. should be prorogued to Dec. 5. C. &c.

On Saturday their Majesties, &c. took the diversion of hunting the stag, in the new park at Richmond, which gave them very good diversion for about three hours, &c. *C.* —— about two hours, *P.* —— The chase lasted near an hour; when the Queen in her chaise came in at the death. *D P.*

The same day his Majesty was pleased to appoint the Hon. Sir Will. Strickland secretary at war, to be master of the buckhounds. C. &c. —— To pay the officers of the buckhounds, till his majesty shall appoint a master. *L E.* 3.

Last week Sir Archibald Grant, Dennis Bond Esq; and others, late directors and managers of the Charitable Corporation, delivered, upon oath to the Barons of the exchequer, duplicates of all their estates and effects. *C.* — Sir Rob. Sutton, knight of the bath, Will. Burroughs Esq; Rich. Wolley, and Tho. Warren, gentlemen. *D J.*

On wednesday Solomon Ashley Esq; was chosen governor of the company of Welsh copper mines, and Pet. Hartopp, Esq; deputy-governor. *D J.*

On saturday the two new sheriffs, Rob. Alsop Esq; and Sir Hen. Hankey Knt. were sworn before the Barons of the exchequer, and inducted into their office. *C. DP.*

On wednesday died, at Nottingham, Tho. White Esq; member of parliament for the said town, and chief clerk of the office of ordnance, under his grace the D. of Argyll. *P.* — On friday night the R. Hon. the L. Lewisham, son to the E. of Dartmouth, at his house in Holles-street, near Cavendish-square. *C. DP. D J.* —— Of the small-pox, at the Earl's house on Black-heath. *P.* —— On saturday morning the Rev. Dr. Edw. Oliver, rector of S. Mary Abchurch, lecturer of S. Augustin's and S. Faith's, and prebendary of S. Paul's. *P.* —— Yesterday morning at Chelsea, the lady Mary Cockburn, eldest sister to the R. Hon. the Earl of Denbigh, and wife to Dr. Will. Cockburn, an eminent physician in S. James's-street. *D P.*

TUESDAY, *Oct.* 3.

Yesterday his Majesty was pleased to appoint Tho. Walker, of Wimbleton in Surrey, Esq. one of the commissioners of the customs, to be surveyor of his Majesty's crown land revenue, in the room of Dr. Sayer, deceased. *D P.*

It is written from Blandford, the 30th ult. that they had received the remainder of the university and city of Oxford's generous donation to their unhappy sufferers, viz. from the university 363 l. 16 s. 6 d. from the city 122 l. 4 s. 6 d. In all 486 l. 1 s. *D J.*

Last night a fire broke out at the house of Mr. Barnes, a cloth-worker in the Old-change; which consumed the top of the said house, and damaged four more. *C.* — Burnt the roofs of two or three houses. *D P.* — Entirely consumed the said house. *P.*

At the close of last week a cabinet courier arrived express to the chevalier de Ossorio, his Sardinian majesty's envoy at this court, with dispatches of great moment: he came to Calais from Turin in five days, and slept but two hours on the way. *S J. L E.*

Stamford, Sept. 26. This day a man flew down a rope from the top of all-saints church to the ball, the iron bar of the window broke, and it was with some difficulty he saved himself; yet he had the hardiness to do it a second time, and went up to the top on the outside of the pinnacle. *W E.*

Edward Burton Esq; was lately appointed receiver-general of his Majesty's revenues in Wales. *W E.* — Thomas Parr, of Datchet in the county of Bucks Esq; is appointed receiver-general of the land-tax and duty on houses for the said county, in the room of William Hartley Esq; who has resigned. *S J.*

Last saturday night, about nine or ten o'clock, a fire broke out in Croucher's-walk, near Burr-street, and burnt down one house to the ground; with several warehouses with pitch, tar, and cables in them, to a considerable value. *S J.*

Last night a gentleman shot himself through the head with a pistol, at the golden-lion tavern in the parish of S. John the evangelist. *S J.* — And died immediately. *L E.* —— With two pistols: one of the slugs is still in his head: it is hoped he will do well. *C.* 4.

WEDNESDAY, *Oct.* 4.

Yeſterday the L. mayor complained to the court of aldermen, againſt the printer of the Daily Poſt-boy, for inſerting in that paper an incoherent ſpeech, alledging it to be ſpoke by his lordſhip on friday laſt, at Guildhall. The court expreſſed a juſt reſentment on the occaſion, and immediately directed a ſummons for the ſaid printer's appearing before them; but not being at home, he is ordered to attend the next court day. *D P.* —— The court was pleaſed to appoint Mr. Ingram, an attorney in Ironmonger-lane [to be] keeper of newgate, in the room of Mr. Pitt; *C.* —— and to make an order for the future, that all priſoners that ſhould be tried at the Old-bailey, and found on their trial to be not guilty, ſhould be immediately diſcharged without paying any fees. *C. DP. DJ.*

The ſpaniſh ambaſſador and his lady, who landed at Dover on ſaturday laſt, lay on monday night at Rocheſter, where three inns were taken up for him and his retinue. His excellency is expected in town this day. *D J.*

Laſt ſaturday counſellor Ford, of Fetter-lane, being a hunting in Buckinghamſhire, was unfortunately thrown off his horſe, by which accident his ſkull was fractured, and he died on the ſpot. *C.* —— He was overturned in a chaiſe; the wheel ran over his head, and bruiſed him ſo that he died ſoon after. *P.*

From the PEGASUS *in Grub-ſtreet.*

THE editors of the pyrated copy of GRUBIANA, *or A compleat collection of all the poems and material letters from the Grub-ſtreet Journals,* &c. *Printed by* J. HUGHS *in High-Holbourn, and ſold by* T. WARNER *in Pater-Noſter-Row. Pr.* 2 *s.* finding their market ſpoiled by the account we gave of that impudent and blundering impoſition on the public, in our 113th and 114th journals; about three months afterwards republiſhed it, under the title of *The Grub-ſtreet Miſcellany,* &c. fairly adding, *Printed for* Mr. BAVIUS, and then, truly, *ſold by* W. HINTON, E. NUTT, *and* J CRITCHLEY. This they advertiſed ſeveral times in an obſcure weekly paper, printed by HINTON; for printing of which, he himſelf is at preſent withdrawn into great obſcurity. But being diſappointed a ſecond time in putting off their ſtolen goods, they have cooked up a third title-page, which runs thus; *Faithful Memoirs of the Grub-ſtreet Society: now firſt publiſhed by* Mr. BAVIUS, &c. *with a picture,* &c. and advertiſed it in the *Daily Poſt-Boy* of laſt Saturday, as ſold by T. DORMER, A. DODD, J. CRICKLY, and W. SHROPSHIRE. In this advertiſement, is inſerted a N.B. *The publick are deſired to take notice, that there was a ſpurious, ill-printed book, publiſhed about three months ago (having the names,* T. WARNER *in the title page) which we advertiſed againſt ſeveral times,* &c. —— In anſwer to which lying advertiſement, The public are deſired to take notice, that this is the very book, which has been publiſhed under three different titles; and is here advertiſed, with the addition of a paltry picture; in which alone the pyratical wretches concerned have any juſt and real property. Who may well laugh at the folly of the buyers, and triumph in their own falſhood, if they can impoſe upon the public a vile edition of a book, even by advertiſing againſt that very edition —— We are not at all ſurprized at any thing which a HUGHS, a HINTON, or a DORMER may do. But we cannot but wonder, that Mr. WARNER, a perſon who has acquired ſo great fame and profit by publiſhing the works of our members, ſhould ſo far countenance ſuch an abominable pyracy, as not only to ſuffer his name to be put to it, and to, permit it to be advertiſed ſeveral times in the *Poſt-Boy*; but even to refuſe to inſert in that paper our advertiſements againſt it. —On this occaſion, we think it very proper to deſire all perſons not raſhly to ſubſcribe for any pretended *New Tranſlations of* JOSEPHUS, PLUTARCH, &c. or for any ſtolen new edition of *The Lives of the Holy Fathers, Book of Martyrs, Burkitt on the New Teſtament,* &c. propoſed weekly; but to inquire firſt into the characters of the perſons who make the propoſals: from whom they can reaſonably expect nothing but pyrated copies vilely printed, if thoſe are principally concerned, whom we have here proved guilty of repeated falſhoods.

A Dialogue betwixt P. *and* W.

P. WHether from France, or Italy, or Spain,
Blow the rough wind, it turns thy fickle vane:
To blunders old, till blunders new ſucceed;
And ſtill blind fortune helps thee at thy need.
W. Let but blind fortune with propitious gales
Favour my courſe, and fill my ſwelling ſails;
Boaſt thou the mighty politician's art,
While ſtill my blunders baffle all thy art.

Edinburgh, Sept. 21. Laſt night Sir Rob. Sinclair, of Sevenſton Bar. was married to Miſs Kerr, daughter to the late Col. Kerr, a lady of great beauty, virtue and merit, and a fortune of 6000 l. *C.* 28. —— Of Stevenſon. *P. DP. DJ.* —— A very handſome fortune. *P.*

Tho. Penn Eſq; proprietor of Penſilvania, landed at Cheſter, ſixteen miles from Philadelphia Aug. 11, and on the 12th made his public entry into that city, being accompanied with 800 horſe, amidſt the acclamations of thouſands of ſpectators. *DP.* —— Moſt of the chiefs of the city had the honour to to ſup with him. *D P.* 2. — *This was much better than only to have kiſſed his hand.*

Woods Rogers Eſq; governor of the Bahama Iſlands, died of the gout in his ſtomach, July 16. in the Iſland of Providence. *DJ.* 30.

The David Brig. Capt. Knox, bound from New England to the bay of Honduras, was lately taken by the Spaniards in the ſaid bay. *DJ. Octob.* 3.

FOREIGN NEWS.

THURSDAY, *Sept.* 28.

Paris, Sept. 29. From Rouergue they tell us a ſad ſtory of a mad wolf, that had bit 21 perſons in the village of Coueſque; and that the Lord of the place having killed it with a fuſee, took the liver and broiled it, and diſtributed it to thoſe that had been bitten. Eleven that eat thereof, recovered; but the other ten, who refuſed, died raving mad. *P.*

Yeſterday arrived the Mail from France.

Paris, Oct. 2. N.S. Mr. O Connor, an Iriſh gentleman, ſet out ſome days ago, with a commiſſion of Inſpector over all the copper and lead mines in Provence. *C. DP. DJ.* — *This office ſhould have been divided into two, and given to an* Iriſh-man *and a* Dutch-man.

FRIDAY, *Sept.* 29.

Amſterdam, Oct. 3. Some private letters from Spain will have it, that the Spaniards have loſt three ſhips, and had a fourth much ſhattered, in a late engagement with ſome Britiſh veſſels, near Jamaica. *D P.*

SATURDAY, *Sept.* 30.

Yeſterday arrived the Mail due from Holland.

Seville, Sept. 12. N. S. They write from Cadiz, that orders are come from Court, for the equipment of 10 men of war; and that eight regiments had received orders to hold themſelves in a readineſs to emberque at an hour's warning; but upon what expedition, we cannot yet learn. *C. DP.*

Genoa, Sept. 16. All that has been hitherto given out, concerning the treaty pretended to have been concluded with the Rebels of Corſica, was without foundation; for 'tis not true that ever any was made with the ſaid rebels and the Republic, nor with the Prince of Wirtemberg, who commanded in chief. *C. DP.*

Genoa, Sept. 26. Yeſterday we received letters from Marſeilles, which ſay, advice was brought thither, that the French Conſul at Algiers and all his domeſtics were cut in pieces; and that the King's ſhips had taken into cuſtody an Algerine Ship of twenty four guns and three hundred men. *P.*

MONDAY, *Octob.* 2.

Yeſterday arrived a Mail from France.

Paris, Octob. 8. N. S. By letters from Madrid, of the 23d paſt, we are informed, that in the night, between the fifth and ſixth, the north part of the roof of the Eſcurial was fired by lightning; and not being perceived till two hours after, the fire got to ſuch a head, that all aſſiſtance was to no purpoſe. The fire ſpread to the center of the college, and conſumed the tower, the patriarch's apartment, and thoſe of the chaplains. At length the Monks brought out the Hoſt; and as ſoon as the prieſt had pronounced the bleſſing, the violence of the flames ceaſed; and thus they got it under. *C. P. DP.*

TUESDAY, *Octob.* 3.

We are adviſed from Lisbon, the 18th paſt, N. S. that they had received the following moſt dreadful news, viz. That what they call a thunder-bolt had penetrated through the tower of the city of Compoſt-Mayor (on the frontiers next Spain, ſituate on the province of Alantejo, and well garriſoned) in which a magazine of powder and warlike ſtores were kept, there being then in it 5700 Arroves of gunpowder, each weighing 32 lb. Engliſh, 400 ſhells filled, &c. which the lightning ſet fire to, by which the greateſt part of the city was laid in ruins, no more than one half of two ſtreets being left ſtanding; above 1000 perſons were miſerably ſhattered and torn, and many deemed incurable. The number buried under the rubbiſh was unknown; tho' undoubtedly very great, only 300 had been dug up. On receipt of this news the King of Portugal ſent all the Surgeons, Apothecaries, &c. that could be found in Lisbon, to take care of theſe wretched people. *DJ.*

WEDNESDAY, *Oct.* 4.

Paris, Oct. 6. N. S. Nothing can be more melancholy, than the news which the two or three laſt Poſts have brought us, by divers ways from Conſtantinople, and other towns in Turky. They repreſent that capital of the eaſtern empire, in the moſt unhappy circumſtances that it has yet known. The plague ravages among the people to that degree, that it carries off thouſands in a day; and, notwithſtanding all the precautions they could take, it has penetrated the ſuburbs of Pera, Galata, to Scutari, and farther into the country and neighbouring villages. The ſeraglio itſelf has not been inacceſſible to this pernicious contagion. —— There is a great buſtle made here about lead and copper-mines. For ſince the fall of charitable corporation ſtock, ſeveral engliſh projectors are come over hither, who are apt to make diſcoveries; and much land has been travelled over for this purpoſe in the provinces of Bretagne, Languedoc, and Province. With theſe adventurers (they ſay) there are concerned, by a private or kind of under-ground contract, two genlemen of great worth, one of charitable, and the other of ſouth-ſea memory. *P.*

BOOKS and PAMPHLETS publiſhed ſince Sept. 22.

23. Remarks upon a pretended Index, in the Courant, Aug. 24 upon Mr. Budgell's late excellent pamphlet, &c. Pr. 6 d.

The civil Magiſtrate's right of inflicting puniſhment, &c. an aſſize Sermon at Kingſton, Aug. 10. by Geo. Osborne, Vicar of Batterſea. Pr. 6 d.

25. Chriſtus ſacræ ſcripturæ nucleus: or Chriſt the ſum and ſubſtance of all the holy ſcriptures, &c.

Hiſtoria literaria: No. 18. Pr. 1 s.

Mr. Gibbs's Rules for drawing the ſeveral parts of architecture, &c.

26. The judgment of Dr. Tho. Burnet, concerning the Trinity, &c. Pr. 1 s.

27. A congratulatory poem on his Majeſt's ſafe arrival. Pr. 6d.

30. The Royal Hermitage: a poem by Mr. Mitchell. Pr. 6 d.

The lives of the moſt remarkable criminals, &c.

Octob. 2. A ſhort view of ſome of the general arts of controverſy made uſe of by the advocates for infidelity: a charge at a primary viſitation at York, by Tho. Hayter. A. M. Archdeacon of York, Pr. 6 d.

The Hiſtorical Regiſter, No. 67.

The London Magazine, No. 6.

3. The Gentleman's Magazine, No. 21.

Eccleſiaſtical Memoirs by M. de Tillemont, No. 7.

The political ſtate of Great Britain, for September.

4. Another volume of miſcellanies in proſe and verſe: by Dr. Swift and Mr. Pope.

The friendly writer and regiſter of truth, &c. by Ruth Collins. Pr. 6 d.

Memoirs of ſecret ſervices of John Macky Eſq; &c.

Limborch's hiſtory of the Inquiſition: tranſlated by Samuel Chandler.

On Tueſday Stocks were

South Sea Stock was 104 3 8ths, to 1 half. South Sea Annuity 111 7 8ths, to 112, for the Opening. Bank 152, for ditto. Bank Circulation 4l. 10 s. Premium. India 155 1 half, 154 1 qr. 155 3 8ths, 155, 155 to 1 qr. Three per Cent. Annuity 100. Royal Exchange Aſſurance 105. London Aſſurance 13 5 8ths, to 3 qrs. for the Opening. York Buildings 5, Books open. African 38. Engliſh Copper 2 l. 2 s. Welch ditto 1 l. 15 s. South Sea Bonds 2 l. 11 s. Premium. India ditto 3 l. 13 s. ditto.

This Day is publish'd,

THE ROYAL HERMITAGE: Or, Temple of Honour. A POEM to her Majesty the Queen-Regent. To which is prefixed, An Epistle to the Right Honourable Sir Robert Walpole. By Mr. Mitchell.

Hic Manus, ob Patriam pugnando vulnera passi
Quique Sacerdotes casti, dum Vita manebat,
Quique pii Vates, & Phœbo digna locuti,
Inventas aut Vitam excoluere per Artes,
Quique sui memores alios fecere merendo:
Omnibus his nivea cinguntur tempora Vitta. VIRG.

Printed for J. Roberts, at the Oxford-Arms in Warwick-Lane, 1732. Price 6d. Where may be had,

An Epistle to the Right Honourable Sir ROBERT WALPOLE, Knight of the most noble Order of the Garter. By RICHARD SAVAGE, Esq.

London, Octob. 2. 1732.

Next Saturday will be publish'd, necessary to be perused by all that read the History of England written by M. RAPIN DE THORAS (*containing six Sheets, at the Price of 6 d.*) *the first Number of a New and Correct Edition of*

THE History of IRELAND: Containing, I. A full and impartial Account of the first Inhabitants of that Kingdom; with the LIVES and REIGNS of an hundred and seventy four succeeding Monarchs of the MILESIAN Race. II. The Original of the GADELIANS; their Travels into Spain, and from thence into Ireland. III. Of the frequent Assistance the Irish afforded the Scots against their Enemies the Romans and Britons, particularly their obliging the Britons to make a Ditch from Sea to Sea between England and Scotland. IV. A genuine Description of the Courage and Liberality of the ancient Irish, their severe Laws to preserve their Records and Antiquities, and the Punishments inflicted upon those Antiquaries who presumed to vary from the Truth; with an Account of the Laws and Customs of the ancient Irish, and their Royal Assemblies at Tara, &c. V. A Relation of the long and bloody Wars of the Irish against the Danes; whose Yoke they at last threw off, and restored Liberty to their Country; which they preserved till the Arrival of HENRY II. King of England. Collected by the learned JEOFFRY KEATING, D. D. Faithfully Translated from the Original IRISH Language. With many curious Amendments, taken from the Psalters of TERA and CASHEL, and other authentick Records. Illustrated with above one hundred and sixty Coats of Arms of the ancient Irish, with particular Genealogies of many noble Families, curiously Engraven upon forty two Copper-Plates. With an Appendix, collected from the Remarks of the learned Dr. ANTHONY RAYMOND of TRIM.

P R O P O S A L S.

I. That the Whole shall consist of about one hundred and seventy Sheets in Folio, on a good Paper and Letter, and will be finished in about seven Months.

II. That six Sheets will be published weekly, stitched up in blue Paper, for Six-pence.

III. Those Gentlemen who are willing to encourage this Undertaking are desired to give in their Names and Places of Abode to B. CREAKE, at the Red-Bible in Ave-Mary-Lane, near Ludgate-Street, or to W. WARING, at the Bible in Jermyn-Street; who will take Care that the Books be carefully delivered.

SUBSCRIPTIONS are taken in by the Booksellers of London and Westminster.

N. B. There are a few printed for the Curious on a Superfine Paper, at Three Halfpence per Sheet.

The Cœlestial Anodyne Tincture: *Or, The* Great Pain-easing Medicine.

F*Am'd and Approv'd of for its wonderful and never-failing Success, in giving immediate Ease and Relief in all manner of Pains, either inward or outward and is the most certain Remedy in the World for a sure and speedy Cure of the Cholick, and expelling Wind, Gripes and Pains in the Stomach, the Pleurisy, Stitches or Pains in the Side, Back, Loins, or any other Part; Rheumatick Ailments, which cause Pain and Dolor. It hath given Ease to a Miracle, when all other Remedies have failed. In the Gravel and Stone in the Kidneys, it gives Ease forthwith, and brings them away to Admiration. It also facilitates and causes a speedy Delivery in Child-Birth. 'Tis no Quack trifling Thing, to allure the World with, but a real and well-experienced Medicine, not acting by Stupefaction, (as Opiates,) But by a friendly, balsamick and subtle Nature, pacifying the most severe and terrible racking Pains, and carries off the Cause, not by purging, but by Transpiration, by Urine, or breaking Wind. No Family ought to be without it. And used outwardly, it cures Swellings, Aches, Pains, Numbness, or Weakness of the Joints: 'Tis excellent for Cramps, and all other aged Infirmities, effecting Wonders in Agues Fevers, Small-Pox, &c. No Family ought to be without it.*

It is Sold only by Mr. PARKER *Printer, at his House in Salisbury-Court, or by such Persons as he shall depute, viz. at Mr. Parker's, a Printer, in Bull Head Court in Jewin-Street; at the White Gally-Pot, a Chandler's Shop in Bandy-Leg Walk, Southwark; and at Mr. Neal's, a Toy-Shop over-against the White-Hart Inn in the Borough, at Eighteen Pence a Bottle, with printed Directions; and if requested, will be brought to any Person by the Hawker who sells his Penny-Post. Sealed as above.*

On Monday, Oct. 2. was publish'd,

The LONDON MAGAZINE: Or, GENTLEMAN'S *Monthly Intelligencer.*

NUMB. VI. for SEPTEMBER. 1732.

To be Continued. [*Price Sixpence each Month*]

CONTAINING.

[*Greater Variety, and more in Quantity, than any* MONTHLY BOOK *extant.*]

I. A VIEW of the WEEKLY ESSAYS, viz. On Flattery, Fear, and Courage; Self-Love and Bigottry; Obstinacy; Anger, Envy, and Malice; Modesty, prudent Reservedness, or moderate Ostentation; Love and Marriage; Coffee-house Conversation; Craftsman's Essay on Ethicks censured; Osborne charged with Inconsistency; Vicissitudes of Fortune; Divine Judgments; Judicial Astrology; a curious Account of the Invention of Printing.

II. POLITICAL SUBJECTS, viz. Debates in Parliament on the Number of Forces, and the Sum granted for maintaining them; Religious and Civil Liberty; the Publick Interest; Condition of Ministers; Competitors for Power; Destruction of the Athenian Liberties; ancient and present Government of France; Parliament of Paris; Nature of just Government; Character of Fog and his Writings; Craftsman answered about Secretaries of State and Messengers; Craftsman, Fog, Osborne, &c. of the Pragmatick Sanction; Hyp-Doctor's Reasoning about the Jacobites; Speech in the Parliament of Paris; Fable of Pan allegorized; Speech of Durham-Yard; Franklin's Petition to a Militia Captain.

III. POETRY: Letter to a Curate versify'd; a noted Song burlesqued; on the Art of Printing; Divine Poetry; Elegy on Lord Chief Baron Dalton; a begging Epistle from a poor Poet; the Milk-Maid, &c.

IV. DOMESTICK OCCURRENCES: Promotions Ecclesiastical, Civil, and Military; Marriages and Births; Deaths, &c.

V. FOREIGN AFFAIRS.

VI. Price of Goods, Grain, Stocks; Monthly Bill of Mortality.

VII. A TABLE of Contents.

To which is added, a Catalogue of Books and Pamphlets, with their Prices; publish'd by the Proprietors of the Monthly Chronicle, now discontinu'd.

MULTUM IN PARVO.

LONDON: Printed for C. Ackers in St. John-Street; for J. Wilford, behind the Chapter-House, near St. Paul's: And sold by W. Meadows, T. Cox, W. Hinchliffe, H. Whitridge, R. Willock, and E. Nutt, in Cornhill; J. Clarke in Duck-Lane; T. Astley in St. Paul's Church-Yard; A. Dodd without Temple-Bar; J. Stagg in Westminster-Hall; J. Jackson in Pall-Mall; J. Jolliffe in St. James's-Street; J. Brindley and W. Shropshire in Bond-Street; and J. Millan near the Admiralty-Office.

Where may be had the former Numbers.

Last Saturday was published,

No. IX. (*containing five Sheets*) *at the Price of 6 d. of*

THE HISTORY of *ENGLAND.* By Mr. RAPIN de THOYRAS. Translated by N. TINDAL, M. A. Vicar of Great Waltham in Essex. The 2d Edition. With the following Improvements:

1. The Translation is thoroughly revised and corrected.
2. The many Errors and Mistakes of the Original are rectified.
3. Several Hundred of Marginal References, accidentally omitted by the Author, are supplied.
4. Additional Notes throughout, with Cuts, Maps, and Genealogical Tables on Copper Plates.

Printed for James, John, and Paul Knapton, removed from St. Paul's Church-Yard, to the Crown in Ludgate-Street, near the West-End of St. Paul's.

Where may be had, the preceding Numbers.

N. B. The Whole will be comprised in 2 Volumes, in Folio, containing 400 Sheets, at the Price of 2 l. 2 s. in Sheets, including the Copper Plates. Five Sheets of the Work will be published every Saturday, 'till the Whole is compleated, at the Price of 6 d. and the said Sheets will be delivered every Week at the Houses of Gentlemen who are pleased to order them.

Proposals at large, with a Specimen of the Work, may be had gratis.

Just imported, and sold by JER. BATLEY, *at the Dove in Pater-Noster-Row.*

HIstoire des Papes depuis St. Pierre jusqu'à Benoit XIII. inclusivement en Deux Volumes 4to, à la Haye, chez Henri Scheurleer, 1732.

Lately published, and sold by J. BATLEY,

Philosophiæ Mathematicæ Newtonianæ Illustratæ Tomi Duo. Quorum prior tradit Elementa Matheseos ad comprehendendam demonstrationem hujus Philosophiæ scitu necessaria: Posterior continet 1) Definitiones & Leges motûs generaliores; 2) Leges virium centripetarum & Theoriam attractionis seu gravitationis corporum in se mutuo; 3) Mundi Systema.

A GEORGIO PETRO DOMCKIO.

October 2. was publish'd, Pr. 6d.

[*Neatly Printed on fine Paper.*]

The GENTLEMAN's MAGAZINE: Or, MONTHLY INTELLIGENCER.

NUMBER XXI. for SEPTEMBER, 1732.

Being the Ninth of VOL. II.

CONTAINING,

[*More in Quantity, and greater Variety, than any Book of the Kind and Price.*]

I. VIews of the WEEKLY ESSAYS, viz. On Flattery, Courage, Bigotry, the Art and Mystery of Printing, Anger, Obstinacy, Ostentation, the Advantages of Coffee-houses, odd Customs, ancient and modern; Origin of Moral Virtue, Divine Judgments, Vicissitude of Fortune, Love and Marriage, Preference of Modesty to Beauty.

II. Political Points: On the Power of Secretaries of State and Messengers; Debates in Parliament; History of the Parliament of Paris; Speech of a Member; the Fable of Pan; Pragmatick Sanction, censur'd and defended; Of Just Government; Treatment of Ministers; Liberties of Athens destroy'd, how; Ancient and Present Government of France; the Selfish Patriot; National Debt; Abjuration Oath; Ambition of Pericles; who pay most Taxes; of Partiality in Quartering the Troops; English and German Generals different way of subsisting; Northern and Sugar Colonies; Abuses of Fees; Merit of Sir Thomas Louther's Invention; Prejudice of Patents.

III. Description of Carolina.

IV. Poetry. The Wary Damsel; Mr. F—'s Letter to his Cartel; to the Memory of a Lady; the Poet's Mistress; Coolon of Asses; Epigrams.

V. Recorder's Speech to their Majesties; Lord Mayor Elect's Speech, &c. Strange Instance of Revenge.

VI. Domestic Occurences; Marriages, Births, Deaths, Promotions, Prices of Goods, Bankrupts, Bill of Mortality.

VII. Foreign Affairs, &c. &c.

VIII. Register of Books.

IX. A Table of Contents.

By *SYLVANUS URBAN* Gent.

London: Printed, and sold at St. John's-Gate, by F. Jefferies in Ludgate-Street; Mrs. Nutt, Mrs. Charlton, Mrs. Cook, at the Royal-Exchange; Mr. Batley, in Pater-Noster-Row; Mr. Midwinter, in St. Paul's Church-Yard; A. Chapman, in Pall-Mall; Mrs. Dodd, and Mr. Bickerton without Temple-Bar; Mr. Critchley, at Charing-Cross; Mr. Stagg, and Mr. King, in Westminster-Hall; Mr. Williamson, in Holborn; Mr. Montague, in Great Queen-Street; Mr. Harding, in St. Martin's-Lane; and most Booksellers in Town and Country.

Where may be had,

All the former Numbers; the twelve first being now reprinted.

N. B. A few are printed on fine Royal Paper, large Margin, for the Curious.

This Day is publish'd,

THE PRESENT STATE of EUROPE: Or, The Historical and Political Monthly Mercury: Giving an Account of all the publick and private Occurrences, Civil, Ecclesiastical, and Military, that are most considerable in every Court. With a more particular Account of the Affairs of Great Britain, &c.

For the Month of AUGUST, 1732.

With Political Reflections upon every State, Vol. XLIV. Continued Monthly, from Originals published at the Hague, by the Authority of the States of Holland and West-Friesland, &c.

Printed for the Assigns of the Executors of H. Rhodes, and Eliz. Harris; and Sold by J. Roberts, in Warwick-Lane.

Where are to be had,

The whole Forty three Volumes, beginning November, 1688, (or single Ones, from July, 1690, to this Time.) Price Six Pence.

This Day is Publish'd,

Printed for *J. Brotherton*, at the *Bible*, next the Fleece-Tavern in Cornhill,

AN Enquiry into the Origin of Honour, and the Usefulness of Christianity in War. By the Author of the FABLE of the BEES.

Where may be had,

1. A Letter to Dion: Being an Answer to a Book, call'd, Alciphron: Or, the Minute Philosopher.
2. The present State of Great Britain and Ireland, for the Year 1731.
3. Traditions of the Jews.
4. Dury's Journal to Madagascar.
5. Religious Courtship.
6. Life of OLIVER CROMWELL, Lord Protector of the Common-wealth.
7. Receipts in Cookery and Surgery. By John Kettilby.

LONDON: Printed by P. SANDERS, *in Crown-Court, Butcher-Row,* without *Temple-Bar*; where Letters and Advertisements are taken in, and by Capt. GULLIVER, near the *Temple*; also at the *Rainbow Coffee-House* in *Cornhill*, and *John's Coffee-House* in *Sheer-Lane*, near *Temple-Bar*. [Price Twopence.]

The Grub-ſtreet Journal.

NUMB. 145.

Thurſday, OCTOBER 12. 1732.

Mr. BAVIUS,

IN my letter to you, about three weeks ago, I endeavoured to ſhew the great uſefulneſs of coffee-houſes, in propagating juſt notions of government and religion; two things neceſſary to be underſtood by all perſons, ſince both their temporal and eternal intereſts depend upon the one and the other. Were there no other evidence, that the generality of mankind are capable of attaining to ſuch juſt notions, the great importance and neceſſity of them would be proof ſufficient. For how is it conſiſtent with the divine goodneſs or juſtice, to place thoſe two things out of their reach, 'in which (to uſe Mr. OSBORNE's words) the 'well-being of men are more concerned, than in all other 'things put together?' But the contrary is fully confirmed by experience, as I have lately obſerved to you; againſt which no valid argument can poſſibly be brought. For we dayly ſee many inſtances of perſons, of all orders and degrees, who, applying themſelves to a careful peruſal of the weekly labours of ſome of your members, become inſenſibly conſummate politicians and divines.

From hence it is natural to infer theſe two concluſions: That the reading of theſe pieces is a religious, as well as a civil duty; and That if this duty be performed, as it ought, upon a ſaturday, there is little or no occaſion for appearing at any place of public inſtruction upon a ſunday. —— If there be any obligation at all to obſerve one day in the week in a different manner from the reſt, to forbear the ordinary works of one's employment, and to appropriate part of it to religious exercices, it ſeems highly reaſonable that it ſhould be left to the diſcretion of every perſon, to chuſe that day, which it may be moſt convenient for him to ſpend in this manner. Agreeably to this, a learned *Philoſophical Enquirer* and great *Comedian*, publicly adviſed the people in the country, in the time of the late harveſt, to carry in their corn on a ſunday, for *fear of bad weather*, rather than to go to church. Whether *this gentleman*'s pious admonitions came into their hands time enough, or not; or whether they followed or neglected them, I cannot tell: but I am certain, that the mechanics in this city, who are leſs prieſt-ridden, are too intelligent to need any advice of this nature, whenever their buſineſs requires more than ordinary haſte.

But neither theſe, nor any perſons of a ſuperior ſtation, either in city, or country, have occaſion at all to be adviſed, not to ſuffer their chriſtian liberty to be reſtrained by a ſuperſtitious performance of religious exercices on this day, in places ſet apart for that purpoſe. Great numbers, eſpecially of the *beau monde*, the people of faſhion, ſeldom or never make their appearance in any of theſe places, unleſs to qualify themſelves to ſerve their country: and yet their notions of religion, as well as of government, are as juſt, and their lives as free from all ſcandalous and notorious vices, as thoſe of many of the conſtant attendants upon religious ordinances. A plain demonſtration this, that theſe things are not ſo efficacious and neceſſary, as a certain ſet of men, whoſe intereſt it is to have them thought ſo, would endeavour to perſuade the world; and likewiſe, that there is ſome other method of inſtruction as effectual, whereby perſons may learn political and religious duties, and become both good ſubjects and good men. And pray, what method can have ſo juſt a claim for approbation, as the conſtant reading of thoſe weekly compoſitions which treat of matters of policy, morality, and religion, with ſuch admirable brevity and perſpicuity? eſpecially if they are read in a place where there is an opportunity of conſulting ingenious and learned perſons, immediately, upon any difficulty which may ariſe. This is a circumſtance, which gives a coffee-houſe the advantage of a church, or of a conventicle, where all perſons are obliged to hear in ſilence whatever abſurdity happens to be dictated from the pulpit.

This indeed, is an advantage which the fair ſex, and people of mean fortune, who do not frequent coffee-houſes, cannot injoy: and therefore it is no wonder, that they do not arrive to ſo high a degree of knowledge in politics and religion. However, it is certain, that all theſe, if it be not their own fault, may attain to ſuch a degree as is neceſſary for them. The papers I have been recommending, which contain this invaluable treaſure of true wiſdom and learning, are offered to ſale in all parts of this great city, and at a low price. The diſadvantage therefore in not reading them at a coffee-houſe may, in a good meaſure, be ſupply'd by carefully peruſing them at home; particularly on a ſaturday night, or ſunday morning: and when any doubts ariſe, they may debate them at leiſure, the former over their tea, and the latter over their tobacco and their ale, on ſunday evening.

All wiſe and good men, Mr. BAVIUS, have long ſeen the inconvenience, not to ſay injuſtice, of maintaining a particular ſet of idle men, at ſo vaſt an expence as the tenth part of the improved value of all lands, which they claim as their due. It is my humble opinion, in which I hope I have the concurrence of all unprejudiced and thinking perſons, that it would be infinitely more for the advantage of the nation in general, and of every individual in particular, if this great revenue was to be applied to the payment of the national debts, and to the reward of ſuch perſons as ſhould diſtinguiſh themſelves weekly in political, moral, and religious diſſertations. One of theſe might be read every morning and afternoon at the public aſſemblies upon a certain day in every week; as homilies were appointed to be read at the beginning of the reformation. Theſe aſſemblies it may be proper to keep up at the uſual times and places; becauſe the generality of perſons have a great regard for thoſe, to which they have been long accuſtomed. The perſon who is to officiate ought to be appointed by the ſtate; and no one ſhould be obliged to contribute to his maintenance, which ſhall ariſe ſolely from voluntary ſubſcriptions, and from the rate of pews. The reading of theſe eſſays may be accompanied with *Expoſitions, Orations, Prælections, Lectures, Poſtills*, &c. after the manner of the ORATORY; which I take to be the beſt plan for the propagating *a religion in which all conſiderate men agree*. In one particular I muſt decline a little from that great pattern, and would have the wedneſday's exercice reſtrained to ſunday evenings; becauſe almoſt all denominations of Chriſtians now agree in ſpending that time in diverſions. But I intirely approve of the ſituation of the ORATORY over a coffe-houſe; and think that all other Oratories ſhould come as near to it as poſſible. And therefore I propoſe, that a coffee-houſe ſhould be opened adjoining to every church. This will be of great advantage both to the orators, and their audiences: the former, who are to have the property of them, may either keep them by their wives, or let them out to others; and the latter may reap all that benefit by converſation, mentioned in the former part of this letter, from, Sir,

Oct. 7. 1732. Your moſt humble ſervant, D. D.

To Bavius, at the ſign of the flying-beaſt, (called by the heathen Poets, a *Pegaſus*) in Grub-ſtreet, London.

Tottenham, the 6th of the 8th Month (otherwiſe termed in the language of heathen *Rome*, *October*) 1732.

Friend BAVIUS,

INaſmuch as thou waſt ſo kind to let my brethren AMINADAB and OBADIAH, have place in thy Paper, I am in hopes thou wilt not neglect a poor handmaid, in reſpect to the following. —— For,

How can I do otherwiſe than cry out as the holy prophet did, *Wo to her that is filthy and polluted*, Zeph. iii. 1. tho' he ſpoke that of a city, yet I cannot but pronounce it of one RUTH COLLINS, who pretending to be one of the houſhold of faith, hath lately put forth a book, called the *Friendly Writer, and Regiſter of Truth*, filled with the marks of the language of the beaſt, and proud titles of men of vain minds; yea, and lies too: of all which together, there are not leſs than twelve dozen inſtances, ſome whereof I ſhall point out.

1. O abomination! ſhe hath cauſed a picture to be made of herſelf; the dreſs and appearance of which hath no reſemblance of a holy ſiſter; but much like that of a whore, yea, a whore of *Babylon*!

2. In the title ſhe hath called the Month of *September*, the *Ninth Month*; which, by the faithful was always reckoned but the *Seventh*. Next, ſhe promiſeth to give an account of thoſe, *who ſpeak evil of dignities*; which is what the ſons of vanity have charged on the children of truth, becauſe they make no diſtinction of ſuch. Alſo, of ſuch *that depart in the fleſh*; a ſaying not uſed by them to ſhew forth *dying*, as ſhe ſeemeth here to intend it. Tho' I really think, according to the outward letter, it ſhould rather be underſtood of ſuch diſhoneſt ſons of darkneſs who run away from their creditors; for this is really a *departing in the fleſh*: and certainly, if ſhe can give accounts of theſe, and of their deeds, it will rejoice the hearts of many. But, the ſpirit of truth giveth me to perceive her to be one of thoſe the wiſe man ſpeaketh of, ſaying, — *a deceitful witneſs ſpeaketh lies*, Prov. xiv. 25. — For ſhe ſayeth, JOHN ISTED, *at the ball of gold*; which ſeemeth to be an untruth; for it is to be queſtioned, whether he hath ſo much of that valuable metal (in the world's eſteem) to ſpare, as to hang it out for a ſign.

3. In the *preface* ſhe ſpeaketh *half in the ſpeech of Aſhdod*, as did the degenerated *Iſraelites* of old, *Neh.* xiii. 24. and therefore certainly is a worſhipper of Dagon, a god of wood: for, behold, ſhe applieth the words, *Majeſty*, and *ſacred Name of Majeſty* to an earthly king and queen; which belong only to the great *Majeſty of heaven*. And alſo ſayeth, that our friend and *Brother*, JOHN HUGGONSON, *putteth forth every Fourth Day, a Paper of Rebuke and Admonition*: whereas he doth not do any ſuch thing. O horrible daughter of *Belial*! bitterneſs and ſorrow will one day be thy portion for theſe things.

4. In p. 5. out of the groſs darkneſs of her heart ſhe uttereth theſe words, *September Month*; in 7. Maſter *Thomas Briand* —— Lord *the King* —— victorious Duke *of Marlborough* — noble *good Woman*, 8 *Worſhipful*; 9 ſhe ſayeth, *the Dogs that are* (I ſuppoſe intended for the vain ſport of hunting) *kept to yield Pleaſure and Delight*; 10. *Reverend Maſter*; 11. *Dame* — *noble Earl* — *Sacriſtan*; 13. *Admiral*; 15. *Sabbath-Day*; p. 20, 21, 22, 23, 24. are full of the language of *Aſhdod*; 25. *honoured with the Title and Renown*; 26. *goodly Order*; 27. *much Rejoicings* — *a coſtly building for our Merriment*; 33. *Paſtime and Delight*; 44. *April Month*.

And becauſe this pretended ſiſter, RUTH, in her vain imagination, thought that nonſenſe was agreeable to the language of the children of the light, ſhe has uttered among many others theſe ſentences following; p. 9. *the Norfolk ſtreet of the Strand*; 11. *the ſquare Building* (meaning Saliſbury court); 15. *Linnen Garments which Men wear next their Skins*; 17. *Leaden Particles* (meaning ſhot); 18. *Parents Jewiſh*; 19. *Maſter Leſtock and his Help-Mate*; 20. *Leathren-Contrivance* (before it was *Leathern Conveniencies*, p. 10.); 15. *Invention for telling the Hour of the Day*, (a Watch); 23. *the Preſider*; 28. *all in like order to live*; 30. *Money-Changers-ſtreet*.

But, oh! ſhe hath committed a more abominable ſin ſtill, in ſpewing forth revilings on the ſons of JACOB, the true ISRAELITES, and beloved of the Lord: for ſhe ſayeth, p. 6. *And the Friends of* JACOB, (*who dwelleth in the Tents of the Whore of Babylon*) *are greatly troubled, becauſe, ſay they — we cannot deviſe againſt the People we have long wiſhed Evil to*: and p. 26. *And none ſhewed any Diſlikings or evil Countenance, but the Friends of Jacob*. What horrible wickedneſs is here? Oh profane RUTH! when did *the friends of Jacob* dwell in the tents of Babylon? No; they are ſuch that depart from the laws of their father JACOB, and pervert the way of the Lord, who abide in her polluted borders: for even Balaam was forced to cry out, *How goodly are thy tents, O Jacob, and thy tabernacles, O Iſrael!* Numb. xxiv. 5. And when did'ſt thou, O vile babler! know *the friends of* JACOB to *wiſh evil* to thoſe that were good? or, to ſhew *Diſlikings, or evil Countenance* at good tidings? No; the true *Iſraelites* (or ſons, or *friends of Jacob*) were the forwardeſt in rejoicing, and bringing the king back, 2 *Sam.* xix, 10, 11, 12. But, verily, verily, thou ſhalt no more be called RUTH, but *Jezebel*, who ſought the deſtruction of *the friends of* JACOB, by ſlaying their prophets, 1 *Kin.* xviii. 13. and other wicked deeds; and who painted and tired herſelf like a harlot, and mocked, and ſcoffed, 2 *Kin.* ix. 30, 31. as even thou doeſt: and ſurely thy portion will be accordingly; for thou plainly appeareſt to be one of that wicked race, the wiſe man hath mentioned, whoſe *houſe is the way to hell, going down to the chambers of death*. Prov. vii. 27.

Now, friend BAVIUS, having a little eaſed my ſpirit of the burthen that lay on it, in relation to this ſpeckled harlot, who hath thus ſported herſelf with the innocent friends of JACOB, and put forth for ſale ſo much merchandize of myſtical *Babylon*, in order to make the ſons and daughters of men drunk with the fornications and ſorceries thereof, I ſhall take my leave:

Who am thy friend in the Truth,
ESTHER ZEA[illegible]

TO the author of a thing, called an Epigram, in the [illegible] *ſtreet Journal*, numb. 144.

Good Sir,

I Am a little at a loſs how to term the verſes you [illegible] pleaſed to make, in anſwer to mine, in the [illegible]

Journal. By the conciseness they should be an *Epigram*; but there is not one of those qualities of which that sort of poetry ought to consist. Where is the exact and apt agreement of the whole, the symmetry, the natural simplicity, the poignant turn of wit? The little education I have had, has enabled me to look over MARTIAL (whom, I hope, you will allow to be a good epigrammatist) and, I do not find one epigram of his, which has not some, and especially the last of these beauties. Well then, 'tis plain it is not an *Epigram*, but an elaborate piece, composed in about five weeks, without reason, and *with very* disputable rhime, merely to cavil at the gentlemen upon whom they verses were written, and not at me. For *sheathe* and *death* can hardly be allowed to be rhime: and then, Sir, you lay down a positive contradiction, with no argument to support it; and lastly conclude, I have murdered a set of gentlemen, because you do not happen to like them.

I did not think either the verses or the author were of so much consequence as to be taken notice of: but since it is otherwise, give me leave to tell you, I am so far from retracting what I have written, that it the more strongly convinces me I am in the right; for nothing less than envy could assert a falsehood, without attempting to maintain it. —— I shall conclude with a line you may perhaps have read, viz.

Invidus alterius rebus macrescit opimis: And am,

Octob. 6. 1732. Dear Sir, yours, PHILO-DIVES.

P. S. I am obliged to you, however, for raising me to the dignity of a constable.

DOMESTIC NEWS.

C. *Courant.*	E P. *Evening Post.*
P. *Post-Boy.*	S J. *St. James's Evening Post.*
D P. *Daily Post.*	W E. *Whitehall Evening Post.*
D J. *Daily Journal.*	L E. *London Evening Post.*

Hyp-Oratorical Advertisements and Puffs in the month of September.

Hyp Advertisements, 4. Oratorical ditto, 9. In all 13 —— Hyp Puffs, 4. Oratorical ditto, 6. In all 10. —— Increased in the Advertisements this month, 1. Decreased in the Puffs, 1.

THURSDAY, *Octob.* 5.

His majesty has given orders for 220 head of male deer to be brought from Hanover, to be put in Windsor forest, Richmond park, &c. *SJ.*

Last night the marq. de Montejo, ambassador from the court of Spain, and monsf. de Chavigny, minister from the court of France, arrived here with very numerous retinues. *P.* — The conde Montejo presented capt. Slaughter, commander of the Hound sloop of war, which brought him, his lady, &c. to Dover, with a gold snuff-box, worth near 70l. *DJ. DP.*

Yesterday began the general quarter-sessions of the peace for the city and liberty of Westminster, at Westminster-hall, when Sir John Gonson gave an incomparable charge to the grand jury. *DJ.* —— A very learned, loyal, and excellent speech or charge, of about half an hour. *DP. LE.* —— A very eloquent and learned charge. *P.* —— Gave a charge. *SJ.* —— On tuesday began the quarter sessions for the royalty of the Tower, when sir John gave a learned and excellent charge, &c. *P.* 6. — My brother D J. *seems to be a little mistaken in calling the* charge *on* wednesday incomparable, *since* that on tuesday *was* excellent, *as well as the other.*

Last night (at 12) the corpse of Robert Wilks Esq; was carried from his late dwelling house, in Bow-street, Covent-garden, and decently interred in the parish church of S. Paul's: the funeral was very private, according to his own desire. The gentlemen of the chappel-royal voluntarily attended at the ceremony, and performed a fine anthem. The pall was supported by John Birket Esq; Mr. Sainthill, Mr. Mills, Colley Cibber Esq; Mr. Coldham, Mr. Theophilus Cibber. *DP.*

Mr. Clarke of Hull has resigned the grammar school there, in order to pursue his studies more closely, and employ his pen more effectually for the service of the public; but continues to reside still in that place. *DP.*

On tuesday night the countess of Albemarle was safely brought to bed of a daughter: the earl is expected every day home from Gibraltar. *LE.*

The only son and child of William Pulteney Esq; lay on tuesday in strong convulsions, so that his life is despaired of. *LE.* —— The small-pox has appeared upon him, and proves to be the kinder sort. *DP.* 6.

The report of the man who flew lately from the monument being dead, is not true. *DJ.*

Yesterday morning, between one and two, a gentleman was knocked down by one street-robber in Holborn, opposite to Hatton-garden, who took his watch, money, &c. the gentleman cry'd, Stop thief, and he was pursued down Shoe-lane. It's remarkable, that a watchman being at his stand, within a few yards, never stirred, nor called for assistance; and, being asked why he did not, replied, It was out of his beat. —— *I am certain, that this* watchman *ought to have been* in the beat *of this* gentleman, *or of any other, who could have* drubbed *him well.*

Yesterday a poor lad in S. James's market, quarelling with a butcher's lad, for a piece of roll and butter, the butcher took a cleaver, which he had in his hand, and gave the lad a cut cross the belly, which let his guts out. The butcher was committed to the Gate-house. *P.* —— About one this morning the coroner's inquest finished their enquiry, in relation to the death of a poor boy killed by a butcher's son in S. James's market, and brought in their verdict wilful murder. *SJ. LE.* 7.

FRIDAY, *Octob.* 6.

Yesterday his excellency count de Montejo was introduced to his majesty at Kensington, when he delivered his credentials, &c. *C. DJ.* He was introduced by his grace the duke of Newcastle. *DP.* —— By the right honourable the lord Harrington. *DJ.* —— He was afterwards introduced to her majesty. *C.* &c.

The youngest daughter of the countess of Deloraine, governess of the princesses Mary and Louisa, lies ill of the smallpox. *DP.*

Paul Cray, Lewis de Vic, James Brothwick, Peter Bell, and Elizabeth Pardoe, are reprieved. *C.* — James Borthwick. *P. DP. DJ.*

The same day the following gentlemen were unanimously chosen by the united company for making hollow sword-blades, for the year ensuing, sir Bibye Lake Bart. *governor*, sir William Billers Knt, *deputy governor. Court of assistants*; Mr. Joseph Browne, James Brooke Esq; sir George Caswall Knt. John Caswall Esq; Mr. John Clark, Peter Cranke Esq; Mr. John Mount, Mr. Thomas Page, Thomas Parker Esq; Mr. Joseph Beachcroft, Mr. John Brassey, Mr. Joseph Davis, Mr. Abraham Henkell junior, Mr. Edward Jasper. *P.*

On wednesday Clifford-William Phillips Esq; and captain Wilkinson, two of the committee of the charitable corporation, found three books belonging to Mr. Thompson, concealed in a cieling of their house on Laurence Pountney-hill, one was a ledger of the whole affair from the time of his entrance into that office, to the day of his going off; the which is hoped, with the other two, may be an inlet into a grand discovery of that iniquitous affair, &c. *DP.*

Yesterday was held a quarterly court of the armourers and braziers company, at their hall in Coleman-street. While they were at dinner a fire happened in the chimney of the court-room: but by timely assistance it was extinguished, without doing much damage. *C.* —— Fires *have frequently* happened *of late at the* courts of companies; *but have not been* extinguished without doing much damage.

Whereas the speeches of the right honourable sir Francis Child knight, the present lord mayor, and of Mr. baron Thomson the recorder, inserted in the Post-Boy, Sept. 30. were grosly misrepresented; I humbly beg pardon of them for the same. *G. James. P. DP.*

SATURDAY, *Octob.* 7.

The king has been pleased to present his royal highness the duke with one of the fine saddle horses newly come from Hanover, called Petit. —— Yesterday the right honourable George earl of Cholmondely kissed the king's hand for the government of the island of Guernsey; and the honourable colonel Edward Montague Esq; for the government of the town of Kingston upon Hull. *DP.*

The same day his excellency the count de Montijo was introduced to his royal highness the prince, and the rest of the royal family. *C. DP. DJ.* —— The same day several eminent Spanish merchants waited on his excellency to compliment him on his arrival. *P. DP.*

The same day at a general court of the York-buildings company it was resolved, that the time allowed to the proprietors for payment of the call of 1 ½ per cent. be further prolonged to Nov. 10. *C. DP.*

On thursday his majesty's plate of 100 guineas was run for at Newmarket, and won by Mr. Griswood's horse *Diamond*, with great ease. *P.* — Against Mr. Kettle, alias Mr. Sanson's *Diamond. DJ.*

Sittings in the court of Common pleas, in and after Michaelmas term.

Middle-sex,	Tues. Oct.	31.	*London,*	Friday, Nov.	3.
	Wednes. Nov.	8		Frid.	10
	Tues.	14		Thurs.	16
	Thurs.	23		Frid.	24
	Wednes.	29		Thurs.	30. *DP.*

On wednesday the right honourable Edward earl of Darnley, with his governour and servants, embarked on board a yatch at Dover for Calais, and from thence [embarqued] directly to the university of Geneva, to finish his studies. *P.* — Geneva *is an odd* university to finish studies in.

The reverend Mr. Pilkington (who sometime since published a collection of poems) is lately come over from Dublin, being appointed chaplain to the lord mayor elect. *DP.*

Yesterday a poor woman, turning the corner of White-cross street into Chitwell-street, a hackney coach turning at the same time, the pole struck her on the body with such violence, that it beat out her bowels. *DP. SJ. WE.* —— A chaise run against her with the pole, and beat her down, and went over her: 'tis thought one, if not two of her ribs are broke. *DJ.*

Last night died George Duckett Esq; one of the commissioners of the excise, and brother to William Duckett Esq; member of parliament for Calne in Wilts. *L. E.*

MONDAY, *Octob.* 9.

The great ball-room in S. James's house has been new fitted, and a fine new canopy of crimson velvet, laced with gold, is fixed up, and the room is all new gilded. *P.*

On saturday their majesties and the royal family took the diversion of hunting the stag in the New-park at Richmond; which gave them much diversion for about three hours, before they killed him. *C.* —— A chase of about two hours and a half. *P.* —— The princess Amelia having strained her ancle, did not go. It rained incessantly all the time; and sir Robert Walpole again acted as master of the buck hounds. *DP.* —— On saturday next a hind is ordered to be turned out on Sunbury common, to be hunted by the king and the royal family. *DP.*

Yesterday a reprieve went to Newgate for Joseph Powis, who was ordered for execution this day. *DP.*

On friday night four prisoners found means to saw off their irons, and made their escape from the Gatehouse, Westminster. *C.*

About ten days ago John Eyres was taken at Sittingbourn in Kent, for smuggling to the value of 800l. Mr. Cumberford, the keeper of Canterbury gaol, kept him three days; when he declared to the sheriff he would not be answerable for any of that gang: which obliged the sheriff to send him up to the Fleet prison on friday last, under a guard of nine dragoons and three of his own officers. *DJ.* —— He is charged in execution upon an extent, at the suit of the crown for 717 l. recovered against him in his majesty's court of exchequer. *P.*

His majesty has been pleased to grant his commission to the right honourable the lords of the admiralty, empowering them to erect a corporation for the relief of the poor widows of the sea officers: which corporation is to consist of the lords of the admiralty for the time being, the commissioners of the navy and victualling for the time being, and so many of the eldest captains and lieutenants in the navy, &c. and they are to meet at the admiralty office for the first time on the 1st of next month. Each officer in the navy is at his pleasure to sign towards it; those that sign are to pay 3 d. per *pound out* of their pay per annum, and those that do not sign are *excluded* the benefit. His majesty has been graciously pleased to grant for the promoting so good a design 10,000 l. and the lords of the admiralty have signed in order to promote it, as have the commissioners of the navy and victualling. The said fund will be settled thus: An admiral's widow to have 50 l. per annum, a captain's 40 l. a lieutenant's 30l. and all other officers widows 20 l. each. There being an officer's chest at Chatham, *which* they pay to monthly, the same will be taken into this corporation, and the widows who are on that chest will be allowed as mentioned. The money that is to be raised by this contribution, will be put out to use, as the commissioners shall think proper at their meeting. *P.*

On Saturday the right honourable the earl of Portmore was married to her grace the dutchess of Leeds; and yesterday morning his lordship, with his new married lady, set out for his seat at Weybridge in Surry. *P. DJ.*

Yesterday morning died suddenly, at her house in great Ormond-street, the lady Boynton, relict of sir Griffith Boynton, of Bramston in Yorkshire, Bar. *DP.*

Yesterday a woman, being in liquor, threw herself into a draw-well in the George inn-yard in Castle-street, the backside of Longacre, and was drowned. *DP.* —— I *believe this poor* woman *got too much* in liquor, *not designedly, but accidentally.*

TUESDAY, *Octob.* 10.

Her majesty is indisposed with a sorethroat, occasioned by a cold, supposed to be taken in the hunting last saturday. *DP.*

Yesterday morning thirteen malefectors were executed at Tyburn: Shelton, the apothecary, went in a mourning coach, and Bumpos in a hackney coach. *C.* —— Bumpus in a mourning coach, and Shelton in a hackney coach. *P. DP. DJ.* —— Attended by two divines. *DJ.* —— Griffith, who was [to be] executed for the murder of Waller in the pillory, made a speech to the populace at his going into the cart, and declared his innocence. *DJ.* —— The bodies of Fleming and Johnson were delivered to the surgeons. *C. DP.*

On friday, at New market, the duke of Devonshire's colt beat the duke of Bridgwater's *colt*, for 200 guineas. — On saturday Mr. Coke's *Hobgoblin* beat the duke of Somerset's *Grey legs*, for 100. *C.* &c.

By letters from Weyhill we learn, that there were about 3500 pockets of hops sold at the fair there, except about 60 Kentish, and 150 of Worcester hops, which lay unsold on saturday night. Farnham hops sold from 7l. to

10 s. and a few superfine at 10 l. Kentish 6 l. 10 s. to 8 l. Worcester, 6 l. to 6 l. 15 s. and 7 l. *D P.*

They write from Doncaster in Yorkshire, that the right honourable the earl of Strafford had the misfortune to break one of his ribs by a fall from his horse, as he was taking the air in his park at Wentworth castle yesterday was se'nnight. *D P.*

On saturday evening ended the general quarter sessions of the peace for the city and liberty of Westminster, where the bench of justices returned thanks to sir John Gonson for his learned, loyal, and excellent charge, and desired him, for the public good, to permit the same to be printed. *D P.* — Francis Geary, keeper of the Gate-house, for not attending the court with the calendar of the prisoners, was fined 10 l. and 40 l. for the escape of John Dawson friday night last. *D P.*

On saturday the reverend Dr. Wright, rector of Christ-church, Spittlefields, was married to miss Merttins, a young lady of an exceeding good character, and about 6000 l. fortune. *D P.*

On thursday night Mr. Wright, a school-master at Grayes in Essex, drinking plentifully at a neighbouring farmer's, went into the yard to make water, but happening to reel, caught hold of the bucket of the well to save his fall, which run down, and carried him with it to the bottom of the well, where he was drowned. *D J.*

Humphery Thayer Esq; inspector general of the duties on coffee, &c. is appointed one of the commissioners of excise, in the room of George Duckett Esq; — Christopher Wyvill Esq; is made inspector general; —— and John Wyndham Esq; succeeds Mr. Wyvill. *L E.* — *D P.* 11. — We hear will be appointed, &c. *C. D J.* 11.

WEDNESDAY, *Octob.* 11.

Yesterday the countess de Montejo was introduced to his majesty, &c. *D P.*

The same day the lady of the right honourable the lord viscount Gage and Mrs. Osborne arrived from France, where they had been some months for the recovery of their health. *D P.*

The same day James Lock Esq; was chosen husband to the Turkey company. *C. D P. D J.*

The same day her grace the dutchess of Buckingham's coaches set out for Dover, in order to bring home her grace, who is now at Calais, where she has been for some months *C.*

Yesterday George James, Printer of the Daily-Post-Boy, according to order appear'd before the court of aldermen; where, after receiving a reprimand from the court, for grossly misrepresenting the speeches spoken by the lord mayor and recorder at Guildhall on Michaelmas-day, in his *Paper of September* the 30th. he acknowledg'd his offence, ask'd pardon of the lord mayor, of Mr. baron *Thomson*, and of the court, and promised never to offend in the like manner for the future. Upon which the court was so favourable to him as to discharge him without any farther prosecution. *D P.*

This day the sessions begins at the Old Baily. *P.*

On friday died Mr. Brevin, the city surveyor. *D P.* — Yesterday died George Woodford Esq; upwards of 90 years of age, worth 50000 l. *C.* —— Formerly a Blackwell-hall-factor. *D P.*

From the PEGASUS *in Grub-street.*

Mr. BAVIUS,

HAving observed in the publick papers, particularly in the Grub-street Journal of the 21st instant a paragraph, which cautions all *clergymen from acting as justices of the peace, whose livings are not rated at* 100 l. *per ann. in the king's books*; and believing it to be inserted there by some malicious pettyfogger, (and not by any gentleman of the long robe,) in order to dissuade several worthy persons from serving their country; I desire you to give the following article a place in your Journal, which will very much oblige

Your constant reader, &c. A. B.

It is the opinion of all persons learned in the law, that glebe and tithes are freeholds, and that the owners of them, whether clergymen or laymen, may act as freeholders according to the value of their estates, viz. as commissioners of sewers, if worth forty marks, and commissioners of the land-tax if worth 100 l. per ann. without any respect had to what their livings are rated at in the *king's books*. And therefore 'tis evident to all *persons of common sense*, that the late *act of parliament*, for qualifying *justices of the peace*, does not disable any *clergyman in commission* from acting as such, if his living be bonâ fide worth 100 l. per ann. Unless these learned persons, out of pique to the order, would disqualify all clergymen, as the *legislature* has thought fit to do all *attorneys and solicitors*, &c. However, if there be no *averring against the king's books*; on condition that the clergy be not taxed higher than they are rated there, (which is equally reasonable,) I'll venture to *aver*, that such as are in the *commission of the peace*, will contentedly leave the *title of worship* to those who are more fond of it, and incumber themselves no longer with so troublesome an office.

ΩΦΕΛΕΙΝ Η ΜΗ ΒΛΑΠΤΕΙΝ

Nihil repugnante natura.

1.

COme listen, good people, both aged and young,
And I'll sing you a merry and innocent song;
For, as long as, genteels, you don't pay for your sport,
If it does you no good, it will do you no hurt.
derry down.

2.

It is of a man, that in title doth vary,
Physician, chirurgeon, and apothecary:
If the meaning of these three hard words you wou'd seek,
He will tell you, no doubt, they're all one in the Greek.

3.

But, however, I rather believe him the last,
Both because he his lawful apprenticeship past;
And because that he talks, ay and talks, and talks on;
'Twill ne'er out of the flesh, for 'twas bred in the bone.

4.

As for Oxford and Cambridge, with all their grave rules,
He left them to dunces, and plodders, and fools;
So discreetly to Leyden his journey he bent,
And came back in a twelve-month, as wise as he went.

5.

Yet at Varsity, lately, he took his degree,
Where he stay'd for nine days, to be seen and to see;
Where the king made him doctor, on humble petition;
But the prince he did more, for he made him physician

6.

He much Greek had digested, so learned, so wise,
That HIPPOCRATES once he wou'd needs methodize;
That were GALEN alive, he would never now know
His transmography'd friend of the island of Co.

7.

But 'ith' street, he thought better his learning to hint,
For a painter makes letters much bigger than print:
So that folks they might wonder whene'er they approach,
He has garnish'd, with Greek, the outside of his coach.

8.

The words are but few; but they tell us, in short,
That if he does us no good, he will do us no hurt:
For he now in good Greek, as doctor, may speak 'em,
Not in gallipot phrase like his old *album græcum.*

9.

'Twas an old woman's charm that an ague cou'd cure,
But, when copy'd in greek, is more safe and more sure:
"For the loaf in my lap, and the pence in my purse,
"If you're never the better, I'm never the worse.

10.

Thus at once, both his reading and judgment are shown,
Where neither the sense nor the words are his own:
And why mayn't he say, like the old woman's charm,
If the bill does no good, yet the fee does no harm?

11.

And not only the motto, but actions will speak,
And the policy tell of our rare merry Greek:
On the state on both sides, ay, and neither, he stood;
He to one does no harm, and to t'other no good.

12.

As for poor paultry Latin, he throws it behind;
As 'tis out of his sight, so 'tis out of his mind:
For a doctor he never had been, to be sure a,
Had he follow'd his *nil repugnante natura.*

FOREIGN NEWS.

THURSDAY, *Oct.* 5.

Yesterday arrived the Mail from Flanders.

Rome, Sept. 20. The chevalier de S. George being upon his departure for his country seat, took leave of his holiness on tuesday, who made him a present of a bill of 9000 scudi. *D P.*

Constantinople, Aug. 28. N.S. This is now the third month since the plague has raged in this capital to such a degree, that not only the houses of the great men are, for the most part, infected; but that amazing distemper has shewn itself in the suburb of Pera, and the prime vizier's palace is not exempt; for we have seen 12 dead men carried out of it in one day; and, some say, it has penetrated even the seraglio. *P.*

This day arrived the Mail from France.

Madrid, Sept. 23. The conferences between the king's commissioners and those of Great Britain, upon the losses sustained on both sides by the late interruption of commerce, have been suspended this fortnight. *P.*

FRIDAY, *Oct.* 6.

Rome, Sept. 17. Mr. Thompson, late warehouse keeper to the charitable corporation in London, has desired to abjure the english religion. *D J.*

SATURDAY, *Oct.* 7.

Naples, Sept. 16. The abbot Vidania, honorary chaplain of this kingdom, died a few days since, in the 110th year of his age. *D P.*

Stockholm, Sept. 14. The directors of the new India company are gone to Gottenburg, to see the cargo of the ship lately arrived from those parts, which is reckoned worth 200,000 livres. *D P.*

Paris, Oct. 10. They write from Fayrac in Agenois, that one Catherine Fort, aged 40, was delivered of four daughters at a birth, who were all baptized. *D J.*

Hague, Sept. 16. Our last letters from Seville advise, that the ambassador of France had had several conferences with don Joseph Patinho, about the affair of the company erected at Cadiz, to trade to the Philippine islands. The answers made by the ministers of France to those of England and Holland, in relation to that affair, were not very favourable; or, if there was any thing that looked so, it was delivered in so loose and equivocal a manner, that it is plain they have no design to thwart that enterprize. *P.*

This day arrived the Mail due from Holland.

Warsaw, Oct. 1. The sessions of last week ended without doing any thing, by reason of the absence of the three Lithuanian deputies of Braslow, Smolensko and Wysepsk, who have protested against holding the dyet. *D P.*

Paris, Oct. 6. We have a report of some british vessels having taken a spanish register ship, with all the letters and merchants accounts on board. *L E. W E.*

MONDAY, *Oct.* 9.

Hague, Sept. 19. N.S. Some letters from Paris insinuate, that a certain ambassador having complained to the cardinal minister of the conduct of the duke de S. Aignan, at Rome, with regard to the chevalier de S. George and his adherents, with whom he maintains a correspondence, which the king his master cannot approve of, the rather, because it is contrary to the conventions and treaties of friendship subsisting between the two kings: the cardinal only answered, with an air of indifference, that that correspondence (if any such there were) between the duke de S. Aignan and the chevalier de S. George, was not a consequence of any order or instruction given to the ambassador of France at Rome; but, in all probability, for some private view or interest of his own, which he knew nothing of. *P.*

WEDNESDAY, *Oct.* 11.

Yesterday arrived the Mail from Holland.

Amsterdam, Oct. 17. From Warsaw it is written, that the general dyet broke up the 2d. *C.*

Seville, Sept. 19. The conferences between the commissioners of Spain and Great Britain continue suspended. *D P.*

BOOKS and PAMPHLETS published since our last.

Octob. 5. A proposal for the improvement of surgery, &c. by John Rushworth.

The 7th, 8th, and 9th volumes of State Trials in 8vo.

Memoirs of the life of Robert Wilks, &c. Pr. 1 s.

A letter to the author of Reflections historical and political, &c. by the right honourable the Lord Lansdowne. Pr. 1 s.

The Comedian or Philosophical Enquirer. No. VI.

7. Some Remarks on the minute Philosopher. Pr. 1 s.

10. Miscellaneous Observations on Authors. No. 22.

11. A congratulatory Poem to his Majesty: by William Collier. Pr. 6 d.

The Perjured Citizen, or Female Revenge. Pr. 1 s.

On Tuesday Stocks were

South Sea Stock was 104 3 8ths South Sea Annuity 111 1 half, for the Opening. Bank 152 3 qrs. Books open. Bank Circulation 4 l. 10 s. Premium. India 154 1 qr. 154 3 qrs. 154 3 8ths Three per Cent. Annuity 99 7 8ths. Royal Exchange Assurance 104 1 half. London Assurance 13 5 8ths, to 3 qrs. York Buildings 4 1 half. African 38. English Copper 2 l. 2 s. Welch ditto 1 l. 15 s. South Sea Bonds 2 l. 9 s. Premium. India ditto 3 l. 9 s. ditto.

THE GRUB-STREET JOURNAL, 145, p. 4

RAMSAY, Surgeon *and* Man-Midwife, *in Castle-Yard, Holbourn,*

HAth, for many Years, successfully practised a Method of RUPTURES and BROKEN BELLIES of all Sorts, peculiar to himself, and hath cured Numbers of Bursten People, who imagin'd themselves incurable; some of whom have been examin'd by Physicians and Surgeons of the greatest Reputation, who have given their Testimony thereof in the publick Prints. There are several Gentlemen to be heard of at Mr. FRANKLIN's in Russel street, Covent-Garden, who are ready to acknowledge their being cured by him.

He performs the Cure within the Compass of three or four Weeks, and without giving the Patient the Trouble or Fatigue of wearing a Truss after the Cure is perfected.

Last Saturday was published,

No. X. (*containing five Sheets*) *at the Price of* 6 d. *of*

THE HISTORY of *ENGLAND*. By Mr. RAPIN de THOYRAS. Translated by N. TINDAL, M. A. Vicar of Great Waltham in Essex. The 2d Edition. With the following Improvements:

1. The Translation is thoroughly revised and corrected.
2. The many Errors and Mistakes of the Original are rectified.
3. Several Hundred of Marginal References, accidentally omitted by the Author, are supplied.
4. Additional Notes throughout, with Cuts, Maps, and Genealogical Tables on Copper Plates.

Printed for James, John, and Paul Knapton, removed from St. Paul's Church-Yard, to the Crown in Ludgate-Street, near the West-End of St. Paul's.

Where may be had, the preceding Numbers.

N. B. The Whole will be comprised in 2 Volumes, in Folio, containing 400 Sheets, at the Price of 2 l. 2 s. in Sheets, including the Copper Plates. Five Sheets of the Work will be published every Saturday, 'till the Whole is compleated, at the Price of 6 d. and the said Sheets will be delivered every Week at the Houses of Gentlemen who are pleased to order them.

Proposals at large, with a Specimen of the Work, may be had gratis.

There is ready for the Press, and will in a short Time be published,

THE Process of the High Court of Chancery. Translated into English. In which Translation Recourse has been constantly had to the original Writs upon Record in the said Court; the Various Readings, and enumerous Errors, of those printed in Latin carefully revised: With a great Number of Writs which have never appeared in Print.

By an Under Clerk of the Six-Clerk's Office.

This Day is published,

MEMOIRS of the Secret Service of JOHN MACKY Esq; (Master of the Pacquet-Boats) during the Reigns of King William, Queen Anne, and King George I. Including also the true Secret History of the English and Scots Nobility, Officers, Civil, Military, Naval, and other Persons of Distinction, from the Revolution, in their respective Characters at large, drawn up by Mr. Macky, pursuant to the Direction of her Royal Highness Princess Sophia, Electoress Dowager of Hanover. With two Letters from her to Mr. Macky. Faithfully published from his Original MS. Attested by his Son Spring Macky Esq; Also an Account of his Father's Sufferings and Death. With an Appendix of Original Papers relating to Dr. Burnet, late Bishop of Salisbury, containing some Pieces omitted in the first Volume of the History of his Own Time.

N. B. These Characters are by him inserted in the second and third Volumes, not yet published.

ATTESTATION.

[*Being inform'd that my Father's Characters of the English and Scots Nobility, &c. drawn up by him at the Request of her Royal Highness Princess Sophia, were in the Press; I thought it became me, as his Son, to prevent any Falsities concerning him; and therefore I have added her own Memoirs, which shew how faithful and active he was in his several Stations.*]

Sept. 12. 1732. SPRING MACKY.

P. S. A Person of the first Rank hath also communicated my Father's View; or, five Years Secret History of the Court of King James II. at St. Germain in France. Of this Tract above 30,000 were sold in the Year 1696.

Sold by W. Mears, at the Lamb on Ludgate-Hill. Pr. 5 s.

October 2. was published, Pr. 6 d.

[*Neatly Printed on fine Paper.*]

The GENTLEMAN's MAGAZINE: Or, MONTHLY INTELLIGENCER. NUMBER XXI. for SEPTEMBER, 1732. *Being the Ninth of* VOL. II.

CONTAINING,

[*More in Quantity, and greater Variety, than any Book of the Kind and Price.*]

I. VIews of the WEEKLY ESSAYS, viz. On Flattery, Courage, Bigotry, the Art and Mystery of Printing, Anger, Obstinacy, Ostentation, the Advantages of Coffee-houses, odd Customs, ancient and modern; Origin of Moral Virtue, Divine Judgments, Vicissitude of Fortune, Love and Marriage, Preference of Modesty to Beauty.

II. Political Points: On the Power of Secretaries of State and Messengers; Debates in Parliament; History of the Parliament of Paris; Speech of a Member; the Fable of Pan; Pragmatick Sanction, censur'd and defended; Of Just Governments; Treatment of Ministers; Liberties of Athens destroy'd, how; Ancient and Present Government of France; the Selfish Patriot; National Debt; Abjuration Oath; Ambition of Pericles; who pay most Taxes; of Partiality in Quartering the Troops; English and German Generals different way of subsisting; Northern and Sugar Colonies; Abuses of Fees; Merit of Sir Thomas Loother's Invention; Prejudice of Patents.

III. Description of Carolina.

IV. Poetry. The Wary Damsel; Mr. F---'s Letter to his Curate; to the Memory of a Lady; the Poet's Mistress; Consort of Asses; Epigrams.

V. Recorder's Speech to their Majesties; Lord Mayor Elect's Speech, &c. Strange Instance of Revenge.

VI. Domestic Occurences; Marriages, Births, Deaths, Promotions, Prices of Goods, Bankrupts, Bill of Mortality.

VII. Foreign Affairs, &c. &c.

VIII. Register of Books.

IX. A Table of Contents.

By *SYLVANUS URBAN* Gent.

London: Printed, and sold at St. John's-Gate, by F. Jefferies in Ludgate-Street; Mrs. Nutt, Mrs. Charlton, Mrs. Cook, at the Royal Exchange; Mr. Batley, in Pater-Noster-Row; Mr. Midwinter, in St. Paul's Church-Yard; A. Chapman, in Pall-Mall; Mrs. Dodd, and Mr. Bickerton without Temple-Bar; Mr. Critchley, at Charing-Cross; Mr. Stagg, and Mr. King, in Westminster-Hall; Mr. Williamson, in Holborn; Mr. Mountague, in Great Queen-Street; Mr. Harding, in St. Martin's-Lane; and most Booksellers in Town and Country.

Where may be had,

All the former Numbers; the twelve first being now reprinted.

N. B. A few are printed on fine Royal Paper, large Margin, for the Curious.

Just imported, and sold by JER. BATLEY, *at the Dove in Pater-Noster-Row.*

HIstoire des Papes depuis St. Pierre jusqu'à Benoit XIII. inclusivement en Deux Volumes 4to, à la Haye, chez Henri Scheurleer, 1732.

Lately published, and sold by J. BATLEY,

Philosophiæ Mathematicæ Newtonianæ Illustratæ Tomi Duo. Quorum prior tradit Elementa Matheseas ad comprehendendam demonstrationem hujus Philosophiæ scitu necessaria: Posterior continet 1) Definitiones & Leges motûs generaliores; 2) Leges virium centripetarum & Theoriam attractionis seu gravitationis corporum in se mutuo; 3) Mundi Systema.

A GEORGIO PETRO DOMCKIO.

BOOKS printed for J. WILFORD, behind the Chapter-House, near St. Paul's,

I. A Collection of several valuable PIECES, which were written by the Right Honourable EDWARD Earl of CLARENDON, exclusive of his History of the Grand Rebellion: With a new and particular Account of his Lordship's Life, Conduct, and Character prefixed. In two Vols. 8vo. Price 10s.

II. Original LETTERS and NEGOTIATIONS of his Excellency Sir Richard Fanshaw, the Earl of Sandwich, the Earl of Sunderland, and Sir William Godolphin, during their respective Embassies in Spain. With the several Letters and Answers of the Lord Chancellor Hyde, the Lord Arlington, Mr Secretary Coventry, Sir Joseph Williamson, Sir Philip Warwick, Sir George Downing, and other chief Ministers of State. In two Vols. 8vo. Price 10s.

III. TULLY's two Essays of Old Age, and of Friendship; with his Stoical Paradoxes, and Scipio's Dream. Done into English by the late Mr. Samuel Parker, of Oxon. Gent. The Third Edition, carefully corrected and revised by the Translator. Price 2 s.

On Monday, Oct. 2. was published,

The LONDON MAGAZINE: Or, GENTLEMAN'S *Monthly Intelligencer.* NUMB. VI. For SEPTEMBER, 1732. To be Continued. [*Price Sixpence each Month.*]

CONTAINING,

[*Greater Variety, and more in Quantity, than any* MONTHLY BOOK *extant.*]

I. A VIEW of the WEEKLY ESSAYS, viz. On Flattery, Fear, and Courage; Self-Love and Bigotry; Obstinacy; Anger, Envy, and Malice; Modesty, prudent Reservedness, or moderate Ostentation; Love and Marriage; Coffee-house Conversation; Craftsman's Essay on Ethicks censured; Osborne charged with Inconsistency; Vicissitudes of Fortune; Divine Judgments; Judicial Astrology; a curious Account of the Invention of Printing.

II. POLITICAL SUBJECTS, viz. Debates in Parliament on the Number of Forces, and the Sum granted for maintaining them; Religious and Civil Liberty; the Publick Interest; Condition of Ministers; Competitors for Power; Destruction of the Athenian Liberties; ancient and present Government of France; Parliament of Paris; Nature of just Government; Character of Fog and his Writings; Craftsman, answered about Secretaries of State and Messengers; Craftsman, Fog, Osborne, &c. of the Pragmatick Sanction; Hyp-Doctor's Reasoning about the Jacobites; Speech in the Parliament of Paris; Fable of Pan allegorized; Speech of Durham-Yard; Franklin's Petition to a Militia Captain.

III. POETRY: Letter to a Curate versify'd; a noted Song burlesqued; on the Art of Printing; Divine Poetry; Elegy on Lord Chief Baron Dalton; a begging Epistle from a poor Poet; the Milk-Maid, &c.

IV. DOMESTICK OCCURRENCES: Promotions Ecclesiastical, Civil, and Military; Marriages and Births; Deaths, &c.

V. FOREIGN AFFAIRS.

VI. Price of Goods, Grain, Stocks; Monthly Bill of Mortality.

VII. A TABLE of Contents.

To which is added, a Catalogue of Books and Pamphlets, with their Prices; published by the Proprietors of the Monthly Chronicle, now discontinu'd.

MULTUM IN PARVO.

LONDON: Printed for C. Ackers in St. John-Street; for J. Wilford, behind the Chapter-House, near St. Paul's: And sold by W. Meadows, T. Cox, W. Hinchliffe, H. Whitridge, R. Willock, and E. Nutt, in Cornhill; J. Clarke in Duck-Lane; T. Astley in St. Paul's Church-Yard; A. Dodd without Temple-Bar; J. Stagg in Westminster-Hall; J. Jackson in Pall-Mall; J. Jolliffe in St. James's-Street; J. Brindley and W. Shropshire in Bond-Street; and J. Millan near the Admiralty-Office.

Where may be had the former Numbers.

Printed for *J. Brotherton*, at the *Bible*, next the Fleece-Tavern in Cornhill,

A Select Collection of NOVELS. In Two Volumes.

Vol. I. contains, The Little Gypsy; Ethelinda; the Amour of Count Palviano and Eleonora; Scanderbeg the Great.

Vol. II. contains, The Life of Castruccio Castracani of Lucca; the Loves of Osmin and Daraxa; the Spanish Lady of England; the Lady Cornelia; the False Dutchess.

Where may be had,

1. The Minute Philosopher.
2. Coke's Detection 3 Vols.
3. The Life of CHARLES the XIIth.
4. Journey from Aleppo to Jerusalem.
5. Lommius's Treatise of Continual Fevers.
6. Bohun's Law of Tythes.
7. Langham's neat Duties of all the Customs.
8. Gay's Fables.
9. Bailey's Justin.
10. Molleir's Plays French and English.

First publish'd this Day,

Another Volume of

MISCELLANIES in PROSE and VERSE. By Dr. SWIFT and Mr. POPE, &c. Consisting of several Pieces Never before Printed, and others Never before Collected together. Which finishes the entire Collection of their MISCELLANIES.

Printed for B. Motte, at the Middle-Temple Gates, Fleet-street: and L. Gilliver, at Homer's Head against St. Dunstan's Church, Where the former Volumes may be had.

And also just published,

I. Lord LANSDOWNE's Works in 4to, never printed before.

II. A New Edition of the Dunciad. With some Additional Notes and Epigrams.

III. The Progress of Love. From the Folio Edition.

IV. STOWE; The Gardens of the Right Honourable the Lord Cobham.

V. The Art of Politicks. With a Curious Frontispiece.

LONDON: Printed by P. SANDERS, *in Crown-Court, Butcher-Row,* without *Temple-Bar*; where Letters and Advertisements are taken in, and by Capt. GULLIVER, near the *Temple*; also at the *Rainbow Coffee-House* in *Cornhill*, and *John's Coffee-House* in *Sheer-Lane*, near *Temple-Bar*. [Price Twopence.]

The Grub-street Journal.

NUMB. 146.

Thursday, OCTOBER 19. 1732.

Animadversions upon Dr. BENTLEY's *edition of* Paradise Lost, *continued.*

BOOK ii. VER. 2. *The wealth of* Ormus *and of* Ind.] Against this reading the doctor objects, that "*Ormus*, "a small island in the persian gulph, "unnamed by antient poets, has no "native wealth, but WHAT is brought "thither as a center of commerce; "and that the words in the next line, "*Or where the gorgeous east*, plainly suppose, that the "two places named before, as the author gave them, were "not in the *east*." — It gives one a just prejudice against this criticism, that, whilst the doctor pretends to correct the inconsistencies of another, he falls into non-sence himself. *Ormus .... has no* NATIVE *wealth, but* WHAT [or *that native wealth, which*] *is brought thither.* But, not to insist upon this slip, tho' not at all excuseable in so severe a critic; if *Ormus* be *a center of commerce*, and consequently very famous for *wealth*, what objection is it, against the use of it in this place, either that it is *unnamed by antient poets*, or that its *wealth* is *not native?* The Arabians, the best judges of that wealth, have so high an opinion of it, that they have this saying among them, *If the world were a ring,* Ormus *ought to be looked upon as the diamond of it.* As to the doctor's objection from the next verse, which, he says, *plainly supposes*, that *the two places named in this, were not in the east*, it will *plainly* appear presently to be founded upon a misunderstanding of MILTON's meaning in the first four lines of this book. However, upon this false supposition, the doctor, instead of *Ormus* and *Ind*, boldly substitutes "*Hermus* and *Tage*, "as two places, proper for the thought, and situate in the "*west*," by way of antithesis to *the gorgeous east* in the next line. But *Hermus* is a river of Lydia, in the *Levant*, which can with no manner of propriety be called by us *the West*: and its wealth is only imaginary, it not having really any *golden*, but only shining *sands*. And as for the gold of the *Tagus*, it is so inconsiderable, that a few poor people can *hardly* get their living by separating it from the sand. —— But supposing, that both these rivers did really abound with *golden sands* without which supposition there could be no manner of reason for the substitution of either of them in this place; yet it unfortunately happens, that this very supposition alone is a sufficient objection against the alteration. For, as the author of the *Review*, &c. has judiciously observed, by *wealth* in the 2d verse is meant *diamonds*, and not *gold*; which is expresly mentioned in the 4th. and is there changed by the doctor into *gem*: as will more fully appear under the next observation.

VER. 3. *Or where the gorgeous east with richest hand* showrs *on her* kings *barbaric pearl and* gold.] The doctor takes these lines in the literal signification, and then is as barbarously witty upon it, as our brother WOOLSTON is upon that of the historical account of miracles in the New Testament. "*Showrs pearl and gold*, as if those dropt "from the clouds, when the one is fetch'd from the bot"tom of the sea, and the other from the basis of mountains." —— But, pray Doctor, to answer you literally, in your own way, Might not these precious things, tho' *fetch'd from the bottom of the sea, and of mountains*, be carried up to the side, or even to the top of one, and from thence be shower'd down upon a person below. — "And "what's that? *showr'd with hands!* as if any poet ever "feign'd, that the hand was the instrument of showring." The *Reviewer* has given you one instance of a *poet*, who has *feigned* this; a poet, whose works, especially that in which the fiction is to be found, one would imagine that you had carefully read. It is MILTON, in whose *Paradise Lost*, v. 640. we find, *Who showr'd with copious hand* —— "*Showr'd gold on her kings*: Did no subjects get a few "drops, the skirts of the golden rain?" Yes, no doubt, some subjects did: for eastern ministers, it is highly probable, are like western, in the time of a golden rain. —— "But the kings would have the worst of it," That is very likely; for they generally have: but this does not render the common reading at all the worse. —— "As *Tarpeia* had, when she was stifled and kill'd under "the presents of the Roman soldiers." No, no, this is mistake, their ministers would take care to secure them from being *stifled*, or even from having their heads broken by such a precious shower —— But as ridiculous as the doctor would represent a shower of this nature, the author of the *Review* gives us a very probable conjecture, that MILTON "alludes here to the custom used at the co"ronation of kings in some countries of the east: for "CHEREFEDDIN ALI the Persian, in his history of Timur"Bec (translated by M. PETIS DE LA CROIX) says, that "when he was crown'd, the princes and emirs *repandirent* "*à pleines mains sur sa tête quantité* d'or *&* *de* pierreries "*selon la coutume*, Liv. ii. Ch. 1. Which I may translate, *shower'd down gold and precious stones upon his head by hand-fulls, according to custom.*

But the doctor, with as much assurance as if he had stood at the poet's elbow, asserts positively, that he gave it thus,

> Sows *on her* clime *barbaric pearl and* gem.

His reasons are, 1. "The best *gems* are peculiar to the "East-Indies, *gold* as common in the West. 2. *Sows* well "accords with *hand*, agreeably to use and nature. 3. Our "author loved those two words, *sowing* and *clime*, as "V. 1, 2.

> *Now morn, her rosie steps in th' eastern* clime
> *Advancing*, sow'd *the earth with orient* pearl.

To the 1. I answer, that it does not so much justifie the doctor's bold alteration of this verse, as the *Reviewer's* explication of the second, who tells us, that "diamonds are "a principal part of the *wealth* of *India*, where they are "found, and of the island *Ormus*, which is the mart for "them." As to the 2. I observe, that it will as well justifie the reading *sews*, as *sows*: for SEWS *as well accords with hand, agreeably to use and nature*; and is much better, according to the doctor's way of criticism, as being more capable of a literal interpretation, which he seems to think most agreeable in poetry. To the 3. the author of the *Review* answers, that "tho' MILTON says "*sow'd the earth with pearl*, yet he never said, *sow'd the* "*clime with pearl.* To which I may add, that these two verses are unluckily quoted by the doctor, to defend his emendation; since in this by *clime* he means a tract of the earth, but in those it signifies a region of the air over it. —— In short, the *Reviewer's* observations upon this place fully confirm and explain the common reading. He says, "*Ormus* and *Ind* being places well known to be in "the east, that circumstance is not mentioned: but when "the poet comes to speak of *pearl* and *gold*, he mentions "the east, because the best kinds of them are found there. "*Barbaric gold* is an imitation of VIRGIL's *barbarico postes* "*auro.* Æn. ii. 504. The distinction is not between the "wealth of the west and of the east; but between three "sorts of riches, all in the east, *diamonds*, *pearls*, and *gold*: "and thus these three are join'd, v. 634.

> *In pearl, in diamond, and massy gold.*

From all which it is evident, that the doctor has pretended to correct three lines in five places, without understanding even the original meaning of one of them.

VER. 130 —————— *That render all access* Impregnable] The doctor says, "No doubt he gave it *Im*"*practicable*; and his reason is, because *access* here does "not signify the place of access, but the action of ac"ceding." This is only assertion, instead of proof. In opposition to which, I assert, that it may signify here the place of access, as well as in i. 761. *all access was throng'd*: and that it does so signify, the epithet *impregnable* is, I think, a sufficient proof. *Recess*, in like manner, denotes the place of recess in v. 254. of this book.

VER. 196. *Chains and these torments? better* these *than worse.*] "*These*, says the doctor, refers to *chains and tor*"*ments*; which deceiv'd the printer. For the author gave "it, *better* thus *than worse*, for they were even then loose "from their *chains*." Yes, answers the author of the *Review*, but not from their *torments*. It was not therefore *the* printer, but the critic, who was *deceiv'd*: and it is the more strange that he should be so, since the poet does not here say, *These chains and torments*, but *Chains and these torments*.

VER. 256. *Hard liberty before the* easie *yoke Of servile pomp.*] The doctor here reads *lazy*, instead of *easy*; because "the yoke was so far from being thought *easy*, "that it was wearisom and unacceptable." To this it has been answered by the *Reviewer*, "To aspiring minds "it was so, but SATAN [MAMMON he means] here speaks "of what it was in itself; and in its nature it was *easy*, as Satan himself allows, iv. 45. *Nor was his service hard*, &c. To this I shall add a quotation from *Samson Agonistes*, which confirms the present reading, VER. 250.

> *To love bondage more than liberty,*
> *Bondage with ease, than strenuous liberty.*

The author of a *Friendly Letter* to the doctor has said very well, on this occasion, p. 38. That "tho' he can "conceive how a *yoke* may be *hard* or *easy*; yet how it "can be *active* or *lazy*, is beyond his apprehension: and "that if the doctor was so fond of *lazy*, he had better "have altered the passage thus;

> *Hard liberty before the* servile *yoke*
> *Of lazy pomp.*

VER. 309. *Or summer's noon-tide* air.] "It was not the "*air*, says the doctor very gravely, that made the silence "and stillness, but the *hour*;" and then very learnedly subjoins three Greek verses from CALLIMACHUS. But I answer, that the *silence and stillness* were *made*, as much by the latter, as by the former; being indeed *made* by neither, but, in hot countries, occasioned in the *air*, at *noon-tide*; when, as the doctor himself tells us, "the sun "shining fierce, both men and animals retire to shade and "rest." But not, as he supposes, occasioned solely by their retirement, but by the calmness of the wind: for, as the *Reviewer* observes, "in hot countries hardly any wind "blows at *noon-tide*, but towards evening the cool breezes "arise. So in x. 93.

> *Now was the sun in western cadence low*
> *From* noon, *and* gentle airs *due at their hour*
> *To fan the earth now wak'd.*

To the doctor's explication of *noon-tide hour* by CALLIMACHUS's μεσαμβριναὶ ὧραι the same ingenious author answers, that the latter "is equivalent only to *noon-hour* "or *noon-tide*, and that no one ever said *noon-tide hour*, "because *tide* is the same as *time* or *hour*." This is confirmed by my learned brother N. BAILEY Φιλόλογος, who under the word TIDE, says only, *Time, Spenc.* so that *noon-tide hour*, *noon-hour tide*, *noon-time tide*, and *noon-tide time*, are all expressions equally just and poetical.

BAVIUS.

The Curate of C——n's answer to Mr. A—— F——'s letter, in the 142d *Journal*, versifyed.

LEST my ill manners you shou'd speak on,
I here begin Mr. A—— D——
And this punctilio being past,
To write of business now I'll haste.

As soon as yours, Sir, came to hand,
I forthwith sent, at your command,
The clerk on foot to A——d town,
From whence he brought the flowers down;
All which I planted with great care,
And over each humm'd a short prayer,
That they might thrive, and be in bloom,
When you to C——R——N shall come.

I must confess, without a bam, Sir,
Had you sent with them, in the hamper,
Some bottles of my lord's good wine,
With cheshire cheese, and flitch of swine;
I then the winter might rub o'er,
Much better than I've heretofore.
For twenty pounds a year, God wot,
Will not buy cloaths, and boil the pot:
And I can hardly make it do,
To keep out cold and hunger too.

Your servant W——KS, I truly say,
Works wondrous hard, both night and day,
And dearly earns what you him pay.

N——W——D his promise doth neglect,
To fetch your wood, as you expect;
And swears, he'll not a cord bring home,
Unless he's pay'd before you come:
And, what is more, doth grinning say,
As he pays you, for him to pray;
He thinks the reason is as good,
That you pay him for fetching wood.

I'll take great care, you well may think,
In brewing of your stock of drink:
For, as your butler, sir, a cup,
When it is tapp'd, I hope to sup.

Your tenants sadly do complain,
That you their rents so high do strain;
That tho' their crops are large, 'tis true,
They're not enough to pay your due.

I travel up and down all day,
And hardly can get time to pray;
And teaze the elves from morn till night,
Without receiving of a doit,
But hope, e'er long, I ſhall prevail;
Or elſe, will ſend them to a jail.

The ſacred coin, you may depend,
I'll either carry, or will ſend,
To Mr. H——K——R, when I get it;
Who will return't, and not forget it:
And not one farthing I'll purloin,
To buy a pint of ale or wine.
But griev'd I am, and often mourn,
At your deep ſighs, at the *return.*
Five ſhillings for each hundred pounds!
Ah me! how very ſad it ſounds!
How great the charge, ſix crowns, to bear,
From but ſix hundred pounds a year!

Laſt ſunday, when the church was done,
I to JOHN H——L——R ſtreight did run;
Who told me, Mrs. R—GE won't give
The new tythe rent of ninety five;
And ſays, already you've undone her,
In raiſing oft her rent upon her:
Therefore will quit the ſame to you,
And ne'er with it have more to do.

You know how much I am you ſlave,
And preach, and walk, and vaunt, and rave,
Your flock to feed, till almoſt ſpent;
And eke to dun them for their rent.
Therefore, I hope, you don't ſuſpect,
That I your buſineſs ſhould neglect;
Who, as your curate, and your bailey,
Will do it faithfully and daily.

But hold; one thing's quite out of head,
The church, well thought, *the church,* you ſaid,
You'd leave to the church-wardens care:
To write of that, my pains I'll ſpare;
And will conclude with adding this,
Your garden in good order is;
And ſo am I: but needs muſt ſay,
In better ſhould be ev'ry day,
If you'd add five pounds to my pay.

In the 2d column of the preceding page, after the 9th line, add from the *Friendly Letter,* " KINGS in this place, " is the only word that could with any propriety be made " uſe of; becauſe the poet was ſpeaking of *Satan's throne,* " as *far outſhining* that of any earthly king whatever.

DOMESTIC NEWS.

C. *Courant.*	E P. *Evening Poſt.*
P. *Poſt-Boy.*	S J. *St. James's Evening Poſt.*
D P. *Daily Poſt.*	W E. *Whitehall Evening Poſt.*
D J. *Daily Journal.*	L E. *London Evening Poſt.*

THURSDAY, *Octob.* 12.

Yeſterday being the anniverſary of his majeſty's coronation, there was a great appearance of nobility, quality, and foreign miniſters, to pay their compliments to their majeſties at Kenſington. C. &c. —— His majeſty ſends a preſent of 100 yards of ſcarlet cloth, beſides gold lace and other things of value, to the dey of Algiers, by his two miniſters, who are preparing to return home. *S J. L E.*

On monday night ſeveral fellows having broke into an empty houſe, near Kenſington, and ſtole ſome of the lead; on tueſday ſome watchmen were placed in the ſaid houſe, with fire arms, and on tueſday three of them came and attempted to remove a copper; but being diſturbed, as they endeavoured to eſcape, one of them, who was a bricklayer belonging to Kenſington, was ſhot dead on the ſpot; the other two eſcaped. C. *D J.* —— Though much wounded *P.* —— They had left the lead in a ditch on monday, and came to carry it off on tueſday night. *DP.*

Glouceſter, Octob. 7. We have an account from Newport in Wales, that as ſome gentlemen were hunting, the dogs ſtopped on a ſudden near the rock and fountain; where the gentlemen found a child buried in the ſand. Search was made ſoon, and the mother diſcovered, and committed to Monmouth goal. *WE.* —— *Theſe dogs were, no doubt,* blood-hounds. *C.*

A few days ſince Mr. Lechmere, couſin and heir to the late lord Lechmere, was married to miſs Charlton, daughter of ſir Blunden Charlton Bar. and niece to the right honourable the lord Foley. *D P.*

FRIDAY, *Octob.* 13.

It having been humbly repreſented to his majeſty by Mr. baron Thomſon, that his majeſty's bounty of 100 l. for apprehending and convicting any highwayman or ſtreet-robber, who hath committed the fact within five miles of London, hath been a temptation to wicked perſons to make a trade of proſecutions for the ſake of ſo large a reward: his majeſty in tender compaſſion to his people, and an abhorrence of ſuch abominable wickedneſs, hath been moſt graciouſly pleaſed to order, that the granting of the ſaid bounty be left entirely ſubject to the diſcretion of the right honourable the lord mayor for the time being, and of the judge who ſhall have tried the convicts, by whom the iſſuing of ſuch reward ſhall be allowed, or diſallowed on every ſeveral conviction, as they ſhall ſee cauſe from the nature of the crime, and from the merits of the proſecution. *P.*

Yeſterday morning a young woman, big with child, was found dead in Hanging-wood, near Charlton, having hanged herſelf on a crab-tree, with her garter and girdle; a guinea, ſome ſilver, and half-pence, were found in her pocket: ſhe appear'd to have been ſervant to a gentleman near Bexley, and being near her time, had come to the father of it, who lived near Charlton, in hopes to induce him to marry her; but he, inſtead of keeping his promiſe, abſconding, it is preſumed, occaſion'd her deſtroying herſelf. *D J.*

On tueſday night ſome rogues found means to break into the houſe of a hog-butcher in Woods-cloſe, and carried off plate to the value of 200 l. *C.* —— *This* hog-butcher *had ſold his hogs at a good market, to get ſo much more plate than he had occaſion for.*

Portſmouth, Octob. 10. Laſt week one Joſeph Baker, a labourer, ſtanding on the collar-beam of the hemp ſtore-houſe, fell down; and tho' by the fall his right-arm was broke ſhort to the wriſt, his left about ſix inches above his elbow, the ſhoulder of the ſame arm diſlocated, his collar-bone of the ſame ſide much hurt, and his head and face greatly bruiſed, he is already capable of going abroad, and is in as fair a way of recovery as is poſſible. *D P.*

SATURDAY, *Octob.* 14.

Yeſterday the clerks of the treaſury removed from the cockpit to the lottery office at Whitehall, it being fitted up for their reception, till ſuch time as the treaſury office be finiſhed, *C. P. D P.*

At New-market on tueſday Mr. Coke's *Bauble* beat Mr. Cotton's *Vulcan* four miles for 500 guineas —— And on wedneſday the lord Gore's *Diana* beat ſir George Oxenden's *Taffy,* for 200 guineas. *C.* &c.

On friday the 6th inſtant, the reverend Dr. Holmes, of S. John's college in Oxford, was elected vice-chancellor of that univerſity. *P.*

Laſt night the ſeſſions ended at the Old-Baily, when four perſons receiv'd ſentence of death; two were burnt on the hand, twenty two order'd for tranſportation, and three to be whipt. *C. DP.* —— Burnt in the hand. *P. DP. D J.* —— *There is ſome difference betwixt* burning on *and* in the hand.

The deſign of riding on the enſuing lord mayor's day, by the lord mayor and aldermen, is entirely laid aſide; not above three or four of them ever intending ſuch a thing. *L E.* —— It is a great mortification to the citizens of London in general, that ſo ancient and laudable a cuſtom ſhould not be received as was intended. *S J.* —— *A great critic reads* revived, *inſtead of* received.

Sittings in the court of King's-bench, *in and after Michaelmas term,* 1732.

London.	Thurſ. Octob.	26	*Middleſex.*	Tueſ. Octob.	31.
	Wedneſ. Nov.	8		Wedneſ. Nov.	15
	Mond.	20		Wedneſ.	22
	Mond.	27		Satur.	25
Aft. Term	Thurſ.	30	*Aft. Term.*	Wedneſ.	29

W J. W E.

The proſecution that ſhould have come on at the laſt ſeſſions againſt Bartholomew Harnett, for wilful and corrupt perjury againſt Holmes the ſawyer, deceas'd, was put off, the widow being ignorant how to proceed in that affair, and made it too late before ſhe applied to have a bill found againſt him; however, he is detained by a ſpecial order till the next ſeſſions when the proſecution will be carried on with the utmoſt ſeverity. *WE.*

On wedneſday, as Mr. Beard's coach and four was bringing two ladies from his ſeat in Suſſex to London, the coach was ſtopped at Croydon by ſeveral dragoons (who followed the coach from Eaſt-grinſtead) on ſuſpicion of having run goods in it: on ſearching the coach, there were two half anchors of brandy and a little tea found; on which the broad R. was immediately clapped on the coach and ſtable-door where the horſes were; and the ladies detained till friday, when the coach and horſes were diſcharged. *L E.* —— *It was hard to deprive* the ladies *of both their* hot *and* cold tea, *at once.*

'Tis written from S. Alban's, that the dutcheſs-dowager of Marlborough has lately been at that place, with an intent to erect a college for a certain number of officers that ſerved under the late duke her conſort in the wars: the place was formerly a fine ſeat, provided with ſome acres of gardening, and, 'tis ſaid, will be endowed with 400 l. per ann. for ever, and built at her ſole charge. *S J.* —— *This will be a better monument of his glory, than* Blenheim-houſe.

Laſt night the corpſe of Thomas Duckett Eſq; was interred in a handſome manner at Kenſington. *C. W E.* —— George Duckett Eſq; *D J. L E.*

MONDAY, *Octob.* 16.

On ſaturday their majeſties, and all the royal family took the diverſion of hunting a hind on Hounſlow-heath, attended by above one hundred gentlemen and ladies: ſhe gave them very good diverſion for above two hours, and was killed at Mr. Vernon's pond at Twickenham. *C. P.* —— Near Moſes Hart's houſe in Iſleworth-fields. *D P.* —— *The* C. *and* P. *tell us, that* all the royal family was there: *but the* DP. *and* DJ. *mention only* the king, queen, prince, duke, and the three eldeſt princeſſes; *which I take to be the trueſt account.* —— The prince, &c. dined with ſir John Sharden at Kempton-park. *D P.* —— His royal highneſs dined at his houſe at Kew-green. *D J.*

Yeſterday in the evening the right honourable the earl of Albemarle, and the honourable captain Dives, arrived here from Gibraltar, but laſt from France. *P.* &c.

On friday laſt an experiment was made on board a ſhip at Black-wall, in the ſervice of the Eaſt-India company, of an engine that is ſo curiouſly contrived, as to tack a large ſhip about at ſea in a calm, which was much approved of by ſeveral preſent; but it was the opinion of ſome, that it would be of more ſervice if it was fixed at the ſtem inſtead of the ſtern: this is chiefly deſigned for the ſervice of the company's ſhips, in caſe they ſhould be attacked by any of Angria the pyrate's grabes in a calm, with which they might be able to defend themſelves, and bring a broadſide to bear upon an enemy almoſt as ſoon as when under a gale of wind. *D P.* —— *The Art of* tacking about at land, *is brought to greater perfection than* that at ſea.

On ſaturday Mr. Hargrove, a noted bricklayer in Prince's-ſtreet, near Stocks-market, fell from a ladder three ſtories high, and fractured his ſkull, ſo that he died immediately. *D P.* — Reputed worth 7000 l. *P.*

TUESDAY, *Octob.* 17.

Yeſterday his excellency the count de Montijo gave a grand entertainment at his houſe in Jermain-ſtreet, on account of the birth-day of the queen of Spain; at which were preſent moſt of the miniſters of ſtate, and a very great appearance of the nobility, quality, and foreign miniſters; and the evening concluded with a very magnificent ball for the entertainment of the ladies, *C. D P.*

The right honourable the lord mayor and court of aldermen having appointed the new houſe adjoining to the cells in Newgate, as a place of reſidence for the ordinary of Newgate, yeſterday he took poſſeſſion of the ſame. *D P.*

The furniture belonging to the right honourable ſir Robert Walpole, is removing from his houſe in Arlington-ſtreet, to the earl of Aſhburnham's houſe in S. James's Square, which he will go to reſide in very ſpeedily. *P.*

Yeſterday an expreſs arrived from Cheſter with the melancholy news, that at the election of a *mayor* on friday laſt, the diſorder ran ſo high, about admitting honorary freemen, that about forty people were kill'd upon the ſpot, and a great many wounded. Two troops of brigadier-general Churchill's dragoons were at the town's end, but did not enter for fear of giving offence: the riot continuing when the expreſs came away, general Wade's regiment of horſe was ſent for to quell the tumult. *D P. S J.*

Briſtol, Oct. 14. In the Letchlade, in the expedition to Oran, was brought over a camelion alive, purchaſed in July laſt, which has ſubſiſted on nothing but the air, and anſwers to the deſcription given by Ariſtotle, Pliny, Scaliger, &c. *P.*

Yeſterday, about four in the morning, died the right honourable the earl of Harborough, at his houſe in Brewer-ſtreet by Golden-ſquare. *C. P.* —— He left no iſſue; and we hear that he has bequeathed the bulk of his eſtate to his ſiſter, the dutcheſs dowager of Rutland. *D J.* —— The honour devolves upon Thomas Sherrard of Wiſſenton, in the county of Leiceſter Eſq; nephew to the deceaſed earl. *S J. L E.*

The ſame day Joſeph Powis was executed at Tyburn for burglary. *C.* — Contrary to his expectation; having declared in the Preſs-yard, that he doubted not of a repreive before he reached the place of execution. *D J.*

His majeſty has been pleaſed to give the regiment of dragoons, vacant by the death of general Roſs, to general Wynne; that commanded by general Wynne, to general Pearce; and that by general Pearce, to colonel Cope; and the lord Effingham Howard, has obtained that commanded by colonel Cope. *S J.*

Yeſterday the right honourable the earl of Portmore and his new-married lady, the dutcheſs of Leeds, were preſented to their majeſties at Kenſington. *C.* &c. —— Yeſterday the counteſs of Portmore was at court, the earl being there the day before. The cuſtom is alter'd of new married people going there together. *S J.*

By a letter from Cheſter, dated on ſaturday laſt, we have the following account, That for near three months paſt there has been vaſt mobbing, and large ſums ſpent, for the election of a mayor, and many broken heads; tho' Mr. Groſvenor's friends, for about theſe three weeks paſt, by their prudent management have prevented mobbing on their part, which the other ſide gave out to proceed from fear and cowardiſe; which greatly exaſperated the Welſh at Wrexham, ſeveral of whom are freemen; ſo that on

wednesday last about five hundred of them, with sticks in their hands, and cockades in their hats, enter'd the town. Mr. Manly's party hearing of their coming, went to meet them; but the Welch overpower'd them, knock'd several down, and put the rest to flight; and it being a wet day, and the Welch fatigu'd, they retired to different alehouses to refresh themselves; and they had not long been there, before the opposite party, to the number of a hundred and fifty, came out again, and about forty armed with broad swords, &c. to fight the Welch, which by Mr. Grosvenor's friends were lock'd up, to prevent mischief, (for had they been suffer'd to come out, their number must have overpower'd the others, and done great mischief,) and at night were sent home very peaceably, tho' with difficulty: But on thursday the Welch at Wrexham and Howarden assembled to the number of near five hundred, arm'd with scythes, pitchforks, &c. and would come to Chester, and attack those cowards, (as they call'd them,) who had two-edg'd swords, &c. given them, to fall on naked men; but several of Mr. Grosvenor's friends got among them, and appeas'd them, and prevented their coming. This affair will be laid before the parliament; for it's very well known who supply'd Mr. Manly's party with swords and fire-arms. There never was known such a grand appearance of gentlemen of the best estates in the country, in Mr. Grosvenor's interest, as at this election. This letter does not mention any persons being kill'd at the election. *L E.*

We hear from Cardiff in Glamorganshire, Octob. 13. that his majesty's coronation day was celebrated at the Red-house, in the said town, in a very elegant and chearful manner, to the honour of the bailiffs of that loyal corporation, and to the satisfaction of every body present; and, when the company broke up, the most visible tokens of joy appeared in every countenance.

WEDNESDAY, *Octob.* 18.

This day the duchess of Buckingham is expected here from France. *P.* —— Last night her grace arrived in good health, at her house in S. James's park. *C.*

Yesterday, at a general court of the york-buildings company, the ballot was taken for and against the proposal made the 12th; the numbers stood thus: for the payment 348, against it 145. *P. C. DJ.*

The same day an order was made by the lord mayor and court of aldermen, that all prisoners that die within Newgate, the two Compters, and Ludgate, shall, as soon as the coroner's jury have sate upon them, be delivered to their friends, to be buried as they shall think proper, without paying any goal fees, or coroner's fees; the expence of the coroner's jury being to be defrayed by the sheriffs. *DP.*

Last friday the Worcester stage-coach was robbed by two highwaymen, well mounted, who took from the passengers the value of 300l. *DJ.*

From the PEGASUS *in Grub-street.*

To PHILO-DIVES.

POOR PHILO-DIVES, in a carping fit,
 Thou damn'st my epigram, as void of wit:
But, as a slouching ass reveals his smart,
And owns the lash by a reluctant start;
So at my epigram thy awkward fling
Confesses both its wit, and poignant sting.

PHILO-HISTORIO.

A short expostulatory Epistle from Mr. SHELTON, *late* Apothecary, *and* Orator *at Tyburn*, to Mr. H —— Hyp-Orator *and* Doctor *in Grubstreet.*

WHY didst thou first seduce my heedless youth,
 From the strait path of piety and truth?
To sabbath-breaking first my heart incline,
By that pernicious eloquence of thine?
Teach me to stroll from church to church, and spark it
At kirk, and conventicle near Clare-market?
This made me want: want made me take a purse.
But, heav'n be prais'd, I scorn'd to do what's worse:
Ne'er, like Quack-Doctor, had the face or conscience
To make fools pay for hearing of my nonsense;
By false advertisements, and lying puff,
Drawn to attend my incoherent stuff:
Nor with vamp'd title-page have ever sold,
For pamphlet new, sad trumpery, vile, and old,
I scorn'd such *Oratorical Transactions*,
Poor, paltry, pilfering, pick-pocket actions.
Unequal lot! that I sublime should hang;
Thou still sublime in gilded tub harangue.

From my cell in Newgate, Octob. 8.

FOREIGN NEWS.

FRIDAY, *Octob.* 13.

Hague, Sept. 23. A person of consideration, tolerably well skilled in politicks, writes to his friend, that he is much deceived, if he imagines that the spanish armada, fitted out this year, was originally designed against a paltry town in Barbary. He rather believes, (he says,) that it was meant against the kingdoms of Naples and Sicily, where the Spaniards have maintained a private correspondence at a vast expence: but France, who was to have acted in concert in that enterprize, drew her neck out of the collar, just as it was upon the point of being executed; the cardinal de Fleury having received intelligence, that the design had taken air at Vienna, and that the imperial ministers had erected batteries to blow the Spaniards and their enterprize to the bottom of the sea. *P.*

TUESDAY, *Octob.* 17.

Yesterday arrived the Mail from Holland.

Bologna, Octob. 7. The infante don Carlos is just arrived from Florence. *C.* —— About four this afternoon. *P.* —In a small post-chaise, preceded by six running foot men, and followed by two other chaises. *DP.*

ADVERTISEMENTS.

This Day is publish'd,

The SECOND PART of

LIBERTY *and* PROPERTY,

A PAMPHLET highly necessary to be read by every Englishman, who has the least Regard for those two Invaluable Blessings. Containing a Curious Account of some Things which have happened since the Publication of the First Part. With An Original Letter from the AUTHOR to the Honourable Mr. Justice FORTESCUE, one of his Majesty's Judges in the Court of Common Pleas. And some Remarks upon Mr. Walsingham's late proper Reply to the First Part of Liberty and Property. The Whole in a Second Letter to a Member of the House of Commons.

By EUSTACE BUDGELL *Esq;*

Tu ne cede Malis, *sed contra audentior ito.* VIRG.

London: Printed for W. MEARS at the Lamb upon Ludgate-Hill. [Price One Shilling.]

Where may be had,

The Fourth Edition of the First Part of LIBERTY and PROPERTY, (Revised, Corrected, and Enlarged by the AUTHOR.) Price stitch'd two Shillings; bound and letter'd three Shillings.

There is now ready for the Press, and in a short Time will be published,

THE Process of the High Court of Chancery in English. In which Translation Recourse has been constantly had to the original Writs remaining of Record in the said Court; the Various Readings; and numerous Errors, of those published in Latin carefully rectified: with the Addition of a great Number of Writs which never appeared in Print.

By an Under-Clerk of the Six Clerks Office.

RAMSAY, Surgeon *and* Man-Midwife, *in Castle-Yard, Holbourn,*

HAth, for many Years, successfully practised a Method of RUPTURES and BROKEN BELLIES of all Sorts, peculiar to himself, and hath cured Numbers of Bursten People, who imagin'd themselves incurable; some of whom have been examin'd by Physicians and Surgeons of the greatest Reputation, who have given their Testimony thereof in the publick Prints. There are several Gentlemen to be heard of at Mr. FRANKLIN's in Russel street, Covent-Garden, who are ready to acknowledge their being cured by him.

He performs the Cure within the Compass of three or four Weeks, and without giving the Patient the Trouble or Fatigue of wearing a Truss after the Cure is perfected.

Lately published,

Curiously Printed in SIX POCKET VOLUMES,

The MUSICAL MISCELLANY; Being a Collection of CHOICE SONGS and LYRICK POEMS. Set to MUSICK by the most Eminent Masters (With the BASSES to each Tune, and Transpos'd for the FLUTE) viz.

Mr Attilio	Mr Geminiani	Mr D. Purcell
Mr Birret	Mr Gough	Mr H. Purcell
Mr Betts	Mr Grano	Mr Ramondon
Mr Bononcini	Mr Graves	Mr Ravenscraft
Mr Bradley	Dr Green	Mr David Rizzio
Mr Brailsford	Mr Handel	Mr Seedo
Mr Burgess	Mr Haym	Mr J. Sheeles
Mr Carey	Mr Holmes	Mr Trevers
Mr Charke	Mr Holcomb	Mr Vincent
Mr Cole	Mr Leveridge	Mr Webber
Dr Croft	Mr Monro	Mr Weldon
Mr Dieupart	Dr Pepusch	Mr Whichello
Mr Flemming	Mr Potter	Mr Anth. Young.
Mr Galliard		

Printed for J. Watts, and sold by the Booksellers both of Town and Country. Of whom may be had the Fourth Edition of

The FAIR CIRCASSIAN, a Dramatick Performance. Done from the Original by a Gentleman-Commoner of Oxford. To which are added several Original Poems, by the same Author. Also the Fifth Edition of

LETTERS of ABELARD and HELOISE. To which is prefixed a particular Account of their Lives, Amours, and Misfortunes, extracted chiefly from Monsieur BAYLE. Translated from the French by the late JOHN HUGHES Esq;

And the Second Edition of

The Works of Mr. Henry Needler; consisting of ORIGINAL POEMS, TRANSLATIONS, ESSAYS, and LETTERS. Nemo parum diu vixit, qui Virtutis perfectæ perfecto functus est munere. Cicero contemnenda Morte. Published by Mr. Duncombe. Also

CHIRON to ACHILLES. A POEM. By HILDEBRAND JACOB Esq; Res est severa Voluptas. Price Six Pence.

Next Week will be published,

Neatly printed in Twelves,

THE fourth Edition of the Ladies Library, in three Volumes: Published by Sir Richard Steele. And,

The third Edition of the History and Adventures of Gil Blas, of Santillane, in three Volumes.

Both printed for J. Tonson in the Strand.

This Day is published,

THE ADVOCATE. A Defence of the Bishop of Litchfield and Coventry, from the Charge of being the Author of a Pamphlet called, The Principles of the Leading Quakers. Including some Remarks on the Writings of the late Mr. CHARLES LESLIE. In a Letter to his Lordship.

Printed by J. Huggonson in Bartholomew-Close; and sold by J. Roberts in Warwick-Lane. Price One Shilling.

This Day is published,

The SIXTH VOLUME *of a* SELECT COLLECTION *of* MOLIERE's COMEDIES, *in* French *and* English, *neatly printed on a Fine Paper, with a Curious Frontispiece to each Comedy.*

The Sixth Volume contains,

Le Misantrope. The Man-Hater.	*Dedicated to his Grace the* Duke *of* Montagu.
M. De Pourceaugnac. Squire Lubberly.	*Dedicated to the Right Hon. the Lady* Mary Wortley Montagu.

The Collection will consist of Eight Pocket Volumes; one Volume to be published every Month, till the Collection be compleated. Printed for, and Sold by J. Wats, at the Printing-Office in Wild-Court, near Lincoln's Inn Fields: And J. Brotherton, in Cornhill; J. Clarke, in Duck-Lane; A. Bettesworth and C. Hitch, J. Osborne and T. Longman, and J. Batley, in Pater-Noster-Row; J. Roberts, in Warwick-Lane; J. Pemberton, L. Gilliver and T. Worral, in Fleet-Street; F. Clay and R. Wellington, without Temple-Bar; A. Millar and P. Dunoyer, in the Strand; J. Batson, in Little Ormond-Street; J. Stagg, in Westminster-Hall; and J. Brindley, in New Bond-Street. Of whom may be had, Just published, with a Curious Frontispiece to each Comedy,

Vol. I. containing,

A General PREFACE to the Whole WORK.

L'AVARE. The MISER.	*Dedicated to* His Royal Highness the Prince of Wales.
Sganarelle ou le Cocu Imaginaire. The Cuckold in Conceit.	*Dedicated to Miss* Wolstenholme.

Vol. II. containing,

Le Bourgeois Gentilhomme. The Cit turn'd Gentleman.	*Dedicated to* His Royal Highness the DUKE.
Le Medecin Malgre Lui. A Doctor and No Doctor.	*Dedicated to* Dr. MEAD.

Vol. III. containing,

L'Etourdi ou les Contre-Tems, The Blunderer: Or the Counter-Plots.	*Dedicated to the Right Honourable* Philip *Earl of* Chesterfield.
Precieuses Ridicules. The Conceited Ladies.	*Dedicated to Miss* Le Bas.

Vol. IV. containing,

L'Ecole des Maris. The School for Husbands.	*Dedicated to the Right Honourable The Lady* Harriot Campbell.
L'Ecole des Femmes. The School for Wives.	*Dedicated to the Right Honourable* Sir Will. Yong, *Knt. of the* Bath.

Vol. V. containing,

Tartuffe, ou L'Imposteur. The Impostor.	*Dedicated to Mr.* Wyndham *of* Clower-Wall *in* Gloucestershire.
George Dandin, ou le Mari Confondu. George Dandin, or the Husband Defeated.	*Dedicated to the Right Honourable the Lady* ***

The Translation is entirely New, and was undertaken by several Gentlemen, who all joined and consulted together about every Part of it. Particular Care has been had to keep as close as possible to the Original, and to observe the very Words of the Author, as well as his Sense, so far as was consistent with giving it a spirited and easy Comick Stile, in order to make it the more serviceable to those of our own Nation, who are Learners of the French Language; as likewise to Foreigners, who desire to be acquainted with ours: To whom the Method we have taken of placing the French and English opposite to each other, will be of no small Benefit. The Work will be printed in a very beautiful Manner, and adorned with new Frontispieces, designed by Monf. COYPEL, Mr. HOGARTH, Mr. DANDRIDGE, Mr. HAMILTON, &c. Price of each Volume, done up in blue Covers, will be Two Shillings and Six Pence.

The SEVENTH and EIGHTH VOLUMES, which finish the Collection, will be published on Friday the Seventeenth of November next.

N. B. A Curious PRINT of the AUTHOR, with his LIFE in French and English, will be delivered (GRATIS) with the Seventh and Eighth Volumes.

In the Press, and will be published with all convenient Speed, Beautifully Printed in Three Pocket Volumes, the TYPES *being all* NEW.

+‡+ A NEW TRANSLATION of HOMER's ILIAD: As this Translation was undertaken by Gentlemen who UNDERSTAND GREEK, the Reader may be sure he has the SENSE of the AUTHOR; and as they have avoided the Fault of other Translators, who leave their Original meerly for the sake of Versification and Gingle, he will generally have his very Words likewise. To this EDITION will be added some Remarks, both on the Beauties and Imperfections of the Author, after the Manner of Mr. ADDISON's REMARKS upon MILTON. Printed by and for John Watts at the Printing-Office in Wild-Court, near Lincoln's-Inn Fields.

N. B. The ODYSSEY will be Printed in the same Manner, in Three more Pocket Volumes.

This Day is published,

A Proper REPLY to a Scurrilous Pamphlet, entitled LIBERTY and PROPERTY. In a Letter to EUSTACE BUDGELL Esq; By CLEOMENES.

If you but hit his Caufe that hurt his Brain,
Then his Teeth gnafh, he foams, he fhakes his Chain,
His Eye-Balls roll, and he is MAD again.

LEE.

London: Printed and Sold by J. ROBERTS at the Oxford-Arms in Warwick-Lane. MDCCXXXII. Pr. 1 s.

Laft Saturday was publifhed,

No. XI. *(containing five Sheets)* at the Price of 6 d. of

THE HISTORY of ENGLAND. By Mr. RAPIN de THOYRAS. Tranflated by N. TINDAL, M. A. Vicar of Great Waltham in Effex. The 2d Edition. With the following Improvements:

1. The Tranflation is thoroughly revifed and corrected.
2. The many Errors and Miftakes of the Original are rectified.
3. Several Hundred of Marginal References, accidentally omitted by the Author, are fupplied.
4. Additional Notes throughout, with Cuts, Maps, and Geneological Tables on Copper Plates.

Printed for James, John, and Paul Knapton, removed from St. Paul's Church-Yard, to the Crown in Ludgate-Street, near the Weft-End of St. Paul's.

Where may be had, the preceding Numbers.

N. B. The Whole will be comprifed in 2 Volumes, in Folio, containing 400 Sheets, at the Price of 2 l. 2 s. In Sheets, including the Copper Plates. Five Sheets of the Work will be publifhed every Saturday, 'till the Whole is completed, at the Price of 6 d. and the faid Sheets will be delivered every Week at the Houfes of Gentlemen who are pleafed to order them.

Propofals at large, with a Specimen of the Work, may be had gratis.

This Day is publifhed,

MEMOIRS of the Secret Service of JOHN MACKY Efq; (Mafter of the Pacquet-Boats) during the Reigns of King William, Queen Anne, and King George I. Including alfo the true Secret Hiftory of the Englifh and Scots Nobility, Officers, Civil, Military, Naval, and other Perfons of Diftinction, from the Revolution, in their refpective Characters at large, drawn up by Mr. Macky, purfuant to the Direction of her Royal Highnefs Princefs Sophia, Electorefs Dowager of Hanover. With two Letters from her to Mr. Macky. Faithfully publifhed from his Original MS. Attefted by his Son Spring Macky Efq; Alfo an Account of his Father's Sufferings and Death. With an Appendix of Original Papers relating to Dr. Burnet, late Bifhop of Salisbury, containing fome Pieces omitted in the firft Volume of the Hiftory of his own Time.

N. B. Thefe Characters are by him inferted in the fecond and third Volumes, not yet publifhed.

ATTESTATION.

[*Being inform'd that my Father's Characters of the Englifh and Scots Nobility, &c. drawn up by him at the Requeft of her Royal Highnefs Princefs Sophia, were in the Prefs; I thought it became me, as his Son, to prevent any Falfities concerning him; and therefore I have added his own Memoirs, which fhew how faithful and alive he was in his feveral Stations.*]

Sept. 12. 1732.
SPRING MACKY.

P. S. A Perfon of the firft Rank hath alfo communicated my Father's View; or, the Years Secret Hiftory of the Court of King James II. at St. Germain in France. Of this Tract above 30,000 were fold in the Year 1696.

Sold by W. Mears, at the Lamb on Ludgate-Hill. Pr. 5 s.

BOOKS printed for J. WILFORD, behind the Chapter-Houfe, near St. Paul's,

I. A Collection of feveral valuable PIECES, which were written by the Right Honourable EDWARD Earl of CLARENDON, exclufive of his Hiftory of the Grand Rebellion: With a new and particular Account of his Lordfhip's Life, Conduct, and Character prefixed. In two Vols. 8vo. Price 10 s.

II. Original LETTERS and NEGOTIATIONS of his Excellency Sir Richard Fanfhaw, the Earl of Sandwich, the Earl of Sunderland, and Sir William Godolphin, during their refpective Embaffies in Spain. With the feveral Letters and Anfwers of the Lord Chancellor Hyde, the Lord Arlington, Mr Secretary Coventry, Sir Jofeph Williamfon, Sir Philip Warwick, Sir George Downing, and other chief Minifters of State. In two Vols. 8vo. Price 10 s.

III. TULLY's two Effays of Old Age, and of Friendfhip; with his fecial Paradoxes, and Scipio's Dream. Done into Englifh by the late Mr. Samuel Parker, of Oxon. Gent. The Third Edition, carefully corrected and revifed by the Tranflator. Price 2 s.

On Monday, Oct. 2. was publifhed,

The LONDON MAGAZINE: Or, GENTLEMAN'S *Monthly Intelligencer.*

NUMB. VI For SEPTEMBER. 1732.

To be Continued. [*Price Sixpence each Month*]

[*Greater Variety, and more in Quantity, than any MONTHLY Book extant.*]

CONTAINING,

I. A VIEW of the WEEKLY ESSAYS, viz. On Flattery, Fear, and Courage; Self-Love and Bigottry; Obftinacy; Anger, Envy, and Malice; Modefty, prudent Referednefs, or moderate Oftentation; Love and Marriage; Coffee-houfe Converfation; Craftfman's Effay on Ethicks cenfured; Ofborne charged with Inconfiftency; Viciffitudes of Fortune; Divine Judgments; Judicial Aftrology; a curious Account of the Inrcation of Printing.

II. POLITICAL SUBJECTS, viz. Debates in Parliament on the Number of Forces, and the Sum granted for maintaining them; Religious and Civil Liberty; the Publick Intereft; Condition of Minifters; Competitors for Power; Deftruction of the Athenian Liberties; ancient and prefent Government of France; Parliament of Paris; Nature of juft Government; Character of Fog and his Writings; Craftfman, anfwered about Secretaries of State and Meffengers; Craftfman, Fog, Ofborne, &c. of the Pragmatick Sanction; Hyp-Doctor's Reafoning about the Jacobites; Speech in the Parliament of Paris; Fable of Pan allegorized; Speech of Durham-Yard; Franklin's Petition to a Militia Captain.

III. POETRY: Letter to a Curate verfify'd; a noted Song burlefqued; on the Art of Printing; Divine Poetry; Elegy on Lord-Chief Baron Dalton; a begging Epiftle from a poor Poet; the Milk-Maid, &c.

IV. DOMESTICK OCCURRENCES: Promotions Ecclefiaftical, Civil, and Military; Marriages and Births; Deaths, &c.

V. FOREIGN AFFAIRS.

VI. Price of Goods, Grain, Stocks; Monthly Bill of Mortality.

VII. A TABLE of Contents.

To which is added, a Catalogue of Books and Pamphlets, with their Prices; publifhed by the Proprietors of the Monthly Chronicle, now difcontinu'd.

MULTUM IN PARVO.

LONDON: Printed for C. Ackers in St. John-Street; for J. Wilford, behind the Chapter-Houfe, near St. Paul's: And fold by W. Meadows, T. Cox, W. Hinchliffe, H. Whitridge, R. Willock, and E. Nutt, in Cornhill; J. Clarke in Duck-Lane; T. Aftley in St. Paul's Church-Yard; A. Dodd without Temple-Bar; J. Stagg in Weftminfter-Hall; J. Jackfon in Pall-Mall; J. Jolliffe in St. James's-Street; J. Brindley and W. Shropfhire in Bond-Street; and J. Millan near the Admiralty-Office.

Where may be had the former Numbers.

Next Saturday will be publifhed, neceffary to be perufed by all that read the Hiftory of England written by M. RAPIN DE THORAS (containing fix Sheets, at the Price of 6 d.) the third Number of a New and Correct Edition of

THE Hiftory of IRELAND: Containing, I. A full and impartial Account of the firft Inhabitants of that Kingdom; with the LIVES and REIGNS of an hundred and feventy four fucceeding Monarchs of the MILESIAN Race. II. The Original of the GADELIANS; their Travels into Spain, and from thence into Ireland. III. Of the frequent Affiftance the Irifh afforded the Scots againft their Enemies the Romans and Britons, particularly their obliging the Britons to make a Ditch from Sea to Sea between England and Scotland. IV. A genuine Description of the Courage and Liberality of the ancient Irifh, their fevere Laws to preferve their Records and Antiquities, and the Punifhments inflicted upon thofe Antiquaries who prefumed to vary from the Truth; with an Account of the Laws and Cuftoms of the ancient Irifh, and their Royal Affemblies at Tara, &c. V. A Relation of the long and bloody wars of the Irifh againft the Danes; whofe Yoke they at laft threw off, and reftored Liberty to their Country; which they preferved till the Arrival of HENRY II. King of England. Collected by the learned JEOFFRY KEATING, D. D. Faithfully Tranflated from the Original IRISH Language. With many curious Amendments, taken from the Pfalters of TERA and CASHEL, and other authentick Records. Illuftrated with above one hundred and fixty Coats of Arms of the ancient Irifh, with particular Genealogies of many noble Families, curioufly Engraven upon forty two Copper-Plates. With an Appendix, collected from the Remarks of the learned Dr. ANTHONY RAYMOND of TRIM.

PROPOSALS.

I. That the Whole fhall confift of about one hundred and feventy Sheets in Folio, on a good Paper and Letter, and will be finifhed in about feven Months.

II. That fix Sheets will be publifhed weekly, flitched up in blue Paper, for Six-pence.

III. Thofe Gentlemen who are willing to encourage this Undertaking are defired to give in their Names and Places of Abode to B. CREAKE, at the Red-Bible in Ave-Mary-Lane, near Ludgate-Street, or to W. WARING, at the Bible in Jermyn-Street; who will take Care that the Books be carefully delivered.

SUBSCRIPTIONS are taken in by the Bookfellers of London and Weftminfter.

N. B. There are a few printed for the Curious on a Superfine Paper, at Three Halfpence per Sheet.

October 2. was publifhed, Pr. 6 d.

[*Neatly Printed on fine Paper.*]

The GENTLEMAN's MAGAZINE: Or, MONTHLY INTELLIGENCER:

NUMBER XXI. for SEPTEMBER. 1732. Being the Ninth of VOL. II.

CONTAINING,

[*More in Quantity, and greater Variety, than any Book of the Kind and Price.*]

I. VIews of the WEEKLY ESSAYS, viz. On Flattery, Courage, Bigotry, the Art and Myftery of Printing, Anger, Obftinacy, Oftentation, the Advantages of Coffee-houfes, odd Cuftoms, ancient and modern; Origin of natural Virtue, Divine Judgments, Viciffitude of Fortune, Love and Marriage, Preference of Modefty to Beauty.

II. Political Points: On the Power of Secretaries of State and Meffengers; Debates in Parliament; Hiftory of the Pragmatick Sanction, cenfur'd and defended; of Juft Government; Treatment of Minifters; Liberties of Athens deftroy'd, how; Ancient and Prefent Government of France; the Selfifh Statefman; National Debt; Abjuration Oath; Ambition of Pericles; who pay moft Taxes; of Partiality in Quartering the Troops; Englifh and German Generals different way of fubfifting; Northern and Sugar Colonies; Abufes of Fees; Merit of Sir Thomas Lombe's Invention; Prejudice of Patents.

III. Defcription of Carolina.

IV. Poetry. The Wary Damfel; Mr. F—'s Letter to his Country; to the Memory of a Lady; the Poet's Miftrefs; Colours of Affes; Epigrams.

V. Recorder's Speech to their Majefties; Lord Mayor Elect's Speech, &c. Strange Inftance of Revenge.

VI. Domeftic Occurrences; Marriages, Births, Deaths, Promotions, Prices of Goods, Bankrupts, Bill of Mortality.

VII. Foreign Affairs, &c. &c.

VIII. Regifter of Books.

IX. A Table of Contents.

By SYLVANUS URBAN Gent.

London: Printed, and fold at St. John's-Gate, by F. Jefferies in Ludgate-Street; Mr. Nutt, Mrs. Charlton, Mrs. Cook, at the Royal Exchange; Mr. Batley, in Pater-Nofter-Row; Mr. Midwinter, in St. Paul's Church-Yard; A Chapman, in Pall-Mall; Mr. Dodd, and Mr. Kickerton without Temple-Bar; Mr. Crichley, Charing-Crofs; Mr. Stagg, and Mr. King, in Weftminfter-Hall; Mr. Williamfon, in Holborn; Mr. Mountague, in Great Queen-Street; Mr. Harding, in St. Martin's-Lane; and moft Bookfellers in Town and Country.

Where may be had,

All the former Numbers; the twelve firft being now reprinted. N. B. A few are printed on fine Royal Paper, large Margin, for the Curious.

Juft publifhed,

A New View and Obfervations on the antient and prefent State of London and Weftminfter; fhewing the Foundation, Walls, Gates, Towers, Bridges, Churches, Rivers, Wards, Places, Halls, Companies, Inns of Court and Chancery, Hofpitals, Schools, Government, Charters, Courts and Privileges thereof. Alfo Hiftorical Remarks thereon. With an Account of the moft remarkable Accidents, as to Wars, Fires, Plagues, and other Occurrences, which have happened therein for above 1400 Years paft, brought down to the prefent Time. Illuftrated with Cuts of the moft confiderable Matters, with the Arms of the fixty fix Companies of London, and the Time of their Incorporation.

By ROBERT BURTON,

Author of the Hiftory of the Wars of England. Continued by an able Hand.

Printed for Jer. Batley, at the Dove in Pater-Nofter-Row.

Printed for J. Brotherton, at the Bible, next the Fleece-Tavern in Cornhill,

A Select Collection of NOVELS In Two Volumes.

Vol. I. contains, The Little Gypfy; Ethelinda; the Amour of Count Palviano and Eleonora; Scanderberg the Great.

Vol. II. contains, The Life of Caftruccio Caftracani of Lucca; the Loves of Ofmio and Daraxa; the Spanifh Lady of England; the Lady Cornelia; the Falfe Dutchefs.

Where may be had,

1. The Minute Philofopher.
2. Coke's Detection 2 Vols.
3. The Life of CHARLES the XIIth.
4. Journey from Aleppo to Jerufalem.
5. Lommius's Treatife of Continual Fevers.
6. Bohun's Law of Tythes.
7. Langham's neat Duties of all the Cuftoms.
8. Gay's Fables.
9. Bailey's Juftin.
10. Molieff's Plays French and Englifh.

LONDON: Printed by P. SANDERS, in Crown-Court, Butcher-Row, without Temple-Bar; where Letters and Advertisements are taken in, and by Capt. GULLIVER, near the Temple; also at the Rainbow Coffee-Houfe in Cornhill, and John's Coffee-Houfe in Sheer-Lane, near Temple-Bar. [Price Twopence.]

The Grub-ſtreet journal.

NUMB. 147.

Thurſday, OCTOBER 26. 1732.

The Art and Myſtery of *Printing* Emblematically Diſplayed.

Devil with Devil damn'd
Firm concord holds ; Men only diſagree,
Of creatures rational. Paradiſe Loſt, B. II. 496.

Mr. BAVIUS,

AS I was going the other day into Lincoln's-inn, under the great gate-way, I met ſeveral lads and boys of different ſizes, loaded moſt of them with great bundles of news-papers, led by a luſty fellow, who turned round and ſtopped them in the paſſage. They were all exceeding black and dirty ; and made ſo very odd a figure, that I could not but ſtop myſelf to gaze upon them. Some that lagged behind and brought up the rear, I ſaw come out of the Stamp-office: from whence I rightly inferred, that they were Printers Devils, carrying from thence the returns of unſold news-papers, after the ſtamps had been cut off. I thought ſomething comical would enſue : nor was I deceived in my expectation by the following Dialogue ; which I committed to writing, as ſoon as I returned to my lodgings. The Dialogiſts I have diſtinguiſhed by names, with as great propriety as I could, either from the appearance the perſons themſelves made, or from the information of others. I have kept as near as poſſible to the thoughts and expreſſions of theſe black gentry ; at both which I was not a little ſurprized at firſt. But when I conſidered, that many perſons in higher life, without ever reading at all, acquire, ſolely by converſation, a faculty of talking, with great fluency, upon variety of ſubjects, tho' they neither underſtand them, nor the language in which they talk ; I did not think it ſo ſtrange, that theſe gentlemen, tho' moving in a lower ſphere, yet having conſtant opportunities of reading the weekly works of our politeſt authors, or at leaſt of hearing them read, ſhould obtain, in ſome degree, their way of thinking and ſpeaking. Thus what they generally carry on the outſide, might get into the inſide of their heads ; from whence it proceeded in the following manner.

POCK-FRETTEN STUMP. Devils, Gentlemen, and Brethren. Let us ſtop here, and lay down our buſineſs for a

while — upon the ground, ſince the bulk is ſhut off, and we are violently debarred from our property. Our property, I ſay, for tho' we at firſt took poſſeſſion of it by force ; yet ſince no body oppoſed us at that time, we may juſtly be ſaid to have had the tacit conſent of every body, And from that time to this, thouſands of paſſengers have given us their expreſs conſent by a laughter of applauſe. — Nor was this to be wondered at, ſince the uſe to which we put this place, was of the ſame nature with that to which it ſerved before, and was a greater improvement of it. It had been for a long while a receptacle of unſalable hiſtory, politics, and poetry ; and therefore a very proper place for us to eaſe our ſhoulders of the weight of all three, which lay ſo heavy upon them. And what company could be more ſuitable to moſt of the preſent writers, than whoſe works we ſwear, than that of PRYN, DEFOE, and OGILBY ? — And ſince therefore our title to this place has been confirmed to us by long poſſeſſion ; and no one can pretend, that we have abuſed it ; why are we thus unjuſtly excluded ? I ſhould be for breaking theſe locks, and demoliſhing theſe ſhutters directly, were not the lawyers much more terrible at the Old Baily, than here in Lincoln's-inn. But they are always on the ſtrongeſt ſide, and thereby make it the legal. Wealth and power, I have heard ſquire STONECASTLE ſay, like two vicious horſes, hurry off the chariot of the law, through thick and thin, through fair and foul ways and weather, juſt as they pleaſe ; while the coach-man in his black livery, ſitting in the box, as it were, for form's ſake, unable to ſtop their career, encourages them in it, with thoſe reins which ought to reſtrain them. Hence we ſometimes ſee thoſe in a coach, who ought to ride only in a cart ; which is frequently aſſigned to honeſter men, who are driven up Holborn-hill by ſome legal coach-man. On which account, I think, it will be better for us to acquieſce under the preſent injurious excluſion, and patiently to lay our burthens down on the ground, than by forcibly re-entring upon our right, expoſe ourſelves to be taken, and perhaps, tucked up. — If you do not expreſs your diſſent to what I have ſaid, I ſhall look upon your ſilence as a token of your concurrence in the ſame opinion with myſelf.

JEREMY TRUDGE. I am heartily glad you are all of my

mind : and aſſure you, had you been of another, as ſoon as ever you had begun your work, I ſhould have ſlipp'd my neck out of the collar, and ſhewed you a fair pair of heels. I think my maſter APPLEBEE, who was the firſt great inventer of *Weekly Journals*, has taken the wiſeſt courſe. As politics is a ſubject which has grown more and more dangerous to meddle with, he has for a long while layed it aſide ; and is become a much more famous biographer than Mr. CURL himſelf. It is no ſmall conſolation to thoſe heroic, but unfortunate gentlemen, who make their exit at the *Oratory* at Tyburn, where all are freely admitted, that a faithful account of their *lives* and *tranſactions*, written or dictated by themſelves, ſhould be printed in a Weekly Journal. It is likewiſe of great advantage to the living in general, as well as to my maſter in particular, to publiſh the *dying ſpeeches* of theſe ORATORS ; which are much more inſtructive to the publick, than copies of laſt wills and teſtaments, which are always added to the CURLEAN *Lives* and *Memoirs*, only to ſwell the volume. Thoſe *Speeches* or *Orations* may be juſtly called *Lectures* or *Sermons*, but moſt properly *Poſtils* : and I have heard, that ſeveral eminent divines have declared, that they contain more ſound divinity, in better language, than any of thoſe delivered at the Coffee-houſe near Clare-market. — But, notwithſtanding all this, I am heartily glad, that you deſiſt from breaking of locks : for ſhould a load of the *laſt dying ſpeeches* of any of you, my brethren, be ever layed upon my back, I ſhould doubly groan under it, as the moſt ſad and heavy burthen I ever carried in my life. — But I beg your pardon, Mr. Preſident, for this long interruption : for you ſeem to have ſomething of great importance in your countenance.

POCK-FRETTEN STUMP. Tho' my ſeniority, who have been Devil to the *Daily Poſt, London Evening Poſt*, and *Univerſal Spectator*, ever ſince their exiſtence ; and my ſtature, which is much ſuperior to yours, might ſeem to give me ſome ſort of right to this Preſidentſhip ; yet I acknowledge the honourable title you have conferred upon me, by a free unbribed election, as a mere inſtance of your favour, tho' undeſerved, yet not altogether unexpected. For it ſeem a natural conſequence of the reſpect you have always ſhewn me, in not taking one cancelled paper

at the Stamp-office, till I was served. Gratitude therefore, as well as interest, obliges me to consult the honour and advantage of our fraternity; and to acquaint you with every thing which may contribute to the promoting of either. — Tho' I think we have no reason at all to be ashamed on account of the vulgar opinion concerning the origin of our name, as I shall presently shew: yet we ought to acknowledge ourselves obliged to the learned herald, who, upon the death of any person of title, constantly gives an exact account of the press-men in my London Evening Post. He says, that there was one Monsieur Deville or De Villa, who came over with

WILLIAM the Conqueror; in company with Delauar, De Vic, De Val, D'Ashwood, D'Urfie, D'Umpling, &c. A descendant of this monsieur De Ville in the direct line being somewhat reduced, one of his sons was taken in by the famous Caxton in 1471. as an errand-boy; who proving very expert, became afterwards his apprentice, and in time an eminent printer, from whom our order took their name. — But suppose they took it from infernal Devils, it was not because they were messengers, frequently sent in darkness, and appeared very black, as our enemies would suggest; but upon a very reputable account; For John Fust or Faustus, of Mentz in Germany was the

first inventer of printing; which so surprized the world, that they thought him a conjurer, and called him Doctor Faustus, and his art his blackart. As he kept a constant succession of boys to run on errands, who were always very black, these they called Devils: some of whom being raised to be his apprentices, and afterwards raising themselves in the world, he was very properly stayed to have raised many a Devil. As to the inferior order among us, called Flies, employed in taking news-papers off from the press for expedition, they are of much later extraction, being no older than news-papers themselves. Mr. Bailey, the Etymologist, is of opinion that their original name was

Lies, taken from the papers which they took off the press, which were generally such. The alteration of which he imagines to have proceeded from the following occasion: To hasten these boys, it was usual for the press-men to cry, Flie Lie; which naturally fell into one single word Flis. This conjecture is confirmed by a like corruption in the true title of the flying Post; tho' this proceeded from a different cause. — Since therefore, my brethren, we are both comprehended under the title of Devils, let us not be ashamed of our name: but discharge our office with diligence; and then, we may justly hope in time to attain, as many of our predecessors have done, to the dignity of Printers; and to have an opportunity of using others, as much like poor Devils, as we ourselves have been used by them, or as they and Authors are used by Booksellers. These I must observe are an upstart profession, who have almost wholly ingrossed to themselves the business of selling books, which originally belonged solely to our masters; and by this means they are become theirs. But I would have them remember, that, if we worship Belial and Beelzebub the god of Flies, as some of them I hear have archly observed, all the world agrees, that their God is Mammon: and therefore our Deities are upon a level. [To be continued.]

DOMESTIC NEWS.

C. Currant.	P. Evening Post.
F. Post-Boy.	S J. St. James's Evening Post.
D P. Daily Post.	W E. Whitehall Evening Post.
D J. Daily Journal.	L E. London Evening Post.

THURSDAY, Octob. 19.

Last night the right honourable the earl of Nottingham, with his lady, arrived in town from Aix la Chapel in France, where her ladyship has been to drink the waters, for the recovery of her health. C.

Yesterday the directors of the East-India company were pleased to appoint Richard Bignion Esq; to be governor of Fort S. George in the East-Indies, in the room of George Morton Pitt Esq; who is ordered home. P. — It is thought governor Pitt will come next year. C. — It is said. D P. S J. W E. L E.

The Happy Return, captain Matthews, which is arrived at Dartmouth, from Madeira, brought in silver to the value of 1800 l. sterling, which had been fished up out of the wreck of the Dutch East-India ship, which was lost near that island in the year 1724. D J. 4 Ev.

The dean and chapter of Winchester have lately given 300 l. for augmenting the vicarage of Litcleton, in the diocese of Winchester. It's hoped this laudable example will be followed by the deans and chapters of other places. D P. 4 Ev.

The reverend Dr. Stebbing, preacher to the honourable society of Gray's inn, is appointed to preach before the lord mayor on the 5th of November. L E.

Last week, as one Richard Wournel, a brewer's servant, was coming with his dray from Anvil-heath to Twickenham, a young black bear came out of the wood, and he perceiving him, took the slings from off the dray and knocked him down; after which he struck out the head of a barrel and put him in, and has him now alive at his house at Twickenham. S J.

FRIDAY, Octob. 20.

Yesterday John Barber Esq; lord mayor elect, was presented to the lord chancellor, at his house in Lincoln's-inn-fields, for his lordship's approbation, according to annual custom. C.

Yesterday morning Mr. Jeremiah Herman, an eminent Hamburgh merchant, was married at the bull and mouth meeting to miss Gurnell, daughter of Mr Jonathan Gurnell, an agreeable young gentlewoman with a fortune of 6000 l. D P. — a young gentlewoman with good accomplishments, with a fortune of 6000 l. C — Mr. Gurnell, an eminent Irish merchant, a fortune of 5000 l. D F.

Last week died at his seat near Doncaster, in Yorkshire, Sir George Cooke, of Wheatly Bar, of a mortification, in his 70th year: he is succeeded in dignity and estate by his eldest son, now Sir Bryan Cooke. D P.

SATURDAY, Octob. 21.

The gentlemen belonging to the parishes of S. Anne's Aldersgate, and S. Martin's le grand, have agreed to build a work-house near the church, for the better employing the poor of those parishes. C.

On thursday Mr. Wicks, an eminent brewer in Whitecross-street, was married to Mrs Ireland of Mile-end, an agreeable widow gentlewoman, of very good accomplishments, and a fortune of 10,000l. C, 4 Ev. — 5000 l. or 6000 l. are only good accomplishments: but 10000 l. are very good.

We have an account from Turin, that the countess of Essex was safely delivered there of a son and heir, to the great joy of that noble family. P. 4 Ev.

William Pulteney Esq; being arrived in town, accompanying the duchess of Buckingham from Dover, set out this morning for Bath. S J. L E.

The honourable Mrs. Anne Vane is removing from S. James's-street to the great house in Grosvenor-square, lately purchased for her. S J. L E.

We hear from Waltham in Leicestershire, near Melton-Mowbray, that a mason's daughter, about 11 years of age, is possessed with an evil spirit, in such a manner, as to throw her out of bed into fits, and pinching bits of flesh out of her arms, &c. and has twice put her collar-bone out: she is thrown into fits often, and lies as one dead, and, at the same time, there is such a knocking, and thundering noise, (sometimes at the door, but oftener near the child, as is terrible to all about her; and if any person bids the spirit knock any number of times at the door, or to any tune, it certainly does so. Most of the clergy, and other people of note thereabouts, particularly the lord How, have had the girl at their own houses, and have all proved it to be no fallacy or imposition. All the account she gives when she comes out of her fits, is, that she is carried into a wood, and tormented by three persons. S J— It is pity, the conjuring Doctor who came from Melton Mowbray, is not in that neighbourhood at this time: tho' some think, he is better at putting the Devil in, than at casting him out.

On Friday last came on the election for a mayor of Chester for the ensuing year. The candidates were alderman Johnson and alderman Ellams, supported by the Grosvenor interest; and alderman Mainwaring and alderman Bennett, set up by Mr. Brereton and Mr. Manley. The poll continued till four o'clock on monday in the afternoon, when the mob obliged them to close the books, and immediately afterwards forced the mayor and recorder into a coffee-house, which they instantly attack'd, and broke open the door with iron crows, seiz'd the sword, mace, and white staff, and carry'd them to alderman Bennett's, committing the vilest outrages imaginable. On tuesday (the insignia being restored) the court sat again; and upon casting up the books the poll stood thus:

For alderman Johnſon 1097	For alder. Mainwaring 858
For alderman Ellams 1095	For alderman Bennett 858

No ſcrutiny being demanded, the former was ſworn into the office. The ſame day Mr. Edward Nichols and Mr. William Edwards, were, without oppoſition, elected ſheriffs. This has been for ſome months the warmeſt conteſt that was ever known in Cheſter: There appear'd in the Groſvenor intereſt eight baronets, five high ſheriffs of counties, and upwards of 120 eſquires; beſides ſeveral members of parliament. Above fifty freemen, friends to the Groſvenor family, were prevented from polling by the violence of the mob, and ſome threaten'd to be murder'd if they ſtirr'd out of their houſes. Alderman Johnſon's election has occaſion'd great joy to thoſe who wiſh well to the true intereſt of that ancient and loyal city; and upon the cockades, worn on that occaſion, was expreſs'd the following motto: CIVITATIS SALUS PATRIA NON VENALIS. *P. DP. SJ. LE.*—The Cheſter news-paper ſays that a ſcrutiny was demanded, and was to begin at 10 next day. *DJ. WE.*

Yeſterday morning a certain Iriſh baronet was taken up by a warrant under the hand and ſeal of ſir John Gonſon, chairman of the ſeſſions of the peace for the city and liberty of Weſtminſter, being charged on oath to have cheated and defrauded a young gentleman of Lincoln's-inn of ſeveral hundred pounds, with falſe dice; the baronet at firſt ſeemed to defy the law, and refuſed to give bail; but his mittimus being made to Newgate, he became bound in a recognizance himſelf in 400 l. with two ſureties in 200 l. to appear at the next ſeſſions, to anſwer to an indictment which will be preferred againſt him for this offence, upon the ſtatute of 9 queen Anne, cap. 14. whereby "Any perſon "that by fraud or ill practice gets or wins at any one "time at play above 10 l. forfeits five times the value, and "is to ſuffer corporal puniſhment as in caſes of perjury, "and be deemed infamous." *DP.*

In the Hyp-Doctor on tueſday next will be, &c. as was laſt tueſday in the ſame [Hyp-Doctor on tueſday next] &c. *DJ.*

MONDAY, *Oct.* 23.

On ſaturday morning their majeſties and all the royal family took the diverſion of hunting a hind on Hounſlow-heath. *C.*—The prince, the duke, and the three eldeſt princeſſes. *P. DP.*—The ſtag gave them good diverſion for about five hours. *C.* His majeſty was ſoon thrown out by a countryman's giving a wrong ſcent, and loſt ſight all the way. *DP.*—The king and queen left the chace at Harrow on the hill. The reſt of the royal family (except *the princeſs* Caroline) purſued the chace, and came in at *the death. P.*—All the royal family and nobility) except his royal highneſs the duke, and the earl of Pomfret, were flung out of the chace, they coming in at the death at Harrow on the hill. *C.*—In a field about eight miles on the other ſide of Harrow on the hill. *P.* The duke and the princeſs royal rode in view till the death. *DP.*

The contribution or bounty-money uſually given to the huntſmen on Holy-rood-day, having not then been collected, Francis Whitworth Eſq; ſurveyor of the king's private roads, held the purſe, and a collection of about 200 l. was made on the ſpot, their majeſties giving 50 guineas, the prince, duke, and princeſſes, 50 gunieas, and the miniſters of ſtate, &c. moſtly five guineas apiece. *DP.*

Yeſterday being the anniverſary of the birth of her royal highneſs the princeſs Anne, the ſame was obſerved throughout the cities of London and Weſtminſter, &c.—Her royal highneſs entered into her 24th year. *P.*—Into her 25th *DP.*

Mr. Meredith, groom of the chambers to the right honourable the earl of Cheſterfield, is appointed by his lordſhip to be one of the gentlemen of the ſcalding-office, in the room of Mr. York, deceaſed. *P.*

On ſaturday, as Dr. Willmot, and Mr. Cheſelden ſurgeon, were paſſing through Chancery-lane in a chariot, by ſome accident they were overturned; but without any further damage than breaking the fore glaſs, and the doctor's receiving a ſmall cut on the forehead. *C.*—*If the* doctor *had* received a great cut, *the* ſurgeon, *no doubt, would have eaſily cured him.*

In the mayoralty of ſir Francis Child Kt. 582 perſons have been indicted at the Old Bailey; of which number 70 have received ſentence of death, 208 been ordered for tranſportation, eight fined, impriſoned or pilloried, four burnt in the hand, four whipp'd, and 288 acquitted by the juries. *DP.*

TUESDAY, *Octob.* 24.

The right honourable lord Wilmington, preſident of the council, has been pleaſed to appoint Mr. Ford, his lordſhip's ſteward, to be chamber keeper of the council, in the room of Mr. Salter, lately deceaſed. *P.*—Mr. Salter's ſon is appointed to ſucceed his father, as one of the clerks of the ſpicery. *P. DP. DJ.*

On ſaturday at Newmarket, the duke of Bolton's *Dreadnought* beat Mr. Panton's *Mouſe*, for 500 guineas. *C.* &c.

We hear that on ſunday laſt there was a collection for the poor perſecuted Saltzburgers made at a diſſenting meeting-houſe in this city, where was collected 58 l. which chriſtian example will, we hope, be followed by all others, who wiſh well to the principles of liberty, and our holy religion. *C.*—Holy religion *will cauſe perſons to* follow this chriſtian example, *whether they* wiſh well to the principles of liberty *here intended, or not.*

Yeſterday, being the firſt day of the term, the right honourable the lord chancellor, &c. went with the uſual ſtate to Weſtminſter-hall. *C.* &c.——The printers of the Daily Advertiſer and the Royal Oak Journal were called upon to anſwer to ſome things they have publiſhed; and againſt the latter a bill was found, for publiſhing ſome ſcandalous reflections againſt the government. *C.*

On ſunday night her grace the dutcheſs of Devonſhire was ſafely delivered of a ſon at the duke's houſe in Piccadilly. *DP.*

A few days ſince died at his houſe at Windſor, Dr. Meighill, an eminent phyſician. *DP.*—and is ſucceeded by Dr. Burton. *DJ.*

Norwich, Oct. 21. On friday night one Mr. Pamont, a young attorney, and heir to an eſtate of 600 l. a year, was moſt barbarouſly murdered at the bell in Swaffam; of which murder Mr. Framingham, an apothecary there, ſtands ſuſpected, and is bound over in very conſiderable recognizances: it ſeems Mr. Pamont and Mr. Framingham had wrangled about the running of their greyhounds, but were ſeemingly very eaſy again; and ſome time after, Mr. Pamont was privately ſtabbed in the belly, ſo that his bowels appeared; and altho' there were eight or ten perſons in the room, no body ſaw who did it, nor had Mr. Framingham (they ſay) any weapon or inſtrument found about him, nor could any be diſcovered in the room.—On monday two convicts, John Bennet, condemned for horſe ſtealing, and Suſan Tyler, for the murder of her baſtard child, were ſent up to Newgate in London, faſtened behind the ſtage coach, in order to be tranſported for 14 years. *P.*

WEDNESDAY, *Octob.* 25.

Whitehall, Octob. 24. His majeſty has been pleaſed to appoint Chriſtopher Montague, John Whetham, Roger Gale, Charles Polhill, John Fowle, Thomas Wilde, James Vernon, Robert Eyre; and Humphry Thayer Eſq, and Humphery Thayer Eſqs, commiſſioners of exciſe. *C. P. DJ.*

The right reverend the lord biſhop of Durham has preſented the reverend doctor Stillingfleet (ſon to the dean of Worceſter, and grandſon to the famous biſhop Stillinfleet) to the rectory of Biſhop's Weremouth in that dioceſe, worth about 400 l. per ann. *DP.*

From the PEGASUS *in Grub-ſtreet.*

Mr BAVIUS,

ERrors of great men, you are ſenſible, are of all others the moſt dangerous, it will therefore be a ſervice to the publick, worthy of your ſociety, to prevent the ſpreading of ſuch miſtakes, by occaſionally recording in the memoirs of Grub-ſtreet

ERRATA *of the* LEARNED.

Dr. MEAD. It is a common opinion, and propagated by authors of great name, that we are uſually viſited with the plague once in thirty or forty years: but this is a mere fancy, without any foundation, either in reaſon or experience. *A diſcourſe concerning peſtilential contagion, p.* 5.—*N.B.* In the ſpace of 100 years, from 1582 to 1682, we have had five great plagues, viz. ann. 1592, 1603, 1625, 1636, 1665. The doctor meant well, to deliver his countrymen from the ſubjection to ſuch vain fears. Yet, I dare ſay, he is no friend to pious frauds; being ſenſible, no doubt, that the knowledge of the truth can never be prejudicial to the intereſts of mankind. Tho' we had been viſited with that dreadful calamity, twice as often, the laſt century; the next, it may pleaſe God to ſpare us.

Mr. CHAMBERS. The colliſion of flint and ſteel *in vacuo*, produces no ſparks. *Vid. Vacuum*——*N.B.* A flint and ſteel ſtrike ſparks of fire as copiouſly *in vacuo* as out of it. *Vid. Air-pump.*

On the liberty of the preſs.

IN good queen ANNA's days, when Tories reign'd,
And the juſt liberty of preſs reſtrain'd,
Sad whigs complain'd in doleful notes and ſundry,
O liberty, O virtue, O my country!
But when themſelves had reach'd the day of grace,
They chang'd their principles, as well as place.
From meſſengers ſecure no printer lies,
They take compoſitors, preſs-men, devils, flies.
What means this change! The ſum of all the ſtory's,
Tories depreſt are Whigs, and Whigs in pow'r are Tories.

MÆVIUS.

FOREIGN NEWS.

Yeſterday arrived the Mail from France.

THURSDAY, *Oct.* 19.

Paris, Oct. 25. Our laſt letters from Madrid aſſure us, that they preſs forward the new levies throughout the kingdom with extraordinary diligence, not only to complete, but conſiderably augment the king's forces; for which purpoſe they ſeize on all paſſengers on the road, eſpecially the pilgrims going to S. James's of Compoſtella, not ſuffering one to eſcape who is found capable to bear arms.—The duke de Chartres is now entirely out of danger of the ſmall pox.—Francis-Hannibal, count de Bethune, formerly admiral of the fleet, died here the 19th, aged 105. *C.* &c.

FRIDAY, *Octob.* 20.

Rome, Sept. 30. The regular canons of the church of S. Mary in the Montferrat, having pulled down ſome old buildings of their houſe, they found in a chamber, the door whereof was walled up, two leaden coffins, in which were the bodies of the popes Alexander VI. and Sixtus II. the place of whoſe burial was not before known. *C.*

Paris, Oct. 24. On friday laſt the old committee of the charitable corporation ſat at Boulogne, when Mr. Thompſon was queſtioned concerning the diſpoſition of a large quantity of capital ſtock. He pretended to make it appear, that the ſaid ſtock was delivered to the uſe of one Mrs. Brown; whereupon Mrs. Brown's character was indecently treated, her honour infamouſly aſperſed, and her perſon foully reflected on. This freedom occaſioned a diſpute; from diſputing they came to wrangling, and from wrangling to quarelling, till they all caned one another round, ſo that the committee broke up without ſettling any accounts. *DJ.*

MONDAY, *Octob.* 23.

Hague, Oct. 7. We have received advice, that there is a ſociety formed at Vienna, of Engliſh, Dutch, and Italians, who have drawn a project for reforming, amending, and improving the commerce of all the emperor's dominions. This plan has been preſented to the imperial court, who have it now actually under conſideration. *P.*

TUESDAY, *Octob.* 24.

Yeſterday arrived the Mail from Holland.

Rome, Octob. 11. N.S. On the 4th, the proviſional ſentence pronounced againſt cardinal Coſcia was communicated to his eminency; the ſubſtance of which was: That he ſhall be again examined in relation to ſome things that he has confeſſed; that he ſhall have two months allowed to furniſh himſelf with materials for his juſtification; that a foreign advocate ſhall plead for him, &c. *C. DP. DJ.*

Parma, Octob. 11. The ſerene infante duke two days ſince made his public entry into this city. *DP. DJ.*

BOOKS and PAMPHLETS publiſhed ſince October 11.

12. The merry thought: 4th part. Price 6 d.

A brief enquiry concerning the dignity of the Lord's ſupper, &c. Price 6 d.

A ſermon before the right honourable the lord mayor, &c. Sept. 29. by John Middleton, D. D.

13. A third part of letters, moral and entertaining, &c.

14. The preſent ſtate of the republick of letters, for September. Price 1 s.

17. A proper reply to a ſcurrilous pamphlet, entitled, liberty and property. Price 1 s.

Another volume of miſcellanies, in verſe and proſe, by Dr. Swift, Mr. Pope, &c.

19. A conference between his excellency Jonathan Belcher Eſq; and the chief Sathems of ſeveral Indian tribes, &c.

Divine truths vindicated, by William Hudelſton.

The great advantage of the uſe of the bark in mortifications, by John Ruſhworth, ſurgeon. Price 6 d.

20. The 2d part of liberty and property, by Euſtace Budgell, Eſq;

21. A philoſophical diſſertation upon death. Pr. 1 s. 6 d.

The political ſtate of Great Britain, for September.

23. Gnomologia, adagies and proverbs, &c. collected by Tho. Fuller, M.D.

24. Remarks upon the right honourable lord Lanſdowne's letter, &c.

Modern hiſtory, by Mr. Salmon, No. 103.

On Tueſday Stocks were

South Sea Stock was 104 1 8th, 103 7 8ths, 103 7 8ths to 104. South Sea Annuity 111 1 qr. for the Opening. Bank 149 1 half. Bank Circulation 4 l. 12 s. 6 d Premium. India 155 1 half, 154 1 half. Three per Cent. Annuity 99 3 qrs. Royal Exchange Aſſurance 104 1 half. London Aſſurance 13 5 8ths, to 3 qrs. for the Opening. York Buildings 4 1 half. African 36. Engliſh Copper 2 l. 1 s. Welch ditto 1 l. 15 s. South Sea Bonds 2 l. 8 s. Premium. India ditto 4 l. 1 s. ditto.

THE GRUB-STREET JOURNAL, 147, p. 4

This Day is publish'd,

(Price Bound 2 s. 6 d.) the Second Edition of

THE GENTLEMAN FARRIER. Containing Instructions for the Choice, and Directions in the Management of Horses, either for Draught or Pleasure, on a Journey, or in the Stable ; with an Account of their Distempers, and Receipts for the Cure of them. To which is added, An Appendix concerning Dogs, either for the Field or the Lap ; wherein their Diseases are describ'd, and the Means to cure them. The Horse Receipts by his late Grace of Devonshire, Earl of Orrery ; Lord Carleton, Sir John Puckington, General Seymour, Portman Seymour Esq; James Nicholson Esq; Thornton Esq; of Bloxham, &c. Published by the Direction of a Person of Quality. Printed for F. COGAN, at the Middle-Temple Gate, Fleet-Street.

N. B.·This Book contains above thirty Pages and thirty Receipts more than Capt. Burdon's, and is sold at half the Price of his.

This Day is publish'd,

A Proper REPLY to a Scurrilous Pamphlet, entitled LIBERTY and PROPERTY. In a Letter to EUSTACE BUDGELL Esq; By CLEOMENES.

If you but hit the Cause that hurts his Brain,
Then his Tooth guess, he foams, he shakes his Chain,
His Eye-Balls roll, and he is MAD again.   LEE.

London : Printed and Sold by J. ROBERTS at the Oxford-Arms in Warwick-Lane. MDCCXXXII. Pr. 1 s.

On Wednesday the 1st of November, will be Published, in 2 Vols. 4to.

AN Anatomical Exposition of the Structure of the Human Body, by JAMES BENIGNUS WINSLOW, Professor of Physick, Anatomy, and Surgery in the University of Paris, Member of the Royal Academy of Sciences, and Royal Society at Berlin, &c.

Translated by G. DOUGLAS, M. D.

And Sold by N. Prevost over-against Southampton-Street in the Strand,

THE Great and Wonderful Cures daily performed by Dr. BATEMAN's Pectoral Drops, in the following Distempers, have gained them so indisputable a Character, that few Families, who have ever heard, or experienced the Virtues thereof, care to be without them in their own Houses, viz. the Gout, Rheumatism, Jaundice, Stone, Gravel, Asthmas, and Cholicks, of what Kind or Nature soever, whether proceeding from Wind, Cold, or Resterik Affecting. Besides which there is no one Secret in the whole Art of Physick of that surprizing, and were it not under the Confirmation of continual Experience almost incredible Effects in Colds, Agues, Fevers, and those endemic Evils which appear in most Constitutions at Spring and Fall. The Price of each Bottle, in which are three moderate Doses, is but one Shilling, and may (by Virtue of the King's Letters Patents) be had at the Printing-Office, Bow-Church-Yard, Cheapside, and no where else within three Quarters of a Mile from thence.

N. B. A Book of the Virtues thereof, with Testimonies of some hundred Cures performed thereby, under the Hands of Persons of known Worth and Credit, may be had gratis with the said Bottles.

Note also, Shopkeepers, &c. in any Town, where they are not already sold, may be supplied with the above Drops (and good Allowance) to fell again, by directing to Wm. Dicey, or Tho. Cobb and Comp. at Dr. Bateman's wholesale Warehouse in Bow-Church-Yard, London.

This Day is publish'd,

The SECOND PART of

LIBERTY and PROPERTY,

A PAMPHLET highly necessary to be read by every Englishman, who has the least Regard for those two Invaluable Blessings. Containing a Curious Account of some Things which have happened since the Publication of the First Part. With An Original Letter from the AUTHOR to the Honourable Mr. Justice FORTESCUE, one of his Majesty's Judges in the Court of Common Pleas. And some Remarks upon Mr. Walsingham's late proper Reply to the First Part of Liberty and Property. The Whole in a Second Letter to a Member of the House of Commons.

By EUSTACE BUDGELL Esq;

Tu ne cede Malis, sed contra audentius ito.   VIRG.

London : Printed for W. MEARS at the Lamb upon Ludgate-Hill. [Price One Shilling.]

Where may be had,

The Fourth Edition of the First Part of LIBERTY and PROPERTY, (Revised, Corrected, and Enlarged by the AUTHOR.) Price stitch'd two Shillings ; bound and letter'd three Shillings.

This Day is publish'd,

THE Great Advantage of the Use of the BARK in MORTIFICATIONS. With several Additions.

By JOHN RUSHWORTH Surgeon.

Printed for Lawton Gilliver, at Homer's Head against St. Dunstan's Church in Fleet-Street.

This Day is Publish'd,

The Fourteenth Edition of,

THE Benefit of FARTING explain'd ; or the Fundament-All Cause of the Distempers of the Fair Sex inquired into, proving A Posteriori most of the Disorders intailed on them, are owing to Flatulencies not seasonably vented. Wrote in Spanish by Don Fart-in-hando Puff-indorst, Professor of Bombast in the University of Crackow, and translated into English at the Request, and for the Use of the Lady Damp-fart, of Her-fart-shire. To which is annexed, A Certificate of the Virtue of Farting, from the Court of the Princess Arsenini. Together with some Verses on Mrs. V——ne's Fart, in the Phillipk Strain, and on Squire Nump's Fart in the Brewers Strain. Also a Meditation on a T——d, wrote in a Place of Ease. Printed for F. Jefferies in Ludgate-Street.

This Day is publish'd,

[Price One Shilling,]

The Second Edition corrected, of

A Practical GRAMMAR of the English TONGUE. In two Parts. Containing, 1. Instructions for the true Spelling, Reading and Writing of English. II. The Principles of Arithmetick, Geography and Chronology, explained and suited to the meanest Capacities. For the Use of Schools.

By THO. DYCHE, late School-Master, at Stratford, Bow,

Printed for J. Clarke, at the Golden-Ball in Duck-Lane, near West-smithfield.

First publish'd this Day,

Another Volume of

MISCELLANIES in PROSE and VERSE by Dr. SWIFT, Mr. POPE, &c. Containing several Pieces never before published ; and others never before collected together ; which finishes the entire Collection of their Miscellanies.

Printed for B. Motte, under the Middle-Temple Gate, and L. Gilliver, at Homer's Head against St. Dunstan's Church, Fleet-street. Where may be had the other Volumes, as also,

1. The Works of the Right Hon. the Lord LANSDOWNE.
2. A new Edition of the DUNCIAD, with some additional Notes and Epigrams. A Collection of Pieces, occasion'd by the DUNCIAD.
3. The Progress of Love, in 8vo. (from the Folio Edition.)
4. An Epistle from Rome to Mr. Pope, by the Author.
5. STOWE : The Gardens of the Lord Viscount Cobham.
6. The Art of Politicks ; with a Curious Frontispiece.
7. An Epistle to Mr. Pope concerning the Authors of the Age, by the Author of Universal Passion.

Last Saturday was publish'd,

No. XII. (containing five Sheets) at the Price of 6 d. of

THE HISTORY of ENGLAND. By Mr. RAPIN de THOYRAS. Translated by N. TINDAL, M. A. Vicar of Great Waltham in Essex. The 2d Edition. With the following Improvements :

1. The Translation is thoroughly revised and corrected.
2. The many Errors and Mistakes of the Original are rectified by the Author, and supplied.
3. Several Hundred of Marginal References, accidentally omitted by the Author, are supplied.
4. Additional Notes throughout, with Cuts, Maps, and Genealogical Tables on Copper Plates.

Printed for James, John, and Paul Knapton, removed from St. Paul's Church-Yard, to the Crown in Ludgate-Street, near the West-End of St. Paul's.

Where may be had, the preceding Numbers.

N. B. The Whole will be comprised in 2 Volumes, in Folio, containing 400 Sheets, at the Price of 11 l. 2 s. in Sheets, including the Copper Plates. Five Sheets of the Work will be published every Saturday, 'till the Whole is completed, and the Price of 6 d. and the said Sheets will be delivered every Week at the Houses of Gentlemen who are pleased to order them.

Proposals at large, with a Specimen of the Work, may be had gratis.

Just published,

A New View and Observations on the antient and present State of London and Westminster, shewing the Foundation, Walls, Gates, Towers, Bridges, Churches, Rivers, Wards, Palaces, Halls, Companies, Inns of Court and Chancery, Hospitals, Schools, Government, Charters, Courts, and Privileges thereof. Also Historical Remarks thereon. With an Account of the most remarkable Accidents, as to Wars, Fires, Plagues, and other Occurrences, which have happened therein for above 1300 Years past, brought down to the present Time. Illustrated with Cuts of the most considerable Matters, with the Arms of the sixty six Companies of London, and the Time of their Incorporation.

By ROBERT BURTON,

Author of the History of the Wars of England. Continued by an able Hand.

Printed for Jer. Batley, at the Dove in Pater-Noster-Row.

BOOKS printed for J. WILFORD, behind the Chapter-House, near St. Paul's,

I. A Collection of several valuable PIECES, which were written by the Right Honourable EDWARD Earl of CLARENDON, exclusive of his History of the Grand Rebellion. With a new and particular Account of his Lordship's Life, Conduct, and Character printed, In two Vols. 8vo. Price 10 s.

II. Original LETTERS and NEGOTIATIONS of his Excellency Sir Richard Fanshaw, the Earl of Sandwich, the Earl of Sunderland, and Sir William Godolphin, during their respective Embassies in Spain. With the several Letters and Answers of the Lord Chancellor Hyde, the Lord Arlington, Mr. Secretary Coventry, Sir Joseph Williamson, Sir Philip Warwick, Sir George Downing, and other chief Ministers of State. In two Vols. 8vo. Price 10 s.

III. TULLY's two Essays of Old Age, and of Friendship ; with his stoical Paradoxes, and Scipio's Dream. Done into English by the late Mr. Samuel Parker, of Oxon. Gent. The Third Edition, carefully corrected and revised by the Translator. price 2 s.

Printed for J. Bretherton, at the Bible, next the Fleece-Tavern in Cornhill,

A Select Collection of NOVELS In Two Volumes.

Vol. I. contains, The Little Gypsy ; Ethelinda ; the History of Count Palviano and Eleonora ; Scanderberg the Great. Vol. II. contains, The Life of Castruccio Castracani of Lucca ; the Loves of Oßmin and Daraxa ; the Spanish Lady of England ; the Lady Cornelia ; the False Dutchess.

Where may be had,

1. The Mizan Philosopher.
2. Coke's Detection 3 Vols.
3. The Life of CHARLES the XIIth.
4. Journey from Aleppo to Jerusalem.
5. Lommius's Treatise of Continual Fevers.
6. Dohun's Law of Tythes.
7. Langham's neat Duties of all the Customs.
8. Gay's Fables.
9. Bailey's Justin.
10. Molliere's Plays French and English.

LONDON : Printed by P. SANDERS, in Crown-Court, Butcher-Row, without Temple-Bar ; where Letters and Advertisements are taken in, and by Capt. GULLIVER, near the Temple ; also at the Rainbow Coffee-House in Cornhill, and John's Coffee-House in Sheer-Lane, near Temple-Bar. [Price Twopence.]

The Grub-street Journal Extraordinary. NUMB. 148.

Monday, OCTOBER 30. 1734.

The Art and Mystery of *Printing* Emblematically Displayed.

Devil with Devil damn'd
Firm concord holds: Men only disagree,
Of creatures rational. Paradise Lost, B. II. 496.

Mr. Bavius,

As I was going the other day into Lincoln's-inn, under the great gate-way, I met several lads and boys of different sizes, loaded most of them with great bundles of news-papers, led by a lusty fellow, who turned round and stopped them in the passage. They were all exceeding black and dirty; and made so very odd a figure, that I could not but stop myself to gaze upon them. Some that lagged behind and brought up the rear, I saw come out of the Stamp-office: from whence I rightly inferred, that they were Printers Devils, carrying from thence the returns of unsold news-papers, after the stamps had been cut off. I thought something comical would ensue: nor was I deceived in my expectation by the following Dialogue; which I committed to writing, as soon as I returned to my lodgings. The Dialogists I have distinguished by names, with as great propriety as I could, either from the appearance the persons themselves made, or from the information of others. I have kept as near as possible to the thoughts and expressions of these black gentry; but when I considered, that many persons in higher life, without ever reading at all, acquire, solely by conversation, a faculty of talking, with great fluency, upon variety of subjects, tho' they neither understand them, nor the language in which they talk; I did not think it so strange, that these gentlemen, tho' moving in a lower sphere, yet having constant opportunities of reading the weekly works of our politest authers, or at least of hearing them read, should obtain, in some degree, their way of thinking and speaking. Thus what they generally carry on the outside, might get into the inside of their heads; from whence it proceeded in the following manner.

Pock-fretten Stump. Devils, Gentlemen, and Brethren. Let us stop here, and lay down our burthens for a

(Price Twopence.)

while — upon the ground, since the bulk is shut off, and we are violently debarred from our property. Our property, I say; for tho' we at first took possession of it by force; yet since no body opposed us at that time, we may justly be said to have had the tacit consent of every body. And from that time to this, thousands of passengers have given us their express consent by a laughter of applause. — Nor was this to be wondered at, since the use to which we put this place, was of the same nature with that to which it served before, and was a greater improvement of it. It had been for a long while a receptacle of unsaleable history, politics, and poetry; and therefore a very proper place for us to ease our shoulders of the weight of all three, which lay so heavy upon them. And what company could be more suitable to most of the present writers, under whose works we sweat, than that of Pryn, Defoe, and Ogilby? — And since therefore our title to this place has been confirmed to us by long possession; and no one can pretend, that we have abused it; why are we thus unjustly excluded? I should be for breaking these locks, and demolishing these shutters directly, were not the lawyers much more terrible at the Old Baily, than here in Lincoln's-inn. But they are always on the strongest side, and therefore make it the legal. Wealth and power, I have heard squire Stonecastle say, like two vicious horses, hurry on the chariot of the law, through thick and thin, through fair and foul ways and weather, just as they please; while the coach-man in his black livery, sitting in the box, as it were, for form's sake, unable to stop their career, encourages them in it, with those reins which ought to restrain them. Hence we sometimes see those in a coach, who ought to ride only in a cart; which is frequently assigned to honester men, who are driven up Holborn-hill by some legal coach-man. On which account, I think, it will be better for us to acquiesce under the present injurious exclusion, and patiently to lay our burthens down on the ground, then by forcibly re-entring upon our right, expose ourselves to be taken, and perhaps, tucked up. — If you do not express your dissent to what I have said, I shall look upon your silence as a token of your concurrence in the same opinion with myself.

Jeremy Trudge. I am heartily glad you are all of my

mind: still assure you, had you been of another, as soon as ever you had begun your work, I should have slipp'd my neck out of the collar, and shewed you a fair pair of heels. I think my master Applebee, who was the first great inventer of Weekly Journals, has taken the wisest course. As politics is a subject which has grown more and more dangerous to meddle with, he has for a long while layed it aside; and is become a much more famous biographer than Mr. Curll himself. It is no small consolation to those heroic, but unfortunate gentlemen, who make their exit at the Oratory at Tyburn, where all are freely admitted, that a faithful account of their lives and translations, written or dictated by themselves, should be printed in a Weekly Journal. It is likewise of great advantage to the living in general, as well as to my master in particular, to publish the dying speeches of these Oratars; which are much more instructive to the publick, than copies of last wills and test aments, which are always added to the Curlean Lives and Memoirs, only to swell the volume. These speeches or Orations may be justly called Lectures or Sermons, but most properly Postills: and I have heard, that several eminent divines have declared, that they contain more sound divinity, in better language, than any of those delivered at the Coffee-house near Clare-market. — But, notwithstanding all this, I am heartily glad, that you desist from breaking of locks: for should a load of the last dying speeches of any of you, my brethren, be ever layed upon my back, I should doubly groan under it, as the most sad and heavy burthen I ever carried in my life. — But I beg your pardon, Mr. President, for this long interruption: for you seem to have something of great importance in your countenance.

Pock-fretten Stump. Tho' my seniority, who have been Devil to the Daily Post, London Evening Post, and Universal Spectator, ever since their existence; and my stature, which is much superior to yours, might seem to give me some sort of right to this Presidentship; yet I acknowledge the honourable title you have conferred upon me, by a free unbribed election, as a mere instance of your favour, tho' undeserved, yet not altogether unexpected. For it seems a natural consequence of the regard you have always shown me, in not thinking me too

Jeremy Trudge. I am heartily glad you are all of my

at the Stamp-office, till I was served. Gratitude therefore, as well as interest, obliges me to consult the honour and advantage of our fraternity ; and to acquaint you with every thing which may contribute to the promoting of either — Tho' I think we have no reason at all to be ashamed on account of the vulgar opinion concerning the origin of our name, as I shall presently shew: yet we ought to acknowledge ourselves obliged to the learned head, who, upon the death of any person of title, constantly gives an exact account of his ancient family in my *London Evening Post*. He says, that there was one Monsieur DEVILE or DE VILLE, who came over with

WILLIAM the conqueror, in company with DALAUNA, DE VIC, DE VAL, D'ASHWOOD, D'URFIE, D'UMPLING, &c. A descendant of this monsieur DE VILLE in the direct line being somewhat reduced, one of his sons was taken in by the famous CAXTON in 1471, as an errand-boy ; who proving very expert, became afterwards his apprentice, and in time an eminent printer, from whom our order took their name. — But suppose they took it from infernal Devils, it was not because they were messengers frequently sent in darkness, and appeared very black, as our enemies would suggest ; but upon a very reputable account. For JOHN FUST or FAUSTUS, of Mentz in Germany, was the

first inventor of printing ; which art so surprized the world, that they thought him a conjurer, and called him Doctor FAUSTUS, and his art *the black art*. As he kept a constant succession of boys to run on errands, who were always very black, these they called Devils: some of whom being paled to be his apprentices, and afterwards raising themselves in the world, he was very properly fayed to have raised many a Devil. As to the inferior order among us, called Flies, employed in taking news-papers off from the press for expedition, they are, I hope, of much later extraction, being no older than news-papers themselves. Mr. BAILEY, the Etymologist, is of opinion that their original name was

Blies, taken from the papers which they took off the press, which were generally such. The alteration of which he imagines to have proceeded from the following occasion : To hasten these boys, it was usual for the press-men to cry, *Flie Lie* ; which naturally fell into one single word *Flie*. This conjecture is confirmed by a like corruption in the true title of the *sLying Post*, tho' this proceeded from a different cause. —— Since therefore, my brethren, we are both comprehended under the title of Devils, let us not be ashamed of our name : but discharge our office with diligence ; and then, we may justly hope in time to attain, as many of our predecessors have done, to the dignity of Printers ; and to have an opportunity of using others, as much like poor Devils, as we ourselves have been used by them, or as they and Authors are used by Booksellers. These I must observe are an upstart profession, who have almost wholly ingrossed to themselves the business of selling books, which originally belonged solely to our masters ; and by this means they are become theirs. But I would have them remember, that, if we worship BELIAL and BEELZEBUB the god of *Flies*, as some of them, I hear, have archly observed, all the world agrees, that their God is MAMMON : and therefore our Deities are upon a level.

As this is a sufficient vindication of our honour from all the scandalous reflections cast upon us, either in jest, or earnest, on account of our common name, by those especially who have risen upon the ruin of our masters ; so I can with pleasure tell you, that our interest begins to revive, in the revival of that of some of our masters ; and that by such a method as promotes at once the advantage and reputation of us all. For a considerable number of young, learned, public-spirited Printers, having observed the great discouragement given to learning by the extravagant prices of books, have undertaken to reprint, weekly, at a very reasonable rate, several books, both original and translated ; the copies of which were purchased by booksellers, and had been vended by them, as their property, secured by an act of parliament, till the late expiration of it. This is properly to fight them with their own weapons ; and that in a double respect: both as the copies are theirs ; and as it has been a common practice among them to print upon one another. But it is to be remarked, that this practice of theirs was a bare-faced,

knavish, stupid piece of piracy, and very frequently executed by very ignorant and indigent persons, whose chief stock lay in impudence: whereas the execution of the modern project requires no small stock of ingenuity and learning. In proof of this there is no occasion to produce any other instances than those of the two *Josephus's* now going forward : in which, only by altering, with care and judgment, the words of the former translators, the authors have made two translations perfectly new, with great propriety, sayed, in the title pages, to be *translated from the original Greek*. I could have wished, that the invention of this way of translating might have been justly attributed to the present undertakers : but I must do Mr Pr sessor B——y the justice to own, that I have been credibly informed, that the glory of it ought to be ascribed to him, who published a few years ago XENOPHON'S *Oeconomics* in English, translated from a translation from the Greek done in the time of queen ELIZABETH. But the great improvement of this invention by weekly publications, at a cheap and easy rate, deserves greater commendation than the invention itself. It has made the benefit of it much more extensive, by alluring multitudes of persons to peruse books, into which they would otherwise never have looked : and it has had a miraculous influence upon some booksellers themselves, inducing them to follow the example by publishing in the same manner, even at a cheaper rate, and to sell a second edition corrected and revised for much less than half the price of the first. The natural consequence of all which must be the propagation of learning among persons of lower rank, who will by this means be rendered as skilful in history, and other parts of literature, as they are already in politics, by the weekly papers here lying before us : concerning the state of which it is now high time that I should inquire. Therefore, DICKY THUMB, pray in what condition is your *Craftsman* ?

DICKY THUMB. You may judge of it by the largeness of my bundle ; which is grown much heavier from the time that Mr. OLDCASTLE fell upon the memory of king CHARLES I. and especially since Mr. D'ANVERS stooped so low as to return an answer to the unintelligible Doctor.

POCK-FRETTEN STUMP. But what sai'st thou, RALPH PHANTOM ; what difference dost thou find betwixt *mily* and *foggy* weather ?

RALPH PHANTOM. Tho' to one of my constitution, one

would think, the difference could not be very great, yet I found the oppression upon my back and lungs greater in the latter. But the taking up of Squire CRAWFURD has given me some ease ; tho', I hope, it will not occasion the laying of a heavier burthen upon my master.

POCK-FRETTEN STUMP. But how comes it to pass, Mr. SPINDLE-SHANKS, that your load is so small ?

OBADIAH SPINDLE-SHANKS. My master, since he has been forced to sink the price of his *Weekly Register* to three half-pence, scarce any body being willing to give two pence for it, has taken an exact list of his customers, who are chiefly alehouse-keepers ; and prints none for casual sale, upon which he has no manner of dependance.

JACK SAUCY. O OBADIAH, your master had better never have undertaken that paper, which he published at first in opposition to my *Grub-street Journal*, almost upon the same model, and on the very same day : but he soon found that would not do, and changed the day to friday ; which proving as unlucky as the other, he passed on to saturday.

OBADIAH SPINDLE-SHANKS. Ay, and he swears he will try every day in the week, before he will lay it down.

JACK SAUCY. Very likely ; and every subject that can be thought on. At first setting out he disclaimed every thing relating to party and politics, and all satirical reflections: then he both fell furiously into party, and abused the persons concerned in my Journal, of whom he gave several false and scandalous accounts: but neither of these methods making the paper sell the better, he now once more declares against every thing political. Instead of which, as if his domestic and foreign news could not furnish lies enough to entertain the public, he presents them with strange stories collected from modern travellers.

OBADIAH SPINDLE-SHANKS. And is not this a likely way to succeed ? Do not the generality of people like what is strange better than what is true ?

JACK SAUCY. Yes. But if your master designs to take the next day in order, and to have his Journal come out on a sunday, it will be proper to revive his political discourses. For then the milk-women may carry about his Journal, without crying it, contrary to law, since it will very properly come under the appellation of MILK : For I have heard, that as the word *Tory* is derived from the Irish *tippa.ees*, so *Whig* signifies sour milk.

OBADIAH SPINDLE-SHANKS. Pray, brother don't be so severe upon people in adversity.

JACK SAUCY. Your people justly deserve it: they were the aggressors upon our authors; who scorned to answer them, and have referred the whole matter to me.

POCK-FRETTEN STUMP. I see plainly how the case stands; therefore pray say no more — But, Mr. DISMAL, how comes your load to be so great? You was not wont to have so large a bundle of *London Journals*.

DANIEL DISMAL. Ever since Mr. OSBORNE set up for a sort of a pope, and asserted "that his authority, as an "honest man, was equal to any man's in the kingdom"; few persons have payed any regard to his authority, and my back has suffered for it.

POCK-FRETTEN STUMP. Hah! WILL DAPPER, What art thou in the same condition too? Thy *Free Briton* seems to have brought thee into some bondage.

WILL DAPPER. King WILLIAM's statue has; we over-printed so much on that occasion, that it requires a back of stone to bear the burthen of the returns. But, JACK SAUCY, I may partly thank your *Grub street* authors for this; who ungratefully repeated their attacks upon a person, who wrote a short, but full vindication of them, in a paper designed in answer to them, Numb. 103. "The "meanest of the people have a natural and lawful right "to examine the transactions of the greatest assembly." [Much more of private persons.] "This is the glory and "the birthright of Englishmen. We Britons have the "boasted privilege of speaking and writing our free opi-"nion, even of the supreme power. Nor are we on-"ly privileged to judge their actions, but their persons "likewise."

NED COPPER. I like this doctrine very well: but it is not expressed in so oratorical a manner, as my *Hyp Doctor* writes, in answer to the *Craftsman*, *Fog*, and *Grub street*. "Calebite, Fog-pate, Tory, Tantivee, Saucy Puppy, Skip "kennel, Tatterdemallion, Raggamuffin, Pygmies, Monkey "Vermin, Rats, Moles, Weazles, Tom-tits, Griggs, Stickle "backs, Newts, Minikins, ———

RALPH PHANTOM. The devil! the devil! the devil!

Upon this PHANTOM took to his heels, being followed by STUMP, THUMB, SAUCY, and TRUDGE: the rest stood their ground, seeing only a messenger, who was their friend; whom the others feared more than their brother the devil.

I am your humble servant, R. B.

Explications of the picture, in which the art and mystery of printing *is* emblematically displayed.

AS the title of this picture professes to exhibit an emblem of the *art and mystery of printing*, the most obvious interpretation is that; which explains the figures in conformity to that art.

In the first part is represented a compositor at work upon a Journal, having the head and ears of an ass; because the compositors are called asses by the press-men, by way of return for their calling them hogs and horses. The work, in which this compositor is concerned, seems to require long ears, that he may hear abundance of news; and likewise the tread of messengers before they come upon him, and so may have time to dispose of his work, and compose himself to give them a proper reception. — The middle part represents the work at the press: in which the first figure, with the face of a hog, is he who works with the balls; and the second, with the horse's face, he who draws the press. This action of drawing gave occasion to the fixing on him the name of horse, but why his companion is called a hog, does not so plainly appear: perhaps it may be, because the hardness of this work inclines the operators to eat and drink like hogs. The third conspicuous figure is an underling sort of devil, called a fly; whose business is to take news-papers off the press, when they are worked in great haste. The next figure, which has the face of a grey-hound, seems to denote a messenger, who carries that animal for his badge, and is kicking the Craftsman out of the chace. The fifth and last figure, with the head of a JANUS, may very well represent the master printer, who is overlooking and hastening of the work: He has two different faces, answerable to the two different weekly papers, which he is supposed to print: but which was designed for the whig face, and which for the tory, it is not easy to discover. One may fancy, that the latter was most probably intended by that, the nose of which is nearest to FOG's Journal: but this is only mere conjecture. The owl, perched upon the press, being the bird of PALLAS, the goddess of arts and sciences very properly presides over the whole work: but whether we suppose it an Athenian, or a Grub-streetian owl, there is no impropriety in either supposition. —— The third division of the picture exhibits to view a lusty errand boy, in the shape of a devil, hanging up upon the poles different papers, books, or pamphlets to dry them.

From this natural explication it is evident, that all the figures are intended to represent characters, and not any particular persons: and consequently, that the figure with the double face is designed only to shew, that Printers in general do not scruple, in political and party controversies, or indeed in any other, to print on both sides. And since there is no person in the world, who ever was concerned in printing the two papers here distinctly specified, the application of that figure to any particular person, who either is at present, or has been formerly a printer, must be the effect of ignorance, or of malice, or of both.

But besides this satyrical explication of this figure, there is another, which is very probable, and which carries with it a tacit, but great commendation of the art of typography. For what statue can more properly be placed in a printing-house, than that of a JANUS; to shew that the professors of this art retrieve the transactions of past ages, and transmit them safe, together with those of the present, down to the latest posterity? So that, as the elder face has a retrospect to all preceding, so the younger has a prospect towards all future generations.

But there is, I hear, a political interpretation, which is this; That by the person with the ass's head is signified an informer, seeming intent on some business, but listening at the same time with his long ass's ears to what passes behind him: that by the three figures with the heads of a dog, a horse, and a swine, the last of which has a glass bottle in each hand, some persons of quality are pointed at, who are censured by the vulgar, as delighting in hunting, or horse-racing, or drinking, or whoring, or in all together: that by the gentleman with the head of a JANUS a great states-man is intended, who could not be fit for that station, unless he had two faces; with one of which he grins in an angry manner at FOG's *Journal*, while his friend with the dog's face, tied wig, and sword, kicks at that of the Craftsman in great indignation: that the press represents the squeezing of the people: lastly, that the meaning of the owl, and one of the devils, is too plain to need any explication; and that by the other is signified some old battered rake, who is a cuckold, and is at last exposed to all the world by a *case of impotency*.

This, I am informed, is the malicious exposition of THE RESTORER OF ANCIENT ELOCUTION, in hopes of drawing a prosecution upon us; who adds, that if no more was intended by the person with the dog's face, than to ridicule one of his majesty's messengers, or even his principal rat-catcher, the design would be *treasonable*. But all this he has sayed in revenge for another interpretation, which has been put upon this picture by some ingenious conjecturers. These say, the figure in the first part represents one of his auditors, and perhaps particularly his clerk: that the JANUS in the second shews him, either according to a former *transaction* of his, of which there is an account in the *Dunciad*, Book iii. 195. "that he offered "the service of his pen, in one morning, to two great "men of opinions and interests directly opposite, but was "unfortunately rejected by both: or else it represents him "in his present two double capacities; in the one of which he appears with his theological or sunday's, and his satyrical or wednesday's face, either as a JACK PRESBYTER or a JACK PUDDING: in the other he is represented as *Orator* and *Hyp-Doctor*. If we look upon him in the former character, we may suppose him to be teaching variety of action to three pupils in a private room: if in the latter, we may imagine him to be in a printing house, taking care that the printers do not print a greater number of his paper than he allows; it being a difficulty, among all those he has explained, which he could never solve to his own satisfaction, How it comes to pass, that, notwithstanding he publishes so few of his paper, and so many daily puffs and advertisements to tell the world what it contains, they should be so stupid as to take so little notice of it, and leave so many upon his hands. The owl is the emblem of the Athenian elocution, which this gentleman has for so many years laboured in vain to restore. As to the two devils, they say, it would be an affront to the understanding of every spectator to illustrate them, the meaning of them being as evident as the *Cases of impotency*, so conspicuous upon the peel of one of them.

There is another explication of some coffee-house wits, which, tho' not so probable, being farther fetched, I shall briefly mention. By this, the whole is applied to the charitable corporation. The poor wretch with the ass's head brings his goods to be pawn'd, and seems intently viewing some ring or jewel of value, and taking his last leave of it. The press stands for the scheme or project of the corporation: The double-faced gentleman may denote a director with his charitable and his cheating face, giving directions to his barbarous, ravenous under-workmen, to screw down and squeeze the poor to death in their engine of extortion and cruelty. The devil with the peel in his hand is their ware-house keeper, disposing and ranging in order the pawn'd goods; which, tho' appearing under the titles of news papers and books, yet if read backward as words ought to be where the devil is concerned, appear to be East-India goods. For instance, the bundle, upon which we see *Examiner*, is exactly like a bale of goods, and that word inverted makes *Renimaxe*, *Free Briton* is *Eerf-notirb*, *Cases of impotency* is *Sesac fo ycnetopmi*, *Hyp Doctor* is *Pyh rotcod*, and so of the rest; words not at all stranger than *Calincour*, *Arreq*, *Armozins*, *Bandanoes*, *Sologeshes*, *Tangebs*, *Allibanees*, *Salempouris*, and *Douriesses*, names of East India goods, which we now and then read in the news-papers.

Tho' there are many other interpretations of single figures, yet it is not requisite to mention them, they explaining them so as to make them bear no conformity or relation at all to the other figures in the picture. I shall therefore conclude with giving my own conjecture on this occasion. — It is my opinion, that the printer had a a double, or perhaps a treble design in this piece. The asinine figure, I think, does very well resemble an author in a musing posture, and perhaps composing a Grub-street, or any other Journal, in a printing-house, and who is properly a compositor, tho' not a compositor. The grand figure I take to be a bookseller, who has as much occasion for two faces in the way of trade, as persons in any other business. To a customer, who asks him how such a book sells, it is proper to answer with a brisk countenance, Extremely well. But if the author asks the same question, he must look grave, shake his head, and say, Very indifferently. What was sayed in relation to the same printer's being concerned in printing weekly papers, pamphlets, or books, written in direct opposition to each other, is equally applicable to booksellers: Nay, they have frequently employed persons to write answers to books printed for themselves, in order to make them sell the better: and sometimes an author has been employed to answer himself. The same bookseller has frequently, printed, at his own charge, religious and impious, godly and lewd books. This sufficiently justifies the application of the figure with two faces — In the attitude in which he is placed, he may be supposed as giving his orders to his slaves the printers, who work like horses, grunt like hogs, and fawn upon him like dogs. Or else he may be considered as giving directions to his authors, to write poetical, political, historical, theological, or bawdy books; which authors are properly represented by the gentlemen who have the heads of a dog, a horse, or a swine, and are accordingly treated by him like spaniels, hackneys, and hogs — The devil in the last division of the picture, seems to denote a particular bookseller, stripped of all his false ornaments of puffs, advertisements, and title pages, and *in propria persona*, putting up his own and other peoples copies, books, some of pious devotions, others of lewd diversion, in his literatory.

BAVIUS.

From the PEGASUS *in Grub-street.*

To the Right Honourable

The LORD MAYOR

OF

The CITY of *LONDON*.

MY LORD,

THE Bard, who with ambitious tongue,
Your two immediate predecessors sung,
For you intends to try a loftier strain,
Tho' he unpension'd and unpay'd remain.
Nor think the street from whence I date these lays
At all can lessen, or obscure the praise:
But lend a willing ear, whilst here I trace
The accidental cause of its disgrace.
When to dethrone their prince the saints combin'd,
In leagues of pious villainy, were join'd;
Against his purple, and the prelates lawn,
Long time their pens, before their swords, were drawn.
The court, provok'd by their audacious spite,
Advanc'd some authors to a proper hight;
Where to the admiring mob their heads were shown,
Whose ears they gain'd by losing of their own.
Grievous the loss to those, who scorn'd to wear
A long, curl'd, useless ornament of hair;
But cropp'd it short, to make their heads seem round,
And shew their ears were large, and long, and sound;
Of which to female saints each gifted brother
Sometimes held forth the one, and sometimes t'other.
These to secure, in this distress, they fly,
And take in Grub-street lodgings near the sky.
Printers attending in this new recess,
In low, dark cellars fix'd the noisy press.
At every pull the sweating press men took,
The engine squeek'd, and all the fabric shook.
No wonder, since his vast Cyclopean hand
He p'd form those bolts which shook the trembling land.

The remaining part of these verses, for want of room, must be deferred till next thursday.

The ARMS of the several Companies of the City of *London*.

1 Mercers, 1393. Honor Deo.
2 Grocers, 1345.
3 Drapers, 1430.
4 Fishmongers, 1509.
5 Goldsmiths, 1571.
6 Skinners, 1327.
7 Merchant-Taylors, 1501.
8 Haberdashers, 1447.
9 Salters, 1530.
10 Ironmongers, 1462.
11 Vintners, 1436.
12 Clothworkers, 1530.

13 Dyers, 39 Hen. VI. Da gloriam Deo.
14 Brewers, 6 Hen. VI. In God is all our trust
15 Leather-Sellers, 6 Rich. II.
16 Pewterers, 15 Ed. IV. In God is all my trust.
17 Barbers-Chirurgeons, 1 Ed. IV. De præcipientia Dei.
18 Cutlers, beg. of Hen V. Pour parvenir à bonne foy.
19 White-Bakers, 1 Hen. VII. Praise God for all.
20 Wax-Chandlers, 2 Rich. III. Truth is the Light.
21 Tallow-Chand. 2 Edw. IV. Ecce agnus Dei qui tollit peccata mundi.
22 Armourers, beg. of Hen VI. Make all sure.
23 Girdlers, 27 Hen. VI. Give Thanks to God.
24 Butchers, 3 James I. Omnia subjecisti sub pedibus, oves & boves.
25 Sadlers, Edw. I. Hold fast, sit sure.
26 Carpenters, 17 Edw. IV. Honour God.
27 Cordwainers, 17 Hen. VI.
28 Painters, 23 Elizabeth. Amor creat obedientiam.
29 Curriers, 3 James I.
30 Masons, 12 Hen. IV. In the Lord is all our trust
31 Plumbers, 9 James I. In God is our Hope.
32 Innholders, 6 Hen. VIII. Come, ye Blessed, when I was harbourless, ye lodged me.
33 Founders, 21 James I. God is the only Founder.
34 Poulterers, 19 Hen. VII.
35 Cooks, 11 Edw. IV.
36 Coopers, 16 Hen. VII. Love as Brethren.

37 Bricklayers and Tylers, 10 Eliz. In God is all our trust.
38 Bowyers, 28 James I.
39 Fletchers.
40 Black-Smiths, 20 Eliz. By Hammer and Hand All Art doth stand
41 Joyners, 13 Elizabeth. Credo videbo.
42 Weavers. Weave Truth with Truth.
43 Wool-packers.
44 Scriveners, 14 James I.
45 Fruiterers, 3 James I.
46 Plaisterers, Hen. VII. Let brotherly Love continue.
47 Stationers 3 and 4 Phil. and Mary. Per bene vatis male vivere.
48 Embroiderers, 4 Eliz. Thou shalt embroider the Goat
49 Upholsters.
50 Musicians.
51 Turners.
52 Glasiers. Lucem tuam, da nobis O Deus.
53 Farriers.
54 Fevin...
55 Apothecaries. Opiferque orbem dicor.
56 Shipwrights.
57 Woodmongers or Fuellers, 3 Jam. I.
58 Gardiners.
59 Sope-Makers. Dii rexque secundeat.
60 Distillers. Drop as Rain, distill as Dew.
61 Hatband-Makers.
62 Tobacco-pipe-Makers.
63 Coach-Makers, 20 Char. II.

Surgit post nubila Phœbus.

LONDON: Printed by P. SANDERS, in *Crown-Court, Butcher-Row*, without *Temple-Bar*; where Letters and Advertisements are taken in, and by Capt. GULLIVER, near the *Temple*; also at the *Rainbow Coffee-House* in *Cornhill*, and *John's Coffee-House* in *Sheer-Lane, Temple-Bar*.

The Grub-ſtreet Journal. NUMB. 149.

Thurſday, NOVEMBER 2. 1732.

Mr. BAVIUS,

I HAVE read your epigram, ſigned PHILO HISTORIO. or, as it ſhould have been, PHILO-HISTRIO. I call it yours; becauſe I fancy ſome of your members made both that and the firſt; and therefore ſhall not go about to ſtop a torrent, but put my wrongs in my pocket. If I ſhould be out in my gueſs, you'll excuſe me, I hope; and as I deſign to drop that ſubject for the preſent, ſhall take it qualis vir, tali oratio. If you think fit to accept of me as a correſpondent, you will, by giving the incloſed a place in your paper, oblige

Your friend, and conſtant reader,
H. W.

Octob. 21. 1732.

THE ſcribendi cacoethes, or itch of writing, has, of late years, ſo epidemically prevailed, as to poſſeſs, even the moſt ignorant, with a notion of their being capable, not only of entertaining, but alſo inſtructing the world. But how capable they have been, will evidently appear from the monſtrous pieces ſome of them have produced. For by attempting to ſoar above their natural capacities, and attain the ſublime, they have either ſwelled into bombaſt, or plunged into an abyſs of nonſence; out of which, the more they labour to extricate themſelves, the lower they ſink into it.

That juſt ſaying, poeta naſcitur, non fit, will hold good, with reſpect to any writer, as well as a poet: for, if a man has not a genius, it is impoſſible he ſhould be a wit. But (as a great man has obſerved, viz. lord SHAFTSBURY) "an Engliſh author would be all genius," which I take to be the reaſon they are ſuch bad wits. Were examples of any effect, we ſhould ſit down contented with our modicum, rather than't endeavouring at more, expoſe ourſelves, and looſe that we have: but the deſire of fame hurries us beyond our reaſon; and we looſe ourſelves before we are aware. An author, 'tis true, may travel for improvement, and ſtretch each clime, and yet (I ſpeak it knowingly) with no other advantage in the end, than changing the cælum, and not the animus.

But muſt I never write then, ſays one, becauſe the degeneracy of people's taſtes can't ſee a fine thing, when it lyes before them? Muſt I quit dear pen, ink, and paper, my very vitals, in compliance to the caprices of the town? Beauties make no impreſſion on the enervate, nor colours on the blind; muſt theſe therefore be none of thoſe? or becauſe the greater part of mankind are illiterate, ſhall the other be ſo too? No, it the age is ſtupified, it is time by writing to endeavour to awaken it, and expel the lethargy.

This is certainly a right way of reaſoning; and could our writers but keep an even pace, might, perhaps, have ſome effect. But, alas! too many have ſuch loads of conceit, which ſeem to magnify their abilities, that they fancy it an eaſy matter to write like a MILTON; and to this end, will raiſe the reader's expectation for the firſt two or three pages; but flagging by degrees, at laſt fall into meer doggrel: like hackneys, they ſet out in a full gallop, but ſoon fall into a dog trot, and ſo come creeping home.

There are others more cautious, indeed, but equally imprudent; who conſcious of their inabilities to rival SWIFT or ADDISON, will rather indulge themſelves in idleneſs, than try their ſtrength: like the man, who, becauſe he was not ſo ſtrong as MILO, would rather ſtarve than carry burthens. But the mind, if it be employed, will always ſupply us with foundations to build upon; and it we take due pains, we may raiſe the ſuperſtructure to a proper height: but if we neglect to cultivate our underſtanding, it will, like ſome growrubſy; or, like unmanur'd land, produce nothing but rank and unwholſome weeds. Want of encouragement is too true an excuſe: for as it is an eaſy matter to oblige beſt vian an author who has taken pains with a piece, and one who has written extempore: ſo certainly the former will be encouraged by all men of ſence, tho' perhaps not meet with univerſal applauſe.

It may be objected, that we have few men of ſence among us, or that thoſe who are ſuch are ſo bigotted to the fiction of the times, as not to encourage literature. This would have been matters even to have ſuſpected a century ago; That the Engliſh nation, inſtead of encouraging true merit, ſhould have deſpiſed a ſet of men, whoſe greateſt talent is nobleneſs and eminence. But we muſt confeſs it is true, that the age, inſtead of refining, grows worſe and worſe: and a man who can furniſh a looſe poem, or

an atheiſtical diſcourſe, is preferred to a ſolid reaſoner, or an impartial hiſtorian.

In anſwer to this gentleman's letter, BAVIUS aſſures him, that he knows PHILO HISTRIO no better than PHILO DIVES: but thought himſelf obliged to publiſh the verſes of the former, as well as thoſe of the latter.

Mr. BAVIUS,

GOing this morning, according to my daily cuſtom, to a neighbouring coffee-houſe, in order to peruſe ſuch papers, as the wit, or neceſſities of my country-men prompt them to preſent to the public. I was more than ſurprized at the horrid appearance of the monſtrous figures. eſpecially thoſe of the two devils, at the head of your journal. As I have, from my infancy, been bred up to the love of God, and a proper fear of the devil, I was ſo ſtartled, and terrified at the ſight, that I could not prevail with myſelf to give your paper a ſecond view. This has made ſo deep an impreſſion upon my imagination that on coming home to my lodgings, I find I cannot reſt 'till I have caſt the devil out of myſelf, i. e. 'till I have ſent you my thoughts on that ſubject.

It is a proverbial expreſſion, not confined to our country, that The devil is not ſo black as he is painted. The uſe of his name among the French is a proof of this: for in their uſual forms of ſpeech he is mentioned with great honour and reſpect Thus when they would commend their wine, or any other thing, they break out into this pious exclamation: "Diables! que cela eſt bon! And when they would repreſent a man as honeſt, ſincere, and ſociable they call him un bon diable.

I know ſome of our own countrymen, who make no ſcruple of ſaying a thing is deviliſh good; and even that a lady is deviliſh pretty. This term is frequently employed by a particular friend of mine, as a high compliment to the witty productions of a poet; and when he would expreſs a mixture of ſurprize at, and approbation of his works, his uſual phraſe is, The devil is in this fellow; or, He is a comical devil.

The generality of mankind, indeed, when they reflect on what they ſay, ſpeak of that apoſtate angel with abhorrence; and apply his name only to things which they diſlike. Thus, nothing is more common than to ſay, ſuch a one is a ſad devil. I remember when I was at S. Germain's, I heard a ſtory of a gentleman, who being in waiting at the court of the unfortunate king James II. and the diſcourſe at ſupper running on dæmons, and apparitions, the king aſked him, whether he had ever ſeen any thing of that ſort. Yes, ſir, replied he, and that no longer ago than laſt night. The whole company grew mighty attentive, expecting ſome conſiderable diſcovery; and his majeſty deſired to know whet he had ſeen. To which he gravely replied, he had ſeen the devil. The devil! ſaid the king; and pray, ſir, in what ſhape did he appear to you? O, ſir, ſaid the gentleman, with a ſigh, in his uſual and natural ſhape. On the king's enquiring farther what ſhape that was, he anſwered, In the ſhape of an empty bottle.

But I have written ſo long about the devil, that my candle burns blue, and I have called for my night-cap, and am reſolved to forget him, if I can. However, Mr. BAVIUS, let me intreat you not to afright the public again with ſuch hideous figures; for I am convinced it will reduce the number of your readers, eſpecially if they are good chriſtians, and as much afraid of the devil, as

Your humble ſervant,
MICO DIABOLUS.

Octob. 29. 1732.
eleven at night.

An ODE for his majeſty's birth day, compoſed by COLLEY CIBBER Eſq; poet laureat, and ſet to muſic by Mr. ECCLES.

LET there be light!
Such was at once the word and work of heav'n,
When, from the void of univerſal night,
Free nature ſprung to the Creator's ſight,
And day to glad the new born world was giv'n.

Air.

Succeeding days to ages roll'd,
And ev'ry age to wonder told:

At length aroſe this glorious morn!
When, to extend his bounteous pow'r,
High heav'n announc'd this inſtant hour
The beſt of monarchs ſhall be born!   12

Born to protect and bleſs the land!
And while the laws his people form,
His ſcepter glories to confirm,
Their wiſhes are his ſole command.   15

The word that form'd the world
In vain had made mankind;
Unleſs his paſſions to reſtrain
Almighty wiſdom had deſign'd,
Sometimes a WILLIAM, or a GEORGE ſhould reign! 20
Yet farther, Britons, caſt your eyes,
Behold a long ſucceſſion riſe
Of future fair felicities.

Air.

Around the royal table ſpread,
See how the brauteous branches ſhine!   25
Sprung from the ſertile genial bed
Of glorious GEORGE, and CAROLINE.

While heav'n with bounteous hand
Has ſo enrich'd her ſtore;
When ſhall this promis'd land   30
In royal heirs be poor?
All we can farther aſk, or heav'n beſtow,
Is, that we long this happineſs may know.

Air.

While o'er our vanquiſh'd hearts alone
Our peaceful prince would gently reign,   35
He binds obedience to his throne,
And haughty Britains hugs her chain.

Her jealous ſons, in GEORGE ſecure,
A happier ſtate than freedom boaſt;
For while his kind commands allure,   40
Freedom in hearts reſign'd is loſt.

Air.

Sing, joyous Britons, ſing
The glorious natal day,
That gave, with ſuch a king,
So great, ſo mild a ſway.   45

Chorus.

His realms around
Diffuſe the ſound!
From ports to fleets the jovial cannon play,
'Till ev'ry peaceful ſhoar
Receives the rolling roar,   50
And joins the joy that crowns the day.

NOTES upon the ODE.

VER. 2. Some carping critics have objected, that the Let there be light was the word, yet it was not the work of Heav'n, which was the creation of light by that word according to Gen 1. 3. Let there be light; and there was light. But if the work immediately followed, or rather accompanied, the words might not the ſame thing be both the word and the work too; and follow or accompany itſelf?

VER. 4. By free nature ſome have thought, that the poet meant the frame of nature, the heaven and the earth, the one formed the ſecond, and the other the third day, called in the 5th verſe the new-born world, to which it is there ſaged, that day was given. But to this it is objected, that this frame of free nature did not ſpring to the ſight of the Creator, when he ſayed, Let there be light: nay, it did not ſpring at all from the void of univerſal night, as is aſſerted in the 3d verſe. For this void of univerſal night had been illuminated by the creation of light the firſt day. — It is therefore thought by others, that free nature, which ſprung to the Creator's ſight means the light itſelf; which is termed free, becauſe it ſprung ſo freely as his word. But then day in the 5th verſe, which was given to the new-born world, cannot mean the ſame light, becauſe the world was not yet born. between theſe two interpretations, of which one muſt be the right, and each is attended with difficulties inſuperable I muſt own myſelf very much in the dark: and can think of no way of clearing up this ſtanza at all, but by reading Then, inſtead of When in the 3d verſe.

VER. 10. To *announce*, is to declare ſome thing to another: and requires in proſe, the expreſs mention of the thing *announced*: but here, to make it more poetical, it is underſtood.

VER. 12. It has been diſputed, whether this ſtanza be part of the annunciation: of *high heaven*, or only that of the poet; by the obſcurity of it, it is more generally thought the latter.

VER. 13. It is not certain, whether the *laws* are to form the *people*, or the *people* the laws. I am inclined to think, that the poet meant the latter: becauſe theſe *laws* are to *confirm the ſcepter glories*, according to the next verſe. So that the intent of both verſes is, *While his people* by their repreſentatives *form laws to confirm* the ſcepter glories of the proteſtant ſucceſſion. But I ſhould rather read *conform*, for the ſake of rime; and I think the ſenſe would be full as good.

VER. 16. I can't imagine, why *the world* ſhould have no rime to it: and therefore humbly offer an emendation; which is *the main*. This, as it ſignifies both the ſea and the land, will agree very well to this place, where the poet is ſpeaking of the government of good kings over mankind.

VER. 30, 31. Were not the LAUREAT's affection to the preſent government above all ſuſpicion, theſe two lines might be liable to miſinterpretation, they being put by way of queſtion; which as frequently implies a wiſh, as it does admiration.

VER. 39, 41. The reaſoning in theſe two lines is this: We *boaſt a happier ſtate than freedom*, becauſe we have *loſt* our *freedom*, by freely *reſigning* up our *hearts* to the king.

FAVIUS,

DOMESTIC NEWS.

C. *Courant.*	E P. *Evening Poſt.*
P. *Poſt-Boy.*	S J. *St. James's Evening Poſt.*
D P. *Daily Poſt.*	W E. *Whitehall Evening Poſt.*
D J. *Daily Journal.*	L E. *London Evening Poſt.*

THURSDAY, *Octob.* 26.

Laſt week a patent was iſſued by the lords of the treaſury, granting to Chriſtopher Wyvill Eſq; and to Mrs. Margaret Purcell, the queen's dreſſer, the place of inſpector general of the duties, on tea, chocolate, &c. in the room of George Duckett Eſq; deceaſed. — John Wyndham Eſq; is made correſpondent, or writer of the circular letters, in the room of Mr. Wyvill. *S J.* —— *The lady is likewiſe to be the beſt inſpector in relation to* tea, coffee, and chocolate.

Yeſterday the ſheriffs of this city waited on their majeſties, and all the royal family, at Kenſington, with a compliment from John Barber Eſq; lord mayor elect, inviting their majeſties and all the royal family to dinner at Guildhall on monday next, &c. *C. DP.*

Yeſterday a committee of directors of the ſouth ſea company, conſiſting of ſir John Eyles and ſix directors attended the Spaniſh ambaſſador, and, in the company's name, complimented him on his arrival in Great Britain. *DJ.* —— They went to wait upon his excellency, on occaſion of the news received a day or two ago, that the king of Spain's orders were come to Vera Cruz for the ſouth-ſea company's factors to depart that place in four months time, becauſe his majeſty's ſhip Deal Caſtle, Capt. Aubin, had ſeized a Spaniſh regiſter ſhip, by way of repriſal. His excellency received them in a moſt courteous and polite manner, and promiſed to write inſtantly to his court upon this ſubject. *DP.* —— We are aſſured the Spaniſh regiſter ſhip is ordered to be ſet at liberty. *DJ.*

His majeſty has been graciouſly pleaſed to order 1000 l. to be paid out of the treaſury, into the hands of the chamberlain of this city, to be diſpoſed of by him, to ſuch decayed perſons of this city, as are deemed proper objects of charity. *SJ.*

A few days ſince, ſir Will. Humble, of Thorpe-underwood, in Northamptonſhire, Bar. was married to Miſs Vane, one of the daughters of the right honourable the L. Barnard. *DP.*

The right reverend the lord biſhop of London has preſented the reverend Mr. Cartwright, one of his lordſhip's chaplains, to the rectory of Hornſey in Middleſex, worth about 300 l. per ann. *SJ.*

Before any perſon caſts an imputation on me, in reference to THE ORATORY, wherein I know no fault but one, that it is a pattern of the trueſt principles of religion, with the moſt various and aſſiduous endeavour to merit, in the capacity of a ſcholar and a clergyman, that is, or ever was, in this iſland, or in the world; before I am reflected upon for this, I would deſire every man who educates a ſon to orders, and him who is ſo educated, to conſider this caſe, and to make it his own.

I waited ſome years ago on a certain PRELATE with a ſollicitation of a pulpit in town, ſignifying my reſolution to cultivate and exert the talent of preaching, which God had given me in the moſt compleat and public manner. His anſwer was, "That I might be of uſe; but before he "could do for me, he muſt have a PLEDGE of my at-"tachment to the government." I was an entire ſtranger to politics, but gave him that PLEDGE. A pledge demanded, given, and accepted for a conſideration, is a contract for that conſideration; the hinge of my intereſt and fortune very much turned upon it: it was the year $172\frac{1}{2}$, a tender criſis, and doubtleſs, he made a job of it to the government. When I applied for the conſideration, he ſhuffled me off: had he any poſitive exception to my intellectual or moral qualifications, (tho' nothing can be more immoral, or ſooner make the world atheiſts, than a perfidious prelate,) he ſhould, before he drew me in, have told me, that if he met with any ſuch exception, he would not do what I ſollicited; and that he would take time to examine. This would have been fair. He aſſigned no exception at all during a whole year, 'till I had ſacrificed my intereſt to him, on his own demand, and it is eaſy to frame exceptions, if a perſon be inclined to break his word. My judgment is, he and his clergy even envied me in the pulpit, and were jealous of my advancement, timorous that at court there might be a patron or a patroneſs of learning, and apprehenſive that I might out ſtrip them there. Was I on my death-bed, I would take the ſacrament, that I know the former part, and believe the latter part (without the leaſt vanity for ſo poor a triumph as excelling them would be) of this advertiſement to be matter of fact.

J. HENLEY. *SJ.*

— *The occaſion of* Mr. Henley's *ſetting up his* Oratory, *if we will believe himſelf, was his being diſappointed in his expectations of preferment from a certain* prelate.

FRIDAY, *Octob.* 27.

A few days ſince, the reverend Mr Boedeker was appointed, by the lord biſhop of London, chaplain to the Lutheran chappel at S. James's. *P.* — Mr. Bleander. *DJ.*

The earl of Portmore's *Daffodil*, which was to have run againſt Mr. Coke's *Silver Locks* on wedneſday laſt for 400 guineas, at Newmarket, paid 100 guineas forfeit. — The duke of Bridgewater's *Nathan* ran againſt Mr Cornwall's *Poſtboy*, for 300 guineas, which was won by the former. *P.*

Laſt week the earl of Deloraine was married to the relict of —— Hearſon Eſq; a Lincolnſhire gentlewoman, and the daughter of —— Liſter, of Burwell, in the ſame county Eſq; *DP.*

Laſt week died, at his brother major Sawle's, in Cornwall, Mr. Francis Sawle, an eminent woollen-draper on the pavement in the Strand, reckoned by ſome worth about 20,000 l. tho' remarkable for being always at law. *DP.* — This alteration is falſe. *DJ. Nov.* 1.

SATURDAY, *Octob.* 28.

The old council chamber at S. James's is repaired and beautified, and a new rich chair fixed, which coſt upwards of 700 l. *C.* —— The council chamber at Whitehall is ordered to be repaired and beautified with the utmoſt expedition, for their lordſhips reception. *C. DP.*

On monday night the will of the late right honourable the earl of Harborough was opened at his houſe in Brewer-ſtreet; there were preſent his two ſiſters, the dutcheſs-dowager of Rutland, and the lady Erwin, and miſs Sherrard, ſiſter to the preſent earl; and, we hear, he has left, viz. to the preſent earl of Harborough, his couſin german, 4000 l. per ann. at ſtapleford in Leiceſterſhire, his lordſhip's ſeat: the dutcheſs dowager of Rutland, 3000 l. per ann. in town, and 2000 l. in Lincolnſhire, [Leiceſterſhire. *DP.*] 2000 l. to each of the dutcheſs's daughters; and to her ſon his jewels: to the lady Erwin his houſe in Brewer-ſtreet, and 500 l. per ann. to Mr. John Battin, his gentleman, [formerly his footman. *DP.*] 100 l. per ann. To all his ſervants handſome legacies, and money for erecting a monument for himſelf at Stapleford in Leiceſterſhire. *C.*

Yeſterday the court of directors of the ſouth-ſea company came to a reſolution, to ſuſpend their trade in the whale-fiſhing (until they receive encouragement from parliament) on account of the great loſſes they have ſuſtained by carrying it on; their fiſhery this laſt ſeaſon, which was one of the beſt they had met with, being far ſhort of a ſaving account. *DJ.*

On thurſday evening the right honourable the earl of Winchelſea and Nottingham, with his lady, came to town to his houſe in Jermyn-ſtreet, from Aix la chapelle, in France, &c. *DJ. LE.* — *It is in* Germany.

This day the lord mayor elect was ſworn into his office at Guildhall, by ſir William Thompſon, the recorder, with the uſual formalities. *SJ.*

On wedneſday laſt, the only ſon of the lord Carteret was taken ill, at his lordſhip's houſe in Arlington ſtreet, in Piccadilly; and on thurſday it appear'd to be the ſmall-pox, &c. *P.*

Yeſterday died John Mowbray, M.D. after a ſhort illneſs, at his houſe in Bond-ſtreet. *C. P. DP.*

MONDAY, *Octob.* 30.

On ſaturday about five in the evening their majeſties, and all the royal family, came from Kenſington to the royal palace at S. James's in good health. *C. P. DJ.* —— Yeſterday the reverend Mr. Ridges preached before their majeſties, his royal highneſs the prince, and the three eldeſt princeſſes, &c. *C. DP.* — The reverend Dr. Briggs [Mr. Biggs *DJ.*] and the reverend Dr. Ridges before the duke of Cumberland, and the two youngeſt princeſſes. *P. DJ.*

On ſaturday laſt his excellency Horatio Walpole Eſq; was pleaſed to preſent Mr. David Barbut to a place worth about 400 l. per ann. in his excellency's gift, as coffer to his majeſty. *DJ.*

We hear from Newmarket, that the noblemen and gentlemen's contribution amounting to 250 l. was run for by five year-old horſes; for which three ſtarted, and was won by a horſe belonging to John Rich Eſq; called Mill-bank. *DP.* — Billank. *C.* — By Mr Fleetwood's horſe. *P. DJ.* —— On the 27th the duke of Bolton's colt beat the duke of Devonſhire's colt, four miles, for 200 guineas. *DP.* — Black colt. *P. DJ.* — Called Cyphax. *C.* —— The ſame day the earl of Portmore's Daffodil beat the duke of Bolton's grey mare the four mile courſe, for 100 guineas. *P. DJ.*

On ſaturday, in the evening, major-general Ruſſell was married at his houſe in Hanover-ſquare to miſs Barton, ſiſter to Mr. Barton, an eminent mercer on Ludgate-hill, and mercer to his royal highneſs the prince; a beautiful young lady, with a good fortune. *C.*

Yeſterday morning died, in an advanced age, the reverend Dr. Oliver, rector of the united pariſhes of S. Mary Abchurch and S. Laurence Pountney, which is in the gift of Corpus Chriſti, or Bennet College in Cambridge. *DJ.* — On ſaturday laſt died Mr. Gryſman, at the wine-celar in the Friery, S. James's, of a bleeding, which was occaſioned by drawing of a tooth a few days before. He had been one of the yeomen of the guard, ever ſince the reign of king William. *DP.*

TUESDAY, *Octob.* 31.

Yeſterday, being the anniverſary of his majeſty's birth-day, there was a great appearance of the nobility and foreign miniſters to pay their compliments to his majeſty, who then entered into the 50th year of his age; and the evening was concluded with a magnificent ball. The ſame was alſo obſerved throughout the cities of London and Weſtminſter, with great rejoicings, &c. and the evening concluded with bonfires, fireworks, and other illuminations. *C. P. DJ* — The ode compoſed by Colley Cibber Eſq; poet laureat, ſet to muſic by Mr. Eccles; was ſung by Mr. Gates, Mr. Row, and the children of his majeſty's chapel, before their majeſties, &c. *in the great council-chamber.* *DP.*

Yeſterday John Barber Eſq; lord mayor elect, went up with the uſual ſtate to the Exchequer-bar at Weſtminſter, and was ſworn lord mayor of this city with the accuſtomed ceremony, &c. *C. P.* —— His lordſhip was ſo lame of the gout, that he was carried in a chair from the water-ſide, and was forced to be held up by two of his domeſticks, whilſt he was taking the oaths. *DJ.* — Afterwards his lordſhip went to a magnificent entertainment provided at Guildhall; and the evening was concluded with a ball. *C. P. DJ.*

On wedneſday a benefaction of 500 l. was paid for the uſe of the publick infirmary for the ſick and needy, in Chapel-ſtreet, Weſtminſter, from the executors of the right honourable the late earl of Thanet. *C.*

They write from Ivelcheſter, that eleven felons under ſentence of tranſportation made their eſcape from the goal the day before they were to be removed, by knocking down the keeper, and getting over the wall: four of them are ſince retaken; but the other ſeven are not yet found, tho' they went off in their irons. *DP.*

We hear from Cheſter, that ſix perſons lately died there of the wounds they received at the late election of an alderman for that city. *DJ.*

This day the right honourable ſir Robert Walpole, accompanied by ſeveral perſons of diſtinction, ſet out for his ſeat at Houghton-hall in Norfolk. *SJ.* — To morrow he will ſet out. *WE.*

This day their majeſties, &c. returned from S. James's to Kenſington to dinner. *WE.* — A rich new canopy and throne is put up in the ſtate-room at S. James's-houſe, for his majeſty to receive the ſpaniſh ambaſſador the day he makes his publick entry thro' London. *LE.*

On thurſday laſt, at a meeting of the royal ſociety, the learned Dr. Allen, an eminent phyſician, and author of ſeveral uſeful books in phyſic, was unanimouſly elected a fellow of that ſociety. *LE.*

We are informed, that John Ellys Eſq; the eminent painter, ſucceeds Mr. Wilks in the management of Drury-lane play-houſe; and that Mr. Cibber, jun. ſucceeds his father, who has reſigned to him. *SJ.*

WEDNESDAY, *Nov.* 1.

Yeſterday the right honourable ſir Robert Walpole's lady came to reſide in the earl of Aſhburnham's houſe in S. James's ſquare. *P.*

By the laſt poſt, letters came from Lyons in France of the ſafe arrival of ſir Thomas Groſvenor in his way to Montpelier, who had received ſo much benefit by the

tention of the climate, that it is hoped a little time may perfect his recovery. *P.*

On monday morning last Mr. Philip Tidd, carpenter of a second rate at Chatham, aged eighty two, was married to a young girl of sixteen years of age; his son having married her sister, who is six years older, some time since *D P.* — *I fear this old fool has embarqued in a leaky bottom, which he cannot stop.*

Last monday as a waterman was endeavouring to land his fare at S. Mary-Overy's Stairs, the boat overturn'd, by which accident four persons were drown'd. *D P.*

From the PEGASUS *in Grub-street.*

To the Right Honourable

The LORD MAYOR

OF

The CITY of *LONDON.*

MY LORD,

THE Bard, who with ambitious tongue,
Your two immediate predecessors sung,
For you intends to try a loftier strain,
Tho' he unpension'd and unpay'd remain.
Nor think the street, from whence I date these lays,
At all can lessen, or obscure the praise:
But lend a willing ear, whilst here I trace
The accidental cause of its disgrace.
When to dethrone their prince the saints combin'd,
In leagues of pious villainy, were join'd;
Against his purple, and the prelates lawn,
Long time their pens, before their swords, were drawn.
The court, provok'd by their audacious spite,
Advanc'd some authors to a proper hight;
Where to the admiring mob their heads were shown,
Whose ears they gain'd by losing of their own.
Grievous the loss to those, who scorn'd to wear
A long, curl'd, useless ornament of hair;
But cropp'd it short, to make their heads seem round,
And shew their ears were large, and long, and sound;
Of which to female saints each gifted brother
Sometimes held forth the one, and sometimes t'other.
These to secure, in this distress, they fly,
And take in Grub street lodgings near the sky.
Printers attending in this new recess,
In low, dark cellars fix'd the noisy press.
At every pull the sweating press men took,
The engine squeek'd, and all the fabric shook.
No wonder; since his vast Cyclopean hand
Help'd forge those bolts which shook the trembling land.
From hence, in secret form'd, incessant flies
A long, dull train of incoherent lies.
Dull as they are, they multitudes deceive,
Finding still duller fools that would believe.
The royal party curs'd the street, whence rose
The fatal cause of all their master's woes.
When some great lye, borne by the popular gale,
Was heard, they cry'd, This is a Grub street tale.
When some vile pamphlet, fraught in every page
With godly nonsence, and fanatic rage,
Run 'mongst the saints, the wicked cavaliers
Swore, 'twas some Grub-street author without ears.
From that blest æra to these learned times,
Whoever in dull prose, or duller rhimes,
Expose their talents, like those sorts of old,
'Mongst Grub-street authors have their names inroll'd.
Nay, tho' they write with greatest sense and skill,
Each party charge their foes, with writing ill:
Still one another in these terms abuse,
Of Grub-street authors writing Grub street news.
But this, my lord, is neither here, nor there:
Of fools and knaves each party has its share.
And one than t'other has no more pretence
T' ingross all honesty, than all the sence
A Grub-street author (to vile pelf no slave)
A tolerable share of both may have:
And some of one, if not of both, I claim;
Tho' chang'd the last, the first is still the same,
As when I sung, twice on this solemn day,
The Two that pass'd in pomp the crouded way:
Whom you in order, principles, and state
Succeeding, close the grand triumvirate.
Instead of things, if persons we compare,
All such comparisons invidious are.
Without offence, in equal ballance lay'd,
One trade against another may be weigh'd.
Those, which alone to body are confin'd,
Must yield to that which cultivates the mind;
Which through the world can art and science spread;
The living keep alive, and raise the dead.
This printing does —— Nor shall my verses flow,
To tell your lordship what you better know:
But change my numbers to the begging strain,
To tell you, that two years I've sung in vain.
For, tho' two Heroes in my verses shine,
Nor Brewer liquor gave, nor Banker coin.
But you, my lord, will one at least impart,
To fix my notions deeper in my heart.
For otherwise, I fear, a twelve month hence,
With my old principles I may dispense,
Tho' sore against my will: for well I know
How odd Whig-Tory principles will show.
As when a press-man, whom some call a horse,
Tugs at the press with all his might and force;
If the thick paper be half dry, half wet,
No fair impression on the sheet is set.
Tho' oft the press-man tugs, he tugs in vain;
The bar flies backward after every strain.
So when a man, to interest inclin'd,
Would print Whig principles on Tory mind:
He forth and backward moves, 'twixt sense and nonsense,
And pulls, and hauls, and tugs in vain his conscience.
Tho' merrily he sings, he's oft'ner dull;
Conscience flies back again at ev'ry pull:
His mind appears, could you within it look,
Like a blurr'd, blotted, and false-printed book.

MÆVIUS.

Musselburgh, Octob. 17. This day, according to old custom, the honourable magistrates and town council, attended by their vassals and the burgesses, in number above 700, rode the marches of the Burgh. But, alas! while they were marshalling, an unlucky difference arose betwixt the weavers and taylors, which should have the precedency, so that in order to prevent the effusion of blood, they agreed to submit the merits of the cause to the magistrates. The taylors argued, that as the precedency had fallen to them by lot, no opposition could now be offered. It was alledged on the other hand, that they (the weavers) were men, and as such, preferable in all events to taylors. This signal affront could not possibly be digested: accordingly to work they went, without waiting the decision of authority: nought was to be seen but heavy blows, hats off, broken heads, bloody noses, and empty saddles; 'till at last the plea of manhood seemed to go in favour of the needlemen, who took Scot, heroe of the weavers, prisoner, disarmed him, and beat them quite out of the field, tho' far more numerous. The weavers allege in excuse of their retreat, that the butchers squadron had been ordered up to assist the taylors; and that they did not incline to imbarque with these men of blood. However, 'tis lucky the fray was got so soon quelied; for already an intolerable stench had almost suffocated the by-standers.

O qualis hurly burly fuit, si forte vidisses
Pypantes arsas, & flavo sanguine breechas
Dripantes, hominumque heartas ad pralia faintas.

HAWTHORNDEN Pol. Middin. *P.* Octob. 27.

Edinburgh, Oct. 23. On the 19th died at his seat at Cathcart near Air, the right honourable Allan, lord Cathcart, in the 85th year of his age; and is succeeded in his honours and estate by his son colonel Charles Cathcart, groom of the bed chamber to his majesty. *C. P. DJ.* 31.

FOREIGN NEWS.

THURSDAY, *Octob.* 26.

Venice, Oct. 18. M. Jerome Justiniani, procurator of S. Mark, died on wednesday, after a long illness, aged 57 years. *C.*

Francfort, Oct. 26. We have received advice, that above 900 families of the bishoprick of Konigsgratz, whereof the prince of Saxe Neustadt is bishop, have declared themselves to be of the confession of Augsburg, demanding the free exercise of their religion. *C.*

FRIDAY, *Octob.* 27.

Yesterday arrived a Mail from France.

Paris, Nov. 1. 'Tis written from Genoa, that the republic had at last ordered the four chiefs of the malecontents of the island of Corsica to be released from the tower, and carried to Savonna, where they are to be delivered to the imperial commissaries. *C.* &c.

SATURDAY, *Octob.* 28.

Yesterday arrived the Mail from Holland.

Madrid, Oct. 14. The preparations for a considerable armament, both by sea and land, are carrying on with great vigour throughout this monarchy; and 'tis reckoned they will be finished by next spring. The army which is to be assembled against that time, will amount to 40,000 men, every parish in the kingdom being to furnish five men, to recruit the old regiments, and to form new. — 'Tis written from Cadiz, that four French men of war were arrived there, belonging to a company erected in France, to fish up the effects of the ships of the Spanish flota destroyed at Vigo, in the year 1702. *C.* &c.

Paris, Oct. 27. Yesterday an express from Turin brought advice of the death of King Victor Amadeus, on the 6th instant, at the castle of Rivoli, in the 66th year of his age. *D P.*

MONDAY, *Octob.* 30.

Yesterday arrived the Mail from France.

Paris, Nov. 5. 'Tis written from Seville of the 17th past, that letters were arrived from the marquis de Santa Cruz, governor of Oran, with advice that the Algerines were come and encamped about that place, to the number of 30 or 40,000 men; and that having formed the siege of Marzalquibir, they made themselves masters of a redoubt, and were as soon beaten out again. — As soon as the king heard this news, he ordered 2000 men to embarque immediately, and reinforce the garrison of Oran. *C.* &c. —— The abbot Reuille, ancient canon of Notre-Dame, prior of Notre Dame, de Donges, died at Auteuil the 28th past. *C.* — *My brother should have said, how* ancient.

TUESDAY, *Octob.* 31.

Hague, Octob 14. N. S. Our last letters from Seville insinuate, that the king of Spain is sicker than ever; but that his distemper, far from being mortal, is not so much as dangerous: they say he lies abed, and will not be shaved; and some add, he has declared, that he will not get up, 'till the coach is at the door, ready to carry him to S. Ildefonso, where he is absolutely resolved to abdicate. The queen will, no doubt, recur to every stratagem to prevent the effect of such a resolution; but has no other resource that we know of, than to find some reason for undertaking the siege of Gibraltar, to which (they say) she is greatly incited by the Pope's nuncio. The holy father has taken it into his head (it seems) that the court of Great Britain designs to introduce the English form of government there, and that this may in time introduce the English religion; which fills his soul with terrible alarms. Wherefore the old gentleman has written a letter to the king of Spain about it, to work upon his timorous conscience; telling him, that he may, if he pleases, alienate the temporalities of any part of his dominions; but that he has no right to alienate any part of the spiritualities, which depend entirely upon the church. —— The instances of the maritime powers at Seville against the new-erected company of the Philippine islands, have produced a declaration from Don Joseph Patinho, That the King, his master, had no intention to do any thing contrary to the treaties, or prejudicial to the commerce and rights of other nations; but was willing that conferences should be entered into, for agreeing upon expedients to obviate all manner of complaint: but this declaration itself seems to be nothing else but an expedient to gain time, during which the company may go on with their enterprize, and make such a progress, as to set them above the fear of any disaster. *P.*

TUESDAY, *Octob.* 31.

This day arrived a Mail from Holland.

Genoa, Octob. 18. By order of the republic the four chiefs of the Corsican rebels are sent, under a guard to Savonna, to be deliver'd to the imperial commissaries. *S J. WE. L E.*

WEDNESDAY, Nov. 1.

Ratisbon, Octob. 30. The Danish minister has notify'd to the dyet the accession of the king his master to the pragmatic sanction, by virtue of a peace concluded between the courts of Denmark and Vienna. *D P. C.*

On Tuesday Stocks were

South Sea Stock was 103 7 8ths, to 104. South Sea Annuity 109 1 qr. Bank 149 3 qrs. to 7 8ths. Bank Circulation 4 l. 12 s. 6 d. Premium. India 155 1 qr. to 1 half. Three per Cent. Annuity 99 3 qrs. Royal Exchange Assurance 104 1 half. London Assurance 13 1 half. York Buildings 4. African 36. English Copper 2 l. Welch ditto 1 l. 15 s. South Sea Bonds 2 l. 8 s. Premium. India ditto 4 l. 5 s. ditto.

RAMSAY, Surgeon and Man-Midwife, in Castle-Yard, Holbourn,

Hath, for many Years, successfully prac-tised a Method of curing RUPTURES and BROKEN BELLIES of all Sorts, peculiar to himself, and hath cured Num-bers of Bursten People, who imagin'd themselves incurable; some of whom have been examin'd by Phy cians and Surgeons of the greatest Reputation, who have given their Testimony thereof in the publick Prints. There are several Gentlemen to be heard of at Mr. FRANKLIN's in Russel-street, Covent-Garden, who are ready to acknowledge their being cured by him.

He performs the Cure within the Compass of three or four Weeks, and without giving the Patient the Trouble or Fatigue of wearing a Truls after the Cure is perfected.

To be Sold, or Lett immediately,

THE Welch-Harp Inn, situate in Ston-nall, in the County of Stafford, three Miles off Litchfield, in a fine Sporting Country, with Land worth 100l. per ann. adjoin-ing and lying contiguous thereto, and with, or without, the Furni-ture of the House, and a good Stock of Hay and Corn.

Enquire of Mr. Theophilus Levett in Litchfield, or at the Welch-Harp, aforesaid.

Last Saturday was published,

No. XIII. *(being five Sheets, containing Part of the Reign of King Henry II. the Reign of King Richard I. and the Beginning of the Reign of King John, at the Price of 6d.)* of

THE HISTORY of ENGLAND. By M. RAPIN DE THOYRAS. Translated by N. TINDAL, M.A. Vicar of Great Waltham in Essex. The Second Edition, with the following Improvements;
1. The Translation is thoroughly revised and corrected.
2. The many Errors and Mistakes of the Original are care-fully retained.
3. Several hundred of Marginal References, accidentally omit-ted by the Author, are supply'd.
4. Additional Notes throughout, with Cuts, Maps and Ge-nealogical Tables, on Copper Plates.

Printed for JAMES, JOHN, and PAUL KNAPTON, re-mov'd from St. Paul's Church-yard, to the Crown in Ludgate-street, near the West End of St. Paul's.

Where may be had, The preceding Numbers.

N.B. The Whole will be comprised in Two Volumes in Folio, containing 400 Sheets, at the Price of Two Guineas in Sheets, including Copper Plates. Five Sheets of the Work will be pub-lish'd every Saturday, till the Whole is compleated, at the Price of 6d. and the said Sheets will be deliver'd every Week at the Houses of Gentlemen who are pleased to order them; and such as take the Weekly Numbers are reckoned as Subscribers; that is, shall pay but Two Guineas, though the Number of Sheets should exceed 400.

Proposals at large, with a Specimen, may be had Gratis.

This Day is published,

(Price Bound Two Shillings, or One Shil-ling and Six Pence Stitch'd,)

A Collection of Heads and Titles, proper for a Common-Place Book in Law and Equity, inter-spers'd with many useful Words for the Benefit of References to the Tales, which renders the Whole a copious Index to the Law.

Printed for J. Worrall, at the Dove in Bell-Yard, near Lincoln's Inn.

Where may be had, lately publish'd,

FOLIO.

Nelson's Abridgment, 3 Vols.
Modern Cases in Law and Equity.
Lilly's Practical Conveyancer, 2d Edit.
Bird's Modern Conveyancer.
Sir Tho. Jones's Reports. 2d Edit.
A general Abridgment of Cases in Equity.

OCTAVO.

Bohun's Practising Attorney, 2 Vols.
Cases concerning Poor's Settlements, 3d Edit.
Bohun's Institutio Legalis, 4th Edit.
English Clerk's Tutor.
Bohun's Law of Tithes. 2d Edit.
Compleat Arbitrator: Or, Law of Awards. By the Author of a General Abridgment of Cases in Equity.
A new Catalogue of all the Law Books extant, to the End of Trinity Term, 1732. giving an Account of their various Editions, Dates and Prices.

This Day is published, Pr. 6d.
[Neatly Printed on fine Paper.]

The GENTLEMAN's MAGAZINE: Or, MONTHLY INTELLIGENCER.

NUMBER XXII. for OCTOBER. 1732.

CONTAINING,

I. A Compendious VIEW of all the pub-lick Papers of the Month, their Essays and Enter-tainments; with the Proceedings, Speeches and Debates in Parlia-ment.
II. A select Pieces of Poetry; among which, MONKTON, a Yorkshire Landskape, Sraad and Carolina, with some others, never before published.
III. Remarkable Transactions and Events, Foreign and Do-mestick, Births, Marriages, and Promotions, Ecclesiastical and Civil.
IV. Prices of Goods, Stocks, &c.
V. Account of CAROLINA concluded; exact List of the Trus-tees and Commissioners for GEORGIA, and their Places of Abode.
VI. A Register of Books and Pamphlets.
VII. A Table of Contents.

By SYLVANUS URBAN Gent.

London; Printed, and sold at St. John's-Gate, by F. Jefferies in Ludgate-street; Mrs. Nutt, Mrs. Charlton, Mrs. Cook, at the Royal-Ex-change; Mr. Bathy, in Pater-Noster Row; Mr. Midwinter, in St. Paul's Church-Yard; A. Chap-man, in Pall Mall; Mr. Dodd, and Mr. Bic-kerton without Temple-Bar; Mr. Crichley, at Charing-Cross; Mr. Stagg, and Mr. Long, in Westminster-Hall; Mr. Williamson, in Holborn, Mr. Montague in Great Queen-Street; S. Harding, in St. Martin's-Lane; and most Booksellers in Town and Country.

Where may be had, All the former Numbers.

This Day is Published,

THE Damerian History of the AFFAIRS of EUROPE, for the memorable Year 1731. with the present State of Gibraltar, and an exact Description of it; and of the Spanish Works before it. Also of Dunkirk, and the late Transactions there. With curious Plans of both those Places. Printed for J. Roberts in Warwick-Lane. Pr. 1s.

This Day is published,

(Humbly Dedicated to the Gentlemen and Ladies, who have frequented the Entertainment of the Ridotto al' Fresco,)

CUPID's GOLDEN AGE: or, The HAPPY ADVENTURES of LOVE. Newly done from the French by HARRY LOVEMORE.
1. Of a Merchant, who, after some considerable Misfortunes which happen'd to him, met with a very lucky Turn of Fortune.
2. Of an Officer, who, by the Means of several sad Acci-dents on his March, surpriz'd a Girl at a Rendezvous, which she had given her Gallant, and of the good Fortune that ensued.
3. Of a young Girl who fell deeply in Love with her Mo-ther's Favourite, and how her Mother serv'd her through Jealousy.
4. Of a Lady who kept Company with a certain Gentle-man, without granting him any Favour, pretending to love him, because she wou'd not lose the Present which he made her from Time to Time; and how she was at length deceiv'd.
5. Of a young Lady who conducted an unknown Person by Night into her Apartment, believing him to be her betrothed Favourite, with whom she had made an Assignation.
6. Of a jealous Woman who had no Complaisance for any Person; and after what Manner Love avenged himself of her Pride.
7. What a faithful Lover did to obtain his Mistress's in Mar-riage, after the Refusal of her Parents.
8. Shewing that a beautiful Woman cannot be in the Wrong.
9. Of an agreeable Turn which happen'd to the Daughter of one of the richest Merchants at Amsterdam.
10. Of a young Soldier, who obtain'd the good Graces of a Citizen's Wife, by pretending to understand the Art of Ne-cromancy.

Printed for J. WILFORD, behind the Chapter-House in St. Paul's Church-yard. Price 2s.

Where may be had,

The Jealous Husband: or, Virtue in Distress. A Novel. By H. Cornwallis, Gent. Price 1s. 6d.

This Day is publish'd,

The LONDON MAGAZINE: Or, GENTLEMAN's *Monthly Intelligencer.*

NUMB. VII. For OCTOBER, 1732.

[Price Sixpence each Month]

CONTAINING,

A Clear and Comprehensive VIEW of the Weekly Essays and Disputes on Political, Moral, and other Pieces: Domestick and Foreign Affairs: Promotions, Ecc-lesiastical, Civil and Military; Marriages and Births; Death; Mortality; together with a Catalogue of Books and Pamphlets with their Prices; published by the Proprietors of the Monthly Chronicle, now discontinu'd.

Printed for C. Ackers in St. John-Street, and sold by J. Wil-ford, behind the Chapter House, near St. Paul's; W. Meadows; T. Cox, W. Hinchliff; H. Whitridge, R. Willock, and E. Nutt, in Cornhill; J. Clarke in Duck-lane; T. Astley in St. Paul's Church-Yard; A. Dodd without Temple-Bar; J. Stagg in West-minster-Hall; J. Jackson in Pall-Mall; J. Jollife in St. James's Street; J. Brindley and W. Shropshire in Bond-Street; and J. Millan, near the Admiralty-Office.

Where may be had the former Numbers.

First publish'd this Day,

Another Volume of

MISCELLANIES in PROSE and VERSE by Dr. SWIFT, Mr. POPE, &c. Containing divers Pieces never before published; and others never before collect-ed together; which baulks an entire Collection of their Miscel-lanies.

Printed for B. Motte, under the Middle-Temple Gate, and L. Gilliver, at Homer's-Head against St. Dunstan's-Church, Fleet-street.

Where may be had the other Volumes, as also,
1. The Works of the Right Hon. the Lord LANSDOWNE.
2. A new Edition of the DUNCIAD, with some additional Notes and Epigrams. A Collection of Pieces, occasion'd by the DUNCIAD.
3. The Progress of Love, in 8vo. (from the Folio Edition.)
4. An Epistle from Rome to Mr. Pope, by the Author.
5. STOWE: The Gardens of the Lord Viscount Cobham.
6. The Art of Politicks; with a Curious Frontispiece.
7. An Epistle to Mr. Pope concerning the Authors of the Age, by the Author of Universal Passion.

Printed for J. Brotherton, at the Bible, next the Fleece-Tavern in Cornhill,

A Select Collection of NOVELS. In Two Volumes.

Vol. I. contains, The Little Gypsy; Ethelinda; the Amour of Count Palviano and Eleonora; Scanderberg the Great.

Vol. II. contains, The Life of Castruccio Castracani of Lucca; the Loves of Oroïn and Durasa; the Spanish Lady of England; the Lady Cornelia; the False Duchess.

Where may be had,
1. The Minute Philosopher.
2. Coke's Detection 3 Vols.
3. The Life of CHARLES the XIIth.
4. Journey from Aleppo to Jerusalem.
5. Lommius's Treatise of Continual Fevers.
6. Bohun's Law of Tythes.
7. Langham's neat Duties of all the Customs.
8. Gay's Fables.
9. Bailey's Justin.
10. Moliere's Plays French and English.

Just published,

A New View and Observations on the antient and present State of London and Westminster, shewing the Foundation, Walls, Gates, Towers, Bridges, Churches, Rivers, Wards, Palaces, Halls, Companies, Inns of Court and Chancery, Hospitals, Schools, Government, Charters, Courts and Privileges thereof. Also Historical Remarks thereon. With an Account of the most remarkable Accidents, as to Wars, Fires, Plagues, and other Occurrences, which have happened therein for above 1400 Years past, brought down to the present Time. Illu-strated with Cuts of the most considerable Matters, with the Arms of the sixty six Companies of London, and the Time of their Incorporation.

By ROBERT BURTON,

Author of the History of the Wars of England. Continued by an able Hand.

Printed for Jer. Batley, at the Dove in Pater-Noster-Row.

LONDON: Printed by P. SANDERS, in Crown-Court, Butcher-Row, without Temple-Bar; where Letters and Advertisements are taken in, and by Capt. GULLIVER, near the Temple; also at the Rainbow Coffee-House in Cornhill, and John's Coffee-House in Sheer-Lane, near Temple-Bar. [Price Twopence.]

The Grub-street Journal.

NUMB. 150.

Thursday, NOVEMBER 9. 1732.

How justly PROTEUS *transmigrations fit*
The monstrous changes of a modern Wit?
Dr. Young's First Epistle.

Mr. BAVIUS,

AS you have frequently declared to the world the impartial conduct of your society; so you have given, it must be confessed, frequent instances thereof, in publishing the different, and sometimes contrary sentiments of your correspondents, together with the contrary reasons by which they defend them. But then you have likewise frequently manifested a greater inclination towards one side, than the other, not at all consistent with that pretended impartiality, of which you have so often boasted. Of this I could produce many instances: but shall at present take notice only of a very late, but a flagrant one. It is in your *Journal extraordinary, Numb.* 148. in the *Explications of the emblematical picture*, which has so much amused the public: of which your own interpretation plainly shews, how much you were blinded by too favourable a regard to your own profession as an author. For tho' you have there justly conjectured, that by the four figures with the heads of brutes authors may be denoted, yet you have very unjustly applied the figures of the JANUS, and of the most conspicuous devil, to booksellers: whom you endeavour to expose, as treating their authors in a very unworthy manner. These indeed you have in general allowed "are properly represented by the gentlemen with the head of a dog, a horse, and a swine:" but you forbore observing in particular the propriety of each of these emblems, which you ought to have done. This defect I shall therefore now supply, by sending you a new and more consistent explication: from which it will appear, that booksellers are not so much to be censured for their conduct towards authors; but that they generally treat them no otherwise than they really deserve. If you publish *this explication*, you will shew your readiness to supply any deficiency of which you are admonished; and I shall take it as a proof of your sincerity and impartiality. But if not, tho' I may perhaps look upon your paper now and then for diversion, I shall have no more regard to any thing that is advanced in it, than I have to the most extravagant assertions and reasonings, which I find in some other papers, written by hirelings to justify every thing, right or wrong, which is done by a particular set of men.

The middle division of this picture, I think, very well represents a consultation of Grubean authors, held at some printer's house; over which Dullness and Wickedness preside, one in the shape of an owl, and the other in that of a devil. The grand figure with two faces may denote all mercenary authors in general, who are ready to undertake any piece of work whatsoever, which a bookseller shall propose to them, upon subjects the most different, and even contrary to one another. For instance, a book to recommend moral virtue, another to propagate immorality; one in defence of the christian religion, another in opposition to it; a collection of devotions, and a collection of novels; a history of the life of Christ and his apostles, and a history of the devil, &c.—If we apply this figure to political authors in particular, it may signify those who pretend to have changed their principles, and now talk and write directly contrary to their former discourse and writings. I say, pretend to have changed, because their conversion, or turning about, has not proceeded from a strict inquiry into the merits of the cause which they now embrace, of which every honest man who is convinced, ought to be converted too; but solely from a prospect of interest and advantage. This is evident from the suddenness of the conversion, the greatness of the profit immediately consequent thereupon, and the weakness of the reasonings advanced in vindication of the new-espoused cause. In so much, that we have seen a person of great volubility of tongue, and velocity of pen, proceed directly from railing against a party, to talking and scribbling for it; from one sort of hackney writing to another: for which being payed in the most generous manner, he pours out a weekly torrent of tautology, in which the arguments are as threadbare as his old coat, the language as glittering as his new, and the sound of it, when read, as ratling as that of his chariot wheels. — The face of the JANUS, which is towards the company, seems to be an artificial one, and looks more like a mask, than a natural countenance; to shew, that hireling authors generally write under a disguise, which they can change at pleasure, and which is most commonly daubed in so deformed a manner, as to make a very frightful appearance —— There is likewise a further propriety in this double figure, as pointing at some particular political authors, if any such there be at present, the genuine successors of the famous DANIEL DE FOE, who, upon very good authority, is believed to have had a great hand at one and the same time, both in a Whig and in a Tory paper. A plain instance of the penetration of persons so violently addicted to any party as to justify all their measures; who by that violence exposed themselves to be directed in things, which they ought to have made a matter of conscience, by a person who seems to have had none, and who was ready to prostitute his pen in any undertaking, at the hire of any bookseller whatsoever.

Nor are mercenary authors less properly represented by the gentleman with the face of a dog. For if we consider the hungry looks of some, their eagerness to satisfy their canine appetites by any means whatsoever; their readiness to bark at and bite, to pursue and hunt harmless and innocent persons, at the instigation of their masters; their servile cringing and fawning, and licking up their spittle; their readiness to leap backward and forward over a stick, especially a white one, at the word of command; we shall plainly perceive in the human species the nature of grey-hounds, spaniels, and harlequins. But there is one quality in which the rational currs seldom or never imitate the irrational, and that is fidelity to their masters in distress.

The person with the head of a horse is a lively emblem of that sort of scribblers, who are employed by booksellers in works of their own projecting. When any of these designs to take a journey into the learned world, he hires one of these hackneys, without inquiring much into his abilities. If he make a pretty tolerable appearance, and be let cheap, scarce any of them are at all sollicitous about the spirit of the beast. Hence it often happens, that they are layed in the dirt, and are either forced to return back, or get to their journey's end in a dismal pickle. But this misfortune, I must own, is frequently owing to the unskilfulness of booksellers themselves in the art of riding; who leading a a sedentary life, and conversing much with books, as well as the clergy, are observed, like them, to be very hard riders, whenever they get on horse-back. These gentlemen must always be at such a place by such a time, tho' they set out never so late; or else they think they might as well stay at home. Hence, trusting to their silver spurs, they strike immediately into a gallop, a pace to which their hacks are not naturally inclined, and which gradually sinks into a dog-trot, and that soon determines in a foot-pace. If the best horse be apt to stumble, when he is almost tired; it is no wonder, that those which stumble on plain ground, and at first setting out, should fall directly down in the dirt, when thus unmercifully ridden beyond their strength —— I knew one of these horses myself, and a jolly nag he was at his first coming to town. His colour was a dark brown; he pranced very prettily; and tho' he had no mane, that defect was more than supplied by the graceful cocking of his head and his tail. But he unfortunately fell into the hands of the book-sellers, who rode him off his legs: with whom however he was even, by frequently causing them to make use of their own against their will. In short, he threw them so often, that not one of them would venture upon his back any more. The butchers of Newport-market had more courage; which soon almost entirely extinguished the remainder of his, they being as hard riders as the booksellers. But hoping to meet with a more civilized sort of them, he removed to a new stable near Clare-market; where he had recourse to a QUACK DOCTOR; who, instead of repairing his broken constitution, has rendered him quite incapable of local motion. So that there he stands, moving only his head and fore-feet, with great variety of action; and is shewn twice a week to all comers for sixpence apiece. And indeed, it must be owned, that the sight for once is worth the money: for tho' he is a battered, spavined, foundered, glandered, broken-winded horse; yet he has a bold, undaunted look, and appears, as MILTON describes SATAN, *Majestic, though in ruin.*

The figure with the swine's head, as you very well intimate, denotes the lewd writers, who are the last and worst sort of hireling authors: with which this kingdom has more abounded for above twenty years last, than ever before. Nor is there any christian country in the world, wherein so many lewd books and pamphlets are publicly sold, as in this. The entertainments of our Theatres have run chiefly in the same strain: and could a goat, or a swine express the sentiments of their hearts in words, and tagg them with rime, they could not do it more properly, than in those of some of our late comedies and ballad operas.

I shall say nothing of the asinine figure in the first part of the picture, since you yourself declare, "that it resembles an author in a musing posture." But as to the devil in the last division, tho' I allow your application of it to a particular book-seller, yet I must observe, that it does not so properly belong to him, as a book-seller, as an author, holding up his own works to the view of the public.

Nov. 3. 1732. I am, Sir, your humble servant,

BIBLIOPOLA.

Mr. BAVIUS,

I Have read in history of a bad poet in ALEXANDER the Great's time, nam'd CHOERILUS, who by dint of a good assurance made interest with the courtiers to be laureat. He sung that conqueror's praise in odes and birthday songs; but with so ill a grace, that he gave his heroe great offence. ALEXANDER cautioned him to be careful for the future. But the conceited scribbler still persisted; and for his next offence proper judges were appointed to try him. Their sentence was, that he should receive a piece of gold for every good verse, and a lash for every bad one. In short, he was rewarded with three pieces of gold, and three hundred lashes. Yours A. B.

This gentleman ought to have mentioned the author's name, who wrote this piece of secret history, which I never met with before. BAVIUS.

SIR,

THE reading of the LAUREAT's *Ode*, put me in mind of a story I have somewhere read of a puppet shew. The scene was the creation; and the master calling out, *Let there be Light!* Punch enters with a farthing candle. Whether Mr. C——R had the same design of being impious, or no, I can't determine: but to put the Almighty's words in the same page with his own ridiculous trash, leaves some grounds for suspicion. But, be that as it will, the rest of the *Ode* had such an influence over me, that I could not be at ease, 'till I had celebrated its *natal day*. The inserting of which will oblige

Your constant Reader, &c.

ODE.

LET *there be light!*
Such was th' Almighty's, such the Laureat's phrase;
When, from the void of his unthinking *head*,
Free Dullness (PALLAS-like) with native *lead*,
Arose *to glad* his heavy, labour'd lays.

Air.

Succeeding songs to odes then *roll'd*,
And every ode surpass'd the *old*.
At length conspicuous o'er the rest,
The laureat *to extend his* pow'r,
Appointed for this *instant hour*,
At once the dullest, and *the best*.

The best that e're did *bless the land!*
And while such nonsence he can *form*,
Her scepter glories to confirm:
The throne of dullness firm will stand.

The Word that form'd the world
Too grave *had made mankind*,
Unless his laughter to constrain,
Almighty wisdom had design'd,
Sometimes a C——R *should* a laureat *reign*.
Yet farther, Britons, cast your eyes,
Behold a long succession rise,
Of future dull stupidities!

Air.

See, when his *table*-cloth is *spread*,
The worthy son of such a sire,
Sprung from a fertile genial bed,
And grac'd with all his father's fire!

While heav'n with bounteous hand,
Has so enrich'd her store;
When shall this promis'd land
In nonsence e'er *be poor?*
All we can farther ask, or heaven bestow,
Is, that we long may such a laureat *know*.

Air.

While o'er our vanquiſh'd hearts alone
Dullneſs (great queen!) *would greatly reign.*
She binds old C—y *to* her *throne,*
And C—r *hugs* the leaden *chain.*

Her jealous ſons, in her ſecure,
A happier ſtate than wiſdom *boaſt;*
For while her *kind commands allure,*
Wiſdom *in hearts reſign'd is loſt.*

Air.

Sound, Grub-ſtreet, ſound the blaſt,
This is the day alone,
In which the laureat has his paſt
Outdoings all undone.

Chorus.

Gin-ſhops around
Diffuſe the ſound!
From cells *to* garrets ſtun us with the noiſe.
Shake, ſhock, and rend the *ſhoar,*
Re-echo *the rolling roar!*
And halloo laureat C—r, boys.

DOMESTIC NEWS.

C. *Courant.*	E P. *Evening Poſt.*
P *Poſt-Boy.*	S J. *St. James's Evening Poſt*
D P. *Daily Poſt.*	W E. *Whitehall Evening Poſt.*
D J *Daily Journal.*	L E. *London Evening Poſt.*

Important articles omitted in our laſt.

Oratorical advertiſements and puffs in the month of ...

... Adv[e]rtiſements, 5 Oratorical ditto, 14. In all, ... — Hyp puffs 7. Oratoric ditto, 5. In all, 12 — Increaſed in the advertiſements this month, 5. Increaſed in the puffs, 2.

We hear that the Grub-ſtreet-mongers having taken their degrees of conjurers at the Devil tavern, the Hyp Doctor to morrow will hit them a ſlap, in a packet from Pluto, &c. D J. Oct 30. —— *Amazing piece of impudence, to endeavour to ſell a ſtupid paper by ſuch a lying puff! there being not one word in that paper relating to the* Grub-ſtreet Journal. *It is, indeed, a larger packet from* Pluto, *as this puff is a ſmall one, they being both* packets of lies.

THURSDAY, *Nov.* 2.

Couthorpe Clayton Eſq; equerry to his majeſty, is appointed avener and clerk-martial, in the room of Col. Negus, deceaſed. *L E.*

Yeſterday a board was held at the admiralty; when his majeſty's commiſſion was opened, relating to ſettling a fund for the widows of all commiſſion and warrant officers of the navy, &c wherein it was found that his majeſty out of his moſt gracious goodneſs towards ſo noble a deſign, had ſubſcribed 10,000 l. which great example gave encouragement to all officers preſent to ſubſcribe to the ſame; and the conditions, we hear, are as follows, viz. that 2 d. per pound be levied out of the ſalaries of all the officers of the navy. 1. That the widows of admirals and commiſſioners be allowed 50 l per ann. 2. To captains, 40 l. per ann. 3. To lieutenants and maſters, 30 l. per ann. 4. To the gunners carpenters, boatſwains, and purſers, 20 l. per ann. C. D P. W E.

They write from S. Weonard's in Herefordſhire, that the wife of a poor man of that pariſh was lately delivered of four girls at a birth, who died ſoon after: it was her firſt lying in, and ſhe had been married but three quarters of a year. *D J*

Great Yarmouth, Oct. 12. Mr. mayor having acquainted the common council, that the right honourable Horatio Walpole Eſq, hath been lately prevailed upon by the gentlemen of Norwich, to ſtand as one of their repreſentatives next election; and that the right honourable ſir Robert Walpole hath kindly propoſed his ſon the honourable Edward Walpole Eſq; to ſtand as candidate at our next election; this aſſembly doth unanimouſly approve the ſaid propoſal, and doth deſire Mr. Mayor to return ſir Robert the thanks of this houſe for the *extraordinary favour*, and doth preſent the ſaid Edward Walpole Eſq; with his freedom, and doth order his burgeſs letter to be preſented to him in a ſilver box. *W E* —— *Had they been as* unanimous at Cheſter, *it would have prevented the diſmal account following,*

They write from Cheſter, that the mayor, &c. had been conſtantly employed ſince the 16th in taking informations and depoſitions, touching the late riots and outrages; that ſeveral were dead of their wounds, beſides others not expected long to ſurvive, and that 1000 l. would ſcarce repair the damage done by the mob to the city. *L E.* —— Eleven perſons were dead: 700 l. or 800 l. *S J.*

Some days ago at Reading, one Richard Boulter, digging in a ſand-pit, with his little ſon by him, perceiving the bank give way, threw him out, ſaying, God bleſs thee, I ſhall never ſee thee more; which he had ſcarce pronounced, before the bank fell in and ſmothered him. *D J.*

On monday one Thomas Caton, about 18 years old, whoſe father is a cabinet-maker in Nine-pin-alley, Noble-ſtreet, purpoſing to ſee the proceſſion of the barges, before he went out, wrote upon a piece of paper his name and place of abode. His mother ſaid, Tommy, what are you writing? He anſwered, Nothing; but in caſe of any miſfortune happening, they may know where I live. The boat in which he was, ſunk by the ſkinners barge, oppoſite to Hungerford-ſtairs, a man and a woman were ſaved, but he was drowned, and brought home next day by the direction found in his pocket. *P.*

FRIDAY, *Nov.* 3.

Yeſterday the lords of the admiralty granted ſeveral Mediterranean paſſes to the Eaſt India company's ſhips outward bound, to make repriſals on all ſhips that attack them on the other ſide the Cape of Good Hope. —— We hear that a ſquadron of five ſail of men of war, with a commadore, will be ordered to the Eaſt Indies to protect the company's commerce againſt Angria the pyrate. *C. DP.*

Chriſtened Males 184 } Females 159 }	343		20 and 30	24
			30 and 40	43
Buried Males 212 } Females 215 }	427		40 and 50	56
			50 and 60	30
Died under 2 years	186		60 and 70	25
Between 2 and 5	24		70 and 80	16
5 and 10	7		80 and 90	8
10 and 20	8		Decreaſed in the burials 15. *P*	

SATURDAY, *Nov* 4.

Yeſterday the right honourable the lord chancellor, the right honourable the dukes of Dorſet and Grafton, &c. with the twelve judges, met at the Exchequer-chamber at Weſtminſter, and pricked down a liſt of three gentlemens names in each county, to ſerve as ſheriffs for the year enſuing. *C. P. D J.*

On thurſday the right honourable the lords, &c. appointed by commiſſion to take a ſurvey of the affairs of the courts of juſtice, to enquire into the fees, met at the right honourable the lord chancellor's cauſe-room, in Lincoln's-inn fields, for the execution of the ſaid commiſſion. *P.*

Yeſterday, at a general court of the India company, it was reſolved, after great debates, to leave the intereſt of the bonds to the conſideration of the court of directors, whether four, or three and a half per cent, ſhould be allowed. *C. D P. D J.* —— It was unanimouſly reſolved to reduce the intereſt to three and a half per cent. *P.*

On wedneſday Mr. Cook's *Bauble* beat my lord Portmore's *Dunkirk*, for 500 guineas. *P.* — 300. *W E.*

Yeſterday morning a fire broke out in the workſhop of Mr. Roſe, a diſtiller, the corner of S Martin's-lane, near Charing-croſs, by the head of the ſtill's flying off, Mr. Roſe, his man, and maid, were burnt in a miſerable manner. The man died in leſs than an hour; and Mr. Roſe's and the maid's life are deſpaired of. *C. D P.* —— The man died about four. *D J.* —— About five. *P.* — It burnt down only the ſhop. *C.*

Lectures to be read every day at Greſham college, during this term, at nine in the morning in latin, and at three in the afternoon in engliſh, by the following gentlemen, viz. *Monday,* John Bruegeen, M. A. divinity. *Tueſday,* John Cuming Eſq; Middle Temple, civil law. *Wedneſday,* John Machin, ſecretary R. S. aſtronomy. *Thurſday* George Newland, L. L. D. geometry. *Friday,* John Ward, F. R. S. rhetoric. *Saturday,* Henry Pemberton, M. D. phyſic; John Gordon, muſic, at four in the afternoon. *S J.* —— Lectures *of this kind are called* Wall lectures *at* Oxford.

We hear from King's Weſton, in Somerſetſhire, the ſeat of the right honourable Edward Southwell Eſq; ſecretary of ſtate for Ireland, that ſeveral workmen being employed to level a large hill there, in order to make a proſpect from his ſeat toward Briſtol, found the remains of the bodies of ſeveral men and women, who had been embalmed and interred there: by the inſcriptions that were engraven on ſeveral copper plates, &c. it is computed that ſome of them have lain there near two thouſand years. *S J.*

MONDAY, *Nov* 6.

His grace the duke of Newcaſtle is gone down to ſir Robert Walpole's ſeat in Norfolk, where ſir Robert keeps open houſe. — William Pulteney Eſq; is taking the houſe adjoining to the earl of Aſhburnham's in S. James's-ſquare, lately taken by ſir Robert. *P*

Laſt thurſday the commiſſioners appointed to take a ſurvey of the offices of the courts of juſtice met, and ordered, that all of them ſhould forthwith lay before them an account of the nature of their reſpective offices and what ſervice, charge, and attendance doth belong unto each of them by virtue of their reſpective offices, and what fees, rewards, and what wages every of the ſaid officers, clerks, and miniſters, and their ſubſtitutes, or under-clerks have, and take for and in reſpect of their ſeveral offices and places The ſaid commiſſioners have appointed Mr. Joſhua Sharp to be their ſecretary. *D J.*

Saturday being the anniverſary of the birth of our great and glorious deliverer King William III. of immortal memory, the ſame was obſerved throughout the cities of London and Weſtminſter with great rejoycings, as ringing of bells, &c. *C. D J.* —— Yeſterday being the anniverſary of the powder plot, and the landing of our great deliverer, the ſame was obſerved, &c. *C.* — The reverend Dr. Stebbing preached a ſermon ſuitable to the occaſion, at the cathedral church of S. Paul's: the lord mayor being indiſpoſed of the gout, was not preſent. *P.*

On thurſday George Lewen of Ewell in Surrey Eſq; one of the repreſentatives in parliament for Wallingford in Buckinghamſhire, was married at Ewell to a ſiſter of Henry Drax Eſq; one of the repreſentatives for Lyme Regis in Dorſetſhire. *D J.*

Yeſterday morning died Dr. Ayliffe, at his lodgings in Crane-court, Fleetſtreet, a very great practitioner in the civil law. *D P.* — Formerly *C.* The ſame morning died Mr Roſe, diſtiller, and his maid, who were both violently burnt by the head of a ſtill flying off. *C.* — The maid's life is not expected *D J. D P.*

TUESDAY, *Nov.* 7.

Yeſterday morning the lady of the right honourable John lord Ruſſel, brother to his grace the duke of Bedford, and grand-daughter to her grace the dutcheſs dowager of Marlborough, was ſafely delivered of a ſon, at his lordſhip's houſe in Groſvenor ſtreet. *D J.* — Between twelve and one. *D P.* —— He died laſt night. *S J. L E.*

We hear the right honourable the lord mayor is much better, and purpoſes, next ſaturday, to take his reſidence at his manſion houſe at Goldſmith's hall *D J.*

Dover, Nov. 5. We hear that Mr. Thompſon, late warehouſe-keeper to the charitable corporation, is now at Boulogne *P.* — *It is hoped he is in his way home.*

Cambridge, Nov. 5, On friday the reverend Dr. Morgan, maſter of Clare hall, was choſen vice-chancellor for the enſuing year. *P.*

On friday died at Norwich, ſir Richard Palgrave Bar. a batchelor, by whoſe death the dignity of a baronet in that family is become extinct. *D P.*

The right honourable Charles L. Cathcart has reſigned his place of groom of the bed-chamber to his Majeſty. *L E.*

WEDNESDAY, *Nov.* 8.

This day their majeſties will remove from Kenſington to Richmond for ten days. *P.* —— To morrow is fixed for the removal. *C. D P.*

Yeſterpay at a court of the Turky company, captain Francis Williams was choſen their conſul at Smyrna. *P.* — In the room of George Boddington Eſq; whom they had removed. *D J.* —— For captain Williams 33. For conſul Purnell 29. *D P.* — For captain Williams 32. For John Purnell Eſq; 23. The company alſo choſe Mr. Barker to be their treaſurer at Conſtantinople, and Mr. Pagan Shaw, treaſurer at Smyrna, for two years. *D J.*

On ſunday night died Mr. Richard Bradley, F.R.S. profeſſor of botany in the univerſity of Cambridge, and author of ſeveral ingenious books of husbandry and gardening. *D P* — *The book ſellers have loſt a good eaſy pad.*

The laſt Hyp Doctor No. 94. on the Grub-ſtreet club, being out of print, and demanded by the town, will be reprinted, and publiſhed on thurſday next, &c. *D J. Nov.* 6. — On thurſday being much called for, will be publiſhed the ſecond edition of the Hyp Doctor, No. 27. on the Grub-ſtreet club. *D J. Nov.* 7. —— On thurſday, being much called for, will be publiſhed the ſecond edition of the Hyp Doctor, No. 97. on the Grub-ſtreet club. *D J. Nov.* 8. —— *How difficult is it, for perſons, accuſtomed to lying, to ſpeak truth?* No. 94, No. 27. *and* No. 97. *being all* demanded, *or* much called for, *are to be* reprinted. *Theſe all equally give a true account of the* Grub-ſtreet club; *tho' only one of them treats of that ſubject. Would the* Doctor *have ſpoken truth, he ſhould have ſayed,* the firſt edition of No 97. republiſhed.

From the PEGASUS *in Grub-ſtreet.*

TO ſhew our impartiality and candor, and how ready we are to retract any error, when diſcovered; we think it proper to declare, that the firſt article of the domeſtic news in our laſt Journal, was miſquoted from a blundering paragraph in *S. James's Evening Poſt* of the 26 h ult. which for want of a proper parentheſis, was not eaſy to be underſtood. And we aſk pardon of the lady and gentleman, as well for incautiouſly inſerting a miſtake, as for the reflection added thereto.

Moſt illuſtrious Grubeans,

THE learned Mr. H. W. alias PHILO DIVES, who now allows my poor productions to be epigrams, by miſtaking them for the compoſition of ſome of the members of your ſociety, has warmed to ſuch a degree, that I am in a fever of delight. I cannot help asking myſelf, What! have I the quaint humour of Mr. CONUNDRUM? Are my lines turned with the elegance and acuteneſs of Mr. MÆVIUS? Or do I appear with the perſpicuity strength and judgment of Mr. BAVIUS? Is it poſſible I ſhould have the leaſt tincture of Grubean literature?

Sublimi feriam sidera vertice.

Let Mr. H. W. who is not infected with the *scribendi ca-*
nibus ; let him, I say,
——*with sense above his peers refin'd,*
Stand up a learn'd dictator to mankind.
D. Young's 2d Epist.

Be it my sole ambition to be regitlered in the Grubean
Memoirs PHILO HISTRIO, F. G. S. Excuse me, gentlemen, if I talk too arrogantly, as if already possessed of the
title. My vanity, perhaps, has carried me on too far ; but
I retreat, and own, with the profoundest submission, that
I am every way unworthy of such an honourable addition
to my obscure name.

Impertinent, bustling, superficial fellows, too often, and,
indeed, with too much ease, obtain an university A. M.
lay, indolent drones the D. D. and fly-catchers the
F. R. S. But your society, to its immortal honour, numerous as it is, admits no member without just pretensions founded upon solid merit. Your exclusion of the
Oratorial Clare-market Dragon, is an admirable instance of
your justice and sagacity. Your pens, like ITHURIEL's
spear, have traced him through all his windings, and detected him in every shape. I need not mention more particulars, when your just abhorrence of atheists, jugglers,
and impostors, of what denomination soever, exalts your reputation, and excites not only in me, but in learned authors,
a laudable ambition of becoming members of your society.
For my own part, I freely confess my heart is smitten with
a fervent desire of a fellowship in your Pegasean Academy.
For should I hereafter publish any piece, what a grand
figure wou'd PHILO HISTRIO, F.G.S. make in my title
page? It would give a sanction to my labour, and provoke
the curiosity of mankind to a perusal of it ; whilst the
HYP DOCTOR, SCRIBLERUS SECUNDUS, and the ferocious
commentator BENTLEIUS are condemned *ad thus & odores* ;
or lie repatched on the bending stalls. What makes the
title to me still more amiable is, that haply friend HOGARTH
may give my face a touch with his immortal pencil ;
and the ingenious Mr. FABER exhibit me to the public
in Mezzo tinto, with PHILO HISTRIO, F.G.S. underwritten ; a mark of honour, which may vie with any
of the above-mentioned distinctions, and stand its ground
against even that of poet laureat. But whilst I consider
the great advantages that may arise on my commencing
a Grubean brother, your strict enquiry into the abilities
of every man aspiring to that dignity, dashes all my hopes
of ever rising so high. However, I am fully satisfied, that
whenever I deserve that inestimable favour, it will be very
readily conferred on,

Temple, Nov. 2d. Gentlemen, your ambitious admirer
1732. PHILO HISTRIO.

EPIGRAM.

DID not th' HYP-ORATOR, with puffing lies,
His weekly non-sense dayly advertise,
No curious fool would go to hear, or read
Th' expiring words of ANDREW almost dead.
Thus when some monster, brought from foreign lands,
Half dead, for pence is shewn ; with face and hands,
Acting his part, some ZANY must contrive
To draw the mob ; and cry, Alive ! Alive !
MÆVIUS.

✦✦✦✦✦✦✦✦✦✦✦✦✦✦✦✦✦✦✦✦✦✦✦✦✦✦✦✦✦✦✦

FOREIGN NEWS.

SATURDAY, *Nov.* 4.
Yesterday arrived the Mail due from Holland.
Oran, Octob. 9. N. S. The Moors, having laid two
months and a half before this place, at last besieged it, toward the end of September, with two armies ; one commanded by Bigorigin, formerly Bey, or governor of Oran ;
and the other by the Dey of Algiers's son : they began
their enterprise by the attack of the fort of Santa Cruz,
which they stormed three times on the 19th, without being able to make themselves masters of an inch of ground.
In the night between the 4th and 5th, 2500 men were sent
to escorte a convoy of provisions, &c. into the fort of
Santa Cruz. The Moors attacked them with 3000 ; and
we lost at the first onset above 100 men : but our troops
having fixed their bayonets in the muzzle s of their muskets
obliged them to retire. The piquet horse coming up, helped to put the Moors entirely to the rout, having lost above
1000 men. C. D?. D?. — A battalion is gone from
Cartagena, and 2000 men from Barcelona, which will be
speedily followed by six men of war and 6000 men from
Cadiz, P. &c. — They write from Seville, that the king
of Spain is indisposed of a cold in his eyes. P.

TUESDAY, Nov. 7.
Yesterday arrived the Mail from France and Holland.
Phoenix, Oct. 25 N.S. On the 23d the infante-duke,
our sovereign, made his public entry into this city. C. DP.
Berlin, Nov. 7. The number of protestants arrived in
Prussia from Salzburgh, amounts to 17,500 persons: about
800 died on the road. C. DP.

WEDNESDAY, Nov. 8.
Moscow, Oct. 17 N.S. Our advices from the frontiers of
Turky say, above 40,000 persons have died of the plague
at Constantinople, and among them 4000 christian slaves,
employed in cleansing the infected houses. G. DP.

*We desire, that the advertisements designed for this paper,
may be sent before twelve of the clock on tuesdays.
otherwise they cannot be inserted.*

ADVERTISEMENTS.

This Day is publiſhed,

(With a Specimen of writing the future Proceedings in Law.)

THE CLERK's ENGLISH TUTOR: Shewing the Practice of the Courts of King's-Bench and Common-Pleas, as they are now ſettled, purſuant to the ſeveral late Acts of Parliament, and the reſpective Rules of both the Courts made conſonant thereto: With great Variety of curious Engliſh Precedents, (never before printed in any Language) drawn by the moſt eminent Counſel of the preſent Age, and done into Engliſh, conformable to the Statute of 4 Geo 2. c. 26. that all Proceedings in the Courts of Juſtice ſhall be in the Engliſh Language; together with ſuch Writs or Proceſs, as well meſne and judicial, as are generally uſed in every Day's Practice. By an Attorney at Law.

Printed for W. Meadows, at the Angel in Cornhill.

Where may be had,

Caſes and Reſolutions of Caſes adjudged in the Court of King's-Bench, concerning Settlements and Removals from the firſt Year of King George I. to the preſent Reign, moſt of them adjudged in the Time when Lord Parker ſate Chief Juſtice there. The Third Edition, with Additions, of a Collection of the like Caſes adjudged when Sir John Holt Knt. was Chief Juſtice. To which is added, An Abſtract of the Statutes concerning Proviſion for the Poor.

This Day is publiſhed,

(Price Bound Two Shillings, or One Shilling and Six Pence Stitch'd,)

A Collection of Heads and Titles, proper for a Common-Place Book in Law and Equity, interſpers'd with many uſeful Words for the Benefit of References to the Titles, which renders the Whole a copious Index to the Law.

Printed for J. Worrall, at the Dove in Bell-Yard, near Lincoln's-Inn.

Where may be had, lately publiſh'd,

FOLIO.

Nelſon's Abridgment, 3 Vols.
Modern Caſes in Law and Equity.
Lilly's Practical Conveyancer, 2d Edit.
Bird's Modern Conveyancer.
Sir Tho. Jones's Reports, 2d Edit.
A general Abridgment of Caſes in Equity.

OCTAVO.

Bohun's Practiſing Attorney, 2 Vols.
Caſes concerning Poor's Settlements, 3d Edit.
Bohun's Inſtitutio Legalis, 4th Edit.
Engliſh Clerk's Tutor.
Bohun's Law of Tithes, 2d Edit.
Compleat Arbitrator: Or, Law of Awards. By the Author of a General Abridgment of Caſes in Equity.

A new Catalogue of all the Law Books extant, to the End of Trinity Term, 1732. giving an Account of their various Editions, Dates and Prices.

PROPOSALS

For Printing by SUBSCRIPTION,

THE HISTORY of the Grand Controverſy between the Secular and Regular Clergy of the Church of Rome, from the Year 1625 to 1634, concerning the Uſurpation of RICHARD SMITH, Titular Biſhop of Chalcedon, who pretended to be ſole Ordinary Biſhop of all England and Scotland. Wrote in Latin by the Preſident of the Engliſh Benedictine Monks, RUDISINDUS BARLO, and faithfully done into Engliſh from the Original, for the Entertainment of the Curious, eſpecially Divines and Lawyers, both Eccleſiaſtick and Civil, of what Religion ſoever.

With the Remonſtrances of the Roman Catholick Laity made to the ſaid Biſhop, and alſo to his Excellency Carolo Coloma, Embaſſador Extraordinary of his moſt Catholick Majeſty, and to the Marquis Fontany, Embaſſador of the moſt Chriſtian King, &c. taken alſo from the Latin Originals: All which Treatiſes have been hitherto ſuppreſt by the Papiſts, for Political Reaſons given therein.

As alſo the famous Bull of Pope URBAN VIII. called PLANTATA, neceſſary for the right Underſtanding of the Whole, wich was never before any where printed.

To which will be added,

A LETTER concerning the Diſputes that have happen'd among the Benedictine Monks ſince the Year 1700. to this preſent Time: Shewing how even they themſelves have varied from their original Principles. By one who was a Member of that Body, and concerned therein.

By JOHN WILLIAMS.

PROPOSALS may be had of (and SUBSCRIPTIONS taken in for the Author by) W. Meadows, at the Angel in Cornhill, T. Aſtley, at the Roſe, and S. Auſten, at the Angel and Bible in St. Paul's Church-Yard; C Davis in Pater-noſter Row; T. Woodward, at the Half-Moon, L. Gilliver, at Homer's Head, and J. Stephens, at the Hand and Star between the Two Temple-Gates, B. Motte, at the Middle-Temple-Gate; T. Worral, at Judge Coke's Head; H. Walthoe, next Door to the Rainbow Coffee-Houſe; W. Reaſon, in Flower-de-Luce-Court; J. Iſted, at the Golden-Ball, near Chancery-Lane, Fleet-Street; F. Gyles, over-againſt Gray's-Inn-Gate, Holborn; O. Payne, in Round-Court; and T. Game, at the Bible, by the New Church, in the Strand, T. Green, Charing-Croſs, J. Jackſon, in Pallmall; J. Jolliffe, at the Bible, in St. James's-Street; J. Brindley, at the King's Arms, and W. Shropſhire, oppoſite to the Duke of Grafton's, New Bond-Street; and J. Stagg, Weſtminſter-Hall, Bookſellers: J. Huggonſon, in Bartholomew-Cloſe, and T. Gover, by Fleet-Ditch, Black-Fryers, Printers.

This Day is publiſh'd,

In a neat Pocket Volume, the Second Edition of

THE BOOK of COMMON-PRAYER, with the Epiſtles and Goſpels at large; the ſame Letter of the large Church Bible printed at Oxford, being the ſame Letter with theſe three Words:

Let us pray.

Printed for R. Ware, at the Bible and Sun in Amen-Corner, near Pater-Noſter-Row. Price 8 s.

Alſo may be had, lately publiſhed, at the ſame Place.

1. A Treatiſe of Architecture, with Remarks and Obſervations, by that excellent Maſter thereof, Sebaſtian le Clerc, Knight of the Empire, Deſigner and Engraver to the Cabinet of the late French King, and Member of the Academy of Arts and Sciences, neceſſary to young People who would apply to that noble Art. Engraved in 200 Copper Plates, by John Sturt. Tranſlated by Mr. Chambers. Price 10 s. 6 d.

2. The large Houſe-Bibles, Folio, with ſix Maps of ſacred Geography, and a brief Concordance for the more eaſy finding out of the Places therein contained. By J. Downame, B. D.

Bound in Calf Leather	1 l. 8 s. per Book.
And with Mr. Sturt's Cuts at	2 l. 5 s. ditto.
On a fine Paper with Cuts	3 l. 3 s. ditto.

3. A Deſcription of 300 Animals, viz. Beaſts, Birds, Fiſhes, Serpents, and Inſects. With a particular Account of the Whale Fiſhery. Extracted out of the beſt Authors, and adapted to the Uſe of all Capacities, eſpecially to allure Children to read. Illuſtrated with Copper Plates, whereon is curiouſly engraven every Beaſt, Bird, Fiſh, Serpent, and Inſect deſcribed in the whole Book. Price 2 s. 6 d.

4. TRADESMAN's GUIDE. Containing a Liſt of all the Stage Coaches and Carriers; with an Account of all the Fairs and Market Towns in England, Price 1 s.

Juſt publiſhed,

A New View and Obſervations on the antient and preſent State of London and Weſtminſter; ſhewing the Foundation, Walls, Gates, Towers, Bridges, Churches, Rivers, Wards, Palaces, Halls, Companies, Inns of Court and Chancery, Hoſpitals, Schools, Government, Charters, Courts, and Privileges thereof. Alſo Hiſtorical Remarks thereon. With an Account of the moſt remarkable Accidents, as to Wars, Fires, Plagues, and other Occurrences, which have happened therein for above 1400 Years paſt, brought down to the preſent Time. Illuſtrated with Cuts of the moſt conſiderable Matters, with the Arms of the ſixty ſix Companies of London, and the Time of their Incorporation.

By ROBERT BURTON,

Author of the Hiſtory of the Wars of England. Continued by an able Hand.

Printed for Jer. Batley, at the Dove in Pater-Noſter-Row.

The Grand Specifick.

For Cleanſing and Strengthning the Reins, &c. that hath been publiſhed, and ſold, ſo many Years, and with ſuch extraordinary Succeſs and Benefit to the Publick, as has been often advertiſed; and lately, an Account at large was given of an extraordinary Cure of a Gentleman in Spain, viz. of a very great Weakneſs and intolerable Pain, mainly occaſioned by a Fall and an over Strain at firſt, that had reduced him to ſo weak and languiſhing a Condition, that he could not ſet one Foot before the other, as he expreſſed it in his Letter; beſides, it brought away above an Ounce of Gravel; and all this by taking but two Bottles: For the Truth of this Great Cure, any Gentleman, for his further Satisfaction, is referred to Mr. Gates in Butolph-Lane, London, the abovesaid Gentleman's Correſpondent.

IT IS

A Medicine that may be depended on as is abſolutely effectual for carying off by Urine, ſafely and ſpeedily, all the Relicks of ſecret Injuries, Remains of pernicious unskilfully prepared Mercurials, Gleets, or Weakneſſes, through tedious or ill manag'd Cures of the Venerial Diſeaſe; or from Self-Pollution, inordinate Coition, &c.

Alſo any Weakneſſes of the Veſſels, from Wrenches, Strains, Blows, or Falls, and all other Obſtructions in the Urinary Paſſages; even Stranguries, Ulcers, &c. are perfectly cured by it, be they of ever ſo long ſtanding: Which Relicks and Ailments are in Part diſcovered by theſe following Symptoms, viz. Weakneſs and Pain in the Back, a Sharpneſs in the Urine, its ſtrong Smell, Films or Hairs (as it were) floating about in it, and in ſome too frequent Occaſion to make it.

This Noble Specifick is alſo of ſingular and very extraordinary Uſe and Efficacy, where there is any Gravel, or even ſmall Stones, Slime, or any other Matter that obſtructs the Urine; bringing all away, in a few Times taking, with Safety, and very great Satiſfaction to the Patients.

It alſo ſtrengthens and recovers, after a particular Manner, all Relaxions of the Veſſels, confirms the Parts, bringing all into right Order, and thereby perfectly cures to Admiration. It's a very pleaſant Medicine, and may be taken with Pleaſure by the moſt ſqueamiſh, and will be found of uncommon Benefit to Mankind, beyond Expectation; which is the Reaſon of its being made publick, and to obviate the Ignorance of Pretenders in all the difficult Caſes above-mentioned. One Bottle, in moſt Caſes, is ſufficient for a perfect Cure, as you will ſee by the Directions given with it. Sold for 7 s. 6 d the Bottle, at Mr. Sindrell's Toy-ſhop, at the Griffin, the Corner of Bucklesbury, in the Poultry.

On Thurſday laſt was publiſhed,

(Beautifully printed on a fine Paper,)

The LONDON MAGAZINE: Or, GENTLEMAN's *Monthly Intelligencer.*

NUMB. VII For OCTOBER, 1732.

To be continued (Price Six-Pence each Month) Containing greater Variety, and more in Quantity, than any Monthly Book extant.

I. A VIEW of the WEEKLY ESSAYS, viz. Humours of Dreſs in the Ladies; Miſchiefs of Flattery; Dedications, Pedigrees, Printer's Devils, Spectres and Apparitions; Fortune-Tellers; Journey on the Tops of Trees, Sagacity of Apes; Advantage of Coffee-Houſes; Animadverſions on Dr. Bentley's Milton; farther Cenſure of Mr. Osborne; Ambition; Love of Fame; Eccleſiaſtical Tyranny; Death of a powerful Inſtructor; Vindication of Clarke, Locke, and Woolaston; Uſefulneſs of Hiſtory, particularly Rapin's.

II. POLLITICAL SUBJECTS, viz. Debates in Parliament about Vacancies in the Army; Sugar Colonies, Fees, Chelſea Hoſpital; Sir Thomas Lombe's Petition, and Account of his Invention; Government compared to a Pyramid; Nature and End of it, and how far it has to do with Religion; National Church, and the Britiſh Conſtitution; the Happineſs of it, and how to preſerve it; Parliament of Paris, and Speech of the Abbé Pucelle; Dialogue between Sir G. Worthy and Mr. Freeman, between Sir Harry Worthy and Mr. D'Anvers; Account of Machiavel, and Fog a Machiavelian; Vindication of Pericles; Articles of Impeachment, &c Governors of Colonies; De Wit, and the Prince of Orange; Pragmatic Sanction; Trade, Fleet, Companies, Laws, Slavery, Political Scandal, Gibraltar, Houſes of Auſtria, and Bourbon, &c.

III. POETRY: On the Death of Mr. Wilks; Death of a beloved Wife; Liberty of the Preſs; Praiſe of Innocence; Ode on the King's Birth-Day; Curate's Letter verſify'd.

IV. DOMESTICK OCCURRENCES: Promotions Eccleſiaſtical, Civil, and Military; Marriages and Births; Deaths, &c.

V. FOREIGN AFFAIRS.

VI. Price of Goods, Grain, Stocks; Monthly Bill of Mortality.

VII. A Table of Contents.

To which is added, A Catalogue of Books and Pamphlets, with their Prices, publiſhed by the Proprietors of the Monthly Chronicle, now diſcontinued.

MULTUM IN PARVO.

Printed for J. Wilford, behind the Chapter-Houſe near S. Paul's; T. Cox, in Cornhill; J. Clarke, in Duck-lane, and T. Aſtley, in S. Paul's Church-Yard.

Where may be had the former Numbers.

The Univerſal Family Medicine,

Still more and more famed;

Is ſold, by the Author's Appointment, by Mr. King, at the Sign of the Globe in the Poultry, near the Royal Exchange, London; at Mr. Hilyard's, Bookſeller in York; and at Mr. Oakey's, Bookſeller in Cardiff, Wales, at 3 s. a Bottle, Retale.

It is to be taken at any Seaſon of the Year, but eſpecially in the Spring and Fall; is ſo very agreeable to Young and Old, that Children take it without Trouble, a few Drops being a Doſe; and ſo gentle, that it weakens not the moſt aged; for it is a ſafe and effectual Alterative (in a leſs Doſe) where purging is not neceſſary; an Excellency inherent in this Medicine, which is a ſingular Property well known to the Learned to be in ſome Cathartick Medicines.

IT is alſo a certain and infallible Cure for the Scurvy, though of the longeſt ſtanding, and attended with the moſt aggravated Circumſtances; being a Cordial Elixir, peculiarly adapted to that Diſeaſe in all its Forms of appearing, from the ſlighteſt itching Humour in the Blood, to its utmoſt or laſt Effort on human Nature.

It is not a rugged Purgative that diſturbs the Patient, but a true Specifick Cordial, that perfectly cures that Diſtemper, by gentle Evacuation by Stool and Urine, the only ſure and effectual Way perfectly to cure the Scurvy, &c. and prevent Relapſes (notwithſtanding what may be dreamt to the contrary;) the Truth of which is witneſſed to daily, by the many Thouſands that have taken this Medicine; it ſo powerfully rectifies the Blood and Juices, that ſcrophulous Caſes are alſo ſpeedily cured by it; and all Spots, Blotches, Pimples, &c. on the Skin, are quickly and entirely taken off, the Patients made lively and briſk, many Chronick Diſeaſes prevented, and a due State of Health ſecured.

It removes all Pains from the Stomach, and helps Digeſtion beyond what all Bitters can do, that have been of late ſo much in Uſe; it opens Obſtructions, and is peculiarly ſerviceable to Maids inclined to, or troubled with the Green Sickneſs. 'Tis the beſt Medicine in the World to deſtroy Worms in Children or grown People, and prevent their Return; and it ſcours away all thoſe ropy viſcid Humours which breed them in their Bowels; and it ſo well adapted to all Conſtitutions, that it is deſervedly eſteemed both in City and Country, the moſt general Family Medicine that ever was known, to preſerve Health; and hinders no Buſineſs or Recreation.

N. B. Good Allowance is given Wholeſale by Mr. King, for ready Money to Country Shop-Keepers, &c. to ſell again. This Medicine will keep many Years, and is ſold no where elſe in London. Therefore beware of pirating Counterfeits, who endeavour to ſhroud under the valid Reputation this ſuperlative Medicament has every where obtained by its known Virtue, for the Purpoſes above mentioned, or any envious Suggeſtions about Names, with an Intent to hinder unwary People the Benefit of this experienced Medicine, too well known to loſe Reputation thereby; but Envy and Intereſt never want Pretences.

The Directions given with it are large and full.

LONDON: Printed for, and Sold by J. ROBERTS, near the *Oxford-Arms* in *Warwick-Lane*; where Letters and Advertiſements are taken in; as alſo by Capt. GULLIVER, near the *Temple*; by P. SANDERS, *in Crown-Court, Butcher-Row,* without *Temple-Bar*; and at the *Rainbow Coffee-Houſe* in *Cornhill.* [Price Twopence.]

The Grub-ſtreet Journal.

NUMB. 151.

Thursday, NOVEMBER 16. 1732.

Difficilis, querulus, laudator temporis acti
Se puero, censor castigatorque minorum.
HOR. *de arte poetica.*

DECORUM, according to TULLY, is a certain gracefulneſs in well timing and properly adapting our words and actions. This beauty and pertinence of behaviour comprehends, in a great meaſure, the perfection of reaſon and humanity. The moſt excellent men, in all ages, have been juſtly diſtinguiſhed for ſo noble and ornamental a ſyſtem, to which the moſt ſignificant offices in life are really and ſubſtantially circumſcribed. The wiſe man tells us, *To every thing there is a ſeaſon* ; and, indeed, in this valuable obſervation the very definition of duty itſelf ſeems to be contained.

It is an obſervation ſome hundred years old, that moſt people are honeſt while they are young. As we advance in years, we advance in the knowledge of the world; which knowledge teaches us diſſimulation and cunning. Hence it comes to paſs, that there are, I fear, but few inſtances of a ſteady honeſty in old men.

I can't help thinking it a remark equally juſt, that the modeſt part of mankind (as the word modeſt is commonly underſtood to import an oppoſition to impudence) conſiſts chiefly of ſuch as are in a progreſſion towards the middle ſtage of life. From the time we come to lay aſide our childiſh follies, we generally begin to ſee into our own weakneſſes and imperfections; and from thence entertain ſuch a diffidence of ourſelves, as is truly neceſſary to preſerve us from the imputation of arrogance and ſelf-conceit. But as we grow older, we fancy mankind has that eſtimation for age, as to imagine it experimentally wiſe; and this preſumption often makes us obſtinate and dogmatical. Women and children, if impudent and headſtrong, are generally ſo from their ignorance : old men ſometimes, as well from ignorance, as pride, but chiefly from the latter.

It is from the implicit reſpect, to which old men lay claim, that many of them think they have a right of committing the moſt enormous indecencies. They expect to be treated with what the world calls good breeding; yet will ſeldom condeſcend to uſe any themſelves. They cenſure the leaſt freedom of ſpeech in others; yet often in their own formal diſcourſes retail out the groſſeſt obſcenity, and moſt antiquated jeſts of bawdry. —— And what renders theſe men ſtill more intolerable, is, that they never make the leaſt allowance to juvenile extravagance, or youthful gaiety. They deſpiſe youth, becauſe they are paſt it, as ſome men, who would be thought philoſophers, condemn wealth, for no other reaſon but becauſe they are poor themſelves.

An old fellow, who is, as it were, monarch in his own houſe, and preſident of a coffee-houſe club, and needs not care for any body, as the expreſſion is, thinks he has an undoubted right of ſaying and acting juſt what he pleaſes. His age, he believes, gives a credit and ſanction to every thing he offers. He ſits in his elbow chair, with a ſagacious pipe in his mouth, interrogates magiſterially concerning other people's buſineſs, aſſerts with boldneſs, and knocks you down with a whiff, or a ſ——, if you aſk for an argument. —— How melancholy is the reflections to think, that age, inſtead of making us wiſer or better, for the moſt part, ſerves only to ſwell us into a tyrannic and preſumptuous behaviour! —— If men were always good and virtuous, in proportion to their years, how beautiful would be the appearance of grey hairs, or of the wrinkles of old age! But, alas! from remarking on the common run of old people, a man of ſenſe would be almoſt glad never to arrive at an age, which is but too generally attended with ſelf-conceit, covetouſneſs, and ill-nature.

I would not, by any thing here ſayed, be underſtood, in the leaſt, to derogate from the reſpect which is due to age, when it is accompanied with a humane and benevolent diſpoſition. I would even have young men imitate the Egyptians and Lacedemonians, in riſing from their ſeats, at the approach of thoſe who are of elder years. But then, in return for ſuch civilities, I would have the treatment of old men to their juniors to be mild and gentle, affable and condeſcending. Their precepts ſhould be inforced with reaſonings; their commands, with love. Severity, as it is the moſt deſperate, ſo it is the laſt remedy that ſhould be uſed. If peace and obedience are equally the reſult of a mild, as of a ſevere government; the former ſhould undoubtedly have the preference, as it ac-tains its end with the leaſt difficulty, and conſequently is moſt agreeable to reaſon.

In perſons of figure, honour is certainly by much the moſt forcible principle of action, except religion. Nay, the law of reputation we find to be in ſome inſtances ſo powerful, as to get the better both of divine and human laws co-operating together. This is but too evident, not only in the caſe of duelling, but many-others. —— How unhappy, therefore, muſt mankind continue, as long as cuſtom can ſo far alter the nature of things, as that a man's character ſhall be impeached for not acting that which is really in itſelf both baſe and diſhoneſt ? Thus a man, who lets ſlip an opportunity with a friend's wife, or ſiſter, is reckoned a dull fellow. As a perſon, who is ſo good a Chriſtian as to forgive an injury, and is, doubtleſs, on that account, the better qualified to anſwer all the ends of civil ſociety, ſhall be hunted, as it were, out of it, as an unworthy wretch, who has not courage enough to lay aſide his humanity, and cut his neighbour's throat.

Could that *decorum*, which TULLY deſcribes, and which that ineſtimable moraliſt makes to be inſeparable from what he calls the *honeſtum* ; I ſay, could that be once eſtabliſhed, as the infallible touch-ſtone for the trying of reputations, we ſhould no longer hear paraſites extolling men in power, and crying them up to the ſkies, for ſuch inglorious qualities as a dexterous diſſimulation, and an artful manner of deceiving. Lawyers would be no longer called ingenious and clever, for underſtanding and practiſing every method of delay, and arguing cunningly, tho' fallaciouſly, on the wrong ſide of the queſtion. The chriſtian clergy would lay claim to no other reſpect, but what they might juſtly demand from the ſanctity of their lives and converſations. In ſhort, a man of virtue would be eſteemed, tho' he were in rags; and a man of quality and fortune, who was vicious and immoral, would be contemned and ſpurned at, tho' he were a peer of the firſt claſs, and could ſpend 20,000 l. per ann. We ſhould no longer ſee ſcraping old dotards, amaſſing up riches, by all manner of diſhoneſt means; arrogant in their converſation; tyrants in their own families; and always aſſuming on account of their grey hairs. The ſatyrical proverb, *Happy is that ſon, whoſe father goes to the devil*, would be ſoon forgotten. Nor would young men any longer be guided by petulant inclinations, or waſte their time and health in debauchery and riot; when by ſuch a conduct they muſt neceſſarily ſuffer in their characters, and become infamous.

Could men be once brought to think indifferently of themſelves, 'tis probable they would be more ready to entertain kind ſentiments of their neighbours; and to ſhew a due ſenſe of the relations they bear to one another, by a conſtant intercourſe of mutual good offices. I believe that inſolence and ill breeding will generally be found to ariſe from the reflection upon a ſuperiority, either of fortune, or of underſtanding; when in truth, if the richeſt, or the moſt knowing of men, conſidered, with a proper attention, their own merits, they would ſoon be informed, that their opulency is nothing but vanity, and their wiſdom but folly. I remember a pretty thought in a french book, in praiſe of which ſir William Temple ſpeaks very largely, I mean the *Plurality of Worlds*. It is there ſayed, that " All men's wiſdom depends upon the " ignorance of their neighbours." This is ſo far true, that whatever the wiſeſt man knows, in compariſon of infinite ſapience, is undoubtedly not of half that conſideration, that a drop of water is in compariſon of the vaſt ocean. The following remarkable ſtory may be ſeen in the Turkiſh Hiſtory : I ſhall give it the reader without making any reflections on it; the moral of it being too obvious, to be miſtaken. SALADIN, the great turkiſh ſultan, commanded, when he was dying, no ſolemnity to be uſed at his burial; but only his ſhirt, in the manner of an enſign, made faſt to the point of a lance, to be carried before his dead body; a plain prieſt going before, and crying thus aloud to the people : " SALADIN, conqueror " of the eaſt, of all the greatneſs and riches he had in " this life, carryeth with him, after his death, nothing " more than his ſhirt to his grave."

Mr. BAVIUS,

THE caſe of Mr. J. HENLEY, printed in your 149th Journal of November 2 under the domeſtic news of thurſday, ſurpriſed me very much. I could hardly imagine, that he would have given a declaration to the world, under his own hand, that a diſappointment in his expectations of preferment was the occaſion of his ſetting up his *Oratory*; as Mr. *Quidnunc* in his reflection has juſtly obſerved he has plainly done. I was a little inclined to think, that it was a caſe drawn up by one of your members, in Mr. HENLEY's ſtile and manner, on purpoſe to ridicule him; and I took the S. J. added after his name to ſignify, not the *S. James's Evening Poſt*, but ſome new honourary title, ſubſtituted inſtead of A. M. I met with ſeveral perſons of the ſame opinion; who agreed, that if that piece was the genuine production of the perſon whoſe name was ſubſcribed to it, he either had removed, or ought to remove his *Oratory*, from Lincoln's-inn-fields to Moor-fields.—I was confirmed in my ſuſpicions on this occaſion, by a N. B. added to the Oratory advertiſement in *Fog's Journal* of ſaturday November 4. " N. B. An advertiſement is pretended to " be Mr. HENLEY's this laſt week, which is only a long puff " of the GRUB-STREET Scribere cum daſho." This I took to be a direct denial, that the caſe printed in the preceding *Grub-ſtreet Journal* was drawn up by J. HENLEY : there being no other puff, or advertiſement, beſides relating to him, inſerted therein; and, I muſt own, I gave ſome credit to this denial. But, to my great amazement, I was ſhewed, a day or two afterwards, this very caſe, in the *S. James's Evening Poſt* of thurſday October 26, in which it ſtood the firſt of the advertiſements, word for word, as it had been reprinted in your 149th Journal. I impatiently expected your anſwer in your next; wherein I was ſtrangely diſappointed, not to find one word relating to this affair.

Tho' I am well ſatisfied, that you had good reaſon for this omiſſion the laſt week; and that neither the honour of the prelate abuſed in the firſt advertiſement, nor that of your ſociety abuſed in the ſecond, can be ſullied by any thing which Mr. ORATOR can either affirm or deny; yet I think it very proper, that ſome anſwer ſhould be returned to ſuch a flagrant double inſtance of affirmative and negative impudence. In which ſentiment, I hope, you will ſhew your concurrence, by publiſhing the following obſervations upon every part thereof.

He aſſerts that in the Oratory he " knows no fault " but one, that it is a pattern of the trueſt principles of " religion, with the moſt various and aſſiduous endeavour " to merit, in the capacity of a ſcholar and a clergyman, " that is, or ever was, in this iſland, or in the world." This, which he ſays is the only *fault*, is certainly none; and conſequently he aſſerts, that it is not only the beſt religious inſtitution *in the world*, but an inſtitution, without even the leaſt *fault* or defect at all. According to which, he has now given the world, for five or ſix years, ocular and auricular demonſtration of his *various* and *aſſiduous endeavour to merit*, as a *ſcholar*, by his buffooneries on the week-day; and as a *clergyman*, by his unintelligible theological effuſions on ſundays.

He then " deſires every man who educates a ſon to or- " ders, and him who is ſo educated, to conſider this caſe, " and to make it his own." The making *his* to refer both to *every man*, and *him*, is a figure of ſpeech uſual with our ORATOR; and an internal mark, that this introduction, and the following caſe, were drawn up by himſelf.

" I waited ſome Years ago on a certain PRELATE, with " a ſollicitation of a pulpit in town." Another inſtance of Oratorian Engliſh, a *ſollicitation of a pulpit*, inſtead of *a ſollicitation for* a prelate FOR a *pulpit*. — " ſignifying " my reſolution to cultivate and exert the talent of preach- " ing, which God had given me, in the moſt compleat " and public manner." Here are two things taken for granted, which are very much queſtioned, by the beſt preachers, and judges of preaching, in this great city, viz. Whether the ORATOR ever had a *talent of preaching*; and Whether God gave him that *talent*, which he now exerts.

" His anſwer was, That I might be of uſe; but be- " fore he could do for me, he muſt have a PLEDGE of my " attachment to the government. I was an entire ſtranger " to politics, but gave him that *pledge*." This, I believe, is the firſt time, that this gentleman ever owned himſelf an entire *ſtranger* to any art or ſcience : however, he was well enough acquainted then with practical *politics*, to give the political *pledge* required of his *attachment to the government*; and he has ſince given many proofs of his intimate acquaintance with ſpeculative *politics*.

" A pledge, demanded, given, and accepted for a con- " ſideration, is a contract; for that conſideration the " pledge itſelf is no *contract*; tho' one may be implied by " the demanding, the giving, and the accepting it. But then this *contract for the conſideration of a pulpit*,

ecclesiastical preferments in the very nature of it, could not be absolute and unconditional.

"The hinge of my interest and fortune very much "turned upon it." *Upon that consideration*, viz. the hinge of the *pulpit*, with *a sollicitation of which* he had waited upon this prelate.

"It was in the year 172½, a tender crisis, and doubt-"less he made a job of it to the government." That *year*, it seems, was a *tender crisis*; and of that *crisis* the prelate *made a job* to the government. A nonsensical and scandalous reflection upon both: insinuating, that the government was ready to incourage dirty jobs, and that a reverend prelate was ready to do them.

"When I applied for the consideration, he shifted me "off: had he any possible exception to my intellectual or "moral qualifications (tho' nothing can be more immoral, "or sooner make the world atheists, than a perfidious pre-"late) he should, before he drew me in, have told me, "that if he met with any such exception, he would not "do what I sollicited; and that he would take time to exa-"mine. This would have been fair." This nonsensical, impudent parenthesis, which intimates, that the person spoken of immediately before was a *perfidious prelate*, is one plain instance of this gentleman's *qualifications*, both *intellectual* and *moral*: to one, or both of which, it is evident, even by this account, that the prelate made an exception. This Mr. ORATOR calls *shifting* him *off*; because the prelate had not expresly told him before, *that if he met with any such exception, he would not do what he sollicited*. There was no manner of occasion for this: for had the prelate even given him an absolute unconditional promise of a pulpit, to which this gentleman does not so much as pretend to lay claim, yet even such a promise must necessarily have implied a supposition, that no discovery should be made in the mean time, in prejudice to his *intellectual or moral qualifications*: because either ignorance, or immorality, renders a man altogether unfit for a pulpit, which he must be supposed not to be at the time of giving him such a promise. As to the intimation, that the prelate *drew him in*, it is plain from what he says himself, that he would have *drawn* the Prelate into a promise of a pulpit by his *sollicitation of* one; and that the prelate *drew him* into nothing, but the giving of *a pledge of his attachment to the government*.

"He assigned no exception at all during a whole year." It was time enough to *assign the exception*, when Mr. HENLEY waited upon him to claim the pulpit — "Till I had "sacrificed my interest to him, on his own demand:" The prelate made no other *demand* on this gentleman, according to this very account, than that he should give *a pledge of his attachment to the government*: and it is very strange, that he should insinuate, that his doing of this was a sacrificing of his interest — "And it is easy to frame "exceptions, if a person be inclined to break his word." Another impudent and scandalous insinuation, that this prelate was *inclined to break his word*. In answer to which, I shall only observe, that in some cases, (of which I take this to be one,) tho' a person be never so much *inclined* to keep his word, it is not only *easy*, but necessary, *to make exceptions*. — But as I have none to the truth of what Mr. ORATOR says, concerning his own *judgment*, in relation to the *envy*, *jealousy*, and *apprehensions* of the *prelate* and *his clergy*; and concerning his own *taking of the sacrament*, in confirmation of the truth of what he either asserts, or believes; I shall only give his own concluding words, and leave them to the reflection of every reader.

"My judgment is, he and his clergy even envied me "in the pulpit, and were jealous of my advancement, "timorous that at court there might might be a patron or "a patroness of learning, and apprehensive that I might "out-strip them there. Was I on my death bed, I would "take the sacrament, that I know the former part, and "believe the latter part (without the least vanity for so "poor a triumph as excelling them would be) of this ad-"vertisement to be matter of fact." J. HENLEY.

I am your humble servant,

ECCLESIATICUS.

DOMESTIC NEWS.

C. *Courant.*	E P. *Evening Post.*
P. *Post-Boy.*	S J. *St. James's Evening Post.*
D P. *Daily Post.*	W E. *Whitehall Evening Post.*
D J. *Daily Journal.*	L E. *London Evening Post.*

THURSDAY, *Nov.* 9.

This day between twelve and one at noon the court removed from Kensington to Richmond. *L E.*

Yesterday his excellency the Spanish embassador gave a magnificent entertainment to several ministers of state, &c. *P.* — On account of the Spaniards having raised the siege of Ceuta, and routed the moorish army. *L E.*

The same day the court of directors of the East India company presented captain Jobson commander of the Okham, with the sum of 200l. as a reward for the service he did in that gallant defence that he made against Angria the pirate's grabbs, on his last voyage home from Bombay; and were likewise pleased to order three months pay to all his ship's company. *C. DP.*

Yesterday a great number of the bond creditors of the East-India company met at the fleece tavern in Cornhill, when it was moved that a committee should be appointed to treat with the court of directors; but this proposal was rejected, and it was resolved to insist upon four per cent. *D J.*

We hear from the seat of the right honourable sir Robert Walpole, in Norfolk, that four oxen were killed, and distributed to the poor of Houghton, and several neighbouring villages; and that there is the greatest plenty in housekeeping that has ever been known before. *S J.* — *Instead of* before *read* of late.

Last thursday Edward Williams, of Yestyn Colwyn in the county of Montgomery Esq; was married to the lady Charlotte Maurice, relict of Edward Maurice, of Penabont in the county of Denbigh Esq; and daughter to the marquis of Powis. *DP.*

Yesterday an express arrived in town from Lisbon, which brought certain advice, that on the 22d of Octob. his grace the duke of Bedford, after a tedious passage to Lisbon, being dangerously ill, landed at the Groin, and died in about two hours after, &c. *C.* — His grace meeting with bad weather at sea, and being exceeding ill, prevailed on the captain to make for the first port he cou'd reach; which was Corunna, where, on Oct. 23. O. S. at five in the evening his grace expired. *D J.* — At Mr. Parker's the English consul. — He was landed the beginning of October. — He was born in 1708. *D P.* ——— Yesterday morning died at his house in Great Queen-street, Thomas Done Esq; reputed worth 50,000l. *D P.* —— A few days since died Mr. Allen, alderman of Chester in the Grosvenor interest: the candidates to succeed him are Thomas Brereton Esq; mayor of Liverpool, and Mr. Nichols, an apothecary in that city; and it is believed the latter, who is in the Grosvenor interest, will carry it by about five to one. *L E.*

Letters from Penzance in Cornwall, *which came t'other day*,
That a vast quantity of pilchards has been lately taken, say;
Enough to fill twenty thousand hogsheads, *or more*;
And each hogshead is worth about half a moidore. *D P.*

FRIDAY, *Nov.* 10.

Yesterday the lords commissioners of the admiralty granted letters of mart to nine captains of ships belonging to the East-India company. *C.*

The same day Mr. Weidle, a learned foreigner, and Mr. Bacon an eminent surgeon in Spittle-fields, were elected members of the royal society. *D J.*

The inducement for erecting the Bank, was a necessary supply of money the government then wanted; and to enable them to effect it, they were incorporated with usual powers to raise money upon credit. They were obliged to divide annually their profits amongst their proprietors, so that there remained no distinct stock of money for the proper sole use of the Bank: but the directors being persons of great merit and integrity, the monied men made the Bank their repository, by which it was enabled to discount tallies, bills of exchange, notes, &c. But as to trade or merchandize it is to be supposed they were not to exercise any, having no stock for that purpose; and to make use of others money in merchandize, that might in any respect prejudice private dealers, could not be thought reasonable. And as to foreign gold or silver, it is as much a merchandize as iron, or lead, or any other commodity; but tho' the Bank may lend money upon gold and silver at the mint or coinage price, yet they are not to deal in it as merchandizes; for so long as they give the least thing above the coinage price, it cannot be supposed any will be carried to the mint. *DP.*

Yesterday the horse militia of the city of Westminster
Paraded in Lincoln's-inn-fields, and marched to *S.* James's square,
From whence they returned to *the first-mentioned place*,
Where they were view'd, *and review'd*, by the duke of Newcastle's grace. *C.*
The Daily Journal *says, (tho' some say that be lyes)*
They marched to Tothill fields, and perform'd a fine exercise.

SATURDAY, *Nov.* 11.

The convocations of Canterbury and York, which were prorogued to the 18th of last month, are farther prorogued to Jan. 9. *P.* — These convocations *seem to meet only in in order to be* PRO-ROGU'D.

By our last letters from Bath we are assured, that Samuel Robinson Esq; chamberlain of this city, is in a fair way of regaining a perfect state of health. *P.*

On thursday afternoon, there was a very numerous meeting of gentlemen, to consider whether the next session will be a proper time to apply to parliament for a repeal of the corporation and test acts; when, after long debates, they unanimously agreed to appoint a committee of twenty one gentlemen, to consider when, and in what manner it may be proper to apply to parliament for repealing or explaining the said corporation or test acts, and the following gentlemen were chosen to be the said committee.

John Holden Esq; Chairman,	Mr. John Hollister,
Joseph Jacob Esq;	Thomas Abney Esq;
Stampt Brooksbanks Esq;	Mr. James Ruck,
John Bance Esq;	Mr. Francis Wilks,
Mr. Richard Coope,	Mr. Peter Hinde,
Dr. Avery,	Mr. George Baker,
Samuel Lessingham Esq;	Mr. Matthew Howard,
Mr. Benjamin Mee,	Mr. Joseph Paice, jun.
Nathaniel Gould Esq;	Lord Barington,
Mr. William Snell,	Mr. Bradley.
Mr. Nathaniel Garland,	Eleven to be a Quorum.

The said committee are to report their opinion at the next meeting of the said Gentlemen, who are to meet again on wednesday the 29th instant. *C.* — *These honest gentlemen are, no doubt, professed enemies to the vile practice of* occasional conformity.

Yesterday a new ship was lauched at Deptford of 700 tons, for the French service, which will be rigg'd and fitted with the utmost expedition for the East-India trade, and carry'd over to France. *D P.*

Norwich, Nov. 6. The pictures of Francis Arnam Esq; our present mayor, and of Robert Marsh Esq; our late mayor, are drawing at full length. They are already judged, by all that have seen them, to be the most beautiful pieces ever done by any hand; the strict likenesses of those gentlemen (which are at least equal to their own reflections in a looking-glass) being thought not to be equalled by any one of that profession now in England, and yet not the greatest beauties in the pieces. *P.*

We hear the right-reverend the lord bishop of Winchester lately sent a hundred guineas to be distributed among the poor Saltzburgers. *L E.*

Yesterday morning early his grace the duke of Newcastle, accompanied by the right honourable the earl of Albermarle, set out for Houghton-hall in Norfolk. *WE.*

We have advice from Falmouth, that thousands in that town and neighbourhood are violently afflicted with an ague, insomuch that many die of it. *D P.*

A few days ago, died at Northampton, Mrs. Katherine Bayles, aged 102, whose father died there in 1706, aged 126. *D J.* — Yesterday died, in an advanced age, at her house in Grosvenor-street, the right honourable the countess-dowager of Strafford. *S J.*

MONDAY, *Nov.* 13.

Yesterday his excellency Horatio Walpole Esq; cofferer to his majesty's houshold, gave a great entertainment at his house at Whitehall to several foreign ministers, &c. *C. DP* —A magnificent entertainment. *P.*

We hear from Derbyshire, that at a great meeting of persons of distinction of all sorts and professions, it was proposed to petition the parliament for a regulation of the practice in the ecclesiastical courts of this kingdom, and for a suppression of the enormities by time and ill management crept into them. *D P.* —— *Never a barrel the better herring.*

TUESDAY, *Nov.* 14.

Bristol, Nov. 12. Letters from Jamaica, of Aug. 12 advise, that the market for Negroes (a great number of whom are lately arrived there) is at a stand in that island, by reason of the trade being stopped at the Havanna, and other places on the main, by the Spanish governors on account of the Deal-castle man of war's taking a Spanish register-ship, as a reprisal for the Woolball. This will prove of great detriment to some merchants of this city; the merchants at Jamaica, to whom their Negroes are consigned, not knowing which way to dispose of them. *P. D P.*

On thursday, at the mine adventurers office in Winchester-street, the following persons were chosen for the year ensuing, viz. sir Tho. Mackworth Bar. governour; Edward Harrison Esq; deputy-governour. *Directors.* Francis Boteler Esq; Mr. Richard Chauncy senior, Mr. deputy John Child, Henry Cooley Esq; Seth Grosvenor Esq; Mr. Henry Hines, Thomas Inwood Esq; William Nichols, Esq; Walter Price Esq; Andrew Robinson Esq; Mr. John Sadlar, Charles Waller Esq; *P.*

The design of the Oxford almanack for next year has given some offence to the enemies of episcopacy, as it represents the sufferings of archbishop Laud and his blessed master: from the top hangs a roll, on which is S. John's college. with a particular view of its second quadrangle, built by archbishop Laud, after the design of Inigo Jones; in three compartments are archbishop Laud at his devotions, the heavens lowering over him, and tempestuous, the mitre reversed, crosier broken, and an hydra of sectaries menacing him: [in the middle, sir Thomas White Knt. lord mayor of London, during Wyat's rebellion, *Temp. Reg. Mariæ*, with the city regalia near him; a roll of his benefactions to the several corporations of this kingdom, with the characters of charity and prudence near him:] the other, a view of the scaffold before the banqueting house, Whitehall, K. Charles led by the Archbishop. [*Præcursor Caroli*] both in a smiling posture, towards the place of his sufferings. *DP.*

On tuesday died at C…

Wake, DD. aged 68 years: he was prebendary of that church, and also of Lincoln, and rector of Wethamstead in Hertfordshire. *DP. DJ.* — By the last letters from Ireland we hear that sir Alexander Cairnes Bart. died there a few days ago. His honour and estate descended to his brother Henry Cairnes Esq; formerly a merchant of this city. C. — An estate of 1200 l. per ann. *DJ.*

The right reverend the lord bishop of Durham has been pleased to appoint the reverend Dr. Sharp, archdeacon of Northumberland, to be one of the prebendaries of Durham in the room of the reverend Mr. Sayer, who has resigned. *LE.*

WEDNESDAY, *Nov.* 15.

Her majesty has been pleased to nominate Miss Paget, daughter to Col. Paget, to be one of her maids of honour in the room of Miss Mordaunt. — On friday their majesties will remove from Richmond to S. James's for the winter season. *P.* — We hear they will remove on saturday sevennight. *D P.*

On monday died of the gout in the stomach, at his seat at Dewshall near Ongar in Essex, Cataline Thorogood Esq; formerly chief factor to the Southsea company. *C.* — At Hews-hall. *DP. DJ.* *Some read* Deuce.

From the PEGASUS *in Grub-street.*

To Mr. BAVIUS.

Renowned Sir,

AS a brother Grubean, I hope you will favour me with a publication in your Journal of the following *Proposals*, and use your interest therein for the advantage of,

Great Sir, your profound admirer,

PIRATICUS.

Proposals for reprinting, by subscription, a book never yet published, containing, *A geographical and historical account of* TERRA INCOGNITA.

Vol. I. An exact description of the extent of their known dominions; with curious cuts and maps of their most noted cities, harbours, and fortifications.

Vol II. Their origine, rise, and continued history, from SNATCHBAC, their first king, nine years before *Adam*, to MORDAVO the *great*, five years hence; with the nature and complexion of the inhabitants, their customs, exercises, religion, marriages, and funeral ceremonies.

Vol. III. The writings of their most celebrated authors, before the use of letters or hieroglyphics.

Vol. IV. Their wars with the *Antipodes*, and the flight of king SOLOCHORUS, through the centre, and miraculous retreat to the remotest part of the *Atmosphere*.

Written originally in Hottentot Hebrew, by JACOBOS ANNIHILATOS; and translated by PETER QUIBUS, who is deaf, dumb, and blind.

Proposals. Imprimis, This book will be printed on a royal paper, in folio, on a new elzivir letter.

2dly. Every subscriber to pay four thousand pounds before he enters his name.

3dly. As an encouragement to those who pay in their money before-hand, they shall pay none afterwards.

4thly. As this work will contain 4000 sheets, one is to be delivered to every subscriber (dead or living) once a year, so that the four volumes will be compleated 732 years after the general conflagration.

Subscriptions are taken in at JONATHAN WILD's pamphlet shop, the corner of DIVES oven in hell; the lawyer's coffee-house next door to heaven on earth; and the bush tavern in the moon. And if any person think that his subscription-money is in danger of being melted down by fire in any of the former places, he may, for his security, pay it in, near the Corner of Water-lane Fleet-street.

Verses occasioned by the LAUREAT's last Ode.

I.

LET *there be light*, th' Almighty said:
  A blazing glory shines;
And o'er the universe was spread,
  Except on C——R's lines.

II.

Unaided by this grant, we find
  Our bard: and thence 'tis plain,
Chaos and darkness were assign'd
  To sleep in C———Y's brain.

III.

One spark of light receiv'd had he,
  We might indeed be sure,
The dullest laureat ne'er could be
  So palpably obscure.

IV.

Ye critics, then blame not the wight,
  Nor let ill words be given;
Since he has lent you all the light
  He e'er receiv'd from heaven.

We desire, that the advertisements design'd for this paper, may be sent before twelve of the clock on tuesdays, otherwise they cannot be inserted.

ADVERTISEMENTS.

To be LETT,

VERY good, dry, and kind Wine Vaults, under the King's-Head Tavern in Wood-Street. Inquire of Mr. Charles Kemp, at the said House.

N. B. You may enter immediately.

This Day is published,

Neatly printed in Twelves,

THE fourth Edition of the Ladies Library, in three Volumes: Published by Sir Richard Steele. And,

The third Edition of the History and Adventures of Gil Blas, of Santillane, in three Volumes.

Both printed for J. Tonson in the Strand.

This Day is published,

A New, Beautiful, and Correct Edition, of

THOMÆ FIENI, Belgij & Bavariæ Ducum Medici Cubicularij, & in Academia Lovaniensi Medicinæ Professoris primarij, Libri Chirurgici Duodecim, de Præcipuis Artis Chirurgicæ Controversiis, viz.

I. De Trepano, sive apertione cranij. II. De Depositione cataractæ. III. De Depositione ungulæ. IV. De Laryngotomia, sive sectione asperæ arteriæ. V. De Paracentesi thoracis. VI. De Paracentesi abdominis. VII. De Arteriotomia, sive sectione arteriæ. VIII. De Hysterotomatocia, sive sectione fœtûs ex utero viventis matris. IX. De sectione calculi. X. De sectione herniæ XI. De amputatione membrorum externorum. XII. De nasi amputati ex carne brachii restitutione.

Opera Posthuma Hermanni Conringij cura edita. Editio Secunda.

Impensis C. DAVIS, in vico vulgo dicto Pater-Noster-Row.

Where may be had, lately published.

I. Glandorpij Opera Omnia Medico Chirurgica, in 4to. II. Jo. Caij Britanni de Canibus Britannicis, Historia Stirpium de Libris Propriis & de Pronuntiatione Gr. Linguæ, 8vo. III. Dr. Lobb's Treatise of the Small-Pox. In two Parts. IV. The compleat City and Country Cook: Or, The Accomplished Housewife, with 50 Copper Plates. By Charles Carter, late Cook to the Duke of Argyll, the Earl of Fontefract, and the lord Cornwallis, 8vo. V. Houghton's Collections for the Improvement of Husbandry and Trade, 4 Vols. 8vo. VI. Dr. Harris's History of Kent, illustrated with above 40 Copper Plates, Folio. VII. Historical and Critical Remarks on the History of Charles XII. King of Sweden, by Mr. De la Motraye.

This Day is published,

(*Price bound 2 s. 6 d. stitched 2 s.*)

(*Adorned with eight excellent Copper Plates, curiously engraved.*)

Translated from the ITALIAN of the celebrated MARINI,
(The Original having passed Ten Editions,)

THE DESPERADOES. An Heroic History. Containing a Series of the most surprizing Adventures of the Princes Formidaur and Florian; the former being in love with Zelinda, whom he takes to be his own Sister; and the latter having married Fidalme, whom he supposes to be his Father's Daughter by a second Wife, and afterwards kills in Disguise in single Combat. With a Relation of the various amazing Accidents and Misfortunes which happened thereon, until the Whole concludes with making them all happy, by a most extraordinary and uncommon Revolution. In Four Books.

Printed by W. R. and sold by T. Astley, at the Rose in St. Paul's Church-Yard; J. Isted, at the Golden-Ball, near Chancery-Lane End; T. Worrall, at the Judge's Head, over-against St. Dunstan's Church, and J. Janeway, at the Golden-Ball, near Water-Lane, Fleet-Street; also by J. Jolliff, in St. James's-Street.

On Saturday will be published No. I. Price 6 d. (To be continued once a Fortnight.)

Dr. COLBBTH's Legacy, or the Family Physician; containing an Account of all the Diseases incident to the human Body; alphabetically digested. With a plain and rational Discussion both of their Causes and their Cures. The Receipts for each Distemper being put into English, and the Method in which the Sick are to be treated carefully explained.

This Day is published,

(With a Specimen of writing the future Proceedings in Law)

THE CLERK's ENGLISH TUTOR: Shewing the Practice of the Courts of King's-Bench and Common-Pleas, as they are now settled, pursuant to the several late Acts of Parliament, and the respective Rules of both the Courts made consonant thereto: With great Variety of curious English Precedents, (never before printed in any Language) drawn by the most eminent Counsel of the present Age, and done into English, conformable to the Statute of 4 Geo. 2. c. 26. that all Proceedings in the Courts of Justice shall be in the English Language; together with such Writs or Process, as well mesne and judicial, as are generally used in every Day's Practice. By an Attorney at Law.

Printed for W. Meadows, at the Angel in Cornhill.

Where may be had,

Cases and Resolutions of Cases adjudged in the Court of King's-Bench, concerning Settlements and Removals from the first Year of King George I. to the present Reign, most of them adjudged in the Time when Lord Parker sate Chief Justice there. The Third Edition, with Additions, of a Collection of the like Cases adjudged when Sir John Holt Knt. was Chief Justice. To which is added, An Abstract of the Statutes concerning Provision for the Poor.

Last Saturday was published,

No. XV. (*containing five Sheets, at the Price of 6 d.*) *of*

THE HISTORY of ENGLAND. By M. RAPIN DE THOYRAS. Translated by N. TINDAL, M. A. Vicar of Great Waltham in Essex. The Second Edition, with the following Improvements:

1. The Translation is thoroughly revised and corrected.

2. The many Errors and Mistakes of the Original are carefully rectified.

3. Several hundred of Marginal References, accidentally omitted by the Author, are supply'd.

4. Additional Notes throughout, with Cuts, Maps and Genealogical Tables, on Copper Plates.

Printed for JAMES, JOHN, and PAUL KNAPTON, remov'd from St. Paul's Church-yard, to the Crown in Ludgate-street, near the West End of St. Paul's.

Where may be had, The preceding Numbers.

N.B. The Whole will be comprised in Two Volumes in Folio, containing 400 Sheets, at the Price of Two Guineas in Sheets, including Copper Plates. Five Sheets of the Work will be publish'd every Saturday, till the Whole is compleated, at the Price of 6 d. and the said Sheets will be deliver'd every Week at the Houses of Gentlemen who are pleased to order them; and such as take the Weekly Numbers are reckoned as Subscribers; that is, shall pay but Two Guineas, though the Number of Sheets should exceed 400.

Proposals at large, with a Specimen, may be had Gratis.

This Day is Published,

THINGS Divine and Supernatural, conceived by Analogy with Things Natural and Human. By the Author of the Procedure Extent, and Limits of Human Understanding.

Printed for William Innys and Richard Manby at the West End of St. Paul's.

Where may be had,

1. The Procedure, Extent, and Limits of Human Understanding. The Second Edition, 8vo.

2. Mr. Law's Practical Treatise on Christian Perfection. The Second Edition, 8vo.

3. ——— Serious Call to a Devout and Holy Life, 8vo.

4. ——— Case of Reason, in Answer to Christianity as old as the Creation, 8vo.

5. An Enquiry into the Evidence of the Christian Religion. The Second Edition, 8vo.

6. Reflections on Reason: The Third Edition, corrected and enlarged, 8vo.

This Day is published,

The POLITICAL STATE *of GREAT BRITAIN.*

For the Month of October, 1732. Containing, in Particular,

I. CONclusion of the Pamphlet lately burnt at Paris, relating to the Power of their Parliaments. II. A Dissertation on Parliaments, Containing, 1. Account given by Tacitus of the Parliaments and Assemblies among the ancient Germans. 2. This German Custom carried into Gaul by the Franks. 3. Power of the first French Kings. 4. Account of the French Assemblies in Campo Martio. 5. Account of the French Parliaments under Charlemain, and the Kings of the second Race. 6. Alterations made afterwards in the Constitution of France. 7. Account of the Assemblies of the Three Estates of France, and of the Difference between them and the Parliament of Paris. 8. Account of what in France is called a Bed of Justice. 9. Origin of the other Parliaments in France. 10. Account of the first Assemblies among us, called Witenagemotes. 11. Parallel between French and English Parliaments. 12. Account of the present State of the Parliament of Paris. III. Disputes occasioned by the late Treaty between Prussia and Orange. IV. A Trick of Priestcraft in Holland. V. Account of the late Proceedings in the Parliament of Paris. VI. Journal of the Proceedings and Debates of last Session of Parliament continued. VII Marriages, &c. VIII. Bill of Mortality. IX. Imports and Exports.

Printed for T. Warner, at the Black-Boy in Pater-Noster-Row. Pr. 1 s. 6 d.

Where may be had,

The POLITICAL STATES for the Months of June, July, August and September, in which are contained the Debates in the last Sessions of Parliament; as also all the former Numbers.

N. B. No other Monthly Account has the Debates in Parliament.

Just published,

A New View and Observations on the antient and present State of London and Westminster; shewing the Foundation, Walls, Gates, Towers, Bridges, Churches, Rivers, Wards, Palaces, Halls, Companies, Inns of Court and Chancery, Hospitals, Schools, Government, Charters, Courts, and Privileges thereof. Also Historical Remarks thereon. With an Account of the most remarkable Accidents, as to Wars, Fires, Plagues, and other Occurrences, which have happened therein for above 1400 Years past, brought down to the present Time. Illustrated with Cuts of the most considerable Matters, with the Arms of the sixty six Companies of London, and the Time of their Incorporation.

By ROBERT BURTON,

Author of the History of the Wars of England. Continued by an able Hand.

Printed for Jer. Batley, at the Dove in Pater-Noster-Row.

Just publisched,

CHristus Sacræ Scripturæ Nucleus : Or CHRIST the Sum and Substance of all the Holy Scriptures in the Old and New Testament. By HERMANNUS FRANCK, D.D. With some Account of the Author's LIFE. Sold by J. Downing in Bartholomew Close.

Where may likewise be had,

An Essay on the Merchandise of Slaves and Souls of Men. With an Application thereof to the Church of Rome. By a Gentleman.

Mr. Hudleston's Divine Truths vindicated in the Church of England.

———— Irresistible Evidence against Popery.

Sir Richard Blackmore's Essay on Divine Eloquence.

An Account of several Work-houses, for Maintaining and Employing the POOR. With their great Usefulness to the Publick.

P R O P O S A L S
For Printing by SUBSCRIPTION,

THE HISTORY of the Grand Controversy between the Secular and Regular Clergy of the Church of Rome, from the Year 1625 to 1634, concerning the Usurpation of RICHARD SMITH, Titular Bishop of Chalcedon, who pretended to be sole Ordinary Bishop of all England and Scotland. Wrote in Latin by the President of the English Benedictine Monks, RUDISINDUS BARLO, and faithfully done into English from the Original, for the Entertainment of the Curious, especially Divines and Lawyers, both Ecclesiastick and Civil, of what Religion soever.

With the Remonstrances of the Roman Catholick Laity made to the said Bishop, and also to his Excellency Carolo Coloma, Embassador Extraordinary of his most Catholick Majesty, and to the Marquis Fontany, Embassador of the most Christian King, &c. taken also from the Latin Originals: All which Treatises have been hitherto supprest by the Papists, for Political Reasons given therein.

As also the famous Bull of Pope URBAN VIII. called PLANTATA, necessary for the right Understanding of the Whole, wich was never before any where printed.

To which will be added,

A LETTER concerning the Disputes that have happen'd among the Benedictine Monks since the Year 1700. to this present Time: Shewing how even they themselves have varied from their original Principles. By one who was a Member of that Body, and concerned therein.

By *JOHN WILLIAMS.*

PROPOSALS may be had of (and SUBSCRIPTIONS taken in for the Author by) W. Meadows, at the Angel in Cornhill; T. Astley, at the Rose, and S. Austen, at the Angel and Bible in St. Paul's Church-Yard; C. Davis in Pater-noster Row; T. Woodward, at the Half-Moon, L. Gilliver, at Homer's Head, and J. Stephens, at the Hand and Star between the Two Temple-Gates; B. Motte, at the Middle-Temple-Gate; T. Worral, at Judge Coke's Head; H. Walthoe, next Door to the Rainbow Coffee-House; W. Reason, in Flower-de-Luce-Court; J. Isted, at the Golden-Ball, near Chancery-Lane, Fleet-Street; F. Gyles, over-against Gray's-Inn-Gate, Holborn; O. Payne, in Round-Court; and T. Game, at the Bible, by the New Church, in the Strand; T. Green, Charing-Cross; J. Jackson, in Pallmall; J. Jolliffe, at the Bible, in St. James's-Street; J. Brindley, at the King's Arms, and W. Shropshire, opposite to the Duke of Grafton's, New Bond-Street; and J. Stagg, Westminster-Hall, Booksellers: J. Huggonson, in Bartholomew-Close, and T. Gover, by Fleet-Ditch, Black-Fryers, Printers.

The INCOMPARABLE POWDER for cleansing the TEETH.

Has withstood, by its most excellent and known Virtues, the Attempts of many repeated Counterfeits; some imitating it by the Name of Powder, others under several other Names; therefore pray take Notice, that the only true, effectual, and Original Powder, is sold no where else, but as mentioned below: It is sent for in large Quantities to the Plantations beyond the Seas, to whom good Allowance is given; and is as effectual in the East or West Indies as at London.

WHich has given so great Satisfaction to most of the Nobility and Gentry in England for above these thirty Years that it hath been published, and vast Quantities of the same still continue to be sold.

It is sold only at Mr. Allcroft's Toyshop at the Blue-coat Boy, against the Royal-Exchange in Cornhill; and at Mrs. Markham's Toyshop, the Seven Stars under St. Dunstan's Church in Fleet-street, and no where else in London; but in the Country, at Mr. Rogers's a Linnen-draper in Warwick, at 1 s. each Box.

At once using it makes the Teeth as white as Ivory, tho' never so black or yellow, and effectually preserves them from rotting or decaying, continuing them sound to exceeding old Age. It wonderfully cures the Scurvy in the Gums, prevents Rheum or Defluction, kills Worms at the Roots of the Teeth, and thereby hinders the Tooth-ach. It admirably fastens loose Teeth, being a neat cleanly Medicine, of a pleasant and grateful Scent, and in Virtue far exceeds any Thing ever yet found out for those Purposes.

All the Nobility, Gentry, &c. who send to Mrs. Markham's for the Powder for Teeth, are desired to give strict Orders, not to mistake the Shop (Markham at length is under the Seven Stars) because most of the Toymen in her Neighbourhood, seeing Multitudes go to her shop for it, have trumpt up Counterfeits, and sell their Stuff in Imitation of our known and approved Powder, in Prejudice to the Publick, &c.

+†+ At the same Place is sold the highly esteemed Lip-Salve, which in two or three Hours Time heals them, though never so rough or chopt; prevents the Skin from peeling, and makes them delicately fair and smooth, giving them a becoming rubicund Colour; the Fragrancy of its Odour also renders the Breath fine and sweet; and it may be eaten for its safety. Price 1 s.

On Thursday Oct. 2. publisched,

(Beautifully printed on a fine Paper,)

The LONDON MAGAZINE: Or, GENTLEMAN's *Monthly Intelligencer.*

NUMB. VII For OCTOBER, 1732.

To be continued (Price Six-Pence each Month)

Containing greater Variety, and more in Quantity, than any Monthly Book extant.

I. A VIEW of the WEEKLY ESSAYS, viz. Humours of Dress in the Ladies; Mischiefs of Flattery; Dedications, Pedigrees, Printer's Devils, Spectres and Apparitions; Fortune-Tellers; Journey on the Tops of Trees, Sagacity of Apes; Advantage of Coffee-Houses; Animadversions on Dr. Bentley's Milton; farther Censure of Mr. Osborne; Ambition; Love of Fame; Ecclesiastical Tyranny; Death of a powerful Instructor; Vindication of Clarke, Locke, and Woolaston; Usefulness of History, particularly Rapin's.

II. POLLITICAL SUBJECTS, viz. Debates in Parliament about Vacancies in the Army; Sugar Colonies, Fees, Chelsea Hospital; Sir Thomas Lombe's Petition, and Account of his Invention; Government compared to a Pyramid; Nature and End of it, and how far it has to do with Religion; National Church, and the British Constitution; the Happiness of it, and how to preserve it; Parliament of Paris, and Speech of the Abbé Pucelle; Dialogue between Sir G. Worthy and Mr. Freeman, between Sir Harry Worthy and Mr. D'Anvers; Account of Machiavel, and Fog a Machiavelian; Vindication of Pericles; Articles of Impeachment, &c. Governors of Colonies; De Wit, and the Prince of Orange; Pragmatic Sanction; Trade, Fleet, Companies, Laws, Slavery, Political Scandal, Gibraltar, Houses of Austria, and Bourbon, &c.

III. POETRY: On the Death of Mr. Wilks; Death of a beloved Wife; Liberty of the Press; Praise of Innocence; Ode on the King's Birth-Day; Curate's Letter versify'd.

IV. DOMESTICK OCCURRENCES: Promotions Ecclesiastical, Civil, and Military; Marriages and Births; Deaths, &c.

V. FOREIGN AFFAIRS.

VI. Price of Goods, Grain, Stocks; Monthly Bill of Mortality.

VII. A Table of Contents.

To which is added, A Catalogue of Books and Pamphlets, with their Prices, published by the Proprietors of the Monthly Chronicle, now discontinued.

MULTUM IN PARVO.

Printed for J. Wilford, behind the Chapter-House near S. Paul's; T. Cox, in Cornhill; J. Clarke, in Duck-lane, and T. Astley, in S. Paul's Church-Yard.

Where may be had the former Numbers.

This Day is publisched,

G*Eodesia Catenea*: Or, SURVEYING by the CHAIN only. (A Method entirely new.) Shewing how to Measure, Plot, and Divide any Parcel of LAND, without any other INSTRUMENT but the CHAIN: With Directions for Mapping and finding the Content of it; and TABLES ready calculated for the more expeditious Performance thereof; as also for measuring TIMBER, &c.

By HENRY WILSON,

Author of several Mathematical Treatises.

Quo facilius eo utilius.

Printed for J. Wilford, behind the Chapter-House in St. Paul's Church-yard. Price 2 s.

This Day is publish'd,

In a neat Pocket Volume, the Second Edition of

THE BOOK of COMMON-PRAYER, with the Epistles and Gospels at large; the same Letter of the large Church Bible printed at Oxford, being the same Letter with these three Words:

Let us pray.

Printed for R. Ware, at the Bible and Sun in Amen-Corner, near Pater-Noster-Row. Price 8 s.

Also may be had, lately published, at the same Place.

1. A Treatise of Architecture, with Remarks and Observations, by that excellent Master thereof, Sebastian le Clerc, Knight of the Empire, Designer and Engraver to the Cabinet of the late French King, and Member of the Academy of Arts and Sciences, necessary to young People who would apply to that noble Art. Engraved in 200 Copper Plates, by John Sturt. Translated by Mr. Chambers. Price 10 s. 6 d.

2. The large House-Bibles, Folio, with six Maps of sacred Geography, and a brief Concordance for the more easy finding out of the Places therein contained. By J. Downame, B. D.

Bound in Calf Leather	1 l. 8 s. per Book.
And with Mr. Sturt's Cuts at	2 l. 5 s. ditto.
On a fine Paper with Cuts	3 l. 3 s. ditto.

3. A Description of 300 Animals, viz. Beasts, Birds, Fishes, Serpents, and Insects. With a particular Account of the Whale Fishery. Extracted out of the best Authors, and adapted to the Use of all Capacities, especially to allure Children to read. Illustrated with Copper Plates, whereon is curiously engraven every Beast, Bird, Fish, Serpent, and Insect described in the whole Book. Price 2 s. 6 d.

4. TRADESMAN's GUIDE. Containing a List of all the Stage Coaches and Carriers; with an Account of all the Fairs and Market Towns in England, Price 1 s.

November 2. was publisched, (Price 6d.)

(Neatly printed on fine Paper.)

The GENTLEMAN's MAGAZINE: Or, MONTHLY INTELLIGENCER.

NUMBER XXII. for OCTOBER, 1732.

To be continued Monthly, Price 6d. each, being a clear and compendious View of all our Public Papers,

CONTAINING,

(More in Quantity, and greater Variety than any Book of the Kind and Price)

I. VIews of the WEEKLY ESSAYS, viz. Of Apparitions; Coffee-Houses; Fortune-telling; Dr. B----y; Ambition; Dress; Flattery; Virtue and Nobility; Printers Devils, their Original and Business; Dr. Clarke, Mr. Locke, and Mr. Wolaston, censured as Atheists and Deists, and vindicated by the Hyp-Doctor.

II. POLITICAL POINTS, viz. Debates in Parliament; on Chelsea Hospital; Charitable Corporation; Pension-Bill; Highland Roads and Forces; Salt Duty; Land Taxes; Pericles vindicated; Secret-Service Money; Effects of a general Excise; Proposal for paying the National Debts; Ruth reproved; Governors for Colonies; Abbe Pucelle's Speech to the Parliament of Paris; the British Constitution; Advantage of Commerce; Reformation of the Laws.

III. POETRY. Anna & Carolina; on his Majesty's Birth-Day; a Taylor's Will; the Expulsion, Curate's Answer; Mock-Lover; Liberty of the Press; an Epistle to N. Paylor Monkton Esq; &c.

IV. DOMESTIC OCCURRENCES: Births, Deaths, Marriages, Promotions, &c.

V. Account of Georgia; Names of the Trustees, and their Places of Abode.

VI. Prices of Goods, Grain, Stocks, in London; Monthly Bill of Mortality.

VII. Foreign Affairs.

VIII. Register of Books.

IX. A Table of Contents.

By *SYLVANUS URBAN* Gent.

London: Printed, and sold at St. John's-Gate, by F. Jefferies in Ludgate-Street; Mrs. Nutt, Mrs. Charlton, Mrs. Cook, at the Royal-Exchange; Mr. Batley, in Pater-Noster-Row; Mr. Midwinter, in St. Paul's Church-Yard; A. Chapman, in Pall-Mall; Mrs. Dodd, without Temple-Bar; Mr. Critchley, at Charing-Cross; Mr. Stagg and Mr. King, in Westminster-Hall; Mr. Williamson, in Holborn; S. Harding, in St. Martin's-Lane; and most Booksellers in Town and Country.

Where may be had, All the former Numbers.

Also a List of Parliament, with blank Pages, more correct and compleat than any other.

The long experienced Chymical Liquor, *to be used externally, and without taking any Thing in at the Mouth, for the Cure of all* Old Gleets, Seminal Weaknesses, *&c.*

IN Consideration of the many PERSONS that have undergone tedious, expensive, and long Courses of Physick, without Success, for the Cure of old Gleets, Seminal Weaknesses of the Vessels from Self-Pollution, &c.

The Author hereof, after a long and laborious Search for an easy and safe Cure, for the several difficult Cases above-mentioned, hath found out an infallible Remedy (being a Chymical Liquor) that, without taking any Thing in at the Mouth, or the least Difficulty or Uneasiness to the Patient, will safely and speedily cure the most severe Gleets, though of many Years standing, in a few Days, as perfectly, as if no such Thing had ever been. Also,

All Seminal Weaknesses of the Vessels, whether from the Secret Disease, Self-Pollution, or inordinate Coition, or from Strains, Blows, Wrenches, Falls, &c. as has been happily experienced in great Numbers of Persons, both Old and Young, in private Practice, without its once failing, in a small Time, and for a small Charge; therefore is this unparalleled Medicine made publick, and sold but for 7 s. the Bottle by the Author's Appointment, only by Mr. Priest, at his House, the Sign of the Tea Canister, in Cock-Lane, near Pye-Corner, West-Smithfield; and is in many Cases more than enough for a perfect Cure.

An Infallible Remedy *for* Broken-winded HORSES, *(and for the present Cold, and great Disorder amongst Horses it is the only quick and sure Remedy extant.)*

WHICH has been publish'd and sold many Years before any Counterfeits in other Forms appeared; and highly commended from one Friend to another: The vast Quantities that have been sold, do also verify the Truth of its Efficacy and Virtues, which most perfectly cures them, after many Things premised have been ineffectual, to a Wonder, in a small Time, without Confinement; by attenuating and opening the Glebules of the Lungs dried up, and all the Passages obstructed by Humours dripping thereon, occasioned by hard Ridings, Colds, &c. It causes presently a free Perspiration, renewing its Force, Vigour, and Length again, as well as ever.

It immediately cures those Horses only a little touched in their Wind, as also continued Coughs, Colds, Wheesing, &c. being excellent in preventing many other Distempers incident unto them, by maintaining, preserving, and continuing a good Breath.

And in a Word, by this very Medicine alone, many Horses have been made so perfectly sound, that they have been sold and valued at 10 or 12 l. which by being broken-winded, could not before be sold for 3 or 4 l. Is sold at Mr. Sandwell's Toyshop at the Griffin, the Corner of Buckler's-Bury in the Poultry, at 4 s. 6 d. the Quart Bottle, with Directions for taking it.

LONDON: Printed for, and Sold by J. ROBERTS, near the *Oxford-Arms* in *Warwick-Lane*; where Letters and Advertisements are taken in; as also by Capt. GULLIVER, near the *Temple*; by P. SANDERS, *in Crown-Court*, *Butcher-Row*, without *Temple-Bar*; and at the *Rainbow Coffee-House* in *Cornhill*. [Price Twopence.]

The Grub-ſtreet Journal.

NUMB. 152.

Thurſday, *NOVEMBER* 23. 1732.

IN our 144th *Journal*, we gave the learned world an account of a Treatiſe in manuſcript, intitled, *The ſtate of the nation*, written by Mr. JOHN GABRIEL; of which we at the ſame time publiſhed the *Preface*, called by the author, A POSTCRIPT *by way of Prolegomena*. The good reception which this met with (the never-failing pretence for the publiſhing of ſecond parts) now occaſions the publication of that which immediately follows the *Poſtſcript*, and which may properly be called an *Introduction* to the Treatiſe.

It being my deſign to proceed in the moſt intelligible and methodical manner, I think it proper to premiſe ſome definitions, axioms, and poſtulata. And this there is the greater occaſion to do, becauſe Politics, as handled by the profeſſors of this age, is become the moſt obſcure ſcience, or, according to Mr. CHAMBERS, a moſt abſtruſe art.

1. OF MAJESTY. By *majeſty* I mean the ſupreme power in the hands of one perſon; whoſe commands, if not contrary to the laws of God, whoſe vice-gerent he or ſhe is, or to the laws of the land, authoriſed by the divine law, we are obliged to obey. If the poſſeſſives *his* or *her* be added, the ſingle perſon inveſted with that ſupreme power is underſtood. But if the plural *their* be prefixed to *majeſty*, it ſignifies the majeſty of the people: who as they are the original, ſo they are the dernier reſort of power, to which *his* or *her majeſty* is accountable, in caſe they act contrary to the original contract between them and the people. Theſe notions were firſt advanced by a ſet of noble patriots, about an hundred years ago, and have prevailed by turns, more or leſs, ever ſince. In ſo much, that it has been the current doctrine, that the king is one of the three eſtates of the realm; tho' our ancient laws expreſſly mention the king and the three eſtates of the realm. But one of thoſe eſtates having graſped at too much power, and domineered over the people by prieſt-craft, it has gradually been, as it were, dropped, and now makes little or no figure in our preſent conſtitution. King, lords, and *commons*, are generally looked upon as the three eſtates of the realm, with little or no regard to the diſtinction of lords ſpiritual and temporal, the former of whom are temporal, as well as ſpiritual.

2. A PRIME MINISTER. He is a perſon, who in the name, and by the authority of the ſupreme power, manages all affairs of ſtate, both at home and abroad, diſpoſes of all preferments, preſides over the receipt and diſburſement of all public money; and, in ſhort, has all the eſſential power of a monarch, without the pomp and the name. Officers of this denomination, who were not ſo much known among the antients, as the moderns, like their nominal maſters, are of two ſorts, good and bad. Both which, like them, are generally extolled to the skies by great parties of men, whilſt they continue in power; and as univerſally exclaimed againſt, when they are out of it. So that if we judge of either prince, or miniſter, by the encomiums given of them by their cotemporary courtiers, we can hardly imagine that there ever was a bad one; and if we give credit to the accounts given after their death, we muſt think, that the number of the good is very ſmall.— The rapines and violences committed by prime miniſters in foreign countries, have given occaſion to many fabulous accounts of the origine of this kind of officers. Some ſay the firſt was begotten by the dog CERBERUS upon ALECTO, one of the Furies, and nurſed up in a ſeraglio of vices; thence ſent into the deſarts of Africa, to learn cunning, cruelty, and rapine, amongſt ſerpents, ſavages, and monſters; from whence he ſwam over into Europe, and became the father of a numerous progeny. Others are of opinion, that he roſe from the blood of the giants, in the ſame manner as the Pythian monſter did. Others affirm, that he ſprung from the head of Ambition, as PALLAS and MARS from the heads of JOVE and JUNO. But the former allegorical pedigree is not ſo natural as the latter. For it is highly probable, that PALLAS, or Wiſdom, ſhould proceed from the head of a God; and nothing is more natural to ſuppoſe, than that a furious female's brain ſhould conceive, and bring forth MARS, or miſchief, war, and blood-ſhed. However, thoſe numerous calamities which have proceeded from the private aims of bad miniſters, may well juſtify the opinion, that the firſt of this ſet of men derived his original from the moſt deſtructive of vices. — There are ſome who aſſert, that they are the genuine off-ſpring of LYCAON, who was turned into a wolf; and that they once infeſted this iſland, but by the care of good king EDGAR, were almoſt totally deſtroyed. But a ſtream of lupine blood, which has flowed now and then in the veins of ſome great miniſters in later centuries, has evidently ſhewed, that the whole race was not quite extinguiſhed in thoſe early times. — Some naturaliſts are of opinion, that the head of the family was firſt brought into the world, and the race ſtill continued and ſupported by the weakneſs or indolence of monarchs; as noxious weeds grow up through the inadvertency or ſluggiſhneſs of the husband-man. —There are about three hundred and fifty different opinions more: but all having ſomething in them like what has been already mentioned, I ſhall not trouble the reader with any of them.

3. PATRIOTS. This name properly denotes thoſe worthy perſons, who prefer the public good to their own private intereſt, and boldly oppoſe all ſuch meaſures as tend to ſubvert, weaken, or diſhonour their country, tho' at the hazard of their fortunes, and even of their lives. There is another ſet of men, who aſſume the ſame title, and talk the ſame language, but either through the prejudices of education, and a furious zeal for what they really think right, or elſe converted by the poſſeſſion or expectation of ſome poſt of honour or advantage, act in direct oppoſition to the true patriots. Such converts, by publick good, mean nothing but their own private intereſt; and by their country's ſafety and honour, the honour and ſafety of the miniſter who pays them. The loweſt and worſt ſort of theſe converts are penſioners, a hungry and ravenous kind of animals, never ſatisfied with their dayly allowance; but always gaping for more. Theſe ſtate quacks, like all others, live by the diſeaſes and death of their fellow-ſubjects; and their whole life is exactly agreeable to their birth; for, like the vipers, which are ſometimes preſcribed to their conſumptive patients, they firſt roſe in o light by eating through the entrails of their mother.

EXPERIMENTS *to illuſtrate the preceding* DEFINITIONS.

EXPERIMENT I. I took oyl of vitriol two ounces, and mixed it with four grains of ſpirits drawn from the moſt voracious animals, ſuch as vulturs, ſharks, and crocodiles: to which I added one grain of *Cancerotlius*, extracted from the name, words, and breath of a Penſioner. I then took ſome *Elixir boni publici*, and tried to mix it with the former compoſition; but after ſeveral repeated attempts, found it to be impoſſible. By accident, I let fall a drop of the *Cancerotieus* upon the copper plate on which *Magna Charta* is engraving, and it immediately eat a hole quite through.

EXPERIMENT II. I took vectigalian ſyrup, with a decoction of *oleum repetundarum*, or oyl of bribery and corruption, and ſhook them together two or three times. Being thus mixed, they formed one body ſo very ſimple, that it was not in the power of chemiſtry to ſeparate them. This ſhews the ſympathy there is between Penſions and Taxes; one can no more ſubſiſt without the other, than a lion without a jack-call, or a mountebank without a merry Andrew.

Here end the DEFINITIONS.

AXIOMS.

When PHILIP king of Macedon, intent upon univerſal monarchy, inquired of APOLLO by what means he might moſt eaſily attain his end, he received this anſwer;

To fight with arms of gold's the ſureſt way,
To riſe in time to univerſal ſway.

The ſucceſs confirmed the truth of the oracle: the Greeks, unable to reſiſt his powerful arms, opened their gates, and PHILIP ſoon ſaw himſelf maſter of all Greece. — Hence we may juſtly wonder, that any miniſters, in any age or country, ſhould fall under the public odium for making war or peace with golden arms. This is ſo far from being any objection to their conduct, that it is the greateſt recommendation of it: and proves the ill judgment, and impotent malice of the objectors. What! would they pretend to be wiſer than APOLLO? Their folly, I think, is much the ſame with that of MIDAS, who judged the divine harmony of that muſical god inferiour to the rough ſqueaking notes of MARSYAS; whom ſome affirm to have been only a Scotch bag-piper, and others a Welch harper. I know not what their ears may be; but I am ſure their judgments, like that of MIDAS, are aſinine. I ſhall therefore boldly lay the following ſentence down as an axiom, or univerſal never-failing maxim; *Aurum belli & pacis elixir eſt catholicum*.

This is likewiſe a ſovereign remedy in all political diſeaſes: but there is ſome difficulty in proportioning the quantity to the ſtomach of the patient; tho' the ſureſt way of having good ſucceſs, is to give a large doſe. The *pilula aurea*, of the weight of a guinea a piece, in great requeſt with all learned phyſicians, cure almoſt all diſtempers, particularly colds, head-achs, heart-burnings, and conſumptions. They agree very well with all tempers and conſtitutions; and are as efficacious a medicine in foreign climates, as in this. A French-man or a Spaniard will ſwallow it like *aurum potabile*: tho' many are of opinion, that *aurum fulminans* would be more proper for the preſent conſtitution of both, but eſpecially of the latter.

Mr. BAVIUS,

THO' nothing but the fair ſubject of the following ſtanzas can poſſibly recommend them to the eye of the Town; as they may chance to ſoften the rigour of a heart, hitherto obſtinate to all entreaties, by letting her know, in this moſt public manner, the extremity of my paſſion, I hope you have humanity enough to favour me with a ſpeedy publication thereof. In return, if through your compliance I make the deſired impreſſion upon the fair, I intend to appoint you god-father to the firſt child. I am, with all becoming reſpect,

Sir, your humble ſervant, J. B.

I.

WHile thoſe who breathe Parnaſſus' air,
And o'er its lofty ſummit flit,
Deign only on ſome high-born fair,
To exerciſe their parts and wit;
Of humble birth a fairer theam I chuſe:
Things humble only ſuit an humble Muſe,

II.

If thoſe great prophets think it ſhame
To ſing their praiſe, where praiſe is due;
Like virtue, beauty is the ſame,
Tho' found, alas! to dwell in few:
To charms and virtue both, in high and low,
Impartial minds with equal rev'rence bow.

III.

'Twas this that did ACHILLES fire;
This haughty AJAX did out-brave;
For this did AGAMEMNON's fire
Become a captive to his ſlave.
The female ſuch that does my numbers grace,
Of beauty brighter, but of equal race.

IV.

Behind the royal place, where meet
All nations, one promiſcuous throng,
To ſtock-job, cozen, and to cheat,
Reigns the dear object of my ſong.
The lamb's your guide: the tender lamb you'll find,
Emblem reverſe of her obdurate mind.

V.

Four ſeveral maids the houſe adorn,
In bus'neſs ſwift, with nimble feet,
'Till night run up and down from morn;
All fair, and as DIANA neat.
CUPID's mamma, like SALLY, does appear;
The reſt to me her lovely GRACES are.

VI.

If faint my lines her beauty ſhow,
What more can ſhe expect to have?
Since her keen eyes have ſhot me through,
One foot is out, one in the grave.
What better colouring can ſhe hope to find
From one thus ſadly abſent to his mind?

VII.

To SALLY's toe from SALLY's face,
Let her conſent to eaſe my pain,
My pencil ſhall each beauty trace,
Soon as my ſenſes I regain.
I'll ſtrive, with all my little skill and ſtrength,
To draw her heav'nly image at full length.

DOMESTIC NEWS.

C. Courant.
P. Poſt-Boy.
DP. Daily Poſt.
DJ. Daily Journal.
EP. Evening Poſt.
SJ. St. James's Evening Poſt.
WE. Whitehall Evening Poſt.
LE. London Evening Poſt.

THURSDAY, *Nov.* 16.

Yeſterday his majeſty, and all the royal family hunted a hind in the new park Richmond: her majeſty being ſlightly indiſpoſed of a cold, did not go abroad. *C. DP.*

On monday count Kelminſeg, ſecond ſon of the late baron Kelminſeg, arrived in town from Hanover. *C. DP.*

Yeſterday the following gentlemen were choſen a committee of managers of the water-works at London-bridge; Mr. Joſeph Beaſlew, Mr. John Bodicoate, Mr. Robert Evans, ſir Bibye Lake Bar. Mr. Samuel Leſingham, Mr. George Monke, Mr. John-Anthony Merle, Mr. Ward Smith, Mr. Thomas Strode; Mr. Thomas Greene, *treaſurer. DP.*

The ſame day, in the court of King's bench, William Rayner was tried for publiſhing an infamous libel, entitled, *Robin's Reign, or Seven's the Main*; conſiſting of ſeveral ſcandalous verſes, printed under a kind of hieroglyphical picture, prefixed to one of the volumes of the Craftſman. *C.*—Being an explanation of Caleb D'Anvers's ſeven Ægyptian hieroglyphics, prefixed to the ſeven volumes of the Craftſman. The trial laſted about four hours, and he was found guilty as to publiſhing. *P.*

His grace the duke of Bedford having cauſed a turnpike upon his rents in Red-lion-ſtreet to be taken down, bonfires, &c. have been made by the inhabitants. *DP.*

On monday night a man was robbed in Moorfields by two footpads. *DJ.* — On tueſday Mr. Lilley, an apothecary in Cheapſide, was robbed by a ſingle highway-man near the Palatine houſes in the road to Newington. *DP.*

The right reverend the lord biſhop of Ely lies very ill at Ely houſe in Holbourn. *SJ. WE. LE.* — Yeſterday his grace the duke of Norfolk was extremely ill. *SJ.* — The lord Villars lay dangerouſly ill. — The earl of Cholmondeley is in a fair way of recovery. *DJ.*

A man did penance in Chelſea church on ſunday laſt,
In time of divine ſervice, for getting a baſt-
Ard child. *For pain, or ſhame, will follow pleaſure paſt.* C.

FRIDAY, *Nov.* 17.

Yeſterday the reverend Dr. Bundy, rector of Eaſt Barnet, prebendary of Weſtminſter, and one of his majeſty's chaplains, *was preſented* by the dean and chapter of Weſtminſter to the vicarage of S. Brides, worth 300l. per ann. *DP.*—Appointed rector of S. Bride's. *P. DJ.*

Yeſterday Robert Walker and John Dormer were taken into cuſtody of two meſſengers, on account of ſome ſcandalous reflections againſt the government, publiſhed in the Royal Oak Journal of laſt ſaturday; the former was admitted to bail. *C.*

On wedneſday in the afternoon, while prayers were reading at S. Botolph Alderſgate, ſome ſharper took a clergyman's new bever hat off the pin, and went off with it. *P.*

The perſon that rode in armour before the company of armourers and braſiers on the lord mayor's day, having taken cold, it brought the fever upon him, of which he died four days ſince. *C.*

On the 3d, died at Oxford Mr. William Muſſendine, M.A. formerly of Magdalen College, and one of the ſuperior faculty bedells; and on the 6th was elected into his place Mr. Herbert Beaver, M.A. formerly fellow of C.C. college. *DP.*

By the lord biſhop of S. David's, the reverend Mr. John Gwyn
Was lately preſented to the vicarage of Lanvihgenel Giynn. *P.*

SATURDAY, *Nov* 18.

The whale fiſhery has proved a trade of ſo much loſs to the South-ſea company, that a reſolution is taken of purſuing it no longer. And many conjectures are whiſpered abroad, ſuſpiciouſly intimating, that the company's trade to America has not been attended with that ſucceſs and advantage, which the proprietors had all along hoped and expected from it. Becauſe, ſay theſe ſcrupulous gentlemen, we do not hear the king of Spain's miniſter has yet received the accounts of his maſter's quarter part intereſt in that trade, which he immediately demanded on his firſt arrival here, and declared to the court of directors, it was his Catholick majeſty's principal motive of ſending him hither. *DJ.*

Yeſterday being the anniverſary of the birth of Queen Elizabeth, of glorious memory, the ſame was obſerved throughout this city by ringing of bells, &c. *C.* — Being the acceſſion of queen Elizabeth to the crown. *P. DJ.*

They write from Lanesborough, the ſeat of the right honourable the earl of Burlington in Yorkſhire, that one day laſt week ſeveral of his lordſhip's ſervants being in a room playing at cards, the floor gave way on a ſudden, and all the company fell through into another apartment; by which Mr. Simpſon, the earl's ſteward, was much hurt. *DP.*

Yeſterday Mr. deputy Smith was elected clerk to the commiſſioners of ſewers in the room of Mr. William Martin, deceaſed. *C. &c.*

Her majeſty having been twice blooded for her cold and rheumatic pains, the latter are gone off. *SJ. LE.*

Letters by the laſt poſt from Lyons in France bring an account, that ſir Thomas Groſvenor Bar. was finely recovered in his health ſince his arrival there; that his ſleep and appetite were greatly mended; and that he was preparing to ſet out thence for Aix, a city in the ſouth of France. *SJ. LE.*

Weſtminſter market is pulling down, in order to be rebuilt and augmented, for the better entertaining of country and town butchers. *SJ.*

Yeſterday morning the lord Palmerſton's porter was drowned in a pond behind his lordſhip's houſe in S. James's ſquare. *P. DJ.*

On thurſday morning, higg'ers ſeveral,
As they were coming unto Leaden-hall,
By three foot-pads were robb'd *of money all.* P.

MONDAY, *Nov.* 20.

On thurſday next their majeſties and all the royal family will remove from Richmond to the palace royal at S. James's, for the winter ſeaſon, neceſſary orders having been given thereto. *C.*—On friday next. *DP. Nov.* 22.

On ſaturday the ſociety of the Inner Temple gave at their hall an entertainment to that of the Middle Temple, on account of their having finally ſettled the boundaries of both houſes, an affair which had been in diſpute for three years. *DP.*

On ſaturday morning the reverend Dr. King, maſter of the Charter houſe, ſet out for Dover, in his way to Montpelier, for the recovery of his health. *P.*

On ſaturday died the right honourable the lady Falconberg, relict of the late lord viſcount Falconberg, at her houſe in Pall-mall. *DJ* — She was daughter of ſir John Gage of Foile near Lewis in Suſſex. *DP.* — Fourle *P.*— The ſame day died at his houſe in Fleet-ſtreet, Mr. Pinchbeck, the famous muſical clock-maker. *C. P. DJ.* — An eminent watch-maker. *DP.*

The ſame day a gentleman's ſervant, behind his maſter's chariot, coming down S. James's-ſtreet, a hackney coach being called, and driving for his fare after the chariot, the poll of the hackney coach ran againſt the footman's back with ſuch violence, that it knocked him off his ſtand, and the coach went over him, and bruiſed him in ſuch a manner, that he died on the ſpot. *P.*

The biſhop of Ely, who has been very ill of the gout in his ſtomach, is in a fair way of recovery. *DP.*

In Biſhopſgate ſtreet, on laſt ſaturday,
A poor woman expir'd, run over by a dray. *P.*

TUESDAY, *Nov.* 21.

On friday the cauſe ſo long depending between Knox Ward Eſq; and miſs Holt, was by arbitration amicably decided to the ſatisfaction of miſs Holt. *P.* — To the ſatisfaction of both parties. *C.* — *Satisfaction upon force, as if they had been married.*

On ſaturday night the barn of Mr. Hawkins at Walham-green was ſet on fire (as it is thought) by ſome evil diſpoſed perſons, which burnt the barn with about four load of wheat. *P.*

Yeſterday morning Mr. Walker, who formerly had a place in the Exchequer, dropt down dead of an apoplectic fit in Channel-row. *C.* — We hear that by his death near 20,000l. goes to his ſiſter's ſon. *DJ.*

Laſt thurſday the Spaniſh-embaſſador was admitted a fellow of the royal ſociety; and on thurſday next he is to be at their weekly meeting at their houſe in Crane Court in Fleetſtreet, when ſeveral curious experiments will be ſhewn him. *LE.*

In the will of Mr. Edward Aleyne, dry ſalter of London, who died lately at Lydd in Kent, are the following remarkable legacies, viz. To Joſeph Day, Eſq; a new years gift, ſuch as my wife ſhall think proper. To Mr. Hatton the protection of the ſaid woman. To Mr. Sutton my ſobriety. To Mrs Sutton, my taciturnity. And to Mr. Edward Berry, attorney at law, my honeſty. *LE.* —— *Theſe were all charitable legacies.*

Yeſterday morning, about ſix o' clock,
A woman in Cannon ſtreet *had a fatal knock*,
For out of a window two ſtory ſhe *got*
Into the ſtreet, and dy'd upon the ſpot. *DJ.*

WEDNESDAY, NOV. 22.

Laſt night Mr. John Dennis the famous critic lay dangerouſly ill at his lodgings, Charing-croſs. *DJ.*

Laſt friday died William Lytton Stroud Robinſon Eſq; at his ſeat at Nebworth in Hertfordſhire, and has left an eſtate of 5000l per ann. to his only ſon, who is about eleven years old. *DJ.* — On monday died ſir Talbot Clerke Bar. a young gentleman at Weſtminſter ſchool. The title deſcends to Talbot Clerke, of Lawnde abbey in the county of Leiceſter, Eſq; *DP.*

On ſaturday laſt Mrs. Empſom was found,
With her head in a waſhing-tub, *unfortunately* drown'd. C.

From the PEGASUS *in Grub-ſtreet.*

Mr. BAVIUS,

THO' you have frequently declared your averſion to all recommendatory accounts of any book newly publiſhed, juſtly diſtinguiſhed by the name of *Puffs*: yet you have profeſſed in your 140th *Journal*, that you do not think it at all improper, that ſome account of a book which is ſoon to be publiſhed, ſhould appear in a News-paper; and conſequently you cannot diſapprove the publication of a ſpecimen of a work, when unaccompanied with any recommendatory account at all. This has incouraged me to ſend you ſome *Odes* of ANACREON, tranſlated into Latin Elegiac verſe. The great uſe and advantage of poetical verſions of the Greek poets; and the propriety of Elegiac verſe for a tranſlation of ANACREON, are ſhewn at large by the author in his *Preface*; which I ſhall not here anticipate. The Odes which ſtand firſt in order are thoſe which I have choſen to ſend; to prevent a ſuſpicion, that I had ſelected ſuch, as I imagined to be turned with the greateſt elegance. I have added an Engliſh tranſlation for the entertainment of the ingenious among your readers, who may not underſtand either Latin or Greek. If you conceive the ſame opinion of this work, from reading this ſpecimen, which I have of it, from reading the whole; which will be certainly preſented to the public in a few weeks: you will, no doubt, in the mean time, allow a place to an Ode or two in your paper, as you ſhall think moſt proper; and thereby oblige

Nov. 18. 1732. Your moſt humble ſervant, D.D.

I.

Εἰς Λύραν.

Θέλω λέγειν Ἀτρείδας,
Θέλω δὲ Κάδμον ᾄδειν·
Ἡ βάρβιτος δὲ χορδαῖς
Ἔρωτα μοῦνον ἠχεῖ.
Ἤμειψα νεῦρα πρώην,
Καὶ τὴν λύρην ἅπασαν·
Κἀγὼ μὲν ᾖδον ἄθλους
Ἡρακλέους· λύρη δὲ
Ἔρωτας ἀντεφώνει.
Χαίροιτε λοιπὸν ἡμῖν,
Ἥρωες· ἡ λύρη γὰρ
Μόνους ἔρωτας ᾄδει.

II.

Εἰς γυναῖκας.

Φύσις κέρατα ταύροις,
Ὁπλὰς δ' ἔδωκεν ἵπποις,
Ποδωκίην λαγωοῖς,
Λέουσι χάσμ' ὀδόντων,
Τοῖς ἰχθύσι τὸ νηκτόν,
Τοῖς ὀρνέοις πέτασθαι,
Τοῖς ἀνδράσι φρόνημα.
Γυναιξὶν οὐκ ἔτ' εἶχεν.
Τί οὖν δίδωσι; κάλλος,
Ἀντ' ἀσπίδων ἁπασῶν,
Ἀντ' ἐγχέων ἁπάντων.
Νικᾷ δὲ καὶ σίδηρον,
Καὶ πῦρ, καλή τις οὖσα.

I

In lyram.

ATridas geminos, Thebanaque dicere bella
Me juvat, ac tenui magna movere lyra.
Illa negat; ſævoſque duces, Martemque ſonantem
Reſpuit: & nervis unicus hæret amor.
Mutavi nuper totam; nova fila protervæ
Affixi; & penitus jam lyra facta nova eſt.
Protinus Herculeos cœpi cantare labores,
Lernæamque hydram, Tartareumque canem.
Illa procax contra teneros ludebat amores;
Et dedit imbelles mollior aura modos.
Heroes valeant, & ferri diſſonus horror:
Solus amor noſtræ dat ſua jura lyræ.

I.

The LUTE.

ARms, and the bloody fields of MARS,
The Trojan and the Theban wars,
I fain would ſing, with epic muſe;
But my untoward ſtrings refuſe:
The ſtrings will not my theme approve,
They have no ſounds for aught but Love.
Thoſe croſs-grain'd things with eager heat
I broke; and tun'd another ſet;
Chang'd ev'ry pin, peg, notch, and skrew,
Chang'd the whole lute —Sure this muſt do:
Strait, big with hopes of new ſucceſs,
I ſing the toils of HERCULES.
The lute, perverſe as ever, plays,
In contradiction, Love's ſoft lays.
Heroes, farewell; in vain your fire
And martial deeds my breaſt inſpire:
'Tis Love alone commands my lyre.

II.

In fœminas.

Fortia belligerum defendunt cornua taurum;
Munit equi validos ungula dura pedes.
Exors pugnandi, præſtat lepus alite curſu;
Armato ſævis dentibus ore, leo.
Dat pinnas piſci natura, alaſque volucri;
Queis ſecat hæc auras, queis ſecat ille lacus.
Dat ſapere, alma, viris, & mentis dona; nec inde
Fœmineo generi quod tribuatur habet.
Quid datur ergo illi? —Pro telo, atque omnibus armis,
Pro galea, & jaculo, forma, decenſque nitor.
Formæ enſes cedunt, rigidique potentia ferri,
Tortaque ab heroïs bellica flamma manu.

II.

WOMEN.

Nature has arm'd with horny force
The fturdy bull, with hoofs the horfe :
The lion with fharp teeth, and claws,
Sinewy ftrength, and knotty paws.
Swift feet to hares fhe gives, that flight
May favour thofe who cannot fight.
Fleetnefs of wings fhe gives to birds,
And fins to fifhes fhe affords.
Wifdom to man fhe has affign'd,
That hidden treafure of the mind:
Wifdom on man fhe lavifh'd fo,
Sh' had none on woman to beftow.
What then have gentle females fhar'd ?
Beauty, the beft, the fafeft guard ;
To which the corflet, helm, and fhield,
The fpear, the fhaft, the jav'lin yield :
Beauty, whofe charms refiftlefs prove
All fire is weak to that of love.

FOREIGN NEWS.

THURSDAY, Nov. 16.

Rome, Nov. 2. Mighty preparations are made at Albano for the reception of the late duke of Ormond, who, they fay, comes from *Paris*, for whom the palace formerly belonging to the queen of *Poland*, is actually hired in this city. *DP.*

FRIDAY, Nov. 17.

Amfterdam, Nov. 21. Letters from Paris of the 14th fay, that the final accommodation between the king and parliament was made at Fontainebleau on the 9th. *DP.*

SATURDAY, Nov. 18.

Hague, Oct. 31. In the fourth article of the treaty, lately concluded between the emperor, the Czarina, and the king of Denmark, the two former, who formerly guarantied to the duke of Holftein his duchy of Slefwick, have thought fit to guaranty the poffeffion of it to the crown of Denmark, upon the latter's paying a million to the duke, with which he is to be content, and renounce in the moft folemn manner the patrimony derived to him from his anceftors, which was taken from him by force of arms, he knows not why, or wherefore. *P.* —— *Military might, Is quickly made right.*

MONDAY, Nov. 20.

Amfterdam, Nov. 23. The preparations are continued in Spain for a great expedition in the fpring. 'Tis computed his catholick majefty has actually above 70 men of war in his fervice. *C. DP. DF.*

We defire, that the advertifements defigned for this paper, may be fent before twelve of the clock on tuefdays, otherwife they cannot be inferted.

ADVERTISEMENTS.

To be LETT,

VERY good, dry, and kind Wine Vaults, under the King's-Head Tavern in Wood-Street. Inquire of Mr. Charles Kemp, at the faid Houfe.
N. B. You may enter immediately.

On *Tueſday* the 21ſt of this Inſtant *November*, 1732, did begin to be ſold very cheap (the Price fixed in each Book) at *Tho. Osborne's* Sho[p] in Gray's-Inn, the Libraries of the late Learned *Thomas Wright*, Eſq; and the late Reverend Mr. *Henry Burton*, M. A.

Among ſeveral Thouſands, are the following Books, viz.

FOLIO.

STate-Trials, 6 vol large and ſm. Paper
— Same, two laſt, to compleat Sets
Selden's Works, 6 vol lar. and ſ. Paper
Howell's Hiſtory of the World, 3 vol
Aſhmole's Order of the Garter, large Pap.
Stow's Survey of London, 2 vol
Hammond's Works, 4 vol
Stillingfleet's Works, 6 vol
Harris's Voyages, 2 vol
Montfaucon's Antiquities, 10 vol in 4to
Rymer's Fœdera, 18 vol
— ſame, 18th vol, to compleat Sets
Du Cheſne Hiſt. Francorum, 5 vol
Hiſpania Illuſtrata, 5 vol
Hiſt. Mariæ Reg. Scotorum, 2 vol
Homeri Opera Euſtathii, 3 vol
Ciceronis Opera P. Manutii, 10 vol
Livii Hiſtoria, Valcoſan
Thucydides, Aldus
Strabonis Geographia
Calmet's Dictionary of the Bible, 3 vol
Collier's Hiſtorical Dictionary, 4 vol
— ſame, Supplement and Appendix to compleat Sets
Hicki's Theſaurus, 2 vol
Hiſt. di Hiſpana, por Mariana, 2 vol
Republicas del Mondo, 3 vol
Hiſtoria del Mondo, por Pineda, 6 vol
Voyages de Mandeſlo, 2 vol
Voyayes du Chardin
Hiſt. & Memoires du Card Richelieu, 3 vol
Bibliotheque de la Croix du Maine
Chroniques de Froiſſart, 2 vol
Voyages de Olearius, 2 vol
Hiſt. de Charles VI. par Laboureur, 2 vol
Antiquité Expliquée, par Montfaucon, 15 vol great Paper
Medailles de Louis XIV
Pozzo's Perſpective
Oxonia & Cantabrigia Illuſtrata, 2 vol
Le Brabant Illuſtre
Deſcription de l'Hoſtel des Invalids
Cours d'Architecture, par Blondel, 2 vol
Cowper's Anatomy, beſt Cuts
Bidlo's Anatomy, large Paper
Annales de la France, par Limiers
Diſcours Hiſtoriques, par Saurin, 2 vol
Edifices Antiques de Rome, par Delgodetz
Scot's Chriſtian Life
Lightfoot's Works, 2 vol
Dart's Antiquities of Weſtminſter
— Antiquities of Canterbury
Breval's Travels, 2 vol
Whitlock's Memorials
Madox's Hiſtory of the Exchequer
Raleigh's Hiſtory of the World, beſt
Salmon's Herbal
Fiddes's Life of Cardinal Wolſey, large and ſmall Paper
Clerici Comm. in totam Scripturam, 4 vol
Camdeni Anglica, Normanica
Critici Sacri, 9 vol
Dion Petavii Opera Theologica, 6 vol
Euſebii, Sozomeni, &c. Hiſt. Eccleſ. 3 vol
Harduini Collectio Conciliorum, 12 vol
St. Chryſoſtomi Opera, 8 vol. Eton
Gibſon's Codex, 2 vol
Domat's Civil Law, 2 vol. l. and ſ. Paper
Bingham's Antiquities, 2 vol
Horſley's Britannia Romana
De la Motraye's Travels, 2 vol
— ſame, 3d vol. to compleat Sets
Locke's Works, 3 vol
Tillotſon's Works, 3 vol
Machiavel's Works
Lindenbrogii Codex Legem Antiq.
Ripamontii Hiſt. Mediolanenſis, 5 vol
Recueil des Traitez des Paix, 4 vol
Etat de la France, par Boulanvilliers, 3 vol
Hiſt. de France, par Mezeray, 3 vol bonne Edit.
— de France, par le Gendre, 3 vol
— de Bretaigne, Par Lobineau, 2 vol
Traite de la Police, 4 vol
Colonna Trajana
Flamſtead's Atlas Cœleſtis
Theatre de la Grand Bretagne, 4 vol
Campbell's Vitruvius, l. and ſ. Paper, 3 vol
— ſame, 3d vol, to compleat Sets
Atlas Maritimus & Commercialis
Meſeo Farneſiano da Pedrui, 4 vol
Sandford's Coronation of King James
Hiſt. d'Angleterre, par du Cheſne, 2 vol grand Papier

Dictionaire de la Bible, par Calmet, 4 vol
Joſephi Opera, Hudſoni, 2 vol
Cooperi Theſaurus Ling. Roman.
Cave Hiſt. Literaria, 2 vol
Poli Synopſis Criticorum, 5 vol
Platonis Opera Serrani, 2 vol
Temple's Works, 2 vol
Puffendorf's Law of Nature
Baker's Chronic. to the end of K. George I.
Beaford's Scripture Chronology
Catrou's Roman Hiſtory, 4 vol
Cudworth's Intellectual Syſtem
Kennet's Hiſtory of England, 3 vol large and ſmall Paper
Camden's Britannia, by Gibſon, large and ſmall Paper, 2 vol
Harris's Hiſtory of Kent, l. and ſm. Paper
Biſhop *Blackhall's* Works, 2 vol
Stebbing's Polemical Tracts
Prideaux's Connection, 2 vol
Cave's Lives of the Fathers and Apoſtles
D'Ewes's Journal of Parliaments
Collection of Voyages and Travels, 6 vol
— ſame, 5 and 6, to compleat Sets
Echard's Hiſt. of England, 3 vol large and ſmall Paper
Patrick, Whitby, and *Lowth's* Comm. 6 vol
Leybourne's Curſus Mathematicus
Fiddes's Body of Divinity, 2 vol
Cambridge Concordance
Barrow's Works, 3 vol
The Religious Ceremonies of the World, by Picart, 3 vol
Burkit on the New Teſtament
Hiſtory of the Conqueſt of Mexico
Kempfer's Hiſtory of Japan, 2 vol
Giannone's Hiſtory of Naple, 2 vol
Gordon's Tacitus, 2 vol
Tyrrel's Bibliotheca Politica, l. and ſ. Pap.
Hackluyt's Voyages, 2 vol
Pope's Homer, 6 vol
The Gentleman's Recreations
Ruſhworth's Collections, 8 vol
Collier's Church Hiſtory, 2 vol
Leſley's Theological Works, l. and ſ. Pap.
Vertot's Hiſtory of the Knights of Malta, 2 vol large and ſmall Paper
L'Eſtrange's Joſephus, large and ſm. Paper
Peck's Antiquities of Standford
Hollingſhed's Chron. with Caſtrations, 2 vol
Polychronicon, very fair
Grafton's Chronicle
Hall's Chronicle
Froiſſart's Chronicle, 2 vol
Heath's Chronicle
Kettlewell's Works, 2 vol
Winwood's Memorial, 3 vol l. and ſ. Paper
Langley's Pomona, large and ſmall Paper
Dryden's Virgil, large Paper
Stackhouſe's Body of Divinity, l. and ſ. Pa.
Sir *L. Jenkins's* Works, 2 vol
Dugdale's Monaſticon, 2 vol
— Baronage, 2 vol
— Antiquities of Warwickſhire, old and new Edition
— Origines Judiciales
— Hiſtory of St. Paul's
— Summons to Parliament
— View of the Troubles
Beveridge's Works, 2 vol
Charnock's Works, 2 vol
Scot's Hiſtory of Scotland
Beaumont and *Fletcher's* Works
Duty of Man's Works
Brandt's Hiſtory of the Reformation in the Low Countries, 4 vol
Spencer's Works
Pocock's Comment. upon Hoſea, Joel, Micah, and Malachi, 2 vol
Mezeray's Hiſtory of France
Gerard's Herbal, by Johnſon
Milton's Works, 3 vol
Weaver's Funeral Monuments, with Tables
Hooke's Micrography
Hayes's Treatiſe of Fluxions
Strype's Memorials, 3 vol
Burnet's Hiſtory of his own Time
— Hiſtory of the Reformation, 3 vol
— ſame, 3d vol to compleat Sets
Joſeph Mead's Works
Du Pin's Eccleſiaſtical Hiſtory, 8 vol
L'Eſtrange's Obſervators, 2 vol
Prynne's King John and Records, 2 vol
Book of Martyrs, 3 vol
Wood's Athenæ Oxonienſes, 2 vol

Young Navigator's Companion, MS. curiouſly writ.
Thuani Hiſt. ſui Temporis, 5 vol
Biblia Polyglotta, cum Caſtelli Lex. 5 vol
Ven. Bedæ Hiſt. Eccleſiaſtica, Chart. max.
Gruteri Corpus Inſcriptionum, 4 vol
H. Wharton Anglia Sacra, 2 vol Ch. max.
Bocharti Opera omnia, 3 vol
Buchanani Opera, 2 vol
D. Wilkins Leges Anglo-Sax. Ch. max.
Corpus Juris Civilis, 2 vol
Spencerus de Legibus Hebræor, 2 vol
Rerum Italicarum Scriptores, 15 vol
Flamſtedii Hiſt. Cœleſtis. 3 vol
Grotii Opera Theologica, 4 vol
Hoſpiniani Opera, 6 vol
Strada de Bello Belgico, 2 vol *Roma*
J. Mabillon de Re Diplomatica
Caniſii Lectiones Antiquæ, 4 vol
Wallis Opera Mathematica, 2 vol
De Chales Curſus Methemat. 3 vol
Dictionaire de Morery, 4 vol
— de Bayle, 4 vol
— Univerſelle, par Furetiere, 4 vol
Stephani Theſaurus Ling. Lat. 2 vol
— Theſaurus Ling. Gr. 5 vol
Harris's Lexicon Technicum, 2 vol
Scapulæ Lexicon
Vocabolario della Cruſca, 2 vol
Portugueſe and Engliſh Dictionary
Bradley's Family Dictionary, 2 vol
Trommii Concordantia Bibliorum, 2 vol
Biſhop *Smalridge's* Sermons
Quintiliani Inſtitut. Oratoriæ. Vaſcoſan
Æſchyli Tragœdiæ T. Stanley
Euripidis Tragœdiæ J. Barnes
Ammianus Marcellinus
Herodotus Gr. Lat. Sylburgii
Thucydides Gr. Lat. H. Steph.
Ciceronis Opera, 2 vol R. Steph.
— Opera, 2 vol C. Steph.
— Opere Lambini, 2 vol
— Opera Verburgii, 2 vol
— Opera, 2 vol. Ch. max. & Ch. min.
Plinii Hiſt. Naturalis, cum Not. Harduini, 3 vol Ch. max.
Ariſtophanis Kuſteri Gr. Lat. Ch. max.
Thucydides Not. Hudſon. 2 vol Ch. max. & Ch. minori
Dionyſius Halicarnaſſenſis Hudſoni, 2 vol Ch. max. & Ch. minori
Quintiliani Inſtitut. Oratoriæ Not. Capparon. Chart. max.
Ariſtotelis Opera Du Val, 2 vol Ch. max. & Ch. minori
Virgilii Opera, by Ogilvium
Spelmanni Gloſſarium
Dionis Caſſii Hiſtoria Gr. Lat. Leunclavii

COMMON-LAW Folio.

Statutes at large, 5 vol beſt Edition.
Comleat Set of the Year-Books, 10 vol with Maynard's Edward II. beſt Edit.

Reports:
Keble's, 3 vol
Modern, 5 vol
Salkeld's, 3 vol
— Same, 3d vol. to be had alone
Carter's
Lutwych's, 2 vol. French
— Same, Engliſh, by Nelſon
Saunders's, 2 vol. Fr. and Eng.
— Same, 2 vol French
Sir *H. Hobart's*, 1724.
— Same, 1678.
Sir *B. Showers's*, 2 vol
Maynard's Edw. IId's, to compleat the Year-Books.
Siderfin's, 1683.
— Same, 1714.
Leving's, French and Engliſh
— Same, French, 2 vol
Sir *T. Jones's*, Fr. and Eng.
Dyer's
Sir *Fr. Moore's*
— Same, large Paper
Foller's, 2 vol
Bulſtrode's, Engliſh
Anderſon's
Owen's
Benloe's and *Dalliſon's*
Leonard's, 4 Parts, 2 vol
Popham's
Modern, in Law and Equity.
Coke's, 12 and 13th
Savile's, French
Hutton's
Davies's, French
Skinner's
Plowden's, French, 1699
— Same, French, 1684
Tolverton's
Fitz Gibbons's
Carthew's
Ventris's
Lilly's
Croke's, 3 vol
Comberbach's
Sir *H. Finch's*
Vernon's, 2 vol
General Table to all the Caſes, printed in the Book of Reports

Abridgments:
Rolles's
— Same, interleav'd, 4 vol
Nelſon's, 3 vol
D'Anvers's, Title Error

Entries:
Cliſt's
Coke's
Hanſard's

Bridgman's Conveyances
Bird's Practiſing Scrivener
Lilly's Practical Conveyancer
Cotton's Abridgment of the Records in the Tower, large and ſmall Paper
Sheppard's Law of Aſſurances
Brownlow's Brevia Judicialia
Caſe of the Quo Warranto
Jacob's Law Dictionary
Blount's Law Dictionary
Cowel's Law Dictionary
Coke's Comment upon Littleton
Wood's Inſtitutes of the Laws of England
— Inſtitutes of the Civil Law

QUARTO.

Hiſt. Eccleſiaſtique, par Fleury, 30 vol
— Romaine, par Catrou, 16 vol
— d'Angleterre, par Rapin, 10 vol
— et Memoires de l'Academie, 4 vol
Le Theatre des Grecs, 3 vol
Hiſt Eccleſiaſtique, 20 Tom. 6. Vol.
Les Eſſais de Montaigne, 3 vol
Verſailles Immortaliſé, 2 vol
Les Vies de Plutarque, par Dacier, 8 vol.
Oeuvres de Marot, 4 vol
Hydra Socinianiſmi Expugnata, 3 vol
Tournefort Inſtitut. Rei Herbariæ, 3 vol
Fabricii Bibliotheca Græca, 14 vol.
Acta Eruditorum, 69 Tom. 37 Vol.
J. Graveſande Phyſ. Elem. Mathem. 3 vol
Philoſoph. Tranſ. 36. vol. in 21 compleat
Lowthorp and *Jones's* Abridgment, 5 vol
Collection of Sermons preach'd before the Sons of the Clergy, 2 vol
Caryl's Expoſition on Job, 12 vol
Addiſon's Works, 4 vol
Wright's Travels, 2 vol
Wells's Comment on the Bible, 5 vol
Trapp's Virgil, 2 vol
Gay's Poems, 2 vol
Cibber's Plays, 2 vol
Waller's Poems
Lanſdown's Poems
Shakeſpear's Works, by Pope, 6 vol
Anderſon's Collections, 4 vol
Opere d'Annibal Caro, 5 vol
Le Vite di Pittori da Vaſſari, 3 vol
Teſoro Britannico di N. Haym, 2 vol
Cumberland's Law of Nature, la. and ſm. Pa.
Dale's Hiſtory of Harwich and Dover-Court, large and ſmall Paper
N. Teſtamentum Copticum

Notis Variorum:
Senecæ Tragœdiæ, Chart. max.
Terentius, 2 vol Chart. max.
Silius Italicus, Chart. max.
Q. Curtius, Chart. max.
Rei Venaticæ Scriptores, C. max.
Quintilianus, Chart, max. 2 vol
Æliani Varia Hiſt. 2 vol

Diogenes Laertius
Plutarchi Vitæ, 5 vol
Horatius Bentleii
Terentius Bentleii
Quintiliani Opera Burmanni, 2 vol.

In Uſum Delphini:
Livii Hiſt. 5 vol
Suetonius
Plinii Hiſt. Naturalis, 5 vol
Manilius
Dictis Cretenſis
Juvenalis
Cæſaris Comment
Apuleius, 2 vol
Pompeius Feſtus
Virgilius
Vel. Paterculus
Terentius
C. Tacitus

Ovidii Opera Burmanni, 4 vol
Suetonius Pitiſci, 2 vol

OCTAVO.

Quincy's Works, 3 vol.
Bradley's Works, 5 vol
Vertot's Works, 5 vol
Clarke's Sermons, 10 vol
Compleat Set of *Hearne's* Works, [illegible] large Paper
Echard's Roman Hiſtory, 5 vol
Plutarch's Lives, 8 vol
Daniel's Hiſtory of France, 5 vol
Religious Philoſopher, 3 vol
Muſical Miſcellany, 6 vol
Salmon's Works, 10 vol
Patrick's Works, 8 vol
Grabe's Septuagint, 8 vol
Vander Linden's Hippocrates, 2 vol
Ciceronis Opera Verburgii, 16 vol
— Opera Lambini, 9 vol
Italia Liberata, 3 vol
Jugemens des Scavans, 17 vol
Bibliotheque Germanique, 18 vol
Tillotſon's Sermons, 14 vol
Ovidii Opera, 3 vol

Notis Variorum:
Plinii Hiſt. Naturalis, 3 vol
Suetonius
Virgilii Opera, 3 vol
Cæſaris Comment. 2 vol
Macrobii Opera
Corn. Nepos
Senecæ Tragœdiæ
Phædri Fabulæ
Grotius de Jure Belli
Terentius Interfoliat. 3 vol
Martialis Epigrammat.
Sulpitius Severus
Horatius
L. Florus
Q. Curtius
Auſonius
Quintiliani Opera, 2 vol
Plautus
Vel. Paterculus
Juſtini Hiſtoria
Juvenalis Satyræ
Eraſmi Colloquia
Pervigilium Veneris
Minucius Felix
Salluſtius
Val. Maximus
Cicer. Epiſt. ad Famil. 2 vol

DUODECIMO.

Ciceronis Opera, 10 vol. Elzev[ir]

Elzev[ir]:
Senecæ Opera, 4 vol
Ovidii Opera
Eraſmi Colloquia
L. Florus
Cæſaris Comment.
Q. Curtius
C. Tacitus
Salluſtius
Virgilius
Senecæ Epiſtolæ
Horatius, Corio Turcico

Oeuvres de Vertot, 5 vol
— de Boileau, 4 vol
— de Moliere, 4 vol
Hiſtoire Eccleſiaſtique, par Fleury[...]
Horace, par Dacier, 10 vol
Hiſt. Eccleſiaſtique, par Tillemont[...]
Voyages de Chardin, 10 vol
—— de Labat, 8 vol
Oeuvres de Fontenelle, 8 vol
Contes Arabes, 12 vol
Jugemens des Scavans, 17 vol
Bibliotheque Françoiſe, 27 vol
Deſcription de la France, 6 vol
Le Mercure Hollandois, 24 vol
Voyages de Careri, 6 vol
Decades de Tite Live, par du Ryer[...]
Voyage de Tavernier, 3 vol
Oeuvres de Rabelais, 5 vol
Hiſtoire d'Alſace, 8 vol
Oeuvres de St. Evremond, 7 vol
Don Quixote, 6 vol
Delices de l'Italie, 6 vol
Oeures de Ville-Dieu, 12 vol.
Delices de Portugal, 6 vol
Oeuvres de Ciceron, par Du Ryer, [...]

With ſeveral Thouſands more in Folio, Quarto, Octavo, and Duodecimo, in Greek, Latin, French, Italian, Spaniſh, and Engliſh. Containing a curious Collection relating to the Hiſtory, Anti[quities], Laws, and Parliamentary Affairs of Great Britain and Ireland, as alſo of divers other Nations. Likewiſe a large Collection of Claſſicks, printed by the moſt eminent Printers. Together with ſeveral [...] of Medals, Coins, Architecture, Sculpture, Painting, Mathematicks, Travels, Voyages, Trade, Husbandry, Civil, Canon, and Common Law, Divinity, Lexicographers, Natural Hiſtory, Phyſ[ick], Surgery. Moſt gilt Backs, and Letter'd, and many large Paper. Catalogues may be had at the Place of Sale, and Money for any Library of Books.

LONDON: Printed for, and Sold by J. ROBERTS, near the *Oxford-Arms* in *Warwick-Lane*; where Letters and Advertiſe[ments] are taken in; as alſo by Capt. GULLIVER, near the *Temple*; by P. SANDERS, *in Crown-Court*, *Butcher-Row*, without *Temple*[-Bar], and at the *Rainbow Coffee-Houſe* in *Cornhill*. [Price Twopence.]

The Grub-street Journal.

NUMB. 153.

Thursday, NOVEMBER 30. 1732.

The northern thistle, whom no hostile hand
Unhurt too nearly may approach.

PRIOR's Ode to the Queen.

THE thirtieth of November being the anniversary commemoration of the apostle S. ANDREW, the tutelar saint of the Scottish nation, in honour of whom all true Scotsmen then constantly wear crosses, an account of the original of this custom cannot be an improper part of the entertainment of our readers for this day. And as this custom, and the honourable order of the thistle, owe their original to one and same cause, an extract of the account given of this order, by Mr. ASHMOLE, in his *Institution of the laws and ceremonies of the most noble order of the garter*, will at the same time shew the rise of this ancient custom.

The occasion of instituting the order of the thistle in Scotland is variously related by different authors. JOHN LESLEY bishop of Ross reports, * that the night before the battle betwixt ATHELSTAN king of England, or rather of Northumberland, and HUNGUS king of the Picts, a bright cross, in fashion of that whereon S. Andrew suffered martyrdom, appeared from heaven to HUNGUS; who having gained the victory, bore the figure of that cross at all times after in his ensigns and banners, from which time all succeeding kings of Scotland have religiously observed the same bearing — Others assert, † that this extraordinary appearance was not to HUNGUS, but to the Scots, whom ACHAIUS king of Scotland sent to his assistance. This victory, it is sayed, was obtained in the year 819, (tho', according to ** BUCHANAN, ACHAIUS died nine years before;) and that HUNGUS and ACHAIUS went barefooted in solemn procession to the kirk of S. ANDREW, to thank God and his apostle, promising that they and all their posterity would ever use in their ensigns the cross of S. ANDREW; which custom prevailed among the Picts, and remains among the Scots to this day: and that both those kings immediately instituted an order, which they named the Order of S. ANDREW.

Others, who allow that ACHAIUS instituted this order, give the following different account of the occasion of it. That ACHAIUS, having made that famous league, offensive and defensive, with CHARLEMAGNE, king of France, against all other princes, (to preserve the memory of which the Scotch Lyon, assumed before by king FERGUS, became then inclosed with a treture of flowers de lis) found himself thereby so strong, that he took for his device the thistle and the rue, which he composed into a collar of his order, and for his motto *Pour ma defence*: intimating thereby, that he feared not the powers of foreign princes, seeing he leaned on the succour and alliance of the French. — And tho' from hence may be inferred, that these two plants, the thistle and the rue, were the united symbols of one order of knighthood, yet ** MENNENIUS divides them into two, making one, whose chief badge was the thistle; whence the knights were so stiled, and the motto, *Nemo me impune lacessit*; and another vulgarly called *Sertum rutæ*, or the garland of rue, the collar of which was composed of two branches or sprigs thereof, or else of many of its leaves: however, at both these collars hung one and the same jewel, to wit, the figure of S. ANDREW, bearing before him the cross of his martyrdom.

But altho' the thistle had been acknowledged for the badge and symbol of the kingdom of Scotland, even from the reign of ACHAIUS, as the rose was of England, the lilly of France, the pomegranate of Spain, &c. yet there are some, who referr the order of the thistle to later times, in the reign of CHARLES VII. of France, when the league of amity was renewed between that kingdom and Scotland, by which the former received great aid and succour from the latter, in a time of extraordinary distress. Others place the foundation still later, even as low as the year 1500.

The chief and principal ensign of this order is a gold collar composed of thistles, interlinked with annulets of gold, having pendant thereunto the image of S. ANDREW with his cross, and this epigraph, *Nemo me impune lacessit*.

This order consisted of thirteen knights, in allusion to the number of our blessed Saviour and his apostles. —— The time of their meeting was heretofore very religiously observed, and celebrated annually, upon the feast day of S. ANDREW, in the church of the town dedicated to his name, in testimony of the high esteem and reverence they bore unto him as their titular saint and patron. During the solemnity, the knights were habited in rich and costly apparel, and wore their parliament robes, having fixed on their left shoulders an azure rundle, on which was embroidered S. ANDREW's cross, environed in center with a crown compos'd of flowers de lis, *or*. —— For the ordinary and common ensign, they used a green ribbon, whereat hung a thistle of gold, crowned with an imperial crown, within a circle of gold, containing also the fore mentioned epigraph or motto.

In this account given by Mr. ASHMOLE, it seems not a little strange, that there should be so great an interval between the times assigned for the rise of this order. The first opinion carries it as high as the year 819: the second places it in 1425, in which year, according to * BUCHANAN, the ancient league between France and Scotland was renewed, by CHARLES VII. of the former, and JAMES I. of the latter: the third opinion brings it down as low as 1500. So that there is above six hundred years difference between the first and second periods of time; and almost an hundred between the second and third: tho' the former of these was but a very little above three centuries, and the latter about thirty years more than two centuries ago. The antiquity therefore of this honourable order is very uncertain, since it is not evident, whether it is about nine hundred, or only two hundred years old.

The occasion likewise is as uncertain, as the time of its institution, and it is not sufficiently manifest, whether that occasion was for the honour of the Scotish nation. As to the story of the miraculous appearance of S ANDREW's cross to HUNGUS and his soldiers, (or of S. ANDREW himself in a dream to HUNGUS, and of the cross in the time of the battel to both armies, as BUCHANAN † relates it,) the present learned age is so far from beleiving any such appearances, that it is rather apt to call in question the truth of S. ANDREW's maytyrdom upon a real cross. But supposing this to be true, and that it gave occasion to the institution of this order; those, who are most zealous to advance the antiquity of it, if they will but impartially attend to the demonstrative reasonings of their countryman the *Independent Whig*, will not think it much for the honour of the order, that it should take its original from an illiterate bigotted fisherman.

If to secure the antiquity of this order, we refer it to the time of king ACHAIUS, who is sayed to have instituted it upon his having concluded a league, offensive and defensive, with CHARLEMAGNE; this occasion seems probable enough: but then it redounds more to his honour, and to that of France, than to the honour of Scotland, and of king ACHAIUS. — If we cut off six hundred years from its antiquity, and, to render this more probable, bring it down to the times of James I. of Scotland, upon his renewing of the league with CHARLES VII. of France; the great assistance given by Scotland to France in the time of her extraordinary distress, which is assigned more especially as the reason for this institution, does not appear from history to be so considerable, as to deserve to be transmitted down to posterity by such a lasting way of commemoration. That assistance was given five or six years before the renewal of this league, and consisted of seven thousand men, as BUCHANAN tells us; tho' the French historians say they were but seven hundred. However, they own, that principally by these auxiliaries the victory at Baugé was gained; where the English under the duke of Clarence were intirely defeated, himself, with several of the nobility and gentry slain, and many more taken prisoners. Had the institution been fixed immediately after the time of this victory, it had seemed more probable, than that it should commence five years after, upon the renewal of the league.

If it be placed no higher than 1500; yet it will be as difficult to ascertain the immediate occasion of its institution. And Mr. CHAMBERLAYNE ** tells us, that being "grown into desuetude by length of time, it was revived by king James VII. [of Scotland, and II. of England;] but his misfortunes preventing the completion of that matter, it was restored by the late queen ANNE."

Nor would it at all have derogated from the honour of this Order, had it derived its original so lately as in her reign; and if instead of removing and restoring, she had first instituted it, and that upon some trivial occasion, so that it had been the effect of her mere will and pleasure. As the soveregin is the sole fountain of this honour, it signifies little upon what occasion the stream was at first let out, or how long it has flowed: nay, this stream, like others, by running a long way, is apt in time to grow muddy. That which makes this order really honourable is neither the antiquity, nor the occasion of its first institution, but the real occasion of its being conferred upon any particular person, as a reward for some signal service, and a mark of the favour of his prince. If we can suppose it to have been ever bestowed upon dishonourable motives, as a sort of wages for giving up the rights of ones country; the ensigns of it are really disgraceful, and like the shoulder-knots of foot-men, are only splendid badges of servitude.

The collar of this order is composed of thistles, interwoven and linked with sprigs or leaves of rue all of gold. Mr. CHAMBERLAYNE asserts, that "the thistle was chosen for its aptness to express one effect of courage, which is threatning:" and by this he vindicates the present motto, which runs in the future, "*Nemo me impune lacesset*, which, he says, is more threatning, and expresses more of courage; tho' he allows the present time *lacessit* makes [denotes] more the nature of the thing." That the thistle is a proper emblem of courage, which will not suffer itself to be insulted, I readily acknowledge; but I cannot think, that the insulting of others by *threatning* is any effect of that virtue. And therefore, the alteration of the motto from the present to the future, if it did run anciently in the present, like all other mottos, I take to have been purely accidental at the first, tho' it may have been continued since by design.

But the thistle is as proper a symbol of the barrenness of any country, as of the courage of its inhabitants: and that country might justly take for its emblem its native thistle, where those two verses of VIRGIL, *Ec.* v. 38, 39. are literally exemplified.

Pro molli viola, pro purpureo narcisso,
Carduus, & *spinis surgit paliurus acutis.*

However, no unfruitfulness of a country, from the disadvantage of its climate, can be just matter of reproach or shame to any people; because it is intirely out of their power to alter it. And therefore that sarcasm of CLEVELAND is too severe and bitter,

Had Cain *been Scot, God would have chang'd his doom,*
Not forc'd him wander, but confin'd him home.

The most barren regions are generally the most fruitful in men of courage: and these are never ashamed of the natural inconveniencies to which their native country is subject; but follow the example of ULYSSES, who preferred the barren rocks of Ithaca, to all the plenty and pleasures of CALYPSO's island. I am therefore inclined to think, that the thistle was originally assumed, as a symbolical representation, both of the infertility of the Scottish soil, and of the intrepidity of its inhabitants.

I do not find any conjectures about the signification of the other symbol, rue. But, as that herb subdues vapours, strengthens the brain, resists poison, and heals the bites of serpents, it might probably be joined with the thistle in the collar of the order, to shew, that those who wear it, are, or ought to be fortified against the whims of spleen and hyp, against the lazy stupidity, the venomous flattery, and the serpentine malice, which abound in warmer, more fertile, and luxurious climates.

BAVIUS.

Mr. BAVIUS,

WIthout staying to see the reasons, why the Translator of ANACREON has chosen Elegiac verse, I am satisfied by the versions of the two Odes which you gave us in your last, that he has copied several beauties of that poet, which he could not have taken in a shorter measure. I am persuaded, that the like observation may be applied to an English version; and hope it will be to the following: in which I have not servilely crept after, either the Greek, or the Latin; but have endeavoured to keep in a middle way betwixt both.

Nov. 25. 1732. I am, sir, your humble servant,

D. D.

---

* *De rebus gestis Scotorum*, L. v. † *Favin, Theat. d'Honneur*, L. v. c. 3. ** *Rerum Scoticarum*, L. v. ** *In Delic. Equest.* p. 143.

* *Rerum Scoticarum.* L. x. † Ibid. L. v. ** *Present State of Great Britain.* p. 421.

Upon his HARP.

I.

ATREUS brave sons, and CADMUS fame to sing
 I try'd, and to my voice I touch'd each string.
To my bold hand the strings rebellious move;
No other sound would they return but Love.
Inrag'd I chang'd 'em all: away I threw
The old; and my whole lyre I strung anew.
Strait I essay'd the great ALCIDES praise,
And sung his labours in heroic lays.
Instead of these, Love's pleasant toils my lyre,
Perverse, resounds from softly tinkling wire.
Heroes farewell; in spheres too high you move:
For my soft lyre will nothing sound but Love.

II.

Upon WOMEN.

Nature strong horns upon the lowing herd;
Upon the generous steed hard hoofs conferr'd;
Swiftness of foot secures the timorous hare;
Vast jaws and teeth the furious lions bear;
To fishes fins she gave through streams to stray;
To birds light wings to cut th' aetherial way;
Of wisdom's gifts exhausted all the store
On man, and left for woman-kind no more.
What gift of nature then the sex has blest?
Beauty, a gift superiour to the rest.
For all defensive and offensive arms,
Shields, spears, and swords, a panoply of charms.
Thus arm'd, e'en pointed steel the beauteous dame,
And fire subdues with fiercer, brighter flame.

DOMESTIC NEWS.

C. *Courant.*	E P. *Evening Post.*
P. *Post-Boy.*	S J. *St. James's Evening Post.*
D P. *Daily Post.*	W E. *Whitehall Evening Post.*
D J. *Daily Journal.*	L E. *London Evening Post.*

THURSDAY, *Nov.* 23.

A passage is to be made from the apartments of the princess royal in S. James's palace to the French chapel adjoining, for the conveniency of her highness going to the same. *S J. WE. L E.*

Yesterday at a general court of the South-sea company, it was agreed to lay aside intirely their Greenland fishery trade: and that their ships and utensils be disposed of to the best advantage: they came to no resolution to the proposal made on the part of Spain, of an equivalent in lieu of the company's right to send an annual ship to New Spain. *C. D P.* — Sir John Eyles took notice, that as the right of sending an annual ship was procured by the crown, he apprehended the company had no power to dispose of it, it being a national concern; and the court agreeing with him, the consideration of that affair was suspended, *D J.*

A rich bed of crimson velvet, with gold fringes and laces of most exquisite workmanship, and other rich ornaments, which is said to have cost 3000 l. is finished, in order to be sent down to sir Robert Walpole's seat at Houghton in Norfolk. *D P.*

On thursday died at Gloucester, after a lingring illness, sir John Guise, of Elmore, Bar. He is succeeded by his only son, now sir John. *DP.*

Yesterday morning 13 or 14 persons were sliding and scating upon Lariman's pond at Newington Butts, when the ice broke, and they were all lost. *D J.*

FRIDAY, *Nov.* 24.

On wednesday a gentleman of Kensington-square, received an anonymous letter by the penny post, demanding ten guineas to be left tied up in a paper at the north corner of the square, under a large stone that he should find there for that purpose, otherwise they would murder him, or set his house on fire the next night. *P.*

Yesterday in the afternoon the rev. Mr. Jackson, curate to Dr Cobden, was chosen by a considerable majority, lecturer of S. Austen's in Watling-street. *D P.* — *This considerable majority was three votes, according* to the *D J.* For Mr. Jackson 101: for Mr Kay 98.

The same day the rev. Mr. Lautane was chosen lecturer of S. Bennet Finck behind the royal-Exchange, in the room of the rev. Mr. Morrison, who resigns at Christmas, by a majority of 13 votes *D P.* — Mr. Laurence by a majority of 15. *C.*

Last week in digging up two old posts in a garden at Tilbury in Essex, there was found a pot full of old silver coin of our ancient kings, to the quantity of near a quarter of a peck. *D J.*

Yesterday morning, at Grosvenor chapel, a marriage was solemnized between Wadham Wyndham, of Lincoln's inn Esq; late chief factor to the south-sea company at La Vera Cruz, and miss Chandler, daughter to the right rev. the lord bishop of Durham, an agreeable young lady of exemplary virtue, and 8000 l. fortune. *D P.*

The same day died - - - - - Wright Esq; at his house in Albemarle street, reputed worth 40,000 l. *P.* — At his house in Crutched Fryers, Mr. Charles Lewen, a very eminent merchant, who formerly resided at Lisbon. *D J.*

SATURDAY, *Nov.* 25.

Yesterday about two in the afternoon, their majesties, and all the royal family, arrived in good health at S. James's. *C. D J.* — About one. *DP.* — About half an hour after two. *P.* — His majesty has been pleased to appoint the hon. James Brudenell Esq; to be groom of the chamber to his majesty, in the room of the hon. colonel Cathcart, now lord Cathcart, *P.*

The right hon. the lord Torrington, first lord of the admiralty, is chosen governour of the Corporation for the relief of the poor sea-officers widows; and the lord Arch. Hamilton, and sir Charles Wager, lords of the admiralty, are chosen deputy-governors, who have chose for their assistants sir George Saunders, assistant to the latter, and Thomas Pearce Esq; assistant to the former. *P.* — The lords of the admiralty appointed the master builder of Sheerness to be master-builder of Chatham, in the room of Mr. Rosewell, who is superannuated; and Mr. Rosewell jun. to be master builder of Sheerness. *D J.*

On thursday Mr. John Belchire, an eminent surgeon, was admitted a fellow of the royal society. *C. D P.* —— Mr John Stephens, surgeon to his royal highness the prince, is appointed surgeon to the first troop of horse-grenadier guards, commanded by Col Fane. *P.* — Commanded by lord Herbert. *D P.*

On wednesday a butcher in Cripplegate parish, going to correct his servant, after he had given him some stripes, a dog that belonged to the servant seized him, and tore him in so violent a manner, that his life is despaired of. *C.* — *This butcher should have been* going to correct his servant BEFORE, *and not* AFTER he had given him some stripes: *this preposterous way of proceeding, I suppose, provoked the dog.*

His Majesty has been pleased to grant leave to the rev. Dr. Henry Herbert, chaplain to the two battalions commanded by the earl of Orkney, to go for some time to Georgia, to assist in settling the affairs relating to religion in that country. *S J. WE.*

Last night a countryman from Derbyshire was picked up by two common women, who put him into a coach, being much in liquor, and stopped at a public house, where one insisted he was to be married to her; but while the parson was sent for, he got out of the other door of the coach, and leaped into Fleet-ditch, and by the assistance of the landlord was happily delivered both from death and marriage. *S J.*

On thursday Stephen Poyntz Esq; governor to his royal highness the duke, and treasurer of the excise, was married at Petersham, to miss Anna Maria Mordaunt. *S J. L E.* — This is a very great mistake. *C,* 28.

The same day Mr. Mears, a bookseller on Ludgatehill, was taken into custody, for publishing a book intituled, *A philosophical dissertation upon death.* S J.

MONDAY, *Nov.* 27.

Yesterday the rev. Dr. Lovell preached before their majesties, &c. in the chapel royal at S. James's. *C. DP.* — The right rev. the lord bishop of Winchester preached the sermon. *P.* — The drawing-room nights are appointed for the winter season on mondays and fridays. *C. DP.* — Her majesty has been pleased to appoint miss Mackenzie, daughter to Col. Mackenzie, to be maid of honour, in the room of miss Mordaunt. Miss Carter, one of the maids of honour, having resigned on account of a great estate lately left her, her majesty has appointed miss Paget, daughter to col. Paget to succeed her. *P.* — Leonard Smelt Esq; representative for Northallerton in Yorshire, is appointed clerk of his majesty's ordinance; James Cockburn Esq; secretary to the master-general; and William Rawlinson Erle Esq; representative for Malmsbury, clerk of the deliveries, in the room of Leonard Smelt Esq; *DP.*

Yesterday morning about nine, the right hon. sir Robert Walpole came to town from his seat in Norfolk, to his house in S. James's Square. *P. D J.* — On sunday evening. *C.* 28.

In the afternoon the count de Passeran and Mr. Joseph Morgan were taken into custody by a messenger, as the supposed author and translator of a pamphlet, intitl'ed, *A philosophical dissertation on death. D J.*

On friday Dr. Boucher made an excellent Latin oration, in the theatre of the college of physicians, before a numerous audience. *P.*

The same day were interred in one grave in S. Leonard's church, Shoreditch, Isaac Thorpe Esq; a Barbadoes merchant, and Joseph Bottom Gent. his companion, who came lately from thence, and were taken ill of a pleurisy. *P.* —— Mr. Bottom, his chief planter, who frequently declared, should his master do otherwise than well, he should die with grief, and accordingly expired within 24 hours after him. *D J.*

TUESDAY, *Nov.* 28.

On wednesday morning a fire broke out at Rack heath hall, in the county of Norfolk, the ancient seat of sir John Pettus, Bar. about three miles from Norwich, and burnt down the said hall, and consumed great part of the furniture. *P. D P.*

On saturday John Braithwaite, Esq; governour in chief over all the royal African company's coasts and factories on the south side of Africa, was married to miss Cole, a lady of great merit and fortune. *DP.*

On tuesday morning died the reverend Dr. Robert Camell, rector of Bradwell in Norfolk. *P. D P.* — On monday died at his house in Golden-Square, Crutched fryers, aged upwards of 80. Charles Sergison Esq; worth 150,000 l. and has left the bulk of his estate to Tho. Warden Esq; of Cockfield in the county of Sussex. *P. DP.* — Aged 82. *D J.* — Yesterday morning died sir Richard Carpenter, formerly an eminent wine-merchant of Mincing Lane, supposed to have died worth 30,000 l. *P.*

This morning died, at the general post-office, Edward Harrison Esq; one of the post-masters general: he was formerly governor of fort S. George in the East-Indies. *WE. L E.* — We hear he has left 50,000 l. to the lady Lynn his daughter, and to his lady 2000 l. per ann. *C.* 29.

WEDNESDAY, *Nov.* 29.

Seals, causes, exceptions and demurrers, after Michaelmas term.

Tuesday, Dec. 5. first general seal.
Wednesday 6. Thursday 7. Friday 8. causes.
Saturday 9. second general seal.
Monday 11. Tuesday 12. rehearings.
Wednesday 13. pleas and demurrers.
Thursday 14. third general seal.
Friday 15. Saturday 16. Monday 18. exceptions.
Tuesday 19. 4th and last general seal.
Wednesday 20. petitions.

The following copy of verses was written by a young lady of twelve years old, the daughter of a gentleman conspicuous for his rank and merit: the occasion was this; her brother being busied in making his school-exercise, she asked him what employed him? Which when he told her, she desired to know, what was meant by an exercise? He answered it was to write verses. If that be all, says she, I'll write some for you. To which when he agreed, she asked, what he would have her write upon? What but paper? replied he smartly. Her answer and performance was in the following lines:

 Oh, spotless paper, fair and white!
On thee by force constrain'd to write;
Is it not hard I shou'd destroy
Thy purity, to please a boy!
Ungrateful I, thus to abuse
The fairest servant of the muse;
Dear friend, to whom I oft impart
The choicest secrets of my heart:
Ah, what atonement can be made
For spotless innocence betray'd?
How fair, how lovely didst thou show,
Like lilly'd banks, or falling snow!
But now, alas! become my prey,
Not floods can wash thy stains away:
Yet this small comfort can I give,
That, when destroy'd, shall make *thee* live.

Yesterday, being the last day of the term, William Rayner was called upon to receive judgment, for publishing a scandalous and seditious pamphlet, entitled *Robin's game,* or *Seven's the main*; but did not appear to his bail. *C.* —— His recognizance was ordered to be estreated. *P.* — *Had he been* called upon to receive *mercy or money, he had* appeared.

On thursday died the right honourable Other-Windsor Hickman, earl of Plymouth, aged 25 years: he has left one son, Other-Lewis-Windsor, about 18 months old. *DP.* — On monday night. *P.*

From the PEGASUS *in Grub-street.*

A letter from ISAAC DE DUOBUS was received; and likewise one concerning marriage; but it was not thought proper to publish the first part, before we see the last.

We return our thanks to Mr. J. N. for his great diligence in carefully inspecting the copper plate on which *Magna Charta* is ingraving; and we are heartily glad to be assured, that it has received no manner of damage by the *Canceroticus.* — We likewise acknowledge ourselves much obliged to the gentleman, who discovered the anachronism in our last. And upon examining the original M S. of Mr. JOHN GABRIEL, we find, that the three lines relating to the copper plate are not there, but were an addition made by the person employed to transcribe a copy for the press; and therefore we desire they may be struck out. The impertinence and ignorance of Amanuenses, Hackney writers, printers, &c. are intolerable. The learned Dr. BENTLEY has justly exposed them in his famous edition of MILTON. Having this timely notice, we shall take care to

ent the like interpolations, in the remaining part of his admirable work of Mr. JOHN GABRIEL.

In the *Daily Journal*, Nov. 22. to the advertisement from the Oratory is added the following N. B.

"IN the first volume of the discourses of the Oratory "lately publish'd, price bound 4 s. is the defence of "it, which is demonstrative and unanswerable; as likewise "the attestation of the reverend and celebrated Dr. BAKER "of Cambridge ; bishop HUTCHESON, and the learned "MONTFAUCON, in favour and recommendation of Mr. "Orator."

This advertisement was drawn up to make the world believe, that those three great men had given an *attestation, in favour and recommendation of* Mr. ORATOR, and consequently of his *Oratory*. But neither of them, at the time of giving this pretended *recommendation*, had ever heard either of the one, or of the other : Mr. HENLEY having then set up only for a *Complete Linguist*, or *Universal Grammarian*, not for an *Orator*.

From Mr. BAKER's (not Dr. BAKER's) letter, which is dated *Oct.* 10. but has no year, it appears that Mr. H. had written to him to desire his assistance in his intended Grammars, and to borrow some books. In answer, Mr. BAKER offers to lend him some books, and concludes his letter ; " I wish they had filled up our fellowships whilst " you was here, that we might have enjoy'd so useful a " member, and one that would have done honour to the " society." Which is no more than a civil compliment to a person engaged in a learned design, who had left the college several years, and whom, it is probable, Mr. BAKER never remembered there : but it contains not one word of *recommendation*, either of the person, or his design.

Dr. HUTCHINSON (not HUTCHENSON) in his letter, dated Dec. 3. 1719. tells Mr. H. that " he has his two Gram-" mars by him, and has ordered his book-seller to send " him the rest, as they come out ; " and then gives him an account of his own design of *making two English grammars*, &c. But he does not add the least *attestation in favour of* Mr. H's abilities, or the least *recommendation* of the *two grammars* he had seen ; which is a good negative argument, that he did not much like them.

MONTFAUCON's letter is dated *Kal. Sept.* 1723, in which he acknowledges the receipt of Mr H's letter informing him of his design of translating his *Diarium Italicum* into English, which, he says, would be a great honour to him ; adding, " that if he would send him any of his *luculen-* " *tisscriptis,* as he had promised, he would do a thing very " gratefully to him." He dignifies him indeed with the titles of *eruditissime* and *clarissime* : but these are words, which, in an epistolary commerce, are given of course to persons, who are neither very learned, nor very famous. So that the whole of all this *attestation* of these three learned gentlemen is faithfully represented in six doggrel verses by Mr. MÆVIUS.

The attestation of the reverend and celebrated Dr. [Mr.] BAKER *of Cambridge ;* Bishop HUTCHENSON ; *and the learned* MONTFAUCON, *its favour and recommendation of* [Mr. HENLEY, *some years before he was*] Mr. ORATOR.

Mr. BAKER. I am ready to lend you any books I have by me :
Then thus fill'd up our fellowships, I wish you'd been nigh me.
Dr. HUTCH. *I have two of your Grammars* now lying on my shelf :
I've a project of making two Grammars my self.
MONTFAUC. You'll do me great honour in translating my Diary :
Send me some of your writings you promise, I desire ye.

✻✻✻✻✻✻✻✻✻✻✻✻✻✻✻✻✻✻✻✻✻✻✻✻✻

FOREIGN NEWS.

FRIDAY, *Nov.* 24.

Bologna, *Nov.* 4. Some days ago, our famous learned mule, Donna Laura Bassa, held public disputations, with great applause, upon several subjects given her by eight philosophers and divines, which lasted several hours, in the presence of 2 cardinals, 6 prelates, and a great number of gentry and other persons of distinction. C.

SATURDAY, *Nov.* 25.

Paris, *Nov.* 26. 'Tis written from Florence, that the emperor had sent a letter to the great duke of Tuscany, to desire him to make void what was done on Mid-sum-mer-day last, when, the infante Don Carlos took the oath to the states of Tuscany, in the name of his royal highness: but that prince answered him, That he had sent him greater lord than himself, and consequently he was not so misled. C. P.

Paris, *Nov.* 29. Letters from Florence of the 8th say, that the pregnancy of the princess of Asturias is no longer doubted of at the court of Spain. DP.

MONDAY, *Nov.* 27.

Vienna, *Nov.* 15. According to our last letters from

Constantinople, the plague continues still to rage very much in that capital, and all the furniture of the horses, where the inhabitants died of that distemper, being carried to the banks of the Red sea, where they are burnt, and the ashes thereof thrown into the same. C. — *I fear my brother does not know where the red sea is.*

TUESDAY, *Nov.* 28.

Petersburgh, Oct. 31. The establishment of the academy for volunteers in this city deserves the applause of the whole world, in which they learn at her imperial majesty's expence, and have both diet and lodging, martial discipline, vaulting, fencing, dancing, music, drawing, geometry, arithmetic, geography, civil law, history, (languages) Latin, French, German, and Rustic : the whole making 325 persons. D J.

WEDNESDAY, *Nov.* 29.

Paris, *Nov.* 24. From Florence they write, that there came to the Great duke and senate, on the part of the emperor, letters *decretal*, containing reprimands against them both, for allowing the infante Don Carlos to use the title of Great Prince, in which he forfeits the feodality which his imperial majesty and the empire have over his estates, and the great duchy of Tuscany. P. — From Amsterdam we hear, that it is perceived that the dykes have been in eity very much damaged by a kind of insect or the figure of a large worm, whose head is so hard, that they cannot break it with the blow of a hammer. P. — *This worm seems to have a thicker skull, than the Dutch themselves.*

BOOKS and PAMPHLETS published in November.

Nov. 1. Tables shewing the prices of liquors, &c Pr. 1 s.
The gentleman's magazine, No. 22. for October. Pr. 6 d.
The London magazine, No. 7. Pr. 6 d.
The friendly writer and register of truth. Pr. 6 d.
Account of a late battle, &c. Pr. 6 d.
3. Historia literaria, No. 19. Pr. 1 s
Dalkeith : a poem. Pr. 4 d.
6. The state of physick, ancient and modern, briefly considered, &c. by Francis Clifton, M. D.
Burnt children dread the fire. Pr. 6 d.
An ode on the birth-day, by Mr. Edward Phillips. Price 6 d.
Things divine and supernatural conceived by analogy with things natural and human.
7. Compendium anatomicum : A. F. Nichols, M. D.
Select tracts relating to colonies.
8. The law of truth. Pr. 1 s.
6. The secret history of the amours of Edward the black prince.
The political state of Great Britain, for October.
The genuine life of Mr. Rob. Wilks, &c. by Mr. Curle. Pr. 1 s. 6 d.
The circle squared : by Thomas Baxter.
Snuff : a poem. Pr. 1 s.
Third part of letters, moral and entertaining.
10. The Desperadoes : an heroic history, from the Italian of Marini. Pr. 1 s.
The court calendar. Pr. 6 d.
The Comedian, or philosophical enquirer. No. 7.
The life of Mrs. M. Moders, the German princess. Pr. 1 s.
14. A sermon before the lord mayor, Sept. 21. by Michael Terrebee, A. M.
Winslow's anatomy, translated by G. Douglas, M. D. 2 vol. 4to.
A dramatic piece, by the Charter-house scholars, in memory of the powder-plot. Pr. 6 d.

Wednesday Stocks were

South Sea Stock was 104 1 half. South Sea Annuity 109 3 qrs. Bank 149 7 8ths. Bank Circulation 4 l 17 s. 6 d. Premium. India 154 7 8ths, 154 1 half. Three per Cent. Annuity 101 to 1 8th. Royal Exchange Assurance 104 1 half. London Assurance 13 1 half to 5 8ths. York Buildings 3 3 qrs. to 4. African 35 to 36. English Copper 1 l. 19 s. Welch ditto 1 l. 14 s. South Sea Bonds 2 l. 6 s. to 7 s. Premium. India ditto 4 l. 12 s. to 13 s. ditto. Three per Cent. ditto 1 l. 16 s. ditto.

✻✻✻✻✻✻✻✻✻✻✻✻✻✻✻✻✻✻✻✻✻✻✻✻✻

ADVERTISEMENTS.

This Day is publish'd,

TERAMINTA : A new English Opera : As it will this Night be performed at the Theatre Royal in Lincoln's-Inn-Fields. Written by Mr. Carey, and set to Musick by Mr. Smith.

Printed for J. Shuckburgh at the Sun, near the Inner-Temple Gate, Fleet-Street. Price One Shilling.

N. B. If Orange Women, or others in the Playhouse demand more, 'tis an Imposition.

This Day is publish'd,

THE PRESENT STATE of EUROPE : Or, The Historical and Political Monthly Mercury : Giving an Account of all the publick and private Occurrence, Civil, Ecclesiastical, and Military, that are most considerable is every Court. With a more Particular Account of the Affairs on Great Britain, &c.

For the Month of October, 1732.
With Political Reflexions upon every State. Vol. XLV. Continued Monthly from Originals published at the Hague by the Authority of the states of Holland and West-Friesland, &c.
Printed for the assigns of the Executors of H. Rhodes, and Eliz. Harris ; and sold by J. Roberts, in Warwick-Lane,
where are to be had the whole Forty-Three Volumes, beginning November, 1688. (Or Single Ones, from July, 1690. to this Time.) Price Six Pence.

Just published,

Ready bound up with Rider's Almanack, and a new List of Parliament.

THE Court Calender : Containing ;
I. The Births of the Sovereign Princes now living ; as also, the Deaths of all since the Year 1700. Together with a short Chronology of the most remarkable Events in some of their Reigns.
II. List of the Cardinals, with the Dates of their Births, and by whom, and when promoted.
III. Remarks Historical and Chronological, concerning the Age of the World.
IV. Of the Derivation of the Names of the Months of the Year.
V. List of the Lord Mayor, Aldermen, Sheriffs, Deputies, and Common-Council-Men of the City of London.
VI. List of the Peers of Scotland at the Union, May 1, 1707.
VII. List of the present Peers of Ireland.
VIII. List of the Lords and others of his Majesty's Most Hon. Privy Council.
IX. List of the Knights of the most Noble Order of the Garter.
X. List of the Knights of the Bath.
Printed and sold by J. Watson, over-against Hungerford Market in the Strand ; F. Jefferies, at the Bible in Ludgate-street ; and J. Brotherton in Cornhill.

Where may be had,
A Letter to the Rector of Fryerning, upon his refusing to pay his Rates to the Parish Assessment. Price 6 d.

Next Saturday at Noon will be published,
(Neatly printed on fine Paper.)

The GENTLEMAN's MAGAZINE : Or, MONTHLY INTELLIGENCER
To be continued, Price 6 d. each Month.
NUMBER XXIII. for NOVEMBER, 1732.

CONtaining, I. A clear and compendious View of all the publick Papers, their Essays and Entertainments ; with the Proceedings and Debates in Parliament. II. Select Pieces of Poetry. III. Remarkable Transaction, Trials at Law, and some particular Pieces never before made publick ; Births, Marriages, and Promotions Civil and Ecclesiastical. IV. Prices of Goods, Stocks, &c. V. A Register of Books, and Pamphlets. VI. A Table of Contents.

London : Printed, and sold at St. John's-Gate by F. Jefferies in Ludgate-Street ; Mrs. Nutt, Mrs. Charlton, Mrs. Cook, at the Royal-Exchange ; Mr. Batley, in Pater-Noster-Row ; Mr. Midwinter, in St. Paul's Church-Yard ; A. Chapman, in Pall-Mall ; Mr. Dodd, without Temple-Bar ; Mr. Crichley, at Charing-Cross; Mr. Stagg and Mr. King, in Westminster-Hall ; Mr. Williamson, in Holborn; S. Harding, in St. Martin's-Lane ; and most Booksellers in Town and Country.

Where may be had, All the former Numbers.

Last Saturday was published,

No. XVII. *(containing five Sheets, at the Price of 6 d.)* of

THE HISTORY of ENGLAND. By M. RAPIN DE THOYRAS. Translated by N. TINDAL, M. A. Vicar of Great Waltham in Essex. The Second Edition, with the following Improvements:

1. The Translation is thoroughly revised and corrected.
2. The many Errors and Mistakes of the Original are carefully rectified.
3. Several hundred of Marginal References, accidentally omitted by the Author, are supply'd.
4. Additional Notes throughout, with Cuts, Maps and Genealogical Tables, on Copper Plates.

Printed for JAMES, JOHN, and PAUL KNAPTON, remov'd from St. Paul's Church-yard, to the Crown in Ludgate-street, near the West End of St. Paul's.

Where may be had, The preceding Numbers.

N.B. The Whole will be comprised in Two Volumes in Folio, containing 400 Sheets, at the Price of Two Guineas in Sheets, including Copper Plates. Five Sheets of the Work will be publish'd every Saturday, till the Whole is compleated, at the Price of 6 d. and the said Sheets will be deliver'd every Week at the Houses of Gentlemen who are pleased to order them; and such as take the Weekly Numbers are reckoned as Subscribers; that is, shall pay but Two Guineas, though the Number of Sheets should exceed 400.

Proposals at large, with a Specimen, may be had Gratis.

This Day is published,

[Price Six Pence.]

A PLAN of EDUCATION for a YOUNG PRINCE.

By the Chevalier RAMSAY,

Author of *The Travels of* CYRUS.

To which is added,

A Thought relating to Education, offered to the Examination of such as have Noblemen or Gentlemen (from the Age of Eight to Twelve, *at* [illegible]) under their Care.

Printed for J. Wilford, behind the Chapter-House in St. Paul's Church Yard.

Where may be had,

A Collection of several valuable PIECES of the Right Hon. EDWARD Earl of CLARENDON, exclusive of his History of the Grand Rebellion. With a large Account of his Life, Conduct, and Character, and his Effigies very neatly engraven. In 2 Vol. 8vo. Price 10s.

Lately published,

THE LIFE of MAHOMET. Translated the French Original; written by the Count of Boulainvilliers, Author of the Present State of France, and of the Historical Memoirs thereto subjoined. Printed for W. Hinchliffe at Dryden's Head under the Royal Exchange.

Where may be had,

1. The Proceedings of the Directors of the South-Sea Company; containing a particular Account of the Debates in the General Courts of the said Company: in the Year 1720. Pr. 1 s.
2. A Letter to Mr. Law, on his Treatise of Christian Perfection. With a Copy of Verses, address'd to the same Author. Price 6d.
3. A View of the Depredations and Ravages committed by the Spaniards on the British Trade and Navigation. Price 1 s.
4. The Monumental Inscription on the Column at Blenheim-House, erected to the Immortal Memory of the late Duke of Marlborough. Price 6 d.

On Saturday Dec. 2. will be publish'd,

The LONDON MAGAZINE: Or, GENTLEMAN's *Monthly Intelligencer.*

NUMB. VII. For NOVEMBER, 1732.

To be continued (Price Six-Pence each Month)

CONTAINING,

A Clear and Comprehensive VIEW of the Weekly Essays and Disputes on Political, Moral, Humourous, and a Variety of other Subjects: Several curious Poetical Pieces; Domestick and Foreign Affairs; Promotions, Ecclesiastical, Civil, and Military; Marriages and Births; Deaths; Bankrupts; Prices of Goods, Grain, Stocks; Monthly Bill of Mortality. Together with a Catalogue of Books and Pamphlets, with their Prices; publish'd by the Proprietors of the Monthly Chronicle, now discontinued.

Printed and Sold by J. Clark, at the Golden Ball, Duck-Lane; T. Cox, at the Lamb under the Royal-Exchange; J. Wilford and T. Astley, in St. Paul's Church-Yard; and C. Ackers, in St. John's-Street.

Just published,

A New View and Observations on the antient and present State of London and Westminster; shewing the Foundation, Walls, Gates, Towers, Bridges, Churches, Rivers, Wards, Palaces, Halls, Companies, Inns of Court and Chancery, Hospitals, Schools, Government, Charters, Courts, and Privileges thereof. Also Historical Remarks thereon. With an Account of the most remarkable Accidents, as to Wars, Fires, Plagues, and other Occurrences, which have happened therein for above 1400 Years past, brought down to the present Time. Illustrated with Cuts of the most considerable Matters, with the Arms of the sixty six Companies of London, and the Time of their Incorporation.

By ROBERT BURTON,

Author of the History of the Wars of England. Continued by an able Hand.

Printed for Jer. Batley, at the Dove in Pater-Noster-Row.

The REAL CORDIAL.

NOT only answers all the Intentions of Plague and Surfeit Waters, but is likewise an excellent Remedy against the Gripes and Cholick. It powerfully expels Wind, provokes Urine gently, and restores Apetite after a Debauch. It keeps off the Gout from the Stomach and Bowels, and drives it out when there. In all Sorts of Loosnesses, and even Bloody-Fluxes; it is of greater Efficacy than any other Medicine besides, that is of the Cordial Kind. It is likewise of Use after the Eating of too much Fruit, and the indiscreet drinking of cooling Liquors, especially in hot Countries; and no Compound Water is more agreeable.

It is sold at Mr. Brotherton's, Bookseller, near the Exchange; Mr. Beauvais, Milliner next to Slaughter's Coffee-house in St. Martin's-Lane; Mrs. Corville, Linnen-draper, in Panton-street Leicester-Fields, at 6 s. per Quart, 3 s. the Pint, and 1 s. the large Phial, with Directions for the Use of it.

The Universal Family Medicine,

Still more and more famed;

Is sold, by the Author's Appointment, by Mr. King, at the Sign of the Globe in the Poultry, near the Royal Exchange, London; at Mr. Hildyard's, Bookseller in York; and at Mr. Oakey's, Bookseller in Cardiff, Wales, at 3 s. a Bottle, Retale,

It is to be taken at any Season of the Year, but especially in the Spring and Fall; is so very agreeable to Young and Old, that Children take it without Trouble, a few Drops being a Dose; and so gentle, that it weakens not the most aged; for it is a safe and effectual Alterative (in a less Dose) where purging is not necessary; an Excellency inherent in this Medicine, which is a singular Property, well known to the Learned to be in some Cathartick Medicines.

IT is also a certain and infallible Cure for the Scurvy, though of the longest standing, and attended with the most aggravated Circumstances; being a Cordial Elixir, peculiarly adapted to that Disease in all its Forms of appearing, from the slightest itching Humour in the Blood, to its utmost or last Effort on human Nature.

It is not a rugged Purgative that disturbs the Patient, but a true specifick Cordial, that perfectly cures that Distemper, by gentle Evacuation by Stool and Urine, the only sure and effectual Way perfectly to cure the Scurvy, &c. and prevent Relapses (notwithstanding what may be dreamt to the contrary;) the Truth of which is witnessed to daily, by the many Thousands that have taken this Medicine; it so powerfully rectifies the Blood and Juices, that Scrophulous Cases are also speedily cured by it; and all Spots, Blotches, Pimples, &c. on the Skin, are quickly and entirely taken off, the Patients made lively and brisk, many Chronick Diseases prevented, and a due State of Health secured.

It removes all Pains from the Stomach, and helps Digestion, beyond what all Bitters can do, that have been of late so much in Use; it opens Obstructions, and is peculiarly serviceable to Maids inclined to, or troubled with the Green Sickness. 'Tis the best Medicine in the World to destroy Worms in Children or grown People, and prevent their Return; and it scours away all those ropy viscid Humours which breed them in their Bowels; and is so well adapted to all Constitutions, that it is deservedly esteemed both in City and Country, the most general Family Medicine that ever was known, to preserve Health; and hinders no Business or Recreation.

N. B. Good Allowance is given Wholesail by Mr. King, for ready Money to Country Shop-Keepers, &c. to sell again. This Medicine will keep many Years, and is so'd no where else in London. Therefore beware of pirating Counterfeitors, who endeavour to shroud under the valid Reputation this superlative Medicament has every where obtained by its known Virtue, for the Purposes above mentioned, or any envious Suggestions about Names, with an Intent to hinder unwary People the Benefit of this experienced Medicine, too well known to lose Reputation thereby; but Envy and Interest never want Pretences.

The Directions given with it are large and full.

This Day is published,

In Two Volumes in Quarto,

AN Anatomical Exposition of the Structure of the Human Body,

By JAMES BENIGNUS WINSLOW,

Professor of Physick, Anatomy and Surgery, in the University of Paris, Member of the Royal Academy of Sciences and Royal Society at Berlin, &c. Translated from the French Original, by G. DOUGLAS, M. D.

Printed for N. PROVOST, at the Ship over-against Southampton-street in the Strand.

N. B. There are a few Copies printed on a fine Paper.

For the PALSY,

An Infallible and speedy Cure, by one entire Medicine, being a most pleasant Chymical Tincture, to be taken in Drops.

WHICH gives instant Relief in any Paralytick or Nervous Indispositions proceeding from what Cause soever; and also all Weaknesses or Decays of Nature, whether from Old Age, or occasioned by continued Illnesses of Body, or any Irregularities of Living, such as hard Drinking, &c. whereby Nature is sorely weakened, and often in a Manner quite spoiled.

This infallible Chymical Tincture is indued with such specifick Qualities, that it instantly enters the Nerves, the principal Seat of all Complaints of a Paralytick Kind, restores natural Heat and Strength to a Degree consistent to a good State of Health; and, in a very little Time, perfectly cures all Paralytick Weaknesses of the longest standing; and also the severest or worst Effects of it, either on old or young, such as Shaking or Trembling of the Limbs, Numbness, or even Deadness on any Part of the Body; as has been happily experienced by great Numbers of both Sexes, and all Ages, before this Publication.

As for any Weaknesses or Decays of Nature, by Age or otherwise, this Tincture has not its Equal; it is so gentle in Operation, as not to give the least Disturbance in taking, but in its Effects so [illegible] and prevalent, that all Decays or Weaknesses of Nature, whether Paralytick, Convulsive, or any other Indispositions attending the Head and Nerves, are instantly relieved, and daily mended; so as in a very little Time a Cure is accomplished.

It is exceeding pleasant to take, safe in Operation, and perfectly agreeable to the Stomach and Palate, greatly helps Digestion, causes a good Appetite, revives and strengthens the whole Human Frame so intirely, as that nothing in the World was ever yet known to come near it, for the safe and regular Cure of all Paralytick, Convulsive, or other Nervous Indisposition, is sold, by special Order of the Author, only at Mrs. Markham's Toyshop, the Seven Stars under St. Dunstan's Church in Fleet-Street, for 3s. 6 d. each Bottle.

The INCOMPARABLE POWDER For cleansing the TEETH,

Has withstood, by its most excellent and known Virtues, the Attempts of many repeated Counterfeits; some imitating it by the Name of Powder, others under several other Names; therefore pray take Notice, that the only true, effectual, and original Powder, is sold no where else, but as mentioned below: It is sent for in large Quantities to the Plantations beyond the Seas, to whom good Allowance is given; and is as effectual in the East or West Indies as at London.

WHich has given so great Satisfaction to most of the Nobility and Gentry in England for above these thirty Years that it hath been published, and vast Quantities of the same still continue to be sold.

It is sold only at Mr. Allcroft's Toyshop at the Blue-coat Boy, against the Royal-Exchange in Cornhill; and at Mrs. Markham's Toyshop, the Seven Stars under St. Dunstan's Church in Fleet-street, and no where else in London; but in the Country, at Mr. Rogers's a Linnen-draper in Warwick, at 1 s. each Box.

At once using it makes the Teeth as white as Ivory, tho' never so black or yellow, and effectually preserves them from rotting or decaying, continuing them sound to exceeding old Age. It wonderfully cures the Scurvy in the Gums, prevents Rheum or Defluction, kills Worms at the Roots of the Teeth, and thereby hinders the Tooth-ach. It admirably fastens loose Teeth, being a neat cleanly Medicine, of a pleasant and grateful Scent, and in Virtue far exceeds any Thing ever yet found out for those Purposes.

All the Nobility, Gentry, &c. who send to Mrs. Markham's for the Powder for Teeth, are desired to give strict Orders, not to mistake the Shop (Markham at length is under the Seven Stars) because most of the Toymen in her Neighbourhood, seeing Multitudes go to her Shop for it, have trumpt up Counterfeits, and sell their Stuff in Imitation of our known and approved Powder, in Prejudice to the Publick, &c.

††† At the same Places is sold the highly esteemed Lip-Salve, which in two or three Hours Time heals them, though never so rough or chopt; prevents the Skin from peeling, and makes them delicately soft and smooth, giving them a becoming rubicund Colour; the Fragrancy of its Odour also renders the Breath fine and sweet; and it may be eaten for its Safety. Price 1 s.

LONDON: Printed for, and Sold by J. ROBERTS, near the *Oxford-Arms* in *Warwick-Lane*; where Letters and Advertisements are taken in; as also by Capt. GULLIVER, near the *Temple*; by P. SANDERS, *in Crown-Court, Butcher-Row,* without *Temple-Bar*; and at the *Rainbow Coffee-House* in *Cornhill.* [Price Twopence.]

The Grub-ſtreet Journal.

NUMB. 154.

Thurſday, DECEMBER 7. 1732.

Mr. BAVIUS,

THE artifices of bookſellers, to give currency to the moſt worthleſs pieces, are ſo numerous, and have occaſioned ſo much vexation in the republic of letters; that I cannot but think ſome of your learned ſociety would be well employed in writing a handſome volume in folio, *de fraudibus bibliopolarum*: which he will eaſily find matter enough to fill, without going beyond the verge of S. Paul's church-yard, for inſtances.

Of all the parts of a book, the title is the moſt important, and that on which moſt depends: 'tis on the *bona fides* of this one page, that half the commerce of literature turns. By this are all future dealings in relation to the book tranſacted; and all bargains ſtruck between author and reader, bookſeller and buyer. Of all parts therefore, the title ſhould be the moſt authentic, and compoſed with the moſt juſtneſs, as well as skill. But the reverſe is known to obtain among us; where no part is ſo much neglected, none ſo ſubject to frauds. The compoſing of them is fallen into the hands of bookſellers; perſons often ignorant and incapable; and at beſt too nearly intereſted in the matter to do ſtrict juſtice. Even authors themſelves are ſcarce fit to be truſted with ſo delicate a province: they are often vain and weak, fond of their own productions, and conſequently liable to over-rate them. In brief, conſidering how large an article in trade books now make, I cannot think it unworthy the wiſdom of the government to take the matter under their care, to appoint ſome perſon, or company (for inſtance, that wherein you, Mr. BAVIUS, make ſo conſpicuous a figure) to give due names and titles to all writings which come from the preſs: that thoſe who have no opportunity of peruſing a book before they purchaſe it, (the caſe of the major part of the book-buyers in *Great Britain*,) may not be impoſed on with *quids pro quo's*; buy chaff for grain; or, to ſpeak in the language of Grub-ſtreet, *pro theſauro carbones*.

The chief rule by which moſt people buy books, is the author's name; which is now become no rule at all: ſince the bookſellers have taken the making of names, as well as titles, into their own hands. 'Tis they who now decide what name an author ſhall bear; and whether he ſhall have any name at all. If his perſon be obſcure, or his name obnoxious, his work ſhall either come out anonymous, that we may have room to ſuppoſe it written by a man of eminence; or ſome ſignificative appellative ſhall be thought of, that imports quite the contrary qualities, to cover the flaw the thicker. Thus, if he be a poor rogue, he ſhall be made a lord; and if an unbeliever, a biſhop: if he be noted for inſincerity, he ſhall be a PHILALETHES, or a PHILELEUTHERUS; if a very coxcomb, perhaps a SOCRATES or a CATO.

The *German* bookſellers give new authors to ſtale books, and print the ſame work under a ſeries of different names, dates, and places of impreſſion, 'till they hit on one to carry it off. The *Dutch* are no leſs dextrous at making the moſt of a good name; and can make a reputable author, who has only written three pages, ſtand as author to ſo many volumes, by a prudent interpoſition of other peoples pieces. For the *Engliſh* bookſellers, there is no ſpecies of legerdemain which certain among them do not practiſe daily, with as much ſucceſs as the heer F——, or minheer W—— themſelves. Generally ſpeaking, however, I find more diſpoſition in our name-brokers to borrow than to make: as who would be at the trouble of framing a new name, which, at beſt, will have its way to make, when he has already ſo many celebrated ones at his mercy? 'Tis but finding ſome author who has excelled on the ſame ſubject, and aſſuming his name, either in its proper form, or, if that be unſafe, with ſome minute variation; ſo as it may ſtill paſs with the generality for the ſame, *yet* ſo as to keep without the ſtatute.

This I take to be the top-part in the whole ſcience of onomotechny. A multitude of things are to be attended to, in order to put it in practice to advantage. Some care is to be taken in the choice of the author, whoſe name is to be borrowed; as that he be one who is dead, or that lives far off, or that holds little correſpondence abroad, or that has *nonchalance* enough to let the thing paſs without an open diſavowal. Then, great skill is to be ſhewn in the manner of making the variation itſelf; as that it turn chiefly on letters which are not heard in the pronunciation, e. gr. final *e's* or double *l's*; or ſuch as are eaſily confounded together, as dipthongs for ſingle vowels, *æ* for *e*; *y* for *i*, and the like. I have obſerved, Mr. BAVIUS, upwards of 30 different forms of this variation in modern books: ſome made by a tranſpoſition of certain letters, as FEILDING for FIELDING; ſome by the ſubſtitution of one letter for another, as in COLBATSH for COLBATCH; ſome by the omiſſion of a letter, as in CHAMBERLEN for CHAMBERLEYN; and ſome by addition, as in ALLEYN for ALLEN. Sometimes again the variation is made in the ſirname; ſometimes in the chriſtian name; where provided the initials be retained, the reſt may be altered ordinarily at pleaſure; thus for JOHN we find JOSEPH, or JAMES, put with good effect. This form has put ſome pounds into E. C—L's pocket: ſeveral editions of ſome of the worſt poems having been ſold, by printing Mr. JOSEPH GAY on the title page, which, the pulic, he knew, would confound with the ingenious author of the paſtorals, Mr. JOHN GAY; on which *the Dunciad* touches very humorouſly.

He caught an empty JOSEPH *for a* JOHN.

On certain occaſions it is found proper to alter both chriſtian and ſirname; of which we have an inſtance in the *New Diſpenſary* juſt publiſhed, where Dr. JAMES ALLEYNE is regularly enough for Dr. JOHN ALLEN. But in all caſes a prudent onomotechniſt will take care to have ſome ſubterfuge or retreat left, in caſe of an open detection; of which we have alſo an inſtance in the book juſt mentioned. Dr. ALLEN hearing, as far as *Bridgewater*, that ſome bookſellers intended to make uſe of his name, proteſted againſt it in the public papers, and diſclaimed any ſhare in the work. Upon this, they prudently drew a little further off, and for JOHN ALLEN took their ſtand in JAMES ALLEYNE: which apparently anſwers the end as well, it being notorious, that notwithſtanding Dr. ALLEN's diſavowal, the book is ſtill bought and ſold for his. One thing is ſtill further neceſſary to make this art compleat, which none but the maſters are capable of; *viz.* to take care there be the due reſemblance between the manners of the two authors; and that their ſtyle, conduct, ſentiments, and ſyſtem be conſiſtent with each other.—On this rock moſt novices who have adventured this way, have ſplit. Thus, notwithſtanding the near alliance between Dr. JOHN ALLEN and Dr. JAMES in point of name, there is too viſible a diſparity in their manners. In the author of the *Synopſis* we find induſtry in compiling, judgment in chuſing, juſtice in quoting, accuracy in deſcribing; an eaſy method, and a ſignificant ſtyle. In the author of the *Diſpenſary* we find, I do not care to ſay what, but plagiary, over-ſight, impertinence, and contradiction in great abundance. For the plagiary, it cries aloud in every page, from the 2d to the 602d. *Stat. contra dicitque tibi tua pagina* FURES. The author does not ſteal at any vulgar rate, by paſſages and paragraphs, but by pages; not by ſingle pages, but by tens and hundreds; in ſhort, of 630 pages, of which his book conſiſts, 500 are fairly tranſcribed from Dr. QUINCY, word for word, without any further artifice than that of tranſpoſing the order, and caſting in now and then a ſpice of the *Hoſpital Diſpenſary*.

Dr. JAMES may reſemble Dr. JOHN, in that both of them copy others: but here commences a difference which ſoon ſets them as far aſunder as eaſt from weſt; one copies with judgment, the other without. You ſhall find Dr. JOHN ſifting his authors, ſeparating what is excellent in them from the reſt; following them ſometimes near, and ſometimes at a diſtance, as occaſion requires. You ſhall find Dr. JAMES groping about in the dark, catching hold of the firſt heap of rubbiſh that lay in his way, and dealing it out as if all jewels. He copies without regarding what, or whom, or how: to copy well, with him, is only to tranſcribe cloſe, to take good with bad; what is for the purpoſe, with what is againſt it. Thus it is he has dealt with QUINCY; copied him in ſeaſon, copied him out of ſeaſon, copied his deſcriptions, copied his recipes, copied his rationales, copied his quotations, copied his very title page, table, and index.—Yet he rails at him, as faſt as he copies him; and having tranſcribed his book, writes a preface to decry him: that the ſaying might be verified, *Spoliavit me, & maledixit mihi.* The ſame perſon is treated in the preface as a pyrate, one who made more blunders than pages; whom in the book we find followed, as if he were infallibility itſelf. Poor QUINCY is here damned for a dunce, who could not tranſlate a recipe without making miſtakes, which I tremble to hear of, after the compliment had been made him, of adopting the worſt parts of his book, with thoſe very miſtakes themſelves, as if it had been all perfection — This brings to mind the practice of certain rogues I have heard of, who, after they have plundered a houſe, ſet it on fire to prevent a diſcovery.

After all, Dr. JAMES is not to blame for copying QUINCY; who in matter of pharmacy, is beyond diſpute the beſt guide he had to follow. Had he copied him more, and given us QUINCY entire, which might ſafely have been done, notwithſtanding any laws now in being, it had been eaſier for himſelf, and better for his readers. Inſtead of this, he has unfortunately let many things eſcape of the greateſt importance, has added others utterly frivolous and foreign to the purpoſe, and altered others ſo exceedingly for the worſe, that the integrity and uſefulneſs of QUINCY's work, are in great meaſure loſt.

To give you a taſte of his additions: the capital one, whereon he values himſelf moſt, is his giving the genitive caſes of the latin Simples, to teach young phyſicians how to decline them; and printing marks over certain ſyllables of the longer names, to denote their quantities, and teach us to read them. I wonder he had not given the genders, and numbers too, of the nouns, and the reſt of the caſes, as well as the genitives; that the *Diſpenſary* might really have done the office of an *Accidence*. This, I ſuppoſe, is an addition reſerved for the next edition; in which young phyſicians will not only be able to learn their *Proſodia*, but their *Orthographia*, *Etymologia*, and *Syntax* too. In earneſt, Mr. BAVIUS, was ever ſuch a ſcheme laid for the improvement of phyſic books, to print them with all the grammatical apparatus of the ſchool books? If it go on, we may ſhortly expect to ſee Dr. SYDENHAM's *Proceſſus integri* printed with one of NATHAN BAILEY's *Numerical Clavis's*.

His omiſſions make worſe work: Of a multitude of articles in QUINCY which he has dropp'd, ſcarce one but leaves an unlucky hole behind, which his reader is left to ſink in, or fill up how he can. QUINCY's work was not ſo excellent throughout, that there was nothing to be found which could better have been ſpared, than thoſe uſeful chapters at the head of each claſs of medicines, as *on Cephalics*, *on Balſamics*, *on Carminatives*, &c. ſo neceſſary to the underſtanding of the particulars which follow; or than thoſe inſtructive articles on the *diſtribution* of ſimples, the rules for *gathering* them, the phyſical *method* of them; or the *hiſtories* of many of them; as *Lapis Hæmatites*, *Kermes*, *Mechoachan*, *Moxa*, and I know not how many more, which are here totally forgotten. Even thoſe two excellent articles of *Water* and *Malt Liquors*, the moſt generally eſteemed of any in the whole book, have periſhed in the croud. — The caſe is not much better with the *preparations* of the ſimples, which are ſo imperfectly delivered in the new QUINCY, in compariſon of the old, that for twenty ſeveral preparations, for inſtance *of Antimony*, in the one, I find but four in the other: for ſeventeen preparations of *Steel* in Q. I find but eight in A; for fifteen of *Nitre* but three; for eighteen of *Opium* but ſix; and of the reſt in proportion. It has fared much at the ſame rate with the extemporaneous *Preſcriptions*, many hundreds of the beſt and moſt approved of which are entirely omitted, and the reſt given twice over to fill up their room. Even the *Operations* of pharmacy have not eſcaped without taxation: no account of *Fermentation*, *Incorporations*, *Filtration*, *Clarification*, and the like.— Dr. ALLEYN's book may, indeed, be a good *Proſodia*, without all theſe; but it will make a very lame *Diſpenſary*.

Hitherto we have only ſeen QUINCY's work mangled; behold it now receives its death's wound: what has hitherto been done, only affected certain parts; Dr. A. has an alteration more, which demoliſhes the whole. The moſt eſſential thing in Q. and that on which he chiefly valued his own work, was the *Method*; in which he had laboured more, and ſucceeded better than any *Diſpenſary* writers before him; many of whom had, indeed, much the ſame materials, but diſpoſed in a manner no wiſe adapted to the occaſions, either of patient, or phyſician. This failing, Q. had the good fortune to ſupply, and to deduce pharmacy to a juſt phyſical order. He ranged his materials ſo, that we have in one view all the ſimples, or all the compounds belonging to any one caſe, or intention of cure; may compare them together; and make a choice moſt ſuitable to the occaſion. By thus interweaving phyſic with pharmacy, the ſtudy of each of thoſe ſciences is much facilitated to thoſe converſant in the other: and what is more, private perſons and families, whoſe circumſtances make it neceſſary, are hereby enabled, in moſt caſes, to do without either. —— All this ſtructure has our new author impiouſly defaced; and thrown QUINCY back into the ſame ſtate of confuſion which other Diſpenſaries were in, when he began to write; and to get out of which it coſt him ſo much pains.

[*The concluſion ſhall follow in our next.*]

The Prologue addressed to the ancient and honourable society of Free Masons, on wednesday, Nov. 29. Written by Mr. HAVARD, and spoken, at the New Theatre in Goodman's-Fields, by Mr. GIFFARD.

PROLOGUE.

IF to delight, to humanize the mind,
The savage world in social ties to bind;
To make the moral virtues all appear,
Improv'd to useful, soften'd from severe;
If these demand the tribute of our praise,
The teacher's honour, or the poet's lays:
How do we view 'em all compriz'd in thee,
Thrice honour'd and mysterious Masonry!

By thee erected, spacious domes arise,
And spires ascending glitter in the skies;
The wond'rous whole by heav'nly art is crown'd,
And order in diversity is found.

Through such a length of ages, still how fair,
How bright, how blooming do thy looks appear!
And still shall bloom — Time, as it glides away,
Fears for it's own, before thy late decay.

The use of accents from thy aid is thrown;
Thou form'st a silent language of thy own;
Disdain'st, that records shou'd contain thy art,
And only liv'st within the faithful heart.
Behold, where kings, and a long shining train
Of garter'd heroes wait upon thy reign:
Ally'd to thee, they are ally'd to fame,
And boast no honour but a Mason's name.

Still in the dark let the unknowing stray;
No matter what they judge, or what they say:
Still may thy mystic secrets be unclear'd;
And still be hid, to be the more rever'd.

DOMESTIC NEWS.

C. *Courant.*	E P. *Evening Post.*
P. *Post-Boy.*	S J. *St James's Evening Post.*
D P. *Daily Post.*	W E. *Whitehall Evening Post.*
D J. *Daily Journal.*	L E. *London Evening Post.*

A monthly bill of Hyp-oratorical mortality for November. Hyp advertisements, 6. Oratorical ditto, 10. In all, 16. — Hyp puffs, 5. Oratorical ditto, 6. In all, 11. — Decreased in the advertisements this month, 3. Decreased in the puffs, 1.

THURSDAY, *Nov.* 30.

N. B. The most important news we'll here rehearse
In lofty strains of various Epic verse.

The right hon. ... has resigned his commission, as lord lieutenant of the county of Salop. *P.*

Mrs. Anne Vane is come to reside at her house in Grosvenor-square, with a great number of servants. *DP.* — Jenkin-Thomas Philips Esq; preceptor to his royal highness the duke of Cumberland, is appointed historiographer to his majesty, in the room of Rob. Stephens Esq; deceased, a place worth 200 l. per ann. *DP.*

Yesterday fifty one causes were entered for tryal at the sittings of *nisi prius* at the court of common-pleas, Westminster, the like having not been known in the memory of man. *DP.* — *This is, no doubt, a plain sign of the great plenty of money.*

The same day the place of one of the coal-meters of this city was sold to Mr. Bramson, formerly a wollen draper, for 4625 l. *P.*

This day, at the annual election of the officers for the royal society, Sir Hans Sloane Bar. was re-elected president, &c. *SJ.*

On monday Mr Kennedy, a young gentleman of Ireland, belonging to the Temple, was married to a young lady of Gloucestershire, with a fortune of 6000 l. *WE.*

The same day a man well dressed, about 60, was found dead in a house at Horsely-down, by some bricklayers going to repair it, it having been uninhabited for several months: he had in his pocket a watch, and some silver, and, in all appearance, had lain there some weeks. *P.*

This morning died at his house in Pall-Mall
Mr. William Belcott, an undertaker of *any* funeral. *SJ.*

FRIDAY, *Dec.* 1.

The committee chosen to consider, when and in what manner to apply for the repeal or explanation of the corporation and test acts, reported to the generality on wednesday, That at present it was not likely to be successful. The majority did not agree therewith, and moved to recommit that opinion. All the committee, except lord Barrington, discharged themselves in a handsome manner from that trust: then he and some others moved for a new committee, which cou'd not be agreed upon. At last it was agreed, that the old committee would reconsider this affair, with an addition of four persons. To avoid the disorders which attend such general meetings, the committee are to report only to two persons deputed by every congregation of the protestant dissenters in and about the city of London; which has put this affair in a good way. ... — The persons added to the committee were Benjamin Burroughs, Thomas Hollis, Edward Leeds, and Martin Bredwell Esqs. *DP.* —— *I hear, that this affair is certainly put in a good way.*

Extract of the chair-man's [John Holden Esq;] *speech on the delivery of the opinion of the committee.* — Your known attachment to his majesty's royal person and family, your persevering zeal for the liberties of your country, your prudent and peaceful behaviour, will, 'tis to be hoped, conciliate the minds of ALL *such who have any real concern for true religion and the welfare of their country*, to promote what is in itself so desirable, and can be opposed by NONE, *but such as are unhappily under the power of bigotry*, or the bials of interest — It must be owned the returns have not been such as might have been REASONABLY *expected.* C. —— *This is a very charitable insinuation, that* ALL who are truely religious *are for this repeal*, *and that* NONE but self-interested persons, or bigots, can *be against it.*

Extract of a Speech intended to have been delivered by, Thomas Bromsall Esq; — I am sure none of us without doors, ever thought we were by that *former favour* secluded from asking the completion of it; as our conduct hath *justly deserved* it, I humbly think, our enemies themselves being judges. — We ought not in the least to diminish our *just* reputation of being the king's *fast friends.* —— And tho' no man more than I, can wish our present *fetters* knocked off, nevertheless I humbly think that the favour should spring from above. *D P.* —— *Since these gentlemen have* justly deserved *to have these supposed* fetters knocked off, *it is great condescension to acknowledge the doing of this to be matter of* favour. *But if this be done, they cannot so well claim the* just reputation *of being* the king's fast friends.

Yesterday his majesty in council was pleased to prorogue the parliament to tuesday Jan. 18. when they will sit. *P.* — Jan. 16. *C. P.* Dec. 6.

Yesterday being S. Andrew's day, the titular saint of Scotland, their majesties, and all the royal family wore crosses. *C. P, DP.*

The same day at a great meeting of the East-India bond-holders it was unanimously agreed, not to take less than four per cent. interest, nor to receive any payment but in ready specie; and then they adjourned to the 13th. *DP.*

Last tuesday night, an undertaker's man,
Between two coaches which together ran,
In Lombard-street, was *squeez'd and* crush'd *so close,*
That the blood gush'd *in streams* out of his nose,
And one arm broke in places two, *as some suppose.* *DJ.*

SATURDAY, *Dec.* 2.

Captain Douglas is made governor of fort S. Philip in Minorca, in the room of Colonel Edward Montagu made governor of Kingston upon Hull. *DJ.*

A general survey of his majesty's Ships of war having been made at Portsmouth and Chatham, several are order'd to be repair'd, and others to be rebuilt, with the utmost expedition. *SJ. LE.*

The dutchess dowager of Malborough's charity house in the town of S. Alban's will be two Stories high, and spacious enough to contain forty families, who are to be provided with all manner of necessaries at her grace's expence, who will endow it for ever. *SJ. LE.*

We hear that on the 20th of next month his excellency the count de Montijo will make his public entry thro' this city in a very magnificent manner. *C. DJ.*

Monday last came on the tryal between Eustace Budgell Esq, and the bailiff who used him in the barbarous manner mentioned in the 2d part of *Liberty and Property.* The court committed the bailiff to the King's bench prison, order'd him to pay the full costs of the suit, and five pounds damages. Mr Budgell pleaded his own cause, and convicted the bailiff upon his own evidence; who, it is thought, will be called to a further account before the house of lords *DJ.*

At the end of the Oratory advertisement *in* Fog's Journal *is this* N.B. *word for word.* " In the scripture, the " rule of preaching, are above a thousand burlesque passages, " WHICH RENDERS IT strictly religious in ITS turn." — *It is hop'd, that* Mr. Orator *gave an* Exposition *of this paradox to the initiated, within doors, which to the profane without seemed as* irreligious, *as* ungrammatical *and* nonsensical.

Yesterday morning, as a higgler did come
To Leadenhall-market, from the town of Rum-
Ford; he was robb'd *(this news was brought by and for owls)*
By two foot-pads, of twelve shillings, a pig, and six fowls.
C. SJ. WE.

MONDAY, *Dec.* 4.

Yesterday the reverend Dr. Crow preached before their majesties, and the three eldest princesses. *C. DJ.* — The reverend Dr. Pierce before his royal highness the duke, and the two youngest princesses. *DJ.*

Charles Towers Esq; member of parliament for Lancaster, and his brother Thomas Towers Esq; member for Wareham in Dorsetshire, hath obtained a grant of the reversion, of the *place* of auditors of his majesty's revenues, after the decease of auditor Harley and auditor Foey. *DP.*

The officers of the royal society for the ensuing year are
Sir Hans Sloane Bar. president.
Members of the old council continued.

Martin Folkes Esq;	John Machin Ast. Pr. Gr. Secr.
Sir John Fortescue Aland.	Richard Mead M D.
Roger Gale Esq. treasurer.	Cromwell Mortimer, M D Se.
John Hadley Esq.	Charles duke of Richmond.
Edm. Halley LL D. Ast. Reg.	James West Esq;

Members of the society added to the council.

Lord Carpenter.	William Jones Esq;
Joseph Andrews Esq;	Smart Lethieullier Esq;
Mr. John Ellis.	Lord Percivall.
Mr George Graham.	Mr. Isaac Rand.
John Jeffreys Esq;	James Theobald Esq; *P.*

On saturday in the afternoon, near Wandsworth, a waggon was overturn'd, and broke a poor woman's leg. *C.*

THURSDAY, *Dec.* 5.

Their majesties being indisposed with a cold, there was no drawing-room at S. James's last night. *P.*

They write from Chester, that last week Watkin Williams Wynn Esq; knight of the shire for Denbigh, was chosen an alderman in the room of alderman Allen deceased. — And that Mr. Manley had begun to make interest to represent that city in the room of sir Richard Grosvenor, deceased. *DP.*

Yesterday a duel was fought in Hyde Park, between a noted distiller near Oxford road, and a gentleman belonging to the life-guards, with sword and pistol; and after a sharp engagement, the latter had one of his legs shatter'd to pieces; and when his antagonist saw him drop, he made off. *P.* — *Had a distiller made* his antagonist *drop by firing a pocket* pistol *charged with brandy, it had not been half so strange*

Yesterday a countryman, who was attending on a cause in the court of Common-pleas at Westminster, had his pocket pick'd of his bag, in which were three guineas and some silver. *P.* — *This* article *is not near so strange as the preceding.*

Last week Richard Vaughan Esq; knight of the shire for the county of Merioneth, was married to miss Nanney, of Nanny hall in the same county, a rich heiress. *DP.* — The latter end of last week Robert Fotherby Esq; an eminent merchant of this city, was married to an agreeable young widow gentlewoman, with a fortune of 30,000 l. *WE.* — Mrs. Chandler. *C. DP. Dec.* 6. — 30,000 l. *would have made* an old widow gentlewoman agreeable *enough.*

On monday the 4th instant dyed of a violent inflamatory fever, at the duke of Queensberry's in Burlington Gardens, Mr. John Gay. He was descended of a gentleman's family in Devonshire, and had been secretary to the embassy to Hanover in the last year of queen Anne, when he had the honour of being personally known by the royal family; to which he express'd his loyalty and affection in some excellent poems. He was one of the most eminent poets; and, in some parts of writing, the most eminent of his age. His personal character was perfectly amiable; the most natural, inoffensive, and disinterested of men: his conversation was sought by all that knew him; and his life chiefly past in the friendship and society of persons of the first rank. He left a moderate fortune, no part owing to any preferment, but wholly to his own labour and prudence, between two sisters. No place is vacant by his death. *L E.*

A few days since died at his seat near Lancaster — Fenwick Esq; a gentleman of about 1000 per ann. *DP.* — Yesterday died at his house at Carshalton, Mr. Benjamin Barker, chief clerk of the bank transfer-books, reputed worth 10,000 l. *DP.*

Yesterday a porter letting down a pipe of wine in a cellar,
The pulley breaking, the pipe upon him fell *there,*
Broke one of his legs, and bruis'd him *more than I can*
tell here. *SJ.*

WEDNESDAY, *Dec.* 6.

Their majesties continuing indisposed with a cold do not see any body except ministers of state. *P.*

The honourable Edward Carteret Esq; has a commission for acting solely as post-master-general, in order to prevent any delay, on account of the joint-commission to himself and the late Edward Harrison Esq; *DJ.*

This day begins the sessions at the Old-Baily, when upwards of sixty persons are to be tried. *DJ.* — Upwards of 120. *P.*

On sunday the son of Mr. Guerney, apothecary in Pall-Mall, was married to the daughter of governor Roberts, an agreeable young lady, and a fortune of 10,000 l. *P.*

On monday died Mr. Whitaker in the Tower. About seven weeks ago he was bit in the hand by a mad dog, and having been dipt twice in the salt water, continued very well till last sunday, when he assured several of his acquaintance he should die next day raving mad: ten or twelve persons attended him, and tied him down in his

led. He retained his senses so far, as to desire them to put on two pair of gloves each, for he should certainly bite them. A small time before he expired, he bark'd ten or twelve times like a dog. *DJ.*
On monday last a young lad, *in the sight of many people,* flew three several times from the top of Lambeth steeple. *DJ.*

From the PEGASUS in Grub-street.

The *EPILOGUE*, written by Mr. HAVARD, and spoken by Mrs. GIFFARD, before the ancient and honourable society of Free-Masons, at the New Theatre in Goodman's-Fields, Nov. 29.

WEll,—here I'm come to let you know my thoughts;
Nay,—ben't allarm'd—I'll not attack your fau'ts—
Alike be safe the cuckold, and the wit.
The cuckold-dubber, and the solemn crit —
I'm in good humour, and am come to prattle —
Han't I a head well turn'd, d'ye think, to rattle ?
But to clear up the point, and to be free —
What think you is my subject ?—Masonry —
Tho' I'm afraid, at lawyers cases clear,
My learn'd debate will leave you as you were.
But I'm a woman — and when I say that,
You know we'll talk—tho' tis — we know not what.
What think you, ladies, an't it dev'lish hard,
That we shou'd from this secret be debarr'd ?
How comes it, that the softest hours of love
To wheedle out this secret fruitless prove ?
For we can wheedle, when we hope to move.
What can it mean ? why all this mighty pother ?
Their mystic signs, and solemn calling Brother ?
That we are qualify'd in signs is known ;
We can keep secrets too — but they're our own.
When my good man first went to be a Mason,
Tho' I resolv'd to put the smoothest face on ;
Yet, to speak truely, I began to fear
He must some dreadful operation bear.
But he return'd to satisfy each doubt,
And brought home every thing he carry'd out :
Nay, came improv'd ; for on his face appear'd
A pleasing smile, that ev'ry scruple clear'd ;
Such added complaisance—so much good nature;
So much, so strangely alter'd for the better, —
That to increase our mutual delight,
Would he were made a Mason every night.

FOREIGN NEWS.

THURSDAY, *Nov.* 30.

Paris, Dec. 6. N.S. His catholic Majesty hath ordered the king of Sardinia's ambassador, to be gone from Seville in 24 hours, and from Spain in a fortnight. *C. &c.*
Vienna, Nov. 22. N.S. The grand seignior has signed the peace with his imperial majesty for 20 years longer. *P.*
Rome, Nov. 15. Last week died the lord Ratcliff, (so called here,) and has left the bulk of his estate, very considerable, to one of his grand nephews; and a curious collection of medals to the chevalier de S. George. *P.*
FRIDAY, *Dec.* 1.
Rome, Nov 15. We learn from Bologne, that the serene infante duke is returned from Placentia to Parma. *DP.* — Not being able to endure the air of Placentia. *C.*
TUESDAY, *Dec.* 5.
Paris, Dec. 1. The parliament was opened this day : but in case the court do not vouchsafe some satisfaction to that illustrious body, it is much feared that the animosities will become more inveterate than ever. *P.*

We desire, that the advertisements designed for this paper may be sent before twelve of the clock on tuesdays, otherwise they cannot be inserted.

BOOKS and PAMPHLETS published in November.

16. A defence of the doctrine of eternal justification : by John Brine. Pr. 1 s.
17. A collection of heads and titles proper for a common place in law and equity, &c.
20. The first volume of the Toast: An epic poem done from the Latin of Frederick Scheffer, by Peregrine O Donald Esq.
21. Teraminta : the last new English opera. Pr. 1 s. The historical Register. No 67.
22. The honour of Christ vindicated. Pr. 1 s. 6 d. The interest of protestant dissenters considered.
23. A plan of education for a young prince. Pr. 6 d. Modern history relating to Great Britain : by Mr Salmon. Vol. V. P. 1.
24. Religious zeal: a sermon preach'd at Bristol, Sep. 15. by John Gardiner, M.A.

ADVERTISEMENTS.

Next Monday will be published,
(*Useful to Gentlemen, Architects, Sculptors, Painters, Workmen, and all Persons concern'd in Building ;*)
NUMBER V.
A Second Edition of the
Magazine of Architecture, Perspective and Sculpture. Collected from the most approved Authors, Ancient and Modern ; particularly PALLADIO, SCAMOZZI, and VIGNOLA.
By EDWARD OAKLEY, Architect.
CONDITIONS.

The whole Work, consisting of Ninety-seven Impressions from Copper Plates, and Thirty-one Sheets and a Half of Common Press-Work, which amounts to Eighty Sheets, and is to be divided into Sixteen Numbers, each Number containing Ten Half-Sheets ; and according to the Precedence in the Volume, it will some times happen that a Number will consist of only Prints, and at other Times of only Common Press Work. The whole Numbers are to be deliver'd in Form following ; viz.

No.	Plates	Sh.		No.	Plates	Sh.		No.	Plates	Sh.		No.	Plates	Sh.
I.	— 4	3		V.	— 6	2		IX.	— 8	1		XIII.	— 2	4
II.	— 4	3		VI.	— 10	0		X.	— 7	1		XIV.	— 8	1
III.	— 2	4		VII.	— 10	0		XI.	— 8	1		XV.	— 10	0
IV.	— 0	5		VIII.	— 12	6		XII.	— 6	2		XVI.	— 2	4

Each Number to be deliver'd stitch'd in blue Paper at 12 d. each every other Monday. And, as no Money is advanc'd for the carrying on the Work, so no Number will be deliver'd without Money.
N. B. A small Number is to be printed for the Curious on Royal Paper, at 1 s. 6 d. each Number.
Each Subscriber is desired to enter his Name, Profession, and Place of Abode, that the Numbers may be deliver'd right.
SUBSCRIPTIONS are taken in by the Author, at the Three Doves in Brewers-street, Golden-Square ; B. Creake, at the Bell Bible in Ave-Mary-Lane, near St. Paul's ; W. Waring, at the Bible in Jermyn-street S. James's ; and by the Booksellers of London and Westminster.

SILK-WORMS.

This Day is Published, in Quarto,
(*Price Two Shillings, stitch'd,*)
A Compendious Account of the whole Art of Breeding, Nursing, and the right Ordering of the Silk-Worm ; illustrated with Figures, beautifully engraven on Six large Copper Plates, wherein is exhibited the whole Management of this profitable Insect.
Note, One of the Plates, curiously representing the several Transformations of that wonderful Creature, was delineated (and is now colour'd) from the Life, by the ingenious ELEAZAR ALBIN.
Printed for J. Worral, at the Dove in Bell-Yard, near Lincoln's Inn ; O. Payne, in Round-Court in the Strand ; T. Boreman, on Ludgate-hill, near the Gate ; and T. Game, at the Bible, facing the East End of the New Church in the Strand.

This Day is published,

In Two Volumes in Quarto,
AN Anatomical Exposition of the Structure of the Human Body.
By JAMES-BENIGNUS WINSLOW.
Professor of Physick, Anatomy, and Surgery, in the University of Paris, Member of the Royal Academy of Sciences and Royal Society at Berlin, &c. Translated from the French Original, by G. DOUGLAS, M.D.
Printed for N. PROVOST, at the Ship over-against Southampton-street in the Strand.
N. B. There are a few Copies printed on a fine Paper.

Whereas many Persons are sorely troubled with Kibes and Chilblains, and at a Loss for an Immediate Cure ;
THIS is to inform all such Persons of either Sex, or of any Age, of a long experienced Balsam, which immediately cures the worst of Kibes or Chilblains, whether broken or whole, so effectually that they will never be troubled with them for the future. It is the best Medicine that ever was known or made use of for those Ailments ; also Womens sore Breasts, and chapped Nipples, whether broken or whole, are safely and speedily cured by it ; and is to be had only at Mrs Markham's Toy-shop, the Seven Stars under St. Dunstan's Church in Fleet-street ; and at Mr. Tichbourn's, a Grinder's Shop, at the Golden-Ball in the Minories, the third House from Vine-street, near Aldgate, Price 3 s. each Gally-pot.

To Morrow will be published,
the SEVENTH and EIGHTH VOLUMES of a SELECT COLLECTION of MOLIERE's COMEDIES, in French and English, *which finish the Collection, being Printed on a Fine Paper, with a Curious Frontispiece to each Come.*

N. B. A Curious PRINT of the AUTHOR; with his LIFE in French and English, extracted from Monsieur Bayle, Rapin, &c. will be deliver'd (GRATIS) with the said Seventh and Eighth Volumes, to compleat the Collection.

The Seventh Volume contains,	
Amphytryon,	Dedicated to the Right Hon.
Amphitryon.	George Dodington Esq;
Le Marriage Forcé.	Dedicated to the Right Hon. the
The Forc'd Marriage.	Lady Harvey.
Le Sicilien, ou L'Amour Peintre.	Dedicated to her Grace the Dutchess
The Sicilian, or Love makes a	of Richmond.
Painter.	

The Eighth Volume contains,	
Le Malade Imaginaire.	Dedicated to his Grace the Duke of
The Hypochondriack.	Argyle.
Les Fâcheux.	Dedicated to the Right Honourable
The Impertinents.	the Lord Carteret.

Printed and Sold by J. Watts at the Printing-Office in Wild-Court, near Lincoln's-Inn Fields : and J. Brotherton in Cornhill ; J. Clarke in Duck-Lane ; A. Betterworth and C. Hitch, J. Osborne and T. Longman, and J. Batley in Pater-Noster-Row ; J. Roberts in Warwick-Lane ; J. Pemberton, L. Gilliver and T. Worrall in Fleet-Street ; F. Clay and K. Wellington without Temple-Bar ; A. Millar and P. Dunoyer in the Strand ; J. Batton in Little Ormond-Street ; J. Stagg in Westminster-Hall ; and J. Brindley in New Bond-Street. Of whom may be had, just published,

Vol. I. containing,	
A General PREFACE to the whole WORK.	
L'AVARE.	Dedicated to his Royal Highness
The MISER.	The Prince of Wales.
Sganarelle ou le Cocu Imaginaire.	
The Cuckold in Conceit.	Dedicated to Miss Wolstenholme.

Vol. II. containing,	
Le Bourgeois Gentilhomme.	Dedicated to his Royal Highness
The Citizen'd Gentleman.	the Duke.
Le Medecin de Malgré Lui.	
A Doctor and no Doctor.	Dedicated to Dr. Mead.

Vol. III. containing,	
L'Etourdi ou les Contre-Tems.	Dedicated to the Right Honourable
The Blunderer : Or, the Counter-Plots.	Philip Earl of Chesterfield.
Précieuses Ridicules.	
The Conceited Ladies.	Dedicated to Miss Le Bass.

Vol. IV. containing,	
L'Ecole des Maris.	Dedicated to the Right Honourable
The School for Husbands.	the Lady Harriot Cambell.
L'Ecole des Femmes.	Dedicated to the Right Honourable
The School for Wives.	Sir Wm. Yong, Knight of the Bath.

Vol. V. containing,	
Tartuffe, ou L'Imposteur.	Dedicated to Mr. Wyndham of
The Impostor.	Clower-Wall, in Gloucestershire
George Dandin, ou le Mari Confondu.	
George Dandin, or the Husband Defeated.	Dedicated to the Right Honourable the Lady ***

Vol. VI. containing,	
Le Misantrope.	Dedicated to his Grace the Duke of
The Man-Hater.	Montagu.
M. De Pourceaugnac.	Dedicated to the Right Hon. the
Squire Lubberly.	Lady Mary Wortley Montagu.

The Translation is entirely new, and was undertaken by several Gentlemen, who all joined and consulted together about every Part of it. Particular Care has been had to keep as close as possible to the Original, and to observe the very words of the Author, as well as his Sense, so far as would consist with giving it a spirited and easy Comick Stile, in order to make it the more serviceable to those of our own Nation who are Learners of the French Language ; as likewise to Foreigners who desire to be acquainted with ours : To whom the Method we had taken of placing the French and English opposite to each other, will be of no small Benefit. The Work is printed in a very beautiful Manner, and adorned with new Frontispieces, designed by Monsieur COYPEL, Mr. HOGARTH, Mr. DANDRIDGE, Mr. HAMILTON, &c. Price of each Volume, done up in blue Covers, Two Shillings and Six Pence.

The Grub-ſtreet Journal. NUMB. 155.

Thursday, *DECEMBER* 14. 1732.

IT will be difficult to ſpeak of the method of the *New Diſpenſary*, ſince, properly ſpeaking, there is no one method in it, unleſs ſomething of unity may have ariſen fortuitouſly from the mixture and colliſion of, I know not how, many contrary methods, which the author has jumbled together. Inſtead, for inſtance, of giving all the medicinal ſimples uniformly, under ſome one point of view, he has ſcattered them under three ; pretending to follow three celebrated authors, Dr. BOERHAAVE in one part, Mr. RAY in another, and Dr. WOODWARD in a third : whereas, in reality, he follows none of them ; unleſs miſtaking their deſigns, and perverting their methods to purpoſes quite remote from their own, may be called following them. He ſhould have conſidered, that thoſe authors wrote with different views from each other, and all of them from his : that they were not writing books of phyſic, but of botany, zoology, and minerology ; and that their meaſures and methods were adopted accordingly, not to the exhibiting things, ſo as we might conceive their medicinal uſes ; but their *General Species* and diſtinctions : and that, had any of them been to write a Diſpenſary, he would have taken a quite different courſe ; as BOERHAAVE has accordingly done in his piece *de Materia Medica*, which is properly his *Diſpenſary*. Dr. JAMES is unhappy at following great men : he concluded he could not go wrong with ſuch guides before him ; forgetting that they were not going his way ; that they were travelling the high road of natural hiſtory, and he the by-way of pharmacy. This has drawn him into the fatal error called by Logicians μετάβασις εἰς ἄλλο γένος, that is, ſetting one ſcience to the tune and pitch of another, and making phyſic and pharmacy dance over hill and dale, after botany, zoology, and I know not what.

As a conſequence hereof, we find all the matters of his book lye acroſs the main deſign of it ; and introduced ſo as to obſtruct, inſtead of aſſiſting, each other. Things neareſt related to each other are ſeparated furtheſt aſunder ; and thoſe brought together, which have no medicinal relation at all. Thus the ſeveral ſimples, e. gr. which agree in being *cardiac*, or *pectoral*, or *vulnerary*, are diſperſed to all points of the compaſs, that others may come together, which agree in certain quaint characters ; as much to the purpoſe of negromancy, as pharmacy. E.gr. The ſeveral plants, which agree in *having one naked ſeed to each flower, and diſcous radiated flowers* : *The ſeveral plants with one naked ſeed to each flower, and diſcous flowers not radiated* : *The ſeveral plants with two naked ſeeds to each flower, and leaves diſpoſed at the joints in form of a radiated ſtar.* — For whoſe uſe may all theſe ſubtilties be calculated ? For botaniſts, you will ſay ! This is too much : the botaniſt himſelf will be at a loſs the next claſs of ſimples that turns up, where he will have to encounter with *all the leſſer animals that are exanguious, and all the greater animals that are exanguious*; and the like : and the zoologiſt, as well as botaniſt, will be caſt out in another claſs, which is only ſuited to the uſe of mineraliſts : for apothecaries, and good women, and ſuch ſort of folks, they ſeem to have no buſineſs in any part.

The like confuſion runs through the preparations of the ſimples : where, inſtead of finding all thoſe procured from the ſame ſubſtance together, they are diſperſed, the *Salt* in one place, the *Water* in another, the *Powder* in another : ſo that it is impoſſible to find what number of preparations any ſimple affords, without, I mean, turning through the whole book. For, as to the *Index*, which ſhould help out on ſuch caſes, inſtead of being a clue to this labyrinth, it makes it more intricate ; as muſt needs be the caſe, conſidering that it is copied from Q. to the ſtructure and method of whoſe book, it was particularly adapted ; ſo that when applied to Dr. A's book, like a key made for another kind of lock, the more you try it, the further you are at a loſs.

Our author cloſes with a *Diſcourſe on the Operations of Medicines*, which fairly overturns the reſt of the book. It is taken from Dr. BOERHAAVE ; whoſe ſyſtem and way of reaſoning on this head are known to be as different from that of Dr. FRIEND, and Dr. QUINCY, which reigns through the body of the work, as Alkali from Acid. The two latter reſolve all into mechanical principles : the former proteſts againſt the ſufficiency thereof, and contends for ſomething immechanical. Theſe oppoſite ſyſtems are both adopted by our author, as if they were conſiſtent : accordingly, all his reaſoning on particular medicines is founded on the one, and his general reaſonings on the other.

But this is not all : In his *Recipes* he every where follows the practice of the London Phyſicians, who are famous for being great compounders ; yet, in the laſt part, he follows one, who is for reducing all phyſic to the uſe of ſimples : ſo that Dr. JAMES has, with his own hand, in his fourth part, ſtruck out all the *Recipes* which make his ſecond and third.

Of all this Author's talents, compoſition ſeems the principal one. For who but himſelf could have thought of making Dr. FRIEND and Dr. BOERHAAVE draw in the ſame yoak ; and the *London* and *Leyden* practice go hand in hand ? *Jungentur jam gryphes equis.* Who but he could have made a book of ſuch jarring elements ? His ſimples look awry on each other ; his *Table of Contents* on itſelf ; his *Index* on the book ; one part of the book claſhes with another ; and the laſt with the whole : general's fight with particulars ; Recipes run counter to reaſonings ; and theory gives the lye to practice.

Thus far I have traced my author, to ſhew how well he was qualified to perſonate Dr. ALLEN ; and to deter others by his example, from aſſuming names they are not fit for.—This brings me back to my firſt propoſal of an *Office for Titles*, as the only effectual method of ſecuring learned men in the quiet poſſeſſion of their own names ; and at the ſame time of making even the worſt writers, if not uſeful, yet innocent : ſince it matters little what their books be, provided their title pages be accordingly. On this condition I will even forgive N. B. the ſuppoſed author, and Meſſ. S. A. and T. A. the publiſhers of the new *Pharmacopœia*, if, within a month from the date of this advertiſement, they reprint their title page after the following model, which they will find drawn up with all the tenderneſs and regard to their intereſt, that a concern for truth and juſtice would admit.

A new edition of Dr. QUINCY's *Diſpenſary*; wherein certain little matters, relating chiefly to grammar, are added ; many great ones relating to phyſic and pharmacy are omitted ; and divers others are ſo altered, as to make a ſurprizing contraſt, and diſcordancy with the reſt. The whole thrown into a new kind of order ; wherein, for certain private reaſons, thoſe things which ought to come firſt are brought laſt ; and ſuch as were before joined together, are ſeparated . . . . By JOHN A-NOKES, M.D.

I am, Sir, your humble Servant,
ISAAC DE DUOBUS, N. M.

AS nothing is more certain, than that induſtry is the mother of wealth : ſo it is as true, that luxury can produce nothing but poverty, which is the direct road to ſlavery. Were not theſe truths ſelf-evident and apparent to every man of common ſenſe, I might bring ſeveral inſtances from hiſtory to prove them. Whatever nation has made a figure in the world, has owed its glory to the ſeverity of its manners, to an induſtry in acquiring, and a frugality in managing wealth. If the people are moderate in their deſires, which they will be while ſuch deſires are regulated by their wants, and induſtrious in their ſeveral profeſſions, it will neceſſarily follow, that their incomes will be greater than their expences ; and conſequently they will have a ſufficient fund or ſtock of money, to anſwer any noble enterprize, in which they ſhall engage ; and wealth and power being in reality the ſame, there is little doubt but they will be ſucceſsful in their undertakings. But when, on the contrary, luxury creeps into the minds of men, they are immediately rendered lazy, expenſive, and effeminate, incapable of all buſineſs ; and, in one word, are uſeleſs members of any ſociety to which they belong. The wantonneſs and luxury of the preſent age affords, indeed, a ſufficient theme for declamation. And I might here take occaſion to preach upon this head ; but that, I think, the learned author of the *London Journal* has a peculiar right to the province ; which he has ſo long enjoy'd, as much to his own honour, as to the edification of his candid and patient readers.

That which threw me into theſe ſerious reflections, was a viſit I lately made to a new Theatre, erected not long ago for the entertainment of certain Wits, that inhabit the purlieus of Lombard-ſtreet and Billingsgate ; who were aſſigned by their indulgent, but miſtaken, parents to ſhops and counting-houſes, when their genius's led them to the Muſes and Parnaſſus. But at length one Mr. G———aroſe, who taking pity on their unhappy condition, having no perſonal intereſt of his own to ſerve, but fir'd with the example of the god-like BRUTUS, in freeing an enſlaved peo-

ple, was reſolv'd likewiſe to ſet at liberty theſe choice ſpirits, and to place them in the ſtation of critics and poetical judges, for which providence had deſigned them.

Upon taking my ſeat in the Pit, I introduced myſelf to the converſation of my neighbour, by communicating to him two or three ſecrets ; which, tho' known to every one, every one thinks himſelf the only maſter of ; ſuch as the temperature of the air, the hour of the day, and ſome other of the like importance. My curioſity naturally led me to inquire what was to be that night's entertainment ; to which my friend readily anſwered, *The Orphan*, or *The Unhappy Marriage*. I was not a little ſurpriſed at this anſwer : for I expected to have been entertain'd with ſome ſtory adapted to the place and audience ; either the *Hiſtory of Wittington and his Cat*, *The London Apprentice*, or *The lamentable Tragedy of George Barnwell*.

It grew towards ſix, when I obſerv'd the company coming into the boxes : the ſplendour of the dreſſes, both of the men and women, made me imagine they were perſons of quality, led by curioſity from the other end of the town, either to ſee the repreſentation, or the audience, which is indeed the more diverting object of the two. But, upon inquiry, I found, they were all citizens ; among whom I obſerved one beau dreſs'd like a bridegroom, whom I had ſeen that very morning ſprinkling a ſhop, and paring his maſter's pavement in Cheapſide. I ſaw one lady in the ſtage-box (which it ſeems is dedicated to women of faſhion) particularly ſplendid in her habit, and loaded with jewels. I could not help demanding of my friend (whom I found to be very converſant in the city) whether he knew that lady, ————he told me he did ; and that ſhe was old ————the Jew's wife : but, ſays he, thoſe diamonds are not her own ; the is a mere daw in peacock's feathers ; thoſe jewels are ſome which have been pawn'd by women of quality, who have had ill luck at play ; and whenever they can redeem them, that lady muſt be ſtripp'd of her ornaments.——Here I could not help objecting to the lady's judgment, in wearing that, of which ſhe muſt ſome day or other be deprived ; and by the diſcovery, lay herſelf open to the ridicule of her acquaintance.——No, no, ſays my friend, ſhe knows a trick worth two of that ; for when they are redeem'd, it is but putting on ſome falſe ſtones, of which her huſband has enough, which he ſells to credulous Chriſtians for real jewels.——But pray, ſays I, who may that young gentleman be, that is ſo very complaiſant and civil to the lady, of whom we have been ſpeaking ?——That, reply'd he, is a Templar, of a ſhort allowance, and an extravagant temper : he is a Chriſtian, or at leaſt reputed ſuch ; but not ſo ſcrupulous but he can ſit at table with publicans and unbelievers, and has no objection to meat, tho' there be no gravy in it ; and the lady is ſo far of his perſuaſion, as to think a man never the worſe gallant for being uncircumciſed. On the contrary, ſhe thinks their great Legiſlator was highly offended with the women, when he enjoined the needleſs ceremony of amputation.

I have often fancied with myſelf, that women were deſign'd for ornament, becauſe nature has given them a genius, which directs them, as it were, by inſtinct, how to order themſelves to the beſt advantage. A girl of fifteen, who has never been educated to dreſs, will put on her clothes ſo as to appear eaſy and agreeable, or what the modern phraſe terms genteel. This I ſaw inſtanced in the ſeveral young beauties in the play-houſe, who appear'd with a gracefulneſs beyond what I expected. But the men, on the contrary, endeavouring to be well dreſs'd, and to reſemble the beaux of St. James's, (as all fools are fond of imitation,) were the moſt awkward, unlick'd cubs I ever beheld. Their habits were indeed expenſive, and faſhion'd according to art ; but ſtill you might diſcover the apprentice, like the aſs under the lion's ſkin, notwithſtanding all their endeavours to conceal it ; which I can impute to nothing but God's judgment upon their arrogance, in attempting to be gentlemen, for which they were never deſign'd.

As I have a great veneration and reſpect for all young lads, commonly known by the name of apprentices, who bear themſelves well in their ſeveral vocations ; as young ſpruce mercers, who do not impoſe upon good country ladies, (too much captivated with their perſons, and allur'd by their eloquence,) in ſelling them old-faſhion'd ſilks, or, as they term them, ſhop-keepers, for the neweſt french faſhions ; for young vintners, that are not too liberal in mixing Alicant in their Port, and lime in their ſack ; I have publiſhed this, which may be intitled *The Apprentices Looking-Glaſs*, deſiring them to mend their behaviour, leſt they oblige me to animadvert upon them again, and publiſh their characters at Temple-Bar and the Royal Exchange.

An EPIGRAM, *occaſioned by reading* the monthly bills of Hyp-oratorical mortality, *in the* Grub-ſtreet Journals.

PUffs and advertiſements, like gaſps of breath,
Drawn in th' approaching agonies of death,
Shew, that the Puffers are but juſt alive;
Tho' ſtill in thoſe they ſay, they're well and thrive.
Whilſt ſuch bold Quacks a dying life inſure,
A living death their patients ſtill endure.
When puffs and advertiſements ceaſe to fly,
The Patients ſoon revive, and Doctors dye.

MÆVIUS.

DOMESTIC NEWS.

C. *Courant.*	E P. *Evening Poſt.*
P. *Poſt-Boy.*	S J. *St. James's Evening Poſt.*
D P. *Daily Poſt.*	W E. *Whitehall Evening Poſt.*
D J. *Daily Journal.*	L E. *London Evening Poſt.*

THURSDAY, *Dec.* 7.

On Friday arrived from Hanover Mr. Curtis, who is appointed riding meſſenger, for managing the great ſaddle horſes belonging to his majeſty. *D J. C.* —— Out of the 60 head of deer arrived from his majeſty's German dominions, 28 died in their paſſage. *C.* — 29. *D J.* — *The* heads *of all* 60, *by this account*, are arrived.]

Yeſterday five private centinels were whipt on the parade for deſertion, three received 300 laſhes, and the two other 200. *C.* — Eight were whipt, and received 200 each. *D J.*

The right honourable the lord mayor being ill of the gout, Mr. baron Thompſon, recorder, went yeſterday to open the ſeſſions at the Old Baily. *D J.*

Yeſterday at the ſale at the South-ſea houſe, cochineal ſold on an average at upwards of 17s. 6d. per pound. *D P.*

The ſame day was to have come on at the court of king's bench, Weſtminſter, the tryal of Mr Lowfield, but the word *caperet* being in the indictment, and *caperit* in the record, the tryal went off. *D P.* — *This miſtake of an* e *for an* i *was of ſtrange conſequence, ſince it made* a tryal go off; *which only* was to have come on, *but did not.*

On tueſday night there was a meeting of about 23 perſons at the Nag's head tavern in Cheapſide, in the room of N° 21; but ſeveral of them having met about petitioning for the repeal of the teſt act, and others for obtaining ſatiſfaction for their loſſes in the Harburgh lottery, purſuant to two advertiſements, they ſtared at one another for two hours, and then paid the reckoning, which came to one ſhilling a-piece; and thereby amicably compromiſed the matter. *C.* — *This* meeting *was more ſilent and unanimous, than that on wedneſday, Nov.* 29.

On tueſday in the afternoon, a man robb'd a poor woman in the fields, between Newington and Clapton, of three pence farthing: he pull'd out a ſhoemaker's knife; which ſhe drew through his hand, and cut it in a deſperate manner. A gardener coming up at the ſame time, took him, and he was committed to Newgate. — At night, about eight, ſome rogues got into Mr. Barker's parlour, a ſaddler in Fetter-lane, and ſtole effects to the value of 40 *l.* *D J.* —— Mr Bates, a weaver in Spittle fields, returning from Newington-green, was beat by two foot-pads, and robb'd of hat, wig, watch, and money. *C.* — Mrs. Harding, at the Chequer-inn in Holborn, ſeized a man in her waſh-houſe, who knock'd her down, and made his eſcape. *D J.*

On ſaturday Mr. Scott, an eminent mercer in Covent-garden, was married to the widow of Mr. Conſtantine, a mercer in that ſtreet, a fortune of 3000 l. *D P.* — On tueſday Mr. Tomkinſon, a noted butcher in Leaden hall market, was married to an agreeable widow gentlewoman, with a fortune of 10 000 l. *S J.*

On Monday died at the Bath, Dr Baker, biſhop of Norwich, and rector of S. Giles's in the fields: he was conſecrated Aug. 11. 1723. biſhop of Bangor, and tranſlated Dec. 19. 1727 to Norwich. *D P.* —— In his 64th year. *D J.* — At night died Mrs. Vernon, who lately kept the ſwan and rummer tavern in Finch-lane. *C.*

FRIDAY, *Dec* 8.

Yeſterday being the anniverſary of the birth of her royal highneſs the princeſs Louiſa, who entered into the 7th year of her age, there was a great appearance at court, &c. *C.* — Into the 9th, being born Dec. 7 1724. *P.*

On monday at Fordwich, John Adams Eſq; the late mayor, was rechoſen in preference to two gentlemen; which choice was ſuppoſed by ſome to be grounded upon an old cuſtom derived from the time of Edward III. who lay there a fortnight wind bound; during which time, a certain foreigner coming thither, wrote a ſmall tract, *de rebus ſuis*, &c. wherein are the following lines:

Hinc in Fordwicum ſera ſub nocte venimus:
[illegible] *mos ductus ab avo;*
[illegible] *eligitur, revoluto tempore, Prætor,*
[illegible] *circa menſam ſtratuuntur aeternam:*
Beſtia, pes, mordax, ſueta [illegible]
Ponitur in medio; tum cujus numine [illegible]
Veſtem adit, toto hinc gratantur murmure fratres,
Atque celebratur ſubjecta per oppida Prætor. P.

Mr. SPONDEE reads in the firſt verſe *ſera*, in the fourth *Plauſtrarii*, and in the fifth *inter creſcere*.

Yeſterday William Pen Eſq; one of the proprietors of Penſilvania, and grandſon of the late Sir William, was married to Miſs Forbes, eldeſt daughter of Mr. Alex Forbes an eminent merchant. *D P.* — Grandaughter to the noted Mr Barclay, author of the Apology. *C.* — At the Quakers meeting-houſe in Devonſhire-ſquare. *P.*

On ſaturday died the lady Pickering, relict of Sir Harry. *C.* —— On wedneſday night died at her houſe in Pall mall, Madam Titus, a maiden gentlewoman, daughter to the late Col. Titus, worth upwards of 60,000 l. — Yeſterday died Mr Odier, an eminent ſurgeon in Pall mall. *P.*

Mr. John Gay is to be interred in Weſtminſter-abbey, at the expence of his grace the duke of Queensberry, who will erect a monument to the memory of ſo facetious and excellent a companion. *D P.* —— A fine monument will be erected by John Rich Eſq; *D J.*

SATURDAY, *Dec.* 6.

The phyſicians have adviſed her majeſty to a change of air. *L E.*

We hear the reverend Dr. Henry Bland, dean of Durham, will be made biſhop of Norwich, and hold his deanery *in commendam*. *P.* — The right reverend Dr. Tanner, biſhop of Aſaph, will be tranſlated to the biſhoprick of Norwich. *D P.*

Yeſterday the reverend Dr. Gally, domeſtic chaplain to the right honourable the lord chancellor, was preſented by his lordſhip to the rectory of S. Giles's in the fields, *P.* — The reverend Dr. Gally will be preſented. *D P.*

This week there was a great meeting of diſſenting miniſters, and others of the ſeveral denominations, at Thame in Oxfordſhire, to conſider of ways and means for obtaining a repeal of the corporation and teſt acts, and after ſigning papers, by way of remonſtrance, &c. they returned to their habitations. *D P.*

Durham, Dec. 3 On friday the reverend Dr. Sharp, rector of Rothbury, and archdeacon of Northumberland, was inſtalled a prebendary, in the room of the reverend Mr. Sayer, who reſigned to him. — The reverend Mr. Bryan Turner, a minor canon, is made precentor. *D P.*

The bill preferred againſt a footman for a rape upon the body of Mrs. St. George's ſiſter, was returned *Ignoramus*. *S J. L E.* — *Want of* knowledge, *makes an* Ignoramus.

On wedneſday died at his houſe on Turnham-Green, Obadiah James Eſq; formerly an eminent Weſt-India merchant. *P.* — On thurſday Mr. Wells, who kept the blue-boar-head-inn in King's-ſtreet, Weſtminſter. *D J.* — At night died at Highgate, Mrs Sheaf, relict of the late Mr. Alex. Sheaf, a noted ſtationer in Bread-ſtreet. *W E.*

MONDAY, *Dec* 11.

On ſaturday in the evening, his majeſty, his royal highneſs the prince, and the princeſs royal, went to the opera. *C.* — Yeſterday the reverend Dr Pearce preached before the king, his royal highneſs the prince, &c and the reverend Dr. Crow, before his royal highneſs the duke, &c. *C.* &c.

On ſaturday an officer belonging to the ſalt office, going a ſhooting, his gun, having been charged before, and by him charged afreſh, in firing burſt, and tore off his thumb and three fingers. *D J.* — *It was very proper the public ſhould know this*

A few days ſince died Sir John Armitage of Kirklees, in the Weſt riding of Yorkſhire, Bart. aged 82. and dying unmarried, the dignity and eſtate (between 3 and 4000 l. per annum,) devolves to his younger brother, now Sir George. *D J.* — On ſaturday Mr. Windman, a noted Goldſmith in Cheapſide. *D J.* — Yeſterday morning, Mr Bawdrey, one of his majeſty's meſſengers. *P.* — In the afternoon, the reverend Dr. Gaskarth, rector of All-hallows, Barkin, near Tower-hill: he was preſented to that living by archbiſhop Sancroft, which he enjoyed 47 years without either ſeeking or getting any other preferment. *D J.* —— *It is no wonder, that he did not* get, *ſince he did not* ſeek any other.

TUESDAY, *Dec.* 12.

Yeſterday her majeſty, being well recovered of her cold, was at the levy, &c. *P.* — We hear, that her majeſty, out of her extenſive goodneſs, and great value for the ſeveral poetical performances that have been wrote as encomiums on the buſtoes of the ſeveral great authors, which her majeſty has been graciouſly pleaſed to fix in the royal hermitage at Richmond, has ordered the ſame to be printed and bound in one volume, in as neat a manner, as can poſſibly be done, in order to perpetuate their memories. *C.* —— *Is only one copy* to be printed; *or are ſeveral copies* to be bound in one volume?

On wedneſday night, the houſe of Mr. Gooding, a ſea-captain in Free-ſchool-ſtreet, Horſleydown, was broke open, and robb'd of plate, &c to the amount of 150 l. *P.* — *My* brother *forgets the ſaying,* Once a captain, and always a captain.

Laſt night the ſeſſions ended at the Old Baily, when ſix perſons received ſentence of death: viz. Henry Neal, Ebenezer Dunn, John Ingram, and William Roberts, alias Hampton, for burglary; William Macclachiane [Macklochlane. *P.* Macclogue. *C. D P.*] late footman to Meſſ. De Vic and Cray, for ſtealing 90 guineas; and William Heath, a cobler in Biſhopſgate-ſtreet, for taking from a woman ſome child bed linen, and three pence farthing. *D J.* — 23 were ordered for tranſportation. *C.* — 33 *D P.* — 35 *P.* — 2 were burnt on the hand. *C.* &c. —— Barth. Harnet was found guilty of wilful and corrupt perjury, for ſwearing a robbery on the highway againſt William Holmes; and ſentenced to ſtand three times in the pillory, to be impriſoned one year, and to be tranſported for ſeven. *D J. C. P.* — Holmes died of the goal diſtemper ſoon after he was diſcharged from Newgate. *D P.*

On the 9th died at Bentley, near Ipſwich, William Beaſton, M. D. aged 60. an able phyſician of great practice. *D J.* —— On ſunday at her houſe in Leiceſter-fields, the right honourable lady Mary Howard, relict of the lord Thomas Howard of Workſop, and mother to his grace the preſent duke of Norfolk. *P.*

Yeſterday came on at Guild-hall a trial, for words, between a merchant and a gentleman; the latter ſaying, *the former would break*: the jury conſidering what a nice thing credit is to merchants and tradeſmen, gave a verdict of 1500 l. damages. *L E.*

A few days ſince counſellor Martin was married to miſs Rogers of Chancery-Lane, an agreeable young lady, endow'd with all the qualifications proper for the *Bar*. *L E.*

WEDNESDAY, *Dec.* 13.

Laſt week died at his ſeat near Portſmouth in Hampſhire, —— Norton Eſq; who hath (as we are credibly inform'd) given all his real eſtate, near 6000 l. per annum, and alſo his perſonal eſtate, upwards of 60,000 l. to the parliament of Great Britain, whom he hath nominated his executors, in truſt to diſpoſe thereof in charitable uſes at their diſcretion; and in caſe the parliament refuſes to accept the ſaid truſt, he then deſires the right reverend the biſhops of England to execute the ſame; and we hear alſo he hath given all his fine collection of pictures to his majeſty. *D P.*

Yeſterday, and the day before, above 200,000 l. India Bonds were carried in and mark'd; and her grace the dutcheſs of Kendall ſent in alſo a conſiderable number; and tis at laſt thought the bondholders will comply, and take three and a half per cent. *D P.* — Mr. Conundrum aſſures *me, that no* Chriſtian *drew up this paragraph: for inſtead of* 200,000 l. bonds, carried in *and* mark'd, *it ſhould have been* 2000 *perſons* went in *to a ſale or* market, *where* ſome Directors *would fain have* indirectly ken'd all, *but could not* ken one *of* the Dutcheſs's bonds; *and that this very day, at a meeting of the* bond-holders, *they confirmed their former repeated reſolution as to four per cent, in* which *her grace the dutcheſs of Marlborough heartily concurs. From whence it is inferred, that our brother, the* Daily Poſt, *who is thus, either undeſignedly, or deſignedly in the dark, ought to change his name to the* K-nightly Poſt.

From the PEGASUS *in Grub-ſtreet.*

IN our laſt, under the domeſtick news of SATURDAY, was inſerted a N. B. taken from the Oratory advertiſement in *Fog's Journal*, of *Dec.* 2.

" In the ſcripture, the rule of preaching, are above a " thouſand burleſque paſſages, WHICH RENDERS IT ſtrictly " religious in ITS turn.' Upon which Mr. QUIDNUNC made a reflection, intimating, that this N. B. was *irreligious, ungrammatical*, and *nonſenſical*.

In anſwer to which reflection, the following article was publiſhed in the *D J.* of *Dec.* 8. " The reverend Mr. Henley has publickly offered a reward of ten guineas to any " perſon that can prove to his face any objection alledg'd " by nameleſs authors hir'd to write againſt him; as to " Buffoonry being ungrammatical, irreligious, illiterate, im- " pudent, &c. which may be ſaid of ANY preach'd what- " ever." —— To this Mr. QUIDNUNC replies, that Mr. H. has altered the ſubject of diſpute betwixt them, which is, not whether *buffoonry*, but whether the N. B. be *irreligious, ungrammatical*, and *nonſenſical*.

He may very fitly offer *ten guineas* for the *proof* of that, which he knows very well can never be *proved*, upon three accounts: 1. He requires, that ſome *objection*, &c. be *proved* TO HIS FACE; which all the world agrees is *proof* againſt any *proof* that can be brought. 2. The *objection* to be *proved* muſt be ſuch as hath been *alledg'd by nameleſs authors hir'd to write againſt him*: but, 'tis probable, there are no ſuch in the world; and if he means any *authors* of our ſociety, concerned in our *Journal*, it is certain, that he is miſtaken. 3. The *objection* to be *proved*, muſt relate to *buffoonry being ungrammatical, irreligious, illiterate, impudent*, &c. an *objection* which no one has made. If he principally intends his own *buffoonry*; to that indeed it has been objected, that it is *ungrammatical*, and *irreligious*, but not that it is *illiterate* and *impudent*. The [illegible]

and impudence may have been *objected* to the *buffoon*, but never to the *buffoonry.* —— " Which may be faid of any preach'd whatever:" that is, of any *buffoonry.* But tho' it may be juftly faid of any buffoonry which is *preach'd,* that it is *irreligious* ; yet it cannot be juftly faid, that it is *un-grammatical, illiterate, impudent,* &c.

To the affiftance of Mr. Orator comes his fecond felf, the *Tuefday* QUACK-DOCTOR, who in a letter, directed to Mr. BA-VIUS, endeavours to clear the N. B. from being *ungrammatical* and *nonfenfical,* by the following *expofition.* " The antecedent " to the relative WHICH, was, not *paffages,* but the whole pre-" ceding fentence." So that the conftruction runs thus ; "The " fcripture, the rule of preaching, has in it above a thou-" fand burlefque paffages, WHICH [its having above a thou-fand burlefque paffages] " RENDERS IT ftrictly religious in " ITS turn." — To this Mr. BAVIUS anfwers, that allow-ing the fentence will admit of this conftruction, yet it is certainly much lefs natural, than to refer the relative WHICH to *paffages,* and to fuppofe *renders* a miftake, either, of the Orator, or of the Printer : and even with this eafier and more natural conftruction, the fenfe is the very fame with that, for which the Doct-Orator contends. — But the misfortune is, that this will clear but half the difficulty. For, where-as Mr. QUIDNUNC had pointed out by fmall capitals four words, which feemed to be *ungrammatical* and *nonfenfical* [WHICH RENDERS IT ftrictly religious in ITS turn] the two little words IT and ITS are left to fhift for themfelves, with-out the leaft care of this great Grammarian, in affigning them any antecedent fubftantive, to which they can relate. Let them be referred, either to *fcripture,* or *rule,* or *preach-ing,* or *burlefque paffages* ; none of thefe can fecure them from being placed here *ungrammatically* and *nonfenfically.*

When Mr. H. has fhewn the contrary, it will be time enough particularly to confider the fyllogifm in this letter ; which, with ufual affurance, it has been twice affirmed in print, that the GRUBS *refufed* to *infert, for fear of us expo-fing them.* In anfwer to which, Mr. BAVIUS, &c. declare, that no fuch *letter* ever came to their hands; nor did any of them ever fee one line of it till it was in print. They wou'd have been fo far from fuppreffing it, *for fear of ex-pofing themfelves,* that they would have publifhed it, on pur-pofe to *expofe* the writer : as they do now the fyllogiftic part of it ; from which, they think, it will evidently ap-pear, to all who underftand language and logic, that this fyllogifm-cobler underftands neither.

The Queftion is, Whether to affert that the *Scripture has in it above a thoufand burlefque paffages* is irreligious ? *Affirm.* In difproof of which this admirable fyllogifm is brought. " Irony is burlefque, the fcripture abounds with " ironical paffages, *ergo* IT is not buffoonery, nor irreligi-" ous." – *Negatur major : negatur conclufio.*

ANACREONTIS TEII.* Ode III.

Εἰς Ἔρωτα.

Μεσονυκτίοις ποθ' ὥραις ;
Στρέφεται' ὅμοτ' ἤδη
Εκτά χεῖρα τὴν Βοώτου,
Μερόπων δὲ φῦλα πάντα
Εἶκται, κόπω δαμέντα'
Τότ' Ἔρως, ἑπισταθεὶς; μὲν
Θυρέων ἐπ.ηἴ σχλημα.
Τίς τὸρων θύρας ἀράσσει,
Κατ' ἐμεων γρίεας, ὁ πίθρους ;
'Ο τ' Ἔρως ἀνωιγε, φησὶ;
Βρέφος ἐιμί, μὴ φόβησαι'
Βρέχομαι δὲ, κἀσέληνον
Κατὰ νύκτα πεπλάνημαι.'
Ἐλέησα τῶντ' ἀκούσας;
'Ανὰ δ' εὐθν λύχνον ἄψας;
'Ανιξια, ἡ βρέφος; μὲν

III.

In CUPIDINEM.

NOX erat, intempefta ; pigri cùm plauftra Bootæ
Radens, per gelidum volvitur uffa polum ;
Dulcis ubi feffos mortales fomnus habebat,
Reclinique toro preftit amica quies :
Ecce venit, ftratus cùm membra fopore jacerem,
Clauf.que, follicitans, oftia pulfat amor.
Quis tam ferò fores ? dixi : quis rumpit iniquus
Non tempeftivis fomnia grata fonis ?
Ille, reclude, inquit lacrimans, & mitte moveri ;
Sum fine luce vagans, obrutus imb re, puer.
Motus ego precibus turgo, accendoque lucem nam ;
Fidus & à portis mox removetur obex.
Alatum vida puerum ; cui corneus arcus,
Et pharetræ ex humero læve pependit ebur.
Sub tectum ducebam, & ad interiora penatium ;
Et tepido admovi frigida membra foco.
Mollitque expreffi noctiunnum è crinibus imbrem ;
Et Jovi manibus terque quaterque manus.
Jam corpus fit mare vigor, jam frigus abire,
Membra animare novus jam rediviva calor.
Exploremus, art, madefactum, fubdolus, arcum ;
Num nervus pluvia langueat udus aqua.

Dixerat hæc, arcum tendens ; miffique fagitt²
Me ferit, & medium vulnerat ufque jecur.
Deinde mihi, faltu gaudens, rifuque maligno,
Mordaci ingratus ingerit ore jocos.
Hofpes, air, mecum lætare ; en ! omnia tuta :
Haud nervus pluvia ladirur udus aqua :
At te (proh pudor & fcelus !) improba ladit arudo
' Quam vellem hofpitii non victaffe fidem

III.
CUPID.

'TWAS midnight ; when the northern bear
Rolls near Bootes' lazy ear,
When weary mortals lie repos'd,
Their eyes in pleafing flumber clos'd.
'Twas then, that mifchief making brat.
CUPID, flood knocking at my gate.
Who's there, faid I, that calls fo late =
What founds unfeafonably moleft
My foothing dreams, and break my reft ²
Sir, with a piteous tone he cry'd,
Pray, be not angry ; do not chide.
I am a poor, weak, helplefs boy ;
Whom wind, and rain, and dirt annoy :
Who without guide, or moonlight ftray,
Wet to the fkin, as cold clay.
I, who his plaints with pity heard,
Rofe, fprung a light, my gates unbar'd.
A lovely boy ftood fhiv'ring there ;
One, whom, I thought, I need not fear.
I view'd him round, and faw ftrange things ;
A bow, a quiver, and two wings.
Him fhudd'ring to the fire I led,
Chaf'd his chill hands, and ftrok'd his head;
Wringing with care its beauteous curls,
Which new-fal'n rain had hung with pearls.
At length, when warm, the yonker faid,
Alas! my bow —— I am afraid
The ftring is damag'd by the wet ;
And that's a damage very great.
Sir, if you pleafe, We'll quickly try ——
—— Ay, by all means ; do, do, faid I.
With that he bent the ftubborn cugh,
And to the head an arrow drew ;
And pierc'd my liver through and through.
Then giggling loud, and with a bound
Jumping, and cap'ring from the ground,
Landlord, he cry'd, the rain, you fee,
Has us'd my bow moft civilly ;
But, Oh ! I fear th' unlucky dart
Has been uncivil to your heart.

FOREIGN NEWS.
THURSDAY, Dec. 7.

Venice, Nov. 15. N.S. We hear from Placentia, that the infante Don Carlos was ftill there. P.

FRIDAY, Dec. 8.

Rome, Nov. 21. On friday the chevalier de S. George, accompany'd with the princes his two fons, had a private audience of the pope, and conferr'd above an hour with his holinefs : after which he was fumptuoufly regaled by car-dinal Aquaviva. DP. P.

Florence, Nov. 22. On the 19th count Caimo, envoy extraordinary of the emperor, fent to the fenate a perfon unknown, who laid a decree upon the table, inclofed like a letter : which the fenate, fufpecting the contents, fent back to the fecretary's office, without opening it. In that decree, " the emperor abolifhes the homage paid to the in-" fante Don Carlos in June laft, by the ftates of Tufcany ; " and forbids the giving him the title of Great Prince of " Tufcany,' P. DP. DF.

Paris, Dec. 10. Letters from Madrid, of the 25th paft, advife, that they had received certain advice, that the blacks of Miquenez, being difgufted with their king for the exe-cution of fome of their countrymen, had fet his brother on throne. C. DP. —— Part of the army is revolted againft Muley-Abdallah, with defign to place a brother of his upon the throne. DP. DF.

MONDAY, Dec. 11.

Paris, Dec. 5. The chancellor addreffed the parliament, on the part of the king, in the following manner : " His " majefty was incenfed againft the parliament; but is in-" clined to look upon their conduct as an effect of their " zeal.' C.

TUESDAY, Dec. 12.

Triers, Dec. 6. Orders are come to Metz, from the French court, to get in readinefs there, and in the other French places, a train of artillery of 180 canon, befides mortars; the French giving out, that there is fome ap-pearances that, during the winter, the tranquillity of Europe may, upon fome incident or other, be interrupted. P.

Yefterday it was currently reported on the Exchange, that the moorifh army before Oran being increafed to 100,000 men, the Spanifh garrifon made a general fally ; but being overpowered, the Moors drove them into the town, entered with them, and put them all to the fword :

---

but that the Spaniards killed near 30,000 Moors before their defeat. DF.

This day arrived a Mail from France.

Paris, Dec. 17. The matter of a veffel arrived at Mar-feilles, who left Oran on the 21ft paft, advifes, that on the fame day the governor ordered fome early in the morning with 10 000 men, and put the Moors to flight, and put feveral them above a league. LE. DF.

Next Monday will be published,

(Useful to Gentlemen, Architects, Sculptors, Painters, Workmen, and all Persons concern'd in Building;)

NUMBER VI.

A Second Edition of the

MAgazine of Architecture, Perspective and Sculpture. Collected from the most approved Authors, Ancient and Modern; particularly PALLADIO, SCAMOZZI, and VIGNOLA.

By EDWARD OAKLEY, Architect.

CONDITIONS.

The whole Work, consisting of Ninety-seven Impressions from Copper Plates, and Thirty-one Sheets and a Half of Common Press Work, which amounts to Eighty Sheets, and is to be divided into Sixteen Numbers, each Number containing Ten Half-Sheets; and according to the Precedence in the Volume, it will some times happen that a Number will consist of only Prints, and at other Times of only Common Press Work. The whole Numbers are to be deliver'd in Form following; viz.

No.	Plates	Sh.	No.	Plates	Sh.	No.	Plates	Sh.	No.	Plates	Sh.
I.	— 4	5	V.	— 6	2	IX.	— 8	1	XIII.	— 2	4
II.	— 4	5	VI.	— 10	2	X.	— 7	1	XIV.	— 8	1
III.	— 2	4	VII.	— 10	2	XI.	— 8	1	XV.	— 10	0
IV.	— 0	5	VIII.	— 10	2	XII.	— 6	2	XVI.	— 2	4

Each Number to be deliver'd stitch'd in blue Paper at 12d. each every other Monday. And, as no Money is advanc'd for the carrying on the Work, [illegible] Number will be deliver'd without Money.

N. B. A small Number is [illegible] printed for the Curious on Royal Paper, at 1 s. 6d. each Number.

Each Subscriber is desired to enter his Name, Profession, and Place of Abode, that the Numbers may be deliver'd right.

SUBSCRIPTIONS are taken in by the Author, at the Three Doves in Brewer-street, Golden-square; B. Creake, at the Red Bible in Ave-Mary-Lane, near St. Paul's; W. Waring, at the Bible in Jermyn-street St. James's, and by the Booksellers of London and Westminster.

This Day is published,

In Two Volumes in Quarto,

AN Anatomical Exposition of the Structure of the Human Body.

By JAMES-BENIGNUS WINSLOW,

Professor of Physick, Anatomy, and Surgery, in the University of Paris, Member of the Royal Academy of Sciences and Royal Society at Berlin, &c. Translated from the French Original, by G. DOUGLAS, M. D.

Printed for N. PREVOST, at the Ship over-against Southampton-street in the Strand.

N. B. There are a few Copies printed on a fine Paper.

This Day is published,

QUO Ruitis Cives: Or, the great Reasonableness and Necessity of chearful and conscientious Loyalty to the present Government; set forth in a Sermon preached Nov. 5. 1732. upon Prov. xxiv. 21, 22. My Son, fear the Lord and the King, &c.

Printed by J. Huggonson, in Bartholomew-Close; and sold by J. Roberts, near the Oxford-Arms in Warwick-Lane.

(Price Four Pence.)

On Saturday will be published,

(To be continued Weekly, Price 2d.)

The MISCELLANY. No. I.

GIVING

AN ACCOUNT of the RELIGION, MORALITY, and LEARNING of the PRESENT TIMES. With OCCURRENCES Foreign and Domestick.

By RICHARD HOOKER, of the Temple, Esq;

The Great Restorative,

Which speedily and infallibly Cures,

ALL Hysterick Diseases, whether Hypocondriack Melancholy in Men, or Vapours in Women, however circumstanc'd, or to what Degree soever advanced, or of ever so long standing, so as never to return again; by a pleasant compound Medicine, chymically prepared of the choicest Anti-Hystericks, [illegible] Art of Chymistry.

This Medicine having cured Thousands of Men and Women of Melancholy and Vapours, may be depended on for a perfect Cure; [illegible] at the first Cause of this Distemper, and [illegible] destroys it Root and Branch, rectifies that vitiated Ferment [illegible], which is generally the first and chief Cause, and [illegible] cures Indigestion, purifies the Blood and Spirits, strengthens the Brain and Nerves, chears the whole Frame, [illegible] Head from confus'd Thoughts, removes [illegible] Sleep, Twitchings of the Arms or Legs, cures [illegible] of the Heart; and indeed all other [illegible] Symptoms that attend this [illegible] Distemper [illegible].

[illegible] the Bottle, at Mr [illegible] the Corner of Bell [illegible] to the [illegible].

Dec. 9. was published, (Price 6 d.

(Neatly printed on fine Paper.)

(With Debates at the last General Meeting of the Dissenters about taking off the Sacramental Test. See p. 1080, 1081.

Also Mr. Thomson's Offers to the Charitable Corporation, p. 1078.)

The GENTLEMAN's MAGAZINE

Or, MONTHLY INTELLIGENCER.

NUMBER XXIII. for NOVEMBER, 1732.

CONTAINING,

(More in Quantity, and greater Variety than any Book of the Kind and Price)

I. VIews of the WEEKLY ESSAYS, viz. Of the Itch of Writing, and quoting the Devil; Hackney Nags; Mercenary Authors, Booksellers, and Butchers; Filial Gratitude; Modesty and Decorum. Power of Custom; Good Laws agreeable to Reason; Love at first Sight; Description of the Hyp, The approved Hyp-Doctor; Of Mythology; Modern Infidelity; Difference of Heathenism and Christianity; The Law of Nature the Law of GOD; St. Andrew's Cross; Golden Arms, &c.

II. POLITICAL POINTS; Debates and Speeches in Parliament about the Salt-Tax; Opposition to Governments; Interest of Money and Trade; Mischief and Benefit of Excise and Excise-Laws canvassed; Blessings of the Revolution; Evil of Precedents; The Czar's Speech to King William; Of the State of the Nation; Of Struggling for Places and Power; The Number of Taxes.

III. POETRY; Advice to the Ladies; The Choice, Greatest Cross; Mister; Birth-Day Ode, and Burlesque; The Country Gentleman; Mitchel to Sir Robert Walpole; Sally at the Chop-House; The Beau's Head and Heels; a NEW DIALOGUE.

IV. DOMESTIC OCCURRENCES, Births, Deaths, Marriages, Promotions, &c.

V. Thomson's Proposals; Account of the Georgians, the Corporation and Test-Act Affair, and of the late Eclipse.

VI. Foreign Affairs.

VII. Register of Books.

VIII. A Table of Contents.

By SYLVANUS URBAN Gent.

London: Printed, and sold at St. John's-Gate: by J. Jefferies in Ludgate-street; Mrs. Nutt, Mrs. Charlton, Mrs. Cook, at the Royal Exchange; Mr. Birkey, in Pater-Noster-Row; Mr. Midwinter, in St. Paul's Church Yard; A. Chapman, in Pall Mall; Mr. Jolliffe, without Temple-Bar; Mr. Crichley, at Charing-Cross; Mr. Stagg and Mr. King, in Westminster-Hall; Mr. Williamson, in Holborn; S. Harding, in St. Martin's-Lane; and most Booksellers.

Where may be had all the former Numbers.

Also a List of Parliament, with blank Pages, more correct than any other.

Note, a few are printed on fine Royal Paper, large Margins for the Curious.

The REAL CORDIAL.

NOT only answers all the Intentions of Plague and Surfeit Waters, but is likewise an excellent Remedy against the Gripes and Cholick. It powerfully expels Wind, provokes Urine gently, and restores Apetite after a Debauch. It keeps off the Gout from the Stomach and Bowels, and drives it out when there. In all Sorts of Loosnesses, and even Bloody-Fluxes; it is of greater Efficacy than any other Medicine besides, that is of the Cordial Kind. It is likewise of Use after the Eating of too much Fruit, and the indiscreet drinking of cooling Liquors, especially in hot Countries; and no Compound Water is more agreeable.

It is sold at Mr. Brotherton's, Bookseller, near the Exchange; Mr. Beaumans, Millener, next to Slaughter's Coffee-house in St. Martin's-Lane, Mrs. Corvisle, Linnen-draper, in Panton-street Leicester-Fields, at 6 s. per Quart, 3 s. the Pint, and 1 s. the large Phial, with Directions for the Use of it.

The long experienced Chymical Liquor, *to be us'd externally, and without taking any Thing in at the Mouth, for the Cure of all* Old Gleets, Seminal Weaknesses, *&c.*

IN Consideration of the many PERSONS that have undergone tedious, expensive, and long Courses of Physick, without Success, for the Cure of old Gleets, Seminal Weaknesses of the Vessels from self-Pollution, &c.

The Author hereof, after a long and laborious Search for an easy and safe Cure, for the several difficult Cases above-mentioned, hath found out an infallible Remedy (being a Chymical Liquor) that, without taking any Thing in at the Mouth, or the least Difficulty or Uneasiness to the Patient, will safely and speedily cure the most severe Gleets, though of many Years standing, in a few Days, as perfectly, as if no such Thing had ever been. Also,

All Seminal Weaknesses of the Vessels, whether from the Secret Disease, Self-Pollution, or inordinate Coition, or from Strains, Bows, Wrenches, Falls, &c. as has been happily experienced in great Numbers of Persons, both Old and Young, in private Practice, without its once failing, in a small Time, and for a small Charge; therefore is this unparalleled Medicine made publick, and sold but for 7 s. the Bottle, by the Author's Appointment, only by Mr. Priest, at his House, the Sign of the Tea Canister, in Cock-Lane, near Pye-Corner, West-Smithfield; and is in many Cases more than enough for a perfect Cure.

On Saturday Dec. 2. was published,

(Beautifully printed on a fine Dutch Paper,)

The LONDON MAGAZINE:

Or, GENTLEMAN's *Monthly Intelligencer,*

NUMB. VIII. For NOVEMBER, 1732.

To be continued (Price Six-Pence each Month)

Containing greater Variety, and more in Quantity, than any Monthly Book extant.

I. A VIEW of the WEEKLY ESSAYS, viz. On the Law of Nature, and State of the Heathen Superstition, and the Principles of some modern Infidels; Decorum in Behaviour; Lenity of Parents; Character of the ancient Romans; a celebrated Comedy censured; the Words Devil and Devilish; a Cure in Love; Authors and their Writings; hireling Authors; the Blunderers; a Cure for the Hyp; Idleness; Luxury; Affectation; the Order of the Thistle.

II. POLITICAL SUBJECTS, viz. Debates in Parliament about Chelsea Hospital; the Charitable Corporation; Pension Bill; Salt Duty, &c. A View of the Oppositions to the present and former Governments; Blessings of the Revolution, and Means of preserving them; the Czar's Speech to King William; Parliament of Paris; Authority and Government; End of Government, and Duty of the Governed; second Dialogue between Sir Harry Worthy and Mr. D'Anvers; De Clerc on the Civil Law, Juries, Excises and Smuggling; Original of Excises; Excise Law; Excise Officers; Trade and Commerce; lowering of Interest, &c.

III. POETRY: Verses of Lord Landsdown; on some Authors honoured by the Queen; to a Lady complaining of her Picture; to the Lord Mayor, a Hymn; two Odes of Anacreon translated; a Rural Lay; the Wish; a new Prologue, and two new Epilogues.

IV. DOMESTICK OCCURRENCES: Promotions Ecclesiastical, Civil, and Military; Marriages and Births; Deaths, &c. A Receipt to cure the Bite of a mad Dog.

V. FOREIGN AFFAIRS.

VI. Prices of Goods, Grain, Stocks; Monthly Bill of Mortality.

VII. A Table of Contents.

To which is added, A Catalogue of Books and Pamphlets, with their Prices, published by the Proprietors of the Monthly Chronicle, now discontinued.

MULTUM IN PARVO.

Printed for J. Wilford, behind the Chapter-House near S. Paul's; T. Cox, in Cornhill; J. Clarke, in Duck-Lane; and T. Astley, in S. Paul's Church-Yard.

Where may be had the former Numbers.

ASTHMA's and CONSUMPTIONS,

The Most Incomparable and never-failing Chymical Drops, *for the Immediate Relief, and Perfect Cure of the most* Confirmed Asthma *of the longest standing:*

And all Sorts of Consumptions, *even when so far advanced, as not to be cured by any other Medicine in the World.*

FOR their VIRTUES vastly exceed any Thing that ever was published, or even known in the whole World, in the Cure of the worst Asthmas, and Consumptions of all Sorts, Coughs, Colds, Catarrhs, &c.

They instantly relieve the Patient in the most suffocating Fit of an Asthma, and make a perfect Cure in a very short Time; for they gently open the Breast, and immediately give Liberty of Breathing, without Danger of taking Cold; they admirably allay the Tickling which provokes frequent Coughing, and takes off the uneasy Sensation of acrimonious Humours, cleanse the small Glands, relax the Fibres; and thereby enlarge the Capacities of the Vessels; thus they regularly and quickly cure the most obstinate Asthma's of the longest Standing.

They speedily, and to Admiration, cure all Sorts of Consumptions, Ulcers of the Lungs, removing all Obstructions of the Breast and Lungs, Hoarseness, Wheesing, Soreness, Shortness of Breath, and all the usual Symptoms which attend the Beginning of a Consumption, and, if taken in Time, will infallibly prevent one when feared. They are also exceeding nutritive and strengthening to persons of weakly Constitutions, and have no other sensible Operation than as mentioned above.

And by Parity of Reasoning, this most excellent Medicine is (and well known to be) the most sovereign Remedy in the World for those troublesome spending Coughs, which many are severely troubled with Night and Morning; also for the Chin-Cough and Hooping-Cough in Children, having cured Thousands; and are so pleasant, and so few Drops to a Dose, that Children take them with Pleasure, and without any Confinement.

In short, these unparallel'd Chymical Drops are the most Infallible Remedy that ever was known (therefore they despise the faint Efforts of any Counterfeiters or Imitators) for the Ailments above-mentioned, and allowed to be so by the most judicious among the Learned in Physick; and confirmed by the largest Experience in private Practice; are therefore made publick for Common Good, and sold for 3 s. 6 d. each Vial, by the Author's Appointment, only at Mr Pairy's, at the Sign of the Golden-Fleece in Boar's Head Court, next the Bolt and Tun Inn in Fleet-street.

LONDON: Printed for, and Sold by J. ROBERTS, near the *Oxford-Arms* in *Warwick-Lane*; where Letters and Advertisements are taken in; as also by Capt. GULLIVER, near the *Temple*; by P. SANDERS, *in Crown-Court, Butcher-Row,* without *Temple-Bar* and at the *Rainbow Coffee-House* in *Cornhill.* [Price Twopence.]

The Grub-ſtreet Journal. NUMB. 156.

Thurſday, *DECEMBER* 21. 1732.

Carpere vel noli noſtra, vel ede tua. Martial.

Mr. BAVIUS,

I Have been not a little ſurpriſed to find your two laſt *Journals* taken up with a moſt virulent and ill-grounded invective, againſt a very uſeful Book juſt publiſh'd, by Dr. JAMES ALLEYNE. The author of it ſeems to have been hired by the propietors of QUINCY's *Diſpenſatory*, to run down this new performance of the ſame kind, for fear of ſpoiling their copy, which indeed muſt neceſſarily very ſoon be the conſequence. And, like a true hireling writer, he ſticks at nothing, but throws his dirt plentifully: tho' (alas, poor man!) he has only dawb'd his own fingers.

This worthy writer ſigns his name ISAAC DE DUOBUS, N.M. which I ſuppoſe he never intended ſhould be taken for a real name; and yet begins his ſcribble with inveighing againſt writing under fictitious names. If this be a crime, many of the beſt writers in all ſciences ; and I believe even you yourſelf, Mr. BAVIUS, are guilty of it. But how is it proved, that JAMES ALLEYNE is a fictitious name? Why truly it muſt be ſo, becauſe a writer under a fictitious name aſſerts it. — He is as poſitive, that it is deſigned to counterfeit the name of one Dr. JOHN, author of the *Synopſis univerſa medicina practica* : but may not JOHN ALLEN be a fictitious name, as well as JAMES? May it not be made to counterfeit the name of ſome others of the ſame name, who have made themſelves known to the world by their writings? I remember I have ſeen ſome phyſical pieces by one Dr. THOMAS ALLEN, and a treatiſe of mineral waters, beſides ſome papers in the *Philoſophical Tranſactions*, by Dr. BENJAMIN ALLEN: ſo that if JOHN ALLEN be a real name, and JAMES fictitious, this laſt may more probably have been made in imitation of thoſe, with whoſe names the public has not been much longer acquainted, than with that of JOHN ALLEN.

But it is very certain, that the Bookſellers never intended to make the world believe this *Diſpenſatory* to be Dr. JOHN's; ſince they publiſhed an advertiſement, ſigned with both their names, wherein they declared to the world, that Dr. JOHN ALLEN was not the author of their *Diſpenſatory*. — And, indeed I think they were in the right : for, as far as appears to me by their different works, it would be more for Dr. JOHN's advantage to be taken for Dr. JAMES, than for Dr. JAMES's to be taken for Dr. JOHN. Mr. DE DUOBUS indeed compliments Dr. JOHN in a very high manner, for his *induſtry in compiling, judgment in chuſing, juſtice in quoting, accuracy in deſcribing, eaſy method, and ſignificant ſtyle*. His induſtry indeed appears from his two octavo volumes, which are chiefly tranſcribed from the works of others ; his judgment in chuſing may admit of a diſpute ; his juſtice in, quoting is not altogether ſo great as Duobus would have us believe. — I ſhall give an inſtance or two. SYDENHAM, ſpeaking of the diſtinct ſmall-pox, tells us, the puſtules generally die quite away on the 14th or 15th day: *in hac variolarum ſpecie, die 14. vel 15 ° fundius pereunt.* Dr. ALLEN, quoting this paſſage, ſticks in *ſi quando, if ever,* which makes it flat nonſenſe : *in hac variolarum ſpecie [ſi quando] die 14 ° vel 15 ° pereunt.* Thus Dr. ALLEN makes the great SYDENHAM doubt, whether the puſtules of the diſtinct ſmall-pox ever die away. Abominable nonſenſe! But in truth, I ſuſpect our accurate quoter miſtook the nominative caſe to *pereunt*; and underſtood SYDENHAM to ſay that of the death of the patient, which he plainly ſaid of the dying of the puſtules. — Another inſtance of his accuracy is in the chapter of Dyſenteries, where he quotes a paſſage from RAY's *Hiſtory*, relating to the virtues of *walnuts*, without ever mentioning the name of the fruit. RAY's words are indeed very faithfully quoted, and as they were in the Chapter *de juglande*, that author had no occaſion to repeat the name of the fruit. But Dr. ALLEN contents himſelf with taking the words juſt as he found them, and ſo gives us a medicine from RAY, but never tells us what it is.

The next charge againſt Dr. ALLEYNE, is, that he is a plagiary ; which is a direct falſhood. He tells us very candidly in his *preface*, from what authors he has compiled his book. QUINCY has been no leſs liberal in tranſcribing, than Dr. ALLEYNE; but he wanted the integrity to acknowledge it: ſo that the charge of being a plagiary will fall, not on Dr. ALLEYNE, but on Dr. QUINCY. — But we are told, that of 630 pages, 500 are fairly tranſcribed word for word, without any further artifice than that of tranſpoſing the order, and caſting in now and then a ſpice of

the *Hoſpital Diſpenſatory.* I muſt needs ſay, I wiſh he had taken leſs from QUINCY, than he has; for I am ſatisfied, that whereſoever he has taken any thing from that author, he could have ſaid ſomething better of his own. But how will Duobus make out his 500 pages ? The firſt part, which contains 157 pages, has very little of QUINCY in it. In the ſecond, which contains 253 pages, there are about 30 pages from FREIND's *Chymiſtry.* all the compoſitions in the *London Diſpenſatory*, all the improvements of the *Edinburgh Diſpenſatory*, a great many preſcriptions from the *Pharmacopœia pauperum*, and a conſiderable number from the *Diſpenſatory of S. Bartholomew's Hoſpital*, never before printed ; not to mention ZWELFER, BATES, &c. whom Dr. ALLEYNE had as much right to copy, as QUINCY had. In the third part, which contains 192 pages, moſt of the preſcriptions are from BATES, FULLER, and the moſt eminent phyſicians now in practice: and when any are taken from QUINCY, his name is always fairly quoted ; a piece of juſtice, of which QUINCY did not uſe to be guilty. The fourth part, which contains 44 pages, has not one word of QUINCY in it. Thus I am afraid Duobus will fall very ſhort of his 500 pages out of 630, he ſhould have ſaid 646; for Dr. ALLEYNE's book contains that number. But had this charge been true, we ſhould however have been obliged to Dr. ALLEYNE for his few emendations, and for rendring his book 130 pages better than that of QUINCY.

Duobus ſeems to be bent upon finding fault with any thing, however excellent ſoever, that Dr. ALLEYNE has done, which is not in QUINCY. Thus he attempts, in an awkard manner, to ridicule that uſeful part of ſetting down the genitive caſes, and marking the quantities of middle ſyllables ; as if none of the readers of *Diſpenſatories* had occaſion for ſuch aſſiſtance. Yet is it very certain, that many words are erroneouſly pronounced by apothecaries ; as may appear by comparing the common pronunciation with Dr. ALLEYNE's corrections. And the marking the genitive uſed in the preſcriptions of phyſicians, for nothing is more common, than to have them miſtaken for the nominative. Thus *Calomelanos*, which is the genitive caſe of *Calomelas*, is mentioned by QUINCY, and others after him, as the nominative. And even Duobus's great oracle, Dr. JOHN ALLEN, has, in his *Synopſis*, miſtaken the genitive caſe of *prunus*, making it *pruna*, inſtead of *pruni* : ſo that, if ſuch prodigies of learning, as Dr. QUINCY and Dr. ALLEN, have fallen into theſe miſtakes, Dr. ALLEYNE might well think, that others had occaſion to be informed of theſe matters. But, ſhould I grant this to be but a ſmall improvement, yet it might be allowed, that Dr. ALLEYNE's *Diſpenſatory* is, in this reſpect, ſome ſmall matter better than QUINCY's.

The omiſſions, it ſeems, *make worſe work.* Dr. ALLEYNE has omitted thoſe uſeful chapters at the head of each claſs of medicines, on *cephalics,* on *balſacnics,* on *carminatives,* &c. Surely it wou'd have been very abſurd to continue theſe heads of chapters, when the very diviſions which QUINCY makes under theſe heads are rejected. But theſe are much better ſupplied in the fourth part ; where the Dr. gives us that excellent abridgment of BOERHAAVE. — The *inſtructive article on the diſtribution of ſimples*, muſt neceſſarily be different from QUINCY's, as the diſtribution itſelf is different. The *rules for gathering them* are not omitted, as Duobus falſely aſſerts; but are in the 153d page of Dr. ALLEYNE's *Diſpenſatory.*—What he means *by the phyſical method* of ſimples, I don't underſtand. He ſays, many ſimples are *totally forgotten* ; which is falſe: He inſtances four, Lapis *Hæmatites, Kermes Meconcan,* and *Moxa.* The *Lapis Hæmatites* is mentioned in page 10. The *Kermes* is indeed *omitted* in the *Index* ; which ſeems to be the greateſt part of our critic's reading, but may be found in page 98. The *Mechoacanna alba* is omitted, but the omiſſion is of no very terrible conſequence. All that Dr. QUINCY has to ſay of the virtues of this drug is, " it " is reckon'd, as the *Hermodactyl*, a very efficacious purge, " but of ſlow operation, the ſeat of its action being chief-" ly in its extreme parts, and therefore *accounted* good in " all arthritic pains: for which purpoſe it ſtands in great " commendation amongſt the ancients, altho' it is rejected " in modern practice." The Doctor might have been excuſed, if he had ſaid nothing at all of Moxa, it not being an official ſimple. It is, however, mentioned in page 35. but not called a *particular ſort* of cotton, as QUINCY has blunderingly made it. Duobus ſeems to lament very feelingly, for the loſs of that excellent article of malt liquors; which, by the way, are not properly the ſubject of a *Diſpenſatory.* I fear, Mr. BAVIUS, the poor man was under

the influence of *malt liquors*, when he ſent you that wretched piece of criticiſm.

I come now to the moſt terrible charge of all, *The death's wound of* QUINCY's *Diſpenſatory*, by altering his method. Here our doubty critic very learnedly deſcants upon method, and would fain be taken for a logician, by bringing in a ſcrap of technical Greek. But, I am afraid he will never be taken for a great maſter of logic, having juſt before unluckily talked of *general ſpecies.* — But let us conſider a little *that ſtructure* which Duobus tells us *our new Author has impiouſly defaced.* QUINCY begins with a theory of pharmacy, then proceeds to the ſimples, which medicines are to be compounded. The ſimples are divided, not according to their obvious properties, but according to an imaginary agreement in their virtues; whence neceſſarily ariſes a very great confuſion. Plants, animals, and minerals are jumbled ſtrangely together ; and of the ſame plant you may find the root in one chapter, the leaves in another, the flowers in a third, and the ſeeds in a fourth ; and his ſubdiviſions are full of blunders. You have *Ambergris* under minerals, which is the production of a whale; *Bitumen Judaicum*, under inſpiſſated juices, which is a mineral balſom ; *Terra Japonica* under minerals, which is an inſpiſſated juice ; and abundance more of the ſame nature — Let us now conſider Dr. ALLEYNE's method. He begins juſtly with ſimples, before he proceeds to compoſition. The ſimples are ranged in ſo eaſy an order, according to the rules of natural hiſtory, that the young ſtudent is led on gradually to the knowledge of their ſtructure ; which will hinder him from having one impoſed on him for another. Thus the learned Mr. DALE treated the ſimples in his *Pharmacologia*, a work compoſed with the approbation and aſſiſtance of as great a judge as ever lived, the celebrated Mr. RAY, who, Duobus boldly affirms, would have taken quite a different way, if he had been to write.—With this, *whirpool oriſs*, the very method followed by the colleges of phyſicians both at London and Edinburgh. Now I appeal to you, Mr. BAVIUS, whether Dr. ALLEYNE is to be cenſured for his impiety in differing from QUINCY ; or Duobus for his *Impudence* in arraigning in ſuch a manner thoſe two learned bodies. Then the doctor gives us examples of extemporaneous preſcriptions, both in Engliſh and Latin ; and concludes with an account of the operation of medicines. Nothing can be more eaſy and natural than this method, Beſides, all the advantage that QUINCY's method can boaſt of is abundantly ſupplied by the copious *Index* of diſeaſes, under each of which both ſimples and compounds are ranged.

Duobus is very angry with Dr. ALLEYNE for following Dr. BOERHAAVE in his diſcourſe on the operations of medicines ; and attempting to reconcile the practice of the London phyſicians, with the rules laid down by that celebrated profeſſor. *Who but himſelf could have thought,* ſays he, *of making* Dr. FREIND *and* Dr. BOERHAAVE *draw in the ſame yoak; and the London and Leyden practice go hand in hand ?* *Fungentur jam gryphes equis.* I will ſatisfy him in this point: Many members of the colleges, both of London and Edinburgh, would have thought this very practicable, who have themſelves been educated under that great man. — But this, it ſeems, is not all ; in his *Recipes* he very often follows the practice of the London *Phyſicians, who are famous for being great compounders; yet in the laſt part he follows one, who is for reducing all phyſic to the uſe of ſimples.* I ſuppoſe our critic thought no body would diſpute the truth of what he aſſerted ſo roundly. But, for my part, I cannot but be complaiſant: He is entirely miſtaken here ; for every one, who is acquainted with Dr. BOERHAAVE's practice, or has ſeen any of his preſcriptions, muſt know they are generally very compound, and contain three times as many ingredients, as thoſe of the moſt celebrated phyſicians now in London.

To concluCARD: I muſt declare my opinion, That Dr. ALLEYNE's book is much better than Dr. QUINCY's. All that is valuable in QUINCY is retained ; the method is more uniform and conſiſtent ; and many excellent things are added, to which QUINCY was entirely a ſtranger.

Dec. 15. 1732. I am, Sir, your humble Servant,

To the Authors of the Grub-ſtreet Journal,

Gentlemen,

FInding my name in capitals in your Journal of 7th, and alſo N. B. in that of the 14th inſtant, ſuppoſed author and compiler of the *Diſpenſ ary* publ in the name of JAMES ALLEYNE ; in order to unde

you. I do ſolemnly declare, I am not the author or compiler of that *Diſpenſary*; nor did ever write one line, or read one page of it; nor do know the compiler, or any thing of that book, directly or indirectly, but what I have obſerved from your animadverſions on it. This I thought proper to let you know, ſuppoſing it would not be unacceptable to you to be undeceiv'd as to this particular.

Stepney, Decem. 14. 1732. I am your Servant,
NATHAN BAILEY.

DOMESTIC NEWS.

C. *Courant.*	E P. *Evening Poſt.*
P. *Poſt-Boy.*	S J. *St. James's Evening Poſt.*
D P. *Daily Poſt.*	W E. *Whitehall Evening Poſt.*
D J. *Daily Journal.*	L E. *London Evening Poſt.*

THURSDAY, *Dec.* 14.

The following gentlemen are appointed to ſettle the corporation for the relief of the poor officers widows, &c. The right honourable George lord viſcount Torrington, firſt lord of the admiralty, *preſident*. The honourable ſir Charles Wager, and the honourable lord Archibald Hamilton, *governors*. — Sir George Saunders and Thomas Pearſe Eſqs, commiſſioners of the navy, *aſſiſtants* to ſir Charles Wager and lord Hamilton — The right honourable the lord Vere Beauclerc, ſir John Jennings Knt. ſir John Norris Knt. ſir George Walton Knt. Philip Cavendiſh Eſq; ——— Balchin Eſq; Charles Stuart Eſq; ——— Mighell's Eſq; ſir Stafford Fairborne, admirals — Beſides five of the eldeſt captains and lieutenants, &c. but theſe are not in the preſent committee. P.

Laſt monday at a ſeſſion of ſewers for the city and liberty of Weſtminſter, ſir John Gonſon gave them a ſhort, but excellent and uſeful charge, C. — A very uſeful and inſtructive charge. D P.

Yeſterday a gentleman met another in Cheapſide, and asked him to go to a coffee-houſe; which he refuſing, the other in a frolick, gave him a blow on the arm, which broke it in pieces. C. — The ſame morning a watchman going off his duty from Cripplegate-watch-houſe, ſlipt aſide in Wood-ſtreet, and broke his leg. D J.—*Two ſtrange and important articles.*

Yeſterday ſir Gilbert Heathcote, Knt. ſenior alderman [illegible] created a baronet. D P.

[illegible] Streatham, and brother-in-law to the reverend Dr. Lynch, is preſented to the rectory of Allhallows Barking by his grace the archbiſhop of Canterbury. L E.

Yeſterday two private centinels met by appointment in one of the quarters in Moor-fields, one was an Engliſhman, and the other an Iriſhman; where they drew their ammunition ſwords, and went to back-ſword, when the latter received two large cuts on the head, and one on the ſword-arm, which diſabled him. WE.

Since the death of the gentleman in the tower by the bite of a mad dog, the lieutenant governor has order'd all dogs whatſoever to be ſhot, that ſhall come within the garriſon. LE.—*Give a dog a bad name, and hang or ſhoot him.*

On tueſday night, about nine, colonel Schutz's gentleman was attacked in Albemarle-ſtreet by five footpads, who robbed him of ſeven pound and his watch. — They juſt before endeavoured to rob a woman, but having nothing worth taking away, they let her go. D J.—*The having of nothing, is the only ſecurity from being robb'd.*

Yeſterday morning died at his lodgings in Finch-lane, Cornhill, William Nutt Eſq; formerly a Weſt-India merchant. He was on the point of marriage with miſs Devereux, a lady of 7000l. fortune. P. — The ſame day Mr. Baker, late an eminent plummer in Fetter-lane, reckon'd worth 12,000l. DP.

A daughter of Mr. Clarke, of Twickenham,
Who for twelve months had *in her tongue been lame,*
Laſt ſaturday recovered the ſame. D P.

FRIDAY, *Dec.* 15.

Yeſterday at a general council his majeſty was pleaſed to nominate the ſeveral ſheriffs for each county. D J.

The ſame day, at a court of lord mayor, aldermen, &c. at Guild-hall, the bill for raiſing 2443l. 14s. on the inhabitants of this city, for maintaining the workhouſe in Biſhopſgate-ſtreet was paſſed; and likewiſe the orphans bill. C. DP. DJ.

The reverſion of one of the ſealers to the broad ſeal, vacant by the death of Edward Dupper Eſq; worth 400l per ann. is given to Samuel Hetherington Eſq; of the Curſitor's office C.

A notorious cheat goes about town, takes lodgings in variety of places, draws bills upon perſons of credit for conſiderable ſums, ſends a porter to receive the money, and borrows money, till his return, of his landord, and goes off with ſome pretence or other. He has taken in five tradeſmen this week: this is inſerted to caution unwary people. D J.

Laſt ſunday died dame Mary Houblon, relict of ſir John Houblon, lord mayor of London in 1695, the firſt governor of the bank. DP. — Aged 92. C. — On wedneſday Robert Jacombe Eſq; one of the repreſentatives for Norfolk. D J. — Yeſterday. D P.

On wedneſday night, ſome rogues broke the ſtone, and
ſtole all
The iron rails from an empty houſe in Stone-cutters alley,
Pall-mall. P.

SATURDAY, *Dec.* 16.

The ſtate-coach late of queen Anne was yeſterday taken out and view'd, in order to be refitted and beautify'd for his excellency count de Montejo, who is to make his publick entry in it. D J.

On tueſday the right honourable ſir Robert Walpole was preſent at a board of treaſury held in the lottery office Whitehall, where he contracted a violent cold. On wedneſday he was much diſordered with a pain in his head, and immediately cauſed himſelf to be let blood: which was followed by a regular ague fit. On thurſday he had a ſhort return of the fever; and was ſo well yeſterday as to ſee ſome company. The phyſicians have preſcribed the bark, and judge him to be in a fair way of recovery. P.

Yeſterday the right honourable the earls of Wilmington and of Burlington, the right honourable Arthur Onſlow Eſq; ſpeaker of the houſe of commons, the right honourable Horatio Walpole Eſq; ſir Thomas Robinſon, &c. met in a room adjoining to the houſe of commons, by the direction of his majeſty, to fix upon a proper place for erecting a ſpacious building for the reception of the Cottonian library: and we hear the ſame is to be built in the middle of Cotton-garden, according to a plan of the right honourable the earl of Burlington. The old Cotton-houſe is to be pulled down. D J.

On thurſday the honourable Benjamin Bathurſt Eſq; eldeſt ſon to the right honourable the lord Bathurſt, was married to the eldeſt daughter of the right honourable the lord Bruce, at his lordſhip's ſeat at Tottenham-park in Wiltſhire. D P.— The ſame day Mr. Robert Turner, an eminent merchant of this city, was married to miſs Lloyd of Holbourn, a beautiful young lady of great merit, and a good fortune. C.

On monday Mr. Henry Smith of Boxworth in the county of Cambridge, got up early, in order to take a journey, in company with a neighbour, and was found hang'd in a cart-lodge near his own houſe. D P.

On tueſday died of a conſumptive illneſs, the right honourable the lord Villers at his houſe in Groſvenor-ſtreet.

An eminent butcher and ſalter for the Eaſt-India company, [illegible] Mr. John Rice, reputed worth upwards of 6000l. C. D P.

Yeſterday Mrs. Poyntz reſigned her place of maid of honour to her majeſty. S J. L E.

All the pilchards taken on the coaſt of Penzance ſince Lady-day has not exceeded 5000 hogſheads: the firſt taken were ſold at 40s. per hogſhead; thoſe taken to Oct. 28. from 40s. to 30s. from thence to Nov. 11. none under 23s. 6d. S J.

On thurſday Mr. Bateman, a draper at Eton, cut his throat. He was a great dealer, of a fair character, and is computed to have died worth 10,000l. This unfortunate accident is ſaid to be attributed to ſome loſſes he lately met with. L E.

A man, in a field at Hoxton, on thurſday evening,
Was robb'd of ſeven ſhillings and two-pence, and a gold ring.
D J.

MONDAY, *Dec.* 18.

Yeſterday the reverend Dr. Cobham preached before their majeſties, his royal highneſs the prince, and the three eldeſt princeſſes: and the reverend Dr. George before his royal highneſs the duke, and the princeſſes Mary and Louiſa. C. DP. DJ. — Dr. Cobden. P. — Their majeſties and the royal family dined in public. D J. P. DP. — The ſame day the court went out of mourning for the king of Sardinia. P. D J. — The right honourable ſir Robert Walpole being perfectly recovered, appeared at court, and was moſt graciouſly received; and received the compliments of the court. C. D P. — Is ſo well received, that yeſterday he quitted his chamber. P.

On ſaturday the right honourable the lord Lovelace, lately arrived from his travels, was introduced to his majeſty, &c. P.

The reverend Mr. Broughton, reader to the honourable ſocieties of the inner and middle Temple, is appointed chaplain to her grace the ſenior dutcheſs of Bedford. DP.

Dover, Dec. 15. Alderman Parſons this morning embarqued for Boulogne: he had a ſtring of fifteen horſes, and two fine coach-horſes. P.

On friday died ſir Thomas Pendergraſs Bar. P. — On friday night the counteſs of Southerland. C. —On ſaturday morning Mr. Noads ſenior, a noted fiſhmonger. C.—The ſame day Mr. Cope his majeſty's card-maker. P. D J. — One William Overan, a cooper, at Huſtchwait, near Black Hamilton in Yorkſhire, died aged 104. To the laſt he worked at his buſineſs, and could read any thing without ſpectacles. D J. — *The age of this* cooper *renders him more eminent, than the* baronet, *the* counteſs, *the* noted fiſhmonger, *or the* card-maker.

Laſt friday night, Mr. Langdell of Alderſgate-ſtreet
Two highway-men at the bottom of Shooter's-hill did *meet,*
Who robb'd him, cut his horſe's girt, and made off very *fleet.* P.

TUESDAY, *Dec.* 19.

Laſt wedneſday the right honourable the lords of the treaſury were pleaſed to appoint —— Tyrone Eſq; brother to the lord Tyrone, of the kingdom of Ireland, to be one of the commiſſioners of his majeſty's cuſtoms. C.

Yeſterday came on a hearing before the court of delegates, at Serjeant's-Inn, Chancery-lane, between a gentleman, who married about four years ſince the daughter of a noble earl, on the lady's complaint of having received ſuch ill treatment as is not uſual to her ſex, eſpecially from men of ſenſe and honour; and after many learned debates, the ſame was adjourned to a further hearing in January next. C.

The body of John Gay Eſq; author of the Beggar's Opera, lies embalmed at the duke of Queensberry's houſe in Burlington-gardens, and will not be interred in the Abbey till his grace's return from Scotland, ſome time in January next. D P.

The reverend Dr. Tyrwhit was yeſterday inſtalled a prebendary of S. Paul's, in the room of the reverend Dr. Olliver, deceaſed. D J.

On friday laſt John Ingram Eſq; was married to Miſs Wilſon of Chiſwick, a lady of great merit, with a fortune of 14,000l. and 400l. per annum; and on ſaturday they ſet out for his ſeat at Kerby in Yorkſhire. C.

Bath, Dec. 16. This day departed this life, the right reverend Dr. William Bradſhaw, biſhop of Briſtol, and dean of Chriſt-Church. D J.

Thomas Paget Eſq; is made colonel of the regiment of foot, late brigadier general Dubourgay's.—Thomas Wentworth Eſq; colonel of the regiment of foot late colonel Cope's ——Richard Onſlow Eſq; lieutenant-colonel to the firſt troop of grenadier guards. L E.

Mr. Hodgſon, fellow of the royal ſociety, the ingenious,
Has ſignify'd his approbation of the new tranſlation of Varenius. S J. W E. L E.

WEDNESDAY, *Dec.* 20.

His majeſty has been pleaſed to appoint Edward Trelawney Eſq; repreſentative in parliament for Weſtlow in Cornwall, to be one of the commiſſioners of the cuſtoms. P.— One of the commiſſioners of the ſalt-office. D J.

An exciſeman came lately to a tallow-chandler's near the Royal-exchange, and ſearching about his cellar, diſcover'd a private door that was lock'd up, which he demanded to be open'd, but was told the perſon was not in town that rented it; but the officer inſiſting upon it, he was anſwered again, he muſt then fetch a conſtable: accordingly he went and brought one with him; but, in the interim, the tallow-chandler perceiving a chimney ſweeper's boy near his door, bid him black his face as much he could, and then put him in and lock'd the door: when the officer and conſtable open'd the ſame, the boy appearing, they both ran out, and tumbled one over the other; the exciſeman was ſo terrified that he fell into fits, and would gladly be removed into another walk. D J.

We are aſſured, that the report of her grace the dutcheſs of Kendal's having ſent in a conſiderable number of India bonds to be mark'd for three and a half per cent, as was inſerted in the news-papers, is intirely groundleſs. DP.— *This report was firſt publiſhed in the* Daily Poſt, *Dec.* 13. *and firſt contradicted in our* laſt Journal: *notwithſtanding which, it was inſerted in the* S J. Dec. 14, *and in* Fog's laſt Journal, *who took it from the* Daily Poſt, *who here accuſes them.*

Yeſterday Bat. Harnet ſtood in the pillory,
At the royal exchange, for wilful perjury,
In ſwearing againſt William Holmes a robbery. C. &c.

From the PEGASUS *in Grub-ſtreet.*

ON occaſion of the controverſy between the late *Orator* and the preſent *Secretary* of GRUB-STREET, the former appealed, in the *Daily Journal, Nov.* 21. to "the "*atteſtation* of Dr. Baker, biſhop Hutchenſon, and the "learned Montfaucon, in his favour and recommendation." This was particularly examined in our 153d *Journal, Novemb.* 30. in which it was ſhewn, that none of theſe *atteſtations were in favour and recommendation of* Mr. ORATOR; and that only two of them were civil compliments, in *favour*, but not in *recommendation*, of Mr. HENLEY, ſeveral years ago.

Upon this Mr. ORATOR changed his ſtyle, and cauſed the following paragraph to be inſerted in the *Daily Journal, Dec.* 1. "In the firſt volume of the Oratory Tracts are "teſtimonies *in favour* of Mr. HENLEY, from the famous "Mr. Baker of S. John's, Cambridge, biſhop Hutchenſon, F. "Montfaucon, the late lord Moleſworth, Dr. Newcomb, the "late E. of Macclesfield, Bp Burſcough, Dr. Pearſe of S. Mar.

re tin's, Dr. Ellis, Dr. Barnard, the late earl of Nottingham,"
" the reverend Mr. Wright, Dr. Gower, Dr. Lambert, ma-
" sters of S. John's; Dr. Edmundson, Mr. Field, Mr. Smales,
" moderators; the university of Cambridge. archbishop
" Wake, bishop Gibson, and the city of London."

All these testimonies are supposed to be contained in a thing intitled *A Narrative by Mr.* WELSTEDE; from which a faithful account of the three first was presented to the public in our 153d *Journal*, tho' the pages were not mentioned where they might be found, which are *pag.* 6, 7, 8, 9, 10, 21. The rest of those testimonies are as follow.

Lord MOLESWORTH's. " The late celebrated lord Molesworth presented him with a scarf, as his chaplain, Mar. " 14, 1721-2." *pag.* 13.——Dr. Newcome's. " Here [at " Melton-school] he was invited by a letter from the re- " verend Mr. Newcome to be a candidate for a fellowship in " S. John's." *pag.* 5.——Earl of MACCLESFIELD's. " His lord " ship gave him a benefice in the county [country] the value " of which to a resident would have been above 80 pounds " year." *pag.* 5.——Bishop BURSCOUGH's. " He was em- " ploy'd as an assistant preacher by Dr. Burscough, now a " bishop." *pag.* 13.—— Dr. PEARSE's, Dr. ELLIS's, Dr. BAR- " NARD's, " Two present convocation-men, Mr. Ellis and " Mr. Barnard, with Dr. Pearce, vicar of S. Martin's, sign'd " his credentials." *pag.* 13.—— Earl of NOTTINGHAM's. " The earl of Nottingham, who has a seat at Burleigh, " near that place, [Okeham in Rutland] often declar'd his " approbation of his juvenile performances." *pag.* 3.—— Mr. WRIGHT's. " From that school [of Melton] he was " remov'd to that of Okeham in Rutland, where, under " Mr. Wright, eminent for his command of the Greek and " Hebrew-Tongues, he still improv'd." *pag.* 2. —— Dr. GOWER's, Dr. LAMBERT's, Dr. EDMUNDSON's. " He was " hence translated, about the age of 17, to S. John's-college " in Cambridge; where, on his examination by Dr. Gower, " then master, Dr. Lambert, Dr. Edmundson, and others, " he was particularly approv'd." *pag.* 3.—— Mr. FIELD's and Mr. SMALES's. " He pass'd his exercises here; and his " examination for the degree of batchelor of arts, with the " particular approbation of Mr. Field and Mr. Smales. *pag.* 4.

The rest is omitted for want of room.

From the Chop-house, the sign of the Lamb, behind the Royal
Mr. BAVIUS, *Exchange.*

AS you was pleased, not long ago, to let me appear in print, I take leave to inform you, that last week a gentleman dined here, who, immediately on his seeing me, took out his pencil, and wrote the following verses, which he left on the table, without saying a word to me. I don't know him; therefore have no other way of acquainting him that I received his favour, than by begging a place for it in your next paper, which I humbly do; and assure you, in return, that whenever you come to our house, you may depend on a kindly welcome, Sir,
From your humble Servant, SALLY.

Dear SALLY, emblem of thy chop-house ware,
As broth reviving, and as white bread fair;
As small beer grateful, and as pepper strong;
As beef-stake tender, as fresh pot-herbs young;
As sharp as knife, and piercing as a fork,
Soft as new butter, white as fairest pork;
Sweet as young mutton, brisk as bottled beer;
Smooth as is oil, juicy as cucumber,
And bright as cruet void of vinegar.
O SALLY! cou'd I turn, and shift my love,
With the same skill that you your stakes can move,
My heart, thus cook'd, might prove a chop-house feast,
And you alone shou'd be the welcome guest.
But, dearest SAL! the flames that you impart,
Like chop on grid-iron, broil my tender-heart;
Which, if thy kindly-helping hand ben't nigh,
Must, like an unturn'd chop, hiss, burn, and fry;
And must at last, thou scorcher of my soul,
Shrink, and become an undistinguish'd coal.

The advertisements left out, came too late to be inserted; which they cannot be, unless sent by tuesday noon.

FOREIGN NEWS.

THURSDAY, Dec. 14.

Paris, Dec. 20. N.S. The marquis de Castellar has received a confirmation of what passed at Oran the 21st and 23d of last month. The marquis de Santa Cruz, governor of that place, caused every quarter of the infidels to be attacked the 21st, and the Moors were forced to fly; but the marquis de Santa Cruz, the marquis de Valdecanas, and some other officers of distinction were killed. The 23d, the commanding officer made a second sally, entirely defeated the Barbarians, levelled all their works, and nailed their cannon. 'Tis computed the infidels lost above 30,000 men, either kill'd or wounded, which is almost the same thing; for as they have neither physician, nor surgeon, if a man be so wounded that he cannot be

soon healed, they take care to knock him on the head. The Spaniards had about 600 men kill'd and 1500 wounded. C. —To knock them in the head, D.F. —To cut off his head. D P.

FRIDAY, Dec. 15.

Vienna, Dec. 6. N.S. 'Tis pretended at court, that new difficulties have arisen, which will retard the investiture and dispensation of age in favour of the infante Don Carlos. C.

Paris, Dec. 19. Don Carlos has demanded of the pope, the restitution of the dutchies of Castro and Ronciglione as dominions belonging to him, but usurped by the holy see. —A hermit, of the family of Caracciolo, a Neapolitan, was received the other day very graciously by the holy father, to whom he recounted his history; which was, That having served many years in the emperor's wars, he took a voyage to Jerusalem, where he stay'd several years; and then retired to a hermitage at Spoletto, from whence he came to Rome, to crave the pope's benediction, and to die in that holy city. Tho' 114 years of age, he appeared chearful, and of a gay disposition —Card. Coscia on thursday called the sacristain of the Minims of S. Andrew della Fratte, and consigned to his hands, by way of alms, all his silver vessels, his gold watch, archiepiscopal ring, &c. saying, he would from hence forward lead the life of a poor monk.
This of his eminency is an unexpected stroke;
But time will discover, how far he'll carry the joke. P.

SATURDAY, Dec. 16.

Hague, Nov. 28. By private advices from good hands, we are assured, that his most christian majesty's circular letter for recalling the exiled presidents and counsellors of the parliament, was short and sweet, being comprised in the following words. —" Mr. N. I have revoked my or- " der of the 7th of September last. God take you into " his holy protection. Signed Lewis. P.

MONDAY, Dec. 18.

Francfort, Dec. 7. Our common discourse is, that a certain potentate is forming an alliance with several princes of the empire, on condition of each supplying 24000 men, to act in concert with him when occasion shall require it. D P.

Hanover, Dec. 12. Some days ago, a considerable sum of money, escorted by three of the life-guards, was sent to Vienna, as 'tis said, at the disposal of our ministers at that court. C.

TUESDAY, Dec. 19.

Paris, Dec. 24. The council of state has lately decided a cause about the vicary and officiality erected in the town of Antibes, by the bulls of popes John XXIII. Martin V. and Eugene IV. This suit has lasted 150 years, and was determined in favour of the bishop of Grasse. C.——Declaring the bulls abusive, and restoring the bishop and his successors to their right. D P. D.F.
His catholic majesty has named the marquis de Villadarias governour of Oran, in the room of the late marquis de Santa Cruz. D P. D.F. —The D.F. of thursday, Dec. 14. kill'd the marquis de Villadarias. P.
A scrivener's daughter, not above eight years and three months old, is unluckily found four months gone with child: the father appears to be a hopeful boy of twelve, who boarded in the house. D P. —— A writing-master's daughter. D.F. C.

On Saturday Dec. 2. was published,

(Beautifully printed on a fine Dutch Paper,)

The LONDON MAGAZINE:

Or, GENTLEMAN's *Monthly Intelligencer.*

NUMB. VIII For NOVEMBER, 1732.

To be continued (Price Six-Pence each Month)

Containing greater Variety, and more in Quantity, than any Monthly Book extant.

I. A VIEW of the WEEKLY ESSAYS, viz. On the Law of Nature, and State of the Heathen Superstition, and the Principles of some modern Infidels; Decorum in Behaviour; Lenity of Parents; Character of the ancient Romans; a celebrated Comedy censured; the Words Devil and Devilish; a Case in Love; Authors and their Writings; hireling Authors; the Blunderers; a Cure for the Hyp; Idleness; Luxury; Affectation; the Order of the Thistle.

II. POLITICAL SUBJECTS, viz. Debates in Parliament about Chelsea Hospital; the Charitable Corporation; Pension Bill; Salt Duty, &c. A View of the Oppositions to the present and former Governments; Blessings of the Revolution, and Means of preserving them; the Czar's Speech to King William; Parliament of Paris; Authority and Government; End of Government, and Duty of the Governed; second Dialogue between Sir Harry Worthy and Mr. D'Anvers; De Clerc on the Civil Laws, Juries; Excises and Smuggling; Original of Excises; Excise Laws; Excise Officers; Trade and Commerce; lowering of Interest, &c.

III. POETRY: Verses of Lord Landsdown; on some Authors honoured by the Queen; to a Lady complaining of her Picture; to the Lord Mayor, a Hymn; two Odes of Anacreon translated; a Rural Lay; the Wish; a new Prologue, and two new Epilogues.

IV. DOMESTICK OCCURRENCES: Promotions Ecclesiastical, Civil, and Military; Marriages and Births; Deaths, &c. A Receipt to cure the Bite of a mad Dog.

V. FOREIGN AFFAIRS.

VI. Price of Goods, Grain, Stocks; Monthly Bill of Mortality.

VII. A Table of Contents.

To which is added, A Catalogue of Books and Pamphlets, with their Prices, published by the Proprietors of the Monthly Chronicle, now discontinued.

MULTUM IN PARVO.

Printed for J. Wilford, behind the Chapter-House near S. Paul's; T. Cox, in Cornhill; J. Clarke, in Duck-Lane; and T. Astley, in S. Paul's Church-Yard.

Where may be had the former Numbers.

To be Sold Cheap,

At HARRISON's Warehouse, the Two Sugar Loaves, Charing-Cross, Mercery Goods bought at the Charitable Corporation, and other Sales, viz.

Black Dutch and Genoa Velvets.
Silk Damasks, half Ell and half Yard.
Tabbies, watered and unwatered.
Unwatered Tabbies as rich as Paudasoys.
Paudasoys and Florellas.
All Sorts of Black Silks.
Rich Brocades.
Italian and English Mantuas.
Shagreens and Turky Silks.
Norwich Crapes, with several Sorts of Washing Things.

READY MADE,

Velvet Manteels.
Velvet Scarfs.
Satten Manteels.
Paudasoy, ditto.
Velvet Hoods.
Short Cloaks.
Quilted Coats.
Mens Morning Gowns.

Just published,

SURVEYING Improv'd:

Or, the whole Art, both in Theory and Practice, fully demonstrated: In Four Parts;

I. ARithmetick, Vulgar and Decimal. II. All Definitions, Theorems, and Problems; with plain Trigonometry, and whatever else is necessary to the Theory of Surveying. III. The Description and Use of Instruments proper to be used in Practical Surveying. IV. How to measure, cast up, plot or divide any Parcel of Land; to take inaccessible Heights and Distances; with Surveying Counties, Roads, Rivers, &c. Also to reduce a Plan to a Prospect; and to correct any Survey by Astronomical Calculation; with Directions for making transparent Colours for Maps. To which is added, An Appendix concerning Levelling, and conveying Water to any possible Place assigned: with 96 Figures engraved on Copper. By HENRY WILSON Price 5 s.

Printed for J Batley, at the Dove in Pater-Noster-Row.

Dec. 1. was published, (Price 6 d.

(Neatly printed on fine Paper.)

(With Debates at the last General Meeting of the Dissenters about taking off the Sacramental Test. See p. 1080, 1081.

Also Mr. Thomson's Offers to the Charitable Corporation, p. 1078.)

The GENTLEMAN's MAGAZINE:

Or, MONTHLY INTELLIGENCER.

NUMBER XXIII. for NOVEMBER, 1732.

CONTAINING,

(More in Quantity, and greater Variety than any Book of the Kind and Price)

I. VIews of the WEEKLY ESSAYS, viz. Of the Itch of Writing, and quoting the Devil; Hackney Nags; Mercenary Authors, Booksellers, and Butchers; Filial Gratitude; Modesty and Decorum, Power of Custom; Good Laws agreeable to Reason; Love at first Sight; Description of the Hyp; The approved Hyp-Doctor; Of Mythology; Modern Infidelity; Difference of Heathenism and Christianity; The Law of Nature the Law of GOD; St. Andrew's Cross; Golden Arms, &c.

II. POLITICAL POINTS: Debates and Speeches in Parliament about the Salt-Tax; Opposition to Governments; Interest of Money and Trade: Mischief and Benefit of Excise and Excise-Laws canvassed; Blessings of the Revolution; Evil of Precedents; The Czar's Speech to King William; Of the State of the Nation; Of struggling for Places and Power; The Number of Taxes.

III. POETRY: Advice to the Lasses; The Choice; Greatest Cross; Miser; Birth-Day Ode, and Burlesque; The Country Gentleman; Mitchel to Sir Robert Walpole; Sally at the Chop-House; The Beau's Head and Heels; a NEW DIALOGUE.

IV. DOMESTIC OCCURRENCES, Births, Deaths, Marriages, Promotions, &c.

V. Thomson's Proposals; Account of the Georgians, the Corporation and Test-Act Affair, and of the late Eclipse.

VI. Foreign Affairs.

VII. Register of Books.

VIII. A Table of Contents.

By *SYLVANUS URBAN* Gent.

London: Printed, and sold at St. John's-Gate: by F. Jefferies in Ludgate-Street; Mrs. Nutt, Mrs. Charlton, Mr. Cook, at the Royal-Exchange; Mr. Batley, in Pater-Noster-Row; Mr. Midwinter, in St. Paul's Church Yard; A. Chapman, in Pall-Mall; Mr. Dodd, without Temple-Bar; Mr. Critchley, at Charing-Cross; Mr. Stagg and Mr. King, in Westminster-Hall; Mr. Williamson, in Holborn; S. Harding, in St. Martin's-Lane; and most Booksellers.

Where may be had all the former Numbers.

Also a List of Parliament, with blank Pages, more correct than any other.

Note, a few are printed on fine Royal Paper, large Margin, for the Curious.

This Day is Published,

(Now first Printed)

FOUR SPEECHES against continuing the ARMY, &c. as they were spoken on several Occasions in the House of Commons. As also, A SPEECH for Relieving the Unhappy Sufferers in the Charitable Corportion, as it was spoken in the House of Commons, May 8, 1732.

By W—— S—— Esq;

Printed for J. Wilford near St. Paul's. Price 1 s.

Where may be had,

The Chevalier RAMSAY's Plan of Education for a young Prince. Price 6 d.

THE Great and Wonderful Cures daily performed by Dr. BATEMAN's Pectoral Drops, in the following Distempers, have gained them so indisputable a Character, that few Families, who have ever heard, or experienced the Virtues thereof, care to be without them in their own Houses, viz. the Gout, Rheumatism, Jaundice, Stone, Gravel, Asthma, and Cholicks, of what Kind or Nature soever, whether proceeding from Wind, Cold, or Hesterick Affection. Besides which there is no one Secret in the whole Art of Physick of that surprizing, and (were it not under the Confirmation of continual Experience) almost incredible Effects in Colds, Agues, Fevers, and those endemic Evils which appear in most Constitutions at Spring and Fall. The Price of each Bottle, in which are three moderate Doses, is but one Shilling, and may (by Virtue of the King's Letters Patents) be had at the Printing-Office, Bow-Church-Yard, Cheapside, and no where else within three Quarters of a Mile from thence.

N. B. A Book of the Virtues thereof, with Testimonies of some hundred Cures performed thereby, under the Hands of Persons of known Worth and Credit, may be had gratis with the said Bottles.

Note also, Shopkeepers, &c. in any Town, where they are not already sold, may be supplied with the above Drops (and good Allowance) to sell again, by directing to Wm. Dicey, or Tho. Cobb and Comp. at Dr. Bateman's Wholesale Warehouse in Bow-Church-Yard, London.

To SMELL to, &c.

The most Noble Volatile Smelling-Bottle in the World, lately much improved:

WHICH smelled to, momentarily fetches the most dismal fainting or swooning Fits, and in a Moment removes Flushings, Vapours, Dulness, Head-ach, Megrims, &c. It takes off all heavy Sleepiness, retards Swooning, keeps up the Spirits to a Miracle, and by its Use admits of no Fainting, but invigorates and enlivens the whole Man; revives and makes chearful, although never so sad, and in a Moment raises all the Sensitive Faculties.

It is also to be taken inwardly by Drops, which effectually takes off and eradicates the very Cause; for it potently relieves, comforts, and strengthens the Brain, creates and corroborates the Stomach, removes Sickness from it, helps Digestion, cleanses the Blood; and, in a word, is the greatest Cephalick Stomachick, Hepatick, and powerful Aromatick possible.

Further, Whereas many Persons of both Sexes perfume their Handkerchiefs with a few Drops of it, and find that in using it so it is of singular Service in all the Cases above mentioned; and many Gentlemen, Ladies, and others use it after this Manner, purely because it gives a most fragrant and delicious Odour, that instantly both delights and relieves the Senses, not only better than any Thing of a musky Kind (which is really hurtful to most Constitutions), but it really takes off what such Things do occasion by their Use; and also relieves the Head and Brain from any ill Effects of common Snuff, and instantly diverts from, and prevents the bad Consequences of any sudden naucеous offensive Smells; therefore is extremely necessary for all Gentlemen, Ladies, &c. always to be carried in their Pockets.

Sold only at Mrs. Markham's Toyshop, at the Seven Stars under St. Dunstan's Church in Fleet-street, and at Mr. King's Toyshop in the Poultry, at 2 s. 6 d. each.

Whereas many Persons are sorely troubled with Kibes and Chilblains, and at a Loss for an Immediate Cure;

THIS is to inform all such Persons of either Sex, or of any Age, of a long experienced Balsam, which immediately cures the worst of Kibes or Chilblains, whether broken or whole, so effectually that they will never be troubled with them for the future. It is the best Medicine that ever was known or made use of for those Ailments; also Womens sore Breasts, and chapped Nipples, whether broken or whole, are safely and speedily cured by it; and is to be had only at Mrs. Markham's Toy-shop, the Seven Stars under St. Dunstan's Church in Fleet-street; and at Mr. Tichbourn's, a Grinder's Shop, at the Golden-Ball in the Minories, the third House from Vine-street, near Aldgate, Price 3 s. each Gally-pot.

The Grand Specifick.

For Cleansing and Strengthening the Reins, &c. that has been published, and sold, so many Years, and with such extraordinary Success and Benefit to the Publick, as has been often advertised; and lately, an Account at large was given of an extraordinary Cure of a Gentleman in Spain, viz. of a very great Weakness and intolerable Pain, mostly occasioned by a Fall and over Strain at first, that had reduced him to so weak and languishing a Condition, that he could not set one Foot before the other, as he expressed it in his Letter; besides, it brought away above an Ounce of Gravel; and all this by taking but two Bottles: For the Truth of this Cure, any Gentleman, for his farther Satisfaction, is referred to Mr. Gates in Botolph-Lane, London, the abovesaid Gentleman's Correspondent.

IT IS

A Medicine that may be depended on as absolutely effectual for carying off by Urine, safely and speedily, all the Relicks of secret Injuries, Remains of pernicious unskilfully prepared Mercurials, Gleets, or Weaknesses, through tedious or ill-manag'd Cures of the Venerial Disease; or from Self-Pollution, inordinate Coition, &c.

Also any Weaknesses of the Vessels, from Wrenches, Strains, Blows, or Falls, and all other Obstructions in the Urinary Passages; even Stranguries, Ulcers, &c. are perfectly cured by it, be they of ever so long standing: Which Relicks and Ailments are in Part discovered by these following Symptoms, viz. Weakness and Pain in the Back, a Sharpness in the Urine, its strong Smell, Films of Hairs (as it were) floating about in it, and is some too frequent Occasion to make it.

This Noble Specifick is also of singular and very extraordinary Use and Efficacy, where there is any Gravel, or even small Stones, Slime, or any other Matter that obstructs the Urine; bringing all away, in a few Times taking, with Safety, and very great Satisfaction to the Patients.

It also strengthens and recovers, after a particular Manner, all Relaxions of the Vessels, confirms the Parts, bringing all into right Order, and thereby perfectly cures to Admiration. It's a very pleasant Medicine, and may be taken with Pleasure by the most squeamish, and will be found of uncommon Benefit to Mankind, beyond Expectation; which is the Reason of its being made publick, and to obviate the Ignorance of Pretenders in all the difficult Cases above-mentioned. One Bottle, in most Cases, is sufficient for a perfect Cure, as you will see by the Directions given with it. Sold for 7 s. 6 d. the Bottle, at Mr. Sandwell's Toyshop, at the Griffin, the Corner of Bucklersbury, in the Poultry.

LONDON: Printed for, and Sold by J. ROBERTS, near the *Oxford-Arms* in *Warwick-Lane*; where Letters and Advertisements are taken in; as also by Capt. GULLIVER, near the *Temple*; by P. SANDERS, *in Crown-Court, Butcher-Row,* without *Temple-Bar*, and at the *Rainbow Coffee-House* in *Cornhill.* [Price Twopence.]

The Grub-street Journal.

NUMB. 157.

Thursday, DECEMBER 28. 1732.

Dear BAVY,

THE other night, as I was sitting in my easy chair by the fire, and amusing myself with my cat; I happen'd to start a thought, which I could not but be very much pleased with, as it might be a means towards rendering our common diversions subservient to good ends and purposes, if put in practice: and therefore could not help communicating it to you, with full power either to publish, or suppress it, as you may think convenient.

Having always the real happiness of my fellow creatures at heart, I can't help being too sensibly affected at the general complaint that is made, with regard to the increase of the poor and miserable, in and about the two cities of *London* and *Westminster*; insomuch, that (as I am credibly inform'd) the assessments of the several parishes fall vastly short of affording a sufficiency towards their maintenance.

Now, as the humour, or rather the fashion, of playing for money prevails every day, not only amongst people of condition, but even amongst such, whose chief interest should be, one would think, to avoid all unnecessary expences in their families; what I was thinking of, is, how to make this very fashion contribute to the benefit of the poor. The tax that is already laid upon every pack of cards, goes only into the exchequer: but what advantage is that to the generality of mankind? The poor are, notwithstanding, as indigent as before: the rich as uselesly extravagant.

I therefore propose to have a wooden box fix'd up in some convenient place in every house, with a slit in the lid, which may contain all money that may be lost from time to time, at cards, or any other games. I would likewise have a proper person appointed in every parish to keep the key, and to collect weekly from each house, what may have been dropt into the box, in order to distribute it among the poor every sunday. This, at the year's end, I am persuaded, would amount to something pretty considerable; and be not only a means of relieving the distress'd and needy, but also of easing the industrious, who are not so polite, from an exorbitant rate, which bears very hard upon them. Besides, I flatter myself, that it can't but be very satisfactory to an ingenious mind to reflect, that from two or three hours amusement, some benefit may accrue to those, who, tho' they are unhappy, are yet of the same species with itself. I am sure there can be no true pleasure in carrying home from a friend's house a guinea or two, and which perhaps can be but ill-spared to be thrown away only upon the prevalency of a fashion.

I would not be mistaken for a churl, by what I have said, or as if I was against any innocent diversion, which may serve to relieve the fatigues of business or study: I like to play at cards myself; and for want of my favourite cat, while I am taking my pipe after supper, often divert myself with a game or two at picquette with my housekeeper, by way of unbending my mind, before I go to bed. But then I never play for any thing: and truly I think my attention is as much kept up, by seeing how the cards run, either for, or against me, as if I play'd for ever so much. This, however, I am sure of, that by this method I don't break in upon the settled serenity of mind I always endeavour to preserve: but I won't say, I should not, were I to run the risque of losing even three or four shillings of a night: for what signifies all the skill in the world, if one holds a bad hand of cards? But if some publick benefit may be carry'd on by the method proposed, the case is otherwise, and I shall not be against playing for some small matter even myself.

The subject I am upon brings to my mind, not altogether unseasonably, the behaviour of a friend of mine; who, that he might not be esteemed unfashionable in a family where he visited, was obliged to play pretty high. He generally had luck, as they term it, on his side, and was wont to carry off something very considerable. In some time, it so happen'd, that the master of the family was extremely embarrassed in the world; when one day he took my friend apart, with whom he was very intimate, and broke the whole affair to him. You must needs think, that he was very much touch'd at so moving a circumstance. Upon going home, he open'd a particular drawer in his cabinet, where he nightly deposited the sums of money that he won from time to time; and returning the next day to his friend, repay'd him only what the family had idly lost at play; which gave him an opportunity of recovering his [illegible] in the world, and was the happy means of saving a whole family from ruin. But that I may not tire you,

I am, dear BAVY, without ceremony,

Dec. 11. 1732. Yours, &c.

JEREMY HINT.

Mr. BAVIUS,

YOUR *Journal* of this day gave me great pleasure. In it you answer fully one of the principal ends of your paper, namely, the detecting a villany in the republick of learning; and will in all probability prevent numbers from being cheated of their money, or what is much more valuable their time; not to mention the justice you do to the character of the much injured Dr QUINCY, so much and so undeservedly attack'd by a vile set of mercenaries in ALLEYNE's *Dispensatory*. And as you are so kind as to promise a conclusion in your next paper upon the same subject, it may not be improper to mention the following particular, as a specimen of the chymistry contained in that book. Speaking of the *Mercurius precipitatus per se*, the compiler tells you, "the Quicksilver is to be put in a glass in a sand heat, and kept "there till it be converted to a red powder; and that it is "a work of some days." — Now, would not any body suppose, from such a slight direction, that it was easily made, attended with few or no difficulties; and that by *some days* he meant no more than a week, or a fortnight at most? On the contrary, it is, perhaps, as nice a thing to make, as any in the whole mercurial tribe; and is attended with so much trouble and expence, that Mr. GODFREY the chymist sells none under two guineas an ounce, tho' there be nothing in the composition but Quicksilver, which, every body knows, is but five shillings per pound. Mr. GODFREY assures me, he has never made any without three months constant fire and attendance; and STAPHORST, who was operator to the hall, and universally esteemed a good chymist, declares, in *page* 62. that "it is about a year in ma-"king." In a word, I refer to all the chymists now alive, or chymical books ever written, for the truth of my assertion: and if this hint do but prove an additional sprig to your rod of chastisement, it will be a singular pleasure to your constant reader.

Dec. 7. 1732. X.

Mr. BAVIUS,

AS you have lately begun to expose the frauds of Booksellers, I hope you will proceed in so laudable an undertaking, 'till you have either redressed the evil, or given the world at least a sufficient caveat against their unjust dealings. This vice is so prevalent in our age, that, in my humble opinion, you cannot employ your time to a more generous purpose, than thus to interest yourself in the cause of honest authors; and to prevent the reader's being imposed upon by the reputable names of sons of APOLLO, of which those false coiners make use at their pleasure, to put off their adulterated metal for current money, and abuse the world with shadows for substance, and sound for sense; while the supposed author is ignorant what mischief his name does to the world, as well as to his own reputation, and can no sooner read a page in the crude and counterfeit composition —— *sed ver'us ructatur*.

There is another set of men, Mr. BAVIUS, which seem worthy your notice; I mean those superficial wits, who, having little or nothing of their own to recommend them to the world, supply their defect by ruining what is other mens, and by some little alterations, additions, and in-corrections, so entirely spoil the piece, that the reader cannot admire what was once admirable, nor the writer claim what was formerly his own. A sermon of TILLOTSON suffers not more, by a young divine, just entered into a cassock and orders, than the most beautiful page in POPE, or ADDISON, by these pretenders to wit. I suppose, you will say, these men have been often reproved already. I know it well; for which reason, if you please, you may bid them remember the following lines of HORACE.

——— *Monitus, multumque monendus,*
Privatas ut quærat opes, et tangere vitet
Scripta Palatinus quæcunque recepit Apollo:
Ne si fortè suas repetitum venerit olim
Grex avium plumas, moveat cornicula risum,
Furtivis nudata coloribus. Epist. Lib. I. 3.

There are some others, Mr. BAVIUS, who, I fear, are too despicable for your animadversion. Yet, if you would condescend to mention them in your paper, (tho' with the very worst of epithets) you would certainly do them an honour they no way deserve. They are a sort of men with rusty tye wigs, and thread bare coats; and may often be seen walking very attentively behind a crowd of courtiers in the Park, but herding oftner among their footmen; with whom, as I hear, they keep a very good intelligence. Sometimes they have the impudence to thrust themselves into the guard-chamber at St. James's; where, with the utmost diligence, they write down every thing they hear in the pocket-book of their memory, till they arrive at the next paultry ale-house, where they transcribe it on paper, in order for the press. By what I can learn, the business of these men, at the first institution of their order, extended no farther than to inform the world of certain useful occurrences; as, what time a ball was opened: — when my lady COSTIVE took physic; how many evacuations she had in a morning; with some other things of the like importance: which (being highly conducive to the improvement of the public) were very requisite to be known. But, alas, Mr. BAVIUS, the most wise and virtuous designs (by the corruption of officers) are converted to most pernicious ends! For these men, not content to act in their own sphere of business, invade the property of other persons, and in such a manner, that they leave them quite incapable of any satisfaction. They now collect scraps of poetry; some entire manuscripts; rase out ends of verses; tag on others; and so hack and maul, and piece, and plaister the most minute production, that when an author sees it in a publick paper, he is ashamed to acknowledge the legitimate issue of his own brain. — I saw an instance of this very lately in a *Copy of Verses on the HERMITAGE*, written by STEVEN DUCK. I happen'd to see him at a coffee-house, not far from the subject of his poem; and while he was very diligently reading the *Daily Post-boy*, (if I mistake not,) I observ'd him to change colour, knit his brows, and sometimes give a disagreeable pish. Seeing these contractions and agitations in his countenance, I took the freedom to ask him what he discover'd in the paper that was able thus to — *distort his visage into frowns?* — What do I discover, said he? I discover a knave and a fool within two letters of one another — I was surpriz'd to observe a man wh[illegible] (as I have heard) is naturally sedate, and not easily provok'd, so suddenly break forth into a passion; and not without some resentment, demanded what he meant by knave and fool? —— Sir, say'd he, (giving me the paper) you shall see. Here is a short copy of verses in my name: true, I writ them, and, doubtless, with some faults; but not so many as they have now. That thief J——s, (you know who I mean, say'd he, the r—e that stole my first poems) is worse than CACUS; for, tho' he stole the cows, he did not cut their tongues out; by which their master knew them, and detected the thief: but this J—s, said he, so murders a thing when he has stolen it, that there is no knowing it again, tho' we meet it in the market. —— Hearing him speak thus, I begg'd him to give me a genuine copy, which he did very willingly. And having read it, I own his resentment seems in some measure reasonable: I therefore, Mr. BAVIUS, communicate his performance to you, (according to the author's own desire,) which, if you will honour with a place in your paper, you will do justice to an honest man, and oblige your constant reader.

On the HERMITAGE. *By* STEPHEN DUCK.

NOW blush, CALYPSO, 'tis but just to yield,
That all your mossy caves are here excell'd.
See how the walls in humble form advance,
With careless pride, and simple elegance.
See art and nature strive with equal grace,
And fancy charm'd with what she can't surpass.
Flow swiftly, THAMES, and flowing still proclaim
This building's beauty, and the builder's fame:
Tell Indian seas thy NAIADS here have seen
The sweetest grotto, and the wisest QUEEN:
Whose royal presence bless'd this humble seat;
How small the mansion, and the guest how great!
So angels sat in Canaan's sweet abodes;
So rural shades were honour'd with the Gods.
Here may her soul th' Almighty's wonders trace,
Far as the worthies that adorn the place;
Whose awful busts around the grot appear,
The brightest stars in learning's hemisphere.
Their fathers dimly view'd the dawning ray:
They rose like suns, and brought a flood of day.

But ceaſe, my muſe, and caſt thy wond'ring eyes
Where PHOEBUS' lofty * domes majeſtic riſe;
Whoſe tuneful train have ſung this grotto's praiſe,
Contending each, till each deſerves the bays.
O pardon me, ye learned ſons of fame,
Who faintly after you attempt the theme:
Nor think I rival your poetic fires;
My QUEEN commands, and gratitude inſpires.
And you, imperial foundreſs, deign to ſmile,
Nor ſcorn the leaſt, the lateſt muſes toil,
Who brings the tardy off'ring of her lays,
The firſt in duty, tho' the laſt in praiſe.

* *Weſtminſter, and Eaton Schools.*

Mr. BENEVOLUS, in a letter publiſhed in the *W E. Dec.* 21. juſtly commends theſe verſes, offering two emendations of them. In line 10th, inſtead of *ſweeteſt*, he would ſubſtitute *faireſt*; becauſe "the word *ſweet* occurs within "two lines:" he ſhould have ſayed, *within three.* But I cannot think *faireſt* ſo good an epither, as *ſweeteſt*. — His other emendation is of the 23d verſe; where he would read *learned ſons*, inſtead of *tuneful ſtrains*: but it appears by the authentic copy here given, that *ſtrains* was a blunder of the tranſcriber.

BAVIUS.

DOMESTIC NEWS.

C. *Courant.*	E P. *Evening Poſt.*
P. *Poſt Boy.*	S J. *St. James's Evening Poſt.*
D P. *Daily Poſt.*	W E. *Whitehall Evening Poſt.*
D J. *Daily Journal.*	L E. *London Evening Poſt.*

THURSDAY, *Dec.* 21.

Nich. Harding, of the Inner-temple, Eſq; clerk to the houſe of commons, is appointed law-reader to his royal highneſs the duke, with a ſalary of 100l. per ann. beſides an allowance for buying books. *S J. L E.* —— We hear Dr. Whiſton is to attend the duke once a day, in order to go through a courſe of philoſophical experiments. *S J.*

Yeſterday the right hon. Sir Rob. Walpole was at S. James's the firſt time ſince his indiſpoſition. *P. W E.* —— *The* C. *and* D P. Dec. 18. *conducted him to* court *laſt* ſunday, *and gave an account of his* gracious reception.

The ſame day 20 of the South-ſea company's Greenland ſhips on an avarage were ſold at 1350l. per ſhip: all being ſold except the Induſtry, for which there were no bidders. C. D. P.

On tueſday was ſold by auction the eſtate of Francis Hawes Eſq; late a South-ſea director, at Marlborough, and purchaſed by her grace the dutcheſs-dowager of Marlborough for 1710l. *S J.*

Col. Wentworth's regiment of foot is arrived from the Weſt-Indies in Ireland, in a ſhattered condition, having ſuffered greatly by death at Jamaica, ſo that there are ſcarce 200 effective men left. *S J.*

On tueſday 3 lace-men coming to town from Buckinghamſhire, were robbed by 2 high-way-men between Acton and the Green-man. — Yeſterday a higgler coming from Stratford, was attacked by a foot-pad, who preſented his piſtol; which the higgler ſtruck out of his hand with his whip, and jumped from his horſe and ſeized him; but his horſe running away, he quitted the fellow, and ran after his horſe: it is thought this was the perſon who killed the pipe-maker laſt week. *P.*

On tueſday Mr. Tagg, an eminent ſurgeon in Weſtminſter, was married to Miſs Napier, a young gentlewoman of good fortune. P. —— *My* brethren, *the news writers, always find perſons* eminent, *or make them ſo.*

FRIDAY, *Dec* 22.

Yeſterday being St. Thomas's day, came on the election of common-council-men: there was very little oppoſition in any ward; tho' in Farringdon without, one Falkner would have put himſelf on the ward for St Bride's pariſh, but met with a juſt contempt, not having above 20 hands out of about 300; ſo that the majority fell on thoſe worthy citizens, who have been remarkable for their attachment to the true intereſt of their country. *D P.* — In Walbrook ward, a poll was begun for Mr. Arnold and Mr. Henſhaw, but given up. — In Vintry ward, Mr. Pitts was choſe in the room of Mr. Whitaker, who is removing out of the ward. — In Aldgate ward, Mr. Lambert in the room of Capt. Hiccox, removed out of the ward. — In Langbourn ward, Mr. Herbert in the room of Mr. Hawys. *D J.*

John Briſtow, Hen. Gautier, Hen. Muilman, Theophilus Salwey, and Rob. Wylde Eſqs, have diſqualify'd themſelves from being directors of the South-ſea company, in order to be examined as witneſſes, in the cauſe, depending in the court of chancery, between the company, and James Delliſſe Eſq, and Capt. Cleland. *D J.*

A watch-maker on Holborn-hill, who had a wife endow'd with ſome faculties diſagreeable to him; ſhe being taken ill, declared to his neighbours, that ſhould it pleaſe God to take her from him, he would entertain them very handſomely: ſhe dy'd, and laſt tueſday he entertain'd a great number, at the Globe ale-houſe on the ſaid hill, very elegantly. *D J.* — *I fear, he was but a bad huſband.*

On tueſday Mr. Weſt, ſon of Mr. Weſt, an apothecary in New Palace-yard, was attacked by 2 highway-men, between Uxbridge and London; but making a ſtout reſiſtance by firing a piſtol, and preſenting another, they rode off. They had juſt before robbed the paſſengers in 2 Waggons. *D J.* — Mr. Weſt, of Old Palace yard, was attack'd by a ſingle highway-man, who demanded his money; Mr. Weſt having a good caſe of piſtols, challeng'd him; upon which the rogue made off as faſt as he could. *D P.*

On ſunday Will Bentley Eſq, of Clapham, was married to Miſs Bennet, eldeſt daughter to Will. Bennet of Lower-Tootin, a beautiful young lady, with a fortune of 5000l. C.

SATURDAY, *Dec.* 23.

Yeſterday on the ballot at the India-houſe, the numbers ſtood thus: for dividing 3 and ½, 188, againſt it, 99. *C. D P. D J.*

The ſame day at a court of directors of the ſouth-ſea company, Sir John Eyles, the ſub-governor, declared his intention of quitting the ſaid poſt at the next election in February. *D J.*

On thurſday in the ward of Farringdon within, Mr Selwyn, an eminent dealer in raw ſilk, and Mr. Mills, an eminent grocer, were choſen common-council-men, in the room of Mr. Bound and Mr. Trollope, who reſigned. *D P.* — Yeſterday, at the poll for common council-men of Allhallows, Lombard ſtreet precinct, in the ward of Biſhopſgate ſtreet within, the numbers were: for Mr. Danſie 324; Mr Cotton, 305; Mr. Weſt, 237. *P.* — The 2 former had a majority by 100. C.

At a meeting of a great number of merchants, traders, and citizens, yeſterday, at the ſwan-tavern in Cornhill, it was unanimouſly *reſolv'd*, "That the merchants, traders, "and citizens, here preſent, will act with the utmoſt unanimity, and by all dutiful and lawful methods ſtrenuouſly oppoſe any new exciſe, or any extenſion of the exciſe laws, under whatever name or pretence it may be "attempted:" and they deputed Sir Will Chapman, Mr. alderman Champion, Mr. alderman Godſchal, Sir John Groſvenor, Mr. Willimot, Mr. Boſworth, Mr. Lambert, Mr. Bradley, Mr. Clarke, Mr. Wilſon, Mr. Chitty, Mr. Pearſe, Mr. Haſwell, Mr. Hyde, Mr. Lockwood, Mr Weyland, Mr. Harris, Mr. Hyam, Mr. Cleaver, Mr. Daſh, Mr. Marſhall, Mr. Newnam, Mr. Sandford, Mr. Fry, and Mr. Duncalf, to wait on the four repreſentatives of this city with the ſaid reſolution, and in the moſt earneſt manner requeſt them, in the name of the merchants, traders, and citizens there met, to oppoſe with the utmoſt vigour and reſolution any motion of that kind in the houſe of commons. *D J.*

A patent has paſſed the ſeals, conſtituting Mr. Hugh Andrews keeper of the chamber to his majeſty's moſt hon. privy council. *L E.*

Yeſterday, at a general court of the charitable corporation, it was reſolved to return thanks to Rob. Holford, John Bennet, James Lightborn, Will. Kynaſton, and Francis Elde, Eſqs, the commiſſioners appointed by the late act for ſtating the claims of the corporation, for their great diſpatch. *L E.*

The ſame day the rev. Mr. Brooks was choſen lecturer of S. Mary hill, in the room of Mr. Gwyn deceaſed, by a majority of 14. There were 14 candidates. C. P.

We hear the author of the tragedy of *Junius Brutus* has withdrawn the ſaid play from Drury-lane houſe. *W E.*

Laſt thurſday 2 boys, the eldeſt not 9 years old, were committed to Newgate for robbing ſeveral ſhops and houſes: and a girl of 10 for receiving goods ſtolen by the boys, and for robbing a cheeſemonger's ſhop. *S J.*

Laſt night his grace the duke of Norfolk was given over by his phyſicians: his grace's brother was ſent for by an expreſs from Suſſex. *D P.* — There was a conſultation of phyſicians at the duke's, in order to conſider of proper means for his grace's recovery: and yeſterday a coach and ſix ſet out for his brother, who is in Nottinghamſhire. *P. D J. W E.* — This morning between 5 and 6 he died of a conſumptive illneſs: he was hereditary earl-marſhal of England, and primier duke, earl, and baron of England next the royal blood. The honours and eſtate devolve upon his only ſurviving brother Philip Howard. *S J. L E.* —— His grace was 49 years of age, on the 9th inſtant. *D P. Dec.* 25.

On wedneſday the 6th inſtant died at Geneva, Nathaniel Norbury Eſq; governor to the right hon. the earl of Darnley. *P.* — On thurſday, of the gout in his ſtomach, at his houſe in Edmonton Sir Will. Jackſon Knt. formerly mayor of York C. —— The ſame day Mr. Willis, maſter of the vintner's company. *D J.*

At the end of the advertiſement from the Oratery in *Fog's Journal*, is this "N. B. In regard to this day [Chriſtmas day] there will be no oration on wedneſday this "week." — *I cannot but wonder at* Mr. Orator's *way of ſhewing his* regard to Chriſtmas day, *by omitting his* duty *on the* wedneſday *following: he having aſſerted in the* Daily Journal *of* Dec. 13. That "a preacher and teacher of God's "word, is bound in conſcience and religion to preach and "teach burleſque."

The DISEASES *and* CASUALTIES *this Year.*

Abortive and ſtilborn	627	Jaundice	11
Aged	1781	Impoſthume	3
Ague	10	Inflammation	14
Apoplexy and ſuddenly	237	Itch	1
Aſthma and Tiſſick	573	Leproſy	2
Bed-ridden	3	Lethargy	3
Bleeding	5	Livergrown	9
Bloody Flux	13	Lunatick	25
Burſten and Rupture	22	Meaſles	30
Cancer	50	Miſcarriage	3
Canker	14	Mortification	49
Child-bed	219	Palſy	36
Cold	1	Pleuriſy	55
Colick, and Twiſting of the Guts	52	Quinſy	11
Conſumption	3719	Raſh	1
Convulſion	7428	Rheumatiſm	19
Cough, and Hooping Cough	65	Rickets	74
Diabetes	5	Riſing of the Lights	54
Dropſy	945	S. Anthony's Fire	2
Evil	19	Scald Head	1
Fever, Malignant Fever, Scarlet Fever, Pu[illegible]s	2939	Small Pox	1197
Fiſtula	17	Sores and Ulcers	45
Flux	32	Spleen	5
French Pox	90	Stoppage in the Stomach	197
Gout	38	Surfeit	4
Gravel, Stone, and Strangury	52	Swelling	1
Grief	14	Teeth	1361
Griping in the Guts	273	Thruſh	65
Headmouldſhot, Horſhoehead, and Water in the Head	81	Tympany	6
		Vapours	5
		Vomiting and Looſeneſs	16
		Worms	11

CASUALTIES.

Broken Leg 3. Burnt 3. Choaked with a Cherry 1. Drowned 98. Exceſſive Drinking 38. Executed 15. Found dead 37. Fractured Skull 1. Kill'd by Falls, and ſeveral other Accidents 55. Kill'd by the Bite of a mad Dog 2. Made away themſelves 52. Murder'd 11. Murdered in the Pillory 1. Overlaid 133. Scalded 1. Smother'd, Strangled, or ſuffocated 3. Starved 1. Total 466.

Chriſtened Males 9144. Females 8644. In all 17788.

Buried Males 11655. Females 11703. In all 23358.

Decreaſed in the Burials this Year 1904.

Whereof have died,

Under two years of age	9502	Fifty and ſixty	1741
Between two and five	1517	Sixty and ſeventy	1581
Five and ten	716	Seventy and eighty	974
Ten and twenty	711	Eighty and ninety	660
Twenty and thirty	1627	Ninety, and upwards of a hundred	133
Thirty and forty	2175		
Forty and fifty	2121		

S J.

MONDAY, *Dec.* 25.

Yeſterday the rev. Dr. George preached before their majeſties, his royal highneſs the prince, and the three eldeſt princeſſes; and the rev. Dr. Cobden before his royal highneſs the duke, and the princeſſes Mary and Louiſa. *C. P. D J.* —— The ſame day their majeſties, &c. dined in publick in the great ball-room at St. James's, before a numerous crowd of ſpectators. C. —— Their majeſties did not dine in publick, on account of their receiving the ſacrament. *P.* — *They did not* receive.

On ſaturday at a general court of the Eaſt-India company, Sir Mat. Decker declared the numbers of the ballot for the dividend, that it had been carried by a great majority, for three and one half per cent. *C.*

The ſame day the right hon. the lord mayor, &c. went through all the great ſtreets and publick markets in the city, and collected charity for the relief of the poor debtors confined in Newgate and the two compters, according to annual cuſtom. *C.*

On ſaturday laſt, the anabaptiſt meeting-houſe in Glaſshouſe ſtreet, S. James's, was broke open in the night-time, and robbed of all the plate and furniture. *P.* — *The rogues, I imagine, thought* plate *too* popiſh *for an* anabaptiſt meeting-houſe.

On ſaturday morning about 2. ſome rogues broke into the houſe of Mr. Sherlock, a lighter-men at the bank-ſide, near S. Saviour's, Southwark, and ſtole all his plate, to the value of 80l. and a large parcel of wearing apparel. *D J.* — Mr. Conundrum *ſays, he was a* lighter man *by* 80 pounds, *and the fitter to* ſwi[illegible]

On friday night, Mr. [illegible]rall an eminent taylor, being at the half-moon tavern in Cheapſide, news was brought him of his niece's being delivered of a baſtard child, which ſhe had put into a box to ſmother it, but was prevented; which ſo ſurprized him, that he died immediately. *D J.*

On ſaturday the corps of Mr. John Gay was interred in the abbey of Weſtminſter. The ſervice was read by the biſhop of Rocheſter, the quire attending, with the uſual ceremonies. The pall was ſupported by the right hon.

the earl of Chesterfield, the right hon. the lord Cornbury, the hon. George Berkley, the hon. Mr. Levison Gower, general Dormer, and Alexander Pope Esq; The funeral was attended by his grace the duke of Queensberry, and other persons of distinction. We hear a monument to his memory will be erected by the duke. P. DP. — On saturday night about 11 o'clock, the corps of John Gay Esq; sunday night lying in state in Exeter-change, &c. was interred &c. after lying in state in Exeter-change, &c. was interred with great pomp and solemnity. D J. — It was at 9.

Bath, Dec. 14. This morning died the rev. Dr. John Davies, rector of Kingsland in Herefordshire, and præcentor of St. David's. D P. —— On saturday died, at his lodgings in Fleet street, Dr. Brown, an eminent physician. D J.

Last night the body of Will. Croombie Esq; was interred in the burying-ground of S. George, whereby he was noted for an ingenious and fair gamester, whereby he acquired an estate of 130,000 l. P. — I believe, he was first, who ever won so much.

TUESDAY, Dec. 26.

Yesterday being Christmas day, was observed as a high festival at court. The rev. Dr. Gilbert, dean of Exeter, sub-almoner and clerk of the closet to his majesty, preached before their majesties, &c. Their majesties, his royal highness the prince, and the three eldest princesses, received the holy communion from the hands of the right rev. the lord bishop of London, dean of the chapel. C P —— The rev. Dr George preached before his royal highness the duke, and the princesses Mary and Louisa. P.

Last week the lord Forbes kiss'd the hands of their majesties, &c. being speedily to set out in quality of envoy extraordinary to the empress of Russia. D P.

The earl of Burlington has prepared a plan for building a stately house in Pall-mall, upon the late lord Carleton's ground, for his royal highness the prince. D P.

Last friday the claimants who had entered a caveat against the will of Rich. Norton Esq; who left near 6000 l. per ann. and also his personal estate, upwards of 60,000 l. to the parliament of Great Britain, to be disposed of for charitable uses, were heard before Dr. John Bettesworth, when a commission of appraisement was decreed, and notice ordered to be given to all the bishops of the said proceedings. D J. P. — Yesterday several chests and boxes of money were brought in a waggon, under a strong guard, to the pay-office at the horse-guards, from the seat of the said Col. Norton, being the personal estate so bequeathed, and deposited in the said office. D J.

The rev. Dr. Willis, bishop of Winchester, lies dangerously ill at Chelsea. D J. — His grace Edward, now duke of Norfolk, lies very much indisposed in S. James's-square. P. — Dangerously ill. D J. — The S J. and L E. Dec. 23. name him Philip.

On friday came advice from Paris of the death of the countess dowager of Seaforth, in the 98th year of her age. P. — By private letters from South Carolina, we hear that a noted broker, late of Exchange-alley, being disordered in his senses, drowned himself, Octob. 13. C. — Mr. Tho. Morrison. D P. — On saturday died Joseph Thurston, of the Inner Temple, Esq; D P.

WEDNESDAY, Dec. 27.

Yesterday his grace the archbishop of Canterbury gave a grand entertainment, at his palace at Lambeth, to all the bishops who are in town. D J.

Yesterday was committed to Newgate by Miles Harper Esq; one Sarah Harper, being charged on the oaths of dame Mary Rich and another person, with cursing their majesties and the rest of the royal family, saying they were all beggars, and came hither to starve the nation; with other opprobrious expressions. DP.

Last saturday evening, a man who works at a wharf at the bottom of Garlick-hill, being at a publick-house there, drank half a pint of geneva; likewise a second, and then a third; after which he went up stairs, and died immediately. D J. — I suppose, he works by proxy.

From the PEGASUS in Grub-street.

IT was asserted by Mr. BAVIUS, in our 155th *Journal,* that a N.B. published by Mr. ORATOR, in Foo's *Journal, Dec. 2.* was *ungrammatical and nonsensical.* " N. B, In the " Scripture, the rule of preaching, are above a thousand " burlesque passages, WHICH RENDERS IT strictly religious " in its turn." The reason assigned was, because the words IT and ITS could not be referred to any of the preceding substantives, either to *scripture,* or *rule,* or *preaching,* or *burlesque passages.*

The same N.B. had been censured by Mr. QUIDNUNC, in our 154th *Journal,* as being *irreligious,* as well as *ungrammatical and nonsensical.* And to prove it not to be *irreligious,* the following syllogism was published in the *Quack-Doctor, Dec. 12.* in a short letter directed to Mr. BAVIUS, which he was falsely charged with refusing to publish. " Irony is burlesque, the scripture abounds with iro-" nical passages, *ergo* IT is not buffoonery, nor irreligious." Of this syllogism Mr. BAVIUS denied both the *major* or first

proposition, and the *conclusion:* and justly expected, that Mr. ORATOR would have endeavoured to prove both, and to vindicate his N.B.

Let us now see what answer he returned. In the *Daily Journal of friday, Dec. 15.* under the title of *Testimonies and patterns of Mr. HENLEY's week-days discourses,* he gave us a catalogue of 83 names of Ancients and Moderns; who have no more right to be placed under such a title, than the lord mayor, aldermen, and common-council of this city. — In the *Daily Journal of Saturday, Dec. 16.* he promised to *prove himself,* on the wednesday following, *a better grammarian and logician* than one of his supposed antagonists. — His way of proof was this: In the *Daily Journals of tuesday and wednesday, Dec. 19, 20.* he advertised, " At the Oratory will be, 1 A thesis offering an " academical disputation in proof that" his N.B. was *strictly grammatical,* and his syllogism *logical.* — In reply to which Mr. BAVIUS says, that as Mr. ORATOR published his N. B. [not in his Oratory, but] in a weekly paper, and likewise endeavoured to vindicate it in another, with the addition of a syllogism to clear it of irreligion; he ought to defend both the N.B. and the syllogism, in the same manner, in which he first presented them to the public. This Mr. BAVIUS now again calls upon him to do, viz. to shew that his N.B. is *strictly grammatical,* and to prove the first proposition and the conclusion of his syllogism. When he has endeavoured to give satisfaction in any of these particulars, Mr. BAVIUS promises, either to acknowledge himself convinced, or to shew the inconclusiveness of Mr. ORATOR's way of reasoning.

Last week Mr. MÆVIUS gave in some verses, written in imitation of those, which the bell-men annually present to their masters and mistresses, at this season of the year: but as we had not room to insert them in our last *Journal;* so we can only give the following specimen of them in this.

On S. THOMAS.

OF all the saints, S. THOMAS sure was best;
His reason greatest, and his faith the least.
Deceiv'd themselves, whilst some were still deceiving,
He wisely thought that seeing was believing.
Now many TOMS there are as wise as he,
Who nothing will believe, but what they see.
Yet bigots censure these as all in head and heart,
And join TOM WOOLSTON still with TOM o' BEDLAM.

On CHRIST-MAS.

OBlessed season! lov'd by saints and sinners,
For long devotions, or for longer dinners,
More grateful still to those who deal in books;
Now not with readers, but with pastry-cooks.
Learn'd works, despis'd by those to merit blind,
By these well weigh'd their certain value find:
Blest lot of paper, falsely called waste,
To bear those cates, which authors seldom taste!

We desire, that the advertisements designed for this paper may be sent before twelve of the clock on tuesdays, otherwise they cannot be inserted.

South Sea Stock was 104 7 8ths. to 105. for the Opening. South Sea Annuity 109 5 8ths. to 3 qrs. Bank 149 3 qrs. to 150. Bank Circulation 5 l. Premium. India 156 1 qr. for the Opening. Three per Cent. Annuity 101 1 half, for ditto. Royal Exchange Assurance 106, for ditto. London Assurance 13 5 8ths. York Buildings 3, for Opening. African 35, for ditto. English Copper 1 l. 19 s. Welch ditto 1 l. 13 s. South Sea Bonds 2 l. 11 s. Premium. India ditto 5 l. 5 s. ditto. Three per Cent. ditto 2 l. 4 s. ditto.

ADVERTISEMENTS.
SILK-WORMS.

This Day is Published, in Quarto, Pr. 2 s. stitch'd.

Humbly dedicated to the Right Honourable the Lord Viscount PERCIVAL, *the Right Honourable the Lord* CARPENTER, *and the rest of the Honourable the Trustees for establishing the Colony of* GEORGIA *in America.*

A Compendious Account of the whole Art of Breeding, Nursing, and the right Ordering of the Silk-Worm; illustrated with Figures, beautifully engraven on Six large Copper Plates, wherein is exhibited the whole Management of this profitable business.

Note, One of the Plates, curiously representing the several Transformations of that wonderful Creature, was delineated (and is now colour'd) from the Life, by the ingenious ELEAZAR ALBIN.

Printed for J. Worral at the Dove in Bell-Yard, near Lincoln's Inn; O Payne, in Round-Court in the Strand; T. Boreman, on Ludgate-Hill, near the Gate; and T. Game, at the Bible, facing the East End of the New Church in the Strand; and Sold by E. Nutt at the Royal Exchange, and A. Dodd without Temple-bar.

Just published,

THE Ancient Physician's LEGACY to his Country; being what he has collected himself in 49 Years Practice: Or, An Account of the several Diseases incident to Mankind, described in so plain a Manner, that any Person may know the Nature of his own Disease. Together with the several Remedies for each Distemper, faithfully set down.

Homines ad Deos nulla in re propiùs accedunt, quàm Salutem Hominibus dando. Cic.

By THOMAS DOVER, M.B.

Printed for the Author, and sold by J. Brotherton at the Bible in Cornhill; A. Bettesworth and C. Hitch, in Pater-noster Row; W. Mears at the Lamb in the Old Baily; and L. Gilliver at Homer's-Head, over-against St. Dunstan's Church in Fleet-Street. Price Stitch'd Five Shillings.

Note, The Doctor is to be heard of, or spoke with, at the Jerusalem Coffee-house in Exchange-Alley.

This Day is published,

*** *The* SEVENTH *and* EIGHTH VOLUMES *of a* SELECT COLLECTION *of* MOLIERE'S COMEDIES, *in* French *and* English, *which finish the Collection, neatly Printed on a Fine Paper, with a Curious Frontispiece to each Comedy.*

N.B. A Curious PRINT of the AUTHOR, with his LIFE in *French* and *English*, extracted from Monsieur *Bayle, Rapin*, &c. will be deliver'd (*GRATIS*) with the said Seventh and Eighth Volumes, to compleat the Collection.

The Seventh Volume contains,

Amphytrion. Amphitryon.	*Dedicated to the Right Hon.* George Doddington Esq;
Le Marriage Forcé. The Forc'd Marriage.	*Dedicated to the Right Hon. the Lady* Harvey.
Le Sicilien, ou L'Amour Peintre. The Sicilian, or Love makes a Painter.	*Dedicated to her Grace the Dutchess of* Richmond.

The Eighth Volume contains,

Le Malade Imaginaire. The Hypochondriack.	*Dedicated to his Grace the Duke of* Argyle.
Les Facheux. The Impertinents.	*Dedicated to the Right Honourable the Lord* Carteret.

Printed for and Sold by J. Watts at the Printing-Office in Wild-Court, near Lincoln's-Inn Fields: And J. Brotherton in Cornhill; J. Clarke in Duck-Lane; A. Bettesworth and C. Hitch, J. Osborne and T. Longman, and J. Batley in Pater-Noster-Row; J. Roberts in Warwick-Lane; J. Pemberton, L. Gilliver and T. Worrall in Fleet-Street; F. Clay and R. Wellington without Temple-Bar; A. Millar and P. Dunoyer in the Strand; J. Baton in Little Ormond-Street; J. Stagg in Westminster-Hall; and J. Brindley in New Bond-Street. Of whom may be had, just published,

Vol. I. containing,
A General PREFACE to the Whole WORK.

L'AVARE. The MISER.	*Dedicated to* his Royal Highness The Prince of Wales.
Sganarelle ou le Cocu Imaginaire. The Cuckold in Conceit.	*Dedicated to Miss* Wolstenholme.

Vol. II. containing,

Le Bourgeois Gentilhomme. The Cit turn'd Gentleman.	*Dedicated to* his Royal Highness the Duke.
Le Medecin de Malgré Lui. A Doctor and no Doctor.	*Dedicated to Dr. Mead.*

Vol. III. containing,

L'Etourdi ou les Contre-Tems. The Blunderer: Or, the Counter-Plots.	*Dedicated to the Right Honourable* Philip *Earl of* Chesterfield.
Precieuses Ridicules. The Conceited Ladies.	*Dedicated to Miss* Le Bass.

Vol. IV. containing,

L'Ecole des Maris. The School for Husbands.	*Dedicated to the Right Honourable the Lady* Harriot Cambell.
L'Ecole des Femmes. The School for Wives.	*Dedicated to the Right Honourable* Sir Wm. Yong, *Knight of the Bath.*

Vol. V. containing,

Tartuffe, ou L'Imposteur. The Impostor.	*Dedicated to Mr.* Wyndham *of* Clower-Wall, *in* Gloucestershire
George Dandin, ou le Mari Confondu. George Dandin, or the Husband Defeated.	*Dedicated to the Right Honourable the Lady ****

Vol. VI. containing,

Le Misantrope. The Man-Hater.	*Dedicated to his Grace the Duke of* Montagu.
M. De Pourceaugnac. Squire Lubberly.	*Dedicated to the Right Hon. the Lady* Mary Wortley Montagu.

The Translation is entirely new, and was undertaken by several Gentlemen, who all joined and consulted together about every Part of it. Particular Care has been had to keep as close as possible to the Original, and to observe the very Words of the Author, as well as his Sense, so far as was consistent with giving it a spirited and easy Comick Stile, in order to make it the more serviceable to those of our own Nation who are Learners of the French Language; as likewise to Foreigners who desire to be acquainted with ours: To whom the Method we had taken of placing the French and English opposite to each other, will be of no small Benefit. The Work is printed in a very beautiful Manner, and adorned with new Frontispieces, designed by Monf. COYPEL, Mr. HOGARTH, Mr. DANDRIDGE, Mr. HAMILTON, &c. Price each Volume, done up in blue Covers, Two Shillings and Six Pence.

RAMSAY, Surgeon and Man-Midwife, in Castle-Yard, Holbourn,

HATH for many Years, successfully practised a Method of RUPTURES and BROKEN BELLIES of all Sorts, peculiar to himself, and hath cured Numbers of Bursten People, who imagin'd themselves incurable; some of whom have been examin'd by Physicians and Surgeons of the greatest Reputation, who have given their Testimony thereof in the publick Prints. There are several Gentlemen to be heard of at Mr. FRANKLIN's in Russel-street, Covent-Garden, who are ready to acknowledge their being cured by him.

He performs the Cure within the Compass of three or four Weeks, and without giving the Patient the Trouble or Fatigue of wearing a Truss after the Cure is perfected.

This Day is Published,

(*Now first Printed*)

FOUR SPEECHES against continuing the ARMY, &c. as they were spoken on several Occasions in the House of Commons. As also, A SPEECH for Relieving the Unhappy Sufferers in the Charitable Corporation, as it was spoken in the House of Commons, May 8. 1732.

By W—— S—— Esq;

Printed for J. Wilford near St. Paul's. Price 1 s.

Where may be had,

The Chevalier RAMSAY's Plan of Education for a young Prince. Price 6 d.

This Day is published,

A New Play, call'd CÆLIA, or, The Perjur'd LOVER, as it is Acted at the Theatre-Royal in Drury-Lane, by his Majesty's Servants.

N. B. This Play is founded on a True Tragical Story in Common Life, and the Incidents very Natural and Moving.

Printed for John Watts, at the Printing-Office in Wild-Court near Lincoln's-Inn Fields. Of whom may be had, Just Publish'd, The Second Edition of The MOCK DOCTOR, Or, the DUMB LADY Cur'd, a Comedy done from Moliere, with Additional SONGS and Alterations.

Lately published,

By Mr. MAITTAIRE, *Curiously and Correctly Printed in Duodecimo, the following Books; viz.*

NOVUM TESTAMENTUM. Græce.

SOPHOCLIS Tragœdiæ septem. Cum Versione Latina & selectis quibusdam variis Lectionibus.

HOMERI Ilias. Adjicitur in Calcem Interpretatio Latina. Scholis in Anglia Celeberrimis; Etonensi, Westmonasteriensi Regiis; Wintoniensi, Carthusianæ, Paulinæ & Mercatorum scissorum, hæc Homeri Editio, in Earum præcipue Usum Concinnata, humilime Offertur Dedicaturque.

P. VIRGILII MARONIS Opera.

Q. HORATII FLACCI Opera.

CATULLI, TIBULLI, & PROPERTII Opera.

P. OVIDII NASONIS Opera, tribus tomis comprehensa.

PUBLII TERENTII Carthaginiensis Afri Comœdiæ sex.

TITI LUCRETII CARI de Rerum Natura libri sex.

M. ANNÆI LUCANI Pharsalia: sive de Bello Civili inter Cæsarem & Pompeium libri decem.

PHÆDRI Aug. Liberti Fabularum Æsopicarum Libri quinque; item Fabulæ quædam ex MS. veteri a Marquardo Gudio descriptæ; cum Indice Vocum & Locutionum. Appendicis loco adjiciuntur Fabulæ Græcæ quædam & Latinæ ex variis Authoribus collectæ; quas claudit Avieni Æsopicarum Fabularum liber unicus.

D. JUNII JUVENALIS, & AULII PERSII FLACCI Satyræ.

M. VALERII MARTIALIS Epigrammata.

CHRISTUS PATIENS. Rapini carmen Heroicum.

MUSARUM ANGLICANARUM ANALECTA: sive Poemata quædam melioris notæ, seu hactenus Inedita, seu sparsim Edita, in duo Volumina congesta. Editio Quarta. Prioribus auctior.

T. LIVII PATAVINI Historiarum ab Urbe condita Libri qui supersunt. In 6 Vol.

C. PLINII CÆCILII Secundi Epistolæ & Panegyricus.

CORNELII NEPOTIS excellentium Imperatorum Vitæ.

LUCIUS ANNÆUS FLORUS. Cui subjungitur Lucii Ampelii liber memorialis.

CAII SALLUSTII CRISPI quæ extant.

VELLEII PATERCULI Historiæ Romanæ quæ supersunt.

JUSTINI Historiarum ex Trogo Pompeio libri XLIV.

Q. CURTIUS RUFUS de rebus gestis Alexandri Magni.

C. JULII CÆSARIS & A. HIRTII de rebus a C. Julio Cæsare gestis Commentarii: Cum C. Jul. Cæsaris fragmentis.

CONCIONES & ORATIONES ex Historicis Latinis excerptæ.

And in Octavo.

TELEMACHUS in French, with Cuts.

C. JULII CÆSARIS quæ extant, accuratissime cum Libris Editis & MSS. optimis Collata, Recognita & Correcta. Accesserunt Annotationes Samuelis Clarke, S. T. P. Item Indices Locorum, Rerumque & Verborum, Utilissimi.

All Printed for Jacob Tonson at Shakespear's Head in the Strand, and John Watts at the Printing-Office in Wild-Court near Lincoln's-Inn Fields; and Sold by the Booksellers of London and Westminster.

This Day is published,

Beautifully Printed in Folio,

No. IX. (Price 2 s. 6 d.) of

ECCLESIASTICAL MEMOIRS of the Six First Centuries, made good by Citations from Original Authors: With a Chronological Table, containing an Abridgment of the principal Things, placed according to Order of Time; and with Notes, clearing the Difficulties of Facts and Chronology. Translated from the French of Lewis Sebastian le Nain de Tillemont. Vol. I. which comprehends the Time of our Lord and the Apostles.

NB. This Number finishes the Notes upon S. Peter, containing those upon S. Paul, and begins those upon S. Andrew; comprehending several curious Dissertations, among many others, upon the following Subjects, viz. That S. Peter and S. Paul probably suffered at the same Time and Place; and that they died on the 29th of June, not on the 22 of February. Upon the tradition of celebrating Easter on Sunday: When, and why S. Paul took the Name of Paul: In what Manner S. Paul saw Jesus Christ at his Conversion: Whether S. Paul was married: Of a Book ascribed to Barjesus against S. Paul: Upon the Decree of the Council of Jerusalem to abstain from Blood and Things strangled: Upon the Altar at Athens, dedicated to the Unknown God: Of S. Paul's fighting with Beasts at Ephesus: Upon S. Paul's saying, that he did not know the High Priest Ananias: Upon the spurious epistle of S. Paul to the Laodiceans: That the Epistle to the Hebrews has been always received by the Greeks, and from the Year 400 by the Latins: What is said of S. Paul's journey into Spain and Gauls is uncertain: That S. Paul returned from Rome into the East: That there is no Proof that S. Andrew founded the Church of Byzantium: An Examination of the Acts of S. Andrew.

Printed for the Author; and Sold by J. Wilford, at the Three Golden Flower de Luces behind the Chapter-House in St. Paul's Church-Yard; and William Clayton, Bookseller in Manchester.

No. IX. is in the Press.

Just published,

SURVEYING Improv'd: *Or, the whole Art, both in Theory and Practice, fully demonstrated: In Four Parts;*

I. ARithmetick, Vulgar and Decimal. II. All Definitions, Theorems, and Problems; with plain Trigonometry, and whatever else is necessary to the Theory of Surveying. III. The Description and Use of Instruments proper to be used in Practical Surveying. IV. How to measure, cast up, plot or divide any Parcel of Land; to take inaccessible Heights and Distances; with Surveying Counties, Roads, Rivers, &c. Also to reduce a Plan to a Prospect; and to correct any Survey by Astronomical Calculation; with Directions for making transparent Colours for Maps. To which is added, An Appendix concerning Levelling, and conveying Water to any possible Place assigned; with 96 Figures engraved on Copper. By HENRY WILSON. Price 5 s.

Printed for J Batley, at the Dove in Pater-Noster-Row.

This Day is publish'd, *Pr. 6 d.*

A LAYMAN'S FAITH: Being a Review of the Principal Evidences of the Truth of the CHRISTIAN RELIGION; interspers'd with several curious Observations, and dedicated to her Majesty.

Nullius addictus jurare in Verba magistri
Amicus SOCRATES, *amicus* PLATO, *sed magis amica* VERITAS.

By a Freethinker, *and a* Christian.

Printed for T. Cooper, at the Globe in Ivy-Lane.

Where may be had,

I. A Vindication of the Old Church of England. In Answer to Mr. Wainhouse's Novelties of the Church of Rome.

In fide vivo filii Dei. Pr. 1 s.

II. An Answer to a Popish Pamphlet, entitled, A Vindication of the Old Church of England. By Richard Wainhouse, M.A. Pr. 6 d.

" Nullum fundamentum aut firmitatem possunt habere, qui " nullis divinarum vocum fulciuntur, oraculis." Lactant.

On Saturday will be published,

THE PRESENT STATE of EUROPE: Or, The Historical and Political Monthly Mercury: Giving an Account of all the publick and private Occurrences Civil, Ecclesiastical, and Military, that are most considerable in every Court. With a more Particular Account of the Affairs of Great Britain, &c.

For the Month of October, 1732. Vol. XLIV.

With Political Reflections upon every State. Continued Monthly, from Originals published at the Hague by the Authority of the States of Holland and West-Friesland, &c.

Printed for the Assigns of the Executors of H. Rhodes, and Eliz. Harris; and sold by J. Roberts, in Warwick-Lane.

Where are to be had the whole Forty-Three Volumes, beginning November, 1688. (Or Single Ones, from July, 1690. to this Time.) Price Six Pence.

LONDON: Printed for, and Sold by J. ROBERTS, near the *Oxford-Arms* in *Warwick-Lane*; where Letters and Advertisements are taken in; as also by Capt. GULLIVER, near the *Temple*; by P. SANDERS, *in Crown-Court*, *Butcher-Row*, without *Temple-Bar*, and at the *Rainbow Coffee-House* in *Cornhill*. [Price Twopence.]

NOTES TO THE *GRUB-STREET JOURNAL*

Although when necessary these notes will refer to secondary and scholarly studies, their primary purpose is explanatory, not bibliographical. The *Grub-street Journal* is dense with allusions to the journalistic, literary, and political figures and events of its time. My purpose in the annotation is to provide a modern, educated, non-specialist reader with all the information needed to enable him or her to understand the issues, the historical and personal contexts, and the satire and humour of these pages in a manner at least approaching the way their original readers did. For the overall scheme of the paper and the background of its editors, readers are strongly recommended to consult the General Introduction in the first volume.

BG

No. 105

P. 1, col. 1, epigraph: Final lines of Matthew Prior's *A Simile* (1707).

P. 1, col. 1, 'An Ode': The Poet Laureate's traditional New Year's Ode; the line-by-line comments that follow are in *Mem.*(slightly revised), signed 'M.' (Russel).

P. 1, col. 2, '*anodyne necklace*': See Pegasus col. of No. 30 and in this issue, p. 3.

P. 1, col. 3, 'Thomas Stiles': See Pegasus col. of No. 104.

No. 106

P. 1, epigraph: Lines 93–94 of 'A Session of the Poets', as reprinted in *Poems on Affairs of State* I (New Haven: Yale U. P., 1963), ed. George deF. Lord, pp. 352–56. Lord dates the poem 1676 and calls the authorship 'uncertain'.

P. 1, col. 2, 'Cloacina': Goddess who presides over sewer systems.

P. 1, col. 3, '*Si quis ... possis*': 'Suppose a man were to speak of wars fought by you on land and sea, and with words like these flatter your attentive care: "May He, to whom both thou and Rome are dear, / Keep secret still, which is the fuller truth, / The love of Rome for thee, or thine for her!" you would see in them the praises of Augustus.' Horace, *Epistles* i. 16. 25–29 (Loeb).

P. 1, col. 3, '*Varius ... Augusti*': 'Indeed Varius had written these things about Augustus; they are, however, from the most noted panegyric of Augustus.'

P. 1, col. 3, '*Falsus honor ...*': 'Whom does false honour delight, whom does lying calumny affright, save the man who is full of flaws and needs the doctor?' (Loeb) but Loeb uses the emendation this writer says is Bentley's, 'medicandum', not 'mendacem' (lying).

P. 1, col. 3, '*egentem ... sanum*': 'Lacking the hellebore, he is not healthy.'

P. 1, col. 3, *'Necquicquam ... collines'*: 'In vain, emboldened by Venus' help, shalt thou comb thy tresses and sing to the music of the unwarlike lyre the songs that women love; vainly in thy chamber's retreat shalt thou shun the heavy spears and darts of Cretan reed, the battle's din, and Ajax fleet to follow. In spite of all, thou shalt yet (alas! too late) defile in the dust thy adulterous locks' (Loeb).

P. 2, col. 1, *'non sola ... Lacaena'*: 'Not Spartan Helen only became inflamed with love, marvelling at a paramour's trim locks, his gold-bespangled raiment, his princely pomp and followers' (Loeb).

P. 2, col. 1, *'adulteres ...* cultus': 'adulterers; gold smeared on clothing; royal refinements'.

P. 2, col. 1, 'Suetonius ... *pueri'*: 'distinguished with respect to the thick hair and most excellent refinement of the boy'.

P. 2, col. 1, 'Cleopatra ... *cultus'*:'she was clothed in the greatest refinements'.

P. 2, col. 1, *'Pour ... bouche'*: I.e., 'to keep the best for the last'; see Russel's note, No. 110, col. 2, n. 5.

P. 2, col. 1, 'Plautus ... *collinunt'*: 'disgusting ways soil a pretty dress more than mud.', Plautus, *Mostellaria* 291 (i. 3) (Loeb).

P. 2, col. 1, *'omnes ... intendere'*: 'to strain every sinew'.

P. 2, col. 1, 'To the King': On the reason for this poem see the note at end of p. 1, col. 3.

P. 3, col. 2, 'Welsted's *Dullness and Scandal'*: Leonard Welsted's attack on the sketch of 'Timon's Villa' in Pope's *Epistle to Burlington*. The line with the 'false Latin' reads 'Pallas' on Welsted's title page, not 'Turnus', and is an adaptation of *Aeneid* xii. 948, so as to render it 'Pallas gives you this wound' (the death of Pallas, son of Evander, killed by Turnus, is being avenged by Aeneas). This item is signed 'A.' in *Mem.*, as an item 'imagined to come' from Pope and his friends.

No. 107

P. 1, col. 1, 'Tonstal ... Ayres': Cuthbert Tonstal (or Tunstall) (1474–1559), Bishop of Durham, wrote *De arte supputandi* (1522), one of the first treatises on arithmetic in England; John Ayres (fl. 1680–1700), calligrapher, was author of *Arithmetic made Easie* (1693).

P. 1, col. 1, *'golden rule'*: Also known and referred to here as the 'Rule of Three', defined as 'a method of finding a fourth number from three given numbers, of which the first is in the same proportion to the second as the third is to the unknown fourth' (*OED*). Another distinction, also referred to in this letter, is between the ordinary form, called the common or direct rule of three, and the indirect, inverse, reverse, or backward form.

P. 1, col. 1, 'NEW METHOD': The author is proposing an algorithm for solving problems involving proportions; the problems are simple when one uses modern notation.

P. 1, col. 2, 'Berkeley... Collier': George Berkeley (1685–1754), Bishop of Cloyne and philosopher; Arthur Collier (1680–1732), metaphysician whose conclusions were less sophisticated but similar to Berkeley's.

P. 1, col. 2, 'Clavis Universalis': 'Universal Key', the title of a work of Collier's (1713).

P. 1, col. 3, 'H. P—r': Not identified.

P. 1, col. 3, 'R—l': Royal.

P. 3, col. 1, Pegasus col., 'following short Letter': This appears to be a serious report, but it is not in the other newspapers for this period.

P. 3, col. 1, 'sound at a *Pun'*: I.e., faint at it (*OED*).

P. 3, col. 1, 'P—r'; 'D—rs': I.e., Proctors and Doctors.

No. 108

P. 1, epigraph: *Dunciad* i. 161–62, Theobald, describing his efforts as an editor.

P. 1, col. 1, 'Milton ... amanuensis': This letter is a critique of Richard Bentley's edition of Milton's *Paradise Lost*, which had just been published; see the news item in the previous number on Bentley's son presenting it to the king and queen. A key part of Bentley's theory involved the supposition that Milton had employed both an amanuensis and an unscrupulous editor.

P. 1, col. 1, 'Chillingworth': William Chillingworth (1602–44), theologian, author of *The Religion of Protestants a Safe Way to Salvation* (1638). The comment about editing this work may refer to the ninth edition of his *Works* (1727), which contained an account of 'the corrections and improvements' made in that impression.

P. 1, col. 1, '*sunt ... illis*': Virgil, *Eclogues* ix. 33–34, 'I too have songs; me also the shepherds call a bard, but I trust them not' (Loeb).

P. 1, col. 3, 'the Hessians': Mercenary troops hired by Walpole and unpopular because they seemed primarily designed to protect Hanover.

P. 1, col. 3, '*The Modish Couple*': A play supposedly written by a Captain Charles Bodens, of the Coldstream Guards, but attributed now to the clergyman poet and playwright James Miller. The epilogue was by Fielding; for an account of the play and the favouritism accorded it by the Court, see Battestin, 125–26. The play's opening night before a politically biassed audience created an uproar.

P. 2, col. 1, 'Nobleman ... formidable party': The Duke of Montagu and the Duke of Richmond invited 200 of their friends to dinner and then brought the group into the theatre (Battestin, 126).

P. 2, col. 1, 'C— B—': Charles Bodens, the pretended author.

P. 2, col. 1, 'T–d': Theobald; 'Bays', of course, refers to Cibber.

P. 3, col. 2, Pegasus col., 'Art of turning a thought': A printing error here; as noted in No. 109, these four lines should have been printed *after* the song on the Peace.

P. 3, col. 2, 'his Majesty's speech': Delivered at the opening of Parliament on 13 Jan., the speech praised the restoration of the 'general Tranquillity' of Europe as a result of the diplomatic moves of the Walpole administration. The versified version given here was doubtless intended to be read ironically.

No. 109

P. 1, col. 1, 'List of Witnesses': In *Mem.* the names, not just the initials, are printed, as they are in No. 115. The agitation in *GSJ* over the Jan. 30 anniversary of the killing of Charles I reflects the 'Carolinism' of Richard Russel; see Pettit, ch. 5.

P. 1, col. 1, Rushworth: *Historical Collections of Private Passages of State* (1659–1701), ed. John Rushworth (?1612–90).

P. 1, col. 2, 'Dr. South's Sermon': Robert South (1634–1716), divine noted for his acerbic, witty style. This excerpt is not reprinted in *Mem.*

P. 1, col. 2, 'One Yeoman ... Cord-strainer': This poem is reprinted in *Mem.*; it is unsigned but the content and style make it almost certainly Richard Russel's.

P. 1, col. 2, 'Bullock ... Penkethman': William Bullock (?1657–?1740) and William Penkethman (1692–1724), both actors; the famous comparison between them is

actually in *Tatler* No. 188 (22 June 1710), and it is that essay, not the *Spectator*, which is quoted at the end of this letter.

P. 1, col. 2, '*vicem gerit ille tonantis*': 'that one conducts the thundering business'.

P. 1, col. 2, '*Corderius*': I.e., Mathurin Cordier (?1480–1564), French schoolmaster who wrote several books in Latin for children.

P. 1, col. 2, '*sententiae Pueriles*': childish thoughts.

P. 1, col. 2, 'Mr. Rowe ... Augustus': Nicholas Rowe (1674–1718), playwright, translated Lucan's *Pharsalia* in 1718; the 'scurvy entertainment' is Cibber's 'Caesar in Aegypt', and 'Augustus' refers to George II, who was 'regaled' with Cibber's birthday and NewYear's odes.

P. 1, col. 2, 'Stephen Bryan': A printer in Worcester (see Foxon S787), printer of the Worcester *Post*.

P. 1, col. 3, '*Ne sutor ultra crepidam*': 'The shoemaker should not go beyond his last' (literally, his slipper).

P. 1, col. 3, 'Pompey ... Nonjurors': On Cibber's borrowings, see No. 3 and note. *The Nonjuror* was based on Molière's *Tartuffe*.

P. 1, col 3, 'Maevius ... Banqueting-house': The poem (signed 'M.' in *Mem.* and by Russel) reflects on the execution of Charles I, who was beheaded on a scaffold next to the walls of the Banqueting House on 30 Jan. 1649. The first stanza refers to the restoration of the building by Inigo Jones after a fire in 1619.

P. 3, col. 1, Pegasus col., 'last new Comedy': *The Modish Couple*; see No. 108, note on p. 1, col. 3.

P. 3, col. 1, '*Boghouse Miscellany*': I.e., *The Merry-Thought: or, the Glass-Window and Bog-House Miscellany ... written in Diamond by Persons of the first Rank and Figure in Great Britain, ... faithfully transcribed from the Drinking-Glasses and Windows in the several noted Taverns, Inns, and other publick Places in the Nation* (1731–32); Roberts was also the publisher of *The Modish Couple*. The intention of 'W. F's' letter seems to be ridicule of the noblemen who led the claque applauding the *Modish Couple* on its opening night (see No. 108) and whose taste and literacy are to be judged by association with bog-house verse and writing on glass, as well as by the illiteracy of this letter. 'Mother Williams' is unidentified but is presumably a bawd or tavern-keeper.

P. 3, col. 1, 'Roman Drama ... Laelius': This passage of fake scholarship is intended as an allegorical analogue to the contrived reception and claques in the opening performance of the *Modish Couple*. *Tibiae* refers to the two pipes or flutes played at the same time with one mouthpiece, *sinistrae* and *dextrae* to the left and right pipes; *impares* to the two pipes of unequal length; and the allusions to the Roman general Gaius Laelius and his famous friend Scipio Africanus are aimed at the Dukes of Montague and Richmond, who headed the claque at the opening of the play (see No. 108, note).

P. 3, col. 1l, 'Whereas some persons ... Apprentices, &c.': A note in *Mem.* explains that Orator Henley had advertised his *Transactions* in the *Daily Journal* making use of most of these words 'excepting only, that instead of *shop*, he had put *place*'.

P. 3, col. 1, '*Fungar ... secandi*': 'I'll play a whetstone's part, which makes steel sharp, but of itself cannot cut', Horace, *Ars Poetica* 304–5 (Loeb).

No. 110

P. 1, col. 1, '*ut si ... frenis*': 'As if one were to train an ass to race upon the Campus obedient to the rein', Horace, *Satires* i. 1. 90–91 (Loeb).

P. 1, col. 1, 'Mr. Baxter': William Baxter (1650–1723), editor of Horace's *Eclogues* in 1701.

P. 1, col. 2, '*Falsus ... mendacem*': See note on quotation of this passage in No. 106; see also that number and its notes on the further emendations discussed in this letter.

P. 1, col. 2, '*introrsum ... decora*': 'foul within, though fair without, under his comely skin', Horace, *Epistles* i. 16. 45 (Loeb).

P. 1, col. 3, 'Doctor of Gainsborough': An obscure label, with no clear reference to 'Philarchaeus' and certainly none to Bentley.

P. 1, col. 3, 'An Act for the Relief of Debtors': 2 Geo II c 22 (1729).

P. 2, col. 1, '*The Orphan*': Frequently performed tragedy (1680) by Thomas Otway (1652–85).

P. 2, col. 1, '*Harlequin ... Cartouch*': names of pantomimes and farces: 'Scaramouch and Harlequin' was a dance; *Harlequin Shepperd* (1724) a pantomime by John Thurmond; and *Cartouche* a farce of 1723 by Louis Legrand. Jonathan Wild as a stage subject has not been located, unless the reference is to Peachum in the *Beggar's Opera*.

P. 2, col. 1, '*Stage-coach ... flying letters*': *Stage-Coach* was an anonymous opera of 1730; *The Coronation* was a stage version at Drury Lane of the procession for the 1727 coronation of George II, burlesqued by Rich (see Miller's *Harlequin Horace*, note on line 369); and *Harlequin Doctor Faustus* (1723) was a pantomime by Thurmond with spectacular effects, though I have not found flying letters among them, only flying limbs.

P. 3, col. 1, Pegasus col., 'a military author': I.e., Capt. Charles Bodens, the pretended author of the *Modish Couple*; see No. 108, p. 1, col. 3, and note.

P. 3, col. 2, 'Penkethman': See No. 109, note.

P. 3, col. 2, 'Historiographer of the Old Baily': I.e., the author of the 'Sessions Papers', which gave accounts of trials at the Old Bailey, the central criminal court. Penkethman apparently actually testified in stilted and inverted diction sounding so much like blank verse that it was printed as such in *Select Trials at the Old-Bailey* (1735), ii. 464–65 and, except for line divisions, the same way in the earlier *Second Part of the Proceedings at the Sessions* (1731–32). The later version of this remarkable incident seems clearly indebted to *GSJ*. Noakes was acquitted.

No. 111

P. 1, 'Chichester, Clarke, Warren': Francis Hare, Alured Clarke, and Robert Warren, whose recent sermons on the anniversary of the execution of Charles I are all presented as representing three different political/religious views on this sensitive occasion, one preached before the House of Lords, the second the Commons, and the third before the Lord Mayor. Clarke's sermon is clearly Whiggish and what might be expected from a Chaplain to King George, Warren's is high-church, hostile to dissenters and deists; but Hare's is problematical, in some way so close to the 'Carolinist' position of someone like Richard Russel that it invited and received attack as exhibiting a high-church spirit. For a full analysis of the issues and of this number of *GSJ*, see Pettit, pp. 151–64.

P. 3, Pegasus col., 'The *Ignoramus*': By George Ruggles; see No. 103, p. 3, note.

P. 3, co. 2, '*In ann ... plain pure English*': 'In the fourth year of George II'; in May 1731 an act was passed (4 George 2, c. 26) which required writs and proceedings in any court of justice in England and in the court of Exchequer in Scotland to be in the

English language and to be written in a legible hand, not in 'court hand'. The new law was not to take effect until 25 March 1733.

P. 3, col. 2, 'Mumpsimus': 'A traditional custom or notion obstinately adhered to however unreasonable it is shown to be' (*OED*).

P. 3, col. 2, '*non compos mentis*': Not of sound mind.

No. 112

P. 1, epigraph, 'Harlequin Horace': By James Miller; see Nos. 59–60 and notes.

P. 1, col. 1, 'Mr. W.': I.e., Robert Wilks, one of the three managers of Drury Lane.

P. 1, col. 1, '*Modish Couple*': See No. 108 and note.

P. 1, col. 2, '*Athelwold*': By Aaron Hill; it ran for three days in Dec. 1731.

P. 1, col. 2, 'a Person ... House': I.e., Cibber.

P. 1, col. 2, '*Injur'd Innocence*': By Pettiplace Bellers; its six nights were in Feb. 1732.

P. 1, col. 2, 'Dramaticus': The identity of this writer, who was to continue his attacks on playwrights (especially Fielding), is unknown. He is not, as Hillhouse supposed, Walpole's henchman Sir William Yonge; see my note in *Notes and Queries* n. s. 19 (June 1972), 226–27.

P. 1, col. 2, 'Reverend SIR': This sarcastic letter is addressed to Alured Clarke, who gave the sort of sermon to be expected of a 'Court Chaplain' on Jan. 31; see No. 111. The writer clearly favours the sermon of Francis Hare, Bishop of Chichester, though it is ironically dismissed as 'Tory notions.' See Pettit, pp. 162–63.

P. 3, col. 2, Pegasus col., 'Narrative ... Welstede': See No. 69, p. 1, and note.

P. 3, col. 2, 'Roberts': John Roberts, publisher of Henley and many other 'Grub Street' writers; see No. 109 and note.

P. 3, col. 2, 'EPIGRAM': Reprinted in *Mem.*, signed 'M.', and by Russel. The subject is Francis Hare's sermon on Jan. 30 (see No. 111), and the tone is ironic at Hare's expense; see discussion by Pettit, p. 163.

No. 113

P. 1, epigraph: Dryden's version of Chaucer's *Nun's Priest's Tale*, 331–32.

P. 1, col. 1, footnote: *Milton Restor'd and Bentley Depos'd*, Numb. I (1732), a short Edmund Curll publication capitalizing on the controversy.

P. 1, col. 2, 'first edition of *Paradise Lost*': Modern scholarship identifies 1667 as the date of the first edition, in ten books; 1674 as the date for the second edition, in twelve books; and 1671 as the date of first edition of *Paradise Regained* and *Samson Agonistes*.

P. 1, col. 3, footnote, '*Review ... Text*': *A Review of the Text of Milton's Paradise Lost in which the chief of Dr. Bentley's Emendations are Consider'd* (1732), by Zachary Pearce (1690–1774).

P. 2, col. 2, footnote, 'Fairfax': Edward Fairfax (d. 1635) published a translation of Tasso's *Jerusalem Delivered* in 1600.

P. 3, col. 2, Pegasus col., '*Grubiana*': The first of a series of unauthorized republications of selections from the *GSJ*, this one mainly of verse from Nos. 1–111; see Hillhouse, pp. 22–24. The actual title was *Faithful Memoirs of the Grubstreet Society*, 'Now first published by Mr. Bavius, Printed for the Benefit of the Grubstreet Society', and the running title was '*Grubiana*'. See the further attack in No. 114.

No. 114

P. 1, epigraph: 'Let him [Achilles on stage] claim that laws are not for him, let him ever make appeal to the sword', Horace, *Ars Poetica* 122 (Loeb).

P. 1, col. 1, 'Brutus ... Lewis': Marcus Brutus (d. 42 BC), conspirator with Cassius against Julius Caesar; Pelopidas (410 - 364 BC), Theban hero, subject of life by Plutarch; and Louis XIV of France.

P. 1, col. 1, '*Prosperum ... vocatur*': 'a successful crime is called a virtue', Seneca, *Hercules Furens*, 251.

P. 1, col. 1, '*Multi ... diadema*': 'Many commit the same crime and fare differently: one man gets a gibbet, another a crown, as the reward of crime', Juvenal, *Sat.* xiii, 103–5 (Loeb).

P. 1, col. 2, 'Voltaire's *History*': I.e., Voltaire's *History of Charles XII, King of Sweden* (1731, trans. 1732); Charles was a common example of 'false greatness' for those like Voltaire and Henry Fielding who attacked common notions of heroic 'greatness'.

P. 1, col. 3, '*in forma pauperis*': 'in the form of a pauper', a legal status granted by which a poor person can plead without fees.

P. 1, col. 3, '*Morning Post ... Hughes*': In this dialogue, *GSJ* attacks those responsible for *Grubiana* (see No. 113). *Morning Post* is the *Coffee-house Morning Post*; *Oedipus* is the *Post Boy Remounted*; John Hughes, a printer in Holborn. In *Mem.* the dialogue is signed 'M.' (Russel).

P. 1, col. 3, '*Scheme ... Enjoyment*': These are all works published by T. Dormer, bookseller in Fleet Street held responsible by Russel for *Grubiana*. 'Curl', mentioned next, is the infamous bookseller; see No. 4, note.

P. 1, col. 3, 'Henley ... *Hyp-Doctor*': 'Orator' John Henley and his paper, attacked throughout; see, e.g., No. 72 and notes.

P. 3, col. 2, Pegasus col, 'Warner ... Hanging': The epigram is ridiculing those concerned in the *Grubiana* project. Russel's note in *Mem.* reads, 'Tho' in the title page of *Grubiana* the names only of *Hughs* in *High-Holborn*, and of *Warner* in *Pater-Noster-Row* appeared; yet in the *Advertisements* those of *Dormer* in *Fleet-street* (who was the chief projector) and of *Hinton* in *High Holborn* were mentioned: with all whom, we were well assured, that one *Hubbard* was deeply concerned in this piracy.' 'Tim Birch' is the persona of a writer for the *Weekly Register*, who on 29 Jan. took on the title of 'The Reformer'.

No. 115

P. 1, epigraph, *Harlequin Horace*: By James Miller; see Nos. 59–60 and notes.

P. 1, col. 1, 'Walsingham ... Hyp-Doctor': Pro-Walpole writers Francis Arnall and 'Orator' Henley.

P. 1, col. 1, 'B—ns ... K—b—rs': 'Bodens', supposed author of the *Modish Couple* and 'Keyber', the Opposition's Germanicised version of 'Cibber' (see No. 74, note).

P. 1, col. 1, 'Master of the New House': John Rich; the 'New House' is his theatre at Lincoln Inn's Fields (his theatre at Covent Garden did not open until Dec. 1732). The letter by 'Tag-Rhime' in the *Daily Courant* (26 Feb. 1731/32) had made a political allegory out of all this: poets who came to Rich because of problems about Cibber now complain of Rich; thus malcontents find they are worse off after a change is made.

P. 1, col. 1, 'Mr. A—b—r', 'Mr. W—ks': 'A—b—r' is no doubt a misprint for 'Cibber', who with Robert Wilks (and Barton Booth) managed Drury Lane.

P. 1, col. 2, 'male qualifications': I.e., 'malqualifications'.

P. 1, col. 2, 'third Manager': Barton Booth, who was ill and had retired from the stage.

P. 1, col. 2, 'Mr. W': Wilks.

P. 1, col. 2, 'C— J—n': Charles Johnson, prolific playwright.

P. 2, col. 1, 'attachment of contempt': Punning on the legal term for being arrested and held for some contempt of court or disobedience of an order in the course of a suit.

P. 2, col. 3, Pegasus col., 'Sharp... Cheselden': Cf. Martyn's ridicule of Cheselden in Nos. 41 and 53.

P. 2, col. 3, 'Stonecastle': The persona of the author of the *Universal Spectator*.

P. 3, col. 1, '*Select Memoirs*': The first mention of the *Memoirs of the Society of Grub-street*, which was actually not published until 1737. For the history of the various collections of material from *GSJ*, see Hillhouse, pp. 21–24.

P. 3, col. 1, 'obscure Weekly Journal': As usual, this means the *Weekly Register*. The lewd poem, entitled 'Verses occasion'd by a Horse's biting a Lady's Breast', is reprinted in *GM* ii (March 1732), p. 672. The epigram is signed 'M.' (Russel) in *Mem.*

P. 3, col. 1, 'Woolston': Thomas Woolston, the deist, now confined to a debtor's prison; see Nos. 13, 19, 22, 27 and notes.

P. 3, col. 1, 'Pamphlet ... Zelim': *A Parallel between Muhamed and Sosem, the Great Deliverer of the Jews*, by 'Zelim Mussulman, in a Letter to *Nathan Rabbi*', listed on this page, col. 3, as published since 4 Mar.

No. 116

P. 1, col. 1, 'To Mr. Bavius': A continuation of the letter on Bentley's edition of Milton in No. 113.

P. 1, col. 1, 'absonous': 'Out of tune, inharmonious' (*OED*).

P. 1, col. 3, '*the thoughts*': I.e., the 'thwarts', the rowers' seats in a boat (*OED*).

P. 1, col. 3, '*—Sunt ... illis*': 'I, too, have songs; me also the shepherds call a bard, but I trust them not' (Loeb). The epigram is in *Mem.*, but unsigned.

P. 3, col. 1, Pegasus' col., 'Osborne': I.e., 'Francis Osborne,' pen name of James Pitt, for whom see No. 20 and note. The poem (in *Mem.* and by Russel) is a response to Pitt's 'Examination of a Doctrine deliver'd in a late Sermon on a Publick Occasion, That the State can't stand without the Church', and the lines in italics are roughly Pitt's words.

P. 3, col. 1, 'No Bishop, no King': The comment of James I on Puritan demands in 1604, attacked throughout the essay by Pitt.

P. 3, col. 1, 'felt a *laudable* stroak': Punning on the name of Archbishop William *Laud*, beheaded in 1645.

No. 117

P. 1, epigraph: William Wycherley, 'An Epistle to Mr. Dryden' (corrected copy of 1706).

P. 1, col. 1, '*The Modern Husband*': Henry Fielding's play had opened on 14 Feb. and had a long and successful run. This essay is the first of a series of attacks on Fielding by the *GSJ* ; see the General Introduction.

P. 1, col. 1, 'Pickled-herring ... Tumbler': A 'Pickle-herring' is 'a clown, a buffoon, a merry-andrew' (*OED*); 'Scaramouch' is a boastful stock-character; and a tumbler is an acrobat.

P. 1, col. 1, '*The Careless Husband ... London*': The first play is by Cibber, the second by Richard Steele, the third a fragment by Vanbrugh.

P. 1, col. 2, 'a great man's levee': Such a scene might cause audiences to suspect a reflection on Sir Robert Walpole, although the printed play was dedicated to him.

P. 2, col. 1, '*mox ... emptor*': 'Soon midst her husband's revels she seeks younger paramours, nor stops to choose on whom she swiftly shall bestow illicit joys when lights are banished; but openly, when bidden, and not without her husband's knowledge, she rises, be it some peddler summons her, or the captain of some Spanish ship, lavish purchaser of shame' (lines 25–32, Loeb).

P. 3, col. 1, Pegasus col., 'Funeral of one Francis': The infamous Francis Charteris, see No. 10 and note.

P. 3, col. 1, 'H—y': Orator Henley, who claimed to have restored the art of ancient elocution. The epigram is signed 'M.' in *Mem.* and is thus assumed to be Russel's.

No. 118

P. 1, col. 1, 'Mr. Fenton': Elijah Fenton (1683–1730), poet and friend of Pope, whose *Life of Milton* was prefixed to the 'fourteenth edition' of *Paradise Lost*, published by Tonson in 1730.

P. 1, col. 1, '*jamdudum ... monuerunt*': 'now for a long time have admonished the memory'

P. 1, col. 1, '*Mitte ... divitiarum*': 'Dismiss airy hopes and the struggle for wealth', Horace, *Epistles* I. v. 8 (Loeb).

P. 1, col. 2, 'Defoedation': I.e., 'defedation', pollution.

P. 3, col. 1, Pegasus col., 'To Mr. Walker': Thomas Walker, actor in Rich's company at Lincoln's Inn Fields, was to act Alexander the Great in a benefit performance on 10 April of Nathaniel Lee's *The Rival Queens, or The Death of Alexander.*

P. 3, col. 1, 'Tyburn ... Tree': The gallows.

P. 3, col. 1, 'Salmoneus': mythological king who, imitating Zeus, demanded sacrifices and made noises like thunder with his chariot, for which he was destroyed with a thunderbolt.

P. 3, col. 1, '*British Senate ... bare*': Probably alluding to Parliamentary investigation into the frauds of the Charitable Corporation.

No. 119

P. 1, epigraph: From the piece by Swift generally known as 'An Argument Against the Abolishing of Christianity'.

P. 1, col. 1, 'a late Writer': Identified in *GM* as author of a pamphlet called 'Reason against Coition, &c. to which are added some observations about the Cause and Cure of the Piles'.

P. 1, col. 1, 'former Correspondent of yours': See the letter on church music in No. 57. The current essay, under the guise of demanding freedom in choice of church music, ironically ridicules dissent and the extremes of religious toleration.

P. 1, col. 1, '*Right womanly ... musick*': Quoted with some adaptations from John Arbuthnot's *John Bull, the Third Part* (1712), ch. ii; in this allegory 'Peg' is the Kirk

of Scotland, an admirer of the Dissenters, and John a son of the Church of England. 'Gundy-guts' means a glutton (*OED*).

P. 1, col. 1, 'Act of Toleration': The Act of 1689 granting freedom of worship to dissenting Protestants who had taken the Oaths of Allegiance.

P. 1, col. 1, 'Sternhold and Hopkins': See No. 2 and note.

P. 1, col. 2, 'H—d—r': John Heidigger (d. 1749), famously ugly opera-house manager.

P. 1, col. 2, 'H—ly': Orator Henley.

P. 1, col. 2, '*Vicar of S. N.*': Referring probably to John Andrews, Vicar of South Newington, author of *Kebla*, a response to *Alkibar* (see notes on No. 121).

P. 1, col. 2, '*un disordine fa un ordine*': 'a disorder creates an order'.

P. 1, col. 2, 'much better judge of decency': Alluding to Rev. William Bowman; see No. 82 and note.

P. 1, col. 2, '*assembling … together*': This language is close to that of Swift's ironic pamphlet used in the epigraph.

P. 1, col. 3, 'W—n … Ass—n': I.e., Woolston, Tindal, Henley, Bowman; 'Ass—n' is unidentified but may refer to William Asplin, Author of *Alkibar* (see note on No. 121).

P. 1, col. 3, 'Mr. W.': Robert Wilks, co-manager of Drury Lane Theatre.

P. 1, col. 3, 'Author … *Husband*': Fielding.

P. 2, col. 1, 'C— J—': Charles Johnson; see his letter in No. 115.

P. 2, col. 1, '*On young Maister K—t*': The name is clearly 'Knight', possibly William Knight, Vicar of Moulton, but not certainly identified.

P. 2, col. 1, 'Bowman … *Whig*': See No 82 and note; on *Independent Whig*, see No. 85 and note.

P. 3, col. 1, Pegasus col., 'the Champion's': Orator Henley; see No. 117. This poem is in *Mem.* signed 'M.' and is probably Russel's.

P. 3, col. 1, 'Corinthian … *Post*': 'Corinthian' not only describes the ornate pillar but also means 'brass', commonly applied to Henley figuratively and literally'; '*Postil*' means 'postillion'. Author of *The Morning Post* (see No. 114) not identified.

No. 120

P. 1, col. 1, 'following Treatise': An ironic series of arguments against reviving the Tithe Bill, which had been abandoned the previous year. The Bill would have prevented suits for tithes in cases where none have been paid in a certain number of years (see No. 68). The *GSJ* , being indeed 'favourers of Priestcraft', naturally satirizes such a bill.

P. 1, col. 1, '*Independent Whig*': See No. 85 and note.

P. 1, col. 2, 'late *London Journal*': Issue of 26 Feb. 1731/2.

P. 1, col. 2, 'make Pork … plentiful': Because there will be no more payment by 'tithe-pigs', a common icon.

P. 1, col. 2, 'Mr. H—': Sir Gilbert Heathcote, who had sponsored the bill; see *GM* 1 (1731), p. 241.

P. 1, col. 3, 'mum … perry': 'Mum' is kind of beer; 'perry' is a fermented cider made from pears.

P. 2, col. 1, 'Bishop B—n—t': Gilbert Burnet, whose *History of my Own Time* is parodied in the passage.

P. 2, col. 1, 'Sinking Fund': A scheme set up by Walpole to set aside revenue to reduce the nation's debt.

P. 2, col. 1, '*onus probandi*': burden of proof.

P. 3, col. 2, Pegasus col., 'Ralph': James Ralph, whose *Muses' Address* was mentioned in No. 21.

No. 121

P. 1, col. 1, 'B—t': On Gilbert Burnet, Bishop of Salisbury, see Nos. 33, 78, and notes.

P. 1, col. 1, '*Memoirs* of the M— of H—': Marquis of Halifax.

P. 1, col. 1, 'B—k of S—': Bishopric of Sarum (Salisbury).

P. 1, col. 1, 'second Part of *Alkibla*': Referring to *Alkibla. Part II. Or, the disquisition upon worshipping towards the East continued from the primitive to the present times* (1731), by William Asplin (1687–1758), vicar of Horley. Asplin signed the Dedication, but the author of the Preface is not given in ESTC. Asplin was answered in *The Kebla* (1728, 1729) by John Andrews, Vicar of South Newington

P. 1, col. 3, 'Reverend and learned Prelate': Richard Smallbrooke (1672–1749).

P. 1, col. 3, 'Buckram-men': Men in buckram, but 'sometimes proverbially for non-existent persons, in allusion to Falstaff's 'four rogues in buckram' in 1 Henry IV. ii. 4 (*OED*).

P. 2, col. 1, 'Grotius … Tony': Hugo Grotius (1583–1645), philosopher of law; a 'Tony' is a foolish person, a simpleton.

P. 2, col. 1, *servanda fides cum latrone*': 'word of honour must be kept with a thief'.

P. 2, col. 1, 'verbo sacerdotis': '[on] the word of a priest'.

P. 2, col. 1, 'Dr. P—': Not identified.

P. 3, col. 1, Pegasus col., 'Woodward': John Woodward (1665–1728), physician, geologist, and antiquarian. The epitaph is as follows: 'Sacred to the Spirit of John Woodward, a most distinguished doctor, a most respected philosopher, whose talents, education, and writings are well known throughout almost the entire earth; truly, the University of Cambridge will declare in perpetuity his generosity and love of country, increased by his liberality, decorated by his wealth. Born 1 May 1665, died 24 April 1728. Richard King, military officer and chief engineer, deservedly as the best of friends, has erected this monument' (trans. H. Nabbefeld).

P. 3, col. 1, '*Aesop's Consort of Animals*': *London Stage* for 25 Apr. lists as 'Music' after a performance of the *Rehearsal* a 'Lapland Entertainment' with this title, and as reported here with instruments played by animals. No indication of authorship is listed.

P. 3, col. 1, 'K—b—r': Cibber, whose 'Son' Theophilus also seems to have been involved.

P. 3, col. 1, '*Ephesian Matron*': By Charles Johnson.

P. 3, col. 1, '*Tears of the Muses*': No such imitation of Spenser has been located; the comment is irony at the expense of the Drury Lane managers.

No. 122

P. 1, epigraph: '[and] cleanliness more animate Love's Fire./ The hair dispos'd, may gain or lose a Grace,/ And much become, or mis-become the Face' (trans. Congreve)

P. 1, col. 3, '*Not that … the fire*': John Sheffield, Duke of Buckinghamshire, *Essay Upon Poetry*, lines 26–29.

P. 1, col. 3, 'Double Contest': On the subject of this 'Lilliputian Poem', as Russel called it in *Mem.*, see No. 115, where the same story is told in prose.

P. 3, col. 1, Pegasus col., 'Characters of King William': Russel's poem (signed 'M.' in *Mem.*) refers to the controversy described in No. 121; the italicized lines are taken from the 'Discourse' by 'Osborne' in the *London Journal* of the date cited.

P. 3, col. 1, 'Hyp': I.e., hypochondria, melancholia.

No. 123

P. 1, col. 2, *'vultu fortis et aere minax'*: 'with a bold face and threatening air'.

P. 1, col. 2, *'exegi ... perennius'*: 'I have finished a monument more lasting than bronze', Horace *Odes* iii. 30. 1. (Loeb).

P. 1, col. 2, 'grammarian of some note': The work, called *The Whetstone*, is by 'Mr. Lowe of Hammersmith' and is advertised in the preceding issue, *GSJ* No. 122.

P. 1, col. 2, *'Rudiments ... Busby'*: *Graecae grammatices rudimenta* (1720), by Richard Busby, famous headmaster of Westminster School.

P. 1, col. 2, *'Tabella ... compositorum'*: 'Table of compound verbs' (see below).

P. 1, col. 2, 'Thomson': George Thompson, schoolmaster at Tottenham; his book was published on 6 April.

P. 1, col. 3, 'Mr. Morland ... Patrick': Apparently these were schoolmasters or scholars who gave testimonials on behalf of Thompson' s work. Benjamin Morland was a 'high master' at St. Paul's School in 1730, according to a notice in the *Daily Post* of 24 Feb; Samuel Patrick was a classical scholar and a master at Charterhouse, who actually collaborated with Thompson on this book (*DNB*); and Thomas Pilgrim was Regius Professor of Greek at Cambridge from 1712–26, then a rector in Lancashire. Ward has not been identified.

P. 3, col. 1, Pegasus col.: The reprint in *Mem.* makes it clear that this is the second part of the Tripos speech at Cambridge, intended to represent the speech of a justice of the peace *'to a mob assembled before a certain College, on pretence of searching for a corps'*. The Latin paragraphs explain the justice's concern over recent episodes of grave-robbing for medical research and set the scene of the self-important J. P. getting ready to speak.

No. 124

P. 1, cols. 1, 2, 3: These columns carry on the controversy discussed in No. 121, between differing newspapers about the relationship between the two Whig heroes Bishop Burnet and King William; see notes to No. 121. 'M— of H—' is Marquis of Halifax. 'Osborne' is the pseudonym of James Pitt (see No. 20 and note).

P. 2, col. 3, *'Higgons'*: Bevil Higgons (1670–1735), historian and poet, whose brother had been arrested in a Jacobite plot; author of *Bishop Burnet's Proofs of the Pretender's Illegitimacy* (1724).

P. 3, col. 2, Pegasus col.,'Astraea: Goddess of justice; daughter of Zeus and Themis. 'Celia' is not identifiable and probably fictitious.

No. 125

P. 1, epigraph: 'whose mind was full of a great store of disorderly words', *Iliad* ii. 213 (describing Thersites) (Loeb).

P. 1, col. 1, 'Ashenhurst': Dr. Ward Grey Ashenhurst (d. 1733), a fellow at Trinity College and a friend and supporter of Bentley in his quarrels at Trinity.

P. 1, col. 1, *'conscia virtus'*: 'consciousness of worth' (*Aeneid*, xii. 668).

P. 1, col. 2, 'mischiefs … committed in prose': I.e., Milton's pamphlets for Cromwell, especially those in defence of the regicide.

P. 1, col. 2, 'Colbatch … Middleton': Bentley attacked John Colbatch (1664–1748), a senior Fellow of Trinity College, because he erroneously thought Colbatch was the author of criticism of his proposals for a new edition of the Greek Testament, criticism actually by Conyers Middleton, another of Bentley's enemies; see *DNB*.

P. 1, col. 3, 'B—y … B—l': Bentley and Charles Boyle; these lines recount the episode which began the so-called 'Battle of the Books' in the 1690s.

P. 1, col. 3, 'Ashburnham House': Actually Abingdon House, formerly Lord Ashburnham's, in Little Dean's Yard, Westminster. It caught fire in Oct. 1731, badly damaging the manuscript of Beowulf as well as other works; the epigram assumes (jokingly ?) that one of those was the manuscript of 'the Epistles of Phalaris' that Boyle had asked to borrow from Bentley long ago at the start of the controversy which Swift recounted in his *Battle of the Books*.

P. 1, col. 3, 'nor Orange … Bishop will make': Punning on 'Bishop', which is 'a sweet drink variously compounded, the chief ingredients being wine, oranges or lemons, and sugar; mulled and spiced port' (*OED*, citing this relevant passage from Swift on women who cry oranges, 'Well roasted, with sugar and wine in a cup, They'll make a sweet bishop'). I am indebted to John D. Baird for pointing me to this pun..

P. 2, col. 3 — p. 3, col. 1, Pegasus col., 'Osborne': This col. continues the controversy presented in Nos. 121 and 124; see the notes on those issues. The 'Extract' from 'Osborne' is more parody than extract, although based on the words actually used in the *London Journal* of 20 May.

P. 3, col. 1, '*Jack Straw*': 'worthless fellow.'

P. 3, col. 1, '*Memoirs* of … H.': Of the Marquis of Halifax.

P. 3, col. 2, 'Figg or Sutton': Professional fighters.

No. 126

P. 1, col. 1, 'appeared to have come from a Quaker': The appearance was less convincing than in this present composition. It may be noted that recently the printer of the *GSJ* had become John Huggonson, a Quaker, who was later to come into conflict with Russel over the content of the paper.

P. 1, col. 1, 'Parson Smith's Preservative': The actual title of the book by Patrick Smith (Vicar of Great Paxton, Huntingtonshire) is *A Preservative against Quakerism; or, a Complication of Deism, Enthusiasm, and divers other Ancient and Modern Dangerous Errors and Heresies* (1732). He was also answered by Joseph Besse, *A Defence of Quakerism* (1732).

P. 1, col. 1, Barclay: Robert Barclay (1648–90), prolific Quaker author.

P. 3, col. 1, 'Pegasus col.': 'Claudia Rufina': The name suggesting both 'lame' (Claudia) and 'red-haired', as noted below. The name is that of a British woman mentioned by Martial in *Epigrams* xi. 53.

P. 3, col. 1, 'reality of longing': This should read 'of her longing', as corrected in the next issue.

P. 3, col. 1, *'Cinna … pauper'*: 'Cinna wishes to appear poor, and he is poor', Martial, *Epigrams* viii. 19 (Loeb).

P. 3, col. 1, *'Register of Grub-street'*: I.e., the *Weekly Register*, the constant enemy of the *GSJ*. A note in *Mem.* on this line says, 'Mr. D. Bellamy, at that time, the Editor of the *Weekly Register.*' See No. 52, note. Their poem is called 'Brat' to continue the metaphor of pregnancy used by 'Claudia Rufina'.

P. 3, col. 1 'honester … *Corporation'*: This should read 'no honester' (corrected in next issue); on the Corporation, see No. 63, note.

P. 3, col. 2, *'Crescit … virtus'*: 'virtue increases under oppression.'

No. 127

P. 1, epigraph: 'one is a big liar' (but see text of leader for other readings of *on*).

P. 1, col. 1, 'Belloni': Russel's note in *Mem.* explains the background. John Thomson, warehouse-keeper to the fraudulent Charitable Corporation, was arrested and confined in Rome at the urging of the Pretender; the incident was described to the Parliamentary Committee investigating the corporation by John Angelo Belloni, a banker in Rome, who added that he had given all the papers found on Thomson to one Arbuthnot, a banker in Paris, and set conditions for their return. Parliament, considering the Belloni letter an affront, had it burned by the Common Hangman on 26 May. All of this, adds Russel, reminded the public of the South Sea Scandal and of the way powerful figures (i.e., Walpole) sacrifice the smaller villains to screen the 'great persons' from inquiry. Another essential point, not mentioned by Russel, is that the government press, such as the *Daily Courant*, claimed that 'Belloni' was a mask for the Pretender himself, who was gloating in this letter over the turn of events. The *Free Briton* also (1 June) took this line, indignant that the Pretender should protect those who had wronged the British public. Hence there is much argument over whether *'on'* is really an 'indeterminate' pronoun or is a cover for the authoritative 'we' of the Stuart Pretender.

P. 1, col. 2, 'Richelet': Pierre Richelet (1626–98), *Dictionnaire de la langue françoise, ancienne et moderne*, 3 vols. (1728).

P. 1, col. 3, 'Gentleman': Russel's note in *Mem.* describes this poem as 'the Substance of the Speech delivered by Sir John Shadwell … at a general court of the Charitable Corporation' on 27 May, as published in the *Daily Journal*, with additional words in italics.

P. 2, col. 1, 'Time … fermented': 'I fear the Greeks, even when bringing gifts', Virgil, *Aeneid* ii. 49 (Loeb).

P. 2, col. 1, *'Babylonish Punk'*: I.e., the Whore of Babylon, here the Church of Rome.

P. 3, col. 1, Pegasus col., 'a fine burlesque piece': Henry Fielding's *Covent-Garden Tragedy*, which opened at Drury Lane on 1 June. On the 'secret history' and 'personal scandal' which amused some audience members, see Battestin, pp. 135–36.

P. 3, col. 1, 'S. George's Chevalier': I.e., James Francis Edward Stuart, the Old Pretender, born on 10 June 1688, an event which helped precipitate the Glorious Revolution. The poem describes various efforts by Whigs to deny the birth of a male heir to James II, including the famous 'warming-pan' story.

P. 3, col. 2, 'Oglethorpe … Gray … Fuller … Shaftoe': Lady Oglethorpe, wife of Sir Theophilus Oglethorpe, a well-known intriguer — her obituary is given at length in No. 130; her supposed role in the alleged pretence is described in *Mrs. Frances*

Shaftoe's narrative: ... an account of her being in Sir Theophilus Oglethorpe's family; where hearing many treasonable things, and among others, that the pretended Prince of Wales was Sir Theophilus's son, she was trick'd into France ... (1707). Gray or Grey was the candidate in a work by William Fuller, a secret agent and informer, who wrote *A brief discovery of the true mother of the pretended Prince of Wales known by the name of Mary Grey* (1696).

No. 128

P. 1, epigraph: See No. 127, and notes, on the epigraph and on the other figures and the controversy discussed here. The essays on this subject were probably written by Russel, since the final one (No. 129) is excerpted in *Mem.* and signed 'M.'.

P. 1, col. 1, 'Walsingham ... Richelet': Pen name of Francis Arnall, chief writer of the pro-Walpole *Free Briton*; on Richelet, see No. 127 and note.

P. 1, col. 1, 'Jonathan Wild': The famous thief, thief-taker, and gang leader who was hanged at Tyburn on 25 May 1725.

P. 1, col. 2, 'Benefit of Clergy': Originally a way of exempting clergymen from secular jurisdiction, this loophole was later extended to laymen who escaped hanging by being able to read; by 1730, however, its use had been considerably limited and restricted to lesser felonies.

P. 3, col. 1, Pegasus col., 'Common Garden Tragedy': I.e., Henry Fielding's *Covent-Garden Tragedy*; this piece by 'Dramaticus' continues the attack by 'Prosaicus' in No. 127. Both authors are unidentified; on the paper war which ensued between the *GSJ* and Fielding, see Battestin, pp. 139–43.

P. 3, col. 1, 'young Managers': Meant ironically; the triumvirate still running Drury Lane were anything but young.

P. 3, col. 1, 'Gonson': See No. 45 and note. Gonson's zeal in prosecuting prostitutes and sending them to Bridewell, the house of correction, was noted by Hogarth in *The Harlot's Progress*, plate 3.

P. 3, col. 1, 'theatrical': Emphasized because of Dramaticus's earlier complaint that his own play had been rejected as insufficiently 'Theatrical'; see No. 119.

P. 3, col. 1, 'Ridotto al Fresco': Reprinted in *Mem.*, signed 'A.', with stanza 10 and its apparent hit at the hypocrisy of Presbyterian dissenters omitted. This 'Ridotto' was held at Spring-Gardens, Vauxhall, on 7 June and 21 June 'At the particular desire of several Persons of Quality' (*Daily Journal*, 2 June). An account in the *Weekly Register* (rptd. in *GM* ii. 802–3), speaks of the soft music and 'unrestrained Licence of the gayest Company'. See also news item for 23 June in No. 130

P. 3, col. 2, 'Satge': Misprint for 'Stage'.

No. 129

P. 1, epigraph: See No. 128, note on epigraph. This essay concludes a series of three leaders, apparently written by Russel, on the *GSJ*'s controversy with the *Free Briton* ('Walsingham') over the role of the Pretender in the affairs of those who absconded from the fraudulent Charitable Corporation; see No. 127 and notes.

P. 1, col. 2, 'Atterbury ... Kelly': Francis Atterbury, Bishop of Rochester and friend of Pope, exiled in 1723 for participating in a Jacobite conspiracy and mentioned frequently in the first 50 numbers of *GSJ* ; he had recently (15 Feb.) died in exile, and

Russel spends the last paragraph of the leader in an encomium on his character. George Kelly was a fellow-conspirator with Atterbury.

P. 3, col. 1, Pegasus col., *'epee … main'*: 'Sword in hand'.

P 3, col. 1, 'Mr. W.': Robert Wilks, one of the Drury Lane managers; obviously 'Poeticus' has not yet seen the assault on Fielding by 'Dramaticus' in No. 128.

P. 3, col. 1, *'Un-theatric'*: See No. 128, note on *'theatrical'*.

No. 130

P. 1, col. 1, epigraph: Lines 187–90 of Dryden's satire (1682) on Thomas Shadwell, here applied to Fielding.

P. 1, col. 1, *'Theatricality'*: On this issue, see No. 119.

P. 1, col. 1, *'with great applause'*: See the comment in the news col. of No. 129, p. 2.

P. 1, col. 1, 'Manager … Players': I.e., John Rich.

P. 1, col. 2, 'Hint the *Candle-snuffer*': A letter in Fielding's defence with this signature had appeared in the *Daily Post* of 21 June, addressed to 'Dramaticus *alias* Prosaicus, *alias* Bavius, *alias* &c. &c. &c.', implying, perhaps correctly, that all the attacks in *GSJ* were by one author. 'Hint' demands proof of indecent dialogue from the text of the play (published 24 June, with a parody of *GSJ* as prolegomena) and claims the Grubeans are attacking him only because in the course of the play a bawd says that her porter is one of the authors of the *GSJ*. For an argument that the 'Hint' letter was by Fielding himself, see W. J. Burling in *Notes and Queries*, 231 (1986), pp. 498–99.

P. 1, col. 3, *'asinus ad lyram'*: Literally, 'an ass at the lyre'; hence a man at odds with himself, something discordant, etc. From fable xiv of Phaedrus.

P. 2, col. 1, 'pretended new Entertainment': Fielding's *The Mock Doctor*, which opened on 23 June.

P. 3, col. 1, 'the *Fleet* … Mr. *J. W.*': The complaints of John Williams, prisoner in the Fleet, began appearing in No. 39; see No. 59 and note, and Hillhouse, pp. 230–31.

P. 3, col. 1, Pegasus col., 'Lady Oglethorpe': See Russel's poem in No. 127 in which Lady Oglethorpe is mentioned as one who, rumours claimed in 1688, was the actual mother of the male infant brought in the 'velvet warming-pan' to pass as the heir of James II. The reason for this elaborate (and duplicated) obituary notice is probably that the Oglethorpes were a 'strong Jacobite family' (Sedgwick).

P. 3, col. 1, 'C— … F…': I.e., Theophilus Cibber and Henry Fielding.

P. 3, col. 1, ' —ld—m's': Not identified, but probably the name of a bawdy house.

No. 131

P. 1, col. 1, 'Dr. B.'s': On Richard Bentley's edition of Milton, see No. 113 and notes.

P. 1, col. 2, 'Ver. 42': Misprint for 46.

P. 1, col. 1, 'learned and ingenious Gentleman': Zachary Pearce; see No. 113, note on p. 1, col. 3.

P. 1, col. 2, *'And laid … Swanswick'*: Samuel Butler's *Hudibras*, Part 3, Canto 2. Supposedly a reference to the famous Puritan William Prynne, born at Swanswick.

P. 1, col. 3, 'Swift's *Letter … Oxford*': I.e., *A Proposal for Correcting, Improving, and Ascertaining the English Tongue* (1712).

P. 2, col. 1, 'Zoilus': Bentley again; see No. 9 and note. This poem mocks his pose as a devout defender of Christianity, which some contemporaries considered opportunistic.

P. 2, col. 1, 'knap': Obsolete form of 'nap'.

P. 3, col. 1, 'Mr. H—': 'Orator' John Henley and his paper the *Hyp-Doctor*, attacked throughout; see e.g., No. 72 and notes.

No. 132

P. 1, col. 1, epigraph: By James Miller; see Nos. 59–60 and notes

P. 1, col. 1, 'Comedian': Monthly periodical, lasting only eight months, dedicated to praise of Walpole and comment on the stage; it was edited by Fielding's friend Thomas Cooke (?1702–56). Defence of both Fielding and Walpole would be a double affront to the writers of the *GSJ*; and Cooke's free-thinking religious views make up a third, as Bavius's column on p. 1 of this issue indicates.

P. 1, col. 1, 'Timoleon ... Devil to pay': Written by the following, in the same order: Benjamin Martyn; John Tracy; Charles Johnson; George Lillo; Pettiplace Bellers; Lillo again; and Charles Coffey.

P. 1, col. 1, 'Modern Husband': Fielding's play, already attacked by 'Dramaticus' in No. 117.

P. 1, col. 2, 'Lady Charlottes': I.e., women like Fielding's character, Lady Charlotte Gaywit.

P. 1, col. 3, 'a Great Man': Walpole.

P. 2, col. 1, 'Old Debauchees': Another play by Fielding, again attacked with sarcasm. It was loosely based on the celebrated case referred to here in which a Jesuit Priest was brought to trial for seducing a young girl. 'Miso-Cleros' (probably Russel – it is signed 'M.' in *Mem*.) is quick to accuse the author of irreligion in general.

P. 2, col. 1, 'Epigram ... F—': 'Young Keyber' (Theophilus Cibber) is spoken to by Fielding, who refers to his moving from the sentimental role of Barnwell in Lillo's *London Merchant* to that of Lovegirlo in the *Covent-Garden Tragedy*.

P. 2, col. 3, Pegasus col., 'Colony of Georgia': This item was of interest to *GSJ* because the moving force behind the establishment of the colony was the son of Lady and Sir Theophilus Oglethorpe; see Pegasus col. in No. 130.

P. 3, col. 1, 'Walsingham': Francis Arnall, writer of the *Free Briton*; see Nos. 127–29.

P. 3, col. 1, 'insani ... scribae': ' the crazy clerk's gewgaws', *Sat*. i. 5. 35 (Loeb).

P. 3, col. 1, 'Satis ... plaudere': ''Tis enough if the knights applaud me', *Sat*. i. 10. 76 (Loeb). I.e., as long as Sir Robert Walpole approves, the view of the Town is irrelevant.

p. 3, col. 1, ''tis called ... Universal': The epigram responds to an attack on the *GSJ* by the *Weekly Register* of 8 July, a paper which since 22 April had taken to calling itself the *Weekly Register or Universal Journal*.

No. 133

P. 1, epigraph: By James Miller; see Nos. 59–60 and notes.

P. 1, col. 1, 'concert of cats': See No. 121, Pegasus col.

P. 1, col. 1, 'Covent-Garden ... Debauchees': This essay continues the attack from the last few issues on the plays of Henry Fielding. 'Publicus' is another in the train of pseudonyms used by the writers attacking Fielding; they are not necessarily dif-

ferent figures, and none can be identified except Russel, writing as 'Bavius' and 'Miso-clerus' in No. 132.

P. 1, col. 2, '*in ... persona*': 'In his own person'.

P. 1, col. 3, 'piece of Moliere's': Fielding's *Mock Doctor* had opened, very successfully, as an afterpiece on 23 June.

P. 2, col. 1, 'Person to whom he dedicates it': Fielding dedicated the *Mock Doctor* (published 11 July) to an actual quack, Dr John Misaubin.

P. 2, col. 1, Epigram, 'Drury Lane': Drury Lane and the surrounding area ('the Hundreds of Drury') were notoriously peopled by prostitutes.

P. 3, col. 1, Pegasus col., 'Georgia': To understand this expression of interest, see note on the Pegasus col. of No. 132.

P. 3, col. 1, '*Philosoph. Trans.*': I.e., *Philosophical Transactions*, the journal of the Royal Society.

No. 134

P. 1, epigraph: Part I, lines 66–67 (1687).

P. 1, col. 1, 'Fancourt ... Bliss': Samuel Fancourt (1678–1768), dissenting minister, whose *Essay Concerning Liberty, Grace, and Prescience* (1729) started the controversy; David Millar (1687/8–1757); John Norman (fl. 1703–57), dissenting minister; and Anthony Bliss, Vicar of Portsmouth.

P. 1, col. 1, 'Chamber's Dictionary': See No. 70, note.

P. 1, col. 1, 'Bayle': See No. 16, note.

P. 1, col. 2, '*in speculo voluntatis*': 'In the image of His Will'.

P. 1, col. 2, '*in mensura propria*'; '*in mensura aliena*': 'in its own capacity', 'in another capacity'.

P. 1, col. 3, '*contumacy*': In law, 'wilful disobedience to the summons or order of a court' (*OED*).

P. 1, col. 3, 'unbecoming a gentleman': An insult which must have been particularly galling to Fielding, who was a gentleman by birth and liked to style himself 'Esq.'. Fielding was stung into defending himself and his background under the name 'Philalethes' in the *Daily Post* of 31 July; Battestin reprints his letter, pp. 140–43.

P. 1, col. 3, 'ridiculous Play': On the *Modish Couple*, see No. 108 and notes.

P. 1, col. 3, '*theatrical*': The reason given for rejecting Dramaticus's own play at Drury Lane; see No 119.

P. 1, col. 3, '*Daily Post ... instant*': The advertisement is in the style of one for professional fighters: at Captain Gulliver's long-room on 20 July will be a trial of skill in which William Hint, Candle-Snuffer (I.e., Fielding), challenges 'one Mr. *Bavius Dramaticus*', Master of 'the Noble Science of Dirty-Work', and so on.

P. 1, col. 3–p. 2, col. 1, '*Nescit ... audientium*': 'A well-known priest, who withdraws his name, newly out of his seat, by the clergymen standing by, delivered this brief phrase, following the bishop, or perhaps before, saying with a resounding voice, *Abbots, the law and the dictates of religion are in opposition*; he had abundant silken vestments swelling out around his neck; this same one was furnished with the important title of "Doctor"; he was wont to speak thunderously, wont to throw among the poor a multitude of verbal thunderbolts, like another Pericles, shaking the forum of the Athenians. But he learns the rules of Prosody (if only admonishing that words must be heard), and he preserves his voice through reasonable breathing, in order to be able to speak more correctly, if he produces words which come from a Greek source under the sacred sanctuary. Nor does he violently

offend the ears of his audience while he invokes the Creeds, which he never reads' (trans. H. Nabbefeld). The title 'Nescit vox missa reverti', 'the word once sent forth can never come back', is quoted from Horace, *Ars Poetica* 390 (Loeb).

P. 3, col. 1, Pegasus col., 'A Paraphrase ... Horace': These lines by Pope, later used in his *Epistle to Dr. Arbuthnot*, were first printed in the *London Evening Post* for 22–25 Jan. 1731/2, entitled 'Horace, Satyr 4. Lib. 1. Paraphrased. Inscribed to the Honourable Mr—'; see *Minor Poems*, ed. Ault (pp. 339–40) for the background and the references. Ault lists the *GSJ* printing but has not found them in the *Whitehall Evening Post*. Couplet no. 4 concerns the charge that Pope had attacked the Duke of Chandos in his Epistle to Burlington, *Of Taste* (Dec. 1731), 'Cannons' being the name of his seat.

No. 135

P. 1, col. 2, '*Comedian*': Thomas Cooke's periodical which defended Fielding; see No. 132.

P. 1, col. 2, 'sorry you chose the *Courant*': The *Daily Courant* was a major outlet of pro-Walpole propaganda. It should be noted that the letter to which 'Dramaticus' is responding was a defence of the *Comedian*, not really of Fielding. The remark here is again evidence of how politically biased critical reaction to plays often was.

P. 1, col. 2, '*Humanum ... errare*': 'To err is human.'

P. 2, col. 3, Pegasus col., '*Daily Post* ... letter': The angry letter was by Henry Fielding, writing under the name 'Philalethes' and strongly attacking the *GSJ* ; Fielding makes it clear that a '*nonjuring Parson*' is involved and hints that only one person may be the author of all the attacks. For the letter, see No. 134, note on p. 1, col. 3.

P. 3, col. 1, Epigram, 'Dryden and Congreve': In his letter to the *Daily Post* Fielding had indeed cited these and the other great Restoration comic dramatists as precedents for his use of 'Indecencies'.

No. 136

P. 1, col. 1, 'Appendix ... Mr. Norman': Samuel Fancourt, *An Appendix to a Letter to Mr. Norman ... shewing ... that the eternal certainty of contingent events cannot be proved* (Sarum, 1730). On Norman and Fancourt, see No. 134. Since a 1733 volume by Fancourt (*The Free Agency of Accountable Creatures*) opens with this letter to *GSJ* reprinted, one may reasonably assume that Fancourt himself is the author of this contribution.

P. 1, col. 2, 'Actor ... Drury-lane': I.e., John Henley and Henry Fielding; this article rehearses the details of the quarrel with Fielding from recent numbers of the *GSJ*. It is signed 'M.' in *Mem.* and is thus probably by Russel, as its extraordinarily vitriolic language also suggests. The Pegasus col. also is signed 'M.'.

P. 1, col. 3, '*Modish Couple*': See No. 108 and notes.

P. 2, col. 1, 'Hurlothrumbo': A famous and ridiculous farce (1729) by Samuel Johnson of Cheshire.

P. 2, col. 1, 'Hurlo-thrumbo, or Hurlo-thumbo': Bavius links Johnson's ridiculous farce with Fielding's own *Tom Thumb* (1730); in *Mem.* he (Russel) calls them 'two wild, extravagant, ridiculous Pieces, which had a great run'.

P. 2, col. 1, 'a Player and a Poet': I.e., Fielding and Theophilus Cibber combined efforts to write as 'Wm. Hint'. Recent scholarship suggests Fielding alone wrote the letter; see No. 130, note on 'Hint'.

No. 137

P. 1, col. 1, 'Eliot': Presumably a pseudonym; as well as No. 134, see No. 136, where another writer, probably Fancourt himself, continues the discussion.

P. 1, col. 1, *'Animadversions ... continued'*: Continued from No. 131.

P. 1, col. 2, *'Reviewer of* Milton's *Text'*: Zachary Pearce; see No. 113, note.

P. 2, col. 1, 'M. Du Cange': Charles du Fresne, sieur Du Cange (1610–88), *Glossarium ad scriptores mediae et infimae graecitatis.*

P. 2, col. 1, 'Johnstonus ... Tom Bostock': Richard Johnson (1656/7–1721), a schoolmaster, parodied Bentley's method in *Aristarchus ... Anti-Bentleianus* (1717) by applying it to a ballad on Tom Bostock, who 'in a sea-fight performed prodigies of valour'; see Boswell's *Life of Samuel Johnson,* ed. Arnold Glover (London, 1925), vol. i, p. 131 note.

P. 2, col. 1, *'Chevy Chace'*: 'Chevy Chase', an old ballad which Addison in his famous criticism on it (*Spectator* Nos. 70, 74) called 'the favourite Ballad of the common People of *England'*.

P. 3, col. 1, Pegasus col.: 'controversy ... Drury-Lane': Russel continues his account begun in the last issue of the *GSJ*'s battle with Fielding.

P. 3, col. 1, *'History ... Sweden'*: Voltaire's account of Charles XII (1731).

P. 3, col. 2, 'Miss Raftor ... *Peachum'*: Gay's *Beggar's Opera* had been playing for the past several weeks at Drury Lane, with Catherine Raftor as Polly. In the epigram, 'Hint and Keyber' are Fielding and Theophilus Cibber; 'Fenton' and 'Rich' refer to Lavinia Fenton and John Rich, the actress who played Polly and the manager of Lincoln's Inn Fields theatre in its first 'smash' run in 1728.

No. 138

P. 1, col. 1, 'conatus': 'An effort, endeavour, striving' (*OED*).

P. 1, col. 1, 'Gomez ... *Teague o' Divelly'*: Referring to Dryden's *Spanish Friar* (1680) and Shadwell's *The Lancashire Witches, and Teague o' Divelly the Irish Priest* (1681).

P. 1, col. 1, *'ridiculum acre'*: Read *'acri'* for *'acre'*; from Horace's comment in *Sat.* i. 10. 14 about 'sharp ridicule' cutting hard knots better than gravity.

P. 1, col. 2, *'Rural Love ... Shepherd'*: An anonymous opera, with only one performance.

P. 1, col. 2, *'Love in a Riddle'*: This play of Colley Cibber's had two performances in 1729.

P. 1, col. 2, *'Devil of a Duke'*: By Robert Drury, it had its first performance 17 Aug. *A Duke and No Duke* (1684) was a play by Nahum Tate.

P. 1, col. 2, 'pretending to ... public Paper': The assumption is again that Theophilus Cibber collaborated with Fielding on the 'William Hint' letter. See No. 130, note on 'Hint'.

P. 1, col. 2, 'Rapin': I.e., Paul Rapin de Thoyras (1661–1725), whose Whiggish *History of England* was published in 1732 in an English translation by Nicholas Tindal.

P. 3, col. 1, Pegasus col., 'Mr. D—': John Dennis; see No. 5 and note.

P. 3, col. 1, 'Hobbinol Lubbin': Both names are commonly used to suggest an unlearned person from the country. This poem was reprinted in *Mem.* with no signature; this issue of the *GSJ* was the last reprinted in that collection of 1737.

P. 3, col. 1, 'Duck': See No. 40 and note.

P. 3, col. 1, 'Pol ... Pye': I.e., the parrot and the magpie.

P. 3, col. 1, 'Col': Colley Cibber, the 'Bays' or Poet Laureate referred to (with his traditional 'butt of sack') at the end of the previous stanza.

No. 139

P. 1, epigraph: 'And ready to make reply', Virgil *Eclogue* vii. 5.

P. 1, col. 1, 'a dissertation ... unseasonable'; this dissertation is one of the contributions attributed to the important divine, Joseph Trapp; see No. 62, second note. Hillhouse calls this essay 'religious argument at its worst' (p. 235); Richard Russel clearly did not share that view.

P. 1, col. 1, 'W—m ... Bowman': I.e., the pro-Walpole political writers 'Walsingham' (see No. 132, note) and 'Osborn' (see No. 121, 124 and notes), the religious zany John Henley, and the heterodox William Bowman, all subject of many previous attacks in the *GSJ*.

P. 1, col. 2, 'P—e': Prelate.

P. 1, col. 2, 'B—': Bishopric.

P. 1, col. 3, 'Curll ... *Westminster*': See No. 4, note on p. 1, col. 2.

P. 1, col. 3, 'S—k, H—e': Thomas Sherlock, Francis Hare, Bishops of Bangor and Chichester, respectively.

P. 1, col. 3, 'S—k—s ... J—k—n': Possibly Thomas Stackhouse (though the date is early for him) and John Jackson, theological writers.

P. 1, col. 3, 'B— ... L—s': 'Bishop', 'Lordship's'.

P. 1, col. 3, 'Bowman': See No. 82 and notes.

P. 2, col. 1, 'Eachard ...T—d—l': John Eachard (?1636–97), who wrote *Mr. Hobb's State of Nature Considered* (1672) and other attacks on Hobbes; and the Deist Matthew Tindal (1657–1733).

P. 3, col. 1, Pegasus col., 'Drurian': I.e., actors at the Theatre Royal, Drury Lane.

P. 3, col. 1, 'Bow street ... rise': The new theatre which Rich was building in Covent Garden and which opened in Dec. 1732.

P. 3, col. 1, 'W— ... C—r's': Wilks, Booth, and Cibber, the old triumvirate managing Drury Lane. The poem asserts one by one the superiority of Rich's company at the 'New House' to the actors of Drury Lane.

P. 3, col. 1, 'great Actor': Barton Booth, who retired because of illness.

P. 3, col. 1, '*Lady Townley*': Townly': In Cibber and Vanbrugh's *Provoked Husband*, a role made famous by Mrs. Oldfield.

P. 3, col. 1, 'H—n ... H—p—y'(lines 28–32): The following names should be supplied: Heron (Mary), Younger (Elizabeth), Chapman (Thomas), Cibbers (Colley and Theophilus), Hippisley (John). For biographical details, see Highfill.

P. 3, col. 2, 'H—l—m ... Th—r—d' (lines 33–40): Hallam (Adam), Ryan (Lacy), Bridgwater (Roger), Walker (Thomas); Marshall, Hulett (Charles), Buchanan (Elizabeth), Thurmond (Sarah).

P. 3, col. 2, '*Lady Grace* ... M—ls'(lines 41–44): Lady Grace is a character in the *Provoked Husband*; other names are Cibber (Susannah), Milward (William), Mills (William).

No. 140

P. 1, col. 1, '*Poeta ... afflatur*': Adapted from Cicero, *pro Archia poeta* viii. 18, 'the poet depends solely on an inborn faculty, is evoked by a purely mental activity, and is infused with a strange supernal inspiration' (adapted from Loeb trans.).

P. 1, col. 2, 'Bubbles': I.e., delusive commercial speculations.

P. 1, col. 2, 'new method of printing': Presumably the writer means by subscription after a published proposal, but that was hardly new in 1732.

P. 1, col. 2, '*The universal ... time &c*': In spite of the writer's doubts, such a book did appear in 1735 by one Patrick Barclay, DD, although only the first volume was published.

P. 1, col. 3, '*hog, smelt, George, teaster*': Slang terms for, respectively, a shilling, a half-crown, a half-guinea, and a sixpence (*OED*).

P. 3, col. 1, Pegasus col., 'Mechell': J. Mechell, a bookseller involved in a controversy over the publication of Rapin's *History of England* (see *Comedian* No. 6).

P. 3, col 1, 'C—'s made Attorney General': Matthew Concanen, pro-Walpole essayist and enemy of Swift and Pope, had just been made attorney general of Jamaica.

P. 3, col. 1, 'Lord of Dawley': Bolingbroke, Opposition leader, attacked in such terms by government propagandists like Concanen.

P. 3, col. 1, 'Coke ...Rawley': In a notorious incident Sir Edward Coke (1552–1634), famous English lawyer, treated Sir Walter Raleigh with harsh invective when representing the Crown in Raleigh's trial of Nov. 1603; he is reputed to have said 'Thou hast an English face, but a Spanish heart!'

No. 141

P. 1, date: 'Sept. 10' is an error for 'Sept. 14'.

P. 1, col. 1, 'obscure Weekly Journal': The usual name in *GSJ* for their enemy the *Weekly Register*.

P. 1, col. 1, 'our defence ... same manner': What follows is a succinct but biting account, undoubtedly by Russel, of the various pieces in the *GSJ* about Fielding and of his efforts to respond.

P. 1, col. 1, 'Mr. C—, or Mr. F—': Theophilus Cibber or Fielding; see No. 130, note on 'Hint'.

P. 1, col. 1, 'Bear– garden': 'A place originally set apart for the baiting of bears, and used for the exhibition of other rough sports, fig. a scene of strife and tumult' (*OED*).

P. 1, col. 3, 'On a poet's pleading ... bawdry': The poem mocks Fielding's claim (in the postscript to his 'Philalethes' letter in the *Daily Post*) that 'all our best Writers of *Comedy*' have used more indecencies in their plays than he has.

P. 3, col. 1, Pegasus col., '*Mock ... lui*': On the charge that the 'Mock Doctor' is a mis-translation of Molière's title, see the postscript to the letter by 'Publicus' in No. 133.

P. 3, col. 1, Pegasus col., 'Smithfield F—g': *The Forc'd Physician* was advertised to be played at 'Fielding and Hippisley's Great Theatrical Booth in the George Inn Yard in West Smithfield during the time of Bartholomew Fair' (*Daily Post*, 22 Aug. 1732). The 'Fielding' is not Henry but Timothy, an actor.

No. 142

P. 1, col. 1, epigraph: From Edward Young, *Two Epistles to Mr. Pope* (1730), Epistle i.

P. 1, col. 1, 'obligations of taking the oaths ... righteousness': When George I succeeded in 1714, a new Oath abjuring the Pretender was imposed; Richard Russel himself gave up his two livings as a vicar rather than take the new oaths.

P. 1, col. 2, '*The rights ... Whig*': Matthew Tindal, *The rights of the Christian Church asserted* (1706); Anthony Collins, *A Discourse of Free-thinking* (1713); on the *Independent Whig*, see No. 85 and note; on its influence on Bowman, mentioned below, see No. 82 and notes.

P. 1, col. 2, *Discourse ... creation*': The first is again by Anthony Collins, published 1724; the second by Tindal, appearing in 1730.

P. 1, col. 2, 'Lipsiensis': I.e., Richard Bentley, who used this name in attacking Collins in 1713; hence the comment about an 'ill-natured Pedant' at the end of the paragraph.

P. 1, col. 2, '*Sirs ... wealth*': Acts 19: 25.

P. 1, col. 2, 'Osborn': See No. 124, first note.

P. 1, col. 3, 'D. D.': Not certainly identified. Circumstantial evidence suggests Joseph Trapp (see No. 152, note), but if so the sarcasm about oaths is odd, since he was not a nonjuror.

P. 1, col. 3, 'Mr. A— F—'s Letter ... versifyed': Although most of the minor personages mentioned in this poem remain unidentified, the main figure satirized is clear: Richard Furney (d. 1753), rector of Cheriton with Tichbourne, Hampshire, since 1729, and Archdeacon of Surrey since 1725. Cheriton is near New Alresford (the 'A—ford' of the poem). The church is one of the richest livings in the Diocese of Winchester (*Victoria County History*, Hampshire). A single-sheet copy of this poem is in the British Library, printed in Salisbury, with no date; BL dates it at 1750 (?), but that seems too late. *The Curate's Answer*, published in *GSJ* No. 146, is also in the BL, again with no date.

P. 2, col. 3, Pegasus col., 'True Turncoats': The letter in *Fog's Journal* (16 Sept.) concerned the epigram on Matthew Concanen in No. 140; the writer is claiming that the *GSJ* writers have joined the ranks of Walpole's hacks by altering the lines in his poem.

P. 3, col. 1, 'Sir R—': Sir Robert (Walpole)

P. 3, col. 1, '*poeta ... fit*': 'The poet is born, not made'.

P. 3, col. 1, 'L— C—': 'Laureate Cibber'.

No. 143

P. 1, col. 2, 'Trenchard': John Trenchard; with Thomas Gordon, author of *Cato's Letters* and *The Independent Whig* (1720–21).

P. 1, col. 3, '*Devil of a Duke*': See No. 138 and note.

P. 1, col. 3, 'Philips ... *Essay on song-writing*': Ambrose Philips, an essay in the *Guardian* (30 March 1713).

P. 3, col. 1, Pegasus col., '*Miscellaneous ... August*': A periodical begun in 1731, ed. John Jortin.

P. 3, col. 1, 'Mr. L. T.': Lewis Theobald, playwright, scholar, and enemy of Pope, whose edition of Shakespeare he had ridiculed in 1726; his own edition was to appear in 1733.

P. 3, col. 1, '*Harlequin Horace*': On Miller's poem, which contains more than a couplet satirizing Theobald, see Nos. 59–60 and notes.

P. 3, col. 2, 'W— to the Aonian mountain came': Leonard Welsted (1688–1747), poet and one of Pope's Dunces, had addressed to Walpole in 1727 a *Discourse*, with Proposals on translating Horace's works into verse, along with a specimen.

P. 3, col. 2, 'Philips … Flaccus': I.e., 'As Ambrose Philips imitated Virgil (Maro) in his pastorals, so I wish to struggle with Horace (Flaccus)'.

P. 3, col. 2, 'Latona's son': Apollo.

P. 3, col. 2, 'Corinthian': I.e., brazen, shameless (*OED*).

P. 3, col. 2, 'Pragmatic bard': I.e., officious, intrusive (*OED*).

No. 144

P. 1, col. 1, 'And the work itself … thought to be mad': Nothing is known of 'one Mr. Gregory', but this leader does imitate *An Essay towards the theory of the intelligible world … Consisting of a preface, a postscript, and a little something between*, itself a parody of an essay with a similar title by the theologian John Norris, appearing 1701–4. The BL attributes the parody, which was signed 'Gabriel John', to Thomas D'Urfey and dates it as probably 1705. This imitation has as its purpose low-key satire on the general political scene.

P. 1, col. 1, '*ex nihilo … fit*': 'Nothing is made from nothing.'

P. 1, col. 2, 'patruelian': A coinage from *patruelis*, Latin for 'descended from a father's brother'.

P. 1, col. 2, 'Grub … Parnassus': They are the bicipital (two-headed) haunts of the modern Muses, since one is the home of hack writers and the other of Bedlam, the home of the mad.

P. 1, col. 2, '*conjunctim … seorsim*': 'conjoined, divided, distinguished from each other, separate'.

P. 1, col. 2, 'hypomastic': Another neologism: 'insufficiently sticking'(?).

P. 1, col. 2, 'What means … of thunder': The lines have not been located elsewhere and are apparently original with this writer.

P. 1, col. 2, '*caput … condit*': 'with head hidden in the clouds', Virgil, *Aeneid* iv. 177 (Loeb).

P. 1, col. 2, 'tellurigenous': 'Produced by the earth', another coinage.

P. 1, col. 2, '*Cedite … Graii*': 'Begone, you Roman writers, begone you Greeks' (parodying the prophecy of Propertius [beginning '*credite*', 'believe it'] of the greatness of Virgil's epic).

P. 1, col. 2, 'Horace's … *monumentum*': Odes iii. 30. 1, 'I have finished a monument [more lasting than bronze]' (Loeb).

P. 1, col. 2, 'Ovid … *exegi*': 'And now I have finished the work', *Metamorphoses* xv. 871; the poet goes on to say that neither Jove nor war nor age will be able to destroy it.

P. 1, col. 2, '*fortemque … Pyracmon*': '[doom of] brave Gyas, and brave Cloanthus'; 'Brontes and Steropes and Pyracmon with bared limbs', *Aeneid* i. 222, viii. 425 (Loeb).

P. 1, col. 2, 'Costarum … Britanus': Stock phrases in political discourse of the 1730s, 'Coast guard, Dunkirk, Gibraltar, Sinking Fund, stock-jobbers,' etc.

P. 1, col. 3, 'Philips … Galligaskins': John Philips, in *The Splendid Shilling* (1703); 'Galligaskins' are long breeches.

P. 1, col. 3, 'Wilks': Robert Wilks, who had been one of the actor-managers of Drury Lane.

P. 2, col. 1, 'by an actor ... heroe': Theophilus Cibber, who played Macduff in the performance on 28 Sept.; he had played Marplot in Centlivre's *Busy Body*, also mentioned, on 22 Sept.

P. 3, col. 1, Pegasus col., 'obscure weekly paper': *GSJ*'s code word for the *Weekly Register*.

P. 3, col. 1, 'P. and W.': Pulteney (leader of Opposition in the Commons) and Walpole.

No. 145

P. 1, col. 1, 'letter to you ... religion': This leader continues the irony of No. 142 and again may be by Joseph Trapp; see No. 152 and note on 'D. D.'

P. 1, col. 1, 'Osborne': See No. 116, note on p. 3, col. 1.

P. 1, col. 1, '*Comedian*': Thomas Cooke; see No. 132, second note.

P. 1, col. 2, 'Oratory': The term used by John Henley for the place where he preached.

P. 1, col. 2, 'Ruth Collins': Pseudonym of a supposed Quaker writer; see No. 47, note. The *Friendly Writer and Register of Truth* was a monthly magazine, intended in part to correct errors of the press.

P. 1, col. 3, 'Huggonson': Partner in the *GSJ* and at this time its printer, also a Quaker. He may have been involved in this burlesque attack on 'Collins'. The *Friendly Register* says he puts forth a paper of rebuke and admonition (*GSJ*), yet 'he doeth the work of Reproof but slothfully'.

P. 1, col. 3, '*friends of Jacob* ... bringing the king back': According to *GM*, the 'Hyp-Doctor' (Henley) thought this line treasonable; 'sons of Jacob' can be read (as it must be in the Collins publication) as 'Jacobites' (*GM* ii, p. 1005).

P. 2, col. 1, '*invidus ... optimis*': 'The envious man grows lean when his neighbour grows fat', Horace, *Epist.* i. 2. 57 (Loeb).

P. 3, col. 2, Greek title, Latin motto: The Greek roughly is the same sense as line 4 of the poem, 'If [though] it does you no good, it will do you no hurt'; the Latin may be rendered, 'As long as nature doesn't repel it', as can the final line of the poem.

P. 3, col. 2, Pegasus col, 'Come listen, good people': This is called by Henley a 'heavy Lampoon on the Prince's Physician' (advertisement in *Daily Journal* for 17 Oct.), in other words on Francis Clifton (d. 1736), who received an MD from Leiden and then an honorary MD from Cambridge, during a visit of George II. He was appointed physician to the Prince of Wales but resigned in 1734 to go to Jamaica, where he died. See also No. 201.

No. 146

P. 1, col. 1, '*Animadversions* ... continued': Continued from No. 131.

P. 1, col. 1, 'Woolston': See No. 115 and note.

P. 1, col. 1, 'the *Reviewer*': Zachary Pearce; see No. 113, note.

P. 1, col. 2, 'Cherefeddin ... Croix': A work about Tammerlane, Emperor of the Moguls, published in Paris in 4 vols. in 1722.

P. 1, col. 3, '*Friendly Letter*': Edmond Miller, *A friendly letter to Dr. Bentley. Occasion'd by his new edition of Paradise Lost by a gentleman of Christ-Church College, Oxon* (1732).

P. 1, col. 3, 'Bailey': See No. 2 for note on Nathaniel Bailey, to whom *GSJ* always assigns the epithet 'Philologist', in Greek.

P. 1, col. 3, 'Curate ... versifyed': A continuation of the satire in No. 142 on Archdeacon Richard Furney; the church is at Cheriton, near New Alresford, Hampshire. See note at No. 142.

P. 3, col. 1, Pegasus col., 'Philo-Dives': See the letter in No. 145.

P. 3, col. 1, 'Shelton ... *Grubstreet*': See the news item in No. 145, for Tuesday, 10 Oct., reporting that 'Shelton, the apothecary, went in a mourning coach' to his execution at Tyburn, where (presumably) he became an 'Orator' as did many about to be hanged, like one Griffith listed in the same story. 'Mr. H—', of course, is John Henley.

P. 3, col. 1, 'Clare-market': The location of Henley's 'Oratory,' where he preached in the 'gilded tub' mentioned in the final line.

No. 147

P. 1, print: There is an 'explication' of the print in No. 148, the first two paragraphs of which are non-ironic and straightforward. Dorothy George also has explained these details: the 'forme' of the *GSJ* is behind the ass-headed man, a sheet of *Fog's Journal* lies on the frame of the press, above which is an owl; the horse-headed man pulls over the frame, the hog's head inks type, the forme of *Craftsman* is kicked out by a greyhound-head; the master printer (two-faced) looks on; and a 'devil' hangs printed sheets to dry (*Cat. Prints and drawings in the Brit. Museum, Div. I: Political and Personal Satires*).

P. 1, col. 1, 'Pock-fretten': A truly unpleasant name, since 'pock' is a skin eruption and 'fretten' is glass waste.

P. 1, col. 2, 'Pryn ... Ogilby': William Prynne, the famous Puritan; Daniel Defoe, another dissenter and Grubean writer; John Ogilby, translator and one of Pope's Dunces. The place which they have in common is slightly obscure, but it is clear from the leader in No. 174 that in the midst of Lincoln's Inn Fields there was a market place for selling 'refuse books, of the past and present age', including newspapers, and that fact explains these derogatory allusions.

P. 1, col. 2, 'Stonecastle': Persona of the *Universal Spectator*.

P. 1, col. 2, 'Hence we sometimes see ... legal coachman': The 'cart' is for those going to be executed; Holborn hill is on the route from Newgate prison to Tyburn.

P. 1, col. 3, 'Applebee': John Applebee was a pioneer in weekly journalism, starting the *Original Weekly Journal* in 1714 (Harris, p. 20); now, the writer points out, he has moved to printing the 'Dying Speeches' of those executed at Tyburn, as indeed he did for the four malefactors, including Jonathan Wild, executed on 24 May 1725. Such are the 'Orators' mentioned a few lines later.

P. 1, col. 3. 'Clare-market': See No. 146, final note.

P. 3, col. 2, Pegasus col., 'Mead': Richard Mead (1673–1754), famous physician and virtuoso.

P. 3, col. 2, 'Chambers': See No. 70, note.

P. 3, col. 2, 'Liberty of the Press': The Tory government under Queen Anne had put into effect the Stamp Act (1712), designed to stifle opposition journalism. The rueful irony of this poem may have been prompted by the recent conviction of Richard Francklin, printer of the *Craftsman*.

No. 148

P. 1, print: Repeated, along with first part of the leader from No. 147; see those notes. In this essay the irony is turned against piracy and dishonest publishing practices. This number is called the *GSJ Extraordinary* because of this print 'designed by Mr. Hemskirk' and also because of the repeat of the print of the arms of the City of London companies from Nos. 43 and 93. Presumably more copies were printed for this issue, though the record is not extant; an advertisement described the issue as 'very proper for those that intend to see his Lordship's Shew with Pleasure and Education' (*Daily Post*, 30 Oct.).

P. 2, col. 2, 'two Josephus's': One was *A compleat collection of the genuine works of Flavius Josephus*, trans. by H. Jackson (printed and sold by D. Henry, 1732), and the other *The works of Flavius Josephus, which are extant*, trans. John Court (printed and sold by R. Penny and J. Janeway, 1733).

P. 2, col. 2, 'Xenophon's … Elizabeth': *The science of good husbandry, or, The oeconomics of Xenophon*, translated from the Greek by R. Bradley (London: printed for Thomas Corbet, 1727). On Bradley see the scathing comments in No. 2; he was succeeded as Professor of Botany at Cambridge by John Martyn.

P. 2, col. 2, 'Oldcastle … D'Anvers': 'Oldcastle' is the persona assumed by Bolingbroke for a series of essays on English history in the *Craftsman*'; 'Caleb D'Anvers' is the pseudonym of the chief writer, Nicholas Amhurst. On Bolingbroke's view of Charles I, see Pettit, pp. 111–14.

P. 2, col. 3, 'Crawfurd': Not identified, but presumably associated with *Fog's Journal*.

P. 3, col. 1, 'King William's Statue': See No. 121 and notes for the controversy with 'Osborne', pen name of Walpole's writer in the *London Journal*, over this issue.

P. 3, col. 1, 'messenger': I.e., a king's messenger, to take them into custody.

P. 3, col. 1, 'Explication of the Picture': See notes for the print in No. 147.

P. 3, col. 2, 'Restorer of Ancient Elocution': Orator Henley. Henley advertised in response that he would publish in the *Hyp Doctor* 'the only true Original Key to the Grub-street, sprinkled lately with Devils, by Dick Russel, in his own Form, from Children's Penny Books' (*Daily Journal*, 30 Oct. 1732).

P. 3, col. 2, 'charitable corporation': See Nos. 127–29 and notes.

P. 3, col. 2, 'read backwards … East India goods': Satirizing the *Free Briton's* over-reading of the letter from Rome; see Nos. 127–29.

P. 3, col. 3, Pegasus col., 'Lord Mayor …London': John Barber (1675–1740), a printer, friend of Jonathan Swift, a Tory with Jacobite leanings and a strong opponent of Walpole. His occupation probably explains the use of a print about printing in Nos. 147–48.

P. 3, col. 3, line 2, 'immediate predecessors': Humphrey Parsons and Francis Child; see Nos. 43, 48, and 95, and notes.

P. 3, col. 3, line 9, 'saints': Puritans in the Commonwealth period, who revolted against the 'purple' (king) and 'lawn' (bishops).

P. 3, col. 3, line 16, 'whose ears … own': I.e., they won an audience by having their ears cut off and becoming Puritan martyrs.

P. 3, col. 3, lines 20–22, 'their ears … t'other': These lines seem closely imitative of Swift's *Tale of a Tub* (1710 edn.), sect. xi.

No. 149

P. 1, col. 1, 'epigram … Philo-Histrio': See No. 146.

P. 1, col. 1, '*qualis ... oratio:*' 'As the man, so the language'.

P. 1, col. 1, '*poeta ... fit*': See No. 142, note.

P. 1, 'Shaftsbury': Anthony Ashley Cooper (1671–1713), third Earl of Shaftesbury, author of *Characteristics of Men, Manners, Opinions, Times* (1711).

P. 1, col. 1, 'Milo': See No. 47, note on epigraph.

P. 1, col. 2, '*Diable ... bon*': 'The devil! how good that is!'

P. 3, col. 1, Pegasus col., 'To ... London': See No. 148 for notes on John Barber, the new Lord Mayor, and on the first thirty lines of this poem (which are here repeated).

P. 3, col. 2, 'Brewer ... Banker': I.e., Parsons and Child, the two predecessors of Barber.

P. 3, col. 2, line 80, 'With my old ... dispense': The speaker (Russel) jokingly threatens that he will turn from Tory to Whig unless Barber (a Tory printer) provides some reward for his verse; the remaining lines develop this point with a strained analogy from a print shop.

No. 150

P. 1, epigraph: Edward Young, *Two Epistles to Mr. Pope* (1730), Epistle i.

P. 1, col. 1, 'Clare market ... Quack Doctor': Alluding to John Henley.

P. 1, col. 3, 'Choerilus': Choerilus, an epic poet of Iasus, mentioned by Horace in *Ars Poetica* 357–58 and *Epistles* ii. 1. 233. The source of the 'secret history' is still secret.

P. 1, col. 3, 'the Laureat's *Ode*': See No. 149 for Cibber's Ode.

P. 2, col. 1, 'Outdoings ... outdone': Alluding to a famously clumsy line of Cibber's; see No. 51, note

P. 3, col. 1, '*sublimi ... vertice*': 'I shall touch the stars with my exalted head', Horace, *Odes* i. 1. 36 (Loeb).

P. 3, col. 1, '*with sense ... mankind*': Young, *Two Epistles to Mr. Pope* (1730), Epistle ii.

P. 3, col. 1, 'Ithuriel's spear': Touching Satan with the spear removed his disguise and returned him to his own form (Milton, *Paradise Lost*, iv. 810–11).

P. 3, col. 1, 'Scriblerus Secundus': A pseudonym used by Fielding for a series of plays in 1730–32, starting with *The Author's Farce*.

P. 3, col. 1, '*ad thus & odores*': 'near the frankincense and perfumes', echoing Horace's last lines of his Epistle to Augustus (*Ep.* ii. 1. 269–70).

P. 3, col. 1, 'Hogarth ... Faber': William Hogarth (1697–1764), the most famous graphic artist of the period; John Faber the younger (?1675–1736), well-known mezzotint engraver.

P. 3, col. 1, epigram, 'Andrew': I.e., 'merry-andrew', buffoon. See also the news items and comments about Henley's *Hyp-Doctor*, p. 2, col. 1, of this issue.

No. 151

P. 1, epigraph: 'peevish, surly, given to praising the days he spent as a boy, and to reproving and condemning the young', Horace, *Ars Poetica* 173–74 (Loeb).

P. 1, col. 1, 'Tully': Cicero.

P. 1, col. 1, '*To ... season*': Ecclesiastes 3:1.

P. 1, col. 2, 'french book ... *Worlds*': Fontenelle's *Conversations on the Plurality of Worlds* (1686). Sir William Temple (1628–99), diplomat and patron of Swift, praises this work in the opening passages of his 'Essay upon the Ancient and Modern Learning' in *Miscellenea: the Second Part* (1690).

P. 1, col. 2, 'case of Mr. J. Henley ... very much': See No. 149, p. 2, cols. 1–2.

P. 1, col. 2, 'Moor-fields': I.e., Bedlam.

P. 3, col. 1, 'Jonathan Wild': See No. 128, note.

P. 3, col. 1, 'Water-Lane Fleet-Street': The joke is merely on the name.

P. 3, col. 1, 'Laureat's last Ode': See No. 149.

No. 152

P. 1, col. 1, 'Gabriel': Fictional name; see notes on No. 144. This essay continues the burlesque with a fairly general discourse on politics; both ministerial and anti-ministerial politicians are lightly ridiculed.

P. 1, col. 1, 'Chambers': See No. 70, note.

P. 1, col. 2, '*Elixir ... publici*' 'Elixir of the good of the public'.

P. 1, col. 2, 'vectigalian ... corruption': 'Vectigalian', a neologism, means 'pertaining to state taxes or revenue'; 'bribery and corruption' is the tag phrase of the Opposition to describe Walpole's way of governing.

P. 1, col. 2, 'Marsyas ... harper': The fable makes him a flutist (Hyginus, Fable 191).

P. 1, col. 2, '*aurum ... catholicum*': 'Gold is the universal elixir of war and peace'.

P. 1, col. 3, '*pilula aurea*' ... '*aurum potabile*' ... '*aurum fulminans*': 'pill of gold', 'drinkable gold', 'thunder-and-lightning gold'.

P. 2, col. 3, Pegasus col., '*Odes* ... elegiac verse': It is unclear who translated the ode into English, but the Latin is the work of Joseph Trapp, whose edition of Anacreon appeared first in 1733 (published by Lawton Gilliver) and again in 1742, published by (among others) Richard Russel's son William. This evidence, however, does not demonstrate that Trapp himself is also the 'D. D.' who signed this and other letters to the *GSJ*.

No. 153

P. 1, epigraph: Matthew Prior, *An Ode ... to the Queen on the Glorious Success of Her Majesty's Arms 1706*, lines 335–36.

P. 1, col. 1, 'Ashmole ... *garter*': Elias Ashmole (1617–92); 1672 and later editions.

P. 1, col. 1, 'Buchanan': George Buchanan (1506–82), *Rerum Scoticarum historia* (1624 and later edns.).

P. 1, col. 1, 'Mennenius': F. Mennenius, writer on heraldry, e.g. *Deliciæ equestrium sive militarium ordinum et eorundem origines, statuta, symbola et insignia* (Cologne,1638).

P. 1, col. 1, '*Nemo ... lacessit*': 'No one provokes me with impunity'.

p. 1, col. 2, '*Independent Whig*': See No. 143, first note.

P. 1, col. 2, 'Chamberlayne': John Chamberlayne (1666–1723), *Angliae notitia: or, The present state of England: with divers remarks upon the ancient state thereof* (an annual reference work from the late seventeenth century onwards; title varies).

P. 1, col. 3, '*Pro ... acutis*': 'Instead of the soft violet, instead of the gleaming narcissus, the thistle rises up and the sharp-spiked thorn', Virgil, *Eclogue* v. 38–39 (Loeb).

P. 1, col. 3, 'Cleveland ... him home': John Cleveland (1613–58), 'The Rebell Scot' (1647), lines 63–64.

P. 1, col. 3, 'Translator of Anacreon': See No. 152, Pegasus col.

P. 2, col. 3, 'John Gabriel': See Nos. 144, 152; since 'Gabriel' is fictitious, this apology for an anachronism is not serious.

P. 3, col. 1, 'Baker ... Hutchinson ... Montfaucon': Thomas Baker (1656–1740), antiquarian scholar and nonjuror; Francis Hutchinson (1660–1739), Bishop of Down
and Connor; Bernard de Montfaucon (1655–1741), renowned French scholar.

No. 154

P. 1, col. 1, '*de fraudibus bibliopolarum*': 'concerning the frauds of booksellers'.

P. 1, col 1, '*pro thesauro carbones*': 'for a treasury of ashes'.

P. 1, col. 1, 'Philalethes ...Phileleutherus': 'Philalethes' is the name Fielding used to
write his letter of self-defence to the *Daily Post* (see No. 135); 'Phileleutherus Lipsiensis' was a pseudonym used by Richard Bentley.

P. 1, col. 1, 'onomotechny': A coinage, 'skill in names'.

P. 1, col. 2, 'C—l ... Gay': Cf. Pope's note to *Dunciad* i. 120, the line quoted here: '*Joseph
Gay*, a fictitious name put by *Curl* before several pamphlets, which made them
pass with many for Mr. *Gay's*'.

P. 1, col. 2, 'Alllen ... Alleyne': John Allen (?1660–1741), FRS, published *Synopsis uni-
versæ medicinæ practicae* in two parts in 1729. The volume by 'James Alleyne' was
entitled *A new English dispensatory, in four parts. Containing, I. A more accurate
account of the simple medicines, ... IV. A rational account of the operation of medicines. To which are added, the quantities of the middle syllables of the Latin names*
(1733).

P. 1, col. 2, '*Bridgewater*': Bridgwater, Somerset, where Allen lived and practised.

P. 1, col. 2, '*Stat ... Fur es*': 'Your page stares you in the face, and calls you "thief"',
Martial, *Epigrams* i. 53. 12 (Loeb).

P. 1, col. 2, 'Dr. Quincy': John Quincy (d. 1722), *The Dispensatory of the Royal College of
Physicians* (1721).

P. 1, col. 2: '*Spoiliavit ... mihi*': 'He plundered me, and he cursed me'.

P. 1, col. 3, 'Simples': A 'simple' is an archaic term for 'a plant or herb employed for
medical purposes' (*OED*).

P. 1, col. 3, '*accidence*': 'That part of Grammar which treats of the Accidents or inflec-
tions of words; a book of the rudiments of grammar' (*OED*).

P. 1 col. 3, 'Sydenham ... Bailey': Referring to the *Processus integri in morbis fere omnibus
curandis* of Thomas Sydenham (1624–89), a famous English physician; and to
Nathan Bailey (d. 1742), well-known lexicographer.

P. 2, col. 1, 'Havard ...Giffard': William Havard (?1710–78), actor and playwright;
Henry Giffard, actor. The play that was performed for the Masons was Cibber and
Vanbrugh's *The Provoked Husband*.

P. 3, col. 1, Pegasus col., 'Epilogue ... Mrs. Giffard': See the previous note. Mrs. Giffard
was Ann Marcella, Mrs. Henry Giffard.

No. 155

P. 1, col. 1, '*New Dispensary*': See No. 154, which is continued here.

P. 1, col. 1, 'Boerhave ... Woodward': On Boerhaave and Woodward, see No. 11 and
notes; John Ray (1627–1705) is considered one of the greatest of early English
botanists.

P. 1, col. 1, 'Dr. James': I.e., 'James Alleyne', supposed author of the patched-together
New Dispensatory.

P. 1, col. 1, 'Dr. Friend': John Friend (Freind) (1675-1728), physician, author of a *History of Physick* (1727) and other works.

P. 1, col. 2, '*Jungentur jam gryphes equis*': 'Griffins now shall mate with mares', Virgil, *Eclogues* viii. 27 (Loeb).

P. 1, col. 2, '*Pharmacopeia*': I.e., the *New Dispensatory* by 'Alleyne', published by Stephen Austin and Thomas Astley ('S. A. and T. A.'). 'N. B.' is unidentified; the lexicographer Nathan Bailey took it personally and in No. 156 denied any connection with the book.

P. 1, col. 2, 'John-a-Nokes': A fictitious name used in legal actions.

P. 1, col. 2, 'Isaac de Duobus': Another fictitious name; *GM* has a puzzling allusion to 'A. M.' as the writer of the leaders thus signed (vol. 2, p. 1100); one could easily believe John Martyn had written them despite his recent departure from *GSJ*, but there is no other evidence that he did.

P. 1, col. 2, 'Mr. G—': Henry Giffard, actor, had built a new playhouse in Ayliffe Street, Goodman's Fields, which opened on 2 Oct. 1732. This letter seems an unpleasant effort to demean the theatre by emphasising its 'City' location and the correspondingly unfashionable nature of its audience, a continuation of the talk that circulated against Odell when he opened the first Goodman's Fields house in 1729. Then, Thomas Lockwood informs me, the complaint was that a Whitechapel location was all wrong for a theatre, because it would lure the nearby apprentices away from their work.

P. 1, col. 3, '*Orphan ... Bardwell*': The writer feigns surprise that the play is a serious one by Otway rather than a play suitable for the instruction or diversion of apprentices.

P. 1, col. 3, 'they were all citizens': I.e., 'Cits', a term used contemptuously to indicate tradesmen or shopkeepers as distinguished from gentlemen (*OED*).

P. 1, col. 3, 'Templar': Someone occupying chambers in the Inner or Middle Temple; a barrister (*OED*).

P. 1, col. 3, 'amputation': I.e., circumcision.

P. 3, col. 1, Pegasus col., '*Quidnunc ... nonsensical*': In his *Daily Journal* notice of 13 Dec. Henley had offered to dispute 'Dick Russel, the Devil-Tavern Chaplain' on the problem, 'A Preacher and teacher of God's Word is "bound in Conscience and Religion to preach and teach Burlesque" on a reciprocal Forfeit of 50 Guineas, in Case of Confrontation or Victory'.

P. 3, col. 1, '*negatur ... conclusio*': 'The major premise is false; the conclusion is false'.

P. 3, col. 1, 'Anacreontis': On the translations of Anacreon into Latin and English, see No. 152, note on Pegasus col.

No. 156

P. 1, epigraph: 'Either do not carp at mine [my poems], or publish your own', Martial, *Epigrams* i. 91. 2 (Loeb).

P. 1, col. 1, 'may not ... as well as James': According to the (old) *DNB*, there has been a more modern controversy about whether 'John Allen' of Bridgwater, Somerset, was 'real'; but the same article dismisses claims of his fictiveness. ESTC records multiple editions of his 'Synopsis' up to the 1760s; the reality of 'James' seems much more doubtful. See also Hillhouse, p. 253; on the other names invoked in this controversy, see Nos. 154–55, and notes.

P. 3, col. 1, Pegasus col., 'Welstede': See No. 69 and note. See also *Dunciad* iii, note on line 195.

No. 157

P. 1, col. 2, 'Dr. Quincy': See Nos. 154–55 and notes.

P. 1, col. 2, 'Godfrey … Staphorst': Ambrose Godfrey (d. 1741), a chemist in Covent Garden; Nicholas Staphorst (1679-1731), author of *Officina chymica Londinensis* (1685).

P. 1, col. 2, '*sed versus ructatur*': 'but the verse is spluttered out' (adapted from Horace, *Ars Poetica* 457).

P. 1, col. 2, 'Tillotson': John Tillotson (1630–94), Archbishop of Canterbury and famous as a preacher and divine.

P. 1, col. 2, '*Monitus … coloribus*': He was warned, and must often be warned to search for home treasures, and to shrink from touching the writings which Apollo on the Palatine has admitted: lest, if some day perchance the flock of birds come to reclaim their plumage, the poor crow, stripped of his stolen colours, awake laughter', Horace, *Epistles* i. 3. 15–20 (Loeb).

P. 1, col. 3, 'Hermitage … Duck': The Hermitage was a structure in Richmond Park built as a retreat for Queen Caroline; on Duck, see No. 40, note.

P. 1, col. 3, 'J—s … r—e': The pirate was one Erasmus Jones; the name he is called is probably 'reprobate'. One of Duck's patrons, Alured Clarke, made this identification, adding that Jones 'gathers news for the London Evening Post' and is 'very poor'. See Katherine Thomson, *Memoirs of Viscountess Sundon* (1847). I. 199, 203, and the discussion by Rose M. Davis, *Stephen Duck the Thresher Poet* (Univ. Press, Orono, Maine: 1926), pp. 40–43.

P. 1, col. 3, 'Cacus': A famous robber in myth, who stole cows from Hercules but was detected and killed when Hercules heard them lowing.

P. 3, col. 2, 'St. Thomas': 'Doubting Thomas'; see John 20: 20–28.

P. 3, col. 2, 'Woolston': See No. 115 and note.

LIST OF ABBREVIATIONS AND
SHORT REFERENCES IN THE NOTES

Ault, *Minor Poems*
Pope, *Minor Poems*, ed. N. Ault and J. Butt, Twickenham Ed. vi (London: Methuen, 1954).

Battestin
Martin C. Battestin with Ruthe R. Battestin, *Henry Fielding: A Life* (London: Routledge, 1989).

BL
The British Library

Capp
Bernard S. Capp, *English Almanacs, 1500-1800: Astrology and the Popular Press* (Ithaca: Cornell University Press, 1979).

DNB
Dictionary of National Biography.

Dunciad
All references are to the 'A' version of Pope's poem in the Twickenham Ed., ed. James Sutherland (London: Methuen, 1963).

ESTC
English Short Title Catalogue.

Foxon
David F. Foxon, *English verse 1701–1750: A Catalogue of Separately Printed Poems* (London: Cambridge Univ. Press, 1975).

GM
The Gentleman's Magazine.

GSJ
The Grub-street Journal.

Harris
Michael Harris, *London Newspapers in the Age of Walpole* (London: Associated Univ. Presses, 1987).

Highfill:
Philip H. Highfill, Jr., Kalman A. Burnim, and Edward A. Langhans, *A Biographical Dictionary of Actors, Actresses, Musicians, Dancers, Managers & Other Stage Personnel in London, 1660–1800* (Carbondale IL: Southern Ill. Univ. Press, 1973–).

Hillhouse
James T. Hillhouse, *The Grub-street Journal* (Durham, NC: Duke Univ. Press, 1928).

Hume
Robert D. Hume, *Henry Fielding and the London Theatre, 1728–1737* (Oxford: Clarendon Press, 1988).

Loeb
translations from volumes of the Loeb Classical Library (Harvard University Press).

London Stage
The London Stage, 1660–1800. Part 3 [1729–47], ed. A. H. Scouten. 2 vols. (Carbondale, IL: Southern Illinois Univ. Press, 1961).

Mem.
Memoirs of the Society of Grub Street (London: 2 vols., 1737).

OED
Oxford English Dictionary.

Pettit
Alexander Pettit, *Illusory Consensus : Bolingbroke and the Polemical Response to Walpole, 1730-1737* (Newark, Del.: Univ. of Delaware Press, 1997).

Pope Corr.
The Correspondence of Alexander Pope, ed. George Sherburn, 5 vols. (Oxford: Clarendon Press, 1956).

Sedgwick   Romney Sedwick, *The House of Commons, 1715–1754* (New York: Published for the History of Parliament Trust, Oxford University Press, 1970).

Twickenham   *The Twickenham Edition of the Poems of Alexander Pope*, ed. John
Ed.   Butt *et al.*, 11 vols. (London: Methuen,1940–69).